Fiction: Craft and Voice

Nicholas Delbanco
University of Michigan

Alan Cheuse
George Mason University

To Our Students

Mc Graw Hill **Higher Education**

Published by McGraw-Hill, an imprint of The McGraw-Hill Companies, Inc., 1221 Avenue of the Americas, New York, NY 10020. Copyright © 2010. All rights reserved. No part of this publication may be reproduced or distributed in any form or by any means, or stored in a database or retrieval system, without the prior written consent of The McGraw-Hill Companies, Inc., including, but not limited to, in any network or other electronic storage or transmission, or broadcast for distance learning.

This book is printed on acid-free paper.

5 6 7 8 9 0 DOW/DOW 0 9

ISBN: 978-0-07-310444-7
MHID: 0-07-310444-2

Editor in Chief: *Michael Ryan*
Publisher: *Lisa Moore*
Executive Marketing Manager: *Allison Jones*
Editorial Coordinator: *Stephen Sachs*
Production Editor: *Leslie LaDow*
Manuscript Editor: *Susan Norton*
Cover Designer: *Jeanne Schreiber*
Interior Designers: *Jeanne Schreiber and Linda Robertson*
Senior Photo Research Coordinator: *Nora Agbayani*
Lead Media Project Manager: *Ron Nelms*
Production Supervisor: *Louis Swaim*
Composition: *9.25/11.25 Miller Roman by Thompson Type*
Printing: *45# Influence Gloss, R. R. Donnelley & Sons/Willard, OH*

Cover: Frog: Photex/Jupiterimages. Dock: Gary John Norman/Getty Images.

Credits: The credits section for this book begins on page C-1 and is considered an extension of the copyright page.

Library of Congress Cataloging-in-Publication Data

Delbanco, Nicholas.
    Literature : craft and voice / Nicholas Delbanco, Alan Cheuse.—1st ed.
        p. cm.
    Includes index.
    3 vols. planned.
    ISBN-13: 978-0-07-310444-7 (v. 1 : acid-free paper)
    ISBN-10: 0-07-310444-2 (v. 1 : acid-free paper)   1. Literature.   I. Cheuse, Alan.   II. Title.
    PN45.D457 2009
    800—dc22

                                                                    2008051003

The Internet addresses listed in the text were accurate at the time of publication. The inclusion of a Web site does not indicate an endorsement by the authors or McGraw-Hill, and McGraw-Hill does not guarantee the accuracy of the information presented at these sites.

www.mhhe.com

Contents

FICTION

1 Reading a Story for Its Elements   2

2 Going Further with Reading   24

3 Writing about Fiction 50

4 Plot 74

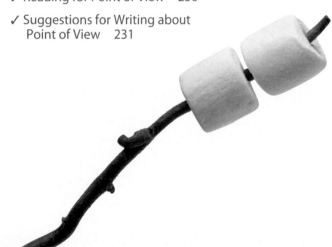

13 Visual Arts, Film, and Fiction   462

14 An Anthology of Stories for Further Reading 483

A HANDBOOK FOR WRITING FROM READING   H-1

6 MLA Documentation Style Guide H-103

Preface for Instructors

W illiam James once called our first glimpse as infants of the paradoxical world we live in "one great blooming, buzzing confusion." Students today, at the outset of their college years, seem to live a much more supercharged technological life than ever before. We see it in our own lives as well. But especially for the students, the buzzing and confusion if unchecked keeps on blooming. Over the years, we have watched our own students struggle with the avalanche of unfiltered information as well as support one another in new families of virtual community, and McGraw-Hill researchers took this further by following thousands of students at hundreds of institutions from sunup to sundown (and well after) as they work, play, and study. We took to heart what we know and what we learned when creating this book. Students need to slow down. They need a private study spot. They need to feel connected, not only to one another but also to their reading. They need different ways of gaining entry to reading and different ways of slowing themselves down mentally so they can concentrate on analysis, synthesis, and interaction with a text.

William Blake urges us to see "a world in a grain of sand." The grains of sand in this book are fiction, poetry, and drama. We poured into this text our combined multiple decades of love for teaching students, our love of reading and discovering new writers, and our experience as writers in the service of what we believe is an extremely effective multimedia pedagogy that brings writers to readers and readers to writing. We have incorporated into that pedagogy various technologies, with an emphasis on video interviews with nearly three dozen writers, scholars, and theater people, which will, we hope, deepen and broaden even further the student's engagement with literature and the growth of his or her own ability to think and write critically.

Reading in a Visual Age and Harnessing the Power of the Media

How do we read in a visual age? We came to this project with a desire to harness the power of media and use it to help students learn the art of sustained reading. This activity may be for pleasure or it may have a specific purpose such as the research paper, but it predates and is not a natural extension of the skim-and-grab reading that permeates our Internet culture. Like you, we believe that, in order to succeed in college, all students need to be able to apply critical thought to complex texts. To do this, they should engage their senses; they must listen as well as look. In this text, each chapter is accompanied by an ancillary video interview (sometimes two) of a featured writer discussing the topic of the chapter as well as what reading and writing have meant to him or her. In this way, we hope a visual and aural approach will enliven student interest in the act of reading.

Bringing Writers to Readers Brings Readers to Writing

Who doesn't appreciate the human voice? In each video, the featured writer reads from a selection of his or her writing included in the chapter and provides a personal insight

---

"Literature: Craft and Voice speaks to students who have grown up in a media-blitzed world who do not really know how or why they should read."

—Shirley Nelson, Chattanooga State Community College

"I think the video is very important for engaging students in discussion. A video is going to be more engaging than text for many people, so there is more opportunity to reach people who wouldn't otherwise participate."

—Kaitlyn Taylor, student, University of Delaware

"I appreciate the effort to appeal to a variety of learning styles. Having authors look students in the eye and talk about their writing has got to appeal and reinforce what teachers are saying in the classroom, whether it's a face-to-face classroom or a cyber classroom."

—April Childress, Greenville Technical College

A Conversation on Writing with Joyce Carol Oates, Chapter 11

A Conversation on Writing with Li-Young Lee, Chapter 17

A Conversation on Writing with Ruben Santiago-Hudson, Chapter 35

"I'm impressed by the thought that has gone into meeting younger 'generation internet students' on their own grounds. I think that "Literature Bibles' sometimes ignore who makes up their audience or marginalize how technology engages the same senses—see/hear/touch—that pen-and-ink fiction, poetry, and drama seek to capture."

—Jennifer Diamond, Bucks County Community College

"I was compelled into reading by the interviews. Once I read the interview, I wanted to continue reading the chapter and the selection for that chapter. It reminded me that I love poetry—I'm not a teacher of poetry but a lover of poetry. Quite a difference huh?"

—Tammy Mata, Tarrant County College

"The use of author interviews not only provides a sense of cohesion but also creates interest as students see and hear professional authors discussing their own writing processes and problems. I also like the emphasis and instruction on sustained reading skills needed for both analyzing and writing about literature."

—Linda Smith, Midlands Technical Community College

"The anthology's treatment of authors and the depth with which the anthology invites students to engage with authors as writers (not unlike themselves) make it a terrifically enabling experience for students."

—Elizabeth Rich, Saginaw Valley State University

into its composition. Actually hearing the voice of the author is one way to experience a text. It is also one way to begin to think independently. With so many writers talking about how they experience writing, there are inevitably exciting differences, such as those who love revision (Joyce Carol Oates) and those who don't revise (Jamaica Kincaid). Discovering writers are real flesh-and-blood people not only makes students more inclined to read but also gives them ideas for writing. These interviews can be important creative energizers for classroom discussion and independent analytical thought for your students.

Providing Media Designed Exclusively for Classroom Use with This Book

These interviews were created exclusively for their application to this project. As mentioned, each interview includes a writer's thoughts on how he or she came to reading; how the writer has worked with the element of craft that is under discussion in the chapter in his or her own work; a reading from the selection included in the chapter; and a personal assessment of what a new reader might find interesting about that work, as well as a discussion of the writing process. Quotations from these interviews and an extended boxed excerpt are included in each chapter. This creates a human connection to each subject and starts a conversation carried through with other quotations from these sessions that are included throughout the book. In this way, these writers' voices are sustained in the pages, along with our unifying discussion, making a complex text more personally inviting to students.

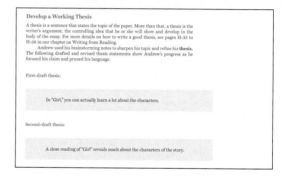

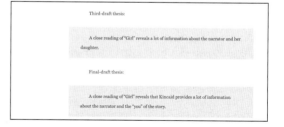

The "Interactive Reading" sections are incredibly useful.... While these models are presented as reading tools, the active reading, deciphering, interpreting, and wordsmithing teach students not only to read but how to write.... They see firsthand how to break down and comment on various aspects of the work, obviously an integral part of research or explication."

—Kristin Le Veness, Nassau Community College

"I was pleased to learn of the emphasis on sustained reading, as this skill will be called upon in every college course these students enter.... *Literature: Craft and Voice* addresses the needs of disengaged readers and writers. It is essential to their success."

—Carol Warren, Georgia Perimeter College

Emphasizing the Kind of Sustained Reading Students Need for College Success

In addition to media enhancement, each section of the book pays significant attention to the skill of sustained reading, with two chapters per genre devoted to developing critical reading skills, one that provides an overview of the reading to analyze elements in a work, and the next that provides an interactive reading—an annotated work that shows an analysis of a work—and a discussion of context. We begin with the reading and writing process so that students are familiar with that set of skills as they approach reading for academic life. This additional guidance is intended to help students develop the tools they need to communicate their thoughts in *writing*.

Making Reading-Writing Connections

Our chapter on writing in each section walks students through how reading interactively with a text is the basis of writing your own interpretation of a text. This is reinforced in the question sets that follow the readings included in the discussion in each chapter, a building block approach to critical thinking from summarizing (for comprehension), to analyzing craft and voice, synthesizing summary and analysis, and using that synthesis to interpret a text. You'll also find tips for interactive reading and As You Read suggestions for most selections. Students responded very positively to this approach in our focus groups.

In addition, we wanted to maintain a wide range of works not only for the instructor to find something interesting to teach but also so that students might go from texts that are assigned to those they might find deeply meaningful personally—the gothic component of Southern literature, perhaps, or the discovery of the role of music in the literature of Langston Hughes. In our suggestions for further reading, we continue to encourage reading with the added enhancement of "If you like this, you might like this" suggestions to draw a student into another selection in the book.

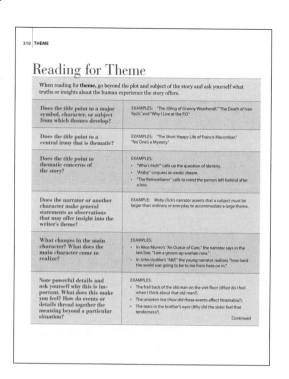

Providing the Vocabulary of Craft for Analysis

As with all things, knowledge of the working pieces of a project will help the student understand it better. Reading is the starting point for most of what is written; therefore, we use our own experience as writers to delve into the craft of composition from the inside out. In every case, some attention to the context, purpose, and genre of a work is needed for sustained response. In fiction, poetry, and drama, we have the opportunity to examine language at its most powerful, to analyze how that power is created and how it affects an individual. The importance of technique in writing is self-evident. Each successful writer employs technique in ways specific to his or her experience of the world in which he or she writes. The effective use of artistic craft and voice creates an overall effect on individual readers living at the same time as the writer, and—if the work is of enduring quality—in readers born centuries later.

Connecting Craft to the Variety of Composition Processes in Student Work

As teachers who have brought our own students to reading and writing by demonstrating a personal connection to the work, we bring an intimate knowledge of the struggles all writers face and the composition process in all its variety. The various featured authors and scholars all have something to say about the composition process that should inspire as well as support a student's own writing process. The following statement by Richard Ford gives a taste of what students will hear in this text about writing, the kind of observation we hope will show them how they themselves can write not just creatively but for every course in the curriculum.

> *People see a story on the page and what they think is that the writer started and then wrote to the end and this is how it looked. And in fact the writer . . . started at the beginning and wrote to the end, and then he started at the end and wrote to the beginning, and then he plucked things out of the middle and closed up the places where he took something out.*

Supporting Writing and Research with Enhanced Coverage of Avoiding Plagiarism

In addition to a chapter on writing that walks a student through three drafts of a student paper in each section, our case studies provide a springboard for research. We include a list of credible sources—both print and online—to get started, secondary sources online, and a research project involving the subject of the case study. Papers written on the subject of our case studies are found in our Handbook for Writing from Reading, which also provides additional support for students who will need to quote, paraphrase, summarize, and document their sources. The specific needs of today's students in writing, not only about literature but across the curriculum, encouraged us to provide pointed and direct guidance on avoiding plagiarism, whether using a single source or multiple sources. You'll find two chapters in our handbook that draw out issues on avoiding plagiarism, along with an MLA documentation style guide, and we believe these aids are crucial in helping students understand the requirements of the college experience.

Selecting Works for Powerful Personal Resonance

Ultimately reading, research, and writing can't exist without a subject: The subject for practicing these skills in this text is, in the broadest sense, literature. It is *alpha* and *omega* here from first to final page. There are many advantages to making literature a jumping-off point for the college experience. First, literature provides a pleasurable and personal place to begin. It offers the kind of complex text that generates, in the best of circumstances, a visceral response. Most people don't read well at first. Most don't write well. But the process does grow simpler when works have been selected to provide a rich introduction to these critical components of college life.

So, a word about selection: We believe in meeting the students halfway, without either blindly adhering to the assumptions of the past or veering too much toward the attractive if fleeting fads of the immediate present. We believe that exercise enhances performance, but that solid performance without the foundation of sound literary taste can be an empty exercise in itself. We believe as most of you do in a practical approach to literary study and that the study of good writing leads to the making of good writers.

This book provides a range of stories, poems, and plays that are testaments to language at its best, examples both well known and new. The selection of contemporary works by writers from a variety of backgrounds should help us demonstrate that literature is alive and well today. And the living, breathing presence of authors on our videos should help dispel the notion that all art is deathly dull and was produced by the dead. But we also wanted to bring to the students' attention enduring works by writers from the past—texts they may only have heard of or studied only glancingly (such as "Beowulf" or Chekhov's fiction) or may read for the first time in this course (such as the poems of Thomas Hardy or the plays of Sophocles). As the table of contents will demonstrate, our examples are numerous and various; their common denominator is that we think them worth sustained attention on the student's part.

Designing a Text for Reading

Enormous thought and care and research has gone into this design, which students tell us makes them want to read further! By beginning with a compelling chapter opener and a quotation from literature itself, students find themselves reading before they've thought about whether they will or want to read this work. This text's design should be an invitation to explore further, think harder, and write. Our student responses have been unanimous and gratifying.

"The bridge from reading to writing . . . provides important information . . . good information on critical approaches, suggestions for writing assignments, documentation, plagiarism, and MLA Guidelines."

—Kathleen A. Carlson, Brevard Community College

"Once students master critical reading skills, they still have great difficulty incorporating others' ideas about texts into their own interpretations."

—John Schaffer, Blinn College

"Well chosen . . . I'm delighted with the inclusion of Ha Jin and a number of stories that could be used to introduce students to multicultural literature."

—Richard C. Taylor, East Carolina University

"The fiction section is outstanding. I like that . . . it has a section on regionalism with authors grouped in the American West and the American South . . . [and] that wonderful chapter 13, Visual Arts, Film, and Fiction, with selections from *Beowulf*, Gardner, and Crichton."

—Grace Haddox, El Paso Community College

"I love the chapter openings! They're not just random pictures—they relate to the text. The spread also includes more than just a plot summary . . . it has a snippet of the text for every kind of reader and personality: a summary, a quote from the text, and a quote from the author."

—Alexandra V. Loizzo, student, Barnard College

4 Plot

"A story like 'Greasy Lake' develops through the opening . . . which is the setup: "I went there one night." . . . *Each of the incidents of the story strings out from that in an escalating way, until we . . . find out what happened. . . . It's not the kind of plot in which they all went to jail . . . the end. No, it ends on a gesture, and that gesture brings you back into the story to rethink what it means. . . ."*

Conversation with T. Coraghessan Boyle, video available at www.mhhe.com/delbancote

THE first mistake, the one that opened the whole floodgate, was losing my grip on the keys. In the excitement, leaping from the car with the gin in one hand and a roach clip in the other, I spilled them in the grass—in the dark, rank, mysterious nighttime grass of Greasy Lake. This was a tactical error, as damaging and irreversible in its way as Westmoreland's decision to dig in at Khe Sanh. I felt it like a jab of intuition, and I stopped there by the open door, peering vaguely into the night that puddled up round my feet.

The second mistake—and this was inextricably bound up with the first—was identifying the car as Tony Lovett's.

—from "Greasy Lake" by T. Coraghessan Boyle

IN the excerpt that begins this chapter, the narrator, a nineteen-year-old and a self-described "dangerous character," identifies the moment when his night of random thrill seeking begins to take shape. He tells the tale in retrospect—so we as readers know "the first" and "the second mistake" won't be fatal—but we also know the "error" will prove "irreversible." He and his two buddies had been cruising their town on the third night of summer vacation, looking for "something we never found." (The reference to "Westmoreland's decision to dig in at Khe Sanh" evokes U.S. Army general William Westmoreland's tactical blunder in Vietnam, and there's a not-so-casual suggestion that "losing my grip on the keys" opens a "floodgate" of trouble in a kind of small-scale war.) Restless with longing, the boys drive up to Greasy Lake and pull in behind the car they think belongs to Tony Lovett. Honking and blinking their headlights, they stumble out of their own car, hoping to catch Tony in the act of whatever he's doing.

And what happens then? This is the moment when the plot of "Greasy Lake" starts in earnest and the real action begins.

CONTINUED ON PAGE 83

75

All would prefer to read from this book when they compare it to the usual suspects. One student brought her sample home to show her sister, as she said, "My sister hates reading but she won't hate it when she sees this." We do hope we have created a twenty-first-century approach to our common task of education.

Our student research also tells us that students don't like a big book. But they don't like it small if all that has happened is that type size is shrunk and more words are crammed onto a page. However, research is clear that a student's ability to toss a book into a backpack makes it more likely he or she can find a quick moment here and there to read. Students in our focus group told us they read on the subway to the New York office because they couldn't wait to see what happened next. They googled authors themselves to find out more after they saw their interviews. This is the kind of engagement we hope this new format brings to the course.

Finally, a word about craft and voice and our names: The wonderful twentieth-century American novelist and poet Robert Penn Warren once described himself to students, when he was in his early eighties, as someone who woke up every day and sat down at his desk and was still trying to be a writer. That's how we both feel about the work of trying to become the best readers and best writers we can. Though we've come a long way from when we first tried "to be a writer," our own work as novelists, essayists, and reviewers brings us face-to-face every day with the hard labor of making sense with words.

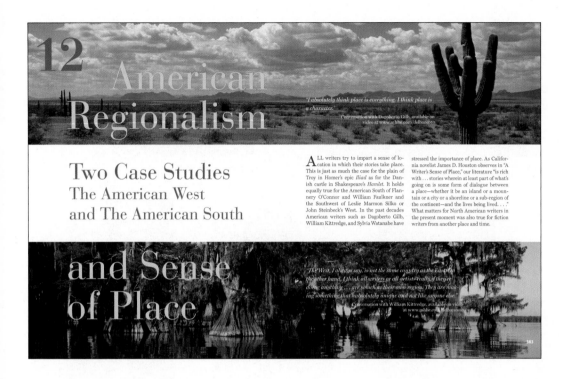

12 American Regionalism

Two Case Studies
The American West
and The American South

and Sense of Place

I absolutely think place is everything. I think place is a character.
— Conversation with Dagoberto Gilb, available on video at www.mhhe.com/delbanco1e

ALL writers try to impart a sense of location in which their stories take place. This is just as much the case for the plain of Troy in Homer's epic *Iliad* as for the Danish castle in Shakespeare's *Hamlet*. It holds equally true for the American South of Flannery O'Connor and William Faulkner and the Southwest of Leslie Marmon Silko or John Steinbeck's West. In the past decades American writers such as Dagoberto Gilb, William Kittredge, and Sylvia Watanabe have stressed the importance of place. As California novelist James D. Houston observes in "A Writer's Sense of Place," our literature "is rich with . . . stories wherein at least part of what's going on is some form of dialogue between a place—whether it be an island or a mountain or a city or a shoreline or a sub-region of the continent—and the lives being lived. . . ." What matters for North American writers in the present moment was also true for fiction writers from another place and time.

The West, I always say, is not the same country as the East. On the other hand, I think all writers or all artists really, if they're doing anything . . . are somehow their own region. They are making something that's absolutely unique and not like anyone else.
— Conversation with William Kittredge, available on video at www.mhhe.com/delbanco1e

The discovery of *craft*—the techniques that taken together engender a work—and its relation to *voice*—the way a story or poem or play sounds to our ear—allows even the novice writer to begin to make his or her mark on the page. This forms the essence of our vision and the central tenet of our text. Remembering where we began has made us better teachers, too, because, as most of you know, nothing helps an instructor help a student so much as firsthand knowledge of the place that student starts from. As writer-teachers, we hope to create an instructive method by which students can help themselves to become better writers. To that end, we, Nicholas Delbanco (pronounced delb-ah-nco) and Alan Cheuse (pronounced *choose*), wish professors and students alike good reading and good writing!

Nicholas Delbanco

Alan Cheuse

"I believe your anthology will be a godsend to students hoping to write better essays and a blessing to professors who are . . . teaching rhetoric."

—William C. Myers, University of Colorado at Colorado Springs

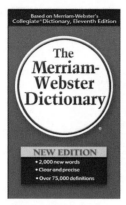 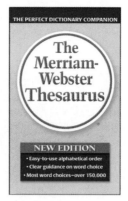 

ISBN: 0-07-310057-9   ISBN: 0-07-310057-9   ISBN: 0-07-310057-9

 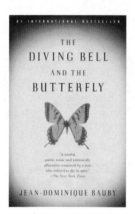  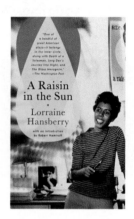

Ancillaries

Instructor Resources for Teaching Literature: Craft and Voice are available online and include an alternate thematic table of contents, sample syllabi, PowerPoints, quizzes (that students can take online), and support for teaching every selection and video associated with *Literature: Craft and Voice*. For students, we put our casebook sources online, to keep our book easy to carry and inviting (which both students and instructors asked for) and provide a reliable place for students to get started on their research. Additional student resources include an interactive tutorial for avoiding plagiarism and evaluating sources, plus resources for conducting research and formatting works cited pages. Blackboard cartridges are available for hybrid and online courses. Our online learning solutions support team can work with qualified adopters to adapt any of these materials to the learning management system at your institution.

Select trade titles and reference sources can be packaged at a discount with *Literature: Craft and Voice*. If you are interested in a dictionary, thesaurus, or any of the following titles, please contact your local McGraw-Hill representative or our Marketing Coordinator for English at English@McGraw-Hill.com.

TRADE TITLES FROM RANDOM HOUSE

Any paperback novel or work of nonfiction published by Random House can be packaged at a discount with *Literature: Craft and Voice*. Below are just a few suggestions. If the work you are looking for is not listed, please contact your McGraw-Hill representative!

Edward Abbey, *The Monkey Wrench Gang*
ISBN: 0-07-243424-4

Chinua Achebe, *Things Fall Apart*
ISBN: 0-07-243518-6

Sherman Alexie, *The Lone Ranger and Tonto Fistfight in Heaven*
ISBN: 0-07-243418-X

Louisa May Alcott, *Little Women*
ISBN: 0-07-724088-X

Maya Angelou, *I Know Why the Caged Bird Sings*
ISBN: 0-07-313592-5

Margaret Atwood, *The Handmaid's Tale*
ISBN: 0-07-724089-8

Jane Austen, *Pride and Prejudice*
ISBN: 0-07-724090-1

H. G. Bissinger, *Friday Night Lights*
ISBN: 0-07-285654-8

Charlotte Brontë, *Jane Eyre*
ISBN: 0-07-724091-X

Sandra Cisneros, *The House on Mango Street*
ISBN: 0-07-243517-8

Joseph Conrad, *Heart of Darkness*
ISBN: 0-07-243513-5

Annie Dillard, *Pilgrim at Tinker Creek*
ISBN: 0-07-243417-1

Buchi Emecheta, *Second-Class Citizen*
ISBN: 0-07-724084-7

Louise Erdrich, *Love Medicine*
ISBN: 0-07-243419-8

Laura Esquivel, *Like Water for Chocolate*
ISBN: 0-07-313589-5

Zora Neale Hurston, *Their Eyes Were Watching God*
ISBN: 0-07-243422-8

Peter Jenkins, *A Walk across America*
ISBN: 0-07-285657-2

Ha Jin, *Waiting*
ISBN: 0-07-313588-7

Jamaica Kincaid, *Lucy*
ISBN: 0-07-724081-2

Maxine Hong Kingston, *Woman Warrior*
ISBN: 0-07-243519-4

Jhumpa Lahiri, *The Namesake*
ISBN: 0-07-724082-0

N. Scott Momaday, *House Made of Dawn*
ISBN: 0-07-243420-1

Toni Morrison, *Beloved*
ISBN: 0-07-313591-7

Azar Nafasi, *Reading Lolita in Tehran*
ISBN: 0-07-313587-9

Jean Rhys, *Wide Sargasso Sea*
ISBN: 0-07-724085-5

Bapsi Sidhwa, *Cracking India*
ISBN: 0-07-724083-9

Art Spiegelman, *Maus,* Vol. 1
ISBN: 0-07-313593-3

Amy Tan, *Joy Luck Club*
ISBN: 0-07-243509-7

Edith Wharton, *The House of Mirth*
ISBN: 0-07-724094-4

E. B. White, *Essays of E. B. White*
ISBN: 0-07-243427-9

Zoë Wicomb, *Playing in the Light*
ISBN: 0-07-724086-3

Virginia Woolf, *Mrs. Dalloway*
ISBN: 0-07-724087-1

MODERN LIBRARY CLASSICS EDITIONS

William Blake, *Selected Poetry and Prose*
ISBN: 0-07-553661-7

James Boswell, *Life of Samuel Johnson*
ISBN: 0-07-553645-5

William Bradford, *Plymouth Plantation 1620-1647*
ISBN: 0-07-554281-1

Albert Camus, *The Plague*
ISBN: 0-07-553649-8

Kate Chopin, *The Awakening and Selected Stories*
ISBN: 0-07-554269-2

Stephen Crane, *The Red Badge of Courage*
ISBN: 0-07-555608-1

John Donne, *Poetry and Prose*
ISBN: 0-07-553663-3

Fyodor Dostoyevsky, *The Brothers Karamazov*
ISBN: 0-07-553575-0

Fyodor Dostoyevsky, *Crime and Punishment*
ISBN: 0-07-553574-2

Frederick Douglass, *Frederick Douglass: The Narrative and Selected Writings*
ISBN: 0-07-554375-3

John Dryden, *Selected Writings of Dryden*
ISBN: 0-07-553553-X

Ralph Waldo Emerson, *The Selected Writings*
ISBN: 0-07-554265-X

William Faulkner, *Absalom, Absalom!*
ISBN: 0-07-553657-9

William Faulkner, *Light in August*
ISBN: 0-07-553648-X

William Faulkner, *The Sound and the Fury*
ISBN: 0-07-553666-8

Gustav Flaubert, *Madame Bovary*
ISBN: 0-07-554378-8

Jacques Guicharnaud, *Seventeenth-Century French Drama*
ISBN: 0-07-553656-0

Allen G. Halline, *Six Modern American Plays*
ISBN: 0-07-553660-9

Alexander Hamilton, John Jay, and James Madison, *The Federalist*
ISBN: 0-07-553644-7

Nathaniel Hawthorne, *The Scarlet Letter and Selected Writings*
ISBN: 0-07-555475-5

Herodotus, *The Persian Wars*
ISBN: 0-07-553640-4

Washington Irving, *Selected Writings*
ISBN: 0-07-554394-X

Henry James, *The Portrait of a Lady*
ISBN: 0-07-553637-4

Roger Sherman Loomis, and Laura Hibbard Loomis, *Medieval Romances*
ISBN: 0-07-553650-1

John Milton, *Paradise Lost*
ISBN: 0-07-553668-4

Frederick Law Olmsted, *The Cotton Kingdom*
ISBN: 0-07-554413-X

Eugene O'Neill, *Later Plays of Eugene O'Neill*
ISBN: 0-07-553664-1

Edgar Allan Poe, *Selected Poetry and Prose*
ISBN: 0-07-553641-2

Marcel Proust, *Swann's Way*
ISBN: 0-07-553647-1

Ricardo Quintana, *Eighteenth-Century Plays*
ISBN: 0-07-553659-5

Jonathan Swift, *Gulliver's Travels*
ISBN: 0-07-553630-7

Henry David Thoreau, *Walden and Other Writings*
ISBN: 0-07-554267-6

Thucydides, *The Peloponnesian War*
ISBN: 0-07-554372-9

Alexis de Tocqueville, *Democracy in America*
ISBN: 0-07-554273-0

Leo Tolstoy, *Anna Karenina*
ISBN: 0-07-553632-3

Walt Whitman, *Leaves of Grass and Selected Prose*
ISBN: 0-07-554263-3

M. L. Wine, *Drama of the English Renaissance*
ISBN: 0-07-553569-6

William Wordsworth, *Selected Poetry*
ISBN: 0-07-553635-8

Acknowledgments

This book is, truly, a collective effort: no single person or pair of authors could have produced it alone. From the first to the final chapter, we have relied upon the work of others; our Table of Contents represents the essence of shared enterprise. The individual voices here became a kind of chorus, and our first debt of gratitude goes to the splendid writers (some of them anonymous) who produced the fiction and poetry and plays that *Literature: Craft and Voice* contains.

We have dedicated this book to our students. In addition to our own students, there were more than 4,000 others at 132 institutions across the country who participated in ethnographic research by letting us into their daily lives and discussing how they live and learn. We thank them for allowing us to observe them at work, at leisure, and in their place of study. To the thousands of young people across the country who participated in this ethnographic research, we thank you, and we extend a special thanks to the several students who gave up their time to provide detailed information and in some cases meet with us personally:

Danielle Crochiere, Colby College; Brittany Davis, University of Southern Mississippi; Alvin Flete, SUNY Stony Brook; Rosellen Flete, SUNY New Paltz; Jane Fountain, Central Piedmont Community College; Drew Henry, New York University; Nancy Kurien, Hunter College; Alex Limanowski, Roosevelt University; Alexandra Loizzo, Barnard College; Selena Poznak, Tulane University; Emily Rejouis, Cornell University; Josie Sayegh, University of California, Santa Cruz; Kaitlyn Taylor, University of Delaware; Liz Wechter, University of Illinois; Brian Yu, University of Michigan.

We also wish to express our gratitude to the professors, colleagues, and students who have contributed to *Literature: Craft and Voice.* Many professors took the time to let some book people from McGraw-Hill into their offices to discuss their challenges with this course. The surveys that emerged from these interviews helped us create a new pedagogical program that we hope these friends recognize as emerging from their thoughtful comments about teaching today.

Heidi Ajrami, Victoria College
Norma Akins, Heart of Georgia Technical College
Frank Albert, Community College of Beaver County
Deborah Albritton, Jefferson Davis Community College–Brewton
Michael Alleman, Louisiana State University–Eunice
Michael Allen, North Central State College
Stephanie Almagno, Piedmont College
Maribeth Anderson, Ivy Tech Community College of Indiana
Helane Androne, Miami University–Middletown
Judith Angona, Ocean County College
Sonia Apgar Begert, Olympic College
Sue Apshaga, Community College of Rhode Island
Saye Atkinson, Georgia Military College
Les Bailey, Saint Martin's University
Ronda Bailey, Fort Scott Community College
Eileen Baland, East Texas Baptist University
John Balcer, Shenandoah University
Allison Bartlett, Wor-Wic Community College

Kathleen Bartlett, Florida Institute of Technology
Jonathan Barz, University of Dubuque
Janice Baskin, Azusa Pacific University
Lynne Belcher, Southern Arkansas University
John Bennett, Lake Land College
Bill Berry, Cape Cod Community College
Ken Bishop, Itawamba Community College
Mark Blaauw-hara, North Central Michigan College
Lawrence Blasco, Wor-Wic Community College
Laura Bloxham, Whitworth University
Paula Bolduc, Salve Regina University
Laurel Bollinger, University of Alabama–Huntsville
Ellen Boose, Bossier Parish Community College
Troy Boucher, Southwestern College
Michelle Bowie, Southern Nazarene University
David Breith, University of the Southwest
Jason Brown, Herkimer County Community College
Kristin Brunnemer, Pierce College
Mitzi Brunsdale, Mayville State University
Laurie Buchanan, Clark State Community College

Dawn Buckey, Charleston Southern University
Suzanne Bufamanti, Niagara County Community College
Dottie Burkhart, Davidson County Community College
Kelly Ann Butterbaugh, Lehigh Carbon Community College
Dona Cady, Middlesex Community College
Mechel Camp, Jackson State Community College
Sarah Canfield-Fuller, Shenandoah University
Robert Canipe, Catawba Valley Community College
Joan Canty, Columbia College
Judith Cavanaugh, Clinton Community College
Sean Cavanaugh, Assumption College
Marlys Cervantes, Cowley County Community College
Diane Chambers, Malone University
Windy Charles, Piedmont College
Maria Chiancola, Salve Regina University
Bill Church, Missouri Western State University
Lori Cinotte, Illinois Valley Community College
Stacy Clanton, Southern Arkansas University
Pam Clark, Frederick Community College
Jessica Cobbs, Bossier Parish Community College
Stanly Coberly, West Virginia University–Parkersburg
Michael Cocchiarale, Widener University
Rose Collins, Dallas Baptist University
Jim Compton, Muscatine Community College
Nancy Corbett, Maysville Community and Technical College
Jean Crockett, Cleveland State Community College
Sarah Dangelantonio, Franklin Pierce University
Judy Daniel, McMurry University
Cherie Dargan, Hawkeye Community College
Rebecca Dark, Dallas Baptist University
Bonita Dattner-Garza, St. Mary's University
Daniel de Roulet, Vanguard University
Laurie Delaney, Kent State University–Stark Campus
Mikee Delony, Abilene Christian University
Louise DeSantis Deutsch, Cape Cod Community College
Anna Crowe Dewart, College of Coastal Georgia
Betty Dobry, Redlands Community College
Scott Douglass, Chattanooga State Technical Community College
Lisa Dresdner, Norwalk Community College
Marilyn Durham, University of Wisconsin–Whitewater
Linda Eicken, Cape Fear Community College
Margaret Ellington, Georgia Southwestern State University
Scott Emmert, University of Wisconsin–Fox Valley
Joseph Ervin, Rend Lake College
Cassandra Falke, East Texas Baptist University
Tyler Farrell, University of Dubuque
William Feeler, Midland College
Sandy Feinstein, Penn State Berks
Maribeth Fell, College of Coastal Georgia
Robin Field, King's College
Jim Fisher, Peninsula College
Michael Flaherty, Triton College

Joey Flamm-Costello, Reading Area Community College
Juliene Forrestal, Olivet Nazarene University
Chriss Foster, San Francisco State University
Deborah Fox, Matanuska-Susitna College
Holly French, Bossier Parish Community College
Julie Fulbright, Cleveland State Community College
Robert Furstoss, Ocean County College
Joanne Gabel, Reading Area Community College
Naomi Gal, Moravian College
Xiongya Gao, Southern University at New Orleans
Maryanne Garbowsky, County College of Morris
Jennifer Garlen, University of Alabama in Huntsville
Vicki Garton, Crowder Community College–Nevada
Tony Giffone, Farmingdale State College
Wayne Gilbert, Community College of Aurora
Michelle Gompf, Concord University
Ron Goulet, Northland Pioneer College
Judith Griffith, Wartburg College
Brian Hale, Chattanooga State Technical Community College
Gary Hall, Victoria College
Carol Harding, Western Oregon University
Simon Hay, Connecticut College
Hunter Hayes, Texas A&M University–Commerce
Catherine Heath, Victoria College
Michael Helfin, Cape Cod University
Sue Henderson, East Central College
Marylou Horn, Middlesex Community College
Dianne Hunter, Trinity College
Deborah Hysell, North Central State College
Adriane Ivey, Oxford College of Emory University
Joanne Jacobs, Shenandoah University
John Jacobs, Shenandoah University
Kathleen Jacquette, Farmingdale State College
Kelli Johnson, Miami University–Hamilton
Dean Karpowicz, University of Wisconsin–Parkside
Robert Kellerman, University of Maine at Augusta
Tim Kelley, Northwest-Shoals Community College
Nora Kindley, Ulster Community College
Mark King, Gordon College
Bette Kirschstein, Pace University
Deborah Klein, Truman State University
John Krafft, Miami University–Hamilton
Theresa Kulbaga, Miami University–Hamilton
Celena Kusch, University of South Carolina Upstate
James Lake, Louisiana State University in Shreveport
Dana Lauro, Ocean County College
David Leigh, Seattle University
Bruce Litte, Northwest Missouri State University
Keming Liu, Medgar Evers College
Megan Lloyd, King's College
Deborah Luoma, Gavilan Community College
Brent Lynn, Wayland Baptist University
Robert Mahon, East Central University
Kathleen Maloney, St. Mary's University
Kelli Maloy, University of Pittsburgh at Greensburg

Beulah Manuel, Columbia Union College
Michael Martin, University of Wisconsin
Cindy McClenagan, Wayland Baptist University
Jeannine McDevitt, Pennsylvania Highlands Community College
Kathleen McDonald, Norwich University
Amy Minervini-Dodson, Arizona Western College
Brooke Mitchell, Wingate University
Kelly Moffett, Kentucky Wesleyan College
D'Juana Montgomery, Southwestern Assemblies of God University
Margaret Morlier, Reinhardt College
David Murdoch, Gadsden State Community College
Josephine Neill-Browning, Holmes Community College
Jeff Nelson, University of Alabama in Huntsville
Ode Ogede, North Carolina Central University
Michael Olendzenski, Cape Cod Community College
Salisa Olmstead, Lake Land College
Kim Overcash, Central Carolina Community College
Renelda Owen, Delta State University
Allison Palumbo, Elizabethtown Community and Technical College
Jeff Patridge, Capital Community College
Michelle Paulsen, Victoria College
Jared Pearce, William Penn University
Shannon Phillips, Lake Land College
Meenakshi Ponnoswami, Bucknell University
Nancy Popkin, Harris-Stowe State University
David Pulling, Louisiana State University–Eunice
Ken Raines, Eastern Arizona College
Wilbur Reames, Erskine College
Shirley Rehberg, Lake City Community College
Margaret Reimer, University of Southern Maine
Chauncey Ridley, Sacramento State University
Nancy Risch, Florence Darlington Technical College
Jason Roberts, Sierra College
Mary Rogerson, West Liberty State College
Patricia Roy, Mount Ida College
Jill Rubinson, University of Maine at Augusta
Wolfgang Runzi, Rogue Community College
Christine Ryan, Middlesex Community College

Elizabeth Sachs, Niagara County Community College
Joe Sarnowski, San Diego Christian College
Jane Schreck, Bismarck State College
Tracy Schrems, St. Bonaventure University
Jolly Sharp, University of the Cumberlands
Maggie Shear, South Suburban College
Deepa Sitaraman, Shawnee State University
Amy Smith, Hilbert College
Matt Smith, University of St. Francis
Amos St. Germain, Wentworth Institute of Technology
Gabriele Stauf, Georgia Southwestern State University
Michael Steven, Wayland Baptist University
Bill Stifler, Chattanooga State Technical Community College
Ron Stormer, Culver-Stockton College
Monnette Sturgill, Big Sandy Community and Technical College
Richard Swanson, University of Wisconsin–Stout
Nannette Tamer, Stevenson University
Richard Terdiman, University of California–Santa Cruz
Jennifer Thompson, Saint Xavier University
Alan Trusky, Florence-Darlington Technical College
Randal Urwiller, Texas College
Scott Vander Ploeg, Madisonville Community College
Leila Wells, Griffin Technical College
Eleanor Welsh, Chesapeake College
Cynthia Wesson, Cowley County Community College
Jeana West, Murray State College
Patricia White, Norwich University
Edward Whitelock, Gordon College
Brenda Williams, University of New Haven
Mary Williams, Midland College
Daniel Wolkow, Eastern New Mexico University–Roswell
Whitney Womack Smith, Miami University–Hamilton
Jane Wood, Park University
P. J. Yongbloed, Springfield Technical Community College
Adam Young, Middle Georgia College
Sarah Young, Baker University
J. B. Zwilling, Allen Community College

In addition, over 175 professors from 113 institutions provided their responses about design, selections, and content by way of WebEx, symposia, focus groups, phone interviews, design surveys, and detailed manuscript reviews. A special thanks to our students Margaret Dean and Valerie Laken, and especially Elizabeth Eshelman, Nicholas Harp, and Anne Stameshkin, who, with Professors Santi Buscemi (Middlesex County College) and Chris Thaiss (University of California, Davis), contributed importantly to the shape and sense of our handbook for writing from reading as well as to the other sections on fiction, poetry, and drama in this book. Tom Kitts (St. John's University) not only reviewed our text but deserves special recognition here for his herculean service to our resources for teaching. We can safely say that every page of this volume has been guided by at least a dozen people dedicated to education and to literature. And for that, to all of you, we offer our sincerest thanks.

Emory Reginald Abbott, Georgia Perimeter College
Kirk Adams, Tarrant Community College
Donna Allego, Gwynedd-Mercy College
Francesco Ancona, Sussex County Community College
Brian Anderson, Central Piedmont Community College
Peter Auski, University of Western Ontario
Beverly Bailey, Seminole Community College
Cynthia Baker-Schverak, Brevard Community College
Elizabeth Barnes, Daytona Beach Community College
Jim Baskin, Joliet Junior College
Amy Beaudry, Quinsigamond Community College
Valerie Belew, Nashville State Community College
Cole Bennett, Abilene Christian University
Randy Blankenship, Valencia Community College
Ethel Bonds, Virginia Western Community College
Debbie Borchers, Pueblo Community College
Patricia Bostian, Central Piedmont Community College
Linda Bow, Blinn College
Steve Brahlek, Palm Beach Community College–Lake Worth
Tamara Brattoli, Joliet Junior College
Joe Bryan, El Paso Community College
JoAnne Bryant, Troy University–Montgomery Campus
Donna Campbell, Washington State University
Patricia Campbell, Lake Sumter Community College
Carlos Campo, College of Southern Nevada
Kathy Carlson, Brevard Community College
Rosa Maria Chacon, California State University, Northridge
Lisbeth Chapin, Gwynedd-Mercy College
April Childress, Greenville Technical College
Kathleen Chrismon, Northeastern Oklahoma A&M University
John Cole, Community College of Rhode Island–Flanagan
Susan Constantine, Keystone College
Linda Cook, Sam Houston State University
Susan Dauer, Valencia Community College
Curtis Derrick, Midlands Technical College
Jason Dew, Georgia Perimeter College
Jennifer Diamond, Bucks County College

Joshua Dickinson, Jefferson Community College
Charles Dielman, Erie Community College
Regina Dilgen, Palm Beach Community College–Lake Worth
Scott Douglass, Chattanooga State Technical Community College
Caroline Dreyer, Pensacola Junior College
Leigh Anne Duck, University of Memphis
Jennifer Duncan, Chattanooga State Community College
Mildred Duprey-Smith, College of Southern Nevada
Heather Elko, Brevard Community College
John Esperian, College of Southern Nevada
Renee Field, Moberly Area Community College
John Freeman, El Paso Community College
Muriel Fuqua, Daytona Beach Community College
Fernando Ganivet, Florida International University
Stephen Gardner, University of South Carolina–Aiken
Richard Gaspar, Hillsboro Community College
Michael Gavin, Prince George's Community College
Joanna Gibson, Texas A&M University
Janine Gilbert, Brigham Young University–Idaho
Kimberly Greenfield, Lorain County Community College
Ross Gresham, U.S. Air Force Academy
Loren Gruber, Missouri Valley College
Frank Gunshanan, Daytona Beach Community College
Grace Haddox, El Paso Community College
Jill Hampton, University of South Carolina–Aiken
Holly Hassel, University of Wisconsin–Marathon County
Levia Hayes, College of Southern Nevada
Joel Henderson, Chattanooga State Community College
Deana Holifield, Pearl River Community College
Matthew Horton, Gainesville State College
Christine Hubbard, Tarrant County Community College
Mary Huffer, Lake Sumter Community College
Rob Hurd, Anne Arundel Community College
Heidi Johnsen, La Guardia Community College
Ken Johnson, Georgia Perimeter College
Theodore Johnston, El Paso Community College
Pamela Kannady, Tulsa Community College–Metro Campus

Barbara Kenney, Texas State Technical College
Nancy Kersell, Northern Kentucky University
Elizabeth Kessler, University of Houston
Rachel Key, East Central University
James Kirkpatrick, Central Piedmont Community College
Tom Kitts, St. John's University
Elaine Kromhout, Indian River Community College
Joseph Kronick, Louisiana State University
Kris Kurrus, Spokane Falls Community College
Angela Laflen, Marist College
James Lake, Louisiana State University
Ilona Law, University of South Carolina–Aiken
Kristin Le Veness, Nassau Community College
Sandy Longhorn, Pulaski Technical College
Joe Lostracco, Austin Community College
Cecilia Macheski, La Guardia Community College
Angela Macri, Pulaski Technical College
Al Maginnes, Wake Technical Community College
Tammy Mata, Tarrant County College
Virgin Mathes, University of New Mexico
Michael Matthews, Central Texas College
Beth Maxfield, Henderson State University
Laura McBride, College of Southern Nevada
Nicole McDaniel, Texas A&M University
Denise McNelly, Old Dominion University
Agnetta Mendoza, Nashville State Community College
Shellie Michael, Volunteer State Community College
Lawrence Milbourn, El Paso Community College
Dorothy Minor, Tulsa Community College–Metro Campus
David Mirchman, Moorpark College
Deborah Montuori, Shippensburg University
Cleatta Morris, Louisiana State University
Jake Morris, Louisiana State University, Shreveport
Kevin Morris, Greenville Technical College
Paul Munn, Saginaw Valley State University
William Myers, University of Colorado
Michelle Navarro, Dallas County Community College
Louise Nayer, City College of San Francisco
Jennifer Nelson, College of Southern Nevada
Shirley Nelson, Chattanooga State Community College
Andrea Neptune, Sierra College
Sally Nielsen, Florida Community College–Jacksonville
Cheryl Nixon, University of Massachusetts
Troy Nordman, Butler Community College
Claire O'Donoghue, St. John's University
Jay O'Leary, Santa Fe Community College
Ben Olguin, University of Texas at San Antonio
Danel Olsen, North Harris College
Thomas O'Neal, St. Johns River Community College
John Padgett, Brevard Community College
Neil Placky, Broward Community College
H. F. Poehlmann, Blinn College

Doranne Polcrack, Kutztown University
Tony Procell, El Paso Community College
Roberta Proctor, Palm Beach Community College–Lake Worth
Jessica Rabin, Anne Arundel Community College
Mary Anne Reiss, Elizabethtown Community and Technical College
Dana Resente, Montgomery County Community College
Elizabeth Rich, Saginaw Valley State University
Nandi Riley, Florida A&M University
Lou Ethel Roliston, Bergen Community College
Valerie Russell, Valencia Community College
Robert Saba, Florida International University
Mark Sanders, Lewis and Clark State College
John Schaffer, Blinn College
Ann Shillinglaw, Moraine Valley Community College
Ronald Shumaker, University of New Mexico
Gerald Siegel, York College
Mary Simpson, Dominican University
Donald Skinner, Indian River Community College
Patrick Slattery, University of Arkansas–Fayetteville
Beverly Slaughter, Brevard Community College
Derek Soles, Drexel University
Jean Sorensen, Grayson Community College
Anne Spurlock, Mississippi State University
Joyce Steelman, Catawba Valley Community College
Greg Stone, Tulsa Community College–Metro Campus
Victor Strandberg, Duke University
Beverly Stroud, Greenville Technical College
Richard Taylor, East Carolina University
Patricia Teel, Victor Valley College
Tracy Teel, California State University–Northridge
Matthew Teutsch, University of Louisiana, Monroe
Amber Flora Thomas, University of Alaska, Fairbanks
Anne-Marie Thomas, Austin Community College
Andrew Tomko, Bergen Community College
Pauline Uchmanowicz, SUNY–New Paltz
Carla Walker, St. Louis Community College
Brad Waltman, College of Southern Nevada
Carol Warren, Georgia Perimeter College
Linda Weeks, Dyersburg State Community College
Bridgette Weir, Nashville State Community College
Bart Welling, University of North Florida
Eleanor Welsh, Chesapeake College
Marian Wernicke, Pensacola Junior College
Sharon Wilson, University of Northern Colorado
Julie Wishart, Butler Community College
Jane Wood, Park University
Daphne Young, College of Southern Nevada
Robyn Younkin, Community College of Rhode Island
John Ziebell, College of Southern Nevada

The video interviews themselves were a labor of love for all those who participated—those interviewed were brought on board by their own deep love of students, writing, and literature. These conversations are as lively and varied and richly engaging as the work of the writers that we've included to represent them in *Literature: Craft and Voice*. Here we want to also add our sincerest thanks for the advice of our board of video advisors, many of whom provided their insight on other aspects of the project as well. These professors from across the country worked with our project for several months to guide the way for its use as part of an effective learning experience.

Paul Andrews, St. Johns River Community College

Christian Clark, College of Southern Nevada–Las Vegas

Chad Hammett, Texas State University

Ruth McAdams, Tarrant County College

Louise McKinney, Georgia Perimeter College–Dunwoody

Roxanne Munch, Joliet Junior College

Deborah Prickett, Jacksonville State University

Linda Smith, Midlands Technical College

Kathy Sanchez, Lone Star College–Tomball

Donna Thomsen, Johnson & Wales University

We are deeply grateful to McGraw-Hill for its many contributions to the development of this new learning program. In particular, we thank Paul Banks (our expert media maven), Betty Chen, David Chodoff, Josh Feldman, Susan Gouijnstook, Meredith Grant, Susan Messer, Andrea Pasquarelli (who took over for Paul Banks midstream and who made sure our videos were nipped and tucked into final shape), Lisa Pinto, and Karen Smith. This list is alphabetical, but Steev Sachs (arigatoo) deserves special mention and to be singled out; for the last weeks and months he seems to have been working twenty-five-hour days. Brian Jones was more than Executive Producer for our media project; he played cameraman, coach, and set designer on more than one occasion, and we were sorry to see him go, but we were also delighted to welcome Aoife Dempsey, Vice President of Digital. Jay Chakrapani, Vice President of Product Development, from the media group also brought information to the table for delivering media to students. The media program at McGraw-Hill has worked hand in hand with the editorial staff to bring out a new kind of program for teaching and learning in composition courses. Thanks also to Patrick Murphy of the University of Michigan for a pair of video interviews and to Laurence Goldstein of MQR and John Darnton of *The New York Times* for assistance with procuring the interviews of Arthur Miller and Edward Albee respectively. For tireless negotiation to make sure our book's permissions came in on budget and just in time to send our pages off to press, we thank the brilliantly efficient and professional Virginia Creeden.

We've had a special opportunity to spend time with many in the marketing and sales group, including the driving force of Suzanne Guinn, Director of Market Development; Allison Jones, Executive Marketing Manager; and Sharon Loeb, Director of Marketing. These muses brought in our sales champions Cristy Acosta, Hector Alvero, Colleen Balco, Jen Edwards, Carolyn Ghazi-Tehrani, Courtney Jones, Matt Parks, and Jack Powers: enthusiasts from the field who took their excitement back to their sales colleagues. With Simon Heathcote's excellent creative direction we looked without blinking at the camera when it came our turn to talk directly into its eye. Some of our field publishers have seen this project through from beginning to end. Byron Hopkins was there at our initial lunch, quoting poetry and wondering if this project would ever come to fruition. Our Senior Field Publisher, Ray Kelley, came to our speeches and sat in on several of our interviews. We met others along the way such as the superreader Barbara Siry and the avid promoter Paula Radosevich; in California, Brian Gore brought his San Francisco style and love of all things literary and musical to support of our project. Jen Nelson, marketing coordinator, has been there on email, at our dress rehearsal, and throughout the marketing effort with good cheer and hard work to keep our marketing efforts running smoothly. Thank you, all.

We've saved for our penultimate note of thanks to McGraw-Hill a special thanks to those who've designed our book. Jeanne Schreiber, Creative Director, brought her tremendous design talent to the look of a new generation of textbooks—along with the midnight oil of many others in the editorial, design, and production group, especially Terri Schiesl, Vice President, Editing, Design, and Production; Leslie LaDow, Senior Production Editor; Nora Agbayani, Photo Research Coordinator; Preston Thomas, Design Manager; and Susan Norton, Copy Editor.

This book would not have come into existence had it not been for Steve Debow, President of Humanities and Social Sciences for McGraw-Hill Higher Education, and Michael Ryan, Editor-in-Chief for the Humanities and Social Sciences. Both lent their ears and time and drive to *Literature: Craft and Voice,* bringing McGraw-Hill's extensive resources to bear on innovation and learning in the twenty-first century.

And finally, our great gratitude to Lisa Moore, our editor and publisher, from whom we learned that writing a textbook is at least as difficult—and as rewarding—as writing novels. Lisa was the first to suggest this project, its tireless supervisor, enthusiastic sponsor, and pitch-perfect voice of experience; without her devotion to detail and eye for quality control we could neither be as proud of nor as pleased with the result.

The authors would like to register their gratitude to their respective agents, Gail Hochman, of Hochman and Brandt, and Timothy Seldes, of Russell & Volkening; they have been careful stewards from the first. Nicholas Delbanco would like to thank the Institute for the Humanities at the University of Michigan (and its director, Daniel Herwitz) for safe haven at this project's start, and Alan Cheuse is grateful to George Mason University for a leave of absence that helped bring it to completion. From the very beginning of this shared enterprise, through the many years of composition and labor, we have had the great good luck of being married to two close critics indeed. Elena Delbanco and Kristin O'Shee were indispensable to this endeavor, as they have long been to our lives; all thanks to each and both of them for everything they do and everything they are.

Foreword to the Student

LITERATURE REWARDS CLOSE READING

There's an important difference between life and art. You only live once. But you can turn and return to the best stories, poems, and plays; the great ones continue to live. So even if they were created in the sixth or the sixteenth century, you learn from the mistakes of characters you read about, revel in their pleasures, and grieve at their dismay. And as you spend time with them, you discover explanations for your own behavior as well.

There are other advantages to making literature a jumping-off point for the college experience. Any work of literature is a complex text. Reading it closely—carefully, analytically, within its own context and tradition—may seem strange at first. Yet it's like learning how to break down and rebuild an automobile engine or construct a defense in football or dance the tango or prepare a meal; you need to study the turns and twists of these various activities.

And there's a difference here too. Unlike taking the controls of an airplane, or performing surgery before you're fully trained, you can read a story and take control of it without doing damage to yourself or someone else in the process. There's reason to hope that you will understand great fiction or poetry or drama in a better and deeper way each time you read it again. By *understanding* we mean *learning* about how works are made up out of language that's carefully crafted and shaped. And learning about the way the characters think and feel. And learning about the world in which they find themselves. In other words, you can acquire all those things that lend depth and breadth to your own sense of life.

READING PREPARES YOU FOR WRITING

So our first article of faith is that *literature rewards close reading*. And as professional writers of many years' experience, we can testify to this book's second article of faith: *reading prepares you for writing*. The ability to read closely and to write clearly about what you've read has practical value; these skills will help you in your other courses as well.

Repeated application—practice—is the key. In sports you know how important it is to practice. If you play a musical instrument, you know you have to practice. If you perform as a singer or actor or work as a salesman or auto mechanic, you know how critical it is to have been taught and, month after month, to rehearse what you do. All these activities have their techniques and depend upon instruction.

Reading literature will help you to think in new and different and powerful ways; writing about it will help you express what you think. It will help you to know yourself and make yourself known to others. Your success in college will depend on your ability to write well, and the better reader you train yourself to be the better you prepare yourself to become a better writer. (Notice, for example, how the previous sentence uses the same word three times; does the repeated "better" seem like a good idea?) It is not easy to read well. It is not easy to write well. But the process does grow simpler when works have been selected to provide a rich introduction to these critical components of your college life.

A FEW FEATURES OF *LITERATURE: CRAFT AND VOICE*

Our Selection of Fiction, Poetry, and Drama

We looked for works you'd enjoy reading as much as your teacher would enjoy teaching. Poetry about love (Pablo Neruda's "Do Not Love You Except Because I Love You") or happiness (Jane Kenyon's "The Suitor"), or grief (Marie Howe's "What the Living Do"). Plays about quick anger and tragic fate (from Sophocles' *Oedipus the King* to Arthur Miller's *Death of a Salesman*). A wide range of fiction from the novella nightmare of Franz Kafka's "The Metamorphosis" to young writers like Chimamanda Ngozi Adichie reporting on a prison cell in Africa, even fiction and film in a section on adaptations of the ancient Beowulf story. We wanted to show you literature at its best, both classic and new. A glance at our table of contents will show you how much we include. But the works here—no matter how numerous and various—have one thing in common: we believe them worth sustained attention on your part. You might not like everything you read, but we'd wager you'll find some that you won't be able to stop thinking about. The professional secret we'll whisper and shout is that reading and writing are fun.

Media Brings Writers to Reading and Readers to Writing

The living, breathing presence of many of the authors we've included in this book is another way we wanted to bring you the full experience of reading literature. For one thing, our accompanying videos should help dispel the notion that all art is deathly dull and was produced by the honored dead. These writers were interviewed exclusively for this book. They prepared for their interviews by thinking about what they wanted to say directly to you. Our authors come in all sizes, ages, shapes, backgrounds. Pulitzer Prize winners, National Book Award winners, PEN/Faulkner Award winners, and Poet Laureates joined us in this endeavor. What they have in common is they wanted to tell you why they love to read, to talk about their trials in coming to love reading, and to reveal how their own writing process might be akin to yours. As has been famously said, every writer is a beginner; we all of us begin again each time we go to the desk.

Designed for Reading

You'll see straightaway that this book doesn't look like other books. We know we live in a visual world. We know that unless you think you might one day be an English major, you're not likely to enjoy page after page of unbroken text, no matter how vivid the pictures the words make in your mind. Literature is not boring, so why should the design not be an invitation to enjoy reading?

We also could have made a thick book, a heavy one, one you would lift or open out of duty not desire. Your teacher tells you to turn to page 7 or 700 or 1700, and you groan and ask yourself why. Those books are doorstops and who knows what your chiropractor would say about your carrying them around. The easier it is to toss your book into your backpack, the more likely it is for you to find that spare moment to read. We wanted this exercise to be a little lighter; it is your intellectual muscles that should be the ones to grow strong.

WHAT'S IN A NAME?

A last word about unusual names: If you have ever listened to National Public Radio, you may already know how to pronounce Alan Cheuse. If not, we invite you to listen to "the voice of books," and we also give you the correct pronunciation here: *Cheuse* sounds like *shoes* and rhymes with *booze* and *choose.* Nicholas Delbanco is quite used to hearing his last name mispronounced; it's *Delb-ah-nco,* as if you're preparing to sneeze. But both of us care less about the way you say our names than that you read these pages (sometimes out loud) and find the kind of pleasure in taking them apart that we ourselves took in putting them together. We wish you great fun and good luck.

Nicholas Delbanco

Alan Cheuse

Literature Fiction

1 Reading a Story for its Elements

THE store's pretty empty, it being Thursday afternoon, so there was nothing much to do except lean on the register and wait for the girls to show up again. The whole store was like a pinball machine and I didn't know which tunnel they'd come out of. After a while they come around out of the far aisle, around the lightbulbs, records at discount of the Caribbean Six or Tony Martin Sings or some such gunk you wonder they waste the wax on, six-packs of candy bars, and plastic toys done up in cellophane that fall apart when a kid looks at them anyway. Around they come, Queenie still leading the way, and holding a little gray jar in her hand. Slots Three through Seven are unmanned and I could see her wondering between Stokes and me, but Stokesie with his usual luck draws an old party in baggy gray pants who stumbles up with four giant cans of pineapple juice (what do these bums do with all that pineapple juice? I've often asked myself) so the girls come to me. Queenie puts down the jar and I take it into my fingers icy cold.

—from "A&P" by John Updike

A FIRST READING

Most of us read *casually* most of the time, not worrying too much about the way the piece—whether fiction or nonfiction—is put together. The first time we read something is one of the most fruitful times. When you first are exposed to a good story, you experience the pleasure of surprise, because the fiction writer has used a sophisticated grasp of technique to create a fresh impression—permitting you to see and feel and recognize something new. Sometimes that first experience will be a physical sensation like those "icy cold" fingers on the jar in the last sentence of the excerpt from "A&P." Sometimes that experience will be something more complex, like the jaded anticipation of the narrator at the cash register as he or she (we don't yet know which) follows the movements of customers at the A&P. You will probably have a gut feeling about the characters and what happens to them. You may feel sympathy with or confusion at the character's thoughts or actions. You may enjoy the tale's beautiful language or find the dialogue between characters amusing. But *why* do you have these responses?

A CRITICAL READING

A writer creates a story out of material he or she has observed in the world and from incidents or feelings in his or her own life. But the result will not hold up well if the writer lacks a firm grasp of the **craft,** or conscious artistry, of fiction. As a noun, craft refers to the elements that comprise a story; as a verb, craft refers to the process of making or fashioning a story out of those elements. When authors write fiction, what they think they know—or believe or dream about or feel—needs to be made clear to others, and that process of transmission requires skill. Among the major elements of the craft of fiction are the following:

- **plot**—the sequence of events in a story (see chapter 4)
- **character**—the depiction of human beings (and nonhumans) within the story (see chapter 5)
- **setting**—when and where a story takes place (see chapter 6)
- **point of view**—who tells the story (see chapter 7)
- **language, tone, and style**—the elements that conjure a story's particular flavor and voice, as achieved because of the words the author chooses and the rhythm with which he or she puts the words together (see chapter 8)
- **theme**—the large meanings and connections explored in a piece of writing. Theme is what a story is "about" beyond the specific characters and events of the story (see chapter 9)
- **symbol**—an object or an event that transcends literal interpretation. A symbol works by using a particular object or event to represent something larger than the object or event itself (see chapter 10)

None of these elements operates in isolation, of course, but focusing on one in each chapter will allow us—as readers and writers—a particular "way in" or way of seeing how the story functions as a whole. By reading deeply and examining not just the obvious content of a story but also its context and form, its craft and voice, you can see beyond the story's surface, beyond merely "what" is happening.

This kind of critical reading begins when you actively engage with the story. As you read a story, mark it up with questions, ideas, and comments. Underline phrases and sentences you admire. Does the main character in a story seem to contradict himself? Does the author suddenly flash forward twenty years on page 2? Ask yourself why. If an author uses the word "idled" instead of "paused," circle the word and ask yourself why she made that choice. If an author titles a story "Would You Please Be Quiet, Please?" ask why he chooses to repeat the word "please." In other words, by formulating questions when you read, you can begin to grasp the techniques that make powerful expression possible.

"The reading habit and the love of books physically, this particular package of words, the smell of the glue, the look of the print, was all that mattered to me to the point that I thought it would be wonderful to create such objects."

Conversation with John Updike, available on video at www.mhhe .com/delbanco1e

CONTINUED ON PAGE 9

Q & A
A Conversation on Writing

John Updike

Writing and the Visual Arts

The pictorial and the verbal are similar in that they both take place in two dimensions on paper or canvas. . . . Drawing was a part of the gentleman's equipment, in fact, in the nineteenth century, just like operating a camera is for a twentieth-century person. . . . Hand-writing is itself a kind of drawing and the letters are in a way visual objects. . . . I wanted to be a cartoonist but I fairly slowly saw that there were others more gifted than I at drawing [, so] I contented myself with being a writer in the theory that in a way you . . . draw with words when you write.

Reading "A&P"

As I read those two paragraphs things come back to me that I'm tempted to share. One was the line "with a good tan and a sweet, soft, broad looking can." Some of the publishers who had to deal with this story in an anthology had great trouble with that *can*. . . . If they wanted to put it in there they should put it all in and let the kids get the shock of the word *can* in print. . . . The parenthetical thought, "Do you really think it's a mind in there or just a little buzz like a bee in a glass jar?" I think has served as the start of a lot of classroom discussions. But to me it seemed true of Sammy's worldview. Your job as a writer of fiction is not to present an ideal world but to try to present the world that you see and hear around you.

Born in Reading, Pennsylvania, John Updike (1932–2009) began writing at a young age; his mother suggested it might cure him of a stammer. By the time of his death from lung cancer, at the age of seventy-six, he had become one of America's most celebrated authors, with abundant honors and a wide-spread readership. He published over fifty titles of fiction, nonfiction, and poetry—including two volumes of art criticism and several children's books. Updike began his career writing "Talk of the Town" pieces for *The New Yorker,* the magazine where his first published story appeared—and where his stories, essays, and book reviews are published to this day. Much (but not all) of Updike's fiction concerns the conflicts—internal and external—among middle-class Protestants in the American Northeast. He is most famous for his "Rabbit" quartet; these four novels follow an ex–basketball player named Harry "Rabbit" Angstrom, who struggles with the lack of fulfillment he feels in the presence of—and when deprived of—his family. (Those novels are, in order of publication, *Rabbit, Run; Rabbit Redux; Rabbit Is Rich;* and *Rabbit at Rest*—notice the pattern of repeated "R"s.) While some of Updike's characters do reprehensible or embarrassing things, the author manages to elicit our sympathy for them. He convinces us, even in the short space of a story, that his characters live and breathe in the American landscape—and that their problems are similar to ours. A number of Updike's short stories, including "A&P" (1961), are considered classic examples of the form.

To watch this entire interview and hear the author read from "A&P," go to **www.mhhe.com/delbanco1e.**

RESEARCH ASSIGNMENT: In his interview, Updike talks about how he originally wrote several more scenes in this story—Sammy leaving the A&P, then going to the beach in order to look for the girls. But his editor at *The New Yorker,* William Maxwell, convinced him that the story should end where it does—thereby preserving the "unities" of time, place, and action. Which would you prefer—the ending as it is, suggesting a continuation of life lived off the page, or the kind of strong resolution the author originally planned? Explain your answer.

AS YOU READ   As you read "A&P," consider who is telling the story and how you feel about this storyteller. Would you want this person for a friend? Why or why not? Does the outcome of this story surprise you? What outcome might you have predicted?

A&P (1961)

1 IN walks these three girls in nothing but bathing suits. I'm in the second checkout slot, with my back to the door, so I don't see them until they're over by the bread. The one that caught my eye first was the one in the plaid green two-piece. She was a chunky kid, with a good tan and a sweet broad soft-looking can with those two crescents of white just under it, where the sun never seems to hit, at the top of the backs of her legs. I stood there with my hand on a box of Hi Ho crackers trying to remember if I rang it up or not. I ring it up again and the customer starts giving me hell. She's one of these cash-register-watchers, a witch about fifty with rouge on her cheekbones and no eyebrows, and I know it made her day to trip me up. She'd been watching cash registers for fifty years and probably never seen a mistake before.

2 By the time I got her feathers smoothed and her goodies into a bag—she gives me a little snort in passing, if she'd been born at the right time they would have burned her over in Salem—by the time I get her on her way the girls had circled around the bread and were coming back, without a pushcart, back my way along the counters, in the aisle between the checkouts and the Special bins. They didn't even have shoes on. There was this chunky one, with the two-piece—it was bright green and the seams on the bra were still sharp and her belly was still pretty pale so I guessed she just got it (the suit)—there was this one, with one of those chubby berry-faces, the lips all bunched together under her nose, this one, and a tall one, with black hair that hadn't quite frizzed right, and one of these sunburns right across under the eyes, and a chin that was too long—you know, the kind of girl other girls think is very "striking" and "attractive" but never quite makes it, as they very well know, which is why they like her so much—and then the third one, who wasn't quite so tall. She was the queen. She kind of led them, the other two peeking around and hunching over a little. She didn't look around, not this queen, she just walked straight on slowly, on these long white prima-donna legs. She came down a little hard on her heels, as if she didn't walk in her bare feet that much, putting down her heels and then letting the weight move along to her toes as if she was testing the floor with every step, putting a little deliberate extra action into it. You never know for sure how girls' minds work (do you really think it's a mind in there or just a little buzz like a bee in a glass jar?) but you got the idea she had talked the other two into coming in here with her, and now she was showing them how to do it, walk slow and hold yourself straight.

3 She had on a kind of dirty-pink—beige maybe, I don't know—bathing suit with a little nubble all over it and, what got me, the straps were down. They were off her shoulders looped loose around the cool tops of her arms, and I guess as a result the suit had slipped a little on her, so all around the top of the cloth there was this shining rim. If it hadn't been there you wouldn't have known there could have been anything whiter than those shoulders. With the straps pushed off, there was nothing between the top of the suit and the top of her head except just *her*, this clean bare plane of the top of her chest down from the shoulder bones like a dented sheet of metal tilted in the light. I mean, it was more than pretty.

4 She had sort of oaky hair that the sun and salt had bleached, done up in a bun that was unravelling, and

a kind of prim face. Walking into the A&P with your straps down, I suppose it's the only kind of face you *can* have. She held her head so high her neck, coming up out of those white shoulders, looked kind of stretched, but I didn't mind. The longer her neck was, the more of her there was.

5   She must have felt in the corner of her eye me and over my shoulder Stokesie in the first slot watching, but she didn't tip. Not this queen. She kept her eyes moving across the racks, and stopped, and turned so slow it made my stomach rub the inside of my apron, and buzzed to the other two, who kind of huddled against her for relief, and then they all three of them went up the cat-and-dog-food-breakfast-cereal-macaroni-rice-raisins-seasonings-spreads-spaghetti-soft-drinks-crackers-and-cookies aisle. From my slot I can look straight up this aisle to the meat counter, and I watched them all the way. The fat one with the tan sort of fumbled with the cookies, but on second thought she put the package back. The sheep pushing their carts down the aisle—the girls were walking against the usual traffic (not that we have one-way signs or anything)—were pretty hilarious. You could see them, when Queenie's white shoulders dawned on them, kind of jerk, or hop, or hiccup, but their eyes snapped back to their own baskets and on they pushed. I bet you could set off dynamite in an A&P and the people would by and large keep reaching and checking oatmeal off their lists and muttering "Let me see, there was a third thing, began with *A*, asparagus, no, ah, yes, applesauce!" or whatever it is they do mutter. But there was no doubt, this jiggled them. A few houseslaves in pin curlers even looked around after pushing their carts past to make sure what they had seen was correct.

6   You know, it's one thing to have a girl in a bathing suit down on the beach, where what with the glare nobody can look at each other much anyway, and another thing in the cool of the A&P, under the fluorescent lights, against all those stacked packages, with her feet paddling along naked over our checkerboard green-and-cream rubber-tile floor.

7   "Oh Daddy," Stokesie said beside me. "I feel so faint."

8   "Darling," I said. "Hold me tight." Stokesie's married, with two babies chalked up on his fuselage already, but as far as I can tell that's the only difference. He's twenty-two, and I was nineteen this April.

9   "Is it done?" he asks, the responsible married man finding his voice. I forgot to say he thinks he's going to be manager some sunny day, maybe in 1990 when

it's called the Great Alexandrov and Petrooshki Tea Company or something.

     What he meant was, our town is five miles from a beach, with a big summer colony out on the Point, but we're right in the middle of town, and the women generally put on a shirt or shorts or something before they get out of the car into the street. And anyway these are usually women with six children and varicose veins mapping their legs and nobody, including them, could care less. As I say, we're right in the middle of town, and if you stand at our front doors you can see two banks and the Congregational church and the newspaper store and three real-estate offices and about twenty-seven old freeloaders tearing up Central Street because the sewer broke again. It's not as if we're on the Cape; we're north of Boston and there's people in this town haven't seen the ocean for twenty years.

10   The girls had reached the meat counter and were asking McMahon something. He pointed, they pointed, and they shuffled out of sight behind a pyramid of Diet Delight peaches. All that was left for us to see was old McMahon patting his mouth and looking after them sizing up their joints. Poor kids, I began to feel sorry for them, they couldn't help it.

12   NOW here comes the sad part of the story, at least my family says it's sad, but I don't think it's so sad myself. The store's pretty empty, it being Thursday afternoon, so there was nothing much to do except lean on the register and wait for the girls to show up again. The whole store was like a pinball machine and I didn't know which tunnel they'd come out of. After a while they come around out of the far aisle, around the lightbulbs, records at discount of the Caribbean Six or Tony Martin Sings or some such gunk you wonder they waste the wax on, six-packs of candy bars, and plastic toys done up in cellophane that fall apart when a kid looks at them anyway. Around they come, Queenie still leading the way, and holding a little gray jar in her hand. Slots Three through Seven are unmanned and I could see her wondering between Stokes and me, but Stokesie with his usual luck draws an old party in baggy gray pants who stumbles up with four giant cans of pineapple juice (what do these bums *do* with all that pineapple juice? I've often asked myself) so the girls come to me. Queenie puts down the jar and I take it into my fingers icy cold. Kingfish Fancy Herring Snacks in Pure Sour Cream: 49¢. Now her hands are empty, not a ring or a bracelet, bare as God made

> The whole store was like a pinball machine . . .

them, and I wonder where the money's coming from. Still with that prim look she lifts a folded dollar bill out of the hollow at the center of her nubbled pink top. The jar went heavy in my hand. Really, I thought that was so cute.

13 Then everybody's luck begins to run out. Lengel comes in from haggling with a truck full of cabbages on the lot and is about to scuttle into that door marked MANAGER behind which he hides all day when the girls touch his eye. Lengel's pretty dreary, teaches Sunday school and the rest, but he doesn't miss that much. He comes over and says,"Girls, this isn't the beach."

14 Queenie blushes, though maybe it's just a brush of sunburn I was noticing for the first time, now that she was so close. "My mother asked me to pick up a jar of herring snacks." Her voice kind of startled me, the way voices do when you see the people first, coming out so flat and dumb yet kind of tony, too, the way it ticked over "pick up" and "snacks." All of a sudden I slid right down her voice into her living room. Her father and the other men were standing around in ice-cream coats and bow ties and the women were in sandals picking up herring snacks on toothpicks off a big glass plate and they were all holding drinks the color of water with olives and sprigs of mint in them. When my parents have somebody over they get lemonade and if it's a real racy affair Schlitz in tall glasses with "They'll Do It Every Time" cartoons stencilled on.

15 "That's all right," Lengel said."But this isn't the beach." His repeating this struck me as funny, as if it had just oc- curred to him, and he had been thinking all these years the A&P was a great big dune and he was the head lifeguard. He didn't like my smiling—as I say, he doesn't miss much—but he concentrates on giving the girls that sad Sunday-school-superintendent stare.

16 Queenie's blush is no sunburn now, and the plump one in plaid, that I liked better from the back—a re- ally sweet can—pipes up, "We weren't doing any shop- ping. We just came in for the one thing."

17 "That makes no difference," Lengel tells her, and I could see from the way his eyes went that he hadn't noticed she was wearing a two-piece before. "We want you decently dressed when you come in here."

18 "We *are* decent," Queenie says suddenly, her lower lip pushing, getting sore now that she remembers her place, a place from which the crowd that runs the A&P must look pretty crummy. Fancy Herring Snacks flashed in her very blue eyes.

19 "Girls, I don't want to argue with you. After this come in here with your shoulders covered. It's our policy." He turns his back. That's policy for you. Policy is what the kingpins want. What the others want is juvenile delinquency.

20 All this while, the customers had been showing up with their carts but, you know, sheep, seeing a scene, they had all bunched up on Stokesie, who shook open a paper bag as gently as peeling a peach, not wanting to miss a word. I could feel in the silence everybody getting nervous, most of all Lengel, who asks me, "Sammy, have you rung up their purchase?"

21 I thought and said "No" but it wasn't about that I was thinking. I go through the punches, 4, 9, GROC, TOT—it's more complicated than you think, and after you do it often enough, it begins to make a little song, that you hear words to, in my case "Hello (*bing*) there, you (*gung*) hap-py *pee*-pul (*splat*)!"—the *splat* being the drawer flying out. I uncrease the bill, tenderly as you may imagine, it just having come from between the two smoothest scoops of vanilla I had ever known were there, and pass a half and a penny into her narrow pink palm, and nestle the herrings in a bag and twist its neck and hand it over, all the time thinking.

22 The girls, and who'd blame them, are in a hurry to get out, so I say "I quit" to Lengel quick enough for them to hear, hoping they'll stop and watch me, their unsuspected hero. They keep right on going, into the electric eye; the door flies open and they flicker across the lot to their car, Queenie and Plaid and Big Tall Goony-Goony (not that as raw material she was so bad), leaving me with Lengel and a kink in his eyebrow.

23 "Did you say something, Sammy?"
24 "I said I quit."
25 "I thought you did."
26 "You didn't have to embarrass them."
27 "It was they who were embarrassing us."
28 I started to say something that came out "Fiddle- de-doo." It's a saying of my grandmother's, and I know she would have been pleased.
29 "I don't think you know what you're saying," Len- gel said.
30 "I know you don't," I said. "But I do." I pull the bow at the back of my apron and start shrugging it off my shoulders. A couple customers that had been

heading for my slot begin to knock against each other, like scared pigs in a chute.

31   Lengel sighs and begins to look very patient and old and gray. He's been a friend of my parents for years. "Sammy, you don't want to do this to your mom and dad," he tells me. It's true, I don't. But it seems to me that once you begin a gesture it's fatal not to go through with it. I fold the apron, "Sammy" stitched in red on the pocket, and put it on the counter, and drop the bow tie on top of it. The bow tie is theirs, if you've ever wondered. "You'll feel this for the rest of your life," Lengel says, and I know that's true, too, but remembering how he made that pretty girl blush makes me so scrunchy inside I punch the No Sale tab and the machine whirs "*pee*-pul" and the drawer splats out. One advantage to this scene taking place in summer, I can follow it up with a clean exit, there's no fumbling around getting your coat and galoshes, I just saunter into the electric eye in my white shirt that my mother ironed the night before, and the door heaves itself open, and outside the sunshine is skating around on the asphalt.

32   I look around for my girls, but they're gone, of course. There wasn't anybody but some young married screaming with her children about some candy they didn't get by the door of a powder-blue Falcon station wagon. Looking back in the big windows, over the bags of peat moss and aluminum lawn furniture stacked on the pavement, I could see Lengel in my place in the slot, checking the sheep through. His face was dark

gray and his back stiff, as if he'd just had an injection of iron, and my stomach kind of fell as I felt how hard the world was going to be to me from here on in.

To hear Updike on the importance of making the reader see, go to **www.mhhe.com/delbanco1e**.

IF you like this story, you may like other initiation stories—stories about growing up and acquiring increased awareness of our relation to the world—James Joyce's "Araby," for example, in chapter 4. You might also want to compare what the future holds for the narrator in "A&P" with the remembrances of the narrator in Alice Munro's "An Ounce of Cure" at the end of this chapter.

GOING FURTHER   John Updike's novels, several of which are listed in the note about the author, may also interest you. In the eyes of many readers and critics, no one surpasses Updike when it comes to describing the manners and way of life of Americans during the last four decades.

Writing from Reading

Summarize

1 What are the literal events—the incidents—of this narrative? How do these events add up to Sammy's decision at the end of the story?

Analyze Craft

2 "A&P" is confined to one setting (the inside of a supermarket) and a brief period of time. How would the *plot* change if it began with Sammy waking up at his house on the morning of the same day?

Analyze Voice

3 Discuss the impact of Sammy's attitude on the narrative. Point to places in the text where Sammy interprets events rather than reports them objectively. What events might be reported differently (or left out altogether) if the story were told by Stokesie, or Queenie?

Synthesize Summary and Analysis

4 In the interview, Updike talks about the importance of making the reader "see." Did he succeed in making you see the scene he was describing? Choose two images that you were able to see very clearly and analyze what Updike did to help you see them.

Interpret the Story

5 Discuss why Sammy quits his job. What does he mean when he recognizes "how hard the world was going to be to me from here on in"?

6 Imagine an alternative ending to "A&P." What ideas in the story lead you to your version of the ending?

CONTINUED FROM PAGE 3

The word *fiction* derives from a Latin word, *fingere*, meaning "to fashion or form." Thus, fiction has to do with shaping, the way a sculptor fashions form. It has to do with making a narrative where nothing existed before. Each work of fiction, as the late Bernard Malamud once wrote, "predicates," or brings to life, an entire world.

Some of the earliest fiction consisted of **fables** and **parables,** short tales designed to impart a moral lesson. In one famous ancient Greek fable, for example, a shepherd boy, tending his family's flock, grows lonely and, to attract company, cries out the alarm signal "wolf!" Villagers come running to the boy's aid, but when they see

"I discovered a world that opened out to me in all kinds of directions. I began to understand things I hadn't understood before. And I began to find other things that I didn't understand yet that I wanted to understand. The world became more interesting to me. Fuller and richer. And I got all of that from reading." Conversation with William Kittredge

STORY AND HISTORY

The words *story* and *history* share a common root, the Latin word *historia,* which means a presumably true account of events and persons from a more or less remote past. In their earliest forms, stories were about purportedly real figures—sometimes gods and goddesses, sometimes human beings. The Latin words in turn go back to the Greek *historia,* meaning "narrative or history," from *histor* or "learned, wise man."

no wolves, they leave. Again the boy cries "wolf!" and once more the neighbors come running but can find no wolves. Eventually, the villagers ignore the boy's cries, and one day, when wolves really do appear, nobody comes to his aid. The moral? No one believes a liar, even when he's telling the truth. This story about seeking attention by deliberately raising a false alarm is the source of the expression "to cry wolf."

"I came to reading, in a way, by way of drawing. I certainly could appreciate cartooning before I could read it, and there was a kind of children's book called 'Big Little Books,' which had a panel of a comic strip opposite a little page of print. And I think it was those books that I first read." Conversation with John Updike

Today, much fiction is referred to according to its contemporary category: horror, spy, romance, etc. Categories such as these have stricter conventions of form than most of contemporary fiction. Horror stories, for example, evoke a world of supernatural or psychological terror:

> *From a private hospital for the insane near Providence, Rhode Island, there recently disappeared an exceedingly singular person. He bore the name of Charles Dexter Ward, and was placed under restraint most reluctantly by the grieving father who had watched his aberration grow from a mere eccentricity to a dark mania involving both a possibility of murderous tendencies and a profound and peculiar change in the apparent contents of his mind. Doctors confess themselves quite baffled by his case, since it presented oddities of a general physiological as well as psychological character.*
>
> *In the first place, the patient seemed oddly older than his twenty-six years would warrant. . . .*
>
> —from "The Case of Charles Dexter Ward,"
> by H. P. Lovecraft

Spy thrillers create a sense of suspense, often involving an international crisis:

> *It took only two minutes from the time Willy's car arrived at the White House grounds to the time he was knocking on Nelson Cummin's door. Willy had done the trip many times. He reckoned that between security checks, registration, elevators, and a little wait in the outer office of the national security advisor, the average entry time to see Nelson—from entering the White House grounds to shaking his hand—was fifteen to twenty minutes. This time his car was waved through and a secretary waited for him at the side door of the building. . . .*
>
> —from *Point of Entry,* by Peter Schechter

Science fiction is set in an imagined future, often on other planets:

> *Got a job for you. Pays a billion.*
> *The message blinked at the top of the screen three times, then dis-*
> *appeared. Rod Morgan smiled. He had been hearing rumors about a quasi-*
> *multigovernment, quasi-commercial consortium that was raising capital to*
> *sponsor a risky trip to Saturn. He closed down his game of WARPWORLD, and*
> *switched to net-mail to read the rest of the message. He'd guessed right, it was*
> *from the consortium. The job must really be risky for them to be offering a bil-*
> *lion dollars. Although the penny was no longer legal tender, a billion dollars*
> *was still a large fortune. . . .*
> —from Saturn Rukh, by Robert L. Forward

Genres like romance, crime, or fantasy help you know what to expect when you read particular texts. Suppose you picked up *Saturn Rukh,* the novel from which we took the preceding example, and you knew it was science fiction. It would not surprise you to see a reference to a trip to Saturn. But if you were unaware of the science fiction genre, you might have a hard time deciding how to approach the information about a trip to Saturn—whether to take it seriously or to laugh at it. Genre fiction is powerful because of the way in which it manipulates your response: What might seem utterly ridiculous or out of place in the real world becomes something we understand if we know to approach it based on the set of expectations created by genre.

Many works of fiction do not fall into a category like crime, horror, or romance; texts that defy this type of classification are generally referred to as mainstream or literary fiction. Most of the stories you will encounter in this book are examples of literary fiction. As with any fashioned form, the art of fiction comes in many sizes, from the briefest story (for an example, see Amy Hempel's couldn't-be-shorter "San Francisco" in our Stories for Further Reading) to novels of a thousand pages or more, such as Leo Tolstoy's *War and Peace.* Novels almost by definition need to tell more than one story, but short stories are dense and intense. Simply put, a **short story** is a brief fictional narrative. It attempts to dramatize or illustrate the effect or meaning of a single incident or small group of incidents in the life of a single character or small group of characters. Even in these compressed lengths, however, you'll find elements of horror (see Edgar Allan Poe's "The Fall of the House of Usher" in chapter 6), science fiction (see Ursula LeGuin's "Kerastion" in Stories for Further Reading), and detective romance (see William Faulkner's "A Rose for Emily" in the casebook on the American South).

"There's a whole range of people writing, and somewhere in there is somebody who respects you, and when you read their stories, you're thinking, "I'm in here, and I can feel myself coming to life." Conversation with Barry Lopez

Whatever the category, reading can expand our emotional range, as Heather King suggests in her memoir, *Parched:*

> *I loved the way books looked, loved the way books smelled, loved that books*
> *made me forget. My favorites were* The Diary of Anne Frank, The Yearling,
> Uncle Tom's Cabin: *tales of grotesque cruelty and unbearable loss. That was*
> *precisely why I liked them. Even back then I understood the real purpose of*
> *literature. I didn't want to hear that people lived happily ever after. I wanted*
> *to know that other people suffered, too.*

You may prefer something with a lighter touch, but reading can give you a view into another world, and the analytical ability you develop from reading critically will stand you in good stead whether you're reading fiction or sociology or a political pamphlet.

WHAT READING FICTION GIVES US

As the early-twentieth-century Austrian writer Robert Musil once put it, when troubled, we like to imagine that there is only one law of life, the law of narrative order. What he meant is that we tend to view our lives as meaningful, and endowed with the same kind of narrative coherence found in good fiction. Fiction allows us a close look

> "Stories console me. If I'm lying in bed at night I'm a little less alone in a lonely universe. Stories connect me not to just other people, but to myself." Conversation with Tim O'Brien

at characters as it explicitly or implicitly tells the stories of their lives in an effort to make sense of them. Reading fiction gives us the opportunity to investigate our own lives by comparison, to notice how we put together the elements of our own stories—our family or friends, our emotions, our decisions, and our hopes—in order to try and understand who we are, where we have come from, and where we might be going. As we delve into good stories in order to understand them better, we come to better understand ourselves.

Kate Chopin (1851–1904)

The daughter of an Irish father and a French Creole mother, Kate Chopin grew up in Saint Louis, where she studied French and English literature at a Catholic school. Her father died in a work-related accident when she was very young, an event that may have inspired this story. By the time she was married to the wealthy businessman Oscar Chopin and living in Louisiana,

she was known as an unconventional woman. She drank, smoked, held her own opinions, and even ran her late husband's business for a year—all the while raising six children. Like many stories in this book, this story follows what some call the "unities" of time, place, and action that are found in classical drama and in a great deal of short fiction. The title suggests that this story will be brief. But when you read

to write, remember that a short story, however brief, is not merely a joke or an anecdote—a funny thing that happened on the way to the parking lot or how your sister's cat got stuck in a tree. The fiction writer must take it further—selecting and arranging events in an artful way to show, for example, how a girl whose cat gets stuck in a tree comes to understand what really matters to her and why she calls for help.

AS YOU READ   Notice the pace of the story. Where does it speed up and slow down? How are you feeling as the pace slows and quickens? Where are the surprises in the story? How do they make you feel?

FOR INTERACTIVE READING . . . "The Story of an Hour" is not written in Louise's voice, but the narrator does seem to know Louise's thoughts. Annotate in the margins instances where the narrator offers insights into Louise's personal thoughts or past. Based on your notes, do you think the narrator tells the story objectively or with a bias?

The Story of an Hour (1894)

1 KNOWING that Mrs. Mallard was afflicted with a heart trouble, great care was taken to break to her as gently as possible the news of her husband's death.

2 It was her sister Josephine who told her, in broken sentences; veiled hints that revealed in half concealing. Her husband's friend Richards was there, too, near her. It was he who had been in the newspaper office when intelligence of the railroad disaster was received, with Brently Mallard's name leading the list of "killed." He had only taken the time to assure himself of its truth by a second telegram, and had hastened to forestall any less careful, less tender friend in bearing the sad message.

3 She did not hear the story as many women have heard the same, with a paralyzed inability to accept its significance. She wept at once, with sudden, wild abandonment, in her sister's arms. When the storm of grief had spent itself she went away to her room alone. She would have no one follow her.

4 There stood, facing the open window, a comfortable, roomy armchair. Into this she sank, pressed down by a physical exhaustion that haunted her body and seemed to reach into her soul.

5 She could see in the open square before her house the tops of trees that were all aquiver with the new spring life. The delicious breath of rain was in the air. In the street below a peddler was crying his wares. The notes of a distant song which some one was singing reached her faintly, and countless sparrows were twittering in the eaves.

6 There were patches of blue sky showing here and there through the clouds that had met and piled one above the other in the west facing her window.

7 She sat with her head thrown back upon the cushion of the chair, quite motionless, except when a sob came up into her throat and shook her, as a child who has cried itself to sleep continues to sob in its dreams.

8 She was young, with a fair, calm face, whose lines bespoke repression and even a certain strength. But now there was a dull stare in her eyes, whose gaze was fixed away off yonder on one of those patches of blue sky. It was not a glance of reflection, but rather indicated a suspension of intelligent thought.

9 There was something coming to her and she was waiting for it, fearfully. What was it? She did not know; it was too subtle and elusive to name. But she felt it, creeping out of the sky, reaching toward her through the sounds, the scents, the color that filled the air.

10 Now her bosom rose and fell tumultuously. She was beginning to recognize this thing that was approaching to possess her, and she was striving to beat it back with her will—as powerless as her two white slender hands would have been.

11 When she abandoned herself a little whispered word escaped her slightly parted lips. She said it over and over under her breath: "free, free, free!" The vacant stare and the look of terror that had followed it went from her eyes. They stayed keen and bright. Her pulses beat fast, and the coursing blood warmed and relaxed every inch of her body.

12   She did not stop to ask if it were or were not a monstrous joy that held her. A clear and exalted perception enabled her to dismiss the suggestion as trivial.

13   She knew that she would weep again when she saw the kind, tender hands folded in death; the face that had never looked save with love upon her, fixed and gray and dead. But she saw beyond that bitter moment a long procession of years to come that would belong to her absolutely. And she opened and spread her arms out to them in welcome.

> ## She breathed a quick prayer that life might be long.

14   There would be no one to live for her during those coming years; she would live for herself. There would be no powerful will bending hers in that blind persistence with which men and women believe they have a right to impose a private will upon a fellow-creature. A kind intention or a cruel intention made the act seem no less a crime as she looked upon it in that brief moment of illumination.

15   And yet she had loved him—sometimes. Often she had not. What did it matter! What could love, the unsolved mystery, count for in face of this possession of self-assertion which she suddenly recognized as the strongest impulse of her being!

16   "Free! Body and soul free!" she kept whispering.

17   Josephine was kneeling before the closed door with her lips to the keyhole, imploring for admission. "Louise, open the door! I beg; open the door—you will make yourself ill. What are you doing, Louise? For heaven's sake open the door."

18   "Go away. I am not making myself ill." No; she was drinking in a very elixir of life through that open window.

19   Her fancy was running riot along those days ahead of her. Spring days, and summer days, and all sorts of days that would be her own. She breathed a quick prayer that life might be long. It was only yesterday she had thought with a shudder that life might be long.

20   She arose at length and opened the door to her sister's importunities. There was a feverish triumph in her eyes, and she carried herself unwittingly like a goddess of Victory. She clasped her sister's waist, and together they descended the stairs. Richards stood waiting for them at the bottom.

21   Some one was opening the front door with a latchkey. It was Brently Mallard who entered, a little travel-stained, composedly carrying his grip-sack and umbrella. He had been far from the scene of accident, and did not even know there had been one. He stood amazed at Josephine's piercing cry; at Richards' quick motion to screen him from the view of his wife.

22   But Richards was too late.

23   When the doctors came they said she had died of heart disease—of joy that kills.

IF you like "The Story of an Hour," you may like other stories with strong heroines who desire more from life than being a wife or mother, such as "The Yellow Wallpaper" by Charlotte Perkins Gilman (in Stories for Further Reading), another classic feminist work.

GOING FURTHER   Although the public responded well to Chopin's less controversial fiction about French Creole life, you may be interested in reading the book that lost her work its critical favor, *The Awakening* (1899), which critics called immoral. It is quite well-regarded today.

Writing from Reading

Summarize

1 Summarize the development of Louise's emotions over the course of the story. Is it ultimately joy or disappointment that causes her death?

Analyze Craft

2 How well has Chopin succeeded in making you *see* the details of this story? Which images are particularly vivid, and how does Chopin make them so?

Analyze Voice

3 How would you describe Chopin's attitude toward her character; does she admire or disdain the way Louise behaves? A "mallard" is a male duck; what does the name "Mrs. Mallard" suggest? What specific language from the story suggests how Chopin wanted the reader to respond to Louise?

Synthesize Summary and Analysis

4 Though "The Story of an Hour" describes only one hour's time, its events are predicated upon the emotions Louise has developed over the course of her entire marriage. Summarize what we know about Louise's relationship with her husband, and discuss whether Chopin provides enough detail to justify Louise's death by the end.

Interpret the Story

5 The first line of the story says that "Mrs. Mallard was afflicted with a heart trouble." Discuss whether Chopin undermines or reinforces the emotional significance of Louise's death by announcing her heart condition so early in the story.

Alice Munro (b. 1931)

Alice Munro (née Laidlaw) was born on a farm in Wingham, Ontario, to a family of fox and potato farmers. She published her first short story at the age of nineteen while attending college and working as a waitress, library clerk, and tobacco picker. After leaving school to marry James Munro, she moved with her husband to British Columbia, where the couple ran a bookstore. In 1968, she published her first collection of stories, *Dance of the Happy Shades,* and in 1971 her first and only novel, *Lives of Girls and Women.* When her marriage ended in 1972, Munro returned to Ontario, remarried (to Gerald Fremlin, a geographer), and went on to publish eleven more collections of short stories (including *The Beggar Maid, The Moons of Jupiter, Friend of My Youth, Open Secrets, Runaway,* and, recently, *The View from Castle Rock,* in 2006). Her work has won many literary awards, including three of Canada's Governor General's Literary Awards and its Giller Prize; the Rea Award for Short Fiction; and the U.S. National Book Critics Circle Award.

Her stories continue to appear in magazines such as *The New Yorker, The Atlantic Monthly,* and *The Paris Review.* Because of her ability to portray everyday human relationships—particularly, though not only, in Ontario—and her clean prose, Munro is widely considered to be one of the most accomplished short story writers alive today. She finds the extraordinary in the ordinary, the strange in the familiar; her influence is large.

An Ounce of Cure (1968)

1   MY parents didn't drink. They weren't rabid about it, and in fact I remember that when I signed the pledge in grade seven, with the rest of that superbly if impermanently indoctrinated class, my mother said, "It's just nonsense and fanaticism, children of that age." My father would drink a beer on a hot day, but my mother did not join him, and—whether accidentally or symbolically—this drink was always consumed *outside* the house. Most of the people we knew were the same way, in the small town where we lived. I ought not to say that it was this which got me into difficulties, because the difficulties I got into were a faithful expression of my own incommodious nature—the same nature that caused my mother to look at me, on any occasion which traditionally calls for feelings of pride and maternal accomplishment (my departure for my first formal dance, I mean, or my hellbent preparations for a descent on college) with an expression of brooding and fascinated despair, as if she could not possibly expect, did not ask, that it should go with me as it did with other girls; the dreamed-of spoils of daughters—orchids, nice boys, diamond rings—would be borne home in due course by the daughters of her friends, but not by me; all she could do was hope for a lesser rather than a greater disaster—an elopement, say, with a boy who could never earn his living, rather than an abduction into the White Slave trade.

2   But ignorance, my mother said, ignorance, or innocence if you like, is not always such a fine thing as people think and I am not sure it may not be dangerous for a girl like you; then she emphasized her point, as she had a habit of doing, with some quotation which had an innocent prompsity and odour of mothballs. I didn't even wince at it, knowing full well how it must have worked wonders with Mr. Berryman.

3   The evening I baby-sat for the Berrymans must have been in April. I had been in love all year, or at least since the first week in September, when a boy named Martin Collingwood had given me a surprised, appreciative, and rather ominously complacent smile in the school assembly. I never knew what surprised him; I was not looking like anybody but me; I had an old blouse on and my home-permanent had turned out badly. A few weeks after that he took me out for the first time, and kissed me

on the dark side of the porch—also, I ought to say, on the mouth; I am sure it was the first time anybody had ever kissed me effectively, and I know that I did not wash my face that night or the next morning, in order to keep the imprint of those kisses intact. (I showed the most painful banality in the conduct of this whole affair, as you will see.) Two months, and a few amatory stages later, he dropped me. He had fallen for the girl who played opposite him in the Christmas production of *Pride and Prejudice*.

> I am sure it was the first time anybody had ever kissed me effectively . . .

4   I said I was not going to have anything to do with that play, and I got another girl to work on Makeup in my place, but of course I went to it after all, and sat down in front with my girl friend Joyce, who pressed my hand when I was overcome with pain and delight at the sight of Mr. Darcy in white breeches, silk waistcoat, and sideburns. It was surely seeing Martin as Darcy that did it for me; every girl is in love with Darcy anyway, and the part gave Martin an arrogance and male splendour in my eyes which made it impossible to remember that he was simply a high-school senior, passably good-looking and of medium intelligence (and with a reputation slightly tainted, at that, by such preferences as the Drama Club and the Cadet *Band*) who happened to be the first boy, the first really presentable boy, to take an interest in me. In the last act they gave him a chance to embrace Elizabeth (Mary Bishop, with a sallow complexion and no figure, but big vivacious eyes) and during this realistic encounter I dug my nails bitterly into Joyce's sympathetic palm.

5   That night was the beginning of months of real, if more or less self-inflicted, misery for me. Why is it a temptation to refer to this sort of thing lightly, with irony, with amazement even, at finding oneself involved with such preposterous emotions in the unaccountable past? That is what we are apt to do, speaking of love; with adolescent love, of course, it's practically obligatory; you would think we sat around, dull afternoons, amusing ourselves with these tidbit recollections of pain. But it really doesn't make me feel very gay—worse still, it doesn't really surprise me—to remember all the stupid, sad, half-ashamed things I did, that people in love always do. I hung around the places where he might be seen, and then pretended not to see him; I made absurdly roundabout approaches, in conversation, to the bitter pleasure of casually mentioning his name. I daydreamed endlessly; in fact if you want to put it mathematically, I spent perhaps ten times as many hours thinking about Martin Collingwood—yes, pining and weeping for him—as I ever spent with him; the idea of him dominated my mind relentlessly and, after a while, against my will. For if at first I had dramatized my feelings, the time came when I would have been glad to escape them; my well-worn daydreams had become depressing and not even temporarily consoling. As I worked my math problems I would torture myself, quite mechanically and helplessly, with an exact recollection of Martin kissing my throat. I had an exact recollection of *everything*. One night I had an impulse to swallow all the aspirins in the bathroom cabinet, but stopped after I had taken six.

6   MY mother noticed that something was wrong and got me some iron pills. She said, "Are you sure everything is going all right at school?" *School!* When I told her that Martin and I had broken up all she said was, "Well so much the better for that. I never saw a boy so stuck on himself." "Martin has enough conceit to sink a battleship," I said morosely and went upstairs and cried.

7   The night I went to the Berrymans was a Saturday night. I baby-sat for them quite often on Saturday nights because they liked to drive over to Baileyville, a much bigger, livelier town about twenty miles away, and perhaps have supper and go to a show. They had been living in our town only two or three years—Mr. Berryman had been brought in as plant manager of the new door-factory—and they remained, I suppose by choice, on the fringes of its society; most of their friends were youngish couples like themselves, born in other places, who lived in new ranch-style houses on a hill outside town where we used to go tobogganing. This Saturday night they had two other couples in for drinks before they all drove over to Baileyville for the opening of a new supper-club; they were all rather festive. I sat in the kitchen and pretended to do Latin. Last night had been the Spring Dance at the High School. I had not gone, since the

only boy who had asked me was Millerd Crompton, who asked so many girls that he was suspected of working his way through the whole class alphabetically. But the dance was held in the Armouries, which was only half a block away from our house; I had been able to see the boys in dark suits, the girls in long pale formals under their coats, passing gravely under the street-lights, stepping around the last patches of snow. I could even hear the music and I have not forgotten to this day that they played "Ballerina," and—oh, song of my aching heart—"Slow Boat to China." Joyce had phoned me up this morning and told me in her hushed way (we might have been discussing an incurable disease I had) that yes, M.C. *had* been there with M.B., and she had on a formal that must have been made out of somebody's old lace tablecloth, it just *hung*.

8   When the Berrymans and their friends had gone I went into the living room and read a magazine. I was mortally depressed. The big softly lit room, with its green and leaf-brown colours, made an uncluttered setting for the development of the emotions, such as you would get on a stage. At home the life of the emotions went on all right, but it always seemed to get buried under the piles of mending to be done, the ironing, the children's jigsaw puzzles and rock collections. It was the sort of house where people were always colliding with one another on the stairs and listening to hockey games and Superman on the radio.

9   I got up and found the Berrymans' "Danse Macabre" and put it on the record player and turned out the living-room lights. The curtains were only partly drawn. A street light shone obliquely on the window-pane, making a rectangle of thin dusty gold, in which the shadows of bare branches moved, caught in the huge sweet winds of spring. It was a mild black night when the last snow was melting. A year ago all this—the music, the wind and darkness, the shadows of the branches—would have given me tremendous happiness; when they did not do so now, but only called up tediously familiar, somehow humiliatingly personal thoughts, I gave up my soul for dead and walked into the kitchen and decided to get drunk.

10   No, it was not like that. I walked into the kitchen to look for a coke or something in the refrigerator, and there on the front of the counter were three tall beautiful bottles, all about half full of gold. But even after I had looked at them and lifted them to feel their weight I had not decided to get drunk; I had decided to have a drink.

Now here is where my ignorance, my disastrous innocence, comes in. It is true that I had seen the Berrymans and their friends drinking their highballs as casually as I would drink a coke, but I did not apply this attitude to myself. No; I thought of hard liquor as something as to be taken in extremities, and relied upon for extravagant results, one way or another. My approach could not have been less casual if I had been the Little Mermaid drinking the witch's crystal potion. Gravely, with a glance at my set face in the black window above the sink, I poured a little whisky from each of the bottles (I think now there were two brands of rye and an expensive Scotch) until I had my glass full. For I had never in my life seen anyone pour a drink and I had no idea that people frequently diluted their liquor with water, soda, et cetera, and I had seen that the glasses the Berrymans' guests were holding when I came through the living room were nearly full.

I drank it off as quickly as possible. I set the glass down and stood looking at my face in the window, half expecting to see it altered. My throat was burning, but I felt nothing else. It was very disappointing, when I had worked myself up to it. But I was not going to let it go at that. I poured another full glass, then filled each of the bottles with water to approximately the level I had seen when I came in. I drank the second glass only a little more slowly than the first. I put the empty glass down on the counter with care, perhaps feeling in my head a rustle of things to come, and went and sat down on a chair in the living room. I reached up and turned on a floor lamp beside the chair, and the room jumped on me.

WHEN I say that I was expecting extravagant results I do not mean that I was expecting this. I had thought of some sweeping emotional change, an upsurge of gaiety and irresponsibility, a feeling of lawlessness and escape, accompanied by a little dizziness and perhaps a tendency to giggle out loud. I did not have in mind the ceiling spinning like a great plate somebody had thrown at me, nor the pale green blobs of the chairs swelling, converging, disintegrating, playing with me a game full of enormous senseless inanimate malice. My head sank back; I closed my eyes. And at once opened them, opened them wide, threw myself out of the chair and down the hall and reached—thank God, thank God!—the Berrymans' bathroom, where I was sick everywhere, everywhere, and dropped like a stone.

From this point on I have no continuous picture of what happened; my memories of the next hour or two are split into vivid and improbable segments, with nothing but murk and uncertainty between. I do remember lying on the bathroom floor looking sideways at the little six-sided white tiles, which lay together in such an admirable and logical pattern, seeing them with the brief broken gratitude and sanity of one who has just been torn to pieces with vomiting. Then I remember sitting on the stool in front of the hall phone, asking weakly for Joyce's number. Joyce was not home. I was told by her mother (a rather rattlebrained woman, who didn't seem to notice a thing the matter—for which I felt weakly, mechanically grateful) that she was at Kay Stringer's house. I didn't know Kay's number so I just asked the operator; I felt I couldn't risk looking down at the telephone book.

Kay Stringer was not a friend of mine but a new friend of Joyce's. She had a vague reputation for wildness and a long switch of hair, very oddly, though naturally, coloured—from soap-yellow to caramel-brown. She knew a lot of boys more exciting than Martin Collingwood, boys who had quit school or been imported into town to play on the hockey team. She and Joyce rode around in these boys' cars, and sometimes went with them—having lied of course to their mothers—to the Gay-la dance hall on the highway north of town.

I got Joyce on the phone. She was very keyed-up, as she always was with boys around, and she hardly seemed to hear what I was saying.

"Oh, I can't tonight," she said. "Some kids are here. We're going to play cards. You know Bill Kline? He's here. Ross Armour—"

"I'm *sick*," I said trying to speak distinctly; it came out an inhuman croak. "I'm *drunk*. Joyce!" Then I fell off the stool and the receiver dropped out of my hand and banged for a while dismally against the wall.

I had not told Joyce where I was, so after thinking about it for a moment she phoned my mother, and using the elaborate and unnecessary subterfuge that young girls delight in, she found out. She and Kay and the boys—there were three of them—told some story about where they were going to Kay's mother, and got into the car and drove out. They found me still lying on the broadloom carpet in the hall; I had been sick again, and this time I had not made it to the bathroom.

It turned out that Kay Stringer, who arrived on this scene only by accident, was exactly the person I needed. She loved a crisis, particularly one like this, which had a shady and scandalous aspect and which must be kept secret from the adult world. She became excited, aggressive, efficient; that energy which was termed wildness was simply the overflow of a great female instinct to manage, comfort and control. I could hear her voice coming at me from all directions, telling me not to worry, telling Joyce to find the biggest coffeepot they had and make it full of coffee (*strong* coffee, she said), telling the boys to pick me up and carry me to the sofa. Later, in the fog beyond my reach, she was calling for a scrub-brush.

Then I was lying on the sofa, covered with some kind of crocheted throw they had found in the bedroom. I didn't want to lift my head. The house was full of the smell of coffee. Joyce came in, looking very pale; she said that the Berryman kids had wakened up but she had given them a cookie and told them to go back to bed, it was all right; she hadn't let them out of their room and she didn't believe they'd remember. She said that she and Kay had cleaned up the bathroom and the hall though she was afraid there was still a spot on the rug. The coffee was ready. I didn't understand anything very well. The boys had turned on the radio and were going through the Berrymans' record collection; they had it out on the floor. I felt there was something odd about this but I could not think what it was.

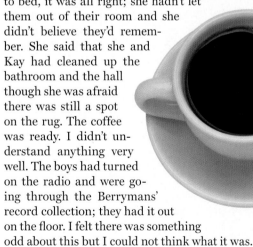

Kay brought me a huge breakfast mug full of coffee.

She loved a crisis, particularly one like this, which had a shady and scandalous aspect and which must be kept secret from the adult world.

14

15

16

17

18

19

20

21

22

23   "I don't know if I can," I said. "Thanks."

24   "Sit up," she said briskly, as if dealing with drunks was an everyday business for her, I had no need to feel myself important. (I met, and recognized, that tone of voice years later, in the maternity ward.) "Now drink," she said. I drank, and at the same time realized that I was wearing only my slip. Joyce and Kay had taken off my blouse and skirt. They had brushed off the skirt and washed out the blouse, since it was nylon; it was hanging in the bathroom. I pulled the throw up under my arms and Kay laughed. She got everybody coffee. Joyce brought in the coffeepot and on Kay's instructions she kept filling my cup whenever I drank from it. Somebody said to me with interest. "You must have really wanted to tie one on."

25   "No," I said rather sulkily, obediently drinking my coffee. "I only had two drinks."

26   Kay laughed, "Well it certainly gets to you, I'll say that. What time do you expect *they*'ll be back?" she said.

27   "Late, after one I think."

28   "You should be all right by that time. Have some more coffee."

29   Kay and one of the boys began dancing to the radio. Kay danced very sexily, but her face had the gently superior and indulgent, rather cold look it had when she was lifting me up to drink the coffee. The boy was whispering to her and she was smiling, shaking her head. Joyce said she was hungry, and she went out to the kitchen to see what there was—potato chips or crackers, or something like that, that you could eat without making too noticeable a dint. Bill Kline came over and sat on the sofa beside me and patted my legs through the crocheted throw. He didn't say anything to me, just patted my legs and looked at me with what seemed to me a very stupid, half-sick, absurd and alarming expression. I felt very uncomfortable; I wondered how it had ever got around that Bill Kline was so good looking, with

an expression like that. I moved my legs nervously and he gave me a look of contempt, not ceasing to pat me. Then I scrambled off the sofa, pulling the throw around me, with the idea of going to the bathroom to see if my blouse was dry. I lurched a little when I started to walk, and for some reason—probably to show Bill Kline that he had not panicked me—I immediately exaggerated this, and calling out, "Watch me walk a straight line!" I lurched and stumbled, to the accompaniment of everyone's laughter, towards the hall. I was standing in the archway between the hall and the living room when the knob of the front door turned with a small matter-of-fact click and everything became silent behind me except the radio of course and the crocheted throw inspired by some delicate malice of its own slithered down around my feet and there—oh, delicious moment in a well-organized farce!—there stood the Berrymans, Mr. and Mrs., with expressions on their faces as appropriate to the occasion as any old-fashioned director of farces could wish. They must have been preparing those expressions, of course; they could not have produced them in the first moment of shock; with the noise we were making, they had no doubt heard us as soon as they got out of the car; for the same reason, we had not heard them. I don't think I ever knew what brought them home so early—a headache, an argument—and I was not really in a position to ask.

30   MR. Berryman drove me home. I don't remember how I got into that car, or how I found my clothes and put them on, or what kind of a good-night, if any, I said to Mrs. Berryman. I don't remember what happened to my friends, though I imagine they gathered up their coats and fled, covering up the ignominy of their departure with a mechanical roar of defiance. I remember Joyce with a box of crackers in her hand, saying that I had become terribly sick from eating—I think she said *sauerkraut*—for supper, and that I had called them for help. (When I asked her later what they made of this she said, "It wasn't any use. You *reeked.*") I remember also her saying, "Oh, no, Mr. Berryman I beg of you, my mother is a terribly nervous person I don't know what the shock might do to her. I will go down on my knees to you if you like but *you must not phone my mother.*" I have no picture of her down on her knees—and she would have done it in a minute—so it seems this threat was not carried out.

31   Mr. Berryman said to me, "Well I guess you know your behaviour tonight is a pretty serious thing." He made it sound as if I might be charged with crimi-

nal negligence or something worse. "It would be very wrong of me to overlook it," he said. I suppose that besides being angry and disgusted with *me*, he was worried about taking me home in this condition to my strait-laced parents, who could always say I got the liquor in his house. Plenty of Temperance people would think that enough to hold him responsible, and the town was full of Temperance people. Good relations with the town were very important to him from a business point of view.

"I have an idea it wasn't the first time," he said. "If it was the first time, would a girl be smart enough to fill three bottles up with water? No. Well in this case, she *was* smart enough, but not smart enough to know I could spot it. What do you say to that?" I opened my mouth to answer and although I was feeling quite sober the only sound that came out was a loud, desolate-sounding giggle. He stopped in front of our house. "Light's on," he said. "Now go in and tell your parents the straight truth. And if you don't, remember I will." He did not mention paying me for my baby-sitting services of the evening and the subject did not occur to me either.

I went into the house and tried to go straight upstairs but my mother called to me. She came into the front hall, where I had not turned on the light, and she must have smelled me at once for she ran forward with a cry of pure amazement, as if she had seen somebody falling, and caught me by the shoulders as I did indeed fall down against the bannister, overwhelmed by my fantastic lucklessness, and I told everything from the start, not omitting even the name of Martin Collingwood and my flirtation with the aspirin bottle, which was a mistake.

On Monday morning my mother took the bus over to Baileyville and found the liquor store and bought a bottle of Scotch whisky. Then she had to wait for a bus back, and she met some people she knew and she was not quite able to hide the bottle in her bag; she was furious with herself for not bringing a proper shopping-bag. As soon as she got back she walked out to the Berrymans'; she had not even had lunch. Mr. Berryman had not gone back to the factory. My mother went in and had a talk with both of them and made an excellent impression and then Mr. Berryman drove her home. She talked to them in the forthright and unemotional way she had, which was always agreeably surprising to people prepared to

> "*. . . I will go down on my knees to you* if you like but *you must not phone my mother.*"

deal with a mother, and she told them that although I seemed to do well enough at school I was extremely backward—or perhaps eccentric—in my emotional development. I imagine that this analysis of my behaviour was especially effective with Mrs. Berryman, a great reader of Child Guidance books. Relations between them warmed to the point where my mother brought up a specific instance of my difficulties, and disarmingly related the whole story of Martin Collingwood.

Within a few days it was all over town and the school that I had tried to commit suicide over Martin Collingwood. But it was already all over school and the town that the Berrymans had come home on Saturday night to find me drunk, staggering, wearing nothing but my slip, in a room with three boys, one of whom was Bill Kline. My mother had said that I was to pay for the bottle she had taken the Berrymans out of my baby-sitting earnings, but my clients melted away like the last April snow, and it would not be paid for yet if newcomers to town had not moved in across the street in July, and needed a baby sitter before they talked to any of their neighbours.

My mother also said that it had been a great mistake to let me go out with boys and that I would not be going out again until well after my sixteenth birthday, if then. This did not prove to be a concrete hardship at all, because it was at least that long before anybody asked me. If you think that news of the Berrymans' adventure would put me in demand for whatever gambols and orgies were going on in and around that town, you could not be more mistaken. The extraordinary publicity which attended my first debauch may have made me seemed marked for a special kind of ill luck, like the girl whose illegitimate baby turns out to be triplets: nobody wants to have anything to do with her. At any rate I had at the same time one of the most silent telephones and positively the most sinful reputation in the whole High School. I had to put up with this until the next fall, when a fat blonde girl in Grade Ten ran away with a married man and was picked up two months later, living in sin—though not with the same man—in the city of Sault Ste. Marie. Then everybody forgot about me.

But there was a positive, a splendidly unexpected, result of this affair: I got completely over Martin Collingwood. It was not only that he at once said, publicly, that he had always thought I was a nut; where he was concerned I had no pride, and my tender fancy could have found a way around that, a month, a week, before. What was it that brought me back into the world again? It was the terrible and fascinating reality of my disaster; it was *the way things happened.* Not that I enjoyed it; I was a self-conscious girl and I suffered a good deal from all this exposure. But the development of events on that Saturday night—that fascinated me; I felt that I had had a glimpse of the shameless, marvellous, shattering absurdity with which the plots of life, though not of fiction, are improvised. I could not take my eyes off it.

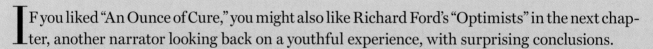

And of course Martin Collingwood wrote his Senior Matric that June, and went away to the city to take a course at a school for Morticians, as I think it is called, and when he came back he went into his uncle's undertaking business. We lived in the same town and we would hear most things that happened to each other but I do not think we met face to face or saw one another, except at a distance, for years. I went to a shower for the girl he married, but then everybody went to everybody else's showers. No, I do not think I really saw him again until I came home after I had been married several years, to attend a relative's funeral. Then I saw him; not quite Mr. Darcy but still very nice-looking in those black clothes. And I saw him looking over at me with an expression as close to a reminiscent smile as the occasion would permit, and I knew that he had been surprised by a memory either of my devotion or my little buried catastrophe. I gave him a gentle uncomprehending look in return. I am a grown-up woman now; let him unbury his own catastrophes.

I F you liked "An Ounce of Cure," you might also like Richard Ford's "Optimists" in the next chapter, another narrator looking back on a youthful experience, with surprising conclusions.

GOING FURTHER Alice Munro is one of many in the group of contemporary Canadian writers with international acclaim. You may also want to look at her work in the context of books by her fellow Canadians, like Michael Ondaatje's *The English Patient* or Margaret Atwood's *The Handmaid's Tale.* Both of these authors are also poets, and samples of their poetry have been included in this book.

Writing from Reading

Summarize

1 The narrator and her mother have very defined views of each other. Summarize their respective opinions, and discuss how they shape (or are shaped by) the events of the story.

Analyze Craft

2 Munro describes the narrator's drunken experience using the same language she uses throughout the story. What words and techniques does she use to convey "drunkenness"?

Analyze Voice

3 Is the description of the narrator's drunken escapade meant to be humorous or tragic? Which aspects of Munro's language create this tone?

Synthesize Summary and Analysis

4 The narrator tells the story as an adult, looking back on an awkward, confusing, and sometimes painful phase in her life. Discuss how the narrator's distance from the story affects the details she presents, and the plot overall.

Interpret the Story

5 "An Ounce of Cure" opens with a description of the narrator's relationship with her parents, and closes with a description of her relationship with Martin Collingwood. Compare and contrast these two relationships, and discuss how both affect and are affected by the narrator's first drinking experience.

Suggestions for Writing

1. The narrator of "A&P" is young and facing forward; the narrator of "An Ounce of Cure" is older, looking back. What might happen, do you think, if the authors had changed their narrative strategies and, for instance, told "A&P" from the vantage point of the store manager or "An Ounce of Cure" as a conversation between the Berrymans?

2. Nothing in "A&P" and "An Ounce of Cure" is *important* in the traditional sense; nobody falls in love eternally or fights to the finish or dies. Discuss what *does* seem to matter in each, and why the authors might have chosen to produce these modest-seeming tales.

3. In the case of "The Story of an Hour," although the situation is also domestic, matters of life and death are indeed under discussion and life itself is at stake. Notice that the narration here comes from "outside" the character and not as a first-person memory. Do you find you know more about the feelings of the first-person narrators in "A&P" and "An Ounce of Cure" than you do about Mrs. Mallard's feelings in "The Story of an Hour"? Or is the outside narrator in "The Story of an Hour" able to convey all that you need to know?

2 Going Further with Reading

YOU can best develop your reading skills by closely examining a piece of literature—whether short story, novel, poem, or any other form—and the craft behind it. In this kind of an examination you will use examples from the work itself as evidence to support your analysis. For example, you might argue that a story's theme is a comment on current day celebrity culture, using quotations from the work itself as evidence. You might argue that the ending of a story is particularly effective or ineffective. Examining the language, characters, and structure of a story helps you write meaningfully about a work. Reading a work critically allows you to make supportable associations that are personally important to you. It can also help you begin to develop your own writing powers and your own voice. Take a moment to look at one student's reading of Anton Chekhov's "Rapture."

A STUDENT'S INITIAL REACTION TO "RAPTURE"

When I first read this, I thought it was amazing how short it is—and how funny it is! Mitya, the main character, doesn't have a clue. He sounds like some of the people I know on campus who like to tell stories about what happened when they were drunk. I had to look up what "Rapture" meant, and I'm still thinking about what it means. When I read this a second time, I plan to make some notes in the margin.

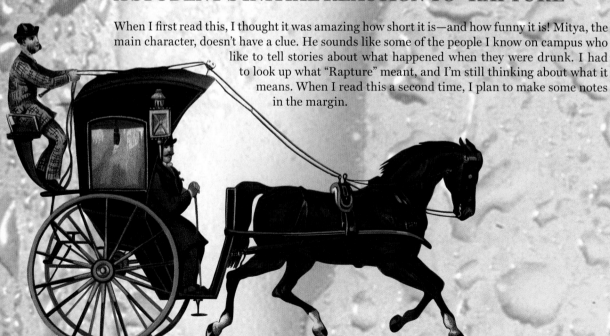

An Interactive Reading of Anton Chekhov's "Rapture"

Rapture

"Rapture" means "ecstasy," "transported to Heaven"—this title tells me the story is about this emotion.

Midnight.

Wild-eyed and disheveled, Mitya Kuldarov burst into his parents' flat and dashed into every room. His parents were about to go to bed. His sister was in bed already and had just got on to the last page of her novel. His schoolboy brothers were asleep.

"Where've you come from?" his parents exclaimed in astonishment. Is something wrong?"

"Oh, I don't know how to tell you! I'm staggered, absolutely staggered. It's . . . it's quite incredible!"

Mitya burst out laughing and collapsed into an armchair, overcome with happiness.

"It's incredible! You'll never believe it! Take a look at this!"

His sister jumped out of bed and came over to him, wrapping a blanket around her. The schoolboys woke up.

"Is something wrong? You look awful."

"I'm so happy, Mum, that's why! Now everyone in Russia knows about me! Everyone! Till now only you knew of the existence of clerical officer of the fourteenth grade, Dimitry Kuldarov, but now everyone in Russia knows! O Lord, Mum!"

Mitya jumped up, ran round every room and sat down again.

"But tell us what's happened, for goodness sake."

"Oh, you lie here like savages, you don't read the papers, you've no ideas what's going on, and the papers are full of such remarkable things! As soon as anything happens, they make it all public, it's down there in black and white! O Lord, I'm so happy! Only famous people get their names in the paper, then all of a sudden—they go and print a story about me!"

"What? Where?"

Dad turned pale. Mum looked up at the icon and crossed herself. The schoolboys jumped out of bed and ran over to their elder brother, wearing nothing but their short little nightshirts.

"They have! About me! Now I'm known all over Russia! You'd better keep this copy, Mum, and we can take it out now and then and read it. Look!"

Mitya pulled the newspaper out of this pocket and handed it to his father, jabbing his finger at a passage ringed with blue pencil. "Read it out!"

Setting: The story takes place in the middle of the night in his parents' apartment. Looks like the stage is set for trouble.

Character: Mitya and his parents are the main characters. Is this a story about their relationship?

Mitya is "wild." Mitya's oblivious to everyone around him. Has he done this before? He is behaving so strangely.

Tone, Language, Style: "burst"—same word, twice.

Tone, Language, Style: Second time Mitya has used word "incredible."

Theme: fame?

Tone, Language, Style: Mitya keeps saying "happy."

Plot: Is this the turning point in the plot?

His parents are worried as if to say "nothing good can come of this." It feels like this isn't the first time they've had to worry about Mitya.

Plot: As the parents see it, there's something "wrong," but the title suggests something else.

Plot: Why is Mitya so happy (when nobody else is)? More uneasy suspense.

Plot: The whole house is in an uproar now.

Plot: Mitya's constant motion contributes to the tension.

Theme: Mitya believes he is famous now. His name is in the paper. This is what has made him rapturous.

Tone, Language, Style: Second time she has done this, as if to imply, My God, what has he gotten himself into this time?

Theme: So he's famous for being intoxicated. Why isn't he embarrassed? Why is he so happy about this? What is the point here?

Point of View: The author really doesn't think much of Mitya.

Character: Mitya is impatient again. Why is it so important to him that he is now "known"? He might have been intoxicated throughout the whole story, accounting for his sloppy collapsing in a chair and wild outbursts.

I don't know if I like this ending. Mitya never grows up. His parents just let him go on like this.

Father put on his glasses.

"Go on, read it!"

Mum looked up at the icon and crossed herself. Dad cleared his throat and began: "On December 29th at 11 p.m. clerical officer of the fourteenth grade, Dimitry Kuldarov—"

"See? See? Go on, Dad!"

"... clerical officer of the fourteenth grade, Dimitry Kuldarov, emerging from the public ale-house situated on the ground floor of Kozikhin's Buildings in Little Bronnaya Street and being in a state of intoxication—"

"It was me and Semyon Petrovich ... They've got all the details! Go on! Now listen, listen to this bit!"

"... and being in a state of intoxication, slipped and fell in front of a cab-horse belonging to Ivan Knoutoff, peasant, from the village of Bumpkino in Pnoff district, which was standing at that spot. The frightened horse, stepping across Kuldarov, dragged over him the sledge in which was seated Ivan Lukov, merchant of the Second Guild in Moscow, bloted down the street and was arrested in its flight by some yard-porters. Kuldarov, being at first in a state of unconsciousness, was taken to the police-station and examined by a doctore. The blow which he had received on the back of the head—"

"I did it on the shaft, Dad. Go on and read the rest of the story."

"... which he had received on the back of his head, was classified as superficial. A police report was drawn up concerning the incident. Medical assistance was rendered to the victim."

"They dabbed the back of my head with cold water. Finished? So what do you say to that, eh? It'll be all over Russia by now! Give it here!"

Mitya grabbed the newspaper, folded it and stuffed it into his pocket.

"Must run now and show the Makarovs ... Then on to the Ivanitsky's, Nataliya Ivanova and Anisim Vasilich ... Can't stop! Bye."

Mitya put on his official cap with the cockade and radiant, triumphant, ran out into the street.

Character: Mitya's impatient. If it's not about him, he doesn't care. He's already played superior to his parents by calling them "savages."

Plot: The story is now winding down.

Character: Mitya is a joke. His "rapture" about his fame shows how comical a character he is.

Plot: His parents read the story instead of telling him off. They play along with his delusion. They let him go on thinking this is a great thing. Why? It looks like the parents didn't really expect much more from him.

Theme: Kind of a sad statement about people. Mitya is a fool. He is proud to be famous for being drunk. He's so deluded that he even wants his parents to know, and his parents do nothing to stop him. He seems ridiculous to me, but he's not acting all that different from how some celebrities act these days.

"Rapture" is one of Anton Chekhov's earliest pieces; it dramatizes the effects of alcohol on a young civil servant's ego, and it demonstrates the multiple ways in which people can perceive experience. If you liked this story, you may also enjoy Chekhov's masterwork "The Lady with the Pet Dog" (in Stories for Further Reading), composed when he had more fully discovered both his craft and his voice.

READING IN CONTEXT

Sometimes while working closely with a story and its meanings, the reader loses sight of the bigger picture, the context. For example, "Rapture" is set in another country, in another century, and was written in another language. Nineteenth-century Russia—with its unpronounceable names and detailed newspaper stories and "official cap with the cockade"—may seem very distant. Yet no piece of writing exists in a vacuum. Each story has an author, a time and place in which it was written, and a tradition of stories

> "I remember reading books about people in Russia, people in India, and people in England, and understanding them—and how surprising this was. Because on the one hand, you realize they're so different from me. But on the other hand, what literature does [is] remind you of how there is that human bond that we all have in common."
>
> Conversation with Chimamanda Ngozi Adichie

and criticism it explicitly or implicitly responds to; taking these aspects into consideration is called **contextual reading.** Traditional research, research that includes multiple sources outside the work itself, can shed light on the context within which a story was written. The most complete analyses of craft and voice push us in the direction of contextual reading, just as the right kind of contextual reading pushes us, throughout the process of analysis, to turn back to the text itself. So reading from the "inside out" in this case means ignoring the fact that we're dealing with a "cab-horse," not a car, and that "Rapture" takes place in Moscow, not Chicago or Los Angeles or Atlanta. Despite the distance, Anton Chekhov's "Rapture" comes nonetheless alive today as an example of the way we may be dazzled by fame. Now, let's look at the critical response paper that is based on the previous reading of "Rapture." In the next chapter we will look more closely at *process* and a set of student drafts; here is the finished *result:*

Lau 1

Liane Lau

Professor Cheuse

Composition 120

23 April 2007

Mitya's False Finale: A Critical Response to Chekhov's "Rapture"

Although it is difficult to talk about language as such in Anton Chekhov's "Rapture," written in Russian in nineteenth-century Moscow, the structure of the story transcends language barriers. Chekhov's setting is domestic: an apartment serves as the location for the entire action, a stage of sorts. The young clerk runs in, stirs up his family and makes them read a newspaper article in which he has been named. Then, still raving about his new-found fame, he runs out again. He is "wild-eyed and disheveled" (25). He runs from room to room. He has laughing outbursts and collapses in a chair. Chekhov paints the portrait of a man out of control, one in an unvoiced conflict with his parents who are "pale" with worry, asking Mitya "Is something wrong? You look awful" (25). Mitya appears to want everyone, beginning with his family, to know his name—he wants to establish himself in the minds of others as someone *important*. However, the young "clerical officer of the fourteenth grade" does not come to any new realization or perception, and therefore, the resolution of the story is not ultimately satisfying (25).

The setting of the story looks like a scene from a play (and it's worth mentioning here that Anton Chekhov would also become a great Russian playwright). The story breaks into three distinct parts. First, the clerk runs in, announcing himself,

Introductory sentence focuses the reader immediately: Essay will center on story elements.

Introduction provides story elements: setting, characters, plot.

Quotes support statements, lend credibility, bring Chekhov's voice to the paper as an ally.

Thesis statement, presents paper's argument: Story elements (listed in paragraph's body) do not add up to a satisfying resolution.

"Three distinct parts": As stated in lead sentence, this argument is based on story structure.

Lau 2

disrupting the household, waking his brothers. Second, Mitya takes out the newspaper and urges his father to read it aloud. He adds his own enthusiastic comments to propel the action forward, and we discover that he was drunk the night before; quite plausibly he remains under the influence now. In the third sequence, a reader may expect something to happen as a result of Mitya's *rapture*, that he has become famous because his name is in the paper and on the police record. The use of the word *rapture* in itself ironically underscores how far it is between Mitya's experience of the truth and the actual truth of his situation. There is nothing elevated about his actions, and to some extent the whole story turns comically on this divide.

However, as the ancient philosopher and critic Aristotle might put it, what is the dramatic purpose here? It looks like Mitya's parents are used to his antics as his mother crosses herself twice in anticipation of Mitya's supposedly "incredible" news (25). His parents and his siblings humor him instead of contradicting or berating him, thus making change less likely for Mitya. Mitya is completely happy with his newfound notoriety, even though it announces to the world that he is a drunkard. As we readers come to understand the nature of Mitya's delusion, we are entitled to wonder what Chekhov is after—what point is he attempting to make? Is "Rapture" a story about the folly of ambition? Is it, perhaps, a presage of our publicity-hungry world and the press agent's promise that any mention in the newspaper is more important than none? Or is it simply poking fun at a simple soul? The reader is left to wonder what the point is, and without that concluding action, the dramatic purpose is unclear, the story is incomplete, and ultimately unsatisfying.

Works Cited

Chekhov, Anton. "Rapture." Trans. Patrick Miles and Harvey Pitcher. *Literature: Craft & Voice*. Eds. Nicholas Delbanco and Alan Cheuse. New York: McGraw-Hill, 2009. Print.

Margin annotations:

Paragraph two critically analyzes elements detailed in intro paragraph.

Conclusion restates the thesis, including logic established by body of the paper.

Critical evidence builds up to the initial debate: Does the story have a clear, satisfying ending.

Topic sentence states the question posed by preceding paragraphs: Do the story elements allow us to determine whether this is a tragedy or a comedy?

Questions reflect the argument that Chekhov has offered no clear resolution.

Quick, challenging question statements build tension that the conclusion sentence relieves.

For more discussion on how to form a text-based argument, refer to the student paper on Jamaica Kincaid (chapter 3).

Whether or not you care more for the factual than the fictional, or ever paid much attention to stories other people made up, or found your way to the library, you can take on the job of forming a text-based argument. You will need to understand what to make of twenty-six separate things (the English alphabet), crack the code of sentences and paragraphs, and solve the mysteries of punctuation. Are the words mostly long or short? Is the text dominated by descriptive prose or lots of dialogue? However you approach the text, you will of necessity go from outside in. Annotate what you read or keep a reading journal. As you grow more comfortable, what was strange becomes familiar, and what was a puzzle gets solved. Reading stories is like passing through a door and entering a world not precisely our own. We meet people in the throes of private trouble or private pleasure, and when our brief exposure to their lives has ended, we relate to them, however briefly, as if they were our family or loved ones or close friends—or ourselves.

"There's only so many people you're going to meet in the world, and so many people who are going to tell you their story, but you know you can multiply that amount of people by whatever degree or whatever number you want to when you're able to go and read a book." Conversation with ZZ Packer

VOICE: LISTENING TO THE PAGE

In every work of fiction, a voice inhabits the page. Try to hear the writers' voices in this book. Each writer will have a special way of using language that sets his or her work apart. Some voices derive from a study of Latin, others from the street, some from the language of the Bible, others from the cadence of the blues. The language in a story may reflect the influence of tribal elders or a beloved teacher. Some writers may rely on the presentation of events, action, or dialogue in brief, condensed form to fill readers in on the story's background, a technique called **exposition.** You are likely to also see

"How different what a Northeasterner hears in his mind and what Faulkner heard in his mind is. We all have to learn to love these irregularities and these personal qualities that fiction has. Fiction's a fairly tough vehicle if it's done right, and it can survive, and engender life in a reader's mind." Conversation with John Updike

moment-by-moment passages, like **scenes** from a movie or play, with characters responding to each other as if onstage in real time. Fiction relies on genuine encounters between characters, usually fully conveyed by the words of a conversation itself. **Dialogue** can signal class, education, intelligence, ethnicity, and attitude—a whole host of characteristics—in the people represented on the page. At its best, it both expresses character and moves the action along.

DIALOGUE AND MONOLOGUE

Dialogue is a by-product of theatrical productions that began in ancient Greece. Even Plato's political treatise *The Republic* is written in dialogue to mimic the famous plays of the period (some critics suggest Plato wanted to be a playwright himself). A *monologue* is a long speech by a single speaker. Whether dialogue or monologue, in fiction as in drama, each line reveals something about the speaker's character as it moves the action forward.

In some ways, any story that is told by the main character is a kind of extended **monologue.** Characters in stories such as "A&P" and "An Ounce of Cure" from the previous chapter are, in effect, speaking to the reader, transmitting what they want the reader to know about what happened to them. (For more on "Point of View," see chapter 7.) Creating dialogue that sounds natural is important in such stories as a way of portraying the world as it exists. This is especially true of **dialect,** which attempts to reproduce the particular sound, accent, cadence, or emphasis of a character's speech. We require dialogue in order to *see* what we *hear*—that is, to visualize in our mind's eye what we have heard in our mind's ear. The *way* a thing is said, or asked, tells us more than the actual words themselves. If a character says, "Get outta my face," he is not likely to remark in another context, "Would you kindly depart our domicile?"

The next two stories, Richard Ford's "Optimists" and Amy Tan's "Two Kinds," examine questions of family. Tan employs dialect in "Two Kinds" in the mother's speech—"Not the best. Because you not trying." Ford discusses his use of dialogue in his interview. Both stories come to us from the perspective of a narrator who looks back. Compare and contrast how Ford and Tan dramatize a young character coming to terms with the adult world—and in particular the behavior of their parents—as you work with the texts and listen to the voices they create.

*I was dyslexic when I was
a little boy . . .*

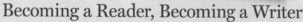

Q&A

*. . . I spend as much time
at my desk as I can.*

A Conversation on Writing

Richard Ford

Richard Ford was born in Jackson, Mississippi, and was raised in Mississippi and Arkansas. He has since lived in New Orleans, Maine, Montana, California, Michigan, New Jersey, and France. Although internationally acclaimed for his fiction, Ford has also committed, as he puts it, "random acts of journalism" and has taught at Harvard, Princeton, and the University of Michigan, among other places. *A Piece of My Heart,* his first book, was published in 1976 and has been followed to date by eight other works of fiction, including both novels and short story collections. His novel *Independence Day* (1995) is the only novel ever to have been accorded both the Pulitzer Prize and the PEN/Faulkner Award. Ford's protagonists are often restless men, adrift and alone; his characteristic first-person narrative mode links action with meditation. In "Optimists," note the span of years that separates the narrator—looking back upon a crucial event of his youth—and the event itself. From his present vantage, the narrator attempts to make sense of the past, seeing not so much an occasion for regret as a mapping of the road not taken, a consideration of what might have been.

Becoming a Reader, Becoming a Writer

I started reading fiction—other than reading *Freddie the Pig* novels when I was a kid—when I was nineteen. I was dyslexic when I was a little boy and am still at age sixty-two, but I've learned how to overcome that. . . . It's often the case with dyslexic kids that they are much better at . . . putting out language than they are given to taking language in. So, it was kind of natural to me . . . to try when I was seventeen. . . . long before I read a book through, to write a story.

On the Writing Process

I go about writing as though it was a job that I liked. I get up in the morning, and I go to work about eight o'clock, and I work all day. And I spend as much time at my desk as I can. And in writing stories, I write with a pen, with a Bic pen, and then after I've written a whole story or whole novel with a Bic pen then I type it all up and work on those typed pages in editing and correcting and making things better.

On Revision

People see a story on the page and what they think is that the writer started and then wrote to the end and this is how it looked. And in fact the writer started at the beginning and wrote to the end, and then he started at the end and wrote to the beginning, and then he plucked things out of the middle and closed up the places where he took something out. Writing stories is much more mosaical than it is linear.

RESEARCH ASSIGNMENT   Richard Ford talks about how in "Optimists" parents and children are equals. Listen to the interview and discuss Ford's own upbringing and how this contributed to this view of family in "Optimists."

To watch this entire interview and hear the author read from "Optimists," go to www.mhhe.com/delbanco1e.

Optimists (1986)

1   ALL of this that I am about to tell happened when I was only fifteen years old, in 1959, the year my parents were divorced, the year when my father killed a man and went to prison for it, the year I left home and school, told a lie about my age to fool the Army, and then did not come back. The year, in other words, when life changed for all of us and forever—ended, really, in a way none of us could ever have imagined in our most brilliant dreams of life.

2   My father was named Roy Brinson, and he worked on the Great Northern Railway, in Great Falls, Montana. He was a switch-engine fireman, and when he could not hold that job on the seniority list, he worked the extra-board as a hostler, or as a hostler's helper, shunting engines through the yard, onto and off the freight trains that went south and east. He was thirty-seven or thirty-eight years old in 1959, a small, young-appearing man, with dark blue eyes. The railroad was a job he liked, because it paid high wages and the work was not hard, and because you could take off days when you wanted to, or even months, and have no one to ask you questions. It was a union shop, and there were people who looked out for you when your back was turned. "It's a workingman's paradise," my father would say, and then laugh.

3   My mother did not work then, though she *had* worked— at waitressing and in the bars in town—and she had liked working. My father thought, though, that Great Falls was

coming to be a rougher town than it had been when he grew up there, a town going downhill, like its name, and that my mother should be at home more, because I was at an age when trouble came easily. We lived in a rented two-story house on Edith Street, close to the freight yards and the Missouri River, a house where from my window at night I could hear the engines as they sat throbbing, could see their lights move along the dark rails. My mother was at home most of her time, reading or watching television or cooking meals, though sometimes she would go out to movies in the afternoon, or would go to the YWCA and swim in the indoor pool. Where she was from— in Havre, Montana, much farther north—there was never such a thing as a pool indoors, and she thought that to swim in the winter, with snow on the ground and the wind howling, was the greatest luxury. And she would come home late in the afternoon, with her brown hair wet and her face flushed, and in high spirits, saying she felt freer.

4   The night that I want to tell about happened in November. It was not then a good time for railroads—not in Montana especially—and for firemen not at all, anywhere. It was the featherbed time, and everyone knew, including my father, that they would—all of them—eventually lose their jobs, though no one knew exactly when, or who would go first, or, clearly, what the future would be. My father had been hired out ten years, and had worked on coal-burners and oil-burners out of Forsythe, Montana, on the

Sheridan spur. But he was still young in the job and low on the list, and he felt that when the cut came young heads would go first. "They'll do something for us, but it might not be enough," he said, and I had heard him say that other times—in the kitchen, with my mother, or out in front, working on his motorcycle, or with me, fishing the whitefish flats up the Missouri. But I do not know if he truly thought that or in fact had any reason to think it. He was an optimist. Both of them were optimists, I think.

5   I know that by the end of summer in that year he had stopped taking days off to fish, had stopped going out along the coulee rims to spot deer. He worked more then and was gone more, and he talked more about work when he was home: about what the union said on this subject and that, about court cases in Washington, D.C., a place I knew nothing of, and about injuries and illnesses to men he knew, that threatened their livelihoods, and by association with them, threatened his own—threatened, he must've felt, our whole life.

6   Because my mother swam at the YWCA she had met people there and made friends. One was a large woman named Esther, who came home with her once and drank coffee in the kitchen and talked about her boyfriend and laughed out loud for a long time, but who I never saw again. And another was a woman named Penny Mitchell whose husband, Boyd, worked for the Red Cross in Great Falls and had an office upstairs in the building with the YWCA, and who my mother would sometimes play canasta with on the nights my father worked late. They would set up a card table in the living room, the three of them, and drink and eat sandwiches until midnight. And I would lie in bed with my radio tuned low to the Calgary station, listening to a hockey match beamed out over the great empty prairie, and could hear the cards snap and laughter downstairs, and later I would hear footsteps leaving, hear the door shut, the dishes rattle in the sink, cabinets close. And in a while the door to my room would open and the light would fall inside, and my mother would set a chair back in. I could see her silhouette. She would always say, "Go back to sleep, Frank." And then the door would shut again, and I would almost always go to sleep in a minute.

7   IT was on a night that Penny and Boyd Mitchell were in our house that trouble came about. My father had been working his regular bid-in job on the switch engine, plus a helper's job off the extra-board—a practice that was illegal by the railroad's rules, but ignored by the union, who could see bad times coming and knew there would be nothing to help it when they came, and so would let men work if they wanted to. I was in the kitchen, eating a sandwich alone at the table, and my mother was in the living room playing cards with Penny and Boyd Mitchell. They were drinking vodka and eating the other sandwiches my mother had made, when I heard my father's motorcycle outside in the dark. It was eight o'clock at night, and I knew he was not expected home until midnight.

8   "Roy's home," I heard my mother say. "I hear Roy. That's wonderful." I heard chairs scrape and glasses tap.

9   "Maybe he'll want to play," Penny Mitchell said. "We can play four-hands."

10   I went to the kitchen door and stood looking through the dining room at the front. I don't think I knew something was wrong, but I think I knew something was unusual, something I would want to know about firsthand.

11   My mother was standing beside the card table when my father came inside. She was smiling. But I have never seen a look on a man's face that was like the look on my father's face at that moment. He looked wild. His eyes were wild. His whole face was. It was cold outside, and the wind was coming up, and he had ridden home from the train yard in only his flannel shirt. His face was red, and his hair was strewn around his bare head, and I remember his fists were clenched white, as if there was no blood in them at all.

12   "My God," my mother said. "What is it, Roy? You look crazy." She turned and looked for me, and I knew she was thinking that this was something I might not need to see. But she didn't say anything. She just looked back at my father, stepped toward him and touched his hand, where he must've been coldest. Penny and Boyd Mitchell sat at the card table, looking up. Boyd Mitchell was smiling for some reason.

13   "Something awful happened," my father said. He reached and took a corduroy jacket off the coat nail and put it on, right in the living room, then sat down on the couch and hugged his arms. His face seemed to get redder then. He was wearing black steel-toe boots, the boots he wore every day, and I stared at them and felt how cold he must be, even in his own house. I did not come any closer.

4   "Roy, what is it?" my mother said, and she sat down beside him on the couch and held his hand in both of hers.

5   My father looked at Boyd Mitchell and at his wife, as if he hadn't known they were in the room until then. He did not know them very well, and I thought he might tell them to get out, but he didn't.

6   "I saw a man be killed tonight," he said to my mother, then shook his head and looked down. He said, "We were pushing into that old hump yard on Ninth Avenue. A cut of coal cars. It wasn't even an hour ago. I was looking out my side, the way you do when you push out a curve. And I could see this one open boxcar in the cut, which isn't unusual. Only this guy was in it and was trying to get off, sitting in the door, scooting. I guess he was a hobo. Those cars had come in from Glasgow tonight. And just the second he started to go off, the whole cut buckled up. It's a thing that'll happen. But he lost his balance just when he hit the gravel, and he fell backwards underneath. I looked right at him. And one set of trucks rolled right over his foot." My father looked at my mother then. "It hit his foot," he said.

7   "My God," my mother said and looked down at her lap.

8   My father squinted. "But then he moved, he sort of bucked himself like he was trying to get away. He didn't yell, and I could see his face. I'll never forget that. He didn't look scared, he just looked like a man doing something that was hard for him to do. He looked like he was concentrating on something. But when he bucked he pushed back, and the other trucks caught his hand." My father looked at his own hands then, and made fists out of them and squeezed them.

19   "What did you do? my mother said. She looked terrified.

20   "I yelled out. And Sherman stopped pushing. But it wasn't that fast."

21   "Did you do anything then," Boyd Mitchell said.

22   "I got down," my father said, "and I went up there. But here's a man cut in three pieces in front of me. What can you do? You can't do very much. I squatted down and touched his good hand. And it was like ice. His eyes were open and roaming all up in the sky."

23   "Did he say anything?" my mother said.

24   "He said, 'Where am I today?' And I said to him, 'It's all right, bud, you're in Montana. You'll be all right.' Though, my God, he wasn't. I took my jacket off and put it over him. I didn't want him to see what had happened."

> He didn't look **scared,** he just looked like a man doing something that was hard for him to do.

25   "You should've put tourniquets on," Boyd Mitchell said gruffly. "That could've helped. That could've saved his life."

26   My father looked at Boyd Mitchell then as if he had forgotten he was there and was surprised that he spoke. "I don't know about that," my father said. "I don't know anything about those things. He was already dead. A boxcar had run over him. He was breathing, but he was already dead to me."

27   "That's only for a licensed doctor to decide," Boyd Mitchell said. "You're morally obligated to do all you can." And I could tell from his tone of voice that he did not like my father. He hardly knew him, but he did not like him. I had no idea why. Boyd Mitchell was a big, husky, red-faced man with curly hair—handsome in a way, but with a big belly—and I knew only that he worked for the Red Cross, and that my mother was a friend of his wife's, and maybe of his, and that they played cards when my father was gone.

28   My father looked at my mother in a way I knew was angry. "Why have you got these people over here now, Dorothy? They don't have any business here."

29   "Maybe that's right," Penny Mitchell said, and she put down her hand of cards and stood up at the table. My mother looked around the room as though an odd noise had occurred inside of it and she couldn't find the source.

30   "Somebody definitely should've done something," Boyd Mitchell said, and he leaned forward on the table toward my father. "That's all there is to say." He was shaking his head *no*. "That man didn't have to die." Boyd Mitchell clasped his big hands on top of his playing cards and stared at my father. "The unions'll cover this up, too, I guess, won't they? That's what happens in these things."

31   My father stood up then, and his face looked wide, though it looked young, still. He looked like a young man who had been scolded and wasn't sure how he should act. "You get out of here," he said in a loud voice. "My God. What a thing to say. I don't even know you."

32   "I know you, though," Boyd Mitchell said angrily. "You're another featherbedder. You aren't good to do anything. You can't even help a dying man. You're bad for this country, and you won't last."

33   "Boyd, my goodness," Penny Mitchell said. "Don't say that. Don't say that to him."

34   Boyd Mitchell glared up at his wife. "I'll say anything I want to," he said. "And he'll listen, because he's helpless. He can't do anything."

35   "Stand up," my father said. "Just stand up on your feet." His fists were clinched again.

36   "All right, I will," Boyd Mitchell said. He glanced up at his wife. And I realized that Boyd Mitchell was drunk, and it was possible that he did not even know what he was saying, or what had happened, and that words just got loose from him this way, and anybody who knew him knew it. Only my father didn't. He only knew what had been said.

37   Boyd Mitchell stood up and put his hands in his pockets. He was much taller than my father. He had on a white Western shirt and whipcords and cowboy boots and was wearing a big silver wristwatch. "All right," he said. "Now I'm standing up. What's supposed to happen?" He weaved a little. I saw that.

38   And my father hit Boyd Mitchell then, hit him from across the card table—hit him with his right hand, square into the chest, not a lunging blow, just a hard, hitting blow that threw my father off balance and made him make a *chuffing* sound with his mouth. Boyd Mitchell groaned, "Oh," and fell down immediately, his big, thick, heavy body hitting the floor already doubled over. And the sound of him hitting the floor in our house was like no sound I had ever heard before. It was the sound of a man's body hitting a floor, and it was only that. In my life I have heard it other places, in hotel rooms and in bars, and it is one you do not want to hear.

> # Maybe she thought about the rest of her life then and what that might be like after tonight.

39   You can hit a man in a lot of ways, I know that, and I knew that then, because my father had told me. You can hit a man to insult him, or you can hit a man to bloody him, or to knock him down, or lay him out. Or you can hit a man to kill him. Hit him that hard. And that is how my father hit Boyd Mitchell—as hard as he could, in the chest and not in the face, the way someone might think who didn't know about it.

40   "Oh my God," Penny Mitchell said. Boyd Mitchell was lying on his side in front of the TV, and she had gotten down on her knees beside him. "Boyd," she said. "Are you hurt? Oh, look at this. Stay where you are, Boyd. Stay on the floor."

41   "Now then. All right," my father said. "Now. All right." He was standing against the wall, over to the side of where he had been when he hit Boyd Mitchell from across the card table. Light was bright in the room, and my father's eyes were wide and touring around. He seemed out of breath and both his fists were clenched, and I could feel his heart beating in my own chest. "All right, now, you son of a bitch," my father said, and loudly. I don't think he was even talking to Boyd Mitchell. He was just saying words that came out of him.

42   "Roy," my mother said calmly. "Boyd's hurt now. He's hurt." She was just looking down at Boyd Mitchell. I don't think she knew what to do.

43   "Oh, no," Penny Mitchell said in an excited voice. "Look up, Boyd. Look up at Penny. You've been hurt." She had her hands flat on Boyd Mitchell's chest, and her skinny shoulders close to him. She wasn't crying, but I think she was hysterical and couldn't cry.

44   All this had taken only five minutes, maybe even less time. I had never even left the kitchen door. And for that reason I walked out into the room where my father and mother were, and where Boyd and Penny Mitchell were both of them on the floor. I looked down at Boyd Mitchell, at his face. I wanted to see what had happened to him. His eyes had cast back up into their sockets. His mouth was open, and I could see his big pink tongue inside. He was breathing heavy breaths, and his fingers—the fingers on both his hands—were moving, moving in the way a man would move them if he was nervous or anxious about something. I think he was dead then, and I think even Penny Mitchell knew he was dead, because she was saying, "Oh please, please, please, Boyd."

45   That is when my mother called the police, and I think it is when my father opened the front door and stepped out into the night.

46   ALL that happened next is what you would expect to happen. Boyd Mitchell's chest quit breathing in a minute, and he turned pale and cold and began to look dead right on our living-room floor. He made a noise in his throat once, and Penny Mitchell cried out, and my mother got down on her knees and held Penny's shoulders while she cried. Then my mother made Penny get up and go into the bedroom—hers and my father's—and lie on the bed. Then she and I sat in the brightly lit living room, with Boyd Mitchell dead on the floor, and simply looked at each other—maybe for ten minutes, maybe for twenty. I don't know what my mother could've been thinking during that time, because she did not say. She did not ask about my father. She did not tell me to leave the room. Maybe she thought

about the rest of her life then and what that might be like after tonight. Or maybe she thought this: that people can do the worst things they are capable of doing and in the end the world comes back to normal. Possibly, she was just waiting for something normal to begin to happen again. That would make sense, given her particular character.

Though what I thought myself, sitting in that room with Boyd Mitchell dead, I remember very well, because I have thought it other times, and to a degree I began to date my real life from that moment and that thought. It is this: that situations have possibilities in them, and we have only to be present to be involved. Tonight was a very bad one. But how were we to know it would turn out this way until it was too late and we had all been changed forever? I realized though, that trouble, real trouble, was something to be avoided, inasmuch as once it has passed by, you have only yourself to answer to, even if, as I was, you are the cause of nothing.

In a little while the police arrived to our house. First one and then two more cars with their red lights turning in the street. Lights were on in the neighbors' houses—people came out and stood in the cold in their front yards watching, people I didn't know and who didn't know us. "It's a circus now," my mother said to me when we looked through the window. "We'll have to move somewhere else. They won't let us alone."

An ambulance came, and Boyd Mitchell was taken away on a stretcher, under a sheet. Penny Mitchell came out of the bedroom and went with them, though she did not say anything to my mother, or to anybody, just got in a police car and left into the dark.

Two policemen came inside, and one asked my mother some questions in the living room, while the other one asked me questions in the kitchen. He wanted to know what I had seen, and I told him. I said Boyd Mitchell had cursed at my father for some reason I didn't know, then had stood up and tried to hit him, and that my father had pushed Boyd, and that was all. He asked me if my father was a violent man, and I said no. He asked if my father had a girlfriend, and I said no. He asked if my mother and father had ever fought, and I said no. He asked me if I loved my mother and father, and I said I did. And then that was all.

I went out into the living room then, and my mother was there, and when the police left we stood at the front door, and there was my father outside, standing by the open door of a police car. He had on handcuffs. And for some reason he wasn't wearing a shirt or his corduroy jacket but was bare-chested in the cold night, holding his shirt behind him. His hair looked wet to me. I heard a policeman say, "Roy, you're going to catch cold," and then my father say, "I wish I was a long way from here right now. China maybe." He smiled at the policeman. I don't think he ever saw us watching, or if he did he didn't want to admit it. And neither of us did anything, because the police had him, and when that is the case, there is nothing you can do to help.

ALL this happened by ten o'clock. At midnight my mother and I drove down to the city jail and got my father out. I stayed in the car while my mother went in—sat and watched the high windows of the jail, which were behind wire mesh and bars. Yellow lights were on there, and I could hear voices and see figures move past the lights, and twice someone called out, "Hello, hello. Marie, are you with me?" And then it was quiet, except for the cars that drove slowly past ours.

On the ride home, my mother drove and my father sat and stared out at the big electrical stacks by the river, and the lights of houses on the other side, in Black Eagle. He had on a checked shirt someone inside had given him, and his hair was neatly combed. No one said anything, but I did not understand why the police would put anyone in jail because he had killed a man and in two hours let him out again. It was a mystery to me, even though I wanted him to be out and for our life to resume, and even though I did not see any way it could and, in fact, knew it never would.

Inside our house, all the lights were burning when we got back. It was one o'clock and there were still lights in some neighbors' houses. I could see a man at the window across the street, both his hands to the glass, watching out, watching us.

My mother went into the kitchen, and I could hear her running water for coffee and taking down cups. My father stood in the middle of the living room and looked around, looking at the chairs, at the card table with cards still on it, at the open doorways to the other rooms. It was as if he had forgotten his own house and now saw it again and didn't like it.

"I don't feel I know what he had against me," my father said. He said this to me, but he said it to anyone, too. "You'd think you'd know what a man had against you, wouldn't you, Frank?"

57 "Yes," I said, "I would." We were both just standing together, my father and I, in the lighted room there. We were not about to do anything.

58 "I want us to be happy here now," my father said. "I want us to enjoy life. I don't hold anything against anybody. Do you believe that?"

59 "I believe that," I said. My father looked at me with his dark blue eyes and frowned. And for the first time I wished my father had not done what he did but had gone about things differently. I saw him as a man who made mistakes, as a man who could hurt people, ruin lives, risk their happiness. A man who did not understand enough. He was like a gambler, though I did not even know what it meant to be a gambler then.

> "'You don't belong in jail. You stand up too straight.'"

60 "It's such a quickly changing time now," my father said. My mother, who had come into the kitchen doorway, stood looking at us. She had on a flowered pink apron, and was standing where I had stood earlier that night. She was looking at my father and at me as if we were one person. "Don't you think it is, Dorothy?" he said. "All this turmoil. Everything just flying by. Look what's happened here."

61 My mother seemed very certain about things then, very precise. "You should've controlled yourself more," she said. "That's all."

62 "I know that," my father said. "I'm sorry. I lost control over my mind. I didn't expect to ruin things, but now I think I have. It was all wrong." My father picked up the vodka bottle, unscrewed the cap and took a big swallow, then put the bottle back down. He had seen two men killed tonight. Who could've blamed him?

63 "When I was in jail tonight," he said, staring at a picture on the wall, a picture by the door to the hallway. He was just talking again. "There was a man in the cell with me. And I've never been in jail before, not even when I was a kid. But this man said to me tonight, 'I can tell you've never been in jail before just by the way you stand up straight. Other people don't stand that way. They stoop. You don't belong in jail. You stand up too straight.'" My father looked back at the vodka bottle as if he wanted to drink more out of it, but he only looked at it. "Bad things happen," he said, and he let his open hands tap against his legs like clappers against a bell. "Maybe he was in love with you, Dorothy," he said. "Maybe that's what the trouble was."

64 And what I did then was stare at the picture on the wall, the picture my father had been staring at, a picture I had seen every day. Probably I had seen it a thousand times. It was two people with a baby on a beach. A man and a woman sitting in the sand with an ocean behind. They were smiling at the camera, wearing bathing suits. In all the times I had seen it I'd thought that it was a picture in which I was the baby, and the two people were my parents. But I realized as I stood there, that it was not me at all; it was my father who was the child in the picture, and the parents there were his parents—two people I'd never known, and who were dead—and the picture was so much older than I had thought it was. I wondered why I hadn't known that before, hadn't understood it for myself, hadn't always known it. Not even that it mattered. What mattered was, I felt, that my father had fallen down now, as much as the man he had watched fall beneath the train just hours before. And I was as helpless to do anything as he had been. I wanted to tell him that I loved him, but for some reason I did not.

65 LATER in the night I lay in my bed with the radio playing, listening to news that was far away, in Calgary and in Saskatoon, and even farther, in Regina and Winnipeg—cold, dark cities I knew I would never see in my life. My window was raised above the sill, and for a long time I had sat and looked out, hearing my parents talk softly down below, hearing their footsteps, hearing my father's steel-toed boots strike the floor, and then their bedsprings squeeze and then be quiet. From out across the sliding river I could hear trucks—stock trucks and grain trucks heading toward Idaho, or down toward Helena, or into the train yards where my father hostled engines. The neighborhood houses were dark again. My father's motorcycle sat in the yard, and out in the night air I felt I could hear even the falls themselves, could hear every sound of them, sounds that found me and whirled and filled my room—could even feel them, cold and wintry, so that warmth seemed like a possibility I would never know again.

66 After a time my mother came in my room. The light fell on my bed, and she set a chair inside. I could see that she was looking at me. She closed the door, came and turned off my radio, then took her chair to the window, closed it, and sat so that I could see her face silhouetted against the streetlight. She lit a cigarette and did not look at me, still cold under the covers of my bed.

67 "How do you feel, Frank," she said, smoking her cigarette.

"I feel all right," I said.

"Do you think your house is a terrible house now?"

"No," I said.

"I hope not," my mother said. "Don't feel it is. Don't hold anything against anyone. Poor Boyd. He's gone."

"Why do you think that happened?" I said, though I didn't think she would answer, and wondered if I even wanted to know.

My mother blew smoke against the window glass, then sat and breathed. "He must've seen something in your father he just hated. I don't know what it was. Who knows? Maybe your father felt the same way." She shook her head and looked out into the street-lamp light. "I remember once," she said. "I was still in Havre, in the thirties. We were living in a motel my father part-owned out Highway Two, and my mother was around then, but wasn't having any of us. My father had this big woman named Judy Belknap as his girl-friend. She was an Assiniboin. Just some squaw. But we used to go on nature tours when he couldn't put up with me any-more. She'd take me. Way up above the Milk River. All this stuff she knew about, animals and plants and ferns—she'd tell me all that. And once we were sitting watching some gadwall ducks on the ice where a creek had made a little turn-out. It was getting colder, just like now. And Judy just all at once stood up and clapped. Just clapped her hands. And all these ducks got up, all except for one that stayed on the ice, where its feet were frozen, I guess. It didn't even try to fly. It just sat. And Judy said to me, 'It's just a coincidence, Dottie. It's wildlife. Some always get left back.' And that seemed to leave her satisfied for some reason. We walked back to the car after that. So," my mother said. "Maybe that's what this is. Just a coincidence."

She raised the window again, dropped her ciga-rette out, blew the last smoke from her throat, and said, "Go to sleep, Frank. You'll be all right. We'll all survive this. Be an optimist."

When I was asleep that night, I dreamed. And what I dreamed was of a plane crashing, a bomber, dropping out of the frozen sky, bouncing as it hit the icy river, sliding and turning on the ice, its wings like knives, and coming into our house where we were sleeping, leveling everything. And when I sat up in bed I could hear a dog in the yard, its collar jingling, and I could hear my father crying, "Boo-hoo-hoo, boo-hoo-hoo,"—like that, quietly—though afterward I could never be sure if I had heard him crying in just that way, or if all of it was a dream, a dream I wished I had never had.

THE most important things of your life can change so suddenly, so unrecoverably, that you can forget even the most important of them and their connections, you are so taken up by the chanciness of all that's happened and by all that could and will happen next. I now no longer remember the exact year of my father's birth, or how old he was when I last saw him, or even when that last time took place. When you're young, these things seem unforgettable and at the heart of everything. But they slide away and are gone when you are not so young.

My father went to Deer Lodge Prison and stayed five months for killing Boyd Mitchell by ac-cident, for using too much force to hit him. In Montana you can-not simply kill a man in your living room and walk off free from it, and what I remember is that my father pleaded no con-test, the same as guilty.

My mother and I lived in our house for the months he was gone. But when he came out and went back on the railroad as a switchman the two of them argued about things, about her wanting us to go someplace else to live—California or Seattle were mentioned. And then they separated, and she moved out. And after that I moved out by joining the Army and adding years to my age, which was sixteen.

I know about my father only that after a time he began to live a life he himself would never have be-lieved. He fell off the railroad, divorced my mother, who would now and then resurface in his life. Drink-ing was involved in that, and gambling, embezzling money, even carrying a pistol, is what I heard. I was apart from all of it. And when you are the age I was then, and loose on the world and alone, you can get along better than at almost any other time, because it's a novelty, and you can act for what you want, and you can think that being alone will not last forever. All I know of my father, finally, is that he was once in Laramie, Wyoming, and not in good shape, and then he simply disappeared from view.

80   A month ago I saw my mother. I was buying groceries at a drive-in store by the interstate in Anaconda, Montana, not far from Deer Lodge itself, where my father had been. It had been fifteen years, I think, since I had seen her, though I am forty-three years old now, and possibly it was longer. But when I saw her I walked across the store to where she was and I said, "Hello, Dorothy. It's Frank."

81   She looked at me and smiled and said, "Oh, Frank. How are you? I haven't seen you in a long time. I'm glad to see you now, though." She was dressed in blue jeans and boots and a Western shirt, and she looked like a woman who could be sixty years old. Her hair was tied back and she looked pretty, though I think she had been drinking. It was ten o'clock in the morning.

82   There was a man standing near her, holding a basket of groceries, and she turned to him and said, "Dick, come here and meet my son, Frank. We haven't seen each other in a long time. This is Dick Spivey, Frank."

83   I shook hands with Dick Spivey, who was a man younger than my mother but older than me—a tall, thin-faced man with coarse blue-black hair—and who was wearing Western boots like hers. "Let me say a word to Frank, Dick," my mother said, and she put her hand on Dick's wrist and squeezed it and smiled at him. And he walked up toward the checkout to pay for his groceries.

84   "So. What are you doing now, Frank," my mother asked, and put her hand on my wrist the way she had on Dick Spivey's, but held it there. "These years," she said.

85   "I've been down in Rock Springs, on the coal boom," I said. "I'll probably go back down there."

86   "And I guess you're married, too."

87   "I was," I said. "But not right now."

88   "That's fine," she said. "You look fine." She smiled at me. "You'll never get anything fixed just right. That's your mother's word. Your father and I had a marriage made in Havre—that was our joke about us. We used to laugh about it. You didn't know that, of course. You were too young. A lot of it was just wrong."

89   "It's a long time ago." I said. "I don't know about that."

90   "I remember those times very well," my mother said. "They were happy enough times. I guess something *was* in the air, wasn't there? Your father was

so jumpy. And Boyd got so mad, just all of a sudden. There was some hopelessness to it, I suppose. All that union business. We were the last to understand any of it, of course. We were trying to be decent people."

91   "That's right," I said. And I believed that was true of them.

92   "I still like to swim," my mother said. She ran her fingers back through her hair as if it were wet. She smiled at me again. "It still makes me feel freer."

93   "Good," I said. "I'm happy to hear that."

94   "Do you ever see your dad?"

95   "No," I said. "I never do."

96   "I don't either," my mother said. "You just reminded me of him." She looked at Dick Spivey, who was standing at the front window, holding a sack of groceries, looking out at the parking lot. It was March, and some small bits of snow were falling onto the cars in the lot. He didn't seem in any hurry. "Maybe I didn't appreciate your father enough," she said. "Who knows? Maybe we weren't even made for each other. Losing your love is the worst thing, and that's what we did." I didn't answer her, but I knew what she meant, and that it was true. "I wish we knew each other better, Frank," my mother said to me. She looked down, and I think she may have blushed. "We have our deep feelings, though, don't we? Both of us."

97   "Yes," I said. "We do."

98   "So. I'm going out now," my mother said. "Frank." She squeezed my wrist, and walked away through the checkout and into the parking lot, with Dick Spivey carrying their groceries beside her.

99   But when I had bought my own groceries and paid, and gone out to my car and started up, I saw Dick Spivey's green Chevrolet drive back into the lot and stop, and watched my mother get out and hurry across the snow to where I was, so that for a moment we faced each other through the open window.

100   "Did you ever think," my mother said, snow freezing in her hair. "Did you ever think back then that I was in love with Boyd Mitchell? Anything like that? Did you ever?"

101   "No," I said. "I didn't."

102   "No, well, I wasn't," she said. "Boyd was in love with Penny. I was in love with Roy. That's how things were. I want you to know it. You have to believe that. Do you?"

103   "Yes," I said. "I believe you."

104   And she bent down and kissed my cheek through the open window and touched my face with both her hands, held me for a moment that seemed like a long time before she turned away, finally, and left me there alone.

RICHARD Ford indicates in his interview that he grew up in the same neighborhood as Eudora Welty and cut his teeth on the novels of fellow Mississipian William Faulkner. Ford doesn't consider himself a Southern writer. His work ranges in location from Montana to New Jersey to Louisiana to New York, but if you like "Optimists," you may enjoy comparing Ford's story to Welty's thoroughly Southern "Why I Live at the P.O." (chapter 6) or the Faulkner stories in the casebook on the American South.

GOING FURTHER   You may also want to read Ford's Pulitzer Prize–winning novel *Independence Day*.

Writing from Reading

Summarize

1 What details does Ford provide about Frank's mother's relationship to Boyd? Based on what you know, discuss whether his mother is telling the truth at the end when she says there was nothing between her and Boyd.

Analyze Craft

2 Where in the story does Ford compress his characters' speech, and where does he let them talk? Where is the stress, the urgency, placed in what's said or left unexpressed? Consider the ways in which the dialogue in "Optimists" *instructs* the reader.

Analyze Voice

3 "Optimists" is told retrospectively from Frank's perspective. All these years later, is it possible that Frank (now forty-three) recalls exactly what was said when he was a child? Are we supposed to believe that the words within the quotation marks are true to the letter? If not, what kind of dramatic license does Ford take with this story's dialogue?

Synthesize Summary and Analysis

4 Consider why Ford has Dick Spivey present during Frank's final encounter with his mother. Why does he have Dick remain silent? Discuss how the final scene would change if Ford had left Dick Spivey out.

Interpret the Story

5 The last words of this story are "and left me there alone." What do we know and what can we deduce about Frank's present life; is he an "optimist"?

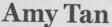

Q&A
A Conversation on Writing
Amy Tan

One of the first serious novelists of the post–Vietnam War era to make her mark on the imagination of a general readership, Amy Tan was born in Oakland, California, to Chinese immigrants. After college she became successful as a business writer and took up jazz piano as a hobby, a young Chinese American woman who had not yet clearly faced the matter of her cultural origins. It wasn't until after her marriage to a Bay Area tax attorney that she eventually began to try to write fiction based on her cultural heritage.

Like many first-generation Americans, Tan had not fully explored her relations to her parents' culture until she had established herself as a successful working adult. After her father and brother died within a year from brain tumors, she and her mother were left to work out their own difficulties. Her troubled relations with her mother eventually smoothed out, and after her mother recovered from a serious illness, the two of them traveled to China. There Tan got a firsthand look at the country of her parents' birth, beginning to explore her origins as possible material for fiction. This led to the composition of a series of stories, which Tan revised and made into the novel *The Joy Luck Club.* That book became a national best seller in 1989, and Tan has since published the novels *The Kitchen God's Wife, The Hundred Secret Senses, The Bonesetter's Daughter, Saving Fish from Drowning,* and two children's books, *The Moon Lady* and *Sagwa.*

Becoming a Reader

I was a very lonely child much of my childhood. Books were a place where I could find someone who understood me. That someone could have lived 200 years ago. Jane Eyre had nothing to do with my life. And yet she did. She was that lonely girl nobody understood . . . and I imagined myself living that life. I realized as a young reader, I could really go anywhere. I could go to the prairie and the big woods, I could be living in a different time. I could wear all these different clothes. I could have romances with the most popular boy. . . . That made me not feel so lonely.

On Voice and the Writing Process

When I started to write, I had this basic question that was posed to me by a woman named Molly Giles, a wonderful writer. She had read my work. And she said, "You know, what you've written here is not a story. It is the beginnings of a dozen stories." And she pointed out these sentences. She said, "This is the beginning of a story, this is the beginning of a story, this is the beginning. This is a voice, this is a voice, this is a voice." And I thought, Well, what is a voice? And what's a story? What are the things that make this up? But I feel now, now that I've been doing this for a while, that the questions are still there. And there's no absolute answer. And that you discover it each time you sit down and write. . . .

To watch this entire interview online and hear the author read from "Two Kinds," go to **www.mhhe.com/ delbanco1e.**

RESEARCH ASSIGNMENT   Amy Tan says in her interview that reading and writing fiction are subversive. Listen to the interview and explain what she means. Do you agree with her?

AS YOU READ As is the case with "Optimists," the narrator here describes her past from a present vantage point; she's a good deal older than the character described. Consider the perspective from which this tale is told.

Two Kinds (1989)

1 MY mother believed you could be anything you wanted to be in America. You could open a restaurant. You could work for the government and get good retirement. You could buy a house with almost no money down. You could become rich. You could become instantly famous.

2 "Of course, you can be prodigy, too," my mother told me when I was nine. "You can be best anything. What does Auntie Lindo know? Her daughter, she is only best tricky."

3 America was where all my mother's hopes lay. She had come here in 1949 after losing everything in China: her mother and father, her family home, her first husband, and two daughters, twin baby girls. But she never looked back with regret. There were so many ways for things to get better

4 WE didn't immediately pick the right kind of prodigy. At first my mother thought I could be a Chinese Shirley Temple. We'd watch Shirley's old movies on TV as though they were training films. My mother would poke my arm and say, *"Ni kan"* —You watch. And I would see Shirley tapping her feet, or singing a sailor song, or pursing her lips into a very round O while saying "Oh, my goodness."

5 *"Ni kan,"* said my mother, as Shirley's eyes flooded with tears. "You already know how. Don't need talent for crying!"

6 Soon after my mother got this idea about Shirley Temple, she took me to a beauty training school in the Mission district and put me in the hands of a student who could barely hold the scissors without shaking. Instead of getting big fat curls, I emerged with an uneven mass of crinkly black fuzz. My mother dragged me off to the bathroom and tried to wet down my hair.

7 "You look like Negro Chinese," she lamented, as if I had done this on purpose.

8 The instructor of the beauty training school had to lop off these soggy clumps to make my hair even again. "Peter Pan is very popular these days," the instructor assured my mother. I now had hair the length of a boy's, with straight-across bangs that hung at a slant two inches above my eyebrows. I liked the haircut and it made me actually look forward to my future fame.

9 In fact, in the beginning, I was just as excited as my mother, maybe even more so. I pictured this prodigy part of me as many different images, trying each one on for size. I was a dainty ballerina girl standing by the curtains, waiting to hear the right music that would send me floating on my tiptoes. I was like the Christ child lifted out of the straw manger, crying with holy indignity. I was Cinderella stepping from her pumpkin carriage with sparkly cartoon music filling the air.

10 In all of my imaginings, I was filled with a sense that I would soon become *perfect*. My mother and father would adore me. I would be beyond reproach. I would never feel the need to sulk for anything.

11 But sometimes the prodigy in me became impatient. "If you don't hurry up and get me out of here, I'm disappearing for good," it warned. "And then you'll always be nothing."

12 EVERY night after dinner, my mother and I would sit at the Formica kitchen table. She would present new tests, taking her examples from stories of amazing children she had read in *Ripley's Believe It or Not*, or *Good Housekeeping, Reader's Digest*, and a dozen other magazines she kept in a pile in our bathroom. My mother got these magazines from people whose houses she cleaned. And since she cleaned many houses each week, we had a great assortment. She would look through them all, searching for stories about remarkable children.

13 The first night she brought out a story about a three-year-old boy who knew the capitals of all the states and even most of the European countries. A teacher was quoted as saying the little boy could also pronounce the names of the foreign cities correctly.

14 "What's the capital of Finland?" my mother asked me, looking at the magazine story.

15 All I knew was the capital of California, because Sacramento was the name of the street we lived on in Chinatown. "Nairobi!" I guessed, saying the most foreign word I could think of. She checked to see if that was possibly one way to pronounce "Helsinki" before showing me the answer.

16 The tests got harder—multiplying numbers in my head, finding the queen of hearts in a deck of cards, trying to stand on my head without using my hands, predicting the daily temperatures in Los Angeles, New York, and London.

17 One night I had to look at a page from the Bible for three minutes and then report everything I could remember. "Now Jehoshaphat had riches and honor in abundance and . . . that's all I remember, Ma," I said.

18 And after seeing my mother's disappointed face once again, something inside of me began to die. I hated the tests, the raised hopes and failed expectations. Before going to bed that night, I looked in the mirror above the bathroom sink and when I saw only my face staring back—and that it would always be this ordinary face—I began to cry. Such a sad, ugly girl! I made high-pitched noises like a crazed animal, trying to scratch out the face in the mirror.

19 And then I saw what seemed to be the prodigy side of me—because I had never seen that face before. I looked at my reflection, blinking so that I could see more clearly. The girl staring back at me was angry, powerful. This girl and I were the same. I had new thoughts, willful thoughts, or rather thoughts filled with lots of won'ts. I won't let her change me, I promised myself. I won't be what I'm not.

I won't let her change me,
I promised myself.

20 So now on nights when my mother presented her tests, I performed listlessly, my head propped on one arm. I pretended to be bored. And I was. I got so bored I started counting the bellows of the foghorns out on the bay while my mother drilled me in other areas. The sound was comforting and reminded me of the cow jumping over the moon. And the next day, I played a game with myself, seeing if my mother would give up on me before eight bellows. After a while I usually counted only one, maybe two bellows at most. At last she was beginning to give up hope.

21 TWO or three months had gone by without any mention of my being a prodigy again. And then one day my mother was watching *The Ed Sullivan Show* on TV. The TV was old and the sound kept shorting out. Every time my mother got halfway up from the sofa to adjust the set, the sound would go back on and Ed would be talking. As soon as she sat down, Ed would go silent again. She got up, the TV broke into loud piano music. She sat down. Silence. Up and down, back and forth, quiet and loud. It was like a stiff embraceless dance between her and the TV set. Finally she stood by the set with her hand on the sound dial.

22 She seemed entranced by the music, a little frenzied piano piece with this mesmerizing quality, sort of quick passages and then teasing lilting ones before it returned to the quick playful parts.

23 "*Ni kan*," my mother said, calling me over with hurried hand gestures, "Look here."

24 I could see why my mother was fascinated by the music. It was being pounded out by a little Chinese girl, about nine years old, with a Peter Pan haircut. The girl had the sauciness of a Shirley Temple. She was proudly modest like a proper Chinese child. And she also did this fancy sweep of a curtsy, so that the fluffy skirt of her white dress cascaded slowly to the floor like the petals of a large carnation.

25 In spite of these warning signs, I wasn't worried. Our family had no piano and we couldn't afford to buy one, let alone reams of sheet music and piano lessons. So I could be generous in my comments when my mother bad-mouthed the little girl on TV.

26 "Play note right, but doesn't sound good! No singing sound," complained my mother.

27 "What are you picking on her for?" I said carelessly. "She's pretty good. Maybe she's not the best, but she's trying hard." I knew almost immediately I would be sorry I said that.

28 "Just like you," she said. "Not the best. Because you not trying." She gave a little huff as she let go of the sound dial and sat down on the sofa.

29 The little Chinese girl sat down also to play an encore of "Anitra's Dance" by Grieg. I remember the song, because later on I had to learn how to play it.

30 THREE days after watching *The Ed Sullivan Show*, my mother told me what my schedule would be for piano lessons and piano practice. She had talked to Mr. Chong, who lived on the first floor of our apartment building. Mr. Chong was a retired piano teacher and my mother had traded housecleaning services for weekly lessons and a piano for me to practice on every day, two hours a day, from four until six.

31 When my mother told me this, I felt as though I had been sent to hell. I whined and then kicked my foot a little when I couldn't stand it anymore.

32 "Why don't you like me the way I am? I'm *not* a genius! I can't play the piano. And even if I could, I wouldn't go on TV if you paid me a million dollars!" I cried.

33 My mother slapped me. "Who ask you to be genius?" she shouted. "Only ask you be your best. For you sake. You think I want you to be genius? Hnnh! What for! Who ask you!"

34 "So ungrateful," I heard her mutter in Chinese. "If she had as much talent as she has temper, she would be famous now."

35 Mr. Chong, whom I secretly nicknamed Old Chong, was very strange, always tapping his fingers to the silent music of an invisible orchestra. He looked ancient in my eyes. He had lost most of the hair on top of his head, and he wore thick glasses and had eyes that always looked tired and sleepy. But he must have been younger than I thought, since he lived with his mother and was not yet married.

36 I met Old Lady Chong once and that was enough. She had this peculiar smell like a baby that had done something in its pants. And her fingers felt like a dead person's, like an old peach I once found in the back of the refrigerator; the skin just slid off the meat when I picked it up.

37 I soon found out why Old Chong had retired from teaching piano. He was deaf. "Like Beethoven!" he shouted to me. "We're both listening only in our head!" And he would start to conduct his frantic silent sonatas.

38 Our lessons went like this. He would open the book and point to different things, explaining their purpose: "Key! Treble! Bass! No sharps or flats! So this is C major! Listen now and play after me!"

39 And then he would play the C scale a few times, a simple chord, and then, as if inspired by an old unreachable itch, he gradually added more notes and running trills and a pounding bass until the music was really something quite grand.

40 I would play after him, the simple scale, the simple chord, and then I just played some nonsense that sounded like a cat running up and down on top of garbage cans. Old Chong smiled and applauded and then said, "Very good! But now you must learn to keep time!"

41 So that's how I discovered that Old Chong's eyes were too slow to keep up with the wrong notes I was playing. He went through the motions in half-time. To help me keep rhythm, he stood behind me, pushing down on my right shoulder for every beat. He balanced pennies on top of my wrists so I would keep them still as I slowly played scales and arpeggios. He had me curve my hand around an apple and keep that shape when playing chords. He marched stiffly to show me how to make each finger dance up and down, staccato like an obedient little soldier.

42 He taught me all these things, and that was how I also learned I could be lazy and get away with mistakes, lots of mistakes. If I hit the wrong notes because I hadn't practiced enough, I never corrected myself. I just kept playing in rhythm. And Old Chong kept conducting his own private reverie.

43 So maybe I never really gave myself a fair chance. I did pick up the basics pretty quickly, and I might have become a good

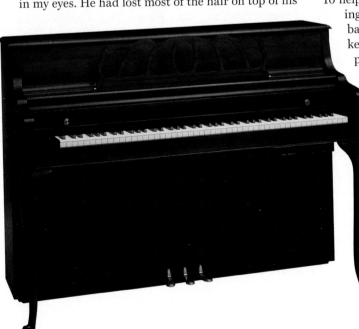

pianist at that young age. But I was so determined not to try, not to be anybody different that I learned to play only the most ear-splitting preludes, the most discordant hymns.

44 Over the next year, I practiced like this, dutifully in my own way. And then one day I heard my mother and her friend Lindo Jong both talking in a loud bragging tone of voice so others could hear. It was after church, and I was leaning against the brick wall wearing a dress with stiff white petticoats. Auntie Lindo's daughter, Waverly, who was about my age, was standing farther down the wall about five feet away. We had grown up together and shared all the closeness of two sisters squabbling over crayons and dolls. In other words, for the most part, we hated each other. I thought she was snotty. Waverly Jong had gained a certain amount of fame as "Chinatown's Littlest Chinese Chess Champion."

45 "She bring home too many trophy," lamented Auntie Lindo that Sunday. "All day she play chess. All day I have no time do nothing but dust off her winnings." She threw a scolding look at Waverly, who pretended not to see her.

46 "You lucky you don't have this problem," said Auntie Lindo with a sigh to my mother.

47 And my mother squared her shoulders and bragged: "Our problem worser than yours. If we ask Jing-mei wash dish, she hear nothing but music. It's like you can't stop this natural talent."

48 And right then I was determined to put a stop to her foolish pride.

49 A FEW weeks later, Old Chong and my mother conspired to have me play in a talent show which would be held in the church hall. By then, my parents had saved up enough to buy me a secondhand piano, a black Wurlitzer spinet with a scarred bench. It was the showpiece of our living room.

50 For the talent show, I was to play a piece called "Pleading Child" from Schumann's *Scenes from Childhood*. It was a simple, moody piece that sounded more difficult than it was. I was supposed to memorize the whole thing, playing the repeat parts twice to make the piece sound longer. But I dawdled over it, playing a few bars and then cheating, looking up to see what notes followed. I never really listened to what I was playing. I daydreamed about being somewhere else, about being someone else.

51 The part I liked to practice best was the fancy curtsy: right foot out, touch the rose on the carpet with a pointed foot, sweep to the side, left leg bends, look up and smile.

My parents invited all the couples from the Joy Luck Club to witness my debut. Auntie Lindo and Uncle Tin were there. Waverly and her two older brothers had also come. The first two rows were filled with children both younger and older than I was. The littlest ones got to go first. They recited simple nursery rhymes, squawked out tunes on miniature violins, twirled Hula Hoops, pranced in pink ballet tutus, and when they bowed or curtsied, the audience would sigh in unison, "Awww," and then clap enthusiastically.

When my turn came, I was very confident. I remember my childish excitement. It was as if I knew, without a doubt, that the prodigy side of me really did exist. I had no fear whatsoever, no nervousness. I remember thinking to myself, This is it! This is it! I looked out over the audience, at my mother's blank face, my father's yawn, Auntie Lindo's stiff-lipped smile, Waverly's sulky expression. I had on a white dress layered with sheets of lace, and a pink bow in my Peter Pan haircut. As I sat down I envisioned people jumping to their feet and Ed Sullivan rushing up to introduce me to everyone on TV.

And I started to play. It was so beautiful. I was so caught up in how lovely I looked that at first I didn't worry how I would sound. So it was a surprise to me when I hit the first wrong note and I realized something didn't sound quite right. And then I hit another and another followed that. A chill started at the top of my head and began to trickle down. Yet I couldn't stop playing, as though my hands were bewitched. I kept thinking my fingers would adjust themselves back, like a train switching to the right track. I played this strange jumble through two repeats, the sour notes staying with me all the way to the end.

When I stood up, I discovered my legs were shaking. Maybe I had just been nervous and the audience, like Old Chong, had seen me go through the right motions and had not heard anything wrong at all. I swept my right foot out, went down on my knee, looked up and smiled. The room was quiet, except for Old Chong, who was beaming and shouting, "Bravo! Bravo! Well done!" But then I saw my mother's face, her stricken face. The audience clapped weakly, and as I walked back to my chair, with my whole face quivering as I tried not to cry, I heard a little boy whisper loudly to his mother, "That was awful," and the mother whispered back, "Well, she certainly tried."

And now I realized how many people were in the audience, the whole world it seemed. I was aware of eyes burning into my back. I felt the shame of my mother and father as they sat stiffly throughout the rest of the show.

We could have escaped during intermission. Pride and some strange sense of honor must have anchored my parents to their chairs. And so we watched it all: the eighteen-year-old boy with a fake mustache who did a magic show and juggled flaming hoops while riding a unicycle. The breasted girl with white makeup who sang from *Madama Butterfly* and got honorable mention. And the eleven-year-old boy who won first prize playing a tricky violin song that sounded like a busy bee.

After the show, the Hsus, the Jongs, and the St. Clairs from the Joy Luck Club came up to my mother and father.

"Lots of talented kids," Auntie Lindo said vaguely, smiling broadly.

"That was somethin' else," said my father, and I wondered if he was referring to me in a humorous way, or whether he even remembered what I had done.

Waverly looked at me and shrugged her shoulders. "You aren't a genius like me," she said matter-of-factly. And if I hadn't felt so bad, I would have pulled her braids and punched her stomach.

But my mother's expression was what devastated me: a quiet, blank look that said she had lost everything. I felt the same way, and it seemed as if everybody were now coming up, like gawkers at the scene of an accident, to see what parts were actually missing. When we got on the bus to go home, my father was humming the busy-bee tune and my mother was silent. I kept thinking she wanted to wait until we got home before shouting at me. But when my father unlocked the door to our apartment, my mother walked in and then went to the back, into the bedroom. No accusations. No blame. And in a way, I felt disappointed. I had been waiting for her to start shouting, so I could shout back and cry and blame her for all my misery.

I ASSUMED my talent-show fiasco meant I never had to play the piano again. But two days later, after school, my mother came out of the kitchen and saw me watching TV.

"Four clock," she reminded me as if it were any other day. I was stunned, as though she were asking me to go through the talent-show torture again. I wedged myself more tightly in front of the TV.

"Turn off TV," she called from the kitchen five minutes later.

I didn't budge. And then I decided. I didn't have to do what my mother said anymore. I wasn't her slave. This wasn't China. I had listened to her before and look what happened. She was the stupid one.

She came out from the kitchen and stood in the arched entryway of the living room. "Four clock," she said once again, louder.

"I'm not going to play anymore," I said nonchalantly. "Why should I? I'm not a genius."

She walked over and stood in front of the TV. I saw her chest was heaving up and down in an angry way.

"No!" I said, and I now felt stronger, as if my true self had finally emerged. So this was what had been inside me all along.

"No! I won't!" I screamed.

She yanked me by the arm, pulled me off the floor, snapped off the TV. She was frighteningly strong, half pulling, half carrying me toward the piano as I kicked the throw rugs under my feet. She lifted me up and onto the hard bench. I was sobbing by now, looking at her bitterly. Her chest was heaving even more and her mouth was open, smiling crazily as if she were pleased I was crying.

"You want me to be someone that I'm not!" I sobbed. "I'll never be the kind of daughter you want me to be!"

"Only two kinds of daughters," she shouted in Chinese. "Those who are obedient and those who follow their own mind! Only one kind of daughter can live in this house. Obedient daughter!"

"Then I wish I wasn't your daughter. I wish you weren't my mother," I shouted. As I said these things I got scared. It felt like worms and toads and slimy things crawling out of my chest, but it also felt good, as if this awful side of me had surfaced, at last.

"Too late to change this," my mother said shrilly.

And I could sense her anger rising to its breaking point. I wanted to see it spill over. And that's when I remembered the babies she had lost in China, the ones we never talked about. "Then I wish I'd never been born!" I shouted. "I wish I were dead! Like them."

It was as if I had said the magic words. Alakazam!— and her face went blank, her mouth closed, her arms went slack, and she backed out of the room, stunned, as if she were blowing away like a small brown leaf, thin, brittle, lifeless.

79   IT was not the only disappointment my mother felt in me. In the years that followed, I failed her so many times, each time asserting my own will, my right to fall short of expectations. I didn't get straight As. I didn't become class president. I didn't get into Stanford. I dropped out of college.

80   For unlike my mother, I did not believe I could be anything I wanted to be. I could only be me.

81   And for all those years, we never talked about the disaster at the recital or my terrible accusations afterward at the piano bench. All that remained unchecked, like a betrayal that was now unspeakable. So I never found a way to ask her why she had hoped for something so large that failure was inevitable.

82   And even worse, I never asked her what frightened me the most: Why had she given up hope?

83   For after our struggle at the piano, she never mentioned my playing again. The lessons stopped. The lid to the piano was closed, shutting out the dust, my misery, and her dreams.

84   So she surprised me. A few years ago, she offered to give me the piano, for my thirtieth birthday. I had not played in all those years. I saw the offer as a sign of forgiveness, a tremendous burden removed.

85   "Are you sure?" I asked shyly. "I mean, won't you and Dad miss it?"

86   "No, this your piano," she said firmly. "Always your piano. You only one can play."

87   "Well, I probably can't play anymore," I said. "It's been years."

88   "You pick up fast," said my mother, as if she knew this was certain. "You have natural talent. You could been genius if you want to."

89   "No, I couldn't."

90   "You just not trying," said my mother. And she was neither angry nor sad. She said it as if to announce a fact that could never be disproved. "Take it," she said.

> ## I played a few bars,
> surprised at how easily the
> notes came back to me.

   But I didn't at first. It was enough that she had offered it to me. And after that, every time I saw it in my parents' living room, standing in front of the bay windows, it made me feel proud, as if it were a shiny trophy I had won back.

   LAST week I sent a tuner over to my parent's apartment and had the piano reconditioned, for purely sentimental reasons. My mother had died a few months before and I had been been getting things in order for my father, a little bit at a time. I put the jewelry in special silk pouches. The sweaters she had knitted in yellow, pink, bright orange—all the colors I hated—I put those in moth-proof boxes. I found some old Chinese silk dresses, the kind with little slits up the sides. I rubbed the old silk against my skin, then wrapped them in tissue and decided to take them home with me.

   After I had the piano tuned, I opened the lid and touched the keys. It sounded even richer than I remembered. Really, it was a very good piano. Inside the bench were the same exercise notes with handwritten scales, the same secondhand music books with their covers held together with yellow tape.

   I opened up the Schumann book to the dark little piece I had played at the recital. It was on the left-hand side of the page, "Pleading Child." It looked more difficult than I remembered. I played a few bars, surprised at how easily the notes came back to me.

   And for the first time, or so it seemed, I noticed the piece on the right-hand side. It was called "Perfectly Contented." I tried to play this one as well. It had a lighter melody but the same flowing rhythm and turned out to be quite easy. "Pleading Child" was shorter but slower; "Perfectly Contented" was longer, but faster. And after I played them both a few times, I realized they were two halves of the same song.

IF you like "Two Kinds," you may also like other stories with distinctive voices, such as that of Bernard Malamud's marriage broker in "The Magic Barrel" (chapter 6) or Gish Jen's irate speaker in "Who's Irish?" (chapter 5).

GOING FURTHER   Amy Tan says in her interview that she is reading writers in translation to get a different point of view. You may be interested in some of these works as well, such as Dai Sijie's *Balzac and the Little Chinese Seamstress*, or *The Sand Child*, by Moroccan Tahar Ben Jelloun.

Writing from Reading

Summarize

1 Some of these memories are comic, some bitter, some loving, some aggrieved. Summarize the daughter's reactions to her mother's expectations and see how and where they change.

Analyze Craft

2 All dialogue by the narrator's mother is written in broken English, even when she is speaking in her native Chinese. What effect does this dialect have on your impression of the mother?

Analyze Voice

3 Tan writes as a first-generation American, a writer from the West Coast. Are there any details in the story that highlight her situation? Is there anything in the way the narrator speaks that calls these facts to mind?

Synthesize Summary and Analysis

4 How does the dialect in the mother's speech reflected in the dialogue between the mother and child establish the narrator's identity as a second-generation Chinese American?

Interpret the Story

5 The first line of "Two Kinds" reads, "My mother believed you could be anything you wanted to be in America." This line is repeated throughout the story. Find instances in the story that prove or refute this statement. Based on the story, do you think Tan believes this idea?

Suggestions for Writing

1. Reread "Optimists." How does your understanding of it differ from the first reading? How did Ford's own comments about the story and his goals as a writer enhance or diminish your responses?

2. Which character do you feel you know better—Mitya or Frank? What elements of craft or voice has the author used to help you know this character? Give examples.

3. Chekhov, a great playwright, envisions "Rapture" almost as a one-act play and sets it up "in scene." How would it be altered if in fact this were a play and not short fiction? What role does dialogue play in "Optimists" and "Two Kinds"? Write an essay that explores the functions of dialogue in the chapter's three stories.

4. Reread the opening sentences of "Optimists," "Two Kinds," and "Rapture." What is the dramatic effect of these opening sentences? How do they work to launch the stories?

3 Writing about Fiction

WASH the white clothes on Monday and put them on the stone heap; wash the color clothes on Tuesday and put them on the clothesline to dry; don't walk barehead in the hot sun; cook pumpkin fritters in very hot sweet oil; soak your little cloths right after you take them off . . .

—*from "Girl" by Jamaica Kincaid*

"I just write. I come to the end, I start again. I come to the end, I start again. And then sometimes I come to the end, and there is no starting again. In my mind there is no question of who will do what and when. Sometimes I've written the end of something before I've written the beginning."

Conversation with Jamaica Kincaid, available on video at www.mhhe.com/delbanco1e

SOME writers, like those interviewed in the previous chapters—John Updike, Richard Ford, and Amy Tan—respond to material from the world around them and present it in a straightforward fashion. Other writers, like Jamaica Kincaid in "Girl," combine realistic and fantastic elements, such as dreams, myths, convoluted plots, and non-naturalistic description. Her "Girl" is an extended monologue, a compilation of lines strung together and remembered but not transcribed as overheard speech. Here the author hopes to highlight aspects of reality that don't mimic everyday life. Kincaid's "Girl" may seem like an unconventional short story. It's quite brief. Also, it is written entirely in the back-and-forth of dialogue, without "objective" descriptive prose or so-called tag lines to alert you to the identity of the speaker. Much of it reads like a repeated instruction; the "girl" has been told all this often. By comparison with such stories as Updike's "A&P" or Ford's "Optimists," this brief, dense summary of a relationship seems less "realistic." However, "Girl" does contain all the components of successful short fiction—from plot and character to theme and symbol.

CONTINUED ON PAGE 54

It's more important to read than to write.

Q & A

I'm really interested in breaking the form....

A Conversation on Writing
Jamaica Kincaid

On Reading and Writing

The advice I always give to people who are going to write is: It's more important to read than to write. I sometimes think I became a writer really to have the opportunity to read some more, because it's the only excuse. It's the only way you are really allowed to read and say, "Well I'm writing. You think I'm reading but really it's part of writing." . . . So, no, reading is the most important thing, and not your own work, reading other things.

On Form, the Voice in "Girl," and Her Mother

Whatever a novel is, I'm not it, and whatever a short story is, I'm not it. If I had to follow these forms, I couldn't write. I'm really interested in breaking the form. . . . With "Girl," I wanted to write something new. . . . Certainly at the time I wrote ["Girl"], I didn't know how to interpret my own experience. I had only the voice . . . of my mother . . . firmly embedded in and interwoven into the way I express myself. . . . I was taught all those instructions. Yes, everything was by her.

On the Writing Process

I generally only have one draft. The first draft is the last draft, but that's because I tend not to commit things to paper before I've fully worked them out in my head. I'm really writing all the time; it sometimes will take me a week to complete a sentence. But that's because it's not right, it doesn't sound right the way I see it in my head. And then when it's completed, and I can judge it, I can see how it works inside my head, I put it to paper and there it is.

To watch this entire interview and hear the author read from "Girl," go to **www.mhhe.com/delbanco1e.**

Jamaica Kincaid was born Elaine Potter Richardson in St. Johns, Antigua, a small Caribbean island in the British West Indies. Images of Kincaid's mother and the close bond they shared run through much of her writing. Kincaid was a precocious child educated in the government school system, which was largely shaped by British influence and which fostered in this particular student a growing disdain for England. Indeed, the British use the expression "don't tell stories" when they reprimand their children for lying—but Jamaica Kincaid has been telling stories ever since.

At the age of seventeen, Kincaid traveled to the United States to work as a nanny for the children of affluent families—an experience reported in her novel *Lucy.* Before long she found her way to New York City, changed her name, and began writing for magazines such as *Ms., Ingenue,* and the *Village Voice.* She became a regular writer for *The New Yorker,* which published her first short stories as well as brief prose pieces in its "Talk of the Town" page; these have been collected in *Talk Stories* (2001).

Kincaid is perhaps best known for turning the facts of her personal history into fictions that blend fantasy and reality, the imagined and the actual. Her first published collection of stories, *At the Bottom of the River* (1983), and novels such as *Annie John* (1985), *Lucy* (1991), *The Autobiography of My Mother* (1996), and *Mr. Potter* (2002) all explore the boundaries of actual and imagined life, or memoir and dream. Her books defy easy classification, falling into the gray area between autobiography and fiction: the incantatory rhythms of her first-person narrator have the quality of song.

RESEARCH ASSIGNMENT In her interview, Kincaid talks about her relationship with her mother. Listen to the interview and comment on how you think this influences the writing of "Girl."

AS YOU READ   As you read "Girl," ask yourself who the main speaker is and how she reveals herself. If she were speaking to you, how would you feel? How do you feel as you listen to her? How does "Girl" achieve the inclusion of all the traditional elements of fiction, from plot to theme, in such limited space?

Girl (1983)

WASH the white clothes on Monday and put them on the stone heap; wash the color clothes on Tuesday and put them on the clothesline to dry; don't walk barehead in the hot sun; cook pumpkin fritters in very hot sweet oil; soak your little cloths right after you take them off; when buying cotton to make yourself a nice blouse, be sure that it doesn't have gum on it, because that way it won't hold up well after a wash; soak salt fish overnight before you cook it; is it true that you sing benna[1] in Sunday school?; always eat your food in such a way that it won't turn someone else's stomach; on Sundays try to walk like a lady and not like the slut you are so bent on becoming; don't sing benna in Sunday school; you mustn't speak to wharf-rat boys, not even to give directions; don't eat fruits on the street—flies will follow you, *but I don't sing benna on Sundays at all and never in Sunday school;* this is how to sew a button; this is how to make a buttonhole for the button you have just sewed on; this is how to hem a dress when you see the hem coming down and so to prevent yourself from looking like the slut I know you are so bent on becoming; this is how you iron your father's khaki shirt so that it doesn't have a crease; this is how you iron your father's khaki pants so that they don't have a crease; this is how you grow okra—far from the house, because okra tree harbors red ants; when you are growing *dasheen,*[2] make sure it gets plenty of water or else it makes your throat itch when you are eating it; this is how you sweep a corner; this is how you sweep a whole house; this is how you sweep a yard; this is how you smile to someone you don't like too much; this is how you smile to someone you don't like at all; this is how you smile to someone you like completely; this is how you set a table for tea; this is how you set a table for dinner; this is how you set a table for dinner with an important guest; this is how you set a table for lunch; this is how you set a table for breakfast; this is how to behave in the presence of men who don't know you very well, and this way they won't recognize immediately the slut I have warned you against becoming; be sure to wash every day, even if it is with your own spit; don't squat down to play marbles—you are not a boy, you know; don't pick people's flowers—you might catch something; don't throw stones at blackbirds, because it might not be a blackbird at all; this is how to make a bread pudding; this is how to make *doukona;*[3] this is how to make *pepper pot;*[4] this is how to make a good medicine for a cold; this is how to make a good medicine to throw away a child before it even becomes a child; this is how to catch a fish; this is how to throw back a fish you don't like, and that way something bad won't fall on you; this is how to bully a man; this is how a man bullies you; this is how to love a man, and if this doesn't work there are other ways, and if they don't work don't feel too bad about giving up; this is how to spit up in the air if you feel like it, and this is how to move quick so that it doesn't fall on you; this is how to make ends meet; always squeeze bread to make sure it's fresh; *but what if the baker won't let me feel the bread?;* you mean to say that after all you are really going to be the kind of woman who the baker won't let near the bread?

> . . . this is how you smile to someone you don't like too much . . .

[1] A form of folk music that originated in the Caribbean islands of Antigua and Barbuda and is usually about lewd or scandalous subjects.

[2] A tropical plant, similar in appearance to elephant ear plants, that grows up to seven feet tall and has edible roots.

[3] A spicy pudding.

[4] A Caribbean stew made of meat, vegetables, and spices.

IF you like "Girl," you might have a taste for magical realism—a style that emerged in the literature of the Caribbean region during the mid-twentieth century and gained practitioners throughout South America—and would enjoy reading the work of Gabriel García Márquez, whose story "The Handsomest Drowned Man in the World" appears in Stories for Further Reading.

GOING FURTHER   In her interview, Kincaid says "Girl" is in a way a condensed version of her novel *Annie John,* which you might like to read in relation to this short work.

Writing from Reading

Summarize

1 Who are the story's characters, and what do you know about them?

Analyze Craft

2 Consider the structure of the story, the order in which the author presents the pieces of advice. How important is the organization of information, and what does it mean?

3 What do you know about the setting of the story? Give examples that reveal and describe it.

4 Is there dialogue in the story? If so, what form does it take and what function does it serve?

Analyze Voice

5 How does the way the girl receives and responds to advice serve to characterize her? Is she a passive character? Why or why not?

Synthesize Summary and Analysis

6 What are the distinct characteristics of the two voices in the story?

Discuss how these two voices help generate the implied setting and motion of the story. How would your mental image of the story change if Kincaid had not included the girl's responses?

Interpret the Story

7 In her interview, Kincaid says that the voice in "Girl" is the voice of her mother, but she also says that there is no difference between her voice and the voice in which she writes. Discuss whether Kincaid has captured her mother's voice, or whether she has filtered that voice through her own.

"I think that you really can't be a writer without being a reader."

Conversation with
ZZ Packer

(CONTINUED FROM PAGE 51)

FROM READING TO WRITING

The first two chapters discussed how reading critically is the means to get your writing started. You look at the title of the work, find out about the author and the context within which a piece was written, and record your impressions by annotating a text or keeping a reading journal about how the elements of craft and the writer's voice work in a particular story. Whatever your assignment—a summary of the work, a short critical response, or a full-fledged research paper requiring multiple sources—one crucial component of writing effectively emerges when you discover something in the subject that is meaningful to *you*. Here is a quick checklist for writing a paper that may help you get started.

Checklist for Writing

✓ **EXPLORE YOUR IDEAS.**

Journal, annotate, brainstorm, freewrite, surf the Web, browse the library, and recognize this: Finding meaning is a complex issue that involves multiple perspectives. Toward what aspect of a story do you find yourself turning in thought? What aspect of the story stirs your emotions the most? These turns of mind and feeling will often alert you to your special interest in a story.

✓ **DEVELOP A WORKING THESIS.**

Make a strong claim that is specific and significant. To maintain a thoughtful tone, you may want to frame your claim as a question you will explore throughout your paper.

✓ **CREATE A PLAN.**

Outlines (formal and informal) can help you support and develop your claim with evidence.

✓ **GENERATE A FIRST DRAFT.**

Avoid straight summary (unless this is the assignment), and, unless you revise in your head like Jamaica Kincaid, give yourself time to go back to revise, edit, and format your paper. At this point you may want to get comments from other readers; their comments may help you revise your paper.

✓ **REVISE YOUR DRAFT.**

Focus on the purpose of your writing and rethink to revise: test your thesis (an exploration of any topic might lead you somewhere you didn't originally set out to go); check that your introduction states your claim; make sure the organization of your paper is clear; note whether your paragraphs are unified and cohesive; check the effectiveness of your transitions; check and double-check your use of quotation and paraphrase; make sure your conclusion answers the question of why your topic (as expressed in your thesis) is important. Save your drafts, label revised drafts with different names, and print hard copies frequently.

✓ **EDIT YOUR SENTENCES.**

Grammar-checkers are unreliable, and editing is more than a spell-check. A spell-check can't tell you if your sentences are correct and clear.

✓ **PROOFREAD AND FORMAT YOUR PAPER.**

Spell-checkers don't always catch your typos. Read over your paper carefully and format it according to the instructions of your instructor, or follow the guidelines outlined by the Modern Language Association. Some tips: Use a 12-point typeface, ragged right margin, one-inch margins on all four sides of your paper, double-space, and assign page numbers. Usually a paper will need your name, the professor's name, and the course and section number at the top of the page.

A SAMPLE STUDENT ESSAY IN PROGRESS

When Andrew Papadopoulis read "Girl," he annotated the story and took notes on his initial responses. Both his annotations and his notes, reproduced here, show him engaged with the text. He reads *actively* to scrutinize the story's language, asks questions about possible meanings, records thoughts and reactions, and notes important insights. By highlighting and annotating the story, this student interacts, or converses, with it, moving back and forth between the story's details and his developing understanding of those details. As he notes in his commentary, "Girl" condenses the elements of fiction into a single paragraph.

"My writing process, I don't really have one. I read. I find that both walk hand in hand, that when I'm writing, I have to read. Somehow I find that it feeds my own work, and not in a direct way." Conversation with Chimamanda Ngozi Adichie

Andrew focuses on the relationship between the story's two main characters—the second-person narrator, who uses *you* and commands ("Wash the white clothes on Monday"), and the listener, the girl of the story's title. He uncovers meaning from the details contained within this brief narrative to understand who the main characters are and where the story takes place. He notes those clues that point to the nature of the relationship between the speaker and the listener—the speaker's repeated use of the word *slut;* her admonitory, accusatory, and sometimes humorous tone; her reference to "your father"; and her advice on how to behave like a proper woman who tends to home and husband. Andrew interprets the story as an interaction between mother and daughter and isolates the details that reveal the story's domestic setting: okra, dasheen, doukona, and a host of household chores. He makes connections between the story's portrayal of domesticity and its broader implications of gender roles, identity, and society.

Next Andrew develops this initial exploration into a full-length essay that examines how Kincaid's distinctive use of literary techniques—especially the way her narrator addresses the readers directly with *you* (second-person point of view, see chapter 7)—allows the reader to feel like a participant in the story, an eavesdropper on a series of telling exchanges between mother and daughter. As this student demonstrates, fiction can be a lens through which we better visualize our relationship to literature and to the world. It can help us to see aspects of our own lives in new ways, or to catch a glimpse of imaginative worlds we find strange and interesting.

"There is a kind of magic to writing. . . . Anybody here who has written a term paper knows that there is a kind of magic to it. You don't know what it will be. You take notes, but the final product is utterly different from your initial conception of it. That's the joy of writing something." Conversation with T. Coraghessan Boyle

We emphasize throughout this text that literary works don't possess a *single* meaning, but rather *multiple* meanings; these are in turn revealed by reading and writing about a story with a close critical eye. We offer this not as a "finished" critique of "Girl" but as a way of demonstrating the process of responding to a text.

The following sections chart Andrew's progress as he works through his response to this writing assignment:

Assignment: Expand the close reading you completed of Jamaica Kincaid's "Girl" into a 4- to 5-page essay in which you analyze one or both of the story's main characters. Your analysis should take into account Kincaid's distinctive voice and use of literary techniques.

An Interactive Reading

Written in second person: directed at whom?

Advice for a variety of situations

Narrator asks a question

Now it's a command: "Don't sing . . ."

Voice change: Listener responds . . .

Loaded term—gender implications?

But completely ignored . . .

Why the repetition?

Suggest mother-daughter conversation

Now "outdoor" directions

No periods anywhere; very tense, intense

Wash the white clothes on Monday and put them on the stone heap; wash the color clothes on Tuesday and put them on the clothesline to dry; don't walk barehead in the hot sun; cook pumpkin fritters in very hot sweet oil; soak your little cloths right after you take them off; when buying cotton to make yourself a nice blouse, be sure that it doesn't have gum on it, because that way it won't hold up well after a wash; soak salt fish overnight before you cook it; is it true that you sing benna in Sunday school?; always eat your food in such a way that it won't turn someone else's stomach; on Sundays try to walk like a lady and not like the slut you are so bent on becoming; don't sing benna in Sunday school; you mustn't speak to wharf-rat boys, not even to give directions; don't eat fruits on the street—flies will follow you; *but I don't sing benna on Sundays at all and never in Sunday school*; this is how to sew a button; this is how to make a buttonhole for the button you have just sewed on; this is how to hem a dress when you see the hem coming down and so to prevent yourself from looking like the slut I know you are so bent on becoming; this is how you iron your father's khaki shirt so that it doesn't have a crease; this is how you iron your father's khaki pants so that they don't have a crease; this is how you grow okra—far from the house, because okra tree harbors red ants; when you are growing dasheen, make sure it gets plenty of water or else it makes your throat itch when you are eating it; this is how you sweep a corner; this is how you sweep a whole house; this is how you sweep a yard; this is how you smile to someone you don't like too much; this is how you smile to someone you don't like at all; this is how you smile to someone you like completely; this is how you set a table for tea; this is how you set a table for dinner; this is how you set a table for dinner with an important guest; this is how you set a table for lunch; this is how you set a table for breakfast; this is how to behave in the presence of men who don't know you very well, and this way they won't recognize immediately the (slut) I have warned you against becoming; be sure to wash every day, even if it is with your own spit; don't squat down to play marbles—you are not a boy, you know, don't pick people's flowers—you might catch something; don't throw stones at blackbirds, because it might not be a blackbird at all; this is how to make a bread pudding; this is how to make doukona, this is how to make pepper pot; this is how to make a good medicine for a cold; this is how to make a good medicine to throw away a child before it becomes a child; this is how to catch a fish; this is how to throw back a fish you don't like, and that way something bad won't fall on you; this is how to bully a man; this is how a man bullies you; this is how to love a man, and if this doesn't work there are other ways, and if they don't work don't feel too bad about giving up; this is how to spit up in the air if you feel like it, and this is how to move quick so that it doesn't fall on you; this is how to make ends meet; always squeeze bread to make sure it's fresh; *but what if the baker won't let me feel the bread?;* you mean to say that after all you are really going to be the kind of woman who the baker won't let near the bread?

Margin notes:

What else would a blackbird be? A soul?

Unwanted fish and child treated the same.

Attitude toward love is same as attitude toward work, etc.

Finally acknowledged at the end . . .

Initial Response

Write an initial response to the text without concern for how formal it sounds or even how logically it flows. In other words, this response is simply your first impressions of the story. Did something stand out to you as important? Were there confusing elements? Don't worry at this point if you don't understand major parts of the story; the more you review the notes you've made and the text itself, the more you will begin to understand.

The first time I read "Girl," I thought it might be difficult to find a lot to say about such a short piece. But after a second and third reading, I realized the story is packed with layers of detail that make it a rich fictional work. I tried to highlight revealing words and phrases and draw connections among sections to show how Kincaid develops elements of craft—like character and setting—and how Kincaid's voice affected my understanding of the story. I found the relationship between the speaker and listener especially interesting; the mother's (I think she's her mother) warnings and advice, and the daughter's sparse, interspersed retorts, define what it means (and doesn't mean) to be a "girl." Being a good "girl," of course, has all sorts of implications about being a good woman, wife, and mother. I'd like to explore these ideas further.

Explore Your Ideas

Freewriting is similar to the initial response—once again, do not worry about the flow of ideas or the language you are using. The difference is that freewriting comes after you have had some time to think about the story and reread it. In a sense, it's your "second response," rather than your initial one, and as such, you may find that you have more ideas and that your freewriting runs longer.

"There's nothing worse than a sheet of blank paper in front of you." Conversation with William Kittredge

After carefully considering his assignment, Andrew reread his close reading of "Girl" and the notes he took during his initial readings of the story. Andrew then moved on to freewrite about the story, writing continuously to get his ideas down on paper, without worrying about making mistakes or whether his initial ideas could be developed into a suitable paper topic. The following excerpt comes from Andrew's freewriting exercise.

> This was a very strange but a very beautiful story. For the first few lines I was def. confused, but the more I read the more I got it. It's a mother talking to her daughter, telling her everything she needs to know. I wonder where this story is set? Need to do some research to find out—need to look up a lot of the terms in the dictionary. But even w/o knowing where the story is set, I liked it. My mother always gives me tons & tons of advice. My mother and this mother are actually pretty similar in a lot of ways, even though my mother doesn't like to cook or garden or anything. It's different, too, that I'm a son not a daughter; must keep the diff. in mind. That's prob. the mark of a good piece of writing, that you can get into it even if it doesn't directly relate to you.

Journaling is a writing exercise that helps you focus the ideas you generated in your notes and freewriting. This is the first step in which you should begin to feel your ideas coming together to form something that will eventually become a paper. The idea you found the most interesting from your reading and notes is a good starting place for a journal entry.

Andrew put aside his freewriting for several hours and returned to the story with a fresh perspective. In the following journal entry, he expands his initial freewriting into a more focused discussion of his growing understanding of the story. He considers how the story's characterizations and point of view create interesting effects.

My initial reaction to the first few lines of "Girl" was confusion. But the further I read, the more I warmed up to the character of the narrator. I realized that she is not totally different from my mother, even though it seems clear that this mother and my mother are from very different worlds. But my mother, like the narrator, is constantly emphasizing the right way (or maybe I should say her way) of doing things. And, like the narrator, although my mother can come across as harsh, I know she cares deeply about my success in life.

What's interesting to me, also, is how or why I assume I know that this story is about a mother talking to her daughter. Maybe it's because of the word "slut"— something my mother wd obviously never say to me! And Kincaid never states this directly. In fact, in "Girl," almost nothing about character is stated directly. And yet, after reading this story, I feel like I have a good idea of who the narrator is, and, just as importantly, who the person being talked to is. It would be interesting to go back and see just where and how Kincaid reveals personality and other character details in this story.

All in all, I really enjoyed "Girl." You don't read many stories written from this perspective (the "you" perspective), and it's an interesting way to experience a narrative. Once I pushed through some initial confusion, I found "Girl" was definitely an engaging piece of writing.

Brainstorming may take the form of a list or a web connecting your thoughts. Once you have used a journal entry to narrow down your interests, use your brainstorming session to generate ideas on how to turn the topics that interest you most into a paper.

Andrew's freewriting and journal entry sparked more and more ideas about how he might develop his character analysis. In the following **brainstorming** excerpt, Andrew lists possible topics for his paper, charts details about the story's characterizations, and works toward a **thesis statement.**

Most interesting topics:

—narrator's personality (funny)

—daughter's personality

—setting (Caribbean)

—WHY does the mother say all this . . .

WHO is the narrator and WHO is the daughter—

Learning WHO the characters are and WHY they do things.

CHARACTERS' ACTION	MOTIVATION
Mother telling about cooking	Teaching girl how to run a household
Mother telling her not to talk to wharf-rat boys	Teaching girl how to behave like a girl. My sister Eleni?
Girl arguing with mother	Being independent, tough

Reading "Girl" = much interesting info

Reading the story "Girl," you can learn a lot about who the characters are and why they do what they do.

Develop a Working Thesis

A thesis is a sentence that states the topic of the paper. More than that, a thesis is the writer's argument, the controlling idea that he or she will show and develop in the body of the essay. For more details on how to write a good thesis, see pages H-35 to H-38 in our chapter on Writing from Reading.

Andrew used his brainstorming notes to sharpen his topic and refine his **thesis.** The following drafted and revised thesis statements show Andrew's progress as he focused his claim and pruned his language.

First-draft thesis:

In "Girl," you can actually learn a lot about the characters.

Second-draft thesis:

A close reading of "Girl" reveals much about the characters of the story.

Third-draft thesis:

> A close reading of "Girl" reveals a lot of information about the narrator and her daughter.

Final-draft thesis:

> A close reading of "Girl" reveals that Kincaid provides a lot of information about the narrator and the "you" of the story.

Revised final-draft thesis:

> A careful, close reading of "Girl" reveals that Kincaid has painted a portrait of both the narrator and the "you" to whom the story is directed.

Create a Plan

With his thesis in mind, Andrew next considered how he would organize his paper to best support his points. He drafted a **topic outline** to guide him through the writing and revising process.

I. Introduction
    a. "Girl" initially confusing
    b. Thesis: A careful, close reading of "Girl" reveals that Kincaid provides a great deal of information about the narrator and the "you" to whom the story is directed.
II. Identity of characters
    a. Discussion of tone
    b. Analysis of clues about gender and relationship of characters
        i. Specific lines directly related to gender
        ii. Nature of narrator's advice

III. Analysis of the narrator
    a. Tone can be humorous
    b. Demonstrates warmth
IV. Analysis of the listener
    a. Independent and uninterested in mother's advice
    b. Actually similar to her mother
V. Narrator's motives
    a. Discussion of story's final line
    b. Mother's advice meant to make daughter a respectable woman
VI. Conclusion
    a. Analysis of setting of "Girl"
    b. Story transcends specific setting

Generate a First Draft

After completing his topic outline, Andrew was now ready to write his first draft. He tried to follow the organization of his outline, making each of the important points he planned to elaborate on and support with examples in subsequent drafts.

FIRST DRAFT

A Mother's Advice

Jamaica Kincaid's short-short story "Girl" can seem weird, if not totally bizarre. But careful, repeated reading reveals that Kincaid provides a great deal of information about the narrator and the person the narrator talks to. In other words, "Girl" hides much beneath its mysterious surface.

The first clues as to the identity of the narrator of "Girl" can be found in the story's tone. The narrator's speech is mean and tough. From the language, it is clear that the speaker is someone who is used to being in charge, believes they know the right way to do things, and believes that the person listening must obey. For these reasons, it is likely that the narrator is a parent, speaking to his or her child.

Further, the narrator is probably a woman talking to her daughter. The narrator even says, at one point, "You are not a boy." The narrator's identity as the girl's mother is suggested by the line: "This is how you iron your father's khaki pants so

Parenthetical citation of page number is not necessary for a story printed on one page. The page reference should appear in the Works Cited only.

that they don't have a crease." This instruction suggests a relationship among the narrator, the girl, and the girl's father. The most obvious characterization of this relationship is that the speaker is the girl's mother. The nature of the advice the narrator gives only reinforces this idea, that "Girl" consists of mother-to-daughter counsel.

Kincaid offers other insight into the characters of the story. As mentioned previously, the tone suggests that the narrator is strict and authoritarian. At times, though, she can be humorous. At other times, the narrator shows affection for her daughter.

What we learn about the listener is of course filtered through the view of the narrator. From the more direct statements her mother makes, one could conclude that the girl is in grave danger of becoming a slut. But beyond this, it is possible to learn something of her personality. The sheer amount of advice she is given suggests that she has a lot to learn, at least about cooking and all of that stuff. Thus, she could very well be independent, disinterested in the traditional activities about which her mother instructs her. Even more interestingly, she is probably very similar to her mother: stubborn and strong-willed.

Why is the narrator giving so much advice? We need to look at the final line to answer that question. After the daughter, in another moment of italicized response, questions whether the baker will let her squeeze the bread to see if it's fresh, the narrator says: "You mean to say that after all you are really going to be the kind of woman who the baker won't let near the bread?" This seems to get at what the mother is trying to teach her daughter: what *kind* of woman she should turn out to be.

All the counsel the mother gives the daughter in "Girl" is specific to the setting, the Caribbean. Nonetheless, in the mother's resolve to make her daughter into the kind of woman she envisions, there is something that transcends the specifics. Every parent wants his or her child to grow up to be a respectable adult, and whether the parent goes about it by saving money for college, exposing the child to different languages and cultures, or, as in the story, giving instructions on how to behave, this drive seems as innate as eating or sleeping. Hence, nearly any mother or father can identify with what the narrator is trying to accomplish.

WRITER'S BLOCK

Sometimes called *the midnight disease,* writer's block can be avoided, especially with freewriting, brainstorming, and other exploratory techniques to get you started. Additional strategies to avoid writer's block include:

Resist the temptation to be a perfectionist. Save getting the right word, the stylish phrase, or even the correct spelling for your revising and editing stages.

Take it "bird by bird." Writer Anne Lamott passes along her father's advice to her brother, who had procrastinated on a report about birds—"Bird by bird, buddy, just take it bird by bird"—when she counsels students to break down writing assignments into manageable units.

Start anywhere. If you're stuck on the beginning, pick another section. Go back later and work out the introduction.

Generate more ideas. If you are drawing a blank, you may need to do some more reading or brainstorming. But don't let yourself use "reading some more" as a stalling tactic.

—from Maimon et al., *A Writer's Resource,* 3rd ed. (New York: McGraw-Hill, 2009).

Revise Your Draft

Andrew's second draft includes his changes and annotations to remind himself to clarify and refine his language, provide more textual evidence to bolster his claims, and format his paper according to MLA guidelines (see chapter 40 in this text).

> "You're asking [for] a reader's time, so to my way of thinking, you owe them. You owe them clarity." Conversation with Barry Lopez

SECOND DRAFT

Andrew Papadopoulis

Professor Delbanco

Composition 102

A Mother's Advice

Jamaica Kincaid's short-short story "Girl" can seem weird, if not totally bizarre. [*Be more specific. More formal language?*] A full appreciation of "Girl" requires careful, and even repeated, reading. [*Why? Explain what's so weird, why you need to be careful.*] Such an approach, though, reveals that Kincaid provides a great deal of information about the narrator and the "you" to whom the story is directed. In other words, "Girl" hides much beneath its initially mysterious surface. [*Much what? Characterization? Details?*]

The first clues as to the identity of the narrator of "Girl" can be found in the story's tone. The narrator's speech is admonitory, domineering, and tough. From [*Quote example from the story.*]

this blunt language, it is clear that the speaker is someone who is used to being in charge, believes he or she knows the right way to do things, and believes that the person listening must obey. For these reasons, it is likely that the narrator is a parent, speaking to his or her child.

Further, it is not difficult to conclude that the narrator is a woman, talking to her daughter. The narrator even says, at one point, "You are not a boy." The narrator's identity as the girl's mother is suggested by a different line. The narrator says: "This is how you iron your father's khaki pants so that they don't have a crease." This instruction, with its casual reference to "your father," suggests a relationship among the narrator, the girl, and the girl's father. The most obvious characterization of this relationship is that the speaker is the girl's mother, and she is telling her daughter how to iron her father's pants. The nature of the advice the narrator gives only reinforces the idea that "Girl" consists of mother-to-daughter counsel.

[margin note: Explain "so what"?]

[margin note: More specific.]

[margin note: Other ways this shows up?]

[margin note: Paragraph's too short. Fill out with text examples.]

Kincaid offers other insight into the characters of the story. As mentioned previously, the tone suggests that the narrator is strict and authoritarian. At times, though, she can be humorous. At other times, the narrator shows affection for her daughter.

What we learn about the listener is of course mainly filtered through the view of the narrator. From the more direct statements her mother makes, one could conclude that the girl is in grave danger of becoming a "slut." But beyond this, it is possible to learn something of her personality. The sheer amount of advice she is given suggests that she has a lot to learn, at least about cooking and all of that stuff. Thus, she could very well be independent, disinterested in the traditional activities about which her mother instructs her. This idea is supported by the brief moments of interaction in the story (the daughter's responses to her mother's words are set off in italics). These show her questioning her mother and arguing with her assertions. For instance, she insists, *"But I don't sing benna on Sundays at all and never in Sunday school."* From this sort of headstrong defense one can conclude that this girl is very much her mother's daughter, strong-willed and determined.

[margin note: Too informal—clean up.]

[margin note: Need to show how mom's strong willed?]

The larger motives of the narrator can be detected in the story's final line. After her daughter, in another moment of italicized response, questions whether the baker will let her squeeze the bread to see if it's fresh, the narrator says: "You mean to say that after all you are really going to be the kind of woman who the baker won't let near the bread?" This seems to get at what the mother is trying to teach her daughter. Ultimately, it is not important *what* the girl knows, but the "kind of woman" the girl becomes.

> Too deep. Need to relate to the thesis—what's hidden?

All the counsel the mother gives the daughter in "Girl" is specific to the setting, the Caribbean. Nonetheless, in the mother's resolve to make her daughter into the kind of woman she envisions, there is something that transcends the specifics. Every parent wants his or her child to grow up to be a respectable adult, and whether the parent goes about it by saving money for college, exposing them to different languages and cultures, or, as in the story, giving instructions on how to behave, this drive seems as innate as eating or sleeping. Hence, nearly any mother or father can identify with what the narrator is trying to accomplish.

> Need text proof?

> Sentence too long—break up or rewrite.

Edit Your Sentences, Proofread and Format Your Paper

Andrew uses these notes to develop his final draft, in which he fleshes out his character analysis and discusses the significance of the story's point of view, tone, and setting. For the final draft, he also checks his spelling, word choice, transitions, and sentences for clarity and grammatical correctness. He also makes sure he has provided ample evidence from the story itself with quotations, and he checks to make sure these quotations are correctly formatted in-text references, which correspond to a Work Cited page at the end of his paper (see the handbook for writing from reading for MLA formatting guidelines). He also incorporates paraphrase and summary where context is needed but quotations are not necessary. Andrew's progress shows his easeful back and forth with the story as he continually revises his interpretation of it.

"I was not a good student. I was not particularly good in English. Yet I am a writer. And this, I think, points to something relevant which is that it's not about talent, necessarily. You [just need to] do whatever is required, because you want it more. That was my experience."

Conversation with Amy Hempel

FINAL DRAFT

Papadopoulis 1

Andrew Papadopoulis

Professor Delbanco

Composition 102

15 April 2008

Student name, instructor name, course number, and date

A Mother's Advice

Essay title

On first encounter, Jamaica Kincaid's short-short story "Girl" can seem enigmatic, if not simply baffling. While most works of fiction are written in either the first or the third person, "Girl" is written in the second person: the "you" voice. This makes the beginning of the story fairly disorienting, as the reader is likely unaccustomed to this narrative perspective. Additionally, because the story is so short, the reader may reach the end before the feeling of disorientation ever goes away. A full appreciation of "Girl" requires careful, and even repeated, reading. Such an approach, though, reveals that Kincaid provides a great deal of information about the narrator and the "you" to whom the story is directed. In other words, "Girl" hides much beneath its initially mysterious surface, mainly, details about the characters.

Introduction leading toward thesis

Thesis

The first clues as to the identity of the narrator of "Girl" can be found in the story's tone. From the first lines, the narrator's speech is admonitory, domineering, and tough. The story begins with "Wash the white clothes on Monday and put them on the stone heap; wash the color clothes on Tuesday and put them on the clothesline to dry; don't walk barehead in the hot sun." From this direct, blunt language, it

Discussion of tone illustrated with example

Papadopoulis 2

is clear that the speaker is someone who is used to being in charge, believes he or she knows the right way to do things, and, importantly, believes that the person listening must obey. For these reasons, it is likely that the narrator is a parent, speaking to his or her child. This interpretation certainly fits the relationship suggested by the story's commanding language.

Further, it is not difficult to conclude that the narrator is a woman, talking to her daughter. The narrator even says, at one point, "You are not a boy." This fairly well clears up any mystery as to the listener's gender! The narrator's identity as the girl's mother is suggested by a line earlier in the story. The narrator says, "This is how you iron your father's khaki pants so that they don't have a crease." This instruction, with its casual reference to "your father," suggests a relationship among the narrator, the girl, and the girl's father. The most obvious characterization of this relationship is that the speaker is the girl's mother, and she is telling her daughter how to iron her father's pants.

> Textual analysis as part of a discussion of the characters' genders.

The nature of the advice the narrator gives only reinforces the idea that "Girl" consists of mother-to-daughter counsel. The narrator has recommendations for cleaning, cooking, gardening, and washing—all domestic chores, traditionally considered women's work. Further, the narrator has plenty of ideas on how to behave like a "lady" and not a "slut." Obviously, this is the sort of gender etiquette one woman would pass on to another, particularly a mother to a daughter.

> Further textual analysis of characters' relationship

Papadopoulis 3

In addition to the familial relationship between the narrator and the listener, Kincaid offers other insight into the characters of the story. As mentioned previously, the tone suggests that the narrator is strict and authoritarian. At times, though, she can be humorous, as when she says, "Always eat your food in such a way that it won't turn someone else's stomach." Although the statement implies criticism (specifically, that the girl eats in a way that *does* turn people's stomachs), the advice cannot be taken as wholly serious. At other times, the narrator demonstrates affection for her daughter. For example, about men, she says, "This is how to love a man, and if this doesn't work there are other ways, and if they don't work don't feel too bad about giving up." There is a warmth to these lines that shows the narrator truly cares that her daughter avoids the deeper pitfalls of love.

What we learn about the listener, the "girl" of the story's title, is of course mainly filtered through the view of the narrator. From the more direct statements her mother makes, one could conclude that the girl is in grave danger of becoming a "slut." But beyond this, it is possible to learn something of her personality. The sheer amount of advice she is given suggests that she has a lot to learn, at least about cooking and such. Thus, she could very well be independent, disinterested in the traditional activities about which her mother instructs her. This idea is supported by the brief moments of interaction in the story (the daughter's responses to her mother's words are set off in italics). These show her questioning her mother and arguing with her assertions. For instance, she insists, *"But I don't sing benna on*

Character analysis of the narrator

Character analysis of the listener

Sundays at all and never in Sunday school." From this sort of headstrong defense one can conclude that this girl is very much her mother's daughter, strong willed and determined.

Given what can be learned about the two characters in the story—mother and daughter—it is interesting to consider *why* the narrator feels compelled to give the girl so much advice. It almost seems as if she wants to tell her daughter every single thing she will need to know, but this of course is impossible. Her larger motives can be detected in the story's final line. After her daughter, in another moment of italicized response, questions whether the baker will let her squeeze the bread to see if it's fresh, the narrator says, "You mean to say that after all you are really going to be the kind of woman who the baker won't let near the bread?" This seems to get at the heart of what the mother is trying to teach her daughter. Ultimately, it is not important *what* the girl knows, but the "kind of woman" the girl becomes. The many lessons of the story represent the accumulated knowledge of a particular type of woman—dignified, competent, capable, wise. These are the qualities the mother hopes to pass on, more than tips about planting okra.

All the counsel the mother gives the daughter in "Girl" is specific to a particular setting. From the details of food (okra, dasheen) and music (*benna*), one can conjecture that this setting is in the Caribbean, where Jamaica Kincaid grew up. Further, all the counsel deals with the rural, domestic realm the mother inhabits and controls. Nonetheless, in the mother's resolve to make her daughter into the kind of

Larger discussion of the narrator's motives

Papadopoulis 5

Conclusion broadening the essay's argument to a more general point

woman she envisions, there is certainly an element that transcends these specifics. Every parent wants his or her child to grow up to be a respectable adult. Whether the parent goes about it by saving money for the child's college, exposing him or her to different languages and cultures, or, as in "Girl," giving instructions on how to behave like a lady, this drive seems as innate as any fundamental parental instinct. Hence, nearly any mother or father, or even anyone who has mentored another in any capacity, can identify with what the narrator is trying to accomplish.

Work Cited

Kincaid, Jamaica. "Girl." *Literature: Craft and Voice*. Eds. Nicholas Delbanco and Alan Cheuse. New York: McGraw-Hill, 2009. 53. Print.

Work Cited page and entry in MLA format

Compiling a Writing Portfolio

If you are compiling a portfolio or just several drafts of a single paper for your instructor, here's some advice:

- Gather your writing.
- Review what you have gathered and make selections.
- Arrange selections in a deliberate order.
- Write a reflective essay or letter to explain what is in your portfolio.
- Suggest who you are as a writer—that is, highlight your strengths and tell how you envision your writing taking shape in future written work.

Your instructor may prefer you to submit your work as an e-portfolio.

- Use the opening screen to establish your purpose and appeal to your audience.
- Provide links to help readers navigate your portfolio.
- Consider using links to connect with related files external to the portfolio like audio or video clips.
- Navigate through it all the way to make sure it's conceptually and structurally right before releasing it.

4 Plot

THE first mistake, the one that opened the whole floodgate, was losing my grip on the keys. In the excitement, leaping from the car with the gin in one hand and a roach clip in the other, I spilled them in the grass—in the dark, rank, mysterious nighttime grass of Greasy Lake. This was a tactical error, as damaging and irreversible in its way as Westmoreland's decision to dig in at Khe Sanh. I felt it like a jab of intuition, and I stopped there by the open door, peering vaguely into the night that puddled up round my feet.

The second mistake—and this was inextricably bound up with the first—was identifying the car as Tony Lovett's.

—from "Greasy Lake" by T. Coraghessan Boyle

"A story like 'Greasy Lake' develops through the opening . . . which is the setup: "I went there one night." . . . Each of the incidents of the story strings out from that in an escalating way, until we . . . find out what happened. . . . It's not the kind of plot in which they all went to jail . . . the end. No, it ends on a gesture, and that gesture brings you back into the story to rethink what it means. . . ."

Conversation with T. Coraghessan Boyle, video available at www.mhhe.com/delbancole

IN the excerpt that begins this chapter, the narrator, a nineteen-year-old and a self-described "dangerous character," identifies the moment when his night of random thrill seeking begins to take shape. He tells the tale in retrospect—so we as readers know "the first" and "the second mistake" won't be fatal—but we also know the "error" will prove "irreversible." He and his two buddies had been cruising their town on the third night of summer vacation, looking for "something we never found." (The reference to "Westmoreland's decision to dig in at Khe Sanh" evokes U.S. Army general William Westmoreland's tactical blunder in Vietnam, and there's a not-so-casual suggestion that "losing my grip on the keys" opens a "floodgate" of trouble in a kind of small-scale war.) Restless with longing, the boys drive up to Greasy Lake and pull in behind the car they think belongs to Tony Lovett. Honking and blinking their headlights, they stumble out of their own car, hoping to catch Tony in the act of whatever he's doing.

And what happens then? This is the moment when the plot of "Greasy Lake" starts in earnest and the real action begins.

CONTINUED ON PAGE 83

I don't consciously make a plot beforehand . . .

Q&A
A Conversation on Writing
T. Coraghessan Boyle

For me it just happens, and it happens slowly . . .

From Music to Writing

As a teenager . . . I wanted to be a serious musician, and I went to music college. I played a saxophone and clarinet. . . . As soon as I got there . . . I realized that I couldn't hack it. The others were so much more advanced and better than I at their instruments. . . . In the first English course I took, which was on the contemporary short story, I discovered Flannery O'Connor, her story "A Good Man Is Hard to Find" [in chapter 12]. And it was a revelation for me, because here was a very funny story about a family going on vacation, and it's hilarious. You've got the brat kids, the old grandmother—she sneaks her cat into the car. The father of the family, Bailey, is overwrought and harassed like any guy on TV. And then the story turns on you and becomes utterly tragic and heartbreaking. And it just woke me up, and I thought, "This is an amazing thing."

On Plot and His Writing Process

I don't consciously make a plot beforehand, nor do I make a plot in revision. . . . I revise as I go along, so that the story that you see is exactly what it was. I don't ever write scenes and change them around or anything like that. . . . For me it just happens, and it happens slowly . . . , and I perfect each line. I couldn't go on if I didn't feel that what is behind me is good. And at some point the end arrives. There's no major revision after that, and there's no detailing for plot, or theme, or symbols, or anything else. They are organic, it all just happens as one whole. So I don't do any revision whatsoever, beyond daily revision of each line till I think it's right.

To watch this entire interview and hear the author read from "Greasy Lake," go to **www.mhhe.com/delbanco1e.**

RESEARCH ASSIGNMENT: In the interview, Boyle says, "Plot is essential to all fiction." After watching the interview, explain why Boyle feels that way. Do you agree with him? What stories can you think of that either support or refute his claim?

T. Coraghessan Boyle (also known as T. C. Boyle), born Thomas John Boyle in Peekskill, New York (1948), is a novelist and short story writer. Boyle earned a B.A. in English and history from the State University of New York at Potsdam in 1968, after which he taught for four years at the high school in his hometown where his mother worked as head secretary and his father as a janitor. After being accepted to the Iowa Writers' Workshop in 1972, Boyle served as fiction editor for the *Iowa Review* and, in 1977, received a Creative Writing Fellowship from the National Endowment for the Arts. In 1988, he received a Guggenheim. Boyle has since received many literary awards, including the PEN/Faulkner Award, the PEN/Malamud Prize, the PEN/West Literary Prize, the Commonwealth Gold Medal for Literature, and the National Academy of Arts and Letters Award for Prose Excellence. His novels include *World's End* (1987, winner of the PEN/Faulkner Award for Fiction); *The Road to Wellville* (1993); and *The Tortilla Curtain* (1995, winner of France's Prix Médicis Étranger). Boyle is also one of America's most accomplished short story writers; his story collections include *Descent of Man* (1979), *Greasy Lake* (1985), *If the River Was Whiskey* (1989), and *Without a Hero* (1994). His short stories regularly appear in major American magazines, including *The New Yorker, Harper's, Esquire, The Atlantic Monthly,* and *Playboy.*

Now the author of nineteen books of fiction, Boyle is known for his imagination and humor as he writes on such subjects as hippies, the environment, illegal immigration, the nineteenth-century health food movement, and identity theft. He describes writing as an addiction and explains that in his own fiction "the themes and obsessions—the search for the father, racism, class and community, predetermination versus free will, cultural imperialism, sexual war and sexual truce—keep repeating. I can see this, but only in retrospect. That's the beauty of this addiction—you have to move on, no retirement here, look out ahead, though you can't see where you're going." Boyle has taught at the University of Southern California since 1978.

AS YOU READ   As you read "Greasy Lake," consider these questions: Where does the tension mount? Why? As the plot unfolds, what does the main character worry about? What do you worry about?

Greasy Lake (1985)

It's about a mile down on the dark side of Route 88.

—Bruce Springsteen

1   THERE was a time when courtesy and winning ways went out of style, when it was good to be bad, when you cultivated decadence like a taste. We were all dangerous characters then. We wore torn-up leather jackets, slouched around with toothpicks in our months, sniffed glue and ether and what somebody claimed was cocaine. When we wheeled our parents' whining station wagons out onto the street we left a patch of rubber half a block long. We drank gin and grape juice, Tango, Thunderbird, and Bali Hai. We were nineteen. We were bad. We read André Gide and struck elaborate poses to show that we didn't give a shit about anything. At night, we went up to Greasy Lake.

2   Through the center of town, up the strip, past the housing developments and shopping malls, street lights giving way to the thin streaming illumination of the headlights, trees crowding the asphalt in a black unbroken wall: that was the way out to Greasy Lake. The Indians had called it Wakan, a reference to the clarity of its waters. Now it was fetid and murky, the mud banks glittering with broken glass and strewn with beer cans and the charred remains of bonfires. There was a single ravaged island a hundred yards from shore, so stripped of vegetation it looked as if the air force had strafed it. We went up to the lake because everyone went there, because we wanted to snuff the rich scent of possibility on the breeze, watch a girl take off her clothes and plunge into the festering murk, drink beer, smoke pot, howl at the stars, savor the incongruous full-throated roar of rock and roll against the primeval susurrus of frogs and crickets. This was nature.

3   I was there one night, late, in the company of two dangerous characters. Digby wore a gold star in his right ear and allowed his father to pay his tuition at Cornell; Jeff was thinking of quitting school to become a painter/musician/head-shop proprietor. They were both expert in the social graces, quick with a sneer, able to manage a Ford with lousy shocks over a rutted and gutted blacktop road at eighty-five while rolling a joint as compact as a Tootsie Roll Pop stick. They could lounge against a bank of booming speakers and trade "man"s with the best of them or roll out across the dance floor as if their joints worked on bearings. They were slick and quick and they wore their mirror shades at breakfast and dinner, in the shower, in closets and caves. In short, they were bad.

4   I drove. Digby pounded the dashboard and shouted along with Toots & the Maytals while Jeff hung his head out the window and streaked the side of my mother's Bel Air with vomit. It was early June, the air soft as a hand on your cheek, the third night of summer vacation. The first two nights we'd been out till dawn, looking for something we never found. On this, the third night, we'd cruised the strip sixty-seven times, been in and out of every bar and club we could think of in a twenty-mile radius, stopped twice for bucket chicken and forty-cent hamburgers, debated going to a party at the house of a girl Jeff's sister knew, and chucked two dozen raw eggs at mailboxes and hitchhikers. It was 2:00 A.M.; the bars were closing. There was nothing to do but take a bottle of lemon-flavored gin up to Greasy Lake.

5   The taillights of a single car winked at us as we swung into the dirt lot with its tufts

of weed and washboard corrugations; '57 Chevy, mint, metallic blue. On the far side of the lot, like the exoskeleton of some gaunt chrome insect, a chopper leaned against its kickstand. And that was it for excitement: some junkie halfwit biker and a car freak pumping his girlfriend. Whatever it was we were looking for, we weren't about to find it at Greasy Lake. Not that night.

6   But then all of a sudden Digby was fighting for the wheel. "Hey, that's Tony Lovett's car! Hey!" he shouted, while I stabbed at the brake pedal and the Bel Air nosed up to the gleaming bumper of the parked Chevy. Digby leaned on the horn, laughing, and instructed me to put my brights on. I flicked on the brights. This was hilarious. A joke. Tony would experience premature withdrawal and expect to be confronted by grim-looking state troopers with flashlights. We hit the horn, strobed the lights, and then jumped out of the car to press our witty faces to Tony's windows; for all we knew we might even catch a glimpse of some little fox's tit, and then we could slap backs with red-faced Tony, roughhouse a little, and go on to new heights of adventure and daring.

7   The first mistake, the one that opened the whole floodgate, was losing my grip on the keys. In the excitement, leaping from the car with the gin in one hand and a roach clip in the other, I spilled them in the grass—in the dark, rank, mysterious nighttime grass of Greasy Lake. This was a tactical error, as damaging and irreversible in its way as Westmoreland's decision to dig in at Khe Sanh. I felt it like a jab of intuition, and I stopped there by the open door, peering vaguely into the night that puddled up round my feet.

8   The second mistake—and this was inextricably bound up with the first—was identifying the car as Tony Lovett's. Even before the very bad character in greasy jeans and engineer boots ripped out of the driver's door, I began to realize that this chrome blue was much lighter than the robin's-egg of Tony's car, and that Tony's car didn't have rear-mounted speakers. Judging from their expressions, Digby and Jeff were privately groping toward the same inevitable and unsettling conclusion as I was.

9   In any case, there was no reasoning with this bad greasy character—clearly he was a man of action. The first lusty Rockette kick of his steel-toed boot caught me under the chin, chipped my favorite tooth, and left me sprawled in the dirt. Like a fool, I'd gone down on one knee to comb the stiff hacked grass for the keys, my mind making connections in the most dragged-out, testudineous way, knowing that things had gone wrong, that I was in a lot of trouble, and

that the lost ignition key was my grail and my salvation. The three or four succeeding blows were mainly absorbed by my right buttock and the tough piece of bone at the base of my spine.

Meanwhile, Digby vaulted the kissing bumpers and delivered a savage kung-fu blow to the greasy character's collarbone. Digby had just finished a course in martial arts for phys-ed credit and had spent the better part of the past two nights telling us apocryphal tales of Bruce Lee types and of the raw power invested in lightning blows shot from coiled wrists, ankles, and elbows. The greasy character was unimpressed. He merely backed off a step, his face like a Toltec mask, and laid Digby out with a single whistling roundhouse blow . . . but by now Jeff had got into the act, and I was beginning to extricate myself from the dirt, a tinny compound of shock, rage, and impotence wadded in my throat.

Jeff was on the guy's back, biting at his ear. Digby was on the ground, cursing. I went for the tire iron I kept under the driver's seat. I kept it there because bad characters always keep tire irons under the driver's seat, for just such an occasion as this. Never mind that I hadn't been involved in a fight since sixth grade, when a kid with a sleepy eye and two streams of mucus depending from his nostrils hit me in the knee with a Louisville slugger, never mind that I'd touched the tire iron exactly twice before, to change tires: it was there. And I went for it.

I was terrified. Blood was beating in my ears, my hands were shaking, my heart turning over like a dirt-bike in the wrong gear. My antagonist was shirtless, and a single cord of muscle flashed across his chest as he bent forward to peel Jeff from his back like a wet overcoat. "Motherfucker," he spat, over and over, and I was aware in that instant that all four of us—Digby, Jeff, and myself included—were chanting "motherfucker, motherfucker," as if it were a battle cry. (What happened next? The detective asks the murderer from beneath the turned-down brim of his porkpie hat. I don't know, the murderer says, something came over me. Exactly.)

13   Digby poked the flat of his hand in the bad character's face and I came at him like a kamikaze, mindless, raging, stung with humiliation—the whole thing, from the initial boot in the chin to this murderous primal instant involving no more than sixty hyperventilating, gland-flooding seconds—I came at him and brought the tire iron down across his ear. The effect was instantaneous, astonishing. He was a stunt man and this was Hollywood, he was a big grimacing toothy balloon and I was a man with a straight pin. He collapsed. Wet his pants. Went loose in his boots.

14   A single second, big as a zeppelin, floated by. We were standing over him in a circle, gritting our teeth, jerking our necks, our limbs and hands and feet twitching with glandular discharges. No one said anything. We just stared down at the guy, the car freak, the lover, the bad greasy character laid low. Digby looked at me; so did Jeff. I was still holding the tire iron, a tuft of hair clinging to the crook like dandelion fluff, like down. Rattled, I dropped it in the dirt, already envisioning the headlines, the pitted faces of the police inquisitors, the gleam of handcuffs, clank of bars, the big black shadows rising from the back of the cell . . . when suddenly a raw torn shriek cut through me like all the juice in all the electric chairs in the country.

15   It was the fox. She was short, barefoot, dressed in panties and a man's shirt. "Animals!" she screamed, running at us with her fists clenched and wisps of blow-dried hair in her face. There was a silver chain round her ankle, and her toenails flashed in the glare of the headlights. I think it was the toenails that did it. Sure, the gin and the cannabis and even the Kentucky Fried may have had a hand in it, but it was the sight of those flaming toes that set us off—the toad emerging from the loaf in *Virgin Spring*, lipstick smeared on a child; she was already tainted. We were on her like Bergman's deranged brothers—see no evil, hear none, speak none—panting, wheezing, tearing at her clothes, grabbing for flesh. We were bad characters, and we were scared and hot and three steps over the line—anything could have happened.

16   It didn't.

17   Before we could pin her to the hood of the car, our eyes masked with lust and greed and the purest primal badness, a pair of headlights swung into the lot. There we were, dirty, bloody, guilty, dissociated from humanity and civilization, the first of the Ur-crimes behind us, the second in progress, shreds of nylon panty and spandex brassiere dangling from our fingers, our flies open, lips licked—there we were, caught in the spotlight. Nailed.

18   We bolted. First for the car, and then, realizing we had no way of starting it, for the woods. I thought nothing. I thought escape. The headlights came at me like accusing fingers. I was gone.

19   Ram-bam-bam, across the parking lot, past the chopper and into the feculent undergrowth at the lake's edge, insects flying up in my face, weeds whipping, frogs and snakes and red-eyed turtles splashing off into the night: I was already ankle-deep in muck and tepid water and still going strong. Behind me, the girl's screams rose in intensity, disconsolate, incriminating, the screams of the Sabine women, the Christian martyrs, Anne Frank dragged from the garret. I kept going, pursued by those cries, imagining cops and bloodhounds. The water was up to my knees when I realized what I was doing: I was going to swim for it. Swim the breadth of Greasy Lake and hide myself in the thick clot of woods on the far side. They'd never find me there.

20   I was breathing in sobs, in gasps. The water lapped at my waist as I looked out over the moon-burnished ripples, the mats of algae that clung to the surface like scabs. Digby and Jeff had vanished. I paused. Listened. The girl was quieter now, screams tapering to sobs, but there were male voices, angry, excited, and the high-pitched ticking of the second car's engine. I waded deeper, stealthy, hunted, the ooze sucking at my sneakers. As I was about to take the plunge—at the very instant I dropped my shoulder for the first slashing stroke—I blundered into something. Something unspeakable, obscene, something soft, wet, mossgrown. A patch of weed? A log? When I reached out to touch it, it gave like a rubber duck, it gave like flesh.

21   In one of those nasty little epiphanies for which we are prepared by films and TV and childhood visits to the funeral home to ponder the shrunken painted forms of dead grandparents, I understood what it was that bobbed there so inadmissibly in the dark. Understood, and stumbled back in horror and revulsion, my mind yanked in six different directions (I was nineteen, a mere child, an infant, and here in the space of five minutes I'd struck down one greasy character and blundered into the waterlogged carcass of a second), thinking, The keys, the keys, why did I have to go and

> We were bad characters, and we were scared and hot and three steps over the line . . .

lose the keys? I stumbled back, but the muck took hold of my feet—a sneaker snagged, balance lost—and suddenly I was pitching face forward into the buoyant black mass, throwing out my hands in desperation while simultaneously conjuring the image of reeking frogs and muskrats revolving in slicks of their own deliquescing juices. AAAAArrrgh! I shot from the water like a torpedo, the dead man rotating to expose a mossy beard and eyes cold as the moon. I must have shouted out, thrashing around in the weeds, because the voices behind me suddenly became animated.

22   "What was that?"

23   "It's them, it's them: they tried to, tried to . . . *rape* me!" Sobs.

24   A man's voice, flat Midwestern accent. "You sons a bitches, we'll kill you!"

25   Frogs, crickets.

26   Then another voice, harsh, *r*-less, Lower East Side: "Motherfucker!" I recognized the verbal virtuosity of the bad greasy character in the engineer boots. Tooth chipped, sneakers gone, coated in mud and slime and worse, crouching breathless in the weeds waiting to have my ass thoroughly and definitively kicked and fresh from the hideous stinking embrace of a three-days-dead-corpse, I suddenly felt a rush of joy and vindication: the son of a bitch was alive! Just as quickly, my bowels turned to ice. "Come on out of there, you pansy mothers!" the bad greasy character was screaming. He shouted curses till he was out of breath.

27   The crickets started up again, then the frogs. I held my breath. All at once was a sound in the reeds, a swishing, a splash: thunk-a-thunk. They were throwing rocks. The frogs fell silent. I cradled my head. Swish, swish, thunk-a-thunk. A wedge of feldspar the size of a cue ball glanced off my knee. I bit my finger.

28   It was then that they turned to the car. I heard a door slam, a curse, and then the sound of the headlights shattering—almost a good-natured sound, celebratory, like corks popping from the necks of bottles. This was succeeded by the dull booming of the fenders, metal on metal, and then the icy crash of the windshield. I inched forward, elbows and knees, my belly pressed to the muck; thinking of guerrillas and commandos and *The Naked and the Dead*. I parted the weeds and squinted the length of the parking lot.

The second car—it was a Trans-Am—was still 29 running, its high beams washing the scene in a lurid stagy light. Tire iron flailing, the greasy bad character was laying into the side of my mother's Bel Air like an avenging demon, his shadow riding up the trunks of the trees. Whomp. Whomp. Whomp-whomp. The other two guys—blond types, in fraternity jackets—were helping out with tree branches and skull-sized boulders. One of them was gathering up bottles, rocks, muck, candy wrappers, used condoms, poptops, and other refuse and pitching it through the window on the driver's side. I could see the fox, a white bulb behind the windshield of the '57 Chevy. "Bobbie," she whined over the thumping, "come on." The greasy character paused a moment, took one good swipe at the left taillight, and then heaved the tire iron halfway across the lake. Then he fired up the '57 and was gone.

Blond head nodded at blond head. One said some- 30 thing to the other, two low for me to catch. They were no doubt thinking that in helping to annihilate my mother's car they'd committed a fairly rash act, and thinking too that there were three bad characters connected with that very car watching them from the woods. Perhaps other possibilities occurred to them as well—police, jail cells, justices of the peace, reparations, lawyers, irate parents, fraternal censure. Whatever they were thinking, they suddenly dropped branches, bottles, and rocks and sprang for their car in unison, as if they'd choreographed it. Five seconds. That's all it took. The engine shrieked, the tires squealed, a cloud of dust rose from the rutted lot and then settled back on darkness.

I don't know how long I lay there, the bad breath 31 of decay all around me, my jacket heavy as a bear, the primordial ooze subtly reconstituting itself to accommodate my upper thighs and testicles. My jaws ached, my knee throbbed, my coccyx was on fire. I contemplated suicide, wondered if I'd need bridgework, scraped the recesses of my brain for some sort of excuse to give my parents—a tree had fallen on the car, I was blinded by a bread truck, hit and run, vandals had got to it while we were playing chess at Digby's. Then I thought of the dead man. He was probably the only person on the planet worse off than I was. I thought about him, fog on the lake, insects chirring eerily, and felt the tug of fear, felt the darkness opening up inside me like a set of jaws. Who was he, I wondered, this victim of time and circumstance bobbing sorrowfully in the lake at my back. The owner of the chopper, no doubt, a bad older character come to this. Shot during a murky drug deal, drowned while drunkenly frolicking in the lake. Another headline. My car was wrecked; he was dead.

When the eastern half of the sky went from black to cobalt and the trees began to separate themselves from the shadows, I pushed myself up from the mud and stepped out into the open. By now the birds had begun to take over for the crickets, and dew lay slick on the leaves. There was a smell in the air, raw and sweet at the same time, the smell of the sun firing buds and opening blossoms. I contemplated the car. It lay there like a wreck along the highway, like a steel sculpture left over from a vanished civilization. Everything was still. This was nature.

I was circling the car, as dazed and bedraggled as the sole survivor of an air blitz, when Digby and Jeff emerged from the trees behind me. Digby's face was cross-hatched with smears of dirt; Jeff's jacket was gone and his shirt was torn across the shoulder. They slouched across the lot, looking sheepish, and silently came up beside me to gape at the ravaged automobile. No one said a word. After a while Jeff swung open the driver's door and began to scoop the broken glass and garbage off the seat. I looked at Digby. He shrugged. "At least they didn't slash the tires," he said.

It was true: the tires were intact. There was no windshield, the headlights were staved in, and the body looked as if it had been sledge-hammered for a quarter a shot at the county fair, but the tires were inflated to regulation pressure. The car was drivable. In silence, all three of us bent to scrape the mud and shattered glass from the interior. I said nothing about the biker. When we were finished, I reached in my pocket for the keys, experienced a nasty stab of recollection, cursed myself, and turned to search the grass. I spotted them almost immediately, no more than five feet from the open door, glinting like jewels in the first tapering shaft of sunlight. There was no reason to get philosophical about it: I eased into the seat and turned the engine over.

It was at that precise moment that the silver Mustang with the flame decals rumbled into the lot. All three of us froze; then Digby and Jeff slid into the car and slammed the door. We watched as the Mustang rocked and bobbed across the ruts and finally jerked to a halt beside the forlorn chopper at the far end of the lot. "Let's go," Digby said. I hesitated, the Bel Air wheezing beneath me.

Two girls emerged from the Mustang. Tight jeans, stiletto heels, hair like frozen fur. They bent over the motorcycle, paced back and forth aimlessly, glanced once or twice at us, and then ambled over to where the reeds sprang up in a green fence round the perimeter of the lake. One of them cupped her hands to her mouth. "Al," she called. "Hey, Al!"

"Come on," Digby hissed. "Let's get out of here."

But it was too late. The second girl was picking her way across the lot, unsteady on her heels, looking up at us and then away. She was older—twenty-five or -six—and as she came closer we could see there was something wrong with her: she was stoned or drunk, lurching now and waving her arms for balance. I gripped the steering wheel as if it were the ejection lever of a flaming jet, and Digby spat out my name, twice, terse and impatient.

"Hi," the girl said.

We looked at her like zombies, like war veterans, like deaf-and-dumb pencil peddlers.

She smiled, her lips cracked and dry. "Listen," she said, bending from the waist to look in the window, "you guys seen Al?" Her pupils were pinpoints, her eyes glass. She jerked her neck. "That's his bike over there—Al's. You seen him?"

Al. I didn't know what to say. I wanted to get out of the car and retch, I wanted to go home to my parents' house and crawl into bed. Digby poked me in the ribs. "We haven't seen anybody," I said.

The girl seemed to consider this, reaching out a slim veiny arm to brace herself against the car. "No matter," she said, slurring the *t*'s, "he'll turn up." And then, as if she'd just taken stock of the whole scene—the ravaged car and our battered faces, the desolation of the place—she said: "Hey, you guys look like some pretty bad characters—been fightin', huh?" We stared straight ahead, rigid as catatonics. She was fumbling in her pocket and muttering something. Finally she held out a handful of tablets in glassine wrappers: "Hey, you want to party, you want to do some of these with me and Sarah?"

I just looked at her. I thought I was going to cry. Digby broke the silence. "No, thanks," he said, leaning over me. "Some other time."

I put the car in gear and it inched forward with a groan, shaking off pellets of glass like an old dog shedding water after a bath, heaving over the ruts on its worn springs, creeping toward the highway. There was a sheen of sun on the lake. I looked back. The girl was still standing there, watching us, her shoulders slumped, hand outstretched.

> # Then I thought of the dead man.
> ## He was probably the only person on the planet worse off than I was.

EACH of the stories in the plot chapter deals with the coming of age, or initiation into adult life, of a young character, somewhat innocent as the story begins and more knowledgeable by the story's end. If you like the way T.C. Boyle treats this subject matter, you might want to compare it with John Updike's disaffected hero in "A&P" in chapter 1.

GOING FURTHER   You can find another comic antihero, like Boyle's, in *Garden State* by Rick Moody, and you may enjoy the comic sensibility in the essays of Steve Almond *(Not That You Asked) Rants, Exploits, and Obsessions.*

"And everybody has been to Greasy Lake" Conversation with T. Coraghessan Boyle

Writing from Reading

Summarize

1 Consider all the plot complications the author introduces to keep the tension in the story mounting. At what point does the story reach its climax (point of greatest tension)? Discuss whether or not the events following the climax decline to a resolution for the story.

2 When the narrator wades into the lake, he "blundered into something. Something unspeakable, obscene." What does he blunder into and what impact does it have on him? How does this plot complication differ from the others?

Analyze Craft

3 Describe how Boyle reveals the characters' context. What is the socioeconomic status of the three main characters in "Greasy Lake"? What clues does Boyle give to reveal this? How is economic status a factor in the plot of this story?

Analyze Voice

4 In the first paragraph of the story, the narrator describes what it means to be "bad." Does his voice throughout the story suggest he thinks of himself as a "bad guy"? How does the narrator's description of events support or refute his idea of himself as a "bad guy"?

Synthesize Summary and Analysis

5 "Greasy Lake" is written in past tense, presumably some time after the events of the story. How does this distance affect the tone of the story? Discuss how the plot and the description of events might change if the story were told in present tense by the narrator at age nineteen.

Interpret the Story

6 Discuss the relationship between plot and character. When the girls arrive at the end of the story, the boys turn down the chance to party with them because, as Boyle says in his interview, "these boys have their tails between their legs." Why do they now have their "tails between their legs"? Use examples from the text to support your answer.

CONTINUED FROM PAGE 75

AN ARTFUL ARRANGEMENT OF INCIDENTS

When we lose ourselves in fiction, are we caught up in the story or its plot? Do *plot* and *story* mean the same thing? In *Aspects of the Novel*, E. M. Forster distinguishes between story and plot with this illustration:

> *"The king died, and then the queen died" is a story. "The king died, and then the queen died of grief" is a plot.*

If an event takes place in a story, we say, "and then?" If it is in a plot we ask, "why?" A **plot** is the artful arrangement of incidents in a story, with each incident building on the next in a series of causes and effects. If the three restless teens in "Greasy Lake" had simply spent the night driving and drinking, stopping at friends' houses, and throwing eggs at mailboxes, the story would be a mere arrangement of chronological events. Once the narrator loses his car keys and taunts the wrong guy, however, the "plot thickens." Event piles on event, succeeding each other in causal but unpredictable ways. The reader becomes engaged, wondering "What next?"

This creates **suspense**—a sense of anticipation or excitement about what will happen and how the characters will deal with their newfound predicament. It's worth remembering that a secondary meaning of the word *plot* is *conspiracy*. In this sense, the word has negative connotations and suggests something faintly illegal, as in: *there was a plot against the king.* What keeps readers enthralled is most often not the root sequence of story, the *and then and then and then* of events; it's the surprise, the *then and therefore* that introduces the idea of motive and permits us to question behavior. Since unexplained behavior lies at the root of mystery, *plot* in its sophisticated manifestations offers the promise of surprise and the excitement of suspense.

As T. C. Boyle says in his interview, "The rest of the story—that's where the plot evolves: what happened that night. Each of the incidents of the story strings out from that in an escalating way, until we try to wrap it up and find out what happened." Authors arrange the incidents of their stories in a variety of ways to show us as readers "what happened."

Crafting Plot

One way writers set up a story and try to draw a reader into the plot is by means of **exposition,** the presentation of necessary information about the character, setting, or characters' history provided to make the reader care what happens to the characters

"Plot is the essential element of all stories."
Conversation with T. Coraghessan Boyle

in the story. In Anton Chekhov's "The Lady with the Pet Dog" (chapter 14), the story starts off with this technique. The opening paragraphs set up the situation: A man alone, on vacation, perhaps restless after two weeks, notices a woman alone and considers approaching her.

> *It was said that a new person had appeared on the sea-front: a lady with a little dog. Dmitri Dmitritch Gurov, who had by then been a fortnight at Yalta, and so was fairly at home there, had begun to take an interest in new arrivals. Sitting in Verney's pavilion, he saw, walking on the sea-front, a fair-haired young lady of medium height, wearing a béret; a white Pomeranian dog was running behind her.*

And afterwards he met her in the public gardens and in the square several times a day. She was walking alone, always wearing the same béret, and always with the same white dog; no one knew who she was, and every one called her simply "the lady with the dog."

"If she is here alone without a husband or friends, it wouldn't be amiss to make her acquaintance," Gurov reflected.

Some stories begin ***in medias res,*** or in the middle of things. In "The Story of an Hour" (chapter 1), for example, we immediately learn what's at stake: Mr. Mallard has died, and someone has to inform the fragile Mrs. Mallard. This is a common technique in dramatic presentations—an almost standard strategy in plays and movies and on TV. The first episode of the popular television show "Lost" began with a plane crash, leaving dozens of survivors stranded on a strange island. The story line was built on a series of **flashbacks,** the device of moving back in time to a point before the primary action of the story, to reveal how and why this particular group of people crashed in this particular place—but the "backstory" is only slowly revealed.

"Characters may not want to do what you want them to do in the story. They may want to do something that's just going to ruin the story. Guess what, they get to do it." Conversation with William Kittredge

Authors also use **foreshadowing,** a hint about plot elements to come, to both advance the plot and build suspense. For example, in "Greasy Lake," Boyle "flashes forward" with this line, about his narrator's "mistakes": "This was a tactical error, as damaging and irreversible in its way as Westmoreland's decision to dig in at Khe Sanh." He's letting the reader know that trouble surely lies ahead, trouble as bad as a bad decision made by a military officer during the Vietnam War.

All stories have a **protagonist,** the main figure (or principal actor) in a work of literature. Like any human being, a protagonist will have desires or objectives. A story's plot hinges equally on the protagonist's efforts to realize his or her desires and to cope with failure if and when plans are thwarted and desires left unfulfilled. Thus, the characters in a story often drive plot development.

The moment of greatest tension in a story is its **climax,** the narrative's turning point in a struggle between opposing forces.

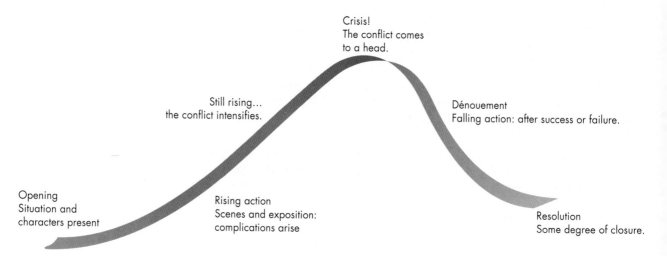

Crisis!
The conflict comes
to a head.

Still rising…
the conflict intensifies.

Dénouement
Falling action: after success or failure.

Opening
Situation and
characters present

Rising action
Scenes and exposition:
complications arise

Resolution
Some degree of closure.

Conflict in a narrative can consist of struggles within the mind and soul of the protagonist, and it can also involve physical struggles. Complications that deepen the protagonist's predicament create the **rising action** of the story. Characters' emotional and psychological conflicts intensify their **conflict** with one or more **antagonists.** The internal and external worlds stand at odds; desires oppose each other; opposition mounts.

In J. R. R. Tolkien's classic story *The Lord of the Rings*, the main character, Frodo, faces a powerful inner struggle: He must resist the corrupting spell of the magic ring so that he can pursue his mission to destroy it and save Middle Earth. He also faces numerous external struggles on his journey, as a series of enemies seeks to kill him and steal the ring. These confrontations with his enemies intensify his internal conflict—the desire to use the ring for his own benefit. The climax in *The Lord of the Rings* occurs when Frodo stands before the Lake of Fire in his mission to destroy the ring forever. Frequently, the climax causes the protagonist to change or at least to gain new understanding.

Gollum (Andy Serkis) plummets into the Lake of Fire holding the magic ring, resolving the overarching conflict of the story and advancing the plot toward the dénouement.

At this moment of internal conflict, Gollum attacks Frodo, and the climax resolves with both the ring and Gollum plunging into the fire toward everlasting destruction.

The conclusion of the story, or the resolution that follows the climactic moment, is referred to as the **dénouement,** the **falling action** and **resolution.** Here conflicts

> "Faulkner said, 'Fiction is the human heart in conflict with itself.' And it does seem to me that the human heart is always in conflict with itself, and that it is the fiction writer's job to understand the nature of that conflict and to make fiction out of it." Conversation with Gish Jen

are resolved and the story comes—at least provisionally—to an end. In the dénouement of *The Lord of the Rings*, peace is restored to Middle Earth, the new king marries his queen, and Frodo and his companions return home to the Shire.

Often, the internal transformation of the protagonist is the focal point of the story. The majority of modern and contemporary short fictions hinge on such moments, in which a significant truth or the essence of something is revealed to a character—and, by extension, the reader. Conflict, in other words, need not consist of a kick in the chin or a battle by a Lake of Fire; its resolution can be as simple as a character saying "Yes" or "No" or "Please stay" or "Go."

It is important to remember that no writer sitting at the work desk (except perhaps a screen-writer) says, "Well, I've had my anticlimax, now I need a falling action and a dénouement," or "I've had my turning point and must write a resolution." The terminology we use to describe the craft of fiction is used to understand how the story makes its impact on us—long after the fact of it being written. The language is useful primarily as a tool for analytic discussion as we share our thoughts about how stories are put together, how they work, and which ones work best.

James Joyce (1882–1941)

Born in Ireland in 1882, James Joyce chose to live much of his life as an expatriate in Paris, Zurich, and Trieste. The country of his birth, however, is the subject of almost all his fiction.

The publication of Joyce's short story collection *Dubliners* (1914) was held up for years for fear of libel; the characters and places of his stories were based on real people and locations in Dublin, and publishers feared readers would recognize them as such. Joyce rendered the Dublin of his novel *Ulysses* so accurately that he once joked the city could be reconstructed solely by consulting the "map" of his book. Ezra Pound wrote of Joyce: "He presents his people swiftly and vividly, he does not sentimentalize over them, he does not weave convulsions. He is a realist. ... He gives the thing as it is. He is not bound by the tiresome convention that any part of life, to be interesting, must be shaped into the conventional form of a 'story.'"

The story "Araby," like the others in *Dubliners*, reflects the influence of nineteenth-century realism, an artistic movement that advocated portraying the world as it is, without idealizing it. His later works—*A Portrait of the Artist As a Young Man, Ulysses,* and *Finnegans Wake*—become progressively more experimental in terms of language and form. Although it is longer than some nineteenth-century epic novels that span generations, the real-time action of *Ulysses* takes place entirely within the span of a single day.

AS YOU READ As you read "Araby," consider these questions: Who is telling the story? What does he want? What complications does he face in getting what he wants? How do these desires and confusions drive the story's plot?

Araby (1914)

1　NORTH Richmond Street, being blind, was a quiet street except at the hour when the Christian Brothers' School set the boys free. An uninhabited house of two storeys stood at the blind end, detached from its neighbours in a square ground. The other houses of the street, conscious of decent lives within them, gazed at one another with brown imperturbable faces.

2　The former tenant of our house, a priest, had died in the back drawing-room. Air, musty from having been long enclosed, hung in all the rooms, and the waste room behind the kitchen was littered with old useless papers. Among these I found a few paper-covered books, the pages of which were curled and damp: *The Abbot*, by Walter Scott, *The Devout Communicant* and *The Memoirs of Vidocq*. I liked the last best because its leaves were yellow. The wild garden behind the house contained a central apple-tree and a few straggling bushes under one of which I found the late tenant's rusty bicycle-pump. He had been a very charitable priest; in his will he had left all his money to institutions and the furniture of his house to his sister.

3　When the short days of winter came dusk fell before we had well eaten our dinners. When we met in the street the houses had grown sombre. The space of sky above us was the colour of ever-changing violet and towards it the lamps of the street lifted their feeble lanterns. The cold air stung us and we played till our bodies glowed. Our shouts echoed in the silent street. The career of our play brought us through the dark muddy lanes behind the houses where we ran the gantlet of the rough tribes from the cottages, to the back doors of the dark dripping gardens where odours arose from the ashpits, to the dark odorous stables where a coachman smoothed and combed the horse or shook music from the buckled harness. When we returned to the street light from the kitchen windows had filled the areas. If my uncle was seen turning the corner we hid in the shadow until we had seen him safely housed. Or if Mangan's sister came out on the doorstep to call her brother in to his tea we watched her from our shadow peer up and down the street. We waited to see whether she would remain or go in and, if she remained, we left our shadow and walked up to Mangan's steps resignedly. She was waiting for us, her figure defined by the light from the half-opened door. Her brother always teased her before he obeyed and I stood by the railings looking at her. Her dress swung as she moved her body and the soft rope of her hair tossed from side to side.

> I had never spoken to her, except for a few casual words, and yet her name was like a summons to all my foolish blood.

4   Every morning I lay on the floor in the front parlour watching her door. The blind was pulled down to within an inch of the sash so that I could not be seen. When she came out on the doorstep my heart leaped. I ran to the hall, seized my books and followed her. I kept her brown figure always in my eye and, when we came near the point at which our ways diverged, I quickened my pace and passed her. This happened morning after morning. I had never spoken to her, except for a few casual words, and yet her name was like a summons to all my foolish blood.

5   Her image accompanied me even in places the most hostile to romance. On Saturday evenings when my aunt went marketing I had to go to carry some of the parcels. We walked through the flaring streets, jostled by drunken men and bargaining women, amid the curses of labourers, the shrill litanies of shop-boys who stood on guard by the barrels of pigs' cheeks, the nasal chanting of street-singers, who sang a *come-all-you* about O'Donovan Rossa, or a ballad about the troubles in our native land. These noises converged in a single sensation of life for me: I imagined that I bore my chalice safely through a throng of foes. Her name sprang to my lips at moments in strange prayers and praises which I myself did not understand. My eyes were often full of tears (I could not tell why) and at times a flood from my heart seemed to pour itself out into my bosom. I thought little of the future. I did not know whether I would ever speak to her or not or, if I spoke to her, how I could tell her of my confused adoration. But my body was like a harp and her words and gestures were like fingers running upon the wires.

6   One evening I went into the back drawing-room in which the priest had died. It was a dark rainy evening and there was no sound in the house. Through one of the broken panes I heard the rain impinge upon the earth, the fine incessant needles of water playing in the sodden beds. Some distant lamp or lighted window gleamed below me. I was thankful that I could see so little. All my senses seemed to desire to veil themselves and, feeling that I was about to slip from them, I pressed the palms of my hands together until they trembled, murmuring: *O love! O love!* many times.

7   At last she spoke to me. When she addressed the first words to me I was so confused that I did not know what to answer. She asked me was I going to *Araby*. I forget whether I answered yes or no. It would be a splendid bazaar, she said; she would love to go.

8   —And why can't you? I asked.

9   While she spoke she turned a silver bracelet round and round her wrist. She could not go, she said, because there would be a retreat that week in her convent. Her brother and two other boys were fighting for their caps and I was alone at the railings. She held one of the spikes, bowing her head towards me. The light from the lamp opposite our door caught the white curve of her neck, lit up her hair that rested there and, falling, lit up the hand upon the railing. It fell over one side of her dress and caught the white border of a petticoat, just visible as she stood at ease.

10   —It's well for you, she said.

11   —If I go, I said, I will bring you something.

12   What innumerable follies laid waste my waking and sleeping thoughts after that evening! I wished to annihilate the tedious intervening days. I chafed against the work of school. At night in my bedroom and by day in the classroom her image came between me and the page I strove to read. The syllables of the word *Araby* were called to me through the silence in which my soul luxuriated and cast an Eastern enchantment over me. I asked for leave to go to the bazaar Saturday night. My aunt was surprised and

hoped it was not some Free-mason affair. I answered few questions in class. I watched my master's face pass from amiability to sternness; he hoped I was not beginning to idle. I could not call my wandering thoughts together. I had hardly any patience with the serious work of life which, now that it stood between me and my desire, seemed to me child's play, ugly monotonous child's play.

13   On Saturday morning I reminded my uncle that I wished to go to the bazaar in the evening. He was fussing at the hallstand, looking for the hat-brush, and answered me curtly:

14   —Yes, boy, I know.

15   As he was in the hall I could not go into the front parlour and lie at the window. I left the house in bad humour and walked slowly towards the school. The air was pitilessly raw and already my heart misgave me.

16   When I came home to dinner my uncle had not yet been home. Still it was early. I sat staring at the clock for some time and, when its ticking began to irritate me, I left the room. I mounted the staircase and gained the upper part of the house. The high cold empty gloomy rooms liberated me and I went from room to room singing. From the front window I saw my companions playing below in the street. Their cries reached me weakened and indistinct and, leaning my forehead against the cool glass, I looked over at the dark house where she lived. I may have stood there for an hour, seeing nothing but the brown-clad figure cast by my imagination, touched discreetly by the lamplight at the curved neck, at the hand upon the railings and at the border below the dress.

17   When I came downstairs again I found Mrs. Mercer sitting at the fire. She was an old garrulous woman, a pawnbroker's widow, who collected used stamps for some pious purpose. I had to endure the gossip of the tea-table. The meal was prolonged beyond an hour and still my uncle did not come. Mrs. Mercer stood up to go: she was sorry she couldn't wait any longer, but it was after eight o'clock and she did not like to be out late, as the night air was bad for her. When she had gone I began to walk up and down the room, clenching my fists. My aunt said:

18   —I'm afraid you may put off your bazaar for this night of Our Lord.

19   At nine o'clock I heard my uncle's latchkey in the halldoor. I heard him talking to himself and heard the hallstand rocking when it had received the weight of his overcoat. I could interpret these signs. When he was midway through his dinner I asked him to give me the money to go to the bazaar. He had forgotten.

—The people are in bed and after their first sleep now, he said.

I did not smile. My aunt said to him energetically:

—Can't you give him the money and let him go? You've kept him late enough as it is.

My uncle said he was very sorry he had forgotten. He said he believed in the old saying: *All work and no play makes Jack a dull boy.* He asked me where I was going and, when I had told him a second time he asked me did I know *The Arab's Farewell to his Steed.* When I left the kitchen he was about to recite the opening lines of the piece to my aunt.

I held a florin tightly in my hand as I strode down Buckingham Street towards the station. The sight of the streets thronged with buyers and glaring with gas recalled to me the purpose of my journey. I took my seat in a third-class carriage of a deserted train. After an intolerable delay the train moved out of the station slowly. It crept onward among ruinous houses and over the twinkling river. At Westland Row Station a crowd of people pressed to the carriage doors; but the porters moved them back, saying that it was a special train for the bazaar. I remained alone in the bare carriage. In a few minutes the train drew up beside an improvised wooden platform. I passed out on to the road and saw by the lighted dial of a clock that it was ten minutes to ten. In front of me was a large building which displayed the magical name.

I could not find any sixpenny entrance and, fearing that the bazaar would be closed, I passed in quickly through a turnstile, handing a shilling to a weary-looking man. I found myself in a big hall girdled at half its height by a gallery. Nearly all the stalls were closed and the greater part of the hall was in darkness. I recognised a silence like that which pervades a church after a service. I walked into the centre of the bazaar timidly. A few people were gathered about the stalls which were still open. Before a curtain, over which the words *Café Chantant* were written in coloured lamps, two men were counting money on a salver. I listened to the fall of the coins.

26   Remembering with difficulty why I had come I went over to one of the stalls and examined porcelain vases and flowered tea-sets. At the door of the stall a young lady was talking and laughing with two young gentlemen. I remarked their English accents and listened vaguely to their conversation.

27   —O, I never said such a thing!

28   —O, but you did!

29   —O, but I didn't!

30   —Didn't she say that?

31   —Yes. I heard her.

32   —O, there's a . . . fib!

33   Observing me the young lady came over and asked me did I wish to buy anything. The tone of her voice was not encouraging; she seemed to have spoken to me out of a sense of duty. I looked humbly at the great jars that stood like eastern guards at either side of the dark entrance to the stall and murmured:

34   —No, thank you.

35   The young lady changed the position of one of the vases and went back to the two young men. They began to talk of the same subject. Once or twice the young lady glanced at me over her shoulder.

36   I lingered before her stall, though I knew my stay was useless, to make my interest in her wares seem the more real. Then I turned away slowly and walked down the middle of the bazaar. I allowed the two pennies to fall against the sixpence in my pocket. I heard a voice call from one end of the gallery that the light was out. The upper part of the hall was now completely dark.

37   Gazing up into the darkness I saw myself as a creature driven and derided by vanity; and my eyes burned with anguish and anger.

IF you liked "Araby," you might like "The Odour of Chrysanthemums" (chapter 9) by D. H. Lawrence, a working-class writer from neighboring England who created a scandal with the publication of his novel *Lady Chatterley's Lover*.

GOING FURTHER   Joyce's stories can be found in his collection *Dubliners*. His novel *A Portrait of the Artist As a Young Man* takes the theme of growing up and enlarges it to include the main character's initiation into matters of family, love, religion, art, and politics.

Writing from Reading

Summarize

1 The story begins with a long expository section in which the narrator describes the setting and his state of mind. Mark the place in the story where it shifts into a scene and the plot is launched.

2 List all the causes and effects you can find in the plot. What role does cause/effect have in the development of the plot?

Analyze Craft

3 Does the terse, isolated dialogue serve to advance the plot of *Araby*? Describe how more detailed interactions would affect the pace of the story.

Analyze Voice

4 The narrator reports this story as he looks back on it from a future time. Based on the language and voice, how distant in time is the narrator from the events he recounts? Using textual evidence, can you piece together the age and social status of the narrator as the story unfolds?

(continued)

Synthesize Summary and Analysis

5 Consider the role of the priest who died in the drawing room in relation to the events of the story. Note the two instances in which the narrator visits the room where the priest died, and discuss these scenes in relation to the rising tension of the story.

Interpret the Story

6 At the end of the story, the narrator recognizes himself as a "creature driven and derided by vanity." Consider whether he is becoming such a person at that moment—whether the events of the story have brought about a change in him—or whether he is having an epiphany about the person he has always been. Which of the narrator's actions in the story support your conclusion?

Naguib Mahfouz (1911–2006)

The first Arab to win the Nobel Prize in Literature, Naguib Mahfouz lived in Cairo, Egypt, his entire life. Mahfouz wrote historical fiction inspired by Sir Walter Scott before turning to social realism to depict everyday life in his native city. *The Cairo Trilogy,* his trilogy about a middle-class family in Cairo, published in the late 1950s and won him widespread fame in the Arab-speaking world. Although many of his works were made into popular Arab films and he was a major influence on Arab literature, Mahfouz never made his living from writing. Instead, he worked as a civil servant for thirty-five years, writing and reading in the evenings after a full day of work. As Mahfouz's work progressed, it increasingly made political statements hidden in allegory and symbolism, combined with elements of realism. Some of his writing was controversial, notably *Children of Gebelawi,* which was banned in Egypt because of its alleged representation of God and the prophets. An outward sign of this controversy came in 1994 when an Islamist extremist stabbed Mahfouz in the neck because he found Mahfouz's portrayal of religion offensive. Although Mahfouz never fully recovered his health, he continued writing and published his last book, *The Seventh Heaven,* in the year preceding his death.

AS YOU READ As you read, notice the way Mahfouz's plot twists transform a simple errand into something far more complex. Why is it so difficult for the narrator to do his mother's bidding? Do you identify with him and his troubles?

FOR INTERACTIVE READING . . . The action of this story is advanced by a series of conflicts and temporary resolutions. As you read, note each new complication and resolution. Based on your notes, draw the plot curve of the story, identifying rising action, the climax, falling action, and the resolution.

The Conjurer Made Off with the Dish (1969)

THE time has come for you to be useful," said my mother to me, and she slipped her hand into her pocket, saying:

"Take this piastre and go off and buy some beans. Don't play on the way, and keep away from the cars."

I took the dish, put on my clogs and went out, humming a tune. Finding a crowd in front of the bean-seller, I waited until I discovered a way through to the marble table.

"A piastre's worth of beans, mister," I called out in my shrill voice.

He asked me impatiently:

"Beans alone? With oil? With cooking butter?"

I didn't answer and he said to me roughly:

"Make way for someone else."

I withdrew, overcome by embarrassment, and returned home defeated.

"Returning with an empty dish?" my mother shouted at me. "What did you do—spill the beans or lose the piastre, you naughty boy?"

"Beans alone? With oil? With cooking butter?— you didn't tell me," I protested.

"You stupid, what do you eat every morning?"

"I don't know."

"You good-for-nothing, ask him for beans with oil."

I went off to the man and said:

"A piastre's worth of beans with oil, mister."

With a frown of impatience he asked:

"Linseed oil? Nut oil? Olive oil?"

I was taken aback and again made no answer:

"Make way for someone else," he shouted at me.

I returned in a rage to my mother, who called out in astonishment:

"You've come back empty-handed—no beans and no oil."

"Linseed oil? Nut oil? Olive oil?—you didn't tell me," I said angrily.

"Beans with oil means beans with linseed oil."

"How should I know?"

"You're a good-for-nothing and he's a tiresome man—tell him beans with linseed oil."

"How should I know?"

I went off quickly and called out to the man while still some yards from his shop:

"Beans with linseed oil, mister."

"Put the piastre on the counter," he said, plunging the ladle into the pot.

I put my hand into my pocket but didn't find the piastre. I searched round for it anxiously. I turned my pocket inside out but found no trace of it. The man withdrew the ladle empty, saying with disgust:

"You've lost the piastre—you're not a boy to be depended on."

"I haven't lost it," I said, looking under my feet and round about me. "It's been in my pocket all the time."

"Make way for someone else and don't make trouble."

I returned to my mother with an empty dish.

"Good grief, you idiot boy!"

"The piastre . . ."

"What of it?"

"It wasn't in my pocket."

"Did you buy sweets with it?"

"I swear I didn't."

"How did you lose it?"

"I don't know."

"Do you swear by the Koran you didn't buy anything with it?"

"I swear."

"There's a hole in your pocket."

"No there isn't."

"Maybe you gave it to the man the first time or the second."

"Maybe."

"Are you sure of nothing?"

"I'm hungry."

She clapped her hands together in a gesture of resignation.

"Never mind," she said. "I'll give you another piastre but I'll take it out of your money-box, and if you come back with an empty dish I'll break your head."

I went off at a run, dreaming of a delicious breakfast. At the turning leading to the alleyway where the bean-seller was I saw a crowd of children and heard merry, festive sounds. My feet dragged as my heart was pulled towards them. At least let me have a fleeting glance. I slipped in amongst them and found the conjurer looking straight at me. A stupefying joy overwhelmed me; I was completely taken out of myself. With the whole of my being I became involved in the tricks of the rabbits and the eggs, and the snakes and the ropes. When the man came up to collect money, I drew back mumbling, "I haven't got any money."

> # A stupefying joy overwhelmed me;
> ## I was completely
> ### taken out of myself.

55 He rushed at me savagely and I escaped only with difficulty. I ran off, my back almost broken by his blow, and yet I was utterly happy as I made my way to the seller of beans.

"Beans with linseed oil for a piastre, mister," I said.

He went on looking at me without moving, so I repeated my request.

"Give me the dish," he demanded angrily.

The dish! Where was the dish? Had I dropped it while running? Had the conjurer made off with it?

60 "Boy, you're out of your mind."

I turned back, searching along the way for the lost dish. The place where the conjurer had been I found empty, but the voices of children led me to him in a nearby lane. I moved round the circle; when the conjurer spotted me he shouted out threateningly:

"Pay up or you'd better scram."

"The dish!" I called out despairingly.

"What dish, you little devil?"

65 "Give me back the dish."

"Scram or I'll make you into food for snakes."

He had stolen the dish, yet fearfully I moved away out of sight and wept. Whenever a passer-by asked me why I was crying I would reply:

"The conjurer made off with the dish."

Through my misery I became aware of a voice saying:

70 "Come along and watch."

I looked behind me and saw a peep-show had been set up. I saw dozens of children hurrying towards it and taking it in turns to stand in front of the peepholes, while the man began making his commentary on the pictures:

"There you've got the gallant knight and the most beautiful of all ladies, Zainat al-Banat."

Drying my tears, I gazed up in fascination at the box, completely forgetting the conjurer and the dish. Unable to overcome the temptation, I paid over the piastre and stood in front of the peephole next to a girl who was standing in front of the other one, and there flowed across our vision enchanting picture stories. When I came back to my own world I realized I had lost both the piastre and the dish, and there was no sign of the conjurer. However, I gave no thought to the loss, so taken up was I with the pictures of chivalry, love and deeds of daring. I forgot my hunger; I forgot the fear of what threatened me back home. I took a few paces back so as to lean against an ancient wall of what had once been a Treasury and the seat of office of the Cadi, and gave myself up wholly to my reveries. For a long while I dreamt of chivalry, of Zainat al-Banat and the ghoul. In my dream I spoke aloud, giving meaning to my words with gestures. Thrusting home the imaginary lance, I said:

"Take that, O ghoul, right in the heart!"

"And he raised Zainat al-Banat up behind him on his horse," came back a gentle voice.

I looked to my right and saw the young girl who had been beside me at the performance. She was wearing a dirty dress and coloured clogs and was playing with her long plait of hair; in her other hand were the red and white sweets called "Lady's fleas," which she was leisurely sucking. We exchanged glances and I lost my heart to her.

"Let's sit down and rest," I said to her.

She appeared to be agreeable to my suggestion, so I took her by the arm and we went through the gateway of the ancient wall and sat down on the step of a stairway that went nowhere, a stairway that rose up until it ended in a platform behind which there could be seen a blue sky and minarets. We sat in silence, side by side. I pressed her hand and we sat on in silence, not knowing what to say. I experienced feelings that were new, strange and obscure. Putting my face close to hers, I breathed in the natural smell of her hair, mingled with an odour of earth, and the fragrance of breath mixed with the aroma of sweets. I kissed her lips. I swallowed my saliva which had taken on a sweetness from the dissolved "Lady's fleas." I put my arm round her, without her uttering a word, kissing her cheek and lips. Her lips grew still as they received the kiss, then went back to sucking at the sweets. At last she decided we should get up. I seized her arm anxiously.

"Sit down," I said.

"I'm going," she said simply.

"Where to?" I asked irritably.

"To the midwife Umm Ali," and she pointed to a house at the bottom of which was a small ironing shop.

"Why?"

"To tell her to come quickly."

"Why?"

"My mother's crying in pain at home. She told me to go to the midwife Umm Ali and to take her along quickly."

"And you'll come back after that?"

She nodded her head in assent. Her mentioning her mother reminded me of my own and my heart missed a beat. Getting up from the ancient stairway, I made my way back home. I wept out loud, a tried method by which I would defend myself. I expected she would come to me but she did not. I wandered from the kitchen to the bedroom but found no trace of her. Where had my mother gone? When would she return? I was bored with being in the empty house. An idea occurred to me: I took a dish from the kitchen and a piastre from my savings and went off immediately to the seller of beans. I found him asleep on a bench outside the shop, his face covered over by his arm. The pots of beans had vanished and the long-necked bottles of oil had been put back on the shelf and the marble top washed down.

"Mister," I whispered, approaching.

Hearing nothing but his snoring, I touched his shoulder. He raised his arm in alarm and looked at me through reddened eyes.

"Mister."

"What do you want?" he asked roughly, becoming aware of my presence and recognizing me.

"A piastre's worth of beans with linseed oil."

"Eh?"

"I've got the piastre and I've got the dish."

"You're crazy, boy," he shouted at me. "Get out or I'll bash your brains in."

When I didn't move he pushed me so violently I went sprawling onto my back. I got up painfully, struggling to hold back the crying that was twisting my lips. My hands were clenched, one on the dish and the other on the piastre. I threw him an angry look. I thought about returning with my hopes dashed, but dreams of heroism and valour altered my plan of action. Resolutely, I made a quick decision and with all my strength threw the dish at him. It flew through the air and struck him on the head, while I took to my heels, heedless of everything. I was convinced I'd killed him, just as the knight had killed the ghoul. I didn't stop running till I was near the ancient wall. Panting, I looked behind me but saw no signs of any pursuit. I stopped to get my breath back, then asked myself what I should do now that the second dish was lost. Something warned me not to return home directly, and soon I had given myself over to a wave of indifference that bore me off where it willed. It meant a beating, neither more nor less, on my return, so let me put it off for a time. Here was the piastre in my hand and I could have some sort of enjoyment with it before being punished. I decided to pretend I had forgotten my having done wrong—but where was the conjurer, where was the peep-show? I looked everywhere for them but to no avail.

Worn out by this fruitless searching, I went off to the ancient stairway to keep my appointment. I sat down to wait, imagining to myself the meeting. I yearned for another kiss redolent with the fragrance of sweets. I admitted to myself that the little girl had given me sensations I had never experienced before. As I waited and dreamed, a whispering sound came to me from far away behind me. I climbed the stairs

95

cautiously and at the final landing I lay down flat on my face in order to see what was behind it, without anyone being able to spot me. I saw some ruins surrounded by a high wall, the last of what remained of the Treasury and the Chief Cadi's house. Directly under the stairs sat a man and a woman, and it was from them that the whispering came. The man looked like a tramp; the woman like one of those gypsies that tend sheep. An inner voice told me that their meeting was similar to the one I had had. Their lips and eyes revealed this, but they showed astonishing expertise in the extraordinary things they did. My gaze became rooted upon them with curiosity, surprise, pleasure, and a certain amount of disquiet. At last they sat down side by side, neither of them taking any notice of the other. After quite a while the man said:

"The money!"

100   "You're never satisfied," she said irritably.

Spitting on the ground, he said: "You're crazy."

"You're a thief."

He slapped her hard with the back of his hand, and she gathered up a handful of earth and threw it in his face. Then he sprang at her, fastening his fingers on her windpipe. In vain she gathered all her strength to escape from his grip. Her voice failed her, her eyes bulged out of their sockets, while her feet struck out at the air. In dumb terror I stared at the scene till I saw a thread of blood trickling down from her nose. A scream escaped from my mouth. Before the man raised his head, I had crawled backwards; descending the stairs at a jump, I raced off like mad to wherever my legs might carry me. I didn't stop running till I was out of breath. Gasping for breath, I was quite unaware of my whereabouts, but when I came to myself I found I was under a raised vault at the middle of a crossroads. I had never set foot there before and had no idea of where I was in relation to our quarter. On both sides sat sightless beggars, and crossing it from all directions were people who paid attention to no one. In terror I realized I had lost my way and that countless difficulties lay in wait for me before I would find my way home. Should I resort to asking one of the passers-by to direct me? What, though, would happen if chance should lead me to a man like the vendor of beans or the tramp of the waste plot? Would a miracle come about whereby I'd see my mother approaching so that I could eagerly hurry towards her? Should I try to make my own way, wandering about till I came across some familiar landmark that would indicate the direction I should take? I told myself that I should be resolute and take a quick decision: the day was passing and soon mysterious darkness would descend.

Translated by Denys Johnson-Davies

IF you liked Mahfouz's "The Conjurer Made Off with the Dish," you might also like a story by a writer whose work, among that of many modernists, including James Joyce in this chapter, influenced Mahfouz: Franz Kafka's "The Metamorphosis" (chapter 10).

GOING FURTHER   Salman Rushdie, like Mahfouz, experienced death threats when he published *The Satanic Verses,* a novel that Mahfouz defended.

Writing from Reading

Summarize

1 What is the boy's level of responsibility for the various complications in the story? At which points is he relatively innocent? At which points does he make decisions that get him into further trouble?

2 Describe the role of the young girl in the story. How does her presence drive the plot?

Analyze Craft

3 Examine the instances of dialogue in the story, and discuss how Mahfouz uses dialogue differently at different points through the story.

4 "The Conjurer Made Off with the Dish" is written in first person. Analyze how the story would change if it were written in third person, and discuss what is gained or lost by hearing events described by the boy narrator.

5 Although the story is named after the conjurer, the boy's complications involve many different characters. Identify one of these characters as the antagonist, citing proof from the story to make your argument.

Analyze Voice

6 Naguib Mahfouz was born in Cairo, and his story takes place in Egypt. How does setting affect the plot and the complications that the narrator encounters? Discuss which elements of the story would differ and which would remain the same if it were told by a boy in a modern American city.

Synthesize Summary and Analysis

7 Consider all the complications and momentary resolutions throughout the story. At what point, if ever,

does the narrator undergo a change? Discuss the events of the story that drive the boy toward, or keep him from, changing by the end of the story.

Interpret the Story

8 In the last line of the story, the boy resolves to make a quick decision. Discuss the irony of this conclusion in light of the events of the story. Consider what, if anything, the boy has learned from the day's events, and argue whether his adventure is finished or just beginning.

Pramoedya Ananta Toer (1925–2006)

Called Indonesia's greatest writer, Pramoedya (Prah-MOO-dia) Ananta Toer spent more than fourteen years in prison because of his political views. A supporter of Indonesian independence at a time when the country was ruled first by the Dutch, then by the Japanese, Pramoedya was beaten so badly upon his arrest that he lost much of his hearing. He suffered other abuses, including no communication with his

wife and children while in prison and the destruction of his manuscripts and notes. Nevertheless, Pramoedya produced novels, short stories, and essays that have been translated into more than thirty languages. His best-known work, the *Buru Quartet,* is a series of four novels about the Indonesian nationalist movement—*This Earth of Mankind* (1980), *Child of All Nations* (1980), *Footsteps* (1985), and *House of Glass* (1988). He began working on the

quartet while imprisoned on the island of Buru, originally telling stories to his fellow prisoners, who enjoyed them so much that they took on Pramoedya's prison labor to allow him to write; he composed on scraps of paper that had to be smuggled from the prison. Although the books were banned in Indonesia, they were well-received internationally, securing Pramoedya's place as the leading literary voice of the Indonesian struggle for independence.

AS YOU READ As you read, notice how straightforward the basic plot is. Notice also how the tension in the story rises and falls as the plot advances. How does the narrator manage his feelings of anxiety? How do the narrator's feelings about events influence your feelings?

Circumcision (1969)

1   **L**IKE other village children, I spent my evenings at the local prayer house learning to recite the Quran. Nothing could have pleased us more than to be there. For recitation lessons we paid two and a half cents per week, which was used to buy oil for the lamps. Lessons began at five thirty in the evening and continued until nine; they were the one and only excuse we had for getting out of doing our homework.

2   What I'm calling recitation lessons was actually nothing more than telling jokes, talking in fevered whispers about sex, and annoying other devotees who came to say their sunset or evening prayers while we waited for our own turn to be called. This was my world at the age of nine.

3   Like my friends, I wanted to be a good Muslim, though few of us, at our age, had been circumcised. But then, one day, one of my friends did get circumcised and a large celebration was held for him. This is when I began to think, if I hadn't been circumcised was I really a Muslim? I mulled over this question but didn't let anyone know what I was thinking.

4   In my small hometown of Blora, boys were usually circumcised somewhere between the ages of eight and thirteen, generally in as grand a style as family circumstances permitted. Girls underwent symbolic circumcision at the age of fifteen days, without any kind of celebration.

5   One night, my father came home and talked to me about circumcision. I had no idea where he had been, but he was in a very buoyant mood. The house was dark; all the lamps had been extinguished except for one in the central hall, where I was sitting with my mother, listening to her tell me a story about an old man—a pious one, presumably, since he had been to Mecca and was called *haji*[1] to indicate that he had made the pilgrimage to Islam's most holy seat—who kept on getting married. The story was a good one, but because of my father's sudden return it died then and there.

6   "Do you think you're brave enough to be circumcised?" he asked me, a hopeful smile on his lips.

7   I didn't know what to say. I wanted to be a good Muslim, but my father's surprise offer terrified me.

Then again, my father always terrified me. But, for some reason, his smile that night made all my fears disappear.

"Yes, I am!" I told him.

His smile broadened and he laughed congenially. "What would you like to wear to your circumcision, a wraparound *kain,*[2] or a sarong?"

"A *kain,*" I answered.

He then turned to my seven-year-old brother, who was also in the room. "And what about you, Tato? Are you brave enough, too?"

Tato laughed happily: "Sure I am!"

Father, too, laughed contentedly and the light from the lamp illuminated his even white teeth and pink gums.

Mother rose from the mat she had rolled out on the floor earlier, before starting her bedtime story.

"When do you want to have them circumcised?" she asked.

"As soon as possible," my father replied.

He then rose from his chair and walked away, into the darkness of the house and his bedroom.

Mother stretched out on the mat again but did not continue her story about the marriage-happy *haji.* Instead, she looked at us: "You boys must give thanks to God that your father is going to have you both circumcised."

"We will, Mother," we answered in unison.

"Your dear departed grandmother and all your other ancestors in heaven will be very pleased to know that you have been circumcised."

"Yes, Mother," we said again.

THAT night I could scarcely sleep as I thought of how much the circumcision would hurt. But then I also began to think of the new *kain* and new pair of sandals I would likely receive—along with all the other new clothes, and a headcloth and prayer mat as well. On top of that, I wouldn't have to go to school and there would be numerous guests. I was almost sure to receive lots of gifts.

I imagined the happiness I would feel from owning my own *kain* and headcloth, for these items were not only a sign of being a good Muslim; they were a

---

[1]A Muslim honorific indicating one has made the pilgrimage to Mecca.

[2]A cloth skirt similar to a sarong, but with the ends sewn together.

sign of being a good Javanese as well, something I also wanted to be.

I was sure to be given at least one sarong, maybe two or even three. My uncircumcised friends would be jealous; that thought, too, gave me a thrill.

The next morning I rose from my bed full of excitement. Tato and I set off for school with plenty of time to spare. Usually, our legs balked at walking to school, but that day they flew. All of our classmates soon heard the news, and the boys who weren't circumcised, especially the older ones, looked on us with newfound respect. Even the teachers cast a kindly gaze on us, for soon we were going to be true Muslims, bona fide circumcised Muslims. And when that happened—and this was the most important thing of all—we would have the right to a place in heaven. We'd no longer have to wish for the many beautiful things that we'd always hoped for but had never been able to obtain, for they would be ours.

> I suddenly felt **taller,** more important than my friends.

At the prayer house, the news also created a sensation among my friends, and our religious teacher gave me the same kindly look that my teachers at school had displayed. I suddenly felt taller, more important than my friends. I could see it very clearly: heaven's gates standing wide open for me. And sure enough, just as our religious teacher had also promised, there they were—the beautiful *houri,* young maidens waiting to tend to my needs. Each one was as beautiful as a certain girl at my school that all the boys talked about.

"After I'm circumcised, I'll be a true Muslim," I told the *kiai.*[3] "I'll have the right to go to heaven!"

The man laughed cheerfully. "And you'll have forty-four *houri* to wait on you!"

"But I don't want any who has six or eight breasts, like a dog," I told him. "I want them to look like Sriati, my classmate at school. She's beautiful."

The *kiai* laughed again.

"And I'll go fishing in rivers of milk every day," Tato chimed in.

Our teacher's mouth opened wider with laughter, baring a disgusting set of teeth that looked like they'd never been brushed.

Our older and uncircumcised friends listened to this conversation silently. I could see fear in their eyes: the fear of missing out on their share of *houri* and the fear of going not to heaven but to hell.

Starting that evening, we followed our recitation lessons diligently and we made sure to finish our homework in short order too. We also fasted, every week, from Monday to Thursday, until the end of the school year. As a result of this extra labor, I easily passed to the next grade.

Two weeks before the end of the school year, my father, the principal of our school, decided to stage a play with the children as actors. Our circumcision ceremony would be held the following day. Father had decided, then and there, to make this an annual event. That way, the poorer boys in school whose parents could not afford to hold a separate celebration would have the chance to get circumcised as well.

For this, my father's first attempt at starting a new tradition, the response of the townspeople was not what Father had expected it to be. Many parents with sons of circumcision age were apparently embarrassed to have someone else pay for their sons' circumcision ceremony. In the end, there were only six boys to be circumcised: my brother Tato and I, a ten-year-old cousin of ours, a sixteen-year-old foster brother, and two boys from poor families who lived outside of town. Another foster brother, who was eighteen and had already had a child with our servant, refused to participate. He insisted that his own father would arrange a ceremony for him.

Five days before the celebration, the boys who were to be circumcised were made to memorize a *panembrama,* a Javanese welcome song. On the night of the play, we were to appear onstage and announce to the audience in song that we were to be circumcised the next day; we were also to request that they offer their prayers for a successful event.

One of our teachers wrote a play about a lost goat in which all the roles were played by the male students.

Finally, the day that we had long awaited approached. The evening before, our grandmother gave Tato and me green silk sarongs. Our mother gave us lacquered wooden sandals and blue shirts. The girls in school gave us switches for keeping flies away during the ceremony, and our father gave us eight Dutch-language children's books. All these gifts made us forget about the pain we were to feel the following day.

O N the night of the play, the school was jam-packed with spectators. Food was served: sweet potatoes and boiled peanuts, fermented cassava, *gemblong*[4] made of sweetened sticky

---

[3]An authority on Islamic religious affairs.

[4]An Indonesian dessert.

rice, and other snacks. Before the performance was to begin, the six of us who were to be circumcised were made to line up on stage. I was outfitted in a *kain* and headcloth, as was my brother, Tato. The other boys were bareheaded. When the curtain opened, the *gamelan*[5] orchestra began to play, and we bowed in respect to the audience. I felt so incredibly proud of myself at that moment. All eyes were focused on us as we sang out that tomorrow we were to be circumcised. The girls looked on us with awe; there would soon be six more eligible men in town.

41   After our song the audience clapped loudly and we took another bow. The curtain was then closed and we were relieved from further responsibility.

42   In my hometown, there was very little public entertainment, which is why, I suppose, people came from all parts of the city to watch our performance of *The Lost Goat*. The school's large central classroom, which was usually subdivided into four sections during the regular school day, had been transformed into one large hall that was now filled with people.

43   The musical entertainment that night varied greatly; besides *gamelan* orchestral works, there were new popular songs such as "Peanut Flower" and "Rose Mary," cowboy songs, theatrical tunes, and older popular songs with a Western influence.

44   After the performance, many people from the audience patted our shoulders or pounded our backs, giving all six of us greater encouragement and making us feel very special. Later that night, after we had returned home, Tato continued to sing in his bed until he could stay awake no longer; his voice grew softer and softer until it finally died and he drifted to sleep.

45   In my hometown, the day of a boy's circumcision was a day of great significance, as important as one's birthday or wedding day, the anniversary of a person's death, or even a public holiday. Although my mother had sent out no formal invitations, news of the ceremony had spread far and wide, and she received contributions for the event from all parts of town.

46   As was usually the case with major life rituals, even though we had stayed up late the night before, on the day of our circumcision we woke up extra early; by four thirty in the morning the house was already very busy. The candidates for circumcision bathed and were then each dressed in his new *kain* and a prayer cap or headcloth. My sisters wore new clothes

and my mother dressed in a new *kain* with a *parang rusak*[6] motif. For a top, she wore a long blouse with embroidered lapels and edging, a gift from an aunt who taught at the girls' school in Rembang. A green rainbow-motif shoulder sash completed her outfit.

My father had on his school uniform: a wrap-around *kain* with a broken dagger motif that matched my mother's and a long-sleeved button-up jacket. As usual he was barefooted. (My father never wore shoes; only at home might he sometimes wear wooden cloppers or sandals.)

As if infected by my family's state of readiness, our neighbors rose early too. All dressed in new clothing as well, they then gathered at our house to escort us to the school, where the ceremony was to be held, about a half kilometer away.

Inside the school a small tentlike shelter with sides made of mosquito netting had been erected for the circumcision ceremony. The six of us who were to be circumcised occupied a row of chairs nearby. As the time for the ceremony approached, the number of visitors around the shelter grew larger, both adults and children too. The girls remained at a slight distance.

Finally, a circumcision specialist, the *calak*, arrived, and proceeded to unwrap three straight-edge blades from their handkerchief covers. As he was doing this, an older man offered us words of advice: "Don't be afraid. It won't hurt. It's a bit like being bitten by a red ant. I laughed when I was circumcised."

His was only one of many comforting voices, but no matter how reassuring the tone, we couldn't completely expunge our anxiety and fear.

Then came the time for the ceremony to begin. My father and mother, who were seated in a pair of large chairs among the crowd of visitors, rose and approached the netted shelter. Pride and elation showed on their faces.

The first boy to enter the hut was my parents' foster son, the sixteen-year-old, because he was the oldest one among us. The other foster son, the one who had refused to be circumcised, was nowhere to be seen in the crowd. The children who had come to witness the ceremony crowded so close to the shelter that the adults were forced to shoo them away.

I was incredibly scared. I wanted to be a good Muslim, but that wasn't enough to still my terror. And when the *calak* suddenly began to bawl out an incom-

> # When my foster brother was led out of the hut, he could scarcely walk.

[5]An Indonesian musical ensemble composed mostly of percussion instruments.

[6]"Broken knife"; a traditional Javanese pattern.

prehensible prayer, the pounding of my heart in my chest grew all the more strong. When my foster brother was led out of the hut, he could scarcely walk. His face was drained of blood and his lips looked almost white. He had no strength. The ushers seated him in his chair and placed a large earthenware saucer that was filled with fine ash from the kitchen hearth between his legs to catch and sop up the blood that was dripping from his penis.

55 One by one, the older boys entered the shelter. As with my foster brother, when they reemerged they looked pale-faced and walked with an unsteady gait. As I stood up to enter the tent, I felt several people take hold of my shoulders, as if they were afraid I would try to run away. I was then ushered inside the hut, where the *calak* was waiting impatiently, with a ferocious gleam in his eye—at least that's how he looked to me.

56 I was placed in a chair and my head pulled backward so that I was now facing up, toward the roof of the tent. While one of the ushers, an older man, held my shoulders tightly to steady me, another pair of old hands attached themselves to my temples so that I could not look down. Below me, on the floor, was an earthenware bowl filled with ash. I felt a hand grope my penis, and then my foreskin being twisted tightly until it began to sting and feel very hot. Just at that moment, a razor severed that knot of my skin. It was over; I was circumcised. The old man who had been holding my temples back released his hands. I looked down to see blood dripping from the end of my penis.

57 "Don't move," one of the men said.

58 "You have to wait until the first flow of blood has stopped," another added.

59 I stared at the stream of blood—a blackened cord as it began to coagulate—and watched it as it slowly fell and disappeared into the fine ash in the saucer directly below.

60 Because Tato was the youngest, he was the last to be circumcised; and when his operation was over, he too was led out from the shelter and put back on the seat beside me. Blood continued to drip into the earthenware dishes below our legs. All eyes were upon us. Mother came to me and kissed my cheeks; her display of affection caused tears to well in my eyes. She kissed Tato on the cheek too. Then Father came over to congratulate us: "Well done, well done."

61 The visitors began to leave, first the children and then the adults, who took their leave one by one. After that, the six of us who had just been circumcised made our way home on foot as well.

62 We were treated like kings that day. Our wishes were commands. The families of the two poor boys who had also been circumcised came to our home bearing gifts of chicken and rice.

63 "Now that you've been circumcised, do you feel that something's changed?" my mother asked me.

64 "I feel really happy," I told her.

65 "And do you feel like a true Muslim?" she then inquired.

66 Her question gave me pause; the fact was, I didn't feel any different.

67 "I feel like I did yesterday," I tried to explain, "... and the day before. I still don't feel like a true Muslim."

68 "Could it be because you don't perform the daily prayers?" Mother then asked.

69 "No, I always do all five," I told her.

70 "Your grandfather's been to Mecca. Maybe if you made the pilgrimage, you'd feel the change, and know that you were a true Muslim."

71 "Would we go by ship?" Tato chirped.

72 "Yes, you'd sail to Arabia," Mother answered.

73 "Wouldn't we have to be really rich to do that?" I then posed.

74 "Yes, you would," Mother said.

75 And with that all my hopes of becoming a true Muslim vanished. I knew that my parents weren't well off and that we could never afford to make the pilgrimage.

76 "Why hasn't Father ever been to Mecca?" I asked.

77 "Because your father doesn't have the money."

78 Although I suddenly wanted to be rich, I also knew that this would never be the case. And after I had healed, the thought of becoming a true Muslim never again entered my mind.

IF you liked this story, "Circumcision," you might also like Chimamanda Ngozi Adichie's "Cell One," about political repression in Nigeria (chapter 9).

GOING FURTHER   The nationalist movement that led to Pramoedya's arrest spawned many Indonesian writers, among them the pioneer in modernizing the Indonesian language, Sutan Takdir Alisjahbana, whose best-known novel is *Open Sail*.

Writing from Reading

Summarize

1 Break down the story into individual events. Does this story follow the traditional pattern described in the chapter? That is, can you identify a conflict or conflicts, rising action, climax, and dénouement or resolution? What are they?

Analyze Craft

2 Does the story have a protagonist and antagonist? Explain.

3 Describe the relationship between the narrator and his father. How does this relationship affect the plot?

Analyze Voice

4 The narrator is relating a deeply personal story, which in some cultures might make for great embarrassment. How would you describe the tone he uses to tell about these events? Does he take a longer view than just focusing on the ritual practice of the title?

Synthesize Summary and Analysis

5 Analyze the relationship between plot and character. How does this story's plot hinge on the protagonist's efforts to realize his desire and his abilities to cope with failure?

6 How do the themes of wealth and poverty affect the characters and the plot of this story? In the narrator's mind, how do economic factors affect his ability to be a "good Muslim"?

7 Reread the paragraphs in which the circumcision occurs. Describe a ceremony or ritual from your own culture, using details and suspense the way this author does.

Interpret the Story

8 What pain does the narrator feel that may be greater than the physical pain? How do you explain the narrator's falling off of devotion at the end?

Reading for Plot

When reading for plot, ask yourself how the author has arranged the incidents in the story for cause and effect leading to the climax and the resolution of the story. We'll use a familiar fairytale as an example.

How does the story begin?	• Is exposition included in the story?	EXAMPLE In those days, it wasn't so unusual for a little girl to walk in the forest by herself—especially since her grandmother's house was close by.
	• Does it begin *in medias res*?	EXAMPLE The forest felt especially dark and creepy, she thought, as she set off in her red cloak with a basket of goodies for her grandmother.

How does the plot unfold?	• Does it include **flashbacks**?	EXAMPLE There had been another time—last spring, when the animals were hungrier than usual, after the long deprivation of winter—that she had felt afraid. She'd seen a wolf, at the bend of the path, and then again, by the pond, drinking. Both times, she passed quickly, not making eye contact, telling herself that so close to grandmother's, nothing could harm her.
	• Does the story include **foreshadowing**?	EXAMPLE Little Red Riding Hood shivered as she walked, drawing her cloak around her, listening for cries of wild animals, wondering whether she really should have come alone, whether that quick movement was the wind . . . or something else.
Which elements of plot can you identify?	• Who is the **protagonist**?	EXAMPLE Little Red Riding Hood
	• Who/what is the **antagonist**?	EXAMPLE the wolf
	• What is the **conflict**?	EXAMPLE The big bad wolf is leading the poor, defenseless Little Red Riding Hood into a trap.
	• What is the **climax**?	EXAMPLE The wolf tore off its cap and leapt from the bed, teeth and claws bared.
	• What is the **dénouement, resolution,** or **conclusion**?	EXAMPLE The woodcutter dusted off the little girl, found the grandmother, and they all had a lovely little snack together.

Suggestions for Writing about Plot

1. Consider the order of incidents in "The Conjurer Made Off with the Dish." Why do you think Mahfouz placed the scenes in this particular order?

2. Compare the setting of "Araby" with that of "Greasy Lake." How do the grim settings of these stories propel the plot?

3. Compare the way each story in this chapter employs plot to achieve its dramatic purpose. What similarities do you see in the writers' techniques? Choose two stories and discuss the elements of plot that are common to both.

4. Make a case for how the young narrators of the stories in this chapter respond to new situations or opportunities. Who takes action and who does not? Which characters reach new levels of perception? Does anyone fulfill his or her desire?

5

IN China, daughter take care of mother. Here it is the other way around. Mother help daughter, mother ask, Anything else I can do? Otherwise daughter complain mother is not supportive. I tell daughter, We do not have this word in Chinese, *supportive*. But my daughter too busy to listen, she has to go to meeting, she has to write memo while her husband go to the gym to be a man. My daughter say otherwise he will be depressed. Seems like all his life he has this trouble, depression.

—*from "Who's Irish?" by Gish Jen*

Chara

WHOSE voice is this, and what can you tell about her from this short excerpt? You can tell quite a bit, actually. It's likely that the first thing you notice is the way the person speaks—with the inaccurate spelling and grammar of a person not native to English. It's also clear from the context that the speaker is female, the mother of a married daughter whose husband is depressed. "Here"—the first word of the second sentence—suggests that the speaker's no longer at home but is instead an immigrant, a stranger in what seems to her a strange land. The character/narrator doesn't use articles or pronouns, and she fails to use appropriate verb forms; her nouns and verbs disagree. The grammatically correct first sentence would have been "In China, *a* daughter *takes* care of *her* mother."

Next, because she knows the ways of China and the Chinese, we can safely guess where the mother comes from and what her native language is. Even the single word "supportive" provides us with much evidence; the speaker tells her daughter that there's no such word in Chinese, and she's evidently repeating a term the daughter—a better English speaker—has previously used. So there's a family disagreement going on; the daughter has complained her mother's not being supportive while she, the younger woman, is earning a living—going to meetings, writing memos "while her husband go to the gym." Jen replicates the sound, accent, and cadence of inflected speech, bringing the character vividly to life.

Even in this brief excerpt, we get a sense of the mother's nature. Her flood of words has an edge. This narrator is not just reporting facts about her life and family; she's *complaining,* even *ranting.* Her daughter's entire way of life is, to the speaker, a puzzle. The mother doesn't approve of a husband who has to "go to the gym to be a man." That phrase, more than any other in the passage, underlines her disapproval and confusion; the behavior of the younger generation is hard for her to swallow, and roles have been reversed. Her child fails to provide her with the respectful attention an elder in China expects. We know that we will read a story about the clash of values, about generations in conflict and cultures at odds with each other.

CONTINUED ON PAGE 111

. . . the character is absolutely the font of all fiction.

Q&A

. . . I am interested in so many questions of ethnicity and identity . . .

A Conversation on Writing

Gish Jen

Using Character to Drive Fiction

I think the character is absolutely the font of all fiction. I think that's where the conflict comes from and I think it's where the plot comes from: that's where the story comes from. And so when I feel that something is not going well, that it doesn't have its own drive, I don't look at the incidents to try to understand what's going wrong. I look at the character, and in particular I look at the character's ambivalence.

Using Humor to Confront Loaded Topics

[Humor] does seem to have a particular use in my writing, because I am interested in so many questions of ethnicity and identity, which are pretty loaded. With humor, it's like everything is just floating on a sea where they can all move around. And things, which perhaps would be crashing into each other in a very unpleasant way, are suddenly able to float.

On the Pleasure of Reading

I at least feel much more alive reading than I do living sometimes. I mean, there is a way in which life itself can be kind of a disappointment, which literature never is.

On the Writing Process

You know, when I was a younger writer, I used to have a system where I kept a little notebook of index cards. These were 4-by-6 index cards that were spiral bound. That was a very useful way of keeping notes because after you write things down you can tear them out and file them. So, all of your thoughts about character, for instance, can be put in one place. . . . Now that I'm an older person and more in need of such devices I actually . . . rely more heavily on my imagination.

"I *am* the kind of person who would make a joke on someone's deathbed, tacky as it may seem," Gish Jen once said in an interview. And while she may have been speaking lightheartedly, she captured one of the essential elements of her craft—her ability to blend tragedy and humor. Born (1955) as Lillian Jen to Chinese immigrant parents in Scarsdale, New York, she changed her first name to "Gish" in honor of the silent film actress Lillian Gish. After graduating from Harvard, Jen taught English to engineers in China, later returning to the United States and earning her M.F.A. from the Iowa Writers' Workshop. She is the author of three novels—*Typical American* (1991), its sequel, *Mona in the Promised Land* (1996), and *The Love Wife* (2004)—as well as a collection of short stories, *Who's Irish?* (2000). In her fiction, Jen explores ideas of ethnic and cultural identity, assimilation, and integration, and how these ideas change for her characters as they adapt to new surroundings or situations. She now lives in Cambridge, Massachusetts, with her husband and two children.

To watch this entire interview and hear the author read from "Who's Irish?" go to www. mhhe.com/delbanco1e.

RESEARCH ASSIGNMENT In Jen's interview, she reflects on this quotation about story writing: "If you don't surprise yourself, you will not surprise the reader." What does this mean to Jen?

AS YOU READ As you read, imagine that you are sitting across the table from the narrator of this story. Imagine that she is speaking directly to you. How do you feel about what she is telling you? What would you like to say to her? Would you say everything you are thinking?

Who's Irish? (1999)

1   IN China, people say mixed children are supposed to be smart, and definitely my granddaughter Sophie is smart. But Sophie is wild, Sophie is not like my daughter Natalie, or like me. I am work hard my whole life, and fierce besides. My husband always used to say he is afraid of me, and in our restaurant, busboys and cooks all afraid of me too. Even the gang members come for protection money, they try to talk to my husband. When I am there, they stay away. If they come by mistake, they pretend they are come to eat. They hide behind the menu, they order a lot of food. They talk about their mothers. Oh, my mother have some arthritis, need to take herbal medicine, they say. Oh, my mother getting old, her hair all white now.

I say, Your mother's hair used to be white, but since she dye it, it become black again. Why don't you go home once in a while and take a look? I tell them, Confucius say a filial son knows what color his mother's hair is.

My daughter is fierce too, she is vice president in the bank now. Her new house is big enough for everybody to have their own room, including me. But Sophie take after Natalie's husband's family, their name is Shea. Irish. I always thought Irish people are like Chinese people, work so hard on the railroad, but now I know why the Chinese beat the Irish. Of course, not all Irish are like the Shea family, of course not. My daughter tell me I should not say Irish this, Irish that.

How do you like it when people say the Chinese this, the Chinese that, she say.

5   You know, the British call the Irish heathen, just like they call the Chinese, she say.

You think the Opium War was bad, how would you like to live right next door to the British, she say.

And that is that. My daughter have a funny habit when she win an argument, she take a sip of something and look away, so the other person is not embarrassed. So I am not embarrassed. I do not call anybody anything either. I just happen to mention about the Shea family, an interesting fact: four brothers in the family, and not one of them work. The mother, Bess, have a job before she got sick, she was executive secretary in a big company. She is handle everything for a big shot, you would be surprised how complicated her job is, not just type this, type that. Now she is a nice woman with a clean house. But her boys, every one of them is on welfare, or so-called severance pay, or so-called disability pay. Something. They say they cannot find work, this is not the economy of the fifties, but I say, Even the black people doing better these days, some of them live so fancy, you'd be surprised. Why the Shea family have so much trouble? They are white people, they speak English. When I come to this country, I have no money and do not speak English. But my husband and I own our restaurant before he die. Free and clear, no mortgage. Of course, I understand I am just lucky; come from a country where the food is popular all over the world. I understand it is not the Shea family's fault they come from a country where everything is boiled. Still, I say.

She's right, we should broaden our horizons, say one brother Jim, at Thanksgiving. Forget about the car business. Think about egg rolls.

Pad thai, say another brother, Mike. I'm going to make my fortune in pad thai. It's going to be the new pizza.

10   I say, You people too picky about what you sell. Selling egg rolls not good enough for you, but at least my husband and I can say, We made it. What can you say? Tell me. What can you say?

Everybody chew their tough turkey.

I especially cannot understand my daughter's husband John, who has no job but cannot take care of Sophie either. Because he is a man, he say, and that's the end of the sentence.

Plain boiled food, plain boiled thinking. Even his name is plain boiled: John. Maybe because I grew up with black bean sauce and hoisin sauce and garlic sauce, I always feel something is missing when my son-in-law talk.

But, okay: so my son-in-law can be man, I am baby-sitter. Six hours a day, same as the old sitter, crazy Amy, who quit. This is not so easy, now that I am sixty-eight, Chinese age almost seventy. Still, I try. In China, daughter take care of mother. Here it is the other way around. Mother help daughter, mother ask, Anything else I can do? Otherwise daughter complain mother is not supportive. I tell daughter, We do not have this word in Chinese, *supportive*. But my daughter too busy to listen, she has to go to meeting, she has to write memo while her husband go to the gym to be a man. My daughter say otherwise he will be depressed. Seems like all his life he has this trouble, depression.

15 No one wants to hire someone who is depressed, she say. It is important for him to keep his spirits up.

Beautiful wife, beautiful daughter, beautiful house, oven can clean itself automatically. No money left over, because only one income, but lucky enough, got the baby-sitter for free. If John lived in China, he would be very happy. But he is not happy. Even at the gym things go wrong. One day, he pull a muscle. Another day, weight room too crowded. Always something.

Until finally, hooray, he has a job. Then he feel pressure.

I need to concentrate, he say. I need to focus.

He is going to work for insurance company. Salesman job. A paycheck, he say, and at least he will wear clothes instead of gym shorts. My daughter buy him some special candy bars from the health-food store. They say THINK! on them, and are supposed to help John think.

20 John is a good-looking boy, you have to say that, especially now that he shave so you can see his face.

I am an old man in a young man's game, say John.

I will need a new suit, say John.

This time I am not going to shoot myself in the foot, say John.

Good, I say.

She means to be supportive, my daughter say. 2▮ Don't start the send her back to China thing, because we can't.

SOPHIE is three years old American age, but already I see her nice Chinese side swallowed up by her wild Shea side. She looks like mostly Chinese. Beautiful black hair, beautiful black eyes. Nose perfect size, not so flat looks like something fell down, not so large looks like some big deal got stuck in wrong face. Everything just right, only her skin is a brown surprise to John's family. So brown, they say. Even John say it. She never goes in the sun, still she is that color, he say. Brown. They say, Nothing the matter with brown. They are just surprised. So brown. Nattie is not that brown, they say. They say, It seems like Sophie should be a color in between Nattie and John. Seems funny, a girl named Sophie Shea be brown. But she is brown, maybe her name should be Sophie Brown. She never go in the sun, still she is that color, they say. Nothing the matter with brown. They are just surprised.

The Shea family talk is like this sometimes, going around and around like a Christmas-tree train.

Maybe John is not her father, I say one day, to stop the train. And sure enough, train wreck. None of the brothers ever say the word *brown* to me again.

Instead, John's mother, Bess, say, I hope you are not offended.

She say, I did my best on those boys. But raising 30 four boys with no father is no picnic.

You have a beautiful family, I say.

I'm getting old, she say.

You deserve a rest, I say. Too many boys make you old.

I never had a daughter, she say. You have a daughter.

I have a daughter, I say. Chinese people don't think a 35 daughter is so great, but you're right. I have a daughter.

I was never against the marriage, you know, she say. I never thought John was marrying down. I always thought Nattie was just as good as white.

I was never against the marriage either, I say. I just wonder if they look at the whole problem.

Of course you pointed out the problem, you are a mother, she say. And now we both have a granddaughter. A little brown granddaughter, she is so precious to me.

I laugh. A little brown granddaughter, I say. To tell you the truth, I don't know how she came out so brown.

We laugh some more. These days Bess need a walker to walk. She take so many pills, she need two glasses of water to get them all down. Her favorite TV show is about bloopers, and she love her bird feeder. All day long, she can watch that bird feeder, like a cat.

I can't wait for her to grow up, Bess say. I could use some female company.

Too many boys, I say.

Boys are fine, she say. But they do surround you after a while.

You should take a break, come live with us, I say. Lots of girls at our house.

Be careful what you offer, say Bess with a wink. Where I come from, people mean for you to move in when they say a thing like that.

NOTHING the matter with Sophie's outside, that's the truth. It is inside that she is like not any Chinese girl I ever see. We go to the park, and this is what she does. She stand up in the stroller. She take off all her clothes and throw them in the fountain.

Sophie! I say. Stop!

But she just laugh like a crazy person. Before I take over as baby-sitter, Sophie has that crazy-person sitter, Amy the guitar player. My daughter thought this Amy very creative—another word we do not talk about in China. In China, we talk about whether we have difficulty or no difficulty. We talk about whether life is bitter or not bitter. In America, all day long, people talk about creative. Never mind that I cannot even look at this Amy, with her shirt so short that her belly button showing. This Amy think Sophie should love her body. So when Sophie take off her diaper, Amy laugh. When Sophie run around naked, Amy say she wouldn't want to wear a diaper either. When Sophie go *shu-shu* in her lap, Amy laugh and say there are no germs in pee. When Sophie take off her shoes, Amy say bare feet is best, even the pediatrician say so. That is why Sophie now walk around with no shoes like a beggar child. Also why Sophie love to take off her clothes.

Turn around! say the boys in the park. Let's see that ass!

Of course, Sophie does not understand. Sophie clap her hands, I am the only one to say, No! This is not a game.

It has nothing to do with John's family, my daughter say. Amy was too permissive, that's all.

But I think if Sophie was not wild inside, she would not take off her shoes and clothes to begin with.

You never take off your clothes when you were little, I say. All my Chinese friends had babies, I never saw one of them act wild like that.

Look, my daughter say. I have a big presentation tomorrow.

John and my daughter agree Sophie is a problem, but they don't know what to do.

You spank her, she'll stop, I say another day.

But they say, Oh no.

In America, parents not supposed to spank the child.

It gives them low self-esteem, my daughter say. And that leads to problems later, as I happen to know.

My daughter never have big presentation the next day when the subject of spanking come up.

I don't want you to touch Sophie, she say. No spanking, period.

Don't tell me what to do, I say.

I'm not telling you what to do, say my daughter. I'm telling you how I feel.

I am not your servant, I say. Don't you dare talk to me like that.

My daughter have another funny habit when she lose an argument. She spread out all her fingers and look at them, as if she like to make sure they are still there.

My daughter is fierce like me, but she and John think it is better to explain to Sophie that clothes are a good idea. This is not so hard in the cold weather. In the warm weather, it is very hard.

Use your words, my daughter say. That's what we tell Sophie. How about if you set a good example.

As if good example mean anything to Sophie. I am so fierce, the gang members who used to come to the restaurant all afraid of me, but Sophie is not afraid.

I say, Sophie, if you take off your clothes, no snack.

I say, Sophie, if you take off your clothes, no lunch.

I say, Sophie, if you take off your clothes, no park.

Pretty soon we are stay home all day, and by the end of six hours she still did not have one thing to eat. You never saw a child stubborn like that.

I'm hungry! she cry when my daughter come home.

What's the matter, doesn't your grandmother feed you? My daughter laugh.

No! Sophie say. She doesn't feed me anything!

My daughter laugh again. Here you go, she say.

She say to John, Sophie must be growing.

Growing like a weed, I say.

Still Sophie take off her clothes, until one day I spank her. Not too hard, but she cry and cry, and when I tell her if she doesn't put her clothes back on I'll spank her again, she put her clothes back on. Then I tell her she is good girl, and give her some food to eat. The next day we go to the park and, like a nice Chinese girl, she does not take off her clothes.

80 She stop taking off her clothes, I report. Finally!

How did you do it? my daughter ask.

After twenty-eight years experience with you, I guess I learned something, I say.

It must have been a phase, John say, and his voice is suddenly like an expert.

His voice is like an expert about everything these days, now that he carry a leather briefcase, and wear shiny shoes, and can go shopping for a new car. On the company, he say. The company will pay for it, but he will be able to drive it whenever he want.

85 A free car, he say. How do you like that.

It's good to see you in the saddle again, my daughter say. Some of your family patterns are scary.

At least I don't drink, he say. He say, And I'm not the only one with scary family patterns.

That's for sure, say my daughter.

EVERYONE is happy. Even I am happy, because there is more trouble with Sophie, but now I think I can help her Chinese side fight against her wild side. I teach her to eat food with fork or spoon or chopsticks, she cannot just grab into the middle of a bowl of noodles. I teach her not to play with garbage cans. Sometimes I spank her, but not too often, and not too hard.

90 Still, there are problems. Sophie like to climb everything. If there is a railing, she is never next to it. Always she is on top of it. Also, Sophie like to hit the mommies of her friends. She learn this from her playground best friend, Sinbad, who is four. Sinbad wear army clothes every day and like to ambush his mommy. He is the one who dug a big hole under the play structure, a foxhole he call it, all by himself. Very hardworking. Now he wait in the foxhole with a shovel full of wet sand. When his mommy come, he throw it right at her.

Oh, it's all right, his mommy say. You can't get rid of war games, it's part of their imaginative play. All the boys go through it.

Also, he like to kick his mommy, and one day he tell Sophie to kick his mommy too.

I wish this story is not true.

Kick her, kick her! Sinbad say.

95 Sophie kick her. A little kick, as if she just so happened was swinging her little leg and didn't realize that big mommy leg was in the way. Still I spank Sophie and make Sophie say sorry, and what does the mommy say?

Really, it's all right, she say. It didn't hurt.

After that, Sophie learn she can attack mommies in the playground, and some will say, Stop, but others will say, Oh, she didn't mean it, especially if they realize Sophie will be punished.

THIS is how, one day, bigger trouble come. The bigger trouble start when Sophie hide in the foxhole with that shovel full of sand. She wait, and when I come look for her, she throw it at me. All over my nice clean clothes.

Did you ever see a Chinese girl act this way?

Sophie! I say. Come out of there, say you're sorry.

But she does not come out. Instead, she laugh. Naaah, naah-na, naaa-naaa, she say.

I am not exaggerate: millions of children in China, not one act like this.

Sophie! I say. Now! Come out now!

But she know she is in big trouble. She know if she come out, what will happen next. So she does not come out. I am sixty-eight, Chinese age almost seventy, how can I crawl under there to catch her? Impossible. So I yell, yell, yell, and what happen? Nothing. A Chinese mother would help, but American mothers, they look at you, they shake their head, they go home. And, of course, a Chinese child would give up, but not Sophie.

I hate you! she yell. I hate you, Meanie!

Meanie is my new name these days.

Long time this goes on, long long time. The foxhole is deep, you cannot see too much, you don't know where is the bottom. You cannot hear too much either. If she does not yell, you cannot even know she is still there or not. After a while, getting cold out, getting dark out. No one left in the playground, only us.

Sophie, I say. How did you become stubborn like this? I am go home without you now.

I try to use a stick, chase her out of there, and once or twice I hit her, but still she does not come out. So finally I leave. I go outside the gate.

Bye-bye! I say. I'm go home now.

But still she does not come out and does not come out. Now it is dinnertime, the sky is black. I think I should maybe go get help, but how can I leave a little girl by herself in the playground? A bad man could come. A rat could come. I go back in to see what is happen to Sophie. What if she have a shovel and is making a tunnel to escape?

Sophie! I say.

No answer.

Sophie!

I don't know if she is alive. I don't know if she is fall asleep down there. If she is crying, I cannot hear her.

So I take the stick and poke.

Sophie! I say. I promise I no hit you. If you come out, I give you a lollipop.

No answer. By now I worried. What to do, what to do, what to do? I poke some more, even harder, so that I am poking and poking when my daughter and John suddenly appear.

What are you doing? What is going on? say my daughter.

Put down that stick! say my daughter.

You are crazy! say my daughter.

John wiggle under the structure, into the foxhole, to rescue Sophie.

She fell asleep, say John the expert. She's okay. That is one big hole.

Now Sophie is crying and crying.

Sophia, my daughter say, hugging her. Are you okay, peanut? Are you okay?

She's just scared, say John.

Are you okay? I say too. I don't know what happen, I say.

She's okay, say John. He is not like my daughter, full of questions. He is full of answers until we get home and can see by the lamplight.

Will you look at her? he yell then. What the hell happened?

Bruises all over her brown skin, and a swollen-up eye.

You are crazy! say my daughter. Look at what you did! You are crazy!

I try very hard, I say.

How could you use a stick? I told you to use your words!

She is hard to handle, I say.

She's three years old! You cannot use a stick! say my daughter.

She is not like any Chinese girl I ever saw, I say.

I brush some sand off my clothes. Sophie's clothes are dirty too, but at least she has her clothes on.

Has she done this before? ask my daughter. Has she hit you before?

She hits me all the time, Sophie say, eating ice cream.

Your family, say John.

Believe me, say my daughter.

A DAUGHTER I have, a beautiful daughter. I took care of her when she could not hold her head up. I took care of her before she could argue with me, when she was a little girl with two pigtails, one of them always crooked. I took care of her when we have to escape from China, I took care of her when suddenly we live in a country with cars everywhere, if you are not careful your little girl get run over. When my husband die, I promise him I will keep the family together, even though it was just two of us, hardly a family at all.

But now my daughter take me around to look at apartments. After all, I can cook, I can clean, there's no reason I cannot live by myself, all I need is a telephone. Of course, she is sorry. Sometimes she cry, I am the one to say everything will be okay. She say she have no choice, she doesn't want to end up divorced. I say divorce is terrible, I don't know who invented this terrible idea. Instead of live with a telephone, though, surprise, I come to live with Bess. Imagine that. Bess make an offer and, sure enough, where she come from, people mean for you to move in when they say things like that. A crazy idea, go to live with someone else's family, but she like to have some female company, not like my daughter, who does not believe in company. These days when my daughter visit, she does not bring Sophie. Bess say we should give Nattie time, we will see Sophie again soon. But seems like my daughter have more presentation than ever before, every time she come she have to leave.

I have a family to support, she say, and her voice is heavy, as if soaking wet. I have a young daughter and a depressed husband and no one to turn to.

When she say no one to turn to, she mean me.

These days my beautiful daughter is so tired she can just sit there in a chair and fall asleep. John lost his job again, already, but still they rather hire a baby-sitter than ask me to help, even they can't afford it. Of course, the new baby-sitter is much younger, can run around. I don't know if Sophie these days is wild or not wild. She call me Meanie, but she like to kiss me too, sometimes. I remember that every time I see a child on TV. Sophie like to grab my hair, a fistful in each hand, and then kiss me smack on the nose. I never see any other child kiss that way.

The satellite TV has so many channels, more channels than I can count, including a Chinese channel from the Mainland and a Chinese channel from

Taiwan, but most of the time I watch bloopers with Bess. Also, I watch the bird feeder—so many, many kinds of birds come. The Shea sons hang around all the time, asking when will I go home, but Bess tell them, Get lost.

She's a permanent resident, say Bess. She isn't going anywhere.

Then she wink at me, and switch the channel with the remote control.

Of course, I shouldn't say Irish this, Irish that, especially now I am become honorary Irish myself, according to Bess. Me! Who's Irish? I say, and she laugh. All the same, if I could mention one thing about some of the Irish, not all of them of course, I like to mention this: Their talk just stick. I don't know how Bess Shea learn to use her words, but sometimes I hear what she say a long time later. *Permanent resident. Not going anywhere.* Over and over I hear it, the voice of Bess.

ASSIMILATION in its widest sense has been a part of our national literature from the start. If you like Gish Jen's "Who's Irish?" you might also like other stories that take up the subject matter of the life of first-generation Americans, such as Sylvia Watanabe's "Talking to the Dead," (chapter 12), Junot Diaz's "How to Date a Browngirl, Blackgirl, Whitegirl, or Halfie" (chapter 8), Amy Tan's "Two Kinds" (chapter 2), Jhumpa Lahiri's "Interpreter of Maladies" (chapter 9), and Dagoberto Gilb's "Romero's Shirt" (chapter 12).

GOING FURTHER   Timothy Mo's *Sour Sweet* and Fae Myenne Ng's *Bone* also explore Asian characters with one foot in one cultural world and the other foot in another.

Writing from Reading

Summarize

1 Summarize the narrator's views of her Irish in-laws at the beginning of the story, then summarize her views at the end. Discuss how these views have changed, and how they've stayed the same.

Analyze Craft

2 Discuss how Jen uses the grandmother's dialect to create her character. What details about the grandmother does this dialect suggest that are never mentioned in the story? Explain how the story would change if it were written in Jen's standard English voice, with only the dialogue in dialect.

Analyze Voice

3 Consider the use of humor in "Who's Irish?" Find and list specific examples of misunderstandings and explore why these are (or are not) used for humorous purposes.

4 Discuss the narrator's view of the words *supportive* and *creative*. What does her view reveal about cultural differences?

Synthesize Summary and Analysis

5 Describe how Jen uses the topic of Sophie's skin color to reveal character.

6 Imagine "Who's Irish?" told by a neutral party. How would your impressions of the various characters change if viewed without the grandmother's direct opinions?

Interpret the Story

7 A central theme of "Who's Irish?" is the speaker's adjustment—as restaurant owner, wife, mother, and grandmother—to the values and systems of behavior in America. Based on her various reactions and interactions throughout the story, do you think she has adjusted?

CONTINUED FROM PAGE 103

THE CRAFT OF CHARACTERIZATION

Characters—the people who inhabit literary works—should capture and hold our attention as they suffer, rejoice, rebel, and sometimes perish within the world of the story. It's the sleeping passenger who makes us care whether her train runs off the tracks and plunges into a ravine; it's the child in the upstairs bedroom who makes us hope the firefighters reach his burning house in time. Theirs are the faces we see, the voices we hear, the decisions we sympathize with or marvel at, and the fates we come to share and care about while we read.

> "I don't sit down in the morning and say, 'Well how am I going to enter this character?' For me it's something which comes naturally, so all I have to do is be quiet. I sit and I listen and the voices come." Conversation with Gish Jen

Characterization, or the way a writer crafts and defines personality, gives us an insight into thoughts and actions that real life rarely permits. We may seek out a story for its plot, admire its setting, and delight in the beauty of its language—but most of us keep turning the page to find out what happens to the characters an author has conjured into life. A character's name, appearance, behavior, words, manner of speech, and inner thoughts all reveal who he or she is. As Gish Jen demonstrates in "Who's Irish?" this process can begin with a tale's opening line. We continue to read to remain in a character's company and understand his or her behavior better, page by page.

> "Fiction really starts with this: I have to understand the people."
> Conversation with William Kittredge

One of the many benefits of fiction is that it allows us to get *inside the minds* of invented characters—something we cannot do, in most cases, even with our closest friends, whose actions may seem mysterious. In "The Jilting of Granny Weatherall," in this chapter, Katherine Anne Porter allows readers to share Granny's thoughts as she lies on her deathbed, listening to her daughter Cornelia and the doctor discuss her condition:

> *Well, and what if she was? She still had ears. It was like Cornelia to whisper around doors. She always kept things secret in such a public way. She was always being tactful and kind. Cornelia was dutiful; that was the trouble with her. Dutiful and good: "So good and dutiful," said Granny, "that I'd like to spank her."*

Together, the few sentences of that paragraph, combined with Granny's one line of dialogue ("So good and dutiful . . . that I'd like to spank her") bring the character to life. She's cantankerous and quarrelsome, impatient with Cornelia, and surprising us as readers with that desire to spank her daughter for being, of all things, "good and dutiful."

In fiction, because we have access to unspoken thoughts, we can understand **motivation,** or what causes people to behave as they do. In Alice Munro's "An Ounce of Cure" (chapter 1), a heartbroken, melancholy teenage girl tells readers one version of what motivated her to act as she did the night she babysat for the Berryman family:

I got up and found the Berrymans' "Danse Macabre" and put it on the record player and turned out the living-room lights. The curtains were only partly drawn. A street light shone obliquely on the windowpane, making a rectangle of thin dusty gold, in which the shadows of bare branches moved, caught in the huge sweet winds of spring. It was a mild black night when the last snow was melting. A year ago all this—the music, the wind and the darkness, the shadows of the branches—would have given me tremendous happiness; when they did not do so now, but only called up tediously familiar, somehow humiliatingly personal thoughts, I gave up my soul for dead and walked into the kitchen and decided to get drunk.

"[Characters] aren't invented for the purposes of function and a plot. . . . They appear as I write." Conversation with Tim O'Brien

In the next paragraph, she changes her story somewhat, leaving readers to assemble their own explanation of her motives:

No, it was not like that. I walked into the kitchen to look for a coke or something in the refrigerator, and there on the front of the counter were three tall beautiful bottles, all about half full of gold. But even after I had looked at them and lifted them to feel their weight I had not decided to get drunk; I had decided to have a drink.

Motivation, she seems to say in these two paragraphs, is a complex matter but something people want and need to understand. It becomes more complex, she might have added, when one is trying to remember one's own motivation many years later—as does the speaker here.

What You See Is What You Get

Because we usually judge people first on their appearance, the writers of prose fiction give great thought to sketching in and filling out a character's looks—the curve of a nose, the crease between brows, the shape of a hulking or a slender frame. However, in literature, physical appearance has meaning beyond a simple list of features. For example, one would make a character seven feet tall and 350 pounds only if the size and heft of the person have some significance signaling the impact he has on those around him, how he views himself, and what frustrations or powers he carries with him as a result. The following portrait of Captain Ahab from *Moby-Dick* uses physical traits to establish character and portend aspects of the plot.

His whole high, broad form, seemed made of solid bronze, and shaped in an unalterable mould. . . . Threading its way out from among his grey hairs, and continuing right down one side of his tawny scorched face and neck, till it disappeared in his clothing, you saw a slender rod-like mark, lividly whitish. It resembled that perpendicular seam sometimes made in the straight, lofty trunk of a great tree, when the upper lightning tearingly darts down it, and without wrenching a single twig, peels and grooves out the bark from top to bottom, ere running off into the soil, leaving the tree still greenly alive, but branded. Whether that mark was born with him, or whether it was the scar left by some desperate wound, no one could certainly say. . . .

Everything about Ahab is striking and distinctive: his statue-like form, his gray hair, his tanned face and neck, and especially the scar that seems to run the length of his body, a scar that Melville compares to a lightning strike. But this passage goes beyond describing his bodily attributes. It also suggests, in the concluding lines about the mark, that his fate may be a product either of his inner nature or of some encounter at sea, which raises the question about the essence of his character.

"Somebody said to me once, 'You know, you'll never write a novel. . . . You care too much about people. You got to use people; you got to put a person in a book and use them for what you need and then get rid of them. But you won't do that, so you're never going to write a novel.'" Conversation with Barry Lopez

What's in a Name?

Authors may reveal aspects of character by their choice of names, though the meaning of those names may often turn ironic. A character named Swift may be slow. A character named Rough may be gentle. A writer may choose a name to suggest a certain nature, as does Nathaniel Hawthorne in the case of Goodman Brown (chapter 10), who enters into a profound struggle between good and evil, thereby earning the "good" part of his name. Katherine Anne Porter's Granny Weatherall is a person who has thus far "weathered all"—meaning she has overcome multiple hardships in her life. Since "clothes make the man," characters can also be known by what they wear. Does a woman wear designer ball gowns or denim overalls? Does she shop at K-Mart or Saks Fifth Avenue or at a showroom for haute couture in Paris? These details allow readers to learn about a character's social class, lifestyle, and in some cases, aspirations.

The Clothes Make the Man

In "Paul's Case," Willa Cather focuses closely on the clothing of her protagonist. She does so because clothing is important to Paul, who envisions himself in a life different and grander than the one he leads. The following description comes near the beginning of the story:

> His clothes were a trifle outgrown, and the tan velvet on the collar of his open overcoat was frayed and worn; but for all that there was something of the dandy about him, and he wore an opal pin in his neatly knotted black four-in-hand, and a red carnation in his buttonhole. The latter adornment the faculty somehow felt was not properly significant of the contrite spirit befitting a boy under the ban of suspension.

Paul, with his outgrown and frayed clothing, is not a wealthy boy. Still, the velvet of the collar suggests an eye for luxury, and he has a certain attitude despite his limitations. He has added the opal pin, the neatly knotted tie, and the red carnation. Notice how Cather gives extra meaning to the carnation by letting us see it through the offended eyes of the teachers.

We Are What We (Repeatedly) Do

What characters do can include a wide array of possibilities that represent who they are: what they eat (brown rice and tofu versus fast-food burgers), what attracts their attention (the bud or the thorns on a rosebush), and how they respond to others—for example, with puzzlement and exasperation, as the narrator does in "Who's Irish?"

They also interact with others, being arrogant or meek or devious, spurring responses that help us as readers know them. For example, we learn about Paul from the way his teachers respond.

Can You Hear Me Now?

Another significant means of understanding characters comes to us through dialogue, or conversation between two or more participants in a scene. We've talked a bit about dialogue in chapter 2, and we will discuss it further in chapter 8 (Language, Tone, and Style). As a way to define a character's behavior, dialogue reveals personality in addition to motivation. When the principal confronts Paul for insulting a teacher, Paul responds by saying, "I don't know. . . . I didn't mean to be polite or impolite, either. I guess it's a sort of way I have of saying things regardless." This is one of the few lines of

"Dialogue in stories is when characters seem the most like real people." Conversation with Richard Ford

dialogue in "Paul's Case," one of the only times we get to hear Paul *in his own words*, and they reinforce the impression that he is a difficult person to understand. His words at least suggest the possibility that he is neither intentionally impertinent nor rude. He is simply being himself and doesn't expect to change or apologize for it.

Dialogue, then, can add dimension to a character. In the bittersweet, teasing voice of Mangan's sister in James Joyce's "Araby" (chapter 4), you can hear the lilt of turn-of-the-century Dublin's middle-class English. The distinctive voice Bernard Malamud achieves with Pinye Salzman in "The Magic Barrel" (chapter 6) emerges from the music of the character's language. At its best—as with dialogue in a stage play—speech both reveals character and advances a story's action. In this exchange in the story "No One's a Mystery" by Elizabeth Tallent (chapter 10), the uninterrupted conversation tells us a lot about what's at stake and what's at risk. Here, Jack, a married man, has just given his teenage girlfriend a diary.

> "Tonight you'll write, 'I love Jack. This is my birthday present from him. I can't imagine anybody loving anybody more than I love Jack.'"
> "I can't."
> "In a year you'll write, 'I wonder what I ever really saw in Jack. I wonder why I spent so many days just riding around in his pickup. It's true he taught me something about sex. It's true there wasn't ever much else to do in Cheyenne.'"
> "I won't write that."
> "In two years you'll write, 'I wonder what that old guy's name was, the one with the curly hair and the filthy dirty pickup truck and time on his hands.'"
> "I won't write that."

The relationship has a certain playfulness. The characters are at ease with each other, comfortable in their shared space. We're getting to know him: he's being clever, flirtatious, playful, as he puts himself in her shoes, imagining what she'll write in the diary. At the same time, he's a realist—projecting into the future, considering how she'll see him as the years pass, revealing somewhat how he may see himself (too old for her, directionless, a diversion). And there's a whiff of self-pity, too, in his prediction that he'll be forgotten, that his girlfriend will remember his "filthy dirty pickup truck" but not his own actual name. So far, she hasn't declared what she *will* write—only what she won't. The exchange moves the plot along because it piques the reader's curiosity—well, what *would* she have to say?

ROUND AND FLAT CHARACTERS

Reading fiction is a bit like eavesdropping or spying; it allows an intimate sense of how people think and live. What gives us that sense of life lived off (as well as on) the page? What makes a character real?

We usually talk about characters in literature in terms of their psychological makeup, the way we speak of family members and friends. *He is a talker. She's a brain. He worries a lot about money. She smokes incessantly and doesn't seem capable of standing up to her mother.* In a story, we come to know characters by way of the sum of their physical and mental attributes or **characteristics.** *He has dark hair, gestures while he speaks, and chews on his lower lip. She wears a silver comb in her hair, taps her right foot while she smokes, and her voice rises into the high upper register when she gets upset.*

If this sum of characteristics is complex and multifaceted, the characters seem real, or, in the terminology of twentieth-century British writer E. M. Forster (in his book *Aspects of the Novel),* they grow **round.** By contrast, in Forster's view, a **flat** character possesses a very narrow range of speech and action; these figures are predictable and do not develop over the course of the plot. In other words, they are **static,** meaning that they are unchanging. Roundness and flatness can be a matter of degree, with characters in a story falling along a spectrum.

This distinction between round and flat characters is a crucial one. Forster suggests, in effect, that no one is either entirely good or entirely bad, completely brave or cowardly, wholly smart or stupid. Instead, we're all a compound or mixture of opposite qualities, and the combination or proportion of these qualities can change. A story's

> "I like characters who have agency, who make the choice to change—who act, rather than having life or having the world act on them." Conversation with Chimamanda Ngozi Adichie

protagonist, or central actor, is almost always round. Such characters are **dynamic,** meaning that their personality and behavior alter over the course of the action in response to challenges and changing circumstances. A protagonist who initially behaves as a coward, for instance, may well become valiant at a crucial moment.

A HISTORY OF CHARACTER

The word *character* comes from *kharakter,* the Greek word for a stamping tool. Thus, the ancient Greeks believed that an individual's character—those defining traits that inform behavior and action—was static. Character made up one's fate or destiny. Whether a person was generous, loving, calm, excitable, level-headed, jittery, easily embarrassed, fearful, or brave, human personalities were seen as stable.

More recent notions of character have grown less absolute. In the nineteenth century, the age of psychology revolutionized and complicated our understanding of the human mind and, consequently, of character. Most people no longer regard personality and behavior as fixed. Instead, a person's behavior could be mutable, contradictory, unpredictable.

Far from a fixed stamp or *kharakter,* characterization and the study of character are, at least in part, ways of exploring an individual's capacity for change within the pages of a story *and* in our own lives.

In most fiction, the developing (or disintegrating) relationship between the protagonist and the antagonist (see chapter 4) has a significant effect on both people. A particular kind of protagonist who often appears in contemporary fiction is referred to as an **antihero**—a main character who acts outside the usual lines of heroic behavior (brave, honest, true). In "Paul's Case" (this chapter) the teachers and principal

> "I think that most of the people that turn up in my stories are somewhat lost. . . . If you have a character who finds herself less than adequate in any situation, that makes that character appealing. You would think that we would see this person as sort of pathetic, but often it doesn't work that way at all."
> Conversation with Amy Hempel

meet with Paul to voice their complaints about his insolence and misbehavior in their classes. If they were only punitive, we might be able to dismiss them, give them less thought. But Cather allows readers access to the teachers' minds and hearts, and in this way shows that they can't help feeling that Paul is sad and damaged, and that they, as adults, bear some blame:

> *His teachers left the building dissatisfied and unhappy; humiliated to have felt so vindictive toward a mere boy, to have uttered this feeling in cutting terms, and to have set each other on, as it were, in the gruesome game of intemperate reproach. Some of them remembered having seen a miserable street cat set at bay by a ring of tormentors.*

In contrast to round characters, flat or **stock characters** represent a concept or type of behavior, such as *mean teacher* or *mischievous student,* and offer readers the comforts of repetition and reliability. Often, such characters are comic and provide us with comic relief—overeating, taking pratfalls, losing their glasses, and bumping into doors. The difference here, as we suggested, is the distinction between characters who are dynamic and those who are static. And it's not always the case that round is desirable and flat is less so; most fictions require both kinds of portrayals to fully establish a plot. Flat characters often play a limited role in a story's plot. As such, they may serve as **foils,** or contrasts, to a central player. A devious friend, for example, might bring out a protagonist's trusting nature, or a happy-go-lucky uncle might make his niece's sadness all the more noticeable.

> "If I have a character walking down the street and all the buildings fall down, it may be reflecting something about a feeling, as opposed to the actual reality of all the buildings falling down."
> Conversation with Aimee Bender

Character in Context

The four stories in this chapter use details to create characters who come to life, emerging from the page—and who do so by being (to some extent) unpredictable. In turn, each story has a distinctive voice that flows from the worlds these figures inhabit. Gish Jen's "Who's Irish?" Katherine Anne Porter's "The Jilting of Granny Weatherall," Willa Cather's "Paul's Case," and Jack London's "A Wicked Woman" focus closely on a single protagonist, but the writers make various choices as to vocabulary, rhythm, and phrasing. Characterization, like personality, does not exist in a vacuum; in each story, consider how other characters influence the protagonist's development. What we learn from these insights into fictional characters helps satisfy our hunger for knowledge about real people in the real world—and, perhaps, may offer insight into our own behavior.

Katherine Anne Porter (1890–1980)

Callie Porter, a girl who grew up motherless and in extreme poverty, was destined to become Katherine Anne Porter, a writer, traveler, and woman of expensive tastes who changed her name after divorcing her first of four husbands. An independent woman with an active interest in life and politics, Porter worked on and off as a journalist, essayist, and book reviewer in a range of places, including Colorado, New York, Washington, D.C., and Mexico. Her work, while not voluminous, is known for its intensity of emotion and its refined and meticulously crafted prose. In her fiction, the personal becomes universal, as her stories are based on her own experiences. Although she lived to age ninety, her zest for life and her perfectionist approach to completing a story hindered her output. She published four collections of short stories—including *Flowering Judas* (1935) and *Pale Horse, Pale Rider* (1939)—and one novel, *Ship of Fools* (1962). Her work was much celebrated in her lifetime, and she won the Pulitzer Prize and the National Book Award in 1966 for her collected stories.

AS YOU READ As you read, notice the way you're drawn into the thoughts of the main character. Notice how her thoughts move back and forth through time, in and out of the present. How well do you get to know her as a result of being allowed to enter the privacy of her mind?

TIP

FOR INTERACTIVE READING . . . Note when Granny Weatherall is experiencing events from the past. Based on your notation, describe Granny as a young woman. Do the events you've noted explain how she's become the woman in the story's present?

The Jilting of Granny Weatherall (1930)

1 SHE flicked her wrist neatly out of Doctor Harry's pudgy careful fingers and pulled the sheet up to her chin. The brat ought to be in knee breeches. Doctoring around the country with spectacles on his nose! "Get along now, take your schoolbooks and go. There's nothing wrong with me."

2 Doctor Harry spread a warm paw like a cushion on her forehead where the forked green vein danced and made her eyelids twitch. "Now, now, be a good girl, and we'll have you up in no time."

3 "That's no way to speak to a woman nearly eighty years old just because she's down. I'd have you respect your elders, young man."

4 "Well, Missy, excuse me." Doctor Harry patted her cheek. "But I've got to warn you, haven't I? You're a marvel, but you must be careful or you're going to be good and sorry."

5 "Don't tell me what I'm going to be. I'm on my feet now, morally speaking. It's Cornelia. I had to go to bed to get rid of her."

6 Her bones felt loose, and floated around in her skin, and Doctor Harry floated like a balloon around the foot of the bed. He floated and pulled down his waistcoat and swung his glasses on a cord. "Well, stay where you are, it certainly can't hurt you."

7 "Get along and doctor your sick," said Granny Weatherall. "Leave a well woman alone. I'll call for you when I want you. . . . Where were you forty years ago when I pulled through milk-leg and double pneumonia? You weren't even born. Don't let Cornelia lead you on," she shouted, because Doctor Harry appeared to float up to the ceiling and out. "I pay my own bills, and I don't throw my money away on nonsense!"

8 She meant to wave good-by, but it was too much trouble. Her eyes closed of themselves, it was like a dark curtain drawn around the bed. The pillow rose and floated under her, pleasant as a hammock in a light wind. She listened to the leaves rustling outside the window. No, somebody was swishing newspapers: no, Cornelia and Doctor Harry were whispering together. She leaped broad awake, thinking they whispered in her ear.

9 "She was never like this, *never* like this!" "Well, what can we expect?" "Yes, eighty years old. . . ."

Well, and what if she was? She still had ears. It was like Cornelia to whisper around doors. She always kept things secret in such a public way. She was always being tactful and kind. Cornelia was dutiful; that was the trouble with her. Dutiful and good: "So good and dutiful," said Granny, "that I'd like to spank her." She saw herself spanking Cornelia and making a fine job of it.

"What'd you say, Mother?"

Granny felt her face tying up in hard knots.

"Can't a body think, I'd like to know?"

"I thought you might want something."

"I do. I want a lot of things. First off, go away and don't whisper."

She lay and drowsed, hoping in her sleep that the children would keep out and let her rest a minute. It had been a long day. Not that she was tired. It was always pleasant to snatch a minute now and then. There was always so much to be done, let me see: tomorrow.

Tomorrow was far away and there was nothing to trouble about. Things were finished somehow when the time came; thank God there was always a little margin over for peace: then a person could spread out the plan of life and tuck in the edges orderly. It was good to have everything clean and folded away, with the hair brushes and tonic bottles sitting straight on the white, embroidered linen: the day started without fuss and the pantry shelves laid out with rows of jelly glasses and brown jugs and white stone-china jars with blue whirligigs and words painted on them: coffee, tea, sugar, ginger, cinnamon, allspice: and the bronze clock with the lion on top nicely dusted off. The dust that lion could collect in twenty-four hours! The box in the attic with all those letters tied up, well, she'd have to go through that tomorrow. All those letters—George's letters and John's letters and her letters to them both—

lying around for the children to find afterwards made her uneasy. Yes, that would be tomorrow's business. No use to let them know how silly she had been once.

8   While she was rummaging around she found death in her mind and it felt clammy and unfamiliar. She had spent so much time preparing for death there was no need for bringing it up again. Let it take care of itself now. When she was sixty she had felt very old, finished, and went around making farewell trips to see her children and grandchildren, with a secret in her mind: This is the very last of your mother, children! Then she made her will and came down with a long fever. That was all just a notion like a lot of other things, but it was lucky too, for she had once for all got over the idea of dying for a long time. Now she couldn't be worried. She hoped she had better sense now. Her father had lived to be one hundred and two years old and had drunk a noggin of strong hot toddy on his last birthday. He told the reporters it was his daily habit, and he owed his long life to that. He had made quite a scandal and was very pleased about it. She believed she'd just plague Cornelia a little.

9   "Cornelia! Cornelia!" No footsteps, but a sudden hand on her cheek. "Bless you, where have you been?"

20   "Here, Mother."

21   "Well, Cornelia, I want a noggin of hot toddy."

22   "Are you cold, darling?"

23   "I'm chilly, Cornelia. Lying in bed stops the circulation. I must have told you that a thousand times."

24   Well, she could just hear Cornelia telling her husband that Mother was getting a little childish and they'd have to humor her. The thing that most annoyed her was that Cornelia thought she was deaf, dumb, and blind. Little hasty glances and tiny gestures tossed around her and over her head saying, "Don't cross her, let her have her way, she's eighty years old," and she sitting there as if she lived in a thin glass cage. Sometimes Granny almost made up her mind to pack up and move back to her own house where nobody could remind her every minute that she was old. Wait, wait, Cornelia, till your own children whisper behind your back!

25   In her day she had kept a better house and had got more work done. She wasn't too old yet for Lydia to be driving eighty miles for advice when one of the children jumped the track, and Jimmy still dropped in and talked things over: "Now, Mammy, you've a good business head, I want to know what you think of this? . . ." Old. Cornelia couldn't change the furniture around without asking. Little things, little things! They had been so sweet when they were little. Granny wished the old days were back again with the children young and

everything to be done over. It had been a hard pull, but not too much for her. When she thought of all the food she had cooked, and all the clothes she had cut and sewed, and all the gardens she had made—well, the children showed it. There they were, made out of her, and they couldn't get away from that. Sometimes she wanted to see John again and point to them and say, Well, I didn't do so badly, did I? But that would have to wait. That was for tomorrow. She used to think of him as a man, but now all the children were older than their father, and he would be a child beside her if she saw him now. It seemed strange and there was something wrong in the idea. Why, he couldn't possibly recognize her. She had fenced in a hundred acres once,

digging the post holes herself and clamping the wires with just a negro boy to help. That changed a woman. John would be looking for a young woman with the peaked Spanish comb in her hair and the painted fan. Digging post holes changed a woman. Riding country roads in the winter when women had their babies was another thing: sitting up nights with sick horses and sick negroes and sick children and hardly ever losing one. John, I hardly ever lost one of them! John would see that in a minute, that would be something he could understand, she wouldn't have to explain anything!

26   It made her feel like rolling up her sleeves and putting the whole place to rights again. No matter if Cornelia was determined to be everywhere at once, there were a great many things left undone on this place. She would start tomorrow and do them. It was good to be strong enough for everything, even if all you made melted and changed and slipped under your hands, so that by the time you finished you almost forgot what you were working for. What was it I set out to do? she asked herself intently, but she could not remember. A fog rose over the valley, she saw it marching across the creek swallowing the trees and moving up the hill

like an army of ghosts. Soon it would be at the near edge of the orchard, and then it was time to go in and light the lamps. Come in, children, don't stay out in the night air.

27 Lighting the lamps had been beautiful. The children huddled up to her and breathed like little calves waiting at the bars in the twilight. Their eyes followed the match and watched the flame rise and settle in a blue curve, then they moved away from her. The lamp was lit, they didn't have to be scared and hang on to mother any more. Never, never, never more. God, for all my life, I thank Thee. Without Thee, my God, I could never have done it. Hail, Mary, full of grace.

28 I want you to pick all the fruit this year and see that nothing is wasted. There's always someone who can use it. Don't let good things rot for want of using. You waste life when you waste good food. Don't let things get lost. It's bitter to lose things. Now, don't let me get to thinking, not when I'm tired and taking a little nap before supper. . . .

29 The pillow rose about her shoulders and pressed against her heart and the memory was being squeezed out of it: oh, push down the pillow, somebody: it would smother her if she tried to hold it. Such a fresh breeze blowing and such a green day with no threats in it. But he had not come, just the same. What does a woman do when she has put on the white veil and set out the white cake for a man and he doesn't come? She tried to remember. No, I swear he never harmed me but in that. He never harmed me but in that . . . and what if he did? There was the day, the day, but a whirl of dark smoke rose and covered it, crept up and over into the bright field where everything was planted so carefully in orderly rows. That was hell, she knew hell when she saw it. For sixty years she had prayed against remembering him and against losing her soul in the deep pit of hell, and now the two things were mingled in one and the thought of him was a smoky cloud from hell that moved and crept in her head when she had just got rid of Doctor Harry and was trying to rest a minute. Wounded vanity, Ellen, said a sharp voice in the top of her mind. Don't let your wounded vanity get the upper hand of you. Plenty of girls get jilted. You were jilted, weren't you? Then stand up to it. Her eyelids wavered and let in streamers of blue-gray light like tissue paper over her eyes. She must get up and pull the shades down or she'd never sleep. She was in bed again and the shades were not down. How could that happen? Better turn over, hide from the light, sleeping in the light gave you nightmares. "Mother, how

> Plenty of girls get jilted.

do you feel now?" and a stinging wetness on her forehead. But I don't like having my face washed in cold water!

Hapsy? George? Lydia? Jimmy? No, Cornelia, and her features were swollen and full of little puddles. "They're coming, darling, they'll all be here soon." Go wash your face, child, you look funny.

Instead of obeying, Cornelia knelt down and put her head on the pillow. She seemed to be talking but there was no sound. "Well, are you tongue-tied? Whose birthday is it? Are you going to give a party?"

Cornelia's mouth moved urgently in strange shapes. "Don't do that, you bother me, daughter."

"Oh, no, Mother. Oh, no . . ."

Nonsense. It was strange about children. They disputed your every word. "No what, Cornelia?"

"Here's Doctor Harry."

"I won't see that boy again. He just left five minutes ago."

"That was this morning, Mother. It's night now. Here's the nurse."

"This is Doctor Harry, Mrs. Weatherall. I never saw you look so young and happy!"

"Ah, I'll never be young again—but I'd be happy if they'd let me lie in peace and get rested."

She thought she spoke up loudly, but no one answered. A warm weight on her forehead, a warm bracelet on her wrist, and a breeze went on whispering, trying to tell her something. A shuffle of leaves in the everlasting hand of God, He blew on them and they danced and rattled. "Mother, don't mind, we're going to give you a little hypodermic." "Look here, daughter, how do ants get in this bed? I saw sugar ants yesterday." Did you send for Hapsy too?

It was Hapsy she really wanted. She had to go a long way back through a great many rooms to find Hapsy standing with a baby on her arm. She seemed to herself to be Hapsy also, and the baby on Hapsy's arm was Hapsy and himself and herself, all at once, and there was no surprise in the meeting. Then Hapsy melted from within and turned flimsy as gray gauze and the baby was a gauzy shadow, and Hapsy came up close and said, "I thought you'd never come," and looked at her very searchingly and said, "You haven't changed a bit!" They leaned forward to kiss, when Cornelia began whispering from a long way off, "Oh, is there anything you want to tell me? Is there anything I can do for you?"

Yes, she had changed her mind after sixty years and she would like to see George. I want you to find George. Find him and be sure to tell him I forgot him. I want him to know I had my husband just the same and my children and my house like any other woman. A good house too and a good husband that I loved and fine children out of him. Better than I had hoped for even. Tell him I was given back everything he took away and more. Oh, no, oh, God, no, there was something else besides the house and the man and the children. Oh, surely they were not all? What was it? Something not given back. . . . Her breath crowded down under her ribs and grew into a monstrous frightening shape with cutting edges; it bored up into her head, and the agony was unbelievable: Yes, John, get the Doctor now, no more talk, my time has come.

When this one was born it should be the last. The last. It should have been born first, for it was the one she had truly wanted. Everything came in good time. Nothing left out, left over. She was strong, in three days she would be as well as ever. Better. A woman needed milk in her to have her full health.

"Mother, do you hear me?"

"I've been telling you—"

"Mother, Father Connolly's here."

"I went to Holy Communion only last week. Tell him I'm not so sinful as all that."

"Father just wants to speak to you."

He could speak as much as he pleased. It was like him to drop in and inquire about her soul as if it were a teething baby, and then stay on for a cup of tea and a round of cards and gossip. He always had a funny story of some sort, usually about an Irishman who made his little mistakes and confessed them, and the point lay in some absurd thing he would blurt out in the confessional showing his struggles between native piety and original sin. Granny felt easy about her soul. Cornelia, where are your manners? Give Father Connolly a chair. She had her secret comfortable understanding with a few favorite saints who cleared a straight road to God for her. All as surely signed and sealed as the papers for the new Forty Acres. Forever . . . heirs and assigns forever. Since the day the wedding cake was not cut, but thrown out and wasted. The whole bottom dropped out of the world, and there she was blind and sweating with nothing under her feet and the walls falling away. His hand had caught her under the breast, she had not fallen, there was the freshly polished floor with the green rug on it, just as before. He had cursed like a sailor's parrot and said, "I'll kill him

for you." Don't lay a hand on him, for my sake leave something to God. "Now, Ellen, you must believe what I tell you. . . ."

So there was nothing, nothing to worry about any more, except sometimes in the night one of the children screamed in a nightmare, and they both hustled out shaking and hunting for the matches and calling, "There, wait a minute, here we are!" John, get the doctor now, Hapsy's time has come. But there was Hapsy standing by the bed in a white cap. "Cornelia, tell Hapsy to take off her cap. I can't see her plain."

Her eyes opened very wide and the room stood out like a picture she had seen somewhere. Dark colors with the shadows rising toward the ceiling in long angles. The tall black dresser gleamed with nothing on it but John's picture, enlarged from a little one, with John's eyes very black when they should have been blue. You never saw him, so how do you know how he looked? But the man insisted the copy was perfect, it was very rich and handsome. For a picture, yes, but it's not my husband. The table by the bed had a linen cover and a candle and a crucifix. The light was blue from Cornelia's silk lampshades. No sort of light at all, just frippery. You had to live forty years with kerosene lamps to appreciate honest electricity. She felt very strong and she saw Doctor Harry with a rosy nimbus around him.

"You look like a saint, Doctor Harry, and I vow that's as near as you'll ever come to it."

"She's saying something."

"I heard you Cornelia. What's all this carrying on?"

"Father Connolly's saying—"

Cornelia's voice staggered and bumped like a cart in a bad road. It rounded corners and turned back again and arrived nowhere. Granny stepped up in the cart very lightly and reached for the reins, but a man sat beside her and she knew him by his hands, driving the cart. She did not look in his face, for she knew without seeing, but looked instead down the road where the trees leaned over and bowed to each other and a thousand birds were singing a Mass. She felt like singing too, but she put her hand in the bosom of her dress and pulled out a rosary, and Father Connolly murmured Latin in a very solemn voice and tickled her feet. My God, will you stop that nonsense? I'm a married woman. What if he did run away and leave me to face the priest by myself? I found another a whole world better. I wouldn't have exchanged my husband for anybody except St. Michael himself, and you may tell him that for me with a thank you in the bargain.

> So, my dear Lord, this is my death
>
> and I wasn't even thinking
>
> about it.

57   Light flashed on her closed eyelids, and a deep roaring shook her. Cornelia, is that lightning? I hear thunder. There's going to be a storm. Close all the windows. Call the children in. . . . "Mother, here we are, all of us." "Is that you, Hapsy?" "Oh, no, I'm Lydia. We drove as fast as we could." Their faces drifted above her, drifted away. The rosary fell out of her hands and Lydia put it back. Jimmy tried to help, their hands fumbled together, and Granny closed two fingers around Jimmy's thumb. Beads wouldn't do, it must be something alive. She was so amazed her thoughts ran round and round. So, my dear Lord, this is my death and I wasn't even thinking about it. My children have come to see me die. But I can't, it's not time. Oh, I always hated surprises. I wanted to give Cornelia the amethyst set—Cornelia, you're to have the amethyst set, but Hapsy's to wear it when she wants, and, Doctor Harry, do shut up. Nobody sent for you. Oh, my dear Lord, do wait a minute. I meant to do some-

thing about the Forty Acres, Jimmy doesn't need it and Lydia will later on, with that worthless husband of hers. I meant to finish the altar cloth and send six bottles of wine to Sister Borgia for her dyspepsia. I want to send six bottles of wine to Sister Borgia, Father Connolly, now don't let me forget.

Cornelia's voice made short turns and tilted over and crashed. "Oh, Mother, oh, Mother, oh, Mother . . ."

"I'm not going, Cornelia. I'm taken by surprise. I can't go."

You'll see Hapsy again. What about her? "I thought you'd never come." Granny made a long journey outward, looking for Hapsy. What if I don't find her? What then? Her heart sank down and down, there was no bottom to death, she couldn't come to the end of it. The blue light from Cornelia's lampshade drew into a tiny point in the center of her brain, it flickered and winked like an eye, quietly it fluttered and dwindled. Granny lay curled down within herself, amazed and watchful, staring at the point of light that was herself; her body was now only a deeper mass of shadow in an endless darkness and this darkness would curl around the light and swallow it up. God, give a sign!

For the second time there was no sign. Again no bridegroom and the priest in the house. She could not remember any other sorrow because this grief wiped them all away. Oh, no, there's nothing more cruel than this—I'll never forgive it. She stretched herself with a deep breath and blew out the light.

DEATH—the darkest theme. If you like Katherine Anne Porter's "The Jilting of Granny Weatherall," you can read another great writer, perhaps the greatest novelist of them all, on the same subject in Leo Tolstoy's "Death of Ivan Ilych" (in the For Further Reading section of this anthology).

GOING FURTHER   Porter concentrates a single life into the briefest of times in the Granny Weatherall story, but she has produced a number of variations on the question of characters living, and dying, over the long years of a life. In her quasi-allegorical novel *Ship of Fools,* she attempts to tell the story of an entire generation of Americans adrift.

Writing from Reading

Summarize

1 How many children did Granny have, and what are their names? Which of them are present in the room with her as she lies on her deathbed?

2 Although the author does not reveal a specific era or place for this story, she provides many details related to setting. Go through the text and find all the details you can that give you a feel for where and when these events occur. Write a paragraph summarizing your findings.

Analyze Craft

3 In revealing Granny's mental/emotional state, Porter sometimes layers past with present or mixes emotional pain with physical pain. Find two examples of this layering and mixing and discuss the effect.

4 How do the minor characters in this story—such as Doctor Harry and Cornelia—add dimension to Granny Weatherall's character? Are these minor characters flat? Support your reasoning with examples from the story.

Analyze Voice

5 How do Porter's use of dialogue and her description of the characters' gestures (particularly Granny's) make them seem real?

Synthesize Summary and Analysis

6 "The Jilting of Granny Weatherall" is written from Granny's limited point of view. How does this limited scope affect your understanding of the major and minor characters?

7 Because of Granny's increasing disorientation, you are able to get a snapshot of all the major moments in her life. Put these events in order and consider them as a story of their own. Is Granny a round or a flat character in this underlying plot? Discuss how her character in the past compares to her character in the present.

Interpret the Story

8 At the end of the story, Granny appears finally to become aware of her impending death. Do you believe she's been ignorant of her situation throughout the whole story? Search the story for evidence of Granny's recognition or ignorance, and discuss how her state of awareness affects your understanding of the story's conclusion.

Willa Cather (1873–1947)

Although any citizen of the United States who publishes fiction could be called an "American writer," some writers, because of a particular mix of subject matter and its presentation, stand out as quintessentially American. Early-twentieth-century writer Willa Cather was one of those—or, as the title of one of her novels puts it, *One of Ours.* Her biography includes some interesting geography, including several locations that affect her work. Born in Virginia, she moved with her family to the Nebraska plains when still a child and lived in the region long enough to attend high school and the University of Nebraska; that state claims her as a "favorite daughter" today. Although she moved to Pittsburgh after graduation and worked as a journalist there and in New York City, she focused in much of her best-known work on life in the small towns and farms of the Great Plains. An independent woman at a time when many were not, Cather never married, preferring instead female friendship. She struggled, however, with the increasingly material society that surrounded her, and some of her later work emphasizes non-materialistic values. Her best-known novels—*My Ántonia, O Pioneers,* and *Death Comes for the Archbishop*—put forward serious themes about identity and life in a masterly prose style, crossing state and regional borders in their subjects. In the story that follows, "Paul's Case," she dramatizes the opposition between disparate locales, dealing with a character who moves from city to city in an attempt to "belong" or feel at home.

AS YOU READ As you read, mark the sections that portray Paul in a negative light—lying, devious, impertinent, ungrateful, or angry—and use a different notation to mark the sections where Paul is portrayed in a positive light—happy, satisfied, gracious, or charming. What do the occasions for these various portrayals say about Paul's temperament?

Paul's Case (1905)

1   IT was Paul's afternoon to appear before the faculty of the Pittsburgh High School to account for his various misdemeanours. He had been suspended a week ago, and his father had called at the Principal's office and confessed his perplexity about his son. Paul entered the faculty room suave and smiling. His clothes were a trifle outgrown, and the tan velvet on the collar of his open overcoat was frayed and worn; but for all that there was something of the dandy about him, and he wore an opal pin in his neatly knotted black four-in-hand, and a red carnation in his buttonhole. This latter adornment the faculty somehow felt was not properly significant of the contrite spirit befitting a boy under the ban of suspension.

2   Paul was tall for his age and very thin, with high, cramped shoulders and a narrow chest. His eyes were remarkable for a certain hysterical brilliancy, and he continually used them in a conscious, theatrical sort of way, peculiarly offensive in a boy. The pupils were abnormally large, as though he were addicted to belladonna, but there was a glassy glitter about them which that drug does not produce.

3   When questioned by the Principal as to why he was there, Paul stated, politely enough, that he wanted to come back to school. This was a lie, but Paul was quite accustomed to lying; found it, indeed, indispensable for overcoming friction. His teachers were asked to state their respective charges against him, which they did with such a rancour and aggrievedness as evinced that this was not a usual case. Disorder and impertinence were among the offences named, yet each of his instructors felt that it was scarcely possible to put into words the real cause of the trouble, which lay in a sort of hysterically defiant manner of the boy's; in the contempt which they all knew he felt for them, and which he seemingly made not the least effort to conceal. Once, when he had been making a synopsis of a paragraph at the blackboard, his English teacher had stepped to his side and attempted to guide his hand. Paul had started back with a shudder and thrust his hands violently behind him. The astonished woman could scarcely have been more hurt and embarrassed had he struck at her. The insult was so involuntary and definitely personal as to be unforgettable. In one way and another, he had made all his teachers, men and women alike, conscious of the same feeling of physical aversion. In one class he habitually sat with his hand shading his eyes; in another he always looked out of the window during the recitation; in another he made a running commentary on the lecture, with humorous intent.

4   His teachers felt this afternoon that his whole attitude was symbolized by his shrug and his flippantly red carnation flower, and they fell upon him without mercy, his English teacher leading the pack. He stood through it smiling, his pale lips parted over his white teeth. (His lips were continually twitching, and he had a habit of raising his eyebrows that was contemptuous and irritating to the last degree.) Older boys than Paul had broken down and shed tears under that ordeal, but his set smile did not once desert him, and his only sign of discomfort was the nervous trembling of the fingers that toyed with the buttons of his overcoat, and an occasional jerking of the other hand which held his hat. Paul was always smiling, always glancing about him, seeming to feel that people might be watching him and trying to detect some-

thing. This conscious expression, since it was as far as possible from boyish mirthfulness, was usually attributed to insolence or "smartness."

As the inquisition proceeded, one of his instructors repeated an impertinent remark of the boy's, and the Principal asked him whether he thought that a courteous speech to make to a woman. Paul shrugged his shoulders slightly and his eyebrows twitched.

"I don't know," he replied. "I didn't mean to be polite or impolite, either. I guess it's a sort of way I have, of saying things regardless."

The Principal asked him whether he didn't think that a way it would be well to get rid of. Paul grinned and said he guessed so. When he was told that he could go, he bowed gracefully and went out. His bow was like a repetition of the scandalous red carnation.

His teachers were in despair, and his drawing master voiced the feeling of them all when he declared there was something about the boy which none of them understood. He added: "I don't really believe that smile of his comes altogether from insolence; there's something sort of haunted about it. The boy is not strong, for one thing. There is something wrong about the fellow."

The drawing master had come to realize that, in looking at Paul, one saw only his white teeth and the forced animation of his eyes. One warm afternoon the boy had gone to sleep at his drawing-board, and his master had noted with amazement what a white, blue-veined face it was; drawn and wrinkled like an old man's about the eyes, the lips twitching even in his sleep.

His teachers left the building dissatisfied and unhappy; humiliated to have felt so vindictive toward a mere boy, to have uttered this feeling in cutting terms, and to have set each other on, as it were, in the grewsome game of intemperate reproach. Some of them remembered having seen a miserable street cat set at bay by a ring of tormentors.

As for Paul, he ran down the hill whistling the Soldiers' Chorus from *Faust,* looking wildly behind him now and then to see whether some of his teachers were not there to witness his

light-heartedness. As it was now late in the afternoon and Paul was on duty that evening as usher at Carnegie Hall, he decided that he would not go home to supper.

When he reached the concert hall the doors were not yet open. It was chilly outside, and he decided to go up into the picture gallery—always deserted at this hour—where there were some of Raffelli's gay studies of Paris streets and an airy blue Venetian scene or two that always exhilarated him. He was delighted to find no one in the gallery but the old guard, who sat in the corner, a newspaper on his knee, a black patch over one eye and the other closed. Paul possessed himself of the place and walked confidently up and down, whistling under his breath. After a while he sat down before a blue Rico and lost himself. When he bethought him to look at his watch, it was after seven o'clock, and he rose with a start and ran downstairs, making a face at Augustus Cæsar, peering out from the cast-room, and an evil gesture at the Venus of Milo as he passed her on the stairway.

When Paul reached the ushers' dressing-room half-a-dozen boys were there already, and he began excitedly to tumble into his uniform. It was one of the few that at all approached fitting, and Paul thought it very becoming—though he knew the tight, straight coat accentuated his narrow chest, about which he was exceedingly sensitive. He was always excited while he dressed, twanging all over to the tuning of the strings and the preliminary flourishes of the horns in the music-room; but tonight he seemed quite beside himself, and he teased and plagued the boys until, telling him that he was crazy, they put him down on the floor and sat on him.

Somewhat calmed by his suppression, Paul dashed out to the front of the house to seat the early comers. He was a model usher. Gracious and smiling he ran up and down the aisles. Nothing was too much trouble for him; he carried messages and brought programs as though it were his greatest pleasure in life, and all the people in his section thought him a charming boy, feeling that he remembered and admired them. As the house filled, he grew more and more vivacious and animated, and the colour came to his cheeks and lips. It was very much as though this were a great reception and Paul were the host. Just as the musicians came out to take their places, his English teacher arrived with checks for the seats which a prominent manufacturer had taken for the season. She betrayed some embarrassment when she handed Paul the tickets, and a *hauteur* which subsequently made her feel very foolish. Paul was startled for a moment, and had the feeling of wanting to put her out; what business had she here among all these fine people and gay colours? He looked her over and decided that she was not appropriately dressed and must be a fool to sit downstairs in such togs. The tickets had probably been sent her out of kindness, he reflected, as he put down a seat for her, and she had about as much right to sit there as he had.

15   When the symphony began Paul sank into one of the rear seats with a long sigh of relief, and lost himself as he had done before the Rico. It was not that symphonies, as such, meant anything in particular to Paul, but the first sigh of the instruments seemed to free some hilarious spirit within him; something that struggled there like the Genius in the bottle found by the Arab fisherman. He felt a sudden zest of life; the lights danced before his eyes and the concert hall blazed into unimaginable splendour. When the soprano soloist came on, Paul forgot even the nastiness of his teacher's being there, and gave himself up to the peculiar intoxication such personages always had for him. The soloist chanced to be a German woman, by no means in her first youth, and the mother of many children; but she wore a satin gown and a tiara, and she had that indefinable air of achievement, that world-shine upon her, which always blinded Paul to any possible defects.

16   After a concert was over, Paul was often irritable and wretched until he got to sleep,—and tonight he was even more than usually restless. He had the feeling of not being able to let down; of its being impossible to give up this delicious excitement which was the only thing that could be called living at all. During the last number he withdrew and, after hastily changing his clothes in the dressing-room, slipped out to the side door where the singer's carriage stood. Here he began pacing rapidly up and down the walk, waiting to see her come out.

17   Over yonder the Schenley, in its vacant stretch, loomed big and square through the fine rain, the windows of its twelve stories glowing like those of a lighted card-board house under a Christmas tree. All the actors and singers of any importance stayed there when they were in the city, and a number of the big manufacturers of the place lived there in the winter. Paul had often hung about the hotel, watching the people go in and out, longing to enter and leave school-masters and dull care behind him for ever.

    At last the singer came out, accompanied by the conductor, who helped her into her carriage and closed the door with a cordial *auf wiedersehen*,—which set Paul to wondering whether she were not an old sweetheart of his. Paul followed the carriage over to the hotel, walking so rapidly as not to be far from the entrance when the singer alighted and disappeared behind the swinging glass doors which were opened by a negro in a tall hat and a long coat. In the moment that the door was ajar, it seemed to Paul that he, too, entered. He seemed to feel himself go after her up the steps, into the warm, lighted building, into an exotic, a tropical world of shiny, glistening surfaces and basking ease. He reflected upon the mysterious dishes that were brought into the dining-room, the green bottles in buckets of ice, as he had seen them in the supper party pictures of the Sunday supplement. A quick gust of wind brought the rain down with sudden vehemence, and Paul was startled to find that he was still outside in the slush of the gravel driveway; that his boots were letting in the water and his scanty overcoat was clinging wet about him; that the lights in front of the concert hall were out, and that the rain was driving in sheets between him and the orange glow of the windows above him. There it was, what he wanted—tangibly before him, like the fairy world of a Christmas pantomime; as the rain beat in his face, Paul wondered whether he were destined always to shiver in the black night outside, looking up at it.

    He turned and walked reluctantly toward the car tracks. The end had to come sometime; his father in his nightclothes at the top of the stairs, explanations that did not explain, hastily improvised fictions that were forever tripping him up, his upstairs room and its horrible yellow wallpaper, the creaking bureau with the greasy plush collar-box, and over his painted wooden bed the pictures of George Washington and John Calvin, and the framed motto, "Feed my Lambs," which had been worked in red worsted by his mother, whom Paul could not remember.

    Half an hour later, Paul alighted from the Negley Avenue car and went slowly down one of the side streets off the main thoroughfare. It was a highly respectable street, where all the houses were exactly alike, and where business men of moderate means begot and reared large families of children, all of whom went to Sabbath-school and learned the shorter catechism, and were interested in arithmetic; all of whom were as exactly alike as their homes, and of a piece with the monotony in which they lived. Paul never went up Cordelia Street without a shudder of loathing. His home was next the house of the Cumberland minister. He approached it tonight with the nerveless sense of defeat, the hopeless feeling of sinking back forever into ugliness and commonness that he had always had when he came home. The moment he turned into Cordelia Street he felt the waters close above his head. After each of these orgies of living, he experienced all the physical depression which follows a debauch; the loathing of respectable beds, of common food, of a house permeated by kitchen odours; a shuddering repulsion for the flavourless, colourless mass of every-day existence; a morbid desire for cool things and soft lights and fresh flowers.

21   The nearer he approached the house, the more absolutely unequal Paul felt to the sight of it all; his ugly sleeping chamber; the cold bath-room with the grimy zinc tub, the cracked mirror, the dripping spiggots; his father, at the top of the stairs, his hairy legs sticking out from his nightshirt, his feet thrust into carpet slippers. He was so much later than usual that there would certainly be inquiries and reproaches. Paul stopped short before the door. He felt that he could not be accosted by his father tonight; that he could not toss again on that miserable bed. He would not go in. He would tell his father that he had no car fare, and it was raining so hard he had gone home with one of the boys and stayed all night.

22   Meanwhile, he was wet and cold. He went around to the back of the house and tried one of the basement windows, found it open, raised it cautiously, and scrambled down the cellar wall to the floor. There he stood, holding his breath, terrified by the noise he had made; but the floor above him was silent, and there was no creak on the stairs. He found a soap-box, and carried it over to the soft ring of light that streamed from the furnace door, and sat down. He was horribly afraid of rats, so he did not try to sleep, but sat looking distrustfully at the dark, still terrified lest he might have awakened his father. In such reactions, after one of the experiences which made days and nights out of the dreary blanks of the calendar, when his senses were deadened, Paul's head was always singularly clear. Suppose his father had heard him getting in at the window and had come down and shot him for a burglar? Then, again, suppose his father had come down, pistol in hand, and he had cried out in time to save himself, and his father had been horrified to think how nearly he had killed him?

Then, again, suppose a day should come when his father would remember that night, and wish there had been no warning cry to stay his hand? With this last supposition Paul entertained himself until daybreak.

23   The following Sunday was fine; the sodden November chill was broken by the last flash of autumnal summer. In the morning Paul had to go to church and Sabbath-school, as always. On seasonable Sunday afternoons the burghers of Cordelia Street usually sat out on their front "stoops," and talked to their neighbours on the next stoop, or called to those across the street in neighbourly fashion. The men sat placidly on gay cushions placed upon the steps that led down to the sidewalk, while the women, in their Sunday "waists," sat in rockers on the cramped porches, pretending to be greatly at their ease. The children played in the streets; there were so many of them that the place resembled the recreation grounds of a kindergarten. The men on the steps—all in their shirt sleeves, their vests unbuttoned—sat with their legs well apart, their stomachs comfortably protruding, and talked of the prices of things, or told anecdotes of the sagacity of their various chiefs and overlords. They occasionally looked over the multitude of squabbling children, listened affectionately to their high-pitched, nasal voices, smiling to see their own proclivities reproduced in their offspring, and interspersed their legends of the iron kings with remarks about their sons' progress at school, their grades in arithmetic, and the amounts they had saved in their toy banks.

24   On this last Sunday of November, Paul sat all the afternoon on the lowest step of his "stoop," staring into the street, while his sisters, in their rockers, were talking to the minister's daughters next door about how many shirt-waists they had made in the last week, and how many waffles some one had eaten at the last church supper. When the weather was warm, and his father was in a particularly jovial frame of mind, the girls made lemonade, which was always brought out in a red-glass pitcher, ornamented with forget-me-nots in blue enamel. This the girls thought very fine, and the neighbours always joked about the suspicious colour of the pitcher.

25   Today Paul's father, on the top step, was talking to a young man who shifted a restless baby from knee to knee. He happened to be the young man who was daily held up to Paul as a model, and after whom it

was his father's dearest hope that he would pattern. This young man was of a ruddy complexion, with a compressed, red mouth, and faded, near-sighted eyes, over which he wore thick spectacles, with gold bows that curved about his ears. He was clerk to one of the magnates of a great steel corporation, and was looked upon in Cordelia Street as a young man with a future. There was a story that, some five years ago—he was now barely twenty-six—he had been a trifle "dissipated," but in order to curb his appetites and save the loss of time and strength that a sowing of wild oats might have entailed, he had taken his chief's advice, oft reiterated to his employés, and at twenty-one had married the first woman whom he could persuade to share his fortunes. She happened to be an angular school-mistress, much older than he, who also wore thick glasses, and who had now borne him four children, all near-sighted, like herself.

> This was Paul's fairy tale, and it had for him all the allurement of a secret love.

26 The young man was relating how his chief, now cruising in the Mediterranean, kept in touch with all the details of the business, arranging his office hours on his yacht just as though he were at home, and "knocking off work enough to keep two stenographers busy." His father told, in turn, the plan his corporation was considering, of putting in an electric railway plant in Cairo. Paul snapped his teeth; he had an awful apprehension that they might spoil it all before he got there. Yet he rather liked to hear these legends of the iron kings, that were told and retold on Sundays and holidays; these stories of palaces in Venice, yachts on the Mediterranean, and high play at Monte Carlo appealed to his fancy, and he was interested in the triumphs of cash boys who had become famous, though he had no mind for the cash-boy stage.

27 After supper was over, and he had helped to dry the dishes, Paul nervously asked his father whether he could go to George's to get some help in his geometry, and still more nervously asked for car-fare. This latter request he had to repeat, as his father, on principle, did not like to hear requests for money, whether much or little. He asked Paul whether he could not go to some boy who lived nearer, and told him that he ought not to leave his school work until Sunday; but he gave him the dime. He was not a poor man, but he had a worthy ambition to come up in the world. His only reason for allowing Paul to usher was that he thought a boy ought to be earning a little.

28 Paul bounded upstairs, scrubbed the greasy odour of the dish-water from his hands with the ill-smelling soap he hated, and then shook over his fingers a few drops of violet water from the bottle he kept hidden in his drawer. He left the house with his geometry conspicuously under his arm, and the moment he got out of Cordelia Street and boarded a downtown car, he shook off the lethargy of two deadening days, and began to live again.

29 The leading juvenile of the permanent stock company which played at one of the downtown theatres was an acquaintance of Paul's, and the boy had been invited to drop in at the Sunday-night rehearsals whenever he could. For more than a year Paul had spent every available moment loitering about Charley Edwards's dressing-room. He had won a place among Edwards's following not only because the young actor, who could not afford to employ a dresser, often found him useful, but because he recognized in Paul something akin to what churchmen term "vocation."

30 It was at the theatre and at Carnegie Hall that Paul really lived; the rest was but a sleep and a forgetting. This was Paul's fairy tale, and it had for him all the allurement of a secret love. The moment he inhaled the gassy, painty, dusty odour behind the scenes, he breathed like a prisoner set free, and felt within him the possibility of doing or saying splendid, brilliant things. The moment the cracked orchestra beat out the overture from *Martha*, or jerked at the serenade from *Rigoletto*, all stupid and ugly things slid from him, and his senses were deliciously, yet delicately fired.

31 Perhaps it was because, in Paul's world, the natural nearly always wore the guise of ugliness, that a certain element of artificiality seemed to him necessary in beauty. Perhaps it was because his experience of life elsewhere was so full of Sabbath-school picnics, petty economies, wholesome advice as to how to succeed in life, and the unescapable odours of cooking, that he found this existence so alluring, these smartly-clad men and women so attractive, that he was so moved by these starry apple orchards that bloomed perennially under the lime-light.

32 It would be difficult to put it strongly enough how convincingly the stage entrance of that theatre was for Paul the actual portal of Romance. Certainly none of the company ever suspected it, least of all Charley Edwards. It was very like the old stories that used to float about London of fabulously rich Jews, who had subterranean halls, with palms, and fountains, and soft lamps and richly apparelled women

who never saw the disenchanting light of London day. So, in the midst of that smoke-palled city, enamoured of figures and grimy toil, Paul had his secret temple, his wishing-carpet, his bit of blue-and-white Mediterranean shore bathed in perpetual sunshine.

Several of Paul's teachers had a theory that his imagination had been perverted by garish fiction; but the truth was, he scarcely ever read at all. The books at home were not such as would either tempt or corrupt a youthful mind, and as for reading the novels that some of his friends urged upon him—well, he got what he wanted much more quickly from music; any sort of music, from an orchestra to a barrel organ. He needed only the spark, the indescribable thrill that made his imagination master of his senses, and he could make plots and pictures enough of his own. It was equally true that he was not stage-struck—not, at any rate, in the usual acceptation of that expression. He had no desire to become an actor, any more than he had to become a musician. He felt no necessity to do any of these things; what he wanted was to see, to be in the atmosphere, float on the wave of it, to be carried out, blue league after blue league, away from everything.

After a night behind the scenes, Paul found the schoolroom more than ever repulsive; the bare floors and naked walls; the prosy men who never wore frock coats, or violets in their buttonholes; the women with their dull gowns, shrill voices, and pitiful seriousness about prepositions that govern the dative. He could not bear to have the other pupils think, for a moment, that he took these people seriously; he must convey to them that he considered it all trivial, and was there only by way of a joke, anyway. He had autograph pictures of all the members of the stock company which he showed his classmates, telling them the most incredible stories of his familiarity with these people, of his acquaintance with the soloists who came to Carnegie Hall, his suppers with them and the flowers he sent them. When these stories lost their effect, and his audience grew listless, he would bid all the boys good-bye, announcing that he was going to travel for awhile; going to Naples, to California, to Egypt. Then, next Mon-

day, he would slip back, conscious and nervously smiling; his sister was ill, and he would have to defer his voyage until spring.

Matters went steadily worse with Paul at school. In the itch to let his instructors know how heartily he despised them, and how thoroughly he was appreciated elsewhere, he mentioned once or twice that he had no time to fool with theorems; adding—with a twitch of the eyebrows and a touch of that nervous bravado which so perplexed them—that he was helping the people down at the stock company; they were old friends of his.

The upshot of the matter was, that the Principal went to Paul's father, and Paul was taken out of school and put to work. The manager at Carnegie Hall was told to get another usher in his stead; the doorkeeper at the theatre was warned not to admit him to the house; and Charley Edwards remorsefully promised the boy's father not to see him again.

The members of the stock company were vastly amused when some of Paul's stories reached them—especially the women. They were hard-working women, most of them supporting indolent husbands or brothers, and they laughed rather bitterly at having stirred the boy to such fervid and florid inventions. They agreed with the faculty and with his father, that Paul's was a bad case.

THE east-bound train was ploughing through a January snow-storm; the dull dawn was beginning to show grey when the engine whistled a mile out of Newark. Paul started up from the seat where he had lain curled in uneasy slumber, rubbed the breath-misted window glass with his hand, and peered out. The snow was whirling in curling eddies above the white bottom lands, and the drifts lay already deep in the fields and along the fences, while here and there the long dead grass and dried weed stalks protruded black above it. Lights shone from the scattered houses, and a gang of labourers who stood beside the track waved their lanterns.

Paul had slept very little, and he felt grimy and uncomfortable. He had made the all-night journey in a day coach because he was afraid if he took a Pullman he might be seen by some Pittsburgh business man who had noticed him in Denny & Carson's office. When the whistle woke him, he clutched quickly at his breast pocket, glancing about him with an uncertain smile. But the little, clay-bespattered Italians were still sleeping, the slatternly women across the aisle were in open-mouthed oblivion, and even the crumby, crying babies were for the nonce stilled. Paul settled back to struggle with his impatience as best he could.

40   When he arrived at the Jersey City station, he hurried through his breakfast, manifestly ill at ease and keeping a sharp eye about him. After he reached the Twenty-third Street station, he consulted a cabman, and had himself driven to a men's furnishing establishment which was just opening for the day. He spent upward of two hours there, buying with endless reconsidering and great care. His new street suit he put on in the fitting-room; the frock coat and dress clothes he had bundled into the cab with his new shirts. Then he drove to a hatter's and a shoe house. His next errand was at Tiffany's, where he selected silver mounted brushes and a scarf-pin. He would not wait to have his silver marked, he said. Lastly, he stopped at a trunk shop on Broadway, and had his purchases packed into various travelling bags.

41   It was a little after one o'clock when he drove up to the Waldorf, and, after settling with the cabman, went into the office. He registered from Washington; said his mother and father had been abroad, and that he had come down to await the arrival of their steamer. He told his story plausibly and had no trouble, since he offered to pay for them in advance, in engaging his rooms; a sleeping-room, sitting-room, and bath.

42   Not once, but a hundred times Paul had planned this entry into New York. He had gone over every detail of it with Charley Edwards, and in his scrap book at home there were pages of description about New York hotels, cut from the Sunday papers.

43   When he was shown to his sitting-room on the eighth floor, he saw at a glance that everything was as it should be; there was but one detail in his mental picture that the place did not realize, so he rang for the bell boy and sent him down for flowers. He moved about nervously until the boy returned, putting away his new linen and fingering it delightedly as he did so. When the flowers came, he put them hastily into water, and then tumbled into a hot bath. Presently he came out of his white bath-room, resplendent in his new silk underwear, and playing with the tassels of his red robe. The snow was whirling so fiercely outside his windows that he could scarcely see across the street; but within, the air was deliciously soft and fragrant. He put the violets and jonquils on the tabouret beside the couch, and threw himself down with a long sigh, covering himself with a Roman blanket. He was thoroughly tired; he had been in such haste, he had stood up to such a strain, covered so much ground in the last twenty-four hours, that he wanted to think how it had all come about. Lulled by the sound of the wind, the warm air, and the cool fragrance of the flowers, he sank into deep, drowsy retrospection.

It had been wonderfully simple; when they had shut him out of the theatre and concert hall, when they had taken away his bone, the whole thing was virtually determined. The rest was a mere matter of opportunity. The only thing that at all surprised him was his own courage—for he realized well enough that he had always been tormented by fear, a sort of apprehensive dread that, of late years, as the meshes of the lies he had told closed about him, had been pulling the muscles of his body tighter and tighter. Until now, he could not remember a time when he had not been dreading something. Even when he was a little boy, it was always there—behind him, or before, or on either side. There had always been the shadowed corner, the dark place into which he dared not look, but from which something seemed always to be watching him—and Paul had done things that were not pretty to watch, he knew.

But now he had a curious sense of relief, as though he had at last thrown down the gauntlet to the thing in the corner.

Yet it was but a day since he had been sulking in the traces; but yesterday afternoon that he had been sent to the bank with Denny & Carson's deposit, as usual—but this time he was instructed to leave the book to be balanced. There was above two thousand dollars in checks, and nearly a thousand in the bank notes which he had taken from the book and quietly transferred to his pocket. At the bank he had made out a new deposit slip. His nerves had been steady enough to permit of his returning to the office, where he had finished his work and asked for a full day's holiday tomorrow, Saturday, giving a perfectly reasonable pretext. The bank book, he knew, would not be returned before Monday or Tuesday, and his father would be out of town for the next week. From the time he slipped the bank notes into his pocket until he boarded the night train for New York, he had not known a moment's hesitation.

How astonishingly easy it had all been; here he was, the thing done; and this time there would be no awakening, no figure at the top of the stairs. He watched the snow flakes whirling by his window until he fell asleep.

WHEN he awoke, it was four o'clock in the afternoon. He bounded up with a start; one of his precious days gone already! He spent nearly an hour in dressing, watching every stage of his toilet carefully in the mirror. Everything was quite perfect; he was exactly the kind of boy he had always wanted to be.

When he went downstairs, Paul took a carriage and drove up Fifth avenue toward the Park. The snow had somewhat abated; carriages and tradesmen's wagons were hurrying soundlessly to and fro in the winter twilight; boys in woollen mufflers were shovelling off the doorsteps; the avenue stages made fine spots of colour against the white street. Here and there on the corners whole flower gardens blooming behind glass windows, against which the snow flakes stuck and melted; violets, roses, carnations, lilies of the valley—somehow vastly more lovely and alluring that they blossomed thus unnaturally in the snow. The Park itself was a wonderful stage winterpiece.

When he returned, the pause of the twilight had ceased, and the tune of the streets had changed. The snow was falling faster, lights streamed from the hotels that reared their many stories fearlessly up into the storm, defying the raging Atlantic winds. A long, black stream of carriages poured down the avenue, intersected here and there by other streams, tending horizontally. There were a score of cabs about the entrance of his hotel, and his driver had to wait. Boys in livery were running in and out of the awning stretched across the sidewalk, up and down the red velvet carpet laid from the door to the street. Above, about, within it all, was the rumble and roar, the hurry and toss of thousands of human beings as hot for pleasure as himself, and on every side of him towered the glaring affirmation of the omnipotence of wealth.

The boy set his teeth and drew his shoulders together in a spasm of realization; the plot of all dramas, the text of all romances, the nerve-stuff of all sensations was whirling about him like the snow flakes. He burnt like a faggot in a tempest.

When Paul came down to dinner, the music of the orchestra floated up the elevator shaft to greet him. As he stepped into the thronged corridor, he sank back into one of the chairs against the wall to get his breath. The lights, the chatter, the perfumes, the bewildering medley of colour—he had, for a moment, the feeling of not being able to stand it. But only for a moment; these were his own people, he told himself. He went slowly about the corridors, through the writing-rooms, smoking-rooms, reception-rooms, as though he were exploring the chambers of an enchanted palace, built and peopled for him alone.

When he reached the dining-room he sat down at a table near a window. The flowers, the white linen, the many-coloured wine glasses, the gay toilettes of the women, the low popping of corks, the undulating repetitions of the *Blue Danube* from the orchestra, all flooded Paul's dream with bewildering radiance. When the roseate tinge of his champagne was added—that cold, precious, bubbling stuff that creamed and foamed in his glass—Paul wondered that there were honest men in the world at all. This was what all the world was fighting for, he reflected; this was what all the struggle was about. He doubted the reality of his past. Had he ever known a place called Cordelia Street, a place where fagged looking business men boarded the early car? Mere rivets in a machine they seemed to Paul,—sickening men, with combings of children's hair always hanging to their coats, and the smell of cooking in their clothes. Cordelia Street—Ah, that belonged to another time and country! Had he not always been thus, had he not sat here night after night, from as far back as he could remember, looking pensively over just such shimmering textures, and slowly twirling the stem of a glass like this one between his thumb and middle finger? He rather thought he had.

He was not in the least abashed or lonely. He had no especial desire to meet or to know any of these people; all he demanded was the right to look on and conjecture, to watch the pageant. The mere stage properties were all he contended for. Nor was he lonely later in the evening, in his loge at the Opera. He was entirely rid of his nervous misgivings, of his forced aggressiveness, of the imperative desire to show himself different from his surroundings. He felt now that his surroundings explained him. Nobody questioned the purple; he had only to wear it passively. He had only to glance down at his dress coat to reassure himself that here it would be impossible for anyone to humiliate him.

55   He found it hard to leave his beautiful sitting-room to go to bed that night, and sat long watching the raging storm from his turret window. When he went to sleep, it was with the lights turned on in his bedroom; partly because of his old timidity, and partly so that, if he should wake in the night, there would be no wretched moment of doubt, no horrible suspicion of yellow wall-paper, or of Washington and Calvin above his bed.

56   On Sunday morning the city was practically snowbound. Paul breakfasted late, and in the afternoon he fell in with a wild San Francisco boy, a freshman at Yale, who said he had run down for a "little flyer" over Sunday. The young man offered to show Paul the night side of the town, and the two boys went off together after dinner, not returning to the hotel until seven o'clock the next morning. They had started out in the confiding warmth of a champagne friendship, but their parting in the elevator was singularly cool. The freshman pulled himself together to make his train, and Paul went to bed. He awoke at two o'clock in the afternoon, very thirsty and dizzy, and rang for ice-water, coffee, and the Pittsburgh papers.

57   On the part of the hotel management, Paul excited no suspicion. There was this to be said for him, that he wore his spoils with dignity and in no way made himself conspicuous. His chief greediness lay in his ears and eyes, and his excesses were not offensive ones. His dearest pleasures were the grey winter twilights in his sitting-room; his quiet enjoyment of his flowers, his clothes, his wide divan, his cigarette and his sense of power. He could not remember a time when he had felt so at peace with himself. The mere release from the necessity of petty lying, lying every day and every day, restored his self-respect. He had never lied for pleasure, even at school; but to make himself noticed and admired, to assert his difference from other Cordelia Street boys; and he felt a good deal more manly, more honest, even, now that he had no need for boastful pretensions, now that he could, as his actor friends used to say, "dress the part." It was characteristic that remorse did not occur to him. His golden days went by without a shadow, and he made each as perfect as he could.

58   On the eighth day after his arrival in New York, he found the whole affair exploited in the Pittsburgh papers, exploited with a wealth of detail which indicated that local news of a sensational nature was at a low ebb. The firm of Denny & Carson announced that the boy's father had refunded the full amount of his theft, and that they had no intention of prosecuting. The Cumberland minister had been interviewed, and expressed his hope of yet reclaiming the motherless lad, and Paul's Sabbath-school teacher declared that she would spare no effort to that end. The rumour had reached Pittsburgh that the boy had been seen in a New York hotel, and his father had gone East to find him and bring him home.

59   Paul had just come in to dress for dinner; he sank into a chair, weak in the knees, and clasped his head in his hands. It was to be worse than jail, even; the tepid waters of Cordelia Street were to close over him finally and forever. The grey monotony stretched before him in hopeless, unrelieved years; Sabbath-school, Young People's Meeting, the yellow-papered room, the damp dishtowels; it all rushed back upon him with sickening vividness. He had the old feeling that the orchestra had suddenly stopped, the sinking sensation that the play was over. The sweat broke out on his face, and he sprang to his feet, looked about him with his white, conscious smile, and winked at himself in the mirror, With something of the childish belief in miracles with which he had so often gone to class, all his lessons unlearned, Paul dressed and dashed whistling down the corridor to the elevator.

60   He had no sooner entered the dining-room and caught the measure of the music, than his remembrance was lightened by his old elastic power of claiming the moment, mounting with it, and finding it all sufficient. The glare and glitter about him, the mere scenic accessories had again, and for the last time, their old potency. He would show himself that he was game, he would finish the thing splendidly. He doubted, more than ever, the existence of Cordelia Street, and for the first time he drank his wine recklessly. Was he not, after all, one of these fortunate beings? Was he not still himself, and in his own place? He drummed a nervous accompaniment to the music and looked about him, telling himself over and over that it had paid.

61   He reflected drowsily, to the swell of the violin and the chill sweetness of his wine, that he might have done it more wisely. He might have caught an outbound steamer and been well out of their clutches before now. But the other side of the world had seemed too far away and too uncertain then; he could not have

> The mere release from the necessity of petty lying, lying every day and every day, restored his self-respect.

waited for it; his need had been too sharp. If he had to choose over again, he would do the same thing tomorrow. He looked affectionately about the dining-room, now gilded with a soft mist. Ah, it had paid indeed!

62   Paul was awakened next morning by a painful throbbing in his head and feet. He had thrown himself across the bed without undressing, and had slept with his shoes on. His limbs and hands were lead heavy, and his tongue and throat were parched. There came upon him one of those fateful attacks of clear-headedness that never occurred except when he was physically exhausted and his nerves hung loose. He lay still and closed his eyes and let the tide of realities wash over him.

63   His father was in New York; "stopping at some joint or other," he told himself. The memory of successive summers on the front stoop fell upon him like a weight of black water. He had not a hundred dollars left; and he knew now, more than ever, that money was everything, the wall that stood between all he loathed and all he wanted. The thing was winding itself up; he had thought of that on his first glorious day in New York, and had even provided a way to snap the thread. It lay on his dressing-table now; he had got it out last night when he came blindly up from dinner,—but the shiny metal hurt his eyes, and he disliked the look of it, anyway.

64   He rose and moved about with a painful effort, succumbing now and again to attacks of nausea. It was the old depression exaggerated; all the world had become Cordelia Street. Yet somehow he was not afraid of anything, was absolutely calm; perhaps because he had looked into the dark corner at last, and knew. It was bad enough, what he saw there; but somehow not so bad as his long fear of it had been. He saw everything clearly now. He had a feeling that he had made the best of it, that he had lived the sort of life he was meant to live, and for half an hour he sat staring at the revolver. But he told himself that was not the way, so he went downstairs and took a cab to the ferry.

65   When Paul arrived at Newark, he got off the train and took another cab, directing the driver to follow the Pennsylvania tracks out of the town. The snow lay heavy on the roadways and had drifted deep in the open fields. Only here and there the dead grass or dried weed stalks projected, singularly black, above it. Once well into the country, Paul dismissed the carriage and walked, floundering along the tracks, his mind a medley of irrelevant things. He seemed to hold in his brain an actual picture of everything he had seen that morning. He remembered every feature of both his drivers, the toothless old woman from whom he had bought the red flowers in his coat, the agent from whom he had got his ticket, and all of his fellow-passengers on the ferry. His mind, unable to cope with vital matters near at hand, worked feverishly and deftly at sorting and grouping these images. They made for him a part of the ugliness of the world, of the ache in his head, and the bitter burning on his tongue. He stooped and put a handful of snow into his mouth as he walked, but that, too, seemed hot. When he reached a little hillside, where the tracks ran through a cut some twenty feet below him, he stopped and sat down.

66   The carnations in his coat were drooping with the cold, he noticed; all their red glory over. It occurred to him that all the flowers he had seen in the show windows that first night must have gone the same way, long before this. It was only one splendid breath they had, in spite of their brave mockery at the winter outside the glass. It was a losing game in the end, it seemed, this revolt against the homilies by which the world is run. Paul took one of the blossoms carefully from his coat and scooped a little hole in the snow, where he covered it up. Then he dozed a while, from his weak condition, seeming insensible to the cold.

67   The sound of an approaching train woke him, and he started to his feet, remembering only his resolution, and afraid lest he should be too late. He stood watching the approaching locomotive, his teeth chattering, his lips drawn away from them in a frightened smile; once or twice he glanced nervously sidewise, as though he were being watched. When the right moment came, he jumped. As he fell, the folly of his haste occurred to him with merciless clearness, the vastness of what he had left undone. There flashed through his brain, clearer than ever before, the blue of Adriatic water, the yellow of Algerian sands.

68   He felt something strike his chest,—his body was being thrown swiftly through the air, on and on, immeasurably far and fast, while his limbs gently relaxed. Then, because the picture making mechanism was crushed, the disturbing visions flashed into black, and Paul dropped back into the immense design of things.

IF you liked this story of a troubled young man in Willa Cather's "Paul's Case," you might look again at "Greasy Lake" by T. Coraghessan Boyle in chapter 4 or at the soldiers of Tim O'Brien's "The Things They Carried" in chapter 10, or the family members in Alice Walker's "Everyday Use" in Stories for Further Reading.

GOING FURTHER   Paul, an ordinary young person moving in a downward spiral, is an interesting variation on the nature of human character, which Willa Cather has explored at length in her many novels. Most of her characters strive upward, such as the immigrant girl Ántonia in *My Ántonia,* the gifted Midwestern opera singer in *The Song of the Lark,* and Father Latour, the nineteenth-century priest, based on an actual historical figure, in the novel *Death Comes for the Archbishop.*

Writing from Reading

Summarize

1 The story's subtitle, "A Study in Temperament," suggests dispassionate analysis—as if we were about to read a clinician's case study or a police report. What are the facts that make up this "case"? Summarize the events.

Analyze Craft

2 Cather first presents Paul from the perspective of his teachers, who see him as smug, flippant, difficult, and beyond their ability to understand. Why does Cather open the story this way, and does this approach affect your response to him as a character?

3 Describe what Paul experiences when he watches the symphony. What, specifically, does he hear, see, and feel? How does his response to the music, especially the soprano soloist, help to characterize him?

4 Compare and contrast the two locations of the story—Pittsburgh and New York—and explore how, in rendering them, Cather also characterizes Paul and the changes in his life. Consider other aspects of setting—times of day, the weather, the season—in your analysis.

Analyze Voice

5 This story raises a series of psychological questions: What motivates Paul to make the choices he does? What does he seek? What is his desire? Discuss how the story's narrator answers these questions.

6 In what ways does Cather's language make this seem more like a "case," a presentation of facts and details, than it does a story?

Synthesize Summary and Analysis

7 Paul is an antihero, a protagonist whose actions do not meet our expectations of courage and honesty. Discuss how Cather makes the reader relate to Paul despite his unacceptable behavior.

Interpret the Story

8 Make a case for Paul as round or flat, and static or dynamic. Consider how Paul has or hasn't changed over the course of the story, citing the events that altered or maintained his character.

Jack London (1876–1916)

Born to an unmarried mother in California, John ("Jack") London sought employment from age ten in order to lessen his family's poverty. In jobs such as working at a cannery, shoveling coal at a power plant, and pirating oysters from commercial oyster operations, London experienced firsthand the life of an average worker and determined to better himself through education. He turned to writing after taking part in the Yukon gold rush, working with a self-imposed rule that he must write 1,000 publishable words every day. His first collection of short stories, *The Son of the Wolf,* appeared in 1900, and within the next several years, he published many of the novels that made him famous, including *The Call of the Wild* (1903), *The Sea Wolf* (1904), and *White Fang* (1906). These novels of survival in a harsh natural world made London famous all over the globe, and he is one of the few early twentieth century writers to have become rich from his fiction. Despite his rags-to-riches life story, London believed in socialism and used his celebrity status to speak and write in favor of it. London was a man of prodigious energy, and his hobbies ranged from sailing to agriculture to building his dream house. He died when just forty years old, of uremia, although some have speculated that his death may have been a suicide.

AS YOU READ As you read, notice your responses to the rather large cast of characters. Which do you get to know best? Do any of them seem familiar to you?

TIP

FOR INTERACTIVE READING . . . As you read, mark the text in the places where Mrs. Hemingway talks about Loretta. How does she describe Loretta to her husband? How does she describe Loretta to Ned Bashford? What do the differences in the descriptions tell you about Mrs. Hemingway?

A Wicked Woman (1906)

1   IT was because she had broken with Billy that Loretta had come visiting to Santa Clara. Billy could not understand. His sister had reported that he had walked the floor and cried all night. Loretta had not slept all night either, while she had wept most of the night. Daisy knew this, because it was in her arms that the weeping had been done. And Daisy's husband, Captain Kitt, knew, too. The tears of Loretta, and the comforting by Daisy, had lost him some sleep.

Now Captain Kitt did not like to lose sleep. Neither did he want Loretta to marry Billy—nor anybody else. It was Captain Kitt's belief that Daisy needed the help of her younger sister in the household. But he did not say this aloud. Instead, he always insisted that Loretta was too young to think of marriage. So it was Captain Kitt's idea that Loretta should be packed off on a visit to Mrs. Hemingway. There wouldn't be any Billy there. 2

3　　Before Loretta had been at Santa Clara a week, she was convinced that Captain Kitt's idea was a good one. In the first place, though Billy wouldn't believe it, she did not want to marry Billy. And in the second place, though Captain Kitt wouldn't believe it, she did not want to leave Daisy. By the time Loretta had been at Santa Clara two weeks, she was absolutely certain that she did not want to marry Billy. But she was not so sure about not wanting to leave Daisy. Not that she loved Daisy less, but that she— had doubts.

He did not believe in the truth of women . . .

4　　The day of Loretta's arrival, a nebulous plan began shaping itself in Mrs. Hemingway's brain. The second day she remarked to Jack Hemingway, her husband, that Loretta was so innocent a young thing that were it not for her sweet guilelessness she would be positively stupid. In proof of which, Mrs. Hemingway told her husband several things that made him chuckle. By the third day Mrs. Hemingway's plan had taken recognizable form. Then it was that she composed a letter. On the envelope she wrote: "Mr. Edward Bashford, Athenian Club, San Francisco."

5　　"Dear Ned," the letter began. She had once been violently loved by him for three weeks in her pre-marital days. But she had covenanted herself to Jack Hemingway, who had prior claims, and her heart as well; and Ned Bashford had philosophically not broken his heart over it. He merely added the experience to a large fund of similarly collected data out of which he manufactured philosophy. Artistically and temperamentally he was a Greek—a tired Greek. He was fond of quoting from Nietzsche, in token that he, too, had passed through the long sickness that follows upon the ardent search for truth; that he too had emerged, too experienced, too shrewd, too profound, ever again to be afflicted by the madness of youths in their love of truth. "To worship appearance," he often quoted; "'to believe in forms, in tones, in words, in the whole Olympus of appearance!'" This particular excerpt he always concluded with, "Those Greeks were superficial—*out of profundity*!"

6　　He was a fairly young Greek, jaded and worn. Women were faithless and unveracious, he held—at such times that he had relapses and descended to pessimism from his wonted high philosophical calm. He did not believe in the truth of women; but, faithful to his German master, he did not strip from them the airy gauzes that veiled their untruth. He was content to accept them as appearances and to make the best of it. He was superficial—*out of profundity*.

7　　"Jack says to be sure to say to you, 'good swimming,'" Mrs. Hemingway wrote in her letter; "and also 'to bring your fishing duds along.'" Mrs. Hemingway wrote other things in the letter. She told him that at last she was prepared to exhibit to him an absolutely true, unsullied, and innocent woman. "A more guileless, immaculate bud of womanhood never blushed on the planet," was one of the several ways in which she phrased the inducement. And to her husband she said triumphantly, "If I don't marry Ned off this time—" leaving unstated the terrible alternative that she lacked either vocabulary to express or imagination to conceive.

8　　Contrary to all her forebodings, Loretta found that she was not unhappy at Santa Clara. True, Billy wrote to her every day, but his letters were less distressing than his presence. Also, the ordeal of being away from Daisy was not so severe as she had expected. For the first time in her life she was not lost in eclipse in the blaze of Daisy's brilliant and mature personality. Under such favorable circumstances Loretta came rapidly to the front, while Mrs. Hemingway modestly and shamelessly retreated into the background.

9　　Loretta began to discover that she was not a pale orb shining by reflection. Quite unconsciously she became a small centre of things. When she was at the piano, there was some one to turn the pages for her and to express preferences for certain songs. When she dropped her handkerchief, there was some one to pick it up. And there was some one to accompany her in ramblings and flower gatherings. Also, she learned to cast flies in still pools and below savage riffles, and how not to entangle silk lines and gut-leaders with the shrubbery.

10　　Jack Hemingway did not care to teach beginners, and fished much by himself, or not at all, thus giving Ned Bashford ample time in which to consider Loretta as an appearance. As such, she was all that his philosophy demanded. Her blue eyes had the direct gaze of a boy, and out of his profundity he delighted in them and forbore to shudder at the duplicity his philosophy bade him to believe lurked in their depths. She had the grace of a slender flower, the fragility of color and line of fine china, in all of which he pleasured greatly, without thought of the Life Force palpitating beneath and in spite of Bernard Shaw—in whom he believed.

11 Loretta bourgeoned. She swiftly developed personality. She discovered a will of her own and wishes of her own that were not everlastingly entwined with the will and the wishes of Daisy. She was petted by Jack Hemingway, spoiled by Alice Hemingway, and devotedly attended by Ned Bashford. They encouraged her whims and laughed at her follies, while she developed the pretty little tyrannies that are latent in all pretty and delicate women. Her environment acted as a soporific upon her ancient desire always to live with Daisy. This desire no longer prodded her as in the days of her companionship with Billy. The more she saw of Billy, the more certain she had been that she could not live away from Daisy. The more she saw of Ned Bashford, the more she forgot her pressing need of Daisy.

12 Ned Bashford likewise did some forgetting. He confused superficiality with profundity, and entangled appearance with reality until he accounted them one. Loretta was different from other women. There was no masquerade about her. She was real. He said as much to Mrs. Hemingway, and more, who agreed with him and at the same time caught her husband's eyelid drooping down for the moment in an unmistakable wink.

13 It was at this time that Loretta received a letter from Billy that was somewhat different from his others. In the main, like all his letters, it was pathological. It was a long recital of symptoms and sufferings, his nervousness, his sleeplessness, and the state of his heart. Then followed reproaches, such as he had never made before. They were sharp enough to make her weep, and true enough to put tragedy into her face. This tragedy she carried down to the breakfast table. It made Jack and Mrs. Hemingway speculative, and it worried Ned. They glanced to him for explanation, but he shook his head.

14 "I'll find out to-night," Mrs. Hemingway said to her husband.

15 But Ned caught Loretta in the afternoon in the big living-room. She tried to turn away. He caught her hands, and she faced him with wet lashes and trembling lips. He looked at her, silently and kindly. The lashes grew wetter.

> There seemed to emanate from her the perfect sweetness of a child—"the aura of a white soul."

16 "There, there, don't cry, little one," he said soothingly.

17 He put his arm protectingly around her shoulder. And to his shoulder, like a tired child, she turned her face. He thrilled in ways unusual for a Greek who has recovered from the long sickness.

18 "Oh, Ned," she sobbed on his shoulder, "if you only knew how wicked I am!"

19 He smiled indulgently, and breathed in a great breath freighted with the fragrance of her hair. He thought of his world-experience of women, and drew another long breath. There seemed to emanate from her the perfect sweetness of a child—"the aura of a white soul," was the way he phrased it to himself.

20 Then he noticed that her sobs were increasing.

21 "What's the matter, little one?" he asked pettingly and almost paternally. "Has Jack been bullying you? Or has your dearly beloved sister failed to write?"

22 She did not answer, and he felt that he really must kiss her hair, that he could not be responsible if the situation continued much longer.

23 "Tell me," he said gently, "and we'll see what I can do."

24 "I can't. You will despise me.—Oh, Ned, I am so ashamed!"

25 He laughed incredulously, and lightly touched her hair with his lips—so lightly that she did not know.

26 "Dear little one, let us forget all about it, whatever it is. I want to tell you how I love—"

27 She uttered a sharp cry that was all delight, and then moaned—

28 "Too late!"

29 "Too late?" he echoed in surprise.

30 "Oh, why did I? Why did I?" she was moaning.

31 He was aware of a swift chill at his heart.

32 "What?" he asked.

33 "Oh, I . . . he . . . Billy.

34 "I am such a wicked woman, Ned. I know you will never speak to me again."

35 "This—er—this Billy," he began haltingly. "He is your brother?"

36 "No . . . he . . . I didn't know. I was so young. I could not help it. Oh, I shall go mad! I shall go mad!"

37 It was then that Loretta felt his shoulder and the encircling arm become limp. He drew away from her gently, and gently he deposited her in a big chair, where she buried her face and sobbed afresh. He twisted his mustache fiercely, then drew up another chair and sat down.

38 "I—I do not understand," he said.

39 "I am so unhappy," she wailed.

40 "Why unhappy?"

41 "Because . . . he . . . he wants me to marry him."

42 His face cleared on the instant, and he placed a hand soothingly on hers.

43 "That should not make any girl unhappy," he remarked sagely. "Because you don't love him is no reason—of course, you don't love him?"

44 Loretta shook her head and shoulders in a vigorous negative.

45 "What?"

46 Bashford wanted to make sure.

47 "No," she asserted explosively. "I don't love Billy! I don't want to love Billy!"

48 "Because you don't love him, "Bashford resumed with confidence, "is no reason that you should be unhappy just because he has proposed to you."

49 She sobbed again, and from the midst of her sobs she cried:—

50 "That's the trouble. I wish I did love him. Oh, I wish I were dead!"

51 "Now, my dear child, you are worrying yourself over trifles." His other hand crossed over after its mate and rested on hers. "Women do it every day. Because you have changed your mind or did not know your mind, because you have—to use an unnecessarily harsh word—jilted a man—"

52 "Jilted!" She had raised her head and was looking at him with tear-dimmed eyes. "Oh, Ned, if that were all!"

53 "All?" he asked in a hollow voice, while his hands slowly retreated from hers. He was about to speak further, then remained silent.

54 "But I don't want to marry him," Loretta broke forth protestingly.

55 "Then I shouldn't," he counselled.

56 "But I ought to marry him."

57 "*Ought* to marry him?"

58 She nodded.

59 "That is a strong word."

60 "I know it is," she acquiesced, while she strove to control her trembling lips. Then she spoke more calmly. "I am a wicked woman, a terribly wicked woman. No one knows how wicked I am—except Billy."

61 There was a pause. Ned Bashford's face was grave, and he looked queerly at Loretta.

62 "He—Billy knows?" he asked finally.

63 A reluctant nod and flaming cheeks was the reply.

64 He debated with himself for a while, seeming, like a diver, to be preparing himself for the plunge.

65 "Tell me about it." He spoke very firmly. "You must tell me all of it."

66 "And will you—ever—forgive me?" she asked in a faint, small voice.

67 He hesitated, drew a long breath, and made the plunge.

68 "Yes," he said desperately. "I'll forgive you. Go ahead."

69 "There was no one to tell me," she began. "We were with each other so much. I did not know anything of the world—then."

70 She paused to meditate. Bashford was biting his lip impatiently.

71 "If I had only known—"

72 She paused again.

73 "Yes, go on," he urged.

74 "We were together almost every evening."

75 "Billy?" he demanded, with a savageness that startled her.

76 "Yes, of course, Billy. We were with each other so much. . . . If I had only known. . . . There was no one to tell me. . . . I was so young—"

77 Her lips parted as though to speak further, and she regarded him anxiously.

78 "The scoundrel!"

79 With the explosion Ned Bashford was on his feet, no longer a tired Greek, but a violently angry young man.

80 "Billy is not a scoundrel; he is a good man," Loretta defended, with a firmness that surprised Bashford.

81 "I suppose you'll be telling me next that it was all your fault," he said sarcastically.

82 She nodded.

83 "What?" he shouted.

84 "It was all my fault," she said steadily. "I should never have let him. I was to blame."

85 Bashford ceased from his pacing up and down, and when he spoke, his voice was resigned.

86 "All right," he said. "I don't blame you in the least, Loretta. And you have been very honest. But Billy is right, and you are wrong. You must get married."

87 "To Billy?" she asked, in a dim, far-away voice.

88 "Yes, to Billy. I'll see to it. Where does he live? I'll make him."

89 "But I don't want to marry Billy!" she cried out in alarm. "Oh, Ned, you won't do that?"

90 "I shall," he answered sternly. "You must. And Billy must. Do you understand?"

91 Loretta buried her face in the cushioned chair back, and broke into a passionate storm of sobs.

92 All that Bashford could make out at first, as he listened, was: "But I don't want to leave Daisy! I don't want to leave Daisy!"

93 He paced grimly back and forth, then stopped curiously to listen.

94 "How was I to know?—Boo-hoo," Loretta was crying. "He didn't tell me. Nobody else ever kissed me. I never dreamed a kiss could be so terrible . . . until,

boo-hoo . . . until he wrote to me. I only got the letter this morning."

His face brightened. It seemed as though light was dawning on him.

"Is that what you're crying about?"

"N-no."

His heart sank.

"Then what are you crying about?" he asked in a hopeless voice.

"Because you said I had to marry Billy. And I don't want to marry Billy. I don't want to leave Daisy. I don't know what I want. I wish I were dead."

He nerved himself for another effort.

"Now look here, Loretta, be sensible. What is this about kisses? You haven't told me everything."

"I—I don't want to tell you everything."

She looked at him beseechingly in the silence that fell.

"Must I?" she quavered finally.

"You must," he said imperatively. 'You must tell me everything."

"Well, then . . . must I?"

"You must."

"He . . . I . . . we . . ." she began flounderingly. Then blurted out, "I let him, and he kissed me."

"Go on," Bashford commanded desperately.

"That's all," she answered.

"All?" There was a vast incredulity in his voice.

"All?" In her voice was an interrogation no less vast.

"I mean—er—nothing worse?" He was overwhelmingly aware of his own awkwardness.

"Worse?" She was frankly puzzled. "As though there could be! Billy said—"

"When did he say it?" Bashford demanded abruptly.

"In his letter I got this morning. Billy said that my . . . our . . . our kisses were terrible if we didn't get married."

Bashford's head was swimming. [118]

"What else did Billy say?" he asked. [119]

"He said that when a woman allowed a man to kiss her, she always married him—that it was terrible if she didn't. It was the custom, he said; and I say it is a bad, wicked custom, and I don't like it. I know I'm terrible," she added defiantly, "but I can't help it." [110]

Bashford absent-mindedly brought out a cigarette. [111]

"Do you mind if I smoke?" he asked, as he struck a match. [1112]

Then he came to himself. [113]

"I beg your pardon," he cried, flinging away match and cigarette. "I don't want to smoke. I didn't mean that at all. What I mean is—" [114]

He bent over Loretta, caught her hands in his, then sat on the arm of the chair and softly put one arm around her. [115]

"Loretta, I am a fool. I mean it. And I mean something more. I want you to be my wife." [116]

He waited anxiously in the pause that followed. [117]

"You might answer me," he urged. [118]

"I will . . . if—" [119]

"Yes, go on. If what?" [120]

"If I don't have to marry Billy." [121]

"You can't marry both of us," he almost shouted. [122]

"And it isn't the custom . . . what . . . what Billy said?" [123]

"No, it isn't the custom. Now, Loretta, will you marry me?" [124]

"Don't be angry with me," she pouted demurely. [125]

He gathered her into his arms and kissed her. [126]

"I wish it were the custom," she said in a faint voice, from the midst of the embrace, "because then I'd have to marry you, Ned . . . dear . . . wouldn't I?" [127]

SUCCESSFUL comedy in fiction is a rare quality. If you like "A Wicked Woman," look at Eudora Welty's "Why I Live at the P.O." (chapter 6), Lorrie Moore's slyly narrated "How to Become a Writer or, Have You Earned This Cliché?" (chapter 7), and the bitter wit in Amy Hempel's "San Francisco" (chapter 14).

GOING FURTHER Although much of London's material came from personal experience, some scholars have claimed he purchased plots and ideas from fellow writer Sinclair Lewis. In his first commercially successful novel, *Main Street,* Lewis provides a realistic picture of small-town America, featuring a strong female protagonist.

Writing from Reading

Summarize

1 List all the characters in this story (including Loretta herself) and summarize their impressions of Loretta.

2 Summarize what Loretta actually wishes for herself, based first on the narrator's exposition in the story, then on Loretta's own spoken confessions. Compare and contrast these two conclusions.

Analyze Craft

3 Do you consider the characters in this story to be round or flat? Why? Place them along a spectrum from roundest to flattest, and explain why you have arranged them in that way.

4 Discuss the character of Loretta. Does she change in the course of the story, and in what ways? Who are her antagonists, and what sort of impact do they have on her development?

Analyze Voice

5 This story was published in 1908. How current does it seem a century later, and how does its date affect the credibility of events in the story?

Synthesize Summary and Analysis

6 Consider the dialogue between Ned and Loretta at the end of the story. What characteristics differentiate the two characters' voices? What aspects of their characters lend to the confusion of their argument? Explain how the same confusion the characters feel is extended to the reader.

Interpret the Story

7 Considering the disparity between the narrator's exposition and Loretta's own assertions, and in light of Loretta's agreement to marry Ned and her final statement, do you think Loretta's behavior with Ned is genuine or preconceived? In other words, has she fooled Ned into a proposal? Provide evidence from the story that supports or denies Loretta's own profession that she is "a wicked woman."

Reading for Character

When reading for character, ask yourself how the author characterizes the personality and motivation that make a character behave in a certain way.

Which elements of characterization can you identify?	
	• What does the physical appearance of the character tell you?
	• Does the name of the character reveal anything?
	• How is the character dressed, and what does this reveal?
	• What actions has a character taken that tell you about his or her motivation?
	• How does the character's voice, by means of either internal thoughts or dialogue, emerge on the page, how does that voice "sound," and what does this tell you about the character?

Is the character complex—exhibiting both good and bad traits—and able to change?	• That character is a *round, dynamic* character.
Does the main character exhibit traits that are sympathetic but not heroic in the traditional sense?	• That character is likely an *antihero.*
Does the character represent primarily one characteristic, such as greed or vanity?	• That character is a *flat, stock* character.
What function do the flat characters play in the story?	• A flat character may be used to reveal the hero more clearly, functioning as the hero's *foil.*

Suggestions for Writing about Character

1. Write an argument for or against the usefulness of flat secondary characters in fiction; back up your main point with examples from at least two stories in this chapter.

2. "Who's Irish?" is told in first person, whereas "The Jilting of Granny Weatherall" is told in third person. (See chapter 7 for a discussion of point of view.) How do the two narrators' biases and personalities affect your responses to the other characters and events in the stories?

3. Consider the role of motivation in a story's protagonist as well as in its antagonist. Choose two stories in this chapter and discuss the thoughts, feelings, beliefs, needs, and wants that drive the main characters.

4. Of the characters in the four stories from this chapter, which seems the most real and the roundest to you? Which seems the least real and the flattest? Compare and contrast these two characters, using examples to show what makes your round character round and your flat one flat.

IN late June 1844, after Foster had begun to despair of ever understanding either the fact or the meaning of the disappearance of the river, after a time of ritual cleansing and dreaming, perhaps agoraphobic or maddened by the interweaving of literalisms and metaphors and forms of proof, Foster began throwing his manuscripts into the river. According to a Pawnee called Wolf Finger, who spoke with the historian Henry Lake, Foster would go down naked in the afternoon, wade out into the Niobrara and hurl a fistful of pages into the water, or from the shore he would skip a journal across the surface like a stone. Eventually he threw everything he'd ever written down into the Niobrara River, turned the pack mules out with the Pawnee horses, and left. He went away to the north, "like a surprised grouse whirring off across the prairie."

—from "The Location of the River" by Barry Lopez

6 Setting

"I don't think of the setting for a story as window dressing, or of anecdotal value. I think setting is often part of what determines the nature of the story, and the nature of the characters. So it's very important for me to have characters involved in a place."

Conversation with Barry Lopez, available on video at www.mhhe.com/delbancole

THIS passage sets us down in a specific place on the earth: western Nebraska, on the banks of the Niobrara River. The year is 1844. In this story, wandering historian Benjamin Foster has set out to solve a mystery. Had, as the Pawnee told him, the upper Niobrara truly disappeared the previous summer? As Foster attempts to understand how or whether such an occurrence was possible, he engages more and more deeply with the surrounding landscape and the people who inhabit it—the Pawnee, the Sioux, the Arapaho, the Arikara, and others. Increasingly preoccupied by what he does and does not know, what he can and cannot prove, he abandons the quest, perhaps half-mad, as portrayed in the excerpt at the beginning of the chapter.

SETTING AS PHYSICAL ENVIRONMENT

Consider the variety of settings you have encountered in the stories in this book: a grim view of Dublin in the early twentieth century in Joyce's "Araby," the crowded streets of Cairo in Mahfouz's "The Conjurer Made Off with the Dish," the 1800s in America in a well-appointed home in Chopin's "The Story of an Hour," the checkout counter of a grocery store in Updike's "A&P," and many more. Each **setting**—each particular time and place—comes with its own sights, sounds, and smells. Each creates a set of expectations among readers for the cast of characters they're likely to encounter and the range of events likely to occur in such a setting; little by little we understand the "local" customs described, as well as the rules of appropriate behavior.

In its most basic sense, the term *setting* refers to the time and place in which a story unfolds. The conceptual meanings of time and place can be various in a work of fiction. Time, of course, can refer to the particular time of day and time of year. It can also refer to the era in which a story occurs—in Lopez's story, the midnineteenth century. Setting also includes weather. For example, the season dictates what characters will wear, what they will eat, see, smell, touch, and hear—what challenges of comfort or survival they will face. All these elements make up the physical environment of the story, and each decision the author makes in this regard shapes the story.

In his essay "A Writer's Sense of Place," novelist James D. Houston describes the power of setting when "the place is profoundly felt, as a feature of the narrative that is working on the characters or through the characters or is somehow bearing upon their lives." "Our literature," he continues, "is rich with such works, stories wherein at least part of what's going on is some form of dialogue between a place—whether it be an island or a mountain or a city or a shoreline or a subregion of the continent—and the lives being lived. I look upon this as one more version of the endless dialogue we're all involved in, between the human imagination and the world we find ourselves inhabiting. . . ."

*. . . I love the idea of making
that place come alive
like another person.*

Q & A

*I can feel it in my mind,
and I can pull it out, . . .*

A Conversation on Writing

Barry Lopez

The Role of Setting in a Story

I'm very comfortable writing a story in which a character just moves through a place, because I love the idea of making that place come alive like another person. . . . It's the thing that's outside the self. . . . And it's not until you get outside the self that you can come alive.

Setting in "The Location of the River"

In a story like "The Location of the River," I can go back and remember a time driving cross-country where I just pulled my truck off the road on the Niobrara River, and slept the night there. . . . So somewhere in my tissues is the sound of that river . . . I can feel it in my mind, and I can pull it out, and it's attached to other things, and then it just unfolds in front of me. It's like the story is inside a little thing that happened when I was young and camping. . . . Years go by, and . . . it pulls all of the things out of my history of observation, and it's turned itself into a world. And then that world is where the story unfolds.

An Intimate Conversation

I feel that push in me all the time, when I'm in a place I've never been before, to have a conversation with it. "Who are you? Talk to me." If I can make myself vulnerable to a place, it senses that, and then it starts to talk to you. You have to trust, because trust is the only way to get to vulnerability, and vulnerability is the only way to get to intimacy. And that's what I want when I'm in a place, that intimate conversation with a place.

To watch this entire interview and hear the author read from "The Location of the River," go to **www.mhhe.com/ delbanco1e.**

Among his many achievements, Barry Lopez counts creating a university major—the B.A. in Natural Sciences and the Humanities at Texas Tech University. The major blends the very elements around which Lopez has built his career as he writes about the relationship between human beings and the physical environments they inhabit: how people are shaped, changed, or haunted by a landscape—and how they, in turn, shape the land. Lopez was born in New York (1945) and grew up both there and in California. After earning his bachelor's and graduate degrees from Notre Dame University, Lopez moved to Oregon, where he has lived ever since, devoting himself full-time to writing. His writing, which includes essay, memoir, and fiction, has earned awards such as the Pushcart Prize for both fiction and nonfiction, and his meditation on life in the northern latitudes, *Arctic Dreams,* received the National Book Award for nonfiction in 1986. Lopez also frequently collaborates with people engaged in other arts, such as the composers John Luther Adams and Arvo Pärt, and the illustrator Tom Pohrt. Above all else, Lopez loves the written word; as one of his characters in *Crow and Weasel* (1998), a children's story, says, "Sometimes a person needs a story more than food to stay alive. That is why we put these stories in each other's memory."

RESEARCH ASSIGNMENT Listen to the interview with Barry Lopez and explain what he means when he talks about a story "fighting" you off. Do you relate to this? Why or why not?

AS YOU READ   As you read this story, picture the setting. In what ways is it hospitable and in what ways inhospitable? Does it seem like an inviting place, one you would like to see for yourself? Why or why not?

TIP

FOR INTERACTIVE READING . . . Go through the story and mark all the details of physical setting, including names of towns or other landmarks, plant and animal life, and geographical features. Consult a map to get a feel for the region where the events in the story took place.

The Location of the River (1986)

1 ACCORDING to a journal kept by Benjamin Foster, a historian returning along the Platte River from the deserts of the Great Basin at the time, the spring of 1844 came early to western Nebraska. He recorded the first notes of a horned lark on the sixteenth of February. This unseasonable good weather induced him to stay a few weeks with a band of Pawnee camped just south of the Niobrara River. One morning he volunteered to go out with two men to look for stray horses. They found the horses grazing near an island of oak and ash trees on the prairie, along the edge of the river. When he saw the current and quicksand Foster was glad the horses had not crossed over.

2 On the way back, writes Foster—little of his last journal survives, but some fragments relevant to this incident are preserved—the Pawnee told him that the previous summer the upper Niobrara had disappeared.

3 At first Foster took this for a figurative statement about a severe drought, but the other Pawnee told him, no, the Niobrara had not run dry—in fact, the spring of 1843 had been very wet. It disappeared. That Foster took this information seriously, that he did not treat it with skepticism or derision, was characteristic of him.

4 The Pawnee, he goes to say, did not associate the disappearance of the river with any one particular phenomenon (Foster, I should say, was a confidant; he spoke fluent Pawnee and I'm sure they felt he was both knowledgeable and trustworthy); they attributed its disappearance to a sort of willful irritation, which they found amusing. They told Foster that the earth, the rivers, did not belong to men but were only to be used by them, and that the earth, though it was pleased with the Pawnee, was very disappointed in the white man. It suited the earth's purpose, they said, to suddenly abandon a river for a while, to confound men who were too dependent on such things always being there.

5 Foster thought this explanation narrow and self-serving and told the Pawnee so. But they were adamant. Foster writes that he himself was increasingly at a loss to understand what had happened, but he had been among Indians long enough to appreciate their sense of humor and to know their strength for allegory. He pointed out to them that if the river had shifted course or disappeared, the Pawnee would be as

affected by it as the white men; but the Pawnee said, no, this was not so, because they saw things like this all the time and were not bothered by them.

6   It is difficult to fathom what happened to the river or to Foster either, once he concluded, as he apparently did, that the Pawnee were literally correct, that sometime during the summer of 1843 the upper reaches of the Niobrara River, above the present town of Marshland and westward into Wyoming, did vanish for four or five months.

7   An initial thought, he wrote, was that the people he was camped with were not Pawnee. He thought they might be a little too far north—in Sioux or possibly Arapaho country. Even though they spoke, ate, dressed, and even played at sleight-of-hand like Pawnee, they could be somebody else, with a cavalier regard for local truth. In others of his papers Foster writes about a rite of imitation in which a band of people from one tribe, Arikara, for example, would imitate a band from some other tribe for long periods of time, fifteen years or more. They began doing this on the northern plains in the 1820s, imitating each other in exacting detail, as a form of amusement. There was no way Foster could be certain he was not among Oglala Sioux pretending to be Pawnee and playing the Long Joke, fooling a white man and making at the same time a joke about their star-gazing neighbors the Pawnee who might not know what was going on at their very feet. But he had been intimate with the Pawnee; after extensive inquiry he believed he was among them, not someone else.

8   It appears Foster tried systematically to establish a basis for belief in the river's disappearance, and pursued this course with increasing determination, as though he intuited the truth of the thing but didn't know how to demonstrate it. I don't know why, but I feel that, by that point, the man had begun to wonder at all he had seen in his life, and what of any of it would be believed.

9   The possibility that the river had simply changed its channel seemed plausible to him, but after reconnoitering extensively through the hills he discounted it. And the river had not switched channels or run dry, it was repeatedly emphasized to him, it had vanished. There were no willows on the islands. There were no islands. There were no mud flats, no smooth places even in the sand, no abandoned channels, nothing. With the aid of survey maps made in 1840, and a theodolite, compass, artificial mercury horizon, and other instruments he borrowed from Fort Laramie some hundred miles to the southwest, Foster tried to compare the present location of the river with its location in November 1840, when the maps were made. The disagreements were too insignificant to have meaning, however, what one would have to expect given the crudeness of tools and methods in those days.

Foster subsequently was unable to find any permanent resident to question, or to learn anything from men garrisoned at Fort Laramie or Fort Platte to the south. He rode as far north as the Sioux Agency in South Dakota looking for people to talk to. Exhausting all these traditional methods, he turned finally to something less conventional. It had long been his personal belief (and he was bolstered in this by some of those with whom he lived) that the history of the earth was revealed anew each spring in the shapes of the towering cumulus clouds that moved over the country from the north and west. If a man were blessed, were *wakan*, and had the patience and watched from the time of the first thunderstorm until the first prairie grass fire, he would see it. There was no sequence; the events unfurled in an order of their own, so Foster prepared himself for a long vigil. One April afternoon, seventeen days after he had begun, he saw on the horizon with the aid of an interpreter, as clear as the blades of blue grama grass and his moccasined feet before him, the fading and disappearance of the upper Niobrara River in the clouds. He judged the time of year to be late June.

This must have been slightly disquieting for Foster, living in two worlds as he did, lying there on his back under the inexorable movement of clouds, feeling the earth turn under him, thinking what he did and did not know, could and could not prove. On the basis of what is a man to be believed?

There is something else here, too. In a letter to Foster dated July 7, 1831, the American explorer and painter George Catlin remarks on his terror of open space in Nebraska. While on foot in the tallgrass prairie, he and his party used a sextant and chronometer, as though at sea. I don't know whether having underlined this passage in Catlin's letter (it survives) means Foster's own perception of the prairie was oceanic—people later spoke of the "coasts of Nebraska"—or whether on his own he had always felt unsettled by the unbounded space, as he might particularly have been that spring.

3 THE disappearance of the upper Niobrara might never have come to light at all had it not been for Foster's breakdown at that point and, much later, the interest of a graduate student at Idaho State University called Anton Breverton. Breverton tried to document Foster's career in the west in his history thesis and he tried especially to clarify this one episode on the Niobrara. I lost touch with Breverton some years ago. He is either living today in obscurity, possibly in Europe, or he has passed on. His thesis, I am sorry to say, is also unavailable. The archival librarian at Pocatello believes his was among some twenty theses lost when the library transferred its collections to a new building in 1948. I read Breverton's thesis at his request when it came out, made a few notes, and returned it. Reconstructing Foster's life had been a preoccupation of mine, too, since coming into possession of the notes and journals he failed to destroy that spring.

I imagine Foster, a brilliant man much troubled by the destruction of native cultures, simply fell prey to a final madness.

4 Breverton read extensively in the literature of western Nebraska, in science and history, from both native and white sources, trying to find some hint of explanation for the disappearance of the river or what was meant by the Pawnee who told Foster this. He combed emigrants' journals, reports from Smithsonian, the Carnegie Institution—all fruitless. He even read regional novels, including those of Mari Sandoz, going so far as to go to New York and interview Miss Sandoz. An unusually sensitive woman who grew up in that country at the turn of the century, Sandoz had been particularly attentive to the stories of the region. But Breverton was unable to corroborate any part of it. He finally left it out of his thesis.

15 I understand a colleague of Breverton, irritated by the entire issue, nearly enraged in fact, secured some military funding to conduct a soil analysis throughout Dawes, Sioux, and Box Butte counties in Nebraska where the river flows, but I do not know what became of this information. I myself have communicated with the Pawnee Tribal Council, with friends among the Arapaho, and with faculty at the University of Nebraska who could be expected to add something, but to no avail.

16 FOR my part, I do not think the river ever disappeared. I imagine Foster, a brilliant man much troubled by the destruction of native cultures, simply fell prey to a final madness.

17 A catalytic event occurred in Foster's life in 1808 when he was living in a large Chippewa village near the present town of Bayfield, Wisconsin. Representatives of the Shawnee Prophet had come among them and instructed the people to extinguish all their fires, to rekindle fire in the old way with sticks, and to never let it go out. They said the old lifeways would return, that the prophet himself would bring back the dead. The psychologically depressed Chippewa enthusiastically adopted the beliefs of these impassioned young men. A demonstration of allegiance they required was that of throwing away one's personal possessions. As an eleven-year-old boy, Foster saw the shore of Lake Superior lined with the medicine bundles of a thousand men, all washed up by the waves. These small bundles, decorated with trade beads, strips of bright cloth, feathers, and quill work, must have been gathered up by someone (perhaps even Foster) and taken somewhere, for one morning the beaches were empty.

18 From this time forward, I am sure Foster was possessed of the idea of recording the beliefs of native tribes before they fell victim to whites or to the panic of their own spiritual leaders. This much is clearly implied by a boyhood friend of Foster who wrote about the incident on the lake in *A Narrative of the Captivity and Adventures of John Tanner*. (It is further substantiated in the private papers of W. W. Warren in the manuscript collection of the Minnesota Historical Society. You can appreciate perhaps the difficulty of piecing together Foster's career, in the wake of the destruction of all his notes.)

19 Foster spent the next thirty years with six or seven different tribes. He is occasionally mentioned in the correspondence of Ogden, Sublette, and others as a translator and Indian expert of exceptional skill. He would apparently live for years with a tribe before moving on. Though loath to do it, he deposited this steady accumulation of field notes periodically at various American and British trading posts for safekeeping, intending one day to collect them all. This is what he was doing in 1844 when he was waylaid by the Pawnee and good weather. He had eleven pack mules with him at the time, all of them burdened with manuscripts. His writings were more detailed, complete, inclusive of fantastic incident, rigorous, and perceptive (to judge from the scraps) than anything Fontenelle, Maximilian, Ruxton, Stewart, or any of the rest ever wrote down. He was en route to

Kansas City, where the great trading family of Chouteau had offered him money for publication. The collection would have equalled in scope and importance the collected volumes on the west edited by Reuben Thwaites some sixty years later. It is one of the great tragedies of American history that he did not arrive and that his manuscripts were ruined.

20 In late June 1844, after Foster had begun to despair of ever understanding either the fact or the meaning of the disappearance of the river, after a time of ritual cleansing and dreaming, perhaps agoraphobic or maddened by the interweaving of literalisms and metaphors and forms of proof, Foster began throwing his manuscripts into the river. According to a Pawnee called

> Eventually he threw everything he'd ever written down into the Niobrara River . . .

Wolf Finger, who spoke with the historian Henry Lake, Foster would go down naked in the afternoon, wade out into the Niobrara and hurl a fistful of pages into the water, or from the shore he would skip a journal across the surface like a stone. Eventually he threw everything he'd ever written down into the Niobrara River, turned the pack mules out with the Pawnee horses, and left. He went away to the north, "like a surprised grouse whirring off across the prairie."

21 WHAT was left of these documents came into my hands though my father, a tax assessor. He found them in a barn near Lusk, Wyoming, in 1901. Among them— there was about enough to fill one cardboard box— was the first page of an essay entitled "Studying the Indian." I have no idea of the date. In the first paragraph Foster says, "I have been among the Absarokee when they left the battlefield like sparrows. I have watched Navajo men run down antelope on foot and smother their last breath in a handful of corn pollen. One bad summer in the Desert of the Black Rocks I saw Shoshoni women go out at sunset and because they were starving call in the quail. I have heard the soft syllables of the Arapaho tongue and the choking sound of the Kiowa and the hissing Cheyenne sounds. A woman called Reaches Deep taught me how to dance, and once I danced until I entered the sun. But already in the

fall of 1826, in Judith Basin, a Piegan called Coyote in the Camp had told me I was learning everything wrong. . . ." Foster goes on, a few words, the rest is washed out and sun bleached.

22 In an attempt to understand what little Foster had written down about the disappearance of the Niobrara (and with a sense of compassion for him), I visited that part of the state in 1963. I stayed in a small hotel, the Plainview, in the town of Box Butte.

I had with me all of Foster's water-stained notes, which I had spread around the room and was examining again for perhaps the hundredth time. During the night a tremendous rainstorm broke over the prairie. The Niobrara threatened to flood and I was awakened by the motel operator. I drove across the river—in the cone of my headlights I could see the fast brown water surging against the bridge supports—and spent the rest of the night in my car on high ground, at some distance from the town, in some hills the name of which I do not remember. In the morning I became confused on farm roads and was unable to find my way back to the river. In desperation I stopped at a place I recognized having been at the day before and proceeded from there on foot toward the river, until I became lost in the fields themselves. I met a man on a tractor who told me the river had never come over in that direction. Ever. And to get away.

23 I have not been back in that country since.

THERE are many stories in this book in which landscape plays a significant role in the meaning of the story. If you enjoyed Barry Lopez's "The Location of the River," you may also enjoy Leslie Marmon Silko's "The Man to Send Rain Clouds" (chapter 12).

GOING FURTHER   Barry Lopez has spent a large part of his career writing about the relationship between landscape—setting—and narrative or story making. His award-winning nonfiction work *Arctic Dreams* was a major step in this direction. *Home Ground,* an anthology he edited with his wife, Debra Gwartney, offers descriptive definitions by dozens of American writers on the various elements of landscape, such as arroyo, swale, muskeg, and so forth.

Writing from Reading

Summarize

1 Compare and contrast the various theories of the river's disappearance—the Native American views and the views of the white researchers: Foster, Breverton, and the narrator.

Analyze Craft

2 Most of this story is related almost as a report. How does this affect the information we receive about the setting? Do we see the place as a scientist would, or as an artist or sightseeing traveler might view it?

Analyze Voice

3 Who is the narrator of this story? When and how does the narrator become an active participant? What is the role of this narrator?

4 Consider the narrator's descriptions of setting compared to Foster's. Discuss the fundamental differences and similarities between the narrator and Foster based on what they see.

Synthesize Summary and Analysis

5 Consider the comparison between open space in Nebraska and the open sea. How does George Catlin's use of a sextant and chronometer in the tallgrass prairie—and Foster's interest in this story—contribute to the story's setting, characterizations, and theme? What effect does this extended metaphor have on you as a reader?

6 List all the things in the story that are lost. Also note the people who get lost or lose their way. Based on your findings, discuss how "loss" operates as a theme in "The Location of the River."

Interpret the Story

7 Consider the passage from the first page of Foster's essay "Studying the Indian," where he is told by an Indian that he has learned everything wrong. Compare this passage to the narrator's study of Foster in the preceding pages. By including the passage, what is Lopez suggesting about the narrator's conclusions?

CONTINUED FROM PAGE 143

SETTING AS SOCIAL ENVIRONMENT

Growing out of the physical environment of a story is something more various called the **social environment.** Elements such as the era and location combined with a character's living and working conditions make up the social environment. To understand social environment, consider the challenges and community being portrayed in any work of fiction. For example, in Lopez's story, Foster is a white man and an historian who is performing research among native peoples on the Great Plains of Wyoming

"I think one of the things that people read for is gossip, curiosity. They want to find out how things work. They want to understand what it's like to be somewhere." Conversation with William Kittredge

and Nebraska in 1844. His physical environment consists of the great, uncharted outdoors, where he is often alone. When he is not alone, the Pawnee and Sioux, Arapaho and Arikara are his companions. Cultural differences, however, make it unclear how much trust exists in these relationships. Thus, Foster inhabits a social environment characterized by a particular kind of isolation.

SETTING AND MOOD

Writers approach setting the way designers use sets for plays or films. Each object is placed deliberately in order to create a particular effect. Consider the following excerpt from the 1957 short story "Wine" by British author Doris Lessing.

> *A man and woman walked toward the boulevard from a little hotel in a side street.*
>
> *The trees were still leafless, black, cold; but the fine twigs were swelling toward spring, so that looking upward it was with an expectation of the first glimmering greenness. Yet everything was calm, and the sky was a calm, classic blue.*
>
> *The couple drifted slowly along. Effort, after days of laziness, seemed impossible; and almost at once they turned into a café and sank down, as if exhausted, in the glass-walled space that was thrust forward into the street.*
>
> *The place was empty. People were seeking the midday meal in the restaurants. Not all: that morning crowds had been demonstrating, a procession had just passed, and its straggling end could still be seen. The sounds of violence, shouted slogans and singing, no longer absorbed the din of Paris traffic; but it was these sounds that had roused the couple from sleep.*

Lessing places the couple in Paris, conjuring up images of romance. They are there in the spring, so we have the promise of new life and the possibility of a new beginning. It is midday, so they are people of leisure, at least at the moment. These details lend a flavor, and the setting sets a mood. These details also hint at plot developments—the demonstrators in the background, the possibility that something is about to change.

SETTING AND CHARACTER

A setting, however, can play a bigger role than simply serving as backdrop and mood. A character's location often shapes his or her identity. A character who lives on a fifty-five-acre farm, for instance, will develop quite differently from a character who takes a crowded subway to work. In James Joyce's novel *A Portrait of the Artist As a Young Man* (1916), the protagonist Stephen Dedalus defines himself as a student, an Irish citizen, and a citizen of the world as he places himself at the top of the list he jots down in his geography book:

> *Stephen Dedalus*
> *Class of Elements*
> *Clongowes Wood College*
> *Sallins*
> *County Kildare*
> *Ireland*
> *Europe*
> *The World*
> *The Universe*

The setting can also explicitly reflect and symbolize the inner lives of characters, as in the opening passage of Edgar Allan Poe's "The Fall of the House of Usher."

> *During the whole of a dull, dark, and soundless day in the autumn of the year, when the clouds hung oppressively low in the heavens, I had been passing alone, on horseback, through a singularly dreary tract of country; and at length found myself, as the shades of the evening drew on, within view of the melancholy House of Usher. . . . I looked upon the scene before me—upon the mere house, and the simple landscape features of the domain—upon the bleak walls—upon the vacant eye-like windows—upon a few rank sedges—and upon a few white trunks of decayed trees—with an utter depression of soul which I can compare to no earthly sensation more properly than to the after-dream of the reveller upon opium—the bitter lapse into everyday life—the hideous dropping off of the veil.*

In this passage, Poe's scene includes lowering clouds and festering vegetation around a "melancholy" mansion, establishing a mood of intense gloom and foreboding. The images shape the reader's experience of the story—showing us not only where it takes place but also how it feels for characters to occupy that space. Just imagine for a moment how the story would change if it opened by saying, "During the whole of a bright, light, and bird-song-filled day in the spring of the year, when no single cloud appeared in the sky, I had been passing . . ." Poe's word choices—"dull, dark," "oppressively low," "dreary tract of country," "melancholy," "bleak," "vacant," and so on—create a sense of dread, foreshadowing terrors to come. More than this, the images reflect the distraught interior life and psyche of his characters, making their flaws and fallibilities

REGIONAL WRITERS

Critics sometimes refer to authors whose work tends to focus on a particular setting and its characters, customs, dialect, and topography as *regional writers*, a term historically used in a negative fashion. Texas writer Larry McMurtry, one of the most popular American writers of his generation, once joked in protest about the way in which Southern writers especially were defined as "regional" and thus put in a pigeonhole by reviewers. He had T-shirts made that said "Regional Writer" and passed them out to his friends. Today, we no longer object to writers merely because of their ties to a particular region. In fact, it's almost impossible *not* to have such ties or a sense of preferred location.

external. Thus, the physical structure of the mansion and the surrounding landscape become a symbol of the disintegration of the family within—the "ancient," "time-honored" Ushers. Even the name Usher stands as a sign pointing to the transitional nature of life and the house stands as a gateway to another world (for more on symbols and symbolism, see chapter 10).

Finally, the setting can itself be a character. Landscape can entwine with personality so that it expresses the soul of the narrator, as it does in Lopez's story. The Great Plains are a vast, unknowable presence baffling Foster and the others who follow him in trying to understand it. Together, the setting, characters, and plot express the writer's feeling about the impossibility of knowing anything with certainty in this vast world.

SETTING IN CONTEXT

Writers locate their stories by selecting particular details that transport us to new places as well as to new ways of seeing familiar ones. As you read, notice how the quite dissimilar stories in this chapter develop from the details of the various landscapes described. The best way to understand the role setting plays with regard to mood, character, or theme is to ask yourself, "Why has the author chosen this particular setting? What would change if the story were set elsewhere?"

The four stories in this chapter explore the ways in which settings shape and reflect mood, character, or theme. Each was composed in America; one in the nineteenth century, the others in the twentieth. There the similarities end. As we've discussed, Barry Lopez's story takes place in the vast, uninhabited lands of the Great Plains. Edgar Allan Poe's story, by contrast, is *interior;* we enter an isolated and decaying mansion. Eudora Welty also confines us to an interior landscape: the conflict-ridden house of a family in the rural South. Bernard Malamud conjures the world of a rabbinical student and a matchmaker in the Yiddish culture of uptown Manhattan and the Bronx.

Together, these stories demonstrate just how much the experience of living can differ from region to region. We should notice also the paradox that despite the differences in time and place and social environment, the problems these characters wrestle with are familiar. These stories, then, help us understand that life anywhere is, simply, life lived everywhere.

Edgar Allan Poe (1809–1849)

Edgar Allan Poe was born Edgar Arnold Poe in Boston. His parents were actors, and both died by 1811, leaving him orphaned. He spent much of his youth in Virginia under the care of John Allan, a tobacco merchant. Allan sent Poe to college at the University of Virginia, but when Poe turned to gambling, Allan withdrew his support, forcing Poe to drop out in 1826. That same year, Poe published his first book of poetry, *Tamerlane and Other Poems.* In the years that followed, Poe wore many hats. He briefly attended West Point Military Academy and served briefly in the U.S. Army. In 1836 he married his thirteen-year-old cousin, Virginia Clem. Editing and contributing to the *Southern Literary Messenger, Graham's Magazine,* and other publications, Poe also wrote book reviews for various periodicals. He published his own writing in popular magazines such as *The Broadway Journal,* and he dreamed of founding his own literary journal. Poe started out as a poet (his most famous poem is "The Raven"), and he did publish one short novel, *The Narrative of Arthur Gordon Pym* (1838), but he mostly devoted himself to short fiction. Today, he is best known for his horror stories (including "The Fall of the House of Usher," "The Masque of the

Red Death," "The Black Cat," "The Tell-Tale Heart," and many others). Critics consider Poe to have invented the genre of the detective mystery with such stories as "The Purloined Letter" and "The Murders in the Rue Morgue."

In his horror stories, Poe uses lush language to render setting in great detail, creating an atmosphere of terror and, often, despair. His unsettling plots rely on suspense and the revelation of terrible secrets, but the settings, as perceived by troubled narrators who are drawn into the horror as actors or observers, are what give these stories their dark and bizarre flavor. In the tale that follows, "The Fall of the House of Usher," a house takes on the literal and symbolic importance of a main character; in such fiction, setting both drives and embodies the plot.

Poe died in Baltimore in 1849 when he was forty years old. The circumstances of his death were mysterious and have been the source of much speculation. His official obituary reported only "a congestion of the brain."

AS YOU READ   As you read, notice the way you enter the world of the story and the interior of the house with the narrator, relying on him for description and interpretation. Does the setting overshadow the characters and/or the plot? How does it make you feel?

The Fall of the House of Usher (1839)

Son cœur est un luth suspendu;
Sitôt qu'on le touche il résonne.[1]

De Béranger

1 DURING the whole of a dull, dark, and soundless day in the autumn of the year, when the clouds hung oppressively low in the heavens, I had been passing alone, on horseback, through a singularly dreary tract of country; and at length found myself, as the shades of evening drew on, within view of the melancholy House of Usher. I know not how it was—but, with the first glimpse of the building, a sense of insufferable gloom pervaded my spirit. I say insufferable; for the feeling was unrelieved by any of that half-pleasurable, because poetic, sentiment, with which the mind usually receives even the sternest natural images of the desolate or terrible. I looked upon the scene before me—upon the mere house, and the simple landscape features of the domain—upon the bleak walls—upon the vacant eye-like windows—and upon a few rank sedges—and upon a few white trunks of decayed trees—with an utter depression of soul which I can compare to no earthly sensation more properly than to the after-dream of the reveller upon opium—the bitter lapse into everyday life—the hideous dropping off of the veil. There was iciness, a sinking, a sickening of the heart—an unredeemed

---

[1] "His heart is a lute hanging (in air) / when touched it resonates."

dreariness of thought which no goading of the imagination could torture into aught of the sublime. What was it—I paused to think—what was it that so unnerved me in the contemplation of the House of Usher? It was a mystery all insoluble; nor could I grapple with the shadowy fancies that crowded upon me as I pondered. I was forced to fall back upon the unsatisfactory conclusion, that while, beyond doubt, there *are* combinations of very simple natural objects which have the power of thus affecting us, still the analysis of this power lies among considerations beyond our depth. It was possible, I reflected, that a mere different arrangement of the particulars of the scene, of the details of the picture, would be sufficient to modify, or perhaps to annihilate its capacity for sorrowful impression; and, acting upon this idea, I reined my horse to the precipitous brink of a black and lurid tarn that lay in unruffled luster by the dwelling, and gazed down—but with a shudder even more thrilling than before—upon the remodelled and inverted images of the gray sedge, and the ghastly tree-stems, and the vacant and eye-like windows.

2 Nevertheless, in this mansion of gloom I now proposed to myself a sojourn of some weeks. Its proprietor, Roderick Usher, had been one of my boon companions in boyhood; but many years had elapsed since our last meeting. A letter, however, had lately reached me in a distant part of the country—a letter from him—which, in its wildly importunate nature, had admitted of no other than a personal reply. The MS. gave evidence of nervous agitation. The writer spoke of acute bodily illness—of a mental disorder which oppressed him—and of an earnest desire to see me, as his best, and indeed his only personal friend, with a view of attempting, by the cheerfulness of my society, some alleviation of his malady. It was the manner in which all this, and much more, was said—it was the apparent *heart* that went with his request—which allowed me no room for hesitation; and I accordingly obeyed forthwith what I still considered a very singular summons.

3 Although, as boys, we had been even intimate associates, yet I really knew little of my friend. His reserve had been always excessive and habitual. I was aware, however, that his very ancient family had been noted, time out of mind, for a peculiar sensibility of temperament, displaying itself, through long ages, in many works of exalted art, and manifested, of late, in repeated deeds of munificent yet unobtrusive char-

… with the first glimpse of the building, a sense of insufferable gloom pervaded my spirit.

ity, as well as in a passionate devotion to the intricacies, perhaps even more than to the orthodox and easily recognizable beauties, of musical science. I had learned, too, the very remarkable fact, that the stem of the Usher race, all time-honored as it was, had put forth, at no period, any enduring branch; in other words, that the entire family lay in the direct line of descent, and had always, with very trifling and very temporary variation, so lain. It was this deficiency, I considered, while running over in thought the perfect keeping of the character of the premises with the accredited character of the people, and while speculating upon the possible influence which the one, in the long lapse of centuries, might have exercised upon the other—it was this deficiency, perhaps, of collateral issue, and the consequent undeviating transmission, from sire to son, of the patrimony with the name, which had, at length, so identified the two as to merge the original title of the estate in the quaint and equivocal appellation of the "House of Usher"—an appellation which seemed to include, in the minds of the peasantry who used it, both the family and the family mansion.

I have said that the sole effect of my somewhat childish experiment—that of looking down within the tarn—had been to deepen the first singular impression. There can be no doubt that the consciousness of the rapid increase of my superstition—for why should I not so term it?—served mainly to accelerate the increase itself. Such, I have long known, is the paradoxical law of all sentiments having terror as a basis. And it might have been for this reason only, that, when I again uplifted my eyes to the house itself, from its image in the pool, there grew in my mind a strange fancy—a fancy so ridiculous, indeed, that I but mention it to show the vivid force of the sensations which oppressed me. I had so worked upon my imagination as really to believe that about the whole mansion and domain there hung an atmosphere peculiar to themselves and their immediate vicinity—an atmosphere which had no affinity with the air of heaven, but which had reeked up from the decayed trees, and the gray wall, and the silent tarn—a pestilent and mystic vapor, dull, sluggish, faintly discernible, and leaden-hued.

Shaking off from my spirit what *must* have been a dream, I scanned more narrowly the real aspect of the building. Its principal feature seemed to be that of an excessive antiquity. The discoloration of ages had been great. Minute fungi overspread the whole exte-

4

5

rior, hanging in a fine tangled web-work from the eaves. Yet all this was apart from any extraordinary dilap-idation. No portion of the masonry had fallen; and there appeared to be a wild inconsistency between its still perfect adaptation of parts, and the crumbling condition of the individ-ual stones. In this there was much that reminded me of the specious totality of old wood-work which has rotted for long years in some neglected vault, with no disturbance from the breath of the external air. Beyond this indication of extensive decay, however, the fabric gave little token of instability. Perhaps the eye of a scrutinizing observer might have discovered a barely perceptible fissure, which, extending from the roof of the building in front, made its way down the wall in a zigzag direction, until it became lost in the sullen waters of the tarn.

Noticing these things, I rode over a short cause-way to the house. A servant in waiting took my horse, and I entered the Gothic archway of the hall. A va-let, of stealthy step, thence conducted me, in silence, through many dark and intricate passages in my progress to the *studio* of his master. Much that I en-countered on the way contributed, I know not how, to heighten the vague sentiments of which I have already spoken. While the objects around me—while the carv-ings of the ceilings, the somber tapestries of the walls, the ebon blackness of the floors, and the phantasma-goric armorial trophies which rattled as I strode, were but matters to which, or to such as which, I had been accustomed from my infancy—while I hesitated not to acknowledge how familiar was all this—I still won-dered to find how unfamiliar were the fancies which ordinary images were stirring up. On one of the stair-cases, I met the physician of the family. His counte-nance, I thought, wore a mingled expression of low cunning and perplexity. He accosted me with trepida-tion and passed on. The valet now threw open a door and ushered me into the presence of his master.

The room in which I found myself was very large and lofty. The windows were long, narrow, and pointed, and at so vast a distance from the black oaken floor as to be altogether inaccessible from within. Feeble gleams of encrimsoned light made their way through the trellised panes, and served to render sufficiently distinct the more prominent objects around; the eye, however, struggled in vain to reach the remoter angles of the chamber, or the recesses of the vaulted and fret-ted ceiling. Dark draperies hung upon the walls. The general furniture was profuse, comfortless, antique, and tat-tered. Many books and musical instruments lay scattered about, but failed to give any vitality to the scene. I felt that I breathed an atmosphere of sorrow. An air of stern, deep, and irredeem-able gloom hung over and per-vaded all.

Upon my entrance, Usher arose from a sofa on which he had been lying at full length, and greeted me with a vivacious warmth which had much in it, I at first thought, of an overdone cordiality—of the constrained effort of the *ennuyé* man of the world. A glance, however, at his countenance, convinced me of his perfect sincerity. We sat down; and for some moments, while he spoke not, I gazed upon him with a feeling half of pity, half of awe. Surely, a man had never before so terribly altered, in so brief a period, as had Roderick Usher! It was with difficulty that I could bring myself to admit the identity of the wan being before me with the companion of my early boy-hood. Yet the character of his face had been at all times remarkable. A cadaverousness of complexion; an eye large, liquid, and luminous beyond comparison; lips somewhat thin and very pallid, but of a surpassingly beautiful curve; a nose of a delicate Hebrew model, but with a breadth of nostril unusual in similar for-mations; a finely moulded chin, speaking, in its want of prominence, of a want of moral energy; hair of a more than web-like softness and tenuity; these fea-tures, with an inordinate expansion above the regions of the temple, made up altogether a countenance not easily to be forgotten. And now in the mere exag-geration of the prevailing character of these features, and of the expression they were wont to convey, lay so much of change that I doubted to whom I spoke. The now ghastly pallor of the skin, and the now mi-raculous luster of the eye, above all things startled and even awed me. The silken hair, too, had been suf-fered to grow all unheeded, and as, in its wild gossa-mer texture, it floated rather than fell about the face, I could not, even with effort, connect its arabesque expression with any idea of simple humanity.

In the manner of my friend I was at once struck with an incoherence—an inconsistency; and I soon found this to arise from a series of feeble and futile struggles to overcome an habitual trepidancy—an ex-cessive nervous agitation. For something of this na-ture I had indeed been prepared, no less by his letter, than by reminiscences of certain boyish traits, and by conclusions deduced from his peculiar physical conformation and temperament. His action was alternatively vivacious and sullen. His voice varied rapidly from a tremulous indecision (when the animal spirits seemed utterly in abeyance) to that of energetic concision—that abrupt, weighty, unhurried, and hollow-sounding enunciation—that leaden, self-balanced and perfectly modulated guttural utterance, which may be observed in the lost drunkard, or the irreclaimable eater of opium, during the periods of his most intense excitement.

10   It was thus that he spoke of the object of my visit, of his earnest desire to see me, and of the solace he expected me to afford him. He entered, at some length, into what he conceived to be the nature of his malady. It was, he said, a constitutional and a family evil, and one for which he despaired to find a remedy—a mere nervous affection, he immediately added, which would undoubtedly soon pass off. It displayed itself in a host of unnatural sensations. Some of these, as he detailed them, interested and bewildered me; although, perhaps, the terms, and the general manner of the narration had their weight. He suffered much from a morbid acuteness of the senses; the most insipid food was alone endurable; he could wear only garments of certain texture; the odors of all flowers were oppressive; his eyes were tortured by even a faint light; and there were but peculiar sounds, and these from stringed instruments, which did not inspire him with horror.

The disease of the lady Madeline
had long baffled the skill of her physicians.

11   To an anomalous species of terror I found him a bounded slave. "I shall perish," said he, "I *must* perish in this deplorable folly. Thus, thus, and not otherwise, shall I be lost. I dread the events of the future, not in themselves but in their results. I shudder at the thought of any, even the most trivial, incident, which may operate upon this intolerable agitation of soul. I have, indeed, no abhorrence of danger, except in its absolute effect—in terror. In this unnerved—in this pitiable condition—I feel that the period will sooner or later arrive when I must abandon life and reason together, in some struggle with the grim phantasm, FEAR."

12   I learned, moreover, at intervals, and through broken and equivocal hints, another singular feature of his mental condition. He was enchained by certain superstitious impressions in regard to the dwelling which he tenanted, and whence, for many years, he had never ventured forth—in regard to an influence whose supposititious force was conveyed in terms too shadowy here to be re-stated—an influence which some peculiarities in the mere form and substance of his family mansion, had, by dint of long sufferance, he said, obtained over his spirit—an effect which the *physique* of the gray walls and turrets, and of the dim tarn into which they all looked down, had, at length, brought about upon the *morale* of his existence.

He admitted, however, although with hesitation, that much of the peculiar gloom which thus afflicted him could be traced to a more natural and far more palpable origin—to the severe and long-continued illness—indeed to the evidently approaching dissolution—of a tenderly beloved sister—his sole companion for long years—his last and only relative on earth. "Her decease," he said, with a bitterness which I can never forget, "would leave him (him the hopeless and the frail) the last of the ancient race of the Ushers." While he spoke, the lady Madeline (for so was she called) passed slowly through a remote portion of the apartment, and, without having noticed my presence, disappeared. I regarded her with an utter astonishment not unmingled with dread—and yet I found it impossible to account for such feelings. A sensation of stupor oppressed me, as my eyes followed her retreating steps. When a door, at length, closed upon her, my glance sought instinctively and eagerly the countenance of the brother—but he had buried his face in his hands, and I could only perceive that a far more than ordinary wanness had overspread the emaciated fingers through which trickled many passionate tears.

The disease of the lady Madeline had long baffled the skill of her physicians. A settled apathy, a gradual wasting away of the person, and frequent although transient affections of a partially cataleptical character, were the unusual diagnosis. Hitherto she had steadily borne up against the pressure of her malady, and had not betaken herself finally to bed; but, on the closing in of the evening of my arrival at the house, she succumbed (as her brother told me at night with inexpressible agitation) to the prostrating power of the destroyer; and I learned that the glimpse I had obtained of her person would thus probably be the last I should obtain—that the lady, at least while living, would be seen by me no more.

For several days ensuing, her name was unmentioned by either Usher or myself: and during this period I was busied in earnest endeavors to alleviate the melancholy of my friend. We painted and read together;

or I listened, as if in a dream, to the wild improvisations of his speaking guitar. And thus, as a closer and still closer intimacy admitted me more unreservedly into the recesses of his spirit, the more bitterly did I perceive the futility of all attempt at cheering a mind from which darkness, as if an inherent positive quality, poured forth upon all objects of the moral and physical universe, in one unceasing radiation of gloom.

I shall ever bear about me a memory of the many solemn hours I thus spent alone with the master of the House of Usher. Yet I should fail in any attempt to convey an idea of the exact character of the studies, or of the occupations, in which he involved me, or led me the way. An excited and highly distempered ideality threw a sulphureous luster over all. His long improvised dirges will ring forever in my ears. Among other things, I hold painfully in mind a certain singular perversion and amplification of the wild air of the last waltz of Von Weber. From the paintings over which his elaborate fancy brooded, and which grew, touch by touch, into vaguenesses at which I shuddered the more thrillingly, because I shuddered knowing not why;—from these paintings (vivid as their images now are before me) I would in vain endeavor to educe more than a small portion which should lie within the compass of merely written words. By the utter simplicity, by the nakedness of his designs, he arrested and over-awed attention. If ever mortal painted an idea, that mortal was Roderick Usher. For me at least—in the circumstances then surrounding me—there arose out of the pure abstractions which the hypochondriac contrived to throw upon his canvas, an intensity of intolerable awe, no shadow of which felt I ever yet in the contemplation of the certainly glowing yet too concrete reveries of Fuseli.

One of the phantasmagoric conceptions of my friend, partaking not so rigidly of the spirit of abstraction, may be shadowed forth, although feebly, in words. A small picture presented the interior of an immensely long and rectangular vault or tunnel, with low walls, smooth, white, and without interruption or device. Certain accessory points of the design served well to convey the idea that this excavation lay at an exceeding depth below the surface of the earth. No outlet was observed in any portion of its vast extent, and no torch, or other artificial source of light was discernible; yet a flood of intense rays rolled throughout, and bathed the whole in a ghastly and inappropriate splendor.

I have just spoken of that morbid condition of the auditory nerve which rendered all music intolerable to the sufferer, with the exception of certain effects of stringed instruments. It was, perhaps, the narrow limits to which he thus confined himself upon the guitar, which gave birth, in great measure, to the fantastic character of his performances. But the fervid *facility* of his *impromptus* could not be so accounted for. They must have been, and were, in the notes, as well as in the words of his wild fantasias (for he not unfrequently accompanied himself with rhymed verbal improvisations), the result of that intense mental collectedness and concentration to which I have previously alluded as observable only in particular moments of the highest artificial excitement. The words of one of these rhapsodies I have easily remembered. I was, perhaps, the more forcibly impressed with it, as he gave it, because, in the under or mystic current of its meaning, I fancied that I perceived, and for the first time, a full consciousness on the part of Usher, of the tottering of his lofty reason upon her throne. The verses, which were entitled "The Haunted Palace," ran very nearly, if not accurately, thus:

I

In the greenest of our valleys,
  By good angels tenanted,
Once a fair and stately palace—
  Radiant palace—reared its head.
In the monarch Thought's dominion—
  It stood there!
Never seraph spread a pinion
  Over fabric half so fair.

II

Banners yellow, glorious, golden,
  On its roof did float and flow;
(This—all this—was in the olden
  Time long ago)
And every gentle air that dallied,
  In that sweet day,
Along the ramparts plumed and pallid,
  A winged odor went away.

III

Wanderers in that happy valley
  Through two luminous windows saw
Spirits moving musically
  To a lute's well-tunèd law,
Round about a throne, where sitting
  (Porphyrogene!)
In state his glory well befitting,
  The ruler of the realm was seen.

IV

And all with pearl and ruby glowing
  Was the fair palace door,
Through which came flowing, flowing, flowing
  And sparkling evermore,
A troop of Echoes whose sweet duty
  Was but to sing,
In voices of surpassing beauty,
  The wit and wisdom of their king.

V

But evil things, in robes of sorrow,
  Assailed the monarch's high estate;
(Ah, let us mourn, for never morrow
  Shall dawn upon him, desolate!)
And, round about his home, the glory
  That blushed and bloomed
Is but a dim-remembered story
  Of the oldtime entombed.

VI

And travellers now within that valley,
  Through the red-litten windows, see
Vast forms that move fantastically
  To a discordant melody;
While, like a rapid ghastly river,
  Through the pale door,
A hideous throng rush out forever,
  And laugh—but smile no more.

I well remember that suggestions arising from this ballad, led us into a train of thought wherein there became manifest an opinion of Usher's which I mention not so much on account of its novelty (for other men that have thought thus), as on account of the pertinacity with which he maintained it. This opinion, in its general form, was that of the sentience of all vegetable things. But, in his disordered fancy, the idea had assumed a more daring character, and trespassed, under certain conditions, upon the kingdom of inorganization. I lack words to express the full extent, of the earnest *abandon* of his persuasion. The belief, however, was connected (as I have previously hinted) with the gray stones of the home of his forefathers. The conditions of the sentience had been here, he imagined, fulfilled in the method of collocation of these stones—in the order of their arrangement, as well as in that of the many *fungi* which overspread them, and of the decayed trees which stood around— above all, in the long undisturbed endurance of this arrangement, and in its reduplication in the still waters of the tarn. Its evidence—the evidence of the sentience—was to be seen, he said (and I here started as he spoke), in the gradual yet certain condensation of an atmosphere of their own about the waters and the walls. The result was discoverable, he added, in that silent, yet importunate and terrible influence which for centuries had moulded the destinies of his family, and which made *him* what I now saw him—what he was. Such opinions need no comment, and I will make none.

Our books—the books which, for years, had formed no small portion of the mental existence of the invalid—were, as might be supposed, in strict keeping with this character of phantasm. We pored together over such works as the Vervet et Chartreuse of Gresset; the Belphegor of Machiavelli; the Heaven and Hell of Swedenborg; the Subterranean Voyage of Nicholas Klimm by Holberg; the Chiromancy of Robert Flud, of Jean D'Indaginé, and of De la Chambre; the Journey into the Blue Distance of Tieck; and the City of the Sun of Campanella. One favorite volume was a small octavo edition of the *Directorium Inquisitorum*, by the Dominican Eymeric de Gironne; and there were passages in Pomponius Mela, about the old African Satyrs and Ægipans, over which Usher would sit dreaming for hours. His chief delight, however, was found in the perusal of an exceedingly rare and curious book in quarto Gothic—the manual of a forgotten church—the *Vigilæ Mortuorum secundum Chorum Ecclesiæ Maguntinæ.*

I could not help thinking of the wild ritual of this work, and of its probable influence upon the hypochondriac, when, one evening, having informed me abruptly that the lady Madeline was no more, he stated his intention of preserving her corpse for a fortnight (previously to its final interment), in one of the numerous vaults within the main walls of the building. The worldly reason, however, assigned for this singular proceeding, was one which I did not feel at liberty to dispute. The brother had been led to his resolution (so he told me) by consideration of the unusual character of the malady of the deceased, of certain obstrusive and eager inquiries on the part of her medical men, and of the remote and exposed situation of the burial-ground of the family. I will not deny that when I called to mind the sinister countenance of the person whom I met upon the staircase, on the day of my arrival at the house, I had no desire to oppose what I regarded as at best but a harmless, and by no means an unnatural, precaution.

At the request of Usher, I personally aided him in the arrangements for the temporary entombment. The body having been encoffined, we two alone bore it to its rest. The vault in which we placed it (and which had been so long unopened that our torches, half smothered in its oppressive atmosphere, gave us little opportunity for investigation) was small, damp, and entirely without means of admission for light; lying, at great depth, immediately beneath that portion of the building in which was my own sleeping apartment. It had been used, apparently, in remote feudal times, for the worst purposes of a donjon-keep, and, in later days, as a place of deposit for powder, or some other highly combustible substance, as a portion of its floor, and the whole interior of a long archway through which we reached it, were carefully sheathed with copper. The door, of massive iron, had been, also, similarly protected. Its immense weight caused an unusually sharp grating sound, as it moved upon its hinges.

Having deposited our mournful burden upon tressels within this region of horror, we partially turned aside the yet unscrewed lid of the coffin, and looked upon the face of the tenant. A striking similitude between the brother and sister now first arrested my attention; and Usher, divining, perhaps, my thoughts, murmured out some few words from which I learned that the deceased and himself had been twins, and that sympathies of a scarcely intelligible nature had always existed between them. Our glances, however, rested not long upon the dead—for we could not regard her unawed. The disease which had thus entombed the lady in the maturity of youth, had left, as usual in all maladies of a strictly cataleptical character, the mockery of a faint blush upon the bosom and the face, and that suspiciously lingering smile upon the lip which is so terrible in death. We replaced and screwed down the lid, and, having secured the door of iron, made our way, with toil, into the scarcely less gloomy apartments of the upper portion of the house.

> The body having been encoffined, we two alone bore it to its rest.

And now, some days of bitter grief having elapsed, an observable change came over the features of the mental disorder of my friend. His ordinary manner had vanished. His ordinary occupations were neglected or forgotten. He roamed from chamber to chamber with hurried, unequal, and objectless step. The pallor of his countenance had assumed, if possible, a more ghastly hue—but the luminousness of his eye had utterly gone out. The once occasional huskiness of his tone was heard no more; and a tremulous quaver, as if of extreme terror, habitually characterized his utterance. There were times, indeed, when I thought his unceasingly agitated mind was laboring with some oppressive secret, to divulge which he struggled for the necessary courage. At times, again, I was obliged to resolve all into the mere inexplicable vagaries of madness, for I beheld him gazing upon vacancy for long hours, in an attitude of the profoundest attention, as if listening to some imaginary sound. It was no wonder that his condition terrified—that it infected me. I felt creeping upon me, by slow yet certain degrees, the wild influences of his own fantastic yet impressive superstitions.

It was, especially, upon retiring to bed late in the night of the seventh or eighth day after the placing of the lady Madeline within the donjon, that I experienced the full power of such feelings. Sleep came not near my couch—while the hours waned and waned away. I struggled to reason off the nervousness which had dominion over me. I endeavored to believe that much, if not all of what I felt, was due to the bewildering influence of the gloomy furniture of the room—of the dark and tattered draperies, which, tortured into motion by the breath of a rising tempest, swayed fitfully to and fro upon the walls, and rustled uneasily about the decorations of the bed. But my efforts were fruitless. An irrepressible tremor gradually pervaded my frame; and, at length, there sat upon my very heart an incubus of utterly causeless alarm. Shaking this off with a gasp and a struggle, I uplifted myself upon the pillows, and, peering earnestly within the intense darkness of the chamber, hearkened—I know not why, except that an instinctive spirit prompted me—to certain low and indefinite sounds which came, through the pauses of the storm, at long intervals, I knew not whence. Overpowered by an intense sentiment of horror, unaccountable yet unendurable, I threw my clothes on with haste (for I felt that I should sleep no more during the night), and endeavored to arouse myself from the pitiable condition into which I had fallen, by pacing rapidly to and fro through the apartment.

25   I had taken but few turns in this manner, when a light step on an adjoining staircase arrested my attention. I presently recognized it as that of Usher. In an instant afterward he rapped, with a gentle touch, at my door, and entered, bearing a lamp. His countenance was, as usual, cadaverously wan—but, moreover, there was a species of mad hilarity in his eyes—an evidently restrained *hysteria* in his whole demeanor. His air appalled me—but anything was preferable to the solitude which I had so long endured, and I even welcomed his presence as a relief.

26   "And you have not seen it?" he said abruptly, after having stared about him for some moments in silence—"you have not then seen it?—but, stay! you shall." Thus speaking, and having carefully shaded his lamp, he hurried to one of the casements, and threw it freely open to the storm.

27   The impetuous fury of the entering gust nearly lifted us from our feet. It was, indeed, a tempestuous yet sternly beautiful night, and one wildly singular in its terror and its beauty. A whirlwind had apparently collected its force in our vicinity; for there were frequent and violent alterations in the direction of the wind; and the exceeding density of the clouds (which hung so low as to press upon the turrets of the house) did not prevent our perceiving the lifelike velocity with which they flew careering from all points against each other, without passing away into the distance. I say that even their exceeding density did not prevent our perceiving this—yet we had no glimpse of the moon or stars—nor was there any flashing forth of the lightening. But the under surfaces of the huge masses of agitated vapor, as well as all terrestrial objects immediately around us, were glowing in the unnatural light of a faintly luminous and distinctly visible gaseous exhalation which hung about and enshrouded the mansion.

28   "You must not—you shall not behold this!" said I, shudderingly, to Usher, as I led him, with a gentle violence, from the window to a seat. "These appearances, which bewilder you, are merely electrical phenomena not uncommon—or it may be that they have their ghastly origin in the rank miasma of the tarn. Let us close this casement;—the air is chilling and dangerous to your frame. Here is one of your favorite romances. I will read, and you shall listen;—and so we will pass away this terrible night together."

29   The antique volume which I had taken up was the "Mad Trist" of Sir Launcelot Canning; but I had called it a favorite of Usher's more in sad jest than in earnest; for, in truth, there is little in its uncouth and unimaginative prolixity which could have had interest for the lofty and spiritual ideality of my friend. It was, however, the only book immediately at hand; and I indulged a vague hope that the excitement which now agitated the hypochondriac, might find relief (for the history of mental disorder is full of similar anomalies) even in the extremeness of the folly which I should read. Could I have judged, indeed, by the wild overstrained air of vivacity with which he hearkened, or apparently hearkened, to the words of the tale, I might well have congratulated myself upon the success of my design.

I had arrived at that well-known portion of the story where Ethelred, the hero of the Trist, having sought in vain for peaceable admission into the dwelling of the hermit, proceeds to make good an entrance by force. Here, it will be remembered, the words of the narrative run thus:

"And Ethelred, who was by nature of a doughty heart, and who was now mighty withal, on account of the powerfulness of the wine which he had drunken, waited no longer to hold parley with the hermit, who, in sooth, was of an obstinate and maliceful turn, but, feeling the rain upon his shoulders, and fearing the rising of the tempest, uplifted his mace outright, and, with blows, made quickly room in the plankings of the door for his gauntleted hand; and now pulling therewith sturdily, he so cracked, and ripped, and tore all asunder, that the noise of the dry and hollow-sounding wood alarumed and reverberated throughout the forest."

At the termination of this sentence I started, and for a moment, paused; for it appeared to me (although I at once concluded that my excited fancy had deceived me)—it appeared to me that, from some very remote portion of the mansion, there came indistinctly, to my ears, what might have been, in its exact similarity of character, the echo (but a stifled and dull one certainly) of the very cracking and ripping sound which Sir Launcelot had so particularly described. It was, beyond doubt, the coincidence alone which had arrested my attention; for, amid the rattling of the sashes of the casements, and the ordinary commingled noises of the still increasing storm, the sound, in itself, had nothing, surely, which should have interested or disturbed me. I continued the story:

"But the good champion Ethelred, now entering within the door, was sore enraged and amazed to perceive no signal of the maliceful hermit; but, in the stead thereof, a dragon of a scaly and prodigious demeanor, and of a fiery tongue, which sate in guard before a palace of gold, with a floor of silver; and upon the wall there hung a shield of shining brass with this legend enwritten—

Who entereth herein, a conqueror hath bin;
Who slayeth the dragon, the shield he shall win;

And Ethelred uplifted his mace, and struck upon the head of the dragon, which fell before him, and gave up his pesty breath, with a shriek so horrid and harsh, and withal so piercing, that Ethelred had fain to close his ears with his hands against the dreadful noise of it, the like whereof was never before heard."

Here again, I paused abruptly, and now with a feeling of wild amazement—for there could be no doubt whatever that, in this instance, I did actually hear (although from what direction it proceeded I found it impossible to say) a low and apparently distant, but harsh, protracted, and most unusual screaming or grating sound—the exact counterpart of what my fancy had already conjured up for the dragon's unnatural shriek as described by the romancer.

Oppressed, as I certainly was, upon the occurrence of the second and most extraordinary coincidence, by a thousand conflicting sensations, in which wonder and extreme terror were predominant, I still retained sufficient presence of mind to avoid exciting, by any observation, the sensitive nervousness of my companion. I was by no means certain that he had noticed the sounds in question; although, assuredly, a strange alteration had, during the last few minutes, taken place in his demeanor. From a position fronting my own, he had gradually brought round his chair, so as to sit with his face to the door of the chamber; and thus I could but partially perceive his features, although I saw that his lips trembled as if he were murmuring inaudibly. His head had dropped upon

We have put her living in the tomb!

his breast—yet I knew that he was not asleep, from the wide and rigid opening of the eye as I caught a glance of it in profile. The motion of his body, too, was at variance with this idea—for he rocked from side to side with a gentle yet constant and uniform sway. Having rapidly taken notice of all this, I resumed the narrative of Sir Launcelot, which thus proceeded:

"And now, the champion, having escaped from the terrible fury of the dragon, bethinking himself of the brazen shield, and of the breaking up of the enchantment which was upon it, removed the carcass from out of the way before him, and approached valorously over the silver pavement of the castle to where the shield was upon the wall; which in sooth tarried not for his full coming, but fell down at his feet upon the silver floor, with a mighty great and terrible ringing sound."

No sooner had these syllables passed my lips, than—as if a shield of brass had indeed, at the moment, fallen heavily upon a floor of silver—I became aware of a distinct, hollow, metallic, and clangorous, yet apparently muffled reverberation. Completely unnerved, I leaped to my feet; but the measured rocking movement of Usher was undisturbed. I rushed to the chair in which he sat. His eyes were bent fixedly before him, and throughout his whole countenance there reigned a stony rigidity. But, as I placed my hand upon his shoulder, there came a strong shudder over his whole person; a sickly smile quivered about his lips; and I saw that he spoke in a low, hurried, and gibbering murmur, as if unconscious of my presence. Bending closely over him, I at length drank in the hideous import of his words.

"Not hear it? —yes, I hear it, and *have* heard it. Long—long—long—many minutes, many hours, many days, have I heard it—yet I dared not—oh, pity me, miserable wretch that I am!—I dared not—I *dared not speak! We have put her living in the tomb!* Said I not that my senses were acute? I *now* tell you that I heard her first feeble movements in the hollow coffin. I heard them—many, many days ago—yet I dared not—*I dared not speak!* And now—to-night—Ethelred—ha! ha! —the breaking of the hermit's door, and the death-cry of the dragon, and the clangor of the shield! —say, rather, the rending of her coffin, and the grating of the iron hinges of her prison, and her struggles within the coppered archway of the vault! Oh whither shall I fly? Will she not be here anon? Is she not hurrying to upbraid me for my haste? Have I not heard her footstep on the stair? Do I not distinguish that heavy and horrible beating of her heart? MADMAN!" here he sprang

furiously to his feet, and shrieked out his syllables, as if in the effort he were giving up his soul—"MADMAN! I TELL YOU THAT SHE NOW STANDS WITHOUT THE DOOR!"

39   As if in the superhuman energy of his utterance there had been found the potency of a spell—the huge antique panels to which the speaker pointed, threw slowly back, upon the instant, their ponderous and ebony jaws. It was the work of the rushing gust—but then without those doors there *did* stand the lofty and enshrouded figure of the lady Madeline of Usher. There was blood upon her white robes, and the evidence of some bitter struggle upon every portion of her emaciated frame. For a moment she remained trembling and reeling to and fro upon the threshold, then, with a low moaning cry, fell heavily inward upon the person of her brother, and in her violent and now final death-agonies, bore him to the floor a corpse, and a victim to the terrors he had anticipated.

40   From that chamber, and from that mansion, I fled aghast. The storm was still abroad in all its wrath as I found myself crossing the old causeway. Suddenly there shot along the path a wild light, and I turned to see whence a gleam so unusual could have issued; for the vast house and its shadows were alone behind me. The radiance was that of the full, setting, and blood-red moon which now shone vividly through that once barely-discernible fissure of which I have before spoken as extending from the roof of the building, in a zigzag direction, to the base. While I gazed, this fissure rapidly widened—there came a fierce breath of the whirlwind—the entire orb of the satellite burst at once upon my sight—my brain reeled as I saw the mighty walls rushing asunder—there was a long tumultuous shouting sound like the voice of a thousand waters—and the deep and dark tarn at my feet closed sullenly and silently over the fragments of the "HOUSE OF USHER."

I F you liked reading Poe's description of the physical setting of the Usher mansion, you may enjoy encountering the dramatic settings in a number of other stories, such as the New York City streets in Bernard Malamud's "The Magic Barrel" in this chapter or in Herman Melville's New York story "Bartleby, the Scrivener" in chapter 14.

GOING FURTHER   In many of his other stories Poe conjures up settings and landscapes somewhere between actual geography and dreamworld. In his novella *The Narrative of Arthur Gordon Pym* he creates a distinctive polar setting without ever having traveled anywhere near the regions he describes.

Writing from Reading

Summarize

1 How would you characterize the relationship between Roderick Usher and his sister Madeline? Use details from the story to back up your claim.

2 Why has the narrator come to visit Roderick Usher? What is his history with the Usher family? How does he feel about entering the house? How has his relationship with the "House of Usher" changed by the time he leaves the house?

Analyze Craft

3 Find the words the narrator uses to describe the valet who guides him through the house and the physician he meets on the stairs. How do these words contribute to your impressions

of the narrator and/or the situation in the house?

4 Describe how the house and its surroundings serve as a character in this story.

Analyze Voice

5 Poe invokes three different voices in this story: the narrator's voice, Roderick's voice in the ballad "The Haunted Palace," and Sir Launcelot's voice in "Mad Trist." Compare and contrast these three different styles and intonations. How is each still uniquely Poe's own voice?

Synthesize Summary and Analysis

6 Discuss the setting of "The Fall of the House of Usher" in relation to the settings within the story of "The Haunted Palace" and the cave where Ethelred confronts his dragon. What is the effect of these three parallel settings?

Interpret the Story

7 Discuss the effect of the storm on your experience at the end of the story. Consider the contrast between the chaotic storm and the stillness that

dominates the rest of the story. How would the ending experience be different if there were no storm to accompany Madeline's appearance and the collapse of the house?

8 How does the overall effect of the story depend on the mood created by the narrator?

9 How might the story, with its emphasis on mood and European-like setting, change your impression of what constitutes "American" literature?

Eudora Welty (1909–2001)

Eudora Welty was born in Jackson, Mississippi, where she lived and worked for most of her life. In the 1930s, she wrote articles for the newspaper *Commercial Appeal,* worked at a Jackson radio station, and became a publicity agent for the Works Progress Administration. Welty began publishing short stories in the mid-1930s. During her long writing career, she received many literary awards, including a Pulitzer Prize. Despite ample opportunities to live abroad or in major cities, Welty always returned to Jackson; arguably, the setting she lived and wrote in was a powerful influence on the timbre of her

writing. Many consider her to be one of the most important stylists of the twentieth century; it is hard to talk about a "southern" voice without mentioning Eudora Welty. (For more on southern writers, see chapter 12, the casebook on the American South.) Always willing to experiment with the voice, tone, and form of her stories, she evoked powerful, often hilarious relationships among eccentric (but recognizable) southern families. In addition to four short story collections, she wrote several books of nonfiction—*One Writer's Beginnings* is about the art of writing—one children's book, and five novels. Welty was also

a photographer and published two books of photographs.

Of her work, and certainly relevant to "Why I Live at the P.O.," she once wrote, "I was trying to write about the way people who live away off from nowhere have to amuse themselves by dramatizing every situation that comes along by exaggerating it—'telling it.' I used the exaggerations and ways of talking I have heard all my life. It's just the way they keep life interesting—they make an experience out of the ordinary. I wasn't trying to do anything but show that. I thought it was cheerful, on the whole."

AS YOU READ As you read this story, notice the manner in which the characters speak to each other—both the tone and the phrasing. Notice other details that relate to the particular place and time in which the story is set.

Why I Live at the P.O. (1941)

1   I was getting along fine with Mama, Papa-Daddy and Uncle Rondo until my sister Stella-Rondo just separated from her husband and came back home again. Mr. Whitaker! Of course I went with Mr. Whitaker first, when he first appeared here in China Grove, taking "Pose Yourself" photos, and Stella-Rondo broke us up. Told him I was one-sided. Bigger on one side than the other, which is a deliberate, calculated falsehood: I'm the same. Stella-Rondo is exactly twelve months to the day younger than I am and for that reason she's spoiled.

2   She's always had anything in the world she wanted and then she'd throw it away. Papa-Daddy gave her this gorgeous Add-a-Pearl necklace when she was eight years old and she threw it away playing baseball when she was nine, with only two pearls.

3   So as soon as she got married and moved away from home the first thing she did was separate! From Mr. Whitaker! This photographer with the popeyes she said she trusted. Came home from one of those towns up in Illinois and to our complete surprise brought this child of two.

4   Mama said she like to made her drop dead for a second. "Here you had this marvelous blonde child and never so much as wrote your mother a word about it," says Mama. "I'm thoroughly ashamed of you." But of course she wasn't.

5   Stella-Rondo just calmly takes off this *hat*, I wish you could see it. She says, "Why, Mama, Shirley-T.'s adopted, I can prove it."

6   "How?" says Mama, but all I says was, "H'm!" There I was over the hot stove, trying to stretch two chickens over five people and a completely unexpected child into the bargain, without one moment's notice.

7   "What do you mean—'H'm!'?" says Stella-Rondo, and Mama says, "I heard that, Sister."

8   I said that oh, I didn't mean a thing, only that whoever Shirley-T. was, she was the spit-image of Papa-Daddy if he'd cut off his beard, which of course he'd never do in the world. Papa-Daddy's Mama's papa and sulks.

9   Stella-Rondo got furious! She said, "Sister, I don't need to tell you you got a lot of nerve and always did have and I'll thank you to make no future reference to my adopted child whatsoever."

10   "Very well," I said. "Very well, very well. Of course I noticed at once she looks like Mr. Whitaker's side too. That frown. She looks like a cross between Mr. Whitaker and Papa-Daddy."

11   "Well, all I can say is she isn't."

12   "She looks exactly like Shirley Temple to me," says Mama, but Shirley-T. just ran away from her. So the first thing Stella-Rondo did at the table was turn Papa-Daddy against me.

13   "Papa-Daddy," she says. He was trying to cut up his meat. "Papa-Daddy!" I was taken completely by surprise. Papa-Daddy is about a million years old and's got this long-long beard. "Papa-Daddy, Sister says she fails to understand why you don't cut off your beard."

So Papa-Daddy l-a-y-s down his knife and fork! He's real rich. Mama says he is, he says he isn't. So he says, "Have I heard correctly? You don't understand why I don't cut off my beard?"

"Why," I says, "Papa-Daddy, of course I understand, I did not say any such of a thing, the idea!"

He says, "Hussy!"

I says, "Papa-Daddy, you know I wouldn't any more want you to cut off your beard than the man in the moon. It was the farthest thing from my mind! Stella-Rondo sat there and made that up while she was eating breast of chicken."

But he says, "So the postmistress fails to understand why I don't cut off my beard. Which job I got you through my influence with the government. 'Bird's nest'—is that what you call it?"

Not that it isn't the next to smallest P.O. in the entire state of Mississippi.

I says, "Oh, Papa-Daddy," I says, "I didn't say any such of a thing, I never dreamed it was a bird's nest, I have always been grateful though this is the next to smallest P.O. in the state of Mississippi, and I do not enjoy being referred to as a hussy by my own grandfather."

But Stella-Rondo says, "Yes, you did say it too. Anybody in the world could of heard you, that had ears."

"Stop right there," says Mama, looking at *me*.

So I pulled my napkin straight back through the napkin ring and left the table.

As soon as I was out of the room Mama says, "Call her back, or she'll starve to death," but Papa-Daddy says, "This is the beard I started growing on the Coast when I was fifteen years old." He would of gone on till nightfall if Shirley-T. hadn't lost the Milky Way she ate in Cairo.

So Papa-Daddy says, "I am going out and lie in the hammock, and you can all sit here and remember my words: I'll never cut off my beard as long as I live, even one inch, and I don't appreciate it in you at all." Passed right by me in the hall and went straight out and got in the hammock.

It would be a holiday. It wasn't five minutes before Uncle Rondo suddenly appeared in the hall in one of Stella-Rondo's flesh-colored kimonos, all cut on the bias, like something Mr. Whitaker probably thought was gorgeous.

"Uncle Rondo!" I says. "I didn't know who that was! Where are you going?"

"Sister," he says, "get out of my way, I'm poisoned."

"If you're poisoned stay away from Papa-Daddy," I says. "Keep out of the hammock. Papa-Daddy will certainly beat you on the head if you come within forty miles of him. He thinks I deliberately said he ought to cut off his beard after he got me the P.O., and I've told him and told him and told him, and he acts like he just don't hear me. Papa-Daddy must of gone stone deaf."

"He picked a fine day to do it then," says Uncle Rondo, and before you could say "Jack Robinson" flew out in the yard.

What he'd really done, he'd drunk another bottle of that prescription. He does it every single Fourth of July as sure as shooting, and it's horribly expensive. Then he falls over in the hammock and snores. So he insisted on zigzagging right on out to the hammock, looking like a half-wit.

Papa-Daddy woke up with this horrible yell and right there without moving an inch he tried to turn Uncle Rondo against me. I heard every word he said. Oh, he told Uncle Rondo I didn't learn to read till I was eight years old and he didn't see how in the world I ever got the mail put up at the P.O., much less read it all, and he said if Uncle Rondo could only fathom the lengths he had gone to to get me that job! And he said on the other hand he thought Stella-Rondo had a brilliant mind and deserved credit for getting out of town. All the time he was just lying there swinging as pretty as you please and looping out his beard, and poor Uncle Rondo was *pleading* with him to slow down the hammock, it was making him as dizzy as a witch to watch it. But that's what Papa-Daddy likes about a hammock. So Uncle Rondo was too dizzy to get turned against me for the time being. He's Mama's only brother and is a good case of a one-track mind. Ask anybody. A certified pharmacist.

Just then I heard Stella-Rondo raising the upstairs window. While she was married she got this peculiar idea that it's cooler with the windows shut and locked. So she has to raise the window before she can make a soul hear her outdoors.

So she raises the window and says, "*Oh!*" You would have thought she was mortally wounded.

Uncle Rondo and Papa-Daddy didn't even look up, but kept right on with what they were doing. I had to laugh.

I flew up the stairs and threw the door open! I says, "What in the wide world's the matter, Stella-Rondo? You mortally wounded?"

37   "No," she says, "I am not mortally wounded but I wish you would do me the favor of looking out that window there and telling me what you see."

38   So I shade my eyes and look out the window.

39   "I see the front yard," I says.

40   "Don't you see any human beings?" she says.

41   "I see Uncle Rondo trying to run Papa-Daddy out of the hammock," I says. "Nothing more. Naturally, it's so suffocating-hot in the house, with all the windows shut and locked, everybody who cares to stay in their right mind will have to go out and get in the hammock before the Fourth of July is over."

42   "Don't you notice anything different about Uncle Rondo?" asks Stella-Rondo.

43   "Why, no, except he's got on some terrible-looking flesh-colored contraption I wouldn't be found dead in, is all I can see," I says.

44   "Never mind, you won't be found dead in it, because it happens to be part of my trousseau, and Mr. Whitaker took several dozen photographs of me in it," says Stella-Rondo. "What on earth could Uncle Rondo *mean* by wearing part of my trousseau out in the broad open daylight without saying so much as 'Kiss my foot,' *knowing* I only got home this morning after my separation and hung my negligee up on the bathroom door, just as nervous as I could be?"

45   "I'm sure I don't know, and what do you expect me to do about it?" I says. "Jump out the window?"

46   "No, I expect nothing of the kind. I simply declare that Uncle Rondo looks like a fool in it, that's all," she says. "It makes me sick to my stomach."

47   "Well, he looks as good as he can," I says. "As good as anybody in reason could." I stood up for Uncle Rondo, please remember. And I said to Stella-Rondo, "I think I would do well not to criticize so freely if I were you and came home with a two-year-old child I had never said a word about, and no explanation whatever about my separation."

48   "I asked you the instant I entered this house not to refer one more time to my adopted child, and you gave me your word of honor you would not," was all Stella-Rondo would say, and started pulling out every one of her eyebrows with some cheap Kress tweezers.

49   So I merely slammed the door behind me and went down and made some green-tomato pickle. Somebody had to do it. Of course Mama had turned both the niggers loose; she always said no earthly power could hold

one anyway on the Fourth of July, so she wouldn't even try. It turned out that Jaypan fell in the lake and came within a very narrow limit of drowning.

    So Mama trots in. Lifts up the lid and says, "H'm! Not very good for your Uncle Rondo in his precarious condition, I must say. Or poor little adopted Shirley-T. Shame on you!"

    That made me tired. I says, "Well, Stella-Rondo had better thank her lucky stars it was her instead of me came trotting in with that very peculiar-looking child. Now if it had been me that trotted in from Illinois and brought a peculiar-looking child of two, I shudder to think of the reception I'd of got, much less controlled the diet of an entire family."

    "But you must remember, Sister, that you were never married to Mr. Whitaker in the first place and didn't go up to Illinois to live," says Mama, shaking a spoon in my face. "If you had I would of been just as overjoyed to see you and your little adopted girl as I was to see Stella-Rondo, when you wound up with your separation and came on back home."

    "You would not," I says.

    "Don't contradict me, I would," says Mama.

    But I said she couldn't convince me though she talked till she was blue in the face. Then I said, "Besides, you know as well as I do that that child is not adopted."

    "She most certainly is adopted," says Mama, stiff as a poker.

    I says, "Why, Mama, Stella-Rondo had her just as sure as anything in this world, and just too stuck up to admit it."

    "Why, Sister," said Mama. "Here I thought we were going to have a pleasant Fourth of July, and you start right out not believing a word your own baby sister tells you!"

    "Just like Cousin Annie Flo. Went to her grave denying the facts of life," I remind Mama.

    "I told you if you ever mentioned Annie Flo's name I'd slap your face," says Mama, and slaps my face.

    "All right, you wait and see," I says.

    "I," says Mama, "I prefer to take my children's word for anything when it's humanly possible." You ought to see Mama, she weighs two hundred pounds and has real tiny feet.

    Just then something perfectly horrible occurred to me.

    "Mama," I says, "can that child talk?" I simply had to whisper! "Mama, I wonder if that child can be—you know—in any way? Do you realize," I says, "that she hasn't spoken one single, solitary word to a human being up to this minute? This is the way she looks," I says, and I looked like this.

Well, Mama and I just stood there and stared at each other. It was horrible!

"I remember well that Joe Whitaker frequently drank like a fish," says Mama. "I believed to my soul he drank *chemicals*." And without another word she marches to the foot of the stairs and calls Stella-Rondo.

"Stella-Rondo? O-o-o-o-o! Stella-Rondo!"

"What?" says Stella-Rondo from upstairs. Not even the grace to get up off the bed.

"Can that child of yours talk?" asks Mama.

Stella-Rondo says, "Can she what?"

"Talk! Talk!" says Mama. "Burdyburdyburdyburdy!"

So Stella-Rondo yells back, "Who says she can't talk?"

"Sister says so," says Mama.

"You didn't have to tell me, I know whose word of honor don't mean a thing in this house," says Stella-Rondo.

And in a minute the loudest Yankee voice I ever heard in my life yells out, "OE'm Pop-OE the Sailor-r-r-r Ma-a-an!" and then somebody jumps up and down in the upstairs hall. In another second the house would of fallen down.

"Not only talks, she can tap-dance!" calls Stella-Rondo. "Which is more than some people I won't name can do."

"Why, the little precious darling thing!" Mama says, so surprised. "Just as smart as she can be!" Starts talking baby talk right there. Then she turns on me. "Sister, you ought to be thoroughly ashamed! Run upstairs this instant and apologize to Stella-Rondo and Shirley-T."

"Apologize for what?" I says. "I merely wondered if the child was normal, that's all. Now that she's proved she is, why, I have nothing further to say."

But Mama just turned on her heel and flew out, furious. She ran right upstairs and hugged the baby. She believed it was adopted. Stella-Rondo hadn't done a thing but turn her against me from upstairs while I stood there helpless over the hot stove. So that made Mama, Papa-Daddy and the baby all on Stella-Rondo's side.

Next, Uncle Rondo.

I must say that Uncle Rondo has been marvelous to me at various times in the past and I was completely unprepared to be made to jump out of my skin, the way it turned out. Once Stella-Rondo did something perfectly horrible to him—broke a chain letter from Flanders Field—and he took the radio back he had given her and gave it to me. Stella Rondo was furious! For six months we all had to call her Stella instead of Stella-Rondo, or she wouldn't answer. I always thought Uncle Rondo had all the brains of the entire family. Another time he sent me to Mammoth Cave, with all expenses paid.

But this would be the day he was drinking that prescription, the Fourth of July.

So at supper Stella-Rondo speaks up and says she thinks Uncle Rondo ought to try to eat a little something. So finally Uncle Rondo said he would try a little cold biscuits and ketchup, but that was all. So *she* brought it to him.

"Do you think it wise to disport with ketchup in Stella-Rondo's flesh-colored kimono?" I says. Trying to be considerate! If Stella-Rondo couldn't watch out for her trousseau, somebody had to.

"Any objections?" asks Uncle Rondo, just about to pour out all the ketchup.

"Don't mind what she says, Uncle Rondo," says Stella-Rondo. "Sister has been devoting this solid afternoon to sneering out my bedroom window at the way you look."

"What's that?" says Uncle Rondo. Uncle Rondo has got the most terrible temper in the world. Anything is liable to make him tear the house down if it comes at the wrong time.

So Stella-Rondo says, "Sister says, 'Uncle Rondo certainly does look like a fool in that pink kimono!'"

Do you remember who it was really said that?

Uncle Rondo spills out all the ketchup and jumps out of his chair and tears off the kimono and throws it down on the dirty floor and puts his foot on it. It had to be sent all the way to Jackson to the cleaners and repleated.

"So that's your opinion of your Uncle Rondo, is it?" he says. "I look like a fool, do I? Well, that's the last straw. A whole day in this house with nothing to do, and then to hear you come out with a remark like that behind my back!"

"I didn't say any such of a thing, Uncle Rondo," I says, "and I'm not saying who did, either. Why, I think you look all right. Just try to take care of yourself and not talk and eat at the same time," I says. "I think you better go lie down."

"Lie down my foot," says Uncle Rondo. I ought to of known by that he was fixing to do something perfectly horrible.

So he didn't do anything that night in the precarious state he was in—just played Casino with Mama and Stella-Rondo and Shirley-T. and gave Shirley-T. a

> "... 'Uncle Rondo certainly does look like a fool
>
> in that pink kimono!'"

nickel with a head on both sides. It tickled her nearly to death, and she called him "Papa." But at 6:30 A.M. the next morning, he threw a whole five-cent package of some unsold one-inch firecrackers from the store as hard as he could into my bedroom and they every one went off. Not one bad one in the string. Anybody else, there'd be one that wouldn't go off.

95   Well, I'm just terribly susceptible to noise of any kind, the doctor has always told me I was the most sensitive person he had ever seen in his whole life, and I was simply prostrated. I couldn't eat! People tell me they heard it as far as the cemetery, and old Aunt Jep Patterson, that had been holding her own so good, thought it was Judgment Day and she was going to meet her whole family. It's usually so quiet here.

96   And I'll tell you it didn't take me any longer than a minute to make up my mind what to do. There I was with the whole entire house on Stella-Rondo's side and turned against me. If I have anything at all I have pride.

97   So I just decided I'd go straight down to the P.O. There's plenty of room there in the back, I says to myself.

98   Well! I made no bones about letting the family catch on to what I was up to. I didn't try to conceal it.

    The first thing they knew, I marched in where they were all playing Old Maid and pulled the electric oscillating fan out by the plug, and everything got real hot. Next I snatched the pillow I'd done the needlepoint on right off the davenport from behind Papa-Daddy. He went "Ugh!" I beat Stella-Rondo up the stairs and finally found my charm bracelet in her bureau drawer under a picture of Nelson Eddy.

> ## "You can just let my mail lie there and *rot,* for all I care ..."

99   "So that's the way the land lies," says Uncle Rondo. There he was, piecing on the ham. "Well, Sister, I'll be glad to donate my army cot if you got any place to set it up, providing you'll leave right this minute and let me get some peace." Uncle Rondo was in France.

100   "Thank you kindly for the cot and 'peace' is hardly the word I would select if I had to resort to firecrackers at 6:30 A.M. in a young girl's bedroom," I says back to him. "And as to where I intend to go, you seem to for-

get my position as postmistress of China Grove, Mississippi," I says. "I've always got the P.O."

    Well, that made them all sit up and take notice.

    I went out front and started digging up some four-o'clocks to plant around the P.O.

    "Ah-ah-ah!" says Mama, raising the window. "Those happen to be my four-o'clocks. Everything planted in that star is mine. I've never known you to make anything grow in your life."

    "Very well," I says. "But I take the fern. Even you, Mama, can't stand there and deny that I'm the one watered that fern. And I happen to know where I can send in a box top and get a packet of one thousand mixed seeds, no two the same kind, free."

    "Oh, where?" Mama wants to know.

    But I says, "Too late. You 'tend to your house, and I'll 'tend to mine. You hear things like that all the time if you know how to listen to the radio. Perfectly marvelous offers. Get anything you want free."

    So I hope to tell you I marched in and got that radio, and they could of all bit a nail in two, especially Stella-Rondo, that it used to belong to, and she well knew she couldn't get it back, I'd sue for it like a shot. And I very politely took the sewing-machine motor I helped pay the most on to give Mama for Christmas back in 1929, and a good big calendar, with the first-aid remedies on it. The thermometer and the Hawaiian ukulele certainly were rightfully mine, and I stood on the step-ladder and got all my watermelon-rind preserves and every fruit and vegetable I'd put up, every jar. Then I began to pull the tacks out of the bluebird wall vases on the archway to the dining room.

    "Who told you you could have those, Miss Priss?" says Mama, fanning as hard as she could.

    "I bought 'em and I'll keep track of 'em," I says. "I'll tack 'em up one on each side the post-office window, and you can see 'em when you come to ask me for your mail, if you're so dead to see 'em."

    "Not I! I'll never darken the door to that post office again if I live to be a hundred," Mama says. "Ungrateful child! After all the money we spent on you at the Normal."

    "Me either," says Stella-Rondo. "You can just let my mail lie there and *rot,* for all I care. I'll never come and relieve you of a single, solitary piece."

    "I should worry," I says. "And who you think's going to sit down and write you all those big fat letters and postcards, by the way? Mr. Whitaker? Just because he was the only man ever dropped down in China Grove and you got him—unfairly—is he going to sit down and write you a lengthy correspondence after you come home giving no rhyme nor reason whatsoever for your separation and no explanation for the presence of that child? I may not have your brilliant mind, but I fail to see it."

So Mama says, "Sister, I've told you a thousand times that Stella-Rondo simply got homesick, and this child is far too big to be hers," and she says, "Now, why don't you all just sit down and play Casino?"

Then Shirley-T. sticks out her tongue at me in this perfectly horrible way. She has no more manners than the man in the moon. I told her she was going to cross her eyes like that some day and they'd stick.

"It's too late to stop me now," I says. "You should have tried that yesterday. I'm going to the P.O. and the only way you can possibly see me is to visit me there."

So Papa-Daddy says, "You'll never catch me setting foot in that post office, even if I should take a notion into my head to write a letter some place." He says, "I won't have you reachin' out of that little old window with a pair of shears and cuttin' off any beard of mine. I'm too smart for you!"

"We all are," says Stella-Rondo.

But I said, "If you're so smart, where's Mr. Whitaker?"

So then Uncle Rondo says, "I'll thank you from now on to stop reading all the orders I get on postcards and telling everybody in China Grove what you think is the matter with them," but I says, "I draw my own conclusions and will continue in the future to draw them." I says, "If people want to write their inmost secrets on penny postcards, there's nothing in the wide world you can do about it, Uncle Rondo."

"And if you think we'll ever *write* another postcard you're sadly mistaken," says Mama.

"Cutting off your nose to spite your face then," I says. "But if you're all determined to have no more to do with the U. S. mail, think of this: What will Stella-Rondo do now, if she wants to tell Mr. Whitaker to come after her?"

"Wah!" says Stella-Rondo. I knew she'd cry. She had a conniption fit right there in the kitchen.

"It will be interesting to see how long she holds out," I says. "And now—I am leaving."

"Good-bye," says Uncle Rondo.

"Oh, I declare," says Mama, "to think that a family of mine should quarrel on the Fourth of July, or the day after, over Stella-Rondo leaving old Mr. Whitaker and having the sweetest little adopted child! It looks like we'd all be glad!"

"Wah!" says Stella-Rondo, and has a fresh conniption fit.

"*He* left *her*—you mark my words," I says. "That's Mr. Whitaker. I know Mr. Whitaker. After all, I knew him first. I said from the beginning he'd up and leave her. I foretold every single thing that's happened."

"Where did he go?" asks Mama.

"Probably to the North Pole, if he knows what's good for him," I says.

But Stella-Rondo just bawled and wouldn't say another word. She flew to her room and slammed the door.

"Now look what you've gone and done, Sister," says Mama. "You go apologize."

"I haven't got time, I'm leaving," I says.

"Well, what are you waiting around for?" asks Uncle Rondo.

So I just picked up the kitchen clock and marched off, without saying "Kiss my foot" or anything, and never did tell Stella-Rondo good-bye.

There was a nigger girl going along on a little wagon right in front.

"Nigger girl," I says, "come help me haul these things down the hill, I'm going to live in the post office."

Took her nine trips in her express wagon. Uncle Rondo came out on the porch and threw her a nickel.

AND that's the last I've laid eyes on my family or my family laid eyes on me for five solid days and nights. Stella-Rondo may be telling the most horrible tales in the world about Mr. Whitaker, but I haven't heard them. As I tell everybody, I draw my own conclusions.

But oh, I like it here. It's ideal, as I've been saying. You see, I've got everything cater-cornered, the way I like it. Hear the radio? All the war news. Radio, sewing machine, book ends, ironing board and

that great big piano lamp—peace, that's what I like. Butter-bean vines planted all along the front where the strings are.

140   Of course, there's not much mail. My family are naturally the main people in China Grove, and if they prefer to vanish from the face of the earth, for all the mail they get or the mail they write, why, I'm not going to open my mouth. Some of the folks here in town are taking up for me and some turned against me. I know which is which. There are always people who will quit buying stamps just to get on the right side of Papa-Daddy.

But here I am, and here I'll stay. I want the world to know I'm happy.

And if Stella-Rondo should come to me this minute, on bended knees, and *attempt* to explain the incidents of her life with Mr. Whitaker, I'd simply put my fingers in both my ears and refuse to listen.

If you like how the physicality of the setting for "Why I Live at the P.O." might be imagined as the setting for a stage play, you may like the way this same treatment could work for the subway platform in Thomas Wolfe's story "Only the Dead Know Brooklyn" in chapter 8.

GOING FURTHER   The American South, with its farms and woods, rural roads and rivers, and, as in "No Place for You, My Love," Welty's passionate celebration of New Orleans and the lower Mississippi Delta provides a distinctive setting for her lifework. In novel after novel she makes the post-Faulknerian landscape come alive.

Writing from Reading

Summarize

1 List details Welty gives about the setting: the house, the town, the season, and the time period.

2 Describe the social environment of these characters. What are these characters' living and working conditions? What are the rhythms and challenges of the community being portrayed?

Analyze Craft

3 Sister's relationship to Mr. Whitaker is mentioned only twice in the story, once at the beginning and once toward the end, but it makes for a conflict central to the story. Explore why Welty chooses in the context to hide this conflict, and discuss how the quarrel between sisters might differ if they were more open.

Analyze Voice

4 How does the narrator's informal voice affect your impression of her? Do you trust her side of the story more or less because she is speaking naturally? How do you think your impression is affected by your familiarity or unfamiliarity with the dialect and the setting of the story?

Synthesize Summary and Analysis

5 Why is it significant that Sister works at (and eventually moves into) a post office? Analyze Welty's choice of this setting and the profession of postmaster.

Interpret the Story

6 Stella-Rondo, unlike Sister, escaped to another place and another life, if only for a short time. What impact might this change of setting have had on Stella-Rondo and her view of her home and family? What impact might

this change have had on her relationship with Sister? Demonstrate this impact with examples.

7 At the end of the story, Sister describes her home at the P.O., telling the reader to experience the setting firsthand. Discuss the narrator's (and Welty's) purpose in involving the reader so directly at the end of the story.

Bernard Malamud (1914–1986)

Bernard Malamud was born in New York City in 1914 and died there in 1986. However, he spent much of his professional life away from the city, teaching writing first at Oregon State College, then at Bennington College in Vermont. In *The Natural* (1952), he wrote about baseball, in *The Fixer* (1966), of Anti-Semitism in Russia. Despite his range of residencies and the variety of fictional locations in his work, Malamud remains best known as a chronicler of urban poverty and the immigrant experience; his characters are city dwellers, often, though not exclusively, Jewish and adrift. In many of his short stories and several of his novels, the world of the New York City tenement frames, as he put it, "my sad and comic tales." Much celebrated in the United States and abroad, Malamud received numerous honors for his work, including the Pulitzer Prize in 1967. *The Magic Barrel,* a collection of stories of which this chapter's selection is the title piece, won the National Book Award for fiction in 1958; he captured this award again in 1967 for *The Fixer.* In 1983 he published *The Stories of Bernard Malamud* and received the American Academy and Institute's Gold Medal for Fiction.

If Richard Ford's characters speak in "standard" English (chapter 2), the spoken utterance of Malamud's characters everywhere betrays its origin and their recent arrival on America's shores. In "The Magic Barrel," the marriage broker Salzman and his wife appear almost to be speaking in translation; their English is recently acquired and poor. In contrast, the seminarian Finkle and the prospective bride Lily Hirschorn are better assimilated, more fluent in the language and therefore "Americanized."

Critics saw Malamud as a Jewish-American writer, but he resisted this label, preferring to be known as a Jew who lived and wrote in America. His fiction reflects his interest in fable and allegory—the way a figure can be both particular and representative, both specific and abstract.

Of this story, he said, "['The Magic Barrel'] has been interpreted in two ways, as realism and as fantasy. I had meant it to be realistic, but two things conditioned some people's reading of it. In the original version Salzman says somewhere, referring to his daughter, 'For her to be poor was a sin. That is why she is dead now.' And the Chagallean imagery of the ending convinces some that it was meant to be fantasy. Either interpretation suits me, I thought, but then in the manuscript I sent to the publisher I altered Salzman's speech so that it now reads, 'This is why to me she is dead now.'"

AS YOU READ As you read, notice the details of setting that Malamud provides. What kind of a world is he leading readers into? Is it a world that seems foreign or familiar to you?

The Magic Barrel (1958)

1   NOT long ago there lived in uptown New York, in a small, almost meager room, though crowded with books, Leo Finkle, a rabbinical student at the Yeshiva University. Finkle, after six years of study, was to be ordained in June and had been advised by an acquaintance that he might find it easier to win himself a congregation if he were married. Since he had no present prospects of marriage, after two tormented days of turning it over in his mind, he called in Pinye Salzman, a marriage broker whose two-line advertisement he had read in the *Forward*.

2   The matchmaker appeared one night out of the dark fourth-floor hallway of the graystone rooming house where Finkle lived, grasping a black, strapped portfolio that had been worn thin with use. Salzman, who had been long in the business, was of slight but dignified build, wearing an old hat, and an overcoat too short and tight for him. He smelled frankly of fish, which he loved to eat, and although he was missing a few teeth, his presence was not displeasing, because of an amiable manner curiously contrasted with mournful eyes. His voice, his lips, his wisp of beard, his bony fingers were animated, but give him a moment of repose and his mild blue eyes revealed a depth of sadness, a characteristic that put Leo a little at ease although the situation, for him, was inherently tense.

3   He at once informed Salzman why he had asked him to come, explaining that but for his parents, who had married comparatively late in life, he was alone in the world. He had for six years devoted himself almost entirely to his studies, as a result of which, understandably, he had found himself without time for a social life and the company of young women. Therefore he thought it the better part of trial and error—of embarrassing fumbling—to call in an experienced person to advise him on these matters. He remarked in passing that the function of the marriage broker was ancient and honorable, highly approved in the Jewish community, because it made practical the necessary without hindering joy. Moreover, his own parents had been brought together by a matchmaker. They had made, if not a financially profitable marriage—since neither had possessed any worldly goods to speak of—at least a successful one in the sense of their everlasting devotion to each other. Salzman listened in embarrassed surprise, sensing a sort of apology. Later, however, he experienced a glow of pride in his work, an emotion that had left him years ago, and he heartily approved of Finkle.

4   The two went to their business. Leo had led Salzman to the only clear place in the room, a table near a window that overlooked the lamp-lit city. He seated himself at the matchmaker's side but facing him, attempting by an act of will to suppress the unpleasant tickle in his throat. Salzman eagerly unstrapped his portfolio and removed a loose rubber band from a thin packet of much-handled cards. As he flipped through them, a gesture and sound that physically hurt Leo, the student pretended not to see and gazed steadfastly out the window. Although it was still February, winter was on its last legs, signs of which he had for the first time in years begun to notice. He now observed the round white moon, moving high in the sky through a cloud menagerie, and watched with half-open mouth as it penetrated a huge hen, and dropped out of her like an egg laying itself. Salzman, though pretending through eyeglasses he had just slipped on to be engaged in scanning the writing on the cards, stole occasional glances at the young man's distinguished face, noting with pleasure the long, severe scholar's nose, brown eyes heavy with learning, sensitive yet ascetic lips, and a certain almost hollow quality of the dark cheeks. He gazed around

> He remarked in passing that the function of the marriage broker was ancient and honorable . . .

at shelves upon shelves of books and let out a soft, contented sigh.

When Leo's eyes fell upon the cards, he counted six spread out in Salzman's hand.

"So few?" he asked in disappointment.

"You wouldn't believe me how much cards I got in my office," Salzman replied. "The drawers are already filled to the top, so I keep them now in a barrel, but is every girl good for a new rabbi?"

Leo blushed at this, regretting all he had revealed of himself in a curriculum vitae he had sent to Salzman. He had thought it best to acquaint him with his strict standards and specifications but, in having done so, felt he had told the marriage broker more than was absolutely necessary.

He hesitantly inquired, "Do you keep photographs of your clients on file?"

"First comes family, amount of dowry, also what kind promises," Salzman replied, unbuttoning his tight coat and settling himself in the chair. "After comes pictures, rabbi."

"Call me Mr. Finkle. I'm not yet a rabbi."

Salzman said he would, but instead called him doctor, which he changed to rabbi when Leo was not listening too attentively.

Salzman adjusted his horn-rimmed spectacles, gently cleared his throat and read in an eager voice the contents of the top card:

"Sophie P. Twenty four years. Widow one year. No children. Educated high school and two years college. Father promises eight thousand dollars. Has wonderful wholesale business. Also real estate. On the mother's side comes teachers, also one actor. Well known on Second Avenue."

Leo gazed up in surprise. "Did you say a widow?"

"A widow don't mean spoiled, rabbi. She lived with her husband maybe four months. He was a sick boy she made a mistake to marry him."

"Marrying a widow has never entered my mind."

"This is because you have no experience. A widow, especially if she is young and healthy like this girl, is a wonderful person to marry. She will be thankful to you the rest of her life. Believe me, if I was looking now for a bride, I would marry a widow."

Leo reflected, then shook his head.

Salzman hunched his shoulders in an almost imperceptible gesture of disappointment. He placed the card down on the wooden table and began to read another:

"Lily H. High school teacher. Regular. Not a substitute. Has savings and new Dodge car. Lived in Paris one year. Father is successful dentist thirty-five years.

Interested in professional man. Well-Americanized family. Wonderful opportunity."

"I know her personally," said Salzman. "I wish you could see this girl. She is a doll. Also very intelligent. All day you could talk to her about books and theayter and whatnot. She also knows current events."

"I don't believe you mentioned her age?"

"Her age?" Salzman said, raising his brows. "Her age is thirty-two years."

Leo said after a while, "I'm afraid that seems a little too old."

Salzman let out a laugh. "So how old are you, rabbi?"

"Twenty-seven."

"So what is the difference, tell me, between twenty-seven and thirty-two? My own wife is seven years older than me. So what did I suffer?— Nothing. If Rothschild's daughter wants to marry you, would you say on account her age, no?"

"Yes," Leo said dryly.

Salzman shook off the no in the yes. "Five years don't mean a thing. I give you my word that when you will live with her for one week you will forget her age. What does it mean five years—that she lived more and knows more than somebody who is younger? On this girl, God bless her, years are not wasted. Each one that it comes makes better the bargain."

"What subject does she teach in high school?"

"Languages. If you heard the way she speaks French, you will think it is music. I am in the business twenty-five years, and I recommend her with my whole heart. Believe me, I know what I'm talking, rabbi."

"What's on the next card?" Leo said abruptly.

Salzman reluctantly turned up the third card:

"Ruth K. Nineteen years. Honor student. Father offers thirteen thousand cash to the right bridegroom. He is a medical doctor. Stomach specialist with marvelous practice. Brother-in-law owns own garment business. Particular people."

Salzman looked as if he had read his trump card.

"Did you say nineteen?" Leo asked with interest.

"On the dot."

"Is she attractive?" He blushed. "Pretty?"

Salzman kissed his fingertips. "A little doll. On this I give you my word. Let me call the father tonight and you will see what means pretty."

But Leo was troubled. "You're sure she's that young?"

"This I am positive. The father will show you the birth certificate."

"Are you positive there isn't something wrong with her?" Leo insisted.

44   "Who says there is wrong?"

45   "I don't understand why an American girl her age should go to a marriage broker."

46   A smile spread over Salzman's face.

47   "So for the same reason you went, she comes."

48   Leo flushed. "I am pressed for time."

49   Salzman, realizing he had been tactless, quickly explained. "The father came, not her. He wants she should have the best, so he looks around himself. When we will locate the right boy he will introduce him and encourage. This makes a better marriage than if a young girl without experience takes for herself. I don't have to tell you this."

50   "But don't you think this young girl believes in love?" Leo spoke uneasily.

51   Salzman was about to guffaw but caught himself and said soberly, "Love comes with the right person, not before."

52   Leo parted dry lips but did not speak. Noticing that Salzman had snatched a glance at the next card, he cleverly asked, "How is her health?"

53   "Perfect," Salzman said, breathing with difficulty. "Of course, she is a little lame on her right foot from an auto accident that it happened to her when she was twelve years, but nobody notices on account she is so brilliant and also beautiful."

54   Leo got up heavily and went to the window. He felt curiously bitter and upbraided himself for having called in the marriage broker. Finally, he shook his head.

55   "Why not?" Salzman persisted, the pitch of his voice rising.

56   "Because I detest stomach specialists."

57   "So what do you care what is his business? After you marry her do you need him? Who says he must come every Friday night in your house?"

58   Ashamed of the way the talk was going, Leo dismissed Salzman, who went home with heavy, melancholy eyes.

59   Though he had felt only relief at the marriage broker's departure, Leo was in low spirits the next day. He explained it as arising from Salzman's failure to produce a suitable bride for him. He did not care for his type of clientele. But when Leo found himself hesitating whether to seek out another matchmaker, one more polished than Pinye, he wondered if it could be—his protestations to the contrary, and although he honored his father and mother—that he did not, in essence, care for the matchmaking institution? This

> "Love comes with the right person, not before."

thought he quickly put out of mind yet found himself still upset. All day he ran around in the woods—missed an important appointment, forgot to give out his laundry, walked out of a Broadway cafeteria without paying and had to run back with the ticket in his hand; had even not recognized his landlady in the street when she passed with a friend and courteously called out, "A good evening to you, Dr. Finkle." By nightfall, however, he had regained sufficient calm to sink his nose into a book and there found peace from his thoughts.

60   Almost at once there came a knock on the door. Before Leo could say enter, Salzman, commercial Cupid, was standing in the room. His face was gray and meager, his expression hungry, and he looked as if he would expire on his feet. Yet the marriage broker managed, by some trick of the muscles, to display a broad smile.

61   "So good evening. I am invited?"

62   Leo nodded, disturbed to see him again, yet unwilling to ask the man to leave.

63   Beaming still, Salzman laid his portfolio on the table, "Rabbi, I got for you tonight good news."

64   "I've asked you not to call me rabbi. I'm still a student."

65   "Your worries are finished. I have for you a first-class bride."

66   "Leave me in peace concerning this subject." Leo pretended lack of interest.

67   "The world will dance at your wedding."

68   "Please, Mr. Salzman, no more."

69   "But first must come back my strength," Salzman said weakly. He fumbled with the portfolio straps and took out of the leather case an oily paper bag, from which he extracted a hard, seeded roll and a small, smoked whitefish. With a quick motion of his hand he stripped the fish out of its skin and began ravenously to chew. "All day in a rush," he muttered.

70   Leo watched him eat.

71   "A sliced tomato you have maybe?" Salzman hesitantly inquired.

72   "No."

73   The marriage broker shut his eyes and ate. When he had finished he carefully cleaned up the crumbs and rolled up the remains of the fish, in the paper bag. His spectacled eyes roamed the room until he discovered, amid some piles of books, a one-burner gas stove. Lifting his hat he humbly asked, "A glass tea you got, rabbi?"

Conscience-stricken, Leo rose and brewed the tea. He served it with a chunk of lemon and two cubes of lump sugar, delighting Salzman.

After he had drunk his tea, Salzman's strength and good spirits were restored.

"So tell me, rabbi," he said amiably, "you considered some more the three clients I mentioned yesterday?"

"There was no need to consider."

"Why not?"

"None of them suits me."

"What then suits you?"

Leo let it pass because he could give only a confused answer.

Without waiting for a reply, Salzman asked, "You remember this girl I talked to you—the high school teacher?"

"Age thirty-two?"

But, surprisingly, Salzman's face lit in a smile. "Age twenty-nine."

Leo shot him a look. "Reduced from thirty-two?"

"A mistake," Salzman avowed. "I talked today with the dentist. He took me to his safety deposit box and showed me the birth certificate. She was twenty-nine years last August. They made her a party in the mountains where she went for her vacation. When her father spoke to me the first time I forgot to write the age and I told you thirty-two, but now I remember this was a different client, a widow."

"The same one you told me about, I thought she was twenty-four?"

"A different. Am I responsible that the world is filled with widows?"

"No, but I'm not interested in them, nor for that matter, in schoolteachers."

Salzman pulled his clasped hands to his breast. Looking at the ceiling he devoutly exclaimed, "Yiddishe kinder, what can I say to somebody that he is not interested in high school teachers? So what then you are interested?"

Leo flushed but controlled himself.

"In what else will you be interested," Salzman went on, "if you not interested in this fine girl that she speaks four languages and has personally in the bank ten thousand dollars? Also her father guarantees further twelve thousand. Also she has a new car, wonderful clothes, talks on all subjects, and she will give you a first-class home and children. How near do we come in our life to paradise?"

"If she's so wonderful, why wasn't she married ten years ago?"

"Why?" said Salzman with a heavy laugh. "—Why? Because she is *partikiler*. This is why. She wants the *best*."

Leo was silent, amused at how he had entangled himself. But Salzman had aroused his interest in Lily H., and he began seriously to consider calling on her. When the marriage broker observed how intently Leo's mind was at work on the facts he had supplied, he felt certain they would soon come to an agreement.

L ATE Saturday afternoon, conscious of Salzman, Leo Finkle walked with Lily Hirschorn along Riverside Drive. He walked briskly and erectly, wearing with distinction the black fedora he had that morning taken with trepidation out of the dusty hat box on his closet shelf, and the heavy black Saturday coat he had thoroughly whisked clean. Leo also owned a walking stick, a present from a distant relative, but quickly put temptation aside and did not use it. Lily, petite and not unpretty, had on something signifying the approach of spring. She was au courant, animatedly, with all sorts of subjects, and he weighed her words and found her surprisingly sound—score another for Salzman, whom he uneasily sensed to be somewhere around, hiding perhaps high in a tree along the street, flashing the lady signals with a pocket mirror; or perhaps a cloven-hoofed Pan, piping nuptial ditties as he danced his invisible way before them, strewing wild buds on the walk and purple grapes in their path, symbolizing fruit of a union, though there was of course still none.

Lily startled Leo by remarking, "I was thinking of Mr. Salzman, a curious figure wouldn't you say?"

Not certain what to answer, he nodded.

She bravely went on, blushing, "I for one am grateful for his introducing us. Aren't you?"

He courteously replied, "I am."

"I mean," she said with a little laugh—and it was all in good taste, or at least gave the effect of being not in bad—"do you mind that we came together so?"

He was not displeased with her honesty, recognizing that she meant to set the relationship aright, and understanding that it took a certain amount of experience in life, and courage, to want to do it quite that way. One had to have some sort of past to make that kind of beginning.

He said that he did not mind. Salzman's function was traditional and honorable—valuable for what it might achieve, which, he pointed out, was frequently nothing.

104   Lily agreed with a sigh. They walked on for a while and she said after a long silence, again with a nervous laugh, "Would you mind if I asked you something a little bit personal? Frankly, I find the subject fascinating." Although Leo shrugged, she went on half-embarrassedly, "How was it that you came to your calling? I mean, was it a sudden passionate inspiration?"

105   Leo, after a time, slowly replied, "I was always interested in the Law."

106   "You saw revealed in it the presence of the Highest?"

107   He nodded and changed the subject. "I understand that you spent a little time in Paris, Miss Hirschorn?"

108   "Oh, did Mr. Salzman tell you, Rabbi Finkle?" Leo winced but she went on, "It was ages ago and almost forgotten. I remember I had to return for my sister's wedding."

109   And Lily would not be put off. "When," she asked in a slightly trembly voice, "did you become enamored of God?"

110   He stared at her. Then it came to him that she was talking about not Leo Finkle but a total stranger, some mystical figure, perhaps even passionate prophet that Salzman had dreamed up for her—no relation to the living or dead. Leo trembled with rage and weakness. The trickster had obviously sold her a bill of goods, just as he had him, who'd expected to become acquainted with a young lady of twenty-nine, only to behold, the moment he had laid eyes upon her strained and anxious face, a woman past thirty-five and aging rapidly. Only his self-control had kept him this long in her presence.

111   "I am not," he said gravely, "a talented religious person," and, in seeking words to go on, found himself possessed by shame and fear. "I think," he said in a strained manner, "that I came to God not because I loved Him but because I did not."

112   This confession he spoke harshly because its unexpectedness shook him.

113   Lily wilted. Leo saw a profusion of loaves of bread go flying like ducks high over his head, not unlike the winged loaves by which he had counted himself to sleep last night. Mercifully, then, it snowed, which he would not put past Salzman's machinations.

114   HE was infuriated with the marriage broker and swore he would throw him out of the room the minute he reappeared. But Salzman did not come that night, and when Leo's anger had subsided, an unaccountable despair grew in its place. At first he thought this was caused by his disappointment in Lily, but before long it became evident that he had involved himself with Salzman without a true knowledge of his own intent. He gradually realized—with an emptiness that seized him with six hands—that he had called in the broker to find him a bride because he was incapable of doing it himself. This terrifying insight he had derived as a result of his meeting and conversation with Lily Hirschorn. Her probing questions had somehow irritated him into revealing—to himself more than her—the true nature of his relationship to God, and from that it had come upon him, with shocking force, that apart from his parents, he had never loved anyone. Or perhaps it went the other way, that he did not love God so well as he might, because he had not loved man. It seemed to Leo that his whole life stood starkly revealed and he saw himself for the first time as he truly was—unloved and loveless. This bitter but somehow not fully unexpected revelation brought him to a point of panic, controlled only by extraordinary effort. He covered his face with his hands and cried.

The week that followed was the worst of his life. He did not eat and lost weight. His beard darkened and grew ragged. He stopped attending seminars and almost never opened a book. He seriously considered leaving the Yeshiva, although he was deeply troubled at the thought of the loss of all his years of study—saw them like pages torn from a book, strewn over the city—and at the devastating effect of this decision upon his parents. But he had lived without knowledge of himself, and never in the Five Books and all the Commentaries—mea culpa—had the truth been revealed to him. He did not know where to turn, and in all this desolating loneliness there was no *to whom*, although he often thought of Lily but not once could bring himself to go downstairs and make the call. He became touchy and irritable, especially with his landlady, who asked him all manner of personal questions; on the other hand, sensing his own disagreeableness, he waylaid her on the stairs and apologized abjectly, until, mortified, she ran from him. Out of this, however, he drew the consolation that he was a Jew and that a Jew suffered. But gradually, as the long and terrible week drew to a close, he regained his composure and some idea of purpose in life: to go on as planned. Although he was imperfect, the ideal was not. As for his quest of a bride, the thought of continuing afflicted him with anxiety and heartburn, yet perhaps with this new knowledge of himself he would be more successful than in the past. Perhaps love would now come to him and a bride to that love. And for this sanctified seeking who needed a Salzman?

The marriage broker, a skeleton with haunted eyes, returned that very night. He looked, withal, the picture of frustrated expectancy—as if he had steadfastly waited the week at Miss Lily Hirschorn's side for a telephone call that never came.

Casually coughing, Salzman came immediately to the point: "So how did you like her?"

Leo's anger rose and he could not refrain from chiding the matchmaker: "Why did you lie to me, Salzman?"

Salzman's pale face went dead white, the world had snowed on him.

"Did you not state that she was twenty-nine?" Leo insisted.

"I give you my word—"

"She was thirty-five, if a day. *At least* thirty-five."

"Of this don't be too sure. Her father told me—"

"Never mind. The worst of it is that you lied to her."

"How did I lie to her, tell me?"

"You told her things about me that weren't true. You made me out to be more, consequently less than I am. She had in mind a totally different person, a sort of semi-mystical Wonder Rabbi."

"All I said, you was a religious man."

"I can imagine."

Salzman sighed. "This is my weakness that I have," he confessed. "My wife says to me I shouldn't be a salesman, but when I have two fine people that they would be wonderful to be married, I am so happy that I talk too much." He smiled wanly. "This is why Salzman is a poor man."

Leo's anger left him. "Well, Salzman, I'm afraid that's all."

The marriage broker fastened hungry eyes on him.

"You don't want anymore a bride?"

"I do," said Leo, "but I have decided to seek her in another way. I am no longer interested in an arranged marriage. To be frank, I now admit the necessity of premarital love. That is, I want to be in love with the one I marry." 133

"Love?" said Salzman, astounded. After a moment he remarked, "For us, our love is our life, not for the ladies. In the ghetto they—" 134

"I know, I know," said Leo. "I've thought of it often. Love, I have said to myself, should be a product of living and worship rather than its own end. Yet for myself I find it necessary to establish the level of my need and fulfill it." 135

Salzman shrugged but answered, "Listen, rabbi, if you want love, this I can find for you also. I have such beautiful clients that you will love them the minute your eyes will see them." 136

Leo smiled unhappily. "I'm afraid you don't understand." 137

But Salzman hastily unstrapped his portfolio and withdrew a manila packet from it. 138

"Pictures," he said, quickly laying the envelope on the table. 139

Leo called after him to take the pictures away, but as if on the wings of the wind, Salzman had disappeared. 140

March came. Leo had returned to his regular routine. Although he felt not quite himself yet—lacked energy—he was making plans for a more active social life. Of course it would cost something, but he was an expert in cutting corners; and when there were no corners left he would make circles rounder. All the while Salzman's pictures had lain on the table, gathering dust. Occasionally as Leo sat studying, or enjoying a cup of tea, his eyes fell on the manila envelope, but he never opened it. 141

The days went by and no social life to speak of developed with a member of the opposite sex—it was difficult, given the circumstances of his situation. One morning Leo toiled up the stairs to his room and stared out the window at the city. Although the day was bright his view of it was dark. For some time he watched the people in the street below hurrying along and then turned with a heavy heart to his little room. On the table was the packet. With a sudden relentless gesture he tore it open. For a half hour he stood by the table in a state of excitement, examining the photographs of the ladies Salzman had included. Finally, with a deep sigh he put them down. There were six, of varying degrees of attractiveness, but look at them long enough and they all became Lily Hirschorn: all past their prime, all starved behind bright smiles, not a true personality in the lot. Life, despite their frantic 142 yoohooings, had passed them by; they were pictures in a briefcase that stank of fish. After a while, however, as Leo attempted to return the photographs into the envelope, he found in it another, a snapshot of the type taken by a machine for a quarter. He gazed at it a moment and let out a low cry.

143 Her face deeply moved him. Why, he could at first not say. It gave him the impression of youth—spring flowers, yet age—a sense of having been used to the bone, wasted; this came from the eyes, which were hauntingly familiar, yet absolutely strange. He had a vivid impression that he had met her before, but try as he might he could not place her although he could almost recall her name, as if he had read it in her own handwriting. No, this couldn't be; he would have remembered her. It was not, he affirmed, that she had an extraordinary beauty—no, though her face was attractive enough; it was that *something* about her moved him. Feature for feature, even some of the ladies of the photographs could do better; but she leaped forth to his heart—had *lived,* or wanted to—more than just wanted, perhaps regretted how she had lived—had somehow deeply suffered: it could be seen in the depths of those reluctant eyes, and from the way the light enclosed and shone from her, and within her, opening realms of possibility: this was her own. Her he desired. His head ached and eyes narrowed with the intensity of his gazing, then as if an obscure fog had blown up in the mind, he experienced fear of her and was aware that he had received an impression, somehow, of evil. He shuddered, saying softly, It is thus with us all. Leo brewed some tea in a small pot and sat sipping it without sugar, to calm himself. But before he had finished drinking, again with excitement he examined the face and found it good: good for Leo Finkle. Only such a one could understand him and help him seek whatever he was seeking. She might, perhaps, love him. How she had happened to be among the discards in Salzman's barrel he could never guess, but he knew he must urgently go find her.

144 Leo rushed downstairs, grabbed up the Bronx telephone book, and searched for Salzman's home address. He was not listed, nor was his office. Neither was he in the Manhattan book. But Leo remembered having written down the address on a slip of paper after he had read Salzman's advertisement in the "personals" column of the *Forward.* He ran up to his room and tore through his papers, without luck. It was exasperating. Just when he needed the matchmaker he was nowhere to be found. Fortunately Leo remembered to look in

He had a vivid impression that he had met her before . . .

his wallet. There on a card he found his name written and a Bronx address. No phone number was listed, the reason—Leo now recalled—he had originally communicated with Salzman by letter. He got on his coat, put a hat on over his skullcap, and hurried to the subway station. All the way to the far end of the Bronx he sat on the edge of his seat. He was more than once tempted to take out the picture and see if the girl's face was as he remembered, but he refrained, allowing the snapshot to remain in his inside coat pocket, content to have her so close. When the train pulled into the station he was waiting at the door and bolted out. He quickly located the street Salzman had advertised.

The building he sought was less than a block from the subway, but it was not an office building, nor even a loft, nor a store in which one could rent office space. It was a very old tenement house. Leo found Salzman's name in pencil on a soiled tag under the bell and climbed three dark flights to his apartment. When he knocked, the door was opened by a thin, asthmatic, gray-haired woman, in felt slippers.

"Yes?" she said, expecting nothing. She listened without listening. He could have sworn he had seen her, too, before but knew it was an illusion.

"Salzman—does he live here? Pinye Salzman," he said, "the matchmaker?"

She stared at him a long minute. "Of course."

He felt embarrassed. "Is he in?"

"No." Her mouth, though left open, offered nothing more.

"The matter is urgent. Can you tell me where his office is?"

"In the air." She pointed upward.

"You mean he has no office?" Leo asked.

"In his socks."

He peered into the apartment. It was sunless and dingy, one large room divided by a half-open curtain, beyond which he could see a sagging metal bed. The near side of the room was crowded with rickety chairs, old bureaus, a three-legged table, racks of cooking utensils, and all the apparatus of a kitchen. But there was no sign of Salzman or his magic barrel, probably also a figment of the imagination. An odor of frying fish made Leo weak to the knees.

"Where is he?" he insisted. "I've got to see your husband."

At length she answered, "So who knows where he is? Every time he thinks a new thought he runs to a different place. Go home, he will find you."

"Tell him Leo Finkle."

She gave no sign she had heard.

He walked downstairs, depressed.

But Salzman, breathless, stood waiting at his door.

Leo was astounded and overjoyed. "How did you get here before me?"

"I rushed."

"Come inside."

They entered. Leo fixed tea, and a sardine sandwich for Salzman. As they were drinking he reached behind him for the packet of pictures and handed them to the marriage broker.

Salzman put down his glass and said expectantly, "You found somebody you like?"

"Not among these."

The marriage broker turned away.

"Here is the one I want." Leo held forth the snapshot.

Salzman slipped on his glasses and took the picture into his trembling hand. He turned ghastly and let out a groan.

"What's the matter?" cried Leo.

"Excuse me. Was an accident this picture. She isn't for you."

Salzman frantically shoved the manila packet into his portfolio. He thrust the snapshot into his pocket and fled down the stairs.

Leo, after momentary paralysis, gave chase and cornered the marriage broker in the vestibule. The landlady made hysterical outcries but neither of them listened.

"Give me back the picture, Salzman."

"No." The pain in his eyes was terrible.

"Tell me who she is then."

"This I can't tell you. Excuse me."

He made to depart, but Leo, forgetting himself, seized the matchmaker by his tight coat and shook him frenziedly.

"Please," sighed Salzman. "*Please*."

Leo ashamedly let him go. "Tell me who she is," he begged. "It's very important for me to know."

"She is not for you. She is a wild one—wild, without shame. This is not a bride for a rabbi."

"What do you mean wild?"

"Like an animal. Like a dog. For her to be poor was a sin. This is why to me she is dead now."

"In God's name, what do you mean?"

"Her I can't introduce to you," Salzman cried.

"Why are you so excited?"

"Why, he asks," Salzman said, bursting into tears. "This is my baby, my Stella, she should burn in hell."

LEO hurried up to bed and hid under the covers. Under the covers he thought his life through. Although he soon fell asleep he could not sleep her out of his mind. He woke, beating his breast. Though he prayed to be rid of her, his prayers went unanswered. Through days of torment he endlessly struggled not to love her; fearing success, he escaped it. He then concluded to convert her to goodness, himself to God. The idea alternately nauseated and exalted him.

He perhaps did not know that he had come to a final decision until he encountered Salzman in a Broadway caferia. He was sitting alone at a rear table, sucking the bony remains of a fish. The marriage broker appeared haggard, and transparent to the point of vanishing.

Salzman looked up at first without recognizing him. Leo had grown a pointed beard and his eyes were weighted with wisdom.

"Salzman," he said, "love has at last come to my heart."

"Who can love from a picture?" mocked the marriage broker.

"It is not impossible."

"If you can love her, then you can love anybody. Let me show you some new clients that they just sent me their photographs. One is a little doll."

"Just her I want," Leo murmured.

"Don't be a fool, doctor. Don't bother with her."

"Put me in touch with her, Salzman," Leo said humbly. "Perhaps I can be of service."

Salzman had stopped eating and Leo understood with emotion that it was now arranged.

Leaving the cafeteria, he was, however, afflicted by a tormenting suspicion that Salzman had planned it all to happen this way.

LEO was informed by letter that she would meet him on a certain corner, and she was there one spring night, waiting under a street lamp. He appeared, carrying a small bouquet of violets and rosebuds. Stella stood by the lamppost, smoking. She wore white with red shoes, which fitted his expectations, although in a troubled moment he had imagined the dress red, and only the shoes white. She waited uneasily and shyly. From afar he saw that her eyes—clearly her father's—were filled with desperate innocence. He pictured, in her, his own redemption. Violins and lit candles revolved in the sky. Leo ran forward with flowers outthrust.

Around the corner, Salzman, leaning against a wall, chanted prayers for the dead.

F ROM reading this story closely you will have noticed that you can consider the interior of a room or apartment a setting in itself. If you like this variety of setting in "The Magic Barrel," you may want to look at the interiors of "Cell One" by Chimamanda Ngozi Adichie in chapter 9 and the interior of the pickup truck in "No One's a Mystery" by Elizabeth Tallent in chapter 10.

GOING FURTHER Malamud is a master of detail and, in the context of our discussion in this chapter, of the creation of settings. From the inside of the small grocery store in his novel *The Assistant* to the Italy of his story-sequence *Pictures of Fidelman* to the Vermont countryside in *Dubin's Lives* and the Pacific island in *God's Grace,* his settings seem absolutely suited to the action of the novels.

Writing from Reading

Summarize

1 Examine Leo's reasoning for rejecting all the various women Salzman presents, then read the description of Stella at the end. Compare and contrast Stella with the ideal Salzman seems to seek at the beginning of the story.

Analyze Craft

2 In many ways, with his "magic" barrel, Pinye Salzman seems more magician than marriage broker. Consider how Malamud constructs the setting and atmosphere of scenes in which Salzman appears to make himself seem larger than life.

Analyze Voice

3 Consider the setting, plot, and characters of the story. How might things differ if Malamud himself weren't a Jew living in America? What details might be omitted or changed?

Synthesize Summary and Analysis

4 Consider the various settings in the story: Leo's and Salzman's apartments, the park, the cafeteria, beneath the streetlamp. Compare and contrast Malamud's description of each. In what ways are Leo's reactions determined by his environment?

Interpret the Story

5 At the end of the story, Leo has the suspicion he has been tricked by Salzman. Use evidence from the story to build a case for Salzman's honesty (or dishonesty). According to your conclusion, who is "the dead" that Salzman prays for at the end?

Reading for Setting

When reading for setting, ask yourself how *time* and *place* create a series of expectations among readers for the cast of characters they're likely to encounter and the range of events likely to occur, and play a role in the overall *effect* of the story.

What *elements* of setting can you identify?	• What is the story's location? • What mood does the setting create? • How is setting a window into character? • How does setting shape character? • Is setting a character itself? • Is setting an expression of the story's theme? • How is setting a window into a particular region?
What is the *physical or social environment* of the setting?	• When does the story occur (day, year, era)? • Is weather a part of the setting? • Is the setting a comfortable one, or is it unpleasant, even brutalizing? • What are the living and working conditions? • What are the social conditions in the era in which the story occurs?

Suggestions for Writing about Setting

1. After reading the introduction to this chapter and the stories within it, what would you add to our definition of "setting"? Use evidence from the stories to illustrate your new definition.

2. "Why I Live at the P.O." and "The Fall of the House of Usher" both feature narrators with distinctive voices. How do Welty and Poe use these voices to establish a sense of place? Give examples.

3. The main events of Lopez's story occur in the first half of the 1800s. What were the conditions for native people in Nebraska at that time? How might those conditions have influenced the relationship between Foster and the Pawnee and other tribes?

4. In Poe's "The Fall of the House of Usher" and Lopez's "The Location of the River," bodies of water take on literal and metaphoric significance. Analyze the role the Niobrara River plays in Lopez's story and the role of the tarn in Poe's.

5. All four stories challenge readers as to what they can or should believe. Write an essay in which you discuss the role of uncertainty and mystery in each story, how they affect the reading experience, and how, possibly, the setting influenced your understanding of these questions.

7

Point of View

> "Brownies" actually
> started out in the first-
> person point of view, and then
> I changed it to the third-person
> point of view, and then I changed
> it back to the first-person point of view.
> ... The first [person] can oftentimes be the
> most personal point of view that a writer can
> employ, but it's also deceptively simple."
>
> Conversation with ZZ Packer, available on
> video at www.mhhe.com/delbancole

D AY HNE?" Arnetta asked. "Are you coming?"
We all looked back at the bending girl, the thin of her back hunch€
like the back of a custodian sweeping a stage, caught in limelight.
strands of her hair were lit near-transparent, thin fiber-optic threads. She
not nod yes to the question, nor did she shake her head no. She abided, be
Then she began again, picking up leaves, wads of paper, the cotton fluff in
from a torn stuffed toy. She did it so methodically, so exquisitely, so humb
must have been trained. I thought of those dresses she wore, faded and ol€
so pressed and clean. I then saw the poverty in them; I then could imagin
mother, cleaning the houses of others, returning home, weary.

—from "Brownies" by Z

THE character whose thoughts are revealed in this passage is Laurel, nicknamed Snot. Laurel is the narrator, or the person who tells the story. The narrator relates events through the filter of her experiences, and it is from her point of view, or perspective, that the reader views the action. As Laurel reflects on Daphne, "the bending girl," she comes to a new understanding of the nature of Daphne's life. As the Brownie troop waits for a response to Arnetta's query—"Are you coming?"—Laurel looks closely at Daphne's movements and clothing and slowly recognizes that the "bending girl" is poor.

NARRATOR AND POINT OF VIEW

When the writer of an autobiography or memoir uses the first-person pronoun *I*, we're entitled to believe that *I* means the person writing the memoir. However, in fiction the narrator of a story is not the same as the writer. Writers create narrators to bring a story to life, and they provide a **point of view** by which to tell the tale. The writer's choice of narrator and point of view determines a great deal about what readers learn and when and how they learn it. Sometimes, as in the case of "Brownies," the story is told by means of a **first-person narrator,** a character in the story identified by use of the pronoun *I* or the plural first-person *we*. In contrast, many stories and novels use a **third-person narrator,** as in Hemingway's story in this chapter, "The Short Happy Life of Francis Macomber," in which the narrator refers to all the characters in the story with the pronouns *he, she,* or *they*. A third option, used less commonly, is for a story to be told via a **second-person narrator,** who addresses the reader directly (you), as is done in the story by Lorrie Moore in this chapter.

CONTINUED ON PAGE 195

... I put it in third person so that I could see some of my blind spots.

... there's almost ... no better way to be a part of the world than to read.

Q & A

A Conversation on Writing

ZZ Packer

Using Point of View to Craft "Brownies"

I found it very good to begin with that [first-person] voice because I felt as though I could just tell the story the way I thought that Laurel/ Snot would. . . . And then I put it in third person so that I could see some of my blind spots. . . . This particular third person could see some things about the rest of the world but might not have access to everything that Laurel had access to. So then that allowed me to see beyond Laurel's point of view. So switching the point of view for me enabled me to get the voice, which I wanted, which was the first-person voice, but also to get the knowledge and range of information that sometimes authors can only get when they travel into the third-person point of view.

The Power of the First-Person Point of View

I like to think of first person [as] here's the "I" that's telling the story. . . . A lot of writers tend to believe that, Oh, it's really me telling the story and so sometimes they just pour everything in . . . [but] they don't realize that the voice, which can be confessional . . . is a storytelling voice, [a storytelling voice that] can easily get out of the writer's grasp because it's so powerful.

Reading to Be a Citizen of the World

I encounter people who don't like to read. I mean to me it doesn't seem to be taking away from your time in the world, but just enriching it. When you read *War and Peace*, it's almost like having lived an extra ten years or something like that. So to me . . . there's almost . . . no better way to be a part of the world than to read. It almost seems the opposite of the way people think of it as a very solitary and even sort of solipsistic kind of activity. But I can't think of any other that would make me more of a citizen of the world.

ZZ Packer was born (1973) Zuwena Packer in Chicago. As she grew up in Atlanta and Louisville, her friends and family shortened Zuwena—Swahili for "good"—to ZZ, the name that she uses today. While attending Yale, Packer considered a career in engineering but ultimately turned to writing. Her debut short story collection, *Drinking Coffee Elsewhere* (2003), received great critical and popular acclaim; named a *New York Times* Notable Book, it was also picked for the *Today Show* Book Club by John Updike. In addition to appearing in *The New Yorker*, *Harper's*, and *Ploughshares*, her work has been anthologized in collections featuring young writers, southern writers, and black women writers, among others. Her stories present a range of characters, most of whom struggle to fit into their community, and she often captures aspects of the African-American experience. Like her varied characters, Packer herself has a résumé that includes stints as a barmaid, a high school teacher, and a coffee shop barista as well as a Stegner Fellow at Stanford University's prestigious writing program. Packer currently lives and writes in San Francisco.

To watch this entire interview and hear the author read from "Brownies," go to www. mhhe .com/delbanco1e.

RESEARCH ASSIGNMENT In her interview, what does ZZ Packer say she is trying to tell a story about? Do you agree this is the subject of the story? How does she get her point across?

AS YOU READ   As you read this story, notice the shifting levels of happiness and unhappiness among the characters. Notice also the shifting alliances among the characters at the center of the story.

TIP

FOR INTERACTIVE READING ... As you read, take note every time the story refers to a father. What is the significance of the various fathers mentioned? How does this tie in with the lesson the girls experience at camp?

Brownies (1999)

1   BY our second day at Camp Crescendo, the girls in my Brownie troop had decided to kick the asses of each and every girl in Brownie Troop 909. Troop 909 was doomed from the first day of camp; they were white girls, their complexions a blend of ice cream: strawberry, vanilla. They turtled out from their bus in pairs, their rolled-up sleeping bags chromatized with Disney characters: Sleeping Beauty, Snow White, Mickey Mouse; or the generic ones cheap parents bought: washed-out rainbows, unicorns, curly-eyelashed frogs. Some clutched Igloo coolers and still others held on to stuffed toys like pacifiers, looking all around them like tourists determined to be dazzled.

2   Our troop was wending its way past their bus, past the ranger station, past the colorful trail guide drawn like a treasure map, locked behind glass.

3   "Man, did you smell them?" Arnetta said, giving the girls a slow once-over, "They smell like Chihuahuas. *Wet* Chihuahuas." Their troop was still at the entrance, and though we had passed them by yards, Arnetta raised her nose in the air and grimaced.

4   Arnetta said this from the very rear of the line, far away from Mrs. Margolin, who always strung our troop behind her like a brood of obedient ducklings. Mrs. Margolin even looked like a mother duck—she had hair cropped close to a small ball of a head, almost no neck, and huge, miraculous breasts. She wore enormous belts that looked like the kind that weight-lifters wear, except hers would be cheap metallic gold or rabbit fur or covered with gigantic fake sunflowers, and often these belts would become nature lessons in and of themselves. "See," Mrs. Margolin once said to us, pointing to her belt, "this one's made entirely from the feathers of baby pigeons."

5   The belt layered with feathers was uncanny enough, but I was more disturbed by the realization that I had never actually *seen* a baby pigeon. I searched weeks for one, in vain—scampering after pigeons whenever I was downtown with my father.

6   But nature lessons were not Mrs. Margolin's top priority. She saw the position of troop leader as an evangelical post. Back at the A.M.E. church where our Brownie meetings were held, Mrs. Margolin was especially fond of imparting religious aphorisms by means of acrostics—"Satan" was the "Serpent Always Tempting and Noisome"; she'd refer to the "Bible" as "Basic Instructions Before Leaving Earth." Whenever she quizzed us on these, expecting to hear the acrostics parroted back to her, only Arnetta's correct replies soared over our vague mumblings. "Jesus?" Mrs. Margolin might ask expectantly, and Arnetta alone would dutifully answer, "Jehovah's Example, Saving Us Sinners."

7   Arnetta always made a point of listening to Mrs. Margolin's religious talk and giving her what she wanted to hear. Because of this, Arnetta could have blared through a megaphone that the white girls of

Troop 909 were "wet Chihuahuas" without so much as a blink from Mrs. Margolin. Once, Arnetta killed the troop goldfish by feeding it a french fry covered in ketchup, and when Mrs. Margolin demanded that she explain what had happened, claimed the goldfish had been eyeing her meal for *hours*, then the fish— giving in to temptation—had leapt up and snatched a whole golden fry from her fingertips.

8   "*Serious* Chihuahua," Octavia added, and though neither Arnetta nor Octavia could *spell* "Chihuahua," had ever *seen* a Chihuahua, trisyllabic words had gained a sort of exoticism within our fourth-grade set at Woodrow Wilson Elementary. Arnetta and Octavia would flip through the dictionary, determined to work the vulgar-sounding ones like "Djibouti" and "asinine" into conversation.

9   "*Caucasian* Chihuahuas," Arnetta said.

10   That did it. The girls in my troop turned elastic: Drema and Elise doubled up on one another like inextricably entwined kites; Octavia slapped her belly; Janice jumped straight up in the air, then did it again, as if to slam-dunk her own head. They could not stop laughing. No one had laughed so hard since a boy named Martez had stuck a pencil in the electric socket and spent the whole day with a strange grin on his face.

11   "Girls, girls," said our parent helper, Mrs. Hedy. Mrs. Hedy was Octavia's mother, and she wagged her index finger perfunctorily, like a windshield wiper. "Stop it, now. Be good." She said this loud enough to be heard, but lazily, bereft of any feeling or indication that she meant to be obeyed, as though she could say these words again at the exact same pitch if a button somewhere on her were pressed.

12   But the rest of the girls didn't stop; they only laughed louder. It was the word "Caucasian" that got them all going. One day at school, about a month before the Brownie camping trip, Arnetta turned to a boy wearing impossibly high-ankled floodwater jeans and said, "What are you? *Caucasian?*" The word took off from there, and soon everything was Caucasian. If you ate too fast you ate like a Caucasian, if you ate too slow you ate like a Caucasian. The biggest feat anyone at Woodrow Wilson could do was to jump off the swing in midair, at the highest point in its arc, and if you fell (as I had, more than once) instead of landing on your feet, knees bent Olympic gymnast–style, Arnetta and Octavia were prepared to comment. They'd look at each other with the silence of passengers who'd narrowly escaped an accident, then nod their heads, whispering with solemn horror, "*Caucasian.*"

The word took off from there, and soon everything was Caucasian.

Even the only white kid in our school, Dennis, got in on the Caucasian act. That time when Martez stuck a pencil in the socket, Dennis had pointed and yelled, "That was *so* Caucasian!"

WHEN you lived in the south suburbs of Atlanta, it was easy to forget about whites. Whites were like those baby pigeons: real and existing, but rarely seen or thought about. Everyone had been to Rich's to go clothes shopping, everyone had seen white girls and their mothers coo-cooing over dresses; everyone had gone to the downtown library and seen white businessmen swish by importantly, wrists flexed in front of them to check the time as though they would change from Clark Kent into Superman at any second. But those images were as fleeting as cards shuffled in a deck, whereas the ten white girls behind us—*invaders*, Arnetta would later call them— were instantly real and memorable, with their long, shampoo-commercial hair, straight as spaghetti from the box. This alone was reason for envy and hatred. The only black girl most of us had ever seen with hair that long was Octavia, whose hair hung past her butt like a Hawaiian hula dancer's. The sight of Octavia's mane prompted other girls to listen to her reverentially, as though whatever she had to say would somehow activate their own follicles. For example, when, on the first day of camp, Octavia made as if to speak, and everyone fell silent. "Nobody," Octavia said, "calls us niggers."

At the end of that first day, when half of our troop made their way back to the cabin after tag-team restroom visits, Arnetta said she'd heard one of the Troop 909 girls call Daphne a nigger. The other half of the girls and I were helping Mrs. Margolin clean up the pots and pans from the campfire ravioli dinner. When we made our way to the restrooms to wash up and brush our teeth, we met up with Arnetta midway.

"Man, I completely heard the girl," Arnetta reported. "Right, Daphne?"

Daphne hardly ever spoke, but when she did, her voice was petite and tinkly, the voice one might expect from a shiny new earring. She'd written a poem once, for Langston Hughes Day, a poem brimming with all the teacher-winning ingredients—trees and oceans, sunsets and moons—but what cinched the poem for the grown-ups, snatching the win from Octavia's musical ode to Grandmaster Flash and the Furious Five, were Daphne's last lines:

> You are my father, the veteran
> When you cry in the dark
> It rains and rains and rains in my heart

She'd always worn clean, though faded, jumpers and dresses when Chic jeans were the fashion, but when she went up to the dais to receive her prize journal, pages trimmed in gold, she wore a new dress with a velveteen bodice and a taffeta skirt as wide as an umbrella. All the kids clapped, though none of them understood the poem. I'd read encyclopedias the way others read comics, and I didn't get it. But those last lines pricked me, they were so eerie, and as my father and I ate cereal, I'd whisper over my Froot Loops, like a mantra, "*You are my father, the veteran. You are my father, the veteran, the veteran, the veteran,*" until my father, who acted in plays as Caliban and Othello and was not a veteran, marched me up to my teacher one morning and said, "Can you tell me what's wrong with this kid?"

I thought Daphne and I might become friends, but I think she grew spooked by me whispering those lines to her, begging her to tell me what they meant, and I soon understood that two quiet people like us were better off quiet alone.

"Daphne? Didn't you hear them call you a nigger?" Arnetta asked, giving Daphne a nudge.

The sun was setting behind the trees, and their leafy tops formed a canopy of black lace for the flame of the sun to pass through. Daphne shrugged her shoulders at first, then slowly nodded her head when Arnetta gave her a hard look.

Twenty minutes later, when my restroom group returned to the cabin, Arnetta was still talking about Troop 909. My restroom group had passed by some of the 909 girls. For the most part, they deferred to us, waving us into the restrooms, letting us go even though they'd gotten there first.

We'd seen them, but from afar, never within their orbit enough to see whether their faces were the way all white girls appeared on TV—ponytailed and full of energy, bubbling over with love and money. All I could see was that some of them rapidly fanned their faces with their hands, though the heat of the day had long passed. A few seemed to be lolling their heads in slow circles, half purposefully, as if exercising the muscles of their necks, half ecstatically, like Stevie Wonder.

24 "We can't let them get away with that," Arnetta said, dropping her voice to a laryngitic whisper. "We can't let them get away with calling us niggers. I say we teach them a lesson." She sat down cross-legged on a sleeping bag, an embittered Buddha, eyes glimmering acrylic-black. "We can't go telling Mrs. Margolin, either. Mrs. Margolin'll say something about doing unto others and the path of righteousness and all. Forget that shit." She let her eyes flutter irreverently till they half closed, as though ignoring an insult not worth returning. We could all hear Mrs. Margolin outside, gathering the last of the metal campware.

25 Nobody said anything for a while. Usually people were quiet after Arnetta spoke. Her tone had an upholstered confidence that was somehow both regal and vulgar at once. It demanded a few moments of silence in its wake, like the ringing of a church bell or the playing of taps. Sometimes Octavia would ditto or dissent to whatever Arnetta had said, and this was the signal that others could speak. But this time Octavia just swirled a long cord of hair into pretzel shapes.

26 "*Well?*" Arnetta said. She looked as if she had discerned the hidden severity of the situation and was waiting for the rest of us to catch up. Everyone looked from Arnetta to Daphne. It was, after all, Daphne who had supposedly been called the name, but Daphne sat on the bare cabin floor, flipping through the pages of the Girl Scout handbook, eyebrows arched in mock wonder, as if the handbook were a catalogue full of bright and startling foreign costumes. Janice broke the silence. She clapped her hands to broach her idea of a plan.

27 "They gone be sleeping," she whispered conspiratorially, "then we gone sneak into they cabin, then we'll put daddy longlegs in they sleeping bags. Then they'll wake up. Then we gone beat 'em up till they're as flat as frying pans!" She jammed her fist into the palm of her hand, then made a sizzling sound.

28 Janice's country accent was laughable, her looks homely, her jumpy acrobatics embarrassing to behold. Arnetta and Octavia volleyed amused, arrogant smiles whenever Janice opened her mouth, but Janice never caught the hint, spoke whenever she wanted, fluttered around Arnetta and Octavia futilely offering her opinions to their departing backs. Whenever Arnetta and Octavia shooed her away, Janice loitered until the two would finally sigh and ask, "What *is* it, Miss Caucausoid? What do you *want*?"

29 "Shut up, Janice," Octavia said, letting a fingered loop of hair fall to her waist as though just the sound of Janice's voice had ruined the fun of her hair twisting.

30 Janice obeyed, her mouth hung open in a loose grin, unflappable, unhurt.

31 "All right," Arnetta said, standing up. "We're going to have a secret meeting and talk about what we're going to do."

32 Everyone gravely nodded her head. The word "secret" had a built-in importance, the modifier form of the word carried more clout than the noun. A secret meant nothing; it was like gossip: just a bit of unpleasant knowledge about someone who happened to be someone other than yourself. A secret *meeting*, or a secret *club* was entirely different.

33 That was when Arnetta turned to me as though she knew that doing so was both a compliment and a charity.

34 "Snot, you're not going to be a bitch and tell Mrs. Margolin, are you?"

35 I had been called "Snot" ever since first grade, when I'd sneezed in class and two long ropes of mucus had splattered a nearby girl.

36 "Hey," I said. "Maybe you didn't hear them right—I mean—"

37 "Are you gonna tell on us or not?" was all Arnetta wanted to know, and by the time the question was asked, the rest of our Brownie troop looked at me as though they'd already decided their course of action, me being the only impediment.

38 CAMP Crescendo used to double as a high-school-band and field hockey camp until an arcing field hockey ball landed on the clasp of a girl's metal barrette, knifing a skull nerve and paralyzing the right side of her body. The camp closed down for a few years and the girl's teammates built a memorial, filling the spot on which the girl fell with hockey balls, on which they had painted—all in nail polish—get-well tidings, flowers, and hearts. The balls were still stacked there, like a shrine of ostrich eggs embedded in the ground.

39 On the second day of camp, Troop 909 was dancing around the mound of hockey balls, their limbs jangling awkwardly, their cries like the constant summer squeal of an amusement park. There was a stream that bordered the field hockey lawn, and the girls from my troop settled next to it, scarfing down the last of lunch: sandwiches made from salami and slices of tomato that had gotten waterlogged from the melting ice in the cooler. From the stream bank, Arnetta eyed the Troop 909 girls, scrutinizing their movements to glean inspiration for battle.

40 "Man," Arnetta said, "we could bumrush them right now if that damn lady would *leave*."

41 The 909 troop leader was a white woman with the severe pageboy hairdo of an ancient Egyptian. She lay on a picnic blanket, sphinx-like, eating a banana, sometimes holding it out in front of her like a microphone. Beside her sat a girl slowly flapping one hand like a bird with a broken wing. Occasionally, the leader would call out the names of girls who'd attempted leapfrogs and flips, or of girls who yelled too loudly or strayed far from the circle.

42 "I'm just glad Big Fat Mama's not following us here," Octavia said. "At least we don't have to worry about her." Mrs. Margolin, Octavia assured us, was having her Afternoon Devotional, shrouded in mosquito netting, in a clearing she'd found. Mrs. Hedy was cleaning mud from her espadrilles in the cabin.

43 "I handled them." Arnetta sucked on her teeth and proudly grinned. "I told her we was going to gather leaves."

44 "Gather leaves," Octavia said, nodding respectfully. "That's a good one. Especially since they're so mad-crazy about this camping thing." She looked from ground to sky, sky to ground. Her hair hung down her back in two braids like a squaw's. "I mean, I really don't know why it's called *camping*—all we ever do with Nature is find some twigs and say something like, 'Wow, this fell from a tree.'" She then studied her sandwich. With two disdainful fingers, she picked out a slice of dripping tomato, the sections congealed with red slime. She pitched it into the stream embrowned with dead leaves and the murky effigies of other dead things, but in the opaque water, a group of small silver-brown fish appeared. They surrounded the tomato and nibbled.

45 "Look!" Janice cried. "Fishes! Fishes!" As she scrambled to the edge of the stream to watch, a covey of insects threw up tantrums from the wheatgrass and nettle, a throng of tiny electric machines, all going at once. Octavia sneaked up behind Janice as if to push her in. Daphne and I exchanged terrified looks. It seemed as though only we knew that Octavia was close enough—and bold enough—to actually push Janice into the stream. Janice turned around quickly, but Octavia was already staring serenely into the still water as though she was gathering some sort of courage from it. "What's so funny?" Janice said, eyeing them all suspiciously.

46 Elise began humming the tune to "Karma Chameleon," all the girls joining in, their hums light and facile. Janice also began to hum, against everyone else, the high-octane opening chords of "Beat It."

47 "I love me some Michael Jackson," Janice said when she'd finished humming, smacking her lips as though Michael Jackson were a favorite meal. "I *will* marry Michael Jackson."

> A secret meant nothing; it was like gossip . . .

Before anyone had a chance to impress upon Janice the impossibility of this, Arnetta suddenly rose, made a sun visor of her hand, and watched Troop 909 leave the field hockey lawn.

"Dammit!" she said. "We've got to get them *alone*."

"They won't ever be alone," I said. All the rest of the girls looked at me, for I usually kept quiet. If I spoke even a word, I could count on someone calling me Snot. Everyone seemed to think that we could beat up these girls; no one entertained the thought that they might fight *back*. "The only time they'll be unsupervised is in the bathroom."

"Oh shut up, Snot," Octavia said.

But Arnetta slowly nodded her head. "The bathroom," she said. "The bathroom," she said, again and again. "The bathroom! The bathroom!"

ACCORDING to Octavia's watch, it took us five minutes to hike to the restrooms, which were midway between our cabin and Troop 909's. Inside, the mirrors above the sinks returned only the vaguest of reflections, as though someone had taken a scouring pad to their surfaces to obscure the shine. Pine needles, leaves, and dirty, flattened wads of chewing gum covered the floor like a mosaic. Webs of hair matted the drain in the middle of the floor. Above the sinks and below the mirrors, stacks of folded white paper towels lay on a long metal counter. Shaggy white balls of paper towels sat on the sinktops in a line like corsages on display. A thread of floss snaked from a wad of tissues dotted with the faint red-pink of blood. One of those white girls, I thought, had just lost a tooth.

> Pine needles, leaves, and dirty, flattened wads of chewing gum covered the floor like a mosaic.

Though the restroom looked almost the same as it had the night before, it somehow seemed stranger now. We hadn't noticed the wooden rafters coming together in great V's. We were, it seemed, inside a whale, viewing the ribs of the roof of its mouth.

"Wow. It's a mess," Elise said.

"You can say that again."

Arnetta leaned against the doorjamb of a restroom stall. "This is where they'll be again," she said. Just seeing the place, just having a plan seemed to satisfy her. "We'll go in and talk to them. You know, 'How you doing? How long'll you be here?' That sort of thing. Then Octavia and I are gonna tell them what happens when they call any one of us a nigger."

"I'm going to say something, too," Janice said.

Arnetta considered this. "Sure," she said. "Of course. Whatever you want."

Janice pointed her finger like a gun at Octavia and rehearsed the line she'd thought up, "'We're gonna teach you a *lesson*!' That's what I'm going to say." She narrowed her eyes like a TV mobster. "'We're gonna teach you little girls a lesson!'"

With the back of her hand, Octavia brushed Janice's finger away. "You couldn't teach me to shit in a toilet."

"But," I said, "what if they say, 'We didn't say that. We didn't call anyone an N-I-G-G-E-R.'"

"Snot," Arnetta said, and then sighed. "Don't think. Just fight. If you even know how."

Everyone laughed except Daphne. Arnetta gently laid her hand on Daphne's shoulder. "Daphne. You don't have to fight. We're doing this for you."

Daphne walked to the counter, took a clean paper towel, and carefully unfolded it like a map. With it, she began to pick up the trash all around. Everyone watched.

"C'mon," Arnetta said to everyone. "Let's beat it." We all ambled toward the doorway, where the sunshine made one large white rectangle of light. We were immediately blinded, and we shielded our eyes with our hands and our forearms.

"Daphne?" Arnetta asked. "Are you coming?"

We all looked back at the bending girl, the thin of her back hunched like the back of a custodian sweeping a stage, caught in limelight. Stray strands of her hair were lit near-transparent, thin fiber-optic threads. She did not nod yes to the question, nor did she shake her head no. She abided, bent. Then she began again, picking up leaves, wads of paper, the cotton fluff innards from a torn stuffed toy. She did it so methodically, so exquisitely, so humbly, she must have been trained. I thought of those dresses she wore, faded and old, yet so pressed and clean. I then saw the poverty in them; I then could imagine her mother, cleaning the houses of others, returning home, weary.

"I guess she's not coming."

We left her and headed back to our cabin, over pine needles and leaves, taking the path full of shade.

"What about our secret meeting?" Elise asked.

Arnetta enunciated her words in a way that defied contradiction: "We just had it."

IT was nearing our bedtime, but the sun had not yet set.

"Hey, your mama's coming," Arnetta said to Octavia when she saw Mrs. Hedy walk toward the cabin, sniffling. When Octavia's mother wasn't giving bored, parochial orders, she sniffled continuously, mourning an imminent divorce from her husband. She might begin a sentence, "I don't know what Robert will do when Octavia and I are gone. Who'll buy him cigarettes?" and Octavia would hotly whisper, *Mama,* in a way that meant: Please don't talk about our problems in front of everyone. Please shut up.

75   But when Mrs. Hedy began talking about her husband, thinking about her husband, seeing clouds shaped like the head of her husband, she couldn't be quiet, and no one could dislodge her from the comfort of her own woe. Only one thing could perk her up—Brownie songs. If the girls were quiet, and Mrs. Hedy was in her dopey, sorrowful mood, she would say, "Y'all know I like those songs, girls. Why don't you sing one?" Everyone would groan, except me and Daphne. I, for one, liked some of the songs.

76   "C'mon, everybody," Octavia said drearily. "She likes the Brownie song best."

77   We sang, loud enough to reach Mrs. Hedy:

> "I've got something in my pocket;
> It belongs across my face.
> And I keep it very close at hand
>   in a most convenient place.
> I'm sure you couldn't guess it
> If you guessed a long, long while.
> So I'll take it out and put it on—
> It's a great big Brownie smile!"

78   The Brownie song was supposed to be sung cheerfully, as though we were elves in a workshop, singing as we merrily cobbled shoes, but everyone except me hated the song so much that they sang it like a maudlin record, played on the most sluggish of rpms.

79   "That was good," Mrs. Hedy said, closing the cabin door behind her. "Wasn't that nice, Linda?"

80   "Praise God," Mrs. Margolin answered without raising her head from the chore of counting out Popsicle sticks for the next day's craft session.

81   "Sing another one," Mrs. Hedy said. She said it with a sort of joyful aggression, like a drunk I'd once seen who'd refused to leave a Korean grocery.

82   "God, Mama, get over it," Octavia whispered in a voice meant only for Arnetta, but Mrs. Hedy heard it and started to leave the cabin.

83   "Don't go," Arnetta said. She ran after Mrs. Hedy and held her by the arm. "We haven't finished singing." She nudged us with a single look. "Let's sing the 'Friends Song.' For Mrs. Hedy."

84   Although I liked some of the songs, I hated this one:

> Make new friends
> But keep the o-old,
> One is silver
> And the other gold.

If most of the girls in the troop could be any type of metal, they'd be bunched-up wads of tinfoil, maybe, or rusty iron nails you had to get tetanus shots for.

"No, no, no," Mrs. Margolin said before anyone could start in on the "Friends Song." "An uplifting song. Something to lift her up and take her mind off all these earthly burdens."

Arnetta and Octavia rolled their eyes. Everyone knew what song Mrs. Margolin was talking about, and no one, no one, wanted to sing it.

"Please, no," a voice called out. "Not 'The Doughnut Song.'"

"Please not 'The Doughnut Song,'" Octavia pleaded.

"I'll brush my teeth two times if I don't have to sing 'The Doughnut—'"

"Sing!" Mrs. Margolin demanded.

We sang:

> "Life without Jesus is like a do-ough-nut!
> Like a do-ooough-nut!
> Like a do-ooough-nut!
> Life without Jesus is like a do-ough-nut!
> There's a hole in the middle of my soul!"

There were other verses, involving other pastries, but we stopped after the first one and cast glances toward Mrs. Margolin to see if we could gain a reprieve. Mrs. Margolin's eyes fluttered blissfully. She was half asleep.

"Awww," Mrs. Hedy said, as though giant Mrs. Margolin were a cute baby, "Mrs. Margolin's had a long day."

"Yes, indeed," Mrs. Margolin answered. "If you don't mind, I might just go to the lodge where the beds are. I haven't been the same since the operation."

I had not heard of this operation, or when it had occurred, since Mrs. Margolin had never missed the once-a-week Brownie meetings, but I could see from Daphne's face that she was concerned, and I could see that the other girls had decided that Mrs. Margolin's operation must have happened long ago in some remote time unconnected to our own. Nevertheless, they put on sad faces. We had all been taught that adulthood was full of sorrow and pain, taxes and bills, dreaded work and dealings with whites, sickness and death. I tried to do what the others did. I tried to look silent.

7 "Go right ahead, Linda," Mrs. Hedy said. "I'll watch the girls." Mrs. Hedy seemed to forget about divorce for a moment; she looked at us with dewy eyes, as if we were mysterious, furry creatures. Meanwhile, Mrs. Margolin walked through the maze of sleeping bags until she found her own. She gathered a neat stack of clothes and pajamas slowly, as though doing so was almost painful. She took her toothbrush, her toothpaste, her pillow. "All right!" Mrs. Margolin said, addressing us all from the threshold of the cabin. "Be in bed by nine." She said it with a twinkle in her voice, letting us know she was allowing us to be naughty and stay up till nine-fifteen.

8 "C'mon everybody," Arnetta said after Mrs. Margolin left. "Time for us to wash up."

9 Everyone watched Mrs. Hedy closely, wondering whether she would insist on coming with us since it was night, making a fight with Troop 909 nearly impossible. Troop 909 would soon be in the bathroom, washing their faces, brushing their teeth—completely unsuspecting of our ambush.

0 "We won't be long," Arnetta said. "We're old enough to go to the restrooms by ourselves."

1 Mrs. Hedy pursed her lips at this dilemma. "Well, I guess you Brownies are almost Girl Scouts, right?"

2 "Right!"

3 "Just one more badge," Drema said.

4 "And about," Octavia droned, "a million more cookies to sell." Octavia looked at all of us, *Now's our chance*, her face seemed to say, but our chance to do *what*, I didn't exactly know.

5 Finally, Mrs. Hedy walked to the doorway where Octavia stood dutifully waiting to say goodbye but looking bored doing it. Mrs. Hedy held Octavia's chin. "You'll be good?"

6 "Yes, Mama."

7 "And remember to pray for me and your father? If I'm asleep when you get back?"

8 "Yes, Mama."

9 WHEN the other girls had finished getting their toothbrushes and washcloths and flashlights for the group restroom trip, I was drawing pictures of tiny birds with too many feathers. Daphne was sitting on her sleeping bag, reading.

0 "You're not going to come?" Octavia asked.

1 Daphne shook her head.

2 "I'm gonna stay, too," I said. "I'll go to the restroom when Daphne and Mrs. Hedy go."

3 Arnetta leaned down toward me and whispered so that Mrs. Hedy, who'd taken over Mrs. Margolin's task of counting Popsicle sticks, couldn't hear. "No, Snot. If

we get in trouble, you're going to get in trouble with the rest of us."

114 WE made our way through the darkness by flashlight. The tree branches that had shaded us just hours earlier, along the same path, now looked like arms sprouting menacing hands. The stars sprinkled the sky like spilled salt. They seemed fastened to the darkness, high up and holy, their places fixed and definite as we stirred beneath them.

115 Some, like me, were quiet because we were afraid of the dark; others were talking like crazy for the same reason.

116 "Wow!" Drema said, looking up. "Why are all the stars out here? I never see stars back on Oneida Street."

117 "It' a camping trip, that's why," Octavia said. "You're supposed to see stars on camping trips."

118 Janice said, "This place smells like my mother's air freshener."

119 "These woods are *pine*," Elise said. "Your mother probably uses *pine* air freshener."

120 Janice mouthed an exaggerated "Oh," nodding her head as though she just then understood one of the world's great secrets.

121 No one talked about fighting. Everyone was afraid enough just walking through the infinite deep of the woods. Even though I didn't fight to fight, was afraid of fighting, I felt I was part of the rest of the troop; like I was defending something. We trudged against the slight incline of the path, Arnetta leading the way.

122 "You know," I said, "their leader will be there. Or they won't even be there. It's dark already. Last night the sun was still in the sky. I'm sure they're already finished."

123 Arnetta acted as if she hadn't heard me. I followed her gaze with my flashlight, and that's when I saw the squares of light in the darkness. The bathroom was just ahead.

124 BUT the girls were there. We could hear them before we could see them.

125 "Octavia and I will go in first so they'll think there's just two of us, then wait till I say, 'We're gonna teach you a lesson,'" Arnetta said. "Then, bust in. That'll surprise them."

126 "That's what I was supposed to say," Janice said.

127 Arnetta went inside, Octavia next to her. Janice followed, and the rest of us waited outside.

128 They were in there for what seemed like whole minutes, but something was wrong. Arnetta hadn't

given the signal yet. I was with the girls outside when I heard one of the Troop 909 girls say, "NO. That did NOT happen!"

129   That was to be expected, that they'd deny the whole thing. What I hadn't expected was *the voice* in which the denial was said. The girl sounded as though her tongue was caught in her mouth. "That's a BAD word!" the girl continued. "We don't say BAD words!"

130   "Let's go in," Elise said.

131   "No," Drema said, "I don't want to. What if we get beat up?"

132   "Snot?" Elise turned to me, her flashlight blinding. It was the first time anyone had asked my opinion, though I knew they were just asking because they were afraid.

133   "I say we go inside, just to see what's going on."

134   "But Arnetta didn't give us the signal," Drema said. "She's supposed to say, 'We're gonna teach you a lesson,' and I didn't hear her say it."

135   "C'mon," I said. "Let's just go in."

136   We went inside. There we found the white girls—about five girls huddled up next to one big girl. I instantly knew she was the owner of the voice we'd heard. Arnetta and Octavia inched toward us as soon as we entered.

137   "Where's Janice?" Elise asked, then we heard a flush. "Oh."

138   "I think," Octavia said, whispering to Elise, "they're retarded."

139   "We ARE NOT retarded!" the big girl said, though it was obvious that she was. That they all were. The girls around her began to whimper.

140   "They're just pretending," Arnetta said, trying to convince herself. "I know they are."

141   Octavia turned to Arnetta. "Arnetta. Let's just leave."

142   Janice came out of a stall, happy and relieved, then she suddenly remembered her line, pointed to the big girl, and said, "We're gonna teach you a lesson."

143   "Shut up, Janice," Octavia said, but her heart was not in it. Arnetta's face was set in a lost, deep scowl. Octavia turned to the big girl and said loudly, slowly, as if they were all deaf, "We're going to leave. It was nice meeting you, O.K.? You don't have to tell anyone that we were here. O.K.?"

144   "Why not?" said the big girl, like a taunt. When she spoke, her lips did not meet, her mouth did not close. Her tongue grazed the roof of her mouth, like a little pink fish. "You'll get in trouble. I know. *I* know."

145   Arnetta got back her old cunning. "If you said anything, then you'd be a tattletale."

146   The girl looked sad for a moment, then perked up quickly. A flash of genius crossed her face. "I *like* tattletale."

IT'S all right, girls. It's gonna be all right!" the 909 troop leader said. All of Troop 909 burst into tears. It was as though someone had instructed them all to cry at once. The troop leader had girls under her arm, and all the rest of the girls crowded about her. It reminded me of a hog I'd seen on a field trip, where all the little hogs gathered about the mother at feeding time, latching onto her teats. The 909 troop leader had come into the bathroom, shortly after the big girl had threatened to tell. Then the ranger came, then, once the ranger had radioed the station, Mrs. Margolin arrived with Daphne in tow.

The ranger had left the restroom area, but everyone else was huddled just outside, swatting mosquitoes.

"Oh. They *will* apologize," Mrs. Margolin said to the 909 troop leader, but she said this so angrily, I knew she was speaking more to us than to the other troop leader. "When their parents find out, every one a them will be on punishment."

"It's all right, it's all right," the 909 troop leader reassured Mrs. Margolin. Her voice lilted in the same way it had when addressing the girls. She smiled the whole time she talked. She was like one of those TV-cooking-show women who talk and dice onions and smile all at the same time.

"See. It could have happened. I'm not calling your girls fibbers or anything." She shook her head ferociously from side to side, her Egyptian-style pageboy flapping against her cheeks like heavy drapes. "It *could* have happened. See. Our girls are *not* retarded. They are *delayed* learners." She said this in a syrupy instructional voice, as though our troop might be delayed learners as well. "We're from the Decatur Children's Academy. Many of them just have special needs."

"Now we won't be able to walk to the bathroom by ourselves!" the big girl said.

"Yes you will," the troop leader said, "but maybe we'll wait till we get back to Decatur—"

"I don't want to wait!" the girl said. "I want my Independence badge!"

The girls in my troop were entirely speechless. Arnetta looked stoic, as though she were soon to be tortured but was determined not to appear weak. Mrs. Margolin pursed her lips solemnly and said, "Bless them, Lord. Bless them."

In contrast, the Troop 909 leader was full of words and energy. "Some of our girls are echolalic—" She smiled and happily presented one of the girls hanging onto her, but the girl widened her eyes in horror, and violently withdrew herself from the center of attention, sensing she was being sacrificed for the village sins. "Echolalic," the troop leader continued. "That means they will say whatever they hear, like an echo—that's where the word comes from. It comes from 'echo.'"

She ducked her head apologetically, "I mean, not all of them have the most *progressive* of parents, so if they heard a bad word, they might have repeated it. But I guarantee it would not have been *intentional*."

Arnetta spoke. "I saw her say the word. I heard her." She pointed to a small girl, smaller than any of us, wearing an oversized T-shirt that read: "Eat Bertha's Mussels."

The troop leader shook her head and smiled, "That's impossible. She doesn't speak. She can, but she doesn't."

Arnetta furrowed her brow. "No. It wasn't her. That's right. It was *her*."

The girl Arnetta pointed to grinned as though she'd been paid a compliment. She was the only one from either troop actually wearing a full uniform: the mocha-colored A-line shift, the orange ascot, the sash covered with badges, though all the same one—the Try-It patch. She took a few steps toward Arnetta and made a grand sweeping gesture toward the sash. "See," she said, full of self-importance, "I'm a Brownie." I had a hard time imagining this girl calling anyone a "nigger"; the girl looked perpetually delighted, as though she would have cuddled up with a grizzly if someone had let her.

ON the fourth morning, we boarded the bus to go home.

The previous day had been spent building miniature churches from Popsicle sticks. We hardly left the cabin. Mrs. Margolin and Mrs. Hedy guarded us so closely, almost no one talked for the entire day.

Even on the day of departure from Camp Crescendo, all was serious and silent. The bus ride began quietly enough. Arnetta had to sit beside Mrs. Margolin; Octavia had to sit beside her mother. I sat beside Daphne, who gave me her prize journal without a word of explanation.

"You don't want it?"

She shook her head no. It was empty.

Then Mrs. Hedy began to weep. "Octavia," Mrs. Hedy said to her daughter without looking at her, "I'm going to sit with Mrs. Margolin. All right?"

Arnetta exchanged seats with Mrs. Hedy. With the two women up front, Elise felt it safe to speak. "Hey," she said, then she set her face into a placid, vacant stare, trying to imitate that of a Troop 909 girl. Emboldened, Arnetta made a gesture of mock pride toward an imaginary sash, the way the girl in full uniform had done. Then they all made a game of it, trying to do the most exaggerated imitations of the Troop 909 girls, all without speaking, all without laughing loud enough to catch the women's attention.

Daphne looked down at her shoes, white with sneaker polish. I opened the journal she'd given me. I looked out the window, trying to decide what to write, searching for lines, but nothing could compare with what Daphne had written, "*My father, the veteran*," my favorite line of all time. It replayed itself in my head, and I gave up trying to write.

By then, it seemed that the rest of the troop had given up making fun of the girls in Troop 909. They were now quietly gossiping about who had passed notes to whom in school. For a moment the gossiping fell off, and all I heard was the hum of the bus as we sped down the road and the muffled sounds of Mrs. Hedy and Mrs. Margolin talking about serious things.

"You know," Octavia whispered, "why did *we* have to be stuck at a camp with retarded girls? You know?"

"*You* know why," Arnetta answered. She narrowed her eyes like a cat. "My mama and I were in the mall in Buckhead, and this white lady just kept looking at us. I mean, like we were foreign or something. Like we were from China."

"What did the woman say?" Elise asked.

"Nothing," Arnetta said. "She didn't say nothing."

A few girls quietly nodded their heads.

"There was this time," I said, "when my father and I were in the mall and—"

"Oh shut up, Snot," Octavia said.

I stared at Octavia, then rolled my eyes from her to the window. As I watched the trees blur, I wanted nothing more than to be through with it all: the bus ride, the troop, school—all of it. But we were going home. I'd see the same girls in school the next day. We were on a bus, and there was nowhere else to go.

"Go on, Laurel," Daphne said to me. It seemed like the first time she'd spoken the whole trip, and she'd said my name. I turned to her and smiled weakly so as not to cry, hoping she'd remember when I'd tried to be her friend, thinking maybe that her gift of the journal was an invitation of friendship. But she didn't smile back. All she said was, "What happened?"

I studied the girls, waiting for Octavia to tell me to shut up again before I even had a chance to utter another word, but everyone was amazed that Daphne had

spoken. The bus was silent. I gathered my voice. "Well," I said. "My father and I were in this mall, but *I* was the one doing the staring." I stopped and glanced from face to face. I continued. "There were these white people dressed like Puritans or something, but they weren't Puritans. They were Mennonites. They're these people who, if you ask them to do a favor, like paint your porch or something, they have to do it. It's in their rules."

180   "That sucks," someone said.

181   "C'mon," Arnetta said. "You're lying."

182   "I am not."

183   "How do you know that's not just some story someone made up?" Elise asked, her head cocked full of daring. "I mean, who's gonna do whatever you ask?"

184   "It's not made up. I know because when I was looking at them, my father said, 'See those people? If you ask them to do something, they'll do it. Anything you want.'"

185   No one would call anyone's father a liar—then they'd have to fight the person. But Drema parsed her words carefully. "How does your *father* know that's not just some story? Huh?"

186   "Because," I said, "he went up to the man and asked him would he paint our porch, and the man said yes. It's their religion."

187   "Man, I'm glad I'm a Baptist," Elise said, shaking her head in sympathy for the Mennonites.

188   "So did the guy do it?" Drema asked, scooting closer to hear if the story got juicy.

189   "Yeah," I said. "His whole family was with him. My dad drove them to our house. They all painted our porch. The woman and girl were in bonnets and long, long skirts with buttons up to their necks. The guy wore this weird hat and these huge suspenders."

"Why," Arnetta asked archly, as though she didn't believe a word, "would someone pick a *porch*? If they'll do anything, why not make them paint the whole *house*? Why not ask for a hundred bucks?"

I thought about it, and then remembered the words my father had said about them painting our porch, though I had never seemed to think about his words after he'd said them.

"He said," I began, only then understanding the words as they uncoiled from my mouth, "it was the only time he'd have a white man on his knees doing something for a black man for free."

I now understood what he meant, and why he did it, though I didn't like it. When you've been made to feel bad for so long, you jump at the chance to do it to others. I remembered the Mennonites bending the way Daphne had bent when she was cleaning the restroom. I remembered the dark blue of their bonnets, the black of their shoes. They painted the porch as though scrubbing a floor. I was already trembling before Daphne asked quietly, "Did he thank them?"

I looked out the window. I could not tell which were the thoughts and which were the trees. "No," I said, and suddenly knew there was something mean in the world that I could not stop.

Arnetta laughed. "If I asked them to take off their long skirts and bonnets and put on some jeans, would they do it?"

And Daphne's voice, quiet, steady: "Maybe they would. Just to be nice."

> **When you've been made to feel bad for so long,** you jump at the chance to do it to others.

Z Z Packer is a young writer who is still experimenting with the use of point of view in her work, and, as with most literary matters, it seems difficult to predict where she will go next. If you like "Brownies," you might also like "Traveling Madness," by another young writer, Ana Menendez (in Stories for Further Reading), who stands at a similar point in her writing career.

GOING FURTHER   As of this writing Packer is at work on her first novel, a story about the "Buffalo Soldiers," black Union Army veterans who went west during and after the Civil War. With her contemporary Danzy Senna (*Caucasia* and *Symptomatic*) and the slightly younger Tayari Jones (*Leaving Atlanta*) and Asali Solomon (*Get Down*), she is carving out space for new black American women writers.

Writing from Reading

Summarize

1 What are Snot/Laurel's feelings about her father? What does she tell the reader directly? What can you infer from what she says and when she says it?

2 Locate all the scenes where Laurel's troop actually encounters Troop 909. What details does Laurel include that foreshadow their later discovery about the white girls? What details are omitted because we get only Laurel's view?

Analyze Craft

3 Packer includes several sets of lyrics in "Brownies," including Daphne's poem, and the songs the girls are asked to sing. What is the effect of including the full text of these lyrics? Why does Packer choose to leave out the lyrics of the Michael Jackson song?

Analyze Voice

4 Analyze the difference between Laurel's voice as narrator of the story and her voice when she speaks in the story. Based on this comparison, do you think Packer was trying to use the voice of a young girl narrator or of a grown-up looking back?

Synthesize Summary and Analysis

5 Compare the descriptions of Laurel's troop members to the descriptions of the girls in Troop 909. Does Packer draw a comparison between the two troops? Examine why Packer chose to distance Troop 909 both racially and mentally.

Interpret the Story

6 Think about the protagonists, antagonists, and foils of this story. Can they be divided evenly into groups by race, age, or troop? What is the overarching conflict the protagonists are up against, and how does the story of the Mennonites help bring resolution to this conflict?

CONTINUED FROM PAGE 183

A PARTICIPANT, OR FIRST-PERSON, NARRATOR

The first-person narrator is always a participant in the story and can be either a major or a minor character. This type of tale telling relies on the perspective of a single character through whose eyes, and by means of whose voice, we come to understand the action in the story. Readers enter the narrator's mind, gaining access to his or her thoughts and emotions. In the opening passage, with Laurel as the first-person narrator, our entry to the narrative comes through her eyes and words.

First person is by its nature limited because we have only one set of eyes. As participants in a story, first-person narrators have their own interests and motivations—

"You have to create a little distance from yourself to make . . . a story; otherwise it's just you talking. . . . As a story . . . you want to be able to walk around in some way. However closely it relates to your own autobiography, it has to be a little different. There has to be some space between you and it and the voice is one way to establish a little space." Conversation with John Updike and, like the rest of us, cannot be entirely objective. They can give only their version of the tale. Often, readers see more than the narrator can, and sometimes this broader vantage point allows us to recognize an **unreliable narrator,** or one who cannot be trusted to present an undistorted account of the action. Not all narrators are unreliable, but those who are have many reasons for their unreliability, ranging from inexperience, ignorance, and personal bias to intentional deceptiveness and even insanity. The narrator of Eudora Welty's story "Why I Live at the P.O." in the previous chapter is so intent on feeling like a victim that she fails to acknowledge any part in or responsibility for the trouble in her family. The reader realizes quickly that her self-pity and jealousy of her younger sister prevent her from understanding anyone else's point of view.

A specific type of unreliable narrator is the **naïve narrator,** who remains unaware of the full complexity of events in the story being told. A narrator may be naïve because of youth, innocence, or lack of cultural alertness. Writers intentionally use naïve narrators to reveal a truth, raise questions in the reader's mind, or otherwise emphasize a point. In Harper Lee's classic novel *To Kill a Mockingbird,* young Scout is the naïve narrator who describes the members of her family and the characters and events in her town. Tom Robinson, a black man, has been falsely accused of raping a white woman. Scout takes us into the courtroom where her father, the town's highly respected lawyer, defends Tom. Scout, an avid observer, still cannot understand how Tom can be convicted when the evidence overwhelmingly supports his innocence. The critical reader, having some knowledge of the social conventions of life in the American South in the 1930s, understands that Tom is the victim of the town's deep-rooted racism. By the use of Scout's perspective, therefore, Harper Lee effectively reveals the injustice of the town's racist attitudes.

A NONPARTICIPANT, OR THIRD-PERSON, NARRATOR

Third-person narrators are never characters in the story. These narrators relate the events of a story as unseen observers, referring to all the characters as *he, she,* or *they.* This particular narrative vantage remains the most common strategy for tale telling, though there are gradations within it, and it's worth spelling them out. Third-person narrators come in three basic varieties:

- **Omniscient narrator.** Omniscient, or all-knowing, third-person narrators observe the thoughts and describe the actions of multiple characters in the story, as does the narrator in Ernest Hemingway's "The Short Happy Life of Francis Macomber" in this chapter.
- **Limited omniscient narrator.** Limited third-person narrators typically enter into the thoughts and emotions of one character, as does the narrator in Kate Chopin's "The Story of an Hour" (chapter 1).
- **Objective point-of-view narrator.** Objective third-person narrators report only what can be seen and heard.

The **omniscient narrator** can see beyond the physical actions and dialogue of characters and is able to reveal the inner thoughts and emotions of anyone in the story. This narrator moves freely between the thoughts of characters and across time and space. The term comes from the Latin *omni scientia, "all-knowing,"* and it suggests a kind of godlike or infallible witness—often one who offers his or her opinion on the action as it unfolds. The omniscient narrator chooses which thoughts are important to the story, and when to tell them.

Using this perspective, for example, Hemingway's narrator at a certain point gives us a glimpse into Mrs. Macomber's thoughts as she sits with Wilson, the safari leader, and her husband, Mr. Macomber: "She looked at both these men as though she had never seen them before. One, Wilson, the white hunter, she knew she had never truly seen before."

At other times, the narrator reveals Wilson's thoughts about Mrs. Macomber: "When she left, Wilson was thinking, when she went off to cry, she seemed a hell of a fine woman. She seemed to understand, to realize, to be hurt for him and for herself and to know how things really stood."

The reader also has access to Mr. Macomber's thoughts, as in the following instance when he lies in bed, unable to fall asleep: "But more than shame he felt cold, hollow fear in him. The fear was still there like a cold slimy hollow in all the emptiness where once his confidence had been and it made him feel sick." The omniscient narrator chooses what should be revealed, and when, providing a deep insight into the nature of each character.

> "Once you break with the first person, then you do discover the wonderful world of multiple view points, and you can fly through space, and go from head to head, and you get out and you become a character in your own right, you become the omniscient author presiding." Conversation with John Updike

Omniscient narrators are not always objective. Sometimes a narrator shows **editorial omniscience,** inserting his or her own commentary about the characters or the events. By contrast, a narrator who shows **impartial omniscience** remains neutral, relating events and characters' thoughts without passing judgment or offering an opinion. Many novels employ the all-knowing third-person (impartial omniscient) approach to their material, as in, for example, the opening of World War II writer James Jones's *The Pistol*. The novel begins on the morning when the Japanese attack Pearl Harbor, and the passage is straightforward enough that you might easily find it in a work of history or general nonfiction:

> When the first bombs hit at Wheeler Field on December 7, 1941, Pfc Richard
> Mast was eating breakfast. He was also wearing a pistol. From where Mast sat,

amidst the bent heads, quiet murmur, and soft, cutlery-against-china sounds of breakfast, in a small company mess in one of the infantry quadrangles of Schofield Barracks, it was perhaps a mile to Wheeler Field, and it took several seconds for the sound of the explosions, followed soon after by the shockwave through the earth, to reach his ears.

Few omniscient narrators are purely editorial or purely impartial, however; in most works of fiction, you will find both kinds of storytelling.

A **limited omniscient narrator** describes the vision and insights of one character only, as if telling the story "over the shoulder" of that character. Unlike a first-person narrator, the limited omniscient narrator is separate from the main character and serves as the interpreter—not the source—of his or her thoughts. The reader can trust that the narrator's observations are more or less objective. Kate Chopin's "The Story of an Hour" uses limited omniscient narration, with the focus on Mrs. Mallard, the only character whose consciousness we enter. In other words, the narrator can relate only what Mrs. Mallard can see and hear, and what she herself feels and thinks.

There were patches of blue sky showing here and there through the clouds that had met and piled one above the other in the west facing her window. . . . There was something coming to her and she was waiting for it, fearfully. What was it? She did not know; it was too subtle and elusive to name. But she felt it, creeping out of the sky, reaching toward her through the sounds, the scents, the color that filled the air.

Now her bosom rose and fell tumultuously. She was beginning to recognize this thing that was approaching to possess her, and she was striving to beat it back with her will—as powerless as her two white slender hands would have been. When she abandoned herself a little whispered word escaped her slightly parted lips. She said it over and over under the breath: "free, free, free!"

In this passage, Mrs. Mallard has left her guests downstairs to go to her room. The narrator describes Mrs. Mallard's movements and feelings in great detail, following her gaze outside the window, as her mind begins to understand what her body has already grasped. She feels as free as the blue sky showing through the clouds.

An omniscient narrator who goes very deeply into the mind of a character may use the technique of interior monologue, in which a character's conscious or unconscious thought processes are narrated as they occur, with only minimal guidance from the narrator. These thoughts can be disconnected, moving rapidly and randomly from one idea to the next. Kate Chopin briefly uses the interior monologue technique in the passage about Mrs. Mallard. A similar but more random-seeming approach is **stream of consciousness,** in which thoughts flow by in free association and the literary convention suggests that there is no writer mediating the consciousness of the subject. The following example comes from James Joyce's novel *Ulysses;* here, the thoughts of a character named Molly Bloom pour onto the page:

. . . and Ronda with the old windows of the posadas glancing eyes a lattice hid for her lover to kiss the iron and the wineshops half open at night and the castanets and the night we missed the boat at Algeciras the watchman going about serene with his lamp and O that awful deepdown torrent O and the sea the sea crimson sometimes like fire and the glorious sunsets and the fig trees in the Alameda gardens yes . . .

In contrast to the narrator with limited omniscience, who delves into the consciousness of a particular character, an **objective point-of-view** narrator seems almost disinterested, relating only what all characters in the story see or hear. This type of narrator is often compared to the "fly on the wall" who sees and hears all. Similarly, the objective narrator provides no insight into the thoughts, emotions, or motivations of any single character. "I am a camera," as the narrator declares in Christopher Isherwood's *Berlin Stories,* suggesting a kind of objective assessment—one that's neither naïve nor editorialized. Reading a story with an objective narrator is much like watching a play, because the reader comes to understand what the characters think and feel based only on what they do and say. An objective narrator never lets the reader enter the consciousness of a particular character, the way Chopin did with Mrs. Mallard. The reader must use the clues of dialogue and behavior to infer what people truly think and feel.

THE SECOND-PERSON NARRATOR

The least commonly used point of view is that of the second-person narrator, who addresses readers directly with the pronoun *you* or with imperatives (*do this and that*). Second-person narration can make a reader feel like a participant in the story. It also creates a sense of closeness to the protagonist—as if the character is talking to himself or herself. In the following selection from Lorrie Moore's "How to Become a Writer," notice how the familiar, conversational use of "you" draws the reader in.

> You spend too much time slouched and demoralized. Your boyfriend suggests bicycling. Your roommate suggests a new boyfriend. You are said to be self-mutilating and losing weight, but you continue writing. The only happiness you have is writing something new, in the middle of the night, armpits damp, heart pounding, something no one has yet seen. You have only those brief, fragile untested moments of exhilaration when you know: you are a genius. Understand what you must do. Switch majors. The kids in your nursery project will be disappointed but you have a calling, an urge, a delusion, an unfortunate habit. You have, as your mother would say, fallen in with a bad crowd.

Drawing the reader directly into the story can prove challenging when creating a work of fiction. For example, not all readers will identify with the "you" being portrayed, thinking, "I don't have a boyfriend," or "My mother would never say something like that." Nevertheless, Lorrie Moore and others have created innovative and compelling fiction by the use of second-person narrators; there's an intimacy (as if we overhear internal monologue) involved.

POINT OF VIEW IN CONTEXT

The stories in this chapter represent points of view from first person in ZZ Packer's "Brownies" to omniscient third person in Hemingway's "The Short Happy Life of Francis Macomber." Each point of view lets you into a different frame of mind and has different powers and limitations. Third person can't feel as intimate as first person. First person can't see as many sides of an issue as third. It's interesting in this regard to notice the role that *fashion* plays in point of view. The omniscient narrator was more common in the eighteenth and nineteenth centuries, for example, than is the case today. In the contemporary moment, we tend to deploy the first-person narrator, either as a reliable or unreliable witness—and the proportion of novels and short stories using the first person, as opposed to the third, has enlarged. Perhaps in the next fifty years the second-person narrator will take center stage.

Lorrie Moore (b. 1957)

Growing up in Glens Falls, New York, Lorrie Moore was so skinny, she feared falling through sidewalk grates. Her fiction, however, has not been lost on critics and readers, who have responded enthusiastically to Moore's ability to blend comedy, pathos, and poignancy. After winning *Seventeen*'s writing contest at age nineteen, Moore's next literary success came when she published *Self-Help* (1985), a collection of stories pulled largely from the graduate thesis she completed at Cornell University. Moore's use of the second-person point of view and witty application of self-help-manual rhetoric in this first collection earned her immediate critical praise. Her stories have since continued to appear in the most prestigious literary venues, including *The New Yorker* and *The Best American Short Stories* series, as she experiments with reverse chronology, sequential accounts, and fragmented narration. A professor of English at the University of Wisconsin since 1984, Moore now boasts two novels, three collections of short stories, and awards including the Rea Award for the Short Story and the O. Henry Prize. Her work treats serious themes such as loneliness and the difficulties of love, both familial and romantic, but in such a way that the darker thematic undertones are highlighted by humor and wit.

AS YOU READ   As you read this story, consider how you feel about being addressed directly by the narrator. What do you think of this narrator? Can you see yourself living the life she is describing?

How to Become a Writer Or, Have You Earned This Cliché? (1985)

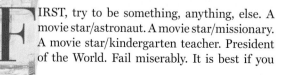

1   FIRST, try to be something, anything, else. A movie star/astronaut. A movie star/missionary. A movie star/kindergarten teacher. President of the World. Fail miserably. It is best if you fail at an early age—say, fourteen. Early, critical disillusionment is necessary so that at fifteen you can write long haiku sequences about thwarted desire. It is a pond, a cherry blossom, a wind brushing against spar-

row wing leaving for mountain. Count the syllables. Show it to your mom. She is tough and practical. She has a son in Vietnam and a husband who may be having an affair. She believes in wearing brown because it hides spots. She'll look briefly at your writing, then back up at you with a face blank as a donut. She'll say: "How about emptying the dishwasher?" Look away. Shove the forks in the fork drawer. Accidentally break one of the freebie gas station glasses. This is the required pain and suffering. This is only for starters.

2   In your high school English class look at Mr. Killian's face. Decide faces are important. Write a villanelle about pores. Struggle. Write a sonnet. Count the syllables: nine, ten, eleven, thirteen. Decide to experiment with fiction. Here you don't have to count syllables. Write a short story about an elderly man and woman who accidentally shoot each other in the head, the result of an inexplicable malfunction of a shotgun which appears mysteriously in their living room one night. Give it to Mr. Killian as your final project. When you get it back, he has written on it: "Some of your images are quite nice, but you have no sense of plot." When you are home, in the privacy of your own room, faintly scrawl in pencil beneath his black-inked comments: "Plots are for dead people, pore-face."

3   Take all the babysitting jobs you can get. You are great with kids. They love you. You tell them stories about old people who die idiot deaths. You sing them songs like "Blue Bells of Scotland," which is their favorite. And when they are in their pajamas and have finally stopped pinching each other, when they are fast asleep, you read every sex manual in the house, and wonder how on earth anyone could ever do those things with someone they truly loved. Fall asleep in a chair reading Mr. McMurphy's *Playboy*. When the McMurphys come home, they will tap you on the shoulder, look at the magazine in your lap, and grin. You will want to die. They will ask you if Tracey took her medicine all right. Explain, yes, she did, that you promised her a story if she would take it like a big girl and that seemed to work out just fine. "Oh, marvelous," they will exclaim.

4   Try to smile proudly.

5   Apply to college as a child psychology major.

6   AS a child psychology major, you have some electives. You've always liked kids. Sign up for something called "The Ornithological Field Trip." It meets Tuesdays and Thursdays at two. When you arrive at Room 134 on the first day of class, everyone is sitting around a seminar table talking about metaphors. You've heard of these. After a short, excruciating while, raise your hand and say diffidently, "Excuse me, isn't this Birdwatching One-oh-one?" The class stops and turns to look at you. They seem to all have one face—giant and blank as a vandalized clock. Someone with a beard booms out, "No, this is Creative Writing." Say: "Oh—right," as if perhaps you knew all along. Look down at your schedule. Wonder how the hell you ended up here. The computer, apparently, has made an error. You start to get up to leave and then don't. The lines at the registrar this week are huge. Perhaps you should stick with this mistake. Perhaps your creative writing isn't all that bad. Perhaps it is fate. Perhaps this is what your dad meant when he said, "It's the age of computers, Francie, it's the age of computers."

7   DECIDE that you like college life. In your dorm you meet many nice people. Some are smarter than you. And some, you notice, are dumber than you. You will continue, unfortunately, to view the world in exactly these terms for the rest of your life.

8   THE assignment this week in creative writing is to narrate a violent happening. Turn in a story about driving with your Uncle Gordon and another one about two old people who are accidentally electrocuted when they go to turn on a badly wired desk lamp. The teacher will hand them back to you with comments: "Much of your writing is smooth and energetic. You have, however, a ludicrous notion of plot." Write another story about a man and a woman who, in the very first paragraph, have their lower torsos accidentally blitzed away by dynamite. In the second paragraph, with the insurance money, they buy a frozen yogurt stand together. There are six more paragraphs. You read the whole thing out loud in class. No one likes it. They say your sense of plot is outrageous and incompetent. After class someone asks you if you are crazy.

9   Decide that perhaps you should stick to comedies. Start dating someone who is funny, someone who has what in high school you called a "really great sense of humor" and what now your creative writing class calls "self-contempt giving rise to comic form." Write down all of his jokes, but don't tell him you are doing this. Make up anagrams of his old girlfriend's name and name all of your socially handicapped characters with

them. Tell him his old girlfriend is in all of your stories and then watch how funny he can be, see what a really great sense of humor he can have.

10   Your child psychology advisor tells you you are neglecting courses in your major. What you spend the most time on should be what you're majoring in. Say yes, you understand.

11   IN creative writing seminars over the next two years, everyone continues to smoke cigarettes and ask the same things: "But does it work?" "Why should we care about this character?" "Have you earned this cliché?" These seem like important questions.

12   On days when it is your turn, you look at the class hopefully as they scour your mimeographs for a plot. They look back up at you, drag deeply, and then smile in a sweet sort of way.

13   YOU spend too much time slouched and demoralized. Your boyfriend suggests bicycling. Your roommate suggests a new boyfriend. You are said to be self-mutilating and losing weight, but you continue writing. The only happiness you have is writing something new, in the middle of the night, armpits damp, heart pounding, something no one has yet seen. You have only those brief, fragile, untested moments of exhilaration when you know: you are a genius. Understand what you must do. Switch majors. The kids in your nursery project will be disappointed, but you have a calling, an urge, a delusion, an unfortunate habit. You have, as your mother would say, fallen in with a bad crowd.

14   WHY write? Where does writing come from? These are questions to ask yourself. They are like: Where does dust come from? Or: Why is there war? Or: If there's a God, then why is my brother now a cripple?

15   These are questions that you keep in your wallet, like calling cards. These are questions, your creative writing teacher says, that are good to address in your journals but rarely in your fiction.

16   The writing professor this fall is stressing the Power of the Imagination. Which means he doesn't want long descriptive stories about your camping trip last July. He wants you to start in a realistic context but then to alter it. Like recombinant DNA. He wants you to let your imagination sail, to let it grow big-bellied in the wind. This is a quote from Shakespeare.

17   TELL your roommate your great idea, your great exercise of imaginative power: a transformation of Melville to contemporary life. It will be about monomania and the fish-eat-fish world of life insurance in Rochester, New York. The first line will be "Call me Fishmeal," and it will feature a menopausal suburban husband named Richard, who because he is so depressed all the time is called "Mopey Dick" by his witty wife Elaine. Say to your roommate: "Mopey Dick, get it?" Your roommate looks at you, her face blank as a large Kleenex. She comes up to you, like a buddy, and puts an arm around your burdened shoulders. "Listen, Francie," she says, slow as speech therapy. "Let's go out and get a big beer."

18   THE seminar doesn't like this one either. You suspect they are beginning to feel sorry for you. They say: "You have to think about what is happening. Where is the story here?"

19   THE next semester the writing professor is obsessed with writing from personal experience. You must write from what you know, from what has happened to you. He wants deaths, he wants camping trips. Think about what has happened to you. In three years there have been three things: you lost your virginity; your parents got divorced; and your brother came home from a forest ten miles from the Cambodian border with only half a thigh, a permanent smirk nestled into one corner of his mouth.

20   About the first you write: "It created a new space, which hurt and cried in a voice that wasn't mine, 'I'm not the same anymore, but I'll be okay.'"

21   About the second you write an elaborate story of an old married couple who stumble upon an unknown land mine in their kitchen and accidentally blow themselves up. You call it: "For Better or for Liverwurst."

22   About the last you write nothing. There are no words for this. Your typewriter hums. You can find no words.

AT undergraduate cocktail parties, people say, "Oh, you write? What do you write about?" Your roommate, who has consumed too much wine, too little cheese, and no crackers at all, blurts: "Oh, my god, she always writes about her dumb boyfriend."

Later on in life you will learn that writers are merely open, helpless texts with no real understanding of what they have written and therefore must half-believe anything and everything that is said of them. You, however, have not yet reached this stage of literary criticism. You stiffen and say, "I do not," the same way you said it when someone in the fourth grade accused you of really liking oboe lessons and your parents really weren't just making you take them.

Insist you are not very interested in any one subject at all, that you are interested in the music of language, that you are interested in—in—syllables, because they are the atoms of poetry, the cells of the mind, the breath of the soul. Begin to feel woozy. Stare into your plastic wine cup.

"Syllables?" you will hear someone ask, voice trailing off, as they glide slowly toward the reassuring white of the dip.

BEGIN to wonder what you do write about. Or if you have anything to say. Or if there even is such a thing as a thing to say. Limit these thoughts to no more than ten minutes a day; like sit-ups, they can make you thin.

You will read somewhere that all writing has to do with one's genitals. Don't dwell on this. It will make you nervous.

YOUR mother will come visit you. She will look at the circles under your eyes and hand you a brown book with a brown briefcase on the cover. It is entitled: *How to Become a Business Executive*. She has also brought the *Names for Baby* encyclopedia you asked for; one of your characters, the aging clown-school teacher, needs a new name. Your mother will shake her head and say: "Francie, Francie, remember when you were going to be a child psychology major?"

Say: "Mom, I like to write."

She'll say: "Sure you like to write. Of course. Sure you like to write."

WRITE a story about a confused music student and title it: "Schubert Was the One with the Glasses, Right?" It's not a big hit, although your roommate likes the part where the two violinists accidentally blow themselves up in a recital room. "I went out with a violinist once," she says, snapping her gum.

Thank god you are taking other courses. You can find sanctuary in nineteenth-century ontological snags and invertebrate courting rituals. Certain globular mollusks have what is called "Sex by the Arm." The male octopus, for instance, loses the end of one arm when placing it inside the female body during intercourse. Marine biologists call it "Seven Heaven." Be glad you know these things. Be glad you are not just a writer. Apply to law school.

FROM here on in, many things can happen. But the main one will be this: you decide not to go to law school after all, and, instead, you spend a good, big chunk of your adult life telling people how you decided not to go to law school after all. Somehow you end up writing again. Perhaps you go to graduate school. Perhaps you work odd jobs and take writing courses at night. Perhaps you are working on a novel and writing down all the clever remarks and intimate personal confessions you hear during the day. Perhaps you are losing your pals, your acquaintances, your balance.

You have broken up with your boyfriend. You now go out with men who, instead of whispering "I love you," shout: "Do it to me baby." This is good for your writing.

Sooner or later you have a finished manuscript more or less. People look at it in a vaguely troubled sort of way and say, "I'll bet becoming a writer was always a fantasy of yours, wasn't it?" Your lips dry to salt. Say that of all the fantasies possible in the world, you can't imagine being a writer even making the top twenty. Tell them you were going to be a child psychology major. "I bet," they always sigh, "you'd be great with kids." Scowl fiercely. Tell them you're a walking blade.

QUIT classes. Quit jobs. Cash in old savings bonds. Now you have time like warts on your hands. Slowly copy all of your friends' addresses into a new address book.

Vacuum. Chew cough drops. Keep a folder full of fragments.

An eyelid darkening sideways.

World as conspiracy.

Possible plot? A woman gets on a bus.

Suppose you threw a love affair and nobody came.

AT home drink a lot of coffee. At Howard Johnson's order the cole slaw. Consider how it looks like the soggy confetti of a map: where you've been, where you're going—"You Are Here," says the red star on the back of the menu.

44   Occasionally a date with a face blank as a sheet of paper asks you whether writers often become discouraged. Say that sometimes they do and sometimes they do. Say it's a lot like having polio.

"Interesting," smiles your date, and then he looks down at his arm hairs and starts to smooth them, all, always, in the same direction.

A STORY about story writing is not to everyone's taste. If you like this one, you should try the Jorge Luis Borges story "The Circular Ruins" in Stories for Further Reading in this anthology.

GOING FURTHER   Moore's comic meta-fiction was influenced early on by the work of Donald Barthelme, a father to many postmodernists, and Gilbert Sorrentino, whose hilarious examination of the literary imagination is captured in his classic novel *Mulligan Stew*.

Writing from Reading

Summarize

1   Make a list of the events and changes that occur in the life of the "you" of this story. Does the narrator reveal how the "you" feels about these events and changes? Give examples.

Analyze Craft

2   Examine the instances of dialogue in the story. Analyze how Moore uses dialogue differently from other authors you have read.

3   What is the plot of this story? Discuss how using the second-person point of view tells a different story than one the same events would describe in third or first person.

Analyze Voice

4   Who is the "you" of this story? Who is the narrator? Who is Francie? Are they all the same person? Does Lorrie Moore provide a clear answer? Explain.

Synthesize Summary and Analysis

5   Which events does the narrator portray in a scene-like way, and which events does she merely refer to in exposition? What effect does dramatizing one event rather than another have on the story?

Interpret the Story

6   Lorrie Moore uses humor in her writing, but she confronts some very serious topics, like self-mutilation, loneliness, and the Vietnam War. Do you think Moore intends this story to be a satire—a joke—or an actual caution to potential writers? Provide examples of instances of Moore being humorous and instances of her being serious, and contrast the two.

Ernest Hemingway (1899–1961)

Born in Oak Park, Illinois, Ernest Hemingway became one of the most influential American authors of the twentieth century. In novels, short stories, and nonfiction alike, Hemingway celebrated the ideal of "grace under pressure" as a way to live and a way to write. He distrusted fancy phrasing and abstract utterance, making a case in much of his work for concrete speech. Under the influence of Gertrude Stein and Sherwood Anderson, he went about the business of renovating the American literary sentence. Writing stories made him into an artist. Novel writing made him famous. His first novel, *The Sun Also Rises* (1926), deals with American expatriates in France and Spain; his novel *A Farewell to Arms* (1929) is set in Italy and Switzerland during World War I. A prolific writer, Hemingway is also the author of *For Whom the Bell Tolls, The Old Man and the Sea, A Moveable Feast,* and numerous other works of fiction and nonfiction. He spent many years abroad and married four times. He was known—and self-described—as writing's "heavyweight champ"; both he and his characters are known for their unapologetic bravado. The men in his fiction are matadors, soldiers, and big-game hunters, a tight-lipped and cool-headed lot in the face of danger. A Nobel laureate and a world-famous public figure, Hemingway was nonetheless prone to suicidal depression; he took his own life in 1961 in Ketchum, Idaho.

AS YOU READ   As you read this story, notice the shifting levels of happiness and unhappiness among the characters. Notice also the shifting alliances in the triangle of characters at the center of the story. Which of them do you most sympathize with and feel compassion for? Why?

TIP

FOR INTERACTIVE READING . . . As you move through the story, mark sections and paragraphs according to whose perspective is represented. What do these glimpses into each character's thoughts reveal about their motivations and weaknesses?

The Short Happy Life of Francis Macomber (1936)

1 IT was now lunch time and they were all sitting under the double green fly of the dining tent pretending that nothing had happened.

2 "Will you have lime juice or lemon squash?" Macomber asked.

3 "I'll have a gimlet," Robert Wilson told him.

4 "I'll have a gimlet too. I need something," Macomber's wife said.

5 "I suppose it's the thing to do," Macomber agreed. "Tell him to make three gimlets."

6 The mess boy had started them already, lifting the bottles out of the canvas cooling bags that sweated wet

in the wind that blew through the trees that shaded the tents.

7   "What had I ought to give them?" Macomber asked.

8   "A quid would be plenty," Wilson told him. "You don't want to spoil them."

9   "Will the headman distribute it?"

10   "Absolutely."

11   Francis Macomber had, half an hour before, been carried to his tent from the edge of the camp in triumph on the arms and shoulders of the cook, the personal boys, the skinner and the porters. The gun-bearers had taken no part in the demonstration. When the native boys put him down at the door of his tent, he had shaken all their hands, received their congratulations, and then gone into the tent and sat on the bed until his wife came in. She did not speak to him when she came in and he left the tent at once to wash his face and hands in the portable wash basin outside and go over to the dining tent to sit in a comfortable canvas chair in the breeze and the shade.

12   "You've got your lion," Robert Wilson said to him, "and a damned fine one too."

13   Mrs. Macomber looked at Wilson quickly. She was an extremely handsome and well kept woman of the beauty and social position which had, five years before, commanded five thousand dollars as the price of endorsing, with photographs, a beauty product which she had never used. She had been married to Francis Macomber for eleven years.

14   "He is a good lion, isn't he?" Macomber said. His wife looked at him now. She looked at both these men as though she had never seen them before.

15   One, Wilson, the white hunter, she knew she had never truly seen before. He was about middle height with sandy hair, a stubby mustache, a very red face and extremely cold blue eyes with faint white wrinkles at the corners that grooved merrily when he smiled. He smiled at her now and she looked away from his face at the way his shoulders sloped in the loose tunic he wore with the four big cartridges held in loops where the left breast pocket should have been, at his big brown hands, his old slacks, his very dirty boots and back to his red face again. She noticed where the baked red of his face stopped in a white line that marked the circle left by his Stetson hat that hung now from one of the pegs of the tent pole.

16   "Well, here's to the lion," Robert Wilson said. He smiled at her again and, not smiling, she looked curiously at her husband.

17   Francis Macomber was very tall, very well built if you did not mind that length of bone, dark, his hair cropped like an oarsman, rather thin-lipped, and was considered handsome. He was dressed in the same sort of safari clothes that Wilson wore except that his were new, he was thirty-five years old, kept himself very fit, was good at court games, had a number of big-game fishing records, and had just shown himself, very publicly, to be a coward.

18   "Here's to the lion," he said. "I can't ever thank you for what you did."

19   Margaret, his wife, looked away from him and back to Wilson.

20   "Let's not talk about the lion," she said.

21   Wilson looked over at her without smiling and now she smiled at him.

22   "It's been a very strange day," she said. "Hadn't you ought to put your hat on even under the canvas at noon? You told me that, you know."

23   "Might put it on," said Wilson.

24   "You know you have a very red face, Mr. Wilson," she told him and smiled again.

25   "Drink," said Wilson.

26   "I don't think so," she said. "Francis drinks a great deal, but his face is never red."

27   "It's red today," Macomber tried a joke.

28   "No," said Margaret. "It's mine that's red today. But Mr. Wilson's is always red."

29   "Must be racial," said Wilson. "I say, you wouldn't like to drop my beauty as a topic, would you?"

30   "I've just started on it."

31   "Let's chuck it," said Wilson.

31   "Conversation is going to be so difficult," Margaret said.

32   "Don't be silly, Margot," her husband said.

33   "No difficulty," Wilson said. "Got a damn fine lion."

34   Margot looked at them both and they both saw that she was going to cry. Wilson had seen it coming for a long time and he dreaded it. Macomber was past dreading it.

35   "I wish it hadn't happened. Oh, I wish it hadn't happened," she said and started for her tent. She made no noise of crying but they could see that her shoul-

ders were shaking under the rose-colored, sun-proofed shirt she wore.

"Women upset," said Wilson to the tall man. "Amounts to nothing. Strain on the nerves and one thing'n another."

"No," said Macomber. "I suppose that I rate that for the rest of my life now."

"Nonsense. Let's have a spot of the giant killer," said Wilson. "Forget the whole thing. Nothing to it anyway."

"We might try," said Macomber. "I won't forget what you did for me though."

"Nothing," said Wilson. "All nonsense."

So they sat there in the shade where the camp was pitched under some wide-topped acacia trees with a boulder-strewn cliff behind them, and a stretch of grass that ran to the bank of a boulder-filled stream in front with forest beyond it, and drank their just-cool lime drinks and avoided one another's eyes while the boys set the table for lunch. Wilson could tell that the boys all knew about it now and when he saw Macomber's personal boy looking curiously at his master while he was putting dishes on the table he snapped at him in Swahili. The boy turned away with his face blank.

"What were you telling him?" Macomber asked.

"Nothing. Told him to look alive or I'd see he got about fifteen of the best."

"What's that? Lashes?"

"It's quite illegal," Wilson said. "You're supposed to fine them."

"Do you still have them whipped?"

"Oh, yes. They could raise a row if they chose to complain. But they don't. They prefer it to the fines."

"How strange!" said Macomber.

"Not strange, really," Wilson said. "Which would you rather do? Take a good birching or lose your pay?"

Then he felt embarrassed at asking it and before Macomber could answer he went on, "We all take a beating every day, you know, one way or another."

This was no better. "Good God," he thought. "I am a diplomat, aren't I?"

"Yes, we take a beating," said Macomber, still not looking at him. "I'm awfully sorry about that lion business. It doesn't have to go any further, does it? I mean no one will hear about it, will they?"

"You mean will I tell it at the Mathaiga Club?" Wilson looked at him now coldly. He had not expected this. So he's a bloody four-letter man as well as a bloody coward, he thought. I rather liked him too until today. But how is one to know about an American?

"No," said Wilson. "I'm a professional hunter. We never talk about our clients. You can be quite easy on that. It's supposed to be bad form to ask us not to talk though."

He had decided now that to break would be much easier. He would eat, then, by himself and could read a book with his meals. They would eat by themselves. He would see them through the safari on a very formal basis—what was it the French called it? Distinguished consideration—and it would be a damn sight easier than having to go through this emotional trash. He'd insult him and make a good clean break. Then he could read a book with his meals and he'd still be drinking their whisky. That was the phrase for it when a safari went bad. You ran into another white hunter and you asked, "How is everything going?" and he answered, "Oh, I'm still drinking their whisky," and you knew everything had gone to pot.

"I'm sorry," Macomber said and looked at him with his American face that would stay adolescent until it became middle-aged, and Wilson noted his crew-cropped hair, fine eyes only faintly shifty, good nose, thin lips and handsome jaw. "I'm sorry I didn't realize that. There are lots of things I don't know."

So what could he do, Wilson thought. He was all ready to break it off quickly and neatly and here the beggar was apologizing after he had just insulted him. He made one more attempt. "Don't worry about me talking," he said. "I have a living to make. You know in Africa no woman ever misses her lion and no white man ever bolts."

"I bolted like a rabbit," Macomber said.

Now what in hell were you going to do about a man who talked like that, Wilson wondered.

Wilson looked at Macomber with his flat, blue, machine-gunner's eyes and the other smiled back at him. He had a pleasant smile if you did not notice how his eyes showed when he was hurt.

"Maybe I can fix it up on buffalo," he said. "We're after them next, aren't we?"

"In the morning if you like," Wilson told him. Perhaps he had been wrong. This was certainly the way to take it. You most certainly could not tell a damned thing about an American. He was all for Macomber again. If you could forget the morning. But, of course, you couldn't. The morning had been about as bad as they come.

"Here comes the Memsahib," he said. She was walking over from her tent looking refreshed and cheerful and quite lovely. She had a very perfect oval face, so perfect that you expected her to be stupid. But she wasn't stupid, Wilson thought, no, not stupid.

> # You most certainly could not tell
> ## a damned thing about
> ### an American.

64   "How is the beautiful red-faced Mr. Wilson? Are you feeling better, Francis, my pearl?"

65   "Oh, much," said Macomber.

66   "I've dropped the whole thing," she said, sitting down at the table. "What importance is there to whether Francis is any good at killing lions? That's not his trade. That's Mr. Wilson's trade. Mr. Wilson is really very impressive killing anything. You do kill anything, don't you?"

67   "Oh, anything," said Wilson. "Simply anything." They are, he thought, the hardest in the world; the hardest, the cruelest, the most predatory and the most attractive and their men have softened or gone to pieces nervously as they have hardened. Or is it that they pick men they can handle? They can't know that much at the age they marry, he thought. He was grateful that he had gone through his education on American women before now because this was a very attractive one.

68   "We're going after buff in the morning," he told her.

69   "I'm coming," she said.

70   "No, you're not."

71   "Oh, yes, I am. Mayn't I, Francis?"

72   "Why not stay in camp?"

73   "Not for anything," she said. "I wouldn't miss something like today for anything."

74   When she left, Wilson was thinking, when she went off to cry, she seemed a hell of a fine woman. She seemed to understand, to realize, to be hurt for him and for herself and to know how things really stood. She is away for twenty minutes and now she is back, simply enamelled in that American female cruelty. They are the damnedest women. Really the damnedest.

75   "We'll put on another show for you tomorrow," Francis Macomber said.

76   "You're not coming," Wilson said.

77   "You're very mistaken," she told him. "And I want *so* to see you perform again. You were lovely this morning. That is if blowing things' heads off is lovely."

78   "Here's the lunch," said Wilson. "You're very merry, aren't you?"

79   "Why not? I didn't come out here to be dull."

80   "Well, it hasn't been dull," Wilson said. He could see the boulders in the river and the high bank beyond with the trees and he remembered the morning.

81   "Oh, no," she said. "It's been charming. And tomorrow. You don't know how I look forward to tomorrow."

82   "That's eland he's offering you," Wilson said.

83   "They're the big cowy things that jump like hares, aren't they?"

84   "I suppose that describes them," Wilson said.

"It's very good meat," Macomber said.

"Did you shoot it, Francis?" she asked.

"Yes."

"They're not dangerous, are they?"

"Only if they fall on you," Wilson told her.

"I'm so glad."

"Why not let up on the bitchery just a little, Margot," Macomber said, cutting the eland steak and putting some mashed potato, gravy and carrot on the down-turned fork that tined through the piece of meat.

"I suppose I could," she said, "since you put it so prettily."

"Tonight we'll have champagne for the lion," Wilson said. "It's a bit too hot at noon."

"Oh, the lion," Margot said. "I'd forgotten the lion!"

> ## How should a woman act when she discovers her husband is a bloody coward?

So, Robert Wilson thought to himself, she *is* giving him a ride, isn't she? Or do you suppose that's her idea of putting up a good show? How should a woman act when she discovers her husband is a bloody coward? She's damn cruel but they're all cruel. They govern, of course, and to govern one has to be cruel sometimes. Still, I've seen enough of their damn terrorism.

"Have some more eland," he said to her politely.

That afternoon, late, Wilson and Macomber went out in the motor car with the native driver and the two gun-bearers. Mrs. Macomber stayed in the camp. It was too hot to go out, she said, and she was going with them in the early morning. As they drove off Wilson saw her standing under the big tree, looking pretty rather than beautiful in her faintly rosy khaki, her dark hair drawn back off her forehead and gathered in a knot low on her neck, her face as fresh, he thought, as though she were in England. She waved to them as the car went off through the swale of high grass and curved around through the trees into the small hills of orchard bush.

In the orchard bush they found a herd of impala, and leaving the car they stalked one old ram with long, wide-spread horns and Macomber killed it with a very creditable shot that knocked the buck down at a good two hundred yards and sent the herd off bounding wildly and leaping over one another's backs in long, leg-drawn-up leaps as unbelievable and as floating as those one makes sometimes in dreams.

"That was a good shot," Wilson said. "They're a small target."

"Is it a worth-while head?" Macomber asked.

"It's excellent," Wilson told him. "You shoot like that and you'll have no trouble."

"Do you think we'll find buffalo tomorrow?"

"There's a good chance of it. They feed out early in the morning and with luck we may catch them in the open."

"I'd like to clear away that lion business," Macomber said. "It's not very pleasant to have your wife see you do something like that."

I should think it would be even more unpleasant to do it, Wilson thought, wife or no wife, or to talk about having done it. But he said, "I wouldn't think about that any more. Any one could be upset by his first lion. That's all over."

But that night after dinner and a whisky and soda by the fire before going to bed, as Francis Macomber lay on his cot with the mosquito bar over him and listened to the night noises it was not all over. It was neither all over nor was it beginning. It was there exactly as it happened with some parts of it indelibly emphasized and he was miserably ashamed at it. But more than shame he felt cold, hollow fear in him. The fear was still there like a cold slimy hollow in all the emptiness where once his confidence had been and it made him feel sick. It was still there with him now.

It had started the night before when he had wakened and heard the lion roaring somewhere up along the river. It was a deep sound and at the end there were sort of coughing grunts that made him seem just outside the tent, and when Francis Macomber woke in the night to hear it he was afraid. He could hear his wife breathing quietly, asleep. There was no one to tell he was afraid, nor to be afraid with him, and, lying alone, he did not know the Somali proverb that says a brave man is always frightened three times by a lion; when he first sees his track, when he first hears him roar and when he first confronts him. Then while they were eating breakfast by lantern light out in the dining tent, before the sun was up, the lion roared again and Francis thought he was just at the edge of camp.

"Sounds like an old-timer," Robert Wilson said, looking up from his kippers and coffee. "Listen to him cough."

"Is he very close?"

"A mile or so up the stream."

"Will we see him?"

"We'll have a look."

"Does his roaring carry that far? It sounds as though he were right in camp."

"Carries a hell of a long way," said Robert Wilson. "It's strange the way it carries. Hope he's a shootable cat. The boys said there was a very big one about here."

"If I get a shot, where should I hit him," Macomber asked, "to stop him?"

"In the shoulders," Wilson said. "In the neck if you can make it. Shoot for bone. Break him down."

"I hope I can place it properly," Macomber said.

"You shoot very well," Wilson told him. "Take your time. Make sure of him. The first one in is the one that counts."

"What range will it be?"

"Can't tell. Lion has something to say about that. Don't shoot unless it's close enough so you can make sure."

"At under a hundred yards?" Macomber asked.

Wilson looked at him quickly.

"Hundred's about right. Might have to take him a bit under. Shouldn't chance a shot at much over that. A hundred's a decent range. You can hit him wherever you want at that. Here comes the Memsahib."

"Good morning," she said. "Are we going after that lion?"

"As soon as you deal with your breakfast," Wilson said. "How are you feeling?"

"Marvellous," she said. "I'm very excited."

"I'll just go and see that everything is ready." Wilson went off. As he left the lion roared again.

"Noisy beggar," Wilson said. "We'll put a stop to that."

"What's the matter, Francis?" his wife asked him.

"Nothing," Macomber said.

"Yes, there is," she said. "What are you upset about?"

"Nothing," he said.

"Tell me," she looked at him. "Don't you feel well?"

"It's that damned roaring," he said. "It's been going on all night, you know."

"Why didn't you wake me," she said. "I'd love to have heard it."

"I've got to kill the damned thing," Macomber said, miserably.

"Well, that's what you're out here for, isn't it?"

"Yes. But I'm nervous. Hearing the thing roar gets on my nerves."

"Well then, as Wilson said, kill him and stop his roaring."

"Yes, darling," said Francis Macomber. "It sounds easy, doesn't it?"

"You're not afraid, are you?"

"Of course not. But I'm nervous from hearing him roar all night."

143 "You'll kill him marvellously," she said. "I know you will. I'm awfully anxious to see it."

144 "Finish your breakfast and we'll be starting."

145 "It's not light yet," she said. "This is a ridiculous hour."

146 Just then the lion roared in a deep-chested moaning, suddenly guttural, ascending vibration that seemed to shake the air and ended in a sigh and a heavy, deep-chested grunt.

147 "He sounds almost here," Macomber's wife said.

148 "My God," said Macomber. "I hate that damned noise."

149 "It's very impressive."

150 "Impressive. It's frightful."

151 Robert Wilson came up then carrying his short, ugly, shockingly big-bored .505 Gibbs and grinning.

152 "Come on," he said. "Your gun-bearer has your Springfield and the big gun. Everything's in the car. Have you solids?"

153 "Yes."

154 "I'm ready," Mrs. Macomber said.

155 "Must make him stop that racket," Wilson said. "You get in front. The Memsahib can sit back here with me."

156 They climbed into the motor car and, in the gray first daylight, moved off up the river through the trees. Macomber opened the breech of his rifle and saw he had metal-cased bullets, shut the bolt and put the rifle on safety. He saw his hand was trembling. He felt in his pocket for more cartridges and moved his fingers over the cartridges in the loops of his tunic front. He turned back to where Wilson sat in the rear seat of the doorless, box-bodied motor car beside his wife, them both grinning with excitement, and Wilson leaned forward and whispered,

157 "See the birds dropping. Means the old boy has left his kill."

158 On the far bank of the stream Macomber could see, above the trees, vultures circling and plummeting down.

159 "Chances are he'll come to drink along here," Wilson whispered. "Before he goes to lay up. Keep an eye out."

160 They were driving slowly along the high bank of the stream which here cut deeply to its boulder-filled bed, and they wound in and out through big trees as they drove. Macomber was watching the opposite bank when he felt Wilson take hold of his arm. The car stopped.

161 "There he is," he heard the whisper. "Ahead and to the right. Get out and take him. He's a marvellous lion."

162 Macomber saw the lion now. He was standing almost broadside, his great head up and turned toward them. The early morning breeze that blew toward them was just stirring his dark mane, and the lion looked huge, silhouetted on the rise of bank in the gray morning light, his shoulders heavy, his barrel of a body bulking smoothly.

"How far is he?" asked Macomber, raising his rifle.

"About seventy-five. Get out and take him."

"Why not shoot from where I am?"

"You don't shoot them from cars," he heard Wilson saying in his ear. "Get out. He's not going to stay there all day."

Macomber stepped out of the curved opening at the side of the front seat, onto the step and down onto the ground. The lion still stood looking majestically and coolly toward this object that his eyes only showed in silhouette, bulking like some super-rhino. There was no man smell carried toward him and he watched the object, moving his great head a little from side to side. Then watching the object, not afraid, but hesitating before going down the bank to drink with such a thing opposite him, he saw a man figure detach itself from it and he turned his heavy head and swung away toward the cover of the trees as he heard a cracking crash and felt the slam of a .30-06 220-grain solid bullet that bit his flank and ripped in sudden hot scalding nausea through his stomach. He trotted, heavy, big-footed, swinging wounded full-bellied, through the trees toward the tall grass and cover, and the crash came again to go past him ripping the air apart. Then it crashed again and he felt the blow as it hit his lower ribs and ripped on through, blood sudden hot and frothy in his mouth, and he galloped toward the high grass where he could crouch and not be seen and make them bring the crashing thing close enough so he could make a rush and get the man that held it.

Macomber had not thought how the lion felt as he got out of the car. He only knew his hands were shaking and as he walked away from the car it was almost impossible for him to make his legs move. They were stiff in the thighs, but he could feel the muscles fluttering. He raised the rifle, sighted on the junction of the lion's head and shoulders and pulled the

trigger. Nothing happened though he pulled until he thought his finger would break. Then he knew he had the safety on and as he lowered the rifle to move the safety over he moved another frozen pace forward, and the lion seeing his silhouette flow clear of the silhouette of the car, turned and started off at a trot, and, as Macomber fired, he heard a whunk that meant that the bullet was home; but the lion kept on going. Macomber shot again and every one saw the bullet throw a spout of dirt beyond the trotting lion. He shot again, remembering to lower his aim, and they all heard the bullet hit, and the lion went into a gallop and was in the tall grass before he had the bolt pushed forward.

. . . a wounded lion's going to charge.

Macomber stood there feeling sick at his stomach, his hands that held the Springfield still cocked, shaking, and his wife and Robert Wilson were standing by him. Beside him too were the two gun-bearers chattering in Wakamba.

"I hit him," Macomber said. "I hit him twice."

"You gut-shot him and you hit him somewhere forward," Wilson said without enthusiasm. The gun-bearers looked very grave. They were silent now.

"You may have killed him," Wilson went on. "We'll have to wait a while before we go in to find out."

"What do you mean?"

"Let him get sick before we follow him up."

"Oh," said Macomber.

"He's a hell of a fine lion," Wilson said cheerfully. "He's gotten into a bad place though."

"Why is it bad?"

"Can't see him until you're on him."

"Oh," said Macomber.

"Come on," said Wilson. "The Memsahib can stay here in the car. We'll go to have a look at the blood spoor."

"Stay here, Margot," Macomber said to his wife. His mouth was very dry and it was hard for him to talk.

"Why?" she asked.

"Wilson says to."

"We're going to have a look," Wilson said. "You stay here. You can see even better from here."

"All right."

Wilson spoke in Swahili to the driver. He nodded and said, "Yes, Bwana."

Then they went down the steep bank and across the stream, climbing over and around the boulders and up the other bank, pulling up by some projecting roots, and along it until they found where the lion had been trotting when Macomber first shot. There was dark blood on the short grass that the gun-bearers pointed out with grass stems, and that ran away behind the river bank trees.

"What do we do?" asked Macomber.

"Not much choice," said Wilson. "We can't bring the car over. Bank's too steep. We'll let him stiffen up a bit and then you and I'll go in and have a look for him."

"Can't we set the grass on fire?" Macomber asked.

"Too green."

"Can't we send beaters?"

Wilson looked at him appraisingly. "Of course we can," he said. "But it's just a touch murderous. You see, we know the lion's wounded. You can drive an unwounded lion—he'll move on ahead of a noise—but a wounded lion's going to charge. You can't see him until you're right on him. He'll make himself perfectly flat in cover you wouldn't think would hide a hare. You can't very well send boys in there to that sort of a show. Somebody bound to get mauled."

"What about the gun-bearers?"

"Oh, they'll go with us. It's their *shauri*. You see, they signed on for it. They don't look too happy though, do they?"

"I don't want to go in there," said Macomber. It was out before he knew he'd said it.

"Neither do I," said Wilson very cheerily. "Really no choice though." Then, as an afterthought, he glanced at Macomber and saw suddenly how he was trembling and the pitiful look on his face.

"You don't have to go in, of course," he said. "That's what I'm hired for, you know. That's why I'm so expensive."

"You mean you'd go in by yourself? Why not leave him there?"

Robert Wilson, whose entire occupation had been with the lion and the problem he presented, and who had not been thinking about Macomber except to note that he was rather windy, suddenly felt as though he had opened the wrong door in a hotel and seen something shameful.

"What do you mean?"

"Why not just leave him?"

"You mean pretend to ourselves he hasn't been hit?"

"No. Just drop it."

"It isn't done."

"Why not?"

"For one thing, he's certain to be suffering. For another, some one else might run onto him."

"I see."

"But you don't have to have anything to do with it."

"I'd like to," Macomber said. "I'm just scared, you know."

"I'll go ahead when we go in," Wilson said, "with Kongoni tracking. You keep behind me and a little to one side. Chances are we'll hear him growl. If we see him we'll both shoot. Don't worry about anything. I'll keep you backed up. As a matter of fact, you know, perhaps you'd better not go. It might be much better. Why don't you go over and join the Memsahib while I just get it over with?"

212 "No, I want to go."

213 "All right," said Wilson. "But don't go in if you don't want to. This is my *shauri* now, you know."

214 "I want to go," said Macomber.

215 They sat under a tree and smoked.

216 "Want to go back and speak to the Memsahib while we're waiting?" Wilson asked.

217 "No."

218 "I'll just step back and tell her to be patient."

219 "Good," said Macomber. He sat there, sweating under his arms, his mouth dry, his stomach hollow feeling, wanting to find courage to tell Wilson to go on and finish off the lion without him. He could not know that Wilson was furious because he had not noticed the state he was in earlier and sent him back to his wife. While he sat there Wilson came up. "I have your big gun," he said. "Take it. We've given him time, I think. Come on."

220 Macomber took the big gun and Wilson said:

221 "Keep behind me and about five yards to the right and do exactly as I tell you." Then he spoke in Swahili to the two gun-bearers who looked the picture of gloom.

222 "Let's go," he said.

223 "Could I have a drink of water?" Macomber asked. Wilson spoke to the older gun-bearer, who wore a canteen on his belt, and the man unbuckled it, unscrewed the top and handed it to Macomber, who took it noticing how heavy it seemed and how hairy and shoddy the felt covering was in his hand. He raised it to drink and looked ahead at the high grass with the flat-topped trees behind it. A breeze was blowing toward them and the grass rippled gently in the wind. He looked at the gun-bearer and he could see the gun-bearer was suffering too with fear.

224 Thirty-five yards into the grass the big lion lay flattened out along the ground. His ears were back and his only movement was a slight twitching up and down of his long, black-tufted tail. He had turned at bay as soon as he had reached this cover and he was sick with the wound through his full belly, and weakening with the wound through his lungs that brought a thin foamy red to his mouth each time he breathed. His flanks were wet and hot and flies were on the little openings the solid bullets had made in his tawny hide, and his big yellow eyes, narrowed with hate, looked straight ahead, only blinking when the pain came as he breathed, and his claws dug in the soft baked earth. All of him, pain, sickness, hatred and all of his remaining strength, was tightening into an absolute concentration for a rush. He could hear the men talking and he waited, gathering all of himself into this preparation for a charge as soon as the men would come into the grass. As he heard their voices his tail stiffened to twitch up and down, and, as they came into the edge of the grass, he made a coughing grunt and charged.

Kongoni, the old gun-bearer, in the lead watching the blood spoor, Wilson watching the grass for any movement, his big gun ready, the second gun-bearer looking ahead and listening, Macomber close to Wilson, his rifle cocked, they had just moved into the grass when Macomber heard the blood-choked coughing grunt, and saw the swishing rush in the grass. The next thing he knew he was running; running wildly, in panic in the open, running toward the stream.

He heard the *ca-ra-wong!* of Wilson's big rifle, and again in a second crashing *carawong!* and turning saw the lion, horrible-looking now, with half his head seeming to be gone, crawling toward Wilson in the edge of the tall grass while the red-faced man worked the bolt on the short ugly rifle and aimed carefully as another blasting *carawong!* came from the muzzle, and the crawling, heavy, yellow bulk of the lion stiffened and the huge, mutilated head slid forward and Macomber, standing by himself in the clearing where he had run, holding a loaded rifle, while two black men and a white man looked back at him in contempt, knew the lion was dead. He came toward Wilson, his tallness all seeming a naked reproach, and Wilson looked at him and said:

"Want to take pictures?"

"No," he said.

That was all any one had said until they reached the motor car. Then Wilson had said:

"Hell of a fine lion. Boys will skin him out. We might as well stay here in the shade."

Macomber's wife had not looked at him nor he at her and he had sat by her in the back seat with Wilson sitting in the front seat. Once he had reached over and taken his wife's hand without looking at her and she had removed her hand from his. Looking across the stream to where the gun-bearers were skinning out the lion he could see that she had been able to see the whole thing. While they sat there his wife had reached forward and put her hand on Wilson's shoulder. He turned and she had leaned forward over the low seat and kissed him on the mouth.

"Oh, I say," said Wilson, going redder than his natural baked color.

"Mr. Robert Wilson," she said. "The beautiful red-faced Mr. Robert Wilson."

Then she sat down beside Macomber again and looked away across the stream to where the lion lay, with uplifted, white-muscled, tendon-marked naked forearms, and white bloating belly, as the black men fleshed away the skin. Finally the gun-bearers brought the skin over, wet and heavy, and climbed in behind with it, rolling it up before they got in, and the motor car started. No one had said anything more until they were back in camp.

That was the story of the lion. Macomber did not know how the lion had felt before he started his rush, nor during it when the unbelievable smash of the .505 with a muzzle velocity of two tons had hit him in the mouth, nor what kept him coming after that, when the second ripping crash had smashed his hind quarters and he had come crawling on toward the crashing, blasting thing that had destroyed him. Wilson knew something about it and only expressed it by saying, "Damned fine lion," but Macomber did not know how Wilson felt abut things either. He did not know how his wife felt except that she was through with him.

His wife had been through with him before but it never lasted. He was very wealthy, and would be much wealthier, and he knew she would not leave him ever now. That was one of the few things that he really knew. He knew about that, about motor cycles—that was earliest—about motor cars, about duck-shooting, about fishing, trout, salmon and big-sea, about sex in books, many books, too many books, about all court games, about dogs, not much about horses, about hanging on to his money, about most of the other things his world dealt in, and about his wife not leaving him. His wife had been a great beauty and she was still a great beauty in Africa, but she was not a great enough beauty any more at home to be able to leave him and better herself and she knew it and he knew it. She had missed the chance to leave him and he knew it. If he had been better with women she would probably have started to worry about him getting another new, beautiful wife; but she knew too much about him to worry about him either. Also, he had always had a great tolerance which seemed the nicest thing about him if it were not the most sinister.

All in all they were known as a comparatively happily married couple, one of those whose disruption is often rumored but never occurs, and as the society columnist put it, they were adding more than a spice of *adventure* to their much envied and ever-enduring *Romance* by a *Safari* in what was known as *Darkest Africa* until the Martin Johnsons lighted it on so many silver screens where they were pursuing *Old Simba* the lion, the buffalo, *Tembo* the elephant and as well collecting specimens for the Museum of Natural History. This same columnist had reported them *on the verge* at least three times in the past and they had been. But they always made it up. They had a sound basis of union. Margot was too beautiful for Macomber to divorce her and Macomber had too much money for Margot ever to leave him.

It was now about three o'clock in the morning and Francis Macomber, who had been asleep a little while after he had stopped thinking about the lion, wakened and then slept again, woke suddenly, frightened in a dream of the bloody-headed lion standing over him, and listening while his heart pounded, he realized that his wife was not in the other cot in the tent. He lay awake with that knowledge for two hours.

At the end of that time his wife came into the tent, lifted her mosquito bar and crawled cozily into bed.

"Where have you been?" Macomber asked in the darkness.

"Hello," she said. "Are you awake?"

"Where have you been?"

"I just went out to get a breath of air."

"You did, like hell."

"What do you want me to say, darling?"

"Where have you been?"

"Out to get a breath of air."

"That's a new name for it. You *are* a bitch."

"Well, you're a coward."

"All right," he said. "What of it?"

"Nothing as far as I'm concerned. But please let's not talk, darling, because I'm very sleepy."

"You think that I'll take anything."

253 "I know you will, sweet."

254 "Well, I won't."

255 "Please, darling, let's not talk. I'm so very sleepy."

256 "There wasn't going to be any of that. You promised there wouldn't be."

257 "Well, there is now," she said sweetly.

258 "You said if we made this trip that there would be none of that. You promised."

259 "Yes, darling. That's the way I meant it to be. But the trip was spoiled yesterday. We don't have to talk about it, do we?"

260 "You don't wait long when you have an advantage, do you?"

261 "Please let's not talk. I'm so sleepy, darling."

262 "I'm going to talk."

263 "Don't mind me then, because I'm going to sleep." And she did.

264 At breakfast they were all three at the table before daylight and Francis Macomber found that, of all the many men that he had hated, he hated Robert Wilson the most.

265 "Sleep well?" Wilson asked in his throaty voice, filling a pipe.

266 "Did you?"

267 "Topping," the white hunter told him.

268 You bastard, thought Macomber, you insolent bastard.

269 So she woke him when she came in, Wilson thought, looking at them both with his flat, cold eyes. Well, why doesn't he keep his wife where she belongs? What does he think I am, a bloody plaster saint? Let him keep her where she belongs. It's his own fault.

270 "Do you think we'll find buffalo?" Margot asked, pushing away a dish of apricots.

271 "Chance of it," Wilson said and smiled at her. "Why don't you stay in camp?"

272 "Not for anything," she told him.

273 "Why not order her to stay in camp?" Wilson said to Macomber.

274 "You order her," said Macomber coldly.

275 "Let's not have any ordering, nor," turning to Macomber, "any silliness, Francis," Margot said quite pleasantly.

276 "Are you ready to start?" Macomber asked.

277 "Any time," Wilson told him. "Do you want the Memsahib to go?"

278 "Does it make any difference whether I do or not?"

279 The hell with it, thought Robert Wilson. The utter complete hell with it. So this is what it's going to be like. Well, this is what it's going to be like, then.

"Makes no difference," he said.

"You're sure you wouldn't like to stay in camp with her yourself and let me go out and hunt the buffalo?" Macomber asked.

"Can't do that," said Wilson. "Wouldn't talk rot if I were you."

"I'm not talking rot. I'm disgusted."

"Bad word, disgusted."

"Francis, will you please try to speak sensibly," his wife said.

"I speak too damned sensibly," Macomber said. "Did you ever eat such filthy food?"

"Something wrong with the food?" asked Wilson quietly.

"No more than with everything else."

"I'd pull yourself together, laddybuck," Wilson said very quietly. "There's a boy waits at table that understands a little English."

"The hell with him."

Wilson stood up and puffing on his pipe strolled away, speaking a few words in Swahili to one of the gun-bearers who was standing waiting for him. Macomber and his wife sat on at the table. He was staring at his coffee cup.

"If you make a scene I'll leave you, darling," Margot said quietly.

"No, you won't."

"You can try it and see."

"You won't leave me."

"No," she said. "I won't leave you and you'll behave yourself."

"Behave myself? That's a way to talk. Behave myself."

"Yes. Behave yourself."

"Why don't *you* try behaving?"

"I've tried it so long. So very long."

"I hate that red-faced swine," Macomber said. "I loathe the sight of him."

"He's really *very* nice."

"Oh, *shut up*," Macomber almost shouted. Just then the car came up and stopped in front of the dining tent and the driver and the two gun-bearers got out. Wilson walked over and looked at the husband and wife sitting there at the table.

"Going, shooting?" he asked.

"Yes," said Macomber, standing up. "Yes."

"Better bring a woolly. It will be cool in the car," Wilson said.

"I'll get my leather jacket," Margot said.

"The boy has it," Wilson told her. He climbed into the front with the driver and Francis Macomber and his wife sat, not speaking, in the back seat.

9 Hope the silly beggar doesn't take a notion to blow the back of my head off, Wilson thought to himself. Women *are* a nuisance on safari.

0 The car was grinding down to cross the river at a pebbly ford in the gray daylight and then climbed, angling up the steep bank, where Wilson had ordered a way shovelled out the day before so they could reach the parklike wooded rolling country on the far side.

1 It was a good morning, Wilson thought. There was a heavy dew and as the wheels went through the grass and low bushes he could smell the odor of the crushed fronds. It was an odor like verbena and he liked this early morning smell of the dew, the crushed bracken and the look of the tree trunks showing black through the early morning mist, as the car made its way through the untracked, parklike country. He had put the two in the back seat out of his mind now and was thinking about buffalo. The buffalo that he was after stayed in the daytime in a thick swamp where it was impossible to get a shot, but in the night they fed out into an open stretch of country and if he could come between them and their swamp with the car, Macomber would have a good chance at them in the open. He did not want to hunt buff with Macomber in thick cover. He did not want to hunt buff or anything else with Macomber at all, but he was a professional hunter and he had hunted with some rare ones in his time. If they got buff today there would only be rhino to come and the poor man would have gone through his dangerous game and things might pick up. He'd have nothing more to do with the woman and Macomber would get over that too. He must have gone through plenty of that before by the look of things. Poor beggar. He must have a way of getting over it. Well, it was the poor sod's own bloody fault.

They were his standards in all except the shooting.

2 He, Robert Wilson, carried a double size cot on safari to accommodate any windfalls he might receive. He had hunted for a certain clientele, the international, fast, sporting set, where the women did not feel they were getting their money's worth unless they had shared that cot with the white hunter. He despised them when he was away from them although he liked some of them well enough at the time, but he made his living by them; and their standards were his standards as long as they were hiring him.

13 They were his standards in all except the shooting. He had his own standards about the killing and they could live up to them or get some one else to hunt them. He knew, too, that they all respected him for this. This Macomber was an odd one though. Damned if he wasn't. Now the wife. Well, the wife. Yes, the wife. Hm, the wife. Well he'd dropped all that. He looked around at them. Macomber sat grim and furious. Margot smiled at him. She looked younger today, more innocent and fresher and not so professionally beautiful. What's in her heart God knows, Wilson thought. She hadn't talked much last night. At that it was a pleasure to see her.

The motor car climbed up a slight rise and went 314 on through the trees and then out into a grassy prairie-like opening and kept in the shelter of the trees along the edge, the driver going slowly and Wilson looking carefully out across the prairie and all along its far side. He stopped the car and studied the opening with his field glasses. Then he motioned to the driver to go on and the car moved slowly along, the driver avoiding warthog holes and driving around the mud castles ants had built. Then, looking across the opening, Wilson suddenly turned and said,

"By God, there they are!" 315

And looking where he pointed, while the car 316 jumped forward and Wilson spoke in rapid Swahili to the driver, Macomber saw three huge, black animals looking almost cylindrical in their long heaviness, like big black tank cars, moving at a gallop across the far edge of the open prairie. They moved at a stiff-necked, stiff bodied gallop and he could see the upswept wide black horns on their heads as they galloped heads out; the heads not moving.

"They're three old bulls," Wilson said. "We'll cut 317 them off before they get to the swamp."

The car was going a wild forty-five miles an hour 318 across the open and as Macomber watched, the buffalo got bigger and bigger until he could see the gray, hairless, scabby look of one huge bull and how his neck was a part of his shoulders and the shiny black of his horns as he galloped a little behind the others that were strung out in that steady plunging gait; and then, the car swaying as though it had just jumped a road, they drew up close and he could see the plunging hugeness of the bull, and the dust in his sparsely haired hide, the wide boss of horn and his outstretched, wide-nostrilled muzzle, and he was raising his rifle when Wilson shouted, "Not from the car, you fool!" and he had no fear, only hatred of Wilson, while the brakes clamped on and the car skidded, plowing sideways to an almost stop and Wilson was out on one side and he on the other, stumbling as his feet hit the still speeding-by of the earth, and then he was shooting at the bull as he moved away, hearing the bullets whunk into him, emptying his rifle at him as he moved steadily away, finally remembering to get his shots forward into the shoulder, and as he fumbled to re-load, he saw the bull was down. Down on his knees, his big head tossing, and seeing the other two still galloping he shot at the leader and hit him. He shot again and missed and he heard the *carawonging* roar as Wilson shot and saw the leading bull slide forward onto his nose.

319   "Get that other," Wilson said. "Now you're shooting!"

320   But the other bull was moving steadily at the same gallop and he missed, throwing a spout of dirt, and Wilson missed and the dust rose in a cloud and Wilson shouted, "Come on. He's too far!" and grabbed his arm and they were in the car again, Macomber and Wilson hanging on the sides and rocketing swayingly over the uneven ground, drawing up on the steady, plunging, heavy-necked, straight-moving gallop of the bull.

321   They were behind him and Macomber was filling his rifle, dropping shells onto the ground, jamming it, clearing the jam, then they were almost up with the bull when Wilson yelled "Stop," and the car skidded so that it almost swung over and Macomber fell forward onto his feet, slammed his bolt forward and fired as far forward as he could aim into the galloping, rounded black back, aimed and shot again, then again, then again, and the bullets, all of them hitting, had no effect on the buffalo that he could see. Then Wilson shot, the roar deafening him, and he could see the bull stagger. Macomber shot again, aiming carefully, and down he came, onto his knees.

322   "All right," Wilson said. "Nice work. That's the three."

323   Macomber felt a drunken elation.

324   "How many times did you shoot?" he asked.

325   "Just three," Wilson said. "You killed the first bull. The biggest one. I helped you finish the other two. Afraid they might have got into cover. You had them killed. I was just mopping up a little. You shot damn well."

326   "Let's go to the car," said Macomber. "I want a drink."

327   "Got to finish off that buff first," Wilson told him. The buffalo was on his knees and he jerked his head furiously and bellowed in pig-eyed, roaring rage as they came toward him.

328   "Watch he doesn't get up," Wilson said. Then, "Get a little broadside and take him in the neck just behind the ear."

329   Macomber aimed carefully at the center of the huge, jerking, rage-driven neck and shot. At the shot the head dropped forward.

"That does it," said Wilson. "Got the spine. They're a hell of a looking thing, aren't they?"

"Let's get the drink," said Macomber. In his life he had never felt so good.

In the car Macomber's wife sat very white-faced. "You were marvellous, darling," she said to Macomber. "What a ride."

"Was it rough?" Wilson asked.

"It was frightful. I've never been more frightened in my life."

"Let's all have a drink," Macomber said.

"By all means," said Wilson. "Give it to the Memsahib." She drank the neat whisky from the flask and shuddered a little when she swallowed. She handed the flask to Macomber who handed it to Wilson.

"It was frightfully exciting," she said. "It's given me a dreadful headache. I didn't know you were allowed to shoot them from cars though."

"No one shot from cars," said Wilson coldly.

"I mean chase them from cars."

"Wouldn't ordinarily," Wilson said. "Seemed sporting enough to me though while we were doing it. Taking more chance driving that way across the plain full of holes and one thing and another than hunting on foot. Buffalo could have charged us each time we shot if he liked. Gave him every chance. Wouldn't mention it to anyone though. It's illegal if that's what you mean."

"It seemed very unfair to me," Margot said, "chasing those big helpless things in a motor car."

"Did it?" said Wilson.

"What would happen if they heard about it in Nairobi?"

"I'd lose my licence for one thing. Other unpleasantnesses," Wilson said, taking a drink from the flask. "I'd be out of business."

"Really?"

"Yes, really."

"Well," said Macomber, and he smiled for the first time all day. "Now she has something on you."

"You have such a pretty way of putting things, Francis," Margot Macomber said. Wilson looked at them both. If a four-letter man marries a five-letter woman, he was thinking, what number of letters would their children be? What he said was, "We lost a gun-bearer. Did you notice it?"

"My God, no," Macomber said.

"Here he comes," Wilson said. "He's all right. He must have fallen off when we left the first bull."

Approaching them was the middle-aged gun-bearer, limping along in his knitted cap, khaki tunic, shorts

> She drank the neat whisky from the flask and shuddered a little when she swallowed.

and rubber sandals, gloomy-faced and disgusted looking. As he came up he called out to Wilson in Swahili and they all saw the change in the white hunter's face.

"What does he say?" asked Margot

"He says the first bull got up and went into the bush," Wilson said with no expression in his voice.

"Oh," said Macomber blankly.

"Then it's going to be just like the lion," said Margot, full of anticipation.

"It's not going to be a damned bit like the lion," Wilson told her. "Did you want another drink, Macomber?"

"Thanks, yes," Macomber said. He expected the feeling he had had about the lion to come back but it did not. For the first time in his life he really felt wholly without fear. Instead of fear he had a feeling of definite elation.

"We'll go and have a look at the second bull," Wilson said. "I'll tell the driver to put the car in the shade."

"What are you going to do?" asked Margaret Macomber.

"Take a look at the buff," Wilson said.

"I'll come."

"Come along."

The three of them walked over to where the second buffalo bulked blackly in the open, head forward on the grass, the massive horns swung wide.

"He's a very good head," Wilson said. "That's close to a fifty-inch spread."

Macomber was looking at him with delight.

"He's hateful looking," said Margot. "Can't we go into the shade?"

"Of course," Wilson said. "Look," he said to Macomber, and pointed. "See that patch of bush?"

"Yes."

"That's where the first bull went in. The gun-bearer said when he fell off the bull was down. He was watching us helling along and the other two buff galloping. When he looked up there was the bull up and looking at him. Gun-bearer ran like hell and the bull went off slowly into that bush."

"Can we go in after him now?" asked Macomber eagerly.

Wilson looked at him appraisingly. Damned if this isn't a strange one, he thought. Yesterday he's scared sick and today he's a ruddy fire eater.

"No, we'll give him a while."

"Let's please go into the shade," Margot said. Her face was white and she looked ill.

They made their way to the car where it stood under a single, wide-spreading tree and all climbed in.

"Chances are he's dead in there," Wilson remarked. "After a little we'll have a look."

Macomber felt a wild unreasonable happiness that he had never known before.

"By God, that was a chase," he said. "I've never felt any such feeling. Wasn't it marvellous, Margot?"

"I hated it."

"Why?"

"I hated it," she said bitterly. "I loathed it."

"You know I don't think I'd ever be afraid of anything again," Macomber said to Wilson. "Something happened in me after we first saw the buff and started after him. Like a dam bursting. It was pure excitement."

"Cleans out your liver," said Wilson. "Damn funny things happen to people."

Macomber's face was shining. "You know something did happen to me," he said. "I feel absolutely different."

His wife said nothing and eyed him strangely. She was sitting far back in the seat and Macomber was sitting forward talking to Wilson who turned sideways talking over the back of the front seat.

"You know, I'd like to try another lion," Macomber said. "I'm really not afraid of them now. After all, what can they do to you?"

"That's it," said Wilson. "Worst one can do is kill you. How does it go? Shakespeare. Damned good. See if I can remember. Oh, damned good. Used to quote it to myself at one time. Let's see. 'By my troth, I care not; a man can die but once; we owe God a death and let it go which way it will, he that dies this year is quit for the next.' Damned fine, eh?"

He was very embarrassed, having brought out this thing he had lived by, but he had seen men come of age before and it always moved him. It was not a matter of their twenty-first birthday.

It had taken a strange chance of hunting, a sudden precipitation into action without opportunity for worrying beforehand, to bring this about with Macomber, but regardless of how it had happened it had most certainly happened. Look at the beggar now, Wilson thought. It's that some of them stay little boys so long, Wilson thought. Sometimes all their lives. Their figures stay boyish when they're fifty. The great Ameri-

can boy-men. Damned strange people. But he liked this Macomber now. Damned strange fellow. Probably meant the end of cuckoldry too. Well, that would be a damned good thing. Damned good thing. Beggar had probably been afraid all his life. Don't know what started it. But over now. Hadn't had time to be afraid with the buff. That and being angry too. Motor car too. Motor cars made it familiar. Be a damn fire eater now. He'd seen it in the war work the same way. More of a change than any loss of virginity. Fear gone like an operation. Something else grew in its place. Main thing a man had. Made him into a man. Women knew it too. No bloody fear.

389   From the far corner of the seat Margaret Macomber looked at the two of them. There was no change in Wilson. She saw Wilson as she had seen him the day before when she had first realized what his great talent was. But she saw the change in Francis Macomber now.

390   "Do you have that feeling of happiness about what's going to happen?" Macomber asked, still exploring his new wealth.

391   "You're not supposed to mention it," Wilson said, looking in the other's face. "Much more fashionable to say you're scared. Mind you, you'll be scared too, plenty of times."

392   But you *have* a feeling of happiness about action to come?"

393   "Yes," said Wilson. "There's that. Doesn't do to talk too much about all this. Talk the whole thing away. No pleasure in anything if you mouth it up too much.

394   "You're both talking rot," said Margot. "Just because you've chased some helpless animals in a motor car you talk like heroes."

395   "Sorry," said Wilson. "I have been gassing too much." She's worried about it already, he thought.

396   "If you don't know what we're talking about why not keep out of it?" Macomber asked his wife.

397   "You've gotten awfully brave, awfully suddenly," his wife said contemptuously, but her contempt was not secure. She was very afraid of something.

398   Macomber laughed, a very natural hearty laugh. "You know I *have*," he said. "I really have."

399   "Isn't it sort of late?" Margot said bitterly. Because she had done the best she could for many years back and the way they were together now was no one person's fault.

400   "Not for me," said Macomber.

401   Margot said nothing but sat back in the corner of the seat.

402   "Do you think we've given him time enough?" Macomber asked Wilson cheerfully.

403   "We might have a look," Wilson said. "Have you any solids left?"

"The gun-bearer has some."

Wilson called in Swahili and the older gun-bearer, who was skinning out one of the heads, straightened up, pulled a box of solids out of his pocket and brought them over to Macomber, who filled his magazine and put the remaining shells in his pocket.

"You might as well shoot the Springfield," Wilson said. "You're used to it. We'll leave the Mannlicher in the car with the Memsahib. Your gun-bearer can carry your heavy gun. I've this damned cannon. Now let me tell you about them." He had saved this until the last because he did not want to worry Macomber. "When a buff comes he comes with his head high and thrust straight out. The boss of the horns covers any sort of a brain shot. The only shot is straight into the nose. The only other shot is into his chest or, if you're to one side, into the neck or the shoulders. After they've been hit once they take a hell of a lot of killing. Don't try anything fancy. Take the easiest shot there is. They've finished skinning out that head now. Should we get started?"

He called to the gun-bearers, who came up wiping their hands, and the older one got into the back.

"I'll only take Kongoni," Wilson said. "The other can watch to keep the birds away."

As the car moved slowly across the open space toward the island of brushy trees that ran in a tongue of foliage along a dry water course that cut the open swale, Macomber felt his heart pounding and his mouth was dry again, but it was excitement, not fear.

"Here's where he went in," Wilson said. Then to the gun-bearer in Swahili, "Take the blood spoor."

The car was parallel to the patch of bush. Macomber, Wilson and the gun-bearer got down. Macomber, looking back, saw his wife, with the rifle by her side, looking at him. He waved to her and she did not wave back.

The brush was very thick ahead and the ground was dry. The middle-aged gun-bearer was sweating heavily and Wilson had his hat down over his eyes and his red neck showed just ahead of Macomber. Suddenly the gun-bearer said something in Swahili to Wilson and ran forward.

"He's dead in there," Wilson said. "Good work," and he turned to grip Macomber's hand and as they shook hands, grinning at each other, the gun-bearer shouted wildly and they saw him coming out of the bush sideways, fast as a crab, and the bull coming, nose out, mouth tight closed, blood dripping, massive head straight out, coming in a charge, his little pig eyes bloodshot as he looked at them. Wilson, who was ahead, was kneeling shooting, and Macomber, as he fired, unhearing his shot in the roaring of Wilson's gun, saw fragments like slate burst from the huge boss of the horns, and the head jerked, he shot again at the wide nostrils and saw the horns jolt again and fragments fly, and he did not see Wilson now and, aiming carefully, shot again with the buffalo's huge bulk almost on him and his rifle almost level with the on-coming head, nose out, and he could see the little wicked eyes and the head started to lower and he felt a sudden white-hot, blinding flash explode inside his head and that was all he ever felt.

Wilson had ducked to one side to get in a shoulder shot. Macomber had stood solid and shot for the nose, shooting a touch high each time and hitting the heavy horns, splintering and chipping them like hitting a slate roof, and Mrs. Macomber, in the car, had shot at the buffalo with the 6.5 Mannlicher as it seemed about to gore Macomber and had hit her husband about two inches up and a little to one side of the base of his skull.

Francis Macomber lay now, face down, not two yards from where the buffalo lay on his side and his wife knelt over him with Wilson beside her.

"I wouldn't turn him over," Wilson said.

The woman was crying hysterically.

"I'd get back in the car," Wilson said. "Where's the rifle?"

She shook her head, her face contorted. The gun-bearer picked up the rifle.

"Leave it as it is," said Wilson. Then, "Go get Abdulla so that he may witness the manner of the accident."

> ". . . Why didn't you poison him? That's what they do in England."

He knelt down, took a handkerchief from his pocket, and spread it over Francis Macomber's crew-cropped head where it lay. The blood sank into the dry, loose earth.

Wilson stood up and saw the buffalo on his side, his legs out, his thinly-haired belly crawling with ticks. "Hell of a good bull," his brain registered automatically. "A good fifty inches, or better. Better." He called to the driver and told him to spread a blanket over the body and stay by it. Then he walked over to the motor car where the woman sat crying in the corner.

"That was a pretty thing to do," he said in a toneless voice. "He *would* have left you too."

"Stop it," she said.

"Of course it's an accident," he said. "I know that."

"Stop it," she said.

"Don't worry," he said. "There will be a certain amount of unpleasantness but I will have some photographs taken that will be very useful at the inquest. There's the testimony of the gun-bearers and the driver too. You're perfectly all right."

"Stop it," she said.

"There's a hell of a lot to be done," he said. "And I'll have to send a truck off to the lake to wireless for a plane to take the three of us into Nairobi. Why didn't you poison him? That's what they do in England."

"Stop it. Stop it. Stop it," the woman cried.

Wilson looked at her with his flat blue eyes.

"I'm through now," he said. "I was a little angry. I'd begun to like your husband."

"Oh, please stop it," she said. "Please stop it."

"That's better," Wilson said. "Please is much better. Now I'll stop."

I F you like "The Short Happy Life of Francis Macomber," you may enjoy looking at some of the other third-person stories and seeing how they dip in and out of the perspective of one or another of the characters besides the main character. Take a look again at Willa Cather's story "Paul's Case" and see if the author herself makes a judgment or two about the situation as the story unfolds.

GOING FURTHER If you like the Hemingway story, you can dive into any one of a number of his novels and story collections. His nonfiction book *The Green Hills of Africa* takes you back to the setting of this story. To read about Africa from the point of view of an African writer, you can find novels that cover the great continent from the work of Tahar Ben Jelloun in the north all the way down to Nadine Gordimer and Zakes Mda in the south.

Writing from Reading

Summarize

1 Summarize the events of the two hunts described in the story, noting their similarities. Discuss the points of view from which Hemingway chooses to describe these parallel events. Do the point-of-view shifts match, or do we see similar events from different points of view?

Analyze Craft

2 The point of view in the story shifts many times. Discuss the ways in which Hemingway signifies this shift to the reader.

3 This story begins *in medias res,* the first hunt of the lion and Macomber's first show of cowardice already having happened. Why does Hemingway choose to begin after the first hunt, rather than before? Explain how the story would change if your introduction to Francis was as a wealthy, attractive American embarking on his first safari.

4 Why does Hemingway choose to show us the lion's point of view? Some readers think of this passage as a triumphant demonstration of Hemingway's narrative style and imaginative reach; others think of it as overreaching or too showy. Criticize or defend the use of the lion's point of view, considering its context in the larger story.

Analyze Voice

5 The story is told by a third-person omniscient narrator who jumps from one character's thoughts to the next. Consider whether the narrator identifies with one character more than the others, and explain your conclusion using clues from the text.

6 Note the parts of the story in which the narrator becomes most objective, acting as an observer who remains outside all the characters. What do these more distant perspectives contribute?

Synthesize Summary and Analysis

7 Thanks to the narrator's omniscient point of view, we are able to see characters in their own minds as well as through the eyes of others. Discuss how Hemingway characterizes Francis Macomber using Francis's thoughts as well as Wilson's impressions of Francis. How does the dual impression affect you as a reader? Are you inclined to believe one source more than the other? Consider how you would view Francis if you never saw him from Wilson's point of view.

Interpret the Story

8 At the end of the story, Wilson accuses Margot of killing her husband on purpose. Do you agree or disagree with Wilson? What evidence from the text supports or denies Wilson's accusations? Consider in your analysis why Hemingway rarely writes from Margot's point of view.

Charlotte Perkins Gilman (1860–1935)

Born in Connecticut, Charlotte Perkins Gilman became a reluctant wife when she was twenty-four—reluctant because she feared the duties of a housewife would interfere with her desire to be active and productive in her own work. When the birth of her first child sent Gilman into depression, her doctor prescribed a rest cure consisting of an entirely domestic life free of physical and intellectual activity. As Gilman explained, "I went home and obeyed those directions for some three months, and came so near the border line of utter mental ruin that I could see over." She recovered by ignoring her doctor's orders and resuming her work as a writer and dedicated feminist. Gilman's most famous short story, "The Yellow Wallpaper," tells the story of a woman secluded from any activity and her consequent descent into madness—the author's way of speaking out against harmful patterns of preventing women's participation in society. In addition to creating stories that promoted feminist ideals, she also wrote nonfiction treatises on behalf of women's rights—most notably, *Women and Economics* (1898)—and lectured widely. Suffering from breast cancer and the loss of her second husband, Gilman ended her own life with chloroform at seventy-five.

AS YOU READ   Notice the images that are repeated—for example, the house, the grounds surrounding it, the journal, the husband, the room where most of the story takes place, and of course, the wallpaper. How does the narrator's view of these crucial images change over the course of the story? How does the narrator herself change over the course of the story?

The Yellow Wallpaper (1892)

1   IT is very seldom that mere ordinary people like John and myself secure ancestral halls for the summer.

2   A colonial mansion, a hereditary estate, I would say a haunted house and reach the height of romantic felicity—but that would be asking too much of fate!

3   Still I will proudly declare that there is something queer about it.

4   Else, why should it be let so cheaply? And why have stood so long untenanted?

5   John laughs at me, of course, but one expects that.

6   John is practical in the extreme. He has no patience with faith, an intense horror of superstition, and he scoffs openly at any talk of things not to be felt and seen and put down in figures.

7   John is a physician, and *perhaps*—(I would not say it to a living soul, of course, but this is dead paper and a great relief to my mind)—*perhaps* that is one reason I do not get well faster.

8   You see, he does not believe I am sick! And what can one do?

9   If a physician of high standing, and one's own husband, assures friends and relatives that there is really nothing the matter with one but temporary nervous depression—a slight hysterical tendency—what is one to do?

10   My brother is also a physician, and also of high standing, and he says the same thing.

11   So I take phosphates or phosphites—whichever it is—and tonics, and air and exercise, and journeys, and am absolutely forbidden to "work" until I am well again.

12   Personally, I disagree with their ideas.

13   Personally, I believe that congenial work, with excitement and change, would do me good.

14   But what is one to do?

15   I did write for a while in spite of them; but it *does* exhaust me a good deal—having to be so sly about it, or else meet with heavy opposition.

16   I sometimes fancy that in my condition, if I had less opposition and more society and stimulus—but John says the very worst thing I can do is to think about my condition, and I confess it always makes me feel bad.

17   So I will let it alone and talk about the house.

18   The most beautiful place! It is quite alone, standing well back from the road, quite three miles from the village. It makes me think of English places that you read about, for there are hedges and walls and

19   gates that lock, and lots of separate little houses for the gardeners and people.

There is a *delicious* garden! I never saw such a garden—large and shady, full of box-bordered paths, and lined with long grape-covered arbors with seats under them.

20   There were greenhouses, but they are all broken now.

21   There was some legal trouble, I believe, something about the heirs and coheirs; anyhow, the place has been empty for years.

22   That spoils my ghostliness, I am afraid, but I don't care— there is something strange about the house—I can feel it.

23   I even said so to John one moonlight evening, but he said what I felt was a *draught,* and shut the window.

24   I get unreasonably angry with John sometimes. I'm sure I never used to be so sensitive. I think it is due to this nervous condition.

25   But John says if I feel so I shall neglect proper self-control; so I take pains to control myself—before him, at least, and that makes me very tired.

26   I don't like our room a bit. I wanted one downstairs that opened onto the piazza and had roses all over the window, and such pretty old-fashioned chintz hangings! But John would not hear of it.

27   He said there was only one window and not room for two beds, and no near room for him if he took another.

28   He is very careful and loving, and hardly lets me stir without special direction.

(29)   I have a schedule prescription for each hour in the day; he takes all care from me, and so I feel basely ungrateful not to value it more.

30   He said he came here solely on my account, that I was to have perfect rest and all the air I could get. "Your exercise depends on your strength, my dear," said he, "and your food somewhat on your appetite; but air you can absorb all the time." So we took the nursery at the top of the house.

31   It is a big, airy room, the whole floor nearly, with windows that look all ways, and air and sunshine galore. It was a nursery first, and then playroom and gymnasium, I should judge, for the windows are barred for little children, and there are rings and things in the walls.

32   The paint and paper look as if a boys' school had used it. It is stripped off—the paper—in great patches all around the head of my bed, about as far as I can reach, and in a great place on the other side of the

room low down. I never saw a worse paper in my life. One of those sprawling, flamboyant patterns committing every artistic sin.

3   It is dull enough to confuse the eye in following, pronounced enough constantly to irritate and provoke study, and when you follow the lame uncertain curves for a little distance they suddenly commit suicide—plunge off at outrageous angles, destroy themselves in unheard-of contradictions.

3   The color is repellent, almost revolting: a smouldering unclean yellow, strangely faded by the slow-turning sunlight. It is a dull yet lurid orange in some places, a sickly sulphur tint in others.

3!   No wonder the children hated it! I should hate it myself if I had to live in this room long.

3(There comes John, and I must put this away— he hates to have me write a word.

> ... there is
> something strange
> about the house—
> I can feel it.

3;   WE have been here two weeks, and I haven't felt like writing before, since that first day.

3!   I am sitting by the window now, up in this atrocious nursery, and there is nothing to hinder my writing as much as I please, save lack of strength.

3!   John is away all day, and even some nights when his cases are serious.

4(I am glad my case is not serious!

41   But these nervous troubles are dreadfully depressing.

4:    John does not know how much I really suffer. He knows there is no *reason* to suffer, and that satisfies him.

4:    Of course it is only nervousness. It does weigh on me so not to do my duty in any way!

44   I meant to be such a help to John, such a real rest and comfort, and here I am a comparative burden already!

4!   Nobody would believe what an effort it is to do what little I am able—to dress and entertain, and order things.

46   It is fortunate Mary is so good with the baby. Such a dear baby!

47   And yet I *cannot* be with him, it makes me so nervous.

48   I suppose John never was nervous in his life. He laughs at me so about this wallpaper!

49   At first he meant to repaper the room, but afterward he said that I was letting it get the better of me, and that nothing was worse for a nervous patient than to give way to such fancies.

He said that after the wallpaper was changed it would be the heavy bedstead, and then the barred windows, and then that gate at the head of the stairs, and so on.

"You know the place is doing you good," he said, "and really, dear, I don't care to renovate the house just for a three months' rental."

"Then do let us go downstairs," I said. "There are such pretty rooms there."

Then he took me in his arms and called me a blessed little goose, and said he would go down to the cellar, if I wished, and have it whitewashed into the bargain.

But he is right enough about the beds and windows and things.

It is as airy and comfortable a room as anyone need wish, and, of course, I would not be so silly as to make him uncomfortable just for a whim.

I'm really getting quite fond of the big room, all but that horrid paper.

Out of one window I can see the garden—those mysterious deep-shaded arbors, the riotous old-fashioned flowers, and bushes and gnarly trees.

Out of another I get a lovely view of the bay and a little private wharf belonging to the estate. There is a beautiful shaded lane that runs down there from the house. I always fancy I see people walking in these numerous paths and arbors, but John has cautioned me not to give way to fancy in the least. He says that with my imaginative power and habit of storymaking, a nervous weakness like mine is sure to lead to all manner of excited fancies, and that I ought to use my will and good sense to check the tendency. So I try.

I think sometimes that if I were only well enough to write a little it would relieve the press of ideas and rest me.

But I find I get pretty tired when I try.

It is so discouraging not to have any advice and companionship about my work. When I get really well, John says we will ask Cousin Henry and Julia down for a long visit; but he says he would as soon put fireworks in my pillow-case as to let me have those stimulating people about now.

I wish I could get well faster.

But I must not think about that. This paper looks to me as if it *knew* what a vicious influence it had!

There is a recurrent spot where the pattern lolls like a broken neck and two bulbous eyes stare at you upside down.

64

I get positively angry with the impertinence of it and the everlastingness. Up and down and sideways they crawl, and those absurd unblinking eyes are everywhere. There is one place where two breadths didn't match, and the eyes go all up and down the line, one a little higher than the other. 65

I never saw so much expression in an inanimate thing before, and we all know how much expression they have! I used to lie awake as a child and get more entertainment and terror out of blank walls and plain furniture than most children could find in a toy-store. 66

I remember what a kindly wink the knobs of our big old bureau used to have, and there was one chair that always seemed like a strong friend. 67

I used to feel that if any of the other things looked too fierce I could always hop into that chair and be safe. 68

The furniture in this room is no worse than inharmonious, however, for we had to bring it all from downstairs. I suppose when this was used as a playroom they had to take the nursery things out, and no wonder! I never saw such ravages as the children have made here. 69

The wallpaper, as I said before, is torn off in spots, and it sticketh closer than a brother—they must have had perseverance as well as hatred. 70

Then the floor is scratched and gouged and splintered, the plaster itself is dug out here and there, and this great heavy bed, which is all we found in the room, looks as if it had been through the wars. 71

But I don't mind it a bit—only the paper. 72

There comes John's sister. Such a dear girl as she is, and so careful of me! I must not let her find me writing. 73

She is a perfect and enthusiastic housekeeper, and hopes for no better profession. I verily believe she thinks it is the writing which made me sick! 74

But I can write when she is out, and see her a long way off from these windows. 75

There is one that commands the road, a lovely shaded winding road, and one that just looks off over the country. A lovely country, too, full of great elms and velvet meadows. 76

This wallpaper has a kind of subpattern in a different shade, a particularly irritating one, for you can only see it in certain lights, and not clearly then. 77

78   But in the places where it isn't faded and where the sun is just so—I can see a strange, provoking, formless sort of figure that seems to skulk about behind that silly and conspicuous front design.

79   THERE'S sister on the stairs!

80   Well, the Fourth of July is over! The people are all gone, and I am tired out. John thought it might do me good to see a little company, so we just had Mother and Nellie and the children down for a week.

81   Of course I didn't do a thing. Jennie sees to everything now.

82   But it tired me all the same.

83   John says if I don't pick up faster he shall send me to Weir Mitchell in the fall.

84   But I don't want to go there at all. I had a friend who was in his hands once, and she says he is just like John and my brother, only more so!

85   Besides, it is such an undertaking to go so far.

86   I don't feel as if it was worthwhile to turn my hand over for anything, and I'm getting dreadfully fretful and querulous.

87   I cry at nothing, and cry most of the time.

88   Of course I don't when John is here, or anybody else, but when I am alone.

89   And I am alone a good deal just now. John is kept in town very often by serious cases, and Jennie is good and lets me alone when I want her to.

90   So I walk a little in the garden or down that lovely lane, sit on the porch under the roses, and lie down up here a good deal.

91   I'm getting really fond of the room in spite of the wallpaper. Perhaps *because* of the wallpaper.

92   It dwells in my mind so!

93   I lie here on this great immovable bed—it is nailed down, I believe—and follow that pattern about by the hour. It is as good as gymnastics, I assure you. I start, we'll say, at the bottom, down in the corner over there where it has not been touched, and I determine for the thousandth time that I *will* follow that pointless pattern to some sort of a conclusion.

94   I know a little of the principle of design, and I know this thing was not arranged on any laws of radiation, or alternation, or repetition, or symmetry, or anything else that I ever heard of.

95   It is repeated, of course, by the breadths, but not otherwise.

96   Looked at in one way, each breadth stands alone; the bloated curves and flourishes—a kind of "debased Romanesque" with *delirium tremens*—go waddling up and down in isolated columns of fatuity.

But, on the other hand, they connect diagonally, and the sprawling outlines run off in great slanting waves of optic horror, like a lot of wallowing seaweeds in full chase.

The whole thing goes horizontally, too, at least it seems so, and I exhaust myself trying to distinguish the order of its going in that direction.

They have used a horizontal breadth for a frieze, and that adds wonderfully to the confusion.

There is one end of the room where it is almost intact, and there, when the crosslights fade and the low sun shines directly upon it, I can almost fancy radiation after all—the interminable grotesque seems to form around a common center and rush off in headlong plunges of equal distraction.

It makes me tired to follow it. I will take a nap, I guess.

I don't know why I should write this.

I don't want to.

I don't feel able.

And I know John would think it absurd. But I *must* say what I feel and think in some way—it is such a relief!

BUT the effort is getting to be greater than the relief.

Half the time now I am awfully lazy, and lie down ever so much. John says I mustn't lose my strength, and has me take cod liver oil and lots of tonics and things, to say nothing of ale and wines and rare meat.

Dear John! He loves me very dearly, and hates to have me sick. I tried to have a real earnest reasonable talk with him the other day, and tell him how I wish he would let me go and make a visit to Cousin Henry and Julia.

But he said I wasn't able to go, nor able to stand it after I got there; and I did not make out a very good case for myself, for I was crying before I had finished.

It is getting to be a great effort for me to think straight. Just this nervous weakness, I suppose.

And dear John gathered me up in his arms, and just carried me upstairs and laid me on the bed, and sat by me and read to me till it tired my head.

He said I was his darling and his comfort and all he had, and that I must take care of myself for his sake, and keep well.

He says no one but myself can help me out of it, that I must use my will and self-control and not let any silly fancies run away with me.

> I'm getting really fond of the room
> in spite of the wallpaper.

There's one comfort—the baby is well and happy, and does not have to occupy this nursery with the horrid wallpaper.

If we had not used it, that blessed child would have! What a fortunate escape! Why, I wouldn't have a child of mine, an impressionable little thing, live in such a room for worlds.

I never thought of it before, but it is lucky that John kept me here after all; I can stand it so much easier than a baby, you see.

Of course I never mention it to them any more—I am too wise—but I keep watch for it all the same.

There are things in the wallpaper that nobody knows about but me, or ever will.

Behind that outside pattern the dim shapes get clearer every day.

It is always the same shape, only very numerous.

And it is like a woman stooping down and creeping about behind that pattern. I don't like it a bit. I wonder—I begin to think—I wish John would take me away from here!

It is so hard to talk with John about my case, because he is so wise, and because he loves me so.

But I tried it last night.

It was moonlight. The moon shines in all around just as the sun does.

I hate to see it sometimes, it creeps so slowly, and always comes in by one window or another.

John was asleep and I hated to waken him, so I kept still and watched the moonlight on that undulating wallpaper till I felt creepy.

The faint figure behind seemed to shake the pattern, just as if she wanted to get out.

I got up softly and went to feel and see if the paper *did* move, and when I came back John was awake.

"What is it, little girl?" he said. "Don't go walking about like that—you'll get cold."

I thought it was a good time to talk, so I told him that I really was not gaining here, and that I wished he would take me away.

"Why, darling!" said he, "Our lease will be up in three weeks, and I can't see how to leave before.

"The repairs are not done at home, and I cannot possibly leave town just now. Of course, if you were in any danger, I could and would, but you really are better, dear, whether you can see it or not. I am a doctor, dear, and I know. You are gaining flesh and color, your appetite is better, I feel really much easier about you."

"I don't weigh a bit more," said I, "nor as much; and my appetite may be better in the evening when you are here but it is worse in the morning when you are away!"

"Bless her little heart!" said he with a big hug. "She shall be as sick as she pleases! But now let's improve the shining hours by going to sleep, and talk about it in the morning!"

"And you won't go away?" I asked gloomily.

"Why, how can I, dear? It is only three weeks more and then we will take a nice little trip for a few days while Jennie is getting the house ready. Really, dear, you are better!"

"Better in body perhaps—" I began, and stopped short, for he sat up straight and looked at me with such a stern, reproachful look that I could not say another word.

"My darling," said he, "I beg you, for my sake and for our child's sake, as well as for your own, that you will never for one instant let that idea enter your mind! There is nothing so dangerous, so fascinating, to a temperament like yours. It is a false and foolish fancy. Can you not trust me as a physician when I tell you so?"

So of course I said no more on that score, and we went to sleep before long. He thought I was asleep first, but I wasn't, and lay there for hours trying to decide whether that front pattern and the back pattern really did move together or separately.

On a pattern like this, by daylight, there is a lack of sequence, a defiance of law, that is a constant irritant to a normal mind.

The color is hideous enough, and unreliable enough, and infuriating enough, but the pattern is torturing.

You think you have mastered it, but just as you get well under way in following, it turns a back-somersault and there you are. It slaps you in the face, knocks you down, and tramples upon you. It is like a bad dream.

The outside pattern is a florid arabesque, reminding one of a fungus. If you can imagine a toadstool in joints, an interminable string of toadstools, budding and sprouting in endless convolutions—why, that is something like it.

That is, sometimes!

There is one marked peculiarity about this paper, a thing nobody seems to notice but myself, and that is that it changes as the light changes.

When the sun shoots in through the east window—I always watch for that first long, straight ray—it changes so quickly that I never can quite believe it.

That is why I watch it always.

148   By moonlight—the moon shines in all night when there is a moon—I wouldn't know it was the same paper.

149   At night in any kind of light, in twilight, candlelight, lamplight, and worst of all by moonlight, it becomes bars! The outside pattern, I mean, and the woman behind it is as plain as can be.

150   I didn't realize for a long time what the thing was that showed behind, that dim subpattern, but now I am quite sure it is a woman.

151   By daylight she is subdued, quiet. I fancy it is the pattern that keeps her so still. It is so puzzling. It keeps me quiet by the hour.

152   I lie down ever so much now. John says it is good for me, and to sleep all I can.

153   Indeed he started the habit by making me lie down for an hour after each meal.

154   It is a very bad habit, I am convinced, for you see, I don't sleep.

155   And that cultivates deceit, for I don't tell them I'm awake—oh, no!

156   The fact is I am getting a little afraid of John.

157   He seems very queer sometimes, and even Jennie has an inexplicable look.

158   It strikes me occasionally, just as a scientific hypothesis, that perhaps it is the paper!

159   I have watched John when he did not know I was looking, and come into the room suddenly on the most innocent excuses, and I've caught him several times *looking at the paper!* And Jennie too. I caught Jennie with her hand on it once.

160   She didn't know I was in the room, and when I asked her in a quiet, a very quiet voice, with the most restrained manner possible, what she was doing with the paper, she turned around as if she had been caught stealing, and looked quite angry—asked me why I should frighten her so!

161   Then she said that the paper stained everything it touched, that she had found yellow smooches on all my clothes and John's and she wished we would be more careful!

162   Did not that sound innocent? But I know she was studying that pattern, and I am determined that nobody shall find it out but myself!

163   LIFE is very much more exciting now than it used to be. You see, I have something more to expect, to look forward to, to watch. I really do eat better, and am more quiet than I was.

> The fact is I am getting a little afraid of John.

John is so pleased to see me improve! He laughed a little the other day, and said I seemed to be flourishing in spite of my wallpaper.

I turned it off with a laugh. I had no intention of telling him it was *because* of the wallpaper—he would make fun of me. He might even want to take me away.

I don't want to leave now until I have found it out. There is a week more, and I think that will be enough.

I'm feeling so much better!

I don't sleep much at night, for it is so interesting to watch developments; but I sleep a good deal during the daytime.

In the daytime it is tiresome and perplexing.

There are always new shoots on the fungus, and new shades of yellow all over it. I cannot keep count of them, though I have tried conscientiously.

It is the strangest yellow, that wallpaper! It makes me think of all the yellow things I ever saw—not beautiful ones like buttercups, but old foul, bad yellow things.

But there is something else about that paper—the smell! I noticed it the moment we came into the room, but with so much air and sun it was not bad. Now we have had a week of fog and rain, and whether the windows are open or not, the smell is here.

It creeps all over the house.

I find it hovering in the dining-room, skulking in the parlor, hiding in the hall, lying in wait for me on the stairs.

It gets into my hair.

Even when I go to ride, if I turn my head suddenly and surprise it—there is that smell!

Such a peculiar odor, too! I have spent hours in trying to analyze it, to find what it smelled like.

It is not bad—at first—and very gentle, but quite the subtlest, most enduring odor I ever met.

In this damp weather it is awful. I wake up in the night and find it hanging over me.

It used to disturb me at first. I thought seriously of burning the house—to reach the smell.

But now I am used to it. The only thing I can think of that it is like is the *color* of the paper! A yellow smell.

There is a very funny mark on this wall, low down, near the mopboard. A streak that runs round the room. It goes behind every piece of furniture, except the bed, a long, straight, even *smooch*, as if it had been rubbed over and over.

I wonder how it was done and who did it, and what they did it for. Round and round and round—round and round and round—it makes me dizzy!

I really have discovered something at last.

Through watching so much at night, when it changes so, I have finally found out.

The front pattern *does* move—and no wonder! The woman behind shakes it!

Sometimes I think there are a great many women behind, and sometimes only one, and she crawls around fast, and her crawling shakes it all over.

Then in the very bright spots she keeps still, and in the very shady spots she just takes hold of the bars and shakes them hard.

And she is all the time trying to climb through. But nobody could climb through that pattern—it strangles so; I think that is why it has so many heads.

They get through and then the pattern strangles them off and turns them upside down, and makes their eyes white!

If those heads were covered or taken off it would not be half so bad.

I think that woman gets out in the daytime!

And I'll tell you why—privately—I've seen her!

I can see her out of every one of my windows!

It is the same woman, I know, for she is always creeping, and most women do not creep by daylight.

I see her in that long shaded lane, creeping up and down. I see her in those dark grape arbors, creeping all round the garden.

I see her on that long road under the trees, creeping along, and when a carriage comes she hides under the blackberry vines.

I don't blame her a bit. It must be very humiliating to be caught creeping by daylight!

I always lock the door when I creep by daylight. I can't do it at night, for I know John would suspect something at once.

And John is so queer now that I don't want to irritate him. I wish he would take another room! Besides, I don't want anybody to get that woman out at night but myself.

I often wonder if I could see her out of all the windows at once.

But, turn as fast as I can, I can only see out of one at one time.

And though I always see her, she *may* be able to creep faster than I can turn! I have watched her sometimes away off in the open country, creeping as fast as a cloud shadow in a wind.

If only that top pattern could be gotten off from the under one! I mean to try it, little by little.

I have found out another funny thing, but I shan't tell it this time! It does not do to trust people too much.

There are only two more days to get this paper off, and I believe John is beginning to notice. I don't like the look in his eyes.

And I heard him ask Jennie a lot of professional questions about me. She had a very good report to give.

She said I slept a good deal in the daytime.

John knows I don't sleep very well at night, for all I'm so quiet!

He asked me all sorts of questions too, and pretended to be very loving and kind.

As if I couldn't see through him!

Still, I don't wonder he acts so, sleeping under this paper for three months.

It only interests me, but I feel sure John and Jennie are affected by it.

HURRAH! This is the last day, but it is enough. John is to stay in town over night, and won't be out until this evening.

Jennie wanted to sleep with me—the sly thing; but I told her I should undoubtedly rest better for a night all alone.

That was clever, for really I wasn't alone a bit! As soon as it was moonlight and that poor thing began to crawl and shake the pattern, I got up and ran to help her.

I pulled and she shook, I shook and she pulled, and before morning we had peeled off yards of that paper.

A strip about as high as my head and half around the room.

And then when the sun came and that awful pattern began to laugh at me, I declared I would finish it today!

We go away tomorrow, and they are moving all my furniture down again to leave things as they were before.

Jennie looked at the wall in amazement, but I told her merrily that I did it out of pure spite at the vicious thing.

She laughed and said she wouldn't mind doing it herself, but I must not get tired.

How she betrayed herself that time!

But I am here, and no person touches this paper but Me—not *alive!*

She tried to get me out of the room—it was too patent! But I said it was so quiet and empty and clean now that I believed I would lie down again and sleep all I could, and not to wake me even for dinner—I would call when I woke.

So now she is gone, and the servants are gone, and the things are gone, and there is nothing left but that great bedstead nailed down, with the canvas mattress we found on it.

227   We shall sleep downstairs tonight, and take the boat home tomorrow.

228   I quite enjoy the room, now it is bare again.

229   How those children did tear about here!

230   This bedstead is fairly gnawed!

231   But I must get to work.

232   I have locked the door and thrown the key down into the front path.

233   I don't want to go out, and I don't want to have anybody come in, till John comes.

234   I want to astonish him.

235   I've got a rope up here that even Jennie did not find. If that woman does get out, and tries to get away, I can tie her!

236   But I forgot I could not reach far without anything to stand on!

237   This bed will *not* move!

238   I tried to lift and push it until I was lame, and then I got so angry I bit off a little piece at one corner—but it hurt my teeth.

239   Then I peeled off all the paper I could reach standing on the floor. It sticks horribly and the pattern just enjoys it! All those strangled heads and bulbous eyes and waddling fungus growths just shriek with derision!

240   I am getting angry enough to do something desperate. To jump out of the window would be admirable exercise, but the bars are too strong even to try.

241   Besides I wouldn't do it. Of course not. I know well enough that a step like that is improper and might be misconstrued.

242   I don't like to *look* out of the windows even—there are so many of those creeping women, and they creep so fast.

243   I wonder if they all come out of that wallpaper as I did!

But I am securely fastened now by my well-hidden rope—you don't get *me* out in the road there!

I suppose I shall have to get back behind the pattern when it comes night, and that is hard!

It is so pleasant to be out in this great room and creep around as I please!

I don't want to go outside. I won't, even if Jennie asks me to.

For outside you have to creep on the ground, and everything is green instead of yellow.

But here I can creep smoothly on the floor, and my shoulder just fits in that long smooch around the wall, so I cannot lose my way.

Why, there's John at the door!

It is no use, young man, you can't open it!

How he does call and pound!

Now he's crying to Jennie for an axe.

It would be a shame to break down that beautiful door!

"John, dear!" said I in the gentlest voice. "The key is down by the front steps, under a plantain leaf!"

That silenced him for a few moments.

Then he said, very quietly indeed, "Open the door, my darling!"

"I can't," said I. "The key is down by the front door under a plantain leaf!" And then I said it again, several times, very gently and slowly, and said it so often that he had to go and see, and he got it of course, and came in. He stopped short by the door.

"What is the matter?" he cried. "For God's sake, what are you doing!"

I kept on creeping just the same, but I looked at him over my shoulder.

"I've got out at last," said I, "in spite of you and Jane. And I've pulled off most of the paper, so you can't put me back!"

Now why should that man have fainted? But he did, and right across my path by the wall, so that I had to creep over him every time!

Y OU can find themes pertaining to the lives of modern women in a number of other stories in the book, including Kate Chopin's "The Story of an Hour" and Amy Tan's "Two Kinds," in chapter 2, and Jamaica Kincaid's "Girl" in chapter 3, among others.

GOING FURTHER One of the classic texts of the modern feminist movement, "The Yellow Wallpaper" points toward a long line of future fiction on similar themes, such as Joan Didion's novels *Run River* and *Play It As It Lays* and Margaret Atwood's *The Handmaid's Tale*.

Writing from Reading

Summarize

1 Describe the wallpaper's pattern in literal terms. What does it look like?

2 The narrator's relationship with the wallpaper goes through various stages. Identify and describe those stages.

Analyze Craft

3 Analyze John's character and his role in the story. How does he help and/or harm his wife?

4 Discuss the themes of censorship, silencing, and imprisonment in this story.

Analyze Voice

5 Consider the use of a first-person narrator in this story. Could the same story be told from a different point of view, or would the effect change entirely? What does your answer to this question say about the narrator's reliability?

Synthesize Summary and Analysis

6 Scan the story for each mention of the narrator's journal, underlining these references when you find them. Form a conclusion about the role of the journal in the story. Why does the narrator have to keep it a secret from John and his sister?

Interpret the Story

7 Identify a conflict central to the story. Discuss how that conflict affects the various characters. Is the conflict resolved by the end?

Reading for Point of View

When reading for point of view, ask yourself, *who is telling the story?*		
• A participant, or first-person narrator? (I/we)	EXAMPLE: I'm still not sure why I agreed to go with him in the first place.
• Is s/he **naïve** because of age, experience, or cultural difference? Is s/he **unreliable** because of bias, character, or mental condition?	EXAMPLE: I was running on only three hours of sleep. Plus, he paid for my coffee, and he had a nice enough smile.
• A nonparticipant, or third-person narrator? (he/she/they)	EXAMPLE: As the lights in the theater dimmed, he reached over and took her hand.
• Is the narrator **omniscient,** or aware of the thoughts of multiple characters?	EXAMPLE: Her heart leaped, and her mind buzzed, so that she missed the entire introduction to the film and had to ask him what was going on. "They're robbing this bank," he replied nonchalantly, silently thrilled she hadn't pulled away.
• Is the narrator **editorial,** inserting judgments about the character?	EXAMPLE: Later she might reflect on the cruelty of excusing herself to go to the bathroom and abandoning him there at the theater, but at the time all she could think about was freedom.
• Is the narrator **impartial,** relating events without judging them?	EXAMPLE: So she left him there, alone, waiting patiently for her return. She went and bought herself a frozen yogurt.
• Is the omniscience limited to one character?	EXAMPLE: There were two cute guys sitting in the bed of the truck next to her car when she exited the ice cream parlor. She tripped as she approached them and experienced a moment of utter terror. The looks on the guys' faces were blank, and she convinced herself they hadn't noticed.
• Does the narrator allow readers into a character's **interior monologue,** following the natural path of the person's thought processes?	EXAMPLE: Don't stare, she told herself. Let them speak to you first. Then a voice in her head reminded her that she'd already blown off one guy tonight, and all she currently had to look forward to was a night of reruns.

CONTINUED

	• Is the narrator **objective**?	EXAMPLE: She said hello, and they said hello back.
	• A second-person narrator, or a narrator who addresses you directly? (you)	EXAMPLE: You taste your frozen yogurt to distract yourself from the race of your heartbeat. You try to look just above and to the right of the nearest guy's eyes—Don't stare into them, you tell yourself, don't show so much interest. You struggle for something to say. They're waiting for you to say something.

Suggestions for Writing about Point of View

1. In her interview, ZZ Packer talks about reading as a way to "live an extra ten years" and become "a citizen of the world." How could reading "The Short Happy Life of Francis Macomber" help you achieve these goals? What did the story teach you about the world? What did it teach you about Africa? What did it teach you about power relationships, including those involving the Africans who work for Wilson?

2. Of the characters you encountered in this chapter's stories, which is the roundest (see chapter 5, Character)? Explain what makes that character particularly round by citing examples from the story you chose. How did the author's use of point of view contribute to your sense of that character's roundness?

3. Write a short profile of the "you" character in "How to Become a Writer" and of the first-person narrator in "The Yellow Wallpaper." Does one type of narration allow you to know more about a character than another type of narration, or are they equally effective in conveying character?

4. Compare the first-person narrator of "Brownies" to the first-person narrator of "The Yellow Wallpaper." Find an example of each narrator's naïveté. By the end of each story, how would you describe their levels of self-awareness?

8 Language, Tone, and Style

"I remember in high school I would play a game with my friends, If you were a color, you would be a light blue . . . if Jenny were an animal, she would be a giraffe. Then we would figure out these reasons why. . . . There's something about tone in that. . . . Every word is going to convey a color, a feeling, a tone like a musical instrument, a mood. . . . If you start to look at the words . . . those are just things that come from the language itself."

Conversation with Aimee Bender, available on video at www.mhhe.com/delbanco1e

MY lover is experiencing reverse evolution. I tell no one. I don't know how it happened, only that one day he was my lover and the next he was some kind of ape. It's been a month and now he's a sea turtle.

I keep him on the counter, in a glass baking pan filled with salt water.

"Ben," I say to his small protruding head, "can you understand me?" and he stares with eyes like little droplets of tar and I drip tears into the pan, a sea of me.

He is shedding a million years a day.

—from "The Rememberer," by Aimee Bender

IN this opening passage, Aimee Bender uses simple, straightforward language. The **language** she has chosen has the narrator sound confessional, a little befuddled, and sad. Of her lover's bizarre transformation, she simply says, "I don't know how it happened." She unblinkingly reports the facts, thereby bringing the reader step by step, word by word, into this odd reality in which a man can devolve into a turtle. In this story, and others that Bender has written, she creates fantastical worlds. This mix of the realistic with the fantastic is a central element of her **style**—meaning the characteristic way in which she, or any writer, uses language and story.

Style is closely related to **tone**—the author's attitude toward his or her characters or subject matter. Think of tone in writing in the same way you think of tone of voice in speech. Depending on the tone of voice your friend uses when she says *Dude*, she may be signaling affection, awe, disdain, pleasure, or disgust. In turn, the tone shapes how you respond to her message. Authors convey tone by word choice and style as well as with their selection of details and images. How do Aimee Bender's style and tone shape our response to her narrator? Readers are likely to feel an odd mix of compassion for her loss and a startled "*What* did she just say about her lover!?"

CONTINUED ON PAGE 238

We need more magic in our imaginative lives . . .

Q&A

There is something . . . about the intimacy of reader and writer . . .

A Conversation on Writing
Aimee Bender

About "The Rememberer"

This story came from a dream. . . . I had had a dream . . . where I was going through reverse evolution with a friend, and we became dolphins, and swam around in a tank. . . . About five years later I was thinking about loss a lot, and I was thinking about it in terms of a relationship that was ending, and somehow that dream came back. And I sat down, and that first line popped into my head, "My lover's going through reverse evolution," and then I followed it to the end.

Fiction and Magic

As a kid I loved books that had magic in them. . . . There was something about that leap into metaphor and into imagination that just thrilled me. I really assumed that part of puberty, and part of growing up, meant a move to realism—that in order to become an adult, you had to give away those trappings of magic. . . . It was only later when I [discovered writers who] were taking on adult issues . . . but were doing it through metaphor, and imaginative leaps, and magical realism. I could start writing things . . . that . . . responded to so much [that I loved] as a kid but now [could write about] with hopefully more depth and perspective. . . . We need more magic in our imaginative lives, because . . . it's freeing, and . . . can be a way to get to feelings that are hard to look at straight on.

The Intimacy of Reading and Writing

There is something . . . about the intimacy of reader and writer, the action of sitting and reading something as one writer, one reader.

 In writing . . . I was trying to put something out there for a future reader, and then it was so satisfying when people read things and responded to them.

In 1998, a *San Francisco Chronicle* review said of Aimee Bender (b. 1969): "Once in a while, a writer comes along who makes you grateful for the very existence of language." Bender's first collection of stories, *The Girl in the Flammable Skirt* (1998), received enthusiastic praise from critics and readers alike. In this book—as in her novel *An Invisible Sign of My Own* (2000) and her second story collection, *Willful Creatures* (2005)—Bender's works push the limits of realism, relaying what seems impossible (a man comes back from the war without lips; a woman gives birth to her own recently deceased mother; a man suffers from an accelerated form of reverse evolution) with a straightforwardness that acknowledges but also fully accepts the fantastic. The surreal subjects of her stories are aided by the lyrical quality of her prose, which combines a straightforward tone with playful diction. Bender holds an M.F.A. from the University of California, Irvine, and she now teaches creative writing at the University of Southern California. She is currently at work on a new novel.

To watch this entire interview and hear Aimee Bender read from "The Rememberer," go to **www.mhhe. com/delbanco1e.**

RESEARCH ASSIGNMENT   In her interview, Aimee Bender talks about realism in fiction. She also talks about fairy tales, magic, and poetry. What is the author's attitude toward realism and fantasy in fiction? Can you relate to what Aimee Bender describes? How did her attitude affect her decision to become a writer? When she did become a writer, and why did she choose to write fiction over other forms, like plays?

AS YOU READ As you read this story, notice the narrator's tone. Does anything that happens seem to surprise her? Do events in the story surprise you? How do you account for the differences, if any, between her responses and yours?

The Rememberer (1997)

1 MY lover is experiencing reverse evolution. I tell no one. I don't know how it happened, only that one day he was my lover and the next he was some kind of ape. It's been a month and now he's a sea turtle.

2 I keep him on the counter, in a glass baking pan filled with salt water.

3 "Ben," I say to his small protruding head, "can you understand me?" and he stares with eyes like little droplets of tar and I drip tears into the pan, a sea of me.

4 He is shedding a million years a day. I am no scientist, but this is roughly what I figured out. I went to the old biology teacher at the community college and asked him for an approximate time line of our evolution. He was irritated at first—he wanted money. I told him I'd be happy to pay and then he cheered up quite a bit. I can hardly read his time line—he should've typed it—and it turns out to be wrong. According to him, the whole process should take about a year, but from the way things are going, I think we have less than a month left.

5 At first, people called on the phone and asked me where was Ben. Why wasn't he at work? Why did he miss his lunch date with those clients? His out-of-print special-ordered book on civilization had arrived at the bookstore, would he please pick it up? I told them he was sick, a strange sickness, and to please stop calling. The stranger thing was, they did. They stopped calling. After a week, the phone was silent and Ben, the baboon, sat in a corner by the window, wrapped up in drapery, chattering to himself.

6 Last day I saw him human, he was sad about the world.

7 This was not unusual. He was always sad about the world. It was a large reason why I loved him. We'd sit together and be sad and think about being sad and sometimes discuss sadness.

8 On his last human day, he said, "Annie, don't you see? We're all getting too smart. Our brains are just getting bigger and bigger, and the world dries up and dies when there's too much thought and not enough heart."

9 He looked at me pointedly, blue eyes unwavering. "Like us, Annie," he said. "We think far too much."

10 I sat down. I remembered how the first time we had sex, I left the lights on, kept my eyes wide open, and concentrated really hard on letting go; then I noticed that his eyes were open too and in the middle of everything we sat down on the floor and had an hour-long conversation about poetry. It was all very peculiar. It was all very familiar.

11 Another time he woke me up in the middle of the night, lifted me off the pale blue sheets, led me outside to the stars and whispered: *Look, Annie, look—there is no space for anything but dreaming.* I listened, sleepily, wandered back to bed and found myself wide awake, staring at the ceiling, unable to dream at all. Ben fell asleep right away, but I crept back outside. I tried to dream up to the stars, but I didn't know how to do that. I tried to find a star no one in all of history had ever wished on before, and wondered what would happen if I did.

12 On his last human day, he put his head in his hands and sighed and I

stood up and kissed the entire back of his neck, covered that flesh, made wishes there because I knew no woman had ever been so thorough, had ever kissed his every inch of skin. I coated him. What did I wish for? I wished for good. That's all. Just good. My wishes became generalized long ago, in childhood; I learned quick the consequence of wishing specific.

13   I took him in my arms and made love to him, my sad man. "See, we're not thinking," I whispered into his ear while he kissed my neck, "we're not thinking at all" and he pressed his head into my shoulder and held me tighter. Afterward, we went outside again; there was no moon and the night was dark. He said he hated talking and just wanted to look into my eyes and tell me things that way. I let him and it made my skin lift, the things in his look. Then he told me he wanted to sleep outside for some reason and in the morning when I woke up in bed, I looked out to the patio and there was an ape sprawled on the cement, great furry arms covering his head to block out the glare of the sun.

14   Even before I saw the eyes, I knew it was him. And once we were face to face, he gave me his same sad look and I hugged those enormous shoulders. I didn't even really care, then, not at first, I didn't panic and call 911. I sat with him outside and smoothed the fur on the back of his hand. When he reached for me, I said No, loudly, and he seemed to understand and pulled back. I have limits here.

15   We sat on the lawn together and ripped up the grass. I didn't miss human Ben right away; I wanted to meet the ape too, to take care of my lover like a son, a pet; I wanted to know him every possible way but I didn't realize he wasn't coming back.

16   Now I come home from work and look for his regular-size shape walking and worrying and realize, over and over, that he's gone. I pace the halls. I chew whole packs of gum in mere minutes. I review my memories and make sure

they're still intact because if he's not here, then it is my job to remember. I think of the way he wrapped his arms around my back and held me so tight it made me nervous and the way his breath felt in my ear: right.

When I go to the kitchen, I peer in the glass and see he's some kind of salamander now. He's small.

"Ben," I whisper, "do you remember me? Do you remember?"

His eyes roll up in his head and I dribble honey into the water. He used to love honey. He licks at it and then swims to the other end of the pan.

This is the limit of my limits: here it is. You don't ever know for sure where it is and then you bump against it and bam, you're there. Because I cannot bear to look down into the water and not be able to find him at all, to search the tiny clear waves with a microscope lens and to locate my lover, the one-celled wonder, bloated and bordered, brainless, benign, heading clear and small like an eye-floater into nothingness.

I put him in the passenger seat of the car, and drive him to the beach. Walking down the sand, I nod at people on towels, laying their bodies out to the sun and wishing. At the water's edge, I stoop down and place the whole pan on the tip of a baby wave. It floats well, a cooking boat, for someone to find washed up on shore and to make cookies in, a lucky catch for a poor soul with all the ingredients but no container.

Ben the salamander swims out. I wave to the water with both arms, big enough for him to see if he looks back.

I turn around and walk back to the car.

Sometimes I think he'll wash up on shore. A naked man with a startled look. Who has been to history and back. I keep my eyes on the newspaper. I make sure my phone number is listed. I walk around the block at night in case he doesn't quite remember which house it is. I feed the birds outside and sometimes before I put my one self to bed, I place my hands around my skull to see if it's growing, and wonder what, of any use, would fill it if it did.

> I walk around the block at night in case he doesn't quite remember which house it is.

IF you like Aimee Bender's "The Rememberer," you may also enjoy other stories in the book that step over the line from realism into the fantastic, such as Jorge Luis Borges's "The Circular Ruins" (chapter 14).

GOING FURTHER In Bender's interview, she mentions that Anne Sexton's *Transformations,* the retelling of fairy tales from a contemporary perspective, was a personal favorite of hers growing up; another version of fairy tales comes in the funny and fantastic *Italian Folktales* by Italo Calvino, whose work influenced Bender. She marches in a line of writers who incorporate the supernatural and the metaphysical into fiction, such as Gabriel García Márquez (*One Hundred Years of Solitude*), Alejo Carpentier (*The Kingdom of This World*), Miguel Angel Asturias (*Men of Maize*), and the American Bernard Malamud (*God's Grace*).

Writing from Reading

Summarize

1 List the different animals we glimpse Ben as throughout the story. Discuss why Bender has chosen these snapshots of de-evolution out of the entire array of animals.

Analyze Craft

2 Briefly describe the narrator's level of vocabulary (i.e., does she use difficult words that you need a dictionary to decode, or simpler words that you might hear in everyday conversation?). Discuss why Bender would write at this level of vocabulary, considering what effect it has on the tone (the emotional effect) of the story.

Analyze Voice

3 "The Rememberer" provides very little background on the characters Annie and Ben. What can you glean about them, their backgrounds, and their style of life from the narrator's voice and the details she provides (or doesn't provide)?

Synthesize Summary and Analysis

4 Discuss Annie's use of the word *limits* throughout the story. What are the different contexts in which she mentions limits? What are her limits, and why?

Interpret the Story

5 The scientist forecasts a year for Ben's de-evolution, but it happens much faster. Why does Bender make a point of mentioning the scientist and his discrepancy? Explore the commentary she might be making about human history, citing the text.

6 Discuss the roles of science, realism, and fantasy in this story. How does Bender use the three to make the world portrayed in this story a convincing place?

CONTINUED FROM PAGE 233

You may have noticed that most chapters in this book focus on a single topic—plot, character, setting, point of view—whereas this chapter groups three topics together. This is because language, tone, and style are difficult to separate from one another. The type of language an author uses establishes his or her tone. In "The Fall of the House of Usher" (chapter 6), for example, Poe uses language that connotes darkness and decay. This, in turn, establishes a melancholy tone, one that suggests the attitude that both narrator and reader take toward the house of Usher is one of sadness at the decline of a once-great family. At the same time, the language of darkness and decay creates a sense of foreboding, even if we don't know at the beginning what causes that feeling. Poe's language, then, gives rise to a tone that we can describe as both melancholy and chilling.

Putting those elements together—the darkness and decay evoked by the language, the melancholy and foreboding tone—you arrive at Poe's style. As you most likely know if you have encountered Poe before, he is famous for his horror stories and mysteries. This reputation is based on a tonal choice, the mood which his work consists of and evokes. Consider his well-known poem "The Raven," which begins with the line "Once upon a midnight dreary." Characteristic of Poe's style, the language here, as in "The Fall of the House of Usher," is dark and immediately sets a melancholy ("dreary"), foreboding ("midnight") tone.

In this chapter, we focus on three stories that we think demonstrate a particularly clear use of language, tone, and style. But remember, all stories contain these three elements—after all, stories are made of language, which in turn creates a tone that combines with the language to form an author's distinctive style.

CRAFTING STYLE AND TONE

Everyone knows what style looks like or feels the effect of it. We see it in the distinctive way a base runner moves, a basketball player goes for a layup, or a kid does turns on a skateboard. We see a person's style in the way she does (or doesn't do) her nails, the choice and placement of a tattoo or a piercing, a particular combination of shirt, jeans, vest, and scarf—with high-top sneakers, cowboy boots, high heels, flip-flops, or anything else in the vast array of potential footwear.

> "I know that there are many things that can open a story, that can start a person working. For me it's language. It's not an idea."
> Conversation with Amy Hempel

The distinctive style combined with the writer's tone molds the reader's impressions. Tone establishes how the narrator regards the story and the people in it—for example, with contempt, longing, passionate curiosity, sympathy, or ambivalence. The writer's tone influences how the reader will relate and respond to the characters and the course of events. Reading a literary work critically comes down to an intense scrutiny of the work's style and tone with these questions in mind:

- *What* is being said, and *how* and *why*?
- What effect does the author wish to create?
- What effect does the writing have on you?

Each of the stories in this chapter evokes a setting or scene and does so with a unique style and tone. As you read them, ask yourself why the authors chose the particular words and images they did. What tone (of voice) do you hear? Where does the style fall on a spectrum of formal to informal, direct to roundabout, concrete to abstract, serious to wry to comedic? Are the sentences long and complex, or short and simple? Does the author use the language of the street or that of academia? Taken together, these are qualities that make up an author's style and tone.

The tone of "The Rememberer" is intimate and informal when the first-person narrator stands weeping over her boyfriend-turned-sea-turtle. Her tone and style arise from her **diction,** an author's or character's distinctive choice of words and style of expression. Now consider a passage written by Ernest Hemingway.

> *You know how it is there early in the morning in Havana with the bums still asleep against the walls of the buildings; before even the ice wagons come by with the ice for the bars? Well, we came across the square from the dock to the Pearl of San Francisco Café to get coffee and there was only one beggar awake in the square and he was getting a drink out of the fountain. But when we got inside the café and sat down, there were the three of them waiting for us. . . .*

—from "One Trip Across" (1934)

In this story, which became the opening lines of his novel *To Have and Have Not* (1937), Hemingway uses the everyday language of his American character, a smuggler living in Cuba. The tone is casual, conversational, and hard-boiled. With that "You know how it is," the narrator speaks to us directly, drawing us in as confederates who are just as street savvy as he is, who have been up that early in the morning. The style is realistic, concrete, and economical, and the details reveal that the place is exotic (Havana), and just a little bit seedy, with its bums and beggars.

"I thought, well what is a voice? And what's a story? What are the things that make this up? And if I know, you know, ABCD, these components, I can sit down and write these things. But I feel now, now that I've been doing this for a while, that the questions are still there. And there's no absolute answer. And that you discover it each time you sit down and write."

Conversation with Amy Tan

Notice what the narrator reveals—in an offhand way. He's been around, the kind of man who has seen enough "bums still asleep against the walls of the buildings" that they barely have an impact on him. There's plenty we don't yet know: why this narrator has come from the dock, who's with him, who's waiting for him at the bar and why. With style, tone, and careful selection of words and details, Hemingway creates an effect: a narrator in motion, leading the reader to a rendezvous with something that seems like trouble. "Follow him," Hemingway seems to say of his narrator. "So he's a little shady. He's still the one to watch."

STYLE AND DICTION

A number of elements contribute to a work's overall style and to the effect it creates on the reader. As we noted, diction, whether formal or informal, is important in writing because of what it reveals about character. Diction, for example, is a central concern of

Thomas Wolfe's "Only the Dead Know Brooklyn." In this story, Wolfe shows how vast the possibilities are for the English language. He wants us to "know Brooklyn" in its own language, in its own words, to know what it's really like to walk those streets and live in that world.

> *Now is the winter of our discontent made glorious by dis mont' of May, and all the long-drowned desolation of our souls in the green fire and radiance of the Springtime buried.*
>
> *We are the dead—ah! We were drowned so long ago—and now we thrust our feelers in distressful ooze upon the sea-floors of the buried world. We are the drowned—blind crawls and eyeless gropes and mindless sucks that swirl and scuttle in the jungle depths, immense and humid skies bend desolately upon us, and our flesh is gray.*
>
> *We are lost, the eyeless atoms of the jungle depth, we grope and crawl and scuttle with blind feelers, and we have no way but this.*
>
> *Dere's no guy livin' dat knows Brooklyn t'roo an' t'roo, (only the dead know Brooklyn t'roo and t'roo), because it'd take a lifetime just to find his way aroun' duh goddam town (—only the dead know Brooklyn t'roo and t'roo, even the dead will quarrel an' bicker over the sprawl and web of jungle desolation that is Brooklyn t'roo and t'roo).*

Part of the first sentence comes from Shakespeare's *Richard III*, which begins with the phrase "Now is the winter of our discontent made glorious summer by this sun of York." But instead of "glorious summer," Wolfe substitutes "dis mont'" (or "this month") of May. The next two paragraphs continue in this Shakespearian-poetic style, but the fourth drops into the exaggeratedly coarse Brooklynese. The contrast between the two

"At some point the sound of the language becomes the story: the sounds of characters talking, what comes out of their mouths, the sound of your own prose as you write a bit of narrative, a bit of description, or whatever. You're discovering meaning as you're doing it through the sound of the prose." Conversation with Tim O'Brien

kinds of language and diction is startling. The opening implies his hope that we would admire the speaker of Brooklynese English as much as we do Shakespeare's speaker, and that the lives of ordinary Brooklynites will have as much resonance and drama as do the lives of kings. Once you've read the story, try to imagine what it would be like if Wolfe had used standard English—how the color and spirit of the story would change. Consider how much flavor you gain because of the work he did to capture the authentic diction of the place.

TONE AND IRONY

Before his transformation, Ben, the narrator's lover in the Bender story, was a melancholy type, always bemoaning the human condition—that people had become too smart, that they thought too much, that they talked too much. So his fate—changing from man, to ape, to sea turtle so that he no longer needs to suffer the human condition—makes "sense," but with a twist. Expecting, as we all do, to live forward in time and evolve as a human being, Ben instead evolves backward, thus experiencing

"Tone is the attitude that the writer lays over the story itself . . . whereas voice is to me the music of the story's intelligence, which is to say it's how the story sounds in your ear—when you're reading it aloud or you're reading it silently—how the story sounds when it's being most itself, when it's being as smart as it is, when it's being as characteristic as it is."

Conversation with Richard Ford

a striking example of ironic reversal. Once you know what it looks and sounds like, **irony** may be the most distinctive and easily recognizable tone to identify. Irony, a difference between what occurs and what you expect to occur or between what is said and what is meant, often involves some sort of reversal in circumstances or fate.

Irony has other manifestations that grow out of the technique of radical reversal. For example, a football player intercepts a pass but becomes confused and runs the ball in the wrong direction, toward his own goal line. A president wants to bring glory to his country but takes actions that lead to disgrace and defeat. A nerdy young man courts a girl by taking acting lessons, buying a new suit, and getting a fresh haircut only to be rejected by the girl who wanted a natural sort of guy. The idea of reversal is central to the fate of Ben in "The Rememberer."

The term *irony* also refers to an incongruity between what someone says and what someone means. For example, your neighbor catches you taking out the garbage in your old wrinkled pajamas, with your hair wildly askew, and says, "You're looking fabulous today." This is an example of **verbal irony**—a person saying one thing and meaning another. When someone speaks in a mean-spirited, critical, or malicious way, we call it **sarcasm.** Sarcasm is not common in literature, but verbal irony is, as in this passage about war by Kurt Vonnegut from his novel *Slaughterhouse Five:*

> *Wherever you went there were women who would do anything for food or protection for themselves and their children and the old people . . . the whole point of war is to put women everywhere in that condition. It's always the men against the women, with the men only pretending to fight among themselves . . . the ones who pretend the hardest get their pictures in the paper and medals afterwards.*

A BRIEF HISTORY OF IRONY

Irony is a concept that comes down to us from the time of Greek tragedy. In that era, it was a philosophical, if not theological, lens through which the Greeks viewed all of life, and it has proved useful to writers throughout the history of literature in the West. While irony was a complex process in the Greek tragedies, the essence of irony is reversal, and reversal is a simple concept: A beggar discovers treasure, or a man at the height of his powers loses everything. In the European Middle Ages, the sign of fortune was a great wheel; irony defined that circling course. The hero's fortune could reside at the top of the wheel, but it could just as easily fall to the bottom. During the thousand years and more when Europe was united in the belief that Christianity was the answer to all questions about life and death, irony became less useful as a general idea. Those who accepted Christ found life after death, so the human outcome was clear.

No one would seriously claim that "the whole point of war" is to turn women's lives into a desperate struggle to protect themselves and others, and Vonnegut does not expect the reader to buy this. He says one thing but means another in order to get at a truth about the *effects* of war and to convey an attitude about war—that it is a horrific and senseless human activity. At the same time, he feigns innocence, as if he is describing a set of simple facts, as if he truly believes that jeopardizing women is "the whole point of war."

"... you draw with words when you write. ... Conrad talked about the need to make the reader see. [Although you also hope to make him or her hear, and smell even, and appeal to all the senses,] nevertheless the seeing seems to be what it's ultimately all about."

Conversation with John Updike

How does a reader know when an author is being ironic? In Vonnegut's case, you know because Vonnegut pushes his point to extremes. When he says "the whole point," and when he talks about "men only pretending to fight," you know that he is up to something other than a straight-faced discussion of war. He also uses an ironic tone—which borders here on sarcasm—because of the extreme points he makes, as if he were saying, "You idiots, can't you see?"

The fable "Appointment in Samarra," retold below by British novelist W. Somerset Maugham, illustrates an aspect of irony that we introduced before—a discrepancy between acts and results, or between what occurs and what the character expected to occur. In this story, the narrator is Death.

> There was a merchant in Bagdad who sent his servant to market to buy provisions and in a little while the servant came back, white and trembling, and said, Master, just now when I was in the marketplace I was jostled by a woman in the crowd and when I turned I saw it was Death that jostled me. She looked at me and made a threatening gesture. Now, lend me your horse, and I will ride away from this city and avoid my fate. I will go to Samarra and there Death will not find me. The merchant lent him his horse, and the servant mounted it, and he dug his spurs in its flanks and as fast as the horse could gallop he went. Then the merchant went down to the marketplace and he saw me standing in the crowd and he came to me and said, Why did you make a threatening gesture to my servant when you saw him this morning? That was not a threatening gesture, I said, it was only a start of surprise. I was astonished to see him in Bagdad, for I had an appointment with him tonight in Samarra.

The outcome for the poor servant is ironic because he hopes to avoid death by leaving his home and going to hide in Samarra. In doing so, however, he unknowingly guarantees that he will be precisely at the place where Death intends to seek him. The reader can see what the outcome will be, but the servant cannot, which gives the reader an advantage but also a feeling of apprehension or, in some cases, sorrow. This literary device is referred to as **dramatic irony,** a situation in which an author or narrator lets the reader know more about a situation than a character does.

LANGUAGE, TONE, AND STYLE IN CONTEXT

For the most part, a prose style, including its tone, is as complex and unique as a fingerprint, as is its genesis. In this chapter, we have looked closely at the topic of style—where it comes from, how to recognize and describe it—and also the faces of irony in literature, and the intricate relationship both style and irony have with tone.

"There are writers that I just deeply admire for the sentences that they write. And they're the ones I go back to read when writing isn't going well." Conversation with Chimamanda Ngozi Adichie

The styles of today's fiction are varied. Its language can be lush or lean, and the language of fiction is *creative;* it provides a window through which we as readers see new worlds, or come to see our own world differently. This chapter offers four short stories, each written in a distinctive literary style. As you read, consider how each writer's voice emerges from the story's tone, style, and language.

Thomas Wolfe (1900–1938)

Thomas Wolfe was born in Asheville, North Carolina, and he attended Harvard, where he read voraciously in the classics. Migrating to New York City, he made a striking figure at literary parties—he was well over six feet tall and broad in girth—and wrote in the kitchen of his Brooklyn apartment by standing in front of his refrigerator and using the top as his writing desk. His work has been lauded primarily for its opulent language and wide range of voices; he was always trying new styles, experimenting with new ways to tell stories that were largely autobiographical. In addition to numerous short stories, Wolfe published two novels, *Look Homeward, Angel* (1929) and *Of Time and the River* (1935); a short-story collection, *From Death to Morning* (1935); and a long essay, *The Story of a Novel* (1936). In 1938, at the age of thirty-eight, after a long, tiring journey through the American West, he succumbed to tuberculosis; it's worth noting that he wrote his entire, relatively small body of work in the span of seven years. After his death, however, dedicated scholars of his work compiled material from his unfinished manuscripts and published four posthumous books: *The Web and the Rock, You Can't Go Home Again, The Hills Beyond,* and—most recently—*The Party at Jack's.*

AS YOU READ As you read this story, let yourself hear the sound of the speaker's voice and the way he pronounces his words. Imagine the sounds of the city and of the train as the two characters travel along together. Imagine or remember how it feels to ask directions in a new place, and all the ways a newcomer stands out from the "natives."

Only the Dead Know Brooklyn (1935)

1 NOW is the winter of our discontent made glorious by dis mont' of May, and all the long-drowned desolation of our souls in the green fire and radiance of Springtime buried.

2 We are the dead—ah! We were drowned so long ago—and now we thrust our feelers in distressful ooze upon the sea-floors of the buried world. We are the drowned—blind crawls and eyeless gropes and mindless sucks that swirl and scuttle in the jungle depths, immense and humid skies bend desolately upon us, and our flesh is gray.

3 We are lost, the eyeless atoms of the jungle depth, we grope and crawl and scuttle with blind feelers, and we have no way but this.

4 DERE'S no guy livin' dat knows Brooklyn t'roo an' t'roo, because it'd take a guy a lifetime just to find his way aroun' duh f——— town.

5 So like I say, I'm waitin' for my train t' come when I sees dis big guy standin' deh—dis is duh foist I eveh see of him. Well, he's lookin' wild, y'know, an' I can see dat he's had plenty, but still he's holdin' it; he talks good an' is walkin' straight enough. So den, dis big guy steps up to a little guy dat's standin' deh, an' says, "How d'yuh get t' Eighteen' Avenoo an' Sixty-sevent' Street?" he says.

6 "Jesus! Yuh got me, chief," duh little guy says to him. "I ain't been heah long myself. Where is duh place?" he says. "Out in duh Flatbush section somewhere?"

7 "Nah," duh big guy says. "It's out in Bensonhoist. But I was neveh deh befoeh. How d'yuh get deh?"

8 "Jesus," duh little guy says, scratchin' his head, y'know—yuh could see duh litle guy didn't know his way about—"yuh got me, chief. I neveh hoid of it. Do any of youse guys know where it is?" he says to me.

9 "Sure," I says. "It's out in Bensonhoist. Yuh take duh Fourt' Avenoo express, get off at Fifty-nint' Street, change to a Sea Beach local deh, get off at Eighteent' Avenoo an' Sixty-toid, an' den walk down foeh blocks. Dat's all yuh got to do," I says.

10 "G'wan!" some wise guy dat I neveh seen befoeh pipes up. "Whatcha talkin' about?" he says—oh, he was wise, y'know. "Duh guy is crazy! I tell yuh what yuh do," he says to duh big guy. "Yuh change to duh West End line at Toity-sixt'," he tells him. "Get off at Noo Utrecht an' Sixteent' Avenoo," he says. "Walk two blocks oveh, foeh blocks up," he says, "an' you'll be right deh." Oh, a *wise* guy, y'know.

11 "Oh, yeah?" I says. "Who told *you* so much?" He got me sore because he was so wise about it. "How long you been livin' heah?" I says.

12 "All my life," he says. "I was bawn in Williamsboig," he says. "An' I can tell you t'ings about dis town you neveh hoid of," he says.

13 "Yeah?" I says.

14 "Yeah," he says.

5 "Well, den, you can tell me t'ings about dis town dat nobody else has eveh hoid of, either. Maybe you make it all up yoehself at night," I says, "befoeh you go to sleep—like cuttin' out papeh dolls, or somp'n."

6 "Oh, yeah?" he says. "You're pretty wise, ain't yuh?"

7 "Oh, I don't know," I says. "Duh boids ain't usin' my head for Lincoln's statue yet," I says. "But I'm wise enough to know a phony when I see one."

8 "Yeah?" he says. "A wise guy, huh? Well, you're so wise dat some one's goin' t'bust yuh one right on duh snoot some day," he says. "Dat's how wise *you* are."

Whatcha gonna do wit a guy
as dumb as dat?

9 WELL, my train was comin', or I'da smacked him den and dere, but when I seen duh train was comin', all I said was, "All right, mugg! I'm sorry I can't stay to take keh of you, but I'll be seein' yuh sometime, I hope, out in duh cemetery." So den I says to duh big guy, who'd been standin' deh all duh time, "You come wit me," I says. So when we gets onto duh train I says to him, "Where yuh goin' out in Bensonhoist?" I says. "What numbeh are yuh lookin' for?" I says. *You* know—I t'ought if he told me duh address I might be able to help him out.

0 "Oh," he says, "I'm not lookin' for no one. I don't know no one out deh."

1 "Then whatcha goin' out deh for?" I says.

2 "Oh," duh guy says, "I'm just goin' out to see duh place," he says. "I like duh sound of duh name—Bensonhoist, y'know—so I t'ought I'd go out an' have a look at it."

3 "Whatcha tryin' t'hand me?" I says. "Whatcha tryin' t'do—kid me?" *You* know, I t'ought duh guy was bein' wise wit me.

4 "No," he says. "I'm tellin' yuh duh troot. I like to go out an' take a look at places wit nice names like dat. I like to go out an' look at all kinds of places," he says.

5 "How'd yuh know deh was such a place," I says, "if yuh neveh been deh befoeh?"

6 "Oh," he says, "I got a map."

7 "A *map?*" I says.

8 "Sure," he says, "I got a map dat tells me about all dese places. I take it wit me every time I come out heah," he says.

9 And Jesus! Wit dat, he pulls it out of his pocket, an' so help me, but he's *got* it—he's tellin' duh troot—a big map of duh whole f——— place with all duh different pahts mahked out. You know—Canarsie an' East Noo Yawk an' Flatbush, Bensonhoist, Sout' Brooklyn, duh Heights, Bay Ridge, Greenpernt—duh whole goddam layout, he's got it right deh on duh map.

30 "You been to any of dose places?" I says.

31 "Sure," he says, "I been to most of 'em. I was down in Red Hook just last night," he says.

32 "Jesus! Red Hook!" I says. "Whatcha do down deh?"

33 "Oh," he says, "nuttin' much. I just walked aroun'. I went into a coupla places an' had a drink," he says, "but most of the time I just walked aroun'."

34 "Just walked aroun'?" I says.

35 "Sure," he says, "just lookin' at t'ings, y'know."

36 "Where'd yuh go?" I asts him.

37 "Oh," he says, "I don't know duh name of duh place, but I could find it on my map," he says. "One time I was walkin' across some big fields where deh ain't no houses," he says, "but I could see ships oveh deh all lighted up. Dey was loadin'. So I walks across duh fields," he says, "to where duh ships are."

38 "Sure," I says, "I know where you was. You was down to duh Erie Basin."

39 "Yeah," he says. "I guess dat was it. Dey had some of dose big elevators an' cranes an' dey was loadin' ships, an' I could see some ships in drydock all lighted up, so I walks across duh fields to where dey are," he says.

40 "Den what did yuh do?" I says.

41 "Oh," he says, "nuttin' much. I came on back across duh fields after a while an' went into a coupla places an' had a drink."

42 "Didn't nuttin' happen while yuh was in dere?" I says.

43 "No," he says. "Nuttin' much. A coupla guys was drunk in one of duh places an' started a fight, but dey bounced 'em out," he says, "an' den one of duh guys stahted to come back again, but duh bartender gets his baseball bat out from under duh counteh, so duh guy goes on."

44 "Jesus!" I said. "Red Hook!"

45 "Sure," he says. "Dat's where it was, all right."

46 "Well, you keep outa deh," I says. "You stay away from deh."

47 "Why?" he says. "What's wrong wit it?"

48 "Oh," I says, "it's a good place to stay away from, dat's all. It's a good place to keep out of."

49 "Why?" he says. "Why is it?"

50 Jesus! Whatcha gonna do wit a guy as dumb as dat? I saw it wasn't no use to try to tell him nuttin', he wouldn't know what I was talkin' about, so I just says to him, "Oh, nuttin'. Yuh might get lost down deh, dat's all."

51   "Lost?" he says. "No, I wouldn't get lost. I got a map," he says.

52   A map! Red Hook! Jesus!

53   SO den duh guy begins to ast me all kinds of nutty questions: how big was Brooklyn an' could I find my way aroun' in it, an' how long would it take a guy to know duh place.

54   "Listen!" I says. "You get dat idea outa yoeh head right now," I says. "You ain't neveh gonna get to know Brooklyn," I says. "Not in a hundred yeahs. I been livin' heah all my life," I says, "an' I don't even know all deh is to know about it, so how do you expect to know duh town," I says, "when you don't even live heah?"

55   "Yes," he says, "but I got a map to help me find my way about."

56   "Map or no map," I says, "yuh ain't gonna get to know Brooklyn wit no map," I says.

57   "Can you swim?" he says, just like dat. Jesus! By dat time, y'know, I begun to see dat duh guy was some kind of nut. He'd had plenty to drink, of course, but he had dat crazy look in his eye I didn't like. "Can you swim?" he says.

58   "Sure," I says. "Can't you?"

59   "No," he says. "Not more'n a stroke or two. I neveh loined good."

60   "Well, it's easy," I says. "All yuh need is a little confidence. Duh way I loined, me older bruddeh pitched me off duh dock one day when I was eight yeahs old, cloes an' all. 'You'll swim,' he says. 'You'll swim all right—or drown.' An', believe me, I *swam*! When yuh know yuh got to, you'll do it. Duh only t'ing yuh need is confidence. An' once you've loined," I says, "you've got nuttin' else to worry about. You'll neveh forget it. It's somp'n dat stays wit yuh as long as yuh live."

61   "Can yuh swim good?" he says.

62   "Like a fish," I tells him. "I'm a regulah fish in duh wateh," I says. "I loined to swim right off duh docks wit all duh oddeh kids," I says.

63   "What would you do if yuh saw a man drownin'?" duh guy says.

64   "Do? Why, I'd jump in an' pull him out," I says. "Dat's what I'd do."

65   "Did yuh eveh see a man drown?" he says.

66   "Sure, " I says. "I see two guys—bot' times at Coney Island. Dey got out too far, an' neider one could swim. Dey drowned befoeh any one could get to 'em."

67   "What becomes of people after dey've drowned out heah?" he says.

68   "Drowned out where?" I says.

69   "Out heah in Brooklyn."

70   "I don't know whatcha mean," I says. "Neveh hoid of no one drownin' heah in Brooklyn, unless you mean a swimmin' pool. Yuh can't drown in Brooklyn," I says. "Yuh gotta drown somewhere else—in duh ocean, where dere's wateh."

71   "Drownin'," duh guy says, lookin' at his map. "Drownin'." Jesus! I could see by den he was some kind of nut, he had dat crazy expression in his eyes when he looked at you, an' I didn't know what he might do. So we was comin' to a station, an' it wasn't my stop, but I got off anyway, an' waited for duh next train.

72   "Well, so long, chief," I says. "Take it easy, now."

73   "Drownin'," duh guy says, lookin' at his map. "Drownin'."

74   Jesus! I've t'ought about dat guy a t'ousand times since den an' wondered what eveh happened to 'm goin' out to look at Bensonhoist because he liked duh name! Walkin' aroun' t'roo Red Hook by himself at night an' lookin' at his map! How many people did I see get drowned out heah in Brooklyn! How long would it take a guy wit a good map to know all deh was to know about Brooklyn!

75   Jesus! What a nut *he* was! I wondeh what eveh happened to 'im, anyway! I wondeh if some one knocked him on duh head, or if he's still wanderin' aroun' in duh subway in duh middle of duh night wit his little map! Duh poor guy! Say, I've got to laugh, at dat, when I t'ink about him! Maybe he's found out by now dat he'll neveh live long enough to know duh whole of Brooklyn. It'd take a guy a lifetime to know Brooklyn t'roo an' t'roo. An' even den, yuh wouldn't know it all.

ONCE the story shifts from the high literary tone in its opening to the low speech of the ordinary Brooklyn subway passenger, you hear a celebration of life and death in the exuberant dialect. You may want to compare this dialect with those you find in the stories by Gish Jen (chapter 5), or Amy Tan (chapter 2), or William Faulkner or Flannery O'Connor (chapter 12).

GOING FURTHER   All this infusion of linguistic energy as a component of American character goes back to Herman Melville's *Moby-Dick* and Mark Twain's *The True Adventures of Huckleberry Finn,* but you may want to read some of Wolfe's contemporaries to see how they handle American speech. "I am an American, Chicago born—Chicago, that somber city . . .": the opening lines of Saul Bellow's 1953 novel *The Adventures of Augie March* explode with much the same exuberance as the Wolfe story does.

Writing from Reading

Summarize

1 Who are the main characters of this story? Describe their personalities and individual traits. Discuss how the narrator's tone changes when he talks about different characters.

2 Who is the "I" of this story? What do you know about him based on the way he speaks and the words he chooses? Use some of his distinctive phrases and expressions as examples to support your view.

Analyze Craft

3 Choose a section of the story and read it aloud. What effect does *hearing* the narrator's voice have? How is it different from imagining how it would sound while reading silently?

Analyze Voice

4 Tone is defined as the author's attitude toward his or her characters or subject matter. Analyze Thomas Wolfe's attitude toward the characters in this story—especially the narrator. How do you think Wolfe would want readers to feel about these people?

Synthesizing Summary and Analysis

5 Describe the tone of the story when the narrator and the big man are discussing Red Hook. Now describe the tone when they discuss swimming and drowning. How are the tones different? Discuss what Wolfe might be showing us through this tone shift that the narrator might be blind to.

Interpret the Story

6 What do you think the man with the map is up to? Why does he ask what happens to men who drown in Brooklyn? What is he looking for—beyond the places on the map? Support your answer by citing instances of tone shifts or uses of irony.

7 What does the story say about the difference between outsiders and insiders? Although all dialogue is delivered in the narrator's native Brooklynese, identify other ways Wolfe makes distinctions between outsiders and insiders.

Ha Jin (b. 1956)

If it hadn't been for the Tiananmen Square Massacre in 1989, Ha Jin—born Jin Xuefei in northern China—most likely would never have written the award-winning short stories, novels, and poetry that he is known for today. In fact, Jin had no plans to be a writer; he had served in the Chinese army for five years before pursuing his education, first in China, then in the United States. But when the massacre occurred, he and his wife decided to remain in the United States to raise their son. Upon Jin's completion of his Ph.D. at Brandeis University, and after several odd jobs, he eventually earned a professorship at Emory University as a result of his success in writing. He kept writing, he says, to keep his job. After publishing two books of poetry, *Between Silences* (1990) and *Facing Shadows* (1996), he published two collections of short stories, *Ocean of Words* (1996) and *Under the Red Flag* (1997), before turning to longer works. His novels *Waiting* (1999) and *War Trash* (2004) were each given the PEN/Faulkner award, making him one of only three writers to win the prestigious award more than once. Although Jin sets much of his work in China and has an interest in immigrant literature, he writes in English, a language he didn't begin learning until he was twenty years old. His precise use of language and detail allows him to fully realize the intersection between characters and society, though he pays attention to the inner lives of his characters above all else. His first work of nonfiction, *The Writer As Migrant* (2008), takes up the question of modern literary exiles and immigrants such as himself. He currently teaches writing and literature at Boston University.

AS YOU READ As you read, pay attention to the details the narrator focuses on—the sights, the sounds, the tastes. Notice your feelings about these details. How does the author's choice of words and details affect your feelings about the events and characters?

Saboteur (2000)

1 MR. CHIU and his bride were having lunch in the square before Muji Train Station. On the table between them were two bottles of soda spewing out brown foam and two paper boxes of rice and sautéed cucumber and pork. "Let's eat," he said to her, and broke the connected ends of the chopsticks. He picked up a slice of streaky pork and put it into his mouth. As he was chewing, a few crinkles appeared on his thin jaw.

2 To his right, at another table, two railroad policemen were drinking tea and laughing; it seemed that the stout, middle-aged man was telling a joke to his young comrade, who was tall and of athletic build. Now and again they would steal a glance at Mr. Chiu's table.

The air smelled of rotten melon. A few flies kept buzzing above the couple's lunch. Hundreds of people were rushing around to get on the platform or to catch buses to downtown. Food and fruit vendors were crying for customers in lazy voices. About a dozen young women, representing the local hotels, held up placards which displayed the daily prices and words as large as a palm, like FREE MEALS, AIR-CONDITIONING, and ON THE RIVER. In the center of the square stood a concrete statue of Chairman Mao, at whose feet peasants were napping, their backs on the warm granite and their faces toward the sunny sky. A flock of pigeons perched on the Chairman's raised hand and forearm.

4   The rice and cucumber tasted good, and Mr. Chiu was eating unhurriedly. His sallow face showed exhaustion. He was glad that the honeymoon was finally over and that he and his bride were heading back for Harbin. During the two weeks' vacation, he had been worried about his liver, because three months ago he had suffered from acute hepatitis; he was afraid he might have a relapse. But he had had no severe symptoms, despite his liver being still big and tender. On the whole he was pleased with his health, which could endure even the strain of a honeymoon; indeed, he was on the course of recovery. He looked at his bride, who took off her wire glasses, kneading the root of her nose with her fingertips. Beads of sweat coated her pale cheeks.

5   "Are you all right, sweetheart?" he asked.

6   "I have a headache. I didn't sleep well last night."

7   "Take an aspirin, will you?"

8   "It's not that serious. Tomorrow is Sunday and I can sleep in. Don't worry."

9   As they were talking, the stout policeman at the next table stood up and threw a bowl of tea in their direction. Both Mr. Chiu's and his bride's sandals were wet instantly.

0   "Hooligan!" she said in a low voice.

1   Mr. Chiu got to his feet and said out loud, "Comrade Policeman, why did you do this?" He stretched out his right foot to show the wet sandal.

2   "Do what?" the stout man asked huskily, glaring at Mr. Chiu while the young fellow was whistling.

3   "See, you dumped tea on our feet."

4   "You're lying. You wet your shoes yourself."

5   "Comrade Policeman, your duty is to keep order, but you purposely tortured us common citizens. Why violate the law you are supposed to enforce?" As Mr. Chiu was speaking, dozens of people began gathering around.

6   With a wave of his hand, the man said to the young fellow, "Let's get hold of him!"

7   They grabbed Mr. Chiu and clamped handcuffs around his wrists. He cried, "You can't do this to me. This is utterly unreasonable."

"Shut up!" The ma[n] out his pistol. "You can u[se your] tongue at our headquarter[s.]

The young fellow added, "[You are] a saboteur, you know that? Y[ou are] disrupting public order."

The bride was too petrifie[d to] say anything coherent. She wa[s a] recent college graduate, had m[a]jored in fine arts, and had neve[r] seen the police make an arrest. All she could say was, "Oh, please, please!"

The policemen were pulling Mr. Chiu, but he refused to go with them, holding the corner of the table and shouting, "We have a train to catch. We already bought the tickets."

22   The stout man punched him in the chest. "Shut up. Let your ticket expire." With the pistol butt he chopped Mr. Chiu's hands, which at once released the table. Together the two men were dragging him away to the police station.

23   Realizing he had to go with them, Mr. Chiu turned his head and shouted to his bride, "Don't wait for me here. Take the train. If I'm not back by tomorrow morning, send someone over to get me out."

24   She nodded, covering her sobbing mouth with her palm.

25   AFTER removing his belt, they locked Mr. Chiu into a cell in the back of the Railroad Police Station. The single window in the room was blocked by six steel bars; it faced a spacious yard, in which stood a few pines. Beyond the trees, two swings hung from an iron frame, swaying gently in the breeze. Somewhere in the building a cleaver was chopping rhythmically. There must be a kitchen upstairs, Mr. Chiu thought.

26   He was too exhausted to worry about what they would do to him, so he lay down on the narrow bed and shut his eyes. He wasn't afraid. The Cultural Revolution was over already, and recently the Party had been propagating the idea that all citizens were equal before the law. The police ought to be a law-abiding model for common people. As long as he remained coolheaded and reasoned with them, they probably wouldn't harm him.

27   Late in the afternoon he was taken to the Interrogation Bureau on the second floor. On his way there, in the stairwell, he ran into the middle-aged policeman who had manhandled him. The man grinned, rolling his bulgy eyes and pointing his fingers at him

as if firing a pistol. Egg of a tortoise! Mr. Chiu cursed mentally.

28   The moment he sat down in the office, he burped, his palm shielding his mouth. In front of him, across a long desk, sat the chief of the bureau and a donkey-faced man. On the glass desk-top was a folder containing in-formation on his case. He felt it bizarre that in just a matter of hours they had accumulated a small pile of writing about him. On second thought he began to wonder whether they had kept a file on him all the time. How could this have happened? He lived and worked in Harbin, more than three hundred miles away, and this was his first time in Muji City.

We can easily prove you are guilty.

29   The chief of the bureau was a thin, bald man who looked serene and intelligent. His slim hands handled the written pages in the folder in the manner of a lec-turing scholar. To Mr. Chiu's left sat a young scribe, with a clipboard on his knee and a black fountain pen in his hand.

30   "Your name?" the chief asked, apparently reading out the question from a form.

31   "Chiu, Maguang."

32   "Age?"

33   "Thirty-four."

34   "Profession?"

35   "Lecturer."

36   "Work unit?"

37   "Harbin University."

38   "Political status?"

39   "Communist Party member."

40   The chief put down the paper and began to speak. "Your crime is sabotage, although it hasn't induced serious consequences yet. Because you are a Party member, you should be punished more. You have failed to be a model for the masses and you—"

41   "Excuse me, sir," Mr. Chiu cut him off.

42   "What?"

43   "I didn't do anything. Your men are the saboteurs of our social order. They threw hot tea on my feet and on my wife's feet. Logically speaking, you should crit-icize them, if not punish them."

44   "That statement is groundless. You have no wit-ness. Why should I believe you?" the chief said matter-of-factly.

45   "This is my evidence." He raised his right hand. "Your man hit my fingers with a pistol."

46   "That doesn't prove how your feet got wet. Be-sides, you could have hurt your fingers yourself."

47   "But I am telling the truth!" Anger flared up in Mr. Chiu. "Your police station owes me an apology. My train ticket has expired, my new leather sandals are ruined, and I am late for a conference in the provin-cial capital. You must compensate me for the damage and losses. Don't mistake me for a common citizen who would tremble when you sneeze. I'm a scholar, a philosopher, and an expert in dialectical material-ism. If necessary, we will argue about this in *The Northeastern Daily*, or we will go to the high-est People's Court in Beijing. Tell me, what's your name?" He got carried away with his harangue, which was by no means trivial and had worked to his advantage on numerous occasions.

"Stop bluffing us," the donkey-faced man broke in. "We have seen a lot of your kind. We can easily prove you are guilty. Here are some of the statements given by eyewitnesses." He pushed a few sheets of pa-per toward Mr. Chiu.

Mr. Chiu was dazed to see the different hand-writings, which all stated that he had shouted in the square to attract attention and refused to obey the police. One of the witnesses had identified herself as a purchasing agent from a shipyard in Shanghai. Something stirred in Mr. Chiu's stomach, a pain ris-ing to his rib. He gave out a faint moan.

"Now you have to admit you are guilty," the chief said. "Although it's a serious crime, we won't punish you severely, provided you write out a self-criticism and promise that you won't disrupt the public order again. In other words, your release will depend on your attitude toward this crime."

"You're daydreaming," Mr. Chiu cried. "I won't write a word, because I'm innocent. I demand that you provide me with a letter of apology so I can explain to my university why I'm late."

Both the interrogators smiled contemptuously. "Well, we've never done that," said the chief, taking a puff at his cigarette.

"Then make this a precedent."

"That's unnecessary. We are pretty certain that you will comply with our wishes." The chief blew a column of smoke toward Mr. Chiu's face.

At the tilt of the chief's head, two guards stepped forward and grabbed the criminal by the arms. Mr. Chiu meanwhile went on saying, "I shall report you to the Provincial Administration. You'll have to pay for this! You are worse than the Japanese military police."

They dragged him out of the room.

AFTER dinner, which consisted of a bowl of millet porridge, a corn bun, and a piece of pickled turnip, Mr. Chiu began to have a fe-ver, shaking with a chill and sweating profusely. He knew that the fire of anger had gotten into his liver and that he was probably having a relapse. No medicine was available, because his briefcase had been left with his bride. At home it would have been time for him to sit in front of their color TV, drinking jasmine tea and watching the evening news. It was so lonesome in here. The orange bulb above the single bed was the only source of light, which enabled the guards to keep him under surveillance at night. A moment ago he had asked them for a newspaper or a magazine to read, but they turned him down.

Through the small opening on the door noises came in. It seemed that the police on duty were playing cards or chess in a nearby office; shouts and laughter could be heard now and then. Meanwhile, an accordion kept coughing from a remote corner in the building. Looking at the ballpoint and the letter paper left for him by the guards when they took him back from the Interrogation Bureau, Mr. Chiu remembered the old saying, "When a scholar runs into soldiers, the more he argues, the muddier his point becomes." How ridiculous this whole thing was. He ruffled his thick hair with his fingers.

He felt miserable, massaging his stomach continually. To tell the truth, he was more upset than frightened, because he would have to catch up with his work once he was back home—a paper that was due at the printers next week, and two dozen books he ought to read for the courses he was going to teach in the fall.

A human shadow flitted across the opening. Mr. Chiu rushed to the door and shouted through the hole, "Comrade Guard, Comrade Guard!"

What do you want?" a voice rasped.

"I want you to inform your leaders that I'm very sick. I have heart disease and hepatitis. I may die here if you keep me like this without medication."

"No leader is on duty on the weekend. You have to wait till Monday."

"What? You mean I'll stay in here tomorrow?"

"Yes."

"Your station will be held responsible if anything happens to me."

"We know that. Take it easy, you won't die."

It seemed illogical that Mr. Chiu slept quite well that night, though the light above his head had been on all the time and the straw mattress was hard and infested with fleas. He was afraid of ticks, mosquitoes, cockroaches—any kind of insect but

fleas and bedbugs. Once, in the country-side, where his school's faculty and staff had helped the peasants harvest crops for a week, his colleagues had joked about his flesh, which they said must have tasted non-human to fleas. Except for him, they were all afflicted with hundreds of bites.

More amazing now, he didn't miss his bride a 69 lot. He even enjoyed sleeping alone, perhaps because the honeymoon had tired him out and he needed more rest.

The backyard was quiet on Sunday morning. Pale 70 sunlight streamed through the pine branches. A few sparrows were jumping on the ground, catching cater-pillars and ladybugs. Holding the steel bars, Mr. Chiu inhaled the morning air, which smelled meaty. There must have been an eatery or a cooked-meat stand nearby. He reminded himself that he should take this detention with ease. A sentence that Chairman Mao had written to a hospitalized friend rose in his mind: "Since you are already in here, you may as well stay and make the best of it."

His desire for peace of mind originated in his fear 71 that his hepatitis might get worse. He tried to remain unperturbed. However, he was sure that his liver was swelling up, since the fever still persisted. For a whole day he lay in bed, thinking about his paper on the na-ture of contradictions. Time and again he was over-whelmed by anger, cursing aloud, "A bunch of thugs!" He swore that once he was out, he would write an article about this experience. He had better find out some of the policemen's names.

It turned out to be a restful day for the most part; 72 he was certain that his university would send some-body to his rescue. All he should do now was remain calm and wait patiently. Sooner or later the police would have to release him, although they had no idea that he might refuse to leave unless they wrote him an apology. Damn those hoodlums, they had ordered more than they could eat!

WHEN he woke up on Monday morning, it 73 was already light. Somewhere a man was moaning; the sound came from the back-yard. After a long yawn, and kicking off the tattered blanket, Mr. Chiu climbed out of bed and went to the window. In the middle of the yard, a young man was fastened to a pine, his wrists handcuffed around the trunk from behind. He was wriggling and swearing loudly, but there was no sight of anyone else in the yard. He looked familiar to Mr. Chiu.

Mr. Chiu squinted his eyes to see who it was. To 74 his astonishment, he recognized the man, who was

Fenjin, a recent graduate from the Law Department at Harbin University. Two years ago Mr. Chiu had taught a course in Marxist materialism, in which Fenjin had enrolled. Now, how on earth had this young devil landed here?

75   Then it dawned on him that Fenjin must have been sent over by his bride. What a stupid woman! A bookworm, who only knew how to read foreign novels! He had expected that she would contact the school's Security Section, which would for sure send a cadre here. Fenjin held no official position; he merely worked in a private law firm that had just two lawyers; in fact, they had little business except for some detective work for men and women who suspected their spouses of having extramarital affairs. Mr. Chiu was overcome with a wave of nausea.

76   Should he call out to let his student know he was nearby? He decided not to, because he didn't know what had happened. Fenjin must have quarreled with the police to incur such a punishment. Yet this could never have occurred if Fenjin hadn't come to his rescue. So no matter what, Mr. Chiu had to do something. But what could he do?

77   It was going to be a scorcher. He could see purple steam shimmering and rising from the ground among the pines. Poor devil, he thought, as he raised a bowl of corn glue to his mouth, sipped, and took a bite of a piece of salted celery.

78   When a guard came to collect the bowl and the chopsticks, Mr. Chiu asked him what had happened to the man in the backyard. "He called our boss 'bandit,'" the guard said. "He claimed he was a lawyer or something. An arrogant son of a rabbit."

79   Now it was obvious to Mr. Chiu that he had to do something to help his rescuer. Before he could figure out a way, a scream broke out in the backyard. He rushed to the window and saw a tall policeman standing before Fenjin, an iron bucket on the ground. It was the same young fellow who had arrested Mr. Chiu in the square two days before. The man pinched Fenjin's nose, then raised his hand, which stayed in the air for a few seconds, then slapped the lawyer across the face. As Fenjin was groaning, the man lifted up the bucket and poured water on his head.

80   "This will keep you from getting sunstroke, boy. I'll give you some more every hour," the man said loudly.

81   Fenjin kept his eyes shut, yet his wry face showed that he was struggling to hold back from cursing the policeman, or, more likely, that he was sobbing in silence. He sneezed, then raised his face and shouted, "Let me go take a piss."

82   "Oh yeah?" the man bawled. "Pee in your pants."

Still Mr. Chiu didn't make any noise, gripping the steel bars with both hands, his fingers white. The policeman turned and glanced at the cell's window; his pistol, partly holstered, glittered in the sun. With a snort he spat his cigarette butt to the ground and stamped it into the dust.

Then the door opened and the guards motioned Mr. Chiu to come out. Again they took him upstairs to the Interrogation Bureau.

The same men were in the office, though this time the scribe was sitting there empty-handed. At the sight of Mr. Chiu the chief said, "Ah, here you are. Please be seated."

After Mr. Chiu sat down, the chief waved a white silk fan and said to him, "You may have seen your lawyer. He's a young man without manners, so our director had him taught a crash course in the backyard."

"It's illegal to do that. Aren't you afraid to appear in a newspaper?"

"No, we are not, not even on TV. What else can you do? We are not afraid of any story you make up. We call it fiction. What we do care about is that you cooperate with us. That is to say, you must admit your crime."

"What if I refuse to cooperate?"

"Then your lawyer will continue his education in the sunshine."

A swoon swayed Mr. Chiu, and he held the arms of the chair to steady himself. A numb pain stung him in the upper stomach and nauseated him, and his head was throbbing. He was sure that the hepatitis was finally attacking him. Anger was flaming up in his chest; his throat was tight and clogged.

The chief resumed, "As a matter of fact, you don't even have to write out your self-criticism. We have your crime described clearly here. All we need is your signature."

Holding back his rage, Mr. Chiu said, "Let me look at that."

With a smirk the donkey-faced man handed him a sheet, which carried these words:

> *I hereby admit that on July 13 I disrupted public order at Muji Train Station, and that I refused to listen to reason when the railroad police issued their warning. Thus I myself am responsible for my arrest. After two days' detention, I have realized the reactionary nature of my crime. From now on, I shall continue to educate myself with all my effort and shall never commit this kind of crime again.*

A voice started screaming in Mr. Chiu's ears, "Lie, lie!" But he shook his head and forced the voice away.

He asked the chief, "If I sign this, will you release both my lawyer and me?"

"Of course, we'll do that." The chief was drumming his fingers on the blue folder—their file on him.

Mr. Chiu signed his name and put his thumbprint under his signature.

"Now you are free to go," the chief said with a smile, and handed him a piece of paper to wipe his thumb with.

Mr. Chiu was so sick that he couldn't stand up from the chair at first try. Then he doubled his effort and rose to his feet. He staggered out of the building to meet his lawyer in the backyard, having forgotten to ask for his belt back. In his chest he felt as though there were a bomb. If he were able to, he would have razed the entire police station and eliminated all their families. Though he knew he could do nothing like that, he made up his mind to do something.

I'M sorry about this torture, Fenjin," Mr. Chiu said when they met.

"It doesn't matter. They are savages." The lawyer brushed a patch of dirt off his jacket with trembling fingers. Water was still dribbling from the bottoms of his trouser legs.

"Let's go now," the teacher said.

The moment they came out of the police station, Mr. Chiu caught sight of a tea stand. He grabbed Fenjin's arm and walked over to the old woman at the table. "Two bowls of black tea," he said and handed her a one-yuan note.

After the first bowl, they each had another one. Then they set out for the train station. But before they walked fifty yards, Mr. Chiu insisted on eating a bowl of tree-ear soup at a food stand. Fenjin agreed. He told his teacher, "You mustn't treat me like a guest."

"No, I want to eat something myself."

As if dying of hunger, Mr. Chiu dragged his lawyer from restaurant to restaurant near the police station, but at each place he ordered no more than two bowls of food. Fenjin wondered why his teacher wouldn't stay at one place and eat his fill.

Mr. Chiu bought noodles, wonton, eight-grain porridge, and chicken soup, respectively, at four restaurants. While eating, he kept saying through his teeth, "If only I could kill all the bastards!" At the last place he merely took a few sips of the soup without tasting the chicken cubes and mushrooms.

Fenjin was baffled by his teacher, who looked ferocious and muttered to himself mysteriously, and whose jaundiced face was covered with dark puckers. For the first time Fenjin thought of Mr. Chiu as an ugly man.

WITHIN a month over eight hundred people contracted acute hepatitis in Muji. Six died of the disease, including two children. Nobody knew how the epidemic had started.

THE direct declarative telling of the story makes this piece by Pulitzer Prize–winner Ha Jin all the more powerful, and you may want to read Ralph Ellison's two stories in the casebook on the American South (chapter 12) in the same light, as fiction dealing with a difficult time in a difficult place.

GOING FURTHER   Modern Chinese life, including that of the army, politics, the professions, and the university, has served as the major focus of Ha Jin's work. However, in *A Free Life,* his 2007 novel, he turned his attention to immigrant life in America, shifting away from his usual material.

Writing from Reading

Summarize

1 Examine the various acts of sabotage in this story and write a description of "saboteur." Now identify the various "saboteurs" (not just those indicated specifically by the story) and name their crimes. Which characters in the story don't commit some act of sabotage?

Analyze Craft

2 What is the narrator's attitude toward Mr. Chiu's plight? How do you know this? What clues does the author provide by use of details and tone?

Analyze Voice

3 Whom does Ha Jin agree with, the narrator or the law system? Cite examples of Jin's use of specific language and tone when describing certain characters and events.

Synthesize Summary and Analysis

4 What is the narrator's attitude toward the police? How do you know this? What clues does the author provide through details and tone? Discuss the ironic aspects of the story.

5 How does the author portray power relations in China? Consider the various roles mentioned—policemen, scholar, lawyer, chief of the bureau.

Interpret the Story

6 Does the story end as you might have expected? Who has won the struggle for power?

7 Does your attitude toward Mr. Chiu change over the course of the story? Discuss how and when, and whether you think Ha Jin has purposely influenced this attitude change.

Junot Diaz (b. 1968)

Today, Junot Diaz's success as both a writer and a professor at MIT may lull others into forgetting the difficulties he faced as a boy who immigrated to the United States from the Dominican Republic when he was six. However, the poverty he experienced in Santo Domingo and the unpleasantness of growing up next door to a landfill in New Jersey left an indelible mark on Diaz and his fiction, which seeks to give voice to the difficulties of the immigrant life. A blend of sharp, slang-filled prose and narrators that include drug dealers and young boys struggling to make their way in an adopted country, Diaz's first book, a collection of stories titled *Drown* (1996), met with such acclaim that Diaz found himself a celebrity overnight; he was named one of *Newsweek*'s "New Faces of 1996." Although Diaz tends to write at a slow pace—ten years elapsed between *Drown* and his first novel, *The Brief Wondrous Life of Oscar Wao*—he has published stories in the most prestigious venues including *The New Yorker*, *The Paris Review*, and the *Best American Short Stories* series. His subject is the immigrant experience in the United States, which he portrays with great detail, right down to the feeling of constant uncertainty and the desire to fit in—a subject that allows his work to be semiautobiographical. And while he writes to set a precedent for future Latino writers, he also helps foster future writers through both his college teaching job and his volunteer work with urban high school students.

AS YOU READ Consider the narrator's tone. What voice do you hear as you're reading? How do you feel about his message? When do you feel comfortable with what he's saying, and when do you feel uncomfortable? What does he hide and what does he reveal?

How to Date a Browngirl, Blackgirl, Whitegirl, or Halfie (1995)

1 WAIT for your brother and your mother to leave the apartment. You've already told them that you're feeling too sick to go to Union City to visit that tía who likes to squeeze your nuts. (He's gotten big, she'll say.) And even though your moms knows you ain't sick you stuck to your story until finally she said, Go ahead and stay, malcriado.

2 Clear the government cheese from the refrigerator. If the girl's from the Terrace stack the boxes behind the milk. If she's from the Park or Society Hill hide the cheese in the cabinet above the oven, way up where she'll never see. Leave yourself a reminder to get it out before morning or your moms will kick your ass. Take down any embarrassing photos of your family in the campo, especially the one with the half-naked kids dragging a goat on a rope leash. The kids are your cousins and by now they're old enough to understand why you're doing what you're doing. Hide the pictures of yourself with an Afro. Make sure the bathroom is presentable. Put the basket with all the crapped-on toilet paper under the sink. Spray the bucket with Lysol, then close the cabinet.

3 Shower, comb, dress. Sit on the couch and watch TV. If she's an outsider her father will be bringing her, maybe her mother. Neither of them want her seeing any boys from the Terrace—people get stabbed in the Terrace—but she's strong-headed and this time will get her way. If she's a white girl you know you'll at least get a hand job.

4 The directions were in your best handwriting, so her parents won't think you're an idiot. Get up from the couch and check the parking lot. Nothing. If the girl's local, don't sweat it. She'll flow over when she's good and ready. Sometimes she'll run into her other friends and a whole crowd will show up at your apartment and even though that means you ain't getting shit it will be fun anyway and you'll wish these people would come over more often. Sometimes the girl won't flow over at all and the next day in school she'll say sorry, smile and you'll be stupid enough to believe her and ask her out again.

5 Wait and after an hour go out to your corner. The neighborhood is full of traffic. Give one of your boys a shout and when he says, Are you still waiting on that bitch? Say, Hell yeah.

6 Get back inside. Call her house and when her father picks up ask if she's there. He'll ask, Who is this? Hang up.

He sounds like a principal or a police chief, the sort of dude with a big neck, who never has to watch his back. Sit and wait. By the time your stomach's ready to give out on you, a Honda or maybe a Jeep pulls in and out she comes.

7   Hey, you'll say.

8   Look, she'll say. My mom wants to meet you. She's got herself all worried about nothing.

9   Don't panic. Say, Hey, no problem. Run a hand through your hair like the whiteboys do even though the only thing that runs easily through your hair is Africa. She will look good. The white ones are the ones you want the most, aren't they, but usually the out-of-towners are black, black-girls who grew up with ballet and Girl Scouts, who have three cars in their driveways. If she's a halfie don't be surprised that her mother is white. Say, Hi. Her moms will say hi and you'll see that you don't scare her, not really. She will say that she needs easier directions to get out and even though she has the best directions in her lap give her new ones. Make her happy.

10   You have choices. If the girl's from around the way, take her to El Cibao for dinner. Order everything in your busted-up Spanish. Let her correct you if she's Latina and amaze her if she's black. If she's not from around the way, Wendy's will do. As you walk to the restaurant talk about school. A local girl won't need stories about the neighborhood but the other ones might. Supply the story about the loco who'd been storing canisters of tear gas in his basement for years, how one day the canisters cracked and the whole neighborhood got a dose of the military-strength stuff. Don't tell her that your moms knew right away what it was, that she recognized its smell from the year the United States invaded your island.

11   Hope that you don't run into your nemesis, Howie, the Puerto Rican kid with the two killer mutts. He walks them all over the neighborhood and every now and then the mutts corner themselves a cat and tear it to shreds, Howie laughing as the cat flips up in the air, its neck twisted around like an owl, red meat showing through the soft fur. If his dogs haven't cornered a cat, he will walk behind you and ask, Hey, Yunior, is that your new fuckbuddy?

12   Let him talk. Howie weighs about two hundred pounds and could eat you if he wanted. At the field he will turn away. He has new sneakers, and doesn't want them muddy. If the girl's an outsider

she will hiss now and say, What a fucking asshole. A homegirl would have been yelling back at him the whole time, unless she was shy. Either way don't feel bad that you didn't do anything. Never lose a fight on a first date or that will be the end of it.

Dinner will be tense. You are not good at talking to people you don't know. A halfie will tell you that her parents met in the Movement, will say, Back then people thought it a radical thing to do. It will sound like something her parents made her memorize. Your brother once heard that one and said, Man, that sounds like a whole lot of Uncle Tomming to me. Don't repeat this.

As you walk to the restaurant
talk about school.

Put down your hamburger and say, It must have been hard.

She will appreciate your interest. She will tell you more. Black people, she will say, treat me real bad. That's why I don't like them. You'll wonder how she feels about Dominicans. Don't ask. Let her speak on it and when you're both finished eating walk back into the neighborhood. The skies will be magnificent. Pollutants have made Jersey sunsets one of the wonders of the world. Point it out. Touch her shoulder and say, That's nice, right?

Get serious. Watch TV but stay alert. Sip some of the Bermúdez your father left in the cabinet, which nobody touches. A local girl may have hips and a thick ass but she won't be quick about letting you touch. She has to live in the same neighborhood you do, has to deal with you being all up in her business. She might just chill with you and then go home. She might kiss you and then go, or she might, if she's reckless, give it up, but that's rare. Kissing will suffice. A whitegirl might just give it up right then. Don't stop her.

She'll take her gum out of her mouth, stick it to the plastic sofa covers and then will move close to you. You have nice eyes, she might say.

Tell her that you love her hair, that you love her skin, her lips, because, in truth, you love them more than you love your own.

She'll say, I like Spanish guys, and even though you've never been to Spain, say, I like you. You'll sound smooth.

You'll be with her until about eight-thirty and then she will want to wash up. In the bathroom she will hum a song from the radio and her waist will keep the beat against the lip of the sink. Imagine her old lady coming to get her, what she would say if she knew her daughter had just lain under you and blown your name, pronounced with her eighth-grade Spanish, into your ear. While she's in the bathroom call one of your boys and say, Lo hice, loco. Or just sit back on the couch and smile.

But usually it won't work this way. Be prepared. She will not want to kiss you. Just cool it, she'll say. The halfie might lean back, breaking away from you. She will cross her arms, say, I hate my tits. Stroke her hair but she will pull away. I don't like anybody touching my hair, she will say. She will act like somebody you don't know. In school she is known for her attention-grabbing laugh, as high and far-ranging as a gull, but here she will worry you. You will not know what to say.

You're the only kind of guy who asks me out, she will say. Your neighbors will start their hyena calls, now that the alcohol is in them. You and the blackboys.

Say nothing. Let her button her shirt, let her comb her hair, the sound of it stretching like a sheet of fire between you. When her father pulls in and beeps, let her go without too much of a good-bye. She won't want it. During the next hour the phone will ring. You will be tempted to pick it up. Don't. Watch the shows you want to watch, without a family around to debate you. Don't go downstairs. Don't fall asleep. It won't help. Put the government cheese back in its place before your moms kills you.

IN many ways this is the most playful story in the book, and if you like the tone of it you may notice it has some affinities to Lorrie Moore's story "How to Become a Writer" (chapter 7)—they both use the second-person point of view—or the story by Sherman Alexie in the Anthology of Stories for Further Reading.

GOING FURTHER Playfulness, even when treating some of the most serious subjects, goes all the way back to Laurence Sterne's *Tristram Shandy* in the eighteenth century and to *Don Quixote*, the classic Spanish novel composed by Miguel de Cervantes and first published in 1605. Today you might find similarities between Diaz's tone and the tone in *Extremely Loud & Incredibly Close* by Jonathan Safran Foer.

Writing from Reading

Summarize

1 Describe the narrator's attitudes toward each kind of girl mentioned in the title. What attracts him about each? What complaints does he have about each?

2 Consider whether this story is meant to be a recipe for *successful* dating. Does the narrator end up where he means to be in each scenario? What is his goal for the date?

Analyze Craft

3 Discuss the use of irony in the story. Are there incongruities (1) between acts and results, (2) between what occurs and what the character expected to occur, or (3) between what is said and what is meant?

Analyze Voice

4 What does the narrator hide and what does he reveal? Discuss how his secrets and confessions affect your attitudes toward him.

Synthesize Summary and Analysis

5 Discuss the attitudes that this narrator reveals about race, class, and ethnicity. Cite examples to demonstrate how Diaz uses tone to affect your response to the narrator's suggestions.

Interpret the Story

6 Consider the form the story would take if written in first person, as a straight-forward dramatic scene. Discuss how the tone and language of the story might change, and what the effect would be on your impression of the boy on the date.

Reading for Language, Tone, and Style

When reading for language, tone, and style, make notes about how the author uses language to express a particular attitude toward the characters and events.

- *What* is being said, and *how* and *why*?
- What effect does the author wish to create?
- What effect does the writing have on you?

What kind of language or diction did the author choose to shape the style and tone of the story?

- Are there particular words that are important to the style and tone of the story?
- Are there key images that have an impact on the style and tone?
- How would you describe the language chosen by the writer?

What tone (of voice) do you hear?	• **Serious or comedic?** • **Distant or intimate?** • **Direct or roundabout?** • **Restrained or emotional?** • **Ominous or lighthearted?** • **Straightforward or ironic?**
Is the author being ironic?	• Is the irony **verbal?** • Is the irony **dramatic?**
How do the language and tone work together to define the writer's style?	• Is the language lush or lean? • Are the sentences long and complex, or short and simple? • What kind of tone is created in the story? • How would you describe the style: elegant? hard-boiled? lyrical? unadorned? ornate? self-conscious?

Suggestions for Writing about Language, Tone, and Style

1. In her interview, Aimee Bender says that she uses her imagination in writing as "a way to get to feelings that are hard to look at straight on." Discuss this aspect of her style as represented by "The Rememberer." How effective is this style for exploring the subject of loss?

2. "The Rememberer" and "How to Date a Browngirl, Blackgirl, Whitegirl, or Halfie" both explore intimate relationships—the limitations and possibilities between members of a couple. Using specific examples, argue how each of the narrators might define love. What words would they use? What kind of language?

3. Briefly describe the style of each story in this chapter, and then compare and contrast the authors' approaches. Why is each style fitting for its particular story?

4. The titles "Only the Dead Know Brooklyn" and "How to Date a Browngirl, Blackgirl, Whitegirl, or Halfie" are both bold declarations. What do these titles suggest about the way language will be used in the stories that follow? How do other lines of dialogue or description reinforce or refute the sense of certainty in the titles?

"THE next day, Nnamabia barely touched his rice. He said that the policemen had splashed soapy water on the floor and walls of the cell, as they usually did, and that the old man, who had not bathed in a week, had yanked his shirt off and rubbed his frail back against the wet floor. The policemen started to laugh when they saw him do this, and then they asked him to take all his clothes off and parade in the corridor outside the cell; as he did, they laughed louder and asked whether his son the thief knew that Papa's buttocks were so shrivelled. Nnamabia was staring at his yellow-orange rice as he spoke, and when he looked up his eyes were filled with tears, my worldly brother, and I felt a tenderness for him that I would not have been able to describe if I had been asked to."

—from "Cell One" by
Chimamanda Ngozi Adichie

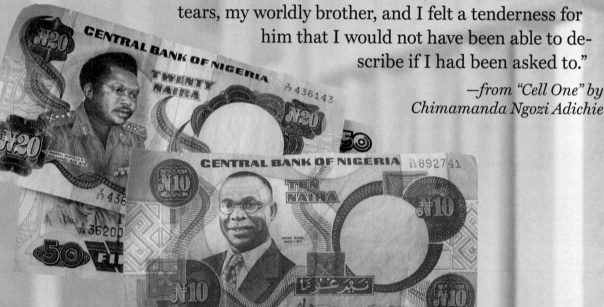

"The germ of the story came from a small story that my brother Okey had told me . . . about an old man in a cell. . . . I was haunted . . . and heartbroken . . . but I knew I wanted to use it . . . and wanted it also to be about my brother. I wanted to write about how my brother was redeemed in the most unlikely way. . . . I think that the story's about redemption—my brother's redemption— but in some ways it also redeemed me."

Conversation with Chimamanda Ngozi Adichie, available on video
at www.mhhe.com/delbancole

9

THEME

NNAMABIA, the young man who is the focus of this passage, is Nigerian. He is handsome, popular, well-educated, from a good family, attractive to women, and he has enjoyed every minute of his privileged life. Now, however, he is in prison because he has been linked, perhaps unjustly, to gang activity and the murder of three students on a college campus. While he is in prison, his mother, father, and sister—who is the narrator of the story—visit him almost daily. During one visit, he tells this story of the old man.

This passage is central to "cell one" because it reveals a change in Nnamabia. The imprisonment has stirred a social consciousness in him, an awareness that life is a serious matter. The passage also reveals the impact this change has on his sister. Nnamabia doesn't say, "I am beginning to understand justice and injustice and human cruelty." His sister certainly doesn't explain why she felt that rush of tenderness. She says that she cannot. Still, as readers, we sense the significance of the old man's mistreatment and its impact on these characters. As we move toward understanding this new situation, we move toward understanding the **theme**—that is, the central or underlying meanings of a literary work.

When we talk about theme, we're talking about broad ideas. Theme is what a story is "about" beyond the specific characters and events of the story. So, we can say that in the passage from Adichie's story, the development of social conscience, the horror of human brutality, and the significance of human connection emerge as thematic concerns. To put these concerns together in a complete thought, we might say that "Cell One" explores the brutal lessons that are sometimes needed to awaken social consciousness and a sense of justice.

CONTINUED ON PAGE 270

Q & A

A Conversation on Writing

Chimamanda Ngozi Adichie

On Multiple Themes in "Cell One"

The notion of just one theme in a story sometimes just reduces a work of fiction. I like to think about multiple themes, that a story can do so many things at the same time. I do think ["Cell One"] is about redemption. . . . but it's also about gender. . . . and also [about] how, in my opinion, unreasonable family love can be. . . . And I wanted to explore middle-class comfort versus wartime deprivation and how it changes how people feel about each other.

Bagels, Longing, and Literature

I grew up in a small university town in western Nigeria. I grew up fortunate enough to be surrounded by books, and I was fascinated by this word *bagel*. . . . because these characters in the books had these things for breakfast. . . . I had never seen one. . . . I think what that showed me was how you don't need to know what it is to long for it. . . . What underlies it all is that human thing that I think is common—that we all long to be loved, and want to love. . . . For me I hope that's really what comes out of my work, and that the other things, the Nigerian food and the language, all of which I love and want to celebrate . . . will be secondary.

On Reading

You don't have to love everything, first of all, and you won't love everything, but . . . you will find something to love. . . . Very often we see literature as something difficult. . . . Sometimes we forget that literature should be something that we enjoy and have fun doing.

To watch this entire interview and hear the author read from "Cell One," go to **www.mhhe.com/delbanco1e.**

When readers think of Nigerian authors, Chinua Achebe is the major name that has come to mind for the past few decades. Today, however, Nigerian writer Chimamanda Ngozi Adichie is following in his footsteps—almost literally, as she grew up in the house where Achebe once lived. Adichie came to the United States when she was nineteen to complete her undergraduate degree; she also earned a master's in creative writing from Johns Hopkins University. Her first novel, *Purple Hibiscus* (2003), met with great success; it was shortlisted for the Orange Fiction Prize and won the Commonwealth Writers' Prize for Best First Book. Like *Purple Hibiscus,* her second novel, *Half of a Yellow Sun,* is set in Nigeria, but whereas her first novel portrayed a Nigerian family and their struggle with religion and authority, this novel takes for its subject the Nigerian Civil War. Adichie's short stories have also met with success; she won an O. Henry Prize in 2003, and her stories have appeared in *Granta, The Iowa Review,* and *The New Yorker.* She was awarded the MacArthur "genius grant" in 2008. She currently divides her time between Nigeria and the United States.

RESEARCH ASSIGNMENT   In her interview, Adichie talks about authenticity in her writing. How does she achieve this authenticity? Do you agree with her about the "ideal of authenticity" in fiction? Why or why not?

AS YOU READ   As you read, notice how these characters change in the course of the story. Which events lead to these changes? How do these changes rise to the level of thematic importance?

 FOR INTERACTIVE READING . . . What is Cell One? Find and mark all references to it in the story. When you are finished reading, describe everything you know about it, including the characters' attitudes about it.

Cell One (2007)

1   THE first time our house was robbed, it was our neighbor Osita who climbed in through the dining-room window and stole our TV and VCR, and the "Purple Rain" and "Thriller" videotapes that my father had brought back from America. The second time our house was robbed, it was my brother Nnamabia, who faked a break-in and stole my mother's jewelry. It happened on a Sunday. My parents had travelled to their home town to visit our grandparents, so Nnamabia and I went to church alone. He drove my mother's green Peugeot 504. We sat together in church as we usually did, but we did not have time to nudge each other and stifle giggles about somebody's ugly hat or threadbare caftan, because Nnamabia left without a word after ten minutes. He came back just before the priest said, "The Mass is ended, go in peace." I was a little piqued. I imagined that he had gone off to smoke or to see some girl, since he had the car to himself for once; but he could at least have told me. We drove home in silence, and when he parked in our long driveway I stayed back to pick some ixora flowers while Nnamabia unlocked the front door. I went inside to find him standing in the middle of the parlor.

2   "We've been robbed!" he said.

3   It took me a moment to take in the room. Even then, I felt that there was a theatrical quality to the way the drawers had been flung open. Or perhaps it was simply that I knew my brother too well. Later, when my parents had come home and neighbors began to troop in to say *ndo*—sorry—and to snap their fingers and heave their shoulders up and down, I sat alone in my room upstairs and realized what the queasiness in my gut was: Nnamabia had done it, I knew. My father knew, too. He pointed out that the window louvres had been slipped out from the inside, rather than from the outside (Nnamabia was usually smarter than that—perhaps he had been in a hurry to get back to church before Mass ended), and that the robber knew exactly where my mother's jewelry was: in the back left corner of her metal trunk. Nnamabia stared at my father with wounded eyes and said that he may have done horrible things in the past, things that had caused my parents pain, but that he had done nothing in this case. He walked out the back door and did not come home that night. Or the next night. Or the night after. Two weeks later, he came home gaunt, smelling of beer, crying, saying he was sorry, that he had pawned the jewelry to the Hausa traders in Enugu, and that all the money was gone.

4   "How much did they give you for my gold?" our mother asked him. And when he told her she placed both hands on her head and cried, "Oh! Oh! *Chi m egbuo m!* My God has killed me!" I wanted to slap her. My father asked Nnamabia to write a report: how he had pawned the jewelry, what he had spent the money on, with whom he had spent it. I didn't think that Nnamabia would tell the truth, and I don't think that my father thought he would, but he liked reports, my professor father, he liked to have things written down and nicely documented. Besides, Nnamabia was seventeen, with

a carefully tended beard. He was already between secondary school and university, and was too old for caning. What else could my father have done? After Nnamabia had written the report, my father filed it in the steel cabinet in his study where he kept our school papers.

5 "That he could hurt his mother like that!" was the last thing my father said on the subject.

6 But Nnamabia hadn't set out to hurt her. He had done it because my mother's jewelry was the only thing of any value in the house: a lifetime's accumulation of solid-gold pieces. He had done it, too, because other sons of professors were doing it. This was the season of thefts on our serene campus. Boys who had grown up watching "Sesame Street," reading Enid Blyton, eating cornflakes for breakfast, and attending the university staff primary school in polished brown sandals were now cutting through the mosquito netting of their neighbors' windows, sliding out glass louvres, and climbing in to steal TVs and VCRs. We knew the thieves. Still, when the professors saw one another at the staff club or at church or at a faculty meeting, they were careful to moan about the riffraff from town coming onto their sacred campus to steal.

7 The thieving boys were the popular ones. They drove their parents' cars in the evening, their seats pushed back and their arms stretched out to reach the steering wheel. Osita, our neighbor who had stolen our TV only weeks before Nnamabia's theft, was lithe and handsome in a brooding sort of way, and walked with the grace of a cat. His shirts were always crisply ironed, and I used to watch him across the hedge, then close my eyes and imagine that he was walking toward me, coming to claim me as his. He never noticed me. When he stole from us, my parents did not go over to Professor Ebube's house to ask for our things back. But they knew it was Osita. Osita was two years older than Nnamabia; most of the thieving boys were a little older than Nnamabia, and maybe that was why Nnamabia had not stolen from another person's house. Perhaps he did not feel old enough, qualified enough, for anything more serious than my mother's jewelry.

8 Nnamabia looked just like my mother—he had her fair complexion and large eyes, and a generous mouth that curved perfectly. When my mother took us to the market, traders would call out, "Hey! Madam, why did you waste your fair skin on a boy and leave the girl so dark? What is a boy doing with all this beauty?" And my mother would chuckle, as though she took a mischievous and joyful responsibility for Nnamabia's looks. When, at eleven, Nnamabia broke the window of his classroom with a stone, my mother gave him the money to replace it and didn't tell my father. When, a few years later, he took the key to my father's car and pressed it into a bar of soap that my father found before Nnamabia could take it to a locksmith, she made vague sounds about how he was just experimenting and it didn't mean anything. When he stole the exam questions from the study and sold them to my father's students, she yelled at him, but then told my father that Nnamabia was sixteen, after all, and really should be given more pocket money.

9 I don't know whether Nnamabia felt remorse for stealing her jewelry. I could not always tell from my brother's gracious, smiling face what he really felt. He and I did not talk about it, and neither did my parents. Even though my mother's sisters sent her their gold earrings, even though she bought a new gold chain from Mrs. Mozie—the glamorous woman who imported gold from Italy—and began to drive to Mrs. Mozie's house once a month to pay in installments, we never talked about what had happened to her jewelry. It was as if by pretending that Nnamabia had not done the things he had done we could give him the opportunity to start afresh. The robbery might never have been mentioned again if Nnamabia had not been arrested two years later, in his second year of university.

10 BY then, it was the season of cults on the Nsukka campus, when signs all over the university read in bold letters, "SAY NO TO CULTS." The Black Axe, the Buccaneers, and the Pirates were the best known. They had once been benign fraternities, but they had evolved, and now eighteen-year-olds who had mastered the swagger of American rap videos were undergoing secret initiations that sometimes left one or two of them dead on Odim Hill. Guns and tortured loyalties became common. A boy would leer at a girl who turned out to be the girlfriend of the Capone of the Black Axe, and that boy, as he walked to a kiosk later to buy a cigarette, would be stabbed in the thigh. He would turn out to be a Buccaneer, and so one of his fellow-Buccaneers would go

to a beer parlor and shoot the nearest Black Axe in the leg, and then the next day another Buccaneer would be shot dead in the refectory, his body falling onto aluminum plates of *garri*, and that evening a Black Axe—a professor's son—would be hacked to death in his room, his CD player splattered with blood. It was inane. It was so abnormal that it quickly became normal. Girls stayed in their rooms after classes, and lecturers quivered, and when a fly buzzed too loudly people jumped. So the police were called in. They sped across campus in their rickety blue Peugeot 505 and glowered at the students, their rusty guns poking out of the car windows. Nnamabia came home from his lectures laughing. He thought that the police would have to do better than that; everyone knew the cult boys had newer guns.

1 My parents watched Nnamabia with silent concern, and I knew that they, too, were wondering if he was in a cult. Cult boys were popular, and Nnamabia was very popular. Boys yelled out his nickname—"The Funk!"—and shook his hand whenever he passed by, and girls, especially the popular ones, hugged him for too long when they said hello. He went to all the parties, the tame ones on campus and the wilder ones in town, and he was the kind of ladies' man who was also a guy's guy, the kind who smoked a packet of Rothmans a day and was reputed to be able to finish a case of Star beer in a single sitting. But it seemed more his style to befriend all the cult boys and yet not be one himself. And I was not entirely sure, either, that my brother had whatever it took—guts or diffidence—to join a cult.

2 The only time I asked him if he was in a cult, he looked at me with surprise, as if I should have known better than to ask, before replying, "Of course not." I believed him. My dad believed him, too, when he asked. But our believing him made little difference, because he had already been arrested for belonging to a cult.

3 THIS is how it happened. On a humid Monday, four cult members waited at the campus gate and waylaid a professor driving a red Mercedes. They pressed a gun to her head, shoved her out of the car, and drove it to the Faculty of Engineering, where they shot three boys who were coming out of the building. It was noon. I was in a class nearby, and when we heard the shots our lecturer was the first to run out the door. There was loud screaming, and suddenly the stairwells were packed with scrambling students unsure where to

Outside, the bodies lay on the lawn.

run. Outside, the bodies lay on the lawn. The Mercedes had already screeched away. Many students hastily packed their bags, and *okada* drivers charged twice the usual fare to take them to the motor park to get on a bus. The vice-chancellor announced that all evening classes would be cancelled and everyone had to stay indoors after 9 P.M. This did not make much sense to me, since the shooting had happened in sparkling daylight, and perhaps it did not make sense to Nnamabia, either, because the first night of the curfew he didn't come home. I assumed that he had spent the night at a friend's; he did not always come home anyway. But the next morning a security man came to tell my parents that Nnamabia had been arrested at a bar with some cult boys and was at the police station.

My mother screamed, *"Ekwuzikwana!* Don't say that!" My father calmly thanked the security man. We drove to the police station in town, and there a constable chewing on the tip of a dirty pen said, "You mean those cult boys arrested last night? They have been taken to Enugu. Very serious case! We must stop this cult business once and for all!"

14 We got back into the car, and a new fear gripped us all. Nsukka, which was made up of our slow, insular campus and the slower, more insular town, was manageable; my father knew the police superintendent. But Enugu was anonymous. There the police could do what they were famous for doing when under pressure to produce results: kill people.

15 THE Enugu police station was in a sprawling, sandy compound. My mother bribed the policemen at the desk with money, and with jollof rice and meat, and they allowed Nnamabia to come out of his cell and sit on a bench under a mango tree with us. Nobody asked why he had stayed out the night before. Nobody said that the police were wrong to walk into a bar and arrest all the boys drinking there, including the barman. Instead, we listened to Nnamabia talk.

16 "If we ran Nigeria like this cell," he said, "we would have no problems. Things are so organized. Our cell has a chief and he has a second-in-command, and when you come in you are expected to give them some money. If you don't, you're in trouble."

17 "And did you have any money?" my mother asked.

18 Nnamabia smiled, his face more beautiful than ever, despite the new pimple-like insect bite on his forehead, and said that he had slipped his money into his anus shortly after the arrest. He knew the policemen would take it if he didn't hide it, and he knew

that he would need it to buy his peace in the cell. My parents said nothing for a while. I imagined Nnamabia rolling hundred-naira notes into a thin cigarette shape and then reaching into the back of his trousers to slip them into himself. Later, as we drove back to Nsukka, my father said, "This is what I should have done when he stole your jewelry. I should have had him locked up in a cell."

19   My mother stared out the window.

20   "Why?" I asked.

21   "Because this has shaken him. Couldn't you see?" my father asked with a smile. I couldn't see it. Nnamabia had seemed fine to me, slipping his money into his anus and all.

22   Nnamabia's first shock was seeing a Buccaneer sobbing. The boy was tall and tough, rumored to have carried out one of the killings and likely to become Capone next semester, and yet there he was in the cell, cowering and sobbing after the chief gave him a light slap on the back of the head. Nnamabia told me this in a voice lined with both disgust and disappointment; it was as if he had suddenly been made to see that the Incredible Hulk was really just painted green. His second shock was learning about the cell farthest away from his, Cell One. He had never seen it, but every day two policemen carried a dead man out of Cell One, stopping by Nnamabia's cell to make sure that the corpse was seen by all.

23   Those in the cell who could afford to buy old plastic paint cans of water bathed every other morning. When they were let out into the yard, the policemen watched them and often shouted, "Stop that or you are going to Cell One now!" Nnamabia could not imagine a place worse than his cell, which was so crowded that he often stood pressed against the wall. The wall had cracks where tiny *kwalikwata* lived; their bites were fierce and sharp, and when he yelped his cellmates mocked him. The biting was worse during the night, when they all slept on their sides, head to foot, to make room for one another, except the chief, who slept with his whole back lavishly on the floor. It was also the chief who divided up the two plates of rice that were pushed into the cell every day. Each person got two mouthfuls.

24   Nnamabia told us this during the first week. As he spoke, I wondered if the bugs in the wall had bitten his face or if the bumps spreading across his forehead were due to an infection. Some of them were tipped with cream-colored pus. Once in a while, he scratched at them. I wanted him to stop talking. He seemed to enjoy his new role as the sufferer of indignities, and he did not understand how lucky he was that the policemen allowed him to come out and eat our food, or how stupid he'd been to stay out drinking that night, and how uncertain his chances were of being released.

W E visited him every day for the first week. We took my father's old Volvo, because my mother's Peugeot was unsafe for trips outside Nsukka. By the end of the week, I noticed that my parents were acting differently—subtly so, but differently. My father no longer gave a monologue, as soon as we were waved through the police checkpoints, on how illiterate and corrupt the police were. He did not bring up the day when they had delayed us for an hour because he'd refused to bribe them, or how they had stopped a bus in which my beautiful cousin Ogechi was travelling and singled her out and called her a whore because she had two cell phones, and asked her for so much money that she had knelt on the ground in the rain begging them to let her go. My mother did not mumble that the policemen were symptoms of a larger malaise. Instead, my parents remained silent. It was as if by refusing to criticize the police they would somehow make Nnamabia's freedom more likely. "Delicate" was the word the superintendent at Nsukka had used. To get Nnamabia out anytime soon would be delicate, especially with the police commissioner in Enugu giving gloating, preening interviews about the arrest of the cultists. The cult problem was serious. Big Men in Abuja were following events. Everybody wanted to seem as if he were doing something.

The second week, I told my parents that we were not going to visit Nnamabia. We did not know how long this would last, and petrol was too expensive for us to drive three hours every day. Besides, it would not hurt Nnamabia to fend for himself for one day.

My mother said that nobody was begging me to come—I could sit there and do nothing while my innocent brother suffered. She started walking toward the car, and I ran after her. When I got outside, I was not sure what to do, so I picked up a stone near the ixora bush and hurled it at the windshield of the Volvo. I heard the brittle sound and saw the tiny lines spreading like rays on the glass before I turned and dashed upstairs and locked myself in my room. I heard my mother shouting. I heard my father's voice. Finally, there was silence. Nobody went to see Nnamabia that day. It surprised me, this little victory.

W E visited him the next day. We said nothing about the windshield, although the cracks had spread out like ripples on a frozen stream. The policeman at the desk, the pleasant dark-skinned one, asked why we had not come the day before—he had missed my mother's jollof rice. I expected Nnamabia to ask, too, even to be upset, but he looked oddly sober. He did not eat all of his rice.

29 "What is wrong?" my mother said, and Nnamabia began to speak almost immediately, as if he had been waiting to be asked. An old man had been pushed into his cell the day before—a man perhaps in his mid-seventies, white-haired, skin finely wrinkled, with an old-fashioned dignity about him. His son was wanted for armed robbery, and when the police had not been able to find his son they had decided to lock up the father.

30 "The man did nothing," Nnamabia said.

31 "But you did nothing, either," my mother said.

32 Nnamabia shook his head as if our mother did not understand. The following days, he was more subdued. He spoke less, and mostly about the old man: how he could not afford bathing water, how the others made fun of him or accused him of hiding his son, how the chief ignored him, how he looked frightened and so terribly small.

33 "Does he know where his son is?" my mother asked.

34 "He has not seen his son in four months," Nnamabia said.

35 "Of course it is wrong," my mother said. "But this is what the police do all the time. If they do not find the person they are looking for, they lock up his relative."

36 "The man is ill," Nnamabia said. "His hands shake, even when he's asleep."

37 He closed the container of rice and turned to my father. "I want to give him some of this, but if I bring it into the cell the chief will take it."

38 My father went over and asked the policeman at the desk if we could be allowed to see the old man in Nnamabia's cell for a few minutes. The policeman was the light-skinned acerbic one who never said thank you when my mother handed over the rice-and-money bribe, and now he sneered in my father's face and said that he could well lose his job for letting even Nnamabia out and yet now we were asking for another person? Did we think this was visiting day at a boarding school? My father came back and sat down with a sigh, and Nnamabia silently scratched at his bumpy face.

39 The next day, Nnamabia barely touched his rice. He said that the policemen had splashed soapy water on the floor and walls of the cell, as they usually did, and that the old man, who had not bathed in a week, had yanked his shirt off and rubbed his frail back against the wet floor. The policemen started to laugh when they saw him do this, and then they asked him to take all his clothes off and parade in the corridor outside the cell; as he did, they laughed louder and asked whether his son the thief knew that Papa's buttocks were so shrivelled. Nnamabia was staring at his yellow-orange rice as he spoke, and when he looked up his eyes were filled with tears, my worldly brother, and I felt a tenderness for him that I would not have been able to describe if I had been asked to.

40 THERE was another attack on campus—a boy hacked another boy with an axe—two days later.

41 "This is good," my mother said. "Now they cannot say that they have arrested all the cult boys." We did not go to Enugu that day; instead my parents went to see the local police superintendent, and they came back with good news. Nnamabia and the barman were to be released immediately. One of the cult boys, under questioning, had insisted that Nnamabia was not a member. The next day, we left earlier than usual, without jollof rice. My mother was always nervous when we drove, saying to my father, *Nekwa ya!* Watch out!," as if he could not see the cars making dangerous turns in the other lane, but this time she did it so often that my father pulled over before we got to Ninth Mile and snapped, "Just who is driving this car?"

42 Two policemen were flogging a man with *koboko* as we drove into the police station. At first, I thought it was Nnamabia, and then I thought it was the old man from his cell. It was neither. I knew the boy on the ground, who was writhing and shouting with each lash. He was called Aboy and had the grave ugly face of a hound; he drove a Lexus around campus and was said to be a Buccaneer. I tried not to look at him as we walked inside. The policeman on duty, the one with tribal marks on his cheeks who always said "God bless you" when he took his bribe, looked away when he saw us, and I knew that something was wrong. My parents

gave him the note from the superintendent. The policeman did not even glance at it. He knew about the release order, he told my father; the barman had already been released, but there was a complication with the boy. My mother began to shout, "What do you mean? Where is my son?"

43 The policeman got up. "I will call my senior to explain to you."

44 My mother rushed at him and pulled on his shirt. "Where is my son? Where is my son?" My father pried her away, and the policeman brushed at his chest, as if she had left some dirt there, before he turned to walk away.

45 "Where is our son?" my father asked in a voice so quiet, so steely, that the policeman stopped.

46 "They took him away, sir," he said.

47 "They took him away? What are you saying?" my mother was yelling. "Have you killed my son? Have you killed my son?"

48 "Where is our son?" my father asked again.

49 "My senior said I should call him when you came," the policeman said, and this time he hurried through a door.

50 It was after he left that I felt suddenly chilled by fear; I wanted to run after him and, like my mother, pull at his shirt until he produced Nnamabia. The senior policeman came out, and I searched his blank face for clues.

51 "Good day, sir," he said to my father.

52 "Where is our son?" my father asked. My mother breathed noisily.

53 "No problem, sir. It is just that we transferred him. I will take you there right away." There was something nervous about the policeman; his face remained blank, but he did not meet my father's eyes.

54 "Transferred him?"

55 "We got the order this morning. I would have sent somebody for him, but we don't have petrol, so I was waiting for you to come so that we could go together."

56 "Why was he transferred?"

57 "I was not here, sir. They said that he misbehaved yesterday and they took him to Cell One, and then yesterday evening there was a transfer of all the people in Cell One to another site."

58 "He misbehaved? What do you mean?"

59 "I was not here, sir."

60 My mother spoke in a broken voice: "Take me to my son! Take me to my son right now!"

61 I sat in the back with the policeman, who smelled of the kind of old camphor that seemed to last forever in my mother's trunk. No one spoke except for the policeman when he gave my father directions. We arrived about fifteen minutes later, my father driving inordinately fast. The small, walled compound looked neglected, with patches of overgrown grass strewn with old bottles and plastic bags. The policeman hardly waited for my father to stop the car before he opened the door and hurried out, and again I felt chilled. We were in a godforsaken part of town, and there was no sign that said "Police Station." There was a strange deserted feeling in the air. But the policeman soon emerged with Nnamabia. There he was, my handsome brother, walking toward us, seemingly unchanged, until he came close enough for my mother to hug him, and I saw him wince and back away—his arm was covered in soft-looking welts. There was dried blood around his nose.

62 "Why did they beat you like this?" my mother asked him. She turned to the policeman. "Why did you people do this to my son? Why?"

63 The man shrugged. There was a new insolence to his demeanor; it was as if he had been uncertain about Nnamabia's well-being but now, reassured, could let himself talk. "You cannot raise your children properly—all of you people who feel important because you work at the university—and when your children misbehave you think they should not be punished. You are lucky they released him."

64 My father said, "Let's go."

65 He opened the door and Nnamabia climbed in, and we drove home. My father did not stop at any of the police checkpoints on the road, and, once, a policeman gestured threateningly with his gun as we sped past. The only time my mother opened her mouth on the drive home was to ask Nnamabia if he wanted us to stop and buy some *okpa*. Nnamabia said no. We had arrived in Nsukka before he finally spoke.

66 "Yesterday, the policemen asked the old man if he wanted a free half bucket of water. He said yes. So they told him to take his clothes off and parade the corridor. Most of my cellmates were laughing. Some of them said it was wrong to treat an old man like that." Nnamabia paused. "I shouted at the policeman. I told him the old man was innocent and ill, and if they kept him here it wouldn't help them find his son, because the man did not even know where his son was. They said that I should shut up immediately, that they would take me to Cell One. I didn't care. I didn't shut up. So they pulled me out and slapped me and took me to Cell One."

> ## My father did not stop at any of the police checkpoints on the road . . .

Nnamabia stopped there, and we asked him nothing else. Instead, I imagined him calling the policeman a stupid idiot, a spineless coward, a sadist, a bastard, and I imagined the shock of the policemen—the chief staring openmouthed, the other cellmates stunned at the audacity of the boy from the university. And I imagined the old man himself looking on with surprised pride and quietly refusing to undress. Nnamabia did not say what had happened to him in Cell One, or what happened at the new site. It would have been so easy for him, my charming brother, to make a sleek drama of his story, but he did not.

IF you like Adichie's "Cell One," you will find similarities in "Saboteur," Ha Jin's story of political turmoil in China.

GOING FURTHER In her interview, Adichie praises the traditional oral storytelling in the work of African writer Ama Ata Aidoo, whose novels include *Our Sister Killjoy; Or, Reflections from a Black-Eyed Squint* and *Changes*. Other novels set on the continent of Africa include Amos Tutuola's *The Palm-Wine Drunkard* and Nigeria's own Chinua Achebe's *Things Fall Apart*. Notable among contemporary Nigerian writers currently living in the United States are Helon Habila and Chris Abani.

Writing from Reading

Summarize

1 Describe Nnamabia. Explain everything you know about him. What does he learn in the course of the story? Do you think he is treated differently from other prisoners because of his social class and level of education?

2 Explain the role of the sister. Why does she break the car windshield? Why is this act important?

Analyze Craft

3 Adichie begins "Cell One" by describing Nnamabia's various trespasses and potential gang involvement. How does her treatment of Nnamabia change once he is imprisoned? Analyze her purpose in including Nnamabia's criminal past.

Analyze Voice

4 Adichie herself grew up in Nigeria. What evidence is there of her own voice coming through in the narrator's description of events? Identify specific phrases or scenes, and describe what sets them apart as more personal to the author.

Synthesize Summary and Analysis

5 Over the course of the story, the narrator seldom takes any action—that is, she mostly remains a detached observer. What single incident turns on the narrator's own actions? Discuss the effect of this scene on the story.

6 Note all the times the narrator expresses her impression of her brother and then says that her father saw the same thing. At what point does the narrator's father think something different from her? Explore what this sudden discrepancy suggests about the theme of the story.

Interpret the Story

7 Adichie named her story after Cell One, a place never glimpsed in the actual story. What is Cell One, literally in the story as well as figuratively? How does the existence of Cell One, and Nnamabia's stay there, influence the theme of the story? Consider how the theme would change if Nnamabia was just beaten up by the guards for his outcry.

CONTINUED FROM PAGE 261

"I figured part of what fiction was, or writing creatively, was to write your view of life." Conversation with Amy Tan

CRAFT AND THEME

Each element of craft—including plot, characterization, setting, and point of view—contributes to the thematic meaning of the tale. Theme connects fiction to the human experience, giving a single story relevance and reach. When we say that we read fiction for the truths or insights it offers—for its ideas—we are reading for theme.

"Fiction's a fairly tough vehicle if it's done right, and it can survive, and engender life in a reader's mind out of a fairly unpromising or difficult base." Conversation with John Updike

WHAT THEME IS NOT

Readers sometimes confuse theme with subject or situation. Take Hemingway's "The Short Happy Life of Francis Macomber" (chapter 7) as an example. We can say that its subject is big-game hunting, but that is not its theme. Similarly, if we say that Hemingway's story is about a man struggling with notions of manhood and cowardice and courage, we are accurately summarizing the situation, but we are still not stating a theme. This statement is too specific to the story to be thematic.

Readers also often confuse theme and plot. Plot tells us in a literal, specific sense *what happens* in a story. To summarize the plot of Hemingway's story, then, you might say that a husband and wife go big-game hunting. The husband struggles with his own cowardice when he faces a lion, but in the end, driven by the complex triangle of relationships among himself, his wife, and their hunting guide, he becomes shockingly bold. In contrast, a theme goes beyond the particulars of the story, revealing something general and universal.

"I'm sort of aware of themes emerging. Sometimes it's helpful for me not to know so much about what themes are coming up, because I think it can get in the way of my investigation." Conversation with Aimee Bender

You can further see the difference between plot and theme by considering other stories in this book. On the level of plot, Alice Munro's "An Ounce of Cure" (chapter 1) is about a high school girl, melancholy over an unrequited love, who gets drunk one night while babysitting. In terms of theme, however, the story raises important questions about adolescents and how they learn the ways of the world. Thematically, the story emphasizes the timeless issue of entry into the world of womanhood. These ideas are organic or intrinsic to the narrative; they don't declare themselves immediately or in a topic sentence.

Finally, a theme, especially in contemporary literature, rarely boils down to a life lesson. Because Hemingway's story encompasses such a complex mix of feelings and events, it would be difficult to reduce it to a simple message or "teaching moment," such as "Don't go big-game hunting if you don't know what you're doing." However, if you dig toward the ideas that link all its elements as well as their meanings, you could articulate a theme such as: "The Short Happy Life of Francis Macomber" is a story about marriage and manhood and the testing of courage in both.

WHAT THEME IS

Some stories do, of course, communicate lessons. "There's no place like home," Dorothy says at the end of *The Wizard of Oz*. This statement is indeed a theme of L. Frank Baum's tale of wonder and danger—because it goes beyond the specific details of the story to a general statement about human life. It is also thematic because it ties elements of the story together, including its beginning, when we see that Dorothy doesn't appreciate her home. Instead, she is frustrated and restless in the confines of that Kansas farm.

> "So [it] was very important for me to understand that people could write about rage and political action, whether it was metaphorical or literal." Conversation with Dagoberto Gilb

A literary work can, of course, put forward multiple themes. Consider Shakespeare's *Hamlet* (chapter 33). Depending on the lens through which we read the work, *Hamlet*'s themes can be seen as the anguish and consequences of indecision, the roots of suicidal melancholy, the repercussions of the Oedipal conflict, the perennial intermingling of power and corruption, or any combination of those ideas. By contrast, on the level of subject or plot, *Hamlet* could be summarized as a play about a man who loves his mother or a melancholic prince who can't make up his mind. The greatness of Shakespeare's play, of course, is that it is all this, and more: Shakespeare gives us a constantly shifting and surprising creation that cannot be reduced to any single reading or meaning.

THEMES THROUGH TIME

Some themes, or thematic questions, persist in literature through the ages. Do we determine the course of our own lives, or do the gods make our fates? From the epics of Homer onward, the Greeks put forward that great question, and fiction writers, poets, and playwrights have taken it up as a theme ever since. Some writers recast this theme as how to live a good life in a world full of turmoil and trouble. Cervantes did so in a semi-comical tone in his seventeenth-century novel *Don Quixote*.

Shakespeare presents a great variety of themes about love and power and the yearning for a meaningful life and asks the audience to draw its own conclusions. Similarly, contemporary story writers and novelists tend to dramatize the quandaries and troubles of their characters—but without drawing any conclusions or suggesting any moralistic answers.

In modern literature, many writers disdain the notion of theme. The pleasure the work offers to the reader becomes everything. Hemingway famously suggested that "if you want a message, go to Western Union." Nevertheless, as we've shown, themes emerge, even in the work of writers, such as Hemingway, who downplay their importance.

IDENTIFYING THEMES

An understanding of theme can come from a work's title. Titles may point to a major symbol, character, or subject from which themes develop, as do "The Jilting of Granny Weatherall," "The Death of Ivan Ilych," and "Why I Live at the P.O." They may also point to a central irony that is thematic, as do "The Short Happy Life of Francis Ma-comber" and "No One's a Mystery." The title "Who's Irish?" calls up the question of identity, while "Araby" conjures an exotic dream, and "The Rememberer" calls to mind the person left behind after a loss—all thematic concerns of those stories.

"I'm trying to create a world in which some of the strange stuff of our life comes to the surface, and we say, "I know that. The circumstances of my life are different from this person's story, but I know that feeling." Conversation with Barry Lopez

As you question the text, notice general statements the narrator or another character makes, because such observations may well offer insight into the writer's theme. In Herman Melville's classic novel *Moby-Dick,* the narrator asserts that a great book needs a great theme—and that a subject must be large to accommodate a large theme. A flea will not do. This novel describes the voyage of Captain Ahab and his crew on a hunt for the great whale. The novel has numerous and wide-ranging subjects and themes: whaling, society, nature, defiance, comradeship, and the human struggle for meaning. The narrator is Ishmael, the sole survivor of that voyage.

Tolstoy's novel *War and Peace,* a surpassing work of fiction that came out of the European realist tradition, demonstrates beyond dispute the truth of Melville's assertion about theme. In its very title, as well as its meticulous execution, it embraces everything there is for us in life and sets it down on the page.

All stories include insights from narrators or characters, and these insights often relate to theme. In Alice Munro's "An Ounce of Cure" (chapter 1), at tale's end, the first-person narrator who got drunk while babysitting says, "I was a self-conscious girl and I suffered a good deal from all the exposure. But the development of events on that Saturday night—that fascinated me." In John Updike's "A&P" (chapter 1), the young narrator realizes "how hard the world was going to be to me from here on in." In both cases, the characters acknowledge a new level of awareness and responsibility; it's not entirely welcome or pleasurable, but it seems to be inevitable, a rite of passage to adulthood.

In music a theme is a recurring motif. In these two stories the theme that recurs calls to our minds the troubles, turmoil, and sometime pleasures of coming of age. At the thematic level, these stories belong to a certain variety of fiction. Theme? Think of a horse as a theme among the general category of land mammals or a whale as a theme among the general category of sea mammals.

THEME IN CONTEXT

Works of serious fiction do not generally give up their meanings easily, and this is why we often feel intimidated or tentative when it comes to articulating a theme. So why, despite the risks and difficulties, should we strive to understand theme? Why not sim-

> "To write a true war story, to write a true story about anything, is difficult—on all kinds of levels. On the most simple level, truth evaporates." Conversation with Tim O'Brien

ply enjoy the plot and the characters and leave it at that? First of all, reading closely enough to gather the threads of theme reveals the greatest potential of a story. Second, delving into the world of a story for its theme can point up truths about the way the world works. Finally, reading with an eye for theme in fiction can teach a great deal about how to get at the essence of other kinds of texts that are required reading in college, and it helps create the skill of linkage and expressiveness in writing for college.

To understand theme, then, readers can ask questions that go beyond the surface and the events. In this chapter you will find four quite different short stories about quite different subjects. Each is rooted in a version of the author's experience. In each, the theme grows seamlessly from plot, setting, style, characterization, and all the other elements of the writer's craft. In each, theme emerges from our reading and questioning of the story in all its twists and permutations. As you saw with the excerpt from "Cell One" at the beginning of the chapter, the theme is not the frail back of the old man on the wet floor or the uneaten rice or even the tears in the brother's eyes. It is embedded in those details and emerges from them. It is the *why* of those details, the thread that ties them together and gives them meaning beyond this particular story and situation. It emerges from asking and answering questions such as, "*How* did these events affect Nnamabia?" and "*Why* did the sister feel that tenderness?" and "*What* do *I* feel when I think about that old man?" and "Why is this important?"

> "So it started off sort of as a memory, and it became, I guess, a story when I began thinking about just the ways in which victims can so easily become victimizers . . ."
> Conversation with ZZ Packer

Common themes in literature include the struggle of justice against injustice, as in Adichie's "Cell One"; comradeship and cooperation, as in "The Open Boat"; the ever-present cycles of life and death, as in "The Odour of Chrysanthemums"; and youth and age, as in "Interpreter of Maladies." But this is stating theme very broadly. Remember that truly identifying theme means paying attention to how that theme is addressed in a specific story. So, for example, you might amend the preceding sentence to say that "Cell One" is about how justice requires a person to think beyond his or her own selfish preoccupations. Or you might refine youth and age in "Interpreter of Maladies" to the theme that age does not necessarily bring wisdom, while youth is capable of being stained by worldly experience. You can probably think of many other broad themes— love and loss, power and powerlessness, freedom and responsibility, death and faith, and love and family. Leaving home, going on a journey, falling in love, proving one's heroism or goodness, making a new start in a new place, or joining with a new family group: these are just a few of the major themes that emerge from the stories in this book, and once you identify them, you can see their variations as you encounter these themes in other courses and in the world after college. In other words, all the most important ideas in life arise as themes in literature.

Stephen Crane (1871–1900)

Stephen Crane was born in Newark, New Jersey. By the time he was sixteen, he was already contributing articles to *The New York Tribune*. Crane moved to New York City, where he conducted extensive research for both fiction and nonfiction projects. To render an accurate account of life in poverty, for example, he lived in the slums while writing his first novel, *Maggie: A Girl of the Streets* (1893). This and Crane's other works—most famously *The Red Badge of Courage* (1895)—are examples of the literary style of *naturalism,* a technique that features characters carried along by fate in realistic, bleak circumstances. The indifference of nature is a popular theme in naturalistic fiction. The story that follows, "The Open Boat," was inspired by Crane's own experience on an 1896 expedition to Cuba. When the ship he was traveling on, the S.S. *Commodore,* was wrecked, Crane and other survivors drifted at sea for two weeks. During this time, he developed what would turn out to be a fatal strain of tuberculosis; he died in 1900. Crane wrote many stories about his experiences in Cuba, among them "Flanagan and His Short Filibustering Adventure" (1897) and "This Majestic Lie" (1900). A poet as well as a prose writer, Crane composed poetry that was experimental in its use of free verse and which put forward a dark view of the human condition. His career was unhappily brief, cut short by his death at age twenty-eight.

AS YOU READ As you read, notice the changes in the relationships among the four characters. Notice their peaks and valleys of hope and despair, of determination and exhaustion. What ideas do you perceive about the struggle for survival and the impact it has on these men?

FOR INTERACTIVE READING . . . Keep track of repeated lines as you read. Consider what effect these repetitions have on the tone of the story, and on your own memory of certain events or characters. Are there any similarities between the repeated phrases?

The Open Boat:

A Tale Intended to Be after the Fact: Being the Experience of Four Men from the Sunk Steamer Commodore (1897)

I

1 None of them knew the color of the sky. Their eyes glanced level, and were fastened upon the waves that swept toward them. These waves were of the hue of slate, save for the tops, which were of foaming white, and all of the men knew the colors of the sea. The horizon narrowed and widened, and dipped and rose, and at all times its edge was jagged with waves that seemed thrust up in points like rocks.

2 Many a man ought to have a bath-tub larger than the boat which here rode upon the sea. These waves were most wrongfully and barbarously abrupt and tall, and each froth-top was a problem in small boat navigation.

3 The cook squatted in the bottom and looked with both eyes at the six inches of gunwale which separated him from the ocean. His sleeves were rolled over his fat forearms, and the two flaps of his unbuttoned vest dangled as he bent to bail out the boat. Often he said: "Gawd! That was a narrow clip." As he remarked it he invariably gazed eastward over the broken sea.

4 The oiler, steering with one of the two oars in the boat, sometimes raised himself suddenly to keep clear of water that swirled in over the stern. It was a thin little oar and it seemed often ready to snap.

5 The correspondent, pulling at the other oar, watched the waves and wondered why he was there.

6 The injured captain, lying in the bow, was at this time buried in that profound dejection and indifference which comes, temporarily at least, to even the bravest and most enduring when, willy nilly, the firm fails, the army loses, the ship goes down. The mind of the master of a vessel is rooted deep in the timbers of her, though he command for a day or a decade, and this captain had on him the stern impression of a scene in the grays of dawn of seven turned faces, and later a stump of a top-mast with a white ball on it that slashed to and fro at the waves, went low and lower, and down. Thereafter there was something strange in his voice. Although steady, it was deep with mourning, and of a quality beyond oration or tears.

7 "Keep'er a little more south, Billie," said he.

8 "'A little more south,' sir," said the oiler in the stern.

9   A seat in this boat was not unlike a seat upon a bucking broncho, and, by the same token, a broncho is not much smaller. The craft pranced and reared, and plunged like an animal. As each wave came, and she rose for it, she seemed like a horse making at a fence outrageously high. The manner of her scramble over these walls of water is a mystic thing, and, moreover, at the top of them were ordinarily these problems in white water, the foam racing down from the summit of each wave, requiring a new leap, and a leap from the air. Then, after scornfully bumping a crest, she would slide, and race, and splash down a long incline and arrive bobbing and nodding in front of the next menace.

> The craft pranced and reared, and plunged like an animal.

10   A singular disadvantage of the sea lies in the fact that after successfully surmounting one wave you discover that there is another behind it just as important and just as nervously anxious to do something effective in the way of swamping boats. In a ten-foot dingey one can get an idea of the resources of the sea in the line of waves that is not probable to the average experience, which is never at sea in a dingey. As each slaty wall of water approached, it shut all else from the view of the men in the boat, and it was not difficult to imagine that this particular wave was the final outburst of the ocean, the last effort of the grim water. There was a terrible grace in the move of the waves, and they came in silence, save for the snarling of the crests.

11   In the wan light, the faces of the men must have been gray. Their eyes must have glinted in strange ways as they gazed steadily astern. Viewed from a balcony, the whole thing would doubtlessly have been weirdly picturesque. But the men in the boat had no time to see it, and if they had had leisure there were other things to occupy their minds. The sun swung steadily up the sky, and they knew it was broad day because the color of the sea changed from slate to emerald-green, streaked with amber lights, and the foam was like tumbling snow. The process of the breaking day was unknown to them. They were aware only of this effect upon the color of the waves that rolled toward them.

12   In disjointed sentences the cook and the correspondent argued as to the difference between a life-saving station and a house of refuge. The cook had said: "There's a house of refuge just north of the Mosquito Inlet Light, and as soon as they see us, they'll come off in their boat and pick us up."

13   "As soon as who see us?" said the correspondent.

"The crew," said the cook.

"Houses of refuge don't have crews," said the correspondent. "As I understand them, they are only places where clothes and grub are stored for the benefit of shipwrecked people. They don't carry crews."

"Oh, yes, they do," said the cook.

"No, they don't," said the correspondent.

"Well, we're not there yet, anyhow," said the oiler, in the stern.

"Well," said the cook, "perhaps it's not a house of refuge that I'm thinking of as being near Mosquito Inlet Light. Perhaps it's a life-saving station."

"We're not there yet," said the oiler, in the stern.

II

As the boat bounced from the top of each wave, the wind tore through the hair of the hatless men, and as the craft plopped her stern down again the spray slashed past them. The crest of each of these waves was a hill, from the top of which the men surveyed, for a moment, a broad tumultuous expanse, shining and wind-riven. It was probably splendid. It was probably glorious, this play of the free sea, wild with lights of emerald and white and amber.

"Bully good thing it's an on-shore wind," said the cook. "If not, where would we be? Wouldn't have a show."

"That's right," said the correspondent.

The busy oiler nodded his assent.

Then the captain, in the bow, chuckled in a way that expressed humor, contempt, tragedy, all in one. "Do you think we've got much of a show, now, boys?" said he.

Whereupon the three were silent, save for a trifle of hemming and hawing. To express any particular optimism at this time they felt to be childish and stupid, but they all doubtless possessed this sense of the situation in their mind. A young man thinks doggedly at such times. On the other hand, the ethics of their condition was decidedly against any open suggestion of hopelessness. So they were silent.

"Oh, well," said the captain, soothing his children, "we'll get ashore all right."

But there was that in his tone which made them think, so the oiler quoth: "Yes! If this wind holds!"

The cook was bailing: "Yes! If we don't catch hell in the surf."

Canton flannel gulls flew near and far. Sometimes they sat down on the sea, near patches of brown sea-weed that rolled over the waves with a movement like carpets on a line in a gale. The birds sat comfortably in groups, and they were envied by some in the dingey, for the wrath of the sea was no more to them than it was to a covey of prairie chickens a thousand miles inland. Often they came very close and stared at the men with black bead-like eyes. At these times they were uncanny and sinister in their unblinking scrutiny, and the men hooted angrily at them, telling them to be gone. One came, and evidently decided to alight on the top of the captain's head. The bird flew parallel to the boat and did not circle, but made short sidelong jumps in the air in chicken-fashion. His black eyes were wistfully fixed upon the captain's head. "Ugly brute," said the oiler to the bird. "You look as if you were made with a jack-knife." The cook and the correspondent swore darkly at the creature. The captain naturally wished to knock it away with the end of the heavy painter, but he did not dare do it, because anything resembling an emphatic gesture would have capsized this freighted boat, and so with his open hand, the captain gently and carefully waved the gull away. After it had been discouraged from the pursuit the captain breathed easier on account of his hair, and others breathed easier because the bird struck their minds at this time as being somehow grewsome and ominous.

In the meantime the oiler and the correspondent rowed. And also they rowed.

They sat together in the same seat, and each rowed an oar. Then the oiler took both oars; then the correspondent took both oars; then the oiler; then the correspondent. They rowed and they rowed. The very ticklish part of the business was when the time came for the reclining one in the stern to take his turn at the oars. By the very last star of truth, it is easier to steal eggs from under a hen than it was to change seats in the dingey. First the man in the stern slid his hand along the thwart and moved with care, as if he were of Sèvres. Then the man in the rowing seat slid his hand along the other thwart. It was all done with the most extraordinary care. As the two sidled past each other, the whole party kept watchful eyes on the coming wave, and the captain cried: "Look out now! Steady there!"

The brown mats of sea-weed that appeared from time to time were like islands, bits of earth. They were travelling, apparently, neither one way nor the other. They were, to all intents, stationary. They informed the men in the boat that it was making progress slowly toward the land.

The captain, rearing cautiously in the bow, after the dingey soared on a great swell, said that he had seen the light-house at Mosquito Inlet. Presently the cook remarked that he had seen it. The correspondent was at the oars, then, and for some reason he too wished to look at the light-house, but his back was toward the far shore and the waves were important, and for some time he could not seize an opportunity to turn his head. But at last there came a wave more gentle than the others, and when at the crest of it he swiftly scoured the western horizon.

"See it?" said the captain.

"No," said the correspondent, slowly, "I didn't see anything."

"Look again," said the captain. He pointed. "It's exactly in that direction."

At the top of another wave, the correspondent did as he was bid, and this time his eyes chanced on a small still thing on the edge of the swaying horizon. It was precisely like the point of a pin. It took an anxious eye to find a light-house so tiny.

"Think we'll make it, Captain?"

"If this wind holds and the boat don't swamp, we can't do much else," said the captain.

The little boat, lifted by each towering sea, and splashed viciously by the crests, made progress that in the absence of sea-weed was not apparent to those in her. She seemed just a wee thing wallowing, miraculously, top-up, at the mercy of five oceans. Occasionally, a great spread of water, like white flames, swarmed into her.

"Bail her, cook," said the captain, serenely.

"All right, captain," said the cheerful cook.

III

It would be difficult to describe the subtle brotherhood of men that was here established on the seas. No one said that it was so. No one mentioned it. But it dwelt in the boat, and each man felt it warm him. They were a captain, an oiler, a cook, and a correspondent, and they were friends, friends in a more curiously iron-bound degree than may be common. The hurt captain, lying against the water-jar in the bow, spoke always in a low voice and calmly, but he could never command a more ready and swiftly obedient crew than the motley three of the dingey. It was more than a mere recognition of what was best for the common safety. There was surely in it a quality that was personal and heartfelt. And after this devotion to the commander of the boat there was this comradeship that the correspondent, for instance, who had been taught to be cynical of men, knew even at the time was the best experience of his life. But no one said that it was so. No one mentioned it.

45   "I wish we had a sail," remarked the captain. "We might try my overcoat on the end of an oar and give you two boys a chance to rest." So the cook and the correspondent held the mast and spread wide the overcoat. The oiler steered, and the little boat made good way with her new rig. Sometimes the oiler had to scull sharply to keep a sea from breaking into the boat, but otherwise sailing was a success.

Slowly and beautifully the land loomed out of the sea.

46   Meanwhile the light-house had been growing slowly larger. It had now almost assumed color, and appeared like a little gray shadow on the sky. The man at the oars could not be prevented from turning his head rather often to try for a glimpse of this little gray shadow.

47   At last, from the top of each wave the men in the tossing boat could see land. Even as the light-house was an upright shadow on the sky, this land seemed but a long black shadow on the sea. It certainly was thinner than paper. "We must be about opposite New Smyrna," said the cook, who had coasted this shore often in schooners. "Captain, by the way, I believe they abandoned that life-saving station there about a year ago."

48   "Did they?" said the captain.

49   The wind slowly died away. The cook and the correspondent were not now obliged to slave in order to hold high the oar. But the waves continued their old impetuous swooping at the dingey, and the little craft, no longer under way, struggled woundily over them. The oiler or the correspondent took the oars again.

50   Shipwrecks are *apropos* of nothing. If men could only train for them and have them occur when the men had reached pink condition, there would be less drowning at sea. Of the four in the dingey none had slept any time worth mentioning for two days and two nights previous to embarking in the dingey, and in the excitement of clambering about the deck of a foundering ship they had also forgotten to eat heartily.

51   For these reasons, and for others, neither the oiler nor the correspondent was fond of rowing at this time. The correspondent wondered ingenuously how in the name of all that was sane could there be people who thought it amusing to row a boat. It was not an amusement; it was a diabolical punishment, and even a genius of mental aberrations could never conclude that it was anything but a horror to the muscles and a crime against the back. He mentioned to the boat in general how the amusement of rowing struck him, and the weary-faced oiler smiled in full sympathy. Previously to the foundering, by the way, the oiler had worked double-watch in the engine-room of the ship.

"Take her easy, now, boys," said the captain. "Don't spend yourselves. If we have to run a surf you'll need all your strength, because we'll sure have to swim for it. Take your time."

Slowly the land arose from the sea. From a black line it became a line of black and a line of white—trees and sand. Finally, the captain said that he could make out a house on the shore. "That's the house of refuge, sure," said the cook. "They'll see us before long, and come out after us."

The distant light-house reared high. "The keeper ought to be able to make us out now, if he's looking through a glass," said the captain. "He'll notify the life-saving people."

"None of those other boats could have got ashore to give word of the wreck," said the oiler, in a low voice. "Else the life-boat would be out hunting us."

Slowly and beautifully the land loomed out of the sea. The wind came again. It had veered from the northeast to the southeast. Finally, a new sound struck the ears of the men in the boat. It was the low thunder of the surf on the shore. "We'll never be able to make the light-house now," said the captain. "Swing her head a little more north, Billie."

"'A little more north,' sir," said the oiler.

Whereupon the little boat turned her nose once more down the wind, and all but the oarsman watched the shore grow. Under the influence of this expansion doubt and direful apprehension was leaving the minds of the men. The management of the boat was still most absorbing, but it could not prevent a quiet cheerfulness. In an hour, perhaps, they would be ashore.

Their back-bones had become thoroughly used to balancing in the boat and they now rode this wild colt of a dingey like circus men. The correspondent thought that he had been drenched to the skin, but happening to feel in the top pocket of his coat, he found therein eight cigars. Four of them were soaked with sea-water; four were perfectly scatheless. After a search, somebody produced three dry matches, and thereupon the four waifs rode impudently in their little boat, and with an assurance of an impending rescue shining in their eyes, puffed at the big cigars and judged well and ill of all men. Everybody took a drink of water.

IV

"Cook," remarked the captain, "there don't seem to be any signs of life about your house of refuge."

"No," replied the cook. "Funny they don't see us!"

A broad stretch of lowly coast lay before the eyes of the men. It was of dunes topped with dark vegetation. The roar of the surf was plain, and sometimes they could see the white lip of a wave as it spun up the

beach. A tiny house was blocked out black upon the sky. Southward, the slim light-house lifted its little gray length.

Tide, wind, and waves were swinging the dingey northward. "Funny they don't see us," said the men.

The surf's roar was here dulled, but its tone was, nevertheless, thunderous and mighty. As the boat swam over the great rollers, the men sat listening to this roar. "We'll swamp sure," said everybody.

It is fair to say here that there was not a life-saving station within twenty miles in either direction, but the men did not know this fact and in consequence they made dark and opprobrious remarks concerning the eyesight of the nation's life-savers. Four scowling men sat in the dingey and surpassed records in the invention of epithets.

"Funny they don't see us."

The light-heartedness of a former time had completely faded. To their sharpened minds it was easy to conjure pictures of all kinds of incompetency and blindness and, indeed, cowardice. There was the shore of the populous land, and it was bitter and bitter to them that from it came no sign.

"Well," said the captain, ultimately, "I suppose we'll have to make a try for ourselves. If we stay out here too long, we'll none of us have strength left to swim after the boat swamps."

And so the oiler, who was at the oars, turned the boat straight for the shore. There was a sudden tightening of muscles. There was some thinking.

"If we don't all get ashore—" said the captain. "If we don't all get ashore, I suppose you fellows know where to send news of my finish?"

They then briefly exchanged some addresses and admonitions. As for the reflections of the men, there was a great deal of rage in them. Perchance they might be formulated thus: "If I am going to be drowned—if I am going to be drowned—if I am going to be drowned, why, in the name of the seven mad gods who rule the sea, was I allowed to come thus far and contemplate sand and trees? Was I brought here merely to have my nose dragged away as I was about to nibble the sacred cheese of life? It is preposterous. If this old ninny-woman, Fate, cannot do better than this, she should be deprived of the management of men's fortunes. She is an old hen who knows not her intention. If she has decided to drown me, why did she not do it in the beginning and save me all this trouble. The whole affair is absurd. . . . But, no, she cannot mean to drown me. She dare not drown me. She cannot drown me. Not after all this work." Afterward the man might have had an impulse to shake his fist at the clouds: "Just you drown me, now, and then hear what I call you!" 71

The billows that came at this time were more formidable. They seemed always just about to break and roll over the little boat in a turmoil of foam. There was a preparatory and long growl in the speech of them. No mind unused to the sea would have concluded that the dingey could ascend these sheer heights in time. The shore was still afar. The oiler was a wily surfman. "Boys," he said, swiftly, "she won't live three minutes more and we're too far out to swim. Shall I take her to sea again, Captain?" 72

"Yes! Go ahead!" said the captain. 73

This oiler, by a series of quick miracles, and fast and steady oarsmanship, turned the boat in the middle of the surf and took her safely to sea again. 74

There was a considerable silence as the boat bumped over the furrowed sea to deeper water. Then somebody in gloom spoke. "Well, anyhow, they must have seen us from the shore by now." 75

The gulls went in slanting flight up the wind toward the gray desolate east. A squall, marked by dingy clouds, and clouds brick-red, like smoke from a burning building, appeared from the southeast. 76

"What do you think of those life-saving people? Ain't they peaches?" 77

"Funny they haven't seen us." 78

"Maybe they think we're out here for sport! Maybe they think we're fishin'. Maybe they think we're damned fools." 79

It was a long afternoon. A changed tide tried to force them southward, but wind and wave said northward. Far ahead, where coast-line, sea, and sky formed their mighty angle, there were little dots which seemed to indicate a city on the shore. 80

81   "St. Augustine?"

82   The captain shook his head. "Too near Mosquito Inlet."

83   And the oiler rowed, and then the correspondent rowed. Then the oiler rowed. It was a weary business. The human back can become the seat of more aches and pains than are registered in books for the composite anatomy of a regiment. It is a limited area, but it can become the theatre of innumerable muscular conflicts, tangles, wrenches, knots, and other comforts.

84   "Did you ever like to row, Billie?" asked the correspondent.

85   "No," said the oiler. "Hang it."

86   When one exchanged the rowing-seat for a place in the bottom of the boat, he suffered a bodily depression that caused him to be careless of everything save an obligation to wiggle one finger. There was cold sea-water swashing to and fro in the boat, and he lay in it. His head, pillowed on a thwart, was within an inch of the swirl of a wave crest, and sometimes a particularly obstreperous sea came in-board and drenched him once more. But these matters did not annoy him. It is almost certain that if the boat had capsized he would have tumbled comfortably out upon the ocean as if he felt sure it was a great soft mattress.

87   "Look! There's a man on the shore!"

88   "Where?"

89   "There! See 'im? See 'im?"

90   "Yes, sure! He's walking along."

91   "Now he's stopped. Look! He's facing us!"

92   "He's waving at us!"

93   "So he is! By thunder!"

94   "Ah, now, we're all right! Now we're all right! There'll be a boat out here for us in half an hour."

95   "He's going on. He's running. He's going up to that house there."

96   The remote beach seemed lower than the sea, and it required a searching glance to discern the little black figure. The captain saw a floating stick and they rowed to it. A bath-towel was by some weird chance in the boat, and, tying this on the stick, the captain waved it. The oarsman did not dare turn his head, so he was obliged to ask questions.

97   "What's he doing now?"

98   "He's standing still again. He's looking, I think. . . . There he goes again. Toward the house. . . . Now he's stopped again."

99   "Is he waving at us?"

100   "No, not now! he was, though."

101   "Look! There comes another man!"

102   "He's running."

103   "Look at him go, would you."

"Why, he's on a bicycle. Now he's met the other man. They're both waving at us. Look!"

"There comes something up the beach."

"What the devil is that thing?"

"Why, it looks like a boat."

"Why, certainly it's a boat."

"No, it's on wheels."

"Yes, so it is. Well, that must be the life-boat. They drag them along shore on a wagon."

"That's the life-boat, sure."

"No, by—, it's—it's an omnibus."

"I tell you it's a life-boat."

"It is not! It's an omnibus. I can see it plain. See? One of these big hotel omnibuses."

"By thunder, you're right. It's an omnibus, sure as fate. What do you suppose they are doing with an omnibus? Maybe they are going around collecting the life-crew, hey?"

"That's it, likely. Look! There's a fellow waving a little black flag. He's standing on the steps of the omnibus. There come those other two fellows. Now they're all talking together. Look at the fellow with the flag. Maybe he ain't waving it!"

"That ain't a flag, is it? That's his coat. Why, certainly, that's his coat."

"So it is. It's his coat. He's taken it off and is waving it around his head. But would you look at him swing it!"

"Oh, say, there isn't any life-saving station there. That's just a winter resort hotel omnibus that has brought over some of the boarders to see us drown."

"What's that idiot with the coat mean? What's he signaling, anyhow?"

"It looks as if he were trying to tell us to go north. There must be a life-saving station up there."

"No! He thinks we're fishing. Just giving us a merry hand. See? Ah, there, Willie."

"Well, I wish I could make something out of those signals. What do you suppose he means?"

"He don't mean anything. He's just playing."

"Well, if he'd just signal us to try the surf again, or to go to sea and wait, or go north, or go south, or go to hell—there would be some reason in it. But look at him. He just stands there and keeps his coat revolving like a wheel. The ass!"

"There come more people."

"Now there's quite a mob. Look! Isn't that a boat?"

"Where? Oh, I see where you mean. No, that's no boat."

"That fellow is still waving his coat."

"He must think we like to see him do that. Why don't he quit it. It don't mean anything."

1   "I don't know. I think he is trying to make us go north. It must be that there's a life-saving station there somewhere."

2   "Say, he ain't tired yet. Look at 'im wave."

3   "Wonder how long he can keep that up. He's been revolving his coat ever since he caught sight of us. He's an idiot. Why aren't they getting men to bring a boat out? A fishing boat—one of those big yawls—could come out here all right. Why don't he do something?"

4   "Oh, it's all right, now."

5   "They'll have a boat out here for us in less than no time, now that they've seen us."

6   A faint yellow tone came into the sky over the low land. The shadows on the sea slowly deepened. The wind bore coldness with it, and the men began to shiver.

7   "Holy smoke!" said one, allowing his voice to express his impious mood, "if we keep on monkeying out here! If we've got to flounder out here all night!"

8   "Oh, we'll never have to stay here all night! Don't you worry. They've seen us now, and it won't be long before they'll come chasing out after us."

9   The shore grew dusky. The man waving a coat blended gradually into this gloom, and it swallowed in the same manner the omnibus and the group of people. The spray, when it dashed uproariously over the side, made the voyagers shrink and swear like men who were being branded.

10   "I'd like to catch the chump who waved the coat. I feel like soaking him one, just for luck."

11   "Why? What did he do?"

12   "Oh, nothing, but then he seemed so damned cheerful."

13   In the meantime the oiler rowed, and then the correspondent rowed, and then the oiler rowed. Gray-faced and bowed forward, they mechanically, turn by turn, plied the leaden oars. The form of the light-house had vanished from the southern horizon, but finally a pale star appeared, just lifting from the sea. The streaked saffron in the west passed before the all-merging darkness, and the sea to the east was black. The land had vanished, and was expressed only by the low and drear thunder of the surf.

14   "If I am going to be drowned—if I am going to be drowned—if I am going to be drowned, why, in the name of the seven mad gods who rule the sea, was I allowed to come thus far and contemplate sand and trees? Was I brought here merely to have my nose dragged away as I was about to nibble the sacred cheese of life?"

15   The patient captain, drooped over the water-jar, was sometimes obliged to speak to the oarsman.

146   "Keep her head up! Keep her head up!"

147   "'Keep her head up,' sir." The voices were weary and low.

148   This was surely a quiet evening. All save the oars-man lay heavily and listlessly in the boat's bottom. As for him, his eyes were just capable of noting the tall black waves that swept forward in a most sinister silence, save for an occasional subdued growl of a crest.

149   The cook's head was on a thwart, and he looked without interest at the water under his nose. He was deep in other scenes. Finally he spoke. "Billie," he murmured, dreamfully, "what kind of pie do you like best?"

V

150   "Pie," said the oiler and the correspondent, agitatedly. "Don't talk about those things, blast you!"

151   "Well," said the cook, "I was just thinking about ham sandwiches, and—"

152   A night on the sea in an open boat is a long night. As darkness settled finally, the shine of the light, lifting from the sea in the south, changed to full gold. On the northern horizon a new light appeared, a small bluish gleam on the edge of the waters. These two lights were the furniture of the world. Otherwise there was nothing but waves.

153   Two men huddled in the stern, and distances were so magnificent in the dingey that the rower was enabled to keep his feet partly warmed by thrusting them under his companions. Their legs indeed extended far under the rowing-seat until they touched the feet of the captain forward. Sometimes, despite the efforts of the tired oarsman, a wave came piling into the boat, an icy wave of the night, and the chilling water soaked them anew. They would twist their bodies for a moment and groan, and sleep the dead sleep once more, while the water in the boat gurgled about them as the craft rocked.

154   The plan of the oiler and the correspondent was for one to row until he lost the ability, and then arouse the other from his sea-water couch in the bottom of the boat.

155   The oiler plied the oars until his head drooped forward, and the overpowering sleep blinded him. And he rowed yet afterward. Then he touched a man in the bottom of the boat, and called his name. "Will you spell me for a little while?" he said, meekly.

156   "Sure, Billie," said the correspondent, awakening and dragging himself to a sitting position. They exchanged places carefully, and the oiler, cuddling

A night on the sea in an open boat is a long night.

down in the sea-water at the cook's side, seemed to go to sleep instantly.

157   The particular violence of the sea had ceased. The waves came without snarling. The obligation of the man at the oars was to keep the boat headed so that the tilt of the rollers would not capsize her, and to preserve her from filling when the crests rushed past. The black waves were silent and hard to be seen in the darkness. Often one was almost upon the boat before the oarsman was aware.

158   In a low voice the correspondent addressed the captain. He was not sure that the captain was awake, although this iron man seemed to be always awake. "Captain, shall I keep her making for that light north, sir?"

159   The same steady voice answered him. "Yes. Keep it about two points off the port bow."

160   The cook had tied a life-belt around himself in order to get even the warmth which this clumsy cork contrivance could donate, and he seemed almost stove-like when a rower, whose teeth invariably chattered wildly as soon as he ceased his labor, dropped down to sleep.

161   The correspondent, as he rowed, looked down at the two men sleeping under foot. The cook's arm was around the oiler's shoulders, and, with their fragmentary clothing and haggard faces, they were the babes of the sea, a grotesque rendering of the old babes in the wood.

162   Later he must have grown stupid at his work, for suddenly there was a growling of water, and a crest came with a roar and a swash into the boat, and it was a wonder that it did not set the cook afloat in his life-belt. The cook continued to sleep, but the oiler sat up, blinking his eyes and shaking with the new cold.

163   "Oh, I'm awful sorry, Billie," said the correspondent, contritely.

164   "That's all right, old boy," said the oiler, and lay down again and was asleep.

165   Presently it seemed that even the captain dozed, and the correspondent thought that he was the one man afloat on all the oceans. The wind had a voice as it came over the waves, and it was sadder than the end.

166   There was a long, loud swishing astern of the boat, and a gleaming trail of phosphorescence, like blue flame, was furrowed on the black waters. It might have been made by a monstrous knife.

167   Then there came a stillness, while the correspondent breathed with the open mouth and looked at the sea.

168   Suddenly there was another swish and another long flash of bluish light, and this time it was alongside the boat, and might almost have been reached

with an oar. The correspondent saw an enormous fin speed like a shadow through the water, hurling the crystalline spray and leaving the long glowing trail.

The correspondent looked over his shoulder at the captain. His face was hidden, and he seemed to be asleep. He looked at the babes of the sea. They certainly were asleep. So, being bereft of sympathy, he leaned a little way to one side and swore softly into the sea.

But the thing did not then leave the vicinity of the boat. Ahead or astern, on one side or the other, at intervals long or short, fled the long sparkling streak, and there was to be heard the whiroo of the dark fin. The speed and power of the thing was greatly to be admired. It cut the water like a gigantic and keen projectile.

The presence of this biding thing did not affect the man with the same horror that it would if he had been a picnicker. He simply looked at the sea dully and swore in an undertone.

Nevertheless, it is true that he did not wish to be alone with the thing. He wished one of his companions to awaken by chance and keep him company with it. But the captain hung motionless over the water-jar and the oiler and the cook in the bottom of the boat were plunged in slumber.

VI

"If I am going to be drowned—if I am going to be drowned—if I am going to be drowned, why, in the name of the seven mad gods who rule the sea, was I allowed to come thus far and contemplate sand and trees?"

During this dismal night, it may be remarked that a man would conclude that it was really the intention of the seven mad gods to drown him, despite the abominable injustice of it. For it was certainly an abominable injustice to drown a man who had worked so hard, so hard. The man felt it would be a crime most unnatural. Other people had drowned at sea since galleys swarmed with painted sails, but still—

When it occurs to a man that nature does not regard him as important, and that she feels she would not maim the universe by disposing of him, he at first wishes to throw bricks at the temple, and he hates deeply the fact that there are no bricks and no temples. Any visible expression of nature would surely be pelleted with his jeers.

Then, if there be no tangible thing to hoot he feels, perhaps, the desire to confront a personification and indulge in pleas, bowed to one knee, and with hands supplicant, saying: "Yes, but I love myself."

A high cold star on a winter's night is the word he feels that she says to him. Thereafter he knows the pathos of his situation.

The men in the dingey had not discussed these matters, but each had, no doubt, reflected upon them in silence and according to his mind. There was seldom any expression upon their faces save the general one of complete weariness. Speech was devoted to the business of the boat.

To chime the notes of his emotion, a verse mysteriously entered the correspondent's head. He had even forgotten that he had forgotten this verse, but it suddenly was in his mind.

> A soldier of the Legion lay dying in Algiers,
> There was lack of woman's nursing, there was
> dearth of woman's tears;
> But a comrade stood beside him, and he took
> that comrade's hand,
> And he said: "I never more shall see my own,
> my native land."

In his childhood, the correspondent had been made acquainted with the fact that a soldier of the Legion lay dying in Algiers, but he had never regarded it as important. Myriads of his school-fellows had informed him of the soldier's plight, but the dinning had naturally ended by making him perfectly indifferent. He had never considered it his affair that a soldier of the Legion lay dying in Algiers, nor had it appeared to him as a matter for sorrow. It was less to him than the breaking of a pencil's point.

Now, however, it quaintly came to him as a human, living thing. It was no longer merely a picture of a few throes in the breast of a poet, meanwhile drinking tea and warming his feet at the grate; it was an actuality—stern, mournful, and fine.

The correspondent plainly saw the soldier. He lay on the sand with his feet out straight and still. While his pale left hand was upon his chest in an attempt to thwart the going of his life, the blood came between his fingers. In the far Algerian distance, a city of low square forms was set against a sky that was faint with the last sunset hues. The correspondent, plying the oars and dreaming of the slow and slower movements of the lips of the soldier, was moved by a profound and perfectly impersonal comprehension. He was sorry for the soldier of the Legion who lay dying in Algiers.

The thing which had followed the boat and waited had evidently grown bored at the delay. There was no longer to be heard the slash of the cut-water, and there was no longer the flame of the long trail. The light in the north still glimmered, but it was apparently no nearer to the boat. Sometimes the boom of the surf rang in the correspondent's ears, and he turned the craft seaward then and rowed harder. Southward, some one had evidently built a watch-fire on the beach. It was too low and too far to be seen, but it made a shimmering, roseate reflection upon the bluff back of it, and this could be discerned from the boat. The wind came stronger, and sometimes a wave suddenly raged out like a mountain-cat and there was to be seen the sheen and sparkle of a broken crest.

The captain, in the bow, moved on his water-jar and sat erect. "Pretty long night," he observed to the correspondent. He looked at the shore. "Those life-saving people take their time."

"Did you see that shark playing around?"

"Yes, I saw him. He was a big fellow, all right."

"Wish I had known you were awake."

Later the correspondent spoke into the bottom of the boat.

"Billie!" There was a slow and gradual disentanglement. "Billie, will you spell me?"

"Sure," said the oiler.

As soon as the correspondent touched the cold comfortable sea-water in the bottom of the boat, and had huddled close to the cook's life-belt he was deep in sleep, despite the fact that his teeth played all the popular airs. This sleep was so good to him that it was but a moment before he heard a voice call his name in a tone that demonstrated the last stages of exhaustion. "Will you spell me?"

"Sure, Billie."

The light in the north had mysteriously vanished, but the correspondent took his course from the wide-awake captain.

Later in the night they took the boat farther out to sea, and the captain directed the cook to take one oar at the stern and keep the boat facing the seas. He was to call out if he should hear the thunder of the surf. This plan enabled the oiler and the correspondent to get respite together. "We'll give those boys a chance to get into shape again," said the captain. They curled down and, after a few preliminary chatterings and trembles, slept once more the dead sleep. Neither knew they had bequeathed to the cook the company of another shark, or perhaps the same shark.

As the boat caroused on the waves, spray occasionally bumped over the side and gave them a fresh soaking, but this had no power to break their repose. The ominous slash of the wind and the water affected them as it would have affected mummies.

196 "Boys," said the cook, with the notes of every reluctance in his voice, "she's drifted in pretty close. I guess one of you had better take her to sea again." The correspondent, aroused, heard the crash of the toppled crests.

197 As he was rowing, the captain gave him some whiskey and water, and this steadied the chills out of him. "If I ever get ashore and anybody shows me even a photograph of an oar—"

198 At last there was a short conversation.

199 "Billie. . . . Billie, will you spell me?"

200 "Sure," said the oiler.

VII

201 When the correspondent again opened his eyes, the sea and the sky were each of the gray hue of the dawning. Later, carmine and gold was painted upon the waters. The morning appeared finally, in its splendor, with a sky of pure blue, and the sunlight flamed on the tips of the waves.

202 On the distant dunes were set many little black cottages, and a tall white wind-mill reared above them. No man, nor dog, nor bicycle appeared on the beach. The cottages might have formed a deserted village.

203 The voyagers scanned the shore. A conference was held in the boat. "Well," said the captain, "if no help is coming, we might better try a run through the surf right away. If we stay out here much longer we will be too weak to do anything for ourselves at all." The others silently acquiesced in this reasoning. The boat was headed for the beach. The correspondent wondered if none ever ascended the tall wind-tower, and if then they never looked seaward. This tower was a giant, standing with its back to the plight of the ants. It represented in a degree, to the correspondent, the serenity of nature amid the struggles of the individual—nature in the wind, and nature in the vision of men. She did not seem cruel to him then, nor beneficent, nor treacherous, nor wise. But she was indifferent, flatly indifferent. It is, perhaps, plausible that a man in this situation, impressed with the unconcern of the universe, should see the innumerable flaws of his life and have them taste wickedly in his mind and wish for another chance. A distinction between right and wrong seems absurdly clear to him, then, in this new ignorance of the grave-edge, and he understands

that if he were given another opportunity he would mend his conduct and his words, and be better and brighter during an introduction, or at a tea.

"Now, boys," said the captain, "she is going to swamp sure. All we can do is to work her in as far as possible, and then when she swamps, pile out and scramble for the beach. Keep cool now, and don't jump until she swamps sure."

It merely occurred to him that if he should drown it would be a shame.

The oiler took the oars. Over his shoulders he scanned the surf. "Captain," he said, "I think I'd better bring her about, and keep her head-on to the seas and back her in."

"All right, Billie," said the captain. "Back her in." The oiler swung the boat then and, seated in the stern, the cook and the correspondent were obliged to look over their shoulders to contemplate the lonely and indifferent shore.

The monstrous inshore rollers heaved the boat high until the men were again enabled to see the white sheets of water scudding up the slanted beach. "We won't get in very close," said the captain. Each time a man could wrest his attention from the rollers, he turned his glance toward the shore, and in the expression of the eyes during this contemplation there was a singular quality. The correspondent, observing the others, knew that they were not afraid, but the full meaning of their glances was shrouded.

As for himself, he was too tired to grapple fundamentally with the fact. He tried to coerce his mind into thinking of it, but the mind was dominated at this time by the muscles, and the muscles said they did not care. It merely occurred to him that if he should drown it would be a shame.

There were no hurried words, no pallor, no plain agitation. The men simply looked at the shore. "Now, remember to get well clear of the boat when you jump," said the captain.

Seaward the crest of a roller suddenly fell with a thunderous crash, and the long white comber came roaring down upon the boat.

"Steady now," said the captain. The men were silent. They turned their eyes from the shore to the comber and waited. The boat slid up the incline, leaped at the furious top, bounced over it, and swung down the long back of the wave. Some water had been shipped and the cook bailed it out.

But the next crest crashed also. The tumbling boiling flood of white water caught the boat and whirled it almost perpendicular. Water swarmed in from all sides. The correspondent had his hands on the gunwale at this time, and when the water entered at that place he swiftly withdrew his fingers, as if he objected to wetting them.

The little boat, drunken with this weight of water, reeled and snuggled deeper into the sea.

"Bail her out, cook! Bail her out," said the captain.

"All right, Captain," said the cook.

"Now, boys, the next one will do for us, sure," said the oiler. "Mind to jump clear of the boat."

The third wave moved forward, huge, furious, implacable. It fairly swallowed the dingey, and almost simultaneously the men tumbled into the sea. A piece of life-belt had lain in the bottom of the boat, and as the correspondent went overboard he held this to his chest with his left hand.

The January water was icy, and he reflected immediately that it was colder than he had expected to find it off the coast of Florida. This appeared to his dazed mind as a fact important enough to be noted at the time. The coldness of the water was sad; it was tragic. This fact was somehow so mixed and confused with his opinion of his own situation that it seemed almost a proper reason for tears. The water was cold.

When he came to the surface he was conscious of little but the noisy water. Afterward he saw his companions in the sea. The oiler was ahead in the race. He was swimming strongly and rapidly. Off to the correspondent's left, the cook's great white and corked back bulged out of the water, and in the rear the captain was hanging with his one good hand to the keel of the overturned dingey.

There is a certain immovable quality to a shore, and the correspondent wondered at it amid the confusion of the sea.

It seemed also very attractive, but the correspondent knew that it was a long journey, and he paddled leisurely. The piece of life-preserver lay under him, and sometimes he whirled down the incline of a wave as if he were on a hand-sled.

But finally he arrived at a place in the sea where travel was beset with difficulty. He did not pause swimming to inquire what manner of current had caught him, but there his progress ceased. The shore was set before him like a bit of scenery on a stage, and he looked at it and understood with his eyes each detail of it.

As the cook passed, much farther to the left, the captain was calling to him, "Turn over on your back, cook! Turn over on your back and use the oar."

"All right, sir." The cook turned on his back, and, paddling with an oar, went ahead as if he were a canoe.

Presently the boat also passed to the left of the correspondent with the captain clinging with one hand to the keel. He would have appeared like a man raising himself to look over a board fence, if it were not for the extraordinary gymnastics of the boat. The correspondent marvelled that the captain could still hold to it.

They passed on, nearer to shore—the oiler, the cook, the captain—and following them went the water-jar, bouncing gayly over the seas.

The correspondent remained in the grip of this strange new enemy—a current. The shore, with its white slope of sand and its green bluff, topped with little silent cottages, was spread like a picture before him. It was very near to him then, but he was impressed as one who in a gallery looks at a scene from Brittany or Holland.

He thought: "I am going to drown? Can it be possible? Can it be possible? Can it be possible?" Perhaps an individual must consider his own death to be the final phenomenon of nature.

But later a wave perhaps whirled him out of this small deadly current, for he found suddenly that he could again make progress toward the shore. Later still, he was aware that the captain, clinging with one hand to the keel of the dingey, had his face turned away from the shore and toward him, and was calling his name. "Come to the boat! Come to the boat!"

In his struggle to reach the captain and the boat, he reflected that when one gets properly wearied, drowning must really be a comfortable arrangement, a cessation of hostilities accompanied by a large degree of relief, and he was glad of it, for the main thing in his mind for some moments had been horror of the temporary agony. He did not wish to be hurt.

Presently he saw a man running along the shore. He was undressing with most remarkable speed. Coat, trousers, shirt, everything flew magically off him.

"Come to the boat," called the captain.

"All right, Captain." As the correspondent paddled, he saw the captain let himself down to bottom and leave the boat. Then the correspondent performed his one little marvel of the voyage. A large wave caught him and flung him with ease and supreme speed completely over the boat and far beyond it. It struck him even then as an event in gymnastics, and a true miracle of the sea. An overturned boat in the surf is not a plaything to a swimming man.

The correspondent arrived in water that reached only to his waist, but his condition did not enable him to stand for more than a moment. Each wave knocked him into a heap, and the under-tow pulled at him.

Then he saw the man who had been running and undressing, and undressing and running, come bounding into the water. He dragged ashore the cook, and then waded toward the captain, but the captain waved him away, and sent him to the correspondent. He was naked, naked as a tree in winter, but a halo was about his head, and he shone like a saint. He gave a strong pull, and a long drag, and a bully heave at the correspondent's hand. The correspondent, schooled in the minor formulae, said: "Thanks, old man." But suddenly the man cried: "What's that?" He pointed a swift finger. The correspondent said: "Go."

> In the shallows, face downward, lay the oiler.

236   In the shallows, face downward, lay the oiler. His forehead touched sand that was periodically, between each wave, clear of the sea.

237   The correspondent did not know all that transpired afterward. When he achieved safe ground he fell, striking the sand with each particular part of his body.

It was as if he had dropped from a roof, but the thud was grateful to him.

It seems that instantly the beach was populated with men with blankets, clothes, and flasks, and women with coffee-pots and all the remedies sacred to their minds. The welcome of the land to the men from the sea was warm and generous, but a still and dripping shape was carried slowly up the beach, and the land's welcome for it could only be the different and sinister hospitality of the grave.

When it came night, the white waves paced to and fro in the moonlight, and the wind brought the sound of the great sea's voice to the men on shore, and they felt that they could then be interpreters.

IF you liked the struggle between human beings and indifferent nature in "The Open Boat," you will also find it in a subtle form in Barry Lopez's "The Location of the River" in chapter 6.

GOING FURTHER   Similar struggles are also found in the short stories and novels of Joseph Conrad, which offer excellent examples of men adrift or with particular goals at sea and in strange lands. The novels of Ernest Hemingway offer similar themes.

Writing from Reading

Summarize

1 The story begins in the middle of things, with the crew already stranded at sea. What details does Crane provide about the shipwreck? Which does he leave out?

2 The swim for shore is described only from the correspondent's point of view. What details are there of the other passengers' swims? Use what information you have to piece together an explanation for the oiler's death.

Analyze Craft

3 Explain what Crane achieves by repeating certain passages of dialogue, reflection, and description within the story. What are some of these repeated lines and how many times do they recur? Do their meanings change with repetition or with the changing contexts in which they occur?

4 Only the oiler is ever called by his name in the story, and then never by the narrator. What is the significance of naming just the one character? Discuss this significance in light of Billie's death.

Analyze Voice

5 This story was written in 1897. Consider how the era in which it was written affected its language. What words appear that you don't know without the aid of a dictionary? Are there any that sound old-fashioned to you?

Synthesize Summary and Analysis

6 What is the narrator's role in this story? How would you describe the narrative distance? In other words, how close is the tale teller to the story and to its characters? Does the distance change over the course of the story? How?

Interpret the Story

7 There are several themes in "The Open Boat," including comrade-ship, the struggle to survive, and nature's indifference. Choose one of these, or identify another theme in the story, and discuss incidents in the story where the theme becomes most clear. Explain how Crane emphasizes the theme, citing passages from the text.

D. H. Lawrence (1855–1930)

David Herbert Lawrence was born in the coal mining district of Eastwood, Nottinghamshire, in the center of England, his father a hard-drinking coal miner and his mother a schoolteacher. He attended high school there and went on to Nottingham University, from which he graduated in his early twenties with a teaching certificate. A few years later, after he had moved to London and taken up a teaching position, he came under the tutelage of writer and magazine editor Ford Madox Ford, who published Lawrence in the *English Review*. By 1910 Lawrence had published his first novel, *The White Peacock,* and was entirely committed to the writing life. After the death of his mother from cancer, he published his autobiographical masterpiece *Sons and Lovers* (1913), and this was followed by other major titles such as *The Rainbow* (1915), *Women in Love* (1920), *Aaron's Rod* (1922), *The Plumed Serpent* (1926), and, perhaps most notoriously, *Lady Chatterley's Lover,* in 1928.

This last book created a scandal, because of its frank sexuality as well as its discussion of class; the "lady's" lover is a gardener, a man beneath her standing in society. In his personal life, as well, Lawrence broke social taboos; he ran off with Frieda von Richthofen Weekley, the wife of his university language professor. Thus began a period of extended travel with only occasional trips back to England; after the end of World War I, he and Frieda embraced a life of self-imposed exile. Mediterranean Europe, Australia, North America, and Mexico became Lawrence's shifting home grounds.

While he was living outside of England, a torrent of language poured forth from his pen; story after story, poem after poem, novel after novel appeared in rapid succession. He wrote travel books and articles and social tracts and plays. Lawrence used Aztec mythology, British social class distinctions, modern history—just about everything in modern life seemed useful to him in the composition of his work. Above all else—and this is truly why he matters to readers and writers of modern fiction—he found a forceful, direct, and appropriate diction by which to dramatize in physical form the volatile nature of interior states of mind and feeling. Upon his death from tuberculosis at the age of forty-four, he left behind one of the great modern bodies of work.

AS YOU READ   Notice the sights and sounds, both of machines and in the natural world, that come to you line by line. Do you get the sense that all of this information points toward some important event? Do you feel this as a premonition of something good or something bad about to occur?

The Odour of Chrysanthemums (1911)

I

1   The small locomotive engine, Number 4, came clanking, stumbling down from Selston with seven full waggons. It appeared round the corner with loud threats of speed, but the colt that it startled from among the gorse, which still flickered indistinctly in the raw afternoon, outdistanced it at a canter. A woman, walking up the railway line to Underwood, drew back into the hedge, held her basket aside, and watched the footplate of the engine advancing. The trucks thumped heavily past, one by one, with slow inevitable movement, as she stood insignificantly trapped between the jolting black waggons and the hedge; then they curved away towards the coppice where the withered oak leaves dropped noiselessly, while the birds, pulling at the scarlet hips beside the track, made off into the dusk that had already crept into the spinney. In the open, the smoke from the engine sank and cleaved to the rough grass. The fields were dreary and forsaken, and in the marshy strip that led to the whimsey, a reedy pit-pond, the fowls had already abandoned their run among the alders, to roost in the tarred fowl-house. The pit-bank loomed up beyond the pond, flames like red sores licking its ashy sides, in the afternoon's stagnant light. Just beyond rose the tapering chimneys and the clumsy black headstocks of Brinsley Colliery. The two wheels were spinning fast up against the sky, and the winding-engine rapped out its little spasms. The miners were being turned up.

2   The engine whistled as it came into the wide bay of railway lines beside the colliery, where rows of trucks stood in harbour.

3   Miners, single, trailing and in groups, passed like shadows diverging home. At the edge of the ribbed level of sidings squat a low cottage, three steps down from the cinder track. A large bony vine clutched at the house, as if to claw down the tiled roof. Round the bricked yard grew a few wintry primroses. Beyond, the long garden sloped down to a bush-covered brook course. There were some twiggy apple trees, winter-crack trees, and ragged cabbages. Beside the path hung dishevelled pink chrysanthemums, like pink cloths hung on bushes. A woman came stooping out of the felt-covered fowl-house, half-way down the garden. She closed and padlocked the door, then drew herself erect, having brushed some bits from her white apron.

4   She was a tall woman of imperious mien, handsome, with definite black eyebrows. Her smooth black hair was parted exactly. For a few moments she stood steadily watching the miners as they passed along the railway: then she turned towards the brook course. Her face was calm and set, her mouth was closed with disillusionment. After a moment she called:

5   "John!" There was no answer. She waited, and then said distinctly:

6   "Where are you?"

7   "Here!" replied a child's sulky voice from among the bushes. The woman looked piercingly through the dusk.

8   "Are you at that brook?" she asked sternly.

9   For answer the child showed himself before the raspberry-canes that rose like whips. He was a small, sturdy boy of five. He stood quite still, defiantly.

10   "Oh!" said the mother, conciliated. "I thought you were down at that wet brook—and you remember what I told you—"

11   The boy did not move or answer.

12   "Come, come on in," she said more gently, "it's getting dark. There's your grandfather's engine coming down the line!"

13   The lad advanced slowly, with resentful, taciturn movement. He was dressed in trousers and waistcoat of cloth that was too thick and hard for the size of the garments. They were evidently cut down from a man's clothes.

14   As they went slowly towards the house he tore at the ragged wisps of chrysanthemums and dropped the petals in handfuls along the path.

"Don't do that—it does look nasty," said his mother. He refrained, and she, suddenly pitiful, broke off a twig with three or four wan flowers and held them against her face. When mother and son reached the yard her hand hesitated, and instead of laying the flower aside, she pushed it in her apron-band. The mother and son stood at the foot of the three steps looking across the bay of lines at the passing home of the miners. The trundle of the small train was imminent. Suddenly the engine loomed past the house and came to a stop opposite the gate.

The engine-driver, a short man with round grey beard, leaned out of the cab high above the woman.

"Have you got a cup of tea?" he said in a cheery, hearty fashion.

It was her father. She went in, saying she would mash. Directly, she returned.

"I didn't come to see you on Sunday," began the little grey-bearded man.

"I didn't expect you," said his daughter.

The engine-driver winced; then, reassuming his cheery, airy manner, he said:

"Oh, have you heard then? Well, and what do you think—?"

"I think it is soon enough," she replied.

At her brief censure the little man made an impatient gesture, and said coaxingly, yet with dangerous coldness:

"Well, what's a man to do? It's no sort of life for a man of my years, to sit at my own hearth like a stranger. And if I'm going to marry again it may as well be soon as late—what does it matter to anybody?"

The woman did not reply, but turned and went into the house. The man in the engine-cab stood assertive, till she returned with a cup of tea and a piece of bread and butter on a plate. She went up the steps and stood near the footplate of the hissing engine.

"You needn't 'a' brought me bread an' butter," said her father. "But a cup of tea"—he sipped appreciatively—"it's very nice." He sipped for a moment or two, then: "I hear as Walter's got another bout on," he said.

"When hasn't he?" said the woman bitterly.

"I heered tell of him in the 'Lord Nelson' braggin' as he was going to spend that b—— afore he went: half a sovereign that was."

"When?" asked the woman.

"A' Sat'day night—I know that's true."

"Very likely," she laughed bitterly. "He gives me twenty-three shillings."

"Aye, it's a nice thing, when a man can do nothing with his money but make a beast of himself!" said the grey-whiskered man. The woman turned her head away. Her father swallowed the last of his tea and handed her the cup.

"Aye," he sighed, wiping his mouth. "It's a settler, it is—"

He put his hand on the lever. The little engine strained and groaned, and the train rumbled towards the crossing. The woman again looked across the metals. Darkness was settling over the spaces of the railway and trucks: the miners, in grey sombre groups, were still passing home. The winding-engine pulsed hurriedly, with brief pauses. Elizabeth Bates looked at the dreary flow of men, then she went indoors. Her husband did not come.

The kitchen was small and full of firelight; red coals piled glowing up the chimney mouth. All the life of the room seemed in the white, warm hearth and the steel fender reflecting the red fire. The cloth was laid for tea; cups glinted in the shadows. At the back, where the lowest stairs protruded into the room, the boy sat struggling with a knife and a piece of whitewood. He was almost hidden in the shadow. It was half-past four. They had but to await the father's coming to begin tea. As the mother watched her son's sullen little struggle with the wood, she saw herself in his silence and pertinacity; she saw the father in her child's indifference to all but himself. She seemed to be occupied by her husband. He had probably gone past his home, slung past his own door, to drink before he came in, while his dinner spoiled and wasted in waiting. She glanced at the clock, then took the potatoes to strain them in the yard. The garden and fields beyond the brook were closed in uncertain darkness. When she rose with the saucepan, leaving the drain steaming into the night behind her, she saw the yellow lamps were lit along the high road that went up the hill away beyond the space of the railway lines and the field.

Then again she watched the men trooping home, fewer now and fewer.

Indoors the fire was sinking and the room was dark red. The woman put her saucepan on the hob, and set a batter pudding near the mouth of the oven. Then she stood unmoving. Directly, gratefully, came quick young steps to the door. Someone hung on the latch a moment, then a little girl entered and began pulling off her outdoor things, dragging a mass of curls, just ripening from gold to brown, over her eyes with her hat.

39   Her mother chid her for coming late from school, and said she would have to keep her at home the dark winter days.

40   "Why, mother, it's hardly a bit dark yet. The lamp's not lighted, and my father's not home."

41   "No, he isn't. But it's a quarter to five! Did you see anything of him?"

42   The child became serious. She looked at her mother with large, wistful blue eyes.

43   "No, mother, I've never seen him. Why? Has he come up an' gone past, to Old Brinsley? He hasn't, mother, 'cos I never saw him."

44   "He'd watch that," said the mother bitterly, "he'd take care as you didn't see him. But you may depend upon it, he's seated in the 'Prince o' Wales.' He wouldn't be this late."

45   The girl looked at her mother piteously.

46   "Let's have our teas, mother, should we?" said she.

47   The mother called John to table. She opened the door once more and looked out across the darkness of the lines. All was deserted: she could not hear the winding-engines.

48   "Perhaps," she said to herself, "he's stopped to get some ripping done."

49   They sat down to tea. John, at the end of the table near the door, was almost lost in the darkness. Their faces were hidden from each other. The girl crouched against the fender slowly moving a thick piece of bread before the fire. The lad, his face a dusky mark on the shadow, sat watching her who was transfigured in the red glow.

50   "I do think it's beautiful to look in the fire," said the child.

51   "Do you?" said her mother. "Why?"

52   "It's so red, and full of little caves—and it feels so nice, and you can fair smell it."

53   "It'll want mending directly," replied her mother, "and then if your father comes he'll carry on and say there never is a fire when a man comes home sweating from the pit. A public-house is always warm enough."

54   There was silence till the boy said complainingly: "Make haste, our Annie."

55   "Well, I am doing! I can't make the fire do it no faster, can I?"

56   "She keeps wafflin' it about so's to make 'er slow," grumbled the boy.

57   "Don't have such an evil imagination, child," replied the mother.

> ## As she reached up, her figure displayed itself just rounding with maternity.

Soon the room was busy in the darkness with the crisp sound of crunching. The mother ate very little. She drank her tea determinedly, and sat thinking. When she rose her anger was evident in the stern unbending of her head. She looked at the pudding in the fender, and broke out:

"It is a scandalous thing as a man can't even come home to his dinner! If it's crozzled up to a cinder I don't see why I should care. Past his very door he goes to get to a public-house, and here I sit with his dinner waiting for him—"

She went out. As she dropped piece after piece of coal on the red fire, the shadows fell on the walls, till the room was almost in total darkness.

"I canna see," grumbled the invisible John. In spite of herself, the mother laughed.

"You know the way to your mouth," she said. She set the dustpan outside the door. When she came again like a shadow on the hearth, the lad repeated, complaining sulkily:

"I canna see."

"Good gracious!" cried the mother irritably, "you're as bad as your father if it's a bit dusk!"

Nevertheless she took a paper spill from a sheaf on the mantelpiece and proceeded to light the lamp that hung from the ceiling in the middle of the room. As she reached up, her figure displayed itself just rounding with maternity.

"Oh, mother—!" exclaimed the girl.

"What?" said the woman, suspended in the act of putting the lamp glass over the flame. The copper reflector shone handsomely on her, as she stood with uplifted arm, turning to face her daughter.

"You've got a flower in your apron!" said the child, in a little rapture at this unusual event.

"Goodness me!" exclaimed the woman, relieved. "One would think the house was afire." She replaced the glass and waited a moment before turning up the wick. A pale shadow was seen floating vaguely on the floor.

"Let me smell!" said the child, still rapturously, coming forward and putting her face to her mother's waist.

"Go along, silly!" said the mother, turning up the lamp. The light revealed their suspense so that the woman felt it almost unbearable. Annie was still bending at her waist. Irritably, the mother took the flowers out from her apron-band.

"Oh, mother—don't take them out!" Annie cried, catching her hand and trying to replace the sprig.

3 "Such nonsense!" said the mother, turning away. The child put the pale chrysanthemums to her lips, murmuring:

4 "Don't they smell beautiful!"

5 Her mother gave a short laugh.

6 "No," she said, "not to me. It was chrysanthemums when I married him, and chrysanthemums when you were born, and the first time they ever brought him home drunk, he'd got brown chrysanthemums in his button-hole."

7 She looked at the children. Their eyes and their parted lips were wondering. The mother sat rocking in silence for some time. Then she looked at the clock.

8 "Twenty minutes to six!" In a tone of fine bitter carelessness she continued: "Eh, he'll not come now till they bring him. There he'll stick! But he needn't come rolling in here in his pit-dirt, for *I* won't wash him. He can lie on the floor—Eh, what a fool I've been, what a fool! And this is what I came here for, to this dirty hole, rats and all, for him to slink past his very door. Twice last week—he's begun now—"

79 She silenced herself, and rose to clear the table.

80 While for an hour or more the children played, subduedly intent, fertile of imagination, united in fear of the mother's wrath, and in dread of their father's home-coming, Mrs. Bates sat in her rocking-chair making a "singlet" of thick cream-coloured flannel, which gave a dull wounded sound as she tore off the grey edge. She worked at her sewing with energy, listening to the children, and her anger wearied itself, lay down to rest, opening its eyes from time to time and steadily watching, its ears raised to listen. Sometimes even her anger quailed and shrank, and the mother suspended her sewing, tracing the footsteps that thudded along the sleepers outside; she would lift her head sharply to bid the children "hush," but she recovered herself in time, and the footsteps went past the gate, and the children were not flung out of their play-world.

81 But at last Annie sighed, and gave in. She glanced at her waggon of slippers, and loathed the game. She turned plaintively to her mother.

82 "Mother!"—but she was inarticulate.

83 John crept out like a frog from under the sofa. His mother glanced up.

84 "Yes," she said, "just look at those shirt-sleeves!"

85 The boy held them out to survey them, saying nothing. Then somebody called in a hoarse voice away down the line, and suspense bristled in the room, till two people had gone by outside, talking.

86 "It is time for bed," said the mother.

87 "My father hasn't come," wailed Annie plaintively. But her mother was primed with courage.

88 "Never mind. They'll bring him when he does come—like a log." She meant there would be no scene. "And he may sleep on the floor till he wakes himself. I know he'll not go to work to-morrow after this!"

89 The children had their hands and faces wiped with a flannel. They were very quiet. When they had put on their nightdresses, they said their prayers, the boy mumbling. The mother looked down at them, at the brown silken bush of intertwining curls in the nape of the girl's neck, at the little black head of the lad, and her heart burst with anger at their father who caused all three such distress. The children hid their faces in her skirts for comfort.

90 When Mrs. Bates came down, the room was strangely empty, with a tension of expectancy. She took up her sewing and stitched for some time without raising her head. Meantime her anger was tinged with fear.

II

91 The clock struck eight and she rose suddenly, dropping her sewing on her chair. She went to the stairfoot door, opened it, listening. Then she went out, locking the door behind her.

92 Something scuffled in the yard, and she started, though she knew it was only the rats with which the place was overrun. The night was very dark. In the great bay of railway lines, bulked with trucks, there was no trace of light, only away back she could see a few yellow lamps at the pit-top, and the red smear of the burning pit-bank on the night. She hurried along the edge of the track, then, crossing the converging lines, came to the stile by the white gates, whence she emerged on the road. Then the fear which had led her shrank. People were walking up to New Brinsley; she saw the lights in the houses; twenty yards further on were the broad windows of the "Prince of Wales," very warm and bright, and the loud voices of men could be heard distinctly. What a fool she had been to imagine that anything had happened to him! He was merely drinking over there at the "Prince of Wales." She faltered. She had never yet been to fetch him, and she never would go. So she continued her walk towards the long straggling line of houses, standing blank on the highway. She entered a passage between the dwellings.

93 "Mr. Rigley?—Yes! Did you want him? No, he's not in at this minute."

94 The raw-boned woman leaned forward from her dark scullery and peered at the other, upon whom fell a dim light through the blind of the kitchen window.

95 "Is it Mrs. Bates?" she asked in a tone tinged with respect.

96 "Yes. I wondered if your Master was at home. Mine hasn't come yet."

97 "'Asn't 'e! Oh, Jack's been 'ome an' 'ad 'is dinner an' gone out. 'E's just gone for 'alf an hour afore bedtime. Did you call at the 'Prince of Wales'?"

98 "No—"

99 "No, you didn't like—! It's not very nice." The other woman was indulgent. There was an awkward pause. "Jack never said nothink about—about your Mester," she said.

100 "No!—I expect he's stuck in there!"

101 Elizabeth Bates said this bitterly, and with recklessness. She knew that the woman across the yard was standing at her door listening, but she did not care. As she turned:

102 "Stop a minute! I'll just go an' ask Jack if 'e knows anythink," said Mrs. Rigley.

103 "Oh, no—I wouldn't like to put—!"

104 "Yes, I will, if you'll just step inside an' see as th' childer doesn't come downstairs and set theirselves afire."

105 Elizabeth Bates, murmuring a remonstrance, stepped inside. The other woman apologized for the state of the room.

106 The kitchen needed apology. There were little frocks and trousers and childish undergarments on the squab and on the floor, and a litter of playthings everywhere. On the black American cloth of the table were pieces of bread and cake, crusts, slops, and a teapot with cold tea.

107 "Eh, ours is just as bad," said Elizabeth Bates, looking at the woman, not at the house. Mrs. Rigley put a shawl over her head and hurried out, saying:

108 "I shanna be a minute."

109 The other sat, noting with faint disapproval the general untidiness of the room. Then she fell to counting the shoes of various sizes scattered over the floor. There were twelve. She sighed and said to herself, "No wonder!"—glancing at the litter. There came the scratching of two pairs of feet on the yard, and the Rigleys entered. Elizabeth Bates rose. Rigley was a big man, with very large bones. His head looked particularly bony. Across his temple was a blue scar, caused by a wound got in the pit, a wound in which the coal-dust remained blue like tattooing.

"'Asna 'e come whoam yit?" asked the man, without any form of greeting, but with deference and sympathy. "I couldna say wheer he is—'e's non ower theer!"—he jerked his head to signify the "Prince of Wales."

"'E's 'appen gone up to th' 'Yew,'" said Mrs. Rigley.

There was another pause. Rigley had evidently something to get off his mind:

"Ah left 'im finishin' a stint," he began. "Loose-all 'ad bin gone about ten minutes when we com'n away, an' I shouted, 'Are ter comin', Walt?' an' 'e said, 'Go on, Ah shanna be but a'ef a minnit,' so we com'n ter th' bottom, me an' Bowers, thinkin' as 'e wor just behint, an' 'ud come up i' th' next bantle—"

He stood perplexed, as if answering a charge of deserting his mate. Elizabeth Bates, now again certain of disaster, hastened to reassure him:

"I expect 'e's gone up to th' 'Yew Tree,' as you say. It's not the first time. I've fretted myself into a fever before now. He'll come home when they carry him."

"Ay, isn't it too bad!" deplored the other woman.

"I'll just step up to Dick's an' see if 'e is theer," offered the man, afraid of appearing alarmed, afraid of taking liberties.

"Oh, I wouldn't think of bothering you that far," said Elizabeth Bates, with emphasis, but he knew she was glad of his offer.

As they stumbled up the entry, Elizabeth Bates heard Rigley's wife run across the yard and open her neighbour's door. At this, suddenly all the blood in her body seemed to switch away from her heart.

"Mind!" warned Rigley. "Ah've said many a time as Ah'd fill up them ruts in this entry, sumb'dy 'll be breakin' their legs yit."

She recovered herself and walked quickly along with the miner.

"I don't like leaving the children in bed, and nobody in the house," she said.

"No, you dunna!" he replied courteously. They were soon at the gate of the cottage.

"Well, I shanna be many minnits. Dunna you be frettin' now, 'e'll be all right," said the butty.

"Thank you very much, Mr. Rigley," she replied.

"You're welcome!" he stammered, moving away. "I shanna be many minnits."

The house was quiet. Elizabeth Bates took off her hat and shawl, and rolled back the rug. When she had finished, she sat down. It was a few minutes past nine. She was startled by the rapid chuff of the winding-engine at the pit, and the sharp whirr of the brakes on the rope as it descended. Again she felt the painful sweep of her blood, and she put her hand to her side, saying aloud, "Good gracious!—it's only the nine o'clock deputy going down," rebuking herself.

She sat still, listening. Half an hour of this, and she was wearied out.

"What am I working myself up like this for?" she said pitiably to herself, "I s'll only be doing myself some damage."

She took out her sewing again.

At a quarter to ten there were footsteps. One person! She watched for the door to open. It was an elderly woman, in a black bonnet and a black woollen shawl—his mother. She was about sixty years old, pale, with blue eyes, and her face all wrinkled and lamentable. She shut the door and turned to her daughter-in-law peevishly.

"Eh, Lizzie, whatever shall we do, whatever shall we do!" she cried.

Elizabeth drew back a little, sharply.

"What is it, mother?" she said.

The elder woman seated herself on the sofa.

"I don't know, child, I can't tell you!"—she shook her head slowly. Elizabeth sat watching her, anxious and vexed.

"I don't know," replied the grandmother, sighing very deeply. "There's no end to my troubles, there isn't. The things I've gone through, I'm sure it's enough—!" She wept without wiping her eyes, the tears running.

"But, mother," interrupted Elizabeth, "what do you mean? What is it?"

The grandmother slowly wiped her eyes. The fountains of her tears were stopped by Elizabeth's directness. She wiped her eyes slowly.

"Poor child! Eh, you poor thing!" she moaned. "I don't know what we're going to do, I don't—and you as you are—it's a thing, it is indeed!"

Elizabeth waited.

"Is he dead?" she asked, and at the words her heart swung violently, though she felt a slight flush of shame at the ultimate extravagance of the question. Her words sufficiently frightened the old lady, almost brought her to herself.

"Don't say so, Elizabeth! We'll hope it's not as bad as that; no, may the Lord spare us that, Elizabeth. Jack Rigley came just as I was sittin' down to a glass afore going to bed, an' 'e said, ''Appen you'll go down th' line, Mrs. Bates. Walt's had an accident. 'Appen you'll go an' sit wi' 'er till we can get him home.' I hadn't time to ask him a word afore he was gone. An' I put my bonnet on an' come straight down, Lizzie. I thought to myself, 'Eh, that poor blessed child, if anybody should come an' tell her of a sudden, there's no knowin' what'll 'appen to 'er.' You mustn't let it upset you, Lizzie—or you

know what to expect. How long is it, six months—or is it five, Lizzie? Ay!"—the old woman shook her head—"time slips on, it slips on! Ay!"

Elizabeth's thoughts were busy elsewhere. If he was killed—would she be able to manage on the little pension and what she could earn?—she counted up rapidly. If he was hurt—they wouldn't take him to the hospital—how tiresome he would be to nurse!—but perhaps she'd be able to get him away from the drink and his hateful ways. She would—while he was ill. The tears offered to come to her eyes at the picture. But what sentimental luxury was this she was beginning? She turned to consider the children. At any rate she was absolutely necessary for them. They were her business.

"Ay!" repeated the old woman, "it seems but a week or two since he brought me his first wages. Ay—he was a good lad, Elizabeth, he was, in his way. I don't know why he got to be such a trouble, I don't. He was a happy lad at home, only full of spirits. But there's no mistake he's been a handful of trouble, he has! I hope the Lord'll spare him to mend his ways. I hope so, I hope so. You've had a sight o' trouble with him, Elizabeth, you have indeed. But he was a jolly enough lad wi' me, he was, I can assure you. I don't know how it is. . . ."

The old woman continued to muse aloud, a monotonous irritating sound, while Elizabeth thought concentratedly, startled once, when she heard the winding-engine chuff quickly, and the brakes skirr with a shriek. Then she heard the engine more slowly, and the brakes made no sound. The old woman did not notice. Elizabeth waited in suspense. The mother-in-law talked, with lapses into silence.

"But he wasn't your son, Lizzie, an' it makes a difference. Whatever he was, I remember him when he was little, an' I learned to understand him and to make allowances. You've got to make allowances for them—"

It was half-past ten, and the old woman was saying: "But it's trouble from beginning to end; you're never too old for trouble, never too old for that—" when the gate banged back, and there were heavy feet on the steps.

"I'll go, Lizzie, let me go," cried the old woman, rising. But Elizabeth was at the door. It was a man in pit-clothes.

"They're bringin' 'im, Missis," he said. Elizabeth's heart halted a moment. Then it surged on again, almost suffocating her.

"Is he—is it bad?" she asked.

The man turned away, looking at the darkness:

153 "The doctor says 'e'd been dead hours. 'E saw 'im i' th' lamp-cabin."

154 The old woman, who stood just behind Elizabeth, dropped into a chair, and folded her hands, crying: "Oh, my boy, my boy!"

155 "Hush!" said Elizabeth, with a sharp twitch of a frown. "Be still, mother, don't waken th' children: I wouldn't have them down for anything!"

156 The old woman moaned softly, rocking herself. The man was drawing away. Elizabeth took a step forward.

157 "How was it?" she asked.

158 "Well, I couldn't say for sure," the man replied, very ill at ease. "'E wor finishin' a stint an' th' butties 'ad gone, an' a lot o' stuff come down atop 'n 'im."

159 "And crushed him?" cried the widow, with a shudder.

160 "No," said the man, "it fell at th' back of 'im. 'E wor under th' face, an' it niver touched 'im. It shut 'im in. It seems 'e wor smothered."

161 Elizabeth shrank back. She heard the old woman behind her cry:

162 "What?—what did 'e say it was?"

163 The man replied, more loudly: "'E wor smothered!"

164 Then the old woman wailed aloud, and this relieved Elizabeth.

165 "Oh, mother," she said, putting her hand on the old woman, "don't waken th' children, don't waken th' children."

166 She wept a little, unknowing, while the old mother rocked herself and moaned. Elizabeth remembered that they were bringing him home, and she must be ready. "They'll lay him in the parlour," she said to herself, standing a moment pale and perplexed.

167 Then she lighted a candle and went into the tiny room. The air was cold and damp, but she could not make a fire, there was no fireplace. She set down the candle and looked round. The candlelight glittered on the lustre-glasses, on the two vases that held some of the pink chrysanthemums, and on the dark mahogany. There was a cold, deathly smell of chrysanthemums in the room. Elizabeth stood looking at the flowers. She turned away, and calculated whether there would be room to lay him on the floor, between the couch and the chiffonier. She pushed the chairs aside. There would be room to lay him down and to step round him. Then she fetched the old red tablecloth, and another old cloth, spreading them down to save her bit of carpet. She shivered on leaving the parlour; so, from the dresser-drawer she took a clean shirt and put it at the fire to air. All the time her mother-in-law was rocking herself in the chair and moaning.

There was a cold, deathly smell

of chrysanthemums

in the room.

"You'll have to move from there, mother," said Elizabeth. "They'll be bringing him in. Come in the rocker."

The old mother rose mechanically, and seated herself by the fire, continuing to lament. Elizabeth went into the pantry for another candle, and there, in the little penthouse under the naked tiles, she heard them coming. She stood still in the pantry doorway, listening. She heard them pass the end of the house, and come awkwardly down the three steps, a jumble of shuffling footsteps and muttering voices. The old woman was silent. The men were in the yard.

Then Elizabeth heard Matthews, the manager of the pit, say: "You go in first, Jim. Mind!"

The door came open, and the two women saw a collier backing into the room, holding one end of a stretcher, on which they could see the nailed pit-boots of the dead man. The two carriers halted, the man at the head stooping to the lintel of the door.

"Wheer will you have him?" asked the manager, a short, white-bearded man.

Elizabeth roused herself and came from the pantry carrying the unlighted candle.

"In the parlour," she said.

"In there, Jim!" pointed the manager, and the carriers backed round into the tiny room. The coat with which they had covered the body fell off as they awkwardly turned through the two doorways, and the women saw their man, naked to the waist, lying stripped for work. The old woman began to moan in a low voice of horror.

"Lay th' stretcher at th' side," snapped the manager, "an' put 'im on th' cloths. Mind now, mind! Look you now—!"

One of the men had knocked off a vase of chrysanthemums. He stared awkwardly, then they set down the stretcher. Elizabeth did not look at her husband. As soon as she could get in the room, she went and picked up the broken vase and the flowers.

"Wait a minute!" she said.

The three men waited in silence while she mopped up the water with a duster.

"Eh, what a job, what a job, to be sure!" the manager was saying, rubbing his brow with trouble and perplexity. "Never knew such a thing in my life, never! He'd no business to ha' been left. I never knew such a thing in my life! Fell over him clean as a whistle, an' shut him in. Not four foot of space, there wasn't—yet it scarce bruised him."

He looked down at the dead man, lying prone, half naked, all grimed with coal-dust.

"'Sphyxiated,' the doctor said. It *is* the most terrible job I've ever known. Seems as if it was done o' purpose. Clean over him, an' shut 'im in, like a mouse-trap"—he made a sharp, descending gesture with his hand.

The colliers standing by jerked aside their heads in hopeless comment.

The horror of the thing bristled upon them all.

Then they heard the girl's voice upstairs calling shrilly: "Mother, mother—who is it? Mother, who is it?"

Elizabeth hurried to the foot of the stairs and opened the door:

"Go to sleep!" she commanded sharply. "What are you shouting about? Go to sleep at once—there's nothing—"

Then she began to mount the stairs. They could hear her on the boards, and on the plaster floor of the little bedroom. They could hear her distinctly:

"What's the matter now?—what's the matter with you, silly thing?"—her voice was much agitated, with an unreal gentleness.

"I thought it was some men come," said the plaintive voice of the child. "Has he come?"

"Yes, they've brought him. There's nothing to make a fuss about. Go to sleep now, like a good child."

They could hear her voice in the bedroom, they waited whilst she covered the children under the bedclothes.

"Is he drunk?" asked the girl, timidly, faintly.

"No! No—he's not! He—he's asleep."

"Is he asleep downstairs?"

"Yes—and don't make a noise."

There was silence for a moment, then the men heard the frightened child again:

"What's that noise?"

"It's nothing, I tell you, what are you bothering for?"

The noise was the grandmother moaning. She was oblivious of everything, sitting on her chair rocking and moaning. The manager put his hand on her arm and bade her "Sh—sh!!"

The old woman opened her eyes and looked at him. She was shocked by this interruption, and seemed to wonder.

"What time is it?"—the plaintive thin voice of the child, sinking back unhappily into sleep, asked this last question.

"Ten o'clock," answered the mother more softly. Then she must have bent down and kissed the children.

Matthews beckoned to the men to come away. They put on their caps and took up the stretcher. Step-ping over the body, they tiptoed out of the house. None of them spoke till they were far from the wakeful children.

When Elizabeth came down she found her mother alone on the parlour floor, leaning over the dead man, the tears dropping on him.

"We must lay him out," the wife said. She put on the kettle, then returning knelt at the feet, and began to unfasten the knotted leather laces. The room was clammy and dim with only one candle, so that she had to bend her face almost to the floor. At last she got off the heavy boots and put them away.

"You must help me now," she whispered to the old woman. Together they stripped the man.

When they arose, saw him lying in the naïve dignity of death, the women stood arrested in fear and respect. For a few moments they remained still, looking down, the old mother whimpering. Elizabeth felt countermanded. She saw him, how utterly inviolable he lay in himself. She had nothing to do with him. She could not accept it. Stooping, she laid her hand on him, in claim. He was still warm, for the mine was hot where he had died. His mother had his face between her hands, and was murmuring incoherently. The old tears fell in succession as drops from wet leaves; the mother was not weeping, merely her tears flowed. Elizabeth embraced the body of her husband, with cheek and lips. She seemed to be listening, inquiring, trying to get some connection. But she could not. She was driven away. He was impregnable.

She rose, went into the kitchen, where she poured warm water into a bowl, brought soap and flannel and a soft towel.

"I must wash him," she said.

Then the old mother rose stiffly, and watched Elizabeth as she carefully washed his face, carefully brushing the big blond moustache from his mouth with the flannel. She was afraid with a bottomless fear, so she ministered to him. The old woman, jealous, said:

"Let me wipe him!"—and she kneeled on the other side drying slowly as Elizabeth washed, her big black bonnet sometimes brushing the dark head of her daughter-in-law. They worked thus in silence for a long time. They never forgot it was death, and the touch of the man's dead body gave them strange emotions, different in each of the women; a great dread possessed them both, the mother felt the lie was given

213 to her womb, she was denied; the wife felt the utter isolation of the human soul, the child within her was a weight apart from her.

213 At last it was finished. He was a man of handsome body, and his face showed no traces of drink. He was blond, full-fleshed, with fine limbs. But he was dead.

214 "Bless him," whispered his mother, looking always at his face, and speaking out of sheer terror. "Dear lad—bless him!" She spoke in a faint, sibilant ecstasy of fear and mother love.

215 Elizabeth sank down again to the floor, and put her face against his neck, and trembled and shuddered. But she had to draw away again. He was dead, and her living flesh had no place against his. A great dread and weariness held her: she was so unavailing. Her life was gone like this.

216 "White as milk he is, clear as a twelve-month baby, bless him, the darling!" the old mother murmured to herself. "Not a mark on him, clear and clean and white, beautiful as ever a child was made," she murmured with pride. Elizabeth kept her face hidden.

217 "He went peaceful, Lizzie—peaceful as sleep. Isn't he beautiful, the lamb? Ay—he must ha' made his peace, Lizzie. 'Appen he made it all right, Lizzie, shut in there. He'd have time. He wouldn't look like this if he hadn't made his peace. The lamb, the dear lamb. Eh, but he had a hearty laugh. I loved to hear it. He had the heartiest laugh, Lizzie, as a lad—"

218 Elizabeth looked up. The man's mouth was fallen back, slightly open under the cover of the moustache. The eyes, half shut, did not show glazed in the obscurity. Life with its smoky burning gone from him, had left him apart and utterly alien to her. And she knew what a stranger he was to her. In her womb was ice of fear, because of this separate stranger with whom she had been living as one flesh. Was this what it all meant—utter, intact separateness, obscured by heat of living? In dread she turned her face away. The fact was too deadly. There had been nothing between them, and yet they had come together, exchanging their nakedness repeatedly. Each time he had taken her, they had been two isolated beings, far apart as now. He was no more responsible than she. The child was like ice in her womb. For as she looked at the dead man, her mind, cold and detached, said clearly: "Who am I? What have I been doing? I have been fighting a husband who did not exist. *He* existed all the time. What wrong have I done? What was that I have been living with? There lies the reality, this man." And her

soul died in her for fear: she knew she had never seen him, he had never seen her, they had met in the dark and had fought in the dark, not knowing whom they met nor whom they fought. And now she saw, and turned silent in seeing. For she had been wrong. She had said he was something he was not; she had felt familiar with him. Whereas he was apart all the while, living as she never lived, feeling as she never felt.

In fear and shame she looked at his naked body, that she had known falsely. And he was the father of her children. Her soul was torn from her body and stood apart. She looked at his naked body and was ashamed, as if she had denied it. After all, it was itself. It seemed awful to her. She looked at his face, and she turned her own face to the wall. For his look was other than hers, his way was not her way. She had denied him what he was—she saw it now. She had refused him as himself. And this had been her life, and his life. She was grateful to death, which restored the truth. And she knew she was not dead.

And all the while her heart was bursting with grief and pity for him. What had he suffered? What stretch of horror for this helpless man! She was rigid with agony. She had not been able to help him. He had been cruelly injured, this naked man, this other being, and she could make no reparation. There were the children—but the children belonged to life. This dead man had nothing to do with them. He and she were only channels through which life had flowed to issue in the children. She was a mother—but how awful she knew it now to have been a wife. And he, dead now, how awful he must have felt it to be a husband. She felt that in the next world he would be a stranger to her. If they met there, in the beyond, they would only be ashamed of what had been before. The children had come, for some mysterious reason, out of both of them. But the children did not unite them. Now he was dead, she knew how eternally he was apart from her, how eternally he had nothing more to do with her. She saw this episode of her life closed. They had denied each other in life. Now he had withdrawn. An anguish came over her. It was finished then: it had become hopeless between them long before he died. Yet he had been her husband. But how little!

"Have you got his shirt, 'Lizabeth?"

Elizabeth turned without answering, though she strove to weep and behave as her mother-in-law expected. But she could not, she was silenced. She went into the kitchen and returned with the garment.

> She felt that in the next world he would be a stranger to her.

"It is aired," she said, grasping the cotton shirt here and there to try. She was almost ashamed to handle him; what right had she or any one to lay hands on him; but her touch was humble on his body. It was hard work to clothe him. He was so heavy and inert. A terrible dread gripped her all the while: that he could be so heavy and utterly inert, unresponsive, apart. The horror of the distance between them was almost too much for her—it was so infinite a gap she must look across.

At last it was finished. They covered him with a 224 sheet and left him lying, with his face bound. And she fastened the door of the little parlour, lest the children should see what was lying there. Then, with peace sunk heavy on her heart, she went about making tidy the kitchen. She knew she submitted to life, which was her immediate master. But from death, her ultimate master, she winced with fear and shame.

IF you like the Lawrence story, you might enjoy comparing it with John Steinbeck's "The Chrysanthemums" (chapter 12) and noting any similarities and differences in the use of the flower in evoking theme.

GOING FURTHER   You can find the renewal of life in the cycle of death and birth at work in D. H. Lawrence's many books, from the early *Sons and Lovers* to later work such as *The Plumed Serpent,* his mystically tinged novel set in rural Mexico.

Writing from Reading

Summarize

1 Explore why Lawrence has Elizabeth's father visit at the beginning of the story. What information do we learn, and what is the effect of our learning it from this specific interaction?

2 Trace Elizabeth's emotions while she awaits her husband's homecoming. Based on this progression, discuss whether or not she truly cares about him.

Analyze Craft

3 What is the setting (place, time period) of the story? Explain how you know, indicating examples from the text.

4 Discuss the techniques Lawrence uses to mount tension as the story progresses. Why is it almost a relief when you finally discover Walter's fate?

Analyze Voice

5 Write a couple of sentences describing the voice of the narrator in terms of diction, tone, and syntax. Discuss why this particular voice complements the theme of longing for beauty in "The Odour of Chrysanthemums."

Synthesize Summary and Analysis

6 Discuss why the setting of a coal mining town seems particularly appropriate for this story. Would the tone and themes of the story remain unchanged if Walt were caught in a factory machine or trampled in a stampede instead of being smothered by coal?

Interpret the Story

7 Consider what the chrysanthemums represent in this story—to Elizabeth and to the children. What does it signify when the men carrying Walter's dead body knock over the vase of chrysanthemums? In light of this image, propose an overarching theme for the story, and try to imagine the future in store for the widow and her children.

Jhumpa Lahiri (b. 1967)

Growing up in Rhode Island as the daughter of South Asian parents, Jhumpa Lahiri struggled with her identity, later reflecting that "my conflicting selves always cancel[ed] each other out." Although she was born in London, her parents moved to the United States when she was two, so Lahiri's two conflicting selves became Indian and American. These identities form the touchstone of her fiction, as she explores issues faced by Indian immigrants (especially Bengalis) as they adapt to new surroundings and cultural expectations. After earning three master's degrees—in English, creative writing, and comparative studies in literature and the arts—and a Ph.D in Renaissance studies from Boston University, Lahiri taught creative writing at Boston University and the Rhode Island School of Art and Design. Her life, however, was disrupted by celebrity when she published *Interpreter of Maladies,* a collection of short stories that won a Pulitzer Prize and the PEN/Hemingway Award, among others, and became an international best seller translated into twenty-nine languages. She became so famous, in fact, that the media had to be held at bay at her wedding to Alberto Vourvoulias, a Guatemalan-Greek journalist. Lahiri published her first novel, *The Namesake,* in 2003. Like her short stories, *The Namesake* focuses on themes such as marital and family difficulties, on the attempts of first- and second-generation immigrants to understand one another, and particularly on what it means to be Indian and to be assimilated. The novel was made into a major motion picture in 2006. Her most recent collection of stories, *Unaccustomed Earth,* was published in 2008.

As she said in an interview, the "question of identity is always a difficult one, but especially so for those who are culturally displaced, as immigrants are, or those who grow up in two worlds simultaneously, as is the case for their children. The older I get, the more I am aware that I have somehow inherited a sense of exile from my parents, even though in many ways I am so much more American than they are. In fact, it is still very hard to think of myself as an American."

AS YOU READ As you read, notice how the personalities and situations of the characters are revealed. How do your feelings about them change as you get to know them better? How do you interpret their maladies?

TIP

FOR INTERACTIVE READING . . . Trace the theme of interpretation and translation over the course of the story. Mark places in the text where any of the characters offers an interpretation.

Interpreter
of Maladies (1999)

1   A T the tea stall Mr. and Mrs. Das bickered about who should take Tina to the toilet. Eventually Mrs. Das relented when Mr. Das pointed out that he had given the girl her bath the night before. In the rearview mirror Mr. Kapasi watched as Mrs. Das emerged slowly from his bulky white Ambassador, dragging her shaved, largely bare legs across the back seat. She did not hold the little girl's hand as they walked to the rest room.

2   They were on their way to see the Sun Temple at Konarak. It was a dry, bright Saturday, the mid-July heat tempered by a steady ocean breeze, ideal weather for sightseeing. Ordinarily Mr. Kapasi would not have stopped so soon along the way, but less than five minutes after he'd picked up the family that morning in front of Hotel Sandy Villa, the little girl had complained. The first thing Mr. Kapasi had noticed when he saw Mr. and Mrs. Das, standing with their children under the portico of the hotel, was that they were very young, perhaps not even thirty. In addition to Tina they had two boys, Ronny and Bobby, who appeared very close in age and had teeth covered in a network of flashing silver wires. The family looked Indian but dressed as foreigners did, the children in stiff, brightly colored clothing and caps with translucent visors. Mr. Kapasi was accustomed to foreign tourists; he was assigned to them regularly because he could speak English. Yesterday he had driven an elderly couple from Scotland, both with spotted faces and fluffy white hair so thin it exposed their sunburnt scalps. In comparison, the tanned youthful faces of Mr. and Mrs. Das were all the more striking. When he'd introduced himself, Mr. Kapasi had pressed his palms together in greeting, but Mr. Das squeezed hands like an American so that Mr. Kapasi felt it in his elbow. Mrs. Das, for her part, had flexed one side of her mouth, smiling dutifully at Mr. Kapasi, without displaying any interest in him.

3   As they waited at the tea stall, Ronny, who looked like the older of the two boys, clambered suddenly out of the back seat, intrigued by a goat tied to a stake in the ground.

4   "Don't touch it," Mr. Das said. He glanced up from his paperback tour book, which said "INDIA" in yellow letters and looked as if it had been published abroad. His voice, somehow tentative and a little shrill, sounded as though it had not yet settled into maturity.

5   "I want to give it a piece of gum," the boy called back as he trotted ahead.

6   Mr. Das stepped out of the car and stretched his legs by squatting briefly to the ground. A clean-shaven man, he looked exactly like a magnified version of Ronny. He had a sapphire blue visor, and was dressed in shorts, sneakers, and a T-shirt. The camera slung around his neck, with an impressive telephoto lens and numerous buttons and markings, was the only complicated thing he wore. He frowned, watching as Ronny rushed toward the goat, but appeared to have no intention of intervening. "Bobby, make sure that your brother doesn't do anything stupid."

7   "I don't feel like it," Bobby said, not moving. He was sitting in the front seat beside Mr. Kapasi, studying a picture of the elephant god taped to the glove compartment.

8   "No need to worry," Mr. Kapasi said. "They are quite tame." Mr. Kapasi was forty-six years old, with receding hair that had gone completely silver, but his butterscotch complexion and his unlined brow, which he treated in spare moments to dabs of lotus-oil balm, made it easy to imagine what he must have looked like at an earlier age. He wore gray trousers and a matching jacket-style shirt, tapered at the waist, with short sleeves and a large pointed collar, made of a thin but durable synthetic material. He had specified both the

cut and the fabric to his tailor—it was his preferred uniform for giving tours because it did not get crushed during his long hours behind the wheel. Through the windshield he watched as Ronny circled around the goat, touched it quickly on its side, then trotted back to the car.

9   "You left India as a child?" Mr. Kapasi asked when Mr. Das had settled once again into the passenger seat.

10   "Oh, Mina and I were both born in America," Mr. Das announced with an air of sudden confidence. "Born and raised. Our parents live here now, in Assansol. They retired. We visit them every couple years." He turned to watch as the little girl ran toward the car, the wide purple bows of her sundress flopping on her narrow brown shoulders. She was holding to her chest a doll with yellow hair that looked as if it had been chopped, as a punitive measure, with a pair of dull scissors. "This is Tina's first trip to India, isn't it, Tina?"

11   "I don't have to go to the bathroom anymore," Tina announced.

12   "Where's Mina?" Mr. Das asked.

13   Mr. Kapasi found it strange that Mr. Das should refer to his wife by her first name when speaking to the little girl. Tina pointed to where Mrs. Das was purchasing something from one of the shirtless men who worked at the tea stall. Mr. Kapasi heard one of the shirtless men sing a phrase from a popular Hindi love song as Mrs. Das walked back to the car, but she did not appear to understand the words of the song, for she did not express irritation, or embarrassment, or react in any other way to the man's declarations.

14   He observed her. She wore a red-and-white-checkered skirt that stopped above her knees, slip-on shoes with a square wooden heel, and a close-fitting blouse styled like a man's undershirt. The blouse was decorated at chest-level with a calico appliqué in the shape of a strawberry. She was a short woman, with small hands like paws, her frosty pink fingernails painted to match her lips, and was slightly plump in her figure. Her hair, shorn only a little longer than her husband's, was parted far to one side. She was wearing large dark brown sunglasses with a pinkish tint to them, and carried a big straw bag, almost as big as her torso, shaped like a bowl, with a water bottle poking out of it. She walked slowly, carrying some puffed rice tossed with peanuts and chili peppers in a large packet made from newspapers. Mr. Kapasi turned to Mr. Das.

15   "Where in America do you live?"

"New Brunswick, New Jersey."

"Next to New York?"

"Exactly. I teach middle school there."

"What subject?"

"Science. In fact, every year I take my students on a trip to the Museum of Natural History in New York City. In a way we have a lot in common, you could say, you and I. How long have you been a tour guide, Mr. Kapasi?"

"Five years."

Mrs. Das reached the car. "How long's the trip?" she asked, shutting the door.

"About two and a half hours," Mr. Kapasi replied.

At this Mrs. Das gave an impatient sigh, as if she had been traveling her whole life without pause. She fanned herself with a folded Bombay film magazine written in English.

"I thought that the Sun Temple is only eighteen miles north of Puri," Mr. Das said, tapping on the tour book.

"The roads to Konarak are poor. Actually it is a distance of fifty-two miles," Mr. Kapasi explained.

Mr. Das nodded, readjusting the camera strap where it had begun to chafe the back of his neck.

Before starting the ignition, Mr. Kapasi reached back to make sure the cranklike locks on the inside of each of the back doors were secured. As soon as the car began to move the little girl began to play with the lock on her side, clicking it with some effort forward and backward, but Mrs. Das said nothing to stop her. She sat a bit slouched at one end of the back seat, not offering her puffed rice to anyone. Ronny and Tina sat on either side of her, both snapping bright green gum.

"Look," Bobby said as the car began to gather speed. He pointed with his finger to the tall trees that lined the road. "Look."

"Monkeys!" Ronny shrieked. "Wow!"

They were seated in groups along the branches, with shining black faces, silver bodies, horizontal eyebrows, and crested heads. Their long gray tails dangled like a series of ropes among the leaves. A few scratched themselves with black leathery hands, or swung their feet, staring as the car passed.

"We call them the hanuman," Mr. Kapasi said. "They are quite common in the area."

As soon as he spoke, one of the monkeys leaped into the middle of the road, causing Mr. Kapasi to brake suddenly. Another bounced onto the hood of the car, then sprang away. Mr. Kapasi beeped his horn. The children began to get excited, sucking in their breath and covering their faces partly with their hands. They had never seen monkeys outside of a zoo, Mr. Das explained. He asked Mr. Kapasi to stop the car so that he could take a picture.

While Mr. Das adjusted his telephoto lens, Mrs. Das reached into her straw bag and pulled out a bottle of colorless nail polish, which she proceeded to stroke on the tip of her index finger.

The little girl stuck out a hand. "Mine too. Mommy, do mine too."

"Leave me alone," Mrs. Das said, blowing on her nail and turning her body slightly. "You're making me mess up."

The little girl occupied herself by buttoning and un-buttoning a pinafore on the doll's plastic body.

"All set," Mr. Das said, replacing the lens cap.

The car rattled considerably as it raced along the dusty road, causing them all to pop up from their seats every now and then, but Mrs. Das continued to polish her nails. Mr. Kapasi eased up on the accelerator, hoping to produce a smoother ride. When he reached for the gearshift the boy in front accommodated him by swinging his hairless knees out of the way. Mr. Kapasi noted that this boy was slightly paler than the other children. "Daddy, why is the driver sitting on the wrong side in this car, too?" the boy asked.

"They all do that here, dummy," Ronny said.

"Don't call your brother a dummy," Mr. Das said. He turned to Mr. Kapasi. "In America, you know . . . it confuses them."

"Oh yes, I am well aware," Mr. Kapasi said. As delicately as he could, he shifted gears again, accelerating as they approached a hill in the road. "I see it on *Dallas*, the steering wheels are on the left-hand side."

"What's *Dallas*?" Tina asked, banging her now naked doll on the seat behind Mr. Kapasi.

"It went off the air," Mr. Das explained. "It's a television show."

They were all like siblings, Mr. Kapasi thought as they passed a row of date trees. Mr. and Mrs. Das behaved like an older brother and sister, not parents. It seemed that they were in charge of the children only for the day; it was hard to believe they were regularly responsible for anything other than themselves. Mr. Das tapped on his lens cap, and his tour book, dragging his thumbnail occasionally across the pages so

that they made a scraping sound. Mrs. Das continued to polish her nails. She had still not removed her sunglasses. Every now and then Tina renewed her plea that she wanted her nails done, too, and so at one point Mrs. Das flicked a drop of polish on the little girl's finger before depositing the bottle back inside her straw bag.

"Isn't this an air-conditioned car?" she asked, still blowing on her hand. The window on Tina's side was broken and could not be rolled down.

"Quit complaining," Mr. Das said. "It isn't so hot."

"I told you to get a car with air-conditioning," Mrs. Das continued. "Why do you do this, Raj, just to save a few stupid rupees. What are you saving us, fifty cents?"

Their accents sounded just like the ones Mr. Kapasi heard on American television programs, though not like the ones on *Dallas*.

"Doesn't it get tiresome, Mr. Kapasi, showing people the same thing every day?" Mr. Das asked, rolling down his own window all the way. "Hey, do you mind stopping the car. I just want to get a shot of this guy."

Mr. Kapasi pulled over to the side of the road as Mr. Das took a picture of a barefoot man, his head wrapped in a dirty turban, seated on top of a cart of grain sacks pulled by a pair of bullocks. Both the man and the bullocks were emaciated. In the back seat Mrs. Das gazed out another window, at the sky, where nearly transparent clouds passed quickly in front of one another.

"I look forward to it, actually," Mr. Kapasi said as they continued on their way. "The Sun Temple is one of my favorite places. In that way it is a reward for me. I give tours on Fridays and Saturdays only. I have another job during the week."

"Oh? Where?" Mr. Das asked.

"I work in a doctor's office."

"You're a doctor?"

"I am not a doctor. I work with one. As an interpreter."

"What does a doctor need an interpreter for?"

"He has a number of Gujarati patients. My father was Gujarati, but many people do not speak Gujarati in this area, including the doctor. And so the doctor asked me to work in his office, interpreting what the patients say."

"Interesting. I've never heard of anything like that," Mr. Das said.

60   Mr. Kapasi shrugged. "It is a job like any other."

61   "But so romantic," Mrs. Das said dreamily, breaking her extended silence. She lifted her pinkish brown sunglasses and arranged them on top of her head like a tiara. For the first time, her eyes met Mr. Kapasi's in the rearview mirror: pale, a bit small, their gaze fixed but drowsy.

62   Mr. Das craned to look at her. "What's so romantic about it?"

63   "I don't know. Something." She shrugged, knitting her brows together for an instant. "Would you like a piece of gum, Mr. Kapasi?" she asked brightly. She reached into her straw bag and handed him a small square wrapped in green-and-white-striped paper. As soon as Mr. Kapasi put the gum in his mouth a thick sweet liquid burst onto his tongue.

64   "Tell us more about your job, Mr. Kapasi," Mrs. Das said.

65   "What would you like to know, madame?"

66   "I don't know," she shrugged, munching on some puffed rice and licking the mustard oil from the corners of her mouth. "Tell us a typical situation." She settled back in her seat, her head tilted in a patch of sun, and closed her eyes. "I want to picture what happens."

67   "Very well. The other day a man came in with a pain in his throat."

68   "Did he smoke cigarettes?"

69   "No. It was very curious. He complained that he felt as if there were long pieces of straw stuck in his throat. When I told the doctor he was able to prescribe the proper medication."

70   "That's so neat."

71   "Yes," Mr. Kapasi agreed after some hesitation.

72   "So these patients are totally dependent on you," Mrs. Das said. She spoke slowly, as if she were thinking aloud. "In a way, more dependent on you than the doctor."

73   "How do you mean? How could it be?"

74   "Well, for example, you could tell the doctor that the pain felt like a burning, not straw. The patient would never know what you had told the doctor, and the doctor wouldn't know that you had told the wrong thing. It's a big responsibility."

75   "Yes, a big responsibility you have there, Mr. Kapasi," Mr. Das agreed.

76   Mr. Kapasi had never thought of his job in such complimentary terms. To him it was a thankless occupation. He found nothing noble in interpreting people's maladies, assiduously translating the symptoms of so many swollen bones, countless cramps of bellies and bowels, spots on people's palms that changed color, shape, or size. The doctor, nearly half his age, had an affinity for bell-bottom trousers and made humorless jokes about the Congress party. Together they worked in a stale little infirmary where Mr. Kapasi's smartly tailored clothes clung to him in the heat, in spite of the blackened blades of a ceiling fan churning over their heads.

The job was a sign of his failings. In his youth he'd been a devoted scholar of foreign languages, the owner of an impressive collection of dictionaries. He had dreamed of being an interpreter for diplomats and dignitaries, resolving conflicts between people and nations, settling disputes of which he alone could understand both sides. He was a self-educated man. In a series of notebooks, in the evenings before his parents settled his marriage, he had listed the common etymologies of words, and at one point in his life he was confident that he could converse, if given the opportunity, in English, French, Russian, Portuguese, and Italian, not to mention Hindi, Bengali, Orissi, and Gujarati. Now only a handful of European phrases remained in his memory, scattered words for things like saucers and chairs. English was the only non-Indian language he spoke fluently anymore. Mr. Kapasi knew it was not a remarkable talent. Sometimes he feared that his children knew better English than he did, just from watching television. Still, it came in handy for the tours.

He had taken the job as an interpreter after his first son, at the age of seven, contracted typhoid—that was how he had first made the acquaintance of the doctor. At the time Mr. Kapasi had been teaching English in a grammar school, and he bartered his skills as an interpreter to pay the increasingly exorbitant medical bills. In the end the boy had died one evening in his mother's arms, his limbs burning with fever, but then there was the funeral to pay for, and the other children who were born soon enough, and the newer, bigger house, and the good schools and tutors, and the fine shoes and the television, and the countless other ways he tried to console his wife and to keep her from crying in her sleep, and so when the doctor offered to pay him twice as much as he earned at the grammar school, he accepted. Mr. Kapasi knew that his wife had little regard for his career as an interpreter. He knew it reminded her of the son she'd lost, and that she resented the other lives he helped, in his own small way, to save. If ever she referred to his position, she used the phrase "doctor's assistant," as if the

> Mr. Kapasi had never thought of his job in such complimentary terms.

71

78

process of interpretation were equal to taking someone's temperature, or changing a bedpan. She never asked him about the patients who came to the doctor's office, or said that his job was a big responsibility.

For this reason it flattered Mr. Kapasi that Mrs. Das was so intrigued by his job. Unlike his wife, she had reminded him of its intellectual challenges. She had also used the word "romantic." She did not behave in a romantic way toward her husband, and yet she had used the word to describe him. He wondered if Mr. and Mrs. Das were a bad match, just as he and his wife were. Perhaps they, too, had little in common apart from three children and a decade of their lives. The signs he recognized from his own marriage were there—the bickering, the indifference, the protracted silences. Her sudden interest in him, an interest she did not express in either her husband or her children, was mildly intoxicating. When Mr. Kapasi thought once again about how she had said "romantic," the feeling of intoxication grew.

He began to check his reflection in the rearview mirror as he drove, feeling grateful that he had chosen the gray suit that morning and not the brown one, which tended to sag a little in the knees. From time to time he glanced through the mirror at Mrs. Das. In addition to glancing at her face he glanced at the strawberry between her breasts, and the golden brown hollow in her throat. He decided to tell Mrs. Das about another patient, and another: the young woman who had complained of a sensation of raindrops in her spine, the gentleman whose birthmark had begun to sprout hairs. Mrs. Das listened attentively, stroking her hair with a small plastic brush that resembled an oval bed of nails, asking more questions, for yet another example. The children were quiet, intent on spotting more monkeys in the trees, and Mr. Das was absorbed by his tour book, so it seemed like a private conversation between Mr. Kapasi and Mrs. Das. In this manner the next half hour passed, and when they stopped for lunch at a roadside restaurant that sold fritters and omelette sandwiches, usually something Mr. Kapasi looked forward to on his tours so that he could sit in peace and enjoy some hot tea, he was disappointed. As the Das family settled together under a magenta umbrella fringed with white and orange tassels, and placed their orders with one of the waiters who marched about in tricornered caps, Mr. Kapasi reluctantly headed toward a neighboring table.

"Mr. Kapasi, wait. There's room here," Mrs. Das called out. She gathered Tina onto her lap, insisting that he accompany them. And so, together, they had bottled mango juice and sandwiches and plates of onions and potatoes deep-fried in graham-flour batter. After finishing two omelette sandwiches Mr. Das took more pictures of the group as they ate.

"How much longer?" he asked Mr. Kapasi as he paused to load a new roll of film in the camera.

"About half an hour more."

By now the children had gotten up from the table to look at more monkeys perched in a nearby tree, so there was a considerable space between Mrs. Das and Mr. Kapasi. Mr. Das placed the camera to his face and squeezed one eye shut, his tongue exposed at one corner of his mouth. "This looks funny. Mina, you need to lean in closer to Mr. Kapasi."

She did. He could smell a scent on her skin, like a mixture of whiskey and rosewater. He worried suddenly that she could smell his perspiration, which he knew had collected beneath the synthetic material of his shirt. He polished off his mango juice in one gulp and smoothed his silver hair with his hands. A bit of the juice dripped onto his chin. He wondered if Mrs. Das had noticed.

She had not. "What's your address, Mr. Kapasi?" she inquired, fishing for something inside her straw bag.

"You would like my address?"

"So we can send you copies," she said. "Of the pictures." She handed him a scrap of paper which she had hastily ripped from a page of her film magazine. The blank portion was limited, for the narrow strip was crowded by lines of text and a tiny picture of a hero and heroine embracing under a eucalyptus tree.

The paper curled as Mr. Kapasi wrote his address in clear, careful letters. She would write to him, asking about his days interpreting at the doctor's office, and he would respond eloquently, choosing only the most entertaining anecdotes, ones that would make her laugh out loud as the read them in her house in New Jersey. In time she would reveal the disappointment of her marriage, and he his. In this way their friendship would grow, and flourish. He would possess a picture of the two of them, eating fried onions under a magenta umbrella, which he would keep, he decided, safely tucked between the pages of his Russian grammar. As his mind raced, Mr. Kapasi experienced a mild and pleasant shock. It was similar to a feeling he used to experience long ago when, after months of translating with the aid of a dictionary, he would finally read a passage from a French novel, or an Italian sonnet, and understand the words, one after another, unencumbered by his own efforts. In those moments Mr. Kapasi used to believe that all was right with the world, that all struggles were rewarded, that all of life's mistakes made sense in the end. The promise that he would hear from Mrs. Das now filled him with the same belief.

90   When he finished writing his address Mr. Kapasi handed her the paper, but as soon as he did so he worried that he had either misspelled his name, or accidentally reversed the numbers of his postal code. He dreaded the possibility of a lost letter, the photograph never reaching him, hovering somewhere in Orissa, close but ultimately unattainable. He thought of asking for the slip of paper again, just to make sure he had written his address accurately, but Mrs. Das had already dropped it into the jumble of her bag.

91   THEY reached Konarak at two-thirty. The temple, made of sandstone, was a massive pyramid-like structure in the shape of a chariot. It was dedicated to the great master of life, the sun, which struck three sides of the edifice as it made its journey each day across the sky. Twenty-four giant wheels were carved on the north and south sides of the plinth. The whole thing was drawn by a team of seven horses, speeding as if through the heavens. As they approached, Mr. Kapasi explained that the temple had been built between A.D. 1243 and 1255, with the efforts of twelve hundred artisans, by the great ruler of the Ganga dynasty, King Narasimhadeva the First, to commemorate his victory against the Muslim army.

92   "It says the temple occupies about a hundred and seventy acres of land," Mr. Das said, reading from his book.

93   "It's like a desert," Ronny said, his eyes wandering across the sand that stretched on all sides beyond the temple.

94   "The Chandrabhaga River once flowed one mile north of here. It is dry now," Mr. Kapasi said, turning off the engine.

95   They got out and walked toward the temple, posing first for pictures by the pair of lions that flanked the steps. Mr. Kapasi led them next to one of the wheels of the chariot, higher than any human being, nine feet in diameter.

96   "'The wheels are supposed to symbolize the wheel of life,'" Mr. Das read. "'They depict the cycle of creation, preservation, and achievement of realization.' Cool." He turned the page of his book. "'Each wheel is divided into eight thick and thin spokes, dividing the day into eight equal parts. The rims are carved with designs of birds and animals, whereas the medallions in the spokes are carved with women in luxurious poses, largely erotic in nature.'"

What he referred to were the countless friezes of entwined naked bodies, making love in various positions, women clinging to the necks of men, their knees wrapped eternally around their lovers' thighs. In addition to these were assorted scenes from daily life, of hunting and trading, of deer being killed with bows and arrows and marching warriors holding swords in their hands.

It was no longer possible to enter the temple, for it had filled with rubble years ago, but they admired the exterior, as did all the tourists Mr. Kapasi brought there, slowly strolling along each of its sides. Mr. Das trailed behind, taking pictures. The children ran ahead, pointing to figures of naked people, intrigued in particular by the Nagamithunas, the half-human, half-serpentine couples who were said, Mr. Kapasi told them, to live in the deepest waters of the sea. Mr. Kapasi was pleased that they liked the temple, pleased especially that it appealed to Mrs. Das. She stopped every three or four paces, staring silently at the carved lovers, and the processions of elephants, and the topless female musicians beating on two-sided drums.

Though Mr. Kapasi had been to the temple countless times, it occurred to him, as he, too, gazed at the topless women, that he had never seen his own wife fully naked. Even when they had made love she kept the panels of her blouse hooked together, the string of her petticoat knotted around her waist. He had never admired the backs of his wife's legs the way he now admired those of Mrs. Das, walking as if for his benefit alone. He had, of course, seen plenty of bare limbs before, belonging to the American and European ladies who took his tours. But Mrs. Das was different. Unlike the other women, who had an interest only in the temple, and kept their noses buried in a guidebook, or their eyes behind the lens of a camera, Mrs. Das had taken an interest in him.

Mr. Kapasi was anxious to be alone with her, to continue their private conversation, yet he felt nervous to walk at her side. She was lost behind her sunglasses, ignoring her husband's requests that she pose for another picture, walking past her children as if they were strangers. Worried that he might disturb her, Mr. Kapasi walked ahead, to admire, as he always did, the three life-sized bronze avatars of Surya, the sun god, each emerging from its own niche on the temple facade to greet the sun at dawn, noon, and evening. They wore elaborate headdresses, their languid, elongated eyes closed, their bare chests draped with carved chains and amulets. Hibiscus petals, offerings from previous visitors, were strewn at their gray-green feet. The last statue, on the northern wall of the temple, was Mr. Kapasi's favorite. This Surya had a tired expression, weary after a hard day of work, sitting astride a horse with folded legs. Even his horse's eyes were drowsy. Around his body were smaller sculptures of women in pairs, their hips thrust to one side.

"Who's that? Mrs. Das asked. He was startled to see that she was standing beside him.

"He is the Astachala-Surya," Mr. Kapasi said. "The setting sun."

"So in a couple of hours the sun will set right here?" She slipped a foot out of one of her square-heeled shoes, rubbed her toes on the back of her other leg.

"That is correct."

She raised her sunglasses for a moment, then put them back on again. "Neat."

Mr. Kapasi was not certain exactly what the word suggested, but he had a feeling it was a favorable response. He hoped that Mrs. Das had understood Surya's beauty, his power. Perhaps they would discuss it further in their letters. He would explain things to her, things about India, and she would explain things to him about America. In its own way this correspondence would fulfill his dream, of serving as an interpreter between nations. He looked at her straw bag, delighted that his address lay nestled among its contents. When he pictured her so many thousands of miles away he plummeted, so much so that he had an overwhelming urge to wrap his arms around her, to freeze with her, even for an instant, in an embrace witnessed by his favorite Surya. But Mrs. Das had already started walking.

"When do you return to America?" he asked, trying to sound placid.

"In ten days."

He calculated: A week to settle in, a week to develop the pictures, a few days to compose her letter, two weeks to get to India by air. According to his schedule, allowing room for delays, he would hear from Mrs. Das in approximately six weeks' time.

THE family was silent as Mr. Kapasi drove them back, a little past four-thirty, to Hotel Sandy Villa. The children had bought miniature granite versions of the chariot's wheels at a souvenir stand, and they turned them round in their hands. Mr. Das continued to read his book. Mrs. Das untangled Tina's hair with her brush and divided it into two little ponytails.

Mr. Kapasi was beginning to dread the thought of dropping them off. He was not prepared to begin his six-week wait to hear from Mrs. Das. As he stole glances at her in the rearview mirror, wrapping elastic bands around Tina's hair, he wondered how he might make the tour last a little longer. Ordinarily he sped back to Puri using a shortcut, eager to return home, scrub his feet and hands with sandalwood soap, and enjoy the evening newspaper and a cup of tea that his wife would serve him in silence. The thought of that silence, something to which he'd long been resigned, now oppressed him. It was then that he suggested visiting the hills at Udayagiri and Khandagiri, where a number of monastic dwellings were hewn out of the ground, facing one another across a defile. It was some miles away, but well worth seeing, Mr. Kapasi told them.

> The thought of that silence, something to which he'd long been resigned, now oppressed him.

Oh yeah, there's something mentioned about it in this book," Mr. Das said. "Built by a Jain king or something."

"Shall we go then?" Mr. Kapasi asked. He paused at a turn in the road. "It's to the left."

Mr. Das turned to look at Mrs. Das. Both of them shrugged.

"Left, left," the children chanted.

Mr. Kapasi turned the wheel, almost delirious with relief. He did not know what he would do or say to Mrs. Das once they arrived at the hills. Perhaps he would tell her what a pleasing smile she had. Perhaps he would compliment her strawberry shirt, which he found irresistibly becoming. Perhaps, when Mr. Das was busy taking a picture, he would take her hand.

He did not have to worry. When they got to the hills, divided by a steep path thick with trees, Mrs. Das refused to get out of the car. All along the path, dozens of monkeys were seated on stones, as well as on the branches of the trees. Their hind legs were stretched out in front and raised to shoulder level, their arms resting on their knees.

"My legs are tired," she said, sinking low in her seat. "I'll stay here."

"Why did you have to wear those stupid shoes?" Mr. Das said. "You won't be in the pictures."

"Pretend I'm there."

"But we could use one of these pictures for our Christmas card this year. We didn't get one of all five of us at the Sun Temple. Mr. Kapasi could take it."

122 "I'm not coming. Anyway, those monkeys give me the creeps."

123 "But they're harmless," Mr. Das said. He turned to Mr. Kapasi. "Aren't they?"

124 "They are more hungry than dangerous," Mr. Kapasi said. "Do not provoke them with food, and they will not bother you."

125 Mr. Das headed up the defile with the children, the boys at his side, the little girl on his shoulders. Mr. Kapasi watched as they crossed paths with a Japanese man and woman, the only other tourists there, who paused for a final photograph, then stepped into a nearby car and drove away. As the car disappeared out of view some of the monkeys called out, emitting soft whooping sounds, and then walked on their flat black hands and feet up the path. At one point a group of them formed a little ring around Mr. Das and the children. Tina screamed in delight. Ronny ran in circles around his father. Bobby bent down and picked up a fat stick on the ground. When he extended it, one of the monkey's approached him and snatched it, then briefly beat the ground.

126 "I'll join them," Mr. Kapasi said, unlocking the door on his side. "There is much to explain about the caves."

127 "No. Stay a minute," Mrs. Das said. She got out of the back seat and slipped in beside Mr. Kapasi. "Raj has his dumb book anyway." Together, through the windshield, Mrs. Das and Mr. Kapasi watched as Bobby and the monkey passed the stick back and forth between them.

128 "A brave little boy," Mr. Kapasi commented.

129 "It's not so surprising," Mrs. Das said.

130 "No?"

131 "He's not his."

"I beg your pardon?"

"Raj's. He's not Raj's son."

Mr. Kapasi felt a prickle on his skin. He reached into his shirt pocket for the small tin of lotus-oil balm he carried with him at all times, and applied it to three spots on his forehead. He knew that Mrs. Das was watching him, but he did not turn to face her. Instead he watched as the figures of Mr. Das and the children grew smaller, climbing up the steep path, pausing every now and then for a picture, surrounded by a growing number of monkeys.

"Are you surprised?" The way she put it made him choose his words with care.

"It's not the type of thing one assumes," Mr. Kapasi replied slowly. He put the tin of lotus-oil balm back in his pocket.

"No, of course not. And no one knows, of course. No one at all. I've kept it a secret for eight whole years." She looked at Mr. Kapasi, tilting her chin as if to gain a fresh perspective. "But now I've told you."

Mr. Kapasi nodded. He felt suddenly parched, and his forehead was warm and slightly numb from the balm. He considered asking Mrs. Das for a sip of water, then decided against it.

"We met when we were very young," she said. She reached into her straw bag in search of something, then pulled out a packet of puffed rice. "Want some?"

"No, thank you."

She put a fistful in her mouth, sank into the seat a little, and looked away from Mr. Kapasi, out the window on her side of the car. "We married when we were still in college. We were in high school when he proposed. We went to the same college, of course. Back then we couldn't stand the thought of being separated, not for a day, not for a minute. Our parents were best friends who lived in the same town. My entire life I saw him every weekend, either at our house or theirs. We were sent upstairs to play together while our parents joked about our marriage. Imagine! They never caught us at anything, though in a way I think it was all more or less a setup. The things we did those Friday and Saturday nights, while our parents sat downstairs drinking tea . . . I could tell you stories, Mr. Kapasi."

As a result of spending all her time in college with Raj, she continued, she did not make many close friends. There was no one to confide in about him at the end of a difficult day, or to share a passing thought or a worry. Her parents now lived on the other side of the world, but she had never been very close to them, anyway. After marrying so young she was overwhelmed by it all, having a child so quickly, and nursing, and warming up bottles of milk and testing their temperature against her wrist while Raj was at work, dressed in sweaters and corduroy pants, teaching his students about rocks and dinosaurs. Raj never looked cross or harried, or plump as she had become after the first baby.

Always tired, she declined invitations from her one or two college girlfriends, to have lunch or shop in Manhattan. Eventually the friends stopped calling her, so that she was left at home all day with the baby, surrounded by toys that made her trip when she walked or wince when she sat, always cross and tired. Only occasionally did they go out after Ronny was born, and even more rarely did they entertain. Raj didn't mind; he looked forward to coming home from teaching and watching television and bouncing Ronny on his knee. She had been outraged when Raj told her that a Punjabi friend, someone whom she had once met but did not remember, would be staying with them for a week for some job interviews in the New Brunswick area.

Bobby was conceived in the afternoon, on a sofa littered with rubber teething toys, after the friend learned that a London pharmaceutical company had hired him, while Ronny cried to be freed from his playpen. She made no protest when the friend touched the small of her back as she was about to make a pot of coffee, then pulled her against his crisp navy suit. He made love to her swiftly, in silence, with an expertise she had never known, without the meaningful expressions and smiles Raj always insisted on afterward. The next day Raj drove the friend to JFK. He was married now, to a Punjabi girl, and they lived in London still, and every year they exchanged Christmas cards with Raj and Mina, each couple tucking photos of their families into the envelopes. He did not know that he was Bobby's father. He never would.

"I beg your pardon, Mrs. Das, but why have you told me this information?" Mr. Kapasi asked when she had finally finished speaking, and had turned to face him once again.

"For God's sake, stop calling me Mrs. Das. I'm twenty-eight. You probably have children my age."

"Not quite." It disturbed Mr. Kapasi to learn that she thought of him as a parent. The feeling he had had toward her, that had made him check his reflection in the rearview mirror as they drove, evaporated a little.

"I told you because of your talents." She put the packet of puffed rice back into her bag without folding over the top.

"I don't understand," Mr. Kapasi said.

"Don't you see? For eight years I haven't been able to express this to anybody, not to friends, certainly not

to Raj. He doesn't even suspect it. He thinks I'm still in love with him. Well, don't you have anything to say?"

"About what?"

"About what I've just told you. About my secret, and about how terrible it makes me feel. I feel terrible looking at my children, and at Raj, always terrible. I have terrible urges, Mr. Kapasi, to throw things away. One day I had the urge to throw everything I own out the window, the television, the children, everything. Don't you think it's unhealthy?"

He was silent.

"Mr. Kapasi, don't you have anything to say? I thought that was your job."

"My job is to give tours, Mrs. Das."

"Not that. Your other job. As an interpreter."

"But we do not face a language barrier. What need is there for an interpreter?"

"That's not what I mean. I would never have told you otherwise. Don't you realize what it means for me to tell you?"

"What does it mean?"

"It means that I'm tired of feeling so terrible all the time. Eight years, Mr. Kapasi, I've been in pain eight years. I was hoping you could help me feel better, say the right thing. Suggest some kind of remedy."

He looked at her, in her red plaid skirt and strawberry T-shirt, a woman not yet thirty, who loved neither her husband nor her children, who had already fallen out of love with life. Her confession depressed him, depressed him all the more when he thought of Mr. Das at the top of the path, Tina clinging to his shoulders, taking pictures of ancient monastic cells cut into the hills to show his students in America, unsuspecting and unaware that one of his sons was not his own. Mr. Kapasi felt insulted that Mrs. Das should ask him to interpret her common, trivial little secret. She did not resemble the patients in the doctor's office, those who came glassy-eyed and desperate, unable to sleep or breathe or urinate with ease, unable, above all, to give words to their pains. Still, Mr. Kapasi believed it was his duty to assist Mrs. Das. Perhaps he ought to tell her to confess the truth to Mr. Das. He would explain that honesty was the best policy. Honesty, surely, would help her feel better, as she'd put it. Perhaps he would offer to preside over the discussion, as a mediator. He decided to begin with the most obvious question, to get to the heart of the matter, and so he asked, "Is it really pain you feel, Mrs. Das, or is it guilt?"

She turned to him and glared, mustard oil thick on her frosty pink lips. She opened her mouth to say something, but as she glared at Mr. Kapasi some

> He thinks I'm still in love with him.

151
152
153
154
155
156
157
158
159
160
161
162

certain knowledge seemed to pass before her eyes, and she stopped. It crushed him; he knew at that moment that he was not even important enough to be properly insulted. She opened the car door and began walking up the path, wobbling a little on her square wooden heels, reaching into her straw bag to eat handfuls of puffed rice. It fell through her fingers, leaving a zigzagging trail, causing a monkey to leap down from a tree and devour the little white grains. In search of more, the monkey began to follow Mrs. Das. Others joined him, so that she was soon being followed by about half a dozen of them, their velvety tails dragging behind.

163   Mr. Kapasi stepped out of the car. He wanted to holler, to alert her in some way, but he worried that if she knew they were behind her, she would grow nervous. Perhaps she would lose her balance. Perhaps they would pull at her bag or her hair. He began to jog up the path, taking a fallen branch in his hand to scare away the monkeys. Mrs. Das continued walking, oblivious, trailing grains of puffed rice. Near the top of the incline, before a group of cells fronted by a row of squat stone pillars, Mr. Das was kneeling on the ground, focusing the lens of his camera. The children stood under the arcade, now hiding, now emerging from view.

164   "Wait for me," Mrs. Das called out. "I'm coming."

165   Tina jumped up and down. "Here comes Mommy!"

166   "Great," Mr. Das said without looking up. "Just in time. We'll get Mr. Kapasi to take a picture of the five of us."

167   Mr. Kapasi quickened his pace, waving his branch so that the monkeys scampered away, distracted, in another direction.

168   "Where's Bobby?" Mrs. Das asked when she stopped.

169   Mr. Das looked up from the camera. "I don't know. Ronny, where's Bobby?"

170   Ronny shrugged. "I thought he was right here."

171   "Where is he?" Mrs. Das repeated sharply. "What's wrong with all of you?"

172   They began calling his name, wandering up and down the path a bit. Because they were calling, they did not initially hear the boy's screams. When they found him, a little farther down the path under a tree, he was surrounded by a group of monkeys, over a dozen of them, pulling at his T-shirt with their long black fingers. The puffed rice Mrs. Das had spilled was scattered at his feet, raked over by the monkeys' hands. The boy was silent, his body frozen, swift tears running down his startled face. His bare legs were dusty and red with welts from where one of the monkeys struck him repeatedly with the stick he had given it earlier.

"Daddy, the monkey's hurting Bobby," Tina said.

Mr. Das wiped his palms on the front of his shorts. In his nervousness he accidentally pressed the shutter on his camera; the whirring noise of the advancing film excited the moneys, and the one with the stick began to beat Bobby more intently. "What are we supposed to do? What if they start attacking?"

"Mr. Kapasi," Mrs. Das shrieked, noticing him standing to one side. "Do something, for God's sake, do something!"

> ## The animals retreated slowly, with a measured gait, obedient but unintimidated.

Mr. Kapasi took his branch and shooed them away, hissing at the ones that remained, stomping his feet to scare them. The animals retreated slowly, with a measured gait, obedient but unintimidated. Mr. Kapasi gathered Bobby in his arms and brought him back to where his parents and siblings were standing. As he carried him he was tempted to whisper a secret into the boy's ear. But Bobby was stunned, and shivering with fright, his legs bleeding slightly where the stick had broken the skin. When Mr. Kapasi delivered him to his parents, Mr. Das brushed some dirt off the boy's T-shirt and put the visor on him the right way. Mrs. Das reached into her straw bag to find a bandage which she taped over the cut on his knee. Ronny offered his brother a fresh piece of gum. "He's fine. Just a little scared, right, Bobby?" Mr. Das said, patting the top of his head.

"God, let's get out of here," Mrs. Das said. She folded her arms across the strawberry on her chest. "This place gives me the creeps."

"Yeah. Back to the hotel, definitely," Mr. Das agreed.

"Poor Bobby," Mrs. Das said. "Come here a second. Let Mommy fix your hair." Again she reached into her straw bag, this time for her hairbrush, and began to run it around the edges of the translucent visor. When she whipped out the hairbrush, the slip of paper with Mr. Kapasi's address on it fluttered away in the wind. No one but Mr. Kapasi noticed. He watched as it rose, carried higher and higher by the breeze, into the trees where the monkeys now sat, solemnly observing the scene below. Mr. Kapasi observed it too, knowing that this was the picture of the Das family he would preserve forever in his mind.

IF you enjoyed "Interpreter of Maladies," you will probably admire "An Astrologer's Day" (in Stories for Further Reading), by R. K. Narayan, an Indian writer to whom Lahiri herself looks for inspiration.

GOING FURTHER Lahiri's more recent fiction, such as *The Namesake* and *Unaccustomed Earth,* belongs to a long line of books that dramatize in universal ways the themes that grow out of immigration to the United States. Examples include Henry Roth's 1934 classic *Call It Sleep,* about immigrant Jews living in New York City's slums, Edwidge Danticat's *The Dew Breaker,* and Junot Diaz's Pulitzer Prize–winning novel of 2007, *The Brief Wondrous Life of Oscar Wao.*

Writing from Reading

Summarize

1 Examine Mr. Kapasi's daydreams of his future with Mrs. Das. What does he expect from their interactions? What is it that he is looking for that he doesn't currently have with his wife?

Analyze Craft

2 Discuss why the story begins with Mr. Kapasi's observations of Mrs. Das, and how they help set up what the story is *about.*

3 Analyze the thematic importance of the story's title. What are the maladies in this story? What does it mean to be an interpreter of maladies?

Analyze Voice

4 Jhumpa Lahiri has referred to her conflicting selves—the Indian and the American. How does this dual cultural background come through in her narration of "Interpreter of Maladies"? What details and themes strike you as more American or more Indian? Explain why.

Synthesize Summary and Analysis

5 Discuss what role the monkeys play in the story. Consider when and where they appear and how various characters respond to them.

Interpret the Story

6 While they wait for Tina and Mrs. Das to emerge from the bathroom, Mr. Das says to Mr. Kapasi: "We have a lot in common, you could say, you and I." Is this true? What do these two men have in common? Explain how the rest of the story serves to prove, disprove, or change the meaning of this statement.

Reading for Theme

When reading for **theme,** go beyond the plot and subject of the story and ask yourself what truths or insights about the human experience the story offers.

Does the title point to a major symbol, character, or subject from which themes develop?	EXAMPLES: "The Jilting of Granny Weatherall," "The Death of Ivan Ilych," and "Why I Live at the P.O."
Does the title point to a central irony that is thematic?	EXAMPLES: "The Short Happy Life of Francis Macomber," "No One's a Mystery."
Does the title point to thematic concerns of the story?	EXAMPLES: • "Who's Irish?" calls up the question of identity. • "Araby" conjures an exotic dream. • "The Rememberer" calls to mind the person left behind after a loss.
Does the narrator or another character make general statements as observations that may offer insight into the writer's theme?	EXAMPLE: *Moby-Dick*'s narrator asserts that a subject must be larger than ordinary or everyday to accommodate a large theme.
What changes in the main character? What does the main character come to realize?	EXAMPLES: • In Alice Munro's "An Ounce of Cure," the narrator says in the last line, "I am a grown-up woman now." • In John Updike's "A&P," the young narrator realizes "how hard the world was going to be to me from here on in."
Note powerful details and ask yourself why this is important. What does this make you feel? How do events or details thread together the meaning beyond a particular situation?	EXAMPLES: • The frail back of the old man on the wet floor (*What* do *I* feel when I think about that old man?). • The uneaten rice (*How* did these events affect Nnamabia?). • The tears in the brother's eyes (*Why* did the sister feel that tenderness?). Continued

A literary work can have multiple themes. Does the proposed theme tie the elements of the story together? Ask questions that go beyond the surface and the events. Theme grows seamlessly from plot, setting, style, characterization, and all the other elements of the writer's craft. In each, theme emerges from our reading and questioning of the story in all its twists and permutations.

| How do you state a theme? | • Formulate a general idea that is not tied to specific details in the story or to a particular character in the story but to all human beings.

• Write a complete sentence that goes beyond the subject and includes some conclusion or attitude about the subject. | **Too limited:** "The Short Happy Life of Francis Macomber" is about a man who struggles with questions of courage during a big-game hunt.
More precise: "The Short Happy Life of Francis Macomber" is a story about marriage and manhood and the testing of courage in both.

Too broad: Adulthood
More precise: Adulthood can be a burden but also a highly prized period of life. |

Suggestions for Writing about Theme

1. How do Stephen Crane and Jhumpa Lahiri raise thematic issues by use of descriptions of setting? Compare the authors' techniques in "The Open Boat" and "Interpreter of Maladies."

2. Select two stories in this chapter and show how, although their plots differ, they explore a similar theme. Throughout, back up your claims with specific lines or passages from the story.

3. Compare and contrast the role of monkeys in "Interpreter of Maladies" with that of the seagulls in "The Open Boat."

4. Compare and contrast the theme of change in Adichie's "Cell One" and Crane's "The Open Boat." In each, how do the characters change and what are the factors that prompt the change?

10

SYM

"**B**RIEFLY, in the rain, Lieutenant Cross saw Martha's gray eyes gazing back at him. He understood.

It was very sad, he thought. The things men carried inside. The things men did or felt they had to do.

He almost nodded at her, but didn't.

Instead he went back to his maps. He was now determined to perform his duties firmly and without negligence. It wouldn't help Lavender, he knew that, but from this point on he would comport himself as an officer. He would dispose of his good-luck pebble. Swallow it, maybe, or use Lee Strunk's slingshot, or just drop it along the trail."

—from "The Things They Carried" by Tim O'Brien

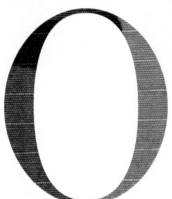

BOL

A YOUNG American lieutenant in Vietnam during the war imagines the eyes of Martha, a girl back home who has become the center of his fantasies. During much of the action, he dreams of her love; now he understands that she has been a distraction and he must focus on duty instead. We've caught him in a sad, contemplative moment—coming to an understanding about the burdens of leadership and how he must "perform his duties firmly and without negligence." The boy at the beginning of the story has "understood" and grown into a man.

This narrative introduces the members of Lieutenant Cross's platoon—describing in an inventory-like manner what each carries on his back as well as in his heart. They trek through jungles and villages; they deal with weather, boredom, and enemy attack. By telling us what the soldiers carry, O'Brien shows us who they are—each with his special burden, each terrified and confused and, in his own way, heroic. If you think beyond the surface of the images in the story—the good-luck pebble, the maps, even the names Cross and Lavender—you enter it in terms of its symbolic resonance. A **symbol,** in the literary sense, is any object, image, character, or action that suggests meaning beyond the everyday literal level. In contemporary literature, symbols don't work in a simple equation of *A = B* or *This means that.* They acquire meaning from a rich matrix of associations. All elements—plot, character, point of view, setting, tone, and theme—contribute to the effect.

CONTINUED ON PAGE 324

Q & A

Art can be born out of playful intent, having fun.

. . . I began to recognize something that mattered . . .

A Conversation on Writing

Tim O'Brien

On Becoming a Writer in Vietnam

I think that somewhere during those months in Vietnam, as I sat in those foxholes at night, was when writing became serious for me. It was serious not in the sense of "I'm going to publish" or "I'm going to be a writer," but the writing itself was serious. It was written partly, I think, as kind of a testament that, if I were to be killed, these words would be found on my person, would be sent to my mom or my dad or my sister, and they would have some sense of their son and brother's personality and spirit during those life-and-death days of war.

On Memory and Writing about War

"The Things They Carried" is organized around, just in terms of locale, foxholes. It takes place largely around men talking and reminiscing about girlfriends and hometowns and religion and the world they don't have . . . in those hours a soldier has that aren't full of horror and violence. . . . Moments in Vietnam were horrible. I don't remember much. I remember saying, "Dear Jesus, dear Jesus," as I was wounded, but I can't remember much before that or much afterwards, for that matter. What I do remember vividly are those quiet moments when you'd reflect back on what happened.

On the Writing Process

I had originally started writing *The Things They Carried* playfully as a game. . . . . . Art can be born out of playful intent, having fun. And my idea was to have fun with the word "carry." I wanted to find how many ways can I use the word: *carry* himself with poise; *carry* yourself with dignity; *carried* in the usual sense; "*carry* on, men."

To watch this entire interview and hear the author read from "The Things They Carried," go to www.mhhe.com/delbanco1e.

Tim O'Brien's biography begins like many American biographies, and a summary might include: He grew up in Minnesota and had a successful college career. However, the summer after graduation, O'Brien was drafted into the Vietnam War and embarked upon an experience that shaped the rest of his life and much of his fiction. He fought for a little over a year, earning both a Purple Heart and a Bronze Star. His first book was a memoir, *If I Die in a Combat Zone: Box Me Up and Ship Me Home* (1973), and two years thereafter he published his first novel, *Northern Lights.*

Like many of the characters in his fiction, O'Brien seems haunted by the experience of combat, unable to relegate it comfortably to the past. Although he has written on other topics, the majority of his books deal in some way with Vietnam and the transforming effects of battle—a battle from which (though the deserter in *Going after Cacciato* literally walks out of Southeast Asia) there's no true escape. Continually, even obsessively, O'Brien describes the condition of life as a soldier and war's aftermath. It is his great subject and recurrent theme.

Such books as *Going after Cacciato* (1978), *The Things They Carried* (1990), and *The Nuclear Age* (1985) masterfully blend short story and memoir, fiction and nonfiction, while exploring themes of courage, morality, love, truth, and ambiguity. In *The Things They Carried,* for example, O'Brien highlights "story truth" as the truth that the reader's stomach believes and "happening truth" as the mere facts of what occurred.

RESEARCH ASSIGNMENT In his interview, O'Brien says he could have set "The Things They Carried" in a different locale. How would this have changed the story, and what do you think the foxholes add to the setting of the story?

AS YOU READ   As you read, notice the differences between "the things" the characters carry on their backs and "the things" they carry in their minds and hearts. How do the two kinds of burdens weigh on these men? What do they carry that inspires or soothes them?

TIPS

FOR INTERACTIVE READING . . .
- Choose three characters and circle all the things they carried. How do these objects characterize them? What do the objects reveal about them? Do these objects complete our understanding of the men or limit it?
- O'Brien introduces a vocabulary of war. Find and circle the special terms the men have for what they do and what they experience.

The Things They Carried (1986)

1   FIRST Lieutenant Jimmy Cross carried letters from a girl named Martha, a junior at Mount Sebastian College in New Jersey. They were not love letters, but Lieutenant Cross was hoping, so he kept them folded in plastic at the bottom of his rucksack. In the late afternoon, after a day's march, he would dig his foxhole, wash his hands under a canteen, unwrap the letters, hold them with the tips of his fingers, and spend the last hour of light pretending. He would imagine romantic camping trips into the White Mountains in New Hampshire. He would sometimes taste the envelope flaps, knowing her tongue had been there. More than anything, he wanted Martha to love him as he loved her, but the letters were mostly chatty, elusive on the matter of love. She was a virgin, he was almost sure. She was an English major at Mount Sebastian, and she wrote beautifully about her professors and roommates and midterm exams, about her respect for Chaucer and her great affection for Virginia Woolf. She often quoted lines of poetry; she never mentioned the war, except to say, Jimmy, take care of yourself. The letters weighed ten ounces. They were signed "Love, Martha," but Lieutenant Cross understood that "Love" was only a way of signing and did not mean what he sometimes pretended it meant. At dusk, he would carefully return the letters to his rucksack. Slowly, a bit distracted, he would get up and move among his men, checking the perimeter, then at full dark he would return to his hole and watch the night and wonder if Martha was a virgin.

2   The things they carried were largely determined by necessity. Among the necessities or near necessities were P-38 can openers, pocket knives, heat tabs, wrist watches, dog tags, mosquito repellant, chewing gum, candy, cigarettes, salt tablets, packets of Kool-Aid, lighters, matches, sewing kits, Military Payment Certificates, C rations, and two or three canteens of water. Together, these items weighed between fifteen and twenty pounds, depending upon a man's habits or rate of metabolism. Henry Dobbins, who was a big man, carried extra rations; he was especially fond of canned peaches in heavy syrup over pound cake. Dave Jensen, who practiced field hygiene, carried a toothbrush, dental floss, and several hotel-size bars of soap he'd stolen on R&R in Sydney, Australia. Ted Lavender, who was scared, carried tranquilizers until he was shot in the head outside the village of Than Khe in mid-April. By necessity, and because it was SOP, they all carried steel helmets that weighed five pounds including the liner and camouflage cover. They carried the standard fatigue jackets and trousers. Very few

carried underwear. On their feet they carried jungle boots—2.1 pounds—and Dave Jensen carried three pairs of socks and a can of Dr. Scholl's foot powder as a precaution against trench foot. Until he was shot, Ted Lavender carried six or seven ounces of premium dope, which for him was a necessity. Mitchell Sanders, the RTO, carried condoms. Norman Bowker carried a diary. Rat Kiley carried comic books. Kiowa, a devout Baptist, carried an illustrated New Testament that had been presented to him by his father, who taught Sunday school in Oklahoma City, Oklahoma. As a hedge against bad times, however, Kiowa also carried his grandmother's distrust of the white man, his grandfather's old hunting hatchet. Necessity dictated. Because the land was mined and booby-trapped, it was SOP for each man to carry a steel-centered, nylon-covered flak jacket, which weighed 6.7 pounds, but which on hot days seemed much heavier. Because you could die so quickly, each man carried at least one large compress bandage, usually in the helmet band for easy access. Because the nights were cold, and because the monsoons were wet, each carried a green plastic poncho that could be used as a raincoat or groundsheet or makeshift tent. With its quilted liner, the poncho weighed almost two pounds, but it was worth every ounce. In April, for instance, when Ted Lavender was shot, they used his poncho to wrap him up, then to carry him across the paddy, then to lift him into the chopper that took him away.

3   THEY were called legs or grunts.

4   To carry something was to "hump" it, as when Lieutenant Jimmy Cross humped his love for Martha up the hills and through the swamps. In its intransitive form, "to hump," meant "to walk," or "to march," but it implied burdens far beyond the intransitive.

5   Almost everyone humped photographs. In his wallet, Lieutenant Cross carried two photographs of Martha. The first was a Kodachrome snapshot signed "Love," though he knew better. She stood against a brick wall. Her eyes were gray and neutral, her lips slightly open as she stared straight-on at the camera. At night, sometimes, Lieutenant Cross wondered who had taken the picture, because he knew she had boyfriends, because he loved her so much, and because he could see the shadow of the picture taker spreading out against the brick wall. The second photograph had been clipped from the 1968 Mount Sebastian yearbook. It was an action shot—women's volleyball—and

Martha was bent horizontal to the floor, reaching, the palms of her hands in sharp focus, the tongue taut, the expression frank and competitive. There was no visible sweat. She wore white gym shorts. Her legs, he thought, were almost certainly the legs of a virgin, dry and without hair, the left knee cocked and carrying her entire weight, which was just over one hundred pounds. Lieutenant Cross remembered touching that left knee. A dark theater, he remembered, and the movie was *Bonnie and Clyde,* and Martha wore a tweed skirt, and during the final scene, when he touched her knee, she turned and looked at him in a sad, sober way that made him pull his hand back, but he would always remember the feel of the tweed skirt and the knee beneath it and the sound of the gunfire that killed Bonnie and Clyde, how embarrassing it was, how slow and oppressive. He remembered kissing her good night at the dorm door. Right then, he thought, he should've done something brave. He should've carried her up the stairs to her room and tied her to the bed and touched that left knee all night long. He should've risked it. Whenever he looked at the photographs, he thought of new things he should've done.

WHAT they carried was partly a function of rank, partly of field specialty.

As a first lieutenant and platoon leader, Jimmy Cross carried a compass, maps, code books, binoculars, and a .45-caliber pistol that weighed 2.9 pounds fully loaded. He carried a strobe light and the responsibility for the lives of his men.

As an RTO, Mitchell Sanders carried the PRC-25 radio, a killer, twenty-six pounds with its battery.

As a medic, Rat Kiley carried a canvas satchel filled with morphine and plasma and malaria tablets and surgical tape and comic books and all the things a medic must carry, including M&M's for especially bad wounds, for a total weight of nearly twenty pounds.

As a big man, therefore a machine gunner, Henry Dobbins carried the M-60, which weighed twenty-three pounds unloaded, but which was almost always loaded. In addition, Dobbins carried between ten and fifteen pounds of ammunition draped in belts across his chest and shoulders.

As PFCs or Spec 4s, most of them were common grunts and carried the standard M-16 gas-operated assault rifle. The weapon weighed 7.5 pounds unloaded, 8.2 pounds with its full twenty-round magazine. Depending on numerous factors, such as topography

> He carried a strobe light and the responsibility for the lives of his men.

6

7

8

9

10

11

and psychology, the riflemen carried anywhere from twelve to twenty magazines, usually in cloth bandoliers, adding on another 8.4 pounds at minimum, fourteen pounds at maximum. When it was available, they also carried M-16 maintenance gear—rods and steel brushes and swabs and tubes of LSA oil—all of which weighed about a pound. Among the grunts, some carried the M-79 grenade launcher, 5.9 pounds unloaded, a reasonably light weapon except for the ammunition, which was heavy. A single round weighed ten ounces. The typical load was twenty-five rounds. But Ted Lavender, who was scared, carried thirty-four rounds when he was shot and killed outside Than Khe, and he went down under an exceptional burden, more than twenty pounds of ammunition, plus the flak jacket and helmet and rations and water and toilet paper and tranquilizers and all the rest, plus the unweighed fear. He was dead weight. There was no twitching or flopping. Kiowa, who saw it happen, said it was like watching a rock fall, or a big sandbag or something—just boom, then down—not like the movies where the dead guy rolls around and does fancy spins and goes ass over teakettle—not like that, Kiowa said, the poor bastard just flat-fuck fell. Boom. Down. Nothing else. It was a bright morning in mid-April. Lieutenant Cross felt the pain. He blamed himself. They stripped off Lavender's canteens and ammo, all the heavy things, and Rat Kiley said the obvious, the guy's dead, and Mitchell Sanders used his radio to report one U.S. KIA and to request a chopper. Then they wrapped Lavender in his poncho. They carried him out to a dry paddy, established security, and sat smoking the dead man's dope until the chopper came. Lieutenant Cross kept to himself. He pictured Martha's smooth young face, thinking he loved her more than anything, more than his men, and now Ted Lavender was dead because he loved her so much and could not stop thinking about her. When the dust-off arrived, they carried Lavender aboard. Afterward they burned Than Khe. They marched until dusk, then dug their holes, and that night Kiowa kept explaining how you had to be there, how fast it was, how the poor guy just dropped like so much concrete, Boom-down, he said. Like cement.

IN addition to the three standard weapons—the M-60, M-16, and M-79—they carried whatever presented itself, or whatever seemed appropriate as a means of killing or staying alive. They carried catch-as-catch-can. At various times, in various situations, they carried M-14s and CAR-15s and Swedish Ks and grease guns and captured AK-47s and ChiCom's and RPGs and Simonov carbines and black-market Uzis and .38-caliber Smith & Wesson handguns and 66 mm LAW's and shotguns and silencers and blackjacks and bayonets and C-4 plastic explosives. Lee Strunk carried a slingshot; a weapon of last resort, he called it. Mitchell Sanders carried brass knuckles. Kiowa carried his grandfather's feathered hatchet. Every third or fourth man carried a Claymore antipersonnel mine—3.5 pounds with its firing device. They all carried fragmentation grenades—fourteen ounces each. They all carried at least one M-18 colored smoke grenade—twenty-four ounces. Some carried CS or tear-gas grenades. Some carried white-phosphorus grenades. They carried all they could bear, and then some, including a silent awe for the terrible power of the things they carried.

In the first week of April, before Lavender died, Lieutenant Jimmy Cross received a good-luck charm from Martha. It was a simple pebble, an ounce at most. Smooth to the touch, it was a milky-white color with flecks of orange and violet, oval-shaped, like a miniature egg. In the accompanying letter, Martha wrote that she had found the pebble on the Jersey shoreline, precisely where the land touched water at high tide, where things came together but also separated. It was this separate-but-together quality, she wrote, that had inspired her to pick up the pebble and to carry it in her breast pocket for several days, where it seemed weightless, and then to send it through the mail, by air, as a token of her truest feelings for him. Lieutenant Cross found this romantic. But he wondered what her truest feelings were, exactly, and what she meant by separate-but-together. He wondered how the tides and waves had come into play on that afternoon along the Jersey shoreline when Martha saw the pebble and bent down to rescue it from geology. He imagined bare feet. Martha was a poet, with the poet's sensibilities, and her feet would be brown and bare, the toenails unpainted, the eyes chilly and somber like the ocean in March, and though it was painful, he wondered who had been with her that afternoon. He imagined a pair of shadows moving along the strip of sand where things came together but also separated. It was phantom jealousy, he knew, but he couldn't help himself. He loved her so much. On the march, through the hot days of early April, he carried the pebble in his mouth, turning it with his tongue, tasting sea salts and moisture. His mind wandered. He had difficulty keeping his attention on the war. On occasion he would yell at his men to spread out the column, to keep their eyes open, but then he would slip away into daydreams, just pretending, walking barefoot along the Jersey shore, with Martha, carrying nothing. He would feel himself rising. Sun and waves and gentle winds, all love and lightness.

14
15 WHAT they carried varied by mission. When a mission took them to the mountains, they carried mosquito netting, machetes, canvas tarps, and extra bug juice.

16   If a mission seemed especially hazardous, or if it involved a place they knew to be bad, they carried everything they could. In certain heavily mined AOs, where the land was dense with Toe Poppers and Bouncing Betties, they took turns humping a twenty-eight-pound mine detector. With its headphones and big sensing plate, the equipment was a stress on the lower back and shoulders, awkward to handle, often useless because of the shrapnel in the earth, but they carried it anyway, partly for safety, partly for the illusion of safety.

17   On ambush, or other night missions, they carried peculiar little odds and ends. Kiowa always took along his New Testament and a pair of moccasins for silence. Dave Jensen carried night-sight vitamins high in carotene. Lee Strunk carried his slingshot; ammo, he claimed, would never be a problem. Rat Kiley carried brandy and M&M's. Until he was shot, Ted Lavender carried the starlight scope, which weighed 6.3 pounds with its aluminum carrying case. Henry Dobbins carried his girlfriend's pantyhose wrapped around his neck as a comforter. They all carried ghosts. When dark came, they would move out single file across the meadows and paddies to their ambush coordinates, where they would quietly set up the Claymores and lie down and spend the night waiting.

18   Other missions were more complicated and required special equipment. In mid-April, it was their mission to search out and destroy the elaborate tunnel complexes in the Than Khe area south of Chu Lai. To blow the tunnels, they carried one-pound blocks of pentrite high explosives; four blocks to a man, sixty-eight pounds in all. They carried wiring, detonators, and battery-powered clackers. Dave Jensen carried earplugs. Most often, before blowing the tunnels, they were ordered by higher command to search them, which was considered bad news, but by and large they just shrugged and carried out orders. Be-

cause he was a big man, Henry Dobbins was excused from tunnel duty. The others would draw numbers. Before Lavender died there were seventeen men in the platoon, and whoever drew the number seventeen would strip off his gear and crawl in head first with a flashlight and Lieutenant Cross's .45-caliber pistol. The rest of them would fan out as security. They would sit down or kneel, not facing the hole, listening to the ground beneath them, imagining cobwebs and ghosts, whatever was down there—the tunnel walls squeezing in—how the flashlight seemed impossibly heavy in the hand and how it was tunnel vision in the very strictest sense, compression in all ways, even time, and how you had to wiggle in—ass and elbows—a swallowed-up feeling—and how you found yourself worrying about odd things—will your flashlight go dead? Do rats carry rabies? If you screamed, how far would the sound carry? Would your buddies hear it? Would they have the courage to drag you out? In some respects, though not many, the waiting was worse than the tunnel itself. Imagination was a killer.

If you screamed, how far would the sound carry?

1   On April 16, when Lee Strunk drew the number seventeen, he laughed and muttered something and went down quickly. The morning was hot and very still. Not good, Kiowa said. He looked at the tunnel opening, then out across a dry paddy toward the village of Than Khe. Nothing moved. No clouds or birds or people. As they waited, the men smoked and drank Kool-Aid, not talking much, feeling sympathy for Lee Strunk but also feeling the luck of the draw, You win some, you lose some, said Mitchell Sanders, and sometimes you settle for a rain check. It was a tired line and no one laughed.

2   Henry Dobbins ate a tropical chocolate bar. Ted Lavender popped a tranquilizer and went off to pee.

2   After five minutes, Lieutenant Jimmy Cross moved to the tunnel, leaned down, and examined the darkness. Trouble, he thought—a cave-in maybe. And then suddenly, without willing it, he was thinking about Martha. The stresses and fractures, the quick collapse, the two of them buried alive under all that weight. Dense, crushing love. Kneeling, watching the hole, he tried to concentrate on Lee Strunk and the war, all the dangers, but his love was too much for him, he felt paralyzed, he wanted to sleep inside her lungs and breathe her blood and be smothered. He wanted her to be a virgin and not a virgin, all at once. He wanted to know her. Intimate secrets—why poetry? Why so sad? Why the grayness in her eyes? Why so alone? Not lonely, just alone—riding her bike across campus or sitting off by herself in the cafeteria. Even dancing, she danced

alone—and it was the aloneness that filled him with love. He remembered telling her that one evening. How she nodded and looked away. And how, later, when he kissed her, she received the kiss without returning it, her eyes wide open, not afraid, not a virgin's eyes, just flat and uninvolved.

22 Lieutenant Cross gazed at the tunnel. But he was not there. He was buried with Martha under the white sand at the Jersey shore. They were pressed together, and the pebble in his mouth was her tongue. He was smiling. Vaguely, he was aware of how quiet the day was, the sullen paddies, yet he could not bring himself to worry about matters of security. He was beyond that. He was just a kid at war, in love. He was twenty-two years old. He couldn't help it.

23 A few moments later Lee Strunk crawled out of the tunnel. He came up grinning, filthy but alive. Lieutenant Cross nodded and closed his eyes while the others clapped Strunk on the back and made jokes about rising from the dead.

24 Worms, Rat Kiley said. Right out of the grave. Fuckin' zombie.

25 The men laughed. They all felt great relief.

26 Spook City, said Mitchell Sanders.

27 Lee Strunk made a funny ghost sound, a kind of moaning, yet very happy, and right then, when Strunk made that high happy moaning sound, when he went *Ahhooooo*, right then Ted Lavender was shot in the head on his way back from peeing. He lay with his mouth open. The teeth were broken. There was a swollen black bruise under his left eye. The cheekbone was gone. Oh shit, Rat Kiley said, the guy's dead. The guy's dead, he kept saying, which seemed profound—the guy's dead. I mean really.

28 THE things they carried were determined to some extent by superstition. Lieutenant Cross carried his good-luck pebble. Dave Jensen carried a rabbit's foot. Norman Bowker, otherwise a very gentle person, carried a thumb that had been presented to him as a gift by Mitchell Sanders. The thumb was dark brown, rubbery to the touch, and weighed four ounces at most. It had been cut from a VC corpse, a boy of fifteen or sixteen. They'd found him at the bottom of an irrigation ditch, badly burned, flies in his mouth and eyes. The boy wore black shorts and sandals. At the time of his death he had been carrying a pouch of rice, a rifle, and three magazines of ammunition.

29 You want my opinion, Mitchell Sanders said, there's a definite moral here.

30 He put his hand on the dead boy's wrist. He was quiet for a time, as if counting a pulse, then he patted the stomach, almost affectionately, and used Kiowa's hunting hatchet to remove the thumb.

31 Henry Dobbins asked what the moral was.

32 Moral?

33 You know. *Moral.*

34 Sanders wrapped the thumb in toilet paper and handed it across to Norman Bowker. There was no blood. Smiling, he kicked the boy's head, watched the files scatter, and said, It's like with that old TV show—Paladin. Have gun, will travel.

35 Henry Dobbins thought about it.

36 Yeah, well, he finally said. I don't see no moral.

37 There it *is*, man.

38 Fuck off.

39 THEY carried USO stationery and pencils and pens. They carried Sterno, safety pins, trip flares, signal flares, spools of wire, razor blades, chewing tobacco, liberated joss sticks and statuettes of the smiling Buddha, candles, grease pencils, *The Stars and Stripes*, fingernail clippers, Psy Ops leaflets, bush hats, bolos, and much more. Twice a week, when the resupply choppers came in, they carried hot chow in green Mermite cans and large canvas bags filled with iced beer and soda pop. They carried plastic water containers, each with a two-gallon capacity. Mitchell Sanders carried a set of starched tiger fatigues for special occasions. Henry Dobbins carried Black Flag insecticide. Dave Jensen carried empty sandbags that could be filled at night for added protection. Lee Strunk carried tanning lotion. Some things they carried in common. Taking turns, they carried the big PRC-77 scrambler radio, which weighed thirty pounds with its battery. They shared the weight of memory. They took up what others could no longer bear. Often, they carried each other, the wounded or weak. They carried infections. They carried chess sets, basketballs, Vietnamese-English dictionaries, insignia of rank, Bronze Stars and Purple Hearts, plastic cards imprinted with the Code of Conduct. They carried diseases, among them malaria and dysentery. They carried lice and ringworm and leeches and paddy algae and various rots and molds. They carried the land itself—Vietnam, the place, the soil—a powdery orange-red dust

that covered their boots and fatigues and faces. They carried the sky. The whole atmosphere, they carried it, the humidity, the monsoons, the stink of fungus and decay, all of it, they carried gravity. They moved like mules. By daylight they took sniper fire, at night they were mortared, but it was not battle, it was just the endless march, village to village, without purpose, nothing won or lost. They marched for the sake of the march. They plodded along slowly, dumbly, leaning forward against the heat, unthinking, all blood and bone, simple grunts, soldiering with their legs, toiling up the hills and down into the paddies and across the rivers and up again and down, just humping, one step and then the next and then another, but no volition, no will, because it was au-tomatic, it was anatomy, and the war was entirely a matter of posture and carriage, the hump was everything, a kind of in-ertia, a kind of emptiness, a dullness of desire and intellect and conscience and hope and human sen-sibility. Their principles were in their feet. Their calculations were biological. They had no sense of strategy or mission. They searched the vil-lages without knowing what to look for, not caring, kicking over jars of rice, frisking children and old men, blowing tunnels, sometimes setting fires and sometimes not, then forming up and moving on to the next village, then other villages, where it would always be the same. They carried their own lives. The pressures were enormous. In the heat of early after-noon, they would remove their helmets and flak jack-ets, walking bare, which was dangerous but which helped ease the strain. They would often discard things along the route of march. Purely for comfort, they would throw away rations, blow their Claymores and grenades, no matter, because by nightfall the re-supply choppers would arrive with more of the same, then a day or two later still more, fresh watermelons and crates of ammunition and sunglasses and woolen sweaters—the resources were stunning—sparklers for the Fourth of July, colored eggs for Easter. It was the great American war chest—the fruits of science, the smokestacks, the canneries, the arsenals at Hartford, the Minnesota forests, the machine shops, the vast fields of corn and wheat—they carried like freight trains; they carried it on their backs and shoulders— and for all the ambiguities of Vietnam, all the mys-teries and unknowns, there was at least the single abiding certainty that they would never be at a loss for things to carry.

AFTER the chopper took Lavender away, Lieu-tenant Jimmy Cross led his men into the vil-lage of Than Khe. They burned everything. They shot chickens and dogs, they trashed the village well, they called in artillery and watched the wreckage, then they marched for several hours through the hot afternoon, and then at dusk, while Kiowa explained how Lavender died, Lieutenant Cross found himself trembling.   **40**

He tried not to cry. With his entrenching tool, which weighed five pounds, he began digging a hole in the earth.   **41**

He felt shame. He hated himself. He had loved Martha more than his men, and as a consequence Lavender was now dead, and this was something he would have to carry like a stone in his stom-ach for the rest of the war.   **42**

All he could do was dig. He used his entrenching tool like an ax, slashing, feeling both love and hate, and then later, when it was full dark, he sat at the bottom of his foxhole and wept. It went on for a long while. In part, he was grieving for Ted Lavender, but mostly it was for Martha, and for himself, because she be-longed to another world, which was not quite real, and because she was a junior at Mount Sebastian College in New Jersey, a poet and a virgin and uninvolved, and because he realized she did not love him and never would.   **43**

LIKE cement, Kiowa whispered in the dark. I swear to God—boom-down. Not a word.   **44**

I've heard this, said Norman Bowker.   **45**

A pisser, you know? Still zipping himself   **46**
up. Zapped while zipping.

All right, fine. That's enough.   **47**
Yeah, but you had to see it, the guy just—   **48**
I *heard*, man. Cement. So why not shut the fuck *up?*   **49**
Kiowa shook his head sadly and glanced over at the   **50**
hole where Lieutenant Jimmy Cross sat watching the night. The air was thick and wet. A warm, dense fog had settled over the paddies and there was the stillness that precedes rain.

After a time Kiowa sighed.   **51**
One thing for sure, he said. The Lieutenant's in   **52**
some deep hurt. I mean that crying jag—the way he was carrying on—it wasn't fake or anything, it was real heavy-duty hurt. The man cares.

Sure, Norman Bowker said.   **53**
Say what you want, the man does care.   **54**

We all got problems.

Not Lavender.

No, I guess not, Bowker said. Do me a favor, though.

Shut up?

That's a smart Indian. Shut up.

Shrugging, Kiowa pulled off his boots. He wanted to say more, just to lighten up his sleep, but instead he opened his New Testament and arranged it beneath his head as a pillow. The fog made things seem hollow and unattached. He tried not to think about Ted Lavender, but then he was thinking how fast it was, no drama, down and dead, and how it was hard to feel anything except surprise. It seemed un-Christian. He wished he could find some great sadness, or even anger, but the emotion wasn't there and he couldn't make it happen. Mostly he felt pleased to be alive. He liked the smell of the New Testament under his cheek, the leather and ink and paper and glue, whatever the chemicals were. He liked hearing the sounds of night. Even his fatigue, it felt fine, the stiff muscles and the prickly awareness of his own body, a floating feeling. He enjoyed not being dead. Lying there, Kiowa admired Lieutenant Jimmy Cross's capacity for grief. He wanted to share the man's pain, he wanted to care as Jimmy Cross cared. And yet when he closed his eyes, all he could think was Boom-down, and all he could feel was the pleasure of having his boots off and the fog curling in around him and the damp soil and the Bible smells and the plush comfort of night.

After a moment Norman Bowker sat up in the dark.

What the hell, he said. You want to talk, *talk*. Tell it to me.

Forget it.

No, man, go on. One thing I hate, it's a silent Indian.

FOR the most part they carried themselves with poise, a kind of dignity. Now and then, however, there were times of panic, when they squealed or wanted to squeal but couldn't, when they twitched and made moaning sounds and covered their heads and said Dear Jesus and flopped around on the earth and fired their weapons blindly and cringed and sobbed and begged for the noise to stop and went wild and made stupid promises to themselves and to God and to their mothers and fathers, hoping not to die. In different ways, it happened to all of them. Afterward, when the firing ended, they would blink and peek up. They would touch their bodies, feeling shame, then quickly hiding it. They would

force themselves to stand. As if in slow motion, frame by frame, the world would take on the old logic—absolute silence, then the wind, then sunlight, then voices. It was the burden of being alive. Awkwardly, the men would reassemble themselves, first in private, then in groups, becoming soldiers again. They would repair the leaks in their eyes. They would check for casualties, call in dust-offs, light cigarettes, try to smile, clear their throats and spit and begin cleaning their weapons. After a time someone would shake his head and say, No lie, I almost shit my pants, and someone else would laugh, which meant it was bad, yes, but the guy had obviously not shit his pants, it wasn't that bad, and in any case nobody would ever do such a thing and then go ahead and talk about it. They would squint into the dense, oppressive sunlight. For a few moments, perhaps, they would fall silent, lighting a joint and tracking its passage from man to man, inhaling, holding in the humiliation. Scary stuff, one of them might say. But then someone else would grin or flick his eyebrows and say, Roger-dodger, almost cut me a new asshole, *almost.*

They were afraid of dying but they were even more afraid to show it.

There were numerous such poses. Some carried themselves with a sort of wistful resignation, others with pride or stiff soldierly discipline or good humor or macho zeal. They were afraid of dying but they were even more afraid to show it.

They found jokes to tell.

They used a hard vocabulary to contain the terrible softness. *Greased*, they'd say. *Offed, lit up, zapped while zipping.* It wasn't cruelty, just stage presence. They were actors and the war came at them in 3-D. When someone died, it wasn't quite dying, because in a curious way it seemed scripted, and because they had their lines mostly memorized, irony mixed with tragedy, and because they called it by other names, as if to encyst and destroy the reality of death itself. They kicked corpses. They cut off thumbs. They talked grunt lingo. They told stories about Ted Lavender's supply of tranquilizers, how the poor guy didn't feel a thing, how incredibly tranquil he was.

There's a moral here, said Mitchell Sanders.

They were waiting for Lavender's chopper, smoking the dead man's dope.

The moral's pretty obvious, Sanders said, and winked. Stay away from drugs. No joke, they'll ruin your day every time.

Cute, said Henry Dobbins.

Mind-blower, get it? Talk about wiggy—nothing left, just blood and brains.

They made themselves laugh.

75 There it is, they'd say, over and over, as if the repetition itself were an act of poise, a balance between crazy and almost crazy, knowing without going. There it is, which meant be cool, let it ride, because oh yeah, man, you can't change what can't be changed, there it is, there it absolutely and positively and fucking well *is*.

76 They were tough.

77 They carried all the emotional baggage of men who might die. Grief, terror, love, longing—these were intangibles, but the intangibles had their own mass and specific gravity, they had tangible weight. They carried shameful memories. They carried the common secret of cowardice barely restrained, the instinct to run or freeze or hide, and in many respects this was the heaviest burden of all, for it could never be put down, it required perfect balance and perfect posture. They carried their reputations. They carried the soldier's greatest fear, which was the fear of blushing. Men killed, and died, because they were embarrassed not to. It was what had brought them to the war in the first place, nothing positive, no dreams of glory or honor, just to avoid the blush of dishonor. They died so as not to die of embarrassment. They crawled into tunnels and walked point and advanced under fire. Each morning, despite the unknowns, they made their legs move. They endured. They kept humping. They did not submit to the obvious alternative, which was simply to close the eyes and fall. So easy, really. Go limp and tumble to the ground and let the muscles unwind and not speak and not budge until your buddies picked you up and lifted you into the chopper that would roar and dip its nose and carry you off to the world. A mere matter of falling, yet no one ever fell. It was not courage, exactly; the object was not valor. Rather, they were too frightened to be cowards.

Men killed, and died, because they were embarrassed not to.

78 By and large they carried these things inside, maintaining the masks of composure. They sneered at sick call. They spoke bitterly about guys who had found release by shooting off their own toes or fingers. Pussies, they'd say. Candyasses. It was fierce, mocking talk, with only a trace of envy or awe, but even so, the image played itself out behind their eyes.

They imagined the muzzle against flesh. They imagined the quick, sweet pain, then the evacuation to Japan, then a hospital with warm beds and cute geisha nurses.

79 They dreamed of freedom birds.

80 At night, on guard, staring into the dark, they were carried away by jumbo jets. They felt the rush of take-off. *Gone!* they yelled. And then velocity, wings and engines, a smiling stewardess—but it was more than a plane, it was a real bird, a big sleek silver bird with feathers and talons and high screeching. They were flying. The weights fell off, there was nothing to bear. They laughed and held on tight, feeling the cold slap of wind and altitude, soaring, thinking *It's over, I'm gone!*—they were naked, they were light and free—it was all lightness, bright and fast and buoyant, light as light, a helium buzz in the brain, a giddy bubbling in the lungs as they were taken up over the clouds and the war, beyond duty, beyond gravity and mortification and global entanglements—*Sin loi!* they yelled, *I'm sorry, motherfuckers, but I'm out of it, I'm goofed, I'm on a space cruise, I'm gone!*—and it was a restful, disencumbered sensation, just riding the light waves, sailing that big silver freedom bird over the mountains and oceans, over America, over the farms and great sleeping cities and cemeteries and highways and the golden arches of McDonald's. It was flight, a kind of fleeing, a kind of falling, falling higher and higher, spinning off the edge of the earth and beyond the sun and through the vast, silent vacuum where there were no burdens and where everything weighed exactly nothing. *Gone!* they screamed, *I'm sorry but I'm gone!* And so at night, not quite dreaming, they gave themselves over to lightness, they were carried, they were purely borne.

ON the morning after Ted Lavender died, First Lieutenant Jimmy Cross crouched at the bottom of his foxhole and burned Martha's letters. Then he burned the two photographs. There was a steady rain falling, which made it difficult, but he used heat tabs and Sterno to build a small fire, screening it with his body, holding the photographs over the tight blue flame with the tips of his fingers.

81 He realized it was only a gesture. Stupid, he thought. Sentimental, too, but mostly just stupid.

82 Lavender was dead. You couldn't burn the blame.

83 Besides, the letters were in his head. And even now, without photographs, Lieutenant Cross could see Martha playing volleyball in her white gym shorts and yellow T-shirt. He could see her moving in the rain.

84 When the fire died out, Lieutenant Cross pulled his poncho over his shoulders and ate breakfast from a can.

85 There was no great mystery, he decided.

86 In those burned letters Martha had never mentioned the war, except to say, Jimmy take care of yourself. She wasn't involved. She signed the letters "Love,"

but it wasn't love, and all the fine lines and technicalities did not matter.

The morning came up wet and blurry. Everything seemed part of everything else, the fog and Martha and the deepening rain.

It was a war, after all.

Half smiling, Lieutenant Jimmy Cross took out his maps. He shook his head hard, as if to clear it, then bent forward and began planning the day's march. In ten minutes, or maybe twenty, he would rouse the men and they would pack up and head west, where the maps showed the country to be green and inviting. They would do what they had always done. The rain might add some weight, but otherwise it would be one more day layered upon all the other days.

He was realistic about it. There was that new hardness in his stomach.

No more fantasies, he told himself.

Henceforth, when he thought about Martha, it would be only to think that she belonged elsewhere. He would shut down the daydreams. This was not Mount Sebastian, it was another world, where there were no pretty poems or midterm exams, a place where men died because of carelessness and gross stupidity. Kiowa was right. Boom-down, and you were dead, never partly dead.

Briefly, in the rain, Lieutenant Cross saw Martha's gray eyes gazing back at him.

He understood.

It was very sad, he thought. The things men carried inside. The things men did or felt they had to do.

He almost nodded at her, but didn't.

Instead he went back to his maps. He was now determined to perform his duties firmly and without negligence. It wouldn't help Lavender, he knew that, but from this point on he would comport himself as a soldier. He would dispose of his good-luck pebble. Swallow it, maybe, or use Lee Strunk's slingshot, or just drop it along the trail. On the march he would impose strict field discipline. He would be careful to send out flank security, to prevent straggling or bunching up, to keep his troops moving at the proper pace and at the proper interval. He would insist on clean weapons. He would confiscate the remainder of Lavender's dope. Later in the day, perhaps, he would call the men together and speak to them plainly. He would accept the blame for what had happened to Ted Lavender. He would be a man about it. He would look them in the eyes, keeping his chin level, and he would issue the new SOPs in a calm, impersonal tone of voice, an officer's voice, leaving no room for argument or discussion. Commencing immediately, he'd tell them, they would no longer abandon equipment along the route of march. They would police up their acts. They would get their shit together, and keep it together, and maintain it neatly and in good working order.

He would not tolerate laxity. He would show strength, distancing himself.

Among the men there would be grumbling, of course, and maybe worse, because their days would seem longer and their loads heavier, but Lieutenant Cross reminded himself that his obligation was not to be loved but to lead. He would dispense with love; it was not now a factor. And if anyone quarreled or complained, he would simply tighten his lips and arrange his shoulders in the correct command posture. He might give a curt little nod. Or he might not. He might just shrug and say Carry on, then they would saddle up and form into a column and move out toward the villages of Than Khe.

IF you enjoyed mulling over the meaning, ultimately mysterious, of the stone in "The Things They Carried," you might also enjoy considering possible interpretations of the grandmother's dance regalia in Sherman Alexie's "What You Pawn I Will Redeem" (in chapter 11) or the car keys in T. Coraghessan Boyle's "Greasy Lake" (chapter 4).

GOING FURTHER War is what Herman Melville (see chapter 14) would call a "great" theme, and in our tumultuous modern age it often serves as literary material, as in, for example, the novels of Joseph Heller (*Catch-22*), Norman Mailer (*The Naked and the Dead*), and James Jones (*The Thin Red Line*). As we suggested, war has emerged in the work of Tim O'Brien as his great subject, sometimes overshadowing the domestic aspects of life in his fiction.

Writing from Reading

Summarize

1 Explain why Cross burns Martha's letters after Lavender's death.

2 O'Brien mentions various reasons why the men carried things. For example, they carried a number of things "by necessity." What are the other reasons given? How does the reason given affect the story that follows?

Analyze Craft

3 Discuss how O'Brien uses lists in this story. How do the lists affect the tone and themes of the story?

4 Consider the names Cross and Lavender. What symbolic meanings do these names suggest?

Analyze Voice

5 Identify passages and details in the story that seem to come from O'Brien's personal experience. What makes them seem this way?

6 The men in this story are soldiers in the Vietnam War. Which of their experiences and the things they carry are specific to that war? Consider reasons of era, culture, climate, and terrain. Which would apply to any war?

Synthesize Summary and Analysis

7 What symbolic meaning does Ted Lavender's death take on? Find each reference to Lavender and to his death and explore the effect the repetition has on you as a reader.

Interpret the Story

8 Consider why O'Brien includes so many detailed passages about Lieutenant Jimmy Cross. How might his thoughts, fears, and fantasies about Martha represent the feelings of all soldiers who served in Vietnam?

CONTINUED FROM PAGE 313

SYMBOLS IN EVERYDAY LIFE AND LITERATURE

We use symbols whenever we speak or write, draw or gesture. Those little icons on your computer screen—the picture of a trash can, the picture of a disk—are symbols. An image represents an idea; a picture stands for a thing. Symbols in literature, however, rarely have single, unambiguous meanings. Symbolism takes us deep into the tangled web of words and characters, incidents and objects in a story. Because symbols are compact and efficient, they can communicate a broad array of feelings and impressions. Moreover, a symbol doesn't boil down to a single "correct" meaning. When a symbolic object or act is successfully embedded in a story, it imbues the story with multiple meanings—and therefore the possibility of multiple interpretations.

In "The Things They Carried," for example, the pebble is a gift from Martha; it's something she has touched, so for Cross it embodies her essence. It comes from a beach back home, so it also carries the essence of "beach"—a place of serenity as well as care-free pleasures. It seems a kind of rabbit's foot, a good-luck charm. Yet it is also a mere piece of stone. Although Martha herself sees symbolic meaning in the stone—she points out the "separate-but-together quality" of the tide line where she found it—anybody else strolling the beach would likely have passed it by as just another ordinary pebble. Now, layered with associations and memories, it becomes symbolic of Cross's longing for romantic love and also with the promise and possibility of escape from brutal war. Lieutenant Cross carries the pebble in his mouth, guarding it, tasting it, absorbing all it carries. Shown in these various lights, the pebble acquires so much significance by the time Cross vows to discard it that we know he's giving a great deal away by doing so.

> "So in this story I take on death—a huge subject. But in this story the way into that huge subject is through the watch that is left behind by a woman who has died, which her daughters are now fighting over." Conversation with Amy Hempel

Just as an object or character can hold many shades of meaning, so can a **symbolic act,** a gesture or action beyond the everyday practical definition. When Lieutenant Cross discards Martha's pebble, he discards an entire dream. In the symbolic act of *carrying*, the weary soldiers not only shoulder a host of physical objects—letters, can openers, pocket knives, salt tablets, ammunition, dental floss—they also bear a host of emotional burdens: the fear of death, the horrors of what they've seen, the fatigue of war.

SYMBOL AND ALLEGORY

Authors have not always used or thought of symbols in this way. Most literature was once allegorical. An **allegory** is a story in which major elements such as characters and settings represent universal truths or moral lessons in a one-to-one correspondence, as they do in the fable of the grasshopper and the ant. In this fable the grasshopper is careless all the way through, frittering away its time, while the ant labors diligently to put away food for the winter. When winter comes, you can guess which one will be secure and which one will suffer. In this allegorical narrative, the lesson to be learned is that it is best to prepare for future necessity. Each character represents a single form of behavior—"irresponsibility" for the grasshopper versus "conscientiousness" for the ant. Allegorical figures are one-dimensional and constant; "what they carry" does not change.

Allegory is a cardboard cutout kind of symbolism; in allegory, a value such as "virtue" or "vice" remains constant from beginning to end. In our discussion of "Character" (chapter 5), we drew the distinction between "flat" and "round" characters; in this regard an allegorical figure would be *flat*, whereas a symbolic figure or object—

THE HISTORY OF SYMBOLISM

The use of allegory stems from the old pagan religions, in which the gods were understood to have created certain constant values—good, evil, heroism, fidelity—in human beings, who were seen as incapable of change. These values gradually adapted to Christian symbols of salvation and redemption. Toward the end of the eighteenth century, poetry and fiction moved largely away from allegory and toward a more multidimensional symbolism. By the mid-nineteenth century, most serious writers produced work that was decidedly symbolic rather than allegorical. Readers, too, took on the new task of interpreting literature in multiple ways, contributing new perspectives and initiating new discussions about the growing literary cannon. What once was myth—an age-old and collective story—became, in time, an individual's tale. If you want to look at these developments in political terms, you might say that allegory is the mode of kings and religious uniformity, while symbolism is the mode of democracy and governments made up of a multiplicity of views.

what O'Brien identifies as "the pebble or the shooting of a baby water buffalo"—would be understood as *round*. In contrast to allegory, symbols convey multiple meanings, and the meaning may expand and become more complex over the course of the story.

RECOGNIZING AND APPRECIATING SYMBOLS

Symbolic meanings are not "hidden," as many readers have come to believe. Their context suggests them, as does the way characters view them. The red carnation the protagonist wears in Willa Cather's "Paul's Case" (chapter 5) becomes far more than a flower in a lapel. The decoration, in one sense, seems a symbol of Paul's aspiration, of his belief that he belongs elsewhere, above the dreary situation he was born into. Yet, from his teachers' perspective, his lapel carnations are a sign of his insubordina-

> "We know from Greek myth and from many mythic structures, the three witches, the three sisters, Cinderella and her two sisters, and on and on. It's just a very organic form, and the triangle is, in general, a very important figure for a fiction writer to have in mind."
> Conversation with John Updike

tion and pretentiousness—precisely what they dislike about him. It's also important to notice that a carnation is scarcely *original* as a flower to wear; it's not as if he puts a sunflower in his buttonhole, or an elaborate orchid; his is a conventional choice. Late in the story, after Paul has escaped into a new life, the carnations embody the futility of his dream.

It's possible to go deeper still. For example, we can ask, "Why, of all flowers, a carnation?" With a little digging, we learn that it is one of the oldest cultivated flowers— dating back to ancient Greece and Rome—and that its botanical name *dianthus* means divine flower. From this comes a feeling that Paul's dreams are ancient, enduring, perhaps even cosmic. Furthermore, in the dictionary, we see that one root of the word is *carne*, or flesh. These images add to and deepen the sense we have of Paul as one who aspires to something grand, something divine, while bound to the earth and the realities of his own flesh. We cannot know whether Cather intended these additional meanings, but we do know that writers choose images carefully, for their resonance.

How can you tell when an image, character, or act is significant in a symbolic sense? First, look at the title of a work. O'Brien sets us up to know what is going to be laden with symbolic importance in his title, "The Things They Carried." Notice also images that you see repeated throughout the story, like the carnations in "Paul's Case." Recurrence, especially, gives an image importance, drawing attention to it, suggesting it has significance beyond the ordinary. Sometimes the author focuses on a precise detail in a way that seems to be saying, "Notice this; it says something important," as in the story in this chapter, "No One's a Mystery," when the narrator describes the manure clinging to Jack's boots. Reflect on how an image is used in a story and how it connects to the characters, especially the protagonist, as in Gregor Samsa in Franz Kafka's "The Metamorphosis" in this chapter.

SYMBOLISM IN CONTEXT

When we read fiction, we are invited—in fact, called upon—to interpret objects, characters, and behavior beyond their literal meanings, and to look for multiple, not simply single, truths or meanings. The four stories in this chapter are filled with richly layered images. As you read, consider how the predominant symbols might be interpreted in multiple ways. How might each symbol be read both literally and figuratively, both as it actually is (a pebble) and as what it represents (longing)? What we learn from reading with symbolic potential in mind not only deepens our reading experience but also prepares us to understand the significance of events in our own lives.

Nathaniel Hawthorne (1804–1864)

Shortly after graduating from Bowdoin College, Nathaniel Hawthorne published his first novel, *Fanshawe* (1828), at his own expense, only to reclaim and destroy nearly every copy. Hawthorne also struggled with holding ordinary jobs—in his case, those of bookkeeper and customs-house employee—while trying to be a writer. Despite these difficulties, Hawthorne became famous with his publication of *The Scarlet Letter* (1850) and has remained in the American canon ever since. A native of Massachusetts and a descendant of prosecutors in the Salem witch trials,

Hawthorne was fascinated with the Puritanical influence in New England, and his work is known for its exploration of sin, punishment, and atonement. Even during his most productive period—when he and his wife lived in Concord, Massachusetts, and maintained friendships with writers Ralph Waldo Emerson and Henry David Thoreau, who were part of a movement called *transcendentalism* and focused on how humans were basically good and connected to the natural world—Hawthorne explored the dark side of human nature in his fiction. To do this, he often turned to a modified form of allegory, making

his characters less like real individuals and more like representations of a theme or concept. His writing is a blend of realism and romanticism, and he is known as a Romantic in the sense that he fused unreal occurrences or situations with his often all-too-human characters. "Young Goodman Brown," a story from his collection *Mosses from an Old Manse* (1846), is quintessential Hawthorne; he uses Goodman Brown's slightly fantastical encounter in the woods to expose the sin present in even the most pious people.

AS YOU READ   As you read, watch for repeated images—concrete details the author wishes to bring to your attention. How do these particular objects or images alter over the course of the story? What kinds of feelings do they stir in you?

FOR INTERACTIVE READING . . . Circle the repeated images. Make brief notes in the margin regarding their portrayal. Based on the context, what feeling or value do you associate with each?

Young Goodman Brown (1835)

1 YOUNG Goodman Brown came forth at sunset into the street of Salem village; but put his head back, after crossing the threshold, to exchange a parting kiss with his young wife. And Faith, as the wife was aptly named, thrust her own pretty head into the street, letting the wind play with the pink ribbons of her cap while she called to Goodman Brown.

2 "Dearest heart," whispered she, softly and rather sadly, when her lips were close to his ear, "prithee put off your journey until sunrise and sleep in your own bed to-night. A lone woman is troubled with such dreams and such thoughts that she's afeard of herself sometimes. Pray tarry with me this night, dear husband, of all nights in the year."

3 "My love and my Faith," replied young Goodman Brown, "of all nights in the year, this one night must I tarry away from thee. My journey, as thou callest it, forth and back again, must needs be done 'twixt now and sunrise. What, my sweet, pretty wife, dost thou doubt me already, and we but three months married?"

4 "Then God bless you!" said Faith, with the pink ribbons; "and may you find all well when you come back."

5 "Amen!" cried Goodman Brown. "Say thy prayers, dear Faith, and go to bed at dusk, and no harm will come to thee."

6 So they parted; and the young man pursued his way until, being about to turn the corner by the meeting house, he looked back and saw the head of Faith still peeping after him with a melancholy air, in spite of her pink ribbons.

7 "Poor little Faith!" thought he, for his heart smote him. "What a wretch am I to leave her on such an errand! She talks of dreams, too. Methought as she spoke there was trouble in her face, as if a dream had warned her what work is to be done to-night. But no, no; 'twould kill her to think it. Well, she's a blessed angel on earth; and after this one night I'll cling to her skirts and follow her to heaven."

8 With this excellent resolve for the future, Goodman Brown felt himself justified in making more haste on his present evil purpose. He had taken a dreary road, darkened by all the gloomiest trees of the forest, which barely stood aside to let the narrow path creep through, and closed immediately behind. It was all as lonely as could be; and there is this peculiarity in such a solitude, that the traveller knows not who may be concealed by the innumerable trunks and thick boughs overhead; so that with lonely footsteps he may yet be passing through an unseen multitude.

9 "There may be a devilish Indian behind every tree," said Goodman Brown to himself; and he glanced fearfully behind him as he added, "What if the devil himself should be at my very elbow!"

10 His head being turned back, he passed a crook of the road, and, looking forward again, beheld the figure of a man, in grave and decent attire, seated at the foot of an old tree. He arose at Goodman Brown's approach and walked onward side by side with him.

11 "You are late, Goodman Brown," said he. "The clock of the Old South was striking as I came through Boston; and that is full fifteen minutes agone."

12 "Faith kept me back a while," replied the young man, with a tremor in his voice, caused by the sudden appearance of his companion, though not wholly unexpected.

13 It was now deep dusk in the forest, and deepest in that part of it where these two were journeying. As nearly as could be discerned, the second traveller was about fifty years old, apparently in the same rank of life as Goodman Brown, and bearing a considerable resemblance to him, though perhaps more in expression than features. Still they might have been taken for father and son. And yet, though the elder person was as simply clad as the younger, and as simple in manner too, he had an indescribable air of one who knew the world, and who would not have felt abashed at the gov-

ernor's dinner table or in King William's court, were it possible that his affairs should call him thither. But the only thing about him that could be fixed upon as remarkable was his staff, which bore the likeness of a great black snake, so curiously wrought that it might almost be seen to twist and wriggle itself like a living serpent. This, of course, must have been an ocular deception, assisted by the uncertain light.

14 "Come, Goodman Brown," cried his fellow-traveller, "this is a dull pace for the beginning of a journey. Take my staff, if you are so soon weary."

15 "Friend," said the other, exchanging his slow pace for a full stop, "having kept covenant by meeting thee here, it is my purpose now to return whence I came. I have scruples touching the matter thou wot'st of."

16 "Sayest thou so?" replied he of the serpent, smiling apart. "Let us walk on, nevertheless, reasoning as we go; and if I convince thee not thou shalt turn back. We are but a little way in the forest yet."

17 "Too far! too far!" exclaimed the goodman, unconsciously resuming his walk. "My father never went into the woods on such an errand, nor his father before him. We have been a race of honest men and good Christians since the days of the martyrs; and shall I be the first of the name of Brown that ever took this path and kept——"

18 "Such company, thou wouldst say," observed the elder person, interpreting his pause. "Well said, Goodman Brown! I have been as well acquainted with your family as with ever a one among the Puritans; and that's no trifle to say. I helped your grandfather, the constable, when he lashed the Quaker woman so smartly through the streets of Salem; and it was I that brought your father a pitch-pine knot, kindled at my own hearth, to set fire to an Indian village, in King Philip's war. They were my good friends, both; and many a pleasant walk have we had along this path, and returned merrily after midnight. I would fain be friends with you for their sake."

19 "If it be as thou sayest," replied Goodman Brown, "I marvel they never spoke of these matters; or, verily, I marvel not, seeing that the least rumor of the sort would have driven them from New England. We are a people of prayer, and good works to boot, and abide no such wickedness."

20 "Wickedness or not," said the traveller with the twisted staff, "I have a very general acquaintance here in New England. The deacons of many a church have drunk the communion wine with me; the selectmen of divers towns make me their chairman; and a majority of the Great and General Court are firm supporters of my interest. The governor and I, too—But these are state secrets."

21 "Can this be so?" cried Goodman Brown, with a stare of amazement at his undisturbed companion. "Howbeit, I have nothing to do with the governor and council; they have their own ways, and are no rule for a simple husbandman like me. But, were I to go on with thee, how should I meet the eye of that good old man, our minister, at Salem village? O, his voice would make me tremble both Sabbath day and lecture day."

22 Thus far the elder traveller had listened with due gravity; but now burst into a fit of irrepressible mirth, shaking himself so violently that his snakelike staff actually seemed to wriggle in sympathy.

23 "Ha! ha! ha!" shouted he again and again; then composing himself. "Well, go on, Goodman Brown, go on; but, prithee, don't kill me with laughing."

24 "Well, then, to end the matter at once," said Goodman Brown, considerably nettled, "there is my wife, Faith. It would break her dear little heart; and I'd rather break my own."

25 "Nay, if that be the case," answered the other, "e'en go thy ways, Goodman Brown. I would not for twenty old women like the one hobbling before us that Faith should come to any harm."

26 As he spoke, he pointed his staff at a female figure on the path, in whom Goodman Brown recognized a very pious and exemplary dame, who had taught him his catechism in youth, and was still his moral and spiritual adviser, jointly with the minister and Deacon Gookin.

27 "A marvel, truly, that Goody Cloyse should be so far in the wilderness at nightfall," said he. "But, with your leave, friend, I shall take a cut through the woods until we have left this Christian woman behind. Being a stranger to you, she might ask whom I was consorting with and whither I was going."

28 "Be it so," said his fellow-traveller. "Betake you to the woods, and let me keep the path."

29 Accordingly the young man turned aside, but took care to watch his companion, who advanced softly along the road until he had come within a staff's length of the old dame. She, meanwhile, was making the best of her way, with singular speed for so aged a woman, and mumbling some indistinct words—a

prayer, doubtless—as she went. The traveller put forth his staff and touched her withered neck with what seemed the serpent's tail.

30 "The devil!" screamed the pious old lady.

31 "Then Goody Cloyse knows her old friend?" observed the traveller, confronting her and leaning on his writhing stick.

32 "Ah, forsooth, and is it your worship indeed?" cried the good dame. "Yea, truly is it, and in the very image of my old gossip, Goodman Brown, the grandfather of the silly fellow that now is. But—would your worship believe it?—my broomstick hath strangely disappeared, stolen, as I suspect, by that unhanged witch, Goody Cory, and that, too, when I was all anointed with the juice of smallage, and cinquefoil, and wolf's bane—"

33 "Mingled with fine wheat and the fat of a new-born babe," said the shape of old Goodman Brown.

34 "Ah, your worship knows the recipe," cried the old lady, cackling aloud. "So, as I was saying, being all ready for the meeting, and no horse to ride on, I made up my mind to foot it; for they tell me there is a nice young man to be taken into communion to-night. But now your good worship will lend me your arm, and we shall be there in a twinkling."

35 "That can hardly be," answered her friend. "I may not spare you my arm, Goody Cloyse; but here is my staff, if you will."

36 So saying, he threw it down at her feet, where, perhaps, it assumed life, being one of the rods which its owner had formerly lent to the Egyptian magi. Of this fact, however, Goodman Brown could not take cognizance. He had cast up his eyes in astonishment, and, looking down again, beheld neither Goody Cloyse nor the serpentine staff, but his fellow-traveller alone, who waited for him as calmly as if nothing had happened.

37 "That old woman taught me my catechism," said the young man; and there was a world of meaning in this simple comment.

38 They continued to walk onward, while the elder traveller exhorted his companion to make good speed and persevere in the path, discoursing so aptly that his arguments seemed rather to spring up in the bosom of his auditor than to be suggested by himself. As they went, he plucked a branch of maple to serve for a walking stick, and began to strip it of the twigs and little boughs, which were wet with evening dew. The moment his fingers touched them they became strangely withered and dried up as with a week's sunshine. Thus the pair proceeded, at a good free pace, until suddenly, in a gloomy hollow of the road, Goodman Brown sat himself down on the stump of a tree and refused to go any farther.

39 "Friend," said he, stubbornly, "my mind is made up. Not another step will I budge on this errand. What if a wretched old woman do choose to go to the devil when I thought she was going to heaven: is that any reason why I should quit my dear Faith and go after her?"

40 "You will think better of this by and by," said his acquaintance, composedly. "Sit here and rest yourself a while; and when you feel like moving again, there is my staff to help you along."

41 Without more words, he threw his companion the maple stick, and was as speedily out of sight as if he had vanished into the deepening gloom. The young man sat a few moments by the roadside, applauding himself greatly, and thinking with how clear a conscience he should meet the minister in his morning walk, nor shrink from the eye of good old Deacon Gookin. And what calm sleep would be his that very night, which was to have been spent so wickedly, but so purely and sweetly now, in the arms of Faith! Amidst these pleasant and praiseworthy meditations, Goodman Brown heard the tramp of horses along the road, and deemed it advisable to conceal himself within the verge of the forest, conscious of the guilty purpose that had brought him thither, though now so happily turned from it.

42 On came the hoof tramps and the voices of the riders, two grave old voices, conversing soberly as they drew near. These mingled sounds appeared to pass along the road, within a few yards of the young man's hidingplace; but, owing doubtless to the depth of the gloom at that particular spot, neither the travellers nor their steeds were visible. Though their figures brushed the small boughs by the wayside, it could not be seen that they intercepted, even for a moment, the faint gleam from the strip of bright sky athwart which they must have passed. Goodman Brown alternately crouched and stood on tiptoe, pulling aside the branches and thrusting forth his head as far as he durst without discerning so much as a shadow. It vexed him the more, because he could have sworn, were such a thing possible, that he recognized the voices of the minister and Deacon Gookin, jogging along quietly, as they were wont to do, when bound to

> **The moment his fingers touched them** they became strangely withered and dried up as with a week's sunshine.

some ordination or ecclesiastical council. While yet within hearing, one of the riders stopped to pluck a switch.

"Of the two, reverend sir," said the voice like the deacon's, "I had rather miss an ordination dinner than to-night's meeting. They tell me that some of our community are to be here from Falmouth and beyond, and others from Connecticut and Rhode Island, besides several of the Indian powwows, who, after their fashion, know almost as much deviltry as the best of us. Moreover, there is a goodly young woman to be taken into communion."

"Mighty well, Deacon Gookin!" replied the solemn old tones of the minister. "Spur up, or we shall be late. Nothing can be done, you know, until I get on the ground."

The hoofs clattered again; and the voices, talking so strangely in the empty air, passed on through the forest, where no church had ever been gathered or solitary Christian prayed. Whither, then, could these holy men be journeying so deep into the heathen wilderness? Young Goodman Brown caught hold of a tree for support, being ready to sink down on the ground, faint and overburdened with the heavy sickness of his heart. He looked up to the sky, doubting whether there really was a heaven above him. Yet there was the blue arch, and the stars brightening in it.

"With heaven above and Faith below, I will yet stand firm against the devil!" cried Goodman Brown.

While he still gazed upward into the deep arch of the firmament and had lifted his hands to pray, a cloud, though no wind was stirring, hurried across the zenith and hid the brightening stars. The blue sky was still visible except directly overhead, where this black mass of cloud was sweeping swiftly northward. Aloft in the air, as if from the depths of the cloud, came a confused and doubtful sound of voices. Once the listener fancied that he could distinguish the accents of townspeople of his own, men and women, both pious and ungodly, many of whom he had met at the communion table, and had seen others rioting at the tavern. The next moment, so indistinct were the sounds, he doubted whether he had heard aught but the murmur of the old forest, whispering without a wind. Then came a stronger swell of those familiar tones, heard daily in the sunshine at Salem village, but never until now from a cloud of night There was one voice, of a young woman, uttering lamentations, yet with an uncertain sorrow, and entreating for some favor, which, perhaps, it would grieve her to obtain; and all the unseen multitude, both saints and sinners, seemed to encourage her onward.

"Faith!" shouted Goodman Brown, in a voice of agony and desperation; and the echoes of the forest mocked him, crying, "Faith! Faith!" as if bewildered wretches were seeking her all through the wilderness.

The cry of grief, rage, and terror was yet piercing the night, when the unhappy husband held his breath for a response. There was a scream, drowned immediately in a louder murmur of voices, fading into far-off laughter, as the dark cloud swept away, leaving the clear and silent sky above Goodman Brown. But something fluttered lightly down through the air and caught on the branch of a tree. The young man seized it, and beheld a pink ribbon.

"My Faith is gone!" cried he, after one stupefied moment. "There is no good on earth; and sin is but a name. Come, devil; for to thee is this world given."

And, maddened with despair, so that he laughed loud and long, did Goodman Brown grasp his staff and set forth again, at such a rate that he seemed to fly along the forest path rather than to walk or run. The road grew wilder and drearier and more faintly traced, and vanished at length, leaving him in the heart of the dark wilderness, still rushing onward with the instinct that guides mortal man to evil. The whole forest was peopled with frightful sounds—the creaking of the trees, the howling of wild beasts, and the yell of Indians; while sometimes the wind tolled like a distant church bell, and sometimes gave a broad roar around the traveller, as if all Nature were laughing him to scorn. But he was himself the chief horror of the scene, and shrank not from its other horrors.

"Ha! ha! ha!" roared Goodman Brown when the wind laughed at him. "Let us hear which will laugh loudest. Think not to frighten me with your deviltry. Come witch, come wizard, come Indian powwow, come devil himself, and here comes Goodman Brown. You may as well fear him as he fear you."

In truth, all through the haunted forest there could be nothing more frightful than the figure of Goodman Brown. On he flew among the black pines, brandishing his staff with frenzied gestures, now giving vent to an inspiration of horrid blasphemy, and now shouting forth such laughter as set all the echoes of the forest laughing like demons around him. The fiend in his own shape is less hideous than when he rages in the breast of man. Thus sped the demoniac

> He looked up to the sky, doubting whether there really was a heaven above him.

on his course, until, quivering among the trees, he saw a red light before him, as when the felled trunks and branches of a clearing have been set on fire, and throw up their lurid blaze against the sky, at the hour of midnight. He paused, in a lull of the tempest that had driven him onward, and heard the swell of what seemed a hymn, rolling solemnly from a distance with the weight of many voices. He knew the tune; it was a familiar one in the choir of the village meeting house. The verse died heavily away, and was lengthened by a chorus, not of human voices, but of all the sounds of the benighted wilderness pealing in awful harmony together. Goodman Brown cried out; and his cry was lost to his own ear by its unison with the cry of the desert.

54   In the interval of silence he stole forward until the light glared full upon his eyes. At one extremity of an open space, hemmed in by the dark wall of the forest, arose a rock, bearing some rude, natural resemblance either to an altar or a pulpit, and surrounded by four blazing pines, their tops aflame, their stems untouched, like candles at an evening meeting. The mass of foliage that had overgrown the summit of the rock was all on fire, blazing high into the night and fitfully illuminating the whole field. Each pendent twig and leafy festoon was in a blaze. As the red light arose and fell, a numerous congregation alternately shone forth, then disappeared in shadow, and again grew, as it were, out of the darkness, peopling the heart of the solitary woods at once.

55   "A grave and dark-clad company," quoth Goodman Brown.

56   In truth they were such. Among them, quivering to and fro between gloom and splendor, appeared faces that would be seen next day at the council board of the province, and others which, Sabbath after Sabbath, looked devoutly heavenward, and benignantly over the crowded pews, from the holiest pulpits in the land. Some affirm that the lady of the governor was there. At least there were high dames well known to her, and wives of honored husbands, and widows, a great multitude, and ancient maidens, all of excellent repute, and fair young girls, who trembled lest their mothers should espy them. Either the sudden gleams of light flashing over the obscure field bedazzled Goodman Brown, or he recognized a score of the church members of Salem village famous for their especial sanctity. Good old Deacon Gookin had arrived, and waited at the skirts of that venerable saint, his revered pastor. But, irreverently consorting with these grave, reputable, and pious people, these elders of the church, these chaste dames and dewy virgins, there were men of dissolute lives and women of spotted fame, wretches given over to all mean and filthy vice, and suspected even of horrid crimes. It was strange to see that the good shrank not from the wicked, nor were the sinners abashed by the saints. Scattered also among their pale-faced enemies were the Indian priests, or powwows, who had often scared their native forest with more hideous incantations than any known to English witchcraft.

> "But where is Faith?" thought Goodman Brown, and, as hope came into his heart, he trembled.

    "But where is Faith?" thought Goodman Brown, and, as hope came into his heart, he trembled.

57   Another verse of the hymn arose, a slow and mournful strain, such as the pious love, but joined to words which expressed all that our nature can conceive of sin, and darkly hinted at far more. Unfathomable to mere mortals is the lore of fiends. Verse after verse was sung; and still the chorus of the desert swelled between the deepest tone of a mighty organ; and with the final peal of that dreadful anthem there came a sound, as if the roaring wind, the rushing streams, the howling beasts, and every other voice of the unconverted wilderness were mingling and according with the voice of guilty man in homage to the prince of all. The four blazing pines threw up a loftier flame, and obscurely discovered shapes and visages of horror on the smoke wreaths above the impious assembly. At the same moment the fire on the rock shot redly forth and formed a glowing arch above its base, where now appeared a figure. With reverence be it spoken, the figure bore no slight similitude, both in garb and manner, to some grave divine of the New England churches.

59   "Bring forth the converts!" cried a voice that echoed through the field and rolled into the forest.

60   At the word, Goodman Brown stepped forth from the shadow of the trees and approached the congregation, with whom he felt a loathful brotherhood by the sympathy of all that was wicked in his heart. He could have well nigh sworn that the shape of his own dead father beckoned him to advance, looking downward from a smoke wreath, while a woman, with dim features of despair, threw out her hand to warn him back. Was it his mother? But he had no power to retreat one step, nor to resist, even in thought, when the minister and good old Deacon Gookin seized his arms and led him to the blazing rock. Thither came also the slender form of a veiled female, led between Goody Cloyse, that pious teacher of the catechism, and Mar-

tha Carrier, who had received the devil's promise to be queen of hell. A rampant hag was she. And there stood the proselytes beneath the canopy of fire.

"Welcome, my children," said the dark figure, "to the communion of your race. Ye have found thus young your nature and your destiny. My children, look behind you!"

They turned; and flashing forth, as it were, in a sheet of flame, the fiend worshippers were seen; the smile of welcome gleamed darkly on every visage.

"There," resumed the sable form, "are all whom ye have reverenced from youth. Ye deemed them holier than yourselves, and shrank from your own sin, contrasting it with their lives of righteousness and prayerful aspirations heavenward. Yet here are they all in my worshipping assembly. This night it shall be granted you to know their secret deeds; how hoary-bearded elders of the church have whispered wanton words to the young maids of their households; how many a woman, eager for widows' weeds, has given her husband a drink at bedtime and let him sleep his last sleep in her bosom; how beardless youths have made haste to inherit their fathers' wealth; and how fair damsels—blush not, sweet ones—have dug little graves in the garden, and bidden me, the sole guest, to an infant's funeral. By the sympathy of your human hearts for sin ye shall scent out all the places—whether in church, bed chamber, street, field, or forest—where crime has been committed, and shall exult to behold the whole earth one stain of guilt, one mighty blood spot. Far more than this. It shall be yours to penetrate, in every bosom, the deep mystery of sin, the fountain of all wicked arts, and which inexhaustibly supplies more evil impulses than human power—than my power at its utmost—can make manifest in deeds. And now, my children, look upon each other."

They did so; and, by the blaze of the hell-kindled torches, the wretched man beheld his Faith, and the wife her husband, trembling before that unhallowed altar.

"Lo, there ye stand, my children," said the figure, in a deep and solemn tone, almost sad with its despairing awfulness, as if his once angelic nature could yet mourn for our miserable race. "Depending upon one another's hearts, ye had still hoped that virtue were not all a dream. Now are ye undeceived. Evil is the nature of mankind. Evil must be your only happiness. Welcome again, my children, to the communion of your race."

"Welcome," repeated the fiend worshippers, in one cry of despair and triumph.

> ## Evil must be your only happiness.

And there they stood, the only pair, as it seemed, who were yet hesitating on the verge of wickedness in this dark world. A basin was hollowed, naturally, in the rock. Did it contain water, reddened by the lurid light? or was it blood? or, perchance, a liquid flame? Herein did the shape of evil dip his hand and prepare to lay the mark of baptism upon their foreheads, that they might be partakers of the mystery of sin, more conscious of the secret guilt of others, both in deed and thought, than they could now be of their own. The husband cast one look at his pale wife, and Faith at him. What polluted wretches would the next glance show them to each other, shuddering alike at what they disclosed and what they saw!

"Faith! Faith!" cried the husband, "look up to heaven, and resist the wicked one."

Whether Faith obeyed, he knew not. Hardly had he spoken when he found himself amid calm night and solitude, listening to a roar of the wind which died heavily away through the forest. He staggered against the rock, and felt it chill and damp; while a hanging twig, that had been all on fire, besprinkled his cheek with the coldest dew.

The next morning young Goodman Brown came slowly into the street of Salem village, staring around him like a bewildered man. The good old minister was taking a walk along the graveyard to get an appetite for breakfast and meditate his sermon, and bestowed a blessing, as he passed, on Goodman Brown. He shrank from the venerable saint as if to avoid an anathema. Old Deacon Gookin was at domestic worship, and the holy words of his prayer were heard through the open window. "What God doth the wizard pray to?" quoth Goodman Brown. Goody Cloyse, that excellent old Christian, stood in the early sunshine at her own lattice, catechizing a little girl who had brought her a pint of morning's milk. Goodman Brown snatched away the child as from the grasp of the fiend himself. Turning the corner by the meeting house, he spied the head of Faith, with the pink ribbons, gazing anxiously forth, and bursting into such joy at sight of him that she skipped along the street and almost kissed her husband before the whole village. But Goodman Brown looked sternly and sadly into her face, and passed on without a greeting.

Had Goodman Brown fallen asleep in the forest and only dreamed a wild dream of a witch meeting?

Be it so, if you will; but, alas; it was a dream of evil omen for young Goodman Brown. A stern, a sad, a darkly meditative, a distrustful, if not a desperate, man did he become from the night of that fearful dream. On the Sabbath day, when the congregation were singing a holy psalm, he could not listen, because an anthem of sin rushed loudly upon his ear and drowned all the blessed strain. When the minister spoke from the pulpit, with power and fervid eloquence and with his hand on the open Bible, of the sacred truths of our religion, and of saintlike lives and triumphant deaths, and of future bliss or misery unutterable, then did Goodman Brown turn pale, dreading lest the roof should thunder down upon the gray blasphemer and his hearers. Often, awaking suddenly at midnight, he shrank from the bosom of Faith; and at morning or eventide, when the family knelt down at prayer, he scowled, and muttered to himself, and gazed sternly at his wife, and turned away. And when he had lived long, and was borne to his grave, a hoary corpse, followed by Faith, an aged woman, and children and grandchildren, a goodly procession, besides neighbors not a few, they carved no hopeful verse upon his tombstone; for his dying hour was gloom.

I F you enjoyed "Young Goodman Brown," you might also look at the dark woods and listen to the voices at one's shoulder in the work of Barry Lopez and William Kittredge, though their landscape is very different from that of New Englander Nathaniel Hawthorne.

GOING FURTHER The world's literature abounds in spiritual quest stories, from the Gilgamesh epic to J. R. R. Tolkien's *Lord of the Rings* novels. You might be interested in the works of C. S. Lewis, another Christian quester given to playing with allegory in the modern world.

Writing from Reading

Summarize

1 What does the story tell you about Goodman Brown's ancestors? What kind of people are they? Does he follow in their footsteps? Explain your answer.

2 What exactly is the wickedness that Goodman Brown witnesses? How does he participate in it? How does Faith?

Analyze Craft

3 Discuss Hawthorne's use of the forest as a symbol. What does the forest represent to Goodman Brown? What does it represent to you as a reader? How and why might those images be different?

4 Discuss the ways in which the scenes that play out for Goodman Brown in the forest reflect his wavering faith. Does Goodman Brown's role as observer of these scenes make the incidents more or less personal, and why?

Analyze Voice

5 Consider the time period in which Hawthorne wrote this story. Identify words and symbols that seem dated or have changed over time. Propose modern equivalents.

Synthesize Summary and Analysis

6 "Faith kept me back a while," says young Goodman Brown, and by "Faith" he means more than his wife. Is her name merely allegorical? Or does she waver in her "faith" and thus become a more complex character? Explore how each character's name makes him or her symbolic—and how he or she lives up to (or defies) this promise.

Interpret the Story

7 When he finally reaches Salem, Goodman Brown finds business as usual. The narrator wonders "Had Goodman Brown fallen asleep . . . and only dreamed a wild dream of a witch meeting?" Does Goodman Brown share this suspicion? Argue yes or no, using evidence from the story. Consider the implications of your argument—that is, how does the story's statement on human nature change when you view Goodman Brown's experience as a dream instead of reality, or vice versa?

Franz Kafka (1883–1924)

Born in Prague to a German-speaking Jewish family, Kafka was relatively unknown during his lifetime but has since come to be recognized internationally as one of the first major modern writers. Kafka, who wrote in German, published a small amount of short fiction in his lifetime and requested that all his unpublished manuscripts be destroyed upon his death. However, his friend and biographer Max Brod disobeyed Kafka's wish, and from the manuscripts he rescued, we have three of Kafka's best-known novels: *The Castle* (1930), *The Trial* (1937), and *Amerika* (1938). An insecure man who never severed his emotional dependency on his parents, Kafka created fiction that uniquely captures the helpless feeling of the individual in a modern, uncaring world. His works are often fantastical or surreal—for example, a man awaking to find he has become a giant insect as in "The Metamorphosis," or a man caught in an inescapable court trial for no clear reason as in *The Trial*—so that the events in his works are symbolic rather than realistic. His clear, direct tone and unreal plots give his fiction the feeling of an unending nightmare, and like a dream, his work can be interpreted in so many ways that a complete understanding eludes even an advanced reader. Kafka never married and spent his life working as a civil servant by day and a writer by night. He contracted tuberculosis in 1917 and died seven years later.

AS YOU READ As you read, picture Gregor Samsa's appearance. He, of course, undergoes a profound metamorphosis, but other things and characters also change in the course of the story. Notice these many changes.

FOR INTERACTIVE READING . . . Scan the text for references to doors. Mark these references. Why do the doors play such an important part in the story? Describe the symbolic ways they are used.

The Metamorphosis (1915)

I

1 When Gregor Samsa awoke in his bed one morning from unquiet dreams, he found himself transformed into an enormous insect. He lay on a back as hard as armor and saw, when he raised his head slightly, a jutting brown underbelly divided into arching segments. The bedcovers could barely cover it; they threatened to slide off altogether. His many legs, pitifully thin in comparison with the rest of his bulk, fluttered helplessly before his eyes.

2 "What has happened to me?" he thought. It wasn't a dream. His room—a decent enough room for a person, if slightly too small—lay quietly between the four familiar walls. Over the table on which was spread his unpacked collections of fabric samples—Samsa was a traveling salesman—hung the picture that he had recently cut out of an illustrated magazine and fit into an attractive gilt frame. The picture was of a woman clad in a fur hat and a fur stole; she sat upright and held out to the viewer a thick fur muff into which her entire forearm disappeared.

3   Gregor's gaze then directed itself to the window. The dreary weather—one could hear raindrops hit the metal awning over the window—made him quite melancholy. "What if I slept a bit longer and forgot all this foolishness," he thought. But that was altogether impossible, because he was used to sleeping on his right side, and his current condition made working himself into this position impossible. No matter how vigorously he swung himself over to the right, he immediately rolled again onto his back. He tried what seemed hundreds of times, closing his eyes in order to avoid having to see his wriggling legs. He finally gave up only when he began to feel in his side a small dull ache that he had never felt before.

4   "Oh, God," he thought, "what a strenuous profession I've chosen—traveling day in, day out! The demands of business are far greater on the road than they are at the home office, and I'm burdened with the annoyances of travel besides: the worry about train connections; the irregular, bad meals; a social life limited to passing acquaintances who never become real friends. To hell with it!" He felt an itch on his belly, and he shoved himself back against the bedpost so he could lift his head more easily. He found the spot that itched: it was covered with small white dots that he couldn't identify. He went to touch the spot with one of his legs but drew it back immediately, because the touch made him shudder.

5   He slid back into his former position. "This early rising," he thought, "can make you into a complete idiot. A man needs his sleep. Other travelers live like women in a harem. When, for example, I go back to my hotel during the course of the morning to write up orders, these gentlemen are just sitting down to breakfast. I should try that with the Director: I'd be fired on the spot. Who knows, though—that might be good for me. If it weren't for my parents, I would have given notice long ago: I would have confronted the Director and given him a piece of my mind. He would have fallen off his chair! It's incredible the way he has of sitting perched at his reading desk and speaking from on high to employees who, on top of everything, have to draw very near owing to his slight deafness. Oh well, I shouldn't give up hope altogether: once I have the money to pay off my parents' debt—it should only be another five or six years—I'll definitely do it. Then I'll make my big break. In the meantime, I have to get up—my train leaves at five."

6   And he looked over at the alarm clock that ticked on the bureau. "God in heaven!" he thought. It was six-thirty, and the hands of the clock went quietly on; it was even later than six-thirty—it was closer to six-forty-five. Shouldn't the alarm have gone off? He could see from the bed that it was correctly set for four o'clock; it must have gone off. But was it possible to sleep peacefully through that furniture-rattling noise? Of course, he hadn't actually slept peacefully, but he had no doubt for that reason slept more deeply. But what should he do now? The next train left at seven o'clock. In order to catch that one, he'd have to rush like a madman, and his samples weren't packed up yet. He hardly felt alert or energetic enough. And even if he caught the train, he wouldn't avoid the Director's wrath, because the office porter had been waiting at the five-o'clock train and would long since have reported his failure to appear. The porter was completely under the Director's thumb—he had neither a backbone nor brains. What if Gregor were to report himself sick? But that would be highly awkward and suspicious, because he had not been sick once in five years of service. The Director would certainly come with the insurance doctor. He would reproach his parents for their lazy son and dismiss all rejoinders by referring them to the doctor, who considered all people completely healthy, but work-averse. And would he be so wrong in this case? Gregor actually felt completely fine, despite a fatigue completely unwarranted after such a long sleep. He even had a powerful appetite.

As he thought all this over hurriedly, without being able to decide whether to leave his bed—the clock had just struck six-forty-five—there was a knock on the door near the head of his bed. "Gregor," he heard—it was his mother—"it's a quarter to seven. Weren't you going on a trip?" What a gentle voice! Gregor was terrified when he heard his answer. It was unmistakably in his old voice, but had mixed in, as if from down deep, an irrepressible, painful, squeaking noise, which allowed words to be heard clearly when first uttered, but as they resonated, distorted them to such an extent that they were difficult to understand. Gregor had wanted to answer in detail and explain everything, but in light of the circumstances he limited himself to saying: "Yes, yes, thanks, Mother, I'm getting up." The wooden door seemed to make the change in Gregor's voice imperceptible outside the room, because his mother was satisfied with his explanation and shuffled away. But through this brief exchange the other family members had become aware that Gregor was unexpectedly still at home, and his father was already knocking on one side door—lightly, but with his fist. "Gregor, Gregor," he called, "What's going on?" And after a short pause he urged again, with a deeper voice: "Gregor! Gregor!" At the other side door, his sister fretted softly: "Gregor? Are you ill? Do you need something?" To both sides, Gregor answered,

"I'm just about ready to go," and he made an effort to ban anything conspicuous from his voice by the most painstaking enunciation and by inserting long pauses between individual words. His father returned to his breakfast, but his sister whispered: "Gregor, open up, I beg you." Gregor had no intention of opening the door, however—instead he gave thanks for his habitual precaution, born of much travel, of locking all doors during the night, even at home.

8 First he wanted to get up, quietly and undisturbed, get dressed, and above all eat breakfast—only then did he want to think over what came next, because he could see that he would come to no reasonable conclusions as along as he lay in bed. In the past he had often felt one mild pain or another while lying in bed, possibly from lying in an awkward position, that proved to be sheer imagination once he got up. He was eager to see how today's fantasies would gradually resolve themselves. He didn't doubt in the least that the change in his voice was nothing more than the harbinger of a hearty cold, one of the occupational hazards of traveling salesmen.

> # He was eager to see
> ## how today's fantasies
> ## would gradually resolve
> ## themselves.

9 Throwing off the covers was perfectly simple: he only needed to puff himself up a bit and they fell off on their own. But doing more than that was difficult, especially because he was so strangely broad. He would normally have used his arms and hands to get up: now, he had only the many little legs which were continuously moving in every direction and which he could not seem to control. If he meant to bend one, it would be the first one to stretch itself out; if he finally succeeded in enforcing his will with one leg, all the rest of them worked furiously, as if liberated, in extreme, painful agitation. "You can't just lie here in bed doing nothing," Gregor said to himself.

10 At first he intended to get out of the bed with the lower part of his body foremost, but this lower part, which he had moreover not yet seen and of which he could not form a proper mental image, proved too difficult to move. It went extremely slowly. When, nearly frantic, he finally gathered his strength and recklessly shoved himself forward, he misjudged the direction and violently struck the lower bed post. The burning pain he felt convinced him that the lower part of his body was at least at the moment the most sensitive part.

11 He afterwards attempted to get his upper body out of bed and carefully turned his head towards the edge of the bed. This he could do easily, and in spite of its bulk and weight, the mass of his body finally slowly followed the direction of his head. But when he held his head at last free of the bed, he became afraid to shift further in this direction, because if he ultimately let himself fall like that, it would be a miracle if his head were not injured. And now, of all times, he could not afford to lose consciousness; he would rather remain in bed.

12 After continued effort, however, he found himself lying exactly as before, and heaved a sigh. He saw his little legs struggling against one another even more furiously, if that were possible, and he saw no way of introducing calm and order to this anarchy. At this point he repeated to himself that he could not possibly lie in bed any longer and that it would be most sensible to risk everything, even if there were only the smallest hope of thereby freeing himself from bed. At the same time, however, he kept reminding himself that calm deliberation was always better than rash decision-making. All the while he tried hard to focus on the view from the window, but unfortunately there was little encouragement or cheer to gain from the sight of the morning fog, which shrouded even the opposite side of the narrow street. "Already seven o'clock," he said to himself with the latest striking of the alarm clock, "already seven o'clock and still such fog." And he lay quiet a short while, breathing shallowly, as if he thought complete stillness might restore things to their true and natural state.

13 After a bit, however, he said to himself, "Before it strikes seven-fifteen, I must without fail be completely out of bed. For one thing, someone from the company will have come by then to inquire after me, because the office opens before seven." And he concentrated his efforts toward swinging his entire body out of the bed all at the same time. If he let himself fall out of bed in this manner, his head, which he would raise sharply during the fall, would presumably remain uninjured. His back seemed to be hard; nothing would happen to it in the fall onto the carpet. His greatest source of misgiving was anticipation of the loud crash that would follow, which would probably arouse anxiety, if not terror, beyond the doors. That would have to be risked, however.

14 When, by rocking back and forth, Gregor moved halfway off of the bed—the new method was more a game than an exertion—it occurred to him how simple everything would be if someone would come help him. Two strong people—he thought of his father and the servant girl—would be more than adequate. They would only have to shove their arms under his domed back, pry him up out of bed, prop up his bulk by crouching low, and then help him complete the turn over onto the floor, where hopefully his little legs would gain some sense of purpose. Quite apart from the fact that the doors were locked, though, should he really call for help? In spite of his predicament he couldn't suppress a smile at the thought.

15 He was already so far along that he could hardly maintain his balance when he rocked forcefully. Very soon he would have to make a final decision, because in five minutes it would be seven-fifteen. Just then the front doorbell rang. "That's someone from the company," he said to himself and virtually froze, though his little legs only danced more hurriedly. Everything remained quiet for a moment. "They're not opening the door," Gregor said to himself, momentarily carried away by some absurd hope. But then, naturally, as always, the servant girl directed her firm step to the door and opened it. Gregor needed to hear only the first word of greeting from the visitor and he already knew who it was—the Deputy Director himself. Why was Gregor condemned to work at a company where the least infraction immediately attracted the greatest suspicion? Were all employees then without exception scoundrels; were there among them no loyal, devoted individuals who, when they had merely missed a few morning hours of service, would become so tormented by pangs of conscience that they would be frankly unable to leave their beds? Wouldn't it really have been enough to send an apprentice to inquire—if indeed this inquiry were necessary at all? Did the Deputy Director himself have to come, thereby showing the entire innocent family that the investigation of this suspicious situation could only be entrusted to the Deputy Director himself? And more as a result of the agitation into which this line of thought transported Gregor, than as a result of a proper decision, he swung himself with all his might out of the bed. There was a loud thump, but no actual crash. The fall was muffled a bit by the carpet, and his back was more elastic than Gregor had thought—these things accounted for the fairly inconspicuous dull thump. He had failed only to raise his head carefully enough and had struck it. He twisted it back and forth and rubbed it into the carpet out of anger and pain.

16 "Something happened inside there," said the Deputy Director in the room to the left. Gregor tried to imagine something similar to what had happened to him today happening to the Deputy Director; it really was possible, after all. But as if in cruel response to this question the Deputy Director took a few decisive steps in the next room, making his patent leather boots creak. From the room to the right Gregor's sister whispered to inform him: "Gregor, the Deputy Director is here." "I know," said Gregor to himself; but he did not dare to raise his voice loud enough for his sister to hear.

"Gregor," his father now said from the room to the left, "the Deputy Director has come and inquires as to why you did not leave with the early morning train. We don't know what we should say to him. Furthermore, he wants to speak to you directly. So please open the door. He will surely have the goodness to excuse the disorder of your room." "Good morning, Mr. Samsa," the Deputy Director called out at the same time in a friendly manner. "He is not well," his mother said to the Deputy Director, while his father still spoke at the door, "he is not well, believe me, sir. Why would Gregor otherwise miss a train? The boy has nothing in his head but the company. I almost worry that he never goes out at night; he has been in the city eight days now, but he was at home every night. He sits with us at the table and quietly reads the newspaper or studies train schedules. Busying himself with woodworking is as far as he goes in the way of amusement. In the course of two, three evenings, for example, he cut himself a small frame; you would be astounded at how pretty it is. It's hanging in his room; you will see it right away, when Gregor opens up. I am happy, in any case, that you're here, Deputy Director. We could not have persuaded Gregor to open the door alone; he is so stubborn; and there's certainly something wrong with him, although he denied it this morning." "I'm coming right away," said Gregor slowly and carefully, while not moving at all, in order not to miss a word of the conversation. "Otherwise, dear woman, I can't explain it myself, either," said the Deputy Director. "Hopefully, it's nothing serious. Though I must say, that we businessmen—either fortunately or unfortunately, as you will—must often ignore a trivial indisposition in the interest of business." "So can the Deputy Director come in to see you?" asked his impatient father, knocking again at the door. "No," said Gregor. In the room to the left there arose an awkward silence; in the room to the right, his sister began sobbing.

18 Why didn't his sister join the others? She had most likely just now arisen from bed and had not yet begun to get dressed. And why was she crying? Because he did not stand up and let the Deputy Director in; because he was in danger of losing his position and because the Director would then persecute his parents

with the old demands? Those were unnecessary worries, for the time being. Gregor was still here and did not in the least contemplate leaving his family. At the moment he was lying on the carpet, and no one who was aware of his condition would seriously request that he let the Deputy Director in. Gregor could not possibly be dismissed just for this minor breach of politeness; he could easily find a suitable excuse later. And it seemed to Gregor far more reasonable to leave him in peace now, instead of disturbing him with tears and entreaties. But it was the uncertainty of it all that distressed the others and so excused their behavior.

"Mr. Samsa," the Deputy Director now called in a raised voice, "what's the matter? You barricade yourself there in your room, answer merely with yes and no, burden your parents with profound, unnecessary worries and—this only mentioned incidentally—neglect your business responsibilities in an unheard-of way. I speak here in the name of your parents and your Director and earnestly request of you an immediate, clear explanation. I am amazed; I am amazed. I thought I knew you as a quiet, reasonable person, and now you suddenly begin to exhibit extraordinary capriciousness. The Director told me early this morning of a possible explanation for your dereliction—it related to the cash account recently entrusted to you—but I actually almost gave him my word of honor that this explanation could not be accurate. Now, however, I see your incomprehensible stubbornness here, and I lose any desire to vouch for you in the least. And your position is not the most secure. I originally had the intention of saying all of this just between the two of us, but since you force me to waste my time here needlessly, I don't know why your parents should not also hear it. Your performance recently has been very unsatisfying. It is not the time of the year, of course, to do extraordinary business, we recognize that; but there is no time of year in which to do *no* business, Mr. Samsa—there cannot be."

"But sir," called out Gregor, beside himself, forgetting everything else in his agitation, "I'll open up immediately, this instant. A mild indisposition—an attack of dizziness—has kept me from getting up. I'm still lying in bed. I'm completely recovered now, though. I'm climbing out of bed right now. Just one moment of patience! I thought things were not quite back to normal yet. But I'm already well again. How it can suddenly come over a person! I was fine yesterday evening, my parents know that, or perhaps I should say that yesterday evening I had a slight premonition of it. It must have been easy to see in me. Why didn't I

report it to the office yesterday! But one always thinks that one can ride out illness without having to stay home. Sir! Spare my parents! There is no basis for all the reproaches you've made against me; no one said anything about them to me before now. Perhaps you haven't seen the latest orders that I sent in. In any case, I will be starting my trip on the eight o'clock train. These few hours of rest have strengthened me. Don't let me hold you up, though, sir; I'll soon be in the office myself, and please have the goodness to say so, and to send my greetings to the Director."

And while Gregor hurriedly blurted all this out, hardly knowing what he said, he moved effortlessly closer to the chest, thanks to the practice he had had in bed, and attempted to raise himself against it to an upright position. He actually wanted to open the door, actually wanted to let them see him and to speak with the Deputy Director. He was eager to know what they all would say to him when they finally saw him, after so much

> ## He ignored the pain in his lower body, despite the fact that it burned.

urging. Would they be afraid? If so, Gregor would be absolved of responsibility and could relax. If they took it all in stride, however, then, too, he would have no cause for worry, and he really could be at the train station at eight, if he hurried. At first he simply slid a few times down the side of the slippery chest; finally, however, he gave himself one last swing and stood upright. He ignored the pain in his lower body, despite the fact that it burned. Now he let himself fall against the back of a nearby chair and held tight to its sides with his legs. This helped him regain his self-control, and he stayed quiet, so that he could hear the Deputy Director speak.

"Did you understand one word?" the Deputy Director asked his parents. "Surely he's making fun of us?" "For God's sake," cried his mother in the midst of tears, "he might be seriously ill, and we're all plaguing him. Grete! Grete!" she then screamed. "Mother?" called his sister from the other side. They were communicating through Gregor's room. "You must go fetch the doctor this minute. Gregor is ill. Quickly, to the doctor. Did you hear Gregor speak just now?" "That was the voice of an animal," said the Deputy Director, noticeably quiet, by contrast with the screaming of his mother. "Anna! Anna!" called his father towards the kitchen, clapping his hands, "Get a locksmith immediately!" And the two girls ran, their skirts rustling, through the foyer—how had his sister gotten dressed so quickly?—and flung the apartment door open. There was no noise of the door slamming; they had probably left it open, as was usual in apartments where some great misfortune had occurred.

23   Gregor had become much calmer, however. It was true that they didn't understand his speech, but it sounded clear enough to him, clearer than previously, perhaps because his ear had adjusted to it. But they did still believe that something was wrong with him, and they were prepared to help him. He was pleased by the confidence and certainty with which the first arrangements had been made. He felt drawn once again into the circle of humanity and expected great things from both the doctor and the locksmith, without really making a distinction between them. In order to develop the clearest possible voice for the decisive discussions to come, he coughed a bit, although he tried to do this in a muted fashion, because this, too, might sound very different from a human cough—he no longer trusted himself to judge. It had now fallen completely silent in the next room. His parents might have been sitting at the table, whispering with the Deputy Director, or perhaps they were all pressed against the door, listening.

24   Using the chair, Gregor slowly shoved himself forward, and then let go, throwing himself against the door, and holding himself upright against it. The balls of his feet had some sticky substance on them. He took a moment to recover from the exertion. Then he applied himself to turning the key in the lock. Unfortunately, it seemed as if he had no real teeth— what then could he grip the key with?—but his jaws, on the other hand, were powerful. With their help he started to turn the key. He paid no attention to the fact that he obviously did some harm to himself in the process—a brown discharge came out from his mouth, flowing over the key and dripping on the floor. "Listen now," said the Deputy Director in the next room, "he's turning the key." That encouraged Gregor greatly, but all of them should have cheered him on, his father and mother, too: "Come on, Gregor," they should have called, "keep at it, keep working the lock!" And imagining that all his efforts were being watched with rapt attention, he recklessly bit down on the key with all his might. He danced around the lock, following the key as it turned; holding himself upright entirely with his mouth, he either pulled up on the key or forced it down with the full weight of his body, as necessary. The crisp click of the lock finally snapping back elated him. Breathing a sigh of relief he said to himself, "I didn't even need the locksmith," and he laid his head on the door handle, in order to open the door.

25   Because he had to open the door in this way, he was not yet visible even when it was opened wide. If he didn't want to fall flat on his back just before his entrance into the next room, he would first have to slowly make his way around the open panel of the double door. He was still busy with this difficult maneuver and had not yet had a moment to think of the others, when he heard the Deputy Director force out a loud "Oh!" It sounded like a gust of wind. Now he could also see the Deputy, who was nearest the door—he pressed his hand to his open mouth and slowly shrank back, as if an invisible, irresistible force drove him. His mother—who stood, despite the presence of the Deputy Director, with her hair still loose, and sticking up in parts from her night's sleep—first looked at his father with her hands clasped; then she walked two steps towards Gregor and sank to the ground in the midst of her billowing skirts, her face completely hidden, sunk upon her breast. His father balled his fist with a fierce expression, as if he wanted to knock Gregor back into his room; then he looked uncertainly around the living room, covered his eyes with his hands, and sobbed so that his powerful chest shook.

26   Gregor had not yet entered the outer room; instead, he leaned from within against the door panel that was still fastened, so that only half of his body and his head, craned to one side in order to see them, were visible. It had become much brighter outside in the meantime: one could clearly see a section of the endless, gray-black building—it was a hospital—that stood across the street, its severe, uniform windows breaking up its facade. The rain still fell, but only in large, singly visible and singly plummeting drops. The table teemed with breakfast dishes; his father considered breakfast the most important meal of the day, and he protracted it for hours reading various periodicals. On the wall just opposite hung a photograph of Gregor from his military days, which showed him dressed as a lieutenant, with a carefree smile, his hand on his dagger, his bearing and his uniform commanding respect. The door to the foyer was open, and because the door to the apartment was open as well, one could see the outer hall and the top of the staircase leading downwards.

27   "Now," said Gregor—and he was well aware that he was the only one remaining calm—"I will just get dressed, pack my samples up, and be off. Will you all allow me to go? Deputy Director, you see that I'm not obstinate and that I want to work. Traveling is demanding, but I couldn't live without it. Where do you intend to go now, Deputy Director? To the office? Yes? Will you report everything accurately? A person might be unable to work for a time, but it is precisely then that one must consider his past accomplishments and keep in mind that once the hindrance is past, he will certainly work even harder and more efficiently. I owe a great deal to the Director—you know that only too well. On the other hand, I have the care of my par-

ents and sister. I'm in a fix, but I'll work my way out again. But please don't make it more difficult for me than it already is. Take my part in the office! I know the traveling salesmen aren't popular. People think we earn a huge amount of money and lead grand lives. People just don't have any particular reason to think this prejudice through carefully. You, however, Deputy Director, you have a better perspective on how things work than most of the staff—I might say, confidentially, a better perspective than even the Director himself, who, in his capacity as owner, as easily be misled in his judgment about an employee. You know very well that the traveling salesman, because he is away from the office the better part of the year, easily falls victim to gossip, to chance misfortune, and groundless complaints. It's impossible for him to defend himself against these complaints, as he ordinarily learns nothing of them; it's only when he comes home at the end of a trip completely exhausted that he feels the terrible consequences, whose origins he can't divine, in his very body. Deputy Director, don't leave without saying one word that shows me that you agree with me at least in part!"

> I'm in a fix, but I'll work my way out again.

But the Deputy Director had turned away at Gregor's first words, and was staring back at Gregor over one twitching shoulder, his mouth agape. During Gregor's speech he had not stood still for a moment, but, never taking his eyes off of Gregor, moved steadily but surreptitiously towards the door, as if there were some secret prohibition against leaving the room. He had already reached the foyer, and judging by the sudden movement with which he pulled his foot out of the room at his last step, one would have thought his sole was on fire. Once in the foyer, he stretched his hand out towards the staircase as if divine deliverance awaited him there.

Gregor realized that the Deputy Director could under no circumstances be allowed to leave this way, if his position at the company were not to be endangered. His parents didn't understand this as well as he did. They had over the years persuaded themselves that he was guaranteed permanent employment in the company, and besides, they had so much to do in dealing with their own distress at the moment, that their foresight had vanished. But Gregor had this foresight. The Deputy Director must be detained, calmed, persuaded, and finally won over—the future of Gregor and his family depended on it. If only his sister were here! She was clever: she was already crying when Gregor was still calmly lying on his back. And the Deputy Director, that ladies' man, would surely have let her sway him: she would have closed the apartment door and talked him out of his fear in the foyer. But his sister was not there, so Gregor would have to handle it himself. And without thinking about the fact that he had no idea yet how well he could move, without thinking that his speech was possibly—well, very probably—incomprehensible, he let go of the door panel, forcing himself through the opening, and headed for the Deputy Director, who was already at the landing in the hall and hugging himself in a comical manner. With a small cry, scrambling in vain for something to hold on to, Gregor immediately fell down onto his many little legs. This had hardly happened, when for the first time that morning he felt a sense of physical well-being. His little legs had solid ground beneath them; they obeyed him completely, as he noted to his delight. They even strove to carry him where he wanted to go. Suddenly, he believed that the ultimate relief of all his suffering was at hand. But at that moment, as he lay on the floor trembling with suppressed energy, close to his mother and directly opposite her, she sprang up—she who had seemed so lost in thought—with her arms outstretched, her fingers splayed, and cried out: "Help, for God's sake, help!" She kept her head turned towards him, as if she wanted to be able to see him better, but, following a contradictory impulse, she ran heedlessly backwards, forgetting that the table full of dishes lay behind her. She quickly sat down when she reached it, as if absent-mindedly, seeming not to notice that next to her the coffeepot had been knocked over and coffee was streaming freely out onto the carpet.

"Mother, Mother," Gregor said softly, and looked up at her. The Deputy Director vanished from his mind momentarily, and he couldn't stop himself from snapping his jaws at the empty air several times at the sight of the flowing coffee. His mother began screaming again over this, fled from the table, and fell into the arms of his father, who was hurrying towards her. But Gregor had no time then for his parents. The Deputy Director was already on the stairs. His chin on the railing, he looked back one last time. Gregor took a running start, in order to have the best chance of catching up to him. The Deputy Director must have sensed something, as he sprang down several steps and then disappeared. "Ahh!" he screamed; it echoed throughout the entire stairwell.

Unfortunately, the flight of the Deputy Director seemed to have completely unhinged his father, who up until then had been relatively self-controlled. Instead of running after the Deputy Director or at least not restraining Gregor from pursuing him, with his right hand he grabbed the walking stick that the Deputy Director had left behind on an armchair together with his hat and coat; with his left hand he picked up a large newspaper from the table; then, stamping his feet, he began to drive Gregor back into his room by swatting at him with the stick and the newspaper. None of Gregor's pleas helped—none of his pleas were understood. The more submissively he bowed his head, the more vigorously his father stamped his feet. Across the room, despite the cool weather, his mother had thrown open a window and, leaning far out of the window, pressed her face into her hands. Between the street and the stairwell there arose a strong cross-draft: the window curtains flew up; the newspapers on the table rustled, and a few pages fluttered to the floor. His father drove him back mercilessly, spitting out hissing noises like a wild beast. Gregor, however, still was unpracticed in moving backwards, so he went very slowly. If he had only been allowed time to turn around, he would have gone immediately back into his room, but he was afraid of making his father impatient. At every moment the stick in his father's hand threatened to deal him a fatal blow to his back or head. Finally, however, Gregor found he had no choice, as he noted with terror that he seemed unable to keep going in the right direction when he moved backwards. He therefore began, with frequent side-glances at his father, to turn around as quickly as he could, which was actually very slowly. His father might have understood his good intentions, because he did not disturb him while he was doing this; in fact, he actually directed him here and there from a distance with the point of his stick. If only there weren't this unbearable hissing from his father! It unnerved Gregor completely. He was already almost completely turned around when, listening to this hissing, he made a mistake and turned a bit in the wrong direction. When he was finally, fortunately, headfirst at the opening of the door, it appeared that his body was too wide to go through without further ado. In his present state of mind it was naturally far from occurring to his father to open the other door panel in order to make a wide enough passageway for Gregor. He was obsessed merely with getting Gregor into his room as quickly as possible. He would never have allowed the preparations necessary for Gregor to raise himself up and possibly go through the door that way. Instead, making a great deal of noise, he drove Gregor forward as if there were no obstacle before him. The noise coming from behind Gregor didn't sound any longer like the voice of his father. It was clearly no laughing matter, so Gregor forced himself—happen what would—through the door. One side of his body was hoisted upwards.

He immediately dunked his head in the milk nearly up to his eyes.

He lay crookedly in the doorway. One of his flanks was rubbed raw, and on the white door ugly smears remained behind. He was soon stuck fast, and couldn't move at all anymore. His little legs hung twitching on one side, and those on the other side were pressed painfully against the floor. Then his father liberated him with a powerful shove from behind, and he flew, bleeding heavily, a long way into his room. The door was slammed shut with the stick, and then it was finally quiet.

II

It was already twilight when Gregor awoke from a deep, dreamless sleep. He would not have arisen much later even without having been disturbed, for he felt well rested and no longer sleepy, but it seemed to him that he had been awakened by the sounds of a fleeting footstep and of the door to the foyer carefully being shut. The glare from the electric street lamp outside lay palely here and there on the ceiling of his room and on the upper surfaces of the furniture, but down by Gregor it was dark. He shoved himself slowly towards the door, awkwardly groping with the feelers he had just then come to appreciate, in order to see what had happened there. His left side seemed to be a single, long, unpleasantly taut scar, and he had to positively limp on his row of legs. One leg had been seriously injured during the events of the morning: it dragged limply behind him.

It was only when he was at the door that he realized what had actually lured him there: it was the smell of something edible. Standing there was a basin filled with fresh milk, swimming with small pieces of white bread. He could almost have laughed for joy, for he was even hungrier than he had been that morning. He immediately dunked his head in the milk nearly up to his eyes. But he soon pulled back, disappointed. It wasn't only that his tender left side made it hard for him to eat—for it seemed he was able to eat only if his entire panting body cooperated—it was rather that the milk, which had always been his favorite drink, and which his sister certainly placed here for that reason, didn't taste good to him at all. He turned away from the basin with something like revulsion and crept back into the middle of the room.

The gas lamps had been turned on in the living room, as Gregor saw through the crack in the door. Whereas ordinarily at this hour his father would read the afternoon paper out loud to his mother and sometimes to his sister, now there wasn't a sound. Perhaps the reading, which his sister had frequently told him and wrote him about, had lately dropped out of their routine. It was completely quiet, though the apartment was certainly not empty. "What a quiet life the family leads," Gregor said to himself and felt great pride, as he stared into the darkness before him, that he had been able to provide his parents and his sister with such a life, in such a nice apartment. But what if terror now drove away all quiet, all prosperity, all contentment? Rather than surrender to such thoughts, Gregor preferred to move about, so he crawled back and forth in the room.

Once during the long evening one of the side doors and later the other was opened a crack and then hastily shut again. Someone had probably needed to come in, but had then thought better of it. Gregor now stopped directly in front of the door to the living room, determined somehow to get the hesitant visitor to come in, or at least to find out who it was, but the doors were not opened again and Gregor waited in vain. Early on, when the doors were locked, everyone had wanted to come in; now, when he had unlocked one door and the others had clearly been unlocked during the day, no one came, and the keys had been moved to the outside.

It was late at night before the light in the living room was turned out, and it was now clear that his parents and sister had been awake until then, for all three could clearly be heard departing on tiptoes. Now surely no one would come to see Gregor until morning; he therefore had quite a while in which to consider undisturbed how he should newly arrange his life. But he was uneasy lying flat on the ground in the high-ceilinged open room. He did not know why this should be, for he had lived in the room for five years already. Half unconsciously, and not without some shame, he scurried under the sofa where, despite the fact that his back was a bit crushed and he could no longer lift his head, he immediately felt more comfortable, regretting only that his body was too broad to fit completely underneath.

He remained there the entire night. He spent part of it in a light sleep, out of which hunger kept jolting him awake, and part of it awake, consumed by worries and by vague hopes that all led to the same conclusion: that for the time being he should keep calm and, by exercising patience and the greatest consideration for his family, try to make bearable the unpleasantness that he would in his present condition inevitably cause them.

Early the next morning—it was nearly still night—Gregor had a chance to test the firmness of his resolve, for his sister, already half-dressed, opened the door

leading from the foyer and looked tensely inside. She couldn't find him right away, but when she noticed him under the sofa—God, he had to be someplace, he couldn't have just flown away—she was so shocked that without being able to stop herself, she slammed the door shut again. But as if she regretted her behavior, she opened the door again immediately, and came inside on tiptoe, as if she were in the presence of someone severely ill, or even a complete stranger. Gregor shoved his head forward just to the edge of the sofa and watched her. He wondered whether she would notice that he had left the milk standing, though not from lack of hunger, and whether she would bring him some other food that suited him better. If she didn't do it on her own, he would rather starve than make her aware of it, although he felt a strong urge to shoot out from beneath the sofa, throw himself at her feet, and beg her for something good to eat. But his sister, with some amazement, right away noticed the still full basin: only a bit of milk had been spilled around its edges. She picked it up immediately, though with a rag, not with her bare hands, and took it away. Gregor was extremely curious to see what she would bring as a replacement and thought a great deal about it. He could never have guessed, however, what his sister in her goodness actually did. In order to test his preferences, she brought him an entire assortment of foods spread out on an old newspaper. There were old, half-rotten vegetables; bones from last night's meal, covered with congealed white sauce; a few raisins and almonds; a cheese that Gregor had declared inedible two days before; a piece of dry bread, a piece of bread smeared with butter, and a piece with butter and salt. Beside this she placed the basin that seemed now to be designated permanently for Gregor, which she had filled with water. And out of tact, because she knew Gregor would not eat in front of her, she departed hastily, even going so far as to turn the key in the lock, just so that Gregor would know that he could make himself as comfortable as he wanted. Gregor's legs quivered, now that the meal lay waiting. His wounds must moreover have completely healed. He felt no impairment now, and was astonished at this, thinking of how he had cut himself very slightly with a knife more than a month ago, and how the wound had still hurt him considerably the day before yesterday. "Am I less sensitive than before?" he wondered, and sucked greedily at the cheese, to which he had found himself urgently drawn, before everything else. In rapid succession, amidst tears of joy, he devoured the cheese, the vegetables, and the sauce. He didn't like the taste of the fresh foods, however—he couldn't even bear their smell, and dragged the foods that he wanted to eat a bit farther away. He had long since finished everything and lay lazily in the same spot when his sister slowly turned the key in the lock, as a sign that he should withdraw. That jolted him awake immediately, though he was almost dozing, and he hurried back under the sofa. But it took great self-control for him to remain under the sofa even for the brief time that his sister was in the room, for his body had swelled a bit with the ample meal, and he could hardly breathe in the narrow space. Half-suffocating, he looked out with slightly bulging eyes as his sister, who noticed nothing, swept up with a broom not just the remainder of the food Gregor had eaten, but also the food that he had not even touched, as if this were no longer useable. She put it all in a container that she closed with a wooden lid, and then carried everything out. She had hardly turned around when Gregor pulled himself out from under the sofa and exhaled.

39   In this way Gregor now received his daily meals: the first in the morning, while his parents and the servant girl still slept, and the second after the common midday meal, for his parents slept a bit afterwards, and his sister sent the serving girl away on one errand or another. It was not that the others wanted him to starve, but experiencing his meals at secondhand might have been all they could bear; or perhaps his sister simply wanted to spare them even this minor source of sorrow, since they were already suffering enough.

40   With what kinds of excuses they had managed to get the doctor and the locksmith out of the apartment the first morning, Gregor didn't manage to find out. Because no one could understand him, it didn't occur to anyone—not even to his sister—that he could understand them, so he had to content himself, when his sister was in his room, with listening to her occasional sighs and appeals to the saints. It was only later, when she had gotten used to things a bit—getting used to them completely was out of the question, of course—that Gregor sometimes seized on a remark that was meant in a friendly way or that could be taken that way. "Today he liked it," she said, if he had made a real dent in the meal, while in the contrary case, which occurred ever more frequently of late, she used to say almost sadly: "Everything untouched again."

41   Though Gregor could not learn any news directly, he overheard some from the rooms next door. The moment he heard voices, he immediately ran to the door and pressed his entire body up against it. Especially in the early days, there was no conversation that did not somehow, if only indirectly, relate to him. For two days

there were consultations at every meal about what they should do; between meals, too, they discussed the same thing. There were always at least two family members at home, because no one wanted to remain home alone, and they couldn't under any circumstances all leave the apartment at the same time. On the very first day the girl who cooked for them had begged his mother on bended knee—it wasn't exactly clear what and how much she knew of what had happened—to dismiss her. As she departed fifteen minutes later, she tearfully thanked them for her dismissal, as if for the greatest favor that had ever been done her, and swore a terrible oath, without anyone having asked her to do so, not to betray the least of what she knew to anyone.

Now his sister had to do the cooking, together with his mother. This didn't take much effort, however, because they ate practically nothing. Gregor heard them again and again urge each other to eat and receive no other answer than "Thanks, I've had enough," or something similar. It seemed they didn't drink anything, either. His sister often asked his father if he would like a beer, cheerfully offering to get it herself. When his father said nothing, she offered to send the porter for it, in case he didn't want to trouble her. When his father finally uttered a firm "No," the subject was dropped.

In the course of the first few days his father explained their entire financial situation and their prospects to his mother and to his sister. Now and then he stood up from the table and took various documents and notebooks out of the small safe that he had rescued from the bankruptcy of his business five years before. He could be heard opening the complicated lock and closing it again after removing what he sought. His father's explanations contained the first heartening news that Gregor had heard since his imprisonment. He had been under the impression that his father had absolutely nothing left over from his business. At least, he had said nothing to the contrary, and Gregor had certainly never asked him about it. Gregor's concern at the time of the bankruptcy had been to arrange everything so that the family could forget as soon as possible the financial misfortune that had brought them to a state of complete despair. And so he had begun to work with pronounced fervor. Practically overnight he was elevated from a minor clerk into a traveling salesman, which naturally gave him completely different financial prospects. His successes at work translated directly into cash that he could lay on the table at home before his astonished and pleased family. Those had been fine times, but they had never recurred, at least not with the same warm feelings, although Gregor later earned so much money that he was in a position to support the entire family, and he did so. They simply got used to it—the family, as well as Gregor. They gratefully accepted his money, and he gladly offered it, but that special warmth did not reappear. Only his sister remained close to Gregor. Because she loved music very much, unlike Gregor, and could play the violin movingly, he secretly planned to send her to the conservatory next year, despite the great cost, which would have to be made up somehow. The conservatory came up often in conversations with his sister during Gregor's brief stays in the city, but only as a beautiful dream whose realization was unthinkable. His parents didn't even like to hear them utter those innocent musings. But Gregor had given it a good deal of thought and intended to announce his decision with due ceremony on Christmas Eve.

These thoughts, completely futile in his present situation, went through his head while he clung to the door and listened. Sometimes, from sheer exhaustion, he could listen no more and would let his head fall against the door, but then immediately catch himself, for even the faint noise that he made in doing so was heard next door and caused them all to fall silent. "What's he doing now?" said his father after a pause, obviously turned towards the door. Only then was the interrupted conversation gradually taken up again.

Gregor now learned—for his father tended to repeat himself often in his explanations, partly because he had not concerned himself with these matters for a long while, and partly, too, because his mother didn't immediately understand everything the first time—that despite all their misfortunes, a certain sum, though a very small one, was left over from the old days. The untouched interest on the sum had moreover in the meantime allowed it to grow a bit. Besides this, the money that Gregor had brought home every month— he had only kept a few florins for himself—had not been completely exhausted and had accumulated into a small amount of capital. Gregor, behind the door, nodded eagerly, overjoyed at this unexpected foresight and thriftiness. It occurred to him that he might have used that extra money to further pay down the debt his father owed the Director, bringing closer the day that he could quit his job, but the way his father had arranged things was no doubt better.

The sum that had been saved was not, however, large enough to allow his family to live off of the interest. It would have been enough to support them for a year, or at most two years, but no longer. The sum really shouldn't be touched; it should be set aside for emergencies. To live, money would have to be earned.

His father was a healthy but old man, who had not worked now for five years and couldn't in any case take on too much. During these five years, which had been the first free time of his hardworking but unsuccessful life, he had put on a great deal of weight and had become downright sluggish. But was his elderly mother supposed to earn money now—his mother, who suffered from asthma, for whom even a stroll through the apartment was considerable exertion, and who spent every other day on the sofa by the open window, gasping for breath? Or his sister, who at seventeen was still a child, and whose lifestyle up to that point had consisted of dressing herself neatly, sleeping late, helping out in the household, taking part in a few modest pleasures, and above all playing the violin? Whenever the conversation turned towards the necessity of earning money, Gregor left the door and threw himself on the leather sofa that stood nearby, for he burned with shame and sorrow.

Often he lay there the long night through, though he was unable to sleep for a moment and just scratched for hours at the leather. Or he would go to great pains to shove an armchair to the window, then crawl up to the windowsill and, bolstered by the armchair, lean against the window. He did so only in some kind of nostalgia for the feeling of freedom he had previously found in looking out the window, for the fact was that every day he saw things that were even a short distance away less and less clearly. He could no longer see the hospital that lay across the way, whose all too massive prospect he had earlier cursed. If he had not known very well that he lived in the quiet, but distinctly urban Charlotte Street, he could have believed that he looked out of his window into a desert in which the gray sky and the gray earth merged indistinguishably. His alert sister only had to see the armchair standing by the window twice before she began to shove the chair precisely back to the spot by the window after she straightened up the room. She even left the inner casement open from then on.

If Gregor had been able to speak to his sister and thank her for everything she had to do for him, he would have been able to bear her assistance more easily; as it was, however, it caused him some pain. His sister tried to hide the awkwardness of the whole thing as much as possible, and the longer it went on, the better she succeeded, but Gregor felt everything more acutely as time went on. Even her entrance was terrible for him. She had hardly entered, when, without even taking the time to shut the doors, though she otherwise took such pains to spare everyone the sight of Gregor's room, she ran to the window and hastily flung it open, as if she were suffocating. Then she remained for a time by the window, cold as it still was, and breathed deeply. With this running and commotion she alarmed Gregor twice daily. He trembled under the sofa the entire time and yet he knew very well that she would gladly have spared him, if only it had been possible to stay in a room where Gregor was with the windows closed.

49   Once—one month had already passed since Gregor's transformation, and there was no longer any reason for his sister to be astonished by his appearance—she came a bit earlier than usual and encountered Gregor as he was staring out the window, motionless and perfectly positioned to frighten someone. Gregor would not have been surprised if she had not come in, since his position hindered her from immediately opening the window, but she not only refrained from coming in, she actually turned around and locked the door. A stranger would have thought that Gregor had lain in wait for her and tried to bite her. Gregor naturally hid himself immediately under the sofa, but he had to wait until midday for her return, and she seemed then more agitated than usual. He realized from this that his appearance was still unbearable to her and that it would remain so—that she had to steel herself to keep from running at the sight of even the small portion of his body that jutted out from beneath the sofa. In order to spare her the sight, one day he dragged a sheet onto the sofa—it took him four hours to do so—and arranged it in such a way that he was completely covered. His sister could not have seen him even if she bent down. If the sheet had not been necessary, in her opinion, she could have removed it, for it obviously couldn't be pleasant for Gregor to block himself off so completely. But she left the sheet where it was, and Gregor thought he even noticed a grateful glance when he once carefully lifted the sheet with his head in order to see how his sister liked the new arrangement.

50   In the first two weeks his parents could not bring themselves to come in to see him, and he often heard them praise his sister's current industry, whereas they had previously complained a great deal about her, as she had then seemed to them a rather idle girl. In those early days, both his father and his mother often waited in front of Gregor's room while his sister straightened up, and as soon as she came out, she had to tell them precisely what it looked like in the room, what Gregor had eaten, how he had behaved, and whether there were perhaps any slight improvement in his condition. His mother also wanted to visit Gregor early on, but his father and sister dissuaded her with sound reasons to which Gregor listened very attentively, and which he completely supported. Later,

> ## He especially liked hanging upside down from the ceiling.

however, she had to be restrained with force. When she cried out, "Let me in to see Gregor; he's my poor son! Don't you understand that I must go to him?" Gregor thought that it might be good if his mother did come in—not every day, of course, but perhaps once a week. After all, she knew how to do things much better than his sister, who, despite her courage, was still only a child, and who likely took on such a heavy burden only out of childish thoughtlessness.

    Gregor's wish to see his mother was soon fulfilled. During the day, for his parents' sake, Gregor did not want to show himself at the window, but he did not have much room to crawl in the few square meters of floor space. It was hard enough for him to bear lying quietly during the night, and eating soon gave him not the least bit of pleasure, so in order to distract himself, he had adopted the habit of crawling across the walls and ceiling. He especially liked hanging upside down from the ceiling. It was completely different from lying on the floor: he could breathe more freely; his entire body swayed gently; and in the nearly happy distraction in which he found himself above, it sometimes happened that he unexpectedly let himself fall and crashed to the ground. But these days he had better control of his body, so he did not hurt himself even in a great fall. His sister immediately noticed the new amusement that Gregor had found for himself—he left a trace of stickiness behind him here and there while crawling—and so she got it in her head to allow him to crawl to his utmost by removing the furniture that hindered it, especially the chest of drawers and desk. She was not capable of doing this herself, however. She didn't dare ask her father for help. The servant girl would certainly not help her: this roughly sixteen-year-old girl had stuck it out quite bravely since the dismissal of the former cook, but she had asked for the privilege of keeping the kitchen door always locked and only having to open it when specifically asked. So his sister had no choice but to enlist her mother one time when her father was absent. With cries of great joy his mother approached, but fell silent at the door of Gregor's room. His sister checked first, of course, to see that the room was in order; only then did she let her mother enter. In great haste Gregor pulled the sheet lower and gathered more material around him. It looked like a sheet had merely been carelessly thrown over the sofa. Gregor also refrained from spying out from under the sheet. He deprived himself of the sight of his mother and took his pleasure entirely from the fact that she had come. "Come on, you can't see him," said his sister, and she apparently led her mother in by the hand. Gregor then heard the two frail women shove the heavy old chest of drawers from its place. His sister reserved the greatest part of the labor for herself, ignoring the warnings of her mother, who feared that she would overexert herself. It took a very long time. After fifteen minutes of work, his mother said that they should just leave the chest where it was, first, because it was too heavy—they wouldn't be finished before his father returned, and so would end up leaving the chest in the middle of the room, where it would block Gregor at every turn—and second, because it was not at all certain that they were doing Gregor a favor by removing the furniture. It seemed to her rather the opposite: the sight of the empty wall oppressed her heart. Why should Gregor not feel the same way? He had been used to the room's furniture for so long, that he would surely feel lost in an empty room. "And isn't it so," concluded his mother very softly—almost whispering, as if she wanted to keep Gregor, of whose precise whereabouts she wasn't certain, from hearing even the sound of her voice, for she was convinced that he could not understand the words—"isn't it so, that by removing the furniture we seem to be saying that we give up all hope of his recovery, and abandon him absolutely? I think it would be best if we left the room in exactly the same condition it was in before, so that when Gregor returns to us, he'll find everything unchanged, and so more easily forget what's happened in the meantime."

In listening to his mother's words, Gregor realized that the lack of any direct human communication over the course of the past two months, together with the monotonous life he led in the midst of the family, must have deranged his mind; otherwise he couldn't explain why he had earnestly desired that his room be emptied. Did he really want to let them transform the warm room, comfortably outfitted with inherited furnishings, into a cave? Granted, he would be able to crawl undisturbed in all directions, but he would at the same time forget, quickly and completely, his human past. He was already close to forgetting it, but his mother's voice, so long unheard, had roused him. Nothing should be removed; everything had to stay. He could not afford to lose the good influence the furniture had on his condition. If the furniture hindered him from carrying on his mindless crawling about, that was no drawback, it was rather a great advantage.

But his sister was unfortunately of a different opinion. She had become accustomed, not completely without justification, to playing the expert when it came to discussing anything that concerned Gregor with her parents. And so her mother's advice now led her to insist on the removal not only of the chest and the desk, which was all she had first intended, but of all of the furniture, with the exception of the indispensable sofa. Of course, it was not just childish stubbornness and the hard-won self-confidence she had recently and unexpectedly acquired that determined her on the this course: she had actually observed that Gregor needed a great deal of room to crawl around in, and that he did not use the furniture at all, as far as she could see. It might also have been the romantic nature of girls of her age, which sought some outlet at every opportunity, and made her want Gregor's situation to be even more terrifying, so that she could do even more than before to help him. For in a space in which Gregor, completely alone, ruled the empty walls, no person but Grete would dare to enter.

And so she did not allow herself to be swayed by her mother, who faltered from sheer uneasiness at being in the room, soon fell silent, and finally helped his sister as much as she was able in shoving the chest out of the room. Gregor could spare the chest if he must, but the desk had to stay. The women had hardly left the room with the chest, pushing at it and gasping for air, when Gregor stuck his head out from under the sofa, in order to see where he could intervene, as carefully and as considerately as possible. But unfortunately it was his mother who returned first, while Grete in the next room gripped the chest and rocked it back and forth alone, without, naturally, being able to move it from its spot. His mother was not, however, used to the sight of Gregor—he might have made her sick—so Gregor, alarmed, rushed back to the opposite end of the sofa. He could not, however, prevent the sheet from moving a bit at the front. That was enough to put his mother on the alert. She froze, stood still a moment, and then returned to Grete.

Though Gregor kept telling himself that nothing extraordinary was happening—a few pieces of furniture were merely being moved around—he soon realized that this continual back and forth on the part of the women, their soft calls to one another, and the scraping of the furniture on the floor affected him like the greatest of commotions closing in on him from all sides. However closely he drew in his head and legs and however firmly he pressed his body to the floor, he realized he couldn't stand it much longer. They were emptying out his room; they were taking from him everything that he held dear. They had carried out the chest which held his fret saw and other tools; they were already working free the desk from the grooves it had worn into the floor—the desk at which he had written his exercises as a student at trade school, at secondary school, and even at primary school. At this point he did not have the patience to contemplate the women's good intentions, the existence of which he had at any rate almost forgotten. Exhausted, they worked now in complete silence, and only the heavy tread of their feet could be heard.

56 And so he burst forth from under the sofa—the women were just leaning against the desk in the next room, in order to catch their breath—though he changed the direction of his charge four times, for he really did not know what to save first. On one otherwise empty wall he distinctly saw the picture of the woman dressed entirely in furs. He crept hurriedly up to it and pressed himself against the glass, which held him fast and soothed his hot belly. At least no one could take away this picture, which Gregor now completely covered with his body. He turned his head towards the door of the living room in order to observe the women on their return.

57 They weren't allowing themselves much rest and so came back directly. Grete had put her arm around her mother and seemed practically to carry her. "Well, what should we take now?" said Grete and looked around. Then her glance met Gregor's as he clung to the wall. She maintained her composure—surely only due to her mother's presence—bent her face to her mother, in order to keep her from looking around, and said hastily, a tremor in her voice, "Come, let's go back in the living room for a moment." Grete's intention was clear to Gregor: she wanted to bring her mother to safety and then chase him down off of the wall. Well, she could try! He would sit on the picture and not give it up. He would rather spring in Grete's face.

58 But Grete's words had for the first time really unsettled his mother. She moved to the side, spotted the giant brown fleck on the flowered wallpaper, and cried out in a screeching, raw voice, before she was really fully conscious that it was Gregor that she saw, "Oh my God; oh my God!" She then fell onto the sofa with widespread arms, as if she were altogether giving up, and didn't move. "Gregor, you—!" cried his sister with a raised fist and piercing gaze. They were the first words she had directly addressed to Gregor since his transformation. She ran into the next room in order to get some scent with which she could wake her mother out of her faint. Gregor wanted to help, too—there was still time to save the picture—but he was stuck to the glass and had to tear himself free. He, too, ran into the next room, as if he could give his sister some advice, as in earlier days, but then he had to stand helplessly behind her while she rummaged through various bottles. She was startled when she turned around; a bottle fell to the floor and broke. A sliver of glass cut Gregor's face, and some burning medicine spilled over him. Grete took as many bottles as she could carry and ran with them in to her mother. She then slammed the door shut with her foot. Gregor was now shut off from his mother, who was through his fault possibly near death.

He couldn't open the door, if he did not want to chase away his sister, who had to remain with his mother. He had nothing left to do but wait. Oppressed by self-reproaches and worry, he began to crawl. He crawled over everything—walls, furniture, and ceiling—and finally, in his despair, he fell, the entire room spinning around him, onto the center of the large table.

A short time passed, and Gregor lay limply there. All around was quiet. Perhaps that was a good sign. Then the bell rang. The servant girl was naturally locked into her kitchen, and so Grete had to go open the door. His father had returned. "What happened?" were his first words. The look on Grete's face betrayed everything to him. Grete answered with a muffled voice—she was obviously pressing her face against her father's chest: "Mother fainted, but she's already better. Gregor broke out." "I was waiting for this," said his father, "I always said it would happen, but you women didn't want to hear it." It was clear to Gregor that his father had interpreted Grete's all-too-brief announcement in the worst possible way, and assumed that Gregor had been guilty of some act of violence. Therefore Gregor had to try to mollify his father, for he had neither the time nor the ability to enlighten him. And so he fled to the door of his room and pressed against it, so that his father could see immediately on leaving the hallway that Gregor had every intention of returning right away to his room. It would not be necessary to drive him back, just to open the door, and he would disappear instantly.

But his father was not in the mood to notice such subtleties: "Ah!" he cried out on entering, in a tone that made him seem at once furious and glad. Gregor drew his head back from the door and turned it toward his father. His father's appearance was different from the way he remembered it. Lately, due to his new habit of crawling about, Gregor had concerned himself less with the goings-on in the rest of the apartment; he should therefore really have been prepared to encounter new developments. But still, still, was this really his father? The same man who lay, tired out, buried deep in his bed, when Gregor was all set to go on a business trip? The man who, dressed in a nightshirt, had greeted him when he returned in the evenings from an easy chair, and, unable to stand up, only raised his arms to show his joy at his return? The man who, on the rare walks he took together with Gregor and his mother on a few Sundays and the most important holidays of the year, walked packed into his old coat even more slowly than they did, though they walked slowly enough, laboring forward with a deliberately placed cane, and who nearly always stopped when he wanted to say something, gathering his companions around him? Now, he was quite well put together. He was dressed in the kind of close-fitting blue uniform with gold buttons that doormen at the banking houses wore; over the high stiff collar of the coat his pronounced double chin protruded; under his bushy eyebrows the glance of his dark eyes sprang forth fresh and alert; the formerly disheveled white hair was combed flat into a painfully exact, shining part. He threw his hat, which bore a gold monogram—probably that of a bank—in an arc across the room and onto the sofa. He moved towards Gregor, the ends of his long coat pushed back, his hands in his pants pockets, his face grim. He probably did not know himself what he planned to do. In any case he lifted his feet unusually high, and Gregor was astonished at the gigantic size of the soles of his boots. But he didn't let his astonishment distract him. He had known from the first day of his new life that his father considered the greatest severity appropriate in dealing with him. And so he ran away from his father. He froze when his father stood still and hurried forward again when his father moved a muscle. In this way they circled the room several times, without anything decisive happening; the whole thing moved at such a slow tempo that it didn't even look like a pursuit. For the time being, Gregor stayed on the floor. He was afraid that his father might consider flight toward the walls or the ceiling as particular wickedness. But Gregor realized that he couldn't keep up even this pace for long, for when his father took a single step, he had to carry out myriad movements. He soon felt short of breath; his lungs had not been reliable even in the old days. As he staggered forward, he could barely keep his eyes open, so hard did he try to concentrate his energy for running. In his dullness he was simply unable to think of any other means of deliverance. He had almost forgotten already that the walls were open to him, though they were obstructed here by painstakingly carved furniture full of points and sharp edges. Suddenly something lightly thrown flew just past him and rolled ahead. It was an apple. Another immediately followed. Gregor froze in fear. Running further was pointless, for his father had decided to bombard him. He had filled his pockets from the fruit bowl on the credenza and now threw apple after apple, without for the time being aiming very carefully. These small red apples rolled around on the ground, knocking into each other as if charged with electricity. A weakly thrown apple strafed Gregor's back, but glanced off without doing any harm. One that flew im-

mediately in its wake actually embedded itself in his back, however. Gregor tried to drag himself forward, as if he could outrun the unbelievable pain by changing position, but he felt as if he were nailed to the spot and lay sprawled upon the ground, in complete distraction of all of his senses. With his last conscious glance he watched as the door to his room was ripped open and, ahead of his screaming sister, his mother ran out of the room in her slip—for his sister had undressed her to let her breathe freely while in her faint—and raced towards his father, her untied skirts slipping down to the floor one after another; he watched as, stumbling on the skirts, she embraced his father, fully at one with him—but Gregor's vision now failed him utterly—and, with her hands clasped around the back of his head, begged him to spare Gregor's life.

> Gregor was a member of the family who should not be treated as an enemy.

III

The deep injury from which Gregor had suffered for over a month—the apple remained embedded in his flesh as a visible memento, as no one had dared to remove it—seemed to have reminded even his father that despite his present sad and repulsive state, Gregor was a member of the family who should not be treated as an enemy. The law of familial obligation dictated, rather, that one had to swallow one's revulsion and be tolerant, simply be tolerant. 61

And though Gregor had probably permanently lost some mobility through his injury, and now, like an invalid, took many, many minutes to cross his room—crawling on high was out of the question—this degeneration in his condition brought with it a compensation that was to his mind completely satisfactory. Toward evening they now opened the living room door so that, lying in the darkness of his room and invisible from the living room, he could watch the entire family at the lighted table and listen to their conversation by general consent, as it were—a complete change from the early days when he used to watch the door like a hawk an hour or two before they gathered. 62

Of course, the conversations were not as lively as in earlier days. Gregor used to recall them longingly in the small hotel rooms where he had had to throw himself, exhausted, into the damp bedclothes. These days everything was mostly very quiet. His father fell asleep in his armchair soon after the evening meal; his mother and sister urged one another to silence. His mother now sewed fine lingerie for a boutique, bend- 63 ing close to her work under the light. His sister, who had taken a job as a salesclerk, studied stenography and French at night, in order to find a better position one day. Sometimes his father awoke and, as if he didn't realize that he had been sleeping, would say to his mother: "How long you're sewing again today!" Then he would fall asleep again immediately, while his mother and sister exchanged tired smiles.

64   With a kind of stubbornness his father refused to take off his work uniform when he returned home, and while his nightshirt hung, useless, on a clothes hook, he dozed at his place fully clothed, as if he were always on duty and awaited the call of his superiors. As a result, the uniform, which hadn't been new in the first place, became less than pristine, despite the care his mother and sister took with it. Gregor often spent whole evenings looking at the badly stained coat, its oft-polished gold buttons shining, in which the old man slept highly uncomfortably, but quietly.

65   As soon as the clock struck ten, his mother tried to wake his father by speaking softly to him, and tried to persuade him to go to bed, for he couldn't sleep well there, and a good sleep was absolutely essential, since he had to be at work by six. But in the stubbornness that had come over him since he became a bank employee, he always insisted on remaining longer where he was, although he regularly fell asleep again, and required much effort to persuade in exchanging the armchair for his bed. His mother and sister could press him with gentle remonstrances as much as they liked—for a quarter of an hour at a time he slowly shook his head, his eyes closed, and refused to stand up. His mother plucked at his sleeve, and whispered endearments in his ear; his sister left her work in order to help her mother, but got nowhere with him. He only sank deeper into his armchair. Only when the women grasped him under the arms would he open his eyes, look in turn at Gregor's mother and sister, and say, "What a life. This is the peace and quiet of my old age." And bracing himself against the women, he hoisted himself up laboriously, as if he were his own greatest burden, and allowed himself to be led to the door. He waved them off then and went on under his own power, but Gregor's mother would hastily throw down her sewing and his sister her quill in order to run after him and be of further help to him.

66   Who in this overworked and overtired family had time to worry about Gregor more than was absolutely necessary? The household was ever more reduced in circumstances. The servant girl had been dismissed, and a gigantic, bony servant with white hair that flut-

> ## What really kept the family from changing apartments was despair . . .

tered about her head came in the mornings and the evenings to do the hardest labor. Everything else his mother took care of, in addition to her abundant sewing work. It even came to pass that various pieces of family jewelry, which his mother and sister had previously worn with pleasure at parties and celebrations, were sold, as Gregor learned one evening from a general conversation about the prices obtained. Their greatest source of complaint, however, was that the apartment, far too large for them under the circumstances, could not be left, because it was unthinkable that Gregor be relocated. But Gregor realized that it was not consideration for him that hindered a relocation, for they could have transported him easily in a suitable carton with a few air holes. What really kept the family from changing apartments was despair, and the thought that they had been afflicted by misfortune such as had struck no one in their circle of relatives and acquaintances. They did everything that the world demanded of poor people—his father fetched breakfast for the junior bank clerks; his mother dedicated herself to making underwear for strangers; his sister ran back and forth behind the counter at the beck and call of customers—but they could do no more than that. And the wound in his back began to hurt Gregor anew when his mother and sister would return from putting his father to bed, let their work lie, and huddle close together, cheek to cheek. His mother, gesturing towards Gregor's room, said, "Close the door, Grete," and Gregor was in the dark again, while next door the women mingled tears or stared, dry-eyed and numb, down at the table.

Gregor passed the days and nights nearly without sleep. Sometimes he considered taking the affairs of the family in hand again, the next time the door was opened. After some time, he thought again about the Director and the Deputy Director, the clerks and the apprentices, the slow-witted porter, two or three friends from other companies, a chambermaid from a hotel in the provinces—a dear, fleeting memory—and a cashier from a hat store whom he had courted seriously, though too slowly. They reappeared in his thoughts together with strangers or people he had already forgotten, but instead of helping him and his family, they all remained detached, and he was glad when they disappeared. At other times, however, he was not in the mood to worry about his family. He was filled with rage at the poor care they took of him, and though he could think of nothing for which he had an appetite, he made plans to reach the pantry and take what was due him, even if he were not hungry. Without considering any longer what might especially please Gregor, mornings and afternoons before returning to the store his sister hurriedly shoved any old kind of food into his room with her foot, only in order to sweep it out with a whisk of the broom in the evenings, indifferent as to whether it might have been merely tasted or—as was usually the case—it remained completely untouched. Her cleaning of the room, which she now always did in the evening, could not have been done any more hastily. Smears of dirt ran along the walls, and here and there lay balls of dust and filth. In the early days Gregor used to position himself upon the arrival of his sister in a particularly grubby corner, in order to reproach her. But he could have remained there for weeks, and his sister would still not have changed her ways. She saw the dirt as well as he did, but she had simply decided to leave it there. At the same time, with a touchiness entirely new to her that had now possessed the entire family, she was vigilant in making sure that the straightening of Gregor's room was left to her. His mother once undertook a thorough cleaning of Gregor's room, which had required several buckets of water—the moisture bothered Gregor, and he lay broad, embittered, and unmoving on top of the sofa—but his mother did not go unpunished. That evening his sister had hardly registered the change in Gregor's room when, highly insulted, she ran into the living room, and despite her mother's beseechingly raised hands, broke into a spasm of tears that his parents—his father had naturally been frightened out of his seat—at first simply watched, helpless with astonishment. Then they, too, were affected: on one side, his father reproached his mother for not leaving the cleaning of Gregor's room to his sister; on the other side, he shouted at his sister that she would never be allowed to clean Gregor's room again. In the meantime, his mother tried to drag his father, who was beside himself with agitation, into the bedroom; his sister, racked by sobs, hammered the table with her small fists; and Gregor hissed loudly with fury that no one thought to close the door and so spare him the scene and the noise.

But even if his sister, exhausted from her work, could no longer manage to care for Gregor as she had earlier, his mother would still not have had to intervene in order to keep Gregor from being neglected. For there was still the servant. This old widow, who had weathered the worst in her long life with the help of a powerful frame, felt no especial revulsion towards Gregor. Without exactly being curious, she had once by chance opened the door to Gregor's room and stood staring at the sight of him, her hands folded across her chest. Gregor was completely taken by surprise, and despite the fact that no one was chasing him, he began to run back and forth. Since that time, she hadn't missed a chance to open the door quickly in the morning and the evening to look in at Gregor. At first she called him over to her with words that she probably considered friendly, like "Come on over here, you old dung beetle!" or "Look at the old dung beetle!" Gregor did not respond to such overtures, but remained motionless in his place, as if the door had not even been opened. If only they would order this servant to clean his room daily, instead of letting her needlessly disturb him at will! Once in the early morning—a hard rain, perhaps already a sign of the coming spring, beat on the windowpanes—Gregor became so embittered when the servant began to speak that he turned towards her, as if to attack, though slowly and feebly. Instead of being afraid, however, the servant simply lifted high into the air a chair that stood in reach of the door. As she stood there with her mouth opened wide, it was clear that she intended to shut her mouth only after the chair in her hands had come down on Gregor's back. "That's it, then?" she asked, as Gregor turned around again, and she put the chair quietly back in its corner.

Gregor now ate almost nothing. When he happened to pass by the food prepared for him, he sometimes idly took a bite and held it in his mouth for an hour or so, only to spit most of it out again. At first he thought that his sorrow over the state of his room kept him from eating, but he had actually reconciled himself very soon to the changes. The family had gotten into the habit of putting into his room things that wouldn't fit anywhere else: there were now many such things, as they had rented one room in the apartment to three lodgers. These three serious gentlemen—all three had full beards, as Gregor discovered once by looking through the crack in the door—were painfully focused on order, not only in their room, but, simply because they had taken lodgings there, in the entire household, especially in the kitchen. They would not put up with useless or dirty things. And in any case, they had brought with them most of their own furnishings. For this reason, many things that were not saleable, but that the family did not want to throw away, had become superfluous. All of this made its way into Gregor's room—even, eventually, the ash bin and the rubbish bin from the kitchen. The servant, who was always in a rush, simply slung anything that was at the moment unuseable into Gregor's room. Fortunately Gregor usually saw only the relevant object and the hand that held it. The servant might once have intended to take the things out again when time and opportunity permitted, or perhaps to throw them all out together once and for all, but in practice they lay wherever they were tossed, unless Gregor wound his way through the clutter and stirred it up—first because he had no other place to crawl, and later with growing pleasure, although after such forays, tired to death and full of sorrow, he could not stir for hours.

70   Because the lodgers sometimes took their evening meal in the common living room, the living room door remained closed on some evenings. Gregor managed without it very well. On some evenings when it was open he did not even take advantage of it, but without the family's knowing it, lay in the darkest corner of his room. Once, however, the servant left the door to his room open a bit, and it remained open, even as the lodgers came in that evening and the light was turned on. They sat at the head of the table, where in former days his father, mother, and Gregor had eaten, unfolded their napkins, and took their knives and forks in hand. His mother immediately appeared in the doorway with a dish of meat and his sister directly behind her with a dish piled high with potatoes. The steaming food gave off a rich smell. The lodgers bent over the dishes placed before them as if they wanted to check them before eating, and the one in the middle, whom the other two appeared to consider an authority, actually cut off a piece of meat still in the serving dish, obviously to test whether it were tender enough, or whether it might perhaps need to be sent back to the kitchen. He was satisfied, and mother and sister, who had watched the proceedings tensely, breathed again and smiled.

71   The family themselves ate in the kitchen. Nevertheless, his father, before he went into the kitchen, came into the room and made a single long bow while circling the table, cap in hand. The lodgers all rose together and murmured something into their beards. When they were alone again, they ate in near total silence. It seemed strange to Gregor that, among all the various sounds of eating, he could pick out the sound of their chewing teeth—it was as if Gregor were thereby reminded that one needed teeth in order to eat, and that one could do nothing with even the most beautiful toothless jaws. "I do have an appetite," said Gregor sorrowfully to himself, "but not for these things. How these lodgers feed themselves, while I'm dying of hunger!"

72   On this very evening, though Gregor did not remember having heard it once before during that whole time, the violin sounded from the kitchen. The lodgers had already finished their meal. The middle one had pulled out a newspaper and given each of the others one page. They now read, leaning back, and smoked. As the violin began to play, they became alert, arose and went on tiptoes to the hall door, where they stood pressed up against one another. They must have heard them in the kitchen, for his father called out: "Do you gentlemen perhaps dislike the playing? It can be stopped immediately." "On the contrary," said the lodger in the middle, "wouldn't the young lady like to come out and play here in this room, where it's much more comfortable and convenient?" "Oh, please!" called his father, as if he were the violin player. The lodgers moved back into the room and waited. His father soon came in with the music stand, his mother with the music, and his sister with the violin. His sister quietly prepared to play. His parents, who had never rented a room out before and so exaggerated the courtesy due the lodgers, did not dare to sit on their own chairs. His father leaned against the door, his right hand stuck between two buttons of his fastened livery coat. His mother, however, accepted a chair offered by one of the lodgers, and sat off in the corner where he had happened to place the chair.

His sister began to play. His father and mother, on either side of her, followed every note, attentive to the movements of her hands. Gregor, drawn by the music, had ventured a bit further forward. His head was already in the living room. He hardly wondered at himself for being so inconsiderate towards the others of late; earlier, this consideration had been a great source of pride. And just now he had more reason than before to hide himself. Because of the dust everywhere in his room that flew up at the least movement, he was himself covered in dust. Threads, hairs, and bits of leftover food stuck to his back and sides. His general apathy was much too great for him now to lie on his back and scrub himself on the carpet, as he used to do several times a day. Despite his condition, however, he had no qualms about advancing a bit onto the immaculate living room floor.

But no one paid any attention to him. His family was entirely absorbed in the playing of the violin. The lodgers, on the other hand, who had at first, their hands in their pants pockets, taken up positions inconveniently close to his sister's music stand, in order to see all the notes, soon withdrew to the window, their heads bowed amidst whispered conversation, and remained there with Gregor's father worriedly observing them. It was now painfully obvious that they were disappointed in what they had assumed would be a beautiful or entertaining performance, and that they were sick of the entire production and now al-

lowed their quiet to be disturbed only out of politeness. They way they all blew their cigar smoke out of
their mouths and noses indicated great irritation. But
his sister played so beautifully! Her face was turned to
the side; her gaze followed the lines of notes, searching and sorrowful. Gregor crept further forward and
held his head close to the floor,
in order to meet her gaze if possible. The music gripped him—
was he then an animal? He felt
as if he were being guided to the
sustenance he had unknowingly
desired. He was determined to
press on all the way to his sister, to pull on her skirt
and let her know that she could come into his room
with her violin. No one here knew how to appreciate
her playing the way he did. He wanted never to let her
out of his room again, at least not as long as he lived.
His terrifying shape would finally be of some use to
him: he would be at all doors of his room at once, hissing at all intruders. His sister, though, would not be
forced, but would rather stay with him willingly. She
would sit next to him on the sofa, her ear inclined towards him, and he would confide in her that he had intended to send her to the conservatory, and that, were
it not for the misfortune that had occurred, he had
intended to announce it to everyone last Christmas—
Christmas had surely passed already?—ignoring any
possible objections. After this declaration, his sister
would surely burst into tears of emotion, and Gregor
would lift himself up to her shoulder and kiss her
neck, which she now left uncovered, without ribbon or
collar, since she had begun working at the store.

"Mr. Samsa!" called the middle lodger and without wasting another word, pointed at Gregor, who was
slowly inching his way forward. The violin fell silent.
The middle lodger smiled at first, shaking his head
at his friends, and then looked down again at Gregor.
His father seemed to consider it more urgent to reassure the lodgers than to drive Gregor back, despite the
fact that they seemed calm and more entertained by
Gregor than by the violin. He hurried over to them
and tried with outspread arms to urge them into their
room; at the same time, he wanted to block their view
of Gregor with his body. They actually became a bit angry now, though it was unclear whether this was over
his father's behavior or over the dawning recognition
that, unbeknownst to them, they had all the while had
a neighbor like Gregor. They asked his father for an explanation, raised their arms, pulled agitatedly at their
beards and only reluctantly retreated into their room.
In the meantime his sister had come out of the trance
into which she had fallen after her playing had been so
suddenly broken off. For a time she had held her violin

The music gripped him—was he then an animal?

and bow in her limply hanging hands and continued to
stare at the music, as if she were still playing. Now, all
at once, she pulled herself together, laid the instrument
in the lap of her mother, who, short of breath and gasping for air, was still seated, and ran into the next room,
which the lodgers were now approaching more quickly
at the urging of her father. Under
her practiced hands, the covers
and pillows flew high in the air
and arranged themselves. Before the lodgers had reached the
room, she was finished readying
the beds and had slipped out.

His father's stubbornness seemed to have returned to
the extent that he forgot all respect that he owed his
lodgers. He kept urging them and urging them, until
finally at the threshold the gentleman in the middle re-
soundingly stamped his foot and so brought his father
to a standstill. "I hereby declare," he said, and, raising
his hand, sought the gaze of Gregor's mother and sister,
as well, "that, in consideration of the revolting conditions existing in this apartment and this family"—and
here, without a moment's hesitation, he spat on the
ground—"I give notice this instant. I will naturally pay
absolutely nothing for the days I have lived here; on the
contrary, I will consider bringing charges against you,
which will—believe me—be very easy to prove." He fell
silent and stared straight ahead, as if he were waiting
for something. His two friends then obliged him by
chiming in with the words: "We, too, give notice this
instant." At that, he seized the door handle and shut
the door with a crash.

His father staggered to his chair, his hands
stretched out before him, and fell into it. It looked as
if he were stretching himself out for his usual evening
nap, but his head, sharply, ceaselessly nodding, showed
that he was not sleeping at all. Gregor had lain all this
time in the same spot where the lodgers had discovered
him. His disappointment at the failure of his plans—
perhaps, though, too, the weakness caused by his long
hunger—made it impossible for him to move. He was
distinctly afraid that in the next moment everything
was going to come crashing down on top of him. He
waited. Not even the violin roused him, which slipped
from his mother's trembling fingers and fell from her
lap, emitting a ringing tone.

"My dear parents," said his sister and struck her
hand on the table by way of preamble, "we can't go on
like this. If you can't see it, I can. I don't want to use
the name of my brother in front of this monster, so let
me just say this: we have to try to get rid of it. We have
tried as much as humanly possible to care for it and
to put up with it. I don't think it could reproach us in
the least."

78   "She is absolutely right," said his father under his breath. His mother, who seemed not to have caught her breath yet, began to emit a muffled cough into the hand she held before her, a crazed expression in her eyes.

79   His sister hurried to his mother and put her hand to her forehead. His sister's words seemed to have put his father's thoughts in a surer course. He sat up straight, fiddling with his uniform cap amongst the plates that still sat on the table from the lodgers' evening meal, and looked for a time down at the quiet Gregor.

80   "We must try to get rid of it," his sister finally said to his father, for his mother heard nothing in the midst of her coughing. "It's going to kill you both; I can see it coming. When people have to work as hard as we do, they can't bear this kind of constant torture at home. I can't bear it any more." And she began crying so hard that her tears flowed down her mother's face, where she began mechanically wiping them away with her hand.

81   "But my child," said his father, sympathetically and with striking compassion, "what should we do?"

82   His sister only shrugged her shoulders as a sign of the helplessness that had during her crying spell taken the place of her former certainty. "But if he understood us—" his father said, questioningly. His sister, in the midst of her tears, waved her hand violently as a sign that that was out of the question.

83   "If he understood us," his father repeated, and by closing his eyes, tried to absorb her certainty that it was impossible, "then we might able be to arrive at some arrangement with him. But as things stand—"

84   "It has to go," cried his sister. "That is the only way, father. You must simply try to rid yourself of the thought that it's Gregor. Our real misfortune is that we believed it for so long. But how can it be Gregor? If it were Gregor, he would have seen long ago that such an animal cannot live with people and he would have left voluntarily. We would then have had no brother, but we could have lived on and honored his memory. But this beast persecutes us, drives off the lodgers, and obviously wants to take over the apartment and force us to sleep out in the alley. Just look, Father," she suddenly screamed, "he's starting again!" And in a state of terror totally incomprehensible to Gregor, his sister abandoned his mother and practically vaulted off her chair, as if she would rather sacrifice her than remain in Gregor's vicinity. She hurried behind her father who, agitated entirely through her behavior, stood up as well and half raised his arms as if to protect her.

85   But it wasn't at all Gregor's intent to upset anyone, especially not his sister. He had just begun to turn himself around in order to make his way back into his room. Of course, that procedure looked peculiar

enough, because his ailing condition meant that in order to turn even with difficulty he had to help with his head, which he lifted repeatedly and braced against the ground. He paused and looked around. His good intentions seemed to be recognized: it had only been a momentary fright. They all looked at him, silent and sorrowful. His mother lay in her chair, her legs stretched before her and pressed together; her eyes were nearly falling shut from exhaustion. His father and sister sat next to one another, his sister with her hand laid around her father's neck.

86   "Maybe they'll allow me to turn around now," thought Gregor, and started to work on it again. He could not suppress the wheezing caused by his exertion, and he had to stop and rest now and then. No one rushed him: he was left to his own devices. When he had completed the turn, he immediately headed straight back. He was astonished by the vast distance that divided him from his room, and he could not grasp how in his weakened condition he had put the entire distance behind him, almost without noticing it. Focused solely on crawling as quickly as possible, he hardly noticed that no word and no outcry from his family disturbed him. He turned his head only when he was already at the door—not all the way, for he felt his neck getting stiff, but enough to see that nothing had changed behind him, except for the fact that his sister had stood up. His last glance fell on his mother, who was now fast asleep.

87   He was hardly in his room when the door was hastily pushed to, bolted fast and locked. The sudden noise behind him frightened Gregor so much that his legs buckled beneath him. It was his sister who had rushed to do it. She had stood, waiting, and had suddenly sprung forward, light-footed—Gregor had not even heard her coming—crying out to her parents "Finally!" as she turned the key in the lock.

88   "And now?" Gregor asked himself, and looked around in the dark. He soon discovered that he could no longer move at all. He didn't wonder at this; on the contrary, it had seemed unnatural to him that he had actually been able to move before on such thin legs. Besides that, however, he felt relatively comfortable. He did have pains all over his body, but it seemed to him that they were becoming weaker and weaker and would finally die away altogether. He could hardly feel the rotten apple in his back or the inflamed surrounding area, which was now completely covered in moist dust. He thought of his family with compassion and love. His conviction that he had to disappear was even more definite than his sister's. He remained in this state of empty and peaceful contemplation until the clock tower struck three. He experienced once more

the approach of daylight outside the window. Then, unwilled, his head sank fully down, and from his nostrils his last breath weakly streamed forth.

89 When the servant came in the early morning—though she had often been asked to refrain from doing so, she slammed all the doors out of sheer vigor and haste, to such an extent that it was not possible to sleep quietly anywhere in the apartment once she had arrived—she noticed nothing unusual at first in her morning visit to Gregor. She thought that he intentionally lay there motionless because he found her behavior insulting; she credited him with all manner of intelligence. As she happened to be holding her long broom in her hand, she tried to tickle Gregor with it from the door. When she met with no response, she became irritated and poked him a bit. Only when she had shoved him from his spot without meeting any resistance did she become alert. She soon understood the situation. Her eyes widened, and she whistled out loud. It wasn't long before she had flung the door of the master bedroom open and called loudly into the darkness: "Look, everyone, it's kicked the bucket; it's lying there, dead as a doornail!"

90 The Samsas sat bolt upright in bed and had first to overcome their alarm at the servant's behavior before they could understand her report. Then, however, they climbed hurriedly out of bed, one on each side. Mr. Samsa threw the blanket over his shoulders; Mrs. Samsa emerged in her nightgown. In this manner they entered Gregor's room. In the meantime Grete had opened the door to the living room, where she had been sleeping since the arrival of the lodgers. She was completely dressed, as if she had not slept; her pale face confirmed the impression. "Dead?" said Mrs. Samsa, and looked questioningly up at the servant, although she could have made her own investigation or even have recognized the fact without making any investigation. "I'd say so," said the servant, and as proof, she pushed Gregor's corpse further to one side with the broom. Mrs. Samsa moved as if she wanted to hold her back, but she didn't. "Well," said Mr. Samsa, "now we can thank God." He crossed himself, and the three women followed his example. Grete, who did not take her eyes from the corpse, said: "Just look at how thin he was. He hadn't eaten anything for so long. The food came out just the way it went in." Gregor's body was indeed completely flat and dry; it was really only possible to see it now that he was off his legs and nothing else distracted the eye.

91 "Come, Grete, come sit with us for a bit," said Mrs. Samsa with a wistful smile, and Grete followed her parents into their bedroom, though not without looking back at the corpse. The servant shut the door and opened the window wide. Despite the early morning the fresh air already had something mild mixed in it. It was, after all, already the end of March.

92 The three lodgers emerged from their room and looked in amazement for their breakfast. It had been forgotten. "Where is breakfast?" the middlemost of the men asked the servant sullenly. She laid a finger to her lips and then silently and hastily signaled to the men that they might come into Gregor's room. They came and stood around Gregor's corpse in the now completely bright room, their hands in the pockets of their somewhat shabby coats.

93 The door to the bedroom opened then, and Mr. Samsa appeared in his livery with his wife on one arm and his daughter on the other. They had all been crying; Grete pressed her face from time to time to her father's arm.

94 "Leave my apartment immediately!" said Mr. Samsa and pointed to the door, without letting the women leave his side. "What do you mean?" said the middle lodger, somewhat dismayed, and smiled mawkishly. The two others held their hands behind their backs and rubbed them together continuously, as if in joyful expectation of a great fight, which would, they were sure, end favorably for them. "I mean exactly what I say," answered Mr. Samsa, and advanced in a line with his companions toward the lodger. He stood quietly, at first, and looked at the ground, as if the things in his head were arranging themselves in a new order. "Then we'll go," he said and looked up at Mr. Samsa, as if a sudden access of humility required him to seek renewed approval even for this decision. Mr. Samsa merely nodded shortly several times, his eyes wide and staring. At this, the man immediately walked with long strides into the foyer. His two friends had listened at first, their hands completely still, and they now skipped after him directly, as if in fear that Mr. Samsa could step in front of them in the foyer and disrupt their connection to their leader. In the hall all three of them took their hats from the rack, drew their walking sticks from the stand, bowed mutely, and left the apartment. In what proved to be a completely unnecessary precaution, Mr. Samsa walked out with the two women onto the landing. Leaning on the railing, they watched as the three men slowly but steadily descended the stairs, disappearing on every floor at the turning of the stairwell, and emerging again after a few moments. The lower they went, the more the

Samsa family lost interest in them, and as a butcher's boy carrying his burden on his head with dignity passed them and then climbed high above them, Mr. Samsa left the landing with the women and they all returned, as if freed from a burden, to their apartment.

95   They decided to spend the day resting and taking a stroll. They had not only earned this rest from work, they absolutely needed it. And so they sat at the table and wrote three letters of excuse, Mr. Samsa to the bank directors, Mrs. Samsa to her employer, and Grete to her supervisor. While they were writing the servant entered in order to say that she was leaving, as her morning work was finished. Writing, the three of them merely nodded at first, without looking up; only when the servant failed to depart did they look up angrily. "Well?" asked Mr. Samsa. The servant stood in the door, smiling, as if she had some great piece of good news to report to the family, but would only do so if she were thoroughly interrogated. The nearly upright little ostrich feather on her hat, which had annoyed Mr. Samsa the entire time she had been employed there, waved freely in all directions. "Well, what do you want?" asked Mrs. Samsa, for whom the servant had the most respect. "Well," the servant answered, and could not say more right away, fairly bursting with friendly laughter, "well, you needn't worry about getting rid of that thing next door. It's all been taken care of." Mrs. Samsa and Grete bent to their letters again, as if they wanted to continue writing. Mr. Samsa, who saw that the servant was about to begin describing everything in great detail, decisively headed this off with an outstretched hand. Since she was not going to be allowed to tell her story, she suddenly remembered her great haste, and, obviously deeply insulted, called out, "Bye, everyone," then spun around wildly and left the apartment amidst a terrific slamming of doors.

96   "Tonight we're firing her," said Mr. Samsa, but received no answer either from his wife or from his daughter, for the servant seemed to have disturbed their but newly restored calm. They rose, went to the window, and remained there, their arms around each other. Mr. Samsa turned in his chair as they went and quietly observed them for a while. Then he called out, "Well, come over here. Let what's past be past. And take some care of me, for once." The women obeyed immediately, hurrying over to him and caressing him, and then quickly finished their letters.

Then all three of them left the apartment together, which they had not done for months, and took a trolley to the open air beyond the city. The car they sat in was drenched with warm sunlight. Leaning back comfortably in their seats, they discussed their future prospects, and it emerged that these were not at all bad on closer inspection, for all three of their positions, were altogether favorable at present and, most importantly, had great potential for the future. The greatest improvement of their present situation would have to come, naturally, from a change of apartments. They would want a smaller and cheaper apartment, but one that was better located and generally more convenient than their current apartment, which Gregor had originally found for them. While they conversed in this way, it occurred to both Mr. and Mrs. Samsa in the same moment in looking at their ever more lively daughter that despite the recent ordeals that had made her cheeks so pale, she had blossomed into a pretty and well-developed young woman. Becoming quieter and almost unconsciously communicating through glances, they realized that it would soon be time to look for a good husband for her. And it seemed to them a confirmation of their new dreams and good intentions, when, at the end of their journey, their daughter rose first and stretched her young body.

translated by Alexis Walker

I F you like the way that Kafka employs the older form of allegory to new ends, leading the reader away from fixed meanings into the world of ambiguity, you may enjoy rereading Thomas Wolfe's "Only the Dead Know Brooklyn" and Stephen Crane's "The Open Boat." "The Gilded Six Bits," by Zora Neale Hurston (see chapter 14) also gives multiple meanings to its titular "six bits."

GOING FURTHER   A few great modern novels waver between—or perhaps encompass both—allegory and symbolism. Among these are Albert Camus's *The Stranger* and Thomas Pynchon's *V.*

Writing from Reading

Summarize

1 Describe how the family viewed Gregor before the metamorphosis. What was his role in the family?

2 Describe each family member's reaction when he or she first discovers Gregor's transformation. What do their responses reveal about them as characters and about their relationship with Gregor?

Analyze Craft

3 Discuss the symbolic aspect of the desk in Gregor's room. What role does it play in his life before and after his metamorphosis?

4 Discuss the three boarders as a symbol. What role do they play in the life of the family? What effect do they have on the family's peculiar situation?

Analyze Voice

5 Gregor's condition is extraordinary, but nobody ever seems to question it. Discuss how Kafka handles this fantastical aspect in his otherwise very practical story. Is he successful in making the surreal believable?

Synthesize Summary and Analysis

6 What happens to the father in the course of the story? Contrast his life before Gregor's metamorphosis with his life afterward.

Interpret the Story

7 Discuss the removal of the furniture in Gregor's room as a symbolic act. In your discussion, contrast the mother's view of the removal with that of Gregor and of his sister.

8 In the original German, Gregor is transformed into an *Ungeziefer*, which does not translate directly to "insect." There are other possible translations, but each fails in some way to capture the same connotations of uncleanness and unpleasantness. Discuss how the use of the word "insect" (as opposed to other possible translations like "pest" or "vermin") affects your reading of the story.

Elizabeth Tallent (b. 1954)

Born in Washington, D.C., Elizabeth Tallent has an impressive teaching record that includes the creative writing programs at the University of California, Irvine, the University of California, Davis, the Iowa Writer's Workshop, and—currently—Stanford University. Although she has published a novel, *Museum Pieces* (1985), and a volume of criticism on John Updike's writing, *Married Men and Magic Tricks* (1982), Tallent is best known for her short stories. She has published three collections—*In Constant Flight* (1983), *Time with Children* (1987), and *Honey* (1993)—each of which chronicles contemporary familial relationships, marriage, and adultery. Tallent's fiction has been featured in a wide variety of literary magazines and journals, including *The New Yorker*, *Grand Street*, and *The Paris Review*, as well as in *The Best American Short Stories*.

AS YOU READ   As you read, note the easy way the two characters talk with each other. Notice what the narrator notices. Where does her eye take you and why?

FOR INTERACTIVE READING…
- Create a marking system and use it to note what's inside the truck, what's outside the truck, and what's in the imaginations of the two characters. How do these three worlds of the story interact with one another?
- Circle the objects in the story that you feel have symbolic resonance. Make brief notes in the margin about associations you have with the circled objects.

No One's a Mystery (1985)

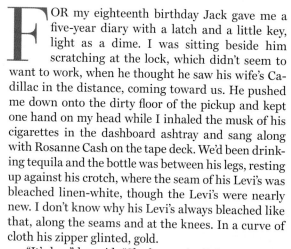

1   FOR my eighteenth birthday Jack gave me a five-year diary with a latch and a little key, light as a dime. I was sitting beside him scratching at the lock, which didn't seem to want to work, when he thought he saw his wife's Cadillac in the distance, coming toward us. He pushed me down onto the dirty floor of the pickup and kept one hand on my head while I inhaled the musk of his cigarettes in the dashboard ashtray and sang along with Rosanne Cash on the tape deck. We'd been drinking tequila and the bottle was between his legs, resting up against his crotch, where the seam of his Levi's was bleached linen-white, though the Levi's were nearly new. I don't know why his Levi's always bleached like that, along the seams and at the knees. In a curve of cloth his zipper glinted, gold.

2   "It's her," he said. "She keeps the lights on in the daytime. I can't think of a single habit in a woman that irritates me more than that." When he saw that I was going to stay still he took his hand from my head and ran it through his own dark hair.

3   "Why does she?" I said.

4   "She thinks it's safer. Why does she need to be safer? She's driving exactly fifty-five miles an hour. She believes in those signs: 'Speed Monitored by Aircraft.' It doesn't matter that you can look up and see that the sky is empty."

5   "She'll see your lips move, Jack. She'll know you're talking to someone."

6   "She'll think I'm singing along with the radio."

7   He didn't lift his head, just raised the fingers in salute while the pressure of his palm steadied the wheel, and I heard the Cadillac honk twice, musically; he was driving easily eighty miles an hour. I studied his boots. The elk heads stitched into the leather were bearded with frayed thread, the toes were scuffed, and there was a compact wedge of muddy manure between the heel and the sole—the same boots he'd been wearing for the two years I'd known him. On the tape deck Rosanne Cash sang, "Nobody's into me, no one's a mystery."

8   "Do you think she's getting famous because of who her daddy is or for herself?" Jack said.

9   "There are about a hundred pop tops on the floor, did you know that? Some little kid could cut a bare foot on one of these, Jack."

10   "No little kids get into this truck except for you."

11   "How come you let it get so dirty?"

12   "'How come,'" he mocked. "You even sound like a kid. You can get back into the seat now, if you want. She's not going to look over her shoulder and see you."

13   "How do you know?"

14   "I just know," he said. "Like I know I'm going to get meat loaf for supper. It's in the air. Like I know what you'll be writing in that diary."

15   "What will I be writing?" I knelt on my side of the seat and craned around to look at the butterfly of dust printed on my jeans. Outside the window Wyoming

was dazzling in the heat. The wheat was fawn and yellow and parted smoothly by the thin dirt road. I could smell the water in the irrigation ditches hidden in the wheat.

"Tonight you'll write, 'I love Jack. This is my birthday present from him. I can't imagine anybody loving anybody more than I love Jack.'"

"I can't."

"In a year you'll write, 'I wonder what I ever really saw in Jack. I wonder why I spent so many days just riding around in his pickup. It's true he taught me something about sex. It's true there wasn't ever much else to do in Cheyenne.'"

"I won't write that."

"In two years you'll write, 'I wonder what that old guy's name was, the one with the curly hair and the filthy dirty pickup truck and time on his hands.'"

"I won't write that."

"No?"

"Tonight I'll write, 'I love Jack. This is my birthday present from him. I can't imagine anybody loving anybody more than I love Jack.'"

"No, you can't," he said. "You can't imagine it."

"In a year I'll write, 'Jack should be home any minute now. The table's set—my grandmother's linen and her old silver and the yellow candles left over from the wedding—but I don't know if I can wait until after the trout à la Navarra to make love to him.'"

"It must have been a fast divorce."

"In two years I'll write, 'Jack should be home by now. Little Jack is hungry for his supper. He said his first word today besides "Mama" and "Papa." He said "kaka."'"

Jack laughed. "He was probably trying to fingerpaint with kaka on the bathroom wall when you heard him say it."

"In three years I'll write, 'My nipples are a little sore from nursing Eliza Rosamund.'" 29

"Rosamund. Every little girl should have a middle name she hates." 30

"'Her breath smells like vanilla and her eyes are just Jack's color of blue.'" 31

"That's nice," Jack said. 32

"So, which one do you like?" 33

"I like yours," he said. "But I believe mine." 34

"It doesn't matter. I believe mine." 35

"Not in your heart of hearts, you don't." 36

"You're wrong." 37

"I'm not wrong," he said. "And her breath would smell like your milk, and it's kind of a bittersweet smell, if you want to know the truth." 38

IF you like "No One's a Mystery," about the education of a young girl bordering on the scandalous, you might also enjoy the casebook on Joyce Carol Oates that includes the cautionary tale "Where Are You Going, Where Have You Been?"

GOING FURTHER Tallent and Oates rank high among a large number of contemporary women who work on material once reserved only for male writers, as in Oates's depiction of a sexually obsessed real-estate salesman in her novel *What I Lived For,* Susanna Moore's focus on violent crime in her novel *In the Cut,* and Alice Walker's depiction of black sexuality in *The Color Purple.*

Writing from Reading

Summarize

1 Describe Jack's life situation as it's suggested by the text. Cite specific details from the text that support your conclusions. Do some details seem incongruous with the Jack portrayed by the narrator?

2 Jack accuses the narrator of acting childish. In what ways does she act childish, and in what ways, if any, does she demonstrate the maturity of the adult she's just become?

Analyze Craft

3 Tallent provides very little physical description of her characters.

Consider the things Tallent does choose to describe: How do these descriptions reflect on the characters and their situation?

Analyze Voice

4 Discuss how having a young woman as a narrator lends extra weight to symbols like the diary and the pop song and breast milk. Would these symbols have the same effect if the story were told from Jack's point of view?

Synthesize Summary and Analysis

5 Compare and contrast the diary entries that the two characters imagine. What do their fantasies reveal about them and the differences between them?

Interpret the Story

6 Discuss the significance of the diary as a central image in this story. Why does Tallent choose to have the diary locked? Does this portend anything for the narrator's future with Jack? Analyze the locked diary by considering other symbols in the story.

Reading for Symbols

When reading for **symbols**—objects, images, characters, or actions that suggest meaning beyond the literal level—notice the images that receive special emphasis. Ask yourself these questions:

Is this an *allegory*—a story in which key elements such as characters and settings represent universal truths or moral lessons in a one-to-one correspondence?		EXAMPLE: the ant and the grasshopper
Is this a *symbolic object* or *symbolic character*—one that appears to have meaning beyond the literal level?		EXAMPLES: the pebble that Martha sent; Paul's red carnation

Is this a *symbolic act*—a gesture or action that conveys something beyond the literal level?		EXAMPLE: Lieutenant Cross discarding the pebble
How do you identify an image with symbolic potential?	• Consider whether it is repeated, portrayed in detail or given emotional weight in the lives of the characters or narrator.	
How do you understand the meanings of a symbol?	• Consider the characters' attitudes about it, the effect it has on the characters, especially the protagonist, or how it changes over the course of the story, and how attitudes toward it change.	

Suggestions for Writing about Symbolism

1. In "The Metamorphosis" and "Young Goodman Brown," what, if any, qualities of an allegory can you identify? Compare the two stories. On the whole, would you label either story as an allegory?

2. Choose any two of the stories in this chapter and articulate their major themes. How do symbols in these stories support and establish the themes? What do these stories suggest about the relationship between theme and symbol in fiction?

3. Exploring the relationship between setting and symbol, "The Things They Carried" and "Young Goodman Brown" both feature characters who find themselves away from home in strange and dangerous places. How does each author establish a sense of place, as in Hawthorne's deep forest in New England and O'Brien's jungle battlefield in Vietnam? Use examples from each story to illustrate how the symbolic resonance of particular details enhances these settings.

11
Fiction As Social Commentary

A Case Study
Joyce Carol Oates

AS a witness to society, Joyce Carol Oates (b. 1938) has few if any equals; for more than forty years she has reported on America, its brightly lit arenas as well as its dark corners. Joyce Carol Oates calls attention to many facets of society, including the dark and violent side, as in "Where Are You Going, Where Have You Been?" A story like "Three Girls" gives a new perspective on celebrity and what our society does to an individual with fame. Her tales are often fringed with menace and their resolutions violent; a storyteller's energy infuses every page. She's—there's no other word for it—prodigious, and though the quality of her written work may vary, the quantity is nearly nonpareil. She produces learned assessments of little-known or long-forgotten authors but is never far away from popular culture in her book reviews, essays, and fiction about figures such as Muhammad Ali, Edward Kennedy, and Marilyn Monroe.

"I like to write about my own time, and I always tell my students that we write for our own time. . . . We can't be writing for people far in the future because we don't know who they are. So, we write for our own time. . . . I address myself to these issues of the present time."

—from a conversation with Joyce Carol Oates, available on video at www.mhhe.com/delbanco1e

Although Oates experiments with different voices in her fiction, she does speak in her own voice in her nonfiction. Deeply intellectual yet not afraid to add a casual personal remark, Oates in her nonfiction voice has commented on a host of topics related to writing in general (as in *The Faith of a Writer*), on her own writing (in *The New York Times*), on other authors' work (as in her collection *Uncensored: Views and (Re)views,* a compilation of Oates's discussions of authors from Emily Brontë to Don DeLillo), and on the sport of boxing, a love of which she acquired as a young girl in the company of her father.

"I've always been very interested in holding a kind of mirror, sometimes a slightly distorting mirror, up to contemporary American society." Conversation with Joyce Carol Oates

The stories reprinted here are among her most famous, and they also exemplify the major themes of much of Oates's work. Here are ordinary people in extraordinary moments; there are questions of identity, the female experience, and the threat of violence. "All my life," Oates says, "I've been fascinated with the mystery of human personality."

CONTINUED ON PAGE 366

CONTINUED ON PAGE 366

I hope readers read without thinking it's a work of fiction.

Q&A

I always felt reading was my freedom.

A Conversation on Writing

Joyce Carol Oates

Falling in Love with Your Subject

You may see something happen and it lodges very deeply in you for a reason that you can't understand. I think it's almost like falling in love. . . . You might see something on television. It makes almost no impression. It just sort of glimmers and goes past you. But once in a while something will enter into you and it imprints itself very deeply into you because it struck a resonance with your own unconscious and your own personal life. I don't think that one can write or create any kind of art that doesn't have a deep resonance in the artist or writer's unconscious.

Daydreaming, Integrity, and the Writing Process

I become really haunted by something. Sometimes I see a photograph; sometimes I'm just drawn by a story. Sometimes it's a dream image. Sometimes it's something that has happened to me. . . . It becomes something of a meditation. . . . I have this meditation, as I say, it can be very haunting. . . . I'm a runner. I just run, and I allow my mind to be very open and kind of loose and sort of in a day-dreaming mode. . . . Then when I come back from this experience I . . . write down what I remember from what I had worked out. . . . So the act of re-membering to me is very thrilling . . . but then the act of writing . . . becomes a very different sort of experience . . . choosing the right language, the right sentences, using maybe compound sentences or complex sentences, long sentences, short sen-

tences—that's the most challenging part of it. The daydreaming part is enjoyable and interesting and has its own integrity. But then the writing part is much more challenging.

The Sport of Revision

Well, the process of revision I find so thrilling. And I encourage my students to deal with revision in a way that's competitive. They take a work of theirs that they've done several weeks ago, and you look through it quickly. And you say to yourself, "I can do better. I can do better than this." And it's true. You can always do better. Every sentence could be rewritten, paragraphs could be rewritten, the whole thing could be kind of restructured. You could have a different opening—more interesting—you could have a different ending, a different title. The whole thing belongs to you, and you say to yourself, "I can make this better." And the fact is that nobody else can touch that except you. You are the sole proprietor and owner of that material.

To watch this entire interview and hear the author read from her work, go to **www.mhhe.com/ delbanco1e**.

RESEARCH ASSIGNMENT In her interview, Oates talks about the original title of "Where Are You Going, Where Have You Been?" and how she originally thought about that story. What made her change her title and with it her story? Do you agree with her decision?

Joyce Carol Oates (b. 1938)

> "I'm very struck by how ordinary people can rise to levels of extraordinary behavior. That people, maybe all of us, could be capable of heroic actions." Conversation with Joyce Carol Oates

First educated in a one-room schoolhouse in rural western New York, Joyce Carol Oates is now a professor of creative writing at Princeton University. For her fourteenth birthday, Oates received a typewriter, began writing, and went on to become one of America's most prominent contemporary authors. At age nineteen, Oates won *Mademoiselle* magazine's prestigious short story contest, continued to write steadily as an undergraduate at Syracuse University, published her first book at the age of twenty-eight, and established a rate of production of at least two books per year. She and her late husband, Raymond Smith, settled at the University of Windsor, near Detroit, after she earned her master's degree from the University of Wisconsin. Together they founded the *Ontario Review,* which they continued to edit after the couple moved to Princeton.

"Genuine artists create their own modes of art and nothing interests them except the free play of the imagination," Oates once said in an interview. From the very beginning, Oates engaged in the "free play" of the imagination—painting and drawing stories before she knew how to read. As she reached her teenage years and began reading great American novelists, she wrote stories in which she mimicked their styles, from Hemingway's spartan prose to Faulkner's lush language. Today, however, her own fiction is it's "own mode of art," and

Oates is often offended when critics call attention to her sex and to the violence that her female protagonists often face. Oates's fiction is concerned with more than female suffering.

While it is often the violence, or suggestion of violence, that draws attention to Oates's writing, this is a single aspect of her fascination with human behavior and the way—even in the face of destructive outside forces—people create identity. "To write," she says in her interview, "you have to have an emotional thread."—an emotional connection between a writer and her work. Oates explains the connection in her interview: "I sometimes write about people who are ordinary people in extraordinary moments because I think that people are much stronger and more interesting than they appear to be. Literature and art take people to places of conflict, where what is buried in them and perhaps even asleep in them is awakened suddenly. . . . And so with all of us I think we awaken from a kind of a sleep of ordinary life by some stressful thing that happens to us."

As a testament to the quality of her prose, twenty-eight of her stories have won O. Henry Prizes for Short Fiction and eleven Pushcart Prizes, and for her work in the form she was awarded the PEN/Malamud Award for Excellence in Short Fiction. Thirty-nine of her books have been *New York Times*

Notable Books of the Year. Oates's literary achievement is both broad—in terms of the number of books, collections, stories, and articles she has published—and deep. Among her better-known novels are *them* (1969), winner of the National Book Award, *Black Water* (1992), a finalist for the Pulitzer Prize, and *We Were the Mulvaneys* (2001), selected for Oprah's Book Club.

Her prizes are as numerous, it sometimes seems, as her titles. Best known as a writer of contemporary gothic fiction that incorporates feminism, violence, the normal and the paranormal, Oates explores the outer limits of human personality and the depths of American society. Her subjects range from the anonymous citizen to the iconic American celebrity; she writes of family life and loneliness, of conviction and delusion, the mall and the family farm.

Additionally, Oates has written in several genres of fiction, including gothic, romance, and mystery. Her celebrity as a writer seems at odds with the humble way she describes her daily writing process: "I have always lived a very conventional life of moderation, absolutely regular hours, nothing exotic, no need, even, to organize my time." The result is an author whose varied awards point to how we might best read her—while some were given to a specific novel or story, others were bestowed for overall influence and ongoing achievement.

"I saw a snapshot of Norma Jean Baker that had been taken when she was sixteen or seventeen years old . . . when you saw her as a high school student, you would not have thought she was anyone that special. . . . I thought it was so interesting how an ordinary girl could be made into a starlet, could become world famous, one day would be called by *Playboy* magazine 'the sexiest female of the twentieth century' . . . how an ordinary person becomes extraordinary." Conversation with Joyce Carol Oates

Three Girls (2002)

1   IN Strand Used Books on Broadway and Twelfth one snowy March early evening in 1956 when the streetlights on Broadway glimmered with a strange sepia glow, we were two NYU girl-poets drifting through the warehouse of treasures as through an enchanted forest. Just past 6:00 P.M. Above the light-riddled Manhattan, opaque night. Snowing, and sidewalks encrusted with ice so there were fewer customers in the Strand than usual at this hour but *there we were*. Among other cranky brooding regulars. In our army-surplus jackets, baggy khaki pants, and zip-up rubber boots. In our matching wool caps (knitted by your restless fingers) pulled down low over our pale-girl foreheads. Enchanted by books. Enchanted by the Strand.

2   No bookstore of merely "new" books with elegant show window displays drew us like the drafty Strand, bins of books untidy and thumbed through as merchants' sidewalk bins on Fourteenth Street, NEW THIS WEEK, BEST BARGAINS, WORLD CLASSICS, ART BOOKS 50% OFF, REVIEWERS' COPIES, HIGHEST PRICE $1.98, REMAINDERS 25¢—$1.00. Hard-cover/paperback. Spotless/battered. Beautiful books/cheaply printed pulp paper. And at the rear and sides in that vast echoing space massive shelves of books books books rising to a ceiling of hammered tin fifteen feet above! Stacked shelves so high they required ladders to negotiate a monkey nimbleness (like yours) to climb.

3   We were enchanted with the Strand and with each other in the Strand. Overseen by surly young clerks who were poets like us, or playwrights/actors/artists. In an agony of unspoken young love I watched you. As always on these romantic evenings at the Strand, prowling the aisles sneering at those luckless books, so many of them, unworthy of your attention. Bestsellers, how-tos, arts and crafts, too-simple *histories of.* Women's romances, sentimental love poems. Patriotic books, middlebrow books, books lacking esoteric covers. We were girl-poets passionately enamored of T. S. Eliot but scornful of Robert Frost whom we'd been made to memorize in high school—slyly we communicated in code phrases from Eliot in the presence of obtuse others in our dining hall and residence. We were admiring of though confused by the poetry of Yeats, we were yet more confused by the lauded worth of Pound, enthusiastically drawn to the bold metaphors of Kafka (that cockroach!) and Dostoevsky (sexy murderer Raskolnikov and the Underground Man were our rebel heroes) and Sartre ("Hell is other people"—we knew this), and had reason to believe that we were their lineage though admittedly we were American middle class, and Caucasian, and female. (Yet we were not "conventional" females. In fact, we shared male contempt for the merely "conventional" female.)

4   Brooding above a tumble of books that quickened the pulse, almost shyly touching Freud's *Civilization and Its Discontents*, Crane Brinton's *The Age of*

Reason, Margaret Mead's *Coming of Age in Samoa,* D. H. Lawrence's *The Rainbow,* Kierkegaard's *Fear and Trembling,* Mann's *Death in Venice*—there suddenly you glided up behind me to touch my wrist (as never you'd done before, had you?) and whispered, "Come here," in a way that thrilled me for its meaning *I have something wonderful/ unexpected/startling to show you.* Like poems these discoveries in the Strand were, to us, found poems to be cherished. And eagerly I turned to follow you though disguising my eagerness, "Yes, what?" as if you'd interrupted me, for possibly we'd had a quarrel earlier that day, a flaring up of tense girl-tempers. Yes, you were childish and self-absorbed and given to sulky silences and mercurial moods in the presence of showy superficial people, and I adored and feared you knowing you'd break my heart, my heart that had never before been broken because never before so exposed.

. . . I saw that she was Marilyn Monroe.

5   So eagerly yet with my customary guardedness I followed you through a maze of book bins and shelves and stacks to the ceiling ANTHROPOLOGY, ART/ANCIENT, ART/RENAISSANCE, ART/MODERN, ART/ASIAN, ART/WESTERN, TRAVEL, PHILOSOPHY, COOKERY, POETRY/MODERN where the way was treacherously lighted only by bare sixty-watt bulbs, and where customers as cranky as we two stood in the aisles reading books, or sat hunched on footstools glancing up annoyed at our passage, and unquestioning I followed you until at POETRY/MODERN you halted, and pushed me ahead and around a corner, and I stood puzzled staring, not knowing what I was supposed to be seeing until impatiently you poked me in the ribs and pointed, and now I perceived an individual in the aisle pulling down books from shelves, peering at them, clearly absorbed by what she read, a woman nearly my height (I was tall for a girl, in 1956) in a man's navy coat to her ankles and with sleeves past her wrists, a man's beige fedora hat on her head, scrunched low as we wore our knitted caps, and most of her hair hidden by the hat except for a six-inch blond plait at the nape of her neck; and she wore black trousers tucked into what appeared to be salt-stained cowboy boots. Someone we knew? An older, good-looking student from one of our classes? *A girl-poet like ourselves?* I was about to nudge you in the ribs in bafflement when the blond woman turned, taking down another book from the shelf (e. e. cummings' *Tulips and Chimneys*— always I would remember that title!), and I saw that she was Marilyn Monroe.

6   Marilyn Monroe. In the Strand. Just like us. And she seemed to be alone.

7   Marilyn Monroe, alone!

8   Wholly absorbed in browsing amid books, oblivious of her surroundings and of us. No one seemed to have recognized her (yet) except you.

9   Here was the surprise: this woman was/was not Marilyn Monroe. For this woman was an individual wholly absorbed in selecting, leafing through, pausing to read books. You could see that this individual was a *reader.* One of those who *reads.* With concentration, with passion. With her very soul. And it was poetry she was reading, her lips pursed, silently shaping words. Absent-mindedly she wiped her nose on the edge of her hand, so intent was she on what she was reading. For when you truly read poetry, poetry reads *you.*

10   Still, this woman was—Marilyn Monroe. And despite our common sense, our scorn for the silly clichés of Hollywood romance, still we halfway expected a Leading Man to join her: Clark Gable, Robert Taylor, Marlon Brando.

11   Halfway we expected the syrupy surge of movie music, to glide us into the scene.

12   But no man joined Marilyn Monroe in her disguise as one of us in the Strand. No Leading Man, no dark prince.

13   Like us (we began to see) this Marilyn Monroe required no man.

14   For what seemed like a long time but was probably no more than half an hour, Marilyn Monroe browsed in the POETRY/MODERN shelves, as from a distance of approximately ten feet two girl-poets watched covertly, clutching each other's hands. We were stunned to see that this woman looked very little like the glamorous "Marilyn Monroe." That figure was a garish blond showgirl, a Hollywood "sexpot" of no interest to intellectuals (*we* thought, we who knew nothing of the secret romance between Marilyn Monroe and Arthur Miller); this figure more resembled us (almost) than she resembled her Hollywood image. We were dying of curiosity to see whose poetry books Marilyn Monroe was examining: Elizabeth Bishop, H. D., Robert Lowell, Muriel Rukeyser, Harry Crosby, Denise Levertov . . . Five or six of these Marilyn Monroe decided to purchase, then moved on, leather bag slung over her shoulder and fedora tilted down on her head.

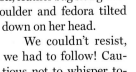

15   We couldn't resist, we had to follow! Cautious not to whisper together like excited schoolgirls, still less to giggle wildly as we were tempted;

you nudged me in the ribs to sober me, gave me a glare signaling *Don't be rude, don't ruin this for all of us.* I conceded: I was the more pushy of the two of us, a tall gawky Rima the Bird Girl with springy carroty-red hair like an exotic bird's crest, while you were petite and dark haired and attractive with long-lashed Semitic sloe eyes, you the wily gymnast and I the aggressive basketball player, you the "experimental" poet and I drawn to "forms," our contrary talents bred in our bones. Which of us would marry, have babies, disappear into "real" life, and which of us would persevere into her thirties before starting to be published and becoming, in time, a "real" poet—could anyone have predicted, this snowy March evening in 1956?

16   Marilyn Monroe drifted through the maze of books and we followed in her wake as through a maze of dreams, past SPORTS, past MILITARY, past WAR, past HISTORY/ANCIENT, past the familiar figures of Strand regulars frowning into books, past surly yawning bearded clerks who took no more heed of the blond actress than they ever did of us, and so to NATURAL HISTORY where she paused, and there again for unhurried minutes (the Strand was open until 9:00 P.M.) Marilyn Monroe in her mannish disguise browsed and brooded, pulling down books, seeking what? at last crouched leafing through an oversized illustrated book (curiosity overcame me! I shoved away your restraining hand; politely I eased past Marilyn Monroe murmuring "excuse me" without so much as brushing against her and without being noticed), Charles Darwin's *Origin of Species* in a deluxe edition. Darwin! *Origin of Species!* We were poet-despisers-of-science, or believed we were, or must be, to be true poets in the exalted mode of T. S. Eliot and William Butler Yeats; such a choice, for Marilyn Monroe, seemed perverse to us. But this book was one Marilyn quickly decided to purchase, hoisting it into her arms and moving on.

17   That rakish fedora we'd come to covet, and that single chunky blonde braid. (Afterward we would wonder: Marilyn Monroe's hair in a braid? Never had we seen Marilyn Monroe with her hair braided in any movie or photo. What did this mean? Did it mean anything? *Had she quit films, and embarked on a new, anonymous life in our midst?*)

18   Suddenly Marilyn Monroe glanced back at us, frowning as a child might frown (had we spoken aloud? had she heard our thoughts?), and there came into her face a look of puzzlement, not alarm or annoyance but a childlike puzzlement: *Who are you? You two? Are you watching me?* Quickly we looked away.

We were engaged in a whispering dispute over a book one of us had fumbled from a shelf, *A History of Botanical Gardens in England.* So we were undetected. We hoped!

But wary now, and sobered. For what if Marilyn   19
Monroe had caught us, and knew that we knew?

She might have abandoned her books and fled the   20
Strand. What a loss for her, and for the books! For us, too.

Oh, we worried at Marilyn Monroe's recklessness!   21
We dreaded her being recognized by a (male) customer or (male) clerk. A girl or woman would have kept her secret (so we thought) but no man could resist staring openly at her, following her, and at last speaking to her. Of course, the blond actress in Strand Used Books wasn't herself, not at all glamorous, or "sexy," or especially blond, in her inconspicuous man's clothing and those salt-stained boots; she might have been anyone, female or male, hardly a Hollywood celebrity, a movie goddess. Yet if you stared, you'd recognize her. If you tried, with any imagination you'd see "Marilyn Monroe." It was like a child's game in which you stare at foliage, grass, clouds in the sky, and suddenly you see a face or a figure, and after that recognition you can't not see the hidden shape, it's staring you in the face. So too with Marilyn Monroe. Once we saw her, it seemed to us she must be seen—and recognized—by anyone who happened to glance at her. If any man saw! We were fearful her privacy would be destroyed. Quickly the blond actress would become surrounded, mobbed. It was risky and reckless of her to have come to Strand Used Books by herself, we thought. Sure, she could shop at Tiffany's, maybe; she could stroll through the lobby of the Plaza, or the Waldorf-Astoria; she'd be safe from fans and unwanted admirers in privileged settings on the Upper East Side, but—here? In the egalitarian Strand, on Broadway and Twelfth?

We were perplexed. Almost, I was annoyed with   22
her. Taking such chances! But you, gripping my wrist, had another, more subtle thought.

"She thinks she's like *us.*"   23

You meant: a human being, anonymous. Female,   24
like us. Amid the ordinary unspectacular customers (predominantly male) of the Strand.

And that was the sadness in it, Marilyn Monroe's   25
wish. To be *like us.* For it was impossible, of course. For anyone could have told Marilyn Monroe, even two young girl-poets, that it was too late for her in history. Already, at age thirty (we could calculate afterward

that this was her age) "Marilyn Monroe" had entered history, and there was no escape from it. Her films, her photos. Her face, her figure, her name. To enter history is to be abducted spiritually, with no way back. As if lightning were to strike the building that housed the Strand, as if an actual current of electricity were to touch and transform only one individual in the great cavernous space and that lone individual, by pure chance it might seem, the caprice of fate, would be the young woman with the blond braid and the fedora slanted across her face. Why? Why her, and not another? You could argue that such a destiny is absurd, and underserved, for one individual among many, and logically you would be correct. And yet: "Marilyn Monroe" has entered history, and you have not. She will endure, though the young woman with the blond braid will die. *And even should she wish to die, "Marilyn Monroe" cannot.*

By this time she—the young woman with the blond braid—was carrying an armload of books. We were hoping she'd almost finished and would be leaving soon, before strangers' rude eyes lighted upon her and exposed her, but no: she surprised us by heading for a section called JUDAICA. In that forbidding aisle, which we'd never before entered, there were books in numerous languages: Hebrew, Yiddish, German, Russian, French. Some of these books looked ancient! Complete sets of the Talmud. Cryptically printed tomes on the cabala. Luckily for us, the titles Marilyn Monroe pulled out were all in English: *Jews of Eastern Europe; The Chosen People: A Complete History of the Jews: Jews of the New World.* Quickly Marilyn Monroe placed her bag and books on the floor, sat on a footstool, and leafed through pages with the frowning intensity of a young girl, as if searching for something urgent, something she knew—knew!—must be there; in this comfortable posture she remained for at least fifteen minutes, wetting her fingers to turn pages that stuck together, pages that had not been turned, still less read, for decades. She was frowning, yet smiling too; fain vertical lines appeared between her eyebrows, in the intensity of her concentration; her eyes moved rapidly along lines of print, then returned, and moved more slowly. By this time we were close enough to observe the blond actress's feverish cheeks and slightly parted moist lips that seemed to move silently. *What is she reading in that ancient book, what can possibly mean so much to her? A secret, revealed? A secret, to save her life?*

7   "Hey you!" a clerk called out in a nasal, insinuating voice.

> But this young woman was **beautiful** without makeup, without even lipstick . . .

28   The three of us looked up, startled.

29   But the clerk wasn't speaking to us. Not to the blond actress frowning over *The Chosen People*, and not to us who were hovering close by. The clerk had caught someone slipping a book into an overcoat pocket, not an unusual sight at the Strand.

30   After this mild upset, Marilyn Monroe became uneasy. She turned to look frankly at us, and though we tried clumsily to retreat, her eyes met ours. *She knows!* But after a moment, she simply turned back to her book, stubborn and determined to finish what she was reading, while we continued to hover close by, exposed now, and blushing, yet feeling protective of her. *She has seen us, she knows. She trusts us.* We saw that Marilyn Monroe was beautiful in her anonymity as she had never seemed, to us, to be beautiful as "Marilyn Monroe." All that was makeup, fakery, cartoon sexiness subtle as a kick in the groin. All that was vulgar and infantile. But this young woman was beautiful without makeup, without even lipstick; in her mannish clothes, her hair in a stubby braid. Beautiful: her skin luminous and pale and her eyes a startling clear blue. Almost shyly she glanced back at us, to note that we were still there, and she smiled. *Yes, I see you two. Thank you for not speaking my name.*

31   Always you and I would remember: that smile of gratitude, and sweetness.

32   Always you and I would remember: that she trusted us, as perhaps we would not have trusted ourselves.

33   So many years later, I'm proud of us. We were so young.

34   Young, headstrong, arrogant, insecure though "brilliant"—or so we'd been let to believe. Not that we thought of ourselves as young: you were nineteen, I was twenty. We were mature for our ages, and we were immature. We were intellectually sophisticated, and emotionally unpredictable. We revered something we called *art*, we were disdainful of something we called *life*. We were overly conscious of ourselves. And yet: how patient, how protective, watching over Marilyn Monroe squatting on a footstool in the JUDAICA stacks as stray customers pushed past muttering "excuse me!" or not even seeming to notice her, or the two of us standing guard. And at last—a relief—Marilyn Monroe shut the unwieldy book, having decided to buy it, and rose from the footstool gathering up her many things. And—this was a temptation!—we held back, not offering to help her carry her things as we so badly wanted to, but only just following at

a discreet distance as Marilyn Monroe made her way through the labyrinth of the bookstore to the front counter. (Did she glance back at us? Did she understand you and I were her protectors?) If anyone dared to approach her, we intended to intervene. We would push between Marilyn Monroe and whomever it was. Yet how strange the scene was: none of the other Strand customers, lost in books, took any special notice of her, any more than they took notice of us. Book lovers, especially used-book lovers, are not ones to stare curiously at others, but only at books. At the front of the store—it was a long hike—the cashiers would be more alert, we thought. One of them seemed to be watching Marilyn Monroe approach. Did he know? Could he guess? Was he waiting for her?

35   Nearing the front counter and the bright fluorescent lights overhead, Marilyn Monroe seemed for the first time to falter. She fumbled to extract out of her shoulder bag a pair of dark glasses and managed to put them on. She turned up the collar of her navy coat. She lowered her hat brim.

36   Still she was hesitant, and it was then that I stepped forward and said quietly, "Excuse me. Why don't I buy your books for you? That way you won't have to talk to anyone."

37   The blond actress stared at me through her oversized dark glasses. Her eyes were only just visible behind the lenses. A shy-girl's eyes, startled and grateful.

38   And so I did. With you helping me. Two girl-poets, side by side, all brisk and businesslike, making Marilyn Monroe's purchases for her: a total of sixteen books!—

hardcover and paperback, relatively new books, old battered thumbed-through books—at a cost of $55.85. A staggering sum! Never in my two years of coming into the Strand had I handed over more than a few dollars to the cashier, and this time my hand might have trembled as I pushed twenty-dollar bills at him, half expecting the bristly bearded man to interrogate me: "Where'd you get so much money?" But as usual the cashier hardly gave me a second glance. And Marilyn Monroe, burdened with no books, had already slipped through the turnstile and was awaiting us at the front door.

There, when we handed over her purchases in two sturdy bags, she leaned forward. For a breathless moment we thought she might kiss our cheeks. Instead she pressed into our surprised hands a slender volume she lifted from one of the bags: *Selected Poems of Marianne Moore*. We stammered thanks, but already the blond actress had pulled the fedora down more tightly over her head and had stepped out into the lightly falling snow, headed south on Broadway. We trailed behind her, unable to resist, waiting for her to hail a taxi, but she did not. We knew we must not follow her. By this time we were giddy with the strain of the past hour, gripping each other's hands in childlike elation. So happy!

"Oh. Oh God. Marilyn Monroe. She gave us a book. Was any of it real?"

It was real: we had *Selected Poems of Marianne Moore* to prove it.

That snowy early evening in March at Strand Used Books. That magical evening of Marilyn Monroe, when I kissed you for the first time.

Questions for Critical Thinking

1 Describe the basic plot of the girls spotting Marilyn Monroe. Then consider the last line, "when I kissed you for the first time." How would you describe this second plot line?

2 Are there conflicts beyond the central conflict of keeping Marilyn Monroe a secret from the outside world? Describe them.

3 Although this is a one-scene story, it contains the elements of a traditional story—conflict, rising action, climax, dénouement. Identify where each of these elements takes place.

4 This story has a specific, carefully described setting. What elements of this setting build toward the sense that something "magical" occurs that evening?

5 The narrator says "we were not 'conventional' females." What does she mean by this? How does her voice as she tells the story prove or refute the statement that she is "unconventional"?

6 As the title suggests, gender plays a large role in this story. The girls clearly have expectations of gender, such as when they expect the Leading Man to join Marilyn Monroe in the bookstore. Considering the three female characters, how are men portrayed in this story?

7 *Three Girls* is as much about creating identity as it is about erasing it. Using examples from the text, create an argument for or against this statement.

"What was so interesting about the original event was not so much that a serial killer had been preying on young people, which is unfortunately all too common, but that the young people had known about it. They had known that some girls had been killed and buried in the desert, but they kept the secret because their allegiance was to this man. And I wanted to write a story about that phenomenon." Conversation with Joyce Carol Oates

Where Are You Going, Where Have You Been? (1970)

For Bob Dylan

1 HER name was Connie. She was fifteen and she had a quick nervous giggling habit of craning her neck to glance into mirrors, or checking other people's faces to make sure her own was all right. Her mother, who noticed everything and knew everything and who hadn't much reason any longer to look at her own face, always scolded Connie about it. "Stop gawking at yourself, who are you? You think you're so pretty?" she would say. Connie would raise her eyebrows at these familiar complaints and look right through her mother, into a shadowy vision of herself as she was right at that moment: she knew she was pretty and that was everything. Her mother had been pretty once too, if

you could believe those old snapshots in the album, but now her looks were gone and that was why she was always after Connie.

2   "Why don't you keep your room clean like your sister? How've you got your hair fixed—what the hell stinks? Hair spray? You don't see your sister using that junk."

3   Her sister June was twenty-four and still lived at home. She was a secretary in the high school Connie attended, and if that wasn't bad enough—with her in the same building—she was so plain and chunky and steady that Connie had to hear her praised all the time by her mother and her mother's sisters. June did this, June did that, she saved money and helped clean the house and cooked and Connie couldn't do a thing, her mind was all filled with trashy daydreams. Their father was away at work most of the time and when he came home he wanted supper and he read the newspaper at supper and after supper he went to bed. He didn't bother talking much to them, but around his bent head Connie's mother kept picking at her until Connie wished her mother was dead and she herself was dead and it was all over. "She makes me want to throw up sometimes," she complained to her friends. She had a high, breathless, amused voice which made everything she said sound a little forced, whether it was sincere or not.

4   There was one good thing: June went places with girl friends of hers, girls who were just as plain and steady as she, and so when Connie wanted to do that her mother had no objections. The father of Connie's best girl friend drove the girls the three miles to town and left them off at a shopping plaza, so that they could walk through the stores or go to a movie, and when he came to pick them up again at eleven he never bothered to ask what they had done.

5   They must have been familiar sights, walking around that shopping plaza in their shorts and flat ballerina slippers that always scuffed the sidewalk, with charm bracelets jingling on their thin wrists; they would lean together to whisper and laugh secretly if someone passed by who amused or interested them. Connie had long dark blond hair that drew anyone's eye to it, and she wore part of it pulled up on her head and puffed out and the rest of it she let fall down her back. She wore a pullover jersey blouse that looked one way when she was at home and another way when she was away from home. Everything about her had two sides to it, one for home and one for anywhere that was not home: her walk that could

He wagged a finger and laughed and said, "Gonna get you, baby."

be childlike and bobbing, or languid enough to make anyone think she was hearing music in her head, her mouth which was pale and smirking most of the time, but bright and pink on these evenings out, her laugh which was cynical and drawling at home—"Ha, ha, very funny"—but high-pitched and nervous anywhere else, like the jingling of the charms on her bracelet.

Sometimes they did go shopping or to a movie, but sometimes they went across the highway, ducking fast across the busy road, to a drive-in restaurant where older kids hung out. The restaurant was shaped like a big bottle, though squatter than a real bottle, and on its cap was a revolving figure of a grinning boy who held a hamburger aloft. One night in mid-summer they ran across, breathless with daring, and right away someone leaned out a car window and invited them over, but it was just a boy from high school they didn't like. It made them feel good to be able to ignore him. They went up through the maze of parked and cruising cars to the bright-lit, fly-infested restaurant, their faces pleased and expectant as if they were entering a sacred building that loomed out of the night to give them what haven and what blessing they yearned for. They sat at the counter and crossed their legs at the ankles, their thin shoulders rigid with excitement, and listened to the music that made everything so good: the music was always in the background like music at a church service, it was something to depend upon.

A boy named Eddie came in to talk with them. He sat backwards on his stool, turning himself jerkily around in semi-circles and then stopping and turning again, and after a while he asked Connie if she would like something to eat. She said she did and so she tapped her friend's arm on her way out—her friend pulled her face up into a brave droll look—and Connie said she would meet her at eleven, across the way. "I just hate to leave her like that," Connie said earnestly, but the boy said that she wouldn't be alone for long. So they went out to his car and on the way Connie couldn't help but let her eyes wander over the windshields and faces all around her, her face gleaming with a joy that had nothing to do with Eddie or even this place; it might have been the music. She drew her shoulders up and sucked in her breath with the pure pleasure of being alive, and just at that moment she happened to glance at a face just a few feet from hers. It was a boy with shaggy black hair, in a convertible jalopy painted gold. He stared at her and then his lips widened into a grin. Connie slit her eyes at him and turned away, but she couldn't help glancing back and there he was still watching her. He wagged a finger and laughed and said, "Gonna get you, baby," and Connie turned away again without Eddie noticing anything.

8 She spent three hours with him, at the restaurant where they ate hamburgers and drank Cokes in wax cups that were always sweating, and then down an alley a mile or so away, and when he left her off at five to eleven only the movie house was still open at the plaza. Her girl friend was there, talking with a boy. When Connie came up the two girls smiled at each other and Connie said, "How was the movie?" and the girl said, "*You* should know." They rode off with the girl's father, sleepy and pleased, and Connie couldn't help but look at the darkened shopping plaza with its big empty parking lot and its signs that were faded and ghostly now, and over at the drive-in restaurant where cars were still circling tirelessly. She couldn't hear the music at this distance.

9 Next morning June asked her how the movie was and Connie said, "So-so."

0 She and that girl and occasionally another girl went out several times a week that way, and the rest of the time Connie spent around the house—it was summer vacation—getting in her mother's way and thinking, dreaming, about the boys she met. But all the boys fell back and dissolved into a single face that was not even a face, but an idea, a feeling, mixed up with the urgent insistent pounding of the music and the humid night air of July. Connie's mother kept dragging her back to the daylight by finding things for her to do or saying, suddenly, "What's this about the Pettinger girl?"

1 And Connie would say nervously, "Oh, her. That dope." She always drew thick clear lines between herself and such girls, and her mother was simple and kindly enough to believe her. Her mother was so simple, Connie thought, that it was maybe cruel to fool her so much. Her mother went scuffling around the house in old bedroom slippers and complained over the telephone to one sister about the other, then the other called up and the two of them complained about the third one. If June's name was mentioned her mother's tone was approving, and if Connie's name was mentioned it was disapproving. This did not really mean she disliked Connie and actually Connie thought that her mother preferred her to June because she was prettier, but the two of them kept up a pretense of exasperation, a sense that they were tugging and struggling over something of little value to either of them. Sometimes, over coffee, they were almost friends, but something would come up—some vexation that was like a fly buzzing suddenly around their heads—and their faces went hard with contempt.

12 One Sunday Connie got up at eleven—none of them bothered with church—and washed her hair so that it could dry all day long, in the sun. Her parents and sister were going to a barbecue at an aunt's house and Connie said no, she wasn't interested, rolling her eyes to let her mother know just what she thought of it. "Stay home alone then," her mother said sharply. Connie sat out back in a lawn chair and watched them drive away, her father quiet and bald, hunched around so that he could back the car out, her mother with a look that was still angry and not at all softened through the windshield, and in the back seat poor old June all dressed up as if she didn't know what a barbecue was, with all the running yelling kids and the flies. Connie sat with her eyes closed in the sun, dreaming and dazed with the warmth about her as if this were a kind of love, the caresses of love, and her mind slipped over onto thoughts of the boy she had been with the night before and how nice he had been, how sweet it always was, not the way someone like June would suppose but sweet, gentle, the way it was in movies and promised in songs; and when she opened her eyes she hardly knew where she was, the back yard ran off into weeds and a fence-line of trees and behind it the sky was perfectly blue and still. The asbestos "ranch house" that was now three years old startled her—it looked small. She shook her head as if to get awake.

13 It was too hot. She went inside the house and turned on the radio to drown out the quiet. She sat on the edge of her bed, barefoot, and listened for an hour and a half to a program called XYZ Sunday Jamboree, record after record of hard, fast, shrieking songs she sang along with, interspersed by exclamations from "Bobby King": "An' look here you girls at Napoleon's—Son and Charley want you to pay real close attention to this song coming up!"

14 And Connie paid close attention herself, bathed in a glow of slow-pulsed joy that seemed to rise mysteriously out of the music itself and lay languidly about the airless little room, breathed in and breathed out with each gentle rise and fall of her chest.

15 After a while she heard a car coming up the drive. She sat up at once, startled, because it couldn't be her father so soon. The gravel kept crunching all the way in from the road—the driveway was long—and Connie ran to the window. It was a car she didn't know. It was an open jalopy, painted a bright gold that caught the sunlight opaquely. Her heart began to pound and her fingers snatched at her hair, checking it, and she

whispered "Christ, Christ," wondering how bad she looked. The car came to a stop at the side door and the horn sounded four short taps as if this were a signal Connie knew.

16   She went into the kitchen and approached the door slowly, then hung out the screen door, her bare toes curling down off the step. There were two boys in the car and now she recognized the driver: he had shaggy, shabby black hair that looked crazy as a wig and he was grinning at her.

17   "I ain't late, am I?" he said.

18   "Who the hell do you think you are?" Connie said.

19   "Toldja I'd be out, didn't I?"

20   "I don't even know who you are."

21   She spoke sullenly, careful to show no interest or pleasure, and he spoke in a fast bright monotone. Connie looked past him to the other boy, taking her time. He had fair brown hair, with a lock that fell onto his forehead. His sideburns gave him a fierce, embarrassed look, but so far he hadn't even bothered to glance at her. Both boys wore sunglasses. The driver's glasses were metallic and mirrored everything in miniature.

22   "You wanta come for a ride?" he said.

23   Connie smirked and let her hair fall loose over one shoulder.

24   "Don'tcha like my car? New paint job," he said. "Hey."

25   "What?"

26   "You're cute."

27   She pretended to fidget, chasing flies away from the door.

28   "Don'tcha believe me, or what?" he said.

29   "Look, I don't even know who you are," Connie said in disgust.

30   "Hey, Ellie's got a radio, see. Mine's broke down." He lifted his friend's arm and showed her the little transistor the boy was holding, and now Connie began to hear the music. It was the same program that was playing inside the house.

31   "Bobby King?" she said.

32   "I listen to him all the time. I think he's great."

33   "He's kind of great," Connie said reluctantly.

34   "Listen, that guy's *great*. He knows where the action is."

35   Connie blushed a little, because the glasses made it impossible for her to see just what this boy was looking at. She couldn't decide if she liked him or if he was just a jerk, and so she dawdled in the doorway and wouldn't come down or go back inside. She said, "What's all that stuff painted on your car?"

> **The way he straightened and recovered** from his fit of laughing showed that it had been all fake.

"Can'tcha read it?" He opened the door very carefully, as if he was afraid it might fall off. He slid out just as carefully, planting his feet firmly on the ground, the tiny metallic world in his glasses slowing down like gelatine hardening and in the midst of it Connie's bright green blouse. "This here is my name, to begin with," he said. ARNOLD FRIEND was written in tarlike black letters on the side, with a drawing of a round grinning face that reminded Connie of a pumpkin, except it wore sunglasses. "I wanta introduce myself, I'm Arnold Friend and that's my real name and I'm gonna be your friend, honey, and inside the car's Ellie Oscar, he's kinda shy." Ellie brought his transistor radio up to his shoulder and balanced it there. "Now these numbers are a secret code, honey," Arnold Friend explained. He read off the numbers 33, 19, 17 and raised his eyebrows at her to see what she thought of that, but she didn't think much of it. The left rear fender had been smashed and around it was written, on the gleaming gold background: DONE BY CRAZY WOMAN DRIVER. Connie had to laugh at that. Arnold Friend was pleased at her laughter and looked up at her. "Around the other side's a lot more—you wanta come and see them?"

36   "No."

37   "Why not?"

38   "Why should I?"

39   "Don'tcha wanta see what's on the car? Don'tcha wanta go for a ride?"

40

41   "I don't know."

42   "Why not?"

43   "I got things to do."

44   "Like what?"

45   "Things."

46   He laughed as if she had said something funny. He slapped his thighs. He was standing in a strange way, leaning back against the car as if he were balancing himself. He wasn't tall, only an inch or so taller than she would be if she came down to him. Connie liked the way he was dressed, which was the way all of them dressed: tight faded jeans stuffed into black, scuffed boots, a belt that pulled his waist in and showed how lean he was, and a white pull-over shirt that was a little soiled and showed the hard small muscles of his arms and shoulders. He looked as if he probably did hard work, lifting and carrying things. Even his neck looked muscular. And his face was a familiar face, somehow: the jaw and chin and cheeks slightly darkened, because he hadn't shaved for a day or two, and the nose long and hawk-like, sniffing as if she were a treat he was going to gobble up and it was all a joke.

"Connie, you ain't telling the truth. This is your day set aside for a ride with me and you know it," he said, still laughing. The way he straightened and recovered from his fit of laughing showed that it had been all fake.

"How do you know what my name is?" she said suspiciously.

"It's Connie."

"Maybe and maybe not."

"I know my Connie," he said, wagging his finger. Now she remembered him even better, back at the restaurant, and her cheeks warmed at the thought of how she sucked in her breath just at the moment she passed him—how she must have looked to him. And he had remembered her. "Ellie and I come out here especially for you," he said. "Ellie can sit in back. How about it?"

"Where?"

"Where what?"

"Where're we going?"

He looked at her. He took off the sunglasses and she saw how pale the skin around his eyes was, like holes that were not in shadow but instead in light. His eyes were chips of broken glass that catch the light in an amiable way. He smiled. It was as if the idea of going for a ride somewhere, to some place, was a new idea to him.

"Just for a ride, Connie sweetheart."

"I never said my name was Connie," she said.

"But I know what it is. I know your name and all about you, lots of things," Arnold Friend said. He had not moved yet but stood still leaning back against the side of his jalopy. "I took a special interest in you, such a pretty girl, and found out all about you like I know your parents and sister are gone somewheres and I know where and how long they're going to be gone, and I know who you were with last night, and your best girl friend's name is Betty. Right?"

He spoke in a simple lilting voice, exactly as if he were reciting the words to a song. His smile assured her that everything was fine. In the car Ellie turned up the volume on his radio and did not bother to look around at them.

"Ellie can sit in the back seat," Arnold Friend said. He indicated his friend with a casual jerk of his chin, as if Ellie did not count and she should not bother with him.

"How'd you find out all that stuff?" Connie said.

"Listen: Betty Schultz and Tony Fitch and Jimmy Pettinger and Nancy Pettinger," he said, in a chant. "Raymond Stanley and Bob Hutter—"

"Do you know all those kids?"

"I know everybody."

"Look, you're kidding. You're not from around here."

"Sure."

"But—how come we never saw you before?"

"Sure you saw me before," he said. He looked down at his boots, as if he were a little offended. "You just don't remember."

"I guess I'd remember you," Connie said.

"Yeah?" He looked up at this, beaming. He was pleased. He began to mark time with the music from Ellie's radio, tapping his fists lightly together. Connie looked away from his smile to the car, which was painted so bright it almost hurt her eyes to look at it. She looked at that name, ARNOLD FRIEND. And up at the front fender was an expression that was familiar—MAN THE FLYING SAUCERS. It was an expression kids had used the year before, but didn't use this year. She looked at it for a while as if the words meant something to her that she did not yet know.

"What're you thinking about? Huh?" Arnold Friend demanded. "Not worried about your hair blowing around in the car, are you?"

"No."

"Think I maybe can't drive good?"

"How do I know?"

"You're a hard girl to handle. How come?" he said. "Don't you know I'm your friend? Didn't you see me put my sign in the air when you walked by?"

"What sign?"

"My sign." And he drew an X in the air, leaning out toward her. They were maybe ten feet apart. After his hand fell back to his side the X was still in the air, almost visible. Connie let the screen door close and stood perfectly still inside it, listening to the music from her radio and the boy's blend together. She stared at Arnold Friend. He stood there so stiffly relaxed, pretending to be relaxed, with one hand idly on the door handle as if he were keeping himself up that way and had no intention of ever moving again. She recognized most things about him, the tight jeans that showed his thighs and buttocks and the greasy leather boots and the tight shirt, and even that slippery friendly smile of his, that sleepy dreamy smile that all the boys used to get across ideas they didn't want to put into words. She recognized all this and also the singsong way he talked, slightly mocking, kidding, but serious and a little melancholy, and she recognized the way he tapped one fist against the other in homage to the perpetual music behind him. But all these things did not come together.

She said suddenly, "Hey, how old are you?"

His smile faded. She could see then that he wasn't a kid, he was much older—thirty, maybe more. At this knowledge her heart began to pound faster.

"That's a crazy thing to ask. Can'tcha see I'm your own age?"

81   "Like hell you are."

82   "Or maybe a coupla years older, I'm eighteen."

83   "Eighteen?" she said doubtfully.

84   He grinned to reassure her and lines appeared at the corners of his mouth. His teeth were big and white. He grinned so broadly his eyes became slits and she saw how thick the lashes were, thick and black as if painted with a black tar-like material. Then he seemed to become embarrassed, abruptly, and looked over his shoulder at Ellie. "*Him,* he's crazy," he said. "Ain't he a riot, he's a nut, a real character." Ellie was still listening to the music. His sunglasses told nothing about what he was thinking. He wore a bright orange shirt unbuttoned halfway to show his chest, which was a pale, bluish chest and not muscular like Arnold Friend's. His shirt collar was turned up all around and the very tips of the collar pointed out past his chin as if they were protecting him. He was pressing the transistor radio up against his ear and sat there in a kind of daze, right in the sun.

> Connie stared at him, another wave of dizziness and fear rising in her . . .

85   "He's kinda strange," Connie said.

86   "Hey, she says you're kinda strange! Kinda strange!" Arnold Friend cried. He pounded on the car to get Ellie's attention. Ellie turned for the first time and Connie saw with shock that he wasn't kid either—he had a fair, hairless face, cheeks reddened slightly as if the veins grew too close to the surface of his skin, the face of a forty-year-old baby. Connie felt a wave of dizziness rise in her at this sight and she stared at him as if waiting for something to change the shock of the moment, make it all right again. Ellie's lips kept shaping words, mumbling along, with the words blasting in his ear.

87   "Maybe you two better go away," Connie said faintly.

88   "What? How come?" Arnold Friend cried. "We come out here to take you for a ride. It's Sunday." He had the voice of the man on the radio now. It was the same voice, Connie thought. "Don'tcha know it's Sunday all day and honey, no matter who you were with last night today you're with Arnold Friend and don't you forget it!—Maybe you better step out here," he said, and this last was in a different voice. It was a little flatter, as if the heat was finally getting to him.

89   "No. I got things to do."

90   "Hey."

91   "You two better leave."

92   "We ain't leaving until you come with us."

93   "Like hell I am—"

94   "Connie, don't fool around with me. I mean, I mean, don't fool *around,*" he said, shaking his head. He laughed incredulously. He placed his sunglasses on top of his head, carefully, as if he were indeed wearing a wig, and brought the stems down behind his ears. Connie stared at him, another wave of dizziness and fear rising in her so that for a moment he wasn't even in focus but was just a blur, standing there against his gold car, and she had the idea that he had driven up the driveway all right but had come from nowhere before that and belonged nowhere and that everything about him and even about the music that was so familiar to her was only half real.

"If my father comes and sees you—"

"He ain't coming. He's at the barbecue."

"How do you know that?"

"Aunt Tillie's. Right now they're—uh—they're drinking. Sitting around," he said vaguely, squinting as if he were staring all the way to town and over to Aunt Tillie's backyard. Then the vision seemed to get clear and he nodded energetically. "Yeah. Sitting around. There's your sister in a blue dress, huh? And high heels, the poor sad bitch—nothing like you, sweetheart! And your mother's helping some fat woman with the corn, they're cleaning the corn—husking the corn—"

"What fat woman?" Connie cried.

"How do I know what fat woman. I don't know every goddam fat woman in the world!" Arnold Friend laughed.

"Oh, that's Mrs. Hornby. . . . Who invited her?" Connie said. She felt a little light-headed. Her breath was coming quickly.

"She's too fat. I don't like them fat. I like them the way you are, honey," he said, smiling sleepily at her. They stared at each other for a while, through the screen door. He said softly, "Now what you're going to do is this: you're going to come out that door. You're going to sit up front with me and Ellie's going to sit in the back, the hell with Ellie, right? This isn't Ellie's date. You're my date. I'm your lover, honey."

"What? You're crazy—"

"Yes, I'm your lover. You don't know what that is but you will," he said. "I know that too. I know all about you. But look: it's real nice and you couldn't ask for nobody better than me, or more polite. I always keep my word. I'll tell you how it is, I'm always nice at first, the first time. I'll hold you so tight you won't think you have to try to get away or pretend anything because you'll know you can't. And I'll come inside you where it's all secret and you'll give in to me and you'll love me—"

"Shut up! You're crazy!" Connie said. She backed away from the door. She put her hands against her ears as if she'd heard something terrible, something not meant for her. "People don't talk like that, you're crazy," she muttered. Her heart was almost too big now for her chest and its pumping made sweat break out all over her. She looked out to see Arnold Friend pause and then take a step toward the porch lurching. He almost fell. But, like a clever drunken man, he managed to catch his balance. He wobbled in his high boots and grabbed hold of one of the porch posts.

"Honey?" he said. "You still listening?"

"Get the hell out of here!"

"Be nice, honey. Listen."

"I'm going to call the police—"

He wobbled again and out of the side of his mouth came a fast spat curse, an aside not meant for her to hear. But even this "Christ!" sounded forced. Then he began to smile again. She watched this smile come, awkward as if he were smiling from inside a mask. His whole face was a mask, she thought wildly, tanned down onto his throat but then running out as if he had plastered makeup on his face but had forgotten about his throat.

"Honey—? Listen, here's how it is. I always tell the truth and I promise you this: I ain't coming in that house after you."

"You better not! I'm going to call the police if you— if you don't—"

"Honey," he said, talking right through her voice, "honey, I'm not coming in there but you are coming out here. You know why?"

She was panting. The kitchen looked like a place she had never seen before, some room she had run inside but which wasn't good enough, wasn't going to help her. The kitchen window had never had a curtain, after three years, and there were dishes in the sink for her to do—probably—and if you ran your hand across the table you'd probably feel something sticky there.

"You listening, honey? Hey?"

"—going to call the police—"

"Soon as you touch the phone I don't need to keep my promise and can come inside. You won't want that."

She rushed forward and tried to lock the door. Her fingers were shaking. "But why lock it," Arnold Friend said gently, talking right into her face. "It's just a screen door. It's just nothing." One of his boots was at a strange angle, as if his foot wasn't in it. It pointed out to the left, bent at the ankle. "I mean, anybody can break through a screen door and glass and wood and iron or anything else if he needs to, anybody at all and specially Arnold Friend. If the place got lit up with a fire honey you'd come running out into my arms, right

into my arms and safe at home—like you knew I was your lover and'd stopped fooling around. I don't mind a nice shy girl but I don't like no fooling around." Part of those words were spoken with a slight rhythmic lilt, and Connie somehow recognized them—the echo of a song from last year, about a girl rushing into her boyfriend's arms and coming home again—

Connie stood barefoot on the linoleum floor, staring at him. "What do you want?" she whispered.

"I want you," he said.

"What?"

"Seen you that night and thought, that's the one, yes sir. I never needed to look any more."

"But my father's coming back. He's coming to get me. I had to wash my hair first—" She spoke in a dry, rapid voice, hardly raising it for him to hear.

"No, your daddy is not coming and yes, you had to wash your hair and you washed it for me. It's nice and shining and all for me, I thank you, sweetheart," he said, with a mock bow, but again he almost lost his balance. He had to bend and adjust his boots. Evidently his feet did not go all the way down; the boots must have been stuffed with something so that he would seem taller. Connie stared out at him and behind him Ellie in the car, who seemed to be looking off toward Connie's right, into nothing. This Ellie said, pulling the words out of the air one after another as if he were just discovering them, "You want me to pull out the phone?"

"Shut your mouth and keep it shut," Arnold Friend said, his face red from bending over or maybe from embarrassment because Connie had seen his boots. "This ain't none of your business."

"What—what are you doing? What do you want?" Connie said. "If I call the police they'll get you, they'll arrest you—"

"Promise was not to come in unless you touch that phone, and I'll keep that promise," he said. He resumed his erect position and tried to force his shoulders back. He sounded like a hero in a movie, declaring something important. He spoke too loudly and it was as if he were speaking to someone behind Connie. "I ain't made plans for coming in that house where I don't belong but just for you to come out to me, the way you should. Don't you know who I am?"

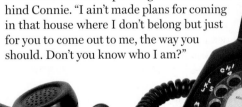

128   "You're crazy," she whispered. She backed away from the door but did not want to go into another part of the house, as if this would give him permission to come through the door. "What do you . . . You're crazy, you . . ."

129   "Huh? What're you saying, honey?"

130   Her eyes darted everywhere in the kitchen. She could not remember what it was, this room.

131   "This is how it is, honey: you come out and we'll drive away, have a nice ride. But if you don't come out we're gonna wait till your people come home and then they're all going to get it."

132   "You want that telephone pulled out?" Ellie said. He held the radio away from his ear and grimaced, as if without the radio the air was too much for him.

133   "I toldja shut up, Ellie," Arnold Friend said, "you're deaf, get a hearing aid, right? Fix yourself up. This little girl's no trouble and's gonna be nice to me, so Ellie keep to yourself, this ain't your date—right? Don't hem in on me. Don't hog. Don't crush. Don't bird dog. Don't trail me," he said in a rapid meaningless voice, as if he were running through all the expressions he'd learned but was no longer sure which one of them was in style, then rushing on to new ones, making them up with his eyes closed, "Don't crawl under my fence, don't squeeze in my chipmunk hole, don't sniff my glue, suck my popsicle, keep your own greasy fingers on yourself!" He shaded his eyes and peered in at Connie, who was backed against the kitchen table. "Don't mind him honey he's just a creep. He's a dope. Right? I'm the boy for you and like I said you come out here nice like a lady and give me your hand, and nobody else gets hurt, I mean, your nice old bald-headed daddy and your mummy and your sister in her high heels. Because listen: why bring them in this?"

134   "Leave me alone," Connie whispered.

135   "Hey, you know that old woman down the road, the one with the chickens and stuff—you know her?"

136   "She's dead!"

137   "Dead? What? You know her?" Arnold Friend said.

138   "She's dead—"

139   'Don't you like her?"

140   "She's dead—she's—she isn't here any more—"

141   "But don't you like her, I mean, you got something against her? Some grudge or something?" Then his voice dipped as if he were conscious of a rudeness. He touched the sunglasses perched on top of his head as if to make sure they were still there. "Now you be a good girl."

142   "What are you going to do?"

143   "Just two things, or maybe three," Arnold Friend said. "But I promise it won't last long and you'll like

me that way you get to like people you're close to. You will. It's all over for you here, so come on out. You don't want your people in any trouble, do you?"

> ## She thought,
> I'm not going to see my mother again.

She turned and bumped against a chair or something, hurting her leg, but she ran into the back room and picked up the telephone. Something roared in her ear, a tiny roaring, and she was so sick with fear that she could do nothing but listen to it—the telephone was clammy and very heavy and her fingers groped down to the dial but were too weak to touch it. She began to scream into the phone, into the roaring. She cried out, she cried for her mother, she felt her breath start jerking back and forth in her lungs as if it were something Arnold Friend were stabbing her with again and again with no tenderness. A noisy sorrowful wailing rose all about her and she was locked inside it the way she was locked inside the house.

After a while she could hear again. She was sitting on the floor with her wet back against the wall.

Arnold Friend was saying from the door, "That's a good girl. Put the phone back." She kicked the phone away from her.

"No, honey. Pick it up. Put it back right."

She picked it up and put it back. The dial tone stopped.

"That's a good girl. Now come outside."

She was hollow with what had been fear, but what was now just an emptiness. All that screaming had blasted it out of her. She sat, one leg cramped under her, and deep inside her brain was something like a pinpoint of light that kept going and would not let her relax. She thought, I'm not going to see my mother again. She thought, I'm not going to sleep in my bed again. Her bright green blouse was all wet.

Arnold Friend said, in a gentle-loud voice that was like a stage voice, "The place where you came from ain't there any more, and where you had in mind to go is cancelled out. This place you are now—inside your daddy's house—is nothing but a cardboard box I can knock down any time. You know that and always did know it. You hear me?"

She thought, I have got to think. I have to know what to do.

"We'll go out to a nice field, out in the country here where it smells so nice and it's sunny," Arnold Friend said. "I'll have my arms around you so you won't need to try to get away and I'll show you what love is like, what it does. The hell with this house! It looks solid all right," he said. He ran a fingernail down the screen and the noise did not make Connie shiver, as it would have the day before. "Now put your hand on your heart, honey. Feel that? That feels solid too but we know better, be nice to me, be sweet like you can because what else is there for a girl like you but to be sweet and pretty and give in?—and get away before her people come back?"

She felt her pounding heart. Her hand seemed to enclose it. She thought for the first time in her life that it was nothing that was hers, that belonged to her, but just a pounding, living thing inside this body that wasn't really hers either.

"You don't want them to get hurt," Arnold Friend went on. "Now get up, honey. Get up all by yourself."

She stood up.

"Now turn this way. That's right. Come over here to me—Ellie, put that away, didn't I tell you? You dope. You miserable creepy dope," Arnold Friend said. His words were not angry but only part of an incantation. The incantation was kindly. "Now come out through the kitchen to me honey and let's see a smile, try it, you're a brave sweet little girl and now they're eating corn and hotdogs cooked to bursting over an outdoor fire, and they don't know one thing about you and never did and honey you're better than them because not a one of them would have done this for you."

Connie felt the linoleum under her feet; it was cool. She brushed her hair back out of her eyes. Arnold Friend let go of the post tentatively and opened his arms for her, his elbows pointing in toward each other and his wrists limp, to show that this was an embarrassed embrace and a little mocking, he didn't want to make her self-conscious. 158

She put out her hand against the screen. She watched herself push the door slowly open as if she were safe back somewhere in the other doorway, watching this body and this head of long hair moving out into the sunlight where Arnold Friend waited. 159

"My sweet little blue-eyed girl," he said, in a half-sung sigh that had nothing to do with her brown eyes but was taken up just the same by the vast sunlit reaches of the land behind him and on all sides of him, so much land that Connie had never seen before and did not recognize except to know that she was going to it. 160

"What was so interesting about the original event was not so much that a serial killer had been preying on young people, which is unfortunately all too common, but that the young people had known about it. They had known that some girls had been killed and buried in the desert, but they kept the secret because their allegiance was to this man. And I wanted to write a story about that phenomenon."
Conversation with Joyce Carol Oates

Questions for Critical Thinking

1 Describe what we know of Arnold Friend when he first appears at Connie's house. Then describe what we know of him by the end of the story. What effect does this change have on us as readers? In other words, how does Oates's pacing build suspense?

2 List the characters besides Connie and Arnold. How are they important to our understanding of Connie?

3 Consider Oates's use of dialogue, particularly the exchange between Arnold and Connie when he comes to her house. What in Arnold's speech suggests who he is and what he is doing? What in Connie's speech contributes to our understanding of her as a teenage girl?

4 Describe the setting—both time and place—of the story. Is it a place where we might expect to find someone like Arnold Friend? Why or why not?

5 The story opens with a bit of background exposition by the narrator. Discuss how this exposition is distinguished from the description of the story's main events. What relationship, if any, does the narrator seem to have or have had with Connie? Cite evidence from the text.

6 Oates builds Connie's character by means of a series of details about her age, her appearance, her habits, her clothes. Which details make Connie believable or familiar to you? Which details represent larger personality traits in Connie?

7 In her interview, Oates suggests Connie's act may be considered heroic in that she sacrifices herself to save her family. What details about Connie suggest her motivation for complying with Arnold Friend? In light of these details, make a case for whether Connie's act is or is not heroic.

8 Much of Oates's fiction deals with violence and the aftermath of such violence. Develop an argument about whether or not this is a violent story; consider the difference between including actual violence and simply suggesting it.

Getting Started: A Research Project

Research is a skill that will carry you through your college career. You can find the research materials you need for this project on our website (**www.mhhe.com/delbanco1e**). Other ideas for research projects and sources appear at the end of this chapter.

A book's initial critical reception, the way reviewers and literary critics first respond to it, can offer some interesting material about the book and the time in which it is published. For example, when *Moby-Dick* was first published in 1851, it was not highly regarded, but today it is recognized as one of the greatest American novels. The best way of studying a critical reception—past or present—is by reading book reviews. Unlike a literary analysis, which builds a complex argument about a particular aspect of a work of literature, a book review gives an overview of what readers will find in the book, as well as the critic's opinion of its strengths and weaknesses. Intended more for a general than an academic audience, today's most influential book reviews are often found in newspapers such as *The Los Angeles Times* or *The New York Times* and on National Public Radio.

Oates's critical reception has been positive overall, as three reviews of *I Am No One You Know,* the short story collection in which "Three Girls" appears, illustrate (reviews available online at **www.mhhe.com/delbanco1e**). While these reviews yield three different views of the book, each compliments Oates's ability. Chanel Lee, writing for the *Village Voice,* draws attention to how Oates "artfully and uncomfortably examines the power of one's inner voice—the one no one can, or is supposed to, hear." An early review in *Publisher's Weekly* similarly points to Oates's intimacy with characters but emphasizes the two major categories those characters comprise: "In Oates's precise psychological renderings, victims are as complex as villains and almost always more interesting." Kevin Bicknell's review in the *Atlanta Journal-Constitution* describes her collection as "post-gothic. That is, Oates is less interested in the grotesque and the doomed than in ordinary people dealing with what Philip Roth called the 'American Berserk,' the sense that anybody's normal, well-ordered life can be thrown into chaos."

Book reviews provide concise summaries of the work so that, for example, after reading the reviews just mentioned here you would know to expect stories with sensational material, stories "populated by serial killers and their victims, murderers, stalkers, pedophiliac teachers, child abusers, the orphaned and the insane" on subjects including "murder, rape, arson and terrorism."

Go to www.mhhe.com/delbanco1e and respond to several book reviews of Oates's work.

1. Explain the ways in which "Three Girls" "artfully and uncomfortably examines the power of one's inner voice—the one no one can, or is supposed to, hear."

2. In what ways is Marilyn Monroe a victim in "Three Girls"? Is there a villain in the story?

3. Explain the notion of the "American Berserk" in relation to Oates's "Three Girls." In what ways are the protagonists' lives "thrown into chaos" with their sighting of Marilyn Monroe?

Further Suggestions for Writing and Research

1. Review the two stories included in this chapter. Write a paragraph or two describing Oates's style—are her sentences short or long, full of metaphors or minimalist? Does she use elevated diction, or everyday expressions? Then research what another critic has to say about Oates's style. How is the critic's view similar to or different from your own?

2. One of Oates's major themes is shaping personal identity. Review the two stories included in this chapter and list details about the main characters' search for identity in each. Then consult other sources to see what critics have said about characters and identity in Oates's work. Do the two stories offer a different insight about identity? If so, explain how those stories show what the critic fails to examine. If not, use specific examples from your choices to support what the critic observes about identity in Oates's other work.

3. Find and read at least three of the dozens of articles on Joyce Carol Oates' website about "Where Are You Going, Where Have You Been?" Incorporating the critical views you found, give and develop your own interpretation of this story.

4. How does the interview with the writer aid your understanding of her work? Read one of the interviews she has given elsewhere about her work. Combining the information from these two sources, consider one of the following new perspectives you gained from hearing about her personal life, her view of her writing, or characteristics of contemporary American life.

Some Sources for Research

5. Johnson, Greg. *Invisible Writer.* New York: Dutton, 1998. The authoritative biography of Joyce Carol Oates.

6. *Celestial Timepiece*, a Joyce Carol Oates homepage, http://jco.usfca.edu/index.html. A website with comprehensive information on Oates's life, work, awards, and schedule of live appearances maintained by a reference librarian at the University of San Francisco.

7. Milazzo, Lee, ed. *Conversations with Joyce Carol Oates.* Jackson, MS: University Press of Mississippi, 1989. Contains interviews with Joyce Carol Oates.

For examples of student papers, see chapter 3, Common Writing Assignments, and chapter 5, Writing the Research Paper, in the Handbook for Writing from Reading.

12

American Regionalism

Two Case Studies
The American West
and The American South

and Sense
of Place

"I absolutely think place is everything. I think place is a character."

Conversation with Dagoberto Gilb, available on video at www.mhhe.com/delbanco1e

ALL writers try to impart a sense of location in which their stories take place. This is just as much the case for the plain of Troy in Homer's epic *Iliad* as for the Danish castle in Shakespeare's *Hamlet*. It holds equally true for the American South of Flannery O'Connor and William Faulkner and the Southwest of Leslie Marmon Silko or John Steinbeck's West. In the past decades American writers such as Dagoberto Gilb, William Kittredge, and Sylvia Watanabe have stressed the importance of place. As California novelist James D. Houston observes in "A Writer's Sense of Place," our literature "is rich with . . . stories wherein at least part of what's going on is some form of dialogue between a place—whether it be an island or a mountain or a city or a shoreline or a sub-region of the continent—and the lives being lived. . . ." What matters for North American writers in the present moment was also true for fiction writers from another place and time.

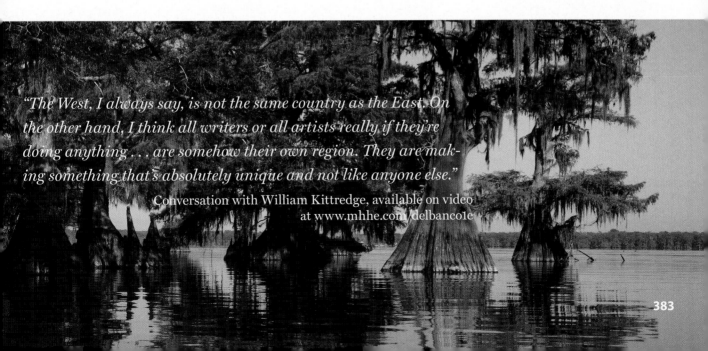

"The West, I always say, is not the same country as the East. On the other hand, I think all writers or all artists really if they're doing anything . . . are somehow their own region. They are making something that's absolutely unique and not like anyone else."

Conversation with William Kittredge, available on video at www.mhhe.com/delbanco1e

The American West

THE last major region of the continental United States to be settled, the West has played a special role in the American imagination. Its vast spaces and wide variety of landscapes—deserts, grazing lands, lush farming valleys, and mountains—have inspired Americans since the Lewis and Clark expedition (1804–1806) to explore the land. With the close of the frontier in the 1890s, the region changed. Cities began to compete with farms and ranches as centers of commercial and cultural experience. New immigrant populations mingled with native inhabitants. Although the romantic image of rugged cowboys and starkly individualistic settlers lives on in twentieth-century Western movies, serious Western literature of the twentieth century has become much more ambiguous—less certain of the good, morally upright settler taming the landscape and more aware of a growing society's willingness to exploit natural resources. With the emergence of Native American writers such as Leslie Marmon Silko, a sense of loss colors the literature; the traditional Native American way of life has long been at risk. Other writers, such as William Kittredge, are deeply attuned to the beauty of surrounding nature, displaying an awareness of the disjunction between the demands of modern life and the environment they so love. From the central plains to southern Texas to the California coast and, beyond, to the islands of Hawaii, the Old West has clearly become a New West, a region to rediscover.

. . . my mother was a woman who valued the arts . . .

Q&A

They're not autobiographical stories at all . . .

A Conversation on Writing

William Kittredge

Books and Cattle

I grew up on a great big cattle ranch in Southeastern Oregon. It was very isolated. The idea of literary culture was pretty nonexistent. We were 300 miles from probably the nearest really functional bookstore. But my mother was a woman who valued the arts, and she was one of those women who . . . belonged to the Book of the Month Club. And I remember when I was about fifteen years old working on the ranch in the summertime and sitting out on the screened-in porch in the evening reading a copy of *Big Sky*, Bud Guthrie's novel. And as I got farther and farther into it, I . . . marveled: How can anybody know this much about the world and their particular piece of the world? I didn't know anything. I didn't know that much about what was within five miles of me and much less all up and down the river and on and on and on. That stayed with me.

Writing "Thirty-Four Seasons of Winter"

Worrying that story through and other stories too. By worrying I mean two things. I was writing about people and places and situations that I cared about deeply, that really were to some degree very close to home to me. They're not autobiographical stories at all, but nevertheless, I know that world and I know people; I had people in my mind's eye when I first started writing about it. And then those people coalesced and came together and became whatever they became in the story.

To watch this entire interview and hear the author read from "Thirty-Four Seasons of Winter," go to **www.mhhe. com/delbanco1e.**

William Kittredge has lived in the West for nearly his entire life; he grew up on a ranch in southeastern Oregon where he farmed into his thirties, after which he taught at the University of Montana for almost thirty years. In between, he studied writing at the Iowa Writers' Workshop and received Stanford University's prestigious Stegner Fellowship. Kittredge's subject is the West—but not the West of tough-grained cowboy heroes or seemingly unlimited resources.

In 2007, at the age of seventy-five, Kittredge published his first novel, *The Willow Trees*. This book deals with the education of a young cowboy whose adventures carry him from the early days of modern ranching to the politics of contemporary Western statehood. In his story collections *We Are Not in This Together* (1984) and *The Van Gogh Field* (1978), Kittredge portrays vulnerable men and complicated love relationships, even as he depicts the Western traditions of farming and ranching as in "Thirty-Four Seasons of Winter."

RESEARCH ASSIGNMENT In his interview, Kittredge says the West is a "museum culture." What does he mean by that? Do you agree? How does that affect how you read "Thirty-Four Seasons of Winter"?

Thirty-Four Seasons of Winter (1984)

1   BEN Alton remembered years in terms of winter. Summers all ran together, each like the last, heat and baled hay and dust. "That was '59," he'd say. "The year I wintered in California." He'd be remembering manure-slick alleys of a feedlot outside Manteca, a flat horizon and constant rain.

2   Or flood years. "March of '64, when the levees went." Or open winters. "We fed cattle the whole of February in our shirtsleeves. For Old Man Swarthout." And then he'd be sad. "One week Art helped. We was done every day by noon and drunk by three." Sad because Art was his stepbrother and dead, and because there'd been nothing but hate between them when Art was killed.

3   Ben and Art fought only once, when they were thirteen. Ben's father, Corrie Alton, moved in with Art's old lady on her dryland place in the hills north of Davanero, and the boys bunked together in a back room. The house was surrounded by a fenced dirt yard where turkeys picked, shaded by three withering peach trees; and the room they shared was furnished with two steel-frame cots and a row of nails where they hung what extra clothing they owned. The first night, while the old people were drinking in town, the boys fought. Ben took a flattened nose and chipped tooth against one of the cot frames and was satisfied and didn't try again.

4   The next year Art's mother sold the place for money to drink on, and when that was gone Ben's old man pulled out, heading for Shafter, down out of Bakersfield, going to see friends and work a season in the spuds. Corrie never came back or sent word, so the next spring the boys took a job setting siphons for an onion farmer, doing the muddy and exhausting work of one man, supporting themselves and Art's mother. She died the spring they were seventeen; and Art began to talk about getting out of town, fighting in the ring, being somebody.

5   So he ran every night, and during the day he and Ben stacked alfalfa bales, always making their thousand a day, twenty bucks apiece, and then in the fall Art went to Portland and worked out in a gym each afternoon, learning to fight, and spent his evenings swimming at the YMCA or watching movies. Early in the winter he began to get some fights; and for at least the first year he didn't lose. People began to know his name in places like Salem and Yakima and Klamath Falls.

6   HE fought at home only once, a January night in the Peterson barn on the edge of town, snow falling steadily. The barn warmed slowly, losing its odor of harness leather and rotting hay; and under a circle of lights that illuminated the fighters in a blue glare, country people smoked and bet and drank. Circling a sweating and tiring Mexican boy, Art tapped his gloves and brushed back his thin blond hair with a quick forearm, sure and quiet. Then he moved under an overhand right, ducking in a quick new way he must have learned in Portland; and then he was inside, forcing, and flat on his feet, grunting as he followed each short chop with his body. The Mexican backed against one of the rough juniper posts supporting the ring, covered his face, gloves fumbling together as he began sink-

ing and twisting, knees folding; and it ended with the Mexican sprawled and cut beneath one eye, bleeding from the nose, and Art in his corner, breathing easily while he flexed and shook his arms as if he weren't loose yet. Art spit the white mouthpiece onto the wet, gray canvas and ducked away under the ropes.

7   That night, Ben sat in the top row of the little grandstand and watched two men drag the other fighter out of the ring and attempt to revive him by pouring water over his head. Ben hugged his knees and watched the crowd settle and heard the silence while everybody watched. Finally the Mexican boy shook his head and stood up, and the crowd moved in a great sigh.

Even tired she looked good.

8   THE next summer Art showed up with Clara, brought her back with him from a string of fights in California. It was an August afternoon, dead hot in the valley hayfields, and dust rose in long spirals from the field ahead where five balers were circling slowly, eating windrows of loose hay and leaving endless and uniform strings of bales. Ben was working the stack, unloading trucks, sweating through his pants every day before noon, shirtless and peeling.

9   The lemon-colored Buick convertible came across the stubble, bouncing and wheeling hard, just ahead of its own dust, and stopped twenty or thirty yards from the stack. Art jumped out holding a can of beer over his head. The girl stood beside the convertible in the dusty alfalfa stubble and squinted into the glaring light, moist and sleepy looking. She was maybe twenty, and her sleeveless white blouse was wrinkled from sleeping in the car and sweat-gray beneath the arms. But she was blond and tan and direct in the 100-degree heat of the afternoon. "Ain't she something?" Art said. "She's a kind of prize I brought home." He laughed and slapped her on the butt.

10   "Hello, Ben," she said. "Art told me about you." They drank a can of beer, iced and metallic tasting, and Art talked about the fighting in California, Fresno, and Tracy, and while he talked he ran his fingers slowly up and down Clara's bare arm. Ben crouched in the shade of the convertible with his beer and tried not to watch the girl. That night he lay awake and thought about her, and everything about that meeting seemed too large and real, like some memory of childhood.

11   Anyway, she was living and traveling with Art. Then the fall he was twenty-five, fighting in Seattle, Art broke his right hand in a way that couldn't be fixed and married Clara and came home to live, driving a logging truck in the summer and drinking in the bars and drawing his unemployment through the winters, letting Clara work as a barmaid when they were broke. The years got away until one afternoon in a tavern called The Tarpaper Shack, when Ben and Art were thirty-one. Art was sitting with a girl named Marie, and when Ben came in and wandered over to the booth she surprised him by being quiet and nice, with brown eyes and dark hair, not the kind Art ran with on his drunks; and by the end of the summer Marie and Ben were engaged.

12   WHICH caused no trouble until Christmas. The stores were open late, but the streets with their decorations were deserted, looking like a carnival at four in the morning, lighted and ready to tear down and move.

13   "You gonna marry that pig?" Art said. Art was drunk. The barkeeper, a woman called Virgie, was leaning on the counter.

14   "I guess I am," Ben said. "But don't sweat it." Then he noticed Virgie looking past them to the far corner of the vaulted room. A worn row of booths ran there, beyond the lighted shuffleboard table and bowling machine. Above the last booth he saw the shadowed back of Clara's head. Just the yellow hair and yet certainly her. Art was grinning.

15   "You see her," he said talking to Ben. "She's got a problem. She ain't getting any."

16   Ben finished the beer and eased the glass back to the wooden counter, wishing he could leave, wanting no more of their trouble. Clara was leaning back, eyes closed and the table in front of her empty except for her clasped hands. She didn't move or look as he approached.

17   "Hello, Clara," he said. And when she opened her eyes it was the same, like herons over the valley swamps, white against green. Even tired she looked good. "All right if I sit?" he asked. "You want a beer?"

18   She sipped from his, taking the glass without speaking, touching his hand with her hand, then smiling and licking the froth from her lips. "Okay," she said, and he ordered another glass and sat down beside her.

19   "How you been?" he said. "All right?"

20   "You know," she said, looking sideways at him, never glancing toward Art. "You got a pretty good idea how I been." Then she smiled. "I hear you're getting married."

21   "Just because you're tied up," he said, and she grinned again, more like her old self now. "I mean it," he said. "Guess I ought to tell you once."

22   "Don't, she said. "For Christ sake. Not with that bastard over there laughing." She drank a little more of the beer. "I mean it," she said, after a moment. "Leave me alone."

23   Ben picked up his empty glass and walked toward the bar, turning the glass in his hand and feeling how it fit his grasp. He stood looking at the back of Art's head, the thin hair, fine and blond; and then he wrapped the glass in his fist and smashed it into the hollow of Art's neck, shattering the glass and driving Art's face into the counter. Then he ran, crashing out the door and onto the sidewalk.

24   His hand was cut and bleeding. He picked glass from his palm and wrapped his hand in his handkerchief as he walked, looking in the store windows, bright and lighted for Christmas.

25   Clara left for Sacramento that night, lived there with her father, worked in a factory southeast of town, making airplane parts and taking care of the old man, not coming back until he died. Sometimes Ben wondered if she would have come back anyway, even if the old man hadn't died. Maybe she's just been waiting for Art to come after her. And then one day on the street he asked, "You and Art going back together?" just hoping he could get her to talk awhile.

26   "I guess not," she said. "That's what he told me."

27   "I'm sorry," Ben said. And he was.

28   "I came back because I wanted," she said. "Guess I lived here too long."

29   THAT spring Ben and Marie were married and began living out of town, on a place her father owned; and the next fall his father was killed, crushed under a hillside combine in Washington, just north of Walla Walla, drunk and asleep at the leveling wheel, dead when they dug him out. And then the summer Art and Ben turned thirty-four Marie got pregnant and that winter Art was killed, shot in the back of the head by a girl named Stephanie Rudd, a thin red-haired girl just out of high school and, so people said, knocked up a little. Art was on the end stool in the The Tarpaper Shack, his usual place, when the girl entered quietly and shot before anyone noticed. He was dead when he hit the floor, face destroyed, blood spattered over the mirror and glasses behind the bar. And all the time music he'd punched was playing on the jukebox. *Trailer for sale or rent;* and *I can't stop loving you;* and *Time to bum again;* and, *That's what you get for loving me:* Roger Miller, Ray Charles, Waylon Jennings.

30   BEN awakened the night of the shooting and heard Marie on the phone, felt her shake him awake in the dim light of the bedroom. She seemed enormously frightened and continued to shake him, as if to awaken herself. She was eight months pregnant.

31   "He's dead." She spoke softly, seeming terrified, as if some idea she feared had been at last confirmed. "He never had a chance," she said.

32   "He had plenty." Ben sat up and put his arm around her, forced from his shock.

33   "They never gave him anything." She bent over and began to cry.

34   Later, it was nearly morning, after coffee and cigarettes, when Marie gave up and went to bed; Ben sat alone at the kitchen table. "Afraid of everything," Art had said. "That's how they are. Every stinking one."

35   Ben saw Art drunk and talking like he was ready for anything, actually involved with nothing except for a string of girls like the one who shot him. And then, somehow, the idea of Art and Marie got hold of Ben. It came from the way she had cried and carried on about Art. There was something wrong. Sitting there at the table, feeling the knowledge seep around his defenses, Ben knew what it was. He got up from the chair.

36   She was in the bedroom, curled under the blankets, crying softly. "What is it?" he asked. "There's something going on." She didn't open her eyes, but the crying seemed to slow a little. Ben waited, standing beside the bed, looking down, all the time wondering, as he became more sure, if it had happened in this bed, and all the time knowing it made no difference where it happened. And it was her fault. Not any fault of Art's. Art was what he was. She could have stopped him. Ben's hands felt strange, as if there was something to be done he couldn't recognize. He asked again, hearing his voice harsh and strained. "What is it, Marie?"

37   She didn't answer. He forced her onto her back and held her there, waiting for her to open her eyes while she struggled silently, twisting her upper body against his grip. His fingers sank into her shoulder

and his wrist trembled. They remained like that, forcing against each other. Then she relaxed and opened her eyes. "What is it?" he asked again. "It was something between you and Art, wasn't it?"

Her eyes were changed, shielded. She shook her head. "No," she said. "No."

"He was screwing you, wasn't he? Is it his kid?"

"It was a long time ago," she said.

"My ass." He let go of her shoulder. "That's why you're so tore up. Because you ain't getting any more from him." He walked around the bed, unable for some reason, because of what he was left with, to ask her if it happened here, in this bed. "Isn't that right?" he said. "How come you married me? He turn you down?"

"Because I was afraid of him. I didn't want him. He was just fooling. I wanted you, not him."

Ben slapped her, and she curled quickly again, her hands pressed to her mouth, crying, shoulders hunching. He made her face him. "You ain't getting away," he said. "So I was a nice tame dog, and you took me."

"You'll hurt the baby."

"His goddamned baby!"

"It all broke off when I met you," she said. "He told me to go ahead, that you'd be good to me." It had surprised him when they met that she was with Art, but somehow he'd never until now gotten the idea they had anything going on. "It was only a few times after I knew you," she said. "He begged me."

"So I got stuck with the leavings." He cursed her again, at the same time listening to at least a little of what she said. "He begged me." That was sad. Remembering Art those last years, after he came home to stay, Ben believed her.

"So he dumped you off onto me," Ben said. "I wish I could thank him."

"It wasn't like that. He loved you. He said for me to marry you and be happy."

"So you did. And I was stupid enough to go for it."

"He was a little boy. It was fun, but he was a little boy."

"I'm happy," Ben said, "things worked out so nice for you." She shook her head and didn't answer. Ben wondered what he should do. It was as if he had never been married, had been right in always imagining his life as single. He'd watched his friends settle, seen their kids start to grow up, and it had seemed those were things he was not entitled to, that he was going to grow old in a habit of taverns, rented rooms, separate from the married world. And now he was

still there, outside. And she'd kept it all a secret. "You stinking pig," he said slowly.

"Ben, it was a long time ago. Ben."

He was tired and his work was waiting. Maybe it was a long time ago and maybe it wasn't. He left her there crying while he dressed to go out and feed her father's cattle.

In the afternoon she had the house picked up and a meal waiting. She watched while he ate, but they didn't talk. He asked if she wanted to go to the funeral, and she said no and that was all. When he was drinking his coffee, calm now, and so tired his chest ached, he started thinking about Clara. He wondered if she'd known. Wouldn't have made any difference, he thought. Not after everything else.

THREE days later, heading for the burial, he was alone and hunched against the wheel, driving through new snow that softly drifted across the highway. His fingers were numb, the broken cracks in the rough calluses ingrained with black. A tire chain ticked a fender, but he kept going. He'd gone out at daylight to feed, a mandatory job that had to be done every day of winter, regardless of other

> "How come you married me? He turn you down?"

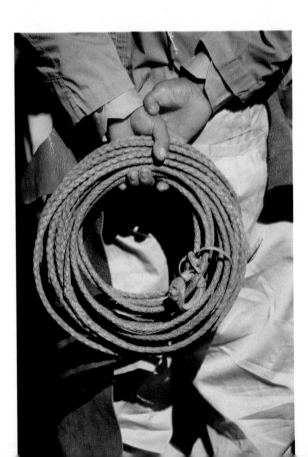

obligations. The rust-streaked Chevrolet swayed on the rutted ice beneath the snow. The steady and lumbering gait of the team he fed with, two massive frost-coated Belgian geldings, the creaking oceanic motion of the hay wagon, was still with him, more real than this.

57   The Derrick County cemetery was just below the road, almost five miles short of town. They were going to bury Art in the area reserved for charity burials, away from the lanes of Lombardy poplars and old-time lilacs. By dark the grave would be covered with snow. Ben parked and got out, and went over to look down in the hole. Far away in town, the bells of the Catholic church were faintly tolling. Ben stood a moment, then started back toward the car. He sat in the front seat with his hands cupped in his crotch, warming them. After a time, he backed slowly out of the graveyard.

58   Davanero was on the east side of the valley, scattered houses hung with ice, windows sealed against wind by tacked-on plastic sheeting. The still smoke of house fires rose straight up. Ben drove between lots heaped with snow-covered junk, past shacks with open, hanging doors where drifters lived in summer, into the center of town. The stores were open and a few people moved toward the coffee shops. He felt cut away from everything, as if this were an island in the center of winter.

59   The OPEN sign hung in the front window of The Tarpaper Shack. Ben wondered if Clara was tending bar and if she intended to go to the funeral. He parked and walked slowly through the snow to the door. The church bells were louder, close and direct now. Inside, the tavern was dark and barn-like, empty except for Clara, who was washing glasses in a metal sink. Ben went to the far end, where Art always sat, and eased onto a stool. "I'd take a shot," he said. "A double. Take one yourself."

60   "I'm closing up," she said. "So there's no use hanging around." She stayed at the sink and continued to wash glasses.

61   "You going to the funeral?" Ben said.

62   "I'm closing up." Her hands were still in the water. "I guess you need a drink," she said. "Go lock the door."

63   She was sitting in one of the booths when he got back. "You ain't going to the funeral?" he asked again.

64   "What good is that?"

65   "I guess you feel pretty bad."

66   "I guess." She drank quietly. "I would have took anything off him. Any damned thing. And that stupid bitch kills him. I would have given anything for his kid."

Ben finished his whiskey, and Clara took his glass and went for some more. "To hell with their goddamned funeral," he said.

Clara played some music on the jukebox, slow country stuff; and they danced staggering against the stools and the shuffleboard table, holding each other. She pushed him away after a few songs. "If you ain't one hell of a dancer," she said. "Art was a pretty dancer." She sat down in the booth and put an arm on the table and then lay her head alongside it, facing the wall. "Goddamn," she said. "I could cry. I ain't cried since I was a little girl," she said. "Not since then. Not since I was a little girl."

Ben wandered around the barroom, carrying his drink. He called his wife on the telephone. "You bet your sweet ass I'm drunk," he shouted when she answered, then hung up.

"Ain't you some hero," Clara said. She drank what whiskey was left in her glass. "You're nothing," she said. "Absolutely nothing."

Outside, the bells had stopped. Nothing. That was what he felt like. Nothing. Like his hands were without strength to steer the car. He sat awhile in the front seat, then drove to the jail, a gray brick building with heavy wire mesh over the windows. The deputy, a small bald man in a gray uniform, sat behind the desk in the center of the main room, coffee cup beside him. He smiled when he saw Ben, but he didn't say anything.

"How's chances of seeing that girl?" Ben asked. He didn't know why he'd come. It was just some idea that because she'd hated Art enough to kill him, because of that, maybe she understood and could tell him, Ben, why he wasn't nothing. He knew, even while he spoke, that it was a stupid, drunk idea.

"Okay," the deputy said, after a minute. "Come on. I guess you got a right."

THEY went through two locked doors, back into a large cinder-block room without any windows. Light came from a long fluorescent tube overhead. Two cells were separated by steel bars six inches apart. The room was warm. The girl was sitting on a cot in the left-hand cell, legs crossed, with red hair straight down over her shoulders and wearing a wrinkled blue smock without any pockets. She was looking at her hands, which were folded in her lap. "What now?" she said when she looked up. Her voice was surprisingly loud.

"Ben wanted to see you," the deputy said.

"Like a zoo, ain't it." The girl grinned and raised and lowered her shoulders.

"And you're not one bit sorry?" Ben said. "Just a little bit sorry for what you did?"

"Not one bit," the girl said. "I've had plenty of time to think about that. I'm not. I'm happy. I feel good."

"He wasn't no bad man," Ben said. "Not really. He never really was."

"He sure as hell wasn't Winston Churchill. He never even *tried* to make me happy." She put her hands in her lap.

"I don't see it," Ben said. "No way I can see you're right. He wasn't that bad."

"The thing I liked about him," she said, "was that he was old enough. He was like you. He was old enough to do anything. He could have been nice if he'd wanted."

The deputy laughed.

"I felt so bad before," the girl said, "killing him was easy. The only thing I feel bad about is that I never got down into him and made him crawl around. That's the only thing. I'm sorry about that, but that's all."

"He didn't owe you nothing," Ben said.

The girl looked at the deputy. "Make him leave," she said.

BEN drove slowly home in the falling snow. He could only see blurred outlines of the trees on either side of the lane that led to his house. He parked the car, kicked the snow from his boots, and went inside the house. Marie was in the bedroom, sleeping. The dim room was gray and cold, the bed a rumpled island. Marie was on her back, her stomach a mound beneath the blankets. Her mouth gaped a little.

After he got out of his clothes, Ben sat on the edge of the bed. Marie sighed in her sleep and moved a little, but she didn't waken. Ben reached to touch her shoulder and then stopped. Her eyelids flickered open. "Come on," she said. "Get under the covers."

"In a minute," Ben said. He went back out to the kitchen and smoked a cigarette. Then he went back into the bedroom and crawled in beside her and put his hand on her belly, hoping to feel the baby move. He remembered a warm, shirtsleeve day in February, working with Art, hurrying while they fed a final load of bales to the cattle that trailed behind, eager to get to town, noon sun glaring off wind-glazed fields of snow.

> "I felt so bad before," the girl said, "killing him was easy. . . ."

Questions for Critical Thinking

1 Think about what you know of the West. Are there details in the story that fit your view of the West? If so, what are they? Are there any that surprised you? Could this story take place in another state or region and still evolve in the same way?

2 Consider the relationships among the four main characters. Which relationship seems to mean the most to Ben? Support your answer with details about the character that suggest his/her importance to Ben.

3 How does the writer portray nature in this story? You might want to consider how the characters are feeling when they are outdoors and what actions they perform while outdoors as opposed to in indoor scenes.

. . . I had no idea that books existed, really.

I loved that you could be angry on the page . . .

Q&A

A Conversation on Writing

Dagoberto Gilb

Growing Up Without Books

I did not grow up with books. . . . I had no idea that books existed, really. And it wasn't part of my own community or culture. I grew up with a mother that was a single mother, a Mexican-American and also as a person from the working class. . . . My friends whether they're black or white basically didn't read; we didn't have any concept of books. So I just came into it late as one of these odd things that seemed to have happened to me.

Discovering Literature

To get through [school], you had to take that freshman comp class. I wasn't really dumb. What do you call that when you're not dumb but you can sort of survive? And you look dumb to all the teachers that are giving you dumb grades. I very wisely took a night class where I looked good because everybody was older and tired. I got a "B". . . . I did have to take one more [course]. I remember reading *Billy Budd* . . . but I had to look up a word every other line. . . . I couldn't believe an American writer wrote so oddly. And I just gave up literature . . . until I started reading others. . . . Luis Valdez . . . Jack Kerouac. . . . I learned, and very gratefully learned, that storytelling was about voice.

Reading As Exercise for Writing

The brain is a muscle. And the muscle that makes the brain the strongest is reading . . . Anybody that sits down to read one book (I don't care if you read it twenty times, it doesn't have to be twenty books, it can be one book twenty times) . . . will get

stronger and . . . see better. You'll breathe deeper. . . . And writing is the same thing. Actually writing doesn't exist without loving books and loving reading.

Born in Los Angeles to a Mexican mother and an American father, Dagoberto Gilb has become an increasingly recognized voice of the Mexican-American, and working-class, experience. Although he graduated with a double major and a master's degree from the University of California, Santa Barbara, Gilb turned to construction for his living and traveled between Los Angeles and El Paso for his work. He began to write during this period, joining a labor union as a class-A journeyman carpenter and working primarily on high-rise buildings. Thus, his writing captures a contemporary working-class perspective, beginning with his first full collection of short stories, *The Magic of Blood* (1993). Gilb has published a novel, *The Last Known Residence of Mickey Acuna* (1994); another collection of short stories, *Woodcuts of Women* (2001); a collection of essays, *Gritos* (1993); and, most recently, a novel, *The Flowers* (2008). His anthology *Hecho En Tejas, An Anthology of Texas-Mexican Literature* appeared in 2007.

To watch this entire interview with Dagoberto Gilb, go to www.mhhe.com/delbanco1e.

RESEARCH ASSIGNMENT In his interview, Gilb says, "I don't think an American white guy can write from a black point of view." What does he mean by this? Do you agree?

"A lot of times the world of books doesn't reflect your own neighborhood. I think in the Rio Grande Valley or in El Paso, Texas, or places like that where the majority of the population, I'd say seventy-five percent of the population, is Mexican-American, first generation to third. . . . They sit there and read about mutton and teapots, and go, ugh, and think, I don't know what I'm going to do in college. . . . There's never gorditas, there's no enchiladas, there's nothing about the neighborhood." Conversation with Dagoberto Gilb

Romero's Shirt (1992)

1   JUAN Romero, a man not unlike many in this country, has had jobs in factories, shops, and stores. He has painted houses, dug ditches, planted trees, hammered, sawed, bolted, snaked pipes, picked cotton and chile and pecans, each and all for wages. Along the way he has married and raised his children and several years ago he finally arranged it so that his money might pay for the house he and his family live in. He is still more than twenty years away from being the owner. It is a modest house even by El Paso standards. The building, in an adobe style, is made of stone which is painted white, though the paint is gradually chipping off or being absorbed by the rock. It has two bedrooms, a den which is used as another, a small dining area, a living room, a kitchen, one bathroom, and a garage which, someday, he plans to turn into another place to live. Although in a development facing a paved street and in a neighborhood, it has the appearance of being on almost half an acre. At the front is a garden of cactus—nopal, ocotillo, and agave—and there are weeds that grow tall with yellow flowers which seed into thorn-hard burrs. The rest is dirt and rocks of various sizes, some of which have been lined up to form a narrow path out of the graded dirt, a walkway to the front porch—where, under a tile and one-by tongue and groove overhang, are a wooden chair and a love seat, covered by an old bedspread, its legless frame on the red cement slab. Once the porch looked onto oak trees. Two of them are dried-out stumps; the remaining one has a limb or two which still can produce leaves, but with so many amputations, its future is irreversible. Romero seldom runs water through a garden hose, though in the back yard some patchy grass can almost seem suburban, at least to him, when he does. Near the corner of his land, in the front, next to the sidewalk, is a juniper shrub, his only bright green plant, and Romero does not want it to yellow and die, so he makes special efforts on its behalf, washing off dust, keeping its leaves neatly pruned and shaped.

2   These days Romero calls himself a handyman. He does odd jobs, which is exactly how he advertises— "no job too small"—in the throwaway paper. He hangs wallpaper and doors, he paints, lays carpet, does just about anything someone will call and ask him to do. It doesn't earn him much, and sometimes it's barely enough, but he's his own boss, and he's had so many bad jobs over those other years, ones no more dependable, he's learned that this suits him. At one time Romero did want more, and he'd believed that he could have it simply through work, but no matter what he did his children still had to be born at the county hospital. Even years later it was there that his oldest son went for serious medical treatment

because Romero couldn't afford the private hospitals. He tried not to worry about how he earned his money. In Mexico, where his parents were born and he spent much of his youth, so many things weren't available, and any work which allowed for food, clothes, and housing was to be honored—by the standards there, Romero lived well. Except this wasn't Mexico, and even though there were those who did worse even here, there were many who did better and had more, and a young Romero too often felt ashamed by what he saw as his failure. But time passed, and he got older. As he saw it, he didn't live in poverty, and *here*, he finally came to realize, was where he was, where he and his family were going to stay. Life in El Paso was much like the land—hard, but one could make do with what was offered. Just as his parents had, Romero always thought it was a beautiful place for a home.

> He denied his wife nothing, but she was a woman who asked for little.

3   Yet people he knew left—to Houston, Dallas, Los Angeles, San Diego, Denver, Chicago—and came back for holidays with stories of high wages and acquisition. And more and more people crossed the river, in rags, taking work, his work, at any price. Romero constantly had to discipline himself by remembering the past, how his parents lived; he had to teach himself to appreciate what he did have. His car, for example, he'd kept up since his early twenties. He'd had it painted three times in that period and he worked on it so devotedly that even now it was in as good a condition as almost any car could be. For his children he tried to offer more—an assortment of clothes for his daughter, lots of toys for his sons. He denied his wife nothing, but she was a woman who asked for little. For himself, it was much less. He owned some work clothes and T-shirts necessary for his jobs as well as a set of good enough, he thought, shirts he'd had since before the car. He kept up a nice pair of custom boots, and in a closet hung a pair of slacks for a wedding or baptism or important mass. He owned two jackets, a leather one from Mexico and a warm nylon one for cold work days. And he owned a wool plaid Pendleton shirt, his favorite piece of clothing, which he'd bought right after the car and before his marriage because it really was good-looking besides being functional. He wore it anywhere and everywhere with confidence that its quality would always be both in style and appropriate.

4   THE border was less than two miles below Romero's home, and he could see, down the dirt street which ran alongside his property, the desert and mountains of Mexico. The street was one of the few in the city which hadn't yet been paved. Romero liked it that way, despite the runoff problems when heavy rains passed by, as they had the day before this day. A night wind had blown hard behind the rains, and the air was so clean he could easily see buildings in Juárez. It was sunny, but a breeze told him to put on his favorite shirt before he pulled the car up alongside the house and dragged over the garden hose to wash it, which was something he still enjoyed doing as much as anything else. He was organized, had a special bucket, a special sponge, and he used warm water from the kitchen sink. When he started soaping the car he worried about getting his shirt sleeves wet, and once he was moving around he decided a T-shirt would keep him warm enough. So he took off the wool shirt and draped it, conspicuously, over the juniper near him, at the corner of his property. He thought that if he couldn't help but see it, he couldn't forget it, and forgetting something outside was losing it. He lived near a school, and teenagers passed by all the time, and also there was regular foot-traffic—many people walked the sidewalk in front of his house, many who had no work.

5   After the car was washed, Romero went inside and brought out the car wax. Waxing his car was another thing he still liked to do, especially on a weekday like this one when he was by himself, when no one in his family was home. He could work faster, but he took his time, spreading with a damp cloth, waiting, then wiping off the crust with a dry cloth. The exterior done, he went inside the car and waxed the dash, picked up some trash on the floorboard, cleaned out the glove compartment. Then he went for some pliers he kept in

a toolbox in the garage, returned and began to wire up the rear license plate which had lost a nut and bolt and was hanging awkwardly. As he did this, he thought of other things he might do when he finished, like prune the juniper. Except his old shears had broken, and he hadn't found another used pair, because he wouldn't buy them new.

An old man walked up to him carrying a garden rake, a hoe, and some shears. He asked Romero if there was some yard work needing to be done. After spring, tall weeds grew in many yards, but it seemed a dumb question this time of year, particularly since there was obviously so little ever to be done in Romero's yard. But Romero listened to the old man. There were still a few weeds over there, and he could rake the dirt so it'd be even and level, he could clip that shrub, and probably there was something in the back if he were to look. Romero was usually brusque with requests such as these, but he found the old man unique and likeable and he listened and finally asked how much he would want for all those tasks. The old man thought as quickly as he spoke and threw out a number. Ten. Romero repeated the number, questioningly, and the old man backed up, saying well, eight, seven. Romero asked if that was for everything. Yes sir, the old man said, excited that he'd seemed to catch a customer. Romero asked if he would cut the juniper for three dollars. The old man kept his eyes on the evergreen, disappointed for a second, then thought better of it. Okay, okay, he said, but, I've been walking all day, you'll give me lunch? The old man rubbed his striped cotton shirt at his stomach.

Romero liked the old man and agreed to it. He told him how he should follow the shape which was already there, to cut it evenly, to take a few inches off all of it just like a haircut. Then Romero went inside, scrambled enough eggs and chile and cheese for both of them and rolled it all in some tortillas. He brought out a beer.

The old man was clearly grateful, but since his gratitude was keeping the work from getting done—he might talk an hour about his little ranch in Mexico, about his little turkeys and his pig—Romero excused himself and went inside. The old man thanked Romero for the food, and, as soon as he was finished with the beer, went after the work sincerely. With dull shears—he sharpened them, so to speak, against a rock wall—the old man snipped garishly, hopping and jumping around the bush, around and around. It gave Romero such great pleasure to watch that this was all he did from his front window.

The work didn't take long, so, as the old man was raking up the clippings, Romero brought out a five-dollar bill. He felt that the old man's dancing around that bush, in those baggy old checkered pants, was more inspiring than religion, and a couple of extra dollars was a cheap price to see old eyes whiten like a boy's.

The old man was so pleased that he invited Romero to that little ranch of his in Mexico where he was sure they could share some aguardiente, or maybe Romero could buy a turkey from him—they were skinny but they could by fattened—but in any case they could enjoy a bottle of tequila together, with some sweet lemons. The happy old man swore he would come back no matter what, for he could do many things for Romero at his beautiful home. He swore he would return, maybe in a week or two, for surely there was work that needed to be done in the back yard.

Romero wasn't used to feeling so virtuous. He so often was disappointed, so often dwelled on the difficulties of life, that he had become hard, guarding against compassion and generosity. So much so that he'd even become spare with his words, even with his family. His wife whispered to the children that this was because he was tired, and, since it wasn't untrue, he accepted it as the explanation too. It spared him that worry, and from having to discuss why he liked working weekends and taking a day off during the week, like this one. But now an old man had made Romero wish his family were there with him so he could give as much, *more*, to them too, so he could watch their spin around dances—he'd missed so many—and Romero swore he would take them all into Juárez that night for dinner. He might even convince them to take a day, maybe two, for a drive to his uncle's house in Chihuahua instead, because he'd promised that so many years ago—so long ago they probably thought about somewhere else by now, like San Diego, or Los Angeles. Then he'd take them there! They'd go for a week, spend whatever it took. No expense could be so great, and if happiness was as easy as some tacos and a five-dollar bill, then how stupid it had been of him not to have offered it all this time.

Romero felt so good, felt such relief, he napped on the couch. When he woke up he immediately remembered his shirt, that it was already gone before the old man had even arrived—he remembered they'd walked around the juniper before it was cut. Nevertheless, the possibility that the old man took it wouldn't leave Romero's mind. Since he'd never believed in letting

> When he woke up he immediately remembered his shirt...

down, giving into someone like that old man, the whole experience became suspect. Maybe it was part of some ruse which ended with the old man taking his shirt, some food, money. This was how Romero thought. Though he held a hope that he'd left it somewhere else, that it was a lapse of memory on his part—he went outside, inside, looked everywhere twice, then one more time after that—his cynicism had flowered, colorful and bitter.

13 UNDERSTAND that it was his favorite shirt, that he'd never thought of replacing it and that its loss was all Romero could keep his mind on, though he knew very well it wasn't a son, or a daughter, or a wife, or a mother or father, not a disaster of any kind. It was a simple shirt, in the true value of things not very much to lose. But understand also that Romero was a good man who tried to do what was right and who would harm no one willfully. Understand that Romero was a man who had taught himself to not care, to not want, to not desire for so long that he'd lost many words, avoided many people, kept to himself, alone, almost always, even when his wife gave him his meals. Understand that it was his favorite shirt and though no more than that, for him it was no less. Then understand how he felt like a fool paying that old man who, he considered, might even have taken it, like a fool for feeling so friendly and generous, happy, when the shirt was already gone, like a fool for having all those and these thoughts for the love of a wool shirt, like a fool for not being able to stop thinking them all, but especially the one reminding him that this was what he had always believed in, that loss was what he was most prepared for. And so then you might understand why he began to stare out the window of his home, waiting for someone to walk by absently with it on, for the thief to pass by, careless. He kept a watch out the window as each of his children came in, then his wife. He told them only what had happened and, as always, they left him alone. He stared out that window onto the dirt street, past the ocotillos and nopales and agaves, the junipers and oaks and mulberries in front of other homes of brick or stone, painted or not, past them to the buildings in Juárez, and he watched the horizon darken and the sky light up with the moon and stars, and the land spread with shimmering lights, so bright in the dark blot of night. He heard dogs barking until another might bark farther away, and then another, back and forth like that, the small rectangles and squares of their fences plotted out distinctly in his mind's eye as his lids closed. Then he heard a gust of wind bend around his house, and then came the train, the metal rhythm getting closer until it was as close as it could be, the steel pounding the earth like a beating heart, until it diminished and then faded away and then left the air to silence, to its quiet and dark, so still it was like death, or rest, sleep, until he could hear a grackle, and then another gust of wind, and then finally a car.

He looked in on his daughter still so young, so beautiful, becoming a woman who would leave that bed for another, his sons still boys when they were asleep, who dreamed like men when they were awake, and his wife, still young in his eyes in the morning shadows of their bed.

Romero went outside. The juniper had been cut just as he'd wanted it. He got cold and came back in and went to the bed and blankets his wife kept so clean, so neatly arranged as she slept under them without him, and he lay down beside her.

Questions for Critical Thinking

1 Notice how character and place interact: If you were called on to testify in court as a character witness for Romero, what might you say? If you were a city official in El Paso and asked to describe Romero's neighborhood, how might you depict it?

2 How much of a part does physical labor play in the story? Does it play a role in other stories you have found in this volume?

3 Where do you see links between geography—location—and symbolic implications about the meaning of Romero's life?

4 "Character and geography— location—are closely bound up together. Where we live says something about who we are." Do you agree or disagree with this statement? Support your answer with examples from the text. Consider how much of Romero's daily life might be the same, and how much might be different, if he were living in Atlanta or New York or Seattle.

John Steinbeck (1902–1968)

The Salinas Valley area of central California, carries the nickname "Steinbeck Country," named, of course, for John Steinbeck, the Nobel Prize–winning author who was born and raised there. Steinbeck's summer job as a ranch hand and his mother's anecdotes about local people rooted him in his home county early on. Although he attended Stanford as an English major, Steinbeck dropped out to pursue his dream of success as a writer, a dream that did not pay off until several novels into his career. Today, his place in the American literary canon is secure with books like *The Grapes of Wrath* (1939), his Pulitzer Prize–winning epic about a family of Oklahomans who migrate to California; *East of Eden* (1952), an account of two families in the Salinas Valley; and *Of Mice and Men* (1937), the tragic tale of a farm laborer and his mentally handicapped friend.

Consider, for a moment, D. H. Lawrence's "The Odour of Chrysanthemums" (chapter 9), another story about the way people Ford Madox Ford called "the other half" live. But the landscape of the north of England is importantly different from the landscape of the American West, and a comparison of these two stories suggests the pervasive effect of a region. A writer conscious of the economic and social problems of his day, Steinbeck portrayed characters who struggle, whether internally with their own psyches or externally with a society permeated by intolerance. Most of the large body of his work—novels, stories, plays, essays, travel books, reportage—has remained in print since his death, a tribute by both publishers and readers to the enduring nature of his vision.

> "Men do change, and change comes like a little wind that ruffles the curtains at dawn, and it comes like the stealthy perfume of wildflowers hidden in the grass." —John Steinbeck

The Chrysanthemums (1938)

1 THE high grey-flannel fog of winter closed off the Salinas Valley from the sky and from all the rest of the world. On every side it sat like a lid on the mountains and made of the great valley a closed pot. On the broad, level land floor the gang plows bit deep and left the black earth shining like metal where the shares had cut. On the foothill ranches across the Salinas River, the yellow stubble fields seemed to be bathed in pale cold sunshine, but there was no sunshine in the valley now in December. The thick willow scrub along the river flamed with sharp and positive yellow leaves.

2 It was a time of quiet and of waiting. The air was cold and tender. A light wind blew up from the southwest

so that the farmers were mildly hopeful of a good rain before long; but fog and rain do not go together.

3   Across the river, on Henry Allen's foothill ranch there was little work to be done, for the hay was cut and stored and the orchards were plowed up to receive the rain deeply when it should come. The cattle on the higher slopes were becoming shaggy and rough-coated.

4   Elisa Allen, working in her flower garden, looked down across the yard and saw Henry, her husband, talking to two men in business suits. The three of them stood by the tractor shed, each man with one foot on the side of the little Fordson. They smoked cigarettes and studied the machine as they talked.

5   Elisa watched them for a moment and then went back to her work. She was thirty-five. Her face was lean and strong and her eyes were as clear as water. Her figure looked blocked and heavy in her gardening costume, a man's black hat pulled low down over her eyes, clod-hopper shoes, a figured print dress almost completely covered by a big corduroy apron with four big pockets to hold the snips, the trowel and scratcher, the seeds and the knife she worked with. She wore heavy leather gloves to protect her hands while she worked.

6   She was cutting down the old year's chrysanthemum stalks with a pair of short and powerful scissors. She looked down toward the men by the tractor shed now and then. Her face was eager and mature and handsome; even her work with the scissors was over-eager, over-powerful. The chrysanthemum stems seemed too small and easy for her energy.

7   She brushed a cloud of hair out of her eyes with the back of her glove, and left a smudge of earth on her cheek in doing it. Behind her stood the neat white farm house with red geraniums close-banked around it as high as the windows. It was a hard-swept looking little house with hard-polished windows, and a clean mud-mat on the front steps.

8   Elisa cast another glance toward the tractor shed. The strangers were getting into their Ford coupe. She took off a glove and put her strong fingers down into the forest of new green chrysanthemum sprouts that were growing around the old roots. She spread the leaves and looked down among the close-growing stems. No aphids were there, no sowbugs or snails or cutworms. Her terrier fingers destroyed such pests before they could get started.

9   Elisa started at the sound of her husband's voice. He had come near quietly, and he leaned over the wire fence that protected her flower garden from cattle and dogs and chickens.

"At it again," he said. "You've got a strong new crop coming."

Elisa straightened her back and pulled on the gardening glove again. "Yes. They'll be strong this coming year." In her tone and on her face there was a little smugness.

"You've got a gift with things," Henry observed. "Some of those yellow chrysanthemums you had this year were ten inches across. I wish you'd work out in the orchard and raise some apples that big."

Her eyes sharpened. "Maybe I could do it, too. I've a gift with things, all right. My mother had it. She could stick anything in the ground and make it grow.

> She could stick anything in the ground and make it grow.

She said it was having planters' hands that knew how to do it."

"Well, it sure works with flowers," he said.

"Henry, who were those men you were talking to?"

"Why, sure, that's what I came to tell you. They were from the Western Meat Company. I sold those thirty head of three-year-old steers. Got nearly my own price, too."

"Good," she said. "Good for you."

"And I thought," he continued, "I thought how it's Saturday afternoon, and we might go into Salinas for dinner at a restaurant, and then to a picture show—to celebrate, you see."

"Good," she repeated. "Oh, yes. That will be good."

Henry put on his joking tone. "There's fights to-night. How'd you like to go to the fights?"

"Oh, no," she said breathlessly. "No, I wouldn't like fights."

"Just fooling, Elisa. We'll go to a movie. Let's see. It's two now. I'm going to take Scotty and bring down those steers from the hill. It'll take us maybe two hours. We'll go in town about five and have dinner at the Cominos Hotel. Like that?"

"Of course I'll like it. It's good to eat away from home."

"All right, then. I'll go get up a couple of horses."

She said, "I'll have plenty of time to transplant some of these sets, I guess."

She heard her husband calling Scotty down by the barn. And a little later she saw the two men ride up the pale yellow hillside in search of the steers.

There was a little square sandy bed kept for rooting the chrysanthemums. With her trowel she turned the soil over and over, and smoothed it and patted it firm. Then she dug ten parallel trenches to receive the sets. Back at the chrysanthemum bed she pulled out the little crisp shoots, trimmed off the leaves of each one with her scissors and laid it on a small orderly pile.

A squeak of wheels and plod of hoofs came from the road. Elisa looked up. The country road ran along the dense bank of willows and cottonwoods that bordered the river, and up this road came a curious vehicle, curiously drawn. It was an old spring-wagon, with a round canvas top on it like the cover of a prairie schooner. It was drawn by an old bay horse and a little grey-and-white burro. A big stubble-bearded man sat between the cover flaps and drove the crawling team. Underneath the wagon, between the hind wheels, a lean and rangy mongrel dog walked sedately. Words were painted on the canvas, in clumsy, crooked letters. "Pots, pans, knives, sisors, lawn mores, Fixed." Two rows of articles, and the triumphantly definitive "Fixed" below. The black paint had run down in little sharp points beneath each letter.

Elisa, squatting on the ground, watched to see the crazy, loose-jointed wagon pass by. But it didn't pass. It turned into the farm road in front of her house, crooked old wheels skirling and squeaking. The rangy dog darted from between the wheels and ran ahead. Instantly the two ranch shepherds flew out at him. Then all three stopped, and with stiff and quivering tails, with taut straight legs, with ambassadorial dignity, they slowly circled, sniffing daintily. The caravan pulled up to Elisa's wire fence and stopped. Now the newcomer dog, feeling out-numbered, lowered his tail and retired under the wagon with raised hackles and bared teeth.

The man on the wagon seat called out, "That's a bad dog in a fight when he gets started."

Elisa laughed. "I see he is. How soon does he generally get started?"

The man caught up her laughter and echoed it heartily. "Sometimes not for weeks and weeks," he said. He climbed stiffly down, over the wheel. The horse and the donkey drooped like unwatered flowers.

Elisa saw that he was a very big man. Although his hair and beard were greying, he did not look old. His worn black suit was wrinkled and spotted with grease. The laughter had disappeared from his face and eyes the moment his laughing voice ceased. His eyes were dark, and they were full of the brooding that gets in the eyes of teamsters and of sailors. The calloused hands he rested on the wire fence were cracked, and every crack was a black line. He took off his battered hat.

"I'm off my general road, ma'am," he said. "Does this dirt road cut over across the river to the Los Angeles highway?"

Elisa stood up and shoved the thick scissors in her apron pocket. "Well, yes, it does, but it winds around and then fords the river. I don't think your team could pull through the sand."

He replied with some asperity. "It might surprise you what them beasts can pull through."

"When they get started?" she asked.

He smiled for a second. "Yes. When they get started."

"Well," said Elisa, "I think you'll save time if you go back to the Salinas road and pick up the highway there."

He drew a big finger down the chicken wire and made it sing. "I ain't in any hurry, ma'am. I go from Seattle to San Diego and back every year. Takes all my time. About six months each way. I aim to follow nice weather."

Elisa took off her gloves and stuffed them in the apron pocket with the scissors. She touched the under edge of her man's hat, searching for fugitive hairs. "That sounds like a nice kind of a way to live," she said.

He leaned confidentially over the fence. "Maybe you noticed the writing on my wagon. I mend pots and sharpen knives and scissors. You got any of them things to do?"

"Oh, no," she said quickly. "Nothing like that." Her eyes hardened with resistance.

"Scissors is the worst thing," he explained. "Most people just ruin scissors trying to sharpen 'em, but I know how. I got a special tool. It's a little bobbit kind of thing, and patented. But it sure does the trick."

"No. My scissors are all sharp."

"All right, then. Take a pot," he continued earnestly, "a bent pot, or a pot with a hole. I can make it like new so you don't have to buy no new ones. That's a saving for you."

"No," she said shortly. "I tell you I have nothing like that for you to do."

His face fell to an exaggerated sadness. His voice took on a whining undertone. "I ain't had a thing to do today. Maybe I won't have no supper tonight. You see I'm off my regular road.

I know folks on the highway clear from Seattle to San Diego. They save their things for me to sharpen up because they know I do it so good and save them money."

49 "I'm sorry," Elisa said irritably. "I haven't anything for you to do."

50 His eyes left her face and fell to searching the ground. They roamed about until they came to the chrysanthemum bed where she had been working. "What's them plants, ma'am?"

51 The irritation and resistance melted from Elisa's face. "Oh, those are chrysanthemums, giant whites and yellows. I raise them every year, bigger than anybody around here."

52 "Kind of a long-stemmed flower? Looks like a quick puff of colored smoke?" he asked.

53 "That's it. What a nice way to describe them."

54 "They smell kind of nasty till you get used to them," he said.

55 "It's a good bitter smell," she retorted, "not nasty at all.

56 He changed his tone quickly. "I like the smell myself."

57 "I had ten-inch blooms this year," she said.

58 The man leaned farther over the fence. "Look. I know a lady down the road a piece, has got the nicest garden you ever seen. Got nearly every kind of flower but no chrysanthemums. Last time I was mending a copper-bottom washtub for her (that's a hard job but I do it good), she said to me, 'If you ever run acrost some nice chrysanthemums I wish you'd try to get me a few seeds.' That's what she told me."

59 Elisa's eyes grew alert and eager. "She couldn't have known much about chrysanthemums. You *can* raise them from seed, but it's much easier to root the little sprouts you see there."

60 "Oh," he said. "I s'pose I can't take none to her, then."

61 "Why yes you can," Elisa cried. "I can put some in damp sand, and you can carry them right along with you. They'll take root in the pot if you keep them damp. And then she can transplant them."

62 "She'd sure like to have some, ma'am. You say they're nice ones?"

63 "Beautiful," she said. "Oh, beautiful." Her eyes shone. She tore off the battered hat and shook out her dark pretty hair. "I'll put them in a flower pot, and you can take them right with you. Come into the yard."

64 While the man came through the picket gate Elisa ran excitedly along the geranium-bordered path to the back of the house. And she returned carrying a big red flower pot. The gloves were forgotten now. She kneeled on the ground by the starting bed and dug up the sandy soil with her fingers and scooped it into the bright new flower pot. Then she picked up the little pile of shoots she had prepared. With her strong fingers she pressed them in the sand and tamped around them with her knuckles. The man stood over her. "I'll tell you what to do," she said. "You remember so you can tell the lady."

65 "Yes, I'll try to remember."

66 "Well, look. These will take root in about a month. Then she must set them out, about a foot apart in good rich earth like this, see?" She lifted a handful of dark soil for him to look at. "They'll grow fast and tall. Now remember this: In July tell her to cut them down, about eight inches from the ground."

67 "Before they bloom?" he asked.

68 "Yes, before they bloom." Her face was tight with eagerness. "They'll grow right up again. About the last of September the buds will start."

69 She stopped and seemed perplexed. "It's the budding that takes the most care," she said hesitantly. "I don't know how to tell you." She looked deep into his eyes, searchingly. Her mouth opened a little, and she seemed to be listening. "I'll try to tell you," she said. "Did you ever hear of planting hands?"

70 "Can't say I have, ma'am."

71 "Well, I can only tell you what it feels like. It's when you're picking off the buds you don't want. Everything goes right down into your fingertips. You watch your fingers work. They do it themselves. You can feel how it is. They pick and pick the buds. They never make a mistake. They're with the plant. Do you see? Your fingers and the plant. You can feel that, right up your arm. They know. They never make a mistake. You can feel it. When you're like that you can't do anything wrong. Do you see that? Can you understand that?"

72 She was kneeling on the ground looking up at him. Her breast swelled passionately.

73 The man's eyes narrowed. He looked away self-consciously. "Maybe I know," he said. "Sometimes in the night in the wagon there—"

74 Elisa's voice grew husky. She broke in on him, "I've never lived as you do, but I know what you mean. When the night is dark—why, the stars are sharp-pointed, and there's quiet. Why, you rise up and up! Every pointed star gets driven into your body. It's like that. Hot and sharp and—lovely."

75 Kneeling there, her hand went out toward his legs in the greasy black trousers. Her hesitant fingers almost touched the cloth. Then her hand dropped to the ground. She crouched low like a fawning dog.

76 He said, "It's nice, just like you say. Only when you don't have no dinner, it ain't."

77 She stood up then, very straight, and her face was ashamed. She held the flower pot out to him and placed

it gently in his arms. "Here. Put it in your wagon, on the seat, where you can watch it. Maybe I can find something for you to do."

At the back of the house she dug in the can pile and found two old and battered aluminum saucepans. She carried them back and gave them to him. "Here, maybe you can fix these."

His manner changed. He became professional. "Good as new I can fix them." At the back of his wagon he set a little anvil, and out of an oily tool box dug a small machine hammer. Elisa came through the gate to watch him while he pounded out the dents in the kettles. His mouth grew sure and knowing. At a difficult part of the work he sucked his under-lip.

"You sleep right in the wagon?" Elisa asked.

"Right in the wagon, ma'am. Rain or shine I'm dry as a cow in there."

"It must be nice," she said. "It must be very nice. I wish women could do such things."

"It ain't the right kind of a life for a woman."

Her upper lip raised a little, showing her teeth. "How do you know? How can you tell?" she said.

"I don't know, ma'am," he protested. "Of course I don't know. Now here's your kettles, done. You don't have to buy no new ones."

"How much?"

"Oh, fifty cents'll do. I keep my prices down and my work good. That's why I have all them satisfied customers up and down the highway."

Elisa brought him a fifty-cent piece from the house and dropped it in his hand. "You might be surprised to have a rival some time. I can sharpen scissors, too. And I can beat the dents out of little pots. I could show you what a woman might do."

He put his hammer back in the oily box and shoved the little anvil out of sight. "It would be a lonely life for a woman, ma'am, and a scarey life, too, with animals creeping under the wagon all night." He climbed over the singletree, steadying himself with a hand on the burro's white rump. He settled himself in the seat, picked up the lines. "Thank you kindly, ma'am," he said. "I'll do like you told me; I'll go back and catch the Salinas road."

"Mind," she called, "if you're long in getting there, keep the sand damp."

"Sand, ma'am? . . . Sand? Oh, sure. You mean around the chrysanthemums. Sure I will." He clucked his tongue. The beasts leaned luxuriously into their collars. The mongrel dog took his place between the back wheels. The wagon turned and crawled out the entrance road and back the way it had come, along the river.

Elisa stood in front of her wire fence watching the slow progress of the caravan. Her shoulders were straight, her head thrown back, her eyes half-closed, so that the scene came vaguely into them. Her lips moved silently, forming the words "Good-bye—good-bye." Then she whispered. "That's a bright direction. There's a glowing there." The sound of her whisper startled her. She shook herself free and looked about to see whether anyone had been listening. Only the dogs had heard. They lifted their heads toward her from their sleeping in the dust, and then stretched out their chins and settled asleep again. Elisa turned and ran hurriedly into the house.

In the kitchen she reached behind the stove and felt the water tank. It was full of hot water from the noonday cooking. In the bathroom she tore off her soiled clothes and flung them into the corner. And then she scrubbed herself with a little block of pumice, legs and thighs, loins and chest and arms, until her skin was scratched and red. When she had dried herself she stood in front of a mirror in her bedroom and looked at her body. She tightened her stomach and threw out her chest. She turned and looked over her shoulder at her back.

After a while she began to dress, slowly. She put on her newest underclothing and her nicest stockings and the dress which was the symbol of her prettiness. She worked carefully on her hair, penciled her eyebrows and rouged her lips.

Before she was finished she heard the little thunder of hoofs and the shouts of Henry and his helper as they drove the red steers into the corral. She heard the gate bang shut and set herself for Henry's arrival.

His step sounded on the porch. He entered the house calling, "Elisa, where are you?"

"In my room, dressing. I'm not ready. There's hot water for your bath. Hurry up. It's getting late."

When she heard him splashing in the tub, Elisa laid his dark suit on the bed, and shirt and socks and tie beside it. She stood his polished shoes on the floor beside the bed. Then she went to the porch and sat primly and stiffly down. She looked toward the river road where the willow-line was still yellow with frosted leaves so that under the high grey fog they seemed a thin band of sunshine. This was the only color in the grey afternoon. She sat unmoving for a long time. Her eyes blinked rarely.

Henry came banging out of the door, shoving his tie inside his vest as he came. Elisa stiffened and her

> "... I wish women could do such things."

face grew tight. Henry stopped short and looked at her. "Why—why, Elisa. You look so nice!"

100   "Nice? You think I look nice? What do you mean by 'nice'?"

101   Henry blundered on. "I don't know. I mean you look different, strong and happy."

102   "I am strong? Yes, strong. What do you mean 'strong'?"

103   He looked bewildered. "You're playing some kind of a game," he said helplessly. "It's a kind of a play. You look strong enough to break a calf over your knee, happy enough to eat it like a watermelon."

104   For a second she lost her rigidity. "Henry! Don't talk like that. You didn't know what you said." She grew complete again. "I'm strong," she boasted. "I never knew before how strong."

105   Henry looked down toward the tractor shed, and when he brought his eyes back to her, they were his own again. "I'll get out the car. You can put on your coat while I'm starting."

106   Elisa went into the house. She heard him drive to the gate and idle down his motor, and then she took a long time to put on her hat. She pulled it here and pressed it there. When Henry turned the motor off she slipped into her coat and went out.

107   The little roadster bounced along on the dirt road by the river, raising the birds and driving the rabbits into the brush. Two cranes flapped heavily over the willow-line and dropped into the river-bed.

108   Far ahead on the road Elisa saw a dark speck. She knew.

109   She tried not to look as they passed it, but her eyes would not obey. She whispered to herself sadly, "He might have thrown them off the road. That wouldn't have been much trouble, not very much. But he kept the pot," she explained. "He had to keep the pot. That's why he couldn't get them off the road."

The roadster turned a bend and she saw the caravan ahead. She swung full around toward her husband so she could not see the little covered wagon and the mismatched team as the car passed them.

In a moment it was over. The thing was done. She did not look back.

She said loudly, to be heard above the motor, "It will be good, tonight, a good dinner."

"Now you're changed again," Henry complained. He took one hand from the wheel and patted her knee. "I ought to take you in to dinner oftener. It would be good for both of us. We get so heavy out on the ranch."

"Henry," she asked, "could we have wine at dinner?"

"Sure we could. Say! That will be fine."

She was silent for a while; then she said, "Henry, at those prize fights, do the men hurt each other very much?"

"Sometimes a little, not often. Why?"

"Well, I've read how they break noses, and blood runs down their chests. I've read how the fighting gloves get heavy and soggy with blood."

He looked around at her. "What's the matter, Elisa? I didn't know you read things like that." He brought the car to a stop, then turned to the right over the Salinas River bridge.

"Do any women ever go to the fights?" she asked.

"Oh, sure, some. What's the matter, Elisa? Do you want to go? I don't think you'd like it, but I'll take you if you really want to go."

She relaxed limply in the seat. "Oh, no. No. I don't want to go. I'm sure I don't." Her face was turned away from him. "It will be enough if we can have wine. It will be plenty." She turned up her coat collar so he could not see that she was crying weakly—like an old woman.

Questions for Critical Thinking

1 Pay attention to Steinbeck's description of the Salinas Valley at the beginning of the story. What pattern of imagery do you notice? How does this contribute to your understanding of Elisa's conflict?

2 What is the conflict in this story? Is it an inner conflict or an external one?

3 Elisa, like Steinbeck, is clearly attuned to the world surrounding her. What does this suggest about her character? In other words, why do you think Steinbeck chose her to be adept at growing plants rather than focusing on other occupations such as sewing or cooking?

Leslie Marmon Silko (b. 1948)

Leslie Marmon Silko grew up in Laguna, New Mexico, a town with a history of conflict between missionaries and the native inhabitants. Her own heritage is a mix of Native American, Hispanic, and Caucasian ancestry. As a young girl, Silko roamed the landscape, traversing it with her horse and her rifle. While an undergraduate at the University of New Mexico, Silko wrote and published "The Man to Send Rain Clouds," which she based on a story she had heard about a priest upset because he had not been asked to take over a Native American's funeral. Silko has been successful in a number of genres, with story collections such as *Storyteller* (1981); poetry like *Laguna Women* (1974); novels including *Ceremony* (1977) and *Almanac of the Dead* (1991); and essays as in *Yellow Woman and a Beauty of the Spirit* (1996). While Silko's subject varies, the heart of her fiction has to do with her mixed identity, her fascination with storytelling, and her reverence for the southwestern landscape and people.

The Man to Send Rain Clouds (1969)

ONE

1 They found him under a big cottonwood tree. His Levi jacket and pants were faded light-blue so that he had been easy to find. The big cottonwood tree stood apart from a small grove of winterbare cottonwoods which grew in the wide, sandy arroyo. He had been dead for a day or more, and the sheep had wandered and scattered up and down the arroyo. Leon and his brother-in-law, Ken, gathered the sheep and left them in the pen at the sheep camp before they returned to the cottonwood tree. Leon waited under the tree while Ken drove the truck through the deep sand to the edge of the arroyo. He squinted up at the sun and unzipped his jacket—it sure was hot for this time of year. But high and northwest the blue mountains were still deep in snow. Ken came sliding down the low, crumbling bank about fifty yards down, and he was bringing the red blanket.

2 Before they wrapped the old man, Leon took a piece of string out of his pocket and tied a small gray feather in the old man's long white hair. Ken gave him the paint. Across the brown wrinkled forehead he drew a streak of white and along the high cheekbones he drew a strip of blue paint. He paused and watched Ken throw pinches of corn meal and pollen into the wind that fluttered the small gray feather. Then Leon painted with yellow under the old man's broad nose, and finally, when he had painted green across the chin, he smiled.

3 "Send us rain clouds, Grandfather." They laid the bundle in the back of the pickup and covered it with with a heavy tarp before they started back to the pueblo.

4 They turned off the highway onto the sandy pueblo road. Not long after they passed the store and post office they saw Father Paul's car coming toward them. When he recognized their faces he slowed his car and

"The oral tradition stays in the human brain and then it is a collective effort in the recollection. So when he is telling a story and she is telling a story and you are telling a story and one of us is listening and there is a slightly different version or a detail, then it is participatory when somebody politely says I remember it this way. It is a collective memory and depends upon the whole community. There is no single entity that controls information or dictates but this oral tradition is a constantly self-correcting process."

—Leslie Marmon Silko (from "An Interview with Leslie Marmon Silko" by Thomas Irmer)

waved for them to stop. The young priest rolled down the car window.

5   "Did you find old Teofilo?" he asked loudly.

6   Leon stopped the truck. "Good morning, Father. We were just out to the sheep camp. Everything is O.K. now."

7   "Thank God for that. Teofilo is a very old man. You really shouldn't allow him to stay at the sheep camp alone."

8   "No, he won't do that any more now."

9   "Well, I'm glad you understand. I hope I'll be seeing you at Mass this week—we missed you last Sunday. See if you can get old Teofilo to come with you." The priest smiled and waved at them as they drove away.

TWO

10   Louise and Teresa were waiting. The table was set for lunch, and the coffee was boiling on the black iron stove. Leon looked at Louise and then at Teresa.

11   "We found him under a cottonwood tree in the big arroyo near sheep camp. I guess he sat down to rest in the shade and never got up again." Leon walked toward the old man's bed. The red plaid shawl had been shaken and spread carefully over the bed, and a new brown flannel shirt and pair of stiff new Levis were arranged neatly beside the pillow. Louise held the screen door open while Leon and Ken carried in the red blanket. He looked small and shriveled, and

after they dressed him in the new shirt and pants he seemed more shrunken.

It was noontime now because the church bells rang the Angelus. They ate the beans with hot bread, and nobody said anything until after Teresa poured the coffee.

Ken stood up and put on his jacket. "I'll see about the gravediggers. Only the top layer of soil is frozen. I think it can be ready before dark."

Leon nodded his head and finished his coffee. After Ken had been gone for a while, the neighbors and clanspeople came quietly to embrace Teofilo's family and to leave food on the table because the gravediggers would come to eat when they were finished.

THREE

The sky in the west was full of pale-yellow light. Louise stood outside with her hands in the pockets of Leon's green army jacket that was too big for her. The funeral was over, and the old men had taken their candles and medicine bags and were gone. She waited until the body was laid into the pickup before she said anything to Leon. She touched his arm, and he noticed that her hands were still dusty from the corn meal that she had sprinkled around the old man. When she spoke, Leon could not hear her.

"What did you say? I didn't hear you."

"I said that I had been thinking about something."

"About what?"

"About the priest sprinkling holy water for Grandpa. So he won't be thirsty."

Leon stared at the new moccasins that Teofilo had made for the ceremonial dances in the summer. They were nearly hidden by the red blanket. It was getting colder, and the wind pushed gray dust down the narrow pueblo road. The sun was approaching the long mesa where it disappeared during the winter. Louise stood there shivering and watching his face. Then he zipped up his jacket and opened the truck door. "I'll see if he's there."

FOUR

Ken stopped the pickup at the church, and Leon got out; and then Ken drove down the hill to the graveyard where people were waiting. Leon knocked at the old carved door with its symbols of the Lamb. While he waited he looked up at the twin bells from the king of Spain with the last sunlight pouring around them in their tower.

The priest opened the door and smiled when he saw who it was. "Come in! What brings you here this evening?"

The priest walked toward the kitchen, and Leon stood with his cap in his hand, playing with the earflaps and examining the living room—the brown sofa, the green armchair, and the brass lamp that hung down from the ceiling by links of chain. The priest dragged a chair out of the kitchen and offered it to Leon.

"No thank you, Father. I only came to ask you if you would bring your holy water to the graveyard."

The priest turned away from Leon and looked out the window at the patio full of shadows and the dining-room windows of the nuns' cloister across the patio. The curtains were heavy, and the light from within faintly penetrated; it was impossible to see the nuns inside eating supper. "Why didn't you tell me he was dead? I could have brought the Last Rites anyway."

Leon smiled. "It wasn't necessary, Father."

The priest stared down at his scuffed brown loafers and the worn hem of his cassock. "For a Christian burial it was necessary."

His voice was distant, and Leon thought that his blue eyes looked tired.

"It's O.K. Father, we just want him to have plenty of water."

The priest sank down into the green chair and picked up a glossy missionary magazine. He turned the colored pages full of lepers and pagans without looking at them.

"You know I can't do that, Leon. There should have been the Last Rites and a funeral Mass at the very least."

Leon put on his green cap and pulled the flaps down over his ears. "It's getting late, Father. I've got to go."

When Leon opened the door Father Paul stood up and said, "Wait." He left the room and came back wearing a long brown overcoat. He followed Leon out the door and across the dim churchyard to the adobe steps in front of the church. They both stooped to fit through the low adobe entrance. And when they started down the hill to the graveyard only half of the sun was visible above the mesa.

The priest approached the grave slowly, wondering how they had managed to dig into the frozen ground; and then he remembered that this was New Mexico, and saw the pile of cold loose sand beside the hole. The people stood close to each other with little clouds of steam puffing from their faces. The priest looked at them and saw a pile of jackets, gloves, and scarves in the yellow, dry tumbleweeds that grew in the graveyard. He looked at the red blanket, not sure that Teofilo was so small, wondering if it wasn't some perverse Indian trick—something they did in March to ensure a good harvest—wondering if maybe old Teofilo was actually at sheep camp corraling the sheep for the night. But there he was, facing into a cold dry wind and squinting at the last sunlight, ready to bury a red wool blanket while the faces of his parishioners were in shadow with the last warmth of the sun on their backs.

His fingers were stiff, and it took him a long time to twist the the lid off the holy water. Drops of water fell on the red blanket and soaked into dark icy spots. He sprinkled the grave and the water disappeared almost before it touched the dim, cold sand; it reminded him of something—he tried to remember what it was, because he thought if he could remember he might understand this. He sprinkled more water; he shook the container until it was empty, and the water fell through the light from sundown like August rain that fell while the sun was still shining, almost evaporating before it touched the wilted squash flowers.

36   The wind pulled at the priest's brown Franciscan robe and swirled away the corn meal and pollen that had been sprinkled on the

> He sprinkled the grave and the water disappeared almost before it touched the dim, cold sand . . .

blanket. They lowered the bundle into the ground, and they didn't bother to untie the stiff pieces of new rope that were tied around the ends of the blanket. The sun was gone, and over on the highway the eastbound lane was full of headlights. The priest walked away slowly. Leon watched him climb the hill, and when he had disappeared within the tall, thick walls, Leon turned to look up at the high blue mountains in the deep snow that reflected a faint red light from the west. He felt good because it was finished, and he was happy about the sprinkling of the holy water; now the old man could send them big thunderclouds for sure.

Questions for Critical Thinking

1 How would you describe the tone of this story? Pay particular attention to the ending. Do you read it as humorous or sad?

2 How large a part does religion play in the story? How much of the priest's actions grow from his official duties, how much from his common humanity?

3 Compare this selection with Sherman Alexie's story ("What You Pawn I Will Redeem") in chapter 14, keeping in mind that both he and Silko are prominent Native American writers. Then make a list of the main similarities and differences between the two.

4 In many places, this story makes history feel as if it bears closely on the present. Where do you see these intersections of time? You might want to begin by listing the details that make it clear the story takes place in the present.

Sylvia Watanabe (b. 1953)

One of the best of a new generation of Hawaiian writers, Sylvia Watanabe was born on the island of Maui and raised on the island of Oahu, a third-generation Japanese-American. After completing her undergraduate degree at the University of Hawaii, she began a long self-imposed exile on the American mainland—doing graduate work at the University of Michigan, marrying a literature scholar, and teaching at various colleges and universities around the country, including Oberlin College in Ohio. In her work she focuses on the region of her birth, examining matters Hawaiian and thus extending the borders of our national literature to include the islands she calls home. Her stories reflect the vital setting of her native grounds and the struggle between traditional beliefs and contemporary necessities as her characters wrestle with personal needs often opposed to the customs of the modern world.

"I first began writing because I wanted to record a way of life which I loved and which seemed in danger of dying away—as the value of island real estate rose, tourism prospered, and the prospect of unlimited development loomed in our future. I wanted to tell how the Lahaina coast looked before it was covered with resorts, how the old-time fishermen went torching at night out on the reefs, and how the iron-rich earth of the canefields smelled in the afternoon sun. I wanted to save my parents' and grandparents' stories."

—from the "Afterword" of "Talking to the Dead"

Talking to the Dead (1992)

1 WE spoke of her in whispers as Aunty Talking to the Dead, the half-Hawaiian kahuna lady. But whenever there was a death in the village, she was the first to be sent for; the priest came second. For it was she who understood the wholeness of things—the significance of directions and colors. Prayers to appease the hungry ghosts. Elixirs for grief. Most times, she'd be out on her front porch, already waiting—her boy, Clinton, standing behind with her basket of spells—when the messenger arrived. People said she could smell a death from clear on the other side of the island, even as the dying person breathed his last. And if she fixed her eyes on you and named a day, you were already as good as six feet under.

2 I went to work as her apprentice when I was eighteen. That was in '48, the year Clinton graduated from mortician school on the GI bill. It was the talk for weeks—how he'd returned to open the Paradise Mortuary in the heart of the village and had bought the scientific spirit of free enterprise to the doorstep of the hereafter. I remember the advertisements for the Grand Opening, promising to modernize the funeral trade with Lifelike Artistic Techniques and Stringent Standards of Sanitation. The old woman, who had waited out the war for her son's return, stoically took his defection in stride and began looking for someone else to help out with her business.

3 At the time, I didn't have many prospects—more schooling didn't interest me, and my mother's attempts at marrying me off inevitably failed when I stood to shake hands with a prospective bridegroom and ended up towering a foot above him. "It would be bad enough if she just looked like a horse," I heard one of them complain, "but she's as big as one, too."

4 My mother dressed me in navy blue, on the theory that dark colors make things look less conspicuous. "Yuri, sit down," she'd hiss, tugging at my skirt as the decisive moment approached. I'd nod, sip my tea, smile through the introductions and small talk, till the time came for sealing the bargain with handshakes. Then, nothing on earth could keep me from

getting to my feet. The go-between finally suggested that I consider taking up a trade. "After all, marriage isn't for everyone," she said. My mother said that that was a fact which remained to be proven, but meanwhile it wouldn't hurt if I took in sewing or learned to cut hair. I made up my mind to apprentice myself to Aunty Talking to the Dead.

5   The old woman's house was on the hill behind the village, just off the road to Chicken Fight Camp. She lived in an old plantation worker's bungalow with peeling green and white paint and a large, well-tended garden—mostly of flowering bushes and strong-smelling herbs.

6   "Aren't you a big one," a voice behind me said.

7   I started, then turned. It was the first time I had ever seen her up close.

8   "Hello, uh, Mrs. Dead," I stammered.

9   She was little, way under five feet, and wrinkled. Everything about her seemed the same color—her skin, her lips, her dress. Everything was just a slightly different shade of the same brown-gray, except her hair, which was absolutely white, and her tiny eyes, which glinted like metal. For a minute those eyes looked me up and down.

10   "Here," she said finally, thrusting an empty rice sack into my hands. "For collecting salt." Then she started down the road to the beach.

11   IN the next few months we walked every inch of the hills and beaches around the village, and then some. I struggled behind, laden with strips of bark and leafy twigs, while Aunty marched three steps ahead, chanting. "This is *a'ali'i* to bring sleep—it must be dried in the shade on a hot day. This is *noni* for the heart, and *awa* for every kind of grief. This is *uhaloa* with the deep roots. If you are like that, death cannot easily take you."

12   "This is where you gather salt to preserve a corpse," I hear her still. "This is where you cut to insert the salt." Her words marked the places on my body, one by one.

13   That whole first year, not a day passed when I didn't think of quitting. I tried to figure out a way of moving back home without making it seem like I was admitting anything.

"You know what people are saying, don't you?" my mother said, lifting the lid of the bamboo steamer and setting a tray of freshly steamed meat buns on the already crowded table before me. It was one of my few visits since my apprenticeship, though I'd never been more than a couple of miles away, and she had stayed up the whole night before, cooking. She'd prepared a canned ham with yellow sweet potatoes, wing beans with pork, sweet and sour mustard cabbage, fresh raw yellowfin, pickled eggplant, and rice with red beans. I had not seen so much food since the night she tried to persuade Uncle Mongoose not to volunteer for the army. He went anyway, and on the last day of training, just before he was to be shipped to Italy, he shot himself in the head while cleaning his gun. "I always knew that boy would come to no good," was all Mama said when she heard the news.

"What do you mean you can't eat another bite?" she fussed now. "Look at you, nothing but a bag of bones."

The truth was, there didn't seem to be much of a future in my apprenticeship. In eleven and a half months I had memorized most of the minor rituals of mourning and learned to identify a couple of dozen herbs and all their medicinal uses, but I had not seen, much less gotten to practice on, a single honest-to-goodness corpse. "People live longer these days," Aunty claimed.

But I knew it was because everyone, even from villages across the bay, had begun taking their business to the Paradise Mortuary. The single event that had established Clinton's monopoly was the untimely death of old Mrs. Parmeter, the plantation owner's mother-in-law, who'd choked on a fishbone in the salmon mousse during a fund-raising luncheon for Famine Relief. Clinton had been chosen to be in charge of the funeral. After that, he'd taken to wearing three-piece suits, as a symbol of his new respectability, and was nominated as a Republican candidate for the village council.

"So, what are people saying?" I asked, finally pushing my plate away.

This was the cue that Mama had been waiting for. "They're saying That Woman has gotten herself a pet donkey, though that's not the word they're using, of course." She paused dramatically; the implication was clear.

I began remembering things about living in my mother's house. The navy-blue dresses. The humiliating weekly tea ceremony lessons at the Buddhist temple.

"Give up this foolishness," she wheedled. "Mrs. Koyama tells me the Barber Shop Lady is looking for help."

"I think I'll stay right where I am," I said.

My mother fell silent. Then she jabbed a meat bun with her serving fork and lifted it onto my plate. "Here, have another helping," she said.

A FEW weeks later Aunty and I were called outside the village to perform a laying-out. It was early afternoon when Sheriff Kanoi came by to tell us that the body of Mustard Hayashi, the eldest of the Hayashi boys, had just been pulled from an irrigation ditch by a team of field workers. He had apparently fallen in the night before, stone drunk, on his way home from the La Hula Rumba Bar and Grill.

I began hurrying around, assembling Aunty's tools and potions, and checking that everything was in working order, but the old woman didn't turn a hair; she just sat calmly rocking back and forth and puffing on her skinny, long-stemmed pipe.

"Yuri, you stop that rattling around back there," she snapped, then turned to the sheriff. "My son Clinton could probably handle this. Why don't you ask him?"

Sheriff Kanoi hesitated before replying, "This looks like a tough case that's going to need some real expertise."

Aunty stopped rocking. "That's true, it was a bad death," she mused.

"Very bad," the sheriff agreed.

"The spirit is going to require some talking to," she continued. "You know, so it doesn't linger."

"And the family asked especially for you," he added.

No doubt because they didn't have any other choice, I thought. That morning, I'd run into Chinky Malloy, the assistant mortician at the Paradise, so I happened to know that Clinton was at a morticians' conference in Los Angeles and wouldn't be back for several days. But I didn't say a word.

When we arrived at the Hayashis', Mustard's body was lying on the green Formica table in the kitchen. It was the only room in the house with a door that faced north. Aunty claimed that a proper laying-out required a room with a north-facing door, so the spirit could find its way home to the land of the dead without getting lost.

Mustard's mother was leaning over his corpse, wailing, and her husband stood behind her, looking white-faced, and absently patting her on the back. The tiny kitchen was jammed with sobbing, nose-blowing mourners, and the air was thick with the smells of grief—perspiration, ladies' cologne, the previous night's cooking, and the faintest whiff of putrefying flesh. Aunty gripped me by the wrist and pushed her way to the front. The air pressed close, like someone's hot, wet breath on my face. My head reeled, and the room broke apart into dots of color. From far away I heard somebody say, "It's Aunty Talking to the Dead."

"Make room, make room," another voice called.

I looked down at Mustard, lying on the table in front of me, his eyes half open in that swollen, purple face. The smell was much stronger close up, and there were flies everywhere.

"We'll have to get rid of some of this bloat," Aunty said, thrusting a metal object into my hand.

People were leaving the room.

She went around to the other side of the table. "I'll start here," she said. "You work over there. Do just like I told you."

I nodded. This was the long-awaited moment. My moment. But it was already the beginning of the end. My knees buckled, and everything went dark.

Aunty performed the laying-out alone and never mentioned the episode again. But it was talk of the village for weeks—how Yuri Shimabukuro, assistant to Aunty Talking to the Dead, passed out under the Hayashis' kitchen table and had to be tended by the grief-stricken mother of the dead boy.

My mother took to catching the bus to the plantation store three villages away whenever she needed to stock up on necessaries. "You're my daughter—how could I *not* be on your side?" was the way she put it, but the air buzzed with her unspoken recriminations. And whenever I went into the village, I was aware of the sly laughter behind my back, and Chinky Malloy smirking at me from behind the shutters of the Paradise Mortuary.

43   SHE'S giving the business a bad name," Clinton said, carefully removing his jacket and draping it across the back of the rickety wooden chair. He dusted the seat, looked at his hand with distaste before wiping it off on his handkerchief, then drew up the legs of his trousers, and sat.

44   Aunty retrieved her pipe from the smoking tray next to her rocker and filled the tiny brass bowl from a pouch of Bull Durham. "I'm glad you found time to drop by," she said. "You still going out with that skinny white girl?"

45   "You mean Marsha?" Clinton sounded defensive. "Sure, I see her sometimes. But I didn't come here to talk about that." He glanced over at where I was sitting on the sofa. "You think we could have some privacy?"

46   Aunty lit her pipe and puffed. "Yuri's my right-hand girl. Couldn't do without her."

47   "The Hayashis probably have their own opinion about that."

48   Aunty dismissed his insinuation with a wave of her hand. "There's no pleasing some people," she said. "Yuri's just young; she'll learn." She reached over and patted me on the knee, then looked him straight in the face. "Like we all did."

49   Clinton turned red. "Damn it, Mama," he sputtered, "this is no time to bring up the past. What counts is now, and right now your right-hand girl is turning you into a laughingstock!" His voice became soft, persuasive. "Look, you've worked hard all your life, and you deserve to retire. Now that my business is taking off, I can help you out. You know I'm only thinking about you."

50   "About the election to village council, you mean." I couldn't help it; the words just burst out of my mouth.

51   Aunty said, "You considering going into politics, son?"

52   "Mama, wake up!" Clinton hollered, like he'd wanted to all along. "You can talk to the dead till you're blue in the face, but *ain't no one listening*. The old ghosts have had it. You either get on the wheel of progress or you get run over."

53   For a long time after he left, Aunty sat in her rocking chair next to the window, rocking and smoking, without saying a word, just rocking and smoking, as the afternoon shadows spread beneath the trees and turned to night.

54   Then she began to sing—quietly, at first, but very sure. She sang the naming chants and the healing chants. She sang the stones, and trees, and stars back into their rightful places. Louder and louder she sang, making whole what had been broken.

EVERYTHING changed for me after Clinton's visit. I stopped going into the village and began spending all my time with Aunty Talking to the Dead. I followed her everywhere, carried her loads without complaint, memorized remedies, and mixed potions till my head spun and I went near blind. I wanted to know what *she* knew; I wanted to make what had happened at the Hayashis' go away. Not just in other people's minds. Not just because I'd become a laughingstock, like Clinton said. But because I knew that I had to redeem myself for that one thing, or my moment—the single instant of glory for which I had lived my entire life—would be snatched beyond my reach forever.

   Meanwhile, there were other layings-out. The kitemaker who hanged himself. The crippled boy from Chicken Fight Camp. The Vagrant. The Blindman. The Blindman's dog.

   "Do like I told you," Aunty would say before each one. Then, "Give it time," when it was done.

   But it was like living the same nightmare over and over—just one look at a body and I was done for. For twenty-five years, people in the village joked about my "indisposition." Last fall, my mother's funeral was held at the Paradise Mortuary. While the service was going on, I stood outside on the cement walk for a long time, but I never made it through the door. Little by little, I'd begun to give up hope that my moment would ever arrive.

   Then, a week ago, Aunty caught a chill, gathering *awa* in the rain. The chill developed into a fever, and for the first time since I'd known her, she took to her bed. I nursed her with the remedies she'd taught me—sweat baths; eucalyptus steam; tea made from *ko'oko'olau*—but the fever worsened. Her breathing became labored, and she grew weaker. My few hours of sleep were filled with bad dreams. Finally, aware of my betrayal, I walked to a house up the road and telephoned for an ambulance.

   "I'm sorry, Aunty," I kept saying, as the flashing red light swept across the porch. The attendants had her on a stretcher and were carrying her out the front door.

   She reached up and grasped my arm, her grip still strong. "You'll do okay, Yuri," the old woman whispered hoarsely. "Clinton used to get so scared, he messed his pants." She chuckled, then began to cough. One of the

> "You can talk to the dead till you're blue in the face, but *ain't no one listening. . . ."*

attendants put an oxygen mask over her face. "Hush," he said. "There'll be plenty of time for talking later."

ON the day of Aunty's wake, the entrance to the Paradise Mortuary was blocked. Workmen had dug up the front walk and carted the old concrete tiles away. They'd left a mound of gravel on the grass, stacked some bags of concrete next to it, and covered the bags with black tarps. There was an empty wheelbarrow parked to one side of the gravel mound. The entire front lawn had been roped off and a sign had been put up that said, "Please follow the arrows around to the back. We are making improvements in Paradise. The Management."

My stomach was beginning to play tricks, and I was feeling shaky. The old panic was mingled with an uneasiness which had not left me ever since I'd decided to call the ambulance. I kept thinking that it had been useless to call it since she'd gone and died anyway. Or maybe I had waited too long. I almost turned back, but I thought of what Aunty had told me about Clinton and pressed ahead. Numbly, I followed the two women in front of me.

"So, old Aunty Talking to the Dead has finally passed on," one of them, whom I recognized as Emi McAllister, said. She was with Pearlie Woo. Both were old classmates of mine.

I was having difficulty seeing—it was getting dark, and my head was spinning so.

"How old do you suppose she was?" Pearlie asked.

"Gosh, even when we were kids it seemed like she was at least a hundred," Emi said.

Pearlie laughed. "'The Undead,' my brother used to call her."

"When we misbehaved," Emi said, "our mother always threatened to abandon us on the hill where Aunty lived. Mama would be beating us with a wooden spoon and hollering, 'This is gonna seem like nothing then.'"

Aunty had been laid out in a room near the center of the mortuary. The heavy, wine-colored drapes had been drawn across the windows and all the wall lamps turned very low, so it was darker indoors than it had been outside. Pearlie and Emi moved off into the front row. I headed for the back.

There were about thirty of us at the viewing, mostly from the old days—those who had grown up on stories about Aunty, or who remembered her from before the Paradise Mortuary. People got up and began filing past the casket. For a moment I felt dizzy again, but I glanced over at Clinton, looking prosperous and self-assured, accepting condolences, and I got into line.

The room was air conditioned and smelled of floor disinfectant and roses. Soft music came from speakers mounted on the walls. I drew nearer and nearer to the casket. Now there were four people ahead. Now three. I looked down at my feet, and I thought I would faint.

Then Pearlie Woo shrieked, "Her eyes!" People behind me began to murmur. "What—whose eyes?" Emi demanded. Pearlie pointed to the body in the casket. Emi cried, "My God, they're open!"

My heart turned to ice.

"What?" voices behind me were asking. "What about her eyes?"

"She said they're open," someone said.

"Aunty Talking to the Dead's eyes are open," someone else said.

Now Clinton was hurrying over.

"That's because she's not dead," still another voice added.

Clinton looked into the coffin, and his face went white. He turned quickly around and waved to his assistants across the room.

"I've heard about cases like this," someone was saying. "It's because she's looking for someone."

"I've heard that too! The old woman is trying to tell us something."

I was the only one there who knew. Aunty was talking to *me*. I clasped my hands together, hard, but they wouldn't stop shaking.

People began leaving the line. Others pressed in, trying to get a better look at the body, but a couple of Clinton's assistants had stationed themselves in front

of the coffin, preventing anyone from getting too close. They had shut the lid, and Chinky Malloy was directing people out of the room.

85   "I'd like to take this opportunity to thank you all for coming here this evening," Clinton was saying. "I hope you will join us at the reception down the hall."

86   WHILE everyone was eating, I stole back into the parlor and quietly—ever so quietly—went up to the casket, lifted the lid, and looked in.

87   At first I thought they had switched bodies on me and exchanged Aunty for some powdered and painted old grandmother, all pink and white, in a pink dress, and clutching a white rose to her chest. But there they were. Open. Aunty's eyes staring up at me.

88   Then I knew. This was *it*: my moment had arrived. Aunty Talking to the Dead had come awake to bear me witness.

89   I walked through the deserted front rooms of the mortuary and out the front door. It was night. I got the wheelbarrow, loaded it with one of the tarps covering the bags of cement, and wheeled it back to the room where Aunty was. It squeaked terribly, and I stopped often to make sure no one had heard. From the back of the building came the clink of glassware and the buzz of voices. I had to work quickly—people would be leaving soon.

> ## Then I knew.
> ## This was *it:* my moment
> ## had arrived.

But this was the hardest part. Small as she was, it was very hard to lift her out of the coffin. She was horribly heavy, and unyielding as a bag of cement. I finally got her out and wrapped her in the tarp. I loaded her in the tray of the wheelbarrow—most of her, anyway; there was nothing I could do about her feet sticking out the front end. Then I wheeled her out of the mortuary, across the village square, and up the road, home.

NOW, in the dark, the old woman is singing. I have washed her with my own hands and worked the salt into the hollows of her body. I have dressed her in white and laid her in flowers.

Aunty, here are the beads you like to wear. Your favorite cakes. A quilt to keep away the chill. Here is *noni* for the heart and *awa* for every kind of grief.

Down the road a dog howls, and the sound of hammering echoes through the still air. "Looks like a burying tomorrow," the sleepers murmur, turning in their warm beds.

I bind the sandals to her feet and put the torch to the pyre.

The sky turns to light. The smoke climbs. Her ashes scatter, filling the wind.

And she sings, she sings, she sings.

Questions for Critical Thinking

1 How does the location affect the characters in "Talking to the Dead"? Can you imagine this story taking place in the village, town, or city where you grew up? If so, how would it remain the same and how would it differ?

2 Note references in the story to a belief in the supernatural. Does the author appear to endorse these views or merely to describe them?

3 Do you agree with the statement "Island cultures are slow to change in comparison with a mainland culture"? Support your answer with examples from the text.

The American South

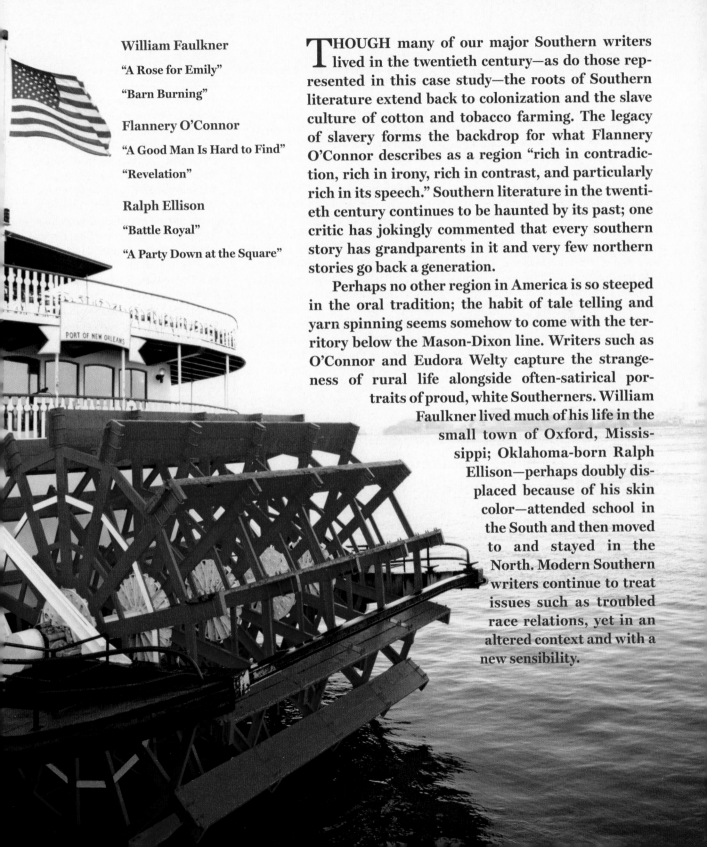

William Faulkner

"A Rose for Emily"

"Barn Burning"

Flannery O'Connor

"A Good Man Is Hard to Find"

"Revelation"

Ralph Ellison

"Battle Royal"

"A Party Down at the Square"

THOUGH many of our major Southern writers lived in the twentieth century—as do those represented in this case study—the roots of Southern literature extend back to colonization and the slave culture of cotton and tobacco farming. The legacy of slavery forms the backdrop for what Flannery O'Connor describes as a region "rich in contradiction, rich in irony, rich in contrast, and particularly rich in its speech." Southern literature in the twentieth century continues to be haunted by its past; one critic has jokingly commented that every southern story has grandparents in it and very few northern stories go back a generation.

Perhaps no other region in America is so steeped in the oral tradition; the habit of tale telling and yarn spinning seems somehow to come with the territory below the Mason-Dixon line. Writers such as O'Connor and Eudora Welty capture the strangeness of rural life alongside often-satirical portraits of proud, white Southerners. William Faulkner lived much of his life in the small town of Oxford, Mississippi; Oklahoma-born Ralph Ellison—perhaps doubly displaced because of his skin color—attended school in the South and then moved to and stayed in the North. Modern Southern writers continue to treat issues such as troubled race relations, yet in an altered context and with a new sensibility.

William Faulkner (1897–1962)

Many of his best-known American contemporaries chose to travel abroad and live as, at least briefly, "expatriates." But William Faulkner lived and wrote in the region in which he was raised. Born in New Albany, Mississippi, he grew up in Oxford, Mississippi, and ultimately settled there. Ten years after dropping out of high school, Faulkner forged a friendship with Sherwood Anderson, who not only helped find a publisher for Faulkner's first novel but also encouraged the young Mississippi writer to take for his subject the people and places of his own life. Consequently, Faulkner wrote about the American South as someone deeply invested in its history and future as well as in its particular language and regional tradition. Much of Faulkner's fiction— including novels such as *The Sound and the Fury* (1929), *As I Lay Dying* (1930), *Absalom, Absalom!* (1936), and *The Unvanquished* (1938)—describes the lives of families in the fictional Yoknapatawpha County, which Faulkner modeled on his own surroundings. He went so far as to draw a map of this imaginary place and call himself "the sole proprietor" of the landscape and region described.

Faulkner is known for his innovative use of language. Many of his characters have no formal education, but they speak and think in a highly stylized English that (although it may not accurately reflect the way people actually converse) gives them a consistent lyric authenticity. In much of his fiction, Faulkner uses the literary technique known as *stream-of-consciousness,* which seeks to capture the disorganized and fleeting way one thought leads to another; we as readers *overhear* the private and unspoken discourse within a character's mind. In both his stories and his novels, Faulkner chronicles the saga of the post–Civil War South, exploring themes of justice, honor, family, racial prejudice, insanity, and decay in a damaged and changing world. Often his characters are troubled; some of them are suicidal, others, crazed. But his final assertions are hopeful, and he laces his books with humor throughout. He was awarded the Nobel Prize in Literature in 1949 "for his powerful and artistically unique contribution to the modern American novel." In his acceptance speech, Faulkner famously declared, "I believe that man will not merely endure: he will prevail."

"I decline to accept the end of man. It is easy enough to say that man is immortal simply because he will endure: that when the last dingdong of doom has clanged and faded from the last worthless rock hanging tideless in the last red and dying evening, that even then there will still be one more sound: that of his puny inexhaustible voice, still talking. I refuse to accept this. I believe that man will not merely endure: he will prevail. He is immortal, not because he alone among creatures has an inexhaustible voice, but because he has a soul, a spirit capable of compassion and sacrifice and endurance. The poet's, the writer's, duty is to write about these things. It is his privilege to help man endure by lifting his heart, by reminding him of the courage and honor and hope and pride and compassion and pity and sacrifice which have been the glory of his past. The poet's voice need not merely be the record of man, it can be one of the props, the pillars to help him endure and prevail." —William Faulkner, speech at the Nobel Banquet at the City Hall in Stockholm, 1949

A Rose for Emily (1932)

I

1 When Miss Emily Grierson died, our whole town went to her funeral: the men through a sort of respectful affection for a fallen monument, the women mostly out of curiosity to see the inside of her house, which no one save an old manservant—a combined gardener and cook—had seen in at least ten years.

2 It was a big, squarish frame house that had once been white, decorated with cupolas and spires and scrolled balconies in the heavily lightsome style of the seventies, set on what had once been our most select street. But garages and cotton gins had encroached and obliterated even the august names of that neighborhood; only Miss Emily's house was left, lifting its stubborn and coquettish decay above the cotton wagons and the gasoline pumps—an eyesore among eyesores. And now Miss Emily had gone to join the representatives of those august names where they lay in the cedar-bemused cemetery among the ranked and anonymous graves of Union and Confederate soldiers who fell at the battle of Jefferson.

3 Alive, Miss Emily had been a tradition, a duty, and a care; a sort of hereditary obligation upon the town, dating from that day in 1894 when Colonel Sartoris, the mayor—he who fathered the edict that no Negro woman should appear on the streets without an apron—remitted her taxes, the dispensation dating from the death of her father on into perpetuity. Not that Miss Emily would have accepted charity. Colonel Sartoris invented an involved tale to the effect that Miss Emily's father had loaned money to the town, which the town, as a matter of business, preferred this way of repaying. Only a man of Colonel Sartoris' generation and thought could have invented it, and only a woman could have believed it.

4 When the next generation, with its more modern ideas, became mayors and aldermen, this arrangement created some little dissatisfaction. On the first of the year they mailed her a tax notice. February came, and there was no reply. They wrote her a formal letter, asking her to call at the sheriff's office at her convenience. A week later the mayor wrote her himself, offering to call or to send his car for her, and received in reply a note on paper of an archaic shape, in a thin, flowing calligraphy in faded ink, to the effect that she no longer went out at all. The tax notice was also enclosed, without comment.

5 They called a special meeting of the Board of Aldermen. A deputation waited upon her, knocked at the door through which no visitor had passed since she ceased giving china-painting lessons eight or ten years earlier. They were admitted by the old Negro into a dim hall from which a stairway mounted into still more shadow. It smelled of dust and disuse—a close, dank smell. The Negro led them into the parlor. It was furnished in heavy, leather-covered furniture. When the Negro opened the blinds of one window, they could see that the leather was cracked; and when they sat down, a faint dust rose sluggishly about their thighs, spinning with slow motes in the single sun-ray. On a tarnished gilt easel before the fireplace stood a crayon portrait of Miss Emily's father.

6 They rose when she entered—a small, fat woman in black, with a thin gold chain descending to her waist and vanishing into her belt, leaning on an ebony cane with a tarnished gold head. Her skeleton was small and spare; perhaps that was why what would have been merely plumpness in another was obesity in her. She looked bloated, like a body long submerged in motionless water, and of that pallid hue. Her eyes, lost in the fatty ridges of her face, looked like two small pieces of coal pressed into a lump of dough as they moved from one face to another while the visitors stated their errand.

7 She did not ask them to sit. She just stood in the door and listened quietly until the spokesman came to a stumbling halt. Then they could hear the invisible watch ticking at the end of the gold chain.

8 Her voice was dry and cold. "I have no taxes in Jefferson. Colonel Sartoris explained

it to me. Perhaps one of you can gain access to the city records and satisfy yourselves."

9   "But we have. We are the city authorities, Miss Emily. Didn't you get a notice from the sheriff, signed by him?"

10   "I received a paper, yes," Miss Emily said. "Perhaps he considers himself the sheriff . . . I have no taxes in Jefferson."

11   "But there is nothing on the books to show that, you see. We must go by the—"

12   "See Colonel Sartoris. I have no taxes in Jefferson."

13   "But, Miss Emily—"

14   "See Colonel Sartoris." (Colonel Sartoris had been dead almost ten years.) "I have no taxes in Jefferson. Tobe!" The Negro appeared. "Show these gentlemen out."

II

15   So she vanquished them, horse and foot, just as she had vanquished their fathers thirty years before about the smell. That was two years after her father's death and a short time after her sweetheart—the one we believed would marry her—had deserted her. After her father's death she went out very little; after her sweetheart went away, people hardly saw her at all. A few of the ladies had the temerity to call, but were not received, and the only sign of life about the place was the Negro man—a young man then—going in and out with a market basket.

16   "Just as if a man—any man—could keep a kitchen properly," the ladies said; so they were not surprised when the smell developed. It was another link between the gross, teeming world and the high and mighty Griersons.

17   A neighbor, a woman, complained to the mayor, Judge Stevens, eighty years old.

18   "But what will you have me do about it, madam?" he said.

19   "Why, send her word to stop it," the woman said. "Isn't there a law?"

20   "I'm sure that won't be necessary," Judge Stevens said. "It's probably just a snake or a rat that nigger of hers killed in the yard. I'll speak to him about it."

21   The next day he received two more complaints, one from a man who came in diffident deprecation. "We really must do something about it, Judge. I'd be the last one in the world to bother Miss Emily, but we've got to do something." That night the Board of Aldermen met—three graybeards and one younger man, a member of the rising generation.

"It's simple enough," he said. "Send her word to have her place cleaned up. Give her a certain time to do it in, and if she don't . . ."

"Dammit, sir," Judge Stevens said, "will you accuse a lady to her face of smelling bad?"

So the next night, after midnight, four men crossed Miss Emily's lawn and slunk about the house like burglars, sniffing along the base of the brickwork and at the cellar openings while one of them performed a regular sowing motion with his hand out of a sack slung from his shoulder. They broke open the cellar door and sprinkled lime there, and in all the outbuildings. As they recrossed the lawn, a window that had been dark was lighted and Miss Emily sat in it, the light behind her, and her upright torso motionless as that of an idol. They crept quietly across the lawn and into the shadow of the locusts that lined the street. After a week or two the smell went away.

That was when people had begun to feel really sorry for her. People in our town, remembering how old lady Wyatt, her great-aunt, had gone completely crazy at last, believed that the Griersons held themselves a little too high for what they really were. None of the young men were quite good enough for Miss Emily and such. We had long thought of them as a tableau, Miss Emily a slender figure in white in the background, her father a spraddled silhouette in the foreground, his back to her and clutching a horsewhip, the two of them framed by the back-flung front door. So when she got to be thirty and was still single, we were not pleased exactly, but vindicated; even with insanity in the family she wouldn't have turned down all of her chances if they had really materialized.

When her father died, it got about that the house was all that was left to her; and in a way, people were glad. At last they could pity Miss Emily. Being left alone, and a pauper, she had become humanized. Now she too would know the old thrill and the old despair of a penny more or less.

The day after his death all the ladies prepared to call at the house and offer condolence and aid, as is our custom. Miss Emily met them at the door, dressed as usual and with no trace of grief on her face. She told them that her father was not dead. She did that for three days, with the ministers calling on her, and the doctors, trying to persuade her to let them dispose of the body. Just as they were about to resort to law and force, she broke down, and they buried her father quickly.

> None of the young men were quite good enough for Miss Emily and such.

We did not say she was crazy then. We believed she had to do that. We remembered all the young men her father had driven away, and we knew that with nothing left, she would have to cling to that which had robbed her, as people will.

III

She was sick for a long time. When we saw her again, her hair was cut short, making her look like a girl, with a vague resemblance to those angels in colored church windows—sort of tragic and serene.

The town had just let the contracts for paving the sidewalks, and in the summer after her father's death they began the work. The construction company came with niggers and mules and machinery, and a foreman named Homer Barron, a Yankee—a big, dark, ready man, with a big voice and eyes lighter than his face. The little boys would follow in groups to hear him cuss the niggers, and the niggers singing in time to the rise and fall of picks. Pretty soon he knew everybody in town. Whenever you heard a lot of laughing anywhere about the square, Homer Barron would be in the center of the group. Presently, we began to see him and Miss Emily on Sunday afternoons driving in the yellow-wheeled buggy and the matched team of bays from the livery stable.

At first we were glad that Miss Emily would have an interest, because the ladies all said, "Of course a Grierson would not think seriously of a Northerner, a day laborer." But there were still others, older people, who said that even grief could not cause a real lady to forget *noblesse oblige*[1]—without calling it *noblesse oblige*. They just said, "Poor Emily. Her kinsfolk should come to her." She had some kin in Alabama; but years ago her father had fallen out with them over the estate of old lady Wyatt, the crazy woman, and there was no communication between the two families. They had not even been represented at the funeral.

And as soon as the old people said, "Poor Emily," the whispering began. "Do you suppose it's really so?" they said to one another. "Of course it is. What else could. . . ." This behind their hands; rustling of craned silk and satin behind jalousies closed upon the sun of Sunday afternoon as the thin, swift clop-clop-clop of the matched team passed: "Poor Emily."

She carried her head high enough—even when we believed that she was fallen. It was as if she demanded more than ever the recognition of her dignity as the

---

[1]French: a term used to describe the obligations and responsibilities of a member of the upper class.

last Grierson; as if it had wanted that touch of earthiness to reaffirm her imperviousness. Like when she bought the rat poison, the arsenic. That was over a year after they had begun to say "Poor Emily," and while the two female cousins were visiting her.

"I want some poison," she said to the druggist. 34 She was over thirty then, still a slight woman, though thinner than usual, with cold, haughty black eyes in a face the flesh of which was strained across the temples and about the eye-sockets as you imagine a lighthouse-keeper's face ought to look. "I want some poison," she said.

"Yes, Miss Emily. What kind? For rats and such? 35 I'd recom—"

"I want the best you have. I don't care what kind." 36

The druggist named several. "They'll kill any- 37 thing up to an elephant. But what you want is—"

"Arsenic," Miss Emily said. "Is that a good one?" 38

"Is . . . arsenic? Yes, ma'am. But what you want—" 39

"I want arsenic." 40

The druggist looked down at her. She looked back 41 at him, erect, her face like a strained flag. "Why, of course," the druggist said. "If that's what you want. But the law requires you to tell what you are going to use it for."

Miss Emily just stared at him, her head tilted back 42 in order to look him eye for eye, until he looked away and went and got the arsenic and wrapped it up. The Negro delivery boy brought her the package; the druggist didn't come back. When she opened the package at home there was written on the box, under the skull and bones: "For rats."

IV

So the next day we all said, "She will kill herself"; and 43 we said it would be the best thing. When she had first begun to be seen with Homer Barron, we had said, "She will marry him." Then we said, "She will persuade him yet," because Homer himself had remarked—he liked men, and it was known that he drank with the younger men in the Elks' Club—that he was not a marrying man. Later we said, "Poor Emily," behind the jalousies as they passed on Sunday afternoon in the glittering buggy, Miss Emily with her head high and Homer Barron with his hat cocked and a cigar in his teeth, reins and whip in a yellow glove.

Then some of the ladies began to say that it was a 44 disgrace to the town and a bad example to the young people. The men did not want to interfere, but at last the ladies forced the Baptist minister—Miss Emily's people were Episcopal—to call upon her. He would never divulge what happened during that interview, but he refused to go back again. The next Sunday they again drove about the streets, and the following day the minister's wife wrote to Miss Emily's relations in Alabama.

45   So she had blood-kin under her roof again and we sat back to watch developments. At first nothing happened. Then we were sure that they were to be married. We learned that Miss Emily had been to the jeweler's and ordered a man's toilet set in silver, with the letters H.B. on each piece. Two days later we learned that she had bought a complete outfit of men's clothing, including a nightshirt, and we said, "They are married." We were really glad. We were glad because the two female cousins were even more Grierson than Miss Emily had ever been.

46   So we were not surprised when Homer Barron—the streets had been finished some time since—was gone. We were a little disappointed that there was not a public blowing-off, but we believed that he had gone on to prepare for Miss Emily's coming, or to give her a chance to get rid of the cousins. (By that time it was a cabal, and we were all Miss Emily's allies to help circumvent the cousins.) Sure enough, after another week they departed. And, as we had expected all along, within three days Homer Barron was back in town. A neighbor saw the Negro man admit him at the kitchen door at dusk one evening.

47   And that was the last we saw of Homer Barron. And of Miss Emily for some time. The Negro man went in and out with the market basket, but the front door remained closed. Now and then we would see her at a window for a moment, as the men did that night when they sprinkled the lime, but for almost six months she did not appear on the streets. Then we knew that this was to be expected too; as if that quality of her father which had thwarted her woman's life so many times had been too virulent and too furious to die.

48   When we next saw Miss Emily, she had grown fat and her hair was turning gray. During the next few years it grew grayer and grayer until it attained an even pepper-and-salt iron-gray, when it ceased turning. Up to the day of her death at seventy-four it was still that vigorous iron-gray, like the hair of an active man.

49   From that time on her front door remained closed, save for a period of six or seven years, when she was about forty, during which she gave lessons in china-painting. She fitted up a studio in one of the downstairs rooms, where the daughters and granddaughters of Colonel Sartoris' contemporaries were

> **A thin, acrid pall as of the tomb** seemed to lie everywhere upon this room decked and furnished as for a bridal . . .

sent to her with the same regularity and in the same spirit that they were sent to church on Sundays with a twenty-five-cent piece for the collection plate. Meanwhile her taxes had been remitted.

Then the newer generation became the backbone and the spirit of the town, and the painting pupils grew up and fell away and did not send their children to her with boxes of color and tedious brushes and pictures cut from the ladies' magazines. The front door closed upon the last one and remained closed for good. When the town got free postal delivery, Miss Emily alone refused to let them fasten the metal numbers above her door and attach a mailbox to it. She would not listen to them.

Daily, monthly, yearly we watched the Negro grow grayer and more stooped, going in and out with the market basket. Each December we sent her a tax notice, which would be returned by the post office a week later, unclaimed. Now and then we would see her in one of the downstairs windows—she had evidently shut up the top floor of the house—like the carven torso of an idol in a niche, looking or not looking at us, we could never tell which. Thus she passed from generation to generation—dear, inescapable, impervious, tranquil, and perverse.

And so she died. Fell ill in the house filled with dust and shadows, with only a doddering Negro man to wait on her. We did not even know she was sick; we had long since given up trying to get any information from the Negro. He talked to no one, probably not even to her, for his voice had grown harsh and rusty, as if from disuse.

She died in one of the downstairs rooms, in a heavy walnut bed with a curtain, her gray head propped on a pillow yellow and moldy with age and lack of sunlight.

V

The Negro met the first of the ladies at the front door and let them in, with their hushed, sibilant voices and their quick, curious glances, and then he disappeared. He walked right through the house and out the back and was not seen again.

The two female cousins came at once. They held the funeral on the second day, with the town coming to look at Miss Emily beneath a mass of bought flowers, with the crayon face of her father musing profoundly above the bier and the ladies sibilant and macabre;

and the very old men—some in their brushed Confederate uniforms—on the porch and the lawn, talking of Miss Emily as if she had been a contemporary of theirs, believing that they had danced with her and courted her perhaps, confusing time with its mathematical progression, as the old do, to whom all the past is not a diminishing road but, instead, a huge meadow which no winter ever quite touches, divided from them now by the narrow bottleneck of the most recent decade of years.

Already we knew that there was one room in that region above stairs which no one had seen in forty years, and which would have to be forced. They waited until Miss Emily was decently in the ground before they opened it.

The violence of breaking down the door seemed to fill this room with pervading dust. A thin, acrid pall as of the tomb seemed to lie everywhere upon this room decked and furnished as for a bridal: upon the valance curtains of faded rose color, upon the rose-shaded lights, upon the dressing table, upon the delicate array of crystal and the man's toilet things backed with tarnished silver, silver so tarnished that the monogram was obscured. Among them lay collar and tie, as if they had just been removed, which, lifted, left upon the surface a pale crescent in the dust. Upon a chair hung the suit, carefully folded; beneath it the two mute shoes and the discarded socks.

The man himself lay in the bed.

For a long while we just stood there, looking down at the profound and fleshless grin. The body had apparently once lain in the attitude of an embrace, but now the long sleep that outlasts love, that conquers even the grimace of love, had cuckolded him. What was left of him, rotted beneath what was left of the nightshirt, had become inextricable from the bed in which he lay; and upon him and upon the pillow beside him lay that even coating of the patient and biding dust.

Then we noticed that in the second pillow was the indentation of a head. One of us lifted something from it, and leaning forward, that faint and invisible dust dry and acrid in the nostrils, we saw a long strand of iron-gray hair.

Questions for Critical Thinking

1 Faulkner is famous for his lush language and imagery. Choose a sentence that you like and which includes a detail unique to the South—whether a description of nature, a chore the characters perform, or a house. What is it about that sentence that speaks to you?

2 There is an element of mystery in this story. How does it affect the plot? What overall effect does it create for you as you read?

3 Imagine adapting the plot to a different time and place. What elements would you have to change in order to make these alterations work?

Barn Burning (1939)

1   THE store in which the Justice of the Peace's court was sitting smelled of cheese. The boy, crouched on his nail keg at the back of the crowded room, knew he smelled cheese, and more: from where he sat he could see the ranked shelves close-packed with the solid, squat, dynamic shapes of tin cans whose labels his stomach read, not from the lettering which meant nothing to his mind but from the scarlet devils and the silver curve of fish—this, the cheese which he knew he smelled and the hermetic meat which his intestines believed he smelled coming in intermittent gusts momentary and brief between the other constant one, the smell and sense just a little of fear because mostly of despair and grief, the old fierce pull of blood. He could not see the table where the Justice sat and before which his father and his father's enemy (*our enemy* he thought in that despair: *ourn! Mine and hisn both! He's my father!*) stood, but he could hear them, the two of them that is, because his father had said no word yet:

2   "But what proof have you, Mr. Harris?"

3   "I told you. The hog got into my corn. I caught it up and sent it back to him. He had no fence that would hold it. I told him so, warned him. The next time I put the hog in my pen. When he came to get it I gave him enough wire to patch up his pen. The next time I put the hog up and kept it. I rode down to his house and saw the wire I gave him still rolled on to the spool in his yard. I told him he could have the hog when he paid me a dollar pound fee. That evening a nigger came with the dollar and got the hog. He was a strange nigger. He said, 'He say to tell you wood and hay kin burn.' I said, 'What?' 'That whut he say to tell you,' the nigger said. 'Wood and hay kin burn.' That night my barn burned. I got the stock out but I lost the barn."

4   "Where's the nigger? Have you got him?"

5   "He was a strange nigger, I tell you. I don't know what became of him."

6   "But that's not proof. Don't you see that's not proof?"

7   "Get that boy up here. He knows." For a moment the boy thought too that the man meant his older brother until Harris said, "Not him. The little one. The boy," and, crouching, small for his age, small and wiry like his father, in patched and faded jeans even too small for him, with straight, uncombed, brown hair and eyes gray and wild as storm scud, he saw the men between himself and the table part and become a lane of grim faces, at the end of which he saw the Justice, a shabby, collarless, graying man in spectacles, beckoning him. He felt no floor under his bare feet; he seemed to walk beneath the palpable weight of the grim turning faces. His father, still in his black Sunday coat donned not for the trial but for the moving, did not even look at him. *He aims for me to lie,* he thought, again with that frantic grief and despair. *And I will have to do hit.*

> ## "Do you want me to question this boy?"

8   "What's your name, boy?" the Justice said.

9   "Colonel Sartoris Snopes," the boy whispered.

10   "Hey?" the Justice said. "Talk louder. Colonel Sartoris? I reckon anybody named for Colonel Sartoris in this country can't help but tell the truth, can they?" The boy said nothing. *Enemy! Enemy!* he thought; for a moment he could not even see, could not see that the Justice's face was kindly nor discern that his voice was troubled when he spoke to the man named Harris: "Do you want me to question this boy?" But he could hear, and during those subsequent long seconds while there was absolutely no sound in the crowded little room save that of quiet and intent breathing it was as if he had swung outward at the end of a grape vine, over a ravine, and at the top of the swing had been caught in a prolonged instant of mesmerized gravity, weightless in time.

11   "No!" Harris said violently, explosively. "Damnation! Send him out of here!" Now time, the fluid world, rushed beneath him again, the voices coming to him again through the smell of cheese and sealed meat, the fear and despair and the old grief of blood:

12   "This case is closed. I can't find against you, Snopes, but I can give you advice. Leave this country and don't come back to it."

13   His father spoke for the first time, his voice cold and harsh, level, without emphasis: "I aim to. I don't figure to stay in a country among people who . . ." he said something unprintable and vile, addressed to no one.

"That'll do," the Justice said. "Take your wagon and get out of this country before dark. Case dismissed."

His father turned, and he followed the stiff black coat, the wiry figure walking a little stiffly from where a Confederate provost's man's musket ball had taken him in the heel on a stolen horse thirty years ago, followed the two backs now, since his older brother had appeared from somewhere in the crowd, no taller than the father but thicker, chewing tobacco steadily, between the two lines of grim-faced men and out of the store and across the worn gallery and down the sagging steps and among the dogs and half-grown boys in the mild May dust, where as he passed a voice hissed:

"Barn burner!"

Again he could not see, whirling; there was a face in a red haze, moonlike, bigger than the full moon, the owner of it half again his size, he leaping in the red haze toward the face, feeling no blow, feeling no shock when his head struck the earth, scrabbling up and leaping again, feeling no blow this time either and tasting no blood, scrabbling up to see the other boy in full flight and himself already leaping into pursuit as his father's hand jerked him back, the harsh, cold voice speaking above him: "Go get in the wagon."

It stood in a grove of locusts and mulberries across the road. His two hulking sisters in their Sunday dresses and his mother and her sister in calico and sunbonnets were already in it, sitting on and among the sorry residue of the dozen and more movings which even the boy could remember—the battered stove, the broken beds and chairs, the clock inlaid with mother-of-pearl, which would not run, stopped at some fourteen minutes past two o'clock of a dead and forgotten day and time, which had been his mother's dowry. She was crying, though when she saw him she drew her sleeve across her face and began to descend from the wagon. "Get back," the father said.

"He's hurt. I got to get some water and wash his . . ."

"Get back in the wagon," his father said. He got in too, over the tail-gate. His father mounted to the seat where the older brother already sat and struck the gaunt mules two savage blows with the peeled willow, but without heat. It was not even sadistic; it was exactly that same quality which in later years would cause his descendants to over-run the engine before putting a motor car into motion, striking and reining back in the same movement. The wagon went on, the store with its quiet crowd of grimly watching men dropped behind; a curve in the road hid it. *Forever* he thought. *Maybe*

... the element of fire spoke to some deep mainspring of his father's being ...

he's done satisfied now, now that he has . . . stopping himself, not to say it aloud even to himself. His mother's hand touched his shoulder.

"Does hit hurt?" she said.

"Naw," he said. "Hit don't hurt. Lemme be."

"Can't you wipe some of the blood off before hit dries?"

"I'll wash to-night," he said. "Lemme be, I tell you."

The wagon went on. He did not know where they were going. None of them ever did or ever asked, because it was always somewhere, always a house of sorts waiting for them a day or two days or even three days away. Likely his father had already arranged to make a crop on another farm before he . . . Again he had to stop himself. He (the father) always did. There was something about his wolflike independence and even courage when the advantage was at least neutral which impressed strangers, as if they got from his latent ravening ferocity not so much a sense of dependability as a feeling that his ferocious conviction in the rightness of his own actions would be of advantage to all whose interest lay with his.

That night they camped, in a grove of oaks and beeches where a spring ran. The nights were still cool and they had a fire against it, of a rail lifted from a nearby fence and cut into lengths—a small fire, neat, niggard almost, a shrewd fire; such fires were his father's habit and custom always, even in freezing weather. Older, the boy might have remarked this and wondered why not a big one; why should not a man who had not only seen the waste and extravagance of war, but who had in his blood an inherent voracious prodigality with material not his own, have burned everything in sight? Then he might have gone a step farther and thought that that was the reason: that niggard blaze was the living fruit of nights passed during those four years in the woods hiding from all men, blue and gray, with his strings of horses (captured horses, he called them). And older still, he might have divined the true reason: that the element of fire spoke to some deep mainspring of his father's being, as the element of steel or of powder spoke to other men, as the one weapon for the preservation of integrity, else breath were not worth the breathing, and hence to be regarded with respect and used with discretion.

But he did not think this now and he had seen those same niggard blazes all his life. He merely ate his supper beside it and was already half asleep over his iron plate when his father called him, and once more he followed the stiff back, the stiff and ruthless limp, up the slope and on to the starlit road where, turning, he could see his father against the stars but without face or depth—a shape black, flat, and bloodless as though cut from tin in the iron folds of the frockcoat which had not been made for him, the voice harsh like tin and without heat like tin:

28   "You were fixing to tell them. You would have told him."

29   He didn't answer. His father struck him with the flat of his hand on the side of the head, hard but without heat, exactly as he had struck the two mules at the store, exactly as he would strike either of them with any stick in order to kill a horse fly, his voice without heat or anger: "You're getting to be a man. You got to learn. You got to learn to stick to your own blood or you ain't going to have any blood to stick to you. Do you think either of them, any man there this morning, would? Don't you know all they wanted was a chance to get at me because they knew I had them beat? Eh?" Later, twenty years later, he was to tell himself, "If I had said they wanted only truth, justice, he would have hit me again." But now he said nothing. He was not crying. He just stood there. "Answer me," his father said.

30   "Yes," he whispered. His father turned.

31   "Get on to bed. We'll be there tomorrow."

32   Tomorrow they were there. In the early afternoon the wagon stopped before a paintless two-room house identical almost with the dozen others it had stopped before even in the boy's ten years, and again, as on the other dozen occasions, his mother and aunt got down and began to unload the wagon, although his two sisters and his father and brother had not moved.

33   "Likely hit ain't fitten for hawgs," one of the sisters said.

34   "Nevertheless, fit it will and you'll hog it and like it," his father said. "Get out of them chairs and help your Ma unload."

35   The two sisters got down, big, bovine, in a flutter of cheap ribbons; one of them drew from the jumbled wagon bed a battered lantern, the other a worn broom. His father handed the reins to the older son and began to climb stiffly over the wheel. "When they get unloaded, take the team to the barn and feed them." Then he said, and at first the boy thought he was still speaking to his brother: "Come with me."

36   "Me?" he said.

37   "Yes," his father said. "You."

38   "Abner," his mother said. His father paused and looked back—the harsh level stare beneath the shaggy, graying, irascible brows.

39   "I reckon I'll have a word with the man that aims to begin tomorrow owning me body and soul for the next eight months."

They went back up the road. A week ago—or before last night, that is—he would have asked where they were going, but not now. His father had struck him before last night but never before had he paused afterward to explain why; it was as if the blow and the following calm, outrageous voice still rang, repercussed, divulging nothing to him save the terrible handicap of being young, the light weight of his few years, just heavy enough to prevent his soaring free of the world as it seemed to be ordered but not heavy enough to keep him footed solid in it, to resist it and try to change the course of its events.

Presently he could see the grove of oaks and cedars and the other flowering trees and shrubs where the house would be, though not the house yet. They walked beside a fence massed with honeysuckle and Cherokee roses and came to a gate swinging open between two brick pillars, and now, beyond a sweep of drive, he saw the house for the first time and at that instant he forgot his father and the terror and despair both, and even when he remembered his father again (who had not stopped) the terror and despair did not return. Because, for all the twelve movings, they had sojourned until now in a poor country, a land of small farms and fields and houses, and he had never seen a house like this before. *Hit's big as a courthouse* he thought quietly, with a surge of peace and joy whose reason he could not have thought into words, being too young for that: *They are safe from him. People whose lives are a part of this peace and dignity are beyond his touch, he no more to them than a buzzing wasp: capable of stinging for a little moment but that's all; the spell of this peace and dignity rendering even the barns and stable and cribs which belong to it impervious to the puny flames he might contrive* . . . this, the peace and joy, ebbing for an instant as he looked again at the still black back, the stiff and implacable limp of the figure which was not dwarfed by the house, for the reason that it had never looked big anywhere and which now, against the serene columned backdrop, had more than ever that impervious quality of something cut ruthlessly from tin, depthless, as though, sidewise to the sun, it would cast no shadow. Watching him, the boy remarked the absolutely undeviating course which his father held and saw the stiff foot come squarely down in a pile of fresh droppings where a horse had stood in the drive and which his father could have avoided by a simple change of stride. But it ebbed only a moment, though he could not have thought this into words either, walking on in the spell of the house, which he could even want but without envy, without sorrow, certainly never with that ravening and jealous rage which unknown to him walked in the ironlike black coat before him: *Maybe he will feel it too. Maybe it will even change him now from what maybe he couldn't help but be.*

They crossed the portico. Now he could hear his father's stiff foot as it came down on the boards with clocklike finality, a sound out of all proportion to the displacement of the body it bore and which was not dwarfed either by the white door before it, as though it had attained to a sort of vicious and ravening minimum not to be dwarfed by anything—the flat, wide, black hat, the formal coat of broadcloth which had once been black but which had now that friction-glazed greenish cast of the bodies of old house flies, the lifted sleeve which was too large, the lifted hand like a curled claw. The door opened so promptly that the boy knew the Negro must have been watching them all the time, an old man with neat grizzled hair, in a linen jacket, who stood barring the door with his body, saying, "Wipe yo foots, white man, fo you come in here. Major ain't home nohow."

"Get out of my way, nigger," his father said, without heat too, flinging the door back and the Negro also and entering, his hat still on his head. And now the boy saw the prints of the stiff foot on the doorjamb and saw them appear on the pale rug behind the machinelike deliberation of the foot which seemed to bear (or transmit) twice the weight which the body compassed. The Negro was shouting "Miss Lula! Miss Lula!" somewhere behind them, then the boy, deluged as though by a warm wave by a suave turn of the carpeted stair and a pendant glitter of chandeliers and a mute gleam of gold frames, heard the swift feet and saw her too, a lady—perhaps he had never seen her like before either—in a gray, smooth gown with lace at the throat and an apron tied at the waist and the sleeves turned back, wiping cake or biscuit dough from her hands with a towel as she came up the hall, looking not at his father at all but at the tracks on the blond rug with an expression of incredulous amazement.

"I tried," the Negro cried. "I tole him to . . ."

"Will you please go away?" she said in a shaking voice. "Major de Spain is not at home. Will you please go away?"

His father had not spoken again. He did not speak again. He did not even look at her. He just stood stiff in the center of the rug, in his hat, the shaggy iron-gray brows twitching slightly above the pebble-colored eyes as he appeared to examine the house with brief deliberation. Then with the same deliberation he turned; the boy watched him pivot on the good leg and saw the stiff foot drag around the arc of the turning, leaving a

. . . the boy watched him pivot on the good leg and saw the stiff foot drag . . .

final long and fading smear. His father never looked at it, he never once looked down at the rug. The Negro held the door. It closed behind them, upon the hysteric and indistinguishable woman-wail. His father stopped at the top of the steps and scraped his boot clean on the edge of it. At the gate he stopped again. He stood for a moment, planted stiffly on the stiff foot, looking back at the house. "Pretty and white, ain't it?" he said. "That's sweat. Nigger sweat. Maybe it ain't white enough yet to suit him. Maybe he wants to mix some white sweat with it."

Two hours later the boy was chopping wood behind the house within which his mother and aunt and the two sisters (the mother and aunt, not the two girls, he knew that; even at this distance and muffled by walls the flat loud voices of the two girls emanated an incorrigible idle inertia) were setting up the stove to prepare a meal, when he heard the hooves and saw the linen-clad man on a fine sorrel mare, whom he recognized even before he saw the rolled rug in front of the Negro youth following on a fat bay carriage horse—a suffused, angry face vanishing, still at full gallop, beyond the corner of the house where his father and brother were sitting in the two tilted chairs; and a moment later, almost before he could have put the axe down, he heard the hooves again and watched the sorrel mare go back out of the yard, already galloping again. Then his father began to shout one of the sisters' names, who presently emerged backward from the kitchen door dragging the rolled rug along the ground by one end while the other sister walked behind it.

"If you ain't going to tote, go on and set up the wash pot," the first said.

"You, Sarty!" the second shouted. "Set up the wash pot!" His father appeared at the door, framed against that shabbiness, as he had been against that other bland perfection, impervious to either, the mother's anxious face at his shoulder.

"Go on," the father said. "Pick it up." The two sisters stooped, broad, lethargic; stooping, they presented an incredible expanse of pale cloth and a flutter of tawdry ribbons.

"If I thought enough of a rug to have to git hit all the way from France I wouldn't keep hit where folks coming in would have to tromp on hit," the first said. They raised the rug.

"Abner," the mother said. "Let me do it."

"You go back and git dinner," his father said. "I'll tend to this."

54   From the woodpile through the rest of the afternoon the boy watched them, the rug spread flat in the dust beside the bubbling wash pot, the two sisters stooping over it with that profound and lethargic reluctance, while the father stood over them in turn, implacable and grim, driving them though never raising his voice again. He could smell the harsh homemade lye they were using; he saw his mother come to the door once and look toward them with an expression not anxious now but very like despair; he saw his father turn, and he fell to with the axe and saw from the corner of his eye his father raise from the ground a flattish fragment of field stone and examine it and return to the pot, and this time his mother actually spoke: "Abner. Abner. Please don't. Please, Abner."

> "It cost a hundred dollars. But you never had a hundred dollars. You never will. . . ."

55   Then he was done too. It was dusk; the whippoorwills had already begun. He could smell coffee from the room where they would presently eat the cold food remaining from the mid-afternoon meal, though when he entered the house he realized they were having coffee again probably because there was a fire on the hearth, before which the rug now lay spread over the backs of the two chairs. The tracks of his father's foot were gone. Where they had been were now long, water-cloudy scoriations resembling the sporadic course of a lilliputian mowing machine.

56   It still hung there while they ate the cold food and then went to bed, scattered without order or claim up and down the two rooms, his mother in one bed, where his father would later lie, the older brother in the other, himself, the aunt, and the two sisters on pallets on the floor. But his father was not in bed yet. The last thing the boy remembered was the depthless, harsh silhouette of the hat and coat bending over the rug and it seemed to him that he had not even closed his eyes when the silhouette was standing over him, the fire almost dead behind it, the stiff foot prodding him awake. "Catch up the mule," his father said.

57   When he returned with the mule his father was standing in the back door, the rolled rug over his shoulder. "Ain't you going to ride?" he said.

58   "No. Give me your foot."

59   He bent his knee into his father's hand, the wiry, surprising power flowed smoothly, rising, he rising with it, on to the mule's bare back (they had owned a saddle once; the boy could remember it though not when or where) and with the same effortlessness his father swung the rug up in front of him. Now in the starlight they retraced the afternoon's path, up the dusty road rife with honeysuckle, through the gate and up the black tunnel of the drive to the lightless house, where he sat on the mule and felt the rough warp of the rug drag across his thighs and vanish.

"Don't you want me to help?" he whispered. His father did not answer and now he heard again that stiff foot striking the hollow portico with that wooden and clocklike deliberation, that outrageous overstatement of the weight it carried. The rug, hunched, not flung (the boy could tell that even in the darkness) from his father's shoulder struck the angle of wall and floor with a sound unbelievably loud, thunderous, then the foot again, unhurried and enormous; a light came on in the house and the boy sat, tense, breathing steadily and quietly and just a little fast, though the foot itself did not increase its beat at all, descending the steps now; now the boy could see him.

"Don't you want to ride now?" he whispered. "We 6 kin both ride now," the light within the house altering now, flaring up and sinking. *He's coming down the stairs now*, he thought. He had already ridden the mule up beside the horse block; presently his father was up behind him and he doubled the reins over and slashed the mule across the neck, but before the animal could begin to trot the hard, thin arm came around him, the hard, knotted hand jerking the mule back to a walk.

In the first red rays of the sun they were in the lot, 6 putting plow gear on the mules. This time the sorrel mare was in the lot before he heard it at all, the rider collarless and even bareheaded, trembling, speaking in a shaking voice as the woman in the house had done, his father merely looking up once before stooping again to the hame he was buckling, so that the man on the mare spoke to his stooping back:

"You must realize you have ruined that rug. Wasn't 63 there anybody here, any of your women . . ." he ceased, shaking, the boy watching him, the older brother leaning now in the stable door, chewing, blinking slowly and steadily at nothing apparently. "It cost a hundred dollars. But you never had a hundred dollars. You never will. So I'm going to charge you twenty bushels of corn against your crop. I'll add it in your contract and when you come to the commissary you can sign it. That won't keep Mrs. de Spain quiet but maybe it will teach you to wipe your feet off before you enter her house again."

Then he was gone. The boy looked at 64 his father, who still had not spoken or even looked up again, who was now adjusting the logger-head in the hame.

"Pap," he said. His father looked at him—the inscrutable face, the shaggy brows beneath where the gray eyes glinted coldly. Suddenly the boy went toward him, fast, stopping as suddenly. "You done the best you could!" he cried. "If he wanted hit done different why didn't he wait and tell you how? He won't git no twenty bushels! He won't git none! We'll gather hit and hide hit! I kin watch . . ."

"Did you put the cutter back in that straight stock like I told you?"

"No, sir," he said.

"Then go do it."

That was Wednesday. During the rest of that week he worked steadily, at what was within his scope and some which was beyond it, with an industry that did not need to be driven nor even commanded twice; he had this from his mother, with the difference that some at least of what he did he liked to do, such as splitting wood with the half-size axe which his mother and aunt had earned, or saved money somehow, to present him with at Christmas. In company with the two older women (and on one afternoon, even one of the sisters), he built pens for the shoat and the cow which were a part of his father's contract with the landlord, and one afternoon, his father being absent, gone somewhere on one of the mules, he went to the field.

They were running a middle buster now, his brother holding the plow straight while he handled the reins, and walking beside the straining mule, the rich black soil shearing cool and damp against his bare ankles, he thought *Maybe this is the end of it. Maybe even that twenty bushels that seems hard to have to pay for just a rug will be a cheap price for him to stop forever and always from being what he used to be;* thinking, dreaming now, so that his brother had to speak sharply to him to mind the mule: *Maybe he even won't collect the twenty bushels. Maybe it will all add up and balance and vanish—corn, rug, fire; the terror and grief; the being pulled two ways like between two teams of horses—gone, done with for ever and ever.*

Then it was Saturday; he looked up from beneath the mule he was harnessing and saw his father in the black coat and hat. "Not that," his father said. "The wagon gear." And then, two hours later, sitting in the wagon bed behind his father and brother on the seat, the wagon accomplished a final curve, and he saw the weathered paintless store with its tattered tobacco- and patent-medicine posters and the tethered wagons and saddle animals below the gallery. He mounted the gnawed steps behind his father and brother, and there again was the lane of quiet, watching faces for the three of them to walk through. He saw the man in spectacles sitting at the plank table and he did not need to be told this was a Justice of the Peace; he sent one glare of fierce, exultant, partisan defiance at the man in collar and cravat now, whom he had seen but twice before in his life, and that on a galloping horse, who now wore on his face an expression not of rage but of amazed unbelief which the boy could not have known was at the incredible circumstance of being sued by one of his own tenants, and came and stood against his father and cried at the Justice: "He ain't done it! He ain't burnt . . ."

"Go back to the wagon," his father said.

"Burnt?" the Justice said. "Do I understand this rug was burned too?"

"Does anybody here claim it was?" his father said. "Go back to the wagon." But he did not, he merely retreated to the rear of the room, crowded as that other had been, but not to sit down this time, instead, to stand pressing among the motionless bodies, listening to the voices:

"And you claim twenty bushels of corn is too high for the damage you did to the rug?"

"He brought the rug to me and said he wanted the tracks washed out of it. I washed the tracks out and took the rug back to him."

"But you didn't carry the rug back to him in the same condition it was in before you made the tracks on it."

His father did not answer, and now for perhaps half a minute there was no sound at all save that of breathing, the faint, steady suspiration of complete and intent listening.

"You decline to answer that, Mr. Snopes?" Again his father did not answer. "I'm going to find against you, Mr. Snopes. I'm going to find that you were responsible for the injury to Major de Spain's rug and hold you liable for it. But twenty bushels of corn seems a little high for a man in your circumstances to have to pay. Major de Spain claims it cost a hundred dollars. October corn will be worth about fifty cents. I figure that if Major de Spain can stand a ninety-five dollar loss on something he paid cash for, you can stand a five-dollar loss you haven't earned yet. I hold you in damages to Major de Spain to the amount of ten bushels of corn over and above your contract with him, to be paid to him out of your crop at gathering time. Court adjourned."

It had taken no time hardly, the morning was but half begun. He thought they would return home and perhaps back to the field, since they were late, far behind all other farmers. But instead his father passed on behind the wagon, merely indicating with his hand for the older brother to follow with it, and crossed the road toward the blacksmith shop opposite, pressing on after his father, overtaking him, speaking, whispering up at the harsh, calm face beneath the weathered hat: "He won't git no ten bushels either. He won't git one. We'll . . ." until his father glanced for an instant down at him, the face absolutely calm, the grizzled eyebrows tangled above the cold eyes, the voice almost pleasant, almost gentle:

81 "You think so? Well, we'll wait till October anyway."

82 The matter of the wagon—the setting of a spoke or two and the tightening of the tires—did not take long either, the business of the tires accomplished by driving the wagon into the spring branch behind the shop and letting it stand there, the mules nuzzling into the water from time to time, and the boy on the seat with the idle reins, looking up the slope and through the sooty tunnel of the shed where the slow hammer rang and where his father sat on an upended cypress bolt, easily, either talking or listening, still sitting there when the boy brought the dripping wagon up out of the branch and halted it before the door.

83 "Take them on to the shade and hitch," his father said. He did so and returned. His father and the smith and a third man squatting on his heels inside the door were talking, about crops and animals; the boy, squatting too in the ammoniac dust and hoof-parings and scales of rust, heard his father tell a long and unhurried story out of the time before the birth of the older brother even when he had been a professional horse-trader. And then his father came up beside him where he stood before a tattered last year's circus poster on the other side of the store, gazing rapt and quiet at the scarlet horses, the incredible poisings and convulsions of tulle and tights and the painted leers of comedians, and said, "It's time to eat."

84 But not at home. Squatting beside his brother against the front wall, he watched his father emerge from the store and produce from a paper sack a segment of cheese and divide it carefully and deliberately into three with his pocket knife and produce crackers from the same sack. They all three squatted on the gallery and ate, slowly, without talking; then in the store again, they drank from a tin dipper tepid water smelling of the cedar bucket and of living beech trees. And still they did not go home. It was a horse lot this time, a tall rail fence upon and along which men stood and sat and out of which one by one horses were led, to be walked and trotted and then cantered back and forth along the road while the slow swapping and buying went on and the sun began to slant westward, they—the three of them—watching and listening, the older brother with his

muddy eyes and his steady, inevitable tobacco, the father commenting now and then on certain of the animals, to no one in particular.

It was after sundown when they reached home. They ate supper by lamplight, then, sitting on the doorstep, the boy watched the night fully accomplish, listening to the whippoorwills and the frogs, when he heard his mother's voice: "Abner! No! No! Oh, God. Oh, God. Abner!" and he rose, whirled, and saw the altered light through the door where a candle stub now burned in a bottle neck on the table and his father, still in the hat and coat, at once formal and burlesque as though dressed carefully for some shabby and ceremonial violence, emptying the reservoir of the lamp back into the five-gallon kerosene can from which it had been filled, while the mother tugged at his arm until he shifted the lamp to the other hand and flung her back, not savagely or viciously, just hard, into the wall, her hands flung out against the wall for balance, her mouth open and in her face the same quality of hopeless despair as had been in her voice. Then his father saw him standing in the door.

"Go to the barn and get that can of oil we were oiling the wagon with," he said. The boy did not move. Then he could speak.

"What . . ." he cried. "What are you . . ."

"Go get that oil," his father said. "Go."

Then he was moving, running, outside the house, toward the stable: this the old habit, the old blood which he had not been permitted to choose for himself, which had been bequeathed him willy nilly and which had run for so long (and who knew where, battening on what of outrage and savagery and lust) before it came to him. *I could keep on,* he thought. *I could run on and on and never look back, never need to see his face again. Only I can't. I can't,* the rusted can in his hand now, the liquid sploshing in it as he ran back to the house and into it, into the sound of his mother's weeping in the next room, and handed the can to his father.

"Ain't you going to even send a nigger?" he cried. "At least you sent a nigger before!"

This time his father didn't strike him. The hand came even faster than the blow had, the same hand which had set the can on the table with almost excruciating care flashing from the can toward him too quick for him to follow it, gripping him by the back of his shirt and on to tiptoe before he had seen it quit the can, the face stooping at him in breathless and frozen ferocity, the cold, dead voice speaking over him to the older brother who leaned against the table, chewing with that steady, curious, sidewise motion of cows:

"Empty the can into the big one and go on. I'll catch up with you."

80

86

87

88

89

90

91

92

"Better tie him up to the bedpost," the brother said.

"Do like I told you," the father said. Then the boy was moving, his bunched shirt and the hard, bony hand between his shoulder-blades, his toes just touching the floor, across the room and into the other one, past the sisters sitting with spread heavy thighs in the two chairs over the cold hearth, and to where his mother and aunt sat side by side on the bed, the aunt's arm about his mother's shoulders.

"Hold him," the father said: The aunt made a startled movement. "Not you," the father said. "Lennie. Take hold of him. I want to see you do it." His mother took him by the wrist. "You'll hold him better than that. If he gets loose don't you know what he is going to do? He will go up yonder." He jerked his head toward the road. "Maybe I'd better tie him."

"I'll hold him," his mother whispered.

"See you do then." Then his father was gone, the stiff foot heavy and measured upon the boards, ceasing at last.

Then he began to struggle. His mother caught him in both arms, he jerking and wrenching at them. He would be stronger in the end, he knew that. But he had no time to wait for it. "Lemme go!" he cried. "I don't want to have to hit you!"

"Let him go!" the aunt said. "If he don't go, before God, I am going up there myself!"

"Don't you see I can't?" his mother cried. "Sarty! Sarty! No! No! Help me, Lizzie!"

Then he was free. His aunt grasped at him but it was too late. He whirled, running, his mother stumbled forward on to her knees behind him, crying to the nearer sister: "Catch him, Net! Catch him!" But that was too late too, the sister (the sisters were twins, born at the same time, yet either of them now gave the impression of being, encompassing as much living meat and volume and weight as any other two of the family) not yet having begun to rise from the chair, her head, face, alone merely turned, presenting to him in the flying instant an astonishing expanse of young female features untroubled by any surprise even, wearing only an expression of bovine interest. Then he was out of the room, out of the house, in the mild dust of the starlit road and the heavy rifeness of honeysuckle, the pale ribbon unspooling with terrific slowness under his running feet, reaching the gate at last and turning in, running, his heart and lungs drumming, on up the drive toward the lighted house, the lighted door. He did not knock, he burst in, sobbing for breath, incapable for the moment of speech; he saw the astonished face of the Negro in the linen jacket without knowing when the Negro had appeared.

"De Spain!" he cried, panted. "Where's . . ." then he saw the white man too emerging from a white door down the hall. "Barn!" he cried. "Barn!"

"What?" the white man said. "Barn?"

"Yes!" the boy cried. "Barn!"

"Catch him!" the white man shouted.

But it was too late this time too. The Negro grasped his shirt, but the entire sleeve, rotten with washing, carried away, and he was out that door too and in the drive again, and had actually never ceased to run even while he was screaming into the white man's face.

Behind him the white man was shouting, "My horse! Fetch my horse!" and he thought for an instant of cutting across the park and climbing the fence into the road, but he did not know the park nor how the vine-massed fence might be and he dared not risk it. So he ran on down the drive, blood and breath roaring; presently he was in the road again though he could not see it. He could not hear either: the galloping mare was almost upon him before he heard her, and even then he held his course, as if the very urgency of his wild grief and need must in a moment more find him wings, waiting until the ultimate instant to hurl himself aside and into the weed-choked roadside ditch as the horse thundered past and on, for an instant in furious silhouette against the stars, the tranquil early summer night sky which, even before the shape of the horse and rider vanished, stained abruptly and violently upward: a long, swirling roar incredible and soundless, blotting the stars, and he springing up and into the road again, running again, knowing it was too late yet still running even after he heard the shot and an instant later, two shots, pausing now without knowing he had ceased to run, crying, "Pap! Pap!", running again before he knew he had begun to run, stumbling, tripping over something and scrabbling up again without ceasing to run, looking backward over his shoulder at the glare as he got up, running on among the invisible trees, panting, sobbing, "Father! Father!"

At midnight he was sitting on the crest of a hill. He did not know it was midnight and he did not know how far he had come. But there was no glare behind him now and he sat now, his back toward what he had called home for four days anyhow, his face toward the dark woods which he would enter when breath was strong again, small, shaking steadily in the chill darkness, hugging himself into the remainder of his thin, rotten shirt, the grief and despair now no longer

102
103
104
105
106
107
108

> He did not know
> it was midnight
> and he did not know how
> far he had come.

terror and fear but just grief and despair. *Father. My father*, he thought. "He was brave!" he cried suddenly, aloud but not loud, no more than a whisper. "He was! He was in the war! He was in Colonel Sartoris' cav'ry!" not knowing that his father had gone to that war a private in the fine old European sense, wearing no uniform, admitting the authority of and giving fidelity to no man or army or flag, going to war as Marlbrouck himself did: for booty—it meant nothing and less than nothing to him if it were enemy booty or his own.

109   The slow constellations wheeled on. It would be dawn and then sun-up after a while and he would be hungry. But that would be tomorrow and now he was only cold, and walking would cure that. His breathing was easier now and he decided to get up and go on, and then he found that he had been asleep because he knew it was almost dawn, the night almost over. He could tell that from the whippoorwills. They were everywhere now among the dark trees below him, constant and inflectioned and ceaseless, so that, as the instant for giving over to the day birds drew nearer and nearer, there was no interval at all between them. He got up. He was a little stiff, but walking would cure that too as it would the cold, and soon there would be the sun. He went on down the hill, toward the dark woods within which the liquid silver voices of the birds called unceasing—the rapid and urgent beating of the urgent and quiring heart of the late spring night. He did not look back.

Questions for Critical Thinking

1 The smells and sounds of country life contribute largely to the effects of this story. Can you catalog these on a second reading of the story? Which senses—smell, touch, etc.—seem the most important?

2 Faulkner's phrases and sentences seem quite distinctive (as in "He went on down the hill, toward the dark woods within which the liquid silver voices of the birds called unceasing— the rapid and urgent beating of the urgent and quiring heart of the late spring night."). Do these seem "Southern" to you? What other terms might you use to describe Faulkner's style?

3 Note the references Faulkner makes to the Civil War. Based on what we learn about the father in the penultimate paragraph of "Barn Burning," how would you describe this author's view of Southern history?

4 Imagine the setting of "Barn Burning" in a northern city. Is it possible? How would it change the story?

"The first and most obvious characteristic of fiction is that it deals with reality through what can be seen, heard, smelt, tasted, and touched. Now this is something that can't be learrned only in the head; it has to be learned in the habits. It has to become a way that you habitually look at things. The fiction writer has to realize that he can't create compassion with compassion, or emotion with emotion, or thought with thought. He has to provide all these things with a body; he has to create a world with weight and extension. . . . The meaning of a story has to be embodied in it, has to be made concrete in it. A story is a way to say something that can't be said any other way, and it takes every word in the story to say what the meaning is." —Flannery O'Connor, 1969 (from "Writing Short Stories")

Flannery O'Connor (1925–1964)

A Southern writer unlike any other, Flannery O'Connor is known for her satire on poor and middle-class Southern whites, her Catholic perspective, and her portrayal of the grotesque. Beyond these signature characteristics, O'Connor's prose jumps off the page with precision, wit, and sharpness—all calculated, as she put it, to show readers moments of God's grace. Born and raised in Savannah, Georgia, O'Connor moved with her parents to the small town of Milledgeville when her father became ill with lupus. She went to college in Georgia and then attended the Iowa Writers' Workshop, where she earned her M.F.A. Her teacher there, Paul Engle, described O'Connor's Georgia accent as so strong when they first met that, after several attempts to comprehend her speech,

he finally had to ask her to write down what she wanted to say.

O'Connor became a shy, silent fixture in the back of the classroom, working hard at stories rooted in Southern culture and Catholic sensibility. The cadences of regional speech course through her fiction, and she urged other writers, too, to "[take] advantage of what's yours." There are traces of the influence of other Southern writers in her work—notably the gothic strain of her great predecessor William Faulkner—but much of her work defies comparison as well as easy imitation; it is, to use a much-overused word, *original.*

Her health—she, too, contracted lupus—forced her to return to the farm in Milledgeville and move in with her mother. She left home only occasionally to lecture or to accept an award; the

rest of her time she spent writing and raising her beloved peacocks. O'Connor is most famous for her short stories, collected in *A Good Man Is Hard to Find* (1955) and *Everything That Rises Must Converge* (1965), but she also wrote two novels before her early death from lupus at age thirty-nine. In 1969 her occasional prose, speeches, and essays were collected in *Mystery and Manners,* and her complete stories were collected in a 1971 edition, which earned her a posthumous National Book Award. O'Connor is remembered not just as a modern master of the short story form but also—from interviews, letters, and speeches—for her wise and witty voice. When asked whether writing programs stifle writers, O'Connor famously replied, "My opinion is that they don't stifle enough of them."

A Good Man Is Hard to Find (1955)

1 THE grandmother didn't want to go to Florida. She wanted to visit some of her connections in east Tennessee and she was seizing at every chance to change Bailey's mind. Bailey was the son she lived with, her only boy. He was sitting on the edge of his chair at the table, bent over the orange sports section of the *Journal.* "Now look here, Bailey," she said, "see here, read this," and she stood with one hand on her thin hip and the other rattling the newspaper at his bald head. "Here this fellow that calls himself The Misfit is aloose from the Federal Pen and headed toward Florida and you read here what it says he did to these people. Just you read it. I wouldn't take my children in any direction with a criminal like that aloose in it. I couldn't answer to my conscience if I did."

2 Bailey didn't look up from his reading so she wheeled around then and faced the children's mother, a young woman in slacks, whose face was as broad and innocent as a cabbage and was tied around with

a green head-kerchief that had two points on the top like a rabbit's ears. She was sitting on the sofa, feeding the baby his apricots out of a jar. "The children have been to Florida before," the old lady said. "You all ought to take them somewhere else for a change so they would see different parts of the world and be broad. They never have been to east Tennessee."

3   The children's mother didn't seem to hear her but the eight-year-old boy, John Wesley, a stocky child with glasses, said, "If you don't want to go to Florida, why dontcha stay at home?" He and the little girl, June Star, were reading the funny papers on the floor.

4   "She wouldn't stay at home to be queen for a day," June Star said without raising her yellow head.

5   "Yes and what would you do if this fellow, The Misfit, caught you?" the grandmother asked.

6   "I'd smack his face," John Wesley said.

7   "She wouldn't stay at home for a million bucks," June Star said. "Afraid she'd miss something. She has to go everywhere we go."

8   "All right, Miss," the grandmother said. "Just remember that the next time you want me to curl your hair."

9   June Star said her hair was naturally curly.

10   The next morning the grandmother was the first one in the car, ready to go. She had her big black valise that looked like the head of a hippopotamus in one corner, and underneath it she was hiding a basket with Pitty Sing, the cat, in it. She didn't intend for the cat to be left alone in the house for three days because he would miss her too much and she was afraid he might brush against one of the gas burners and accidentally asphyxiate himself. Her son, Bailey, didn't like to arrive at a motel with a cat.

11   She sat in the middle of the back seat with John Wesley and June Star on either side of her. Bailey and the children's mother and the baby sat in front and they left Atlanta at eight forty-five with the mileage on the car at 55890. The grandmother wrote this down because she thought it would be interesting to say how many miles they had been when they got back. It took them twenty minutes to reach the outskirts of the city.

12   The old lady settled herself comfortably, removing her white cotton gloves and putting them up with her purse on the shelf in front of the back window. The children's mother still had on slacks and still had her head tied up in a green kerchief, but the grandmother had on a navy blue straw sailor hat with a bunch of white violets on the brim and a navy blue dress with a small white dot in the print. Her collars and cuffs were white organdy trimmed with lace and at her neckline she had pinned a purple spray of cloth violets containing a sachet. In case of an accident, anyone seeing her dead on the highway would know at once that she was a lady.

1   She said she thought it was going to be a good day for driving, neither too hot nor too cold, and she cautioned Bailey that the speed limit was fifty-five miles an hour and that the patrolmen hid themselves behind billboards and small clumps of trees and sped out after you before you had a chance to slow down. She pointed out interesting details of the scenery: Stone Mountain; the blue granite that in some places came up to both sides of the highway; the brilliant red clay banks slightly streaked with purple; and the various crops that made rows of green lace-work on the ground. The trees were full of silver-white sunlight and the meanest of them sparkled. The children were reading comic magazines and their mother had gone back to sleep.

14   "Let's go through Georgia fast so we won't have to look at it much," John Wesley said.

15   "If I were a little boy," said the grandmother, "I wouldn't talk about my native state that way. Tennessee has the mountains and Georgia has the hills."

16   "Tennessee is just a hillbilly dumping ground," John Wesley said, "and Georgia is a lousy state too."

17   "You said it," June Star said.

18   "In my time," said the grandmother, folding her thin veined fingers, "children were more respectful of their native states and their parents and everything else. People did right then. Oh look at the cute little pickaninny!" she said and pointed to a Negro child standing in the door of a shack. "Wouldn't that make a picture, now?" she asked and they all turned and looked at the little Negro out of the back window. He waved.

19   "He didn't have any britches on," June Star said.

20   "He probably didn't have any," the grandmother explained. "Little niggers in the country don't have things like we do. If I could paint, I'd paint that picture," she said.

21   The children exchanged comic books.

22   The grandmother offered to hold the baby and the children's mother passed him over the front seat to her.

> In case of an accident, anyone seeing her dead on the highway would know at once that she was a lady.

She set him on her knee and bounced him and told him about the things they were passing. She rolled her eyes and screwed up her mouth and stuck her leathery thin face into his smooth bland one. Occasionally he gave her a faraway smile. They passed a large cotton field with five or six graves fenced in the middle of it, like a small island. "Look at the graveyard!" the grandmother said, pointing it out. "That was the old family burying ground. That belonged to the plantation."

"Where's the plantation?" John Wesley asked.

"Gone With the Wind," said the grandmother. "Ha. Ha."

When the children finished all the comic books they had brought, they opened the lunch and ate it. The grandmother ate a peanut butter sandwich and an olive and would not let the children throw the box and the paper napkins out the window. When there was nothing else to do they played a game by choosing a cloud and making the other two guess what shape it suggested. John Wesley took one of the shape of a cow and June Star guessed a cow and John Wesley said, no, an automobile, and June Star said he didn't play fair, and they began to slap each other over the grandmother.

The grandmother said she would tell them a story if they would keep quiet. When she told a story, she rolled her eyes and waved her head and was very dramatic. She said once when she was a maiden lady she had been courted by a Mr. Edgar Atkins Teagarden from Jasper, Georgia. She said he was a very good-looking man and a gentleman and that he brought her a watermelon every Saturday afternoon with his initials cut in it, E. A. T. Well, one Saturday, she said, Mr. Teagarden brought the watermelon and there was nobody at home and he left it on the front porch and returned in his buggy to Jasper, but she never got the watermelon, she said, because a nigger boy ate it when he saw the initials, E. A. T.! This story tickled John Wesley's funny bone and he giggled and giggled but June Star didn't think it was any good. She said she wouldn't marry a man that just brought her a watermelon on Saturday. The grandmother said she would have done well to marry Mr. Teagarden because he was a gentle-

man and had bought Coca-Cola stock when it first came out and that he had died only a few years ago, a very wealthy man.

They stopped at The Tower for barbecued sandwiches. The Tower was a part stucco and part wood filling station and dance hall set in a clearing outside of Timothy. A fat man named Red Sammy Butts ran it and there were signs stuck here and there on the building and for miles up and down the highway saying, TRY RED SAMMY'S FAMOUS BARBECUE. NONE LIKE FAMOUS RED SAMMY'S! RED SAM! THE FAT BOY WITH THE HAPPY LAUGH! A VETERAN! RED SAMMY'S YOUR MAN! 27

Red Sammy was lying on the bare ground outside The Tower with his head under a truck while a gray monkey about a foot high, chained to a small chinaberry tree, chattered nearby. The monkey sprang back into the tree and got on the highest limb as soon as he saw the children jump out of the car and run toward him. 28

Inside, The Tower was a long dark room with a counter at one end and tables at the other and dancing space in the middle. They sat down at a board table next to the nickelodeon and Red Sam's wife, a tall burnt-brown woman with hair and eyes lighter than her skin, came and took their order. The children's mother put a dime in the machine and played "The Tennessee Waltz," and the grandmother said that tune always made her want to dance. She asked Bailey if he would like to dance but he only glared at her. He didn't have a naturally sunny disposition like she did and trips made him nervous. The grandmother's brown eyes were very bright. She swayed her head from side to side and pretended she was dancing in her chair. June Star said play something she could tap to so the children's mother put in another dime and played a fast number and June Star stepped out onto the dance floor and did her tap routine. 29

"Ain't she cute?" Red Sam's wife said, leaning over the counter. "Would you like to come be my little girl?" 30

"No I certainly wouldn't," June Star said. "I wouldn't live in a broken-down place like this for a million bucks!" and she ran back to the table. 31

"Ain't she cute?" the woman repeated, stretching her mouth politely. 32

"Aren't you ashamed?" hissed the grandmother. 33

Red Sam came in and told his wife to quit lounging on the counter and hurry up with these people's order. His khaki trousers reached just to his hip bones and his stomach hung over them like a sack of meal swaying under his shirt. He came over and sat down at a table nearby and let out a combination sigh and yodel. "You can't win," he said. "You can't win," and he wiped his sweating red face off with a gray handkerchief. 34

"These days you don't know who to trust," he said. "Ain't that the truth?"

35 "People are certainly not nice like they used to be," said the grandmother.

36 "Two fellers come in here last week," Red Sammy said, "driving a Chrysler. It was a old beat-up car but it was a good one and these boys looked all right to me. Said they worked at the mill and you know I let them fellers charge the gas they bought? Now why did I do that?"

37 "Because you're a good man!" the grandmother said at once.

38 "Yes'm, I suppose so," Red Sam said as if he were stuck with this answer.

39 His wife brought the orders, carrying the five plates all at once without a tray, two in each hand and one balanced on her arm. "It isn't a soul in this green world of God's that you can trust," she said. "And I don't count nobody out of that, not nobody," she repeated, looking at Red Sammy.

40 "Did you read about that criminal, The Misfit, that's escaped?" asked the grandmother.

41 "I wouldn't be a bit surprised if he didn't attact this place right here," said the woman. "If he hears about it being here, I wouldn't be none surprised to see him. If he hears it's two cent in the cash register, I wouldn't be a tall surprised if he . . ."

42 "That'll do," Red Sam said. "Go bring these people their Co'-Colas," and the woman went off to get the rest of the order.

43 "A good man is hard to find," Red Sammy said. "Everything is getting terrible. I remember the day you could go off and leave your screen door unlatched. Not no more."

44 He and the grandmother discussed better times. The old lady said that in her opinion Europe was entirely to blame for the way things were now. She said the way Europe acted you would think we were made of money and Red Sam said it was no use talking about it, she was exactly right. The children ran outside into the white sunlight and looked at the monkey in the lacy chinaberry tree. He was busy catching fleas on himself and biting each one carefully between his teeth as if it were a delicacy.

45 They drove off again into the hot afternoon. The grandmother took cat naps and woke up every few minutes with her own snoring. Outside of Toombsboro she woke up and recalled an old plantation that she had visited in this neighborhood once when she was a young lady. She said the house had six white columns across the front and that there was an avenue of oaks leading up to it and two little wooden trellis arbors on either side in front where you sat down with your suitor after a stroll in the garden. She recalled exactly which road to turn off to get to it. She knew that Bailey would not be willing to lose any time looking at an old house, but the more she talked about it, the more she wanted to see it once again and find out if the little twin arbors were still standing. "There was a secret panel in this house," she said craftily, not telling the truth but wishing that she were, "and the story went that all the family silver was hidden in it when Sherman came through but it was never found . . ."

"Hey!" John Wesley said. "Let's go see it! We'll find it! We'll poke all the woodwork and find it! Who lives there? Where do you turn off at? Hey Pop, can't we turn off there?"

"We never have seen a house with a secret panel!" June Star shrieked. "Let's go to the house with the secret panel! Hey Pop, can't we go see the house with the secret panel!"

"It's not far from here, I know," the grandmother said. "It wouldn't take over twenty minutes."

Bailey was looking straight ahead. His jaw was as rigid as a horseshoe. "No," he said.

The children began to yell and scream that they wanted to see the house with the secret panel. John Wesley kicked the back of the front seat and June Star hung over her mother's shoulder and whined desperately into her ear that they never had any fun even on their vacation, that they could never do what THEY wanted to do. The baby began to scream and John Wesley kicked the back of the seat so hard that his father could feel the blows in his kidney.

"All right!" he shouted and drew the car to a stop at the side of the road. "Will you all shut up? Will you all just shut up for one second? If you don't shut up, we won't go anywhere."

"It would be very educational for them," the grandmother murmured.

"All right," Bailey said, "but get this: this is the only time we're going to stop for anything like this. This is the one and only time."

"The dirt road that you have to turn down is about a mile back," the grandmother directed. "I marked it when we passed."

"A dirt road," Bailey groaned.

After they had turned around and were headed toward the dirt road, the grandmother recalled other points about the house, the beautiful glass over the front doorway and the candle-lamp in the hall. John Wesley said that the secret panel was probably in the fireplace.

"You can't go inside this house," Bailey said. "You don't know who lives there."

"While you all talk to the people in front, I'll run around behind and get in a window," John Wesley suggested.

"We'll all stay in the car," his mother said.

They turned onto the dirt road and the car raced roughly along in a swirl of pink dust. The grandmother recalled the times when there were no paved roads and thirty miles was a day's journey. The dirt road was hilly and there were sudden washes in it and sharp curves on dangerous embankments. All at once they would be on a hill, looking down over the blue tops of trees for miles around, then the next minute, they would be in a red depression with the dust-coated trees looking down on them.

"This place had better turn up in a minute," Bailey said, "or I'm going to turn around."

The road looked as if no one had traveled on it in months.

"It's not much farther," the grandmother said and just as she said it, a horrible thought came to her. The thought was so embarrassing that she turned red in the face and her eyes dilated and her feet jumped up, upsetting her valise in the corner. The instant the valise moved, the newspaper top she had over the basket under it rose with a snarl and Pitty Sing, the cat, sprang onto Bailey's shoulder.

The children were thrown to the floor and their mother, clutching the baby, was thrown out the door onto the ground; the old lady was thrown into the front seat. The car turned over once and landed right-side-up in a gulch off the side of the road. Bailey remained in the driver's seat with the cat—gray-striped with a broad white face and an orange nose—clinging to his neck like a caterpillar.

As soon as the children saw they could move their arms and legs, they scrambled out of the car, shouting, "We've had an ACCIDENT!" The grandmother was curled up under the dashboard, hoping she was injured so that Bailey's wrath would not come down on her all at once. The horrible thought she had had before the accident was that the house she had remembered so vividly was not in Georgia but in Tennessee.

Bailey removed the cat from his neck with both hands and flung it out the window against the side of a pine tree. Then he got out of the car and started looking for the children's mother. She was sitting against the side of the red gutted ditch, holding the screaming baby, but she only had a cut down her face and a broken shoulder. "We've had an ACCIDENT!" the children screamed in a frenzy of delight.

"But nobody's killed," June Star said with disappointment as the grandmother limped out of the car, her hat still pinned to her head but the broken front brim standing up at a jaunty angle and the violet spray hanging off the side. They all sat down in the ditch, except the children, to recover from the shock. They were all shaking.

"Maybe a car will come along," said the children's mother hoarsely.

"I believe I have injured an organ," said the grandmother, pressing her side, but no one answered her. Bailey's teeth were clattering. He had on a yellow sport shirt with bright blue parrots designed in it and his face was as yellow as the shirt. The grandmother decided that she would not mention that the house was in Tennessee.

The road was about ten feet above and they could see only the tops of the trees on the other side of it. Behind the ditch they were sitting in there were more woods, tall and dark and deep. In a few minutes they saw a car some distance away on top of a hill, coming slowly as if the occupants were watching them. The grandmother stood up and waved both arms dramatically to attract their attention. The car continued to come on slowly, disappeared around a bend and appeared again, moving even slower, on top of the hill they had gone over. It was a big black battered hearse-like automobile. There were three men in it.

It came to a stop just over them and for some minutes, the driver looked down with a steady expressionless gaze to where they were sitting, and didn't speak. Then he turned his head and muttered something to the other two and they got out. One was a fat boy in black trousers and a red sweat shirt with a silver stallion embossed on the front of it. He moved around on the right side of them and stood staring, his mouth

partly open in a kind of loose grin. The other had on khaki pants and a blue striped coat and a gray hat pulled down very low, hiding most of his face. He came around slowly on the left side. Neither spoke.

72   The driver got out of the car and stood by the side of it, looking down at them. He was an older man than the other two. His hair was just beginning to gray and he wore silver-rimmed spectacles that gave him a scholarly look. He had a long creased face and didn't have on any shirt or undershirt. He had on blue jeans that were too tight for him and was holding a black hat and a gun. The two boys also had guns.

73   "We've had an ACCIDENT!" the children screamed.

74   The grandmother had the peculiar feeling that the bespectacled man was someone she knew. His face was as familiar to her as if she had known him all her life but she could not recall who he was. He moved away from the car and began to come down the embankment, placing his feet carefully so that he wouldn't slip. He had on tan and white shoes and no socks, and his ankles were red and thin. "Good afternoon," he said. "I see you all had you a little spill."

75   "We turned over twice!" said the grandmother.

76   "Oncet," he corrected. "We seen it happen. Try their car and see will it run, Hiram," he said quietly to the boy with the gray hat.

77   "What you got that gun for?" John Wesley asked. "Whatcha gonna do with that gun?"

78   "Lady," the man said to the children's mother, "would you mind calling them children to sit down by you? Children make me nervous. I want all you to sit down right together there where you're at."

79   "What are you telling US what to do for?" June Star asked.

80   Behind them the line of woods gaped like a dark open mouth. "Come here," said their mother.

81   "Look here now," Bailey began suddenly, "we're in a predicament! We're in . . ."

82   The grandmother shrieked. She scrambled to her feet and stood staring. "You're The Misfit!" she said. "I recognized you at once!"

83   "Yes'm," the man said, smiling slightly as if he were pleased in spite of himself to be known, "but it would have been better for all of you, lady, if you hadn't of reckernized me."

84   Bailey turned his head sharply and said something to his mother that shocked even the children. The old lady began to cry and The Misfit reddened.

> ## Behind them the line of woods gaped like a dark open mouth.

"Lady," he said, "don't you get upset. Sometimes a man says things he don't mean. I don't reckon he meant to talk to you thataway."

"You wouldn't shoot a lady, would you?" the grandmother said and removed a clean handkerchief from her cuff and began to slap at her eyes with it.

The Misfit pointed the toe of his shoe into the ground and made a little hole and then covered it up again. "I would hate to have to," he said.

"Listen," the grandmother almost screamed, "I know you're a good man. You don't look a bit like you have common blood. I know you must come from nice people!"

"Yes mam," he said, "finest people in the world." When he smiled he showed a row of strong white teeth. "God never made a finer woman than my mother and my daddy's heart was pure gold," he said. The boy with the red sweat shirt had come around behind them and was standing with his gun at his hip. The Misfit squatted down on the ground. "Watch them children, Bobby Lee," he said. "You know they make me nervous." He looked at the six of them huddled together in front of him and he seemed to be embarrassed as if he couldn't think of anything to say. "Ain't a cloud in the sky," he remarked, looking up at it. "Don't see no sun but don't see no cloud neither."

"Yes, it's a beautiful day," said the grandmother. "Listen," she said, "you shouldn't call yourself The Misfit because I know you're a good man at heart. I can just look at you and tell."

"Hush!" Bailey yelled. "Hush! Everybody shut up and let me handle this!" He was squatting in the position of a runner about to sprint forward but he didn't move.

"I pre-chate that, lady," The Misfit said and drew a little circle in the ground with the butt of his gun.

"It'll take a half a hour to fix this here car," Hiram called, looking over the raised hood of it.

"Well, first you and Bobby Lee get him and that little boy to step over yonder with you," The Misfit said, pointing to Bailey and John Wesley. "The boys want to ast you something," he said to Bailey. "Would you mind stepping back in them woods there with them?"

"Listen," Bailey began, "we're in a terrible predicament! Nobody realizes what this is," his voice cracked. His eyes were as blue and intense as the parrots in his shirt and he remained perfectly still.

The grandmother reached up to adjust her hat brim as if she were going to the woods with him but it came

off in her hand. She stood staring at it and after a second she let it fall on the ground. Hiram pulled Bailey up by the arm as if he were assisting an old man. John Wesley caught hold of his father's hand and Bobby Lee followed. They went off toward the woods and just as they reached the dark edge, Bailey turned and supporting himself against a gray naked pine trunk, he shouted, "I'll be back in a minute, Mamma, wait on me!"

"Come back this instant!" his mother shrilled but they all disappeared into the woods.

"Bailey Boy!" the grandmother called in a tragic voice but she found she was looking at The Misfit squatting on the ground in front of her. "I just know you're a good man," she said desperately. "You're not a bit common!"

"Nome, I ain't a good man," The Misfit said after a second as if he had considered her statement carefully, "but I ain't the worst in the world neither. My daddy said I was a different breed of dog from my brothers and sisters. 'You know,' Daddy said, 'it's some that can live their whole life out without asking about it and it's others has to know why it is, and this boy is one of the latters. He's going to be into everything!'" He put on his black hat and looked up suddenly and then away deep into the woods as if he were embarrassed again. "I'm sorry I don't have on a shirt before you ladies," he said, hunching his shoulders slightly. "We buried our clothes that we had on when we escaped and we're just making do until we can get better. We borrowed these from some folks we met," he explained.

"That's perfectly all right," the grandmother said. "Maybe Bailey has an extra shirt in his suitcase."

"I'll look and see terrectly," The Misfit said.

"Where are they taking him?" the children's mother screamed.

"Daddy was a card himself," The Misfit said. "You couldn't put anything over on him. He never got in trouble with the Authorities though. Just had the knack of handling them."

"You could be honest too if you'd only try," said the grandmother. "Think how wonderful it would be to settle down and live a comfortable life and not have to think about somebody chasing you all the time."

The Misfit kept scratching in the ground with the butt of his gun as if he were thinking about it. "Yes'm, somebody is always after you," he murmured.

The grandmother noticed how thin his shoulder blades were just behind his hat because she was standing up looking down on him. "Do you ever pray?" she asked.

He shook his head. All she saw was the black hat wiggle between his shoulder blades. "Nome," he said.

There was a pistol shot from the woods, followed closely by another. Then silence. The old lady's head jerked around. She could hear the wind move through the tree tops like a long satisfied insuck of breath. "Bailey Boy!" she called.

"I was a gospel singer for a while," The Misfit said. "I been most everything. Been in the arm service, both land and sea, at home and abroad, been twice married, been an undertaker, been with the railroads, plowed Mother Earth, been in a tornado, seen a man burnt alive oncet," and looked up at the children's mother and the little girl who were sitting close together, their faces white and their eyes glassy; "I even seen a woman flogged," he said.

"Pray, pray," the grandmother began, "pray, pray . . ."

"I never was a bad boy that I remember of," The Misfit said in an almost dreamy voice, "but somewheres along the line I done something wrong and got sent to the penitentiary. I was buried alive," and he looked up and held her attention to him by a steady stare.

""That's when you should have started to pray," she said. "What did you do to get sent to the penitentiary that first time?"

"Turn to the right, it was a wall," The Misfit said, looking up again at the cloudless sky. "Turn to the left, it was a wall. Look up it was a ceiling, look down it was a floor. I forget what I done, lady. I set there and set there, trying to remember what it was I done and I ain't recalled it to this day. Oncet in a while, I would think it was coming to me, but it never come."

"Maybe they put you in by mistake," the old lady said vaguely.

"Nome," he said. "It wasn't no mistake. They had the papers on me."

103
104
105
106
107
108
109
110
111
112
113
114
115

97
98
99
100
101
102

116   "You must have stolen something," she said.

117   The Misfit sneered slightly. "Nobody had nothing I wanted," he said. "It was a head-doctor at the penitentiary said what I had done was kill my daddy but I know that for a lie. My daddy died in nineteen ought nineteen of the epidemic flu and I never had a thing to do with it. He was buried in the Mount Hopewell Baptist churchyard and you can go there and see for yourself."

118   "If you would pray," the old lady said, "Jesus would help you."

119   "That's right," The Misfit said.

120   "Well then, why don't you pray?" she asked trembling with delight suddenly.

121   "I don't want no hep," he said. "I'm doing all right by myself."

122   Bobby Lee and Hiram came ambling back from the woods. Bobby Lee was dragging a yellow shirt with bright blue parrots in it.

123   "Throw me that shirt, Bobby Lee," The Misfit said. The shirt came flying at him and landed on his shoulder and he put it on. The grandmother couldn't name what the shirt reminded her of. "No, lady," The Misfit said while he was buttoning it up, "I found out the crime don't matter. You can do one thing or you can do another, kill a man or take a tire off his car, because sooner or later you're going to forget what it was you done and just be punished for it."

124   The children's mother had begun to make heaving noises as if she couldn't get her breath. "Lady," he asked, "would you and that little girl like to step off yonder with Bobby Lee and Hiram and join your husband?"

125   "Yes, thank you," the mother said faintly. Her left arm dangled helplessly and she was holding the baby, who had gone to sleep, in the other. "Hep that lady up, Hiram," The Misfit said as she struggled to climb out of the ditch, "and Bobby Lee, you hold onto that little girl's hand."

126   "I don't want to hold hands with him," June Star said. "He reminds me of a pig."

127   The fat boy blushed and laughed and caught her by the arm and pulled her off into the woods after Hiram and her mother.

128   Alone with The Misfit, the grandmother found that she had lost her voice. There was not a cloud in the sky nor any sun. There was nothing around her but woods. She wanted to tell him that he must pray. She opened and closed her mouth several times before anything came out. Finally she found herself saying, "Jesus, Jesus," meaning, Jesus will help you, but the way she was saying it, it sounded as if she might be cursing.

        "Yes'm," The Misfit said as if he agreed. "Jesus thrown everything off balance. It was the same case with Him as with me except He hadn't committed any crime and they could prove I had committed one because they had the papers on me. Of course," he said, "they never shown me my papers. That's why I sign myself now. I said long ago, you get you a signature and sign everything you do and keep a copy of it. Then you'll know what you done and you can hold up the crime to the punishment and see do they match and in the end you'll have something to prove you ain't been treated right. I call myself The Misfit," he said, "because I can't make what all I done wrong fit what all I gone through in punishment."

        There was a piercing scream from the woods, followed closely by a pistol report. "Does it seem right to you, lady, that one is punished a heap and another ain't punished at all?"

        "Jesus!" the old lady cried. "You've got good blood! I know you wouldn't shoot a lady! I know you come from nice people! Pray! Jesus, you ought not to shoot a lady. I'll give you all the money I've got!"

        "Lady," The Misfit said, looking beyond her far into the woods, "there never was a body that give the undertaker a tip."

        There were two more pistol reports and the grandmother raised her head like a parched old turkey hen crying for water and called, "Bailey Boy, Bailey Boy!" as if her heart would break.

        "Jesus was the only One that ever raised the dead." The Misfit continued, "and He shouldn't have done it. He thrown everything off balance. If He did what He said, then it's nothing for you to do but throw away everything and follow Him, and if He didn't, then it's nothing for you to do but enjoy the few minutes you got left the best way you can—by killing somebody or burning down his house or doing some other meanness to him. No pleasure but meanness," he said and his voice had become almost a snarl.

        "Maybe He didn't raise the dead," the old lady mumbled, not knowing what she was saying and feeling so dizzy that she sank down in the ditch with her legs twisted under her.

        "I wasn't there so I can't say He didn't," The Misfit said. "I wisht I had of been there," he said, hitting the ground with his fist. "It ain't right I wasn't there be-

> There was a piercing scream from the woods, followed closely by a pistol report.

cause if I had of been there I would of known. Listen lady," he said in a high voice, "if I had of been there I would of known and I wouldn't be like I am now." His voice seemed about to crack and the grandmother's head cleared for an instant. She saw the man's face twisted close to her own as if he were going to cry and she murmured, "Why you're one of my babies. You're one of my own children!" She reached out and touched him on the shoulder. The Misfit sprang back as if a snake had bitten him and shot her three times through the chest. Then he put his gun down on the ground and took off his glasses and began to clean them.

Hiram and Bobby Lee returned from the woods and stood over the ditch, looking down at the grandmother who half sat and half lay in a puddle of blood with her legs crossed under her like a child's and her face smiling up at the cloudless sky.

Without his glasses, The Misfit's eyes were red-rimmed and pale and defenseless looking. "Take her off and throw her where you thrown the others," he said, picking up the cat that was rubbing itself against his leg. **138**

"She was a talker, wasn't she?" Bobby Lee said, sliding down the ditch with a yodel. **139**

"She would have been a good woman," The Misfit said, "if it had been somebody there to shoot her every minute of her life." **140**

"Some fun!" Bobby Lee said. **141**

"Shut up, Bobby Lee," The Misfit said. "It's no real pleasure in life." **142**

Questions for Critical Thinking

1 What is the grandmother's attitude toward the South as opposed to the rest of her family's attitude, particularly her grandson's? How do you account for the difference?

2 "It is the grandmother's 'Southern Pride' that leads to the family's downfall." In a short essay, explain whether you agree or disagree with this statement. Support your answer with examples from the text.

3 Review the story and mark the margins whenever you find an example of humor. How would you describe O'Connor's humor? What role does humor play in the story?

4 How much of a role does irony play in the story? How should we take The Misfit's final statement about the grandmother?

Revelation (1965)

THE doctor's waiting room, which was very small, was almost full when the Turpins entered and Mrs. Turpin, who was very large, made it look even smaller by her presence. She stood looming at the head of the magazine table set in the center of it, a living demonstration that the room was inadequate and ridiculous. Her little bright black eyes took in all the patients as she sized up the seating situation. There was one vacant chair and a place on a sofa occupied by a blond child in a dirty blue romper who should have been told to move over and make room for the lady. He was five or six, but Mrs. Turpin saw at once that no one was going to tell him to move over. He was slumped down in the seat, his arms idle at his sides and his eyes idle in his head; his nose ran unchecked.

Mrs. Turpin put a firm hand on Claud's shoulder and said in a voice that included anyone who wanted **2** to listen, "Claud, you sit in that chair there," and gave him a push down into the vacant one. Claud was florid and bald and sturdy, somewhat shorter than Mrs. Turpin, but he sat down as if he were accustomed to doing what she told him to.

3   Mrs. Turpin remained standing. The only man in the room besides Claud was a lean stringy old fellow with a rusty hand spread out on each knee, whose eyes were closed as if he were asleep or dead or pretending to be so as not to get up and offer her his seat. Her gaze settled agreeably on a well-dressed grey-haired lady whose eyes met hers and whose expression said: if that child belonged to me, he would have some manners and move over—there's plenty of room there for you and him too.

4   Claud looked up with a sigh and made as if to rise.

5   "Sit down," Mrs. Turpin said. "You know you're not supposed to stand on that leg. He has an ulcer on his leg," she explained.

6   Claud lifted his foot onto the magazine table and rolled his trouser leg up to reveal a purple swelling on a plump marble-white calf.

7   "My!" the pleasant lady said. "How did you do that?"

8   "A cow kicked him," Mrs. Turpin said.

9   "Goodness!" said the lady.

10   Claud rolled his trouser leg down.

11   "Maybe the little boy would move over," the lady suggested, but the child did not stir.

12   "Somebody will be leaving in a minute," Mrs. Turpin said. She could not understand why a doctor—with as much money as they made charging five dollars a day to just stick their head in the hospital door and look at you—couldn't afford a decent-sized waiting room. This one was hardly bigger than a garage. The table was cluttered with limp-looking magazines and at one end of it there was a big green glass ash tray full of cigaret butts and cotton wads with little blood spots on them. If she had had anything to do with the running of the place, that would have been emptied every so often. There were no chairs against the wall at the head of the room. It had a rectangular-shaped panel in it that permitted a view of the office where the nurse came and went and the secretary listened to the radio. A plastic fern in a gold pot sat in the opening and trailed its fronds down almost to the floor. The radio was softly playing gospel music.

13   Just then the inner door opened and a nurse with the highest stack of yellow hair Mrs. Turpin had ever seen put her face in the crack and called for the next patient. The woman sitting beside Claud grasped the two arms of her chair and hoisted herself up; she pulled her dress free from her legs and lumbered through the door where the nurse had disappeared.

Mrs. Turpin eased into the vacant chair, which held her tight as a corset. "I wish I could reduce," she said, and rolled her eyes and gave a comic sigh.

"Oh, *you* aren't fat," the stylish lady said.

"Ooooo I am too," Mrs. Turpin said. "Claud he eats all he wants to and never weighs over one hundred and seventy-five pounds, but me I just look at something good to eat and I gain some weight," and her stomach and shoulders shook with laughter. "You can eat all you want to, can't you, Claud?" she asked, turning to him.

Claud only grinned.

"Well, as long as you have such a good disposition," the stylish lady said, "I don't think it makes a bit of difference what size you are. You just can't beat a good disposition."

Next to her was a fat girl of eighteen or nineteen, scowling into a thick blue book which Mrs. Turpin saw was entitled *Human Development*. The girl raised her head and directed her scowl at Mrs. Turpin as if she did not like her looks. She appeared annoyed that anyone should speak while she tried to read. The poor girl's face was blue with acne and Mrs. Turpin thought how pitiful it was to have a face like that at that age. She gave the girl a friendly smile but the girl only scowled the harder. Mrs. Turpin herself was fat but she had always had good skin, and, though she was forty-seven years old, there was not a wrinkle in her face except around her eyes from laughing too much.

Next to the ugly girl was the child, still in exactly the same position, and next to him was a thin leathery old woman in a cotton print dress. She and Claud had three sacks of chicken feed in their pump house that was in the same print. She had seen from the first that the child belonged with the old woman. She could tell by the way they sat—kind of vacant and white-trashy, as if they would sit there until Doomsday if nobody called and told them to get up. And at right angles but next to the well-dressed pleasant lady was a lank-faced woman who was certainly the child's mother. She had on a yellow sweat shirt and wine-colored slacks, both gritty-looking, and the rims of her lips were stained with snuff. Her dirty yellow hair was tied behind with a little piece of red paper ribbon. Worse than niggers any day, Mrs. Turpin thought.

The gospel hymn playing was, "When I looked up and He looked down," and Mrs. Turpin, who knew it, supplied the last line mentally, "And wona these days I know I'll we-eara crown."

Without appearing to, Mrs. Turpin always noticed people's feet. The well-dressed lady had on red and grey suede shoes to match her dress. Mrs. Turpin had on her good black patent leather pumps. The ugly girl had on Girl Scout shoes and heavy socks. The old woman had on tennis shoes and the white-trashy mother had on what appeared to be bedroom slippers, black straw with gold braid threaded through them—exactly what you would have expected her to have on.

Sometimes at night when she couldn't go to sleep, Mrs. Turpin would occupy herself with the question of who she would have chosen to be if she couldn't have been herself. If Jesus had said to her before he made her, "There's only two places available for you. You can either be a nigger or white-trash," what would she have said? "Please, Jesus, please," she would have said, "just let me wait until there's another place available," and he would have said, "No, you have to go right now and I have only those two places so make up your mind." She would have wiggled and squirmed and begged and pleaded but it would have been no use and finally she would have said, "All right, make me a nigger then—but that don't mean a trashy one." And he would have made her a neat clean respectable Negro woman, herself but black.

Next to the child's mother was a red-headed youngish woman, reading one of the magazines and working a piece of chewing gum, hell for leather, as Claud would say. Mrs. Turpin could not see the woman's feet. She was not white-trash, just common. Sometimes Mrs. Turpin occupied herself at night naming the classes of people. On the bottom of the heap were most colored people, not the kind she would have been if she had been one, but most of them; then next to them—not above, just away from—were the white-trash; then above them were the home-owners, and above them the home-and-land owners, to which she and Claud belonged. Above she and Claud were people with a lot of money and much bigger houses and much more land. But here the complexity of it would begin to bear in on her, for some of the people with a lot of money were common and ought to be below she and Claud and some of the people who had good blood had lost their money and had to rent and then there were colored people who owned their homes and land as well. There was a colored dentist in town who had two red Lincolns and a swimming pool and a farm with registered white-face cattle on it. Usually by the time she had fallen asleep all the classes of people were moiling and roiling around in her head, and she would dream they were all crammed in together in a box car, being ridden off to be put in a gas oven.

> ### Sometimes Mrs. Turpin occupied herself at night
> naming the classes of people.

"That's a beautiful clock," she said and nodded to her right. It was a big wall clock, the face encased in a brass sunburst.

"Yes, it's very pretty," the stylish lady said agreeably. "And right on the dot too," she added, glancing at her watch.

The ugly girl beside her cast an eye upward at the clock, smirked, then looked directly at Mrs. Turpin and smirked again. Then she returned her eyes to her book. She was obviously the lady's daughter because, although they didn't look anything alike as to disposition, they both had the same shape of face and the same blue eyes. On the lady they sparkled pleasantly but in the girl's seared face they appeared alternately to smolder and to blaze.

What if Jesus had said, "All right, you can be white-trash or a nigger or ugly"!

Mrs. Turpin felt an awful pity for the girl, though she thought it was one thing to be ugly and another to act ugly.

The woman with the snuff-stained lips turned around in her chair and looked up at the clock. Then she turned back and appeared to look a little to the side of Mrs. Turpin. There was a cast in one of her eyes. "You want to know wher you can get you one of them ther clocks?" she asked in a loud voice.

"No, I already have a nice clock," Mrs. Turpin said. Once somebody like her got a leg in the conversation, she would be all over it.

"You can get you one with green stamps," the woman said. "That's most likely wher he got hisn. Save you up enough, you can get you most anythang. I got me some joo'ry."

Ought to have got you a wash rag and some soap, Mrs. Turpin thought.

"I get contour sheets with mine," the pleasant lady said.

The daughter slammed her book shut. She looked straight in front of her, directly through Mrs. Turpin and on through the yellow curtain and the plate glass window which made the wall behind her. The girl's eyes seemed lit all of a sudden with a peculiar light, an unnatural light like night road signs give. Mrs. Turpin turned her head to see if there was anything going on outside that she should see, but she could not see anything. Figures passing cast only a pale shadow through the curtain. There was no reason the girl should single her out for her ugly looks.

"Miss Finley," the nurse said, cracking the door. The gum-chewing woman got up and passed in front of her and Claud and went into the office. She had on red high-heeled shoes.

37 Directly across the table, the ugly girl's eyes were fixed on Mrs. Turpin as if she had some very special reason for disliking her.

38 "This is wonderful weather, isn't it?" the girl's mother said.

39 "It's good weather for cotton if you can get the niggers to pick it," Mrs. Turpin said, "but niggers don't want to pick cotton any more. You can't get the white folks to pick it and now you can't get the niggers—because they got to be right up there with the white folks."

40 "They gonna *try* anyways," the white-trash woman said, leaning forward.

41 "Do you have one of those cotton-picking machines?" the pleasant lady asked.

42 "No," Mrs. Turpin said, "they leave half the cotton in the field. We don't have much cotton anyway. If you want to make it farming now, you have to have a little of everything. We got a couple of acres of cotton and a few hogs and chickens and just enough white-face that Claud can look after them himself."

43 "One thang I don't want," the white-trash woman said, wiping her mouth with the back of her hands. "Hogs. Nasty stinking things, a-gruntin and a-rootin all over the place."

44 Mrs. Turpin gave her the merest edge of her attention. "Our hogs are not dirty and they don't stink," she said. "They're cleaner than some children I've seen. Their feet never touch the ground. We have a pig-parlor—that's where you raise them on concrete," she explained to the pleasant lady, "and Claud scoots them down with the hose every afternoon and washes off the floor." Cleaner by far than that child right there, she thought. Poor nasty little thing. He had not moved except to put the thumb of his dirty hand into his mouth.

45 The woman turned her face away from Mrs. Turpin. "I know I wouldn't scoot down no hog with no hose," she said to the wall.

46 You wouldn't have no hog to scoot down, Mrs. Turpin said to herself.

47 "A-gruntin and a-rootin and a-groanin," the woman muttered.

48 "We got a little of everything," Mrs. Turpin said to the pleasant lady. "It's no use in having more than you can handle yourself with help like it is. We found enough niggers to pick our cotton this year but Claud he has to go after them and take them home again in the evening. They can't walk that half a mile. No

they can't. I tell you," she said and laughed merrily. "I sure am tired of buttering up niggers, but you got to love em if you want em to work for you. When they come in the morning, I run out and I say, 'Hi yawl this morning?' and when Claud drives them off to the field I just wave to beat the band and they just wave back." And she waved her hand rapidly to illustrate.

"Like you read out of the same book," the lady said, showing she understood perfectly.

"Child, yes," Mrs. Turpin said. "And when they come in from the field, I run out with a bucket of icewater. That's the way it's going to be from now on," she said. "You may as well face it."

"One thang I know," the white-trash woman said. "Two thangs I ain't going to do: love no niggers or scoot down no hog with no hose." And she let out a bark of contempt.

The look that Mrs. Turpin and the pleasant lady exchanged indicated they both understood that you had to *have* certain things before you could *know* certain things. But every time Mrs. Turpin exchanged a look with the lady, she was aware that the ugly girl's peculiar eyes were still on her, and she had trouble bringing her attention back to the conversation.

"When you got something," she said, "you got to look after it." And when you ain't got a thing but breath and britches, she added to herself, you can afford to come to town every morning and just sit on the Court House coping and spit.

A grotesque revolving shadow passed across the curtain behind her and was thrown palely on the opposite wall. Then a bicycle clattered down against the outside of the building. The door opened and a colored boy glided in with a tray from the drug store. It had two large red and white paper cups on it with tops on them. He was a tall, very black boy in discolored white pants and a green nylon shirt. He was chewing gum slowly, as if to music. He set the tray down in the office opening next to the fern and stuck his head through to look for the secretary. She was not in there. He rested his arms on the ledge and waited, his narrow bottom stuck out, swaying slowly to the left and right. He raised a hand over his head and scratched the base of his skull.

"You see that button there, boy?" Mrs. Turpin said. "You can punch that and she'll come. She's probably in the back somewhere."

"Is thas right?" the boy said agreeably, as if he had never seen the button before. He leaned to the right

> ... they both understood that you had to *have* certain things before you could *know* certain things.

and put his finger on it. "She sometime out," he said and twisted around to face his audience, his elbows behind him on the counter. The nurse appeared and he twisted back again. She handed him a dollar and he rooted in his pocket and made the change and counted it out to her. She gave him fifteen cents for a tip and he went out with the empty tray. The heavy door swung to slowly and closed at length with the sound of suction. For a moment no one spoke.

"They ought to send all them niggers back to Africa," the white-trash woman said. "That's wher they come from in the first place."

"Oh, I couldn't do without my good colored friends," the pleasant lady said.

"There's a heap of things worse than a nigger," Mrs. Turpin agreed. "It's all kinds of them just like it's all kinds of us."

"Yes, and it takes all kinds to make the world go round," the lady said in her musical voice.

As she said it, the raw-complexioned girl snapped her teeth together. Her lower lip turned downwards and inside out, revealing the pale pink inside of her mouth. After a second it rolled back up. It was the ugliest face Mrs. Turpin had ever seen anyone make and for a moment she was certain that the girl had made it at her. She was looking at her as if she had known and disliked her all her life—all of Mrs. Turpin's life, it seemed too, not just all the girl's life. Why, girl, I don't even know you, Mrs. Turpin said silently.

She forced her attention back to the discussion. "It wouldn't be practical to send them back to Africa," she said. "They wouldn't want to go. They got it too good here."

"Wouldn't be what they wanted—if I had anything to do with it," the woman said.

"It wouldn't be a way in the world you could get all the niggers back over there," Mrs. Turpin said. "They'd be hiding out and lying down and turning sick on you and wailing and hollering and raring and pitching. It wouldn't be a way in the world to get them over there."

"They got over here," the trashy woman said. "Get back like they got over."

"It wasn't so many of them then," Mrs. Turpin explained.

The woman looked at Mrs. Turpin as if here was an idiot indeed but Mrs. Turpin was not bothered by the look, considering where it came from.

"Nooo," she said, "they're going to stay here where they can

go to New York and marry white folks and improve their color. That's what they all want to do, every one of them, improve their color."

69 "You know what comes of that, don't you?" Claud asked.

70 "No, Claud, what?" Mrs. Turpin said.

71 Claud's eyes twinkled. "White-faced niggers," he said with never a smile.

72 Everybody in the office laughed except the white-trash and the ugly girl. The girl gripped the book in her lap with white fingers. The trashy woman looked around her from face to face as if she thought they were all idiots. The old woman in the feed sack dress continued to gaze expressionless across the floor at the hightop shoes of the man opposite her, the one who had been pretending to be asleep when the Turpins came in. He was laughing heartily, his hands still spread out on his knees. The child had fallen to the side and was lying now almost face down in the old woman's lap.

73 While they recovered from their laughter, the nasal chorus on the radio kept the room from silence.

> "You go to blank blank
> And I'll go to mine
> But we'll all blank along
> To-geth-ther,
> And all along the blank
> We'll hep each other out
> Smile-ling in any kind of
> Weath-ther!"

74 Mrs. Turpin didn't catch every word but she caught enough to agree with the spirit of the song and it turned her thoughts sober. To help anybody out that needed it was her philosophy of life. She never spared herself when she found somebody in need, whether they were white or black, trash or decent. And of all she had to be thankful for, she was most thankful that this was so. If Jesus had said, "You can be high society and have all the money you want and be thin and svelte-like, but you can't be a good woman with it," she would have had to say, "Well don't make me that then. Make me a good woman and it don't matter what else, how fat or how ugly or how poor!" Her heart rose. He had not made her a nigger or white-trash or ugly! He had made her herself and given her a little of everything. Jesus, thank you! she said. Thank you thank you thank you! Whenever she counted her blessings she felt as buoyant as if she weighed one hundred and twenty-five pounds instead of one hundred and eighty.

75   "What's wrong with your little boy?" the pleasant lady asked the white-trashy woman.

76   "He has a ulcer," the woman said proudly. "He ain't give me a minute's peace since he was born. Him and her are just alike," she said, nodding at the old woman, who was running her leathery fingers through the child's pale hair. "Look like I can't get nothing down them two but Co' Cola and candy."

77   That's all you try to get down em, Mrs. Turpin said to herself. Too lazy to light the fire. There was nothing you could tell her about people like them that she didn't know already. And it was not just that they didn't have anything. Because if you gave them everything, in two weeks it would all be broken or filthy or they would have chopped it up for lightwood. She knew all this from her own experience. Help them you must, but help them you couldn't.

78   All at once the ugly girl turned her lips inside out again. Her eyes were fixed like two drills on Mrs. Turpin. This time there was no mistaking that there was something urgent behind them.

79   Girl, Mrs. Turpin exclaimed silently, I haven't done a thing to you! The girl might be confusing her with somebody else. There was no need to sit by and let herself be intimidated. "You must be in college," she said boldly, looking directly at the girl. "I see you reading a book there."

80   The girl continued to stare and pointedly did not answer.

81   Her mother blushed at this rudeness. "The lady asked you a question, Mary Grace," she said under her breath.

82   "I have ears," Mary Grace said.

83   The poor mother blushed again. "Mary Grace goes to Wellesley College," she explained. She twisted one of the buttons on her dress. "In Massachusetts," she added with a grimace. "And in the summer she just keeps right on studying. Just reads all the time, a real book worm, She's done real well at Wellesley; she's taking English and Math and History and Psychology and Social Studies," she rattled on, "and I think it's too much. I think she ought to get out and have fun."

84   The girl looked as if she would like to hurl them all through the plate glass window.

85   "Way up north," Mrs. Turpin murmured and thought, well, it hasn't done much for her manners.

86   "I'd almost rather to have him sick," the white-trash woman said, wrenching the attention back to herself. "He's so mean when he ain't. Look like some children just take natural to meanness. It's some gets bad when they get sick but he was the opposite. Took sick and turned good. He don't give me no trouble now. It's me waitin to see the doctor," she said.

If I was going to send anybody back to Africa, Mrs. Turpin thought, it would be your kind, woman. "Yes, indeed," she said aloud, but looking up at the ceiling, "it's a heap of things worse than a nigger." And dirtier than a hog, she added to herself.

"I think people with bad dispositions are more to be pitied than anyone on earth," the pleasant lady said in a voice that was decidedly thin.

"I thank the Lord he has blessed me with a good one," Mrs. Turpin said. "The day has never dawned that I couldn't find something to laugh at."

"Not since she married me anyways," Claud said with a comical straight face.

Everybody laughed except the girl and the white-trash.

Mrs. Turpin's stomach shook. "He's such a caution," she said, "that I can't help but laugh at him."

The girl made a loud ugly noise through her teeth.

Her mother's mouth grew thin and straight. "I think the worst thing in the world," she said, "is an ungrateful person. To have everything and not appreciate it. I know a girl," she said, "who has parents who would give her anything, a little brother who loves her dearly, who is getting a good education, who wears the best clothes, but who can never say a kind word to anyone, who never smiles, who just criticizes and complains all day long."

"Is she too old to paddle?" Claud asked.

The girl's face was almost purple.

"Yes," the lady said, "I'm afraid there's nothing to do but leave her to her folly. Some day she'll wake up and it'll be too late."

"It never hurt anyone to smile," Mrs. Turpin said. "It just makes you feel better all over."

"Of course," the lady said sadly, "but there are just some people you can't tell anything to. They can't take criticism."

"If it's one thing I am," Mrs. Turpin said with feeling, "it's grateful. When I think who all I could have been besides myself and what all I got, a little of everything, and a good disposition besides, I just feel like shouting, 'Thank you, Jesus, for making everything the way it is!' It could have been different!" For one thing, somebody else could have got Claud. At the thought of this, she was flooded with gratitude and a terrible pang of joy ran through her. "Oh thank you, Jesus, Jesus, thank you!" she cried aloud.

> There was nothing you could tell her about people like them that she didn't know already.

The book struck her directly over her left eye. It struck almost at the same instant that she realized the girl was about to hurl it. Before she could utter a sound, the raw face came crashing across the table toward her, howling. The girl's fingers sank like clamps into the soft flesh of her neck. She heard the mother cry out and Claud shout, "Whoa!" There was an instant when she was certain that she was about to be in an earthquake.

All at once her vision narrowed and she saw everything as if it were happening in a small room far away, or as if she were looking at it through the wrong end of a telescope. Claud's face crumpled and fell out of sight. The nurse ran in, then out, then in again. Then the gangling figure of the doctor rushed out of the inner door. Magazines flew this way and that as the table turned over. The girl fell with a thud and Mrs. Turpin's vision suddenly reversed itself and she saw everything large instead of small. The eyes of the white-trashy woman were staring hugely at the floor. There the girl, held down on one side by the nurse and on the other by her mother, was wrenching and turning in their grasp. The doctor was kneeling astride her, trying to hold her arm down. He managed after a second to sink a long needle into it.

Mrs. Turpin felt entirely hollow except for her heart which swung from side to side as if it were agitated in a great empty drum of flesh.

"Somebody that's not busy call for the ambulance," the doctor said in the offhand voice young doctors adopt for terrible occasions.

Mrs. Turpin could not have moved a finger. The old man who had been sitting next to her skipped nimbly into the office and made the call, for the secretary still seemed to be gone.

"Claud!" Mrs. Turpin called.

He was not in his chair. She knew she must jump up and find him but she felt like someone trying to catch a train in a dream, when everything moves in slow motion and the faster you try to run the slower you go.

"Here I am," a suffocated voice, very unlike Claud's, said.

He was doubled up in the corner on the floor, pale as paper, holding his leg. She wanted to get up and go to him but she could not move. Instead, her gaze was drawn slowly downward to the churning face on the floor, which she could see over the doctor's shoulder.

110 The girl's eyes stopped rolling and focused on her. They seemed a much lighter blue than before, as if a door that had been tightly closed behind them was now open to admit light and air.

111 Mrs. Turpin's head cleared and her power of motion returned. She leaned forward until she was looking directly into the fierce brilliant eyes. There was no doubt in her mind that the girl did know her, knew her in some intense and personal way, beyond time and place and condition. "What you got to say to me?" she asked hoarsely and held her breath, waiting, as for a revelation.

112 The girl raised her head. Her gaze locked with Mrs. Turpin's. "Go back to hell where you came from, you old wart hog," she whispered. Her voice was low but clear. Her eyes burned for a moment as if she saw with pleasure that her message had struck its target.

113 Mrs. Turpin sank back in her chair.

114 After a moment the girl's eyes closed and she turned her head wearily to the side.

115 The doctor rose and handed the nurse the empty syringe. He leaned over and put both hands for a moment on the mother's shoulders, which were shaking. She was sitting on the floor, her lips pressed together, holding Mary Grace's hand in her lap. The girl's fingers were gripped like a baby's around her thumb. "Go on to the hospital," he said. "I'll call and make the arrangements."

116 "Now let's see that neck," he said in a jovial voice to Mrs. Turpin. He began to inspect her neck with his first two fingers. Two little moon-shaped lines like pink fish bones were indented over her windpipe. There was the beginning of an angry red swelling above her eye. His fingers passed over this also.

117 "Lea'me be," she said thickly and shook him off. "See about Claud. She kicked him."

118 "I'll see about him in a minute," he said and felt her pulse. He was a thin gray-haired man, given to pleasantries. "Go home and have yourself a vacation the rest of the day," he said and patted her on the shoulder.

119 Quit your pattin me, Mrs. Turpin growled to herself.

120 "And put an ice pack over that eye," he said. Then he went and squatted down beside Claud and looked at his leg. After a moment he pulled him up and Claud limped after him into the office.

121   Until the ambulance came, the only sounds in the room were the tremulous moans of the girl's mother, who continued to sit on the floor. The white-trash woman did not take her eyes off the girl. Mrs. Turpin looked straight ahead at nothing. Presently the ambulance drew up, a long dark shadow, behind the curtain. The attendants came in and set the stretcher down beside the girl and lifted her expertly onto it and carried her out. The nurse helped the mother gather up her things. The shadow of the ambulance moved silently away and the nurse came back in the office.

122   "That ther girl is going to be a lunatic, ain't she?" the white-trash woman asked the nurse, but the nurse kept on to the back and never answered her.

123   "Yes, she's going to be a lunatic," the white-trash woman said to the rest of them.

124   "Po' critter," the old woman murmured. The child's face was still in her lap. His eyes looked idly out over her knees. He had not moved during the disturbance except to draw one leg up under him.

125   "I thank Gawd," the white-trash woman said fervently, "I ain' a lunatic."

126   Claud came limping out and the Turpins went home.

127   As their pick-up truck turned into their own dirt road and made the crest of the hill, Mrs. Turpin gripped the window ledge and looked out suspiciously. The land sloped gracefully down through a field dotted with lavender weeds and at the start of the rise their small yellow frame house, with its little flower beds spread out around it like a fancy apron, sat primly in its accustomed place between two giant hickory trees. She would not have been startled to see a burnt wound between two blackened chimneys.

128   Neither of them felt like eating so they put on their house clothes and lowered the shade in the bedroom and lay down, Claud with his leg on a pillow and herself with a damp washcloth over her eye. The instant she was flat on her back, the image of a razor-backed hog with warts on its face and horns coming out behind its ears snorted into her head. She moaned, a low quiet moan.

129   "I am not," she said tearfully, "a wart hog. From hell." But the denial had no force. The girl's eyes and her words, even the tone of her voice, low but clear, directed only to her, brooked no repudiation. She had been singled out for the message, though there was trash in the room to whom it might justly have been applied. The full force of this fact struck her only now. There was a woman there who was neglecting her own child but she had been overlooked. The message had been given to Ruby Turpin, a respectable, hardworking, church-going woman. The tears dried. Her eyes began to burn instead with wrath.

She rose on her elbow and the washcloth fell into her hand. Claud was lying on his back, snoring. She wanted to tell him what the girl had said. At the same time, she did not wish to put the image of herself as a wart hog from hell into his mind.

"Hey, Claud," she muttered and pushed his shoulder.

Claud opened one pale baby blue eye.

She looked into it warily. He did not think about anything. He just went his way.

"Wha, whasit?" he said and closed the eye again.

"Nothing," she said. Does your leg pain you?"

"Hurts like hell," Claud said.

"It'll quit terreckly," she said and lay back down. In a moment Claud was snoring again. For the rest of the afternoon they lay there. Claud slept. She scowled at the ceiling. Occasionally she raised her fist and made a small stabbing motion over her chest as if she was defending her innocence to invisible guests who were like the comforters of Job, reasonable-seeming but wrong.

About five-thirty Claud stirred. "Got to go after those niggers," he sighed, not moving.

She was looking straight up as if there were unintelligible handwriting on the ceiling. The protuberance over her eye had turned a greenish-blue. "Listen here," she said.

"What?"

"Kiss me."

Claud leaned over and kissed her loudly on the mouth. He pinched her side and their hands interlocked. Her expression of ferocious concentration did not change. Claud got up, groaning and growling, and limped off. She continued to study the ceiling.

She did not get up until she heard the pick-up truck coming back with the Negroes. Then she rose and thrust her feet in her brown oxfords, which she did not bother to lace, and stumped out onto the back porch and got her red plastic bucket. She emptied a tray of ice cubes into it and filled it half full of water and went out into the back yard. Every afternoon after Claud brought the hands in, one of the boys helped him put out hay and the rest waited in the back of the truck until he was ready to take them home. The truck was parked in the shade under one of the hickory trees.

"Hi yawl this evening?" Mrs. Turpin asked grimly, appearing with the bucket and the dipper. There were three women and a boy in the truck.

"Us doin nicely," the oldest woman said. "Hi you doin?" and her gaze stuck immediately on the dark lump on Mrs. Turpin's forehead. "You done fell down, ain't you?" she asked in a solicitous voice. The old woman was dark and almost toothless. She had on an old felt hat of Claud's set back on her head. The other two women were younger and lighter and they both had new bright green sun hats. One of them had hers on her head; the other had taken hers off and the boy was grinning beneath it.

Mrs. Turpin set the bucket down on the floor of the truck. "Yawl hep yourselves," she said. She looked around to make sure Claud had gone. "No. I didn't fall down," she said, folding her arms. "It was something worse than that."

"Ain't nothing bad happen to you!" the old woman said. She said it as if they all knew Mrs. Turpin was protected in some special way by Divine Providence. "You just had you a little fall."

"We were in town at the doctor's office for where the cow kicked Mr. Turpin," Mrs. Turpin said in a flat tone that indicated they could leave off their foolishness. "And there was this girl there. A big fat girl with her face all broke out. I could look at that girl and tell she was peculiar but I couldn't tell how. And me and her mama were just talking and going along and all of a sudden WHAM! She throws this big book she was reading at me and . . ."

"Naw!" the old woman cried out.

"And then she jumps over the table and commences to choke me."

"Naw!" they all exclaimed, "naw!"

"Hi come she do that?" the old woman asked. "What ail her?"

Mrs. Turpin only glared in front of her.

"Somethin ail her," the old woman said.

"They carried her off in an ambulance," Mrs. Turpin continued, "but before she went she was rolling on the floor and they were trying to hold her down to give her a shot and she said something to me." She paused. "You know what she said to me?"

"What she say?" they asked.

"She said," Mrs. Turpin began, and stopped, her face very dark and heavy. The sun was getting whiter and whiter, blanching the sky overhead so that the

leaves of the hickory tree were black in the face of it. She could not bring forth the words. "Something real ugly," she muttered.

"She sho shouldn' said nothing ugly to you," the old woman said. "You so sweet. You the sweetest lady I know." 158

"She pretty too," the one with the hat on said. 159

"And stout," the other one said. "I never knowed no sweeter white lady." 160

"That's the truth befo' Jesus," the old woman said. "Amen! You des as sweet and pretty as you can be." 161

Mrs. Turpin knew just exactly how much Negro flattery was worth and it added to her rage: "She said," she began again and finished this time with a fierce rush of breath, "that I was an old wart hog from hell." 162

There was an astounded silence. 163

"Where she at?" the youngest woman cried in a piercing voice. 164

"Lemme see her. I'll kill her!" 165

"I'll kill her with you!" the other one cried. 166

"She b'long in the sylum," the old woman said emphatically. "You the sweetest white lady I know." 167

"She pretty too," the other two said. "Stout as she can be and sweet. Jesus satisfied with her!" 168

"Deed he is," the old woman declared. 169

Idiots! Mrs. Turpin growled to herself. You could never say anything intelligent to a nigger. You could talk at them but not with them. "Yawl ain't drunk your water," she said shortly. "Leave the bucket in the truck when you're finished with it. I got more to do than just stand around and pass the time of day," and she moved off and into the house. 170

She stood for a moment in the middle of the kitchen. The dark protuberance over her eye looked like a miniature tornado cloud which might any moment sweep across the horizon of her brow. Her lower lip protruded dangerously. She squared her massive shoulders. Then she marched into the front of the house and out the side door and started down the road to the pig parlor. She had the look of a woman going single-handed, weaponless, into battle. 171

The sun was a deep yellow now like a harvest moon and was riding westward very fast over the far tree line as if it meant to reach the hogs before she did. The road was rutted and she kicked several good-sized stones out of her path as she strode along. The pig parlor was on a little knoll at the end of a lane that ran off from the side of the barn. It was a square of concrete as large as a small room, with a board fence about four feet high around it. The concrete floor sloped slightly so that the hog wash could drain off into a trench where it was carried to the field for fertilizer. Claud was standing on the outside, on the edge of the concrete, hanging onto the top board, hosing 172 down the floor inside. The hose was connected to the faucet of a water trough nearby.

173 Mrs. Turpin climbed up beside him and glowered down at the hogs inside. There were seven long-snouted bristly shoats in it—tan with liver-colored spots—and an old sow a few weeks off from farrowing. She was lying on her side grunting. The shoats were running about shaking themselves like idiot children, their little slit pig eyes searching the floor for anything left. She had read that pigs were the most intelligent animal. She doubted it. They were supposed to be smarter than dogs. There had even been a pig astronaut. He had performed his assignment perfectly but died of a heart attack afterwards because they left him in his electric suit, sitting upright throughout his examination when naturally a hog should be on all fours.

174 A-gruntin and a-rootin and a-groanin.

175 "Gimme that hose," she said, yanking it away from Claud. "Go on and carry them niggers home and then get off that leg."

176 "You look like you might have swallowed a mad dog," Claud observed, but he got down and limped off. He paid no attention to her humors.

177 Until he was out of earshot, Mrs. Turpin stood on the side of the pen, holding the hose and pointing the stream of water at the hind quarters of any shoat that looked as if it might try to lie down. When he had had time to get over the hill, she turned her head slightly and her wrathful eyes scanned the path. He was nowhere in sight. She turned back again and seemed to gather herself up. Her shoulder rose and she drew in her breath.

"What do you send me a message like that for?" she said in a low fierce voice, barely above a whisper but with the force of a shout in its concentrated fury. "How am I hog and me both? How am I saved from hell too?" Her free fist was knotted and with the other she gripped the hose, blindly pointing the stream of water in and out of the eye of the old sow whose outraged squeal she did not hear.

The pig parlor commanded a view of the back pasture where their twenty beef cows were gathered around the hay-bales Claud and the boy had put out. The freshly cut pasture sloped down to the highway. Across it was their cotton field and beyond that a dark green dusty wood which they owned as well. The sun was behind the wood, very red, looking over the paling of trees like a farmer inspecting his own hogs.

"Why me?" she rumbled. "It's no trash around here, black or white, that I haven't given to. And break my back to the bone every day working. And do for the church."

She appeared to be the right size woman to command the arena before her. "How am I a hog?" she demanded. "Exactly how am I like them?" and she jabbed the stream of water at the shoats. "There was plenty of trash there. It didn't have to be me.

"If you like trash better, go get yourself some trash then," she railed. "You could have made me trash. Or a nigger. If trash is what you wanted why didn't you make me trash?" She shook her fist with the hose in it and a watery snake appeared momentarily in the air. "I could quit working and take it easy and be filthy,"

she growled. "Lounge about the sidewalks all day drinking root beer. Dip snuff and spit in every puddle and have it all over my face. I could be nasty.

"Or you could have made me a nigger. It's too late for me to be a nigger," she said with deep sarcasm, "but I could act like one. Lay down in the middle of the road and stop traffic. Roll on the ground."

In the deepening light everything was taking on a mysterious hue. The pasture was growing a peculiar glassy green and the streak of highway had turned lavender. She braced herself for a final assault and this time her voice rolled out over the pasture. "Go on," she yelled, "call me a hog! Call me a hog again. From hell. Call me a wart hog from hell. Put that bottom rail on top. There'll still be a top and bottom!"

A garbled echo returned to her.

A final surge of fury shook her and she roared, "Who do you think you are?"

The color of everything, field and crimson sky, burned for a moment with a transparent intensity. The question carried over the pasture and across the highway and the cotton field and returned to her clearly like an answer from beyond the wood.

She opened her mouth but no sound came out of it.

A tiny truck, Claud's, appeared on the highway, heading rapidly out of sight. Its gears scraped thinly. It looked like a child's toy. At any moment a bigger truck might smash into it and scatter Claud's and the niggers' brains all over the road.

Mrs. Turpin stood there, her gaze fixed on the highway, all her muscles rigid, until in five or six minutes the truck reappeared, returning. She waited until it had had time to turn into their own road. Then like a monumental statue coming to life, she bent her head slowly and gazed, as if through the very heart of mystery, down into the pig parlor at the hogs. They had settled all in one corner around the old sow who was grunting softly. A red glow suffused them. They appeared to pant with a secret life.

Until the sun slipped finally behind the tree line, Mrs. Turpin remained there with her gaze bent to them as if she were absorbing some abysmal life-giving knowledge. At last she lifted her head. There was only a purple streak in the sky, cutting through a field of crimson and leading, like an extension of the highway, into the descending dusk. She raised her hands from the side of the pen in a gesture hieratic and profound. A visionary light settled in her eyes. She saw the streak as a vast swinging bridge extending upward from the earth through a field of living fire. Upon it a vast horde of souls were rumbling toward heaven. There were whole companies of white-trash, clean for the first time in their lives, and bands of black niggers in white robes, and battalions of freaks and lunatics shouting and clapping and leaping like frogs. And bringing up the end of the procession was a tribe of people whom she recognized at once as those who, like herself and Claud, had always had a little of everything and the God-given wit to use it right. She leaned forward to observe them closer. They were marching behind the others with great dignity, accountable as they had always been for good order and common sense and respectable behavior. They alone were on key. Yet she could see by their shocked and altered faces that even their virtues were being burned away. She lowered her hands and gripped the rail of the hog pen, her eyes small but fixed unblinkingly on what lay ahead. In a moment the vision faded but she remained where she was, immobile.

At length she got down and turned off the faucet and made her slow way on the darkening path to the house. In the woods around her the invisible cricket choruses had struck up, but what she heard were the voices of the souls climbing upward into the starry field and shouting hallelujah.

Questions for Critical Thinking

1 What does the title tell you about the theme of the story? How would you distinguish between Mrs. Turpin's final revelation in the story and the revelation of the overall story itself? Flannery O'Connor was a devout Catholic. How does that color her view of her characters, if at all?

2 What is the significance of the names chosen for the characters in this story?

3 What is the central conflict of the story and how does race play a role in defining that conflict?

Ralph Ellison (1914–1994)

"If I'm going to be remembered as a novelist, I'd better produce a few more books," Ralph Ellison said in a 1981 interview. Indeed, Ellison failed to complete a second novel in his lifetime, but the quality and importance of his first novel, *Invisible Man,* was so great that his literary reputation remains intact long after his death. *Invisible Man* follows the life of an unnamed black man in New York City who is "invisible" because white 1940s society refuses to see him. Although Ellison was insistent that the book was first and foremost a piece of literature, it is difficult to read it without paying attention to its comment on race.

Invisible Man responds to life in the Jim Crow era, the time period from 1877 to the mid-1960s in which blacks were the victims of widespread racism. A phenomenon primarily of the Southern states, Jim Crow laws (the name comes from a black, servile character in a popular minstrel show) kept blacks legally segregated from whites with the idea of "separate but equal." In effect, facilities for blacks were rarely equal in quality to those for whites. Segregation was only one manifestation of the prevailing mentality that blacks were inferior to whites. At its worst, racist behavior took the form of lynching, a term that refers to the execution of an individual carried out by a mob, rather than by legal authorities. Blacks were often lynched without any reason and in brutal ways. Ellison's fiction captures both this overtly cruel form of racism, as in his story that appears in this chapter, "A Party Down at the Square," and the subtler, once-commonplace discrimination that leads the black protagonist of *Invisible Man* to believe his path ought to be humility.

Unlike his protagonist, who was born in the Deep South, Ellison was raised in Oklahoma City, then educated at Tuskegee Institute, where he studied music and became friends with important jazz musicians of the day. He went to New York City to earn money before his senior year at Tuskegee but never returned. Ellison wrote essays and reviews, edited publications such as *The Negro Quarterly,* and taught creative writing later in his life. In addition to *Invisible Man,* which won the National Book Award in 1953, Ellison published two books of essays, *Shadow and Act* (1964) and *Going to the Territory* (1986), and a number of short stories. His collection *Flying Home* appeared posthumously in 1996. Three years thereafter, literary scholar John Callahan published a highly edited version of Ellison's second novel as *Juneteenth.*

A kindly and gracious man, intense with his friends and patient with his students, Ellison suffered some harsh criticism from later generations of African-American writers, who wanted him to be more overtly political in his prose. He never faltered, however, in his belief that literature was one of the highest callings a human being might follow. And, although he died at eighty with just one published novel, he remained devoted to the craft. Music—jazz in particular—was a clear influence on this writer; he once described *Invisible Man* as having the structure of a jazz composition—a beginning theme and bass line with variations and improvised solos.

"The act of writing requires a constant plunging back into the shadow of the past where time hovers ghostlike." —Ralph Ellison

Battle Royal (1952)

IT goes a long way back, some twenty years. All my life I had been looking for something, and everywhere I turned someone tried to tell me what it was. I accepted their answers too, though they were often in contradiction and even self-contradictory. I was naïve. I was looking for myself and asking everyone except myself questions which I, and only I, could answer. It took me a long time and much painful boomeranging of my expectations to achieve a realization everyone else appears to have been born with: That I am nobody but myself. But first I had to discover that I am an invisible man!

And yet I am no freak of nature, nor of history. I was in the cards, other things having been equal (or unequal) eighty-five years ago. I am not ashamed of my grandparents for having been slaves. I am only ashamed of myself for having at one time been ashamed. About eighty-five years ago they were told they were free, united with others of our country in everything pertaining to the common good, and, in everything social, separate like the fingers of the hand. And they believed it. They exulted in it. They stayed in their place, worked hard, and brought up my father to do the same. But my grandfather is the one. He was an odd old guy, my grandfather, and I am told I take after him. It was he who caused the trouble. On his deathbed he called my father to him and said, "Son, after I'm gone I want you to keep up the good fight. I never told you, but our life is a war and I have been a traitor all my born days, a spy in the enemy's country ever since I give up my gun back in the Reconstruction. Live with your head in the lion's mouth. I want you to overcome 'em with yeses, undermine 'em with grins, agree 'em to death and destruction, let 'em swoller you till they vomit or bust wide open." They thought the old man had gone out of his mind. He had been the meekest of men. The younger children were rushed from the room, the shades drawn and the flame of the lamp turned so low that it sputtered on the wick like the old man's breathing. "Learn it to the younguns," he whispered fiercely; then he died.

But my folks were more alarmed over his last words than over his dying. It was as though he had not died at all, his words caused so much anxiety. I was warned emphatically to forget what he had said and, indeed, this is the first time it has been mentioned outside the family circle. It had a tremendous effect upon me, however. I could never be sure of what he meant. Grandfather had been a quiet old man who never made any trouble, yet on his deathbed he had called himself a traitor and a spy, and he had spoken of his meekness as a dangerous activity. It became a constant puzzle which lay unanswered in the back of my mind. And whenever things went well for me I remembered my grandfather and felt guilty and uncomfortable. It was as though I was carrying out his advice in spite of myself. And to make it worse, everyone loved me for it. I was praised by the most lily-white men in town. I was considered an example of desirable conduct—just as my grandfather had been. And what puzzled me was that the old man had defined it as *treachery*. When I was praised for my conduct I felt a guilt that in some way I was doing something that was really against the wishes of the white folks, that if they had understood they would have desired me to act just the opposite, that I should have been sulky and mean, and that that really would have been what they wanted, even though they were fooled and thought they wanted me to act as I did. It made me afraid that some day they would look upon me as a traitor and I would be lost. Still I was more afraid to act any other way because they didn't like that at all. The old man's words were like a curse. On my graduation day I delivered an oration in which I showed that humility was the secret, indeed, the very essence of progress. (Not that I believed this—how could I, remembering my grandfather?—I only believed that it worked.) It was a great success. Everyone praised me and I was invited to give the speech at a gathering of the town's leading white citizens. It was a triumph for the whole community.

4   It was in the main ballroom of the leading hotel. When I got there I discovered that it was on the occasion of a smoker, and I was told that since I was to be there anyway I might as well take part in the battle royal to be fought by some of my schoolmates as part of the entertainment. The battle royal came first.

5   All of the town's big shots were there in their tuxedoes, wolfing down the buffet foods, drinking beer and whiskey and smoking black cigars. It was a large room with a high ceiling. Chairs were arranged in neat rows around three sides of a portable boxing ring. The fourth side was clear, revealing a gleaming space of polished floor. I had some misgivings over the battle royal, by the way. Not from a distaste for fighting but because I didn't care too much for the other fellows who were to take part. They were tough guys who seemed to have no grandfather's curse worrying their minds. No one could mistake their toughness. And besides, I suspected that fighting a battle royal might detract from the dignity of my speech. In those pre-invisible days I visualized myself as a potential Booker T. Washington. But the other fellows didn't care too much for me either, and there were nine of them. I felt superior to them in my way, and I didn't like the manner in which we were all crowded together in the servants' elevator. Nor did they like my being there. In fact, as the warmly lighted floors flashed past the elevator we had words over the fact that I, by taking part in the fight, had knocked one of their friends out of a night's work.

6   We were led out of the elevator through a rococo hall into an anteroom and told to get into our fighting togs. Each of us was issued a pair of boxing gloves and ushered out into the big mirrored hall, which we entered looking cautiously about us and whispering, lest we might accidentally be heard above the noise of the room. It was foggy with cigar smoke. And already the whiskey was taking effect. I was shocked to see some of the most important men of the town quite tipsy. They were all there—bankers, lawyers, judges, doctors, fire chiefs, teachers, merchants. Even one of the more fashionable pastors. Something we could not see was going on up front. A clarinet was vibrating sensuously and the men were standing up and moving eagerly forward. We were a small tight group, clustered together, our bare upper bodies touching and shining with anticipatory sweat: while up front the big shots were becoming increasingly excited over something we still could not see. Suddenly I heard the school superintendent, who had told me to come, yell, "Bring up the shines, gentlemen! Bring up the little shines!"

7   We were rushed up to the front of the ballroom, where it smelled even more strongly of tobacco and whiskey. Then we were pushed into place. I almost wet my pants. A sea of faces, some hostile, some amused, ringed around us, and in the center, facing us, stood a magnificent blonde—stark naked. There was dead silence. I felt a black of cold air chill me. I tried to back away, but they were behind me and around me. Some of the boys stood with lowered heads, trembling. I felt a wave of irrational guilt and fear. My teeth chattered, my skin turned to goose flesh, my knees knocked. Yet I was strongly attracted and looked in spite of myself. Had the price of looking been blindness, I would have looked. The hair was yellow like that of a circus kewpie doll, the face heavily powdered and rouged, as though to form an abstract mask, the eyes hollow and smeared a cool blue, the color of a baboon's butt. I felt a desire to spit upon her as my eyes brushed slowly over her body. Her breasts were firm and round as the domes of East Indian temples, and I stood so close as to see the fine skin texture and beads of pearly perspiration glistening like dew around the pink and erected buds of her nipples. I wanted at one and the same time to run from the room, to sink through the floor, or go to her and cover her from my eyes and the eyes of the others with my body; to feel the soft thighs, to caress her and destroy her, to love her and to murder her, to hide from her and yet to stroke where below the small American flag tattooed upon her belly her thighs formed a capital V. I had a notion that of all in the room she saw only me with her impersonal eyes.

And then she began to dance, a slow sensuous movement; the smoke of a hundred cigars clinging to her like the thinnest of veils. She seemed like a fair bird-girl girdled in veils calling to me from the angry surface of some gray and threatening sea. I was transported. Then I became aware of the clarinet playing and the big shots yelling at us. Some threatened us if we looked and others if we did not. On my right I saw one boy faint. And now a man grabbed a silver pitcher from a table and stepped close as he dashed ice water upon him and stood him up and forced two of us to support him as his head hung and moans issued from his thick bluish lips. Another boy began to plead to go home. He was the largest of the group, wearing dark red fighting trunks much too small to conceal the erection which projected from him as though in answer to the insinuating low-registered moaning of the clarinet. He tried to hide himself with his boxing gloves.

And all the while the blonde continued dancing, smiling faintly at the big shots who watched her with fascination, and faintly smiling at our fear. I noticed a certain merchant who followed her hungrily, his lips loose and drooling. He was a large man who wore diamond studs in a shirtfront which swelled with the ample paunch underneath, and each time the blonde swayed her undulating hips he ran his hand through the thin hair of his bald head and, with his arms upheld, his posture clumsy like that of an intoxicated panda, wound his belly in a slow and obscene grind. This creature was completely hypnotized. The music had quickened. As the dancer flung herself about with a detached expression on her face, the men began reaching out to touch her. I could see their beefy fingers sink into her soft flesh. Some of the others tried to stop them and she began to move around the floor in graceful circles, as they gave chase, slipping and sliding over the polished floor. It was mad. Chairs went crashing, drinks were spilt, as they ran laughing and howling after her. They caught her just as she reached a door, raised her from the floor, and tossed her as college boys are tossed at a hazing, and above her red, fixed-smiling lips I saw the terror and disgust in her eyes, almost like my own terror and that which I saw in some of the other boys. As I watched, they tossed her twice and her soft breasts seemed to flatten against the air and her legs flung wildly as she spun. Some of the more sober ones helped her to escape. And I started off the floor, heading for the anteroom with the rest of the boys.

Some were still crying and in hysteria. But as we tried to leave we were stopped and ordered to get into the ring. There was nothing to do but what we were told. All ten of us climbed under the ropes and allowed ourselves to be blindfolded with broad bands of white cloth. One of the men seemed to feel a bit sympathetic and tried to cheer us up as we stood with our backs against the ropes. Some of us tried to grin. "See that boy over there?" one of the men said. "I want you to run across at the bell and give it to him right in the belly. If you don't get him, I'm going to get you. I don't like his looks." Each of us was told the same. The blindfolds were put on. Yet even then I had been going over my speech. In my mind each word was as bright as a flame. I felt the cloth pressed into place, and frowned so that it would be loosened when I relaxed.

But now I felt a sudden fit of blind terror. I was unused to darkness, it was as though I had suddenly found myself in a dark room filled with poisonous cottonmouths. I could hear the bleary voices yelling insistently for the battle royal to begin. 11

"Get going in there!" 12

"Let me at that big nigger!" 13

I strained to pick up the school superintendent's voice, as though to squeeze some security out of that slightly more familiar sound. 14

"Let me at those black sonsabitches!" someone yelled. 15

"No, Jackson, no!" another voice yelled. "Here, somebody, help me hold Jack." 16

"I want to get at that ginger-colored nigger. Tear him limb from limb," the first voice yelled. 17

I stood against the ropes trembling. For in those days I was what they called ginger-colored, and he sounded as though he might crunch me between his teeth like a crisp ginger cookie. 18

Quite a struggle was going on. Chairs were being kicked about and I could hear voices grunting as with terrific effort. I wanted to see, to see more desperately than ever before. But the blindfold was as tight as a thick skin-puckering scab and when I raised my gloved hands to push the layers of white aside a voice yelled, "Oh, no you don't, black bastard! Leave that alone!" 19

"Ring the bell before Jackson kills him a coon!" someone boomed in the sudden silence. And I heard the bell clang and the sound of the feet scuffling forward. 20

A glove smacked against my head. I pivoted, striking out stiffly as someone went past, and felt the jar ripple along the length of my arm to my shoulder. Then it seemed as though all nine of the boys had turned upon me at once. Blows pounded me from all sides while I struck out as best I could. So many blows landed upon me that I wondered if I were not the only blindfolded fighter in the ring, or if the man called Jackson hadn't succeeded in getting me after all. 21

Blindfolded, I could no longer control my motions. I had no dignity. I stumbled about like a baby or a drunken man. The smoke had become thicker and with each new blow it seemed to sear and further restrict my lungs. My saliva became like hot bitter glue. A glove connected with my head, filling my mouth with warm blood. It was everywhere. I could not tell if the moisture I felt upon my body was sweat or blood. A blow landed hard against the nape of my neck. I felt myself going over, my head hitting the floor. Streaks of blue light filled the black world behind the blindfold. I lay prone, pretending that I was knocked out, but felt myself seized by hands and yanked to my feet. "Get going, black boy! Mix it up!" My arms were like 22 lead, my head smarting from blows. I managed to feel my way to the ropes and held on, trying to catch my breath. A glove landed in my midsection and I went over again, feeling as though the smoke had become a knife jabbed into my guts. Pushed this way and that by the legs milling around me, I finally pulled erect and discovered that I could see the black, sweat-washed forms weaving in the smoky-blue atmosphere like drunken dancers weaving to the rapid drum-like thuds of blows.

23   Everyone fought hysterically. It was complete anarchy. Every-body fought everybody else. No group fought together for long. Two, three, four, fought one, then turned to fight each other, were themselves attacked. Blows landed below the belt and in the kidney, with the gloves open as well as closed, and with my eye partly opened now there was not so much terror. I moved carefully, avoiding blows, although not too many to attract attention, fighting group to group. The boys groped about like blind, cautious crabs crouching to protect their midsections, their heads pulled in short against their shoulders, their arms stretched nervously before them, with their fists testing the smoke-filled air like the knobbed feelers of hypersensitive snails. In one corner I glimpsed a boy violently punching the air and heard him scream in pain as he smashed his hand against a ring post. For a second I saw him bent over holding his hand, then going down as a blow caught his unprotected head. I played one group against the other, slipping in and throwing a punch then stepping out of range while pushing the others into the melee to take the blows blindly aimed at me. The smoke was agonizing and there were no rounds, no bells at three minute intervals to relieve our exhaustion. The room spun round me, a swirl of lights, smoke, sweating bodies surrounded by tense white faces. I bled from both nose and mouth, the blood spattering upon my chest.

24   The men kept yelling, "Slug him, black boy! Knock his guts out!"

25   "Uppercut him! Kill him! Kill that big boy!"

26   Taking a fake fall, I saw a boy going down heavily beside me as though we were felled by a single blow, saw a sneaker-clad foot shoot into his groin as the two who had knocked him down stumbled upon him. I rolled out of range, feeling a twinge of nausea.

27   The harder we fought the more threatening the men became. And yet, I had begun to worry about my speech again. How would it go? Would they recognize my ability? What would they give me?

> I wanted to deliver my speech more than anything else in the world . . .

I was fighting automatically when suddenly I noticed that one after another of the boys was leaving the ring. I was surprised, filled with panic, as though I had been left alone with an unknown danger. Then I understood. The boys had arranged it among themselves. It was the custom for the two men left in the ring to slug it out for the winner's prize. I discovered this too late. When the bell sounded two men in tuxedoes leaped into the ring and removed the blindfold. I found myself facing Tatlock, the biggest of the gang. I felt sick at my stomach. Hardly had the bell stopped ringing in my ears than it clanged again and I saw him moving swiftly toward me. Thinking of nothing else to do I hit him smash on the nose. He kept coming, bringing the rank sharp violence of stale sweat. His face was a black blank of a face, only eyes alive—with hate of me and aglow with a feverish terror from what had happened to us all. I became anxious. I wanted to deliver my speech and he came at me as though he meant to beat it out of me. I smashed him again and again, taking his blows as they came. Then on a sudden impulse I struck him lightly and we clinched. I whispered, "Fake like I knocked you out, you can have the prize."

"I'll break your behind," he whispered hoarsely.

"For *them*?"

"For *me*, sonofabitch!"

They were yelling for us to break it up and Tatlock spun me half around with a blow, and as a joggled camera sweeps in a reeling scene, I saw the howling red faces crouching tense beneath the cloud of blue-gray smoke. For a moment the world wavered, unraveled, flowed, then my head cleared and Tatlock bounced before me. That fluttering shadow before my eyes was his jabbing left hand. Then falling forward, my head against his damp shoulder, I whispered.

"I'll make it five dollars more."

"Go to hell!"

But his muscles relaxed a trifle beneath my pressure and I breathed, "Seven?"

"Give it to your ma," he said, ripping me beneath the heart.

And while I still held him I butted him and moved away. I felt myself bombarded with punches. I fought back with hopeless desperation. I wanted to deliver my speech more than anything else in the world, because I felt that only these men could judge truly my ability, and now this stupid clown was ruining my chances. I began fighting carefully now, moving in to punch him and out again with my greater speed. A lucky blow to his chin and I had him going too—until I heard a loud voice yell, "I got my money on the big boy."

Hearing this, I almost dropped my guard. I was confused: Should I try to win against the voice out there? Would not this go against my speech, and was not this a moment for humility, for nonresistance? A blow to my head as I danced about sent my right eye popping like a jack-in-the-box and settled my dilemma. The room went red as I fell. It was a dream fall, my body languid and fastidious as to where to land, until the floor became impatient and smashed up to meet me. A moment later I came to. An hypnotic voice and said FIVE emphatically. And I lay there, hazily watching a dark red spot of my own blood shaping itself into a butterfly, glistening and soaking into the soiled gray world of the canvas.

When the voice drawled TEN I was lifted up and dragged to a chair. I sat dazed. My eye pained and swelled with each throb of my pounding heart and I wondered if now I would be allowed to speak. I was wringing wet, my mouth still bleeding. We were grouped along the wall now. The other boys ignored me as they congratulated Tatlock and speculated as to how much they would be paid. One boy whimpered over his smashed hand. Looking up front, I saw attendants in white jackets rolling the portable ring away and placing a small square rug in the vacant space surrounded by chairs. Perhaps, I thought, I will stand on the rug to deliver my speech.

Then the M.C. called to us. "Come on up here boys and get your money."

We ran forward to where the men laughed and talked in their chairs, waiting. Everyone seemed friendly now.

"There it is on the rug," the man said. I saw the rug covered with coins of all dimensions and a few crumpled bills. But what excited me, scattered here and there, were the gold pieces.

"Boys, it's all yours," the man said. "You get all you grab."

"That's right, Sambo," a blond man said, winking at me confidentially.

I trembled with excitement, forgetting my pain. I would get the gold and the bills. I thought. I would use both hands. I would throw my body against the boys nearest me to block them from the gold.

"Get down around the rug now," the man commanded, "and don't anyone touch it until I give the signal."

"This ought to be good," I heard.

As told, we got around the square rug on our knees. Slowly the man raised his freckled hand as we followed it upward with our eyes.

I heard, "These niggers look like they're about to pray!"

Then, "Ready," the man said. "Go!"

I lunged for a yellow coin lying on the blue design of the carpet, touching it and sending a surprised shriek to join those around me. I tried frantically to remove my hand but could not let go. A hot, violent force tore through my body, shaking me like a wet rat. The rug was electrified. The hair bristled up on my head as I shook myself free. My muscles jumped, my nerves jangled, writhed. But I saw that this was not stopping the other boys. Laughing in fear and embarrassment, some were holding back and scooping up the coins knocked off by the painful contortions of others. The men roared above us as we struggled.

"Pick it up, goddamnit, pick it up!" someone called like a bass-voiced parrot. "Go on, get it!"

I crawled rapidly around the floor, picking up the coins, trying to avoid the coppers and to get greenbacks and the gold. Ignoring the shock by laughing, as I brushed the coins off quickly, I discovered that I could contain the electricity—a contradiction but it works. Then the men began to push us onto the rug. Laughing embarrassedly, we struggled out of their hands and kept after the coins. We were all wet and slippery and hard to hold. Suddenly I saw a boy lifted into the air, glistening with sweat like a circus seal, and dropped, his wet back landing flush upon the charged rug, heard him yell and saw him literally dance upon his back, his elbows beating a frenzied tattoo upon the floor, his muscles twitching like the flesh of a horse stung by many flies. When he finally rolled off, his face was gray and no one stopped him when he ran from the floor amid booming laughter.

"Get the money," the M.C. called. "That's good hard American cash!"

And we snatched and grabbed, snatched and grabbed. I was careful not to come too close to the rug now, and when I felt the hot whiskey breath descend upon me like a cloud of foul air I reached out and grabbed the leg of a chair. It was occupied and I held on desperately.

"Leggo, nigger! Leggo!"

The huge face wavered down to mine as he tried to push me free. But my body was slippery and he was too drunk. It was Mr. Colcord, who owned a chain of movie houses and "entertainment palaces." Each time he grabbed me I slipped out of his hands. It became a real struggle. I feared the rug more than I did the drunk, so I held on, surprising myself for a moment by trying to topple *him* upon the rug. It was such an enormous idea that I found myself actually carrying it out. I tried not to be obvious, yet when I grabbed his leg, trying to tumble him out of the chair, he raised up, roaring with laughter, and, looking at me with soberness dead in the eye, kicked me viciously in the chest. The chair leg flew out of my hand and I felt myself going and rolled. It was as though I had rolled through a bed of hot coals. It seemed a whole century would pass before I would roll free, a century in which I was seared through the deepest levels of my body to the fearful breath within me and the breath seared and heated to the point of explosion. It'll all be over in a flash, I thought as I rolled clear. It'll all be over in a flash.

58   But not yet, the men on the other side were waiting, red faces swollen as though from apoplexy as they bent forward in their chairs. Seeing their fingers coming toward me I rolled away as a fumbled football rolls off the receiver's fingertips, back into the coals. That time I luckily sent the rug sliding out of place and heard the coins ringing against the floor and the boys scuffling to pick them up and the M.C. calling, "All right, boys, that's all. Go get dressed and get your money."

59   I was limp as a dish rag. My back felt as though it had been beaten with wires.

60   When we had dressed the M.C. came in and gave us each five dollars, except Tatlock, who got ten for being the last in the ring. Then he told us to leave. I was not to get a chance to deliver my speech, I thought. I was going out into the dim alley in despair when I was stopped and told to go back. I returned to the ballroom, where the men were pushing back their chairs and gathering in small groups to talk.

61   The M.C. knocked on a table for quiet. "Gentlemen," he said, "we almost forgot an important part of the program. A most serious part, gentlemen. This boy was brought here to deliver a speech which he made at his graduation yesterday . . ."

62   "Bravo!"

63   "I'm told that he is the smartest boy we've got out there in Greenwood. I'm told that he knows more big words than a pocket-sized dictionary."

64   Much applause and laughter.

65   "So now, gentlemen, I want you to give him your attention."

66   There was still laughter as I faced them, my mouth dry, my eyes throbbing. I began slowly, but evidently my throat was tense, because they began shouting. "Louder! Louder!"

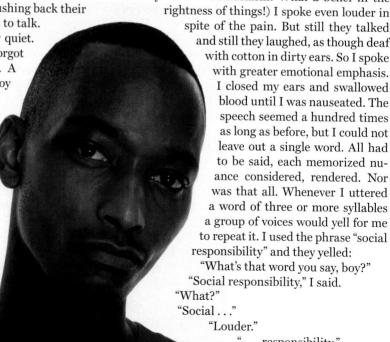

"We of the younger generation extol the wisdom of that great leader and educator," I shouted, "who first spoke these flaming words of wisdom: 'A ship lost at sea for many days suddenly sighted a friendly vessel. From the mast of the unfortunate vessel was seen a signal: "Water, water, we die of thirst!" The answer from the friendly vessel came back: "Cast down your bucket where you are." The captain of the distressed vessel, at last heeding the injunction, cast down his bucket, and it came up full of fresh sparkling water from the mouth of the Amazon River.' And like him I say, and in his words, 'To those of my race who depend upon bettering their condition in a foreign land, or who underestimate the importance of cultivating friendly relations with the Southern white man, who is his next-door neighbor, I would say: "Cast down your bucket where you are"—cast it down in making friends in every manly way of the people of all races by whom we are surrounded . . .'"

I spoke automatically and with such fervor that I did not realize that the men were still talking and laughing until my dry mouth, filling up with blood from the cut, almost strangled me. I coughed, wanting to stop and go to one of the tall brass, sand-filled spittoons to relieve myself, but a few of the men, especially the superintendent, were listening and I was afraid. So I gulped it down, blood, saliva and all, and continued. (What powers of endurance I had during those days! What enthusiasm! What a belief in the rightness of things!) I spoke even louder in spite of the pain. But still they talked and still they laughed, as though deaf with cotton in dirty ears. So I spoke with greater emotional emphasis. I closed my ears and swallowed blood until I was nauseated. The speech seemed a hundred times as long as before, but I could not leave out a single word. All had to be said, each memorized nuance considered, rendered. Nor was that all. Whenever I uttered a word of three or more syllables a group of voices would yell for me to repeat it. I used the phrase "social responsibility" and they yelled:

"What's that word you say, boy?"

"Social responsibility," I said.

"What?"

"Social . . ."

"Louder."

" . . . responsibility."

"More!"

"Respon—"

"Repeat!"

"—sibility."

The room filled with the uproar of laughter until, no doubt, distracted by having to gulp down my blood, I made a mistake and yelled a phrase I had often seen denounced in newspaper editorials, heard debated in private.

"Social . . ."

"What?" they yelled.

". . . equality—"

The laughter hung smokelike in the sudden stillness. I opened my eyes, puzzled. Sounds of displeasure filled the room. The M.C. rushed forward. They shouted hostile phrases at me. But I did not understand.

A small dry mustached man in the front row blared out, "Say that slowly, son!"

"What, sir?"

"What you just said!"

"Social responsibility, sir," I said.

"You weren't being smart, were you, boy?" he said, not unkindly.

"No, sir!"

"You sure that about 'equality' was a mistake?"

"Oh, yes, sir," I said. "I was swallowing blood."

"Well, you had better speak more slowly so we can understand. We mean to do right by you, but you've got to know your place at all times. All right, now, go on with your speech."

I was afraid. I wanted to leave but I wanted also to speak and I was afraid they'd snatch me down.

"Thank you, sir," I said, beginning where I had left off, and having them ignore me as before.

Yet when I finished there was a thunderous applause. I was surprised to see the superintendent come forth with a package wrapped in white tissue paper, and, gesturing for quiet, address the men.

"Gentlemen, you see that I did not overpraise the boy. He makes a good speech and some day he'll lead his people in the proper paths. And I don't have to tell you that this is important in these days and times. This is a good, smart boy, and so to encourage him in the right direction, in the name of the Board of Education I wish to present him a prize in the form of this . . ."

He paused, removing the tissue paper and revealing a gleaming calfskin briefcase.

> "... We mean to do right by you, but you've got to know your place at all times. ..."

". . . in the form of this first-class article from Shad Whitmore's shop."

"Boy," he said, addressing me, "take this prize and keep it well. Consider it a badge of office. Prize it. Keep developing as you are and some day it will be filled with important papers that will help shape the destiny of your people."

I was so moved that I could hardly express my thanks. A rope of bloody saliva forming a shape like an undiscovered continent drooled upon the leather and I wiped it quickly away. I felt an importance that I had never dreamed.

"Open it and see what's inside," I was told.

My fingers a-tremble, I complied, smelling fresh leather and finding an official-looking document inside. It was a scholarship to the state college for Negroes. My eyes filled with tears and I ran awkwardly off the floor.

I was overjoyed; I did not even mind when I discovered the gold pieces I had scrambled for were brass pocket tokens advertising a certain make of automobile.

When I reached home everyone was excited. Next day the neighbors came to congratulate me. I even felt safe from grandfather, whose deathbed curse usually spoiled my triumphs. I stood beneath his photograph with my briefcase in hand and smiled triumphantly into his stolid black peasant's face. It was a face that fascinated me. The eyes seemed to follow everywhere I went.

That night I dreamed I was at a circus with him and that he refused to laugh at the clowns no matter what they did. Then later he told me to open my briefcase and read what was inside and I did, finding an official envelope stamped with the state seal: and inside the envelope I found another and another, endlessly, and I thought I would fall of weariness. "Them's years," he said. "Now open that one." And I did and in it I found an engraved stamp containing a short message in letters of gold. "Read it," my grandfather said. "Out loud."

"To Whom It May Concern," I intoned. "Keep This Nigger-Boy Running."

I awoke with the old man's laughter ringing in my ears.

Questions for Critical Thinking

1 Unlike most writers who lived in the South (such as Faulkner and O'Connor), Ralph Ellison was not born there. What about "Battle Royal" makes it a Southern story? You might want to consider which, if any, themes it shares with the Faulkner and O'Connor selections.

2 Reread the protagonist's dream recounted at the end of the story. Given the time and place in which this story's action occurs, what do you think the boy's dream stands for or means?

3 The narrator tells his story from a future point in time, looking back

on the occurrence of this battle royal. Identify the ironies you see in the story that are created from this disjuncture of point of view. How does the point of view of the non-Southern narrator of the second story affect its meaning?

A Party Down at the Square (1966)

1   I DON'T know what started it. A bunch of men came by my Uncle Eds place and said there was going to be a party down at the Square, and my uncle hollered for me to come on and I ran with them through the dark and rain and there we were at the Square. When we got there everybody was mad and quiet and standing around looking at the nigger. Some of the men had guns, and one man kept goosing the nigger in his pants with the barrel of a shotgun, saying he ought to pull the trigger, but he never did. It was right in front of the courthouse, and the old clock in the tower was striking twelve. The rain was falling cold and freezing as it fell. Everybody was cold, and the nigger kept wrapping his arms around himself trying to stop the shivers.

2   Then one of the boys pushed through the circle and snatched off the nigger's shirt, and there he stood, with his black skin all shivering in the light from the fire, and looking at us with a scaired look on his face and putting his hands in his pants pockets. Folks started yelling to hurry up and kill the nigger. Somebody yelled: "Take your hands out of your pockets,

nigger; we gonna have plenty heat in a minnit." But the nigger didn't hear him and kept his hands where they were.

3   I tell you the rain was cold. I had to stick my hands in my pockets they got so cold. The fire was pretty small, and they put some logs around the platform they had the nigger on and then threw on some gasoline, and you could see the flames light up the whole Square. It was late and the streetlights had been off for a long time. It was so bright that the bronze statue of the general standing there in the Square was like something alive. The shadows playing on his moldy green face made him seem to be smiling down at the nigger.

4   They threw on more gas, and it made the Square bright like it gets when the lights are turned on or when the sun is setting red. All the wagons and cars were standing around the curbs. Not like Saturday though—the niggers weren't there. Not a single nigger was there except this Bacote nigger and they dragged him there tied to the back of Jed Wilson's truck. On Saturday there's as many niggers as white folks.

5 Everybody was yelling crazy 'cause they were about to set fire to the nigger, and I got to the rear of the circle and looked around the Square to try to count the cars. The shadows of the folks was flickering on the trees in the middle of the Square. I saw some birds that the noise had woke up flying through the trees. I guess maybe they thought it was morning. The ice had started the cobblestones in the street to shine where the rain was falling and freezing. I counted forty cars before I lost count. I knew folks must have been there from Phenix City by all the cars mixed in with the wagons.

6 God, it was a hell of a night. It was some night all right. When the noise died down I heard the nigger's voice from where I stood in the back, so I pushed my way up front. The nigger was bleeding from his nose and ears, and I could see him all red where the dark blood was running down his black skin. He kept lifting first one foot and then the other, like a chicken on a hot stove. I looked down to the platform they had him on, and they had pushed a ring of fire up close to his feet. It must have been hot to him with the flames almost touching his big black toes. Somebody yelled for the nigger to say his prayers, but the nigger wasn't saying anything now. He just kinda moaned with his eyes shut and kept moving up and down on his feet, first one foot and then the other.

7 I watched the flames burning the logs up closer and closer to the nigger's feet. They were burning good now, and the rain had stopped and the wind was rising, making the flames flare higher. I looked, and there must have been thirty-five women in the crowd, and I could hear their voices clear and shrill mixed in with those of the men. Then it happened. I heard the noise about the same time everyone else did. It was like the roar of a cyclone blowing up from the gulf, and everyone was looking up into the air to see what it was. Some of the faces looked surprised and scaired, all but the nigger. He didn't even hear the noise. He didn't even look up. Then the roar came closer, right above our heads and the wind was blowing higher and higher and the sound seemed to be going in circles.

8 Then I saw her. Through the clouds and fog I could see a red and green light on her wings. I could see them just for a second: then she rose up into the low clouds. I looked out for the beacon over the tops of the buildings in the direction of the airfield that's forty miles away, and it wasn't circling around. You usually could see it sweeping around the sky at night, but it wasn't there. Then, there she was again, like a big bird lost in the fog. I looked for the red and green lights, and they weren't there anymore. She was flying even closer to the tops of the buildings than before. The wind was blowing harder, and leaves started flying about, making funny shadows on the ground, and tree limbs were cracking and falling.

9 It was a storm all right. The pilot must have thought he was over the landing field. Maybe he thought the fire in the Square was put there for him to land by. Gosh, but it scaired the folks. I was scaired too. They started yelling: "He's going to land. He's going to land."

And: "He's going to fall." A few started for their cars and wagons. I could hear the wagons creaking and chains jangling and cars spitting and missing as they started the engines up. Off to my right, a horse started pitching and striking his hooves against a car.

> **I wanted to run,** and I wanted to stay and see what was going to happen.

10 I didn't know what to do. I wanted to run, and I wanted to stay and see what was going to happen. The plane was close as hell. The pilot must have been trying to see where he was at, and her motors were drowning out all the sounds. I could even feel the vibration, and my hair felt like it was standing up under my hat. I happened to look over at the statue of the general standing with one leg before the other and leaning back on a sword, and I was fixing to run over and climb between his legs and sit there and watch when the roar stopped some, and I looked up and she was gliding just over the top of the trees in the middle of the Square.

11 Her motors stopped altogether and I could hear the sound of branches cracking and snapping off below her landing gear. I could see her plain now, all silver and shining in the light of the fire with T.W.A. in black letters under her wings. She was sailing smoothly out of the Square when she hit the high power lines that follow the Birmingham highway through the town. It made a loud crash. It sounded like the wind blowing the door of a tin barn shut. She only hit with her landing gear, but I could see the sparks flying, and the wires knocked loose from the poles were spitting blue sparks and whipping around like a bunch of snakes and leaving circles of blue sparks in the darkness.

12 The plane had knocked five or six wires loose, and they were dangling and swinging, and every time they touched they threw off more sparks. The wind was making them swing, and when I got over there, there was a crackling and spitting screen of blue haze across the highway. I lost my hat running over, but I didn't stop to look for it. I was among the first and I could hear the others pounding behind me across the grass

of the Square. They were yelling to beat all hell, and they came up fast, pushing and shoving, and someone got pushed against a swinging wire. It made a sound like when a blacksmith drops a red hot horseshoe into a barrel of water, and the steam comes up. I could smell the flesh burning. The first time I'd ever smelled it. I got up close and it was a woman. It must have killed her right off. She was lying in a puddle stiff as a board, with pieces of glass insulators that the plane had knocked off the poles lying all around her. Her white dress was torn, and I saw one of her tits hanging out in the water and her thighs. Some woman screamed and fainted and almost fell on a wire, but a man caught her. The sheriff and his men were yelling and driving folks back with guns shining in their hands, and everything was lit up blue by the sparks. The shock had turned the woman almost as black as the nigger. I was trying to see if she wasn't blue too, or if it was just the sparks, and the sheriff drove me away. As I backed off trying to see, I heard the motors of the plane start up again somewhere off to the right in the clouds.

13   The clouds were moving fast in the wind and the wind was blowing the smell of something burning over to me. I turned around, and the crowd was headed back to the nigger. I could see him standing there in the middle of the flames. The wind was making the flames brighter every minute. The crowd was running. I ran too. I ran back across the grass with the crowd. It wasn't so large now that so many had gone when the plane came. I tripped and fell over the limb of a tree lying in the grass and bit my lip. It ain't well yet I bit it so bad. I could taste the blood in my mouth as I ran over. I guess that's what made me sick. When I got there, the fire had caught the nigger's pants, and the folks were standing around watching, but not too close on account of the wind blowing the flames. Somebody hollered, "Well, nigger, it ain't so cold now, is it? You don't need to put your hands in your pockets now." And the nigger looked up with his great white eyes looking like they was 'bout to pop out of his head, and I had enough. I didn't want to see anymore. I wanted to run somewhere and puke, but I stayed. I stayed right there in the front of the crowd and looked.

14   The nigger tried to say something I couldn't hear for the roar of the wind in the fire, and I strained my ears. Jed Wilson hollered, "What you say there, nigger?" And it came back through the flames in his nigger voice: "Will one a you gentlemen please cut my throat?" he said. "Will somebody please cut my throat like a Christian?" And Jed hollered back, "Sorry, but ain't no Christians around tonight. Ain't no Jew-boys neither. We're just one hundred percent Americans."

    Then the nigger was silent. Folks started laughing at Jed. Jed's right popular with the folks, and the next year, my uncle says, they plan to run him for sheriff. The heat was too much for me, and the smoke was making my eyes to smart. I was trying to back away when Jed reached down and brought up a can of gasoline and threw it in the fire on the nigger. I could see the flames catching the gas in a puff as it went in in a silver sheet and some of it reached the nigger, making spurts of blue fire all over his chest.

    Well, that nigger was tough. I have to give it to that nigger; he was really tough. He had started to burn like a house afire and was making the smoke smell like burning hides. The fire was up around his head, and the smoke was so thick and black we couldn't see him. And him not moving—we thought he was dead. Then he started out. The fire had burned the ropes they had tied him with, and he started jumping and kicking about like he was blind, and you could smell his skin burning. He kicked so hard that the platform, which was burning too, fell in, and he rolled out of the fire at my feet. I jumped back so he wouldn't get on me. I'll never forget it. Every time I eat barbeque I'll remember that nigger. His back was just like a barbecued hog. I could see the prints of his ribs where they start around from his backbone and curve down and around. It was a sight to see, that nigger's back. He was right at my feet, and somebody behind pushed me and almost made me step on him, and he was still burning.

    I didn't step on him though, and Jed and somebody else pushed him back in the burning planks and logs and poured on more gas. I wanted to leave, but the folks were yelling and I couldn't move except to look around and see the statue. A branch the wind had broken was resting on his hat. I tried to push out and get away because my guts were gone, and all I got was spit and hot breath in my face from the woman and two men standing directly behind me. So I had to turn back around. The nigger rolled out of the fire again. He wouldn't stay put. It was on the other side this time. I couldn't see him very well through the flames and smoke. They got some tree limbs and held him there this time and he stayed there till he was ashes. I guess he stayed there. I know he burned to ashes because I saw Jed a week later, and he laughed and showed me some white finger bones still held together with little pieces of the nigger's skin. Anyway, I left when somebody moved around to see the nigger. I pushed my way through the crowd, and a woman in the rear scratched my face as she yelled and fought to get up close.

I ran across the Square to the other side, where the sheriff and his deputies were guarding the wires that were still spitting and making a blue fog. My heart was pounding like I had been running a long ways, and I bent over and let my insides go. Everything came up and spilled in a big gush over the ground. I was sick, and tired, and weak, and cold. The wind was still high, and large drops of rain were beginning to fall. I headed down the street to my uncle's place past a store where the wind had broken a window, and glass lay over the sidewalk. I kicked it as I went by. I remember somebody's fool rooster crowing like it was morning in all that wind.

The next day I was too weak to go out, and my uncle kidded me and called me "the gutless wonder from Cincinnati." I didn't mind. He said you get used to it in time. He couldn't go out hisself. There was too much wind and rain. I got up and looked out of the window, and the rain was pouring down and dead sparrows and limbs of trees were scattered all over the yard. There had been a cyclone all right. It swept a path right through the county, and we were lucky we didn't get the full force of it.

It blew for three days steady, and put the town in a hell of a shape. The wind blew sparks and set fire to the white-and-green-rimmed house on Jackson Avenue that had the big concrete lions in the yard and burned it down to the ground. They had to kill another nigger who tried to run out of the county after they burned this Bacote nigger. My Uncle Ed said they always have to kill niggers in pairs to keep the other niggers in place. I don't know though, the folks seem a little skittish of the niggers. They all came back, but they act pretty sullen. They look mean as hell when you pass them down at the store. The other day I was down to Brinkley's store, and a white cropper said it didn't do no good to kill the niggers 'cause things don't get no better. He looked hungry as hell. Most of the croppers look hungry. You'd be surprised how hungry white folks can look. Somebody said that he'd better shut his damn mouth, and he shut up. But from the look on his face he won't stay shut long. He went out of the store muttering to himself and spit a big chew of tobacco right down on Brinkley's floor. Brinkley said he was sore 'cause he wouldn't let him have credit. Anyway, it didn't seem to help things. First it was the nigger and the storm, then the plane, then the woman and the wires, and now I hear the airplane line is investigating to find who set the fire that almost wrecked their plane. All that in one night, and all of it but the storm over one nigger. It was some night all right. It was some party too. I was right there, see. I was right there watching it all. It was my first party and my last. God, but that nigger was tough. That Bacote nigger was some nigger!

> ## He said you get used to it in time.

Questions for Critical Thinking

1 What role does setting play in this story?

2 Why does Ellison use the first-person narrator of a young boy? What does this accomplish?

3 Ellison asks readers to bear witness to this event. What does the title of the story reveal?

4 What is the point of the airplane in the story? What is Ellison trying to suggest to us by including this incident?

Getting Started: A Research Project

Research is a skill that will carry you through your college career. You can find the research materials you need for this project on our website (**www.mhhe.com/delbanco1e**). Other ideas for research projects and sources appear at the end of this chapter.

Between the South and the West, decide which region's literature you liked the most in this chapter. Then, use one of the sources found at **www.mhhe.com/delbanco1e** to read more selections from that region. Formulate a thesis in which you identify what you believe to be the defining feature of literature from that region. But as you do this, take note of your own understanding or personally held myths about the region before you began and after you completed the reading. Consider how much of the region's identity comes from within, from its own inhabitants, and how much outside observers impose on it. For example, race relations in the South as depicted in fiction emerge as complex and painful on all sides; the heritage and memory of the Civil War—popularly known in the South as the War Between the States—holds different meanings for different races, and different meanings within social classes as well. In our national literature the war was a mostly subterranean subject, or as critic Daniel Aaron referred to it, an "unwritten war." The West has its own myths, some coming from within—as we noticed about the South—and some imposed on it from out-side the region. The fairy-tale-large notion of "cowboys and Indians," for example, is something we grow up with. How realistic a view of the West does that image convey once you've read even a few selections about the country between the western bank of the Mississippi River and the Pacific Ocean?

Go to www.mhhe.com/delbanco1e and respond to story selections from the South and the West.

1. Choose a figure particular to one of the regions—the white farmer, say, in the South or the black fieldworker or the small-town shop-owner, or the western ranch owner or a Native American schoolteacher or reservation policeman—and, working with your instructor, draw up a reading list that will help you to flesh out a portrait of a person rooted in the region who seems recognizable to people living outside the region. Try to establish how much of that person's habits and views comes from local and regional influences and what aspect pertains to the national way of seeing the world.

2. Work from the outside in, beginning with a stereotype out of American popular or commercial culture, the Marlboro Man, for example, or the Southern Rebel soldier, and see how much the actual literature of the time, the stories and novels, lends support to these stereotypes.

Further Suggestions for Writing and Research

1. Consider the three Southern authors you read in this chapter. Based on their fiction, how would you describe their attitudes toward the South? What characteristics of the region or its people do you see recur in more than one of the authors' works? Which aspects differ from author to author?

2. Are there such things as "regional" writers, or do all writers, even those from major cities, belong to a particular place, with habits and speech patterns and ways of seeing all their own?

3. Apply Thomas Wolfe's notion that "only the dead know Brooklyn" (from his story of the same name in chapter 8) to the South. Apply it to the West. Is there a particular place where you might imagine setting a Southern story equivalent to Wolfe's Brooklyn subway station? A Western story?

Some Sources for Research

Ayers, Edward L., and Bradley Mittendorf, eds. *The Oxford Book of the American South: Testimony, Memory, and Fiction.* New York: Oxford University Press, 1997.

Bercovitch, Sacvan. *Rites of Assent: Transformations in the Symbolic Construction of America.* New York: Routledge, 1993.

Fetterley, Judith, and Marjorie Pryse. *Regionalism, Women, and American Literary Culture.* Champaign, IL: University of Illinois Press, 2003. Especially chapters 1 and 2 and the Works Cited section.

Kittredge, William, ed. *The Portable Western Reader.* New York: Penguin, 1997.

Stegner, Wallace. "Western Record and Romance." *Literary History of the United States.* Ed. William Kittredge. New York: Penguin, 1997.

Work, James C., ed. *Prose and Poetry of the American West.* Lincoln: University of Nebraska Press, 1990.

For examples of student papers, see chapter 3, Common Writing Assignments, and chapter 5, Writing the Research Paper, in the Handbook for Writing from Reading.

13 Visual Arts,

AS you have seen throughout this textbook, writers use all aspects of technique—tone, point of view, character, symbols—to create a text. However, at the heart of their craft is the desire to tell a tale. Human beings have always delighted in telling and listening to stories, and that basic urge has lasted from the Greek epics to Biblical accounts to Elizabethan drama to the present day of TV, movies, email, text messages, and the Internet. The modes of delivery may have changed, but the hunger for story—both to tell it and hear it—remains.

As a result of these technologies, our culture has become increasingly based on visual media. Accordingly, we have found more visual ways to tell stories—including comics, television, movies, and—one of the newest and fastest growing formats—graphic novels. This chapter asks you to

Film, & Fiction

think about the intersection between visual storytelling and the textual storytelling we have presented up to this point, with the hope of both learning about new ways to tell stories and illuminating what is unique to the written word. We will begin with comics, a hybrid of images and text, and their recent descendent, graphic novels. Then we'll explore adaptation—that is, how an old story is retold and reshaped into contemporary formats—as we chart *Beowulf* from its original epic poem format to current novel versions, to a major motion picture. In so doing, we hope you'll see how narratives, both old and new, really live all around us.

COMICS

In his seminal book *Understanding Comics*, Scott McCloud traces comics all the way back to 1300 B.C. in Egyptian art. Although he admits that he cannot be sure where or when comics actually started, the point is that using a series of pictures to depict an action or a story is an age-old form. In the late 1930s and through the 1940s, however, comic books were marketed specifically for children, with superheroes like Superman and Wonder Woman high in popularity in the World War II era. Later, in the 1950s, comics became far more controversial as they began to take on adult themes with content closer to the hard-boiled edge of film noir and crime fiction than to stories suitable for children. As time passed, comics for adults continued to grow, even though adult comics today still fight the stereotype that they are a children's format.

Narrative prose requires time over which the story unfolds; in comics, however, space becomes an important element. Comics have their own set of techniques that the cartoonist can manipulate to create effects. One of the most important features of comics is the panel. Panels can be differently sized to create emphasis on certain images or moments. The gutter (the space between the panels) usually signals a time change from one panel to the next, and since not all minutiae of action are drawn, readers must fill in the gap between two panels as they read across the strip. Where a panel is positioned on the page generally determines where that panel occurs in time.

GRAPHIC NOVELS

The term "graphic novel" is problematic in the eyes of many who create them. "Graphic" is all too easily and errantly associated with pornography, while many graphic novels are actually graphic memoirs or other genres like biography. Yet it is the term most widely used to describe a book-length comic that develops serious subject matter in roughly the length and depth of a novel. More than that, "graphic novel" signifies one of the fastest growing formats in terms of popularity and book sales; *Publisher's Weekly* estimated that graphic novels generated $330 million in sales in 2006, up from $75 million just five years earlier.

The first graphic novels were published in the late 1970s. In 1986, the first volume of Art Spiegelman's landmark graphic novel *Maus* was published, followed by the second volume in 1991. In 1992, the complete *Maus* won the Pulitzer Prize Special Award. *Maus* is at the heart of the graphic novel canon; a memoir more than a novel, it recounts Spiegelman's parents' survival of concentration camps during the Holocaust and the lasting effect the experience had on both them and on Spiegelman himself. Other widely known graphic novels include *The Sandman* (serialized 1989 to 1996) by Neil Gaiman, *Jimmy Corrigan* (2000) by Chris Ware, *Sin City* (serialized 1991–1992)

GRAPHIC POETRY

Putting images with text is not, of course, a new invention. One of many artists to have done so is the early Romantic poet William Blake (1757-1827). In addition to a highly ornate style created by a unique printing process he invented, Blake's work is notable for the way that text and image work together to create meaning. For more on this topic, and to see samples of Blake's mix of graphics and poetry, see the William Blake casebook (chapter 26). For step-by-step help in "reading" graphics, refer to the "Learning to Read Images" exercise in that chapter.

by Frank Miller, *V for Vendetta* (originally serialized 1982–1985) by Alan Moore and David Lloyd, and *Persepolis* by Marjane Satrapi. *Sin City, V for Vendetta*, and *Persepolis* were adapted into major motion pictures. In the tradition of *Maus, Persepolis* is really a graphic memoir rather than a graphic novel. Like *Maus, Persepolis* also deals with political oppression and its effect on the people who live through it. Satrapi tells the story of her own childhood in Iran during the tumultuous times of the Shah's downfall and the installation of Islamic rule. Other graphic novels are themselves adaptations of previously told stories; a notable example is *Gemma Bovary (1999)*, Posy Simmond's modern recasting of Flaubert's classic novel *Madame Bovary*.

Stills from the movie *Persepolis* (2007) by Marjane Satrapi and Vincent Paronnaud; based on the graphic novel by Marjane Satrapi

Graphic novels are as diverse in craft as are literary novels. Much has to do with the artist's individual style: Chris Ware's meticulous detail and his use of straight lines make for a clean, precise look that seems to reflect the isolation his characters feel, while Marjane Satrapi's stark black-and-white illustrations confront the reader in the same bold manner that her characters negotiate life in Iran. Compare the graphics from *Persepolis* to those by Gareth Hinds, who created *Beowulf: A Graphic Novel* in 2007, featuring full-color illustrations of the classic epic.

Gareth Hinds (b. 1971)

Beowulf:
A Graphic Novel

[Grendel's Attack] (2007)

Questions for Critical Thinking

1 A graphic novel usually brings text and pictures together. Describe the balance between text and images in Hinds's *Beowulf*. How effective do you find his visual rendition? What, if anything, would you change if you were the artist?

2 What details of Beowulf's depiction allow you to read him as a hero figure? What details of Grendel make it clear he is a villain?

3 Note the physical features of Beowulf and Grendel that are emphasized in the drawings. Are certain unique features emphasized for each character? Are certain features hidden? How do the two characters' portrayals influence your impressions of them?

FILM ADAPTATIONS

When you hear the titles *Field of Dreams, Gone with the Wind,* and *Jaws,* you most likely think of Kevin Costner in a whispering cornfield, Clark Gable as Rhett Butler taking Vivien Leigh as Scarlett O'Hara into his arms, and the threatening bass music of the shark's approach. What you may not as readily think of are the novels these movies are based on—*Shoeless Joe* by Canadian novelist William P. Kinsella, *Gone with the Wind* by Margaret Mitchell, and *Jaws* by Peter Benchley—but each of these classic movies were novels first. Although estimates vary, it is safe to say that more than half of all movies made are drawn from literary sources. Screenwriters and filmmakers have adapted narratives and novels, and sometimes short stories, from Homer through Shakespeare, Tolstoy, and Hemingway into film. The transition from prose to the movie screen has advantages and disadvantages. Novels are frequently trimmed down, while filmmakers often plump up a short story, usually by presenting additional material about major characters. Certain aspects of a writer's voice or a narrator's presence can be difficult, if not impossible, to translate into film; often the closest approximation of a narrator is a voice-over in film. Almost by definition, the visual aspects of a work of literature come to life on the screen.

People who study film adaptation get frustrated with the oft-heard audience criticism that "it wasn't like that in the book." They would point out that there are several types of adaptation. Some do seek to be absolutely faithful to the original source. A frequently cited example is the BBC's production of Jane Austen's *Pride and Prejudice,* which takes approximately five hours to watch. Many adaptations incorporate differences to offer a reinterpretation of the original. A popular example you might be familiar with is *10 Things I Hate about You,* which is a contemporary interpretation of Shakespeare's *The Taming of the Shrew.* Reinterpretation doesn't have to be as dramatically different as placing a sixteenth-century drama in a modern-day high school; it can be as subtle as emphasizing a particular character more than the original does, or creating a mood or atmosphere that is augmented from the literary version.

A third type of adaptation is one in which the film uses a literary work as the germ of an idea, but takes it in such a different direction that the adaptation becomes its own work. A famous example is the 1979 film *Apocalypse Now,* which stands alone as a comment on the Vietnam War, yet clearly has at its heart Joseph Conrad's 1899 novella *Heart of Darkness.*

Those who study film adaptation lament that the criticism "It wasn't like the book" shows how thoughtlessly prejudiced many viewers are toward the original reading experience. The truth is that reading a book and watching a movie are completely different experiences, and comparing the two is most useful for understanding the story from various angles, rather than trying to precisely replicate one experience in another medium.

CHARTING *BEOWULF:* FROM REINTERPRETATION TO FILM ADAPTATION

Stories are so important to a culture that writers and poets and playwrights tell them and retell them, over and over again. In the English and American literary tradition, one such story is *Beowulf,* an epic poem written around 1000 A.D. (although it likely existed in oral form as early as 700 A.D.). *Beowulf,* an epic poem in Old English by an anonymous author, tells the story of the Danes and the Geats, early Germanic tribes who lived in Denmark and southern Sweden. The poem was recorded by a Christian scribe, and so references to Christianity are inserted in an otherwise pagan society.

BEOWULF STORY

King Hrothgar has built a magnificent hall named Heorot. But the hall is soon attacked by Grendel, a monster who is described as a descendant of Cain. Beowulf and his group of warriors arrive at Heorot from their homeland, and Beowulf offers to rid Hrothgar of his cursed monster. Beowulf fights Grendel hand-to-hand, and mortally wounds Grendel by tearing off his arm. Hrothgar's people are celebrating Beowulf's victory when another attack occurs, this time by Grendel's mother. Beowulf follows her to her lair and kills her as well. Victorious, Beowulf takes leave of Hrothgar and returns to his homeland. Years pass, and Beowulf eventually becomes king of the Geats. When Beowulf is old, a thief disturbs a nearby treasure trove that is guarded by a fierce dragon. The dragon threatens Beowulf's kingdom, and Beowulf sets out for one last fight. He is successful at slaying the dragon, but at the cost of his own life. Beowulf is mourned and honored as a hero by his people.

Beowulf

[Grendel's attack and the fight with Beowulf] (circa 1000 A.D.)

1 THE king's men lived, blissful and happy, until a certain one, a fiend of hell, began to plot mischief. This wrathful spirit was called Grendel, a mighty stalker of the marches, who haunted the moors, the fens and fastnesses. The wretched being had long inhabited the abode of the monster kind, e'er since the Creator had condemned him. The Lord eternal wreaked vengeance upon the kindred of Cain, because of the murder—the slaying of Abel. He got no pleasure in the feud, but the Lord banished him for that wicked deed far from mankind. From him there woke to life all the evil broods, monsters and elves and sea-beasts, and giants too, who long time strove with God. He gave them their reward! [. . .]

A thane of Hygelac,[1] great among the Geats, heard of these deeds of Grendel in his native land. In his strength he was the best of men in the day of this life, noble and mighty. He bade make ready for him a goodly ship, he said that he would go over the ocean-road unto that war-king, the great prince, since he had need of men. Little did his prudent thanes blame him for that journey, though he was dear to them; they encouraged him in his high purpose, and looked for good omens. The hero had warriors, chosen from among the Geats, the keenest he could find. Fifteen in all went down unto the ship. [. . .]

> In his strength he was the best of men in the day of this life, noble and mighty.

[Beowulf arrives at Hrothgar's Kingdom.]

Then the mighty one arose with many a warrior round him,—it was a noble group of thanes! Some remained and guarded the armor as the chief bade them. The heroes hastened on, as the guide led them under the roof of Heorot. The great-hearted man, bold under his helmet, went on until he stood within the hall. Beowulf spoke,—on him gleamed his byrnie, his coat of mail linked by the smith's craft—: "Hail to thee, Hrothgar! I am Hygelac's kinsman and thane. Many an exploit have I undertaken in the days of my youth. In my native land I learned of Grendel's deeds; for seafarers say that this hall, this best of houses, stands empty and useless for all men, as soon as evening light is hidden under the vault of heaven. And my people, e'en the best and wisest men among them, urged me, king Hrothgar, to come unto thee, for they knew the strength of my might. They had themselves looked on when I came from the fight, stained with the blood of my foes. There I bound five of my enemies, destroyed a giant race, and slew by night the sea-beasts on the wave. I endured great distress, avenged the affliction of the Weder people,—they who had suffered woes! I ground the angry foe in pieces. And now I alone will decide the fight with Grendel, the giant monster. [. . .]

[Night falls.]

Then from the moorland, 'neath the misty hillsides, came Grendel drawing near; and God's anger was on him. The deadly foe was thinking to ensnare some man in that high hall. On he strode beneath the clouds, until he could see full well the wine-hall, the gilded house of men, all bright with gold. [. . .] The door, though fast in fire-hardened bands, sprang open straightway, soon as he touched it with his hands.

Thus, plotting evil, he burst open the entrance to the hall, for he was swollen with rage. Quickly thereafter the fiend was treading upon the bright-paved floor, moving on in wrathful mood. Out of his eyes started a loathsome light, most like to flame. He saw in the hall many warriors, a kindred band together, a group of clansmen all asleep. And he laughed in his heart. The cursèd monster thought to take the life from each body, ere the day broke; for the hope of a plenteous feast was come to him. But it was not fated that he should devour any more of the race of men after that night.

The mighty kinsman of Hygelac was watching to see how the deadly foe would go about his swift attacks. The monster thought not of tarrying, but sudden, for his first move, he seized upon a sleeping thane, rent him in pieces unawares, bit into the flesh, drank the blood from the veins, and swallowed him in huge pieces. In a moment he had devoured the whole corpse, even the hands and feet. He stepped on nearer and seized with his hands the great-hearted warrior on his bed. The fiend clutched at him with his claw, but Beowulf quickly grasped it with deadly purpose, fastening upon the arm. Straightway that master of evils discovered that never in this world in all the corners of the earth, had he met in any man a mightier hand-grip. But he could get away never the faster for that. He was eager to be gone; he wished to flee away into the darkness, to rejoin the horde of devils. He was not faring there as in the former days. Then the good kinsman of Hygelac bethought him of his speech at even; he stood upright and grappled him fast; his fingers cracked. The giant was making off. The hero followed him close. The monster was minded to fling loose, if he could, and flee away thence to the fenhollows; but he knew that the strength of his arm was in the grasp of an angry foe. It was a dire journey that the destroyer had made to Heorot.

[. . .] Upon his shoulder a gaping wound appeared; the sinews sprang asunder, the flesh was rent apart. The glory of the fight was given unto Beowulf. Grendel, sick to death, was doomed to flee thence and find out his joyless abode 'neath the fen-banks. Full well he knew that the end of his life was come, the appointed number of his days. By that deadly fight the desire of all the Danes was satisfied.

5

6

---

[1] "A thane of Hygelac" refers to Beowulf. A thane is a general term for a warrior; Hygelac is the name of Beowulf's kinsman.

Questions for Critical Thinking

1 Grendel's physical appearance is one of the great mysteries of the Beowulf epic because very few direct details are provided in the text. How did you envision Grendel while reading the text?

2 Examine how Beowulf fits the traditional role of the hero. In what ways does he conform to typical conceptions of the hero? In what ways, if any, does he differ? Before you write, you may want to brainstorm qualities of heroes; in your introduction, offer a definition of the hero as you understand that archetype.

3 In what ways is Grendel a villain? Are there any ways in which he is sympathetic?

TWO NOVEL ADAPTATIONS OF BEOWULF

The ancient epic has been reinterpreted in two contemporary novels, *Grendel* by John Gardner (1971) and *Eaters of the Dead* by Michael Crichton (1976). Popular novelist Crichton takes *Beowulf* and tells it from an outsider's perspective—Ibn Fadlan, an Arab who is conscripted into Beowulf's group of warriors. Crichton searches for the rational explanation of the events recounted in *Beowulf* and puts forth a story in which Grendel is not a single monster, but a group of Neanderthals who are ransacking the nearby village of the evolved Norsemen. He makes the novel read like the tenth-century eyewitness account of Ibn Fadlan; it includes many observations of Viking habits and way of life. Gardner provides another "outsider" perspective, telling the Beowulf tale through the eyes of the monster Grendel—whose tale is more a tragic coming-of-age story than an heroic epic. As you read, pay careful attention to the ways in which these modern interpretations adhere to the original epic, and to the ways in which they differ. Could these be, as Michael Crichton suggests, merely different accounts of the same actual event?

John Gardner (1933–1982)
Grendel (1971)

GRENDEL'S ISOLATION

1 The sky ignores me, forever unimpressed. Him too I hate, the same as I hate these brainless budding trees, these brattling birds.

Not, of course, that I fool myself with thoughts that I'm more noble. Pointless, ridiculous monster crouched in the shadows, stinking of dead men, murdered children, martyred cows. (I am neither proud nor ashamed, understand. One more dull victim, leering at seasons that never were meant to be observed.) "Ah, sad one, poor old freak!" I cry, and hug myself, and laugh, letting out salt tears, he he! till I fall down gasping and sobbing. (It's mostly fake.) The sun spins mindlessly overhead, the shadows lengthen and shorten as if by plan. Small birds, with a high-pitched yelp, lay eggs. The tender grasses peek up, innocent yellow, through the ground: the children of the dead. (It was just here, this shocking green, that once when the moon was tombed in clouds, I tore off sly old Athelgard's head. Here, where the startling tiny jaws of crocuses snap at the late-winter sun like the heads of baby watersnakes, here I killed the old woman with the iron-gray hair. She tasted of urine and spleen, which made me spit. Sweet mulch for yellow blooms. Such are the tiresome memories of a shadow-shooter, earth-rim-roamer, walker of the world's weird wall.) "Waaah!" I cry, with another quick, nasty face at the sky, mournfully observing the way it is, bitterly remembering the way it was, and idiotically casting tomorrow's nets. "Aargh! Yaww!" I reel, smash trees. Disfigured son of lunatics. The big-boled oaks gaze down at me yellow with morning, beneath complexity. "No offense," I say, with a terrible, sycophantish smile, and tip an imaginary hat.

3   It was not always like this, of course. On occasion, it's been worse.

BEOWULF'S ARRIVAL

4   I am mad with joy.—At least I think it's joy. Strangers have come, and it's a whole new game. I kiss the ice on the frozen creeks, I press my ear to it, honoring the water that rattles below, for by water they came: the icebergs parted as if gently pushed back by enormous hands, and the ship sailed through, sea-eager, foamy-necked, white sails riding the swan-road, flying like a bird! O happy Grendel! Fifteen glorious heroes, proud in their battle dress, fat as cows! [. . .]

[Grendel watches as Hrothgar's coast guard questions Beowulf as to who he is.]

5   At last the coastguard's voice gave out—he bent over the pommel, coughing into his fist—and the leader answered. His voice, though powerful, was mild. Voice of a dead thing, calm as dry sticks and ice when the wind blows over them. He had a strange face that, little by little, grew unsettling to me: it was

a face, or so it seemed for an instant, from a dream I had almost forgotten. The eyes slanted downward, never blinking, unfeeling as a snake's. He had no more beard than a fish. He smiled as he spoke, but it was as if the gentle voice, the childlike yet faintly ironic smile were holding something back, some magician-power that could blast stone cliffs to ashes as lightning blasts trees.

> The eyes slanted downward, never blinking, unfeeling as a snake's.

6   "We're Geats," he said, "the hearth-companions of King Hygilac. You've heard of my father. A famous old man named Ecgtheow." His mind, as he spoke, seemed far away, as if, though polite, he were indifferent to all this—an outsider not only among the Danes but everywhere.

FIGHT WITH BEOWULF

7   I touch the door with my fingertips and it bursts, for all its fire-forged bands—it jumps away like a terrified deer—and I plunge into the silent, hearth-lit hall with a laugh that I wouldn't much care to wake up to myself. I trample the planks that a moment before protected the hall like a hand raised in horror to a terrified mouth (sheer poetry, ah!) and the broken hinges rattle like swords down the timbered walls. The Geats are like stones, and whether it's because they're numb with terror or stiff from too much mead, I cannot tell. I am swollen with excitement, bloodlust and joy and a strange fear that mingle in my chest like the twisting rage of a bone-fire. I step onto the brightly shining floor and angrily advance on them. They're all asleep, the whole company! I can hardly believe my luck, and my wild heart laughs, but I let out no sound. Swiftly, softly, I will move from bed to bed and destroy them all, swallow every last man. I am blazing, half-crazy with joy. For pure, mad prank, I snatch a cloth from the nearest table and tie it around my neck to make a napkin. I delay no longer. I seize up a sleeping man, tear at him hungrily, bite through his bone-locks and suck hot, slippery blood. He goes down in huge morsels, head, chest, hips, legs, even the hands and feet. My face and arms are wet, matted. The napkin is sopping. The dark floor steams. I move on at once and I reach for another one (whispering, whispering, chewing the universe down to words), and I seize a wrist. A shock goes through me. Mistake!

8   It's a trick! His eyes are open, were open all the time, cold-bloodedly watching to see how I work. The eyes nail me now as his hand nails down my arm. I

jump back without thinking (whispering wildly: *jump back without thinking*). Now he's out of his bed, his hand still closed like a dragon's jaw on mine. Nowhere on middle-earth, I realize, have I encountered a grip like his. My whole arm's on fire, incredible, searing pain—it's as if his crushing fingers are charged like fangs with poison. I scream, facing him, grotesquely shaking hands—dear long-lost brother, kinsman-thane—and the timbered hall screams back at me. I feel the bones go, ground from their sockets, and I scream again. [. . .]

9   The room goes suddenly white, as if struck by lightning. I stare down, amazed. He has torn off my arm at the shoulder! Blood pours down where the limb was. I cry, I bawl like a baby. He stretched his blinding white wings and breathes out fire. I run for the door and through it. I move like wind. I stumble and fall, get up again. I'll die! I howl. The night is aflame with winged men. *No, no! Think!* I come suddenly awake once more from the nightmare. Darkness. I really will die! Every rock, every tree, every crystal of snow cries out cold-blooded objectness. Cold, sharp outlines, everything around me: distinct, detached as dead men. I understand. "Mama!" I bellow. "Mama, Mama! I'm dying!" But her love is history. His whispering follows me into the woods, though I've outrun him. "It was an accident," I bellow back. I will cling to what is true. "Blind, mindless, mechanical. Mere logic of chance." I am weak from loss of blood. No one follows me now. I stumble again and with my one weak arm I cling to the huge twisted roots of an oak. I look down past stars to a terrifying darkness. I seem to recognize the place, but it's impossible. "Accident," I whisper. I will fall. I seem to desire the fall, and though I fight it with all my will I know in advance that I can't win. Standing baffled, quaking with fear, three feet from the edge of a nightmare cliff, I find myself, incredibly, moving toward it. I look down, down, into bottomless blackness, feeling the dark power moving in me like an ocean current, some monster inside me, deep sea wonder, dread night monarch astir in his cave, moving me slowly to my voluble tumble into death.

Questions for Critical Thinking

1 Write a description of Grendel as he appears in Gardner's novel. What can you say about his personality and attitude? Support your description with quotes from the excerpt.

2 How does being in Grendel's point of view affect the way you see Beowulf in Gardner's version? How similar or different do you find Beowulf from the original epic in which he was the main character?

3 Compare Gardner's Grendel to the monster in the original epic. Is he a more sympathetic character in Gardner's rendering? If so, formulate a thesis explaining what makes him more sympathetic in your view. If not, create a thesis in which you argue why he is not.

4 Read the excerpts from Michael Crichton's *Eaters of the Dead* below. Compare and contrast the Grendel monster from the original epic, Gardner's interpretation, and Crichton's depiction of the wendol. Are the various authors describing different characters altogether, or are they emphasizing different traits of the same creature?

A FACTUAL NOTE ON ADAPTING *BEOWULF* FOR

Eaters of the Dead by Michael Crichton

I started from the scholarly tradition that examined epic poetry and mythology as if it might have some underlying basis in fact. Heinrich Schliemann assumed the *Iliad* was true, and found what he claimed was Troy and Mycenae; Arthur Evans believed there was something to the myth of the Minotaur, and uncovered the Palace of Knossos on Crete; M. I. Finley and others had traced the route of Ulysses in the *Odyssey;* Lionel Casson had written about the real journeys that might underlie the myth of Jason and the Argonauts. Thus it seemed reasonable, within this tradition, to imagine that *Beowulf,* too, had originally been based on an actual event.

That event had been embellished over centuries of oral retelling, producing the fantastic narrative we read today. But I thought it might be possible to reverse the process, peeling away the poetic invention, and returning to a kernel of genuine human experience—something that had actually happened. . . .

Clearly, I wanted an eyewitness account. I could not extract it from the existing *Beowulf* narrative, and I did not want to invent it. That was my impasse. But at some point, I realized I did not have to invent it—I could *discover* it instead.

Suppose, I thought, a contemporary observer had been present at these battles, and had written an account of the events that were later transformed into a poem. Suppose, too, that this account *already existed,* but had never been recognized for what it was. If this were so, then no invention on my part would be necessary. I could merely reproduce the eyewitness narrative, and annotate it for the reader. . . .

What sort of narrative would be most desirable? I concluded the most useful account would be written by an outsider—someone not part of the culture, who could report objectively on the events as they occurred. But who would this outside observer have been? Where would he have come from?

On reflection, I realized I already knew of such a person. In the tenth century, an Arab named Ibn Fadlan had traveled north from Baghdad into what is now Russia, where he came in contact with the Vikings. His manuscript, well-known to scholars, provides one of the earliest eyewitness accounts of Viking life and culture. As a college undergraduate, I had read portions of the manuscript. Ibn Fadlan had a distinct voice and style. He was imitable. He was believable. He was unexpected. And after a thousand years, I felt that Ibn Fadlan would not mind being revived in a new role, as a witness to the events that led to the epic poem of *Beowulf.* . . .

I obtained the existing manuscript fragments and combined them, with only slight modifications, into the first three chapters of *Eaters of the Dead.* I then wrote the rest of the novel in the style of the manuscript to carry Ibn Fadlan on the rest of his now-fictional journey. . . .

Michael Crichton (1942–2008)
Eaters of the Dead (1976)

FIRST GLIMPSE OF BULIWYF

1   Now, one of their number, a young noble called Buliwyf, was chosen to be their new leader, but he was not accepted while the sick chieftan still lived. This was the cause of uneasiness, at the time of our arrival. Yet also there was no aspect of sorrow or weeping among the people encamped on the Volga.

2   The Northmen place great importance on the duty of the host. They greet every visitor with warmth and hospitality, much food and clothing, and the earls and nobles compete for the honor of the greatest hospitality. The party of our caravan was brought before Buliwyf and a great feast was given us. Over this Buliwyf himself presided, and I saw him to be a tall man, and strong, with skin and hair and beard of pure white. He had the bearing of a leader.

BATTLE WITH THE WENDOL

3   Now I noticed that Buliwyf and all his company did not drink that night, or only sparingly, and Rothgar took this as no insult, but rather acknowledged it as the natural course of things. There was no wind that night; the candles and flames of Hurot Hall did not flicker, and yet it was damp, and chill. I saw with my own eyes that out of doors the mist was rolling in from the hills, blocking the silvered light of the moon, cloaking all in blackness.

4   As the night continued, King Rothgar and his Queen departed for sleep, and the massive doors of Hurot Hall were locked and barred, and the nobles and earls remaining there fell into a drunken stupor and snored loudly.

5   Then Buliwyf and his men, still wearing their armor, went about the room, dousing the candles and seeing to the fires, that they should burn low and weak. I asked Herger the meaning of this, and he told me to pray for my life, and to feign sleep. I was given a weapon, a short sword, but it was little comfort to me; I was not a warrior and knew it full well.

Verily, all the men feigned sleep. Buliwyf and his men joined the slumbering bodies of the King Rothgar's earls, who were truly snoring. How long we waited I do not know, for I think I slept awhile myself. Then all at once I was awake, in a manner of unnatural sharp alertness; I was not drowsy but instantly tense and alert, still lying on a bearskin cloth on the floor of the great hall. It was dark night; the candles in the hall burned low, and a faint breeze whispered through the hall and fluttered the yellow flames.

And then I heard a low grunting sound, like the rooting of a pig, carried to me by the breeze, and I smelled a rank odor like the rot of a carcass after a month, and I feared greatly. This rooting sound, for I can call it none else, this grumbling, grunting, snorting sound, grew louder and more excited. It came from outdoors, at one side of the hall. Then I heard it from another side, and then another, and another. Verily the hall was surrounded.

I sat up on one elbow, my heart pounding, and I looked about the hall. No man among the sleeping warriors moved, and yet there was Herger, lying with his eyes wide open. And there, too, Buliwyf, breathing in a snore, with his eyes also wide open. From this I gathered that all the warriors of Buliwyf were waiting to do battle with the wendol, whose sounds now filled the air. [. . .]

Then came the most fearsome moment. All sounds ceased. There was utter silence, except for the snoring of the men and the low crackle of the fire. Still none of the warriors of Buliwyf stirred.

And then there was a mighty crash upon the solid doors of the hall of Hurot, and these doors burst open, and a rush of reeking air gutted all the lights, and the black mist entered the room. I did not count their number: verily it seemed thousands of black grunting shapes, and yet it might have been no more than five or six, huge black shapes hardly in the manner of men, and yet also manlike. The air stank of blood and death; I was cold beyond reason, and shivered. Yet still no warrior moved.

Then, with a curdling scream to wake the dead, Buliwyf leapt up, and in his arms he swung the giant sword Runding, which sang like a sizzling flame as it cut the air. And his warriors leapt up with him, and all joined in battle. The shouts of the men mingled with the pig-grunts and the odors of the black mist, and there was terror and confusion and great wracking and rending of the Hurot Hall. [. . .]

The air stank of blood and death;

I remember, most distinctly, the touch of these monsters upon me, especially the furry aspect of the bodies, for these mist monsters have hair as long as a hairy dog, and as thick, on all parts of their bodies. And then the black mist was gone, slunk away, grunting and panting and stinking, leaving behind destruction and death that we could not know until we had lighted fresh tapers. [. . .]

Herger said thus: "I saw two of their number carrying a third, who was dead." Perhaps this was so, for all generally agreed upon it. I learned that the mist monsters never leave one of their kind to the society of men, but rather will risk great dangers to retrieve him from human purview. So also will they go to extreme lengths to keep a victim's head, and we could not find the head of Edgtho in any place; the monsters had carried it off with them.

Then Buliwyf spoke, and Herger told me his words thus: "Look, I have retained a trophy of the night's bloody deeds. See, here is an arm of one of the fiends." 14

And, true to his word, Buliwyf held the arm of one of the mist monsters, cut off at the shoulder by the great sword Runding. All the warriors crowded around to examine it. I perceived it thusly: it appeared to be small, with a hand of abnormally large size. But the forearm and upper arm were not large to match it, although the muscles were powerful. There was long black matted hair on all parts of the arm except the palm of the hand. Finally it is to say that the arm stank as the whole beast stank, with the fetid smell of the black mist. 15

Now all the warriors cheered Buliwyf, and his sword Runding. The fiend's arm was hung from the rafters of the great hall of Hurot, and marveled at by all the people of the kingdom of Rothgar. Thus ended the first battle with the wendol. 16

Questions for Critical Thinking

1 Compare Grendel in the original version to the wendol of *Eaters of the Dead*. In it, examine what is gained, as well as what is lost, by making these changes.

2 Crichton shifts the point of view of the story by making it a first-person account from an Arab—an outsider to the Northman tribe. Note the places in which you see the outsider status of the narrator giving Crichton the opportunity to expand on the details of Buliwyf's tribe. How do these details change your view of Beowulf and his brave warriors?

3 Take a small portion of Grendel's fight with Beowulf from the original epic and underline all the descriptions the author includes. Do the same for the wendol attack in *Eaters of the Dead*. In your opinion, which version more clearly brings the battle to life on the page?

4 Both Crichton and Gardner offer an "outsider's" view of Beowulf. Compare Crichton's Arab narrator's impression of Buliwyf to Grendel's first impression of Beowulf. What feelings do they share about him? What do the differences between their impressions say about their characters?

TWO FILM ADAPTATIONS OF *BEOWULF*

Buliwyf, his sword bloody from battling his way into the subterranean wendol lair, prepares to do battle with the wendol queen. Contrast his weary expression and dirty clothes with the naked, glistening bravura of Beowulf from *Beowulf: The Movie*.

The wendol queen, adorned in snakes and human bones, casts a baleful look at Buliwyf. How does her warped humanity compare to the twisted, gigantic form of Grendel from *Beowulf: The Movie*?

Beowulf, naked and unarmed, steps forward to challenge Grendel in combat. In what ways is he "larger than life" compared to Buliwyf from *The 13th Warrior*? What effect does computer rendering of a real actor have on your perception of the Beowulf character?

The hulking, twisted Grendel bursts into Hrothgar's mead hall, intent on a feast of human flesh. Compare his bent posture to the coiled crouch of the wendol queen. Which "monster" seems more threatening?

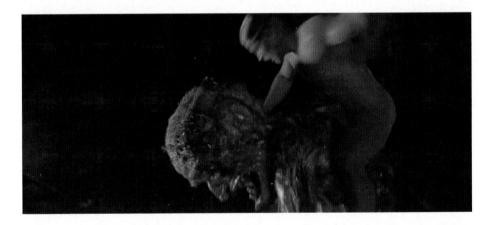

Beowulf gains the advantage over the giant Grendel and pummels him with his bare fists. Which version of the epic presented in this chapter does this representation remind you most of? Is this how you imagined the fight when you read the original epic?

Buliwyf wields the mighty sword Huring in a fatal blow to the wendol leader. By using weapons and fighting foes his own size, does Buliwyf appear to be more or less heroic? Does he or the Beowulf of *Beowulf: The Movie* seem more believable?

The 13th Warrior (1999)

Adapted from the novel Eaters of the Dead *by Michael Crichton*
Screenplay by: William Wisher Jr. and Warren Lewis
Director: John McTiernan
Starring: Antonio Banderas (Ibn Fadlan), Vladimir Kulich (Buliwyf)

1   AHMED Ibn Fadlan, an Arab charged to be an ambassador to the north, comes across a band of Vikings. They have been asked to help a far-off kingdom, and they cast lots to see which thirteen men will be sent. Since the thirteenth man must be a foreigner, Ahmed is conscripted to go along with the group, led by Buliwyf.

2   Disgusted by the Vikings' habits and hygiene, Ahmed is at first on the outskirts of the group. He begins to prove himself by picking up their language, showing off his horsemanship and maintaining his dignity as an Arab devoted to Allah.

3   When the warriors arrive in Hrothgar's land, they come upon a house in which all the inhabitants have been killed and their bodies gnawed on. They speak with Hrothgar and understand that it is the wendol, a group that comes with the mist, who have attacked his kingdom repeatedly. That night, Buliwyf's group feigns sleep and are alert and ready when the wendol come. Ahmed takes part in the fight, even though he does not want to. Bulywif takes the arm of one of the wendol, which are portrayed as hairy men with bear skins that cover their heads.

4   It is Ahmed who pieces together that they must fight the source of the wendol in order to get rid of them, and so Buliwyf's men find the wendol's cave. In the cave, they see the remains of human victims who have been eaten by the wendol. Bulywif sneaks into the innermost room where the wendol's queen is kept. He kills her, but in so doing is himself wounded. Pursued by wendol, he escapes with his men by swimming under the cave and out into the sea (another of Ahmed's ideas).

5   Back at Hrothgar's hall, they prepare for a final attack from the wendol. With his waning strength, Buliwyf fights in the battle and kills the leader of the wendol before dying himself. Ahmed fights, too, as he has become a brave warrior.

6   The movie ends with Ahmed, now a friend of the Vikings, setting sail for home.

Questions for Critical Thinking

1   In *Eaters of the Dead,* Ibn Fadlan and Buliwyf have a growing friendship over the course of the novel. In *The 13th Warrior,* Buliwyf remains far more distant. How does this alter the reader's/viewer's perception of Buliwyf? Why might the moviemakers have changed this aspect of Crichton's book?

2   *The 13th Warrior* is, in a way, twice removed from the original *Beowulf*—that is, it is a movie adaptation of a reinterpretation of the original. Can you trace similarities between the original epic and this reinterpreted movie adaptation? List any similarities you see, from the overall plot to the smallest detail. Does the number of similarities, whether small or large, surprise you?

3   After reading Michael Crichton's process in "A Factual Note on *Eaters of the Dead,*" evaluate whether the movie represents what Crichton was trying to do or takes the book in a new direction. What, if anything, does the film add to further Crichton's idea?

Beowulf: The Movie (2007)

Written by: Roger Avary and Neil Gaiman
Director: Robert Zemeckis
Starring: Anthony Hopkins (Hrothgar), Ray Winstone (Beowulf),
Crispin Glover (Grendel), Angelina Jolie (Grendel's mother)

1   RELEASED in 2007, the movie uses motion capture animation—that is, a technique in which infrared light captures the movements of real actors, which are then put into computer animation to create the look and color desired by the animators—and was originally released as a 3D movie. The major change to the plot of the original epic is that Beowulf is seduced by Grendel's mother, and their offspring is the dragon that Beowulf later fights. Other changes include that Hrothgar was also seduced by Grendel's mother, and—tormented by the fact that Grendel is his offspring—Hrothgar commits suicide, making Beowulf king of the Danes, not the Geats.

2   *Note:* This movie adaptation is not to be confused with the 2005 movie *Beowulf & Grendel. Beowulf: The Movie* begins with Grendel's attack on the mead hall, showing the destruction and death he causes, even though Grendel clearly avoids harming Hrothgar. Next, Beowulf arrives with his men and is taken to meet with Hrothgar, where he pledges to rid the king of his monster. After feasting, Beowulf strips off his armor to go to bed, reasoning that he will fight Grendel hand to hand. When Grendel bursts in, Beowulf fights him and breaks off Grendel's arm.

3   Grendel, who speaks Old English, returns to his mother's cave where he laments his missing arm and assures her he did not kill Hrothgar. All the movie shows of his mother at this point is a soft, seductive voice with flashes of a snake's tail. When Beowulf comes to the cave to slay Grendel's mother, he finds that she is a beautiful seductress.

4   After Beowulf returns and refuses to directly tell Hrothgar whether or not he killed Grendel's mother, Hrothgar—tormented by his concealment of the fact that he was himself seduced by Grendel's mother years ago and that Grendel is their love child—commits suicide, making Beowulf king.

5   The movie jumps ahead many years to show that Beowulf, though an adored king, is bothered by a former guilt. Only the queen seems to understand that guilt, and she is cold to Beowulf because of what she knows about his relation with Grendel's mother. It becomes clear that Beowulf, like Hrothgar before him, was seduced by Grendel's mother, and that their love child is a dragon. In the end, Beowulf slays the dragon—his own offspring—but is mortally wounded in the fight and dies. As Beowulf tells the queen before he dies, "Keep a memory of me, not as a king or a hero, but as a man, fallible and flawed."

An Interview on Adapting *Beowulf* for the movie with Roger Avary & Neil Gaiman

(from http://www.moviesonline.ca/movienews_13367.html)

Roger Avary: The original genesis of the project began with questioning. You know when I read the eulogy itself, who is Grendel's father? Why has no one in academia ever addressed that? Why does Beowulf emerge from the cave with the head of Grendel and not the head of the mother and why was he in there for eight days? You know, these were questions that I didn't see anybody answering. . . .

And then I had heard much theorizing about the themes of the last half but no one had ever united it properly into a single story and so I was talking with Neil ten years ago in May and telling him my theories on Beowulf and the problem I was having with the second half, and Neil said, "But don't you see? If this and this and this that you say are true about Beowulf, if Hrothgar is Grendel's father and if Beowulf did indeed give in to the mother, don't you see the dragon is Beowulf's son come back to haunt him for his sins?" And it was like, had it been a snake it would have bit me. I stood up and I immediately told Neil, "When are you available? Let's go work on this."

Neil Gaiman: [. . .] [T]he problem with Beowulf is that we only have one manuscript and that manuscript, the Cotton Vitellius document, has frankly come to us through luck more than anything else. It was written over a thousand years ago. The manuscript has scorch marks on it from where it was rescued from a fire and thrown out of a window. Is it incomplete? Well no, it's not like we're missing pages of that version of Beowulf. Is that the only version of Beowulf that has that story that ever existed or was ever told? Obviously not. This was part of the oral tradition that was at the end of it. . . .

You know so it's like do we think that? When you tell a story in the oral tradition, you tend to adapt it to your audience. If your audience wants blood, you give them blood. If they want sex, you give them sex. If you are a Christian monk writing something down, if there were sexual elements, you're not going to put them in and they didn't. . . .

Roger Avary: So you can imagine that many changes could have occurred over it. And for us it was a matter of investigating why . . . were we not privy to the actual battles with Grendel's mother? Why was it told by Beowulf afterwards?

Neil Gaiman: Taking concepts like just the idea of an unreliable narrator and saying we think that the story of Beowulf is told by an unreliable narrator. And one of the things that our Beowulf is about is the idea of okay, at the end of it, we are told his song is going to be sung and this is the song of Beowulf but it's very obvious by the end of our film that the song of Beowulf that is being sung even then is not actually what happened. It's already changing and shifting. It's about the relationship between a man and his story in some ways.

Questions for Critical Thinking

1 After watching Grendel's attack in *Beowulf* and the battle scenes in *The 13th Warrior,* compare the strengths of the movies. Which effects are particularly stimulating visually? How realistic or fantastic is each version? How do the effects build that sense of reality or fantasy?

2 Contrast the duels between Beowulf and Grendel from *Beowulf* the movie and from Gareth Hinds's graphic novel. How are the two battles different? Discuss how the differing dynamics of the battles impact your impressions of the Beowulf and Grendel characters.

3 Observe the Grendel character in the *Beowulf* movie. Is he sympathetic or a villain? Compare him to the Grendel characters from Crichton's and Gardner's versions, as well as from the original epic. Which "Grendel" does he have most in common with? Explain your answer with examples from the movie.

Getting Started: A Research Project

Research is a skill that will carry you through your college career. You can find the research materials you need for this project on our website (www.mhhe.com/delbanco1e). Other ideas for research projects and sources appear at the end of this chapter.

As you've witnessed, when it comes to the classics, adaptation is a major way of honoring the original. We see this in the thousands-of-years-old tradition of staging and restaging Greek tragedy (see chapter 32) and Shakespeare's plays (see chapter 33) and in the adaptation of the Beowulf epic. Another long heroic poem that has gone through a number of changes and permutations is Homer's *Odyssey*. Its ancient original oral form—which was chanted by a group of rhetors or reciters at Greek religious festivals four times a year in the centuries leading up to the birth of writing—became a literary form. The story of Odysseus and the Trojan War was copied down on papyrus and read by Greek scholars up until the present moment. There have been a number of translations over the centuries (from say, that of Alexander Pope to Chapman's and Murray's), and some striking and powerful contemporary versions of the poem (Lattimore, Fitzgerald, Fagles); there was also a Classics Illustrated comic book version, and, with the advent of film technology, a number of cinematic versions.

An adventurous student may want to take on the task of reading the *Odyssey* in a few different translations and plotting the course of this epic's evolution from English version of the classical Greek poem to comic book to the movies. Focusing on a particular incident or scene in the original poem, such as Odysseus's trick of employing the so-called Trojan Horse to gain entry into the heavily fortified city of Troy, you can observe and comment upon the various changes and transformations. Add to this the various cinematic versions of the epic. From Italian costume epics to the 1997 TV movie made here in the United States and such variations on the story as we find in "O Brother, Where Art Thou?" the possibilities are rich for studying how a timeless story became adapted over time. A similarly rich trail of versions of Jane Austen's novels is something you can follow as well, or Shakespeare's *Othello* or *Hamlet*.

Further Suggestions for Writing and Research

The Research in the World box at the end of each casebook directs you toward secondary sources available at www.mhhe.com/delbanco1e that enhance your understanding of the work or author by giving you another perspective. This casebook also offers another kind of research: working in depth with the literature itself. While the excerpts in this chapter have given you an idea of each work and its major similarities with and differences from the original epic, the topics below will ask you to read or watch a couple of works from this casebook in their entirety. Studying the entire work will give you the chance to make your own connections and form your own ideas.

1. The poet who recorded *Beowulf* was Christian, even if those who recited the epic in earlier centuries were not. There is an interesting mix, then, of Christian references and pagan norms. *Eaters of the Dead, The Thirteenth Warrior, Beowulf* the movie, and *Grendel* all involve the presence of religion in different ways. Along with the original epic, choose one of

continued

these adaptations to read or watch in its entirety. Then write a five-page paper in which you examine the portrayal of religion in each work. A good starting place for a thesis would be to state where you see the conflict between 1) religious belief and action, or 2) different religions within one work.

2. The hero is an important character to literature. After brainstorming your ideas about hero characters—and you may want to consider heroes from Odysseus all the way up to current heroes like Superman—write a paragraph that defines the hero and lists his qualities. Keep this paragraph handy as you read the original *Beowulf* and one other work or movie of your choice from this chapter. Then write a five-page paper in which you discuss who the hero is and how he is portrayed in the adaptation you chose. How do these versions of the hero complicate and expand your original definition? In other words, formulate a thesis that states how the concept of the hero is used in *Beowulf* and in an adaptation.

3. In addition to the original *Beowulf*, read one book and watch one movie presented in this chapter. Then write a five-page essay in which you place the three versions on a continuum of adaptation from the most to the least like the original epic. Make a decision about which of the adaptations you feel is most stimulating to a modern audience. What are the major differences? What is the effect of these differences? Do these differences enhance readers' experience of the epic or diminish it?

4. After reading the original *Beowulf* and viewing one of its reinterpretations, imagine what your own reinterpretation of *Beowulf* might look like. In five pages, outline your ideas, including decisions such as the medium you would use (i.e., book or movie or something else), the point of view or main character, the setting and time period, etc.

Some Sources for Research

5. A contemporary version of graphic poetry has recently developed around Billy Collins, U.S. poet laureate from 2001–2003. Independent animators have created short animation to accompany Collins's own reading of his poems. To sample some of this animated poetry, this poetry can be found at *www.bcactionpoet.org*. (Poems we particularly recommend: "Budapest" and "Forgetfulness")

6. "Why They Changed the Beowulf Story"
http://www.moviesonline.ca/movienews_13367.html

7. The field is quite new and still truly wide open, so you can perform raw field research on your own by taking a character from your reading and seeing what adaptations you can find on the Web, reading the new versions, viewing the films, and writing down your own findings.

For examples of student papers, see chapter 3, Common Writing Assignments, and chapter 5, Writing the Research Paper, in the Handbook for Writing from Reading.

14

An Anthology
of Stories for
Further Reading

*I'll read stories where
the stakes are high . . .*

*I don't like to see a bad
sentence on the page.*

Q&A

A Conversation on Writing

Amy Hempel

The Allure of Reading

I will read any story about somebody getting through a hard thing. Anybody who comes out the other side of a difficult experience— I want to know how that person did it. I'll read stories where the stakes are high, where it matters if things turn out right or not. I read people who are incredibly inventive with language, people who say things I've never heard before. People who have sentences with kind of a rhythm like music. I like the sounds of a sentence, the acoustics of a sentence, not just what it's saying or the information in it. In fact, information for me is often the least important part of the story. I'm interested in who it happened to and what he or she is making of it.

Writing from Experience

One of the things that interests me most in story writing is that, even though you start maybe with things that really happened to you, people that you know, if you're paying attention there's a point where it stops being your story and becomes the story's story. It will veer off. And if you're paying attention and open to invention, that's when story really comes into being, I think. We mythologize ourselves, so even when you try to tell a true story, you tell a friend about a close call, you find yourself embellishing it, because it could have been a closer call. And I think everybody's alert to that without even trying. So I usually start with something that did happen with people I know. But almost without trying, it changes. They change. And they become somebody else or anybody else.

Reading As a Refuge

My earliest memory of reading fiction is taking *The Secret Garden* into a fort that I had built in a family's home in Denver. It was a basement fort next to a crawl space. . . . I remember taking couch cushions off the couch and using sheets and building a fort. And I could just stay there for hours and hours.

San Francisco (1985)

Do you know what I think?

I think it was the tremors. That's what must have done it. The way the floor rolled like bongo boards under our feet? Remember it was you and Daddy and me having lunch? "I guess that's not an earthquake," you said. "I guess you're shaking the table?"

That's when it must have happened. A watch on a dresser, a small thing like that—it must have been shaken right off, onto the floor.

And how would Maidy know? Maidy at the doctor's office? All those years on a psychiatrist's couch and suddenly the couch is *moving.*

Good God, she is on that couch when the big one hits.

Maidy didn't tell you, but you know what her doctor said? When she sprang from the couch and said, "My God, was that an earthquake?"

The doctor said this: "Did it *feel* like an earthquake to you?"

I think we are agreed, you have to look on the light side.

So that's when I think it must have happened. Not that it matters to me. Maidy is the one who wants to know. She thinks she has it coming, being the older daughter. Although where was the older daughter when it happened? Which daughter was it that found you?

When Maidy started asking about your watch, I felt I had to say it. I said, "With the body barely cold?"

Maidy said the body is not the person, that the *essence* is the person, and that the essence leaves the body behind it, along with the body's possessions—for example, its watch?

"Time flies," I said. "Like an arrow.

"*Fruit flies,*" I said, and Maidy said, "What?"

"Fruit flies," I said again. "Fruit flies like a banana."

That's how easy it is to play a joke on Maidy.

Remember how easy?

Now Maidy thinks I took your watch. She thinks because I got there first, my first thought was to take it. Maidy keeps asking, "Who took Mama's watch?" She says, "Did *you* take Mama's watch?"

If you like the exquisitely crafted "San Francisco," you may also like another spare, trim story, thought of as "minimalist" by some contemporary critics—"Cathedral" by Raymond Carver (in this section).

GOING FURTHER   You might also enjoy the novelist Mary Robison's *Why Did I Ever*, also of the "less is more" school of writing, and the elegantly spare novels, particularly *Play It As It Lays*, of Joan Didion.

Sherman Alexie (b. 1966)

SHERMAN ALEXIE GREW UP on the Spokane Indian Reservation in Washington (he is of Spokane/Coeur d'Alene Indian descent). He attended college with the goal of becoming a doctor. His career as a poet took off shortly after graduation; by 1993, he had re-ceived two major fellowships and published two books of poetry. Next, he returned to short stories with *The Lone Ranger and Tonto Fistfight In Heaven* (1993) and then produced a novel, *Reservation Blues* (1995). He also wrote the screenplay for the award-winning,

independently produced film *Smoke Signals* (1998). His signature blend of irony, humor, cynicism, and critique of modern Native American life has won him many honors including the PEN/Hemingway award, the PEN/Malamud award, and the Pushcart Prize. In 2007 he received the National Book Award for Young People's Literature with *The Absolutely True Diary of a Part-Time Indian.* He calls Seattle home.

What You Pawn I Will Redeem (2003)

NOON

1   One day you have a home and the next you don't, but I'm not going to tell you my particular reasons for being homeless, because it's my secret story, and Indians have to work hard to keep secrets from hungry white folks.

    I'm a Spokane Indian boy, an Interior Salish, and my people have lived within a hundred-mile radius of Spokane, Washington, for at least ten thousand years. I grew up in Spokane, moved to Seattle twenty-three years ago for college, flunked out after two semesters, worked various blue- and bluer-collar jobs, married two or three times, fathered two or three kids, and then went crazy. Of course, crazy is not the official definition of my mental problem, but I don't think asocial disorder fits it, either, because that makes me sound like I'm a serial killer or something. I've never hurt another human being, or, at least, not physically. I've broken a few hearts in my time, but we've all done that, so I'm nothing special in that regard. I'm a boring heartbreaker, too. I never dated or married more than one woman at a time. I didn't break hearts into pieces overnight. I broke them slowly and carefully. And I didn't set any land-speed records running out the door. Piece by piece, I disappeared. I've been disappearing ever since.

    I've been homeless for six years now. If there's such a thing as an effective homeless man, then I suppose I'm effective. Being homeless is probably the only thing I've ever been good at. I know where to get the best free food. I've made friends with restaurant and convenience-store managers who let me use their bathrooms. And I don't mean the public bathrooms, either. I mean the employees' bathrooms, the clean ones hidden behind the kitchen or the pantry or the cooler. I know it sounds strange to be proud of this, but it means a lot to me, being trustworthy enough to piss in somebody else's clean bathroom. Maybe you don't understand the value of a clean bathroom, but I do.

    Probably none of this interests you. Homeless Indians are everywhere in Seattle. We're common and boring, and you walk right on by us, with maybe a look of anger or disgust or even sadness at the terrible fate of the noble savage. But we have dreams and families. I'm friends with a homeless Plains Indian man whose son is the editor of a big-time newspaper back East. Of course, that's his story, but we Indians are great storytellers and liars and mythmakers, so maybe that Plains Indian hobo is just a plain old everyday Indian. I'm kind of suspicious of him, because he identifies himself only as Plains Indian, a generic term, and not by a specific tribe. When I asked him why he wouldn't tell me exactly what he is, he said, "Do any of us know exactly what we are?" Yeah, great, a philosophizing Indian. "Hey," I said, "you got to have a home to be that homely." He just laughed and flipped me the eagle and walked away.

5   I wander the streets with a regular crew—my teammates, my defenders, my posse. It's Rose of Sharon, Junior, and me. We matter to each other if we don't matter to anybody else. Rose of Sharon is a big woman, about seven feet tall if you're measuring over-all effect and about five feet tall if you're only talking about the physical. She's a Yakama Indian of the Wishram variety. Junior is a Colville, but there are about a hundred and ninety-nine tribes that make up the Colville, so he could be anything. He's good-looking, though, like he just stepped out of some "Don't Litter the Earth" public-service advertisement. He's got those great big cheekbones that are like planets, you know, with little moons orbiting them. He gets me jealous, jealous, and jealous. If you put Junior and me next to each other, he's the Before Columbus Arrived Indian and I'm the After Columbus

Arrived Indian. I am living proof of the horrible damage that colonialism has done to us Skins. But I'm not going to let you know how scared I sometimes get of history and its ways. I'm a strong man, and I know that silence is the best method of dealing with white folks.

This whole story really started at lunchtime, when Rose of Sharon, Junior, and I were panning the handle down at Pike Place Market. After about two hours of negotiating, we earned five dollars—good enough for a bottle of fortified courage from the most beautiful 7-Eleven in the world. So we headed over that way, feeling like warrior drunks, and we walked past this pawnshop I'd never noticed before. And that was strange, because we Indians have built-in pawnshop radar. But the strangest thing of all was the old powwow-dance regalia I saw hanging in the window.

"That's my grandmother's regalia," I said to Rose of Sharon and Junior.

"How you know for sure?" Junior asked.

I didn't know for sure, because I hadn't seen that regalia in person ever. I'd only seen photographs of my grandmother dancing in it. And those were taken before somebody stole it from her, fifty years ago. But it sure looked like my memory of it, and it had all the same color feathers and beads that my family sewed into our powwow regalia.

"There's only one way to know for sure," I said.

So Rose of Sharon, Junior, and I walked into the pawnshop and greeted the old white man working behind the counter.

"How can I help you?" he asked.

"That's my grandmother's powwow regalia in your window," I said. "Somebody stole it from her fifty years ago, and my family has been searching for it ever since."

The pawnbroker looked at me like I was a liar. I understood. Pawnshops are filled with liars.

"I'm not lying," I said. "Ask my friends here. They'll tell you."

"He's the most honest Indian I know," Rose of Sharon said.

"All right, honest Indian," the pawnbroker said. "I'll give you the benefit of the doubt. Can you prove it's your grandmother's regalia?"

Because they don't want to be perfect, because only God is perfect, Indian people sew flaws into their powwow regalia. My family always sewed one yellow bead somewhere on our regalia. But we always hid it so that you had to search really hard to find it.

"If it really is my grandmother's," I said, "there will be one yellow bead hidden somewhere on it."

"All right, then," the pawnbroker said. "Let's take a look."

He pulled the regalia out of the window, laid it down on the glass counter, and we searched for that yellow bead and found it hidden beneath the armpit.

"There it is," the pawnbroker said. He didn't sound surprised. "You were right. This is your grandmother's regalia."

"It's been missing for fifty years," Junior said.

"Hey, Junior," I said. "It's my family's story. Let me tell it."

"All right," he said. "I apologize. You go ahead."

"It's been missing for fifty years," I said.

"That's his family's sad story," Rose of Sharon said. "Are you going to give it back to him?"

"That would be the right thing to do," the pawnbroker said. "But I can't afford to do the right thing. I paid a thousand dollars for this. I can't just give away a thousand dollars."

"We could go to the cops and tell them it was stolen," Rose of Sharon said.

"Hey," I said to her. "Don't go threatening people."

The pawnbroker sighed. He was thinking about the possibilities.

"Well, I suppose you could go to the cops," he said. "But I don't think they'd believe a word you said."

He sounded sad about that. As if he was sorry for taking advantage of our disadvantages.

"What's your name?" the pawnbroker asked me.

"Jackson," I said.

"Is that first or last?"

"Both," I said.

"Are you serious?"

"Yes, it's true. My mother and father named me Jackson Jackson. My family nickname is Jackson Squared. My family is funny."

40   "All right, Jackson Jackson," the pawnbroker said. "You wouldn't happen to have a thousand dollars, would you?"

"We've got five dollars total," I said.

"That's too bad," he said, and thought hard about the possibilities. "I'd sell it to you for a thousand dollars if you had it. Heck, to make it fair, I'd sell it to you for nine hundred and ninety-nine dollars. I'd lose a dollar. That would be the moral thing to do in this case. To lose a dollar would be the right thing."

"We've got five dollars total," I said again.

"That's too bad," he said once more, and thought harder about the possibilities. "How about this? I'll give you twenty-four hours to come up with nine hundred and ninety-nine dollars. You come back here at lunchtime tomorrow with the money and I'll sell it back to you. How does that sound?"

45   "It sounds all right," I said.

"All right, then," he said. "We have a deal. And I'll get you started. Here's twenty bucks."

He opened up his wallet and pulled out a crisp twenty-dollar bill and gave it to me. And Rose of Sharon, Junior, and I walked out into the daylight to search for nine hundred and seventy-four more dollars.

1 P.M.

Rose of Sharon, Junior, and I carried our twenty-dollar bill and our five dollars in loose change over to the 7-Eleven and bought three bottles of imagination. We needed to figure out how to raise all that money in only one day. Thinking hard, we huddled in an alley beneath the Alaska Way Viaduct and finished off those bottles—one, two, and three.

2 P.M.

Rose of Sharon was gone when I woke up. I heard later that she had hitchhiked back to Toppenish and was living with her sister on the reservation.

50   Junior had passed out beside me and was covered in his own vomit, or maybe somebody else's vomit, and my head hurt from thinking, so I left him alone and walked down to the water. I love the smell of ocean water. Salt always smells like memory.

When I got to the wharf, I ran into three Aleut cousins, who sat on a wooden bench and stared out at the bay and cried. Most of the homeless Indians in Seattle come from Alaska. One by one, each of them hopped a big working boat in Anchorage or Barrow or Juneau, fished his way south to Seattle, jumped off the boat with a pocketful of cash to party hard at one of the highly sacred and traditional Indian bars, went broke and broker, and has been trying to find his way back to the boat and the frozen North ever since.

These Aleuts smelled like salmon, I thought, and they told me they were going to sit on that wooden bench until their boat came back.

"How long has your boat been gone?" I asked.

"Eleven years," the elder Aleut said.

55   I cried with them for a while.

"Hey," I said. "Do you guys have any money I can borrow?"

They didn't.

3 P.M.

I walked back to Junior. He was still out cold. I put my face down near his mouth to make sure he was breathing. He was alive, so I dug around in his bluejeans pockets and found half a cigarette. I smoked it all the way down and thought about my grandmother.

Her name was Agnes, and she died of breast cancer when I was fourteen. My father always thought Agnes caught her tumors from the uranium mine on the reservation. But my mother said the disease started when Agnes was walking back from a powwow one night and got run over by a motorcycle. She broke three ribs, and my mother always said those ribs never healed right, and tumors take over when you don't heal right.

Sitting beside Junior, smelling the smoke and the salt and the vomit, I wondered if my grandmother's cancer started when somebody stole her powwow regalia. Maybe the cancer started in her broken heart and then leaked out into her breasts. I know it's crazy, but I wondered whether I could bring my grandmother back to life if I bought back her regalia.

I needed money, big money, so I left Junior and walked over to the Real Change office.

4 P.M.

Real Change is a multifaceted organization that publishes a newspaper, supports cultural projects that empower the poor and the homeless, and mobilizes the public around poverty issues. Real Change's mission is to organize, educate, and build alliances to create solutions to homelessness and poverty. It exists to provide a voice for poor people in our community.

I memorized Real Change's mission statement because I sometimes sell the newspaper on the streets. But you have to stay sober to sell it, and I'm not always good at staying sober. Anybody can sell the paper. You buy each copy for thirty cents and sell it for a dollar, and you keep the profit.

"I need one thousand four hundred and thirty papers," I said to the Big Boss.

"That's a strange number," he said. "And that's a lot of papers."

"I need them."

The Big Boss pulled out his calculator and did the math.

"It will cost you four hundred and twenty-nine dollars for that many," he said.

"If I had that kind of money, I wouldn't need to sell the papers."

"What's going on, Jackson-to-the-Second-Power?" he asked. He is the only person who calls me that. He's a funny and kind man.

I told him about my grandmother's powwow regalia and how much money I needed in order to buy it back.

"We should call the police," he said.

"I don't want to do that," I said. "It's a quest now. I need to win it back by myself."

"I understand," he said. "And, to be honest, I'd give you the papers to sell if I thought it would work. But the record for the most papers sold in one day by one vender is only three hundred and two."

"That would net me about two hundred bucks," I said.

The Big Boss used his calculator. "Two hundred and eleven dollars and forty cents," he said.

"That's not enough," I said.

"And the most money anybody has made in one day is five hundred and twenty-five. And that's because somebody gave Old Blue five hundred-dollar bills for some dang reason. The average daily net is about thirty dollars."

"This isn't going to work."

"No."

"Can you lend me some money?"

"I can't do that," he said. "If I lend you money, I have to lend money to everybody."

"What can you do?"

"I'll give you fifty papers for free. But don't tell anybody I did it."

"O.K.," I said.

He gathered up the newspapers and handed them to me. I held them to my chest. He hugged me. I carried the newspapers back toward the water.

5 P.M.

Back on the wharf, I stood near the Bainbridge Island Terminal and tried to sell papers to business commuters boarding the ferry.

I sold five in one hour, dumped the other forty-five in a garbage can, and walked into McDonald's, ordered four cheeseburgers for a dollar each, and slowly ate them.

After eating, I walked outside and vomited on the sidewalk. I hated to lose my food so soon after eating it. As an alcoholic Indian with a busted stomach, I always hope I can keep enough food in me to stay alive.

6 P.M.

90 With one dollar in my pocket, I walked back to Junior. He was still passed out, and I put my ear to his chest and listened for his heartbeat. He was alive, so I took off his shoes and socks and found one dollar in his left sock and fifty cents in his right sock.

With two dollars and fifty cents in my hand, I sat beside Junior and thought about my grandmother and her stories.

When I was thirteen, my grandmother told me a story about the Second World War. She was a nurse at a military hospital in Sydney, Australia. For two years, she healed and comforted American and Australian soldiers.

One day, she tended to a wounded Maori soldier, who had lost his legs to an artillery attack. He was very dark-skinned. His hair was black and curly and his eyes were black and warm. His face was covered with bright tattoos.

"Are you Maori?" he asked my grandmother.

95 "No," she said. "I'm Spokane Indian. From the United States."

"Ah, yes," he said. "I have heard of your tribes. But you are the first American Indian I have ever met."

"There's a lot of Indian soldiers fighting for the United States," she said. "I have a brother fighting in Germany, and I lost another brother on Okinawa."

"I am sorry," he said. "I was on Okinawa as well. It was terrible."

"I am sorry about your legs," my grandmother said.

100 "It's funny, isn't it?" he said.

"What's funny?"

"How we brown people are killing other brown people so white people will remain free."

"I hadn't thought of it that way."

"Well, sometimes I think of it that way. And other times I think of it the way they want me to think of it. I get confused."

105 She fed him morphine.

"Do you believe in Heaven?" he asked.

"Which Heaven?" she asked.

"I'm talking about the Heaven where my legs are waiting for me."

They laughed.

110 "Of course," he said, "my legs will probably run away from me when I get to Heaven. And how will I ever catch them?"

"You have to get your arms strong," my grandmother said. "So you can run on your hands."

They laughed again.

Sitting beside Junior, I laughed at the memory of my grandmother's story. I put my hand close to Junior's mouth to make sure he was still breathing. Yes, Junior was alive, so I took my two dollars and fifty cents and walked to the Korean grocery store in Pioneer Square.

7 P.M.

At the Korean grocery store, I bought a fifty-cent cigar and two scratch lottery tickets for a dollar each. The maximum cash prize was five hundred dollars a ticket. If I won both, I would have enough money to buy back the regalia.

115 I loved Mary, the young Korean woman who worked the register. She was the daughter of the owners, and she sang all day.

"I love you," I said when I handed her the money.

"You always say you love me," she said.

"That's because I will always love you."

"You are a sentimental fool."

"I'm a romantic old man."

"Too old for me."

"I know I'm too old for you, but I can dream."

"O.K.," she said. "I agree to be a part of your dreams, but I will only hold your hand in your dreams. No kissing and no sex. Not even in your dreams."

"O.K.," I said. "No sex. Just romance."

"Goodbye, Jackson Jackson, my love. I will see you soon."

I left the store, walked over to Occidental Park, sat on a bench, and smoked my cigar all the way down.

Ten minutes after I finished the cigar, I scratched my first lottery ticket and won nothing. I could only win five hundred dollars now, and that would only be half of what I needed.

Ten minutes after I lost, I scratched the other ticket and won a free ticket—a small consolation and one more chance to win some money.

I walked back to Mary.

"Jackson Jackson," she said. "Have you come back to claim my heart?"

"I won a free ticket," I said.

"Just like a man," she said. "You love money and power more than you love me."

"It's true," I said. "And I'm sorry it's true."

She gave me another scratch ticket, and I took it outside. I like to scratch my tickets in private. Hopeful and sad, I scratched that third ticket and won real money. I carried it back inside to Mary.

"I won a hundred dollars," I said.

She examined the ticket and laughed.

"That's a fortune," she said, and counted out five twenties. Our fingertips touched as she handed me the money. I felt electric and constant.

"Thank you," I said, and gave her one of the bills.

"I can't take that," she said. "It's your money."

"No, it's tribal. It's an Indian thing. When you win, you're supposed to share with your family."

"I'm not your family."

"Yes, you are."

She smiled. She kept the money. With eighty dollars in my pocket, I said goodbye to my dear Mary and walked out into the cold night air.

8 P.M.

I wanted to share the good news with Junior. I walked back to him, but he was gone. I heard later that he had hitchhiked down to Portland, Oregon, and died of exposure in an alley behind the Hilton Hotel.

9 P.M.

Lonesome for Indians, I carried my eighty dollars over to Big Heart's in South Downtown. Big Heart's is an all-Indian bar. Nobody knows how or why Indians migrate to one bar and turn it into an official Indian bar. But Big Heart's has been an Indian bar for twenty-three years. It used to be way up on Aurora Avenue, but a crazy Lummi Indian burned that one down, and the owners moved to the new location, a few blocks south of Safeco Field.

I walked into Big Heart's and counted fifteen Indians—eight men and seven women. I didn't know any of them, but Indians like to belong, so we all pretended to be cousins.

"How much for whiskey shots?" I asked the bartender, a fat white guy.

"You want the bad stuff or the badder stuff?"

"As bad as you got."

150 "One dollar a shot."

I laid my eighty dollars on the bar top.

"All right," I said. "Me and all my cousins here are going to be drinking eighty shots. How many is that apiece?"

"Counting you," a woman shouted from behind me, "that's five shots for everybody."

I turned to look at her. She was a chubby and pale Indian woman, sitting with a tall and skinny Indian man.

155 "All right, math genius," I said to her, and then shouted for the whole bar to hear. "Five drinks for everybody!"

All the other Indians rushed the bar, but I sat with the mathematician and her skinny friend. We took our time with our whiskey shots.

"What's your tribe?" I asked.

"I'm Duwamish," she said. "And he's Crow."

"You're a long way from Montana," I said to him.

160 "I'm Crow," he said. "I flew here."

"What's your name?" I asked them.

"I'm Irene Muse," she said. "And this is Honey Boy."

She shook my hand hard, but he offered his hand as if I was supposed to kiss it. So I did. He giggled and blushed, as much as a dark-skinned Crow can blush.

"You're one of them two-spirits, aren't you?" I asked him.

165 "I love women," he said. "And I love men."

"Sometimes both at the same time," Irene said.

We laughed.

"Man," I said to Honey Boy. "So you must have about eight or nine spirits going on inside you, enit?"

"Sweetie," he said. "I'll be whatever you want me to be."

170 "Oh, no," Irene said. "Honey Boy is falling in love."

"It has nothing to do with love," he said.

We laughed.

"Wow," I said. "I'm flattered, Honey Boy, but I don't play on your team."

"Never say never," he said.

175 "You better be careful," Irene said. "Honey Boy knows all sorts of magic."

"Honey Boy," I said, "you can try to seduce me, but my heart belongs to a woman named Mary."

"Is your Mary a virgin?" Honey Boy asked.

We laughed.

And we drank our whiskey shots until they were gone. But the other Indians bought me more whiskey shots, because I'd been so generous with my money. And Honey Boy pulled out his credit card, and I drank and sailed on that plastic boat.

180 After a dozen shots, I asked Irene to dance. She refused. But Honey Boy shuffled over to the jukebox, dropped in a quarter, and selected Willie Nelson's "Help Me Make It Through the Night." As Irene and I sat at the table and laughed and drank more whiskey, Honey Boy danced a slow circle around us and sang along with Willie.

"Are you serenading me?" I asked him.

He kept singing and dancing.

"Are you serenading me?" I asked him again.

"He's going to put a spell on you," Irene said.

185 I leaned over the table, spilling a few drinks, and kissed Irene hard. She kissed me back.

10 P.M.

Irene pushed me into the women's bathroom, into a stall, shut the door behind us, and shoved her hand down my pants. She was short, so I had to lean over to kiss her. I grabbed and squeezed her everywhere I could reach, and she was wonderfully fat, and every part of her body felt like a large, warm, soft breast.

MIDNIGHT

Nearly blind with alcohol, I stood alone at the bar and swore I had been standing in the bathroom with Irene only a minute ago.

"One more shot!" I yelled at the bartender.

"You've got no more money!" he yelled back.

"Somebody buy me a drink!" I shouted.

"They've got no more money!"

"Where are Irene and Honey Boy?"

"Long gone!"

2 A.M.

"Closing time!" the bartender shouted at the three or four Indians who were still drinking hard after a long, hard day of drinking. Indian alcoholics are either sprinters or marathoners.

"Where are Irene and Honey Boy?" I asked.

"They've been gone for hours," the bartender said.

"Where'd they go?"

"I told you a hundred times, I don't know."

"What am I supposed to do?"

"It's closing time. I don't care where you go, but you're not staying here."

"You are an ungrateful bastard. I've been good to you."

"You don't leave right now, I'm going to kick your ass."

"Come on, I know how to fight."

He came at me. I don't remember what happened after that.

4 A.M.

I emerged from the blackness and discovered myself walking behind a big warehouse. I didn't know where I was. My face hurt. I felt my nose and decided that it might be broken. Exhausted and cold, I pulled a plastic tarp from a truck bed, wrapped it around me like a faithful lover, and fell asleep in the dirt.

6 A.M.

Somebody kicked me in the ribs. I opened my eyes and looked up at a white cop.

"Jackson," the cop said. "Is that you?"

"Officer Williams," I said. He was a good cop with a sweet tooth. He'd given me hundreds of candy bars over the years. I wonder if he knew I was diabetic.

"What the hell are you doing here?" he asked.

"I was cold and sleepy," I said. "So I lay down."

"You dumb-ass, you passed out on the railroad tracks."

I sat up and looked around. I was lying on the railroad tracks. Dockworkers stared at me. I should have been a railroad-track pizza, a double Indian pepperoni with extra cheese. Sick and scared, I leaned over and puked whiskey.

"What the hell's wrong with you?" Officer Williams asked. "You've never been this stupid."

"It's my grandmother," I said. "She died."

"I'm sorry, man. When did she die?"

"Nineteen seventy-two."

"And you're killing yourself now?"

"I've been killing myself ever since she died."

He shook his head. He was sad for me. Like I said, he was a good cop.

"And somebody beat the hell out of you," he said. "You remember who?"

"Mr. Grief and I went a few rounds."

"It looks like Mr. Grief knocked you out."

"Mr. Grief always wins."

"Come on," he said. "Let's get you out of here."

225 He helped me up and led me over to his squad car. He put me in the back. "You throw up in there and you're cleaning it up," he said.

"That's fair."

He walked around the car and sat in the driver's seat. "I'm taking you over to detox," he said.

"No, man, that place is awful," I said. "It's full of drunk Indians."

We laughed. He drove away from the docks.

230 "I don't know how you guys do it," he said.

"What guys?" I asked.

"You Indians. How the hell do you laugh so much? I just picked your ass off the railroad tracks, and you're making jokes. Why the hell do you do that?"

"The two funniest tribes I've ever been around are Indians and Jews, so I guess that says something about the inherent humor of genocide."

We laughed.

235 "Listen to you, Jackson. You're so smart. Why the hell are you on the street?"

"Give me a thousand dollars and I'll tell you."

"You bet I'd give you a thousand dollars if I knew you'd straighten up your life."

He meant it. He was the second-best cop I'd ever known.

"You're a good cop," I said.

240 "Come on, Jackson," he said. "Don't blow smoke up my ass."

"No, really, you remind me of my grandfather."

"Yeah, that's what you Indians always tell me."

"No, man, my grandfather was a tribal cop. He was a good cop. He never arrested people. He took care of them. Just like you."

"I've arrested hundreds of scumbags, Jackson. And I've shot a couple in the ass."

245 "It don't matter. You're not a killer."

"I didn't kill them. I killed their asses. I'm an ass-killer."

We drove through downtown. The missions and shelters had already released their overnighters. Sleepy homeless men and women stood on street corners and stared up at a gray sky. It was the morning after the night of the living dead.

"Do you ever get scared?" I asked Officer Williams.

"What do you mean?"

250 "I mean, being a cop, is it scary?"

He thought about that for a while. He contemplated it. I liked that about him.

"I guess I try not to think too much about being afraid," he said. "If you think about fear, then you'll be afraid. The job is boring most of the time. Just driving and looking into dark corners, you know, and seeing nothing. But then things get heavy. You're chasing somebody, or fighting them or walking around a dark house, and you just know some crazy guy is hiding around a corner, and hell, yes, it's scary."

"My grandfather was killed in the line of duty," I said.

"I'm sorry. How'd it happen?"

255 I knew he'd listen closely to my story.

"He worked on the reservation. Everybody knew everybody. It was safe. We aren't like those crazy Sioux or Apache or any of those other warrior tribes. There've only been three murders on my reservation in the last hundred years."

"That is safe."

"Yeah, we Spokane, we're passive, you know. We're mean with words. And we'll cuss out anybody. But we don't shoot people. Or stab them. Not much, anyway."

"So what happened to your grandfather?"

260 "This man and his girlfriend were fighting down by Little Falls."

"Domestic dispute. Those are the worst."

"Yeah, but this guy was my grandfather's brother. My great-uncle."

"Oh, no."

"Yeah, it was awful. My grandfather just strolled into the house. He'd been there a thousand times. And his brother and his girlfriend were drunk and beating on each other. And my grandfather stepped between them, just as he'd done a hundred times before. And the girlfriend tripped or something. She fell down and hit her head and started crying. And my grandfather kneeled down beside her to make sure she was all right. And for some reason my great-uncle reached down, pulled my grandfather's pistol out of the holster, and shot him in the head."

"That's terrible. I'm sorry."

"Yeah, my great-uncle could never figure out why he did it. He went to prison forever, you know, and he always wrote these long letters. Like fifty pages of tiny little handwriting. And he was always trying to figure out why he did it. He'd write and write and write and try to figure it out. He never did. It's a great big mystery."

"Do you remember your grandfather?"

"A little bit. I remember the funeral. My grandmother wouldn't let them bury him. My father had to drag her away from the grave."

"I don't know what to say."

"I don't, either."

We stopped in front of the detox center.

"We're here," Officer Williams said.

"I can't go in there," I said.

"You have to."

"Please, no. They'll keep me for twenty-four hours. And then it will be too late."

"Too late for what?"

I told him about my grandmother's regalia and the deadline for buying it back.

"If it was stolen, you need to file a report," he said. "I'll investigate it myself. If that thing is really your grandmother's, I'll get it back for you. Legally."

"No," I said. "That's not fair. The pawnbroker didn't know it was stolen. And, besides, I'm on a mission here. I want to be a hero, you know? I want to win it back, like a knight."

"That's romantic crap."

"That may be. But I care about it. It's been a long time since I really cared about something."

Officer Williams turned around in his seat and stared at me. He studied me.

"I'll give you some money," he said. "I don't have much. Only thirty bucks. I'm short until payday. And it's not enough to get back the regalia. But it's something."

"I'll take it," I said.

"I'm giving it to you because I believe in what you believe. I'm hoping, and I don't know why I'm hoping it, but I hope you can turn thirty bucks into a thousand somehow."

"I believe in magic."

"I believe you'll take my money and get drunk on it."

"Then why are you giving it to me?"

"There ain't no such thing as an atheist cop."

"Sure, there is."

"Yeah, well, I'm not an atheist cop."

He let me out of the car, handed me two fivers and a twenty, and shook my hand.

"Take care of yourself, Jackson," he said. "Stay off the railroad tracks."

"I'll try," I said.

He drove away. Carrying my money, I headed back toward the water.

8 A.M.

On the wharf, those three Aleuts still waited on the wooden bench.

"Have you seen your ship?" I asked.

"Seen a lot of ships," the elder Aleut said. "But not our ship."

I sat on the bench with them. We sat in silence for a long time. I wondered if we would fossilize if we sat there long enough.

I thought about my grandmother. I'd never seen her dance in her regalia. And, more than anything, I wished I'd seen her dance at a powwow.

"Do you guys know any songs?" I asked the Aleuts.

"I know all of Hank Williams," the elder Aleut said.

"How about Indian songs?"

"Hank Williams is Indian."

305 "How about sacred songs?"

"Hank Williams is sacred."

"I'm talking about ceremonial songs. You know, religious ones. The songs you sing back home when you're wishing and hoping."

"What are you wishing and hoping for?"

"I'm wishing my grandmother was still alive."

310 "Every song I know is about that."

"Well, sing me as many as you can."

The Aleuts sang their strange and beautiful songs. I listened. They sang about my grandmother and about their grandmothers. They were lonesome for the cold and the snow. I was lonesome for everything.

10 A.M.

After the Aleuts finished their last song, we sat in silence for a while. Indians are good at silence.

"Was that the last song?" I asked.

315 "We sang all the ones we could," the elder Aleut said. "The others are just for our people."

I understood. We Indians have to keep our secrets. And these Aleuts were so secretive they didn't refer to themselves as Indians.

"Are you guys hungry?" I asked.

They looked at one another and communicated without talking.

"We could eat," the elder Aleut said.

11 A.M.

320 The Aleuts and I walked over to the Big Kitchen, a greasy diner in the International District. I knew they served homeless Indians who'd lucked into money.

"Four for breakfast?" the waitress asked when we stepped inside.

"Yes, we're very hungry," the elder Aleut said.

She took us to a booth near the kitchen. I could smell the food cooking. My stomach growled.

"You guys want separate checks?" the waitress asked.

325 "No, I'm paying," I said.

"Aren't you the generous one," she said.

"Don't do that," I said.

"Do what?" she asked.

"Don't ask me rhetorical questions. They scare me."

330 She looked puzzled, and then she laughed.

"O.K., Professor," she said. "I'll only ask you real questions from now on."

"Thank you."

"What do you guys want to eat?"

"That's the best question anybody can ask anybody," I said. "What have you got?"

335 "How much money you got?" she asked.

"Another good question," I said. "I've got twenty-five dollars I can spend. Bring us all the breakfast you can, plus your tip."

She knew the math.

"All right, that's four specials and four coffees and fifteen per cent for me."

The Aleuts and I waited in silence. Soon enough, the waitress returned and poured us four coffees, and we sipped at them until she returned again, with four plates of food. Eggs, bacon, toast, hash-brown potatoes. It's amazing how much food you can buy for so little money.

340 Grateful, we feasted.

NOON

I said farewell to the Aleuts and walked toward the pawnshop. I heard later that the Aleuts had waded into the salt water near Dock 47 and disappeared. Some Indians swore they had walked on the water and headed north. Other Indians saw the Aleuts drown. I don't know what happened to them.

I looked for the pawnshop and couldn't find it. I swear it wasn't in the place where it had been before. I walked twenty or thirty blocks looking for the pawnshop, turned corners and bisected intersections, and looked up its name in the phone books and asked people walking past me if they'd ever heard of it. But that pawnshop seemed to have sailed away like a ghost ship. I wanted to cry. And just when I'd given up, when I turned one last corner and thought I might die if I didn't find that pawnshop, there it was, in a space I swear it hadn't occupied a few minutes ago.

I walked inside and greeted the pawnbroker, who looked a little younger than he had before.

"It's you," he said.

"Yes, it's me," I said.

"Jackson Jackson."

"That is my name."

"Where are your friends?"

"They went travelling. But it's O.K. Indians are everywhere."

"Do you have the money?"

"How much do you need again?" I asked, and hoped the price had changed.

"Nine hundred and ninety-nine dollars."

It was still the same price. Of course, it was the same price. Why would it change?

"I don't have that," I said.

"What do you have?"

"Five dollars."

I set the crumpled Lincoln on the countertop. The pawnbroker studied it.

"Is that the same five dollars from yesterday?"

"No, it's different."

He thought about the possibilities.

"Did you work hard for this money?" he asked.

"Yes," I said.

He closed his eyes and thought harder about the possibilities. Then he stepped into the back room and returned with my grandmother's regalia.

"Take it," he said, and held it out to me.

"I don't have the money."

"I don't want your money."

"But I wanted to win it."

"You did win it. Now take it before I change my mind."

Do you know how many good men live in this world? Too many to count!

I took my grandmother's regalia and walked outside. I knew that solitary yellow bead was part of me. I knew I was that yellow bead in part. Outside, I wrapped myself in my grandmother's regalia and breathed her in. I stepped off the sidewalk and into the intersection. Pedestrians stopped. Cars stopped. The city stopped. They all watched me dance with my grandmother. I was my grandmother, dancing.

If you enjoyed "What You Pawn I Will Redeem," you may enjoy "The Man to Send Rainclouds" by Leslie Marmon Silko in chapter 12, The Casebook on the American West.

GOING FURTHER Alexie and Silko come from a long line of American Indian fiction writers that includes Pulitzer Prize winner N. Scott Momaday and his lyrical work of fiction *The Way to Rainy Mountain.* You also might enjoy Louise Erdrich's novels *Tracks* or *The Beet Queen.*

Margaret Atwood (b. 1939)

BORN IN TORONTO, Margaret Atwood has been, along with short story writer Alice Munro, one of the few Canadian writers with a major impact on the contemporary American reading public. A driving force in the literature scene to our north, she works in a wide range of genres and styles—seeming equally at home in the mode of historical fiction as that of science fiction. Her novels such as *Surfacing* (1972), *The Handmaid's Tale* (1985), and the Booker Prize–winning *The Blind Assassin* (2000) have won her great acclaim. Atwood is also a poet (see Poetry, chapter 21), essayist, and short story writer. In each of these genres and forms, she demonstrates keen attention to craft as well as theme.

Happy Endings (1983)

1   John and Mary meet.
    What happens next?
    If you want a happy ending, try A.

A

John and Mary fall in love and get married. They both have worthwhile and remunerative jobs which they find stimulating and challenging. They buy a charming house. Real estate values go up. Eventually, when they can afford live-in help, they have two children, to whom they are devoted. The children turn out well. John and Mary have a stimulating and challenging sex life and worthwhile friends. They go on fun vacations together. They retire. They both have hobbies which they find stimulating and challenging. Eventually they die. This is the end of the story.

B

5   Mary falls in love with John but John doesn't fall in love with Mary. He merely uses her body for selfish pleasure and ego gratification of a tepid kind. He comes to her apartment twice a week and she cooks him dinner, you'll notice that he doesn't even consider her worth the price of a dinner out, and after he's eaten the dinner he fucks her and after that he falls asleep, while she does the dishes so he won't think she's untidy, having all those dirty dishes lying around, and puts on fresh lipstick so she'll look good when he wakes up, but when he wakes up he doesn't even notice, he puts on his socks and his shorts and his pants and his shirt and his tie and his shoes, the reverse order from the one in which he took them off. He doesn't take off Mary's clothes, she takes them off herself, she acts as if she's dying for it every time, not because she likes sex exactly, she doesn't, but she wants John to think she does because if they do it often enough surely he'll get used to her, he'll come to depend on her and they will get married, but John goes out the door with hardly so much as a good-night and three days later he turns up at six o'clock and they do the whole thing over again.

    Mary gets run-down. Crying is bad for your face, everyone knows that and so does Mary but she can't stop. People at work notice. Her friends tell her John is a rat, a pig, a dog, he isn't good enough for her, but she can't believe it. Inside John, she thinks, is another John, who is much nicer. This other John will emerge like a butterfly from a cocoon, a Jack from a box, a pit from a prune, if the first John is only squeezed enough.

    One evening John complains about the food. He has never complained about the food before. Mary is hurt.

Her friends tell her they've seen him in a restaurant with another woman, whose name is Madge. It's not even Madge that finally gets to Mary; it's the restaurant. John has never taken Mary to a restaurant. Mary collects all the sleeping pills and aspirins she can find, and takes them and a half a bottle of sherry. You can see what kind of a woman she is by the fact that it's not even whiskey. She leaves a note for John. She hopes he'll discover her and get her to the hospital in time and repent and then they can get married, but this fails to happen and she dies.

John marries Madge and everything continues as in A.

C

John, who is an older man, falls in love with Mary, and Mary, who is only twenty-two, feels sorry for him because he's worried about his hair falling out. She sleeps with him even though she's not in love with him. She met him at work. She's in love with someone called James, who is twenty-two also and not yet ready to settle down.

John on the contrary settled down long ago: this is what is bothering him. John has a steady, respectable job and is getting ahead in his field, but Mary isn't impressed by him, she's impressed by James, who has a motorcycle and a fabulous record collection. But James is often away on his motorcycle, being free. Freedom isn't the same for girls, so in the meantime Mary spends Thursday evenings with John. Thursdays are the only days John can get away.

John is married to a woman called Madge and they have two children, a charming house which they bought just before the real estate values went up, and hobbies which they find stimulating and challenging, when they have the time. John tells Mary how important she is to him, but of course, he can't leave his wife because a commitment is a commitment. He goes on about this more than is necessary and Mary finds it boring, but older men can keep it up longer so on the whole she has a fairly good time.

One day James breezes in on his motorcycle with some top-grade California hybrid and James and Mary get higher than you'd believe possible and they climb into bed. Everything becomes very underwater, but along comes John, who has a key to Mary's apartment. He finds them stoned and entwined. He's hardly in any position to be jealous, considering Madge, but nevertheless he's overcome with despair. Finally he's middle-aged, in two years he'll be bald as an egg and he can't stand it. He purchases a handgun, saying he needs it for target practice—this is the thin part of the plot, but it can be dealt with later—and shoots the two of them and himself.

Madge, after a suitable period of mourning, marries an understanding man called Fred and everything continues as in A, but under different names.

D

Fred and Madge have no problems. They get along exceptionally well and are good at working out any little difficulties that may arise. But their charming house is by the seashore and one day a giant tidal wave approaches. Real estate values go down. The rest of the story is about what caused the tidal wave and how they escape from it. They do, though thousands drown, but Fred and Madge are virtuous and lucky. Finally on high ground they clasp each other, wet and dripping and grateful, and continue as in A.

E

Yes, but Fred has a bad heart. The rest of the story is about how kind and understanding they both are until Fred dies. Then Madge devotes herself to charity work until the end of A. If you like, it can be "Madge," "cancer," "guilty and confused," and "bird watching."

F

If you think this is all too bourgeois, make John a revolutionary and Mary a counterespionage agent and see how far that gets you. Remember, this is Canada. You'll still end up with A, though in between you may get a lustful brawling saga of passionate involvement, a chronicle of our times, sort of.

Y ou'll have to face it, the endings are the same however you slice it. Don't be deluded by any other endings, they're all fake, either deliberately fake, with malicious intent to deceive, or just motivated by excessive optimism if not by downright sentimentality.

The only authentic ending is the one provided here:

20   *John and Mary die. John and Mary die. John and Mary die.*

S o much for endings. Beginnings are almost more fun. True connoisseurs, however, are known to favor the stretch in between, since it's the hardest to do anything with.

T hat's about all that can be said for plots, which anyway are just one thing after another, a what and a what and a what.

Now try How and Why.

If you like this story, you may also like "An Ounce of Cure" (chapter 1) by Atwood's fellow Canadian writer Alice Munro.

GOING FURTHER   Atwood's literary mentor was a novelist and story writer named Margaret Laurence. Laurence's novel *The Diviners* is one of the finest examples you'll find of a female coming-of-age story, a powerful and important novel set mainly in western Canada.

James Baldwin (1924–1987)

BORN IN NEW York City, James Baldwin grew up in Harlem, the mostly black section at the north end of Manhattan. Though his formal education ended in high school, he asserted his place in contemporary letters before the age of thirty with a powerful debut novel about childhood in a Pentecostal Harlem church, *Go Tell It on the Mountain* (1953). For the next three decades Baldwin made a place for himself in American letters as both a fiction writer and an essayist, gaining a place as well in the unfolding saga of the American Civil Rights movement. His novels *Giovanni's Room* (1956) and *Another Country* (1962) drew solid readerships, but his polemical essay *The Fire Next Time* (1955)—which first appeared in the pages of *The New Yorker* magazine and then as a book—brought him national attention.

He never relinquished it. Like his sometime mentor Richard Wright, Baldwin exiled himself in France—living first in Paris, then in the village of St. Paul de Vence—for a large part of his adult life. His focus was always on America, however, and while living abroad he continued to write about politics and race at home. The Civil War and the Civil Rights Movement were, to this writer, two chapters of the one story. Such nonfiction texts as *No Name in the Street* (1972) and *Evidence of Things Not Seen* (1985) focus both on race and politics; his final fiction and essays about black-and-white life in America attested equally to his sharp eye and a troubled dream of harmony.

A lifelong adept of jazz, Baldwin wrote that when he first moved to Paris he took along a phonograph record of the jazz singer Bessie Smith in order to remind himself of what he'd left behind. "Sonny's Blues" attests to this fascination with music, its sorrows and delights.

Sonny's Blues (1957)

I read about it in the paper, in the subway, on my way to work. I read it, and I couldn't believe it, and I read it again. Then perhaps I just stared at it, at the newsprint spelling out his name, spelling out the story. I stared at it in the swinging lights of the subway car, and in the faces and bodies of the people, and in my own face, trapped in the darkness which roared outside.

It was not to be believed and I kept telling myself that, as I walked from the subway station to the high school. And at the same time I couldn't doubt it. I was scared, scared for Sonny. He became real to me again. A great block of ice got settled in my belly and kept melting there slowly all day long, while I taught my classes algebra. It was a special kind of ice. It kept melting, sending trickles of ice water all up and down my veins, but it never got less. Sometimes it hardened and seemed to expand until I felt my guts were going to come spilling out or that I was going to choke or scream. This would always be at a moment when I was remembering some specific thing Sonny had once said or done.

When he was about as old as the boys in my classes his face had been bright and open, there was a lot of copper in it; and he'd had wonderfully direct brown eyes, and great gentleness and privacy. I wondered what he looked like now. He had been picked up, the evening before, in a raid on an apartment downtown, for peddling and using heroin.

I couldn't believe it: but what I mean by that is that I couldn't find any room for it anywhere inside me. I had kept it outside me for a long time. I hadn't wanted to know. I had had suspicions, but I didn't name them, I kept putting them away. I told myself that Sonny was wild, but he wasn't crazy. And he'd always been a good boy, he hadn't ever turned hard or evil or disrespectful, the way kids can, so quick, so quick, especially in Harlem. I didn't want to believe that I'd ever see my brother going down, coming to nothing, all that light in his face gone out, in the condition I'd already seen so many others. Yet it had happened and here I was, talking about algebra to a lot of boys who might, every one of them for all I knew, be popping off needles every time they went to the head. Maybe it did more for them than algebra could.

I was sure that the first time Sonny had ever had horse, he couldn't have been much older than these boys were now. These boys, now, were living as we'd been living then, they were growing up with a rush and their heads bumped abruptly against the low ceiling of their actual possibilities. They were filled with rage. All they really knew were two darknesses, the darkness of their lives, which was now closing in on them, and the darkness of the movies, which had blinded them to that other darkness, and in which they now, vindictively, dreamed, at once more together than they were at any other time, and more alone.

When the last bell rang, the last class ended, I let out my breath. It seemed I'd been holding it for all that time. My clothes were wet—I may have looked as though I'd been sitting in a steam bath, all dressed up, all afternoon. I sat alone in the classroom a long time. I listened to the boys outside, downstairs, shouting and cursing and laughing. Their laughter struck me for perhaps the first time. It was not the joyous laughter which—God knows why—one associates with children. It was mocking and insular, its intent was to denigrate. It was disenchanted, and in this, also, lay the authority of their curses. Perhaps I was listening to them because I was thinking about my brother. And myself.

One boy was whistling a tune, at once very complicated and very simple, it seemed to be pouring out of him as though he were a bird, and it sounded very cool and moving through all that harsh, bright air, only just holding its own through all those other sounds.

I stood up and walked over to the window and looked down into the courtyard. It was the beginning of the spring and the sap was rising in the boys. A teacher passed through them every now and again, quickly, as though he or she couldn't wait to get out of that courtyard, to get those boys out of their sight and off their minds. I started collecting my stuff. I thought I'd better get home and talk to Isabel.

The courtyard was almost deserted by the time I got downstairs. I saw this boy standing in the shadow of a doorway, looking just like Sonny. I almost called his name. Then I saw that it wasn't

Sonny, but somebody we used to know, a boy from around our block. He'd been Sonny's friend. He'd never been mine, having been too young for me, and, anyway, I'd never liked him. And now, even though he was a grown-up man, he still hung around that block, still spent hours on the street corners, was always high and raggy. I used to run into him from time to time and he'd often work around to asking me for a quarter or fifty cents. He always had some real good excuse, too, and I always gave it to him, I don't know why.

10   But now, abruptly, I hated him. I couldn't stand the way he looked at me, partly like a dog, partly like a cunning child. I wanted to ask him what the hell he was doing in the school courtyard.

He sort of shuffled over to me, and he said, "I see you got the papers. So you already know about it."

"You mean about Sonny? Yes, I already know about it. How come they didn't get you?"

He grinned. It made him repulsive and it also brought to mind what he'd looked like as a kid. "I wasn't there. I stay away from them people."

"Good for you." I offered him a cigarette and I watched him through the smoke. "You come all the way down here just to tell me about Sonny?"

15   "That's right." He was sort of shaking his head and his eyes looked strange, as though they were about to cross. The bright sun deadened his damp dark brown skin and it made his eyes look yellow and showed up the dirt in his kinked hair. He smelled funky. I moved a little away from him and I said, "Well, thanks. But I already know about it and I got to get home."

"I'll walk you a little ways," he said. We started walking. There were a couple of kids still loitering in the courtyard and one of them said goodnight to me and looked strangely at the boy beside me.

"What're you going to do?" he asked me. "I mean, about Sonny?"

"Look. I haven't seen Sonny for over a year, I'm not sure I'm going to do anything. Anyway, what the hell *can* I do?"

"That's right," he said quickly, "ain't nothing you can do. Can't much help old Sonny no more, I guess."

20   It was what I was thinking and so it seemed to me he had no right to say it.

"I'm surprised at Sonny, though," he went on—he had a funny way of talking, he looked straight ahead as though he were talking to himself—"I thought Sonny was a smart boy, I thought he was too smart to get hung."

"I guess he thought so too," I said sharply, "and that's how he got hung. And how about you? You're pretty goddamn smart, I bet."

Then he looked directly at me, just for a minute. "I ain't smart," he said. "If I was smart, I'd have reached for a pistol a long time ago."

"Look. Don't tell *me* your sad story, if it was up to me, I'd give you one." Then I felt guilty—guilty, probably, for never having supposed that the poor bastard *had* a story of his own, much less a sad one, and I asked, quickly, "What's going to happen to him now?"

25   He didn't answer this. He was off by himself some place. "Funny thing," he said, and from his tone we might have been discussing the quickest way to get to Brooklyn, "when I saw the papers this morning, the first thing I asked myself was if I had anything to do with it. I felt sort of responsible."

I began to listen more carefully. The subway station was on the corner, just before us, and I stopped. He stopped, too. We were in front of a bar and he ducked slightly, peering in, but whoever he was looking for didn't seem to be there. The juke box was blasting away with something black and bouncy and I half watched the barmaid as she danced her way from the juke box to her place behind the bar. And I watched her face as she laughingly responded to something someone said to her, still keeping time to the music. When she smiled one saw the little girl, one sensed the doomed, still-struggling woman beneath the battered face of the semi-whore.

"I never *give* Sonny nothing," the boy said finally, "but a long time ago I come to school high and Sonny asked me how it felt." He paused, I couldn't bear to watch him, I watched the barmaid, and I listened to the music which seemed to be causing the pavement to shake. "I told him it felt great." The music stopped, the barmaid paused and watched the juke box until the music began again. "It did."

All this was carrying me some place I didn't want to go. I certainly didn't want to know how it felt. It filled everything, the people, the houses, the music, the dark, quicksilver barmaid, with menace; and this menace was their reality.

"What's going to happen to him now?" I asked again.

"They'll send him away some place and they'll try to cure him." He shook his head. "Maybe he'll even think he's kicked the habit. Then they'll let him loose"—he gestured, throwing his cigarette into the gutter. "That's all."

"What do you mean, that's *all*?"

But I knew what he meant.

"I *mean*, that's *all*." He turned his head and looked at me, pulling down the corners of his mouth. "Don't you know what I mean?" he asked, softly.

"How the hell *would* I know what you mean?" I almost whispered it, I don't know why.

"That's right," he said to the air, "how would *he* know what I mean?" He turned toward me again, patient and calm, and yet I somehow felt him shaking, shaking as though he were going to fall apart. I felt that ice in my guts again, the dread I'd felt all afternoon; and again I watched the barmaid, moving about the bar, washing glasses, and singing. "Listen. They'll let him out and then it'll just start all over again. That's what I mean."

"You mean—they'll let him out. And then he'll just start working his way back in again. You mean he'll never kick the habit. Is that what you mean?"

"That's right," he said, cheerfully. "*You* see what I mean."

"Tell me," I said at last, "why does he want to die? He must want to die, he's killing himself, why does he want to die?"

He looked at me in surprise. He licked his lips. "He don't want to die. He wants to live. Don't nobody want to die, ever."

Then I wanted to ask him—too many things. He could not have answered, or if he had, I could not have borne the answers. I started walking. "Well, I guess it's none of my business."

"It's going to be rough on old Sonny," he said. We reached the subway station. "This is your station?" he asked. I nodded. I took one step down. "Damn!" he said, suddenly. I looked up at him. He grinned again. "Damn it if I didn't leave all my money home. You ain't got a dollar on you, have you? Just for a couple of days, is all."

All at once something inside gave and threatened to come pouring out of me. I didn't hate him any more. I felt that in another moment I'd start crying like a child.

"Sure," I said. "Don't sweat." I looked in my wallet and didn't have a dollar, I only had a five. "Here," I said. "That hold you?"

He didn't look at it—he didn't want to look at it. A terrible, closed look came over his face, as though he were keeping the number on the bill a secret from him and me. "Thanks," he said, and now he was dying to see me go. "Don't worry about Sonny. Maybe I'll write him or something."

"Sure," I said. "You do that. So long."

"Be seeing you," he said. I went on down the steps.

And I didn't write Sonny or send him anything for a long time. When I finally did, it was just after my little girl died, he wrote me back a letter which made me feel like a bastard.

Here's what he said:

> *Dear brother,*
>
> *You don't know how much I needed to hear from you. I wanted to write you many a time but I dug how much I must have hurt you and so I didn't write. But now I feel like a man who's been trying to climb up out of some deep, real deep and funky hole and just saw the sun up there, outside. I got to get outside.*
>
> *I can't tell you much about how I got here. I mean I don't know how to tell you. I guess I was afraid of something or I was trying to escape from something and you know I have never been very strong in the head (smile). I'm glad Mama and Daddy are dead and can't see what's happened to their son and I swear if I'd known what I was doing I would never have hurt you so, you and a lot of other fine people who were nice to me and who believed in me.*

I don't want you to think it had anything to do with me being a musician. It's more than that. Or maybe less than that. I can't get anything straight in my head down here and I try not to think about what's going to happen to me when I get outside again. Sometime I think I'm going to flip and never get outside and sometime I think I'll come straight back. I tell you one thing, though, I'd rather blow my brains out than go through this again. But that's what they all say, so they tell me. If I tell you when I'm coming to New York and if you could meet me, I sure would appreciate it. Give my love to Isabel and the kids and I was sure sorry to hear about little Gracie. I wish I could be like Mama and say the Lord's will be done, but I don't know it seems to me that trouble is the one thing that never does get stopped and I don't know what good it does to blame it on the Lord. But maybe it does some good if you believe it.

> *Your brother,*
> *Sonny*

55   Then I kept in constant touch with him and I sent him whatever I could and I went to meet him when he came back to New York. When I saw him many things I thought I had forgotten came flooding back to me. This was because I had begun, finally, to wonder about Sonny, about the life that Sonny lived inside. This life, whatever it was, had made him older and thinner and it had deepened the distant stillness in which he had always moved. He looked very unlike my baby brother. Yet, when he smiled, when we shook hands, the baby brother I'd never known looked out from the depths of his private life, like an animal waiting to be coaxed into the light.

"How you been keeping?" he asked me.

"All right. And you?"

"Just fine." He was smiling all over his face. "It's good to see you again."

"It's good to see you."

60   The seven years' difference in our ages lay between us like a chasm: I wondered if these years would ever operate between us as a bridge. I was remembering, and it made it hard to catch my breath, that I had been there when he was born; and I had heard the first words he had ever spoken. When he started to walk, he walked from our mother straight to me. I caught him just before he fell when he took the first steps he ever took in this world.

"How's Isabel?"

"Just fine. She's dying to see you."

"And the boys?"

"They're fine, too. They're anxious to see their uncle."

65   "Oh, come on. You know they don't remember me."

"Are you kidding? Of course they remember you."

He grinned again. We got into a taxi. We had a lot to say to each other, far too much to know how to begin.

As the taxi began to move, I asked, "You still want to go to India?"

He laughed. "You still remember that. Hell, no. This place is Indian enough for me."

70   "It used to belong to them," I said.

And he laughed again. "They damn sure knew what they were doing when they got rid of it."

Years ago, when he was around fourteen, he'd been all hipped on the idea of going to India. He read books about people sitting on rocks, naked, in all kinds of weather, but mostly bad, naturally, and walking barefoot through hot coals and arriving at wisdom. I used to say that it sounded to me as though they were getting away from wisdom as fast as they could. I think he sort of looked down on me for that.

"Do you mind," he asked, "if we have the driver drive alongside the park? On the west side— I haven't seen the city in so long."

"Of course not," I said. I was afraid that I might sound as though I were humoring him, but I hoped he wouldn't take it that way.

75   So we drove along, between the green of the park and the stony, lifeless elegance of hotels and apartment buildings, toward the vivid, killing streets of our childhood. These streets hadn't changed, though housing projects jutted up out of them now like rocks in the middle of a boiling sea. Most of the houses in which we had grown up had vanished, as had the stores from which we

had stolen, the basements in which we had first tried sex, the rooftops from which we had hurled tin cans and bricks. But houses exactly like the houses of our past yet dominated the landscape, boys exactly like the boys we once had been found themselves smothering in these houses, came down into the streets for light and air and found themselves encircled by disaster. Some escaped the trap, most didn't. Those who got out always left something of themselves behind, as some animals amputate a leg and leave it in the trap. It might be said, perhaps, that I had escaped, after all, I was a school teacher; or that Sonny had, he hadn't lived in Harlem for years. Yet, as the cab moved uptown through streets which seemed, with a rush, to darken with dark people, and as I covertly studied Sonny's face, it came to me that what we both were seeking through our separate cab windows was that part of ourselves which had been left behind. It's always at the hour of trouble and confrontation that the missing member aches.

We hit 110th Street and started rolling up Lenox Avenue. And I'd known this avenue all my life, but it seemed to me again, as it had seemed on the day I'd first heard about Sonny's trouble, filled with a hidden menace which was its very breath of life.

"We almost there," said Sonny.

"Almost." We were both too nervous to say anything more.

We live in a housing project. It hasn't been up long. A few days after it was up it seemed uninhabitably new, now, of course, it's already rundown. It looks like a parody of the good, clean, faceless life—God knows the people who live in it do their best to make it a parody. The beat-looking grass lying around isn't enough to make their lives green, the hedges will never hold out the streets, and they know it. The big windows fool no one, they aren't big enough to make space out of no space. They don't bother with the windows, they watch the TV screen instead. The playground is most popular with the children who don't play at jacks, or skip rope, or roller skate, or swing, and they can be found in it after dark. We moved in partly because it's not too far from where I teach, and partly for the kids; but it's really just like the houses in which Sonny and I grew up. The same things happen, they'll have the same things to remember. The moment Sonny and I started into the house I had the feeling that I was simply bringing him back into the danger he had almost died trying to escape.

Sonny has never been talkative. So I don't know why I was sure he'd be dying to talk to me when supper was over the first night. Everything went fine, the oldest boy remembered him, and the youngest boy liked him, and Sonny had remembered to bring something for each of them; and Isabel, who is really much nicer than I am, more open and giving, had gone to a lot of trouble about dinner and was genuinely glad to see him. And she's always been able to tease Sonny in a way that I haven't. It was nice to see her face so vivid again and to hear her laugh and watch her make Sonny laugh. She wasn't, or, anyway, she didn't seem to be, at all uneasy or embarrassed. She chatted as though there were no subject which had to be avoided and she got Sonny past his first, faint stiffness. And thank God she was there, for I was filled with that icy dread again. Everything I did seemed awkward to me, and everything I said sounded freighted with hidden meaning. I was trying to remember everything I'd heard about dope addiction and I couldn't help watching Sonny for signs. I wasn't doing it out of malice. I was trying to find out something about my brother. I was dying to hear him tell me he was safe.

"Safe!" my father grunted, whenever Mama suggested trying to move to a neighborhood which might be safer for children. "Safe, hell! Ain't no place safe for kids, nor nobody."

He always went on like this, but he wasn't, ever, really as bad as he sounded, not even on weekends, when he got drunk. As a matter of fact, he was always on the lookout for "something a little better," but he died before he found it. He died suddenly, during a drunken weekend in the middle of the war, when Sonny was fifteen. He and Sonny hadn't ever got on too well. And this was partly because Sonny was the apple of his father's eye. It was because he loved Sonny so much and was frightened for him, that he was always fighting with him. It doesn't do any good to fight with Sonny. Sonny just moves back, inside himself, where he can't be reached. But the principal reason that they never hit it off is that they were so much alike. Daddy was big and rough and loud-talking, just the opposite of Sonny, but they both had—that same privacy.

Mama tried to tell me something about this, just after Daddy died. I was home on leave from the army.

This was the last time I ever saw my mother alive. Just the same, this picture gets all mixed up in my mind with pictures I had of her when she was younger. The way I always see her is the way she used to be on a Sunday afternoon, say, when the old folks were talking after the big Sunday dinner. I always see her wearing pale blue. She'd be sitting on the sofa. And my father would be sitting in the easy chair, not far from her. And the living room would be full of church folks and relatives. There they sit, in chairs all around the living room, and the night is creeping up outside, but nobody knows it yet. You can see the darkness growing against the windowpanes and you hear the street noises every now and again, or maybe the jangling beat of a tambourine from one of the churches close by, but it's real quiet in the room. For a moment nobody's talking, but every face looks darkening, like the sky outside. And my mother rocks a little from the waist, and my father's eyes are closed. Everyone is looking at something a child can't see. For a minute they've forgotten the children. Maybe a kid is lying on the rug, half asleep. Maybe somebody's got a kid in his lap and is absent-mindedly stroking the kid's head. Maybe there's a kid, quiet and big-eyed, curled up in a big chair in the corner. The silence, the darkness coming, and the darkness in the faces frightens the child obscurely. He hopes that the hand which strokes his forehead will never stop—will never die. He hopes that there will never come a time when the old folks won't be sitting around the living room, talking about where they've come from, and what they've seen, and what's happened to them and their kinfolk.

85   But something deep and watchful in the child knows that this is bound to end, is already ending. In a moment someone will get up and turn on the light. Then the old folks will remember the children and they won't talk any more that day. And when light fills the room, the child is filled with darkness. He knows that every time this happens he's moved just a little closer to that darkness outside. The darkness outside is what the old folks have been talking about. It's what they've come from. It's what they endure. The child knows that they won't talk any more because if he knows too much about what's happened to *them*, he'll know too much too soon, about what's going to happen to *him*.

The last time I talked to my mother, I remember I was restless. I wanted to get out and see Isabel. We weren't married then and we had a lot to straighten out between us.

There Mama sat, in black, by the window. She was humming an old church song, *Lord, you brought me from a long ways off*. Sonny was out somewhere. Mama kept watching the streets.

"I don't know," she said, "if I'll ever see you again, after you go off from here. But I hope you'll remember the things I tried to teach you."

"Don't talk like that," I said, and smiled. "You'll be here a long time yet."

90   She smiled, too, but she said nothing. She was quiet for a long time. And I said, "Mama, don't you worry about nothing. I'll be writing all the time, and you be getting the checks. . . ."

"I want to talk to you about your brother," she said, suddenly. "If anything happens to me he ain't going to have nobody to look out for him."

"Mama," I said, "ain't nothing going to happen to you *or* Sonny. Sonny's all right. He's a good boy and he's got good sense."

"It ain't a question of his being a good boy," Mama said, "nor of his having good sense. It ain't only the bad ones, nor yet the dumb ones that gets sucked under." She stopped, looking at me. "Your Daddy once had a brother," she said, and she smiled in a way that made me feel she was in pain. "You didn't never know that, did you?"

"No," I said, "I never knew that," and I watched her face.

95   "Oh, yes," she said, "your Daddy had a brother." She looked out of the window again. "I know you never saw your Daddy cry. But *I* did—many a time, through all these years."

I asked her, "What happened to his brother? How come nobody's ever talked about him?"

This was the first time I ever saw my mother look old.

"His brother got killed," she said, "when he was just a little younger than you are now. I knew him. He was a fine boy. He was maybe a little full of the devil, but he didn't mean nobody no harm."

Then she stopped and the room was silent, exactly as it had sometimes been on those Sunday afternoons. Mama kept looking out into the streets.

100   "He used to have a job in the mill," she said, "and, like all young folks, he just liked to perform on Saturday nights. Saturday nights, him and your father would drift around to different places,

go to dances and things like that, or just sit around with people they knew, and your father's brother would sing, he had a fine voice, and play along with himself on his guitar. Well, this particular Saturday night, him and your father was coming home from some place, and they were both a little drunk and there was a moon that night, it was bright like day. Your father's brother was feeling kind of good, and he was whistling to himself, and he had his guitar slung over his shoulder. They was coming down a hill and beneath them was a road that turned off from the highway. Well, your father's brother, being always kind of frisky, decided to run down this hill, and he did, with that guitar banging and clanging behind him, and he ran across the road, and he was making water behind a tree. And your father was sort of amused at him and he was still coming down the hill, kind of slow. Then he heard a car motor and that same minute his brother stepped from behind the tree, into the road, in the moonlight. And he started to cross the road. And your father started to run down the hill, he says he don't know why. This car was full of white men. They was all drunk, and when they seen your father's brother they let out a great whoop and holler and they aimed the car straight at him. They was having fun, they just wanted to scare him, the way they do sometimes, you know. But they was drunk. And I guess the boy, being drunk, too, and scared, kind of lost his head. By the time he jumped it was too late. Your father says he heard his brother scream when the car rolled over him, and he heard the wood of that guitar when it give, and he heard them strings go flying, and he heard them white men shouting, and the car kept on a-going and it ain't stopped till this day. And, time your father got down the hill, his brother weren't nothing but blood and pulp."

Tears were gleaming on my mother's face. There wasn't anything I could say.

"He never mentioned it," she said, "because I never let him mention it before you children. Your Daddy was like a crazy man that night and for many a night thereafter. He says he never in his life seen anything as dark as that road after the lights of that car had gone away. Weren't nothing, weren't nobody on that road, just your Daddy and his brother and that busted guitar. Oh, yes. Your Daddy never did really get right again. Till the day he died he weren't sure but that every white man he saw was the man that killed his brother."

She stopped and took out her handkerchief and dried her eyes and looked at me.

"I ain't telling you all this," she said, "to make you scared or bitter or to make you hate nobody. I'm telling you this because you got a brother. And the world ain't changed."

I guess I didn't want to believe this. I guess she saw this in my face. She turned away from me, toward the window again, searching those streets.

"But I praise my Redeemer," she said at last, "that He called your Daddy home before me. I ain't saying it to throw no flowers at myself, but, I declare, it keeps me from feeling too cast down to know I helped your father get safely through this world. Your father always acted like he was the roughest, strongest man on earth. And everybody took him to be like that. But if he hadn't had *me* there—to see his tears!"

She was crying again. Still, I couldn't move. I said, "Lord, Lord, Mama, I didn't know it was like that."

"Oh, honey," she said, "there's a lot that you don't know. But you are going to find it out." She stood up from the window and came over to me. "You got to hold on to your brother," she said, "and don't let him fall, no matter what it looks like is happening to him and no matter how evil you gets with him. You going to be evil with him many a time. But don't you forget what I told you, you hear?"

"I won't forget," I said. "Don't you worry, I won't forget. I won't let nothing happen to Sonny."

My mother smiled as though she were amused at something she saw in my face. Then, "You may not be able to stop nothing from happening. But you got to let him know you's *there*."

Two days later I was married, and then I was gone. And I had a lot of things on my mind and I pretty well forgot my promise to Mama until I got shipped home on a special furlough for her funeral.

And, after the funeral, with just Sonny and me alone in the empty kitchen, I tried to find out something about him.

"What do you want to do?" I asked him.

"I'm going to be a musician," he said.

115   For he had graduated, in the time I had been away, from dancing to the juke box to finding out who was playing what, and what they were doing with it, and he had bought himself a set of drums.

"You mean, you want to be a drummer?" I somehow had the feeling that being a drummer might be all right for other people but not for my brother Sonny.

"I don't think," he said, looking at me very gravely, "that I'll ever be a good drummer. But I think I can play a piano."

I frowned. I'd never played the role of the older brother quite so seriously before, had scarcely ever, in fact, *asked* Sonny a damn thing. I sensed myself in the presence of something I didn't really know how to handle, didn't understand. So I made my frown a little deeper as I asked: "What kind of musician do you want to be?"

He grinned. "How many kinds do you think there are?"

120   "Be *serious*," I said.

He laughed, throwing his head back, and then looked at me. "I *am* serious."

"Well, then, for Christ's sake, stop kidding around and answer a serious question. I mean, do you want to be a concert pianist, you want to play classical music and all that, or—or what?" Long before I finished he was laughing again. "For Christ's *sake,* Sonny!"

He sobered, but with difficulty. "I'm sorry. But you sound so—*scared!*" and he was off again.

"Well, you may think it's funny now, baby, but it's not going to be so funny when you have to make your living at it, let me tell you *that*." I was furious because I knew he was laughing at me and I didn't know why.

125   "No," he said, very sober now, and afraid, perhaps, that he'd hurt me, "I don't want to be a classical pianist. That isn't what interests me. I mean"—he paused, looking hard at me, as though his eyes would help me to understand, and then gestured helplessly, as though perhaps his hand would help—"I mean, I'll have a lot of studying to do, and I'll have to study *everything,* but, I mean, I want to play *with*—jazz musicians." He stopped. "I want to play jazz," he said.

Well, the word had never before sounded as heavy, as real, as it sounded that afternoon in Sonny's mouth. I just looked at him and I was probably frowning a real frown by this time. I simply couldn't see why on earth he'd want to spend his time hanging around nightclubs, clowning around on bandstands, while people pushed each other around a dance floor. It seemed—beneath him, somehow. I had never thought about it before, had never been forced to, but I suppose I had always put jazz musicians in a class with what Daddy called "good-time people."

"Are you *serious?*"

"Hell, *yes,* I'm serious."

He looked more helpless than ever, and annoyed, and deeply hurt.

130   I suggested, helpfully: "You mean—like Louis Armstrong?"

His face closed as though I'd struck him. "No. I'm not talking about none of that old-time, down home crap."

"Well, look, Sonny, I'm sorry, don't get mad. I just don't altogether get it, that's all. Name somebody—you know, a jazz musician you admire."

"Bird."

"Who?"

135   "Bird! Charlie Parker! Don't they teach you nothing in the goddamn army?"

I lit a cigarette. I was surprised and then a little amused to discover that I was trembling. "I've been out of touch," I said. "You'll have to be patient with me. Now. Who's this Parker character?"

"He's just one of the greatest jazz musicians alive," said Sonny, sullenly, his hands in his pockets, his back to me. "Maybe *the* greatest," he added, bitterly, "that's probably why *you* never heard of him."

"All right," I said, "I'm ignorant. I'm sorry. I'll go out and buy all the cat's records right away, all right?"

"It don't," said Sonny, with dignity, "make any difference to me. I don't care what you listen to. Don't do me no favors."

I was beginning to realize that I'd never seen him so upset before. With another part of my mind I was thinking that this would probably turn out to be one of those things kids go through and that I shouldn't make it seem important by pushing it too hard. Still, I didn't think it would do any harm to ask: "Doesn't all this take a lot of time? Can you make a living at it?"

He turned back to me and half leaned, half sat, on the kitchen table. "Everything takes time," he said, "and—well, yes, sure, I can make a living at it. But what I don't seem to be able to make you understand is that it's the only thing I want to do."

"Well, Sonny," I said, gently, "you know people can't always do exactly what they *want* to do—"

"*No*, I don't know that," said Sonny, surprising me. "I think people *ought* to do what they want to do, what else are they alive for?"

"You getting to be a big boy," I said desperately, "it's time you started thinking about your future."

"I'm thinking about my future," said Sonny, grimly. "I think about it all the time."

I gave up. I decided, if he didn't change his mind, that we could always talk about it later. "In the meantime," I said, "you got to finish school." We had already decided that he'd have to move in with Isabel and her folks. I knew this wasn't the ideal arrangement because Isabel's folks are inclined to be dicty and they hadn't especially wanted Isabel to marry me. But I didn't know what else to do. "And we have to get you fixed up at Isabel's."

There was a long silence. He moved from the kitchen table to the window. "That's a terrible idea. You know it yourself."

"Do you have a *better* idea?"

He just walked up and down the kitchen for a minute. He was as tall as I was. He had started to shave. I suddenly had the feeling that I didn't know him at all.

He stopped at the kitchen table and picked up my cigarettes. Looking at me with a kind of mocking, amused defiance, he put one between his lips. "You mind?"

"You smoking already?"

He lit the cigarette and nodded, watching me through the smoke. "I just wanted to see if I'd have the courage to smoke in front of you." He grinned and blew a great cloud of smoke to the ceiling. "It was easy." He looked at my face. "Come on, now. I bet you was smoking at my age, tell the truth."

I didn't say anything but the truth was on my face, and he laughed. But now there was something very strained in his laugh. "Sure. And I bet that ain't all you was doing."

He was frightening me a little. "Cut the crap," I said. "We already decided that you was going to go and live at Isabel's. Now what's got into you all of a sudden?"

"*You* decided it," he pointed out. "*I* didn't decide nothing." He stopped in front of me, leaning against the stove, arms loosely folded. "Look, brother. I don't want to stay in Harlem no more, I really don't." He was very earnest. He looked at me, then over toward the kitchen window. There was something in his eyes I'd never seen before, some thoughtfulness, some worry all his own. He rubbed the muscle of one arm. "It's time I was getting out of here."

"Where do you want to *go*, Sonny?"

"I want to join the army. Or the navy, I don't care. If I say I'm old enough, they'll believe me."

Then I got mad. It was because I was so scared. "You must be crazy. You goddamn fool, what the hell do you want to go and join the *army* for?"

"I just told you. To get out of Harlem."

"Sonny, you haven't even finished *school*. And if you really want to be a musician, how do you expect to study if you're in the *army*?"

He looked at me, trapped, and in anguish. "There's ways. I might be able to work out some kind of deal. Anyway, I'll have the G.I. Bill when I come out."

"*If* you come out." We stared at each other. "Sonny, please. Be reasonable. I know the setup is far from perfect. But we got to do the best we can."

"I ain't learning nothing in school," he said. "Even when I go." He turned away from me and opened the window and threw his cigarette out into the narrow alley. I watched his back. "At least, I ain't learning nothing you'd want me to learn." He slammed the window so hard I thought the glass would fly out, and turned back to me. "And I'm sick of the stink of these garbage cans!"

"Sonny," I said, "I know how you feel. But if you don't finish school now, you're going to be sorry later that you didn't." I grabbed him by the shoulders. "And you only got another year. It ain't so bad. And I'll come back and I swear I'll help you do *whatever* you want to do. Just try to put up with it till I come back. Will you please do that? For me?"

165   He didn't answer and he wouldn't look at me.

"Sonny. You hear me?"

He pulled away. "I hear you. But you never hear anything *I* say."

I didn't know what to say to that. He looked out of the window and then back at me. "OK," he said, and sighed. "I'll try."

Then I said, trying to cheer him up a little, "They got a piano at Isabel's. You can practice on it."

170   And as a matter of fact, it did cheer him up for a minute. "That's right," he said to himself. "I forgot that." His face relaxed a little. But the worry, the thoughtfulness, played on it still, the way shadows play on a face which is staring into the fire.

But I thought I'd never hear the end of that piano. At first, Isabel would write me, saying how nice it was that Sonny was so serious about his music and how, as soon as he came in from school, or wherever he had been when he was supposed to be at school, he went straight to that piano and stayed there until suppertime. And, after supper, he went back to that piano and stayed there until everybody went to bed. He was at the piano all day Saturday and all day Sunday. Then he bought a record player and started playing records. He'd play one record over and over again, all day long sometimes, and he'd improvise along with it on the piano. Or he'd play one section of the record, one chord, one change, one progression, then he'd do it on the piano. Then back to the record. Then back to the piano.

Well, I really don't know how they stood it. Isabel finally confessed that it wasn't like living with a person at all, it was like living with sound. And the sound didn't make any sense to her, didn't make any sense to any of them—naturally. They began, in a way, to be afflicted by this presence that was living in their home. It was as though Sonny were some sort of god, or monster. He moved in an atmosphere which wasn't like theirs at all. They fed him and he ate, he washed himself, he walked in and out of their door; he certainly wasn't nasty or unpleasant or rude, Sonny isn't any of those things; but it was as though he were all wrapped up in some cloud, some fire, some vision all his own; and there wasn't any way to reach him.

At the same time, he wasn't really a man yet, he was still a child, and they had to watch out for him in all kinds of ways. They certainly couldn't throw him out. Neither did they dare to make a great scene about that piano because even they dimly sensed, as I sensed, from so many thousands of miles away, that Sonny was at that piano playing for his life.

But he hadn't been going to school. One day a letter came from the school board and Isabel's mother got it—there had, apparently, been other letters but Sonny had torn them up. This day, when Sonny came in, Isabel's mother showed him the letter and asked where he'd been spending his time. And she finally got it out of him that he'd been down in Greenwich Village, with musicians and other characters, in a white girl's apartment. And this scared her and she started to scream at him and what came up, once she began—though she denies it to this day—was what sacrifices they were making to give Sonny a decent home and how little he appreciated it.

175   Sonny didn't play the piano that day. By evening, Isabel's mother had calmed down but then there was the old man to deal with, and Isabel herself. Isabel says she did her best to be calm but she broke down and started crying. She says she just watched Sonny's face. She could tell, by watching him, what was happening with him. And what was happening was that they penetrated his cloud, they had reached him. Even if their fingers had been a thousand times more gentle than human fingers ever are, he could hardly help feeling that they had stripped him naked and were spitting on that nakedness. For he also had to see that his presence, that music, which was life or death to him, had been torture for them and that they had endured it, not at all for his sake, but only for mine. And Sonny couldn't take that. He can take it a little better today than he could then but he's still not very good at it and, frankly, I don't know anybody who is.

The silence of the next few days must have been louder than the sound of all the music ever played since time began. One morning, before she went to work, Isabel was in his room for something and she suddenly realized that all of his records were gone. And she knew for certain that he was gone. And he was. He went as far as the navy would carry him. He finally sent me a postcard from some place in Greece and that was the first I knew that Sonny was still alive. I didn't see him any more until we were both back in New York and the war had long been over.

He was a man by then, of course, but I wasn't willing to see it. He came by the house from time to time, but we fought almost every time we met. I didn't like the way he carried himself, loose and dreamlike all the time, and I didn't like his friends, and his music seemed to be merely an excuse for the life he led. It sounded just that weird and disordered.

Then we had a fight, a pretty awful fight, and I didn't see him for months. By and by I looked him up, where he was living, in a furnished room in the Village, and I tried to make it up. But there were lots of other people in the room and Sonny just lay on his bed, and he wouldn't come downstairs with me, and he treated these other people as though they were his family and I weren't. So I got mad and then he got mad, and then I told him that he might just as well be dead as live the way he was living. Then he stood up and he told me not to worry about him any more in life, that he *was* dead as far as I was concerned. Then he pushed me to the door and the other people looked on as though nothing were happening, and he slammed the door behind me. I stood in the hallway, staring at the door. I heard somebody laugh in the room and then the tears came to my eyes. I started down the steps, whistling to keep from crying, I kept whistling to myself, *You going to need me, baby, one of these cold, rainy days.*

I read about Sonny's trouble in the spring. Little Grace died in the fall. She was a beautiful little girl. But she only lived a little over two years. She died of polio and she suffered. She had a slight fever for a couple of days, but it didn't seem like anything and we just kept her in bed. And we would certainly have called the doctor, but the fever dropped, she seemed to be all right. So we thought it had just been a cold. Then, one day, she was up, playing, Isabel was in the kitchen fixing lunch for the two boys when they'd come in from school, and she heard Grace fall down in the living room. When you have a lot of children you don't always start running when one of them falls, unless they start screaming or something. And, this time, Grace was quiet. Yet, Isabel says that when she heard that *thump* and then that silence, something happened in her to make her afraid. And she ran to the living room and there was little Grace on the floor, all twisted up, and the reason she hadn't screamed was that she couldn't get her breath. And when she did scream, it was the worst sound, Isabel says, that she'd ever heard in all her life, and she still hears it sometimes in her dreams. Isabel will sometimes wake me up with a low, moaning, strangled sound and I have to be quick to awaken her and hold her to me and where Isabel is weeping against me seems a mortal wound.

I think I may have written Sonny the very day that little Grace was buried. I was sitting in the living room in the dark, by myself, and I suddenly thought of Sonny. My trouble made his real.

One Saturday afternoon, when Sonny had been living with us, or, anyway, been in our house, for nearly two weeks, I found myself wandering aimlessly about the living room, drinking from a can of beer, and trying to work up the courage to search Sonny's room. He was out, he was usually out whenever I was home, and Isabel had taken the children to see their grandparents. Suddenly I was standing still in front of the living room window, watching Seventh Avenue. The idea of searching Sonny's room made me still. I scarcely dared to admit to myself what I'd be searching for. I didn't know what I'd do if I found it. Or if I didn't.

On the sidewalk across from me, near the entrance to a barbecue joint, some people were holding an old-fashioned revival meeting. The barbecue cook, wearing a dirty white apron, his conked hair reddish and metallic in the pale sun, and a cigarette between his lips, stood in the doorway, watching them. Kids and older people paused in their errands and stood there, along with some older men and a couple of very tough-looking women who watched everything that happened on the avenue, as though they owned it, or were maybe owned by it. Well, they were watching this, too. The revival was being carried on by three sisters in black, and a brother. All they had were their voices and their Bibles and a tambourine. The brother was testifying and while he testified two of the sisters stood together, seeming to say, amen, and the third sister walked around with the tambourine outstretched and a couple of people dropped coins into it. Then the brother's testimony ended and the sister who had been taking up the collection dumped the coins into her palm and transferred them to the pocket of her long black robe. Then she raised both hands, striking the tambourine against the air, and then against one hand, and she started to sing. And the two other sisters and the brother joined in.

It was strange, suddenly, to watch, though I had been seeing these street meetings all my life. So, of course, had everybody else down there. Yet, they paused and watched and listened and I stood still at the window. "*Tis the old ship of Zion,*" they sang, and the sister with the tambourine kept a steady, jangling beat, "*it has rescued many a thousand!*" Not a soul under the sound of their voices was hearing this song for the first time, not one of them had been rescued. Nor had they seen much in the way of rescue work being done around them. Neither did they especially believe in the holiness of the three sisters and the brother, they knew too much about them, knew where they lived, and how. The woman with the tambourine, whose voice dominated the air, whose face was bright with joy, was divided by very little from the woman who stood watching her, a cigarette between her heavy, chapped lips, her hair a cuckoo's nest, her face scarred and swollen from many beatings, and her black eyes glittering like coal. Perhaps they both knew this, which was why, when, as rarely, they addressed each other, they addressed each other as Sister. As the singing filled the air the watching, listening faces underwent a change, the eyes focusing on something within; the music seemed to soothe a poison out of them; and time seemed, nearly, to fall away from the sullen, belligerent, battered faces, as though they were fleeing back to their first condition, while dreaming of their last. The barbecue cook half shook his head and smiled, and dropped his cigarette and disappeared into his joint. A man fumbled in his pockets for change and stood holding it in his hand impatiently, as though he had just remembered a pressing appointment further up the avenue. He looked furious. Then I saw Sonny, standing on the edge of the crowd. He was carrying a wide, flat notebook with a green cover, and it made him look, from where I was standing, almost like a schoolboy. The coppery sun brought out the copper in his skin, he was very faintly smiling, standing very still. Then the singing stopped, the tambourine turned into a collection plate again. The furious man dropped in his coins and vanished, so did a couple of the women, and Sonny dropped some change in the plate, looking directly at the woman with a little smile. He started across the avenue, toward the house. He has a slow, loping walk, something like the way Harlem hipsters walk, only he's imposed on this his own half-beat. I had never really noticed it before.

I stayed at the window, both relieved and apprehensive. As Sonny disappeared from my sight, they began singing again. And they were still singing when his key turned in the lock.

185 "Hey," he said.

"Hey, yourself. You want some beer?"

"No. Well, maybe." But he came up to the window and stood beside me, looking out. "What a warm voice," he said.

They were singing *If I could only hear my mother pray again!*

"Yes," I said, "and she can sure beat that tambourine."

190 "But what a terrible song," he said, and laughed. He dropped his notebook on the sofa and disappeared into the kitchen. "Where's Isabel and the kids?"

"I think they went to see their grandparents. You hungry?"

"No." He came back into the living room with his can of beer. "You want to come some place with me tonight?"

I sensed, I don't know how, that I couldn't possibly say no. "Sure. Where?"

He sat down on the sofa and picked up his notebook and started leafing through it. "I'm going to sit in with some fellows in a joint in the Village."

195 "You mean, you're going to play, tonight?"

"That's right." He took a swallow of his beer and moved back to the window. He gave me a sidelong look. "If you can stand it."

"I'll try," I said.

He smiled to himself and we both watched as the meeting across the way broke up. The three sisters and the brother, heads bowed, were singing *God be with you till we meet again.* The faces around them were very quiet. Then the song ended. The small crowd dispersed. We watched the three women and the lone man walk slowly up the avenue.

"When she was singing before," said Sonny, abruptly, "her voice reminded me for a minute of what heroin feels like sometimes—when it's in your veins. It makes you feel sort of warm and cool at the same time. And distant. And—and sure." He sipped his beer, very deliberately not looking at me. I watched his face. "It makes you feel—in control. Sometimes you've got to have that feeling."

"Do you?" I sat down slowly in the easy chair.

"Sometimes." He went to the sofa and picked up his notebook again. "Some people do."

"In order," I asked, "to play?" And my voice was very ugly, full of contempt and anger.

"Well"—he looked at me with great, troubled eyes, as though, in fact, he hoped his eyes would tell me things he could never otherwise say—"they *think* so. And *if* they think so—!"

"And what do *you* think?" I asked.

He sat on the sofa and put his can of beer on the floor. "I don't know," he said, and I couldn't be sure if he were answering my question or pursuing his thoughts. His face didn't tell me. "It's not so much to *play*. It's to *stand* it, to be able to make it at all. On any level." He frowned and smiled: "In order to keep from shaking to pieces."

"But these friends of yours," I said, "they seem to shake themselves to pieces pretty goddamn fast."

"Maybe." He played with the notebook. And something told me that I should curb my tongue, that Sonny was doing his best to talk, that I should listen. "But of course you only know the ones that've gone to pieces. Some don't—or at least they haven't *yet* and that's just about all *any* of us can say." He paused. "And then there are some who just live, really, in hell, and they know it and they see what's happening and they go right on. I don't know." He sighed, dropped the notebook, folded his arms. "Some guys, you can tell from the way they play, they on something *all* the time. And you can see that, well, it makes something real for them. But of course," he picked up his beer from the floor and sipped it and put the can down again, "they *want* to, too, you've got to see that. Even some of them that say they don't—*some*, not all."

"And what about you?" I asked—I couldn't help it. "What about you? Do *you* want to?"

He stood up and walked to the window and remained silent for a long time. Then he sighed. "Me," he said. Then: "While I was downstairs before, on my way here, listening to that woman sing, it struck me all of a sudden how much suffering she must have had to go through—to sing like that. It's *repulsive* to think you have to suffer that much."

I said: "But there's no way not to suffer—is there, Sonny?"

"I believe not," he said and smiled, "but that's never stopped anyone from trying." He looked at me. "Has it?" I realized, with this mocking look, that there stood between us, forever, beyond the power of time or forgiveness, the fact that I had held silence—so long!—when he had needed human speech to help him. He turned back to the window. "No, there's no way not to suffer. But you try all kinds of ways to keep from drowning in it, to keep on top of it, and to make it seem— well, like *you*. Like you did something, all right, and now you're suffering for it. You know?" I said nothing. "Well you know," he said, impatiently, "why *do* people suffer? Maybe it's better to do something to give it a reason, *any* reason."

"But we just agreed," I said, "that there's no way not to suffer. Isn't it better, then, just to— take it?"

"But nobody just takes it," Sonny cried, "that's what I'm telling you! *Everybody* tries not to. You're just hung up on the *way* some people try—it's not *your* way!"

The hair on my face began to itch, my face felt wet. "That's not true," I said, "that's not true. I don't give a damn what other people do, I don't even care how they suffer. I just care how *you* suffer." And he looked at me. "Please believe me," I said, "I don't want to see you—die—trying not to suffer."

"I won't," he said, flatly, "die trying not to suffer. At least, not any faster than anybody else."

"But there's no need," I said, trying to laugh, "is there? in killing yourself."

I wanted to say more, but I couldn't. I wanted to talk about will power and how life could be—well, beautiful. I wanted to say that it was all within; but was it? or, rather, wasn't that exactly the trouble? And I wanted to promise that I would never fail him again. But it would all have sounded—empty words and lies.

So I made the promise to myself and prayed that I would keep it.

"It's terrible sometimes, inside," he said, "that's what's the trouble. You walk these streets, black and funky and cold, and there's not really a living ass to talk to, and there's nothing shaking, and there's no way of getting it out—that storm inside. You can't talk it and you can't make love with it, and when you finally try to get with it and play it, you realize *nobody's* listening. So *you've* got to listen. You got to find a way to listen."

220   And then he walked away from the window and sat on the sofa again, as though all the wind had suddenly been knocked out of him. "Sometimes you'll do *anything* to play, even cut your mother's throat." He laughed and looked at me. "Or your brother's." Then he sobered. "Or your own." Then: "Don't worry. I'm all right now and I think I'll *be* all right. But I can't forget—where I've been. I don't mean just the physical place I've been, I mean where I've *been*. And *what* I've been."

"What have you been, Sonny?" I asked.

He smiled—but sat sideways on the sofa, his elbow resting on the back, his fingers playing with his mouth and chin, not looking at me. "I've been something I didn't recognize, didn't know I could be. Didn't know anybody could be." He stopped, looking inward, looking helplessly young, looking old. "I'm not talking about it now because I feel *guilty* or anything like that—maybe it would be better if I did, I don't know. Anyway, I can't really talk about it. Not to you, not to anybody," and now he turned and faced me. "Sometimes, you know, and it was actually when I was most *out* of the world, I felt that I was in it, that I was *with* it, really, and I could play or I didn't really have to *play,* it just came out of me, it was there. And I don't know how I played, thinking about it now, but I know I did awful things, those times, sometimes, to people. Or it wasn't that I *did* anything to them—it was that they weren't real." He picked up the beer can; it was empty; he rolled it between his palms: "And other times—well, I needed a fix, I needed to find a place to lean, I needed to clear a space to *listen*—and I couldn't find it, and I—went crazy, I did terrible things to *me,* I was terrible *for* me." He began pressing the beer can between his hands, I watched the metal begin to give. It glittered, as he played with it, like a knife, and I was afraid he would cut himself, but I said nothing. "Oh well. I can never tell you. I was all by myself at the bottom of something, stinking and sweating and crying and shaking, and I smelled it, you know? *my* stink, and I thought I'd die if I couldn't get away from it and yet, all the same, I knew that everything I was doing was just locking me in with it. And I didn't know," he paused, still flattening the beer can, "I didn't know, I still *don't* know, something kept telling me that maybe it was good to smell your own stink, but I didn't think that *that* was what I'd been trying to do—and—who can stand it?" and he abruptly dropped the ruined beer can, looking at me with a small, still smile, and then rose, walking to the window as though it were the lodestone rock. I watched his face, he watched the avenue. "I couldn't tell you when Mama died—but the reason I wanted to leave Harlem so bad was to get away from drugs. And then, when I ran away, that's what I was running from—really. When I came back, nothing had changed, *I* hadn't changed, I was just—older." And he stopped, drumming with his fingers on the windowpane. The sun had vanished, soon darkness would fall. I watched his face. "It can come again," he said, almost as though speaking to himself. Then he turned to me. "It can come again," he repeated. "I just want you to know that."

"All right," I said, at last. "So it can come again. All right."

He smiled, but the smile was sorrowful. "I had to try to tell you," he said.

225   "Yes," I said. "I understand that."

"You're my brother," he said, looking straight at me, and not smiling at all.

"Yes," I repeated, "yes. I understand that."

He turned back to the window, looking out. "All that hatred down there," he said, "all that hatred and misery and love. It's a wonder it doesn't blow the avenue apart."

We went to the only nightclub on a short, dark street, downtown. We squeezed through the narrow, chattering, jam-packed bar to the entrance of the big room, where the bandstand was. And we stood there for a moment, for the lights were very dim in this room and we couldn't see. Then, "Hello, boy," said a voice and an enormous black man, much older than Sonny or myself, erupted out of all that atmospheric lighting and put an arm around Sonny's shoulder. "I been sitting right here," he said, "waiting for you."

He had a big voice, too, and heads in the darkness turned toward us.

Sonny grinned and pulled a little away, and said, "Creole, this is my brother. I told you about him."

Creole shook my hand. "I'm glad to meet you, son," he said, and it was clear that he was glad to meet me *there,* for Sonny's sake. And he smiled, "You got a real musician in *your* family," and he took his arm from Sonny's shoulder and slapped him, lightly, affectionately, with the back of his hand.

"Well. Now I've heard it all," said a voice behind us. This was another musician, and a friend of Sonny's, a coal-black, cheerful-looking man, built close to the ground. He immediately began confiding to me, at the top of his lungs, the most terrible things about Sonny, his teeth gleaming like a lighthouse and his laugh coming up out of him like the beginning of an earthquake. And it turned out that everyone at the bar knew Sonny, or almost everyone; some were musicians, working there, or nearby, or not working, some were simply hangers-on, and some were there to hear Sonny play. I was introduced to all of them and they were all very polite to me. Yet, it was clear that, for them, I was only Sonny's brother. Here, I was in Sonny's world. Or, rather: his kingdom. Here, it was not even a question that his veins bore royal blood.

They were going to play soon and Creole installed me, by myself, at a table in a dark corner. Then I watched them, Creole, and the little black man, and Sonny, and the others, while they horsed around, standing just below the bandstand. The light from the bandstand spilled just a little short of them and, watching them laughing and gesturing and moving about, I had the feeling that they, nevertheless, were being most careful not to step into that circle of light too suddenly: that if they moved into the light too suddenly, without thinking, they would perish in flame. Then, while I watched, one of them, the small, black man, moved into the light and crossed the bandstand and started fooling around with his drums. Then—being funny and being, also, extremely ceremonious—Creole took Sonny by the arm and led him to the piano. A woman's voice called Sonny's name and a few hands started clapping. And Sonny, also being funny and being ceremonious, and so touched, I think, that he could have cried, but neither hiding it nor showing it, riding it like a man, grinned, and put both hands to his heart and bowed from the waist.

Creole then went to the bass fiddle and a lean, very bright-skinned brown man jumped up on the bandstand and picked up his horn. So there they were, and the atmosphere on the bandstand and in the room began to change and tighten. Someone stepped up to the microphone and announced them. Then there were all kinds of murmurs. Some people at the bar shushed others. The waitress ran around, frantically getting in the last orders, guys and chicks got closer to each other, and the lights on the bandstand, on the quartet, turned to a kind of indigo. Then they all looked different there. Creole looked about him for the last time, as though he were making certain that all his chickens were in the coop, and then he—jumped and struck the fiddle. And there they were.

All I know about music is that not many people ever really hear it. And even then, on the rare occasions when something opens within, and the music enters, what we mainly hear, or hear corroborated, are personal, private, vanishing evocations. But the man who creates the music is hearing something else, is dealing with the roar rising from the void and imposing order on it as it hits the air. What is evoked in him, then, is of another order, more terrible because it has no words, and triumphant, too, for that same reason. And his triumph, when he triumphs, is ours. I just watched Sonny's face. His face was troubled, he was working hard, but he wasn't with it. And I had the feeling that, in a way, everyone on the bandstand was waiting for him, both waiting for him and pushing him along. But as I began to watch Creole, I realized that it was Creole who held them all back. He had them on a short rein. Up there, keeping the beat with his whole body, wailing on the fiddle, with his eyes half closed, he was listening to everything, but he was listening to Sonny. He was having a dialogue with Sonny. He wanted Sonny to leave the shoreline and strike out for the deep water. He was Sonny's witness that deep water and drowning were not the same thing—he had been there, and he knew. And he wanted Sonny to know. He was waiting for Sonny to do the things on the keys which would let Creole know that Sonny was in the water.

And, while Creole listened, Sonny moved, deep within, exactly like someone in torment. I had never before thought of how awful the relationship must be between the musician and his instrument. He has to fill it, this instrument, with the breath of life, his own. He has to make it do what he wants it to do. And a piano is just a piano. It's made out of so much wood and wires and little hammers and big ones, and ivory. While there's only so much you can do with it, the only way to find this out is to try; to try and make it do everything.

And Sonny hadn't been near a piano for over a year. And he wasn't on much better terms with his life, not the life that stretched before him now. He and the piano stammered, started one way, got scared, stopped; started another way, panicked, marked time, started again; then seemed to have found a direction, panicked again, got stuck. And the face I saw on Sonny I'd never seen before. Everything had been burned out of it, and, at the same time, things usually hidden were being burned in, by the fire and fury of the battle which was occurring in him up there.

Yet, watching Creole's face as they neared the end of the first set, I had the feeling that something had happened, something I hadn't heard. Then they finished, there was scattered applause, and then, without an instant's warning, Creole started into something else, it was almost sardonic, it was *Am I Blue*. And, as though he commanded, Sonny began to play. Something began to happen. And Creole let out the reins. The dry, low, black man said something awful on the drums, Creole answered, and the drums talked back. Then the horn insisted, sweet and high, slightly detached perhaps, and Creole listened, commenting now and then, dry, and driving, beautiful and calm and old. Then they all came together again, and Sonny was part of the family again. I could tell this from his face. He seemed to have found, right there beneath his fingers, a damn brand-new piano. It seemed that he couldn't get over it. Then, for awhile, just being happy with Sonny, they seemed to be agreeing with him that brand-new pianos certainly were a gas.

240   Then Creole stepped forward to remind them that what they were playing was the blues. He hit something in all of them, he hit something in me, myself, and the music tightened and deepened, apprehension began to beat the air. Creole began to tell us what the blues were all about. They were not about anything very new. He and his boys up there were keeping it new, at the risk of ruin, destruction, madness, and death, in order to find new ways to make us listen. For, while the tale of how we suffer, and how we are delighted, and how we may triumph is never new, it always must be heard. There isn't any other tale to tell, it's the only light we've got in all this darkness.

And this tale, according to that face, that body, those strong hands on those strings, has another aspect in every country, and a new depth in every generation. Listen, Creole seemed to be saying, listen. Now these are Sonny's blues. He made the little black man on the drums know it, and the bright, brown man on the horn. Creole wasn't trying any longer to get Sonny in the water. He was wishing him Godspeed. Then he stepped back, very slowly, filling the air with the immense suggestion that Sonny speak for himself.

Then they all gathered around Sonny and Sonny played. Every now and again one of them seemed to say, amen. Sonny's fingers filled the air with life, his life. But that life contained so many others. And Sonny went all the way back, he really began with the spare, flat statement of the opening phrase of the song. Then he began to make it his. It was very beautiful because it wasn't hurried and it was no longer a lament. I seemed to hear with what burning he had made it his, with what burning we had yet to make it ours, how we could cease lamenting. Freedom lurked around us and I understood, at last, that he could help us to be free if we would listen, that he would never be free until we did. Yet, there was no battle in his face now. I heard what he had gone through, and would continue to go through until he came to rest in earth. He had made it his: that long line, of which we knew only Mama and Daddy. And he was giving it back, as everything must be given back, so that, passing through death, it can live forever. I saw my mother's face again, and felt, for the first time, how the stones of the road she had walked on must have bruised her feet. I saw the moonlit road where my father's brother died. And it brought something else back to me, and carried me past it. I saw my little girl again and felt Isabel's tears again, and I felt my own tears begin to rise. And I was yet aware that this was only a moment, that the world waited outside, as hungry as a tiger, and that trouble stretched above us, longer than the sky.

Then it was over. Creole and Sonny let out their breath, both soaking wet, and grinning. There was a lot of applause and some of it was real. In the dark, the girl came by and I asked her to take drinks to the bandstand. There was a long pause, while they talked up there in the indigo light and after awhile I saw the girl put a Scotch and milk on top of the piano for Sonny. He didn't seem to notice it, but just before they started playing again, he sipped from it and looked toward me, and nodded. Then he put it back on top of the piano. For me, then, as they began to play again, it glowed and shook above my brother's head like the very cup of trembling.

If you like this story you may also like Ralph Ellison's "Battle Royal" and "A Party Down at the Square" (chapter 12) as well as "Everyday Use," by black fiction writer and essayist Alice Walker (at the end of this section), and ZZ Packer's "Brownies" (chapter 7).

GOING FURTHER Baldwin's predecessor Richard Wright, the author of *Native Son*, *Uncle Tom's Children*, and *Eight Men*, is one of the most important writers of the twentieth century. Both Wright and Baldwin fled America and settled in France. Wright nurtured Ralph Ellison and his work, and Ellison's "Battle Royal" is one of the opening scenes in his award-winning novel *Invisible Man*. Another major black novelist and story writer worth considering in relation to James Baldwin is John Edgar Wideman, particularly his novel *Sent for You Yesterday*.

Jorge Luis Borges (1899–1986)

JORGE LUIS BORGES was born in Buenos Aires and spent most of his childhood there. When his family moved to Geneva he enrolled in the equivalent of a high school, returning only in the early 1920s to Argentina, where he began a career as a poet and then took to writing short fiction as well. Over the decades his reputation as a poet, story writer, and essayist continued to grow; his work made an enormous impact not only in Latin America but also around the world. As Mexican novelist Carlos Fuentes has noted, Borges renovated twentieth-century Latin American literary language and cleared the way for the new narrative styles of prose in New World Spanish.

By the end of his life he was clinically blind, but he never lost the inner vision that marked his learned imagination; as one of his titles—*The Book of Imaginary Beings*—suggests, he loved libraries and delighted in textual complexity. Questions about the nature of reality, time, personal identity, and history stand at the center of his concentrated "ficciones" or "fictions," his way of describing his version of the short story form.

The Circular Ruins (1949)

And if he left off dreaming about you . . .
—Through the Looking Glass, VI.

1   No one saw him disembark in the unanimous night, no one saw the bamboo canoe sink into the sacred mud, but in a few days there was no one who did not know that the taciturn man came from the South and that his home had been one of those numberless villages upstream in the deeply cleft side of the mountain, where the Zend language has not been contaminated by Greek and where leprosy is infrequent. What is certain is that the gray man kissed the mud, climbed up the bank without pushing aside (probably, without feeling) the blades which were lacerating his flesh, and crawled, nauseated and bloodstained, up to the circular enclosure crowned with a stone tiger or horse, which sometimes was the color of flame and now was that of ashes. This circle was a temple which had been devoured by ancient fires, profaned by the miasmal jungle, and whose god no longer received the homage of men. The stranger stretched himself out beneath the pedestal. He was awakened by the sun high overhead. He was not astonished to find that his wounds had healed; he closed his pallid eyes and slept, not through weakness of flesh but through determination of will. He knew that this temple was the place required for his invincible intent; he knew that the incessant trees had not succeeded in strangling the ruins of

another propitious temple downstream which had once belonged to gods now burned and dead; he knew that his immediate obligation was to dream. Toward midnight he was awakened by the inconsolable shriek of a bird. Tracks of bare feet, some figs and a jug warned him that the men of the region had been spying respectfully on his sleep, soliciting his protection or afraid of his magic. He felt a chill of fear, and sought out a sepulchral niche in the dilapidated wall where he concealed himself among unfamiliar leaves.

The purpose which guided him was not impossible, though supernatural. He wanted to dream a man; he wanted to dream him in minute entirety and impose him on reality. This magic project had exhausted the entire expanse of his mind; if some one had asked him his name or to relate some event of his former life, he would not have been able to give an answer. This uninhabited, ruined temple suited him, for it contained a minimum of visible world; the proximity of the workmen also suited him, for they took it upon themselves to provide for his frugal needs. The rice and fruit they brought him were nourishment enough for his body, which was consecrated to the sole task of sleeping and dreaming.

At first his dreams were chaotic; then in a short while they became dialectic in nature. The stranger dreamed that he was in the center of a circular amphitheater which was more or less the burnt temple; clouds of taciturn students filled the tiers of seats; the faces of the farthest ones hung at a distance of many centuries and as high as the stars, but their features were completely precise. The man lectured his pupils on anatomy, cosmography, and magic: the faces listened anxiously and tried to answer understandingly, as if they guessed the importance of that examination which would redeem one of them from his condition of empty illusion and interpolate him into the real world. Asleep or awake, the man thought over the answers of his phantoms, did not allow himself to be deceived by impostors, and in certain perplexities he sensed a growing intelligence. He was seeking a soul worthy of participating in the universe.

After nine or ten nights he understood with a certain bitterness that he could expect nothing from those pupils who accepted his doctrine passively, but that he could expect something from those who occasionally dared to oppose him. The former group, although worthy of love and affection, could not ascend to the level of individuals; the latter pre-existed to a slightly greater degree. One afternoon (now afternoons were also given over to sleep, now he was only awake for a couple of hours at daybreak) he dismissed the vast illusory student body for good and kept only one pupil. He was a taciturn, sallow boy, at times intractable, and whose sharp features resembled those of his dreamer. The brusque elimination of his fellow students did not disconcert him for long; after a few private lessons, his progress was enough to astound the teacher. Nevertheless, a catastrophe took place. One day, the man emerged from his sleep as if from a viscous desert, looked at the useless afternoon light which he immediately confused with the dawn, and understood that he had not dreamed. All that night and all day long, the intolerable lucidity of insomnia fell upon him. He tried exploring the forest, to lose his strength; among the hemlock he barely succeeded in experiencing several short snatches of sleep, veined with fleeting, rudimentary visions that were useless. He tried to assemble the student body but scarcely had he articulated a few brief words of exhortation when it became deformed and was then erased. In his almost perpetual vigil, tears of anger burned his old eyes.

5   He understood that modeling the incoherent and vertiginous matter of which dreams are composed was the most difficult task that a man could undertake, even though he should penetrate all the enigmas of a superior and inferior order; much more difficult than weaving a rope out of sand or coining the faceless wind. He swore he would forget the enormous hallucination which had thrown him off at first, and he sought another method of work. Before putting it into execution, he spent a month recovering his strength, which had been squandered by his delirium. He abandoned all premeditation of dreaming and almost immediately succeeded in sleeping a reasonable part of each day. The few times that he had dreams during this period, he paid no attention to them. Before resuming his task, he waited until the moon's disk was perfect. Then, in the afternoon, he purified himself in the waters of the river, worshiped the planetary gods, pronounced the prescribed syllables of a mighty name, and went to sleep. He dreamed almost immediately, with his heart throbbing.

He dreamed that it was warm, secret, about the size of a clenched fist, and of a garnet color within the penumbra of a human body as yet without face or sex; during fourteen lucid nights he dreamt of it with meticulous love. Every night he perceived it more clearly. He did not touch it; he only permitted himself to witness it, to observe it, and occasionally to rectify it with a glance. He perceived it and lived it from all angles and distances. On the fourteenth night he lightly touched the pulmonary artery with his index finger, then the whole heart, outside and inside. He was satisfied with the examination. He deliberately did not dream for a night; he then took up the heart again, invoked the name of a planet, and undertook the vision of another of the principal organs. Within a year he had come to the skeleton and the eyelids. The innumerable hair was perhaps the most difficult task. He dreamed an entire man—a young man, but who did not sit up or talk, who was unable to open his eyes. Night after night, the man dreamt him asleep.

In the Gnostic cosmogonies, demiurges fashion a red Adam who cannot stand; as clumsy, crude and elemental as this Adam of dust was the Adam of dreams forged by the wizard's nights. One afternoon, the man almost destroyed his entire work, but then changed his mind. (It would have been better had he destroyed it.) When he had exhausted all supplications to the deities of the earth, he threw himself at the feet of the effigy which was perhaps a tiger or perhaps a colt and implored its unknown help. That evening, at twilight, he dreamt of the statue. He dreamt it was alive, tremulous: it was not an atrocious bastard of a tiger and a colt, but at the same time these two fiery creatures and also a bull, a rose, and a storm. This multiple god revealed to him that his earthly name was Fire, and that in this circular temple (and in others like it) people had once made sacrifices to him and worshiped him, and that he would magically animate the dreamed phantom, in such a way that all creatures, except Fire itself and the dreamer, would believe it to be a man of flesh and blood. He commanded that once this man had been instructed in all the rites, he should be sent to the other ruined temple whose pyramids were still standing downstream, so that some voice would glorify him in that deserted edifice. In the dream of the man that dreamed, the dreamed one awoke.

The wizard carried out the orders he had been given. He devoted a certain length of time (which finally proved to be two years) to instructing him in the mysteries of the universe and the cult of fire. Secretly, he was pained at the idea of being separated from him. On the pretext of pedagogical necessity, each day he increased the number of hours dedicated to dreaming. He also remade the right shoulder, which was somewhat defective. At times, he was disturbed by the impression that all this had already happened. . . . In general, his days were happy; when he closed his eyes, he thought: *Now I will be with my son*. Or, more rarely: *The son I have engendered is waiting for me and will not exist if I do not go to him*.

Gradually, he began accustoming him to reality. Once he ordered him to place a flag on a faraway peak. The next day the flag was fluttering on the peak. He tried other analogous experiments, each time more audacious. With a certain bitterness, he understood that his son was ready to be born—and perhaps impatient. That night he kissed him for the first time and sent him off to the other temple whose remains were turning white downstream, across many miles of inextricable jungle and marshes. Before doing this (and so that his son should never know that he was a phantom, so that he should think himself a man like any other) he destroyed in him all memory of his years of apprenticeship.

His victory and peace became blurred with boredom. In the twilight times of dusk and dawn, he would prostrate himself before the stone figure, perhaps imagining his unreal son carrying out identical rites in other circular ruins downstream; at night he no longer dreamed, or dreamed as any man does. His perceptions of the sounds and forms of the universe became somewhat pallid: his absent son was being nourished by these diminutions of his soul. The purpose of his life had been fulfilled; the man remained in a kind of ecstasy. After a certain time, which some chroniclers prefer to compute in years and others in decades, two oarsmen awoke him at midnight; he could not see their faces, but they spoke to him of a charmed man in a temple of the North, capable of walking on fire without burning himself. The wizard suddenly remembered the words of the god. He remembered that of all the creatures that people the earth, Fire was the only one who knew his son to be a phantom. This memory, which at first calmed him, ended by tormenting him. He feared lest his son should meditate on this abnormal privilege and by some means find out he was a mere simulacrum. Not to be a man, to be a projection of another man's dreams—what an incomparable humiliation, what madness! Any father is interested in the sons he has procreated (or permitted) out of the mere confusion of happiness; it was natural that the wizard should fear for the future of that son whom he had thought out entrail by entrail, feature by feature, in a thousand and one secret nights.

His misgivings ended abruptly, but not without certain forewarnings. First (after a long drought) a remote cloud, as light as a bird, appeared on a hill; then, toward the South, the sky took on the rose color of leopard's gums; then came clouds of smoke which rusted the metal of the nights; afterwards came the panic-stricken flight of wild animals. For what had happened many centuries before was repeating itself. The ruins of the sanctuary of the god of Fire was destroyed by fire. In a dawn without birds, the wizard saw the concentric fire licking the walls. For a moment, he thought of taking refuge in the water, but then he understood that death was coming to crown his old age and absolve him from his labors. He walked toward the sheets of flame. They did not bite his flesh, they caressed him and flooded him without heat or combustion. With relief, with humiliation, with terror, he understood that he also was an illusion, that someone else was dreaming him.

—Translated by Anthony Bonner

If you like this story, you may also like "The Handsomest Drowned Man in the World" (in this section) by another Latin American writer, Gabriel García Márquez. The work of Borges and García Márquez has had a large impact on North American readers.

GOING FURTHER If you discover you have a taste for the Borgesian style you may also want to read works such as *Hopscotch* by the late Argentinian writer Julio Cortázar.

Raymond Carver (1938–1988)

RAYMOND CARVER WAS born into a working-class family in the Pacific Northwest and spent most of his childhood in Yakima, Washington, before moving to California in his early twenties and attending classes at California State College, Chico. There he studied fiction writing with John Gardner and began the apprenticeship that would lead to his creation of some of the most celebrated short fiction of his time. Critics pointed to his stories about working-class and lower-middle-class people in desperate straits as evidence of the so-called minimalist style. Carver himself often pointed out that he saw his work in the tradition of Sherwood Anderson, Ernest Hemingway, and Anton Chekhov.

Carver was also a practicing poet and essayist; perhaps in keeping with the aesthetic of minimalism, however, he never wrote a novel. He possessed a keen sense of dialogue, and the director Robert Altman joined several of his short stories together for the 1993 film *Short Cuts*.

Cathedral (1984)

1   This blind man, an old friend of my wife's, he was on his way to spend the night. His wife had died. So he was visiting the dead wife's relatives in Connecticut. He called my wife from his in-laws'. Arrangements were made. He would come by train, a five-hour trip, and my wife would meet him at the station. She hadn't seen him since she worked for him one summer in Seattle ten years ago. But she and the blind man had kept in touch. They made tapes and mailed them back and forth. I wasn't enthusiastic about his visit. He was no one I knew. And his being blind

bothered me. My idea of blindness came from the movies. In the movies, the blind moved slowly and never laughed. Sometimes they were led by seeing-eye dogs. A blind man in my house was not something I looked forward to.

That summer in Seattle she had needed a job. She didn't have any money. The man she was going to marry at the end of the summer was in officers' training school. He didn't have any money, either. But she was in love with the guy, and he was in love with her, etc. She'd seen something in the paper: HELP WANTED—*Reading to Blind Man,* and a telephone number. She phoned and went over, was hired on the spot. She'd worked with this blind man all summer. She read stuff to him, case studies, reports, that sort of thing. She helped him organize his little office in the county social-service department. They'd become good friends, my wife and the blind man. How do I know these things? She told me. And she told me something else. On her last day in the office, the blind man asked if he could touch her face. She agreed to this. She told me he touched his fingers to every part of her face, her nose—even her neck! She never forgot it. She even tried to write a poem about it. She was always trying to write a poem. She wrote a poem or two every year, usually after something really important had happened to her.

When we first started going out together, she showed me the poem. In the poem, she recalled his fingers and the way they had moved around over her face. In the poem, she talked about what she had felt at the time, about what went through her mind when the blind man touched her nose and lips. I can remember I didn't think much of the poem. Of course, I didn't tell her that. Maybe I just don't understand poetry. I admit it's not the first thing I reach for when I pick up something to read.

Anyway, this man who'd first enjoyed her favors, the officer-to-be, he'd been her childhood sweetheart. So okay. I'm saying that at the end of the summer she let the blind man run his hands over her face, said goodbye to him, married her childhood etc., who was now a commissioned officer, and she moved away from Seattle. But they'd kept in touch, she and the blind man. She made the first contact after a year or so. She called him up one night from an Air Force base in Alabama. She wanted to talk. They talked. He asked her to send him a tape and tell him about her life. She did this. She sent the tape. On the tape, she told the blind man about her husband and about their life together in the military. She told the blind man she loved her husband but she didn't like it where they lived and she didn't like it that he was a part of the military-industrial thing. She told the blind man she'd written a poem about what it was like to be an Air Force officer's wife. The poem wasn't finished yet. She was still writing it. The blind man made a tape. He sent her the tape. She made a tape. This went on for years. My wife's officer was posted to one base and then another. She sent tapes from Moody AFB, McGuire, McConnell, and finally Travis, near Sacramento, where one night she got to feeling lonely and cut off from people she kept losing in that moving-around life. She got to feeling she couldn't go it another step. She went in and swallowed all the pills and capsules in the medicine chest and washed them down with a bottle of gin. Then she got into a hot bath and passed out.

5   But instead of dying, she got sick. She threw up. Her officer—why should he have a name? he was the childhood sweetheart, and what more does he want?—came home from somewhere, found her, and called the ambulance. In time, she put it all on a tape and sent the tape to the blind man. Over the years, she put all kinds of stuff on tapes and sent the tapes off lickety-split. Next to writing a poem every year, I think it was her chief means of recreation. On one tape, she told the blind man she'd decided to live away from her officer for a time. On another tape, she told him about her divorce. She and I began going out, and of course she told her blind man about it. She told him everything, or so it seemed to me. Once she asked me if I'd like to hear the latest tape from the blind man. This was a year ago. I was on the tape, she said. So I said okay, I'd listen to it. I got us drinks and we settled down in the living room. We made ready to listen. First she inserted the tape into the player and adjusted a couple of dials. Then she pushed a lever. The tape squeaked and someone began to talk in this loud voice. She lowered the volume. After a few minutes of harmless chitchat, I heard my own name in the mouth of this stranger, this blind man I didn't even know! And then this: "From all you've said about him, I can only conclude—" But we were interrupted, a knock at the door, something, and we didn't ever get back to the tape. Maybe it was just as well. I'd heard all I wanted to.

Now this same blind man was coming to sleep in my house.

"Maybe I could take him bowling," I said to my wife. She was at the draining board doing scalloped potatoes. She put down the knife she was using and turned around.

"If you love me," she said, "you can do this for me. If you don't love me, okay. But if you had a friend, any friend, and the friend came to visit, I'd make him feel comfortable." She wiped her hands with the dish towel.

"I don't have any blind friends," I said.

10   "You don't have *any* friends," she said. "Period. Besides," she said, "goddamn it, his wife's just died! Don't you understand that? The man's lost his wife!"

I didn't answer. She'd told me a little about the blind man's wife. Her name was Beulah. Beulah! That's a name for a colored woman.

"Was his wife a Negro?" I asked.

"Are you crazy?" my wife said. "Have you just flipped or something?" She picked up a potato. I saw it hit the floor, then roll under the stove. "What's wrong with you?" she said. "Are you drunk?"

"I'm just asking," I said.

15   Right then my wife filled me in with more detail than I cared to know. I made a drink and sat at the kitchen table to listen. Pieces of the story began to fall into place.

Beulah had gone to work for the blind man the summer after my wife had stopped working for him. Pretty soon Beulah and the blind man had themselves a church wedding. It was a little wedding—who'd want to go to such a wedding in the first place?—just the two of them, plus the minister and the minister's wife. But it was a church wedding just the same. It was what Beulah had wanted, he'd said. But even then Beulah must have been carrying the cancer in her glands. After they had been inseparable for eight years—my wife's word, *inseparable*—Beulah's health went into a rapid decline. She died in a Seattle hospital room, the blind man sitting beside the bed and holding on to her hand. They'd married, lived and worked together, slept together—had sex, sure—and then the blind man had to bury her. All this without his having ever seen what the goddamned woman looked like. It was beyond my understanding. Hearing this, I felt sorry for the blind man for a little bit. And then I found myself thinking what a pitiful life this woman must have led. Imagine a woman who could never see herself as she was seen in the eyes of her loved one. A woman who could go on day after day and never receive the smallest compliment from her beloved. A woman whose husband could never read the expression on her face, be it misery or something better. Someone who could wear makeup or not—what difference to him? She could, if she wanted, wear green eye-shadow around one eye, a straight pin in her nostril, yellow slacks and purple shoes, no matter. And then to slip off into death, the blind man's hand on her hand, his blind eyes streaming tears—I'm imagining now—her last thought maybe this: that he never even knew what she looked like, and she on an express to the grave. Robert was left with a small insurance policy and half of a twenty-peso Mexican coin. The other half of the coin went into the box with her. Pathetic.

So when the time rolled around, my wife went to the depot to pick him up. With nothing to do but wait—sure, I blamed him for that—I was having a drink and watching the TV when I heard the car pull into the drive. I got up from the sofa with my drink and went to the window to have a look.

I saw my wife laughing as she parked the car. I saw her get out of the car and shut the door. She was still wearing a smile. Just amazing. She went around to the other side of the car to where the blind man was already starting to get out. This blind man, feature this, he was wearing a full beard! A beard on a blind man! Too much, I say. The blind man reached into the back seat and dragged out a suitcase. My wife took his arm, shut the car door, and, talking all the way, moved him down the drive and then up the steps to the front porch. I turned off the TV. I finished my drink, rinsed the glass, dried my hands. Then I went to the door.

My wife said, "I want you to meet Robert. Robert, this is my husband. I've told you all about him." She was beaming. She had this blind man by his coat sleeve.

20   The blind man let go of his suitcase and up came his hand.

I took it. He squeezed hard, held my hand, and then he let it go.

"I feel like we've already met," he boomed.

"Likewise," I said. I didn't know what else to say. Then I said, "Welcome. I've heard a lot about you." We began to move then, a little group, from the porch into the living room, my wife guiding him by the arm. The blind man was carrying his suitcase in his other hand. My wife said things like, "To your left here, Robert. That's right. Now watch it, there's a chair. That's it. Sit down right here. This is the sofa. We just bought this sofa two weeks ago."

I started to say something about the old sofa. I'd liked that old sofa. But I didn't say anything. Then I wanted to say something else, small-talk, about the scenic ride along the Hudson. How going *to* New York, you should sit on the right-hand side of the train, and coming *from* New York, the left-hand side.

"Did you have a good train ride?" I said. "Which side of the train did you sit on, by the way?"

"What a question, which side!" my wife said. "What's it matter which side?" she said.

"I just asked," I said.

"Right side," the blind man said. "I hadn't been on a train in nearly forty years. Not since I was a kid. With my folks. That's been a long time. I'd nearly forgotten the sensation. I have winter in my beard now," he said. "So I've been told, anyway. Do I look distinguished, my dear?" the blind man said to my wife.

"You look distinguished, Robert," she said. "Robert," she said. "Robert, it's just so good to see you."

My wife finally took her eyes off the blind man and looked at me. I had the feeling she didn't like what she saw. I shrugged.

I've never met, or personally known, anyone who was blind. This blind man was late forties, a heavy-set, balding man with stooped shoulders, as if he carried a great weight there. He wore brown slacks, brown shoes, a light-brown shirt, a tie, a sports coat. Spiffy. He also had this full beard. But he didn't use a cane and he didn't wear dark glasses. I'd always thought dark glasses were a must for the blind. Fact was, I wished he had a pair. At first glance, his eyes looked like anyone else's eyes. But if you looked close, there was something different about them. Too much white in the iris, for one thing, and the pupils seemed to move around in the sockets without his knowing it or being able to stop it. Creepy. As I stared at his face, I saw the left pupil turn in toward his nose while the other made an effort to keep in one place. But it was only an effort, for that eye was on the roam without his knowing it or wanting it to be.

I said, "Let me get you a drink. What's your pleasure? We have a little of everything. It's one of our pastimes."

"Bub, I'm a Scotch man myself," he said fast enough in this big voice.

"Right," I said. Bub! "Sure you are. I knew it."

He let his fingers touch his suitcase, which was sitting alongside the sofa. He was taking his bearings. I didn't blame him for that.

"I'll move that up to your room," my wife said.

"No, that's fine," the blind man said loudly. "It can go up when I go up."

"A little water with the Scotch?" I said.

"Very little," he said.

"I knew it," I said.

He said, "Just a tad. The Irish actor, Barry Fitzgerald? I'm like that fellow. When I drink water, Fitzgerald said, I drink water. When I drink whiskey, I drink whiskey." My wife laughed. The blind man brought his hand up under his beard. He lifted his beard slowly and let it drop.

I did the drinks, three big glasses of Scotch with a splash of water in each. Then we made ourselves comfortable and talked about Robert's travels. First the long flight from the West Coast to Connecticut, we covered that. Then from Connecticut up here by train. We had another drink concerning that leg of the trip.

I remembered having read somewhere that the blind didn't smoke because, as speculation had it, they couldn't see the smoke they exhaled. I thought I knew that much and that much only about blind people. But this blind man smoked his cigarette down to the nubbin and then lit another one. This blind man filled his ashtray and my wife emptied it.

When we sat down at the table for dinner, we had another drink. My wife heaped Robert's plate with cube steak, scalloped potatoes, green beans. I buttered him up two slices of bread. I said, "Here's bread and butter for you." I swallowed some of my drink. "Now let us pray," I said, and the blind man lowered his head. My wife looked at me, her mouth agape. "Pray the phone won't ring and the food doesn't get cold," I said.

45 We dug in. We ate everything there was to eat on the table. We ate like there was no tomorrow. We didn't talk. We ate. We scarfed. We grazed that table. We were into serious eating. The blind man had right away located his foods, he knew just where everything was on his plate. I watched with admiration as he used his knife and fork on the meat. He'd cut two pieces of meat, fork the meat into his mouth, and then go all out for the scalloped potatoes, the beans next, and then he'd tear off a hunk of buttered bread and eat that. He'd follow this up with a big drink of milk. It didn't seem to bother him to use his fingers once in a while, either.

We finished everything, including half a strawberry pie. For a few moments, we sat as if stunned. Sweat beaded on our faces. Finally, we got up from the table and left the dirty plates. We didn't look back. We took ourselves into the living room and sank into our places again. Robert and my wife sat on the sofa. I took the big chair. We had us two or three more drinks while they talked about the major things that had come to pass for them in the past ten years. For the most part, I just listened. Now and then I joined in. I didn't want him to think I'd left the room, and I didn't want her to think I was feeling left out. They talked of things that had happened to them— to them!—these past ten years. I waited in vain to hear my name on my wife's sweet lips: "And then my dear husband came into my life"—something like that. But I heard nothing of the sort. More talk of Robert. Robert had done a little of everything, it seemed, a regular blind jack-of-all-trades. But most recently he and his wife had had an Amway distributorship, from which, I gathered, they'd earned their living, such as it was. The blind man was also a ham radio operator. He talked in his loud voice about conversations he'd had with fellow operators in Guam, in the Philippines, in Alaska, and even in Tahiti. He said he'd have a lot of friends there if he ever wanted to go visit those places. From time to time, he'd turn his blind face toward me, put his hand under his beard, ask me something. How long had I been in my present position? (Three years.) Did I like my work? (I didn't.) Was I going to stay with it? (What were the options?) Finally, when I thought he was beginning to run down, I got up and turned on the TV.

My wife looked at me with irritation. She was heading toward a boil. Then she looked at the blind man and said, "Robert, do you have a TV?"

The blind man said, "My dear, I have two TVs. I have a color set and a black-and-white thing, an old relic. It's funny, but if I turn the TV on, and I'm always turning it on, I turn on the color set. It's funny, don't you think?"

I didn't know what to say to that. I had absolutely nothing to say to that. No opinion. So I watched the news program and tried to listen to what the announcer was saying.

50 "This is a color TV," the blind man said. "Don't ask me how, but I can tell."

"We traded up a while ago," I said.

The blind man had another taste of his drink. He lifted his beard, sniffed it, and let it fall. He leaned forward on the sofa. He positioned his ashtray on the coffee table, then put the lighter to his cigarette. He leaned back on the sofa and crossed his legs at the ankles.

My wife covered her mouth, and then she yawned. She stretched. She said, "I think I'll go upstairs and put on my robe. I think I'll change into something else. Robert, you make yourself comfortable," she said.

"I'm comfortable," the blind man said.

55 "I want you to feel comfortable in this house," she said.

"I am comfortable," the blind man said.

After she'd left the room, he and I listened to the weather report and then to the sports roundup. By that time, she'd been gone so long I didn't know if she was going to come back. I thought she might have gone to bed. I wished she'd come back downstairs. I didn't want to be left alone with

a blind man. I asked if he wanted to smoke some dope with me. I said I'd just rolled a number. I
hadn't, but I planned to do so in about two shakes.

"I'll try some with you," he said.

"Damn right," I said. "That's the stuff."

I got our drinks and sat down on the sofa with him. Then I rolled us two fat numbers. I lit one
and passed it. I brought it to his fingers. He took it and inhaled.

"Hold it as long as you can," I said. I could tell he didn't know the first thing.

My wife came back downstairs wearing her pink robe and her pink slippers.

"What do I smell?" she said.

"We thought we'd have us some cannabis," I said.

My wife gave me a savage look. Then she looked at the blind man and said, "Robert, I didn't
know you smoked."

He said, "I do now, my dear. There's a first time for everything. But I don't feel anything yet."

"This stuff is pretty mellow," I said. "This stuff is mild. It's dope you can reason with," I said.
"It doesn't mess you up."

"Not much it doesn't, bub," he said, and laughed.

My wife sat on the sofa between the blind man and me. I passed her the number. She took
it and toked and then passed it back to me. "Which way is this going?" she said. Then she said,
"I shouldn't be smoking this. I can hardly keep my eyes open as it is. That dinner did me in. I
shouldn't have eaten so much."

"It was the strawberry pie," the blind man said. "That's what did it," he said, and he laughed
his big laugh. Then he shook his head.

"There's more strawberry pie," I said.

"Do you want some more, Robert?" my wife said.

"Maybe in a little while," he said.

We gave our attention to the TV. My wife yawned again. She said, "Your bed is made up when
you feel like going to bed, Robert. I know you must have had a long day. When you're ready to go
to bed, say so." She pulled his arm. "Robert?"

He came to and said, "I've had a real nice time. This beats tapes, doesn't it?"

I said, "Coming at you," and I put the number between his fingers. He inhaled, held the
smoke, and then let it go. It was like he'd been doing it since he was nine years old.

"Thanks, bub," he said. "But I think this is all for me. I think I'm beginning to feel it," he said.
He held the burning roach out for my wife.

"Same here," she said. "Ditto. Me, too." She took the roach and passed it to me. "I may just sit
here for a while between you two guys with my eyes closed. But don't let me bother you, okay?
Either one of you. If it bothers you, say so. Otherwise, I may just sit here with my eyes closed until
you're ready to go to bed," she said. "Your bed's made up, Robert, when you're ready. It's right next
to our room at the top of the stairs. We'll show you up when you're ready. You wake me up now,
you guys, if I fall asleep." She said that and then she closed her eyes and went to sleep.

The news program ended. I got up and changed the channel. I sat back down on the sofa.
I wished my wife hadn't pooped out. Her head lay across the back of the sofa, her mouth open.
She'd turned so that her robe had slipped away from her legs, exposing a juicy thigh. I reached
to draw her robe back over her, and it was then that I glanced at the blind man. What the hell! I
flipped the robe open again.

"You say when you want some strawberry pie," I said.

"I will," he said.

I said, "Are you tired? Do you want me to take you up to your bed? Are you ready to hit
the hay?"

"Not yet," he said. "No, I'll stay up with you, bub. If that's all right. I'll stay up until you're
ready to turn in. We haven't had a chance to talk. Know what I mean? I feel like me and her
monopolized the evening." He lifted his beard and he let it fall. He picked up his cigarettes and
his lighter.

"That's all right," I said. Then I said, "I'm glad for the company."

85   And I guess I was. Every night I smoked dope and stayed up as long as I could before I fell asleep. My wife and I hardly ever went to bed at the same time. When I did go to sleep, I had these dreams. Sometimes I'd wake up from one of them, my heart going crazy.

Something about the church and the Middle Ages was on the TV. Not your run-of-the-mill TV fare. I wanted to watch something else. I turned to the other channels. But there was nothing on them, either. So I turned back to the first channel and apologized.

"Bub, it's all right," the blind man said. "It's fine with me. Whatever you want to watch is okay. I'm always learning something. Learning never ends. It won't hurt me to learn something tonight. I got ears," he said.

We didn't say anything for a time. He was leaning forward with his head turned at me, his right ear aimed in the direction of the set. Very disconcerting. Now and then his eyelids dropped and then they snapped open again. Now and then he put his fingers into his beard and tugged, like he was thinking about something he was hearing on the television.

On the screen, a group of men wearing cowls was being set upon and tormented by men dressed in skeleton costumes and men dressed as devils. The men dressed as devils wore devil masks, horns, and long tails. This pageant was part of a procession. The Englishman who was narrating the thing said it took place in Spain once a year. I tried to explain to the blind man what was happening.

90   "Skeletons," he said. "I know about skeletons," he said, and he nodded.

The TV showed this one cathedral. Then there was a long, slow look at another one. Finally, the picture switched to the famous one in Paris, with its flying buttresses and its spires reaching up to the clouds. The camera pulled away to show the whole of the cathedral rising above the skyline.

There were times when the Englishman who was telling the thing would shut up, would simply let the camera move around over the cathedrals. Or else the camera would tour the countryside, men in fields walking behind oxen. I waited as long as I could. Then I felt I had to say something. I said, "They're showing the outside of this cathedral now. Gargoyles. Little statues carved to look like monsters. Now I guess they're in Italy. Yeah, they're in Italy. There's paintings on the walls of this one church."

"Are those fresco paintings, bub?" he asked, and he sipped from his drink.

I reached for my glass. But it was empty. I tried to remember what I could remember. "You're asking me are those frescoes?" I said. "That's a good question. I don't know."

95   The camera moved to a cathedral outside Lisbon. The differences in the Portuguese cathedral compared with the French and Italian were not that great. But they were there. Mostly the interior stuff. Then something occurred to me, and I said, "Something has occurred to me. Do you have any idea what a cathedral is? What they look like, that is? Do you follow me? If somebody says cathedral to you, do you have any notion what they're talking about? Do you know the difference between that and a Baptist church, say?"

He let the smoke dribble from his mouth. "I know they took hundreds of workers fifty or a hundred years to build," he said. "I just heard the man say that, of course. I know generations of the same families worked on a cathedral. I heard him say that, too. The men who began their life's work on them, they never lived to see the completion of their work. In that wise, bub, they're no different from the rest of us, right?" He laughed. Then his eyelids drooped again. His head nodded. He seemed to be snoozing. Maybe he was imagining himself in Portugal. The TV was showing another cathedral now. This one was in Germany. The Englishman's voice droned on. "Cathedrals," the blind man said. He sat up and rolled his head back and forth. "If you want the truth, bub, that's about all I know. What I just said. What I heard him say. But maybe you could describe one to me? I wish you'd do it. I'd like that. If you want to know, I really don't have a good idea."

I stared hard at the shot of the cathedral on the TV. How could I even begin to describe it? But say my life depended on it. Say my life was being threatened by an insane guy who said I had to do it or else.

I stared some more at the cathedral before the picture flipped off into the countryside. There was no use. I turned to the blind man and said, "To begin with, they're very tall." I was looking around the room for clues. "They reach way up. Up and up. Toward the sky. They're so big, some of them, they have to have these supports. To help hold them up, so to speak. These supports are called buttresses. They remind me of viaducts, for some reason. But maybe you don't know viaducts, either? Sometimes the cathedrals have devils and such carved into the front. Sometimes lords and ladies. Don't ask me why this is," I said.

He was nodding. The whole upper part of his body seemed to be moving back and forth.

"I'm not doing so good, am I?" I said.

He stopped nodding and leaned forward on the edge of the sofa. As he listened to me, he was running his fingers through his beard. I wasn't getting through to him, I could see that. But he waited for me to go on just the same. He nodded, like he was trying to encourage me. I tried to think what else to say. "They're really big," I said. "They're massive. They're built of stone. Marble, too, sometimes. In those olden days, when they built cathedrals, men wanted to be close to God. In those olden days, God was an important part of everyone's life. You could tell this from their cathedral-building. I'm sorry," I said, "but it looks like that's the best I can do for you. I'm just no good at it."

"That's all right, bub," the blind man said. "Hey, listen. I hope you don't mind my asking you. Can I ask you something? Let me ask you a simple question, yes or no. I'm just curious and there's no offense. You're my host. But let me ask if you are in any way religious? You don't mind my asking?"

I shook my head. He couldn't see that, though. A wink is the same as a nod to a blind man. "I guess I don't believe in it. In anything. Sometimes it's hard. You know what I'm saying?"

"Sure, I do," he said.

"Right," I said.

The Englishman was still holding forth. My wife sighed in her sleep. She drew a long breath and went on with her sleeping.

"You'll have to forgive me," I said. "But I can't tell you what a cathedral looks like. It just isn't in me to do it. I can't do any more than I've done."

The blind man sat very still, his head down, as he listened to me.

I said, "The truth is, cathedrals don't mean anything special to me. Nothing. Cathedrals. They're something to look at on late-night TV. That's all they are."

It was then that the blind man cleared his throat. He brought something up. He took a handkerchief from his back pocket. Then he said, "I get it, bub. It's okay. It happens. Don't worry about it," he said. "Hey, listen to me. Will you do me a favor? I got an idea. Why don't you find us some heavy paper? And a pen. We'll do something. We'll draw one together. Get us a pen and some heavy paper. Go on, bub, get the stuff," he said.

So I went upstairs. My legs felt like they didn't have any strength in them. They felt like they did after I'd done some running. In my wife's room, I looked around. I found some ballpoints in a little basket on her table. And then I tried to think where to look for the kind of paper he was talking about.

Downstairs, in the kitchen, I found a shopping bag with onion skins in the bottom of the bag. I emptied the bag and shook it. I brought it into the living room and sat down with it near his legs. I moved some things, smoothed the wrinkles from the bag, spread it out on the coffee table.

The blind man got down from the sofa and sat next to me on the carpet.

He ran his fingers over the paper. He went up and down the sides of the paper. The edges, even the edges. He fingered the corners.

"All right," he said. "All right, let's do her."

He found my hand, the hand with the pen. He closed his hand over my hand. "Go ahead, bub, draw," he said. "Draw. You'll see. I'll follow along with you. It'll be okay. Just begin now like I'm telling you. You'll see. Draw," the blind man said.

So I began. First I drew a box that looked like a house. It could have been the house I lived in. Then I put a roof on it. At either end of the roof, I drew spires. Crazy.

"Swell," he said. "Terrific. You're doing fine," he said. "Never thought anything like this could happen in your lifetime, did you, bub? Well, it's a strange life, we all know that. Go on now. Keep it up."

I put in windows with arches. I drew flying buttresses. I hung great doors. I couldn't stop. The TV station went off the air. I put down the pen and closed and opened my fingers. The blind man felt around over the paper. He moved the tips of his fingers over the paper, all over what I had drawn, and he nodded.

120   "Doing fine," the blind man said.

I took up the pen again, and he found my hand. I kept at it. I'm no artist. But I kept drawing just the same.

My wife opened up her eyes and gazed at us. She sat up on the sofa, her robe hanging open. She said, "What are you doing? Tell me, I want to know."

I didn't answer her.

The blind man said, "We're drawing a cathedral. Me and him are working on it. Press hard," he said to me. "That's right. That's good," he said. "Sure. You got it, bub. I can tell. You didn't think you could. But you can, can't you? You're cooking with gas now. You know what I'm saying? We're going to really have us something here in a minute. How's the old arm?" he said. "Put some people in there now. What's a cathedral without people?"

125   My wife said, "What's going on? Robert, what are you doing? What's going on?"

"It's all right," he said to her. "Close your eyes now," the blind man said to me.

I did it. I closed them just like he said.

"Are they closed?" he said. "Don't fudge."

"They're closed," I said.

130   "Keep them that way," he said. He said, "Don't stop now. Draw."

So we kept on with it. His fingers rode my fingers as my hand went over the paper. It was like nothing else in my life up to now.

Then he said, "I think that's it. I think you got it," he said. "Take a look. What do you think?"

But I had my eyes closed. I thought I'd keep them that way for a little longer. I thought it was something I ought to do.

"Well?" he said. "Are you looking?"

135   My eyes were still closed. I was in my house. I knew that. But I didn't feel like I was inside anything.

"It's really something," I said.

Critics coined the term "minimalism" to describe a pared down type of realistic story. Carver didn't like the term. Nor did some of the other writers associated with this group, such as Amy Hempel. If you like "Cathedral," you may also want to read Hempel's "San Francisco" (in this chapter).

GOING FURTHER   Jayne Anne Phillips writes stories made up of brief lyrical bursts of events. *Black Tickets* is a collection of her stories that may be of interest to those who like Carver.

Anton Chekhov (1860–1904)

RUSSIAN WRITER ANTON Chekhov was born into poverty but trained to become a physician. Even at the start of his medical practice, he was trying out short fictional sketches on magazine editors in Moscow, discovering that he had a talent for creating characters with a few brief lines of prose. Around 1888 Chekhov began writing more extended pieces of fiction, such as "The Kiss" and "Gusev," that were acclaimed for their artistic merit, not just their entertainment value. Well known to his contemporaries as a writer of numerous stories, Chekhov counted Leo Tolstoy among his early admirers. Later in life, Chekhov wrote plays, including *The Seagull* (1896) and *The Cherry*

Orchard (1904); his stage works have become nearly as influential as his short stories, affecting playwrights such as George Bernard Shaw and Tennessee Williams. Today, Chekhov's work is even more widely read than during his lifetime, and many consider him to be the "father" of the modern short story (see his "Rapture" in chapter 2).

The Lady with the Pet Dog (1899)

I

1   A new person, it was said, had appeared on the esplanade: a lady with a pet dog. Dmitry Dmitrich Gurov, who had spent a fortnight at Yalta and had got used to the place, had also begun to take an interest in new arrivals. As he sat in Vernet's confectionery shop, he saw, walking on the esplanade, a fair-haired young woman of medium height, wearing a beret; a white Pomeranian was trotting behind her.

And afterwards he met her in the public garden and in the square several times a day. She walked alone, always wearing the same beret and always with the white dog; no one knew who she was and everyone called her simply "the lady with the pet dog."

"If she is here alone without husband or friends," Gurov reflected, "it wouldn't be a bad thing to make her acquaintance."

He was under forty, but he already had a daughter twelve years old, and two sons at school. They had found a wife for him when he was very young, a student in his second year, and by now she seemed half as old again as he. She was a tall, erect woman with dark eyebrows, stately and dignified and, as she said of herself, intellectual. She read a great deal, used simplified spelling in her letters, called her husband, not Dmitry, but Dimitry, while he privately considered her of limited intelligence, narrow-minded, dowdy, was afraid of her, and did not like to be at home. He had begun being unfaithful to her long ago—had been unfaithful to her often and, probably for that reason, almost always spoke ill of women, and when they were talked of in his presence used to call them "the inferior race."

5   It seemed to him that he had been sufficiently tutored by bitter experience to call them what he pleased, and yet he could not have lived without "the inferior race" for two days together. In the company of men he was bored and ill at ease, he was chilly and uncommunicative with them; but when he was among women he felt free, and knew what to speak to them about and how to comport himself; and even to be silent with them was no strain on him. In his appearance, in his character, in his whole makeup there was something attractive and elusive that disposed women in his favor and allured them. He knew that, and some force seemed to draw him to them, too.

Oft-repeated and really bitter experience had taught him long ago that with decent people—particularly Moscow people—who are irresolute and slow to move, every affair which at first seems a light and charming adventure inevitably grows into a whole problem of extreme complexity, and in the end a painful situation is created. But at every new meeting with an interesting woman this lesson of experience seemed to slip from his memory, and he was eager for life, and everything seemed so simple and diverting.

One evening while he was dining in the public garden the lady in the beret walked up without haste to take the next table. Her expression, her gait, her dress, and the way she did her hair told him that she belonged to the upper class, that she was married, that she was in Yalta for the first time and alone, and that she was bored there. The stories told of the immorality in Yalta are to a great extent untrue; he despised them, and knew that such stories were made up for the most part by persons who would have been glad to sin themselves if they had had the chance; but when the lady sat down at the next table three paces from him, he recalled these stories of easy conquests, of trips to the mountains, and the tempting thought of swift, fleeting liaison, a romance with an unknown woman of whose very name he was ignorant suddenly took hold him.

He beckoned invitingly to the Pomeranian, and when the dog approached him, shook his finger at it. The Pomeranian growled; Gurov threatened it again.

The lady glanced at him and at once dropped her eyes.

10 "He doesn't bite," she said and blushed.

"May I give him a bone?" he asked; and when she nodded he inquired affably, "Have you been in Yalta long?"

"About five days."

"And I am dragging out the second week here."

There was a short silence.

15 "Time passes quickly, and yet it is so dull here!" she said, not looking at him.

"It's only the fashion to say it's dull here. A provincial will live in Belyov or Zhizdra and not be bored, but when he comes here it's 'Oh, the dullness! Oh, the dust!' One would think he came from Granada."

She laughed. Then both continued eating in silence, like strangers, but after dinner they walked together and there sprang up between them the light banter of people who are free and contented, to whom it does not matter where they go or what they talk about. They walked and talked of the strange light on the sea; the water was a soft, warm, lilac color, and there was a golden band of moonlight upon it. They talked of how sultry it was after a hot day. Gurov told her that he was a native of Moscow, that he had studied languages and literature at the university, but had a post in a bank; that at one time he had trained to become an opera singer but had given it up, that he owned two houses in Moscow. And he learned from her that she had grown up in Petersburg, but had lived in S——— since her marriage two years previously, that she was going to stay in Yalta for about another month, and that her husband, who needed a rest, too, might perhaps come to fetch her. She was not certain whether her husband was a member of a Government Board or served on a Zemstvo Council, and this amused her. And Gurov learned too that her name was Anna Sergeyevna.

Afterwards in his room at the hotel he thought about her—and was certain that he would meet her the next day. It was bound to happen. Getting into bed he recalled that she had been a schoolgirl only recently, doing lessons like his own daughter; he thought how much timidity and angularity there was still in her laugh and her manner of talking with a stranger. It must have been the first time in her life that she was alone in a setting in which she was followed, looked at, and spoken to for one secret purpose alone, which she could hardly fail to guess. He thought of her slim, delicate throat, her lovely gray eyes.

"There's something pathetic about her, though," he thought, and dropped off.

II

20 A week had passed since they had struck up an acquaintance. It was a holiday. It was close indoors, while in the street the wind whirled the dust about and blew people's hats off. One was thirsty all day, and Gurov often went into the restaurant and offered Anna Sergeyevna a soft drink or ice cream. One did not know what to do with oneself.

In the evening when the wind had abated they went out on the pier to watch the steamer come in. There were a great many people walking about the dock; they had come to welcome someone and they were carrying bunches of flowers. And two peculiarities of a festive Yalta crowd stood out: the elderly ladies were dressed like young ones and there were many generals.

Owing to the choppy sea, the steamer arrived late, after sunset, and it was a long time tacking about before it put in at the pier. Anna Sergeyevna peered at the steamer and the passengers through her lorgnette as though looking for acquaintances, and whenever she turned to Gurov her eyes were shining. She talked a great deal and asked questions jerkily, forgetting the next moment what she had asked; then she lost her lorgnette in the crush.

The festive crowd began to disperse; it was now too dark to see people's faces; there was no wind any more, but Gurov and Anna Sergeyevna still stood as though waiting to see someone else come off the steamer. Anna Sergeyevna was silent now, and sniffed her flowers without looking at Gurov.

"The weather has improved this evening," he said. "Where shall we go now? Shall we drive somewhere?"

She did not reply.

Then he looked at her intently, and suddenly embraced her and kissed her on the lips, and the moist fragrance of her flowers enveloped him; and at once he looked round him anxiously, wondering if anyone had seen them.

"Let us go to your place," he said softly. And they walked off together rapidly.

The air in her room was close and there was the smell of the perfume she had bought at the Japanese shop. Looking at her, Gurov thought: "What encounters life offers!" From the past he preserved the memory of carefree, good-natured women whom love made gay and who were grateful to him for the happiness he gave them, however brief it might be; and of women like his wife who loved without sincerity, with too many words, affectedly, hysterically, with an expression that it was not love or passion that engaged them but something more significant; and of two or three others, very beautiful, frigid women, across whose faces would suddenly flit a rapacious expression—an obstinate desire to take from life more than it could give, and these were women no longer young, capricious, unreflecting, domineering, unintelligent, and when Gurov grew cold to them their beauty aroused his hatred, and the lace on their lingerie seemed to him to resemble scales.

But here there was the timidity, the angularity of inexperienced youth, a feeling of awkwardness; and there was a sense of embarrassment, as though someone had suddenly knocked at the door. Anna Sergeyevna, "the lady with the pet dog," treated what had happened in a peculiar way, very seriously, as though it were her fall—so it seemed, and this was odd and inappropriate. Her features drooped and faded, and her long hair hung down sadly on either side of her face; she grew pensive and her dejected pose was that of a Magdalene in a picture by an old master.

"It's not right," she said. "You don't respect me now, you first of all."

There was a watermelon on the table. Gurov cut himself a slice and began eating it without haste. They were silent for at least half an hour.

There was something touching about Anna Sergeyevna; she had the purity of a well-bred, naive woman who has seen little of life. The single candle burning on the table barely illumined her face, yet it was clear that she was unhappy.

"Why should I stop respecting you, darling?" asked Gurov. "You don't know what you're saying."

"God forgive me," she said, and her eyes filled with tears. "It's terrible."

"It's as though you were trying to exonerate yourself."

"How can I exonerate myself? No. I am a bad, low woman; I despise myself and I have no thought of exonerating myself. It's not my husband but myself I have deceived. And not only just now; I have been deceiving myself for a long time. My husband may be a good, honest man, but he is a flunkey! I don't know what he does, what his work is, but I know he is a flunkey! I was twenty when I married him. I was tormented by curiosity; I wanted something better. 'There must be a different sort of life,' I said to myself. I wanted to live! To live, to live! Curiosity kept eating at me—you don't understand it, but I swear to God I could no longer control myself; something was going on in me: I could not be held back. I told my husband I was ill, and came here. And here I have been walking about as though in a daze, as though I were mad; and now I have become a vulgar, vile woman whom anyone may despise."

Gurov was already bored with her; he was irritated by her naive tone, by her repentance, so unexpected and so out of place; but for the tears in her eyes he might have thought she was joking or play-acting.

"I don't understand, my dear," he said softly. "What do you want?"

She hid her face on his breast and pressed close to him.

"Believe me, believe me, I beg you," she said, "I love honesty and purity, and sin is loathsome to me; I don't know what I'm doing. Simple people say, 'The Evil One has led me astray.' And I may say of myself now that the Evil One has led me astray."

"Quiet, quiet," he murmured.

He looked into her fixed, frightened eyes, kissed her, spoke to her softly and affectionately, and by degrees she calmed down, and her gaiety returned; both began laughing.

Afterwards when they went out there was not a soul on the esplanade. The town with its cypresses looked quite dead, but the sea was still sounding as it broke upon the beach; a single launch was rocking on the waves and on it a lantern was blinking sleepily.

They found a cab and drove to Oreanda.

45 "I found out your surname in the hall just now: it was written on the board—von Dideritz," said Gurov. "Is your husband German?"

"No; I believe his grandfather was German, but he is Greek Orthodox himself."

At Oreanda they sat on a bench not far from the church, looked down at the sea, and were silent. Yalta was barely visible through the morning mist; white clouds rested motionlessly on the mountaintops. The leaves did not stir on the trees, cicadas twanged, and the monotonous muffled sound of the sea that rose from below spoke of the peace, the eternal sleep awaiting us. So it rumbled below when there was no Yalta, no Oreanda here; so it rumbles now, and it will rumble as indifferently and as hollowly when we are no more. And in this constancy, in this complete indifference to the life and death of each of us, there lies, perhaps, a pledge of our eternal salvation, of the unceasing advance of life upon earth, of unceasing movement towards perfection. Sitting beside a young woman who in the dawn seemed so lovely, Gurov, soothed and spellbound by these magical surroundings—the sea, the mountains, the clouds, the wide sky—thought how everything is really beautiful in this world when one reflects: everything except what we think or do ourselves when we forget the higher aims of life and our own human dignity.

A man strolled up to them—probably a guard—looked at them and walked away. And this detail, too, seemed so mysterious and beautiful. They saw a steamer arrive from Feodosia, its lights extinguished in the glow of dawn.

"There is dew on the grass," said Anna Sergeyevna, after a silence.

50 "Yes, it's time to go home."

They returned to the city.

Then they met every day at twelve o'clock on the esplanade, lunched and dined together, took walks, admired the sea. She complained that she slept badly, that she had palpitations, asked the same questions, troubled now by jealousy and now by the fear that he did not respect her sufficiently. And often in the square or the public garden, when there was no one near them, he suddenly drew her to him and kissed her passionately. Complete idleness, these kisses in broad daylight exchanged furtively in dread of someone's seeing them, the heat, the smell of the sea, and the continual flitting before his eyes of idle, well-dressed, well-fed people, worked a complete change in him; he kept telling Anna Sergeyevna how beautiful she was, how seductive, was urgently passionate; he would not move a step away from her, while she was often pensive and continually pressed him to confess that he did not respect her, did not love her in the least, and saw in her nothing but a common woman. Almost every evening rather late they drove somewhere out of town, to Oreanda or to the waterfall; and the excursion was always a success, the scenery invariably impressed them as beautiful and magnificent.

They were expecting her husband, but a letter came from him saying that he had eye-trouble, and begging his wife to return home as soon as possible. Anna Sergeyevna made haste to go.

"It's a good thing I am leaving," she said to Gurov. "It's the hand of Fate!"

55 She took a carriage to the railway station, and he went with her. They were driving the whole day. When she had taken her place in the express, and when the second bell had rung, she said, "Let me look at you once more—let me look at you again. Like this."

She was not crying but was so sad that she seemed ill, and her face was quivering.

"I shall be thinking of you—remembering you," she said. "God bless you; be happy. Don't remember evil against me. We are parting forever—it has to be, for we ought never to have met. Well, God bless you."

The train moved off rapidly, its lights soon vanished, and a minute later there was no sound of it, as though everything had conspired to end as quickly as possible that sweet trance, that madness. Left alone on the platform, and gazing into the dark distance, Gurov listened to the twang of the grasshoppers and the hum of the telegraph wires, feeling as though he had just waked up. And he reflected, musing, that there had now been another episode or adventure in his life, and it, too, was at an end, and nothing was left of it but a memory. He was moved, sad, and slightly remorseful: this young woman whom he would never meet again had not been happy with him; he had been warm and affectionate with her, but yet in his manner, his tone, and his caresses there had been a shade of light irony, the slightly coarse arrogance of a happy male who was, besides, almost twice her age. She had constantly called him kind, exceptional, high-minded; obviously he had seemed to her different from what he really was, so he had involuntarily deceived her.

Here at the station there was already a scent of autumn in the air; it was a chilly evening.

"It is time for me to go north, too," thought Gurov as he left the platform. "High time!"

III

At home in Moscow the winter routine was already established: the stoves were heated, and in the morning it was still dark when the children were having breakfast and getting ready for school, and the nurse would light the lamp for a short time. There were frosts already. When the first snow falls, on the first day the sleighs are out, it is pleasant to see the white earth, the white roofs; one draws easy, delicious breaths, and the season brings back the days of one's youth. The old limes and birches, white with hoar-frost, have a good-natured look; they are closer to one's heart than cypresses and palms, and near them one no longer wants to think of mountains and the sea.

Gurov, a native of Moscow, arrived there on a fine frosty day, and when he put on his fur coat and warm gloves and took a walk along Petrovka, and when on Saturday night he heard the bells ringing, his recent trip and the places he had visited lost all charm for him. Little by little he became immersed in Moscow life, greedily read three newspapers a day, and declared that he did not read the Moscow papers on principle. He already felt a longing for restaurants, clubs, formal dinners, anniversary celebrations, and it flattered him to entertain distinguished lawyers and actors, and to play cards with a professor at the physicians' club. He could eat a whole portion of meat stewed with pickled cabbage and served in a pan, Moscow style.

A month or so would pass and the image of Anna Sergeyevna, it seemed to him, would become misty in his memory, and only from time to time he would dream of her with her touching smile as he dreamed of others. But more than a month went by, winter came into its own, and everything was still clear in his memory as though he had parted from Anna Sergeyevna only yesterday. And his memories glowed more and more vividly. When in the evening stillness the voices of his children preparing their lessons reached his study, or when he listened to a song or to an organ playing in a restaurant, or when the storm howled in the chimney, suddenly everything would rise up in his memory: what had happened on the pier and the early morning with the mist on the mountains, and the steamer coming from Feodosia, and the kisses. He would pace about his room a long time, remembering and smiling; then his memories passed into reveries, and in his imagination the past would mingle with what was to come. He did not dream of Anna Sergeyevna, but she followed him about everywhere and watched him. When he shut his eyes he saw her before him as though she were there in the flesh; and she seemed to him lovelier, younger, tenderer than she had been; and he imagined himself a finer man than he had been in Yalta. Of evenings she peered out at him from the bookcase, from the fireplace, from the corner—he heard her breathing, the caressing rustle of her clothes. In the street he followed the women with his eyes, looking for someone who resembled her.

Already he was tormented by a strong desire to share his memories with someone. But in his home it was impossible to talk of his love, and he had no one to talk to outside; certainly he could not confide in his tenants or in anyone at the bank. And what was there to talk to about? He hadn't loved her then, had he? Had there been anything beautiful, poetical, edifying, or simply interesting in his relations with Anna Sergeyevna? And he was forced to talk vaguely of love, of women, and no one guessed what he meant; only his wife would twitch her black eyebrows and say, "The part of a philanderer does not suit you at all, Dimitry."

One evening, coming out of the physician's club with an official with whom he had been playing cards, he could not resist saying:

"If you only knew what a fascinating woman I became acquainted with at Yalta!"

The official got into his sledge and was driving away, but turned suddenly and shouted: "Dmitry Dmitrich!"

"What is it?"

"You were right this evening: the sturgeon was a bit high."

70   These words, so commonplace, for some reason moved Gurov to indignation, and struck him as degrading and unclean. What savage manners, what mugs! What stupid nights, what dull, humdrum days! Frenzied gambling, gluttony, drunkenness, continual talk always about the same things! Futile pursuits and conversations always about the same topics take up the better part of one's time, the better part of one's strength, and in the end there is left a life clipped and wingless, an absurd mess, and there is no escaping or getting away from it—just as though one were in a madhouse or a prison.

Gurov, boiling with indignation, did not sleep all night. And he had a headache all the next day. And the following nights too he slept badly; he sat up in bed, thinking, or paced up and down his room. He was fed up with his children, fed up with the bank; he had no desire to go anywhere or to talk of anything.

In December during the holidays he prepared to take a trip and told his wife he was going to Petersburg to do what he could for a young friend—and he set off for S———. What for? He did not know, himself. He wanted to see Anna Sergeyevna and talk with her, to arrange a rendezvous if possible.

He arrived at S——— in the morning, and at the hotel took the best room, in which the floor was covered with gray army cloth, and on the table there was an inkstand, gray with dust and topped by a figure on horseback, its hat in its raised hand and its head broken off. The porter gave him the necessary information: von Dideritz lived in a house of his own on Staro-Goncharnaya Street, not far from the hotel: he was rich and lived well and kept his own horses; everyone in the town knew him. The porter pronounced the name: "Dridiritz."

Without haste Gurov made his way to Staro-Goncharnaya Street and found the house. Directly opposite the house stretched a long gray fence studded with nails.

75   "A fence like that would make one run away," thought Gurov, looking now at the fence, now at the windows of the house.

He reflected: this was a holiday, and the husband was apt to be at home. And in any case, it would be tactless to go into the house and disturb her. If he were to send her a note, it might fall into her husband's hands, and that might spoil everything. The best thing was to rely on chance. And he kept walking up and down the street and along the fence, waiting for the chance. He saw a beggar go in at the gate and heard the dogs attack him; then an hour later he heard a piano, and the sound came to him faintly and indistinctly. Probably it was Anna Sergeyevna playing. The front door opened suddenly, and an old woman came out, followed by the familiar white Pomeranian. Gurov was on the point of calling to the dog, but his heart began beating violently, and in his excitement he could not remember the Pomeranian's name.

He kept walking up and down, and hated the gray fence more and more, and by now he thought irritably that Anna Sergeyevna had forgotten him, and was perhaps already diverting herself with another man, and that that was very natural in a young woman who from morning till night had to look at that damn fence. He went back to his hotel room and sat on the couch for a long while, not knowing what to do, then he had dinner and a long nap.

"How stupid and annoying all this is!" he thought when he woke and looked at the dark windows: it was already evening. "Here I've had a good sleep for some reason. What am I going to do at night?"

He sat on the bed, which was covered with a cheap gray blanket of the kind seen in hospitals, and he twitted himself in his vexation:

80   "So there's your lady with the pet dog. There's your adventure. A nice place to cool your heels in."

That morning at the station a playbill in large letters had caught his eye. *The Geisha* was to be given for the first time. He thought of this and drove to the theater.

"It's quite possible that she goes to first nights," he thought.

The theater was full. As in all provincial theaters, there was a haze above the chandelier, the gallery was noisy and restless; in the front row, before the beginning of the performance the local dandies were standing with their hands clasped behind their backs; in the Governor's box the Governor's daughter, wearing a boa, occupied the front seat, while the Governor himself hid modestly behind the portiere and only his hands were visible; the curtain swayed; the orchestra was a long time tuning up. While the audience were coming in and taking their seats, Gurov scanned the faces eagerly.

Anna Sergeyevna, too, came in. She sat down in the third row, and when Gurov looked at her his heart contracted, and he understood clearly that in the whole world there was no human being so near, so precious, and so important to him; she, this little, undistinguished woman, lost in a provincial crowd, with a vulgar lorgnette in her hand, filled his whole life now, was his sorrow and his joy, the only happiness that he now desired for himself, and to the sounds of the bad orchestra, of the miserable local violins, he thought how lovely she was. He thought and dreamed.

A young man with small side-whiskers, very tall and stooped, came in with Anna Sergeyevna and sat down beside her; he nodded his head at every step and seemed to be bowing continually. Probably this was the husband whom at Yalta, in an excess of bitter feeling, she had called a flunkey. And there really was in his lanky figure, his side-whiskers, his small bald patch, something of a flunkey's retiring manner; his smile was mawkish, and in his buttonhole there was an academic badge like a waiter's number.

During the first intermission the husband went out to have a smoke; she remained in her seat. Gurov, who was also sitting in the orchestra, went up to her and said in a shaky voice, with a forced smile:

"Good evening!"

She glanced at him and turned pale, then looked at him again in horror, unable to believe her eyes, and gripped the fan and the lorgnette tightly together in her hands, evidently trying to keep herself from fainting. Both were silent. She was sitting, he was standing, frightened by her distress and not daring to take a seat beside her. The violins and the flute that were being tuned up sang out. He suddenly felt frightened: it seemed as if all the people in the boxes were looking at them. She got up and went hurriedly to the exit; he followed her, and both of them walked blindly along the corridors and up and down stairs, and figures in the uniforms prescribed for magistrates, teachers, and officials of the Department of Crown Lands, all wearing badges, flitted before their eyes, as did also ladies, and fur coats on hangers; they were conscious of drafts and the smell of stale tobacco. And Gurov, whose heart was beating violently, thought:

"Oh, Lord! Why are these people here and this orchestra!"

And at that instant he suddenly recalled how when he had seen Anna Sergeyevna off at the station he had said to himself that all was over between them and that they would never meet again. But how distant the end still was!

On the narrow, gloomy staircase over which it said "To the Amphitheatre," she stopped.

"How you frightened me!" she said, breathing hard, still pale and stunned. "Oh, how you frightened me! I am barely alive. Why did you come? Why?"

"But do understand, Anna, do understand—" he said hurriedly, under his breath. "I implore you, do understand—"

She looked at him with fear, with entreaty, with love; she looked at him intently, to keep his features more distinctly in her memory.

"I suffer so," she went on, not listening to him. "All this time I have been thinking of nothing but you; I live only by the thought of you. And I wanted to forget, to forget; but why, oh, why have you come?"

On the landing above them two high school boys were looking down and smoking, but it was all the same to Gurov; he drew Anna Sergeyevna to him and began kissing her face and her hands.

"What are you doing, what are you doing!" she was saying in horror, pushing him away. "We have lost our senses. Go away today; go away at once—I conjure you by all that is sacred, I implore you—People are coming this way!"

Someone was walking up the stairs.

"You must leave," Anna Sergeyevna went on in a whisper. "Do you hear, Dmitry Dmitrich? I will come and see you in Moscow. I have never been happy; I am unhappy now, and I never, never shall be happy, never! So don't make me suffer still more! I swear I'll come to Moscow. But now let us part. My dear, good, precious one, let us part!"

100   She pressed his hand and walked rapidly downstairs, turning to look round at him, and from her eyes he could see that she really was unhappy. Gurov stood for a while, listening, then when all grew quiet, he found his coat and left the theater.

IV

And Anna Sergeyevna began coming to see him in Moscow. Once every two or three months she left S————, telling her husband that she was going to consult a doctor about a woman's ailment from which she was suffering—and her husband did and did not believe her. When she arrived in Moscow she would stop at the Slavyansky Bazar Hotel, and at once send a man in a red cap to Gurov. Gurov came to see her, and no one in Moscow knew of it.

Once he was going to see her in this way on a winter morning (the messenger had come the evening before and not found him in). With him walked his daughter, whom he wanted to take to school: it was on the way. Snow was coming down in big wet flakes.

"It's three degrees above zero,[1] and yet it's snowing," Gurov was saying to his daughter. "But this temperature prevails only on the surface of the earth; in the upper layers of the atmosphere there is quite a different temperature."

"And why doesn't it thunder in winter, papa?"

105   He explained that, too. He talked, thinking all the while that he was on his way to a rendezvous, and no living soul knew of it, and probably no one would ever know. He had two lives: an open one, seen and known by all who needed to know it, full of conventional truth and conventional falsehood, exactly like the lives of his friends and acquaintances; and another life that went on in secret. And through some strange, perhaps accidental, combination of circumstances, everything that was of interest and importance to him, everything that was essential to him, everything about which he felt sincerely and did not deceive himself, everything that constituted the core of his life, was going on concealed from others; while all that was false, the shell in which he hid to cover the truth—his work at the bank, for instance, his discussions at the club, his references to the "inferior race," his appearances at anniversary celebrations with his wife—all that went on in the open. Judging others by himself, he did not believe what he saw, and always fancied that every man led his real, most interesting life under cover of secrecy as under cover of night. The personal life of every individual is based on secrecy, and perhaps it is partly for that reason that civilized man is so nervously anxious that personal privacy should be respected.

Having taken his daughter to school, Gurov went on to the Slavyansky Bazar Hotel. He took off his fur coat in the lobby, went upstairs, and knocked gently at the door. Anna Sergeyevna, wearing his favorite gray dress, exhausted by the journey and by waiting, had been expecting him since the previous evening. She was pale, and looked at him without a smile, and he had hardly entered when she flung herself on his breast. Their kiss was a long, lingering one, as though they had not seen one another for two years.

"Well, darling, how are you getting on there?" he asked. "What news?"

"Wait; I'll tell you in a moment—I can't speak."

She could not speak; she was crying. She turned away from him, and pressed her handkerchief to her eyes.

110   "Let her have her cry; meanwhile I'll sit down," he thought, and he seated himself in an armchair.

Then he rang and ordered tea, and while he was having his tea she remained standing at the window with her back to him. She was crying out of sheer agitation, in the sorrowful consciousness that their life was so sad; that they could only see each other in secret and had to hide from people like thieves! Was it not a broken life?

"Come, stop now, dear!" he said.

It was plain to him that this love of theirs would not be over soon, that the end of it was not in sight. Anna Sergeyevna was growing more and more attached to him. She adored him, and it

---

[1]Equal to approximately thirty-seven degrees Fahrenheit (Russia uses the Celsius scale).

was unthinkable to tell her that their love was bound to come to an end some day; besides, she would not have believed it!

He went up to her and took her by the shoulders, to fondle her and say something diverting, and at that moment he caught sight of himself in the mirror.

His hair was already beginning to turn gray. And it seemed odd to him that he had grown so much older in the last few years, and lost his looks. The shoulders on which his hands rested were warm and heaving. He felt compassion for this life, still so warm and lovely, but probably already about to begin to fade and wither like his own. Why did she love him so much? He always seemed to women different from what he was, and they loved in him not himself, but the man whom their imagination created and whom they had been eagerly seeking all their lives; and afterwards, when they saw their mistake, they loved him nevertheless. And not one of them had been happy with him. In the past he had met women, come together with them, parted from them, but he had never once loved; it was anything you please, but not love. And only now when his head was gray he had fallen in love, really, truly—for the first time in his life.

Anna Sergeyevna and he loved each other as people do who are very close and intimate, like man and wife, like tender friends; it seemed to them that Fate itself had meant them for one another, and they could not understand why he had a wife and she had a husband; and it was as though they were a pair of migratory birds, male and female, caught and forced to live in different cages. They forgave each other what they were ashamed of in their past, they forgave everything in the present, and felt that this love of theirs had altered them both.

Formerly in moments of sadness he had soothed himself with whatever logical arguments came into his head, but now he no longer cared for logic; he felt profound compassion, he wanted to be sincere and tender.

"Give it up now, my darling," he said. "You've had your cry; that's enough. Let us have a talk now, we'll think up something."

Then they spent a long time taking counsel together, they talked of how to avoid the necessity for secrecy, for deception, for living in different cities, and not seeing one another for long stretches of time. How could they free themselves from these intolerable fetters?

"How" How?" he asked, clutching his head. "How?"

And it seemed as though in a little while the solution would be found, and then a new and glorious life would begin; and it was clear to both of them that the end was still far off, and that what was to be most complicated and difficult for them was only just beginning.

—Translated by Avrahm Yarmolinsky

Most contemporary short story writers would agree that Chekhov's work is the source and inspiration of a large part of their own work. If you like this story you may want to read "Optimists" by Richard Ford (chapter 2), who served as editor for a recent collection of Chekhov's prose.

GOING FURTHER Works by the French Guy de Maupassant and the Russian Isaac Babel contribute, like Chekhov's stories, to the European legacy of the modern short story. Working in this tradition are also some Irish writers such as Frank O'Connor and William Trevor. The latter's *Collected Stories* offers a feast of modern short fiction.

Gabriel García Márquez (b. 1928)

THE WINNER OF the 1982 Nobel Prize for Literature, Gabriel García Márquez was born in the small northern Colombian town of Aracataca. Originally a student of law, he ended his studies and went to work as a journalist, a profession that took him to Europe and eventually to the United States. There he made a pilgrimage to Oxford,

Mississippi, the hometown of his literary idol William Faulkner, whom he referred to in his Nobel Prize acceptance speech in laudatory terms. Márquez declared that the writer's goal was to create a "new and sweeping utopia of life, where no one will be able to decide for others how they die, where love will prove true and happiness be possible, and where the races condemned to one hundred years of solitude will have, at last and forever, a second opportunity on earth."

His style is that of "magical realism," in which supernatural events occur in otherwise natural contexts and settings. Marquez is famous for his ability to span decades in a sentence, to bring the dead to life, and to make even the cruelest fates a matter of course—all with utmost fluidity and believability. Along with his many other works of fiction and nonfiction, his masterwork, the novel *One Hundred Years of Solitude,* has illuminated life in the Americas for millions of readers.

The Handsomest Drowned Man in the World (1972)

A TALE FOR CHILDREN

1   The first children who saw the dark and slinky bulge approaching through the sea let themselves think it was an enemy ship. Then they saw it had no flags or masts and they thought it was a whale. But when it washed up on the beach, they removed the clumps of seaweed, the jellyfish tentacles, and the remains of fish and flotsam, and only then did they see that it was a drowned man.

They had been playing with him all afternoon, burying him in the sand and digging him up again, when someone chanced to see them and spread the alarm in the village. The men who carried him to the nearest house noticed that he weighed more than any dead man they had ever known, almost as much as a horse, and they said to each other that maybe he'd been floating too long and the water had got into his bones. When they laid him on the floor they said he'd been taller than all other men because there was barely enough room for him in the house, but they thought that maybe the ability to keep on growing after death was part of the nature of certain drowned men. He had the smell of the sea about him and only his shape gave one to suppose that it was the corpse of a human being, because the skin was covered with a crust of mud and scales.

They did not even have to clean off his face to know that the dead man was a stranger. The village was made up of only twenty-odd wooden houses that had stone courtyards with no flowers and which were spread about on the end of a desertlike cape. There was so little land that mothers always went about with the fear that the wind would carry off their children and the few dead that the years had caused among them had to be thrown off the cliffs. But the sea was calm and bountiful and all the men fit into seven boats. So when they found the drowned man they simply had to look at one another to see that they were all there.

That night they did not go out to work at sea. While the men went to find out if anyone was missing in neighboring villages, the women stayed behind to care for the drowned man. They took the mud off with grass swabs, they removed the underwater stones entangled in his hair, and they scraped the crust off with tools used for scaling fish. As they were doing that they noticed that the vegetation on him came from faraway oceans and deep water and that his clothes were in tatters, as if he had sailed through labyrinths of coral. They noticed too that he bore his death with pride, for he did not have the lonely look of other drowned men who came out of the sea or that haggard, needy look of men who drowned in rivers. But only when they finished cleaning him off did they become aware of the kind of man he was and it left them breathless. Not only was he the tallest, strongest, most virile, and best built man they had ever seen, but even though they were looking at him there was no room for him in their imagination.

They could not find a bed in the village large enough to lay him on nor was there a table solid enough to use for his wake. The tallest men's holiday pants would not fit him, nor the fattest ones' Sunday shirts, nor the shoes of the one with the biggest feet. Fascinated by his huge size and his beauty, the women then decided to make him some pants from a large piece of sail and a shirt from some bridal brabant linen so that he could continue through his death with dignity. As they sewed, sitting in a circle and gazing at the corpse between stitches, it seemed to them that the wind had never been so steady nor the sea so restless as on that night and they supposed that the change had something to do with the dead man. They thought that if that magnificent man had lived in the village, his house would have had the widest doors, the highest ceiling, and the strongest floor, his bedstead would have been made from a midship frame held together by iron bolts, and his wife would have been the happiest woman. They thought that he would have had so much authority that he could have drawn fish out of the sea simply by calling their names and that he would have put so much work into his land that springs would have burst forth from among the rocks so that he would have been able to plant flowers on the cliffs. They secretly compared him to their own men, thinking that for all their lives theirs were incapable of doing what he could do in one night, and they ended up dismissing them deep in their hearts as the weakest, meanest, and most useless creatures on earth. They were wandering through that maze of fantasy when the oldest woman, who as the oldest had looked upon the drowned man with more compassion than passion, sighed:

"He has the face of someone called Esteban."

It was true. Most of them had only to take another look at him to see that he could not have any other name. The more stubborn among them, who were the youngest, still lived for a few hours with the illusion that when they put his clothes on and he lay among the flowers in patent leather shoes his name might be Lautaro. But it was a vain illusion. There had not been enough canvas, the poorly cut and worse sewn pants were too tight, and the hidden strength of his heart popped the buttons on his shirt. After midnight the whistling of the wind died down and the sea fell into its Wednesday drowsiness. The silence put an end to any last doubts: he was Esteban. The women who had dressed him, who had combed his hair, had cut his nails and shaved him were unable to hold back a shudder of pity when they had to resign themselves to his being dragged along the ground. It was then that they understood how unhappy he must have been with that huge body since it bothered him even after death. They could see him in life, condemned to going through doors sideways, cracking his head on crossbeams, remaining on his feet during visits, not knowing what to do with his soft, pink, sea lion hands while the lady of the house looked for her most resistant chair and begged him, frightened to death, sit here, Esteban, please, and he, leaning against the wall, smiling, don't bother, ma'am, I'm fine where I am, his heels raw and his back roasted from having done the same thing so many times whenever he paid a visit, don't bother, ma'am, I'm fine where I am, just to avoid the embarrassment of breaking up the chair, and never knowing perhaps that the ones who said don't go, Esteban, at least wait till the coffee's ready, were the ones who later on would whisper the big boob finally left, how nice, the handsome fool has gone. That was what the women were thinking beside the body a little before dawn. Later, when they covered his face with a handkerchief so that the light would not bother him, he looked so forever dead, so defenseless, so much like their men that the first furrows of tears opened in their hearts. It was one of the younger ones who began the weeping. The others, coming to, went from sighs to wails, and the more they sobbed the more they felt like weeping, because the drowned man was becoming all the more Esteban for them, and so they wept so much, for he was the most destitute, most peaceful, and most obliging man on earth, poor Esteban. So when the men returned with the news that the drowned man was not from the neighboring villages either, the women felt an opening of jubilation in the midst of their tears.

"Praise the Lord," they sighed, "he's ours!"

The men thought the fuss was only womanish frivolity. Fatigued because of the difficult nighttime inquiries, all they wanted was to get rid of the bother of the newcomer once and for all before the sun grew strong on that arid, windless day. They improvised a litter with the remains of foremasts and gaffs, tying it together with rigging so that it would bear the weight of the body until they reached the cliffs. They wanted to tie the anchor from a cargo ship to him so that he would sink easily into the deepest waves, where fish are blind and divers die of nostalgia, and bad currents would not bring him back to shore, as had happened with other bodies. But the more they hurried, the more the women thought of ways to waste time. They walked about like startled hens, pecking with the sea charms on their breasts, some interfering on one side to put a scapular of the good wind on the drowned man, some on the other side to put a wrist compass on him, and after a great deal of *get away from there, woman, stay out of the way, look, you almost made me fall on top of the dead man,* the men began to feel mistrust in their livers and started grumbling about why so many main-altar decorations for a stranger, because no matter how many nails and holy-water jars he had on him, the sharks would chew him all the same, but the women kept piling on their junk relics, running back and forth, stumbling, while they released in sighs what they did not in tears, so that the men finally exploded with *since when has there ever been such a fuss over a drifting corpse, a drowned nobody, a piece of cold Wednesday meat.* One of the women, mortified by so much lack of care, then removed the handkerchief from the dead man's face and the men were left breathless too.

10   He was Esteban. It was not necessary to repeat it for them to recognize him. If they had been told Sir Walter Raleigh, even they might have been impressed with his gringo accent, the macaw on his shoulder, his cannibal-killing blunderbuss, but there could be only one Esteban in the world and there he was, stretched out like a sperm whale, shoeless, wearing the pants of an undersized child, and with those stony nails that had to be cut with a knife. They only had to take the handkerchief off his face to see that he was ashamed, that it was not his fault that he was so big or so heavy or so handsome, and if he had known that this was going to happen, he would have looked for a more discreet place to drown in, seriously, I even would have tied the anchor off a galleon around my neck and staggered off a cliff like someone who doesn't like things in order not to be upsetting people now with this Wednesday dead body, as you people say, in order not to be bothering anyone with this filthy piece of cold meat that doesn't have anything to do with me. There was so much truth in his manner that even the most mistrustful men, the ones who felt the bitterness of endless nights at sea fearing that their women would tire of dreaming about them and begin to dream of drowned men, even they and others who were harder still shuddered in the marrow of their bones at Esteban's sincerity.

That was how they came to hold the most splendid funeral they could ever conceive of for an abandoned drowned man. Some women who had gone to get flowers in the neighboring villages returned with other women who could not believe what they had been told, and those women went back for more flowers when they saw the dead man, and they brought more and more until there were so many flowers and so many people that it was hard to walk about. At the final moment it pained them to return him to the waters as an orphan and they chose a father and mother from among the best people, and aunts and uncles and cousins, so that through him all the inhabitants of the village became kinsmen. Some sailors who heard the weeping from a distance went off course and people heard of one who had himself tied to the mainmast, remembering ancient fables about sirens. While they fought for the privilege of carrying him on their shoulders along the steep escarpment by the cliffs, men and women became aware for the first time of the desolation of their streets, the dryness of their courtyards, the narrowness of their dreams as they faced the splendor and beauty of their drowned man. They let him go without an anchor so that he could come back if he wished and whenever he wished, and they all held their breath for the fraction of centuries the body took to fall into the abyss. They did not need to look at one another to realize that they were no longer all present, that they would never be. But they also knew that everything would be different from then on, that their houses would have wider doors, higher ceilings, and stronger floors so that Esteban's memory could go everywhere without bumping into beams and so that no one in the future would dare whisper the big boob finally died, too bad, the handsome fool has finally died, because they were going to paint their house fronts gay colors to make Esteban's memory eternal and they were going to break their backs digging for springs among the stones and planting flowers on the cliffs so that in future years at dawn the passengers on great liners would awaken, suffocated by the smell of gardens on the high seas, and the captain would have to come down from the bridge in his dress uniform, with his astrolabe, his pole star, and his row of war medals and, pointing to the promontory of roses on the horizon, he would say in fourteen languages, look there, where the wind is so peaceful now that it's gone to sleep beneath the beds, over there, where the sun's so bright that the sunflowers don't know which way to turn, yes, over there, that's Esteban's village.

If you like this story, you can find affinities with the style in the work of Franz Kafka, whose long story "The Metamorphosis" you can find in chapter 10, and in "The Rememberer" by Aimee Bender (chapter 8).

GOING FURTHER A number of U.S. writers have found themselves influenced by García Márquez's so-called magical realist style, among them Toni Morrison in her novel *Song of Solomon* and younger writers such as Mark Helprin in the stories collected in *A Dove of the East* and Jonathan Safran Foer in his 2005 novel *Extremely Loud and Incredibly Close.*

Zora Neale Hurston (1891–1960)

GROWING UP IN Eatonville, Florida—an all-black town—Zora Neale Hurston did not experience racial prejudice. Instead, she saw examples of black role models, such as her father, who served as the town mayor. She began her education at Howard University in Washington, D.C., and finished her B.A. in anthropology at Barnard College in New York City. Her love of folk culture and literature led her to write novels, short stories, and collections of folklore that captured the common black person; unlike her contemporaries, including Langston Hughes, Hurston cared more about authenticity than about how her depictions made blacks appear to white audiences. An important figure of the Harlem Renaissance, Hurston is famous for her charming, vibrant personality that made her the center of parties and social life in Harlem. Some of her early fiction was published in *Opportunity,* a black magazine of the Harlem Renaissance. Her best work appeared in the 1930s and '40s with books such as *Mules and Men* (1935), which was the fruit of her ethnographic studies of blacks in Florida, and *Their Eyes Were Watching God* (1937), Hurston's classic novel about an African-American woman who forges her identity in relation to three different husbands. Although these works found an audience, Hurston sank into obscurity toward the end of her life. However, interest in her writing revived in the 1970s, thanks to Alice Walker's article "In Search of Zora Neale Hurston," which appeared in *Ms.* magazine. Today, Hurston is recognized as the most important African-American woman in early-twentieth-century literature.

The Gilded Six-Bits (1933)

1   It was a Negro yard around a Negro house in a Negro settlement that looked to the payroll of the G and G Fertilizer works for its support.

But there was something happy about the place. The front yard was parted in the middle by a sidewalk from gate to door-step, a sidewalk edged on either side by quart bottles driven neck down into the ground on a slant. A mess of homey flowers planted without a plan but blooming cheerily from their helter-skelter places. The fence and house were whitewashed. The porch and steps scrubbed white.

The front door stood open to the sunshine so that the floor of the front room could finish drying after its weekly scouring. It was Saturday. Everything clean from the front gate to the privy house. Yard raked so that the strokes of the rake would make a pattern. Fresh newspaper cut in fancy edge on the kitchen shelves.

Missie May was bathing herself in the galvanized washtub in the bedroom. Her dark-brown skin glistened under the soapsuds that skittered down from her wash rag. Her stiff young breasts thrust forward aggressively, like broad-based cones with the tips lacquered in black.

5 She heard men's voices in the distance and glanced at the dollar clock on the dresser.

"Humph! Ah'm way behind time t'day! Joe gointer be heah 'fore Ah git mah clothes on if Ah don't make haste."

She grabbed the clean meal sack at hand and dried herself hurriedly and began to dress. But before she could tie her slippers, there came the ring of singing metal on wood. Nine times.

Missie May grinned with delight. She had not seen the big tall man come stealing in the gate and creep up the walk grinning happily at the joyful mischief he was about to commit. But she knew that it was her husband throwing silver dollars in the door for her to pick up and pile beside her plate at dinner. It was this way every Saturday afternoon. The nine dollars hurled into the open door, he scurried to a hiding place behind the cape jasmine bush and waited.

Missie May promptly appeared at the door in mock alarm.

10 "Who dat chunkin' money in mah do'way?" she demanded. No answer from the yard. She leaped off the porch and began to search the shrubbery. She peeped under the porch and hung over the gate to look up and down the road. While she did this, the man behind the jasmine darted to the chinaberry tree. She spied him and gave chase.

"Nobody ain't gointer be chunkin' money at me and Ah not do 'em nothin'," she shouted in mock anger. He ran around the house with Missie May at his heels. She overtook him at the kitchen door. He ran inside but could not close it after him before she crowded in and locked with him in a rough and tumble. For several minutes the two were a furious mass of male and female energy. Shouting, laughing, twisting, turning, tussling, tickling each other in the ribs; Missie May clutching onto Joe and Joe trying, but not too hard, to get away.

"Missie May, take yo' hand out mah pocket!" Joe shouted out between laughs.

"Ah ain't, Joe, not lessen you gwine gimme whateve' it is good you got in yo' pocket. Turn it go, Joe, do Ah'll tear yo' clothes."

"Go on tear 'em. You de one dat pushes de needles round heah. Move yo' hand Missie May."

15 "Lemme git dat paper sack out yo' pocket. Ah bet it's candy kisses."

"Taint. Move yo' hand. Woman ain't got no business in a man's clothes no how. Go way."

Missie May gouged way down and gave an upward jerk and triumphed.

"Unhhunh! Ah got it! It 'tis so candy kisses. Ah knowed you had somethin' for me in yo' clothes. Now Ah got to see whut's in every pocket you got."

Joe smiled indulgently and let his wife go through all of his pockets and take out the things that he had hidden there for her to find. She bore off the chewing gum, the cake of sweet soap, the pocket handkerchief as if she had wrested them from him, as if they had not been bought for the sake of this friendly battle.

20 "Whew! dat play-fight done got me all warmed up," Joe exclaimed. "Got me some water in de kittle?"

"Yo' water is on de fire and yo' clean things is cross de bed. Hurry up and wash yo'self and git changed so we kin eat. Ah'm hongry." As Missie said this, she bore the steaming kettle into the bedroom.

"You ain't hongry, sugar," Joe contradicted her. "Youse jes' a little empty. Ah'm de one whut's hongry. Ah could eat up camp meetin', back off 'ssociation, and drink Jurdan dry. Have it on de table when Ah git out de tub."

"Don't you mess wid mah business, man. You git in yo' clothes. Ah'm a real wife, not no dress and breath. Ah might not look lak one, but if you burn me, you won't git a thing but wife ashes."

Joe splashed in the bedroom and Missie May fanned around in the kitchen. A fresh red and white checked cloth on the table. Big pitcher of buttermilk beaded with pale drops of butter from the churn. Hot fried mullet, crackling bread, ham hock atop a mound of string beans and new potatoes, and perched on the window-sill a pone of spicy potato pudding.

25 Very little talk during the meal but that little consisted of banter that pretended to deny affection but in reality flaunted it. Like when Missie May reached for a second helping of the tater pone. Joe snatched it out of her reach.

After Missie May had made two or three unsuccessful grabs at the pan, she begged, "Aw, Joe gimme some mo' dat tater pone."

"Nope, sweetenin' is for us men-folks. Y'all pritty lil frail eels don't need nothin' lak dis. You too sweet already."

"Please, Joe."

"Naw, naw. Ah don't want you to git no sweeter than whut you is already. We goin' down de road a lil piece t'night so you go put on yo' Sunday-go-to-meetin' things."

Missie May looked at her husband to see if he was playing some prank. "Sho nuff, Joe?"

"Yeah. We goin' to de ice cream parlor."

"Where de ice cream parlor at, Joe?"

"A new man done come heah from Chicago and he done got a place and took and opened it up for a ice cream parlor, and bein' as it's real swell, Ah wants you to be one de first ladies to walk in dere and have some set down."

"Do Jesus, Ah ain't knowed nothin' 'bout it. Who de man done it?"

"Mister Otis D. Slemmons, of spots and places—Memphis, Chicago, Jacksonville, Philadelphia and so on."

"Dat heavy-set man wid his mouth full of gold teethes?"

"Yeah. Where did you see 'im at?"

"Ah went down to de sto' tuh git a box of lye and Ah seen 'im standin' on de corner talkin' to some of de mens, and Ah come on back and went to scrubbin' de floor, and he passed and tipped his hat whilst Ah was scourin' de steps. Ah thought Ah never seen *him* befo'."

Joe smiled pleasantly. "Yeah, he's up to date. He got de finest clothes Ah ever seen on a colored man's back."

"Aw, he don't look no better in his clothes than you do in yourn. He got a puzzlegut on 'im and he so chuckle-headed, he got a pone behind his neck."

Joe looked down at his own abdomen and said wistfully: "Wisht Ah had a build on me lak he got. He ain't puzzlegutted, honey. He jes' got a corperation. Dat make 'm look lak a rich white man. All rich mens is got some belly on 'em."

"Ah seen de pitchers of Henry Ford and he's a spare-built man and Rockefeller look lak he ain't got but one gut. But Ford and Rockefeller and dis Slemmons and all de rest kin be as many-gutted as dey please, Ah'm satisfied wid you jes' lak you is, baby. God took pattern after a pine tree and built you noble. Youse a pritty man, and if Ah knowed any way to make you mo' pritty still Ah'd take and do it."

Joe reached over gently and toyed with Missie May's ear. "You jes' say dat cause you love me, but Ah know Ah can't hold no light to Otis D. Slemmons. Ah ain't never been nowhere and Ah ain't got nothin' but you."

Missie May got on his lap and kissed him and he kissed back in kind. Then he went on. "All de womens is crazy 'bout 'im everywhere he go."

"How you know dat, Joe?"

"He tole us so hisself."

"Dat don't make it so. His mouf is cut cross-ways, ain't it? Well, he kin lie jes' lak anybody else."

"Good Lawd, Missie! You womens sho is hard to sense into things. He's got a five-dollar gold piece for a stick-pin and he got a ten-dollar gold piece on his watch chain and his mouf is jes' crammed full of gold teethes. Sho wisht it wuz mine. And whut make it so cool, he got money 'cumulated. And womens give it all to 'im."

"Ah don't see whut de womens see on 'im. Ah wouldn't give 'im a wink if de sheriff wuz after 'im."

"Well, he tole us how de white womens in Chicago give 'im all dat gold money. So he don't 'low nobody to touch it at all. Not even put dey finger on it. Dey tole 'im not to. You kin make 'miration at it, but don't tetch it."

"Whyn't he stay up dere where dey so crazy 'bout 'im?"

"Ah reckon dey done made 'im vast-rich and he wants to travel some. He says dey wouldn't leave 'im hit a lick of work. He got mo' lady people crazy 'bout him than he kin shake a stick at."

"Joe, Ah hates to see you so dumb. Dat stray nigger jes' tell y'all anything and y'all b'lieve it."

"Go 'head on now, honey and put on yo' clothes. He talkin' 'bout his pritty womens—Ah want 'im to see *mine*."

55   Missie May went off to dress and Joe spent the time trying to make his stomach punch out like Slemmons' middle. He tried the rolling swagger of the stranger, but found that his tall bone-and-muscle stride fitted ill with it. He just had time to drop back into his seat before Missie May came in dressed to go.

On the way home that night Joe was exultant. "Didn't Ah say ole Otis was swell? Can't he talk Chicago talk? Wuzn't dat funny whut he said when great big fat ole Ida Armstrong come in? He asted me, 'Who is dat broad wid de forte shake?' Dat's a new word. Us always thought forty was a set of figgers but he showed us where it means a whole heap of things. Sometimes he don't say forty, he jes' say thirty-eight and two and dat mean de same thing. Know whut he tole me when Ah wuz payin' for our ice cream? He say, 'Ah have to hand it to you, Joe. Dat wife of yours is jes' thirty-eight and two. Yessuh, she's forte!' Ain't he killin'?"

"He'll do in case of a rush. But he sho is got uh heap uh gold on 'im. Dat's de first time Ah ever seed gold money. It lookted good on him sho nuff, but it'd look a whole heap better on you."

"Who, me? Missie May, youse crazy! Where would a po' man lak me git gold money from?"

Missie May was silent for a minute, then she said, "Us might find some goin' long de road some time. Us could."

60   "Who would be losin' gold money round heah? We ain't even seen none dese white folks wearin' no gold money on dey watch chain. You must be figgerin' Mister Packard or Mister Cadillac goin' pass through heah."

"You don't know whut been lost 'round heah. Maybe somebody way back in memorial times lost they gold money and went on off and it ain't never been found. And then if we wuz to find it, you could wear some 'thout havin' no gang of womens lak dat Slemmons say he got."

Joe laughed and hugged her. "Don't be so wishful 'bout me. Ah'm satisfied de way Ah is. So long as Ah be yo' husband, Ah don't keer 'bout nothin' else. Ah'd ruther all de other womens in de world to be dead than for you to have de toothache. Less we go to bed and git our night rest."

It was Saturday night once more before Joe could parade his wife in Slemmons' ice cream parlor again. He worked the night shift and Saturday was his only night off. Every other evening around six o'clock he left home, and dying dawn saw him hustling home around the lake where the challenging sun flung a flaming sword from east to west across the trembling water.

That was the best part of life—going home to Missie May. Their whitewashed house, the mock battle on Saturday, the dinner and ice cream parlor afterwards, church on Sunday nights when Missie outdressed any woman in town—all, everything was right.

65   One night around eleven the acid ran out at the G and G. The foreman knocked off the crew and let the steam die down. As Joe rounded the lake on his way home, a lean moon rode the lake in a silver boat. If anybody had asked Joe about the moon on the lake, he would have said he hadn't paid it any attention. But he saw it with his feelings. It made him yearn painfully for Missie. Creation obsessed him. He thought about children. They had been married more than a year now. They had money put away. They ought to be making little feet for shoes. A little boy child would be about right.

He saw a dim light in the bedroom and decided to come in through the kitchen door. He could wash the fertilizer dust off himself before presenting himself to Missie May. It would be nice for her not to know that he was there until he slipped into his place in bed and hugged her back. She always liked that.

He eased the kitchen door open slowly and silently, but when he went to set his dinner bucket on the table he bumped it into a pile of dishes, and something crashed to the floor. He heard his wife gasp in fright and hurried to reassure her.

"Iss me, honey. Don't git skeered."

There was a quick, large movement in the bedroom. A rustle, a thud, and a stealthy silence. The light went out.

70   What? Robbers? Murderers? Some varmint attacking his helpless wife, perhaps. He struck a match, threw himself on guard and stepped over the door-sill into the bedroom

The great belt on the wheel of Time slipped and eternity stood still. By the match light he could see the man's legs fighting with his breeches in his frantic desire to get them on. He had both chance and time to kill the intruder in his helpless condition—half in and half out of his pants—but he was too weak to take action. The shapeless enemies of humanity that live in the hours of Time had waylaid Joe. He was assaulted in his weakness. Like Samson awakening after his haircut. So he just opened his mouth and laughed.

The match went out and he struck another and lit the lamp. A howling wind raced across his heart, but underneath its fury he heard his wife sobbing and Slemmons pleading for his life. Offering to buy it with all that he had. "Please, suh, don't kill me. Sixty-two dollars at de sto'. Gold money."

Joe just stood. Slemmons looked at the window, but it was screened. Joe stood out like a rough-backed mountain between him and the door. Barring him from escape, from sunrise, from life.

He considered a surprise attack upon the big clown that stood there laughing like a chessy cat. But before his fist could travel an inch, Joe's own rushed out to crush him like a battering ram. Then Joe stood over him.

"Git into yo' damn rags, Slemmons, and dat quick."

Slemmons scrambled to his feet and into his vest and coat. As he grabbed his hat, Joe's fury overrode his intentions and he grabbed at Slemmons with his left hand and struck at him with his right. The right landed. The left grazed the front of his vest. Slemmons was knocked a somersault into the kitchen and fled through the open door. Joe found himself alone with Missie May, with the golden watch charm clutched in his left fist. A short bit of broken chain dangled between his fingers.

Missie May was sobbing. Wails of weeping without words. Joe stood, and after awhile he found out that he had something in his hand. And then he stood and felt without thinking and without seeing with his natural eyes. Missie May kept on crying and Joe kept on feeling so much and not knowing what to do with all his feelings, he put Slemmons' watch charm in his pants pocket and took a good laugh and went to bed.

"Missie May, whut you cryin' for?"

"Cause Ah love you so hard and Ah know you don't love *me* no mo'."

Joe sank his face into the pillow for a spell then he said huskily, "You don't know de feelings of dat yet, Missie May."

"Oh Joe, honey, he said he wuz gointer give me dat gold money and he jes' kept on after me—"

Joe was very still and silent for a long time. Then he said, "Well, don't cry no mo', Missie May. Ah got yo' gold piece for you."

The hours went past on their rusty ankles. Joe still and quiet on one bed-rail and Missie May wrung dry of sobs on the other. Finally the sun's tide crept upon the shore of night and drowned all its hours. Missie May with her face stiff and streaked towards the window saw the dawn come into her yard. It was day. Nothing more. Joe wouldn't be coming home as usual. No need to fling open the front door and sweep off the porch, making it nice for Joe. Never no more breakfast to cook; no more washing and starching of Joe's jumper-jackets and pants. No more nothing. So why get up?

With this strange man in her bed, she felt embarrassed to get up and dress. She decided to wait till he had dressed and gone. Then she would get up, dress quickly and be gone forever beyond reach of Joe's looks and laughs. But he never moved. Red light turned to yellow, then white.

From beyond the no-man's land between them came a voice. A strange voice that yesterday had been Joe's.

"Missie May, ain't you gonna fix me no breakfus'?"

She sprang out of bed. "Yeah, Joe. Ah didn't reckon you wuz hongry."

No need to die today. Joe needed her for a few more minutes anyhow.

Soon there was a roaring fire in the cook stove. Water bucket full and two chickens killed. Joe loved fried chicken and rice. She didn't deserve a thing and good Joe was letting her cook him some breakfast. She rushed hot biscuits to the table as Joe took his seat.

He ate with his eyes in his plate. No laughter, no banter.

"Missie May, you ain't eatin' yo' breakfus'."

"Ah don't choose none, Ah thank yuh."

His coffee cup was empty. She sprang to refill it. When she turned from the stove and bent to set the cup beside Joe's plate, she saw the yellow coin on the table between them.

She slumped into her seat and wept into her arms.

95 Presently Joe said calmly, "Missie May, you cry too much. Don't look back lak Lot's wife and turn to salt."

The sun, the hero of every day, the impersonal old man that beams as brightly on death as on birth, came up every morning and raced across the blue dome and dipped into the sea of fire every evening. Water ran down hill and birds nested.

Missie knew why she didn't leave Joe. She couldn't. She loved him too much, but she could not understand why Joe didn't leave her. He was polite, even kind at times, but aloof.

There were no more Saturday romps. No ringing silver dollars to stack beside her plate. No pockets to rifle. In fact the yellow coin in his trousers was like a monster hiding in the cave of his pockets to destroy her.

She often wondered if he still had it, but nothing could have induced her to ask nor yet to explore his pockets to see for herself. Its shadow was in the house whether or no.

100 One night Joe came home around midnight and complained of pains in the back. He asked Missie to rub him down with liniment. It had been three months since Missie had touched his body and it all seemed strange. But she rubbed him. Grateful for the chance. Before morning, youth triumphed and Missie exulted. But the next day, as she joyfully made up their bed, beneath her pillow she found the piece of money with the bit of chain attached.

Alone to herself, she looked at the thing with loathing, but look she must. She took it into her hands with trembling and saw first thing that it was no gold piece. It was a gilded half dollar. Then she knew why Slemmons had forbidden anyone to touch his gold. He trusted village eyes at a distance not to recognize his stick-pin as a gilded quarter, and his watch charm as a four-bit piece.

She was glad at first that Joe had left it there. Perhaps he was through with her punishment. They were man and wife again. Then another thought came clawing at her. He had come home to buy from her as if she were any woman in the long house. Fifty cents for her love. As if to say that he could pay as well as Slemmons. She slid the coin into his Sunday pants pocket and dressed herself and left his house.

Halfway between her house and the quarters she met her husband's mother, and after a short talk she turned and went back home. Never would she admit defeat to that woman who prayed for it nightly. If she had not the substance of marriage she had the outside show. Joe must leave *her*. She let him see she didn't want his gold four-bits too.

She saw no more of the coin for some time though she knew that Joe could not help finding it in his pocket. But his health kept poor, and he came home at least every ten days to be rubbed.

105 The sun swept around the horizon, trailing its robes of weeks and days. One morning as Joe came in from work, he found Missie May chopping wood. Without a word he took the ax and chopped a huge pile before he stopped.

"You ain't got no business choppin' wood, and you know it."

"How come? Ah been choppin' it for de last longest."

"Ah ain't blind. You makin' feet for shoes."

"Won't you be glad to have a lil baby chile, Joe?"

110 "You know dat 'thout astin' me."

"Iss gointer be a boy chile and de very spit of you."

"You reckon, Missie May?"

"Who else could it look lak?"

Joe said nothing, but he thrust his hand deep into his pocket and fingered something there.

115 It was almost six months later Missie May took to bed and Joe went and got his mother to come wait on the house.

Missie May was delivered of a fine boy. Her travail was over when Joe came in from work one morning. His mother and the old women were drinking great bowls of coffee around the fire in the kitchen.

The minute Joe came into the room his mother called him aside.

"How did Missie May make out?" he asked quickly.

"Who, dat gal? She strong as a ox. She gointer have plenty mo'. We done fixed her wid de sugar and lard to sweeten her for de nex' one."

Joe stood silent awhile.

"You ain't ast 'bout de baby, Joe. You oughter be mighty proud cause he sho is de spittin' image of yuh, son. Dat's yourn all right, if you never git another one, dat un is yourn. And you know Ah'm mighty proud too, son, cause Ah never thought well of you marryin' Missie May cause her ma used tuh fan her foot round right smart and Ah been mighty skeered dat Missie May wuz gointer git misput on her road."

Joe said nothing. He fooled around the house till late in the day then just before he went to work, he went and stood at the foot of the bed and asked his wife how she felt. He did this every day during the week.

On Saturday he went to Orlando to make his market. It had been a long time since he had done that.

Meat and lard, meal and flour, soap and starch. Cans of corn and tomatoes. All the staples. He fooled around town for awhile and bought bananas and apples. Way after while he went around to the candy store.

"Hello, Joe," the clerk greeted him. "Ain't seen you in a long time."

"Nope, Ah ain't been heah. Been round in spots and places."

"Want some of them molasses kisses you always buy?"

"Yessuh." He threw the gilded half dollar on the counter. "Will dat spend?"

"What is it, Joe? Well, I'll be doggone! A gold-plated four-bit piece. Where'd you git it, Joe?"

"Offen a stray nigger dat come through Eatonville. He had it on his watch chain for a charm—goin' round making out iss gold money. Ha ha! He had a quarter on his tie pin and it wuz all golded up too. Tryin' to fool people. Makin' out he so rich and everything. Ha! Ha! Tryin' to tole off folkses wives from home."

"How did you git it, Joe? Did he fool you, too?"

"Who, me? Naw suh! He ain't fooled me none. Know whut Ah done? He come round me wid his smart talk. Ah hauled off and knocked 'im down and took his old four-bits way from 'im. Gointer buy my wife some good ole lasses kisses wid it. Gimme fifty cents worth of dem candy kisses."

"Fifty cents buys a mighty lot of candy kisses, Joe. Why don't you split it up and take some chocolate bars, too? They eat good, too."

"Yessuh, dey do, but Ah wants all dat in kisses. Ah got a lil boy chile home now. Tain't a week old yet, but he kin suck a sugar tit and maybe eat one them kisses hisself."

Joe got his candy and left the store. The clerk turned to the next customer. "Wisht I could be like these darkies. Laughin' all the time. Nothin' worries 'em."

Back in Eatonville, Joe reached his own front door. There was the ring of singing metal on wood. Fifteen times. Missie May couldn't run to the door, but she crept there as quickly as she could.

"Joe Banks, Ah hear you chunkin' money in mah do'way. You wait till Ah got mah strength back and Ah'm gointer fix you for dat."

Hurston is a Southern writer whose work you might consider in context with that of William Faulkner, Flannery O'Connor, and Ralph Ellison, all in the case study on the American South in chapter 12.

GOING FURTHER Hurston, a native of Alabama, did primary anthropological research among black populations in Florida and hobnobbed with the New York intellectual crowd in Manhattan during the period known as the Harlem Renaissance. Contemporary black American women writers such as Alice Walker and Toni Morrison point to her as an ancestor; the former's *The Color Purple* and the latter's *Song of Solomon* and *Beloved* owe much to the example of *Their Eyes Were Watching God*.

Ursula K. Le Guin (b. 1929)

ONE OF THE foremost writers of imaginative fiction in our time, Ursula K. Le Guin was born Ursula Kroeber in Berkeley, California. Her parents were the anthropologist Alfred Kroeber and the writer Theodora Kroeber, author of *Ishi*. Although Le Guin is widely known as a science-fiction writer, her most successful and best-known books—novels such as *The Left Hand of Darkness* (1969) and *The Dispossessed* (1974), and her short fiction in collections such as *The Wind's Twelve Quarters* (1975) and *The Compass Rose* (1982)—have always expressed a certain anthropological cast of mind reminiscent of her parents' scientific study of human habits and customs.

Few writers working in a particular genre—in Le Guin's case, science fiction—have had such success as a "cross-over" writer, publishing stories in both popular and genre magazines, from *Galaxy* and *Fantasy & Science Fiction* to *The New Yorker,* and winning Hugo and Nebula awards for outstanding science fiction while garnering such prestigious literary prizes as the PEN/Malamud Award for Excellence in the Short Story. Le Guin has also written many volumes of fantasy fiction, childrens' books, and essays.

The Kerastion (1994)
FOR ROUSSEL SARGENT, WHO INVENTED IT

1 The small caste of the Tanners was a sacred one. To eat food prepared by a Tanner would entail a year's purification to a Tinker or a Sculptor, and even low-power castes such as the Traders had to be cleansed by a night's ablutions after dealing for leather goods. Chumo had been a Tanner since she was five years old and had heard the willows whisper all night long at the Singing Sands. She had had her proving day, and since then had worn a Tanner's madder-red and blue shirt and doublet, woven of linen on a willow-wood loom. She had made her masterpiece, and since then had worn the Master Tanner's neckband of dried vauti-tuber incised with the double line and double circles. So clothed and ornamented she stood among the willows by the burying ground, waiting for the funeral procession of her brother, who had broken the law and betrayed his caste. She stood erect and silent, gazing towards the village by the river and listening for the drum.

She did not think; she did not want to think. But she saw her brother Kwatewa in the reeds down by the river, running ahead of her, a little boy too young to have caste, too young to be polluted by the sacred, a crazy little boy pouncing on her out of the tall reeds shouting, "I'm a mountain lion!"

A serious little boy watching the river run, asking, "Does it ever stop? Why can't it stop running, Chumo?"

A five-year-old coming back from the Singing Sands, coming straight to her, bringing her the joy, the crazy, serious joy that shone in his round face—"Chumo! I heard the sand singing! I heard it! I have to be a Sculptor, Chumo!"

5 She had stood still. She had not held out her arms. And he had checked his run towards her and stood still, the light going out of his face. She was only his wombsister. He would have truesibs, now. He and she were of different castes. They would not touch again.

Ten years after that day she had come with most of the townsfolk to Kwatewa's proving day, to see the sand-sculpture he had made in the Great Plain Place where the Sculptors performed their art. Not a breath of wind had yet rounded off the keen edges or leveled the lovely curves of the classic form he had executed with such verve and sureness, the Body of Amakumo. She saw admiration and envy in the faces of his truebrothers and truesisters. Standing aside among the sacred castes, she heard the speaker of the Sculptors dedicate Kwatewa's proving piece to Amakumo. As his voice ceased a wind came out of the desert north, Amakumo's wind, the maker hungry for the made—Amakumo the Mother eating her body, eating herself. Even while they watched, the wind destroyed Kwatewa's sculpture. Soon there was only a shapeless lump and a feathering of white sand blown across the proving ground. Beauty had gone back to the Mother. That the sculpture had been destroyed so soon and so utterly was a great honor to the maker.

The funeral procession was approaching. She heard or imagined she heard the drumbeat, soft, no more than a heartbeat.

Her own proving piece had been the traditional one for Tanner women, a drumhead. Not a funeral drum but a dancing drum, loud, gaudy with red paint and tassels. "Your drumhead, your maidenhead!" her truebrothers called it, and made fierce teasing jokes, but they couldn't make her blush. Tanners had no business blushing. They were outside shame. It had been an excellent drum, chosen at once from the proving ground by an old Musician, who had played it so much she soon wore off the bright paint and lost the red tassels; but the drumhead lasted through the winter and till the Roppi Ceremony, when it finally split wide open during the drumming for the all-night dancing under the moons, when Chumo and Karwa first twined their wristplaits. Chumo had been proud all winter when she heard the voice of her drum loud and clear across the dancing ground, she had been proud when it split and gave itself to the Mother; but that had been nothing to the pride she had felt in Kwatewa's sculptures. For if the work be well done and the thing made be powerful, it belongs to the Mother. She will desire it; she will not wait for it to give itself, but will take it. So the child dying young is called the Mother's Child. Beauty, the most sacred of all things, is hers; the body of the Mother is the most beautiful of all things. So all that is made in the likeness of the Mother is made in sand.

To keep your work, to try to keep it for yourself, to take her body from her. Kwatewa! How could you, how could you, my brother? her heart said. But she put the question back into the silence and stood silent among the willows, the trees sacred to her caste, watching the funeral procession come between the flaxfields. It was his shame, not hers. What was shame to a Tanner? It was pride she felt, pride. For that was her masterpiece that Dastuye the Musician held now and raised to his lips as he walked before the procession, guiding the new ghost to its body's grave.

She had made that instrument, the kerastion, the flute that is played only at a funeral. The kerastion is made of leather, and the leather is tanned human skin, and the skin is that of the womb-mother or the foremother of the dead.

When Wekuri, wombmother of Chumo and Kwatewa, had died two winters ago, Chumo the Tanner had claimed her privilege. There had been an old, old kerastion to play at Wekuri's funeral, handed down from her grandmothers; but the Musician, when he had finished playing it, laid it on the mats that wrapped Wekuri in the open grave. For the night before, Chumo had flayed the left arm of the body, singing the songs of power of her caste as she worked, the songs that ask the dead mother to put her voice, her song into the instrument. She had kept and cured the piece of rawhide, rubbing it with the secret cures, wrapping it round a clay cylinder to harden, wetting it, oiling it, forming it and refining its form, till the clay went to powder and was knocked from the tube, which she then cleaned and rubbed and oiled and finished. It was a privilege which only the most powerful, the most truly shameless of the Tanners took, to make a kerastion of the mother's skin. Chumo had claimed it without fear or doubt. As she worked she had many times pictured the Musician leading the procession, playing the flute, guiding her own spirit to its grave. She had wondered which of the Musicians it might be, and who would follow her, walking in her funeral procession. Never once had she thought that it would be played for Kwatewa before it was played for her. How was she to think of him, so much younger, dying first?

He had killed himself out of shame. He had cut his wrist veins with one of the tools he had made to cut stone.

His death itself was no shame, since there had been nothing for him to do but die. There was no fine, no ablution, no purification, for what he had done.

Shepherds had found the cave where he had kept the stones, great marble pieces from the cave walls, carved into copies of his own sandsculptures, his own sacred work for the Solstice and the Hariba: sculptures of stone, abominable, durable, desecrations of the body of the Mother.

15   People of his caste had destroyed the things with hammers, beaten them to dust and sand, swept the sand down into the river. She had thought Kwatewa would follow them, but he had gone to the cave at night and taken the sharp tool and cut his wrists and let his blood run. Why can't it stop running, Chumo?

    The Musician had come abreast of her now as she stood among the willows by the burying ground. Dastuye was old and skillful; his slow dancewalk seemed to float him above the ground in rhythm with the soft heartbeat of the drum that followed. Guiding the spirit and the body on its litter borne by four casteless men, he played the kerastion. His lips lay light on the leather mouthpiece, his fingers moved lightly as he played, and there was no sound at all. The kerastion flute has no stops and both its ends are plugged with disks of bronze. Tunes played on it are not heard by living ears. Chumo, listening, heard the drum and the whisper of the north wind in the willow leaves. Only Kwatewa in his woven grass shroud on the litter heard what song the Musician played for him, and knew whether it was a song of shame, or of grief, or of welcome.

If you like this story, you may also enjoy the use of the fantastic in Franz Kafka's "The Metamorphosis" and in Nathaniel Hawthorne's "Young Goodman Brown" (both in chapter 10).

GOING FURTHER The ranks of interesting American science-fiction writers are broad and deep. A British novelist who, like Le Guin, employs science-fiction motifs for other purposes is the prize-winning writer Jeanette Winterson, whose novel *The Stone Gods* (2008) crosses over into mainstream fiction.

Katherine Mansfield (1888–1923)

KATHERINE MANSFIELD, ONE of the finest practitioners of the modern short story in English, was born Kathleen Mansfield Beauchamp in Wellington, New Zealand. As an adolescent she traveled to England to study and eventually left New Zealand permanently to make a life in bohemian literary circles in London and Europe.

Her short stories, influenced by Chekhov but glowing with a mastery all their own, won her both the praise and the envy of such modernist writers as Virginia Woolf. She died too young to leave behind a major body of work, but her eye for detail and sense of nuanced emotion have assured her a place in the circle of important writers of the twentieth century.

Miss Brill (1920)

1   Although it was so brilliantly fine—the blue sky powdered with gold and great spots of light like white wine splashed over the Jardins Publiques—Miss Brill was glad that she had decided on her fur. The air was motionless, but when you opened your mouth there was just a faint chill, like a chill from a glass of iced water before you sip, and now and again a leaf came drifting—from nowhere, from the sky. Miss Brill put up her hand and touched her fur. Dear little thing! It was nice to feel it again. She had taken it out of its box that afternoon, shaken out the moth powder, given it a good brush, and rubbed the life back into the dim little eyes. "What has been happening to me?" said the sad little eyes. Oh, how sweet it was to see them snap at her again from the red eiderdown! . . . But the nose, which was of some black composition, wasn't at all firm. It must have had a knock, somehow. Never mind—a little dab of black sealing-wax when the time came—when it was absolutely necessary . . . Little rogue! Yes, she really felt like that

about it. Little rogue biting its tail just by her left ear. She could have taken it off and laid it on her lap and stroked it. She felt a tingling in her hands and arms, but that came from walking, she supposed. And when she breathed, something light and sad—no, not sad, exactly—something gentle seemed to move in her bosom.

There were a number of people out this afternoon, far more than last Sunday. And the band sounded louder and gayer. That was because the Season had begun. For although the band played all the year round on Sundays, out of season it was never the same. It was like some one playing with only the family to listen; it didn't care how it played if there weren't any strangers present. Wasn't the conductor wearing a new coat, too? She was sure it was new. He scraped with his foot and flapped his arms like a rooster about to crow, and the bandsmen sitting in the green rotunda blew out their cheeks and glared at the music. Now there came a little "flutey" bit—very pretty!—a little chain of bright drops. She was sure it would be repeated. It was; she lifted her head and smiled.

Only two people shared her "special" seat: a fine old man in a velvet coat, his hands clasped over a huge carved walking-stick, and a big old woman, sitting upright, with a roll of knitting on her embroidered apron. They did not speak. This was disappointing, for Miss Brill always looked forward to the conversation. She had become really quite expert, she thought, at listening as though she didn't listen, at sitting in other people's lives just for a minute while they talked round her.

She glanced, sideways, at the old couple. Perhaps they would go soon. Last Sunday, too, hadn't been as interesting as usual. An Englishman and his wife, he wearing a dreadful Panama hat and she button boots. And she'd gone on the whole time about how she ought to wear spectacles; she knew she needed them; but that it was no good getting any; they'd be sure to break and they'd never keep on. And he'd been so patient. He'd suggested everything—gold rims, the kind that curve round your ears, little pads inside the bridge. No, nothing would please her. "They'll always be sliding down my nose!" Miss Brill had wanted to shake her.

5   The old people sat on the bench, still as statues. Never mind, there was always the crowd to watch. To and fro, in front of the flower beds and the band rotunda, the couples and groups paraded, stopped to talk, to greet, to buy a handful of flowers from the old beggar who had his tray fixed to the railings. Little children ran among them, swooping and laughing; little boys with big white silk bows under their chins, little girls, little French dolls, dressed up in velvet and lace. And sometimes a tiny staggerer came suddenly rocking into the open from under the trees, stopped, stared, as suddenly sat down "flop," until its small high-stepping mother, like a young hen, rushed scolding to its rescue. Other people sat on the benches and green chairs, but they were nearly always the same, Sunday after Sunday, and—Miss Brill had often noticed—there was something funny about nearly all of them. They were odd, silent, nearly all old, and from the way they stared they looked as though they'd just come from dark little rooms or even—even cupboards!

Behind the rotunda the slender trees with yellow leaves down drooping, and through them just a line of sea, and beyond the blue sky with gold-veined clouds.

Tum-tum-tum tiddle-um! tiddle-um! tum tiddley-um tum ta! blew the band.

Two young girls in red came by and two young soldiers in blue met them, and they laughed and paired and went off arm-in-arm. Two peasant women with funny straw hats passed, gravely, leading beautiful smoke-colored donkeys. A cold, pale nun hurried by. A beautiful woman came along and dropped her bunch of violets, and a little boy ran after to hand them to her, and she took them and threw them away as if they'd been poisoned. Dear me! Miss Brill didn't know whether to admire that or not! And now an ermine toque and a gentleman in gray met just in front of her. He was tall, stiff, dignified, and she was wearing the ermine toque she'd bought when her hair was yellow. Now everything, her hair, her face, even her eyes, was the same color as the shabby ermine, and her hand, in its cleaned glove, lifted to dab her lips, was a tiny yellowish paw. Oh, she was so pleased to see him—delighted! She rather thought they were going to meet that afternoon. She described where she'd been—everywhere, here, there, along by the sea. The day was so charming—didn't he agree? And wouldn't he, perhaps? . . . But he shook his head, lighted a cigarette, slowly breathed a great deep puff into her face, and, even while she was still talking and laughing, flicked the match away and walked on. The ermine toque was alone; she smiled more brightly than ever. But even the band seemed to know what she was feeling and played more softly, played tenderly, and the drum beat, "The Brute! The Brute!" over and over. What would she do? What was going to happen now? But as Miss Brill wondered, the ermine toque turned, raised her hand as though she'd seen some one else, much nicer, just over there, and pattered away. And the band changed again and played more quickly, more gayly than ever, and the old couple on Miss Brill's seat got up and marched away, and such a funny old man with long whiskers hobbled along in time to the music and was nearly knocked over by four girls walking abreast.

Oh, how fascinating it was! How she enjoyed it! How she loved sitting here, watching it all! It was like a play. It was exactly like a play. Who could believe the sky at the back wasn't painted? But it wasn't till a little brown dog trotted on solemn and then slowly trotted off, like a little "theater" dog, a little dog that had been drugged, that Miss Brill discovered what it was that made it so exciting. They were all on stage. They weren't only the audience, not only looking on; they were acting. Even she had a part and came every Sunday. No doubt somebody would have noticed if she hadn't been there; she was part of the performance after all. How strange she'd never thought of it like that before! And yet it explained why she made such a point of starting from home at just the same time each week—so as not to be late for the performance—and it also explained why she had quite a queer, shy feeling at telling her English pupils how she spent her Sunday afternoons. No wonder! Miss Brill nearly laughed out loud. She was on the stage. She thought of the old invalid gentleman to whom she read the newspaper four afternoons a week while he slept in the garden. She had got quite used to the frail head on the cotton pillow, the hollowed eyes, the open mouth and the high pinched nose. If he'd been dead she mightn't have noticed for weeks; she wouldn't have minded. But suddenly he knew he was having the paper read to him by an actress! "An actress!" The old head lifted; two points of light quivered in the old eyes. "An actress—are ye?" And Miss Brill smoothed the newspaper as though it were the manuscript of her part and said gently: "Yes, I have been an actress for a long time."

10   The band had been having a rest. Now they started again. And what they played was warm, sunny, yet there was just a faint chill—a something, what was it?—not sadness—no, not sadness—a something that made you want to sing. The tune lifted, lifted, the light shone; and it seemed to Miss Brill that in another moment all of them, all the whole company, would begin singing. The young ones, the laughing ones who were moving together, they would begin, and the men's voices, very resolute and brave, would join them. And then she too, she too, and the others on the benches—they would come in with a kind of accompaniment—something low, that scarcely rose or fell, something so beautiful—moving . . . And Miss Brill's eyes filled with tears and she looked smiling at all the other members of the company. Yes, we understand, we understand, she thought—though what they understood she didn't know.

Just at that moment a boy and girl came and sat down where the old couple had been. They were beautifully dressed; they were in love. The hero and heroine, of course, just arrived from his father's yacht. And still soundlessly singing, still with that trembling smile, Miss Brill prepared to listen.

"No, not now," said the girl. "Not here, I can't."

"But why? Because of that stupid old thing at the end there?" asked the boy. "Why does she come here at all—who wants her? Why doesn't she keep her silly old mug at home?"

"It's her fu-fur which is so funny," giggled the girl. "It's exactly like a fried whiting."

15   "Ah, be off with you!" said the boy in an angry whisper. Then: "Tell me, ma petite chère—"

"No, not here," said the girl. "Not *yet*."

On her way home she usually bought a slice of honeycake at the baker's. It was her Sunday treat. Sometimes there was an almond in her slice, sometimes not. It made a great difference. If there was an almond it was like carrying home a tiny present—a surprise—something that might very well not have been there. She hurried on the almond Sundays and struck the match for the kettle in quite a dashing way.

But today she passed the baker's by, climbed the stairs, went into the little dark room—her room like a cupboard—and sat down on the red eiderdown. She sat there for a long time. The box that the fur came out of was on the bed. She unclasped the necklet quickly; quickly, without looking, laid it inside. But when she put the lid on she thought she heard something crying.

If you like this story, you may also like Katherine Anne Porter's "The Jilting of Granny Weatherall" and other character studies in chapter 5. You might ask yourself how Mansfield's drawing of character compares with those found in that chapter.

GOING FURTHER You may want to read her work alongside the dark psychological portraits, in *Mrs. Dalloway* or *To the Lighthouse,* by her contemporary Virginia Woolf.

Herman Melville (1819–1891)

WHEN HERMAN MELVILLE died of a heart attack in 1891, his name was virtually unknown. His obituary in *Harper's* magazine consisted of only one line—and they got his age wrong: *September 27—In New York City, Herman Melville, aged seventy-three years* (he was actually seventy-two). Today he is considered one of our greatest writers, known for having produced what many critics consider America's most important novel, *Moby-Dick; or The Whale.* When he was a young man his desire for independence (financial and personal) led him to find work as a sailor. The sea and the ships that travel upon it were major subjects for many of Melville's fictions—including the novels *Typee* and *Omoo*, which report on his adventures in the South Seas, and his last brief masterpiece, the novella *Billy Budd.*

Melville spent much of the middle of his life in New England, where he forged a strong friendship with Nathaniel Hawthorne. As Melville's writing matured, his interest in metaphysics (the philosophy of being and reality) increasingly influenced his work. However, the complexity of his fiction was unappreciated if not unnoticed, and after the publication of several commercially unsuccessful novels, among them *Moby-Dick,* Melville stopped writing prose and took a job as a customs inspector in New York City. His description, here, of city life reads almost like a clinical analysis of both depression and the impersonal, corporate world; the famous phrase "I prefer not to" has become an emblem of passive resistance. It is the oppressiveness of this conventional, urban existence that Melville captures so poignantly in "Bartleby, the Scrivener."

Bartleby, the Scrivener (1853)

A STORY OF WALL STREET

1   I am a rather elderly man. The nature of my avocations, for the last thirty years, has brought me into more than ordinary contact with what would seem an interesting and somewhat singular set of men, of whom, as yet, nothing, that I know of, has ever been written—I mean, the law-copyists, or scriveners. I have known very many of them, professionally and privately, and, if I pleased, could relate divers histories, at which good-natured gentlemen might smile, and sentimental souls might weep. But I waive the biographies of all other scriveners, for a few passages in the life of Bartleby, who was a scrivener, the strangest I ever saw, or heard of. While, of other law-copyists, I might write the complete life, of Bartleby nothing of that sort can be done. I believe that no materials exist, for a full and satisfactory biography of this man. It is an irreparable loss to literature. Bartleby was one of those beings of whom nothing is ascertainable, except from the original sources, and in

his case, those are very small. What my own astonished eyes saw of Bartleby, *that* is all I know of him, except, indeed, one vague report, which will appear in the sequel.

Ere introducing the scrivener, as he first appeared to me, it is fit I make some mention of myself, my *employés,* my business, my chambers, and general surroundings, because some such description is indispensable to an adequate understanding of the chief character about to be presented. Imprimis: I am a man who, from his youth upwards, has been filled with a profound conviction that the easiest way of life is the best. Hence, though I belong to a profession proverbially energetic and nervous, even to turbulence, at times, yet nothing of that sort have I ever suffered to invade my peace. I am one of those unambitious lawyers who never address a jury, or in any way draw down public applause; but, in the cool tranquillity of a snug retreat, do a snug business among rich men's bonds and mortgages and title-deeds. All who know me consider me an eminently *safe* man. The late John Jacob Astor, a personage little given to poetic enthusiasm, had no hesitation in pronouncing my first grand point to be prudence; my next, method. I do not speak it in vanity, but simply record the fact, that I was not unemployed in my profession by the late John Jacob Astor; a name which, I admit, I love to repeat; for it hath a rounded and orbicular sound to it, and rings like unto bullion. I will freely add, that I was not insensible to the late John Jacob Astor's good opinion.

Some time prior to the period at which this little history begins, my avocations had been largely increased. The good old office, now extinct in the State of New York, of a Master in Chancery, had been conferred upon me. It was not a very arduous office, but very pleasantly remunerative. I seldom lose my temper; much more seldom indulge in dangerous indignation at wrongs and outrages; but I must be permitted to be rash here and declare, that I consider the sudden and violent abrogation of the office of Master of Chancery, by the new Constitution, as a —— premature act; inasmuch as I had counted upon a life-lease of the profits, whereas I only received those of a few short years. But this is by the way.

My chambers were up stairs at No. —— Wall Street. At one end, they looked upon the white wall of the interior of a spacious skylight shaft, penetrating the building from top to bottom.

5   This view might have been considered rather tame than otherwise, deficient in what landscape painters call "life." But, if so, the view from the other end of my chambers offered, at least, a contrast, if nothing more. In that direction, my windows commanded an unobstructed view of a lofty brick wall, black by age and everlasting shade; which wall required no spyglass to bring out its lurking beauties, but, for the benefit of all near-sighted spectators, was pushed up to within ten feet of my window-panes. Owing to the great height of the surrounding buildings, and my chambers being on the second floor, the interval between this wall and mine not a little resembled a huge square cistern.

At the period just preceding the advent of Bartleby, I had two persons as copyists in my employment, and a promising lad as an office-boy. First, Turkey; second, Nippers; third, Ginger Nut. These may seem names, the like of which are not usually found in the Directory. In truth, they were nicknames, mutually conferred upon each other by my three clerks, and were deemed expressive of their respective persons or characters. Turkey was a short, pursy Englishman, of about my own age—that is, somewhere not far from sixty. In the morning, one might say, his face was of a fine florid hue, but after twelve o'clock, meridian—his dinner hour—it blazed like a grate full of Christmas coals; and continued blazing—but, as it were, with a gradual wane— till six o'clock, P.M., or thereabouts; after which, I saw no more of the proprietor of the face, which, gaining its meridian with the sun, seemed to set with it, to rise, culminate, and decline the following day, with the like regularity and undiminished glory. There are many singular coincidences I have known in the course of my life, not the least among which was the fact, that, exactly when Turkey displayed his fullest beams from his red and radiant countenance, just then, too, at that critical moment, began the daily period when I considered his business capacities as seriously disturbed for the remainder of the twenty-four hours. Not that he was absolutely idle, or averse to business then; far from it. The difficulty was, he was apt to be altogether too energetic. There was a strange, inflamed, flurried, flighty recklessness of activity about him. He would be incautious in dipping his pen into his inkstand. All his blots upon my documents were dropped there after twelve o'clock, meridian. Indeed, not only would he be reckless, and sadly given to making blots in the afternoon, but, some days, he went further, and was rather noisy. At such times, too, his face flamed with augmented blazonry, as if cannel coal had been heaped on anthracite. He made an unpleasant racket with his chair; spilled his sand-box; in mending his pens, impatiently split them all to pieces, and threw them on the floor in a sudden passion; stood up, and leaned over his table, boxing his papers about in a most indecorous manner, very sad to behold in an elderly man like him. Nevertheless, as he was in many ways a most valuable person to me, and all the time before twelve o'clock, meridian, was the quickest, steadiest creature, too, accomplishing a great deal of work in a style not easily to be matched—for these reasons, I was willing to overlook his eccentricities, though, indeed, occasionally, I remonstrated with him. I did this very gently, however, because, though the civilest, nay, the blandest and most reverential of men in the morning, yet, in the afternoon, he was disposed, upon provocation, to be slightly rash with his tongue—in fact, insolent. Now, valuing his morning services as I did, and resolved not to lose them—yet, at the same time, made uncomfortable by his inflamed ways after twelve o'clock—and being a man of peace, unwilling by my admonitions to call forth unseemly retorts from him, I took upon me, one Saturday noon (he was always worse on Saturdays) to hint to him, very kindly, that, perhaps, now that he was growing old, it might be well to abridge his labors; in short, he need not come to my chambers after twelve o'clock, but, dinner over, had best go home to his lodgings, and rest himself till tea-time. But no; he insisted upon his afternoon devotions. His countenance became intolerably fervid, as he oratorically assured me—gesticulating with a long ruler at the other end of the room—that if his services in the morning were useful, how indispensable, then, in the afternoon?

"With submission, sir," said Turkey, on this occasion, "I consider myself your right-hand man. In the morning I but marshal and deploy my columns; but in the afternoon I put myself at their head, and gallantly charge the foe, thus"—and he made a violent thrust with the ruler.

"But the blots, Turkey," intimated I.

"True; but, with submission, sir, behold these hairs! I am getting old. Surely, sir, a blot or two of a warm afternoon is not to be severely urged against gray hairs. Old age—even if it blot the page—is honorable. With submission, sir, we *both* are getting old."

10 This appeal to my fellow-feeling was hardly to be resisted. At all events, I saw that go he would not. So, I made up my mind to let him stay, resolving, nevertheless, to see to it that, during the afternoon, he had to do with my less important papers.

Nippers, the second on my list, was a whiskered, sallow, and, upon the whole, rather piratical-looking young man of about five-and-twenty. I always deemed him the victim of two evil powers—ambition and indigestion. The ambition was evinced by a certain impatience of the duties of a mere copyist, an unwarrantable usurpation of strictly professional affairs such as the original drawing up of legal documents. The indigestion seemed betokened in an occasional nervous testiness and grinning irritability, causing the teeth to audibly grind together over mistakes committed in copying; unnecessary maledictions, hissed, rather than spoken, in the heat of business; and especially by a continual discontent with the height of the table where he worked. Though of a very ingenious mechanical turn, Nippers could never get this table to suit him. He put chips under it, blocks of various sorts, bits of pasteboard, and at last went so far as to attempt an exquisite adjustment, by final pieces of folded blotting-paper. But no invention would answer. If, for the sake of easing his back, he brought the table-lid at a sharp angle well up towards his chin, and wrote there like a man using the steep roof of a Dutch house for his desk, then he declared that it stopped the circulation in his arms. If now he lowered the table to his waistbands, and stooped over it in writing, then there was a sore aching in his back. In short, the truth of the matter was, Nippers knew not what he wanted. Or, if he wanted anything, it was to be rid of a scrivener's table altogether. Among the manifestations of his diseased ambition was a fondness he had for receiving visits from certain ambiguous-looking fellows in seedy coats, whom he called his clients. Indeed, I was aware that not only was he, at times, considerable of a ward-politician, but he occasionally did a little business at the justices' courts, and was not unknown on the steps of the Tombs. I have good reason to believe, however, that one individual who called upon him at my chambers, and who, with a grand air, he insisted was his client, was no other than a dun, and the alleged title-deed, a bill. But, with all his failings, and the annoyances he caused me, Nippers, like his compatriot Turkey, was a very useful man to me; wrote a neat, swift hand; and, when he chose, was not deficient in a gentlemanly sort of deportment. Added to this, he always dressed in a gentlemanly sort of way; and so, incidentally, reflected credit upon my chambers. Whereas, with respect to Turkey, I had much ado to keep him from being a reproach to me. His clothes were apt to look oily, a smell of eating-houses. He wore his pantaloons very loose and baggy in summer. His coats were execrable, his hat not to be handled. But while the hat was a thing of indifference to me, inasmuch as his natural civility and deference, as a dependent Englishman, always led him to doff it the moment he entered the room, yet his coat was another matter. Concerning his coats, I reasoned with him; but with no effect. The truth was, I suppose, that a man with so small an income, could not afford to sport such a lustrous face and a lustrous coat at one and the same time. As Nippers once observed, Turkey's money went chiefly for red ink. One winter day, I presented Turkey with a highly respectable-looking coat of my own—a padded gray coat, of a most comfortable warmth, and which buttoned straight up from the knee to the neck. I thought Turkey would appreciate the favor, and abate his rashness and obstreperousness of afternoons. But no; I verily believe that buttoning himself up in so downy and blanket-like a coat had a pernicious effect upon him—upon the same principle that too much oats are bad for horses. In fact, precisely as a rash, restive horse is said to feel his oats, so Turkey felt his coat. It made him insolent. He was a man whom prosperity harmed.

Though, concerning the self-indulgent habits of Turkey, I had my own private surmises, yet, touching Nippers, I was well persuaded that, whatever might be his faults in other respects, he was, at least, a temperate young man. But indeed, nature herself seemed to have been his vintner, and, at his birth, charged him so thoroughly with an irritable, brandy-like disposition, that all subsequent potations were needless. When I consider how, amid the stillness of my chambers, Nippers would sometimes impatiently rise from his seat, and stooping over his table, spread his arms wide apart, seize the whole desk, and move it, and jerk it, with a grim, grinding motion on the floor, as if the table were a perverse voluntary agent, intent on thwarting and vexing him, I plainly perceive that, for Nippers, brandy-and-water were altogether superfluous.

It was fortunate for me that, owing to its peculiar cause—indigestion—the irritability and consequent nervousness of Nippers were mainly observable in the morning, while in the afternoon he was comparatively mild. So that, Turkey's paroxysms only coming on about twelve o'clock, I never had to do with their eccentricities at one time. Their fits relieved each other, like guards. When Nippers' was on, Turkey's was off; and *vice versa.* This was a good natural arrangement under the circumstances.

Ginger Nut, the third on my list, was a lad, some twelve years old. His father was a carman, ambitious of seeing his son on the bench instead of a cart, before he died. So he sent him to my office, as student at law, errand-boy, cleaner, and sweeper, at the rate of one dollar a week. He had a little desk to himself, but he did not use it much. Upon inspection, the drawer exhibited a great array of the shells of various sorts of nuts. Indeed, to this quick-witted youth, the whole noble science of the law was contained in a nutshell. Not the least among the employments of Ginger Nut, as well as one which he discharged with the most alacrity, was his duty as cake and apple purveyor for Turkey and Nippers. Copying lawpapers being proverbially a dry, husky sort of business, my two scriveners were fain to moisten their mouths very often with Spitzenbergs, to be had at the numerous stalls nigh the Custom House and Post Office. Also, they sent Ginger Nut very frequently for that peculiar cake—small, flat, round, and very spicy—after which he had been named by them. Of a cold morning, when business was but dull, Turkey would gobble up scores of these cakes, as if they were mere wafers—indeed, they sell them at the rate of six or eight for a penny—the scrape of his pen blending with the crunching of the crisp particles in his mouth. Of all the fiery afternoon blunders and flurried rashness of Turkey, was his once moistening a ginger-cake between his lips, and clapping it on to a mortgage, for a seal. I came within an ace of dismissing him then. But he mollified me by making an oriental bow, and saying—

15   "With submission, sir, it was generous of me to find you in stationery on my own account."

Now my original business—that of a conveyancer and title hunter, and drawer-up of recondite documents of all sorts—was considerably increased by receiving the master's office. There was now great work for scriveners. Not only must I push the clerks already with me, but I must have additional help.

In answer to my advertisement, a motionless young man one morning stood upon my office threshold, the door being open, for it was summer. I can see that figure now—pallidly neat, pitiably respectable, incurably forlorn! It was Bartleby.

After a few words touching his qualifications, I engaged him, glad to have among my corps of copyists a man of so singularly sedate an aspect, which I thought might operate beneficially upon the flighty temper of Turkey, and the fiery one of Nippers.

I should have stated before that ground-glass folding-doors divided my premises into two parts, one of which was occupied by my scriveners, the other by myself. According to my humor, I threw open these doors, or closed them. I resolved to assign Bartleby a corner by the folding-doors, but on my side of them, so as to have this quiet man within easy call, in case any trifling thing was to be done. I placed his desk close up to a small side-window in that part of the room, a window which originally had afforded a lateral view of certain grimy brickyards and bricks, but which, owing to subsequent erections, commanded at present no view at all, though it gave some light. Within three feet of the panes was a wall, and the light came down from far above, between two lofty buildings, as from a very small opening in a dome. Still further to a satisfactory arrangement, I procured a high green folding screen, which might entirely isolate Bartleby from my sight, though not remove him from my voice. And thus, in a manner, privacy and society were conjoined.

At first, Bartleby did an extraordinary quantity of writing. As if long famishing for something to copy, he seemed to gorge himself on my documents. There was no pause for digestion. He ran a day and night line, copying by sunlight and by candle-light. I should have been quite delighted with his application, had be been cheerfully industrious. But he wrote on silently, palely, mechanically.

It is, of course, an indispensable part of a scrivener's business to verify the accuracy of his copy, word by word. Where there are two or more scriveners in an office, they assist each other in this examination, one reading from the copy, the other holding the original. It is a very dull, wearisome, and lethargic affair. I can readily imagine that, to some sanguine temperaments, it would be altogether intolerable. For example, I cannot credit that the mettlesome poet, Byron, would have contentedly sat down with Bartleby to examine a law document of, say five hundred pages, closely written in a crimpy hand.

Now and then, in the haste of business, it had been my habit to assist in comparing some brief document myself, calling Turkey or Nippers for this purpose. One object I had, in placing Bartleby so handy to me behind the screen, was, to avail myself of his services on such trivial occasions. It was on the third day, I think, of his being with me, and before any necessity had arisen for having his own writing examined, that, being much hurried to complete a small affair I had in hand, I abruptly called to Bartleby. In my haste and natural expectancy of instant compliance, I sat with my head bent over the original on my desk, and my right hand sideways, and somewhat nervously extended with the copy, so that, immediately upon emerging from his retreat, Bartleby might snatch it and proceed to business without the least delay.

In this very attitude did I sit when I called to him, rapidly stating what it was I wanted him to do—namely, to examine a small paper with me. Imagine my surprise, nay, my consternation, when, without moving from his privacy, Bartleby, in a singularly mild, firm voice, replied, "I would prefer not to."

I sat awhile in perfect silence, rallying my stunned faculties. Immediately it occurred to me that my ears had deceived me, or Bartleby had entirely misunderstood my meaning. I repeated my request in the clearest tone I could assume; but in quite as clear a one came the previous reply, "I would prefer not to."

"Prefer not to," echoed I, rising in high excitement, and crossing the room with a stride. "What do you mean? Are you moonstruck? I want you to help me compare this sheet here—take it," and I thrust it towards him.

"I would prefer not to," said he.

I looked at him steadfastly. His face was leanly composed; his gray eye dimly calm. Not a wrinkle of agitation rippled him. Had there been the least uneasiness, anger, impatience, or impertinence in his manner; in other words, had there been anything ordinarily human about him, doubtless I should have violently dismissed him from the premises. But as it was, I should have as soon thought of turning my pale plaster-of-paris bust of Cicero out of doors. I stood gazing at him awhile, as he went on with his own writing, and then reseated myself at my desk. This is very strange, thought I. What had one best do? But my business hurried me. I concluded to forget the matter for the present, reserving it for my future leisure. So, calling Nippers from the other room, the paper was speedily examined.

A few days after this, Bartleby concluded four lengthy documents, being quadruplicates of a week's testimony taken before me in my High Court of Chancery. It became necessary to examine them. It was an important suit, and great accuracy was imperative. Having all things arranged, I called Turkey, Nippers, and Ginger Nut, from the next room, meaning to place the four copies in the hands of my four clerks, while I should read from the original. Accordingly, Turkey, Nippers, and Ginger Nut had taken their seats in a row, each with his document in his hand, when I called to Bartleby to join this interesting group.

"Bartleby! quick, I am waiting."

30   I heard a slow scrape of his chair legs on the uncarpeted floor, and soon he appeared standing at the entrance of his hermitage.

"What is wanted?" said he, mildly.

"The copies, the copies," said I, hurriedly. "We are going to examine them. There"—and I held towards him the fourth quadruplicate.

"I would prefer not to," he said, and gently disappeared behind the screen.

For a few moments I was turned into a pillar of salt, standing at the head of my seated column of clerks. Recovering myself, I advanced towards the screen, and demanded the reason for such extraordinary conduct.

35   "*Why* do you refuse?"

"I would prefer not to."

With any other man I should have flown outright into a dreadful passion, scorned all further words, and thrust him ignominiously from my presence. But there was something about Bartleby that not only strangely disarmed me, but, in a wonderful manner, touched and disconcerted me. I began to reason with him.

"These are your own copies we are about to examine. It is labor saving to you, because one examination will answer for your four papers. It is common usage. Every copyist is bound to help examine his copy. Is it not so? Will you not speak? Answer!"

"I prefer not to," he replied in a flute-like tone. It seemed to me that, while I had been addressing him, he carefully revolved every statement that I made; fully comprehended the meaning; could not gainsay the irresistible conclusion; but, at the same time, some paramount consideration prevailed with him to reply as he did.

40   "You are decided, then, not to comply with my request—a request made according to common usage and common sense?"

He briefly gave me to understand that on that point my judgment was sound. Yes: his decision was irreversible.

It is not seldom the case that, when a man is browbeaten in some unprecedented and violently unreasonable way, he begins to stagger in his own plainest faith. He begins, as it were, vaguely to surmise that, wonderful as it may be, all the justice and all the reason is on the other side. Accordingly, if any disinterested persons are present, he turns to them for some reinforcement for his own faltering mind.

"Turkey," said I, "what do you think of this? Am I not right?"

"With submission, sir," said Turkey, in his blandest tone, "I think that you are."

45   "Nippers," said I, "what do *you* think of it?"

"I think I should kick him out of the office."

(The reader of nice perceptions will have perceived that, it being morning, Turkey's answer is couched in polite and tranquil terms, but Nippers replies in ill-tempered ones. Or, to repeat a previous sentence, Nippers' ugly mood was on duty, and Turkey's off.)

"Ginger Nut," said I, willing to enlist the smallest suffrage in my behalf, "what do *you* think of it?"

"I think, sir, he's a little *luny*," replied Ginger Nut, with a grin.

"You hear what they say," said I, turning towards the screen, "come forth and do your duty."

But he vouchsafed no reply. I pondered a moment in sore perplexity. But once more business hurried me. I determined again to postpone the consideration of this dilemma to my future leisure. With a little trouble we made out to examine the papers without Bartleby, though at every page or two Turkey deferentially dropped his opinion, that this proceeding was quite out of the common; while Nippers, twitching in his chair with a dyspeptic nervousness, ground out, between his set teeth, occasional hissing maledictions against the stubborn oaf behind the screen. And for his (Nippers') part, this was the first and the last time he would do another man's business without pay.

Meanwhile Bartleby sat in his hermitage, oblivious to every thing but his own peculiar business there.

Some days passed, the scrivener being employed upon another lengthy work. His late remarkable conduct led me to regard his ways narrowly. I observed that he never went to dinner; indeed, that he never went anywhere. As yet I had never, of my personal knowledge, known him to be outside of my office. He was a perpetual sentry in the corner. At about eleven o'clock though, in the morning, I noticed that Ginger Nut would advance toward the opening in Bartleby's screen, as if silently beckoned thither by a gesture invisible to me where I sat. The boy would then leave the office, jingling a few pence, and reappear with a handful of ginger-nuts, which he delivered in the hermitage, receiving two of the cakes for his trouble.

He lives, then, on ginger-nuts, thought I; never eats a dinner, properly speaking; he must be a vegetarian, then, but no; he never eats even vegetables, he eats nothing but ginger-nuts. My mind then ran on in reveries concerning the probable effects upon the human constitution of living entirely on ginger-nuts. Ginger-nuts are so called, because they contain ginger as one of their peculiar constituents, and the final flavoring one. Now, what was ginger? A hot, spicy thing. Was Bartleby hot and spicy? Not at all. Ginger, then, had no effect upon Bartleby. Probably he preferred it should have none.

Nothing so aggravates an earnest person as a passive resistance. If the individual so resisted be of a not inhumane temper, and the resisting one perfectly harmless in his passivity, then, in the better moods of the former, he will endeavor charitably to construe to his imagination what proves impossible to be solved by his judgment. Even so, for the most part, I regarded Bartleby and his ways. Poor fellow! thought I, he means no mischief; it is plain he intends no insolence; his aspect sufficiently evinces that his eccentricities are involuntary. He is useful to me. I can get along with him. If I turn him away, the chances are he will fall in with some less indulgent employer, and then he will be rudely treated, and perhaps driven forth miserably to starve. Yes. Here I can cheaply purchase a delicious self-approval. To befriend Bartleby; to humor him in his strange wilfulness, will cost me little or nothing, while I lay up in my soul what will eventually prove a sweet morsel for my conscience. But this mood was not invariable with me. The passiveness of Bartleby sometimes irritated me. I felt strangely goaded on to encounter him in new opposition— to elicit some angry spark from him answerable to my own. But, indeed, I might as well have essayed to strike fire with my knuckles against a bit of Windsor soap. But one afternoon the evil impulse in me mastered me, and the following little scene ensued:

"Bartleby," said I, "when those papers are all copied, I will compare them with you."

"I would prefer not to."

"How? Surely you do not mean to persist in that mulish vagary?"

No answer.

I threw open the folding-doors nearby, and turning upon Turkey and Nippers, exclaimed:

"Bartleby a second time says, he won't examine his papers. What do you think of it, Turkey?"

It was afternoon, be it remembered. Turkey sat glowing like a brass boiler; his bald head steaming; his hands reeling among his blotted papers.

"Think of it?" roared Turkey. "I think I'll just step behind his screen, and black his eyes for him!"

So saying, Turkey rose to his feet and threw his arms into a pugilistic position. He was hurrying away to make good his promise, when I detained him, alarmed at the effect of incautiously rousing Turkey's combativeness after dinner.

65   "Sit down, Turkey," said I, "and hear what Nippers has to say. What do you think of it, Nippers? Would I not be justified in immediately dismissing Bartleby?"

"Excuse me, that is for you to decide, sir. I think his conduct quite unusual, and, indeed, unjust, as regards Turkey and myself. But it may only be a passing whim."

"Ah," exclaimed I, "you have strangely changed your mind, then—you speak very gently of him now."

"All beer," cried Turkey; "gentleness is effects of beer—Nippers and I dined together to-day. You see how gentle *I* am, sir. Shall I go and black his eyes?"

"You refer to Bartleby, I suppose. No, not to-day, Turkey," I replied; "pray, put up your fists."

70   I closed the doors, and again advanced towards Bartleby. I felt additional incentives tempting me to my fate. I burned to be rebelled against again. I remembered that Bartleby never left the office.

"Bartleby," said I, "Ginger Nut is away; just step around to the Post Office, won't you?" (it was but a three minutes' walk) "and see if there is anything for me."

"I would prefer not to."

"You *will* not?"

"I *prefer* not."

75   I staggered to my desk, and sat there in a deep study. My blind inveteracy returned. Was there any other thing in which I could procure myself to be ignominiously repulsed by this lean, penniless wight?—my hired clerk? What added thing is there, perfectly reasonable, that he will be sure to refuse to do?

"Bartleby!"

No answer.

"Bartleby," in a louder tone.

No answer.

80   "Bartleby," I roared.

Like a very ghost, agreeably to the laws of magical invocation, at the third summons, he appeared at the entrance of his hermitage.

"Go to the next room, and tell Nippers to come to me."

"I prefer not to," he respectfully and slowly said, and mildly disappeared.

"Very good, Bartleby," said I, in a quiet sort of serenely-severe self-possessed tone, intimating the unalterable purpose of some terrible retribution very close at hand. At the moment I half intended something of the kind. But upon the whole, as it was drawing towards my dinner-hour, I thought it best to put on my hat and walk home for the day, suffering much from perplexity and distress of mind.

85   Shall I acknowledge it? The conclusion of this whole business was, that it soon became a fixed fact of my chambers, that a pale young scrivener, by the name of Bartleby, had a desk there; that he copied for me at the usual rate of four cents a folio (one hundred words); but he was permanently exempt from examining the work done by him, that duty being transferred to Turkey and Nippers, out of compliment, doubtless, to their superior acuteness; moreover, said Bartleby was never, on any account, to be dispatched on the most trivial errand of any sort; and that even if entreated to take upon him such a matter, it was generally understood that he would "prefer not to"—in other words, that he would refuse point-blank.

As days passed on, I became considerably reconciled to Bartleby. His steadiness, his freedom from all dissipation, his incessant industry (except when he chose to throw himself into a standing revery behind his screen), his great stillness, his unalterableness of demeanor under all circumstances, made him a valuable acquisition. One prime thing was this—*he was always there*—first in the morning, continually through the day, and the last at night. I had a singular confidence in his honesty. I felt my most precious papers perfectly safe in his hands. Sometimes, to be sure, I could not, for the very soul of me, avoid falling into sudden spasmodic passions with him. For it was exceeding difficult to bear in mind all the time those strange peculiarities, privileges, and unheard-of exemptions, forming the tacit stipulations on Bartleby's part under which he remained in my office. Now and then, in the eagerness of dispatching pressing business, I would inadvertently summon Bartleby, in a short, rapid tone, to put his finger, say, on the incipient tie of a bit of red tape with which I was about compressing some papers. Of course, from behind the screen the usual answer, "I prefer not to," was sure to come; and then, how could a human creature, with the common infirmities of our nature, refrain from bitterly exclaiming upon such perverseness—such unreasonableness? However, every added repulse of this sort which I received only tended to lessen the probability of my repeating the inadvertence.

Here is must be said, that, according to the custom of most legal gentlemen occupying chambers in densely populated law buildings, there were several keys to my door. One was kept by a woman residing in the attic, which person weekly scrubbed and daily swept and dusted my apartments. Another was kept by Turkey for convenience sake. The third I sometimes carried in my own pocket. The fourth I knew not who had.

Now, one Sunday morning I happened to go to Trinity Church, to hear a celebrated preacher, and finding myself rather early on the ground I thought I would walk round to my chambers for a while. Luckily I had my key with me; but upon applying it to the lock, I found it resisted by something inserted from the inside. Quite surprised, I called out; when to my consternation a key was turned from within; and thrusting his lean visage at me, and holding the door ajar, the apparition of Bartleby appeared, in his shirt-sleeves, and otherwise in a strangely tattered *deshabille,* saying quietly that he was sorry, but he was deeply engaged just then, and—preferred not admitting me at present. In a brief word or two, he moreover added, that perhaps I had better walk round the block two or three times, and by that time he would probably have concluded his affairs.

Now, the utterly unsurmised appearance of Bartleby, tenanting my law-chambers of a Sunday morning, with his cadaverously gentlemanly *nonchalance,* yet withal firm and self-possessed, had such a strange effect upon me, that incontinently I slunk away from my own door, and did as desired. But not without sundry twinges of impotent rebellion against the mild effrontery of this unaccountable scrivener. Indeed, it was his wonderful mildness chiefly, which not only disarmed me, but unmanned me, as it were. For I consider that one, for the time, is sort of unmanned when he tranquilly permits his hired clerk to dictate to him, and order him away from his own premises. Furthermore, I was full of uneasiness as to what Bartleby could possibly be doing in my office in his shirt-sleeves, and in an otherwise dismantled condition of a Sunday morning. Was anything amiss going on? Nay, that was out of the question. It was not to be thought of for a moment that Bartleby was an immoral person. But what could he be doing there?—copying? Nay again, whatever might be his eccentricities, Bartleby was an eminently decorous person. He would be the last man to sit down to his desk in any state approaching to nudity. Besides, it was Sunday; and there was something about Bartleby that forbade the supposition that he would by any secular occupation violate the proprieties of the day.

0   Nevertheless, my mind was not pacified; and full of a restless curiosity, at last I returned to the door. Without hindrance I inserted my key, opened it, and entered. Bartleby was not to be seen. I looked round anxiously, peeped behind his screen; but it was very plain that he was gone. Upon more closely examining the place, I surmised that for an indefinite period Bartleby must have ate, dressed, and slept in my office, and that too without plate, mirror, or bed. The cushioned seat of a rickety old sofa in one corner bore the faint impress of a lean, reclining form. Rolled away under his desk, I found a blanket; under the empty grate, a blacking box and brush; on a chair, a tin basin, with soap and a ragged towel; in a newspaper a few crumbs of ginger-nuts and a morsel of cheese. Yes, thought I, it is evident enough that Bartleby has been making his home here, keeping bachelor's hall all by himself. Immediately then the thought came sweeping across me, what miserable friendlessness and loneliness are here revealed! His poverty is great; but his solitude, how horrible! Think of it. Of a Sunday, Wall Street is deserted as Petra; and every night of every day it is an emptiness. This building, too, which of week-days hums with industry and life, at nightfall echoes with sheer vacancy, and all through Sunday is forlorn. And here Bartleby

makes his home; sole spectator of a solitude which he has seen all populous—a sort of innocent and transformed Marius brooding among the ruins of Carthage?

For the first time in my life a feeling of overpowering stinging melancholy seized me. Before, I had never experienced aught but a not unpleasing sadness. The bond of a common humanity now drew me irresistibly to gloom. A fraternal melancholy! For both I and Bartleby were sons of Adam. I remembered the bright silks and sparkling faces I had seen that day, in gala trim, swan-like sailing down the Mississippi of Broadway; and I contrasted them with the pallid copyist, and thought to myself, Ah, happiness courts the light, so we deem the world is gay; but misery hides aloof, so we deem that misery there is none. These sad fancyings—chimeras, doubtless, of a sick and silly brain—led on to other and more special thoughts, concerning the eccentricities of Bartleby. Presentiments of strange discoveries hovered round me. The scrivener's pale form appeared to me laid out, among uncaring strangers, in its shivering winding-sheet.

Suddenly I was attracted by Bartleby's closed desk, the key in open sight left in the lock.

I mean no mischief, seek the gratification of no heartless curiosity, thought I; besides, the desk is mine, and its contents, too, so I will make bold to look within. Everything was methodically arranged, the papers smoothly placed. The pigeon-holes were deep, and removing the files of documents, I groped into their recesses. Presently I felt something there, and dragged it out. It was an old bandanna handkerchief, heavy and knotted. I opened it, and saw it was a saving's bank.

I now recalled all the quiet mysteries which I had noted in the man. I remembered that he never spoke but to answer; that, though at intervals he had considerable time to himself, yet I had never seen him reading—no, not even a newspaper; that for long periods he would stand looking out, at his pale window behind the screen, upon the dead brick wall; I was quite sure he never visited any refectory or eating-house; while his pale face clearly indicated that he never drank beer like Turkey, or tea and coffee even, like other men; that he never went anywhere in particular that I could learn; never went out for a walk, unless, indeed, that was the case at present; that he had declined telling who he was, or whence he came, or whether he had any relatives in the world; that though so thin and pale, he never complained of ill-health. And more than all, I remembered a certain unconscious air of pallid—how shall I call it?—of pallid haughtiness, say, or rather an austere reserve about him, which had positively awed me into my tame compliance with his eccentricities, when I had feared to ask him to do the slightest incidental thing for me, even though I might know, from his long-continued motionlessness, that behind his screen he must be standing in one of those dead-wall reveries of his.

95 Revolving all these things, and coupling them with the recently discovered fact, that he made my office his constant abiding place and home, and not forgetful of his morbid moodiness; revolving all these things, a prudential feeling began to steal over me. My first emotions had been those of pure melancholy and sincerest pity; but just in proportion as the forlornness of Bartleby grew and grew to my imagination, did that same melancholy merge into fear, that pity into repulsion. So true it is, and so terrible, too, that up to a certain point the thought or sight of misery enlists our best affections; but, in certain special cases, beyond that point it does not. They err who would assert that invariably this is owing to the inherent selfishness of the human heart. It rather proceeds from a certain hopelessness of remedying excessive and organic ill. To a sensitive being, pity is not seldom pain. And when at last it is perceived that such pity cannot lead to effectual succor, common sense bids the soul be rid of it. What I saw that morning persuaded me that the scrivener was the victim of innate and incurable disorder. I might give alms to his body; but his body did not pain him; it was his soul that suffered, and his soul I could not reach.

I did not accomplish the purpose of going to Trinity Church that morning. Somehow, the things I had seen disqualified me for the time from church-going. I walked homeward, thinking what I would do with Bartleby. Finally, I resolved upon this—I would put certain calm questions to him the next morning, touching his history, etc., and if he declined to answer then openly and unreservedly (and I supposed he would prefer not), then to give him a twenty dollar bill over and above whatever I might owe him, and tell him his services were no longer required; but that if in any other way I could assist him, I would be happy to do so, especially if he desired to return to his native place, wherever that might be, I would willingly help to defray the expenses. Moreover, if, after reaching home, he found himself at any time in want of aid, a letter from him would be sure of a reply.

The next morning came.

"Bartleby," said I, gently calling to him behind his screen.

No reply.

"Bartleby," said I, in a still gentler tone, "come here; I am not going to ask you to do anything you would prefer not to do—I simply wish to speak to you."

Upon this he noiselessly slid into view.

"Will you tell me, Bartleby, where you were born?"

"I would prefer not to."

"Will you tell me *anything* about yourself?"

"I would prefer not to."

"But what reasonable objection can you have to speak to me? I feel friendly towards you."

He did not look at me while I spoke, but kept his glance fixed upon my bust of Cicero, which, as I then sat, was directly behind me, some six inches above my head.

"What is your answer, Bartleby?" said I, after waiting a considerable time for a reply, during which his countenance remained immovable, only there was the faintest conceivable tremor of the white attenuated mouth.

"At present I prefer to give no answer," he said, and retired into his hermitage.

It was rather weak in me I confess, but his manner, on this occasion, nettled me. Not only did there seem to lurk in it a certain calm disdain, but his perverseness seemed ungrateful, considering the undeniable good usage and indulgence he had received from me.

Again I sat ruminating what I should do. Mortified as I was at his behavior, and resolved as I had been to dismiss him when I entered my office, nevertheless I strangely felt something superstitious knocking at my heart, and forbidding me to carry out my purpose, and denouncing me for a villain if I dared to breathe one bitter word against this forlornest of mankind. At last, familiarly drawing my chair behind his screen, I sat down and said: "Bartleby, never mind, then, about revealing your history; but let me entreat you, as a friend, to comply as far as may be with the usages of this office. Say now, you will help to examine papers tomorrow or next day: in short, say now, that in a day or two you will begin to be a little reasonable:—say so, Bartleby."

"At present I would prefer not to be a little reasonable," was his mildly cadaverous reply.

Just then the folding-doors opened, and Nippers approached. He seemed suffering from an unusually bad night's rest, induced by severer indigestion than common. He overheard those final words of Bartleby.

"*Prefer not*, eh?" gritted Nippers—"I'd *prefer* him, if I were you, sir," addressing me—"I'd *prefer* him; I'd give him preferences, the stubborn mule! What is it, sir, pray, that he *prefers* not to do now?"

Bartleby moved not a limb.

"Mr. Nippers," said I, "I'd prefer that you would withdraw for the present."

Somehow, of late, I had got into the way of involuntarily using this word "prefer" upon all sorts of not exactly suitable occasions. And I trembled to think that my contact with the scrivener had already and seriously affected me in a mental way. And what further and deeper aberration might it not yet produce? This apprehension had not been without efficacy in determining me to summary measures.

As Nippers, looking very sour and sulky, was departing, Turkey blandly and deferentially approached.

"With submission, sir," said he, "yesterday I was thinking about Bartleby here, and I think that if he would but prefer to take a quart of good ale every day, it would do much towards mending him, and enabling him to assist in examining his papers."

"So you have got the word, too," said I, slightly excited.

"With submission, what word, sir?" asked Turkey, respectfully crowding himself into the contracted space behind the screen, and by so doing, making me jostle the scrivener. "What word, sir?"

"I would prefer to be left alone here," said Bartleby, as if offended at being mobbed in his privacy.

"*That's* the word, Turkey," said I—"*that's* it."

"Oh, *prefer?* oh yes—queer word. I never use it myself. But, sir, as I was saying, if he would but prefer—"

125 "Turkey," interrupted I, "you will please withdraw."

"Oh certainly, sir, if you prefer that I should."

As he opened the folding-door to retire, Nippers at his desk caught a glimpse of me, and asked whether I would prefer to have a certain paper copied on blue paper or white. He did not in the least roguishly accent the word "prefer." It was plain that it involuntarily rolled from his tongue. I thought to myself, surely I must get rid of a demented man, who already has in some degree turned the tongues, if not the heads of myself and clerks. But I thought it prudent not to break the dismission at once.

The next day I noticed that Bartleby did nothing but stand at his window in his dead-wall revery. Upon asking him why he did not write, he said that he had decided upon doing no more writing.

"Why, how now? what next?" exclaimed I, "do no more writing?"

130 "No more."

"And what is the reason?"

"Do you not see the reason for yourself?" he indifferently replied.

I looked steadfastly at him, and perceived that his eyes looked dull and glazed. Instantly it occurred to me, that his unexampled diligence in copying by his dim window for the first few weeks of his stay with me might have temporarily impaired his vision.

I was touched. I said something in condolence with him. I hinted that of course he did wisely in abstaining from writing for a while; and urged him to embrace that opportunity of taking wholesome exercise in the open air. This, however, he did not do. A few days after this, my other clerks being absent, and being in a great hurry to dispatch certain letters by the mail, I thought that, having nothing else earthly to do, Bartleby would surely be less inflexible than usual, and carry these letters to the Post Office. But he blankly declined. So, much to my inconvenience, I went myself.

135 Still added days went by. Whether Bartleby's eyes improved or not, I could not say. To all appearance, I thought they did. But when I asked him if they did, he vouchsafed no answer. At all events, he would do no copying. At last, in replying to my urgings, he informed me that he had permanently given up copying.

"What!" exclaimed I; "suppose your eyes should get entirely well—better than ever before—would you not copy then?"

"I have given up copying," he answered, and slid aside.

He remained as ever, a fixture in my chamber. Nay—if that were possible—he became still more of a fixture than before. What was to be done? He would do nothing in the office; why should he stay there? In plain fact, he had now become a millstone to me, not only useless as a necklace, but afflictive to bear. Yet I was sorry for him. I speak less than truth when I say that, on his own account, he occasioned me uneasiness. If he would but have named a single relative or friend, I would instantly have written, and urged their taking the poor fellow away to some convenient retreat. But he seemed alone, absolutely alone in the universe. A bit of wreck in the mid-Atlantic. At length, necessities connected with my business tyrannized over all other considerations. Decently as I could, I told Bartleby that in six days' time he must unconditionally leave the office. I warned him to take measures, in the interval, for procuring some other abode. I offered to assist him in this endeavor, if he himself would but take the first step towards a removal. "And when you finally quit me, Bartleby," added I, "I shall see that you go not away entirely unprovided. Six days from this hour, remember."

At the expiration of that period, I peeped behind the screen, and lo! Bartleby was there.

140 I buttoned up my coat, balanced myself; advanced slowly towards him, touched his shoulder, and said, "The time has come; you must quit this place; I am sorry for you; here is money; but you must go."

"I would prefer not," he replied, with his back still towards me.

"You *must.*"

He remained silent.

Now I had an unbounded confidence in this man's common honesty. He had frequently restored to me sixpences and shillings carelessly dropped upon the floor, for I am apt to be very reckless in such shirt-button affairs. The proceeding, then, which followed will not be deemed extraordinary.

"Bartleby," said I, "I owe you twelve dollars on account; here are thirty-two, the odd twenty are yours—Will you take it?" and I handed the bills towards him.

But he made no motion.

"I will leave them here, then," putting them under a weight on the table. Then taking my hat and cane and going to the door, I tranquilly turned and added—"After you have removed your things from these offices, Bartleby, you will of course lock the door—since every one is now gone for the day but you—and if you please, slip your key underneath the mat, so that I may have it in the morning. I shall not see you again; so good-bye to you. If, hereafter, in your new place of abode, I can be of any service to you, do not fail to advise me by letter. Good-bye, Bartleby, and fare you well."

But he answered not a word; like the last column of some ruined temple, he remained standing mute and solitary in the middle of the otherwise deserted room.

As I walked home in a pensive mood, my vanity got the better of my pity. I could not but highly plume myself on my masterly management in getting rid of Bartleby. Masterly I call it, and such it must appear to any dispassionate thinker. The beauty of my procedure seemed to consist in its perfect quietness. There was no vulgar bullying, no bravado of any sort, no choleric hectoring, and striding to and fro across the apartment, jerking out vehement commands for Bartleby to bundle himself off with his beggarly traps. Nothing of the kind. Without loudly bidding Bartleby depart—as an inferior genius might have done—I *assumed* the ground that depart he must; and upon that assumption built all I had to say. The more I thought over my procedure, the more I was charmed with it. Nevertheless, next morning, upon awakening, I had my doubts—I had somehow slept off the fumes of vanity. One of the coolest and wisest hours a man has, is just after he awakes in the morning. My procedure seemed as sagacious as ever—but only in theory. How it would prove in practice—there was the rub. It was truly a beautiful thought to have assumed Bartleby's departure; but, after all, that assumption was simply my own, and none of Bartleby's. The great point was, not whether I had assumed that he would quit me, but whether he would prefer to do so. He was more a man of preferences than assumptions.

After breakfast, I walked down town, arguing the probabilities *pro* and *con.* One moment I thought it would prove a miserable failure, and Bartleby would be found all alive at my office as usual; the next moment it seemed certain that I should find his chair empty. And so I kept veering about. At the corner of Broadway and Canal Street, I saw quite an excited group of people standing in earnest conversation.

"I'll take odds he doesn't," said a voice as I passed.

"Doesn't go?—done!" said I, "put up your money."

I was instinctively putting my hand in my pocket to produce my own, when I remembered that this was an election day. The words I had overheard bore no reference to Bartleby, but to the success or non-success of some candidate for the mayoralty. In my intent frame of mind, I had, as it were, imagined that all Broadway shared in my excitement, and were debating the same question with me. I passed on, very thankful that the uproar of the street screened my momentary absent-mindedness.

As I had intended, I was earlier than usual at my office door. I stood listening for a moment. All was still. He must be gone. I tried the knob. The door was locked. Yes, my procedure had worked to a charm; he indeed must be vanished. Yet a certain melancholy mixed with this: I was almost sorry for my brilliant success. I was fumbling under the door mat for the key, which Bartleby was to have left there for me, when accidentally my knee knocked against a panel, producing a summoning sound, and in response a voice came to me from within—"Not yet; I am occupied."

It was Bartleby.

I was thunderstruck. For an instant I stood like the man who, pipe in mouth, was killed one cloudless afternoon long ago in Virginia, by summer lightning; at his own warm open window he was killed, and remained leaning out there upon the dreamy afternoon, till some one touched him, when he fell.

"Not gone!" I murmured at last. But again obeying that wondrous ascendancy which the inscrutable scrivener had over me, and from which ascendancy, for all my chafing, I could not completely escape, I slowly went down stairs and out into the street, and while walking round the block, considered what I should next do in this unheard-of perplexity. Turn the man out by an actual thrusting I could not; to drive him away by calling him hard names would not do; calling in the police was an unpleasant idea; and yet, permit him to enjoy his cadaverous triumph over me—this, too, I could not think of. What was to be done? or, if nothing could be done, was there anything further that I could *assume* in the matter? Yes, as before I had prospectively assumed that Bartleby would depart, so now I might retrospectively assume that departed he was. In the legitimate carrying out of this assumption, I might enter my office in a great hurry, and pretending not to see Bartleby at all, walk straight against him as if he were air. Such a proceeding would in a singular degree have the appearance of a home-thrust. It was hardly possible that Bartleby could withstand such an application of the doctrine of assumption. But upon second thoughts the success of the plan seemed rather dubious. I resolved to argue the matter over with him again.

"Bartleby," said I, entering the office, with a quietly severe expression, "I am seriously displeased. I am pained, Bartleby. I had thought better of you. I had imagined you of such a gentlemanly organization, that in any delicate dilemma a slight hint would suffice—in short, an assumption. But it appears I am deceived. Why," I added, unaffectedly starting, "you have not even touched that money yet," pointing to it, just where I had left it the evening previous.

He answered nothing.

160　　"Will you, or will you not, quit me?" I now demanded in a sudden passion, advancing close to him.

"I would prefer *not* to quit you," he replied, gently emphasizing the *not*.

"What earthly right have you to stay here? Do you pay any rent? Do you pay my taxes? Or is this property yours?"

He answered nothing.

"Are you ready to go on and write now? Are your eyes recovered? Could you copy a small paper for me this morning? or help examine a few lines? or step round to the Post Office? In a word, will you do anything at all, to give a coloring to your refusal to depart the premises?"

165　　He silently retired into his hermitage.

I was now in such a state of nervous resentment that I thought it but prudent to check myself at present from further demonstrations. Bartleby and I were alone. I remembered the tragedy of the unfortunate Adams and the still more unfortunate Colt in the solitary office of the latter; and how poor Colt, being dreadfully incensed by Adams, and imprudently permitting himself to get wildly excited, was at unawares hurried into his fatal act—an act which certainly no man could possibly deplore more than the actor himself. Often it had occurred to me in my ponderings upon the subject that had that altercation taken place in the public street, or at a private residence, it would not have terminated as it did. It was the circumstance of being alone in a solitary office, up stairs, of a building entirely unhallowed by humanizing domestic associations—an uncarpeted office, doubtless, of a dusty, haggard sort of appearance—this it must have been, which greatly helped to enhance the irritable desperation of the hapless Colt.

But when this old Adam of resentment rose in me and tempted me concerning Bartleby, I grappled him and threw him. How? Why, simply by recalling the divine injunction: "A new commandment give I unto you, that ye love one another." Yes, this it was that saved me. Aside from higher considerations, charity often operates as a vastly wise and prudent principle—a great safeguard to its possessor. Men have committed murder for jealousy's sake, and anger's sake, and hatred's sake, and selfishness' sake, and spiritual pride's sake; but no man, that ever I heard of, ever committed a diabolical murder for sweet charity's sake. Mere self-interest, then, if no better motive can be enlisted, should, especially with high-tempered men, prompt all beings to charity and philanthropy. At any rate, upon the occasion in question, I strove to drown my exasperated feelings towards the scrivener by benevolently construing his conduct. Poor fellow, poor fellow! thought I, he don't mean anything; and besides, he has seen hard times, and ought to be indulged.

I endeavored, also, immediately to occupy myself, and at the same time to comfort my despondency. I tried to fancy, that in the course of the morning, at such time as might prove agreeable to him, Bartleby, of his own free accord, would emerge from his hermitage and take up some decided line of march in the direction of the door. But no. Half-past twelve o'clock came; Turkey began to glow in the face, overturn his inkstand, and become generally obstreperous; Nippers abated down into quietude and courtesy; Ginger Nut munched his noon apple; and Bartleby remained standing at his window in one of his profoundest dead-wall reveries. Will it be credited? Ought I to acknowledge it? That afternoon I left the office without saying one further word to him.

Some days now passed, during which, at leisure intervals I looked a little into "Edwards on the Will," and "Priestley on Necessity." Under the circumstances, those books induced a salutary feeling. Gradually I slid into the persuasion that these troubles of mine, touching the scrivener, had been all predestined from eternity, and Bartleby was billeted upon me for some mysterious purpose of an all-wise Providence, which it was not for a mere mortal like me to fathom. Yes, Bartleby, stay there behind your screen, thought I; I shall persecute you no more; you are harmless and noiseless as any of these old chairs; in short, I never feel so private as when I know you are here. At least I see it, I feel it; I penetrate to the predestined purpose of my life. I am content. Others may have loftier parts to enact; but my mission in this world, Bartleby, is to furnish you with office-room for such period as you may see fit to remain.

I believe that this wise and blessed frame of mind would have continued with me, had it not been for the unsolicited and uncharitable remarks obtruded upon me by my professional friends who visited the rooms. But thus it often is, that the constant friction of illiberal minds wears out at last the best resolves of the more generous. Though to be sure, when I reflected upon it, it was not strange that people entering my office should be struck by the peculiar aspect of the unaccountable Bartleby, and so be tempted to throw out some sinister observations concerning him. Sometimes an attorney, having business with me, and calling at my office, and finding no one but the scrivener there, would undertake to obtain some sort of precise information from him touching my whereabouts; but without heeding his idle talk, Bartleby would remain standing immovable in the middle of the room. So after contemplating him in that position for a time, the attorney would depart, no wiser than he came.

Also, when a reference was going on, and the room full of lawyers and witnesses, and business driving fast, some deeply-occupied legal gentleman present, seeing Bartleby wholly unemployed, would request him to run round to his (the legal gentleman's) office and fetch some papers for him. Thereupon, Bartleby would tranquilly decline, and yet remain idle as before. Then the lawyer would give a great stare, and turn to me. And what could I say? At last I was made aware that all through the circle of my professional acquaintance, a whisper of wonder was running round, having reference to the strange creature I kept at my office. This worried me very much. And as the idea came upon me of his possibly turning out a long-lived man, and keeping occupying my chambers, and denying my authority; and perplexing my visitors; and scandalizing my professional reputation; and casting a general gloom over the premises; keeping soul and body together to the last upon his savings (for doubtless he spent but half a dime a day), and in the end perhaps outlive me, and claim possession of my office by right of his perpetual occupancy: as all these dark anticipations crowded upon me more and more, and my friends continually intruded their relentless remarks upon the apparition in my room; a great change was wrought in me. I resolved to gather all my faculties together, and forever rid me of this intolerable incubus.

Ere revolving any complicated project, however, adapted to this end, I first simply suggested to Bartleby the propriety of his permanent departure. In a calm and serious tone, I commended the idea to his careful and mature consideration. But, having taken three days to meditate upon it, he apprised me, that his original determination remained the same; in short, that he still preferred to abide with me.

What shall I do? I now said to myself, buttoning up my coat to the last button. What shall I do? what ought I to do? what does conscience say I *should* do with this man, or, rather, ghost. Rid myself of him, I must; go, he shall. But how? You will not thrust him, the poor, pale, passive mortal—you will not thrust such a helpless creature out of your door? you will not dishonor yourself by such cruelty? No, I will not, I cannot do that. Rather would I let him live and die here, and then mason up his remains in the wall. What, then, will you do? For all your coaxing, he will not budge. Bribes he leaves under your own paperweight on your table; in short, it is quite plain that he prefers to cling to you.

Then something severe, something unusual must be done. What! surely you will not have him collared by a constable, and commit his innocent pallor to the common jail? And upon what ground could you procure such a thing to be done?—a vagrant, is he? What! he a vagrant, a wanderer, who refuses to budge? It is because he will *not* be a vagrant, then, that you seek to count him *as* a vagrant. That is too absurd. No visible means of support: there I have him. Wrong again: for indubitably he *does* support himself, and that is the only unanswerable proof that any man can show of his possessing the means so to do. No more, then. Since he will not quit me, I must quit him. I will change my offices; I will move elsewhere, and give him fair notice, that if I find him on my new premises I will then proceed against him as a common trespasser.

175 Acting accordingly, next day I thus addressed him: "I find these chambers too far from the City Hall; the air is unwholesome. In a word, I propose to remove my offices next week, and shall no longer require your services. I tell you this now, in order that you may seek another place."

He made no reply, and nothing more was said.

On the appointed day I engaged carts and men, proceeded to my chambers, and having but little furniture, everything was removed in a few hours. Throughout, the scrivener remained standing behind the screen, which I directed to be removed the last thing. It was withdrawn; and, being folded up like a huge folio, left him the motionless occupant of a naked room. I stood in the entry watching him a moment, while something from within me upbraided me.

I re-entered, with my hand in my pocket—and—and my heart in my mouth.

"Good-bye, Bartleby; I am going—good-bye, and God some way bless you; and take that," slipping something in his hand. But it dropped upon the floor, and then—strange to say—I tore myself from him whom I had so longed to be rid of.

180 Established in my new quarters, for a day or two I kept the door locked, and started at every footfall in the passages. When I returned to my rooms, after any little absence, I would pause at the threshold for an instant, and attentively listen, ere applying my key. But these fears were needless. Bartleby never came nigh me.

I thought all was going well, when a perturbed-looking stranger visited me, inquiring whether I was the person who had recently occupied rooms at No. — Wall Street.

Full of forebodings, I replied that I was.

"Then, sir," said the stranger, who proved a lawyer, "you are responsible for the man you left there. He refuses to do any copying; he refuses to do anything; he says he prefers not to; and he refuses to quit the premises."

"I am very sorry, sir," said I, with assumed tranquillity, but an inward tremor, "but, really, the man you allude to is nothing to me—he is no relation or apprentice of mine, that you should hold me responsible for him."

185 "In mercy's name, who is he?"

"I certainly cannot inform you. I know nothing about him. Formerly I employed him as a copyist; but he has done nothing for me now for some time past."

"I shall settle him, then—good morning, sir."

Several days passed, and I heard nothing more; and though I often felt a charitable prompting to call at the place and see poor Bartleby, yet a certain squeamishness, of I know not what, withheld me.

All is over with him, by this time, thought I, at last, when, through another week, no further intelligence reached me. But, coming to my room the day after, I found several persons waiting at my door in a high state of nervous excitement.

"That's the man—here he comes," cried the foremost one, whom I recognized as the lawyer who had previously called upon me alone.

"You must take him away, sir, at once," cried a portly person among them, advancing upon me, and whom I knew to be the landlord of No. — Wall Street. "These gentlemen, my tenants, cannot stand it any longer; Mr. B————," pointing to the lawyer, "has turned him out of his room, and he now persists in haunting the building generally, sitting upon the banisters of the stairs by day, and sleeping in the entry by night. Everybody is concerned; clients are leaving the offices; some fears are entertained of a mob; something you must do, and that without delay."

Aghast at this torrent, I fell back before it, and would fain have locked myself in my new quarters. In vain I persisted that Bartleby was nothing to me—no more than to any one else. In vain—I was the last person known to have anything to do with him, and they held me to the terrible account. Fearful, then, of being exposed in the papers (as one person present obscurely threatened), I considered the matter, and, at length, said, that if the lawyer would give me a confidential interview with the scrivener, in his (the lawyer's) own room, I would, that afternoon, strive my best to rid them of the nuisance they complained of.

Going up stairs to my old haunt, there was Bartleby silently sitting upon the banister at the landing.

"What are you doing here, Bartleby?" said I.

"Sitting upon the banister," he mildly replied.

I motioned him into the lawyer's room, who then left us.

"Bartleby," said I, "are you aware that you are the cause of great tribulation to me, by persisting in occupying the entry after being dismissed from the office?"

No answer.

"Now one of two things must take place. Either you must do something, or something must be done to you. Now what sort of business would you like to engage in? Would you like to re-engage in copying for some one?"

"No; I would prefer not to make any change."

"Would you like a clerkship in a dry-goods store?"

"There is too much confinement about that. No, I would not like a clerkship; but I am not particular."

"Too much confinement," I cried, "why, you keep yourself confined all the time!"

"I would prefer not to take a clerkship," he rejoined, as if to settle that little item at once.

"How would a bar-tender's business suit you? There is no trying of the eye-sight in that."

"I would not like it at all; though, as I said before, I am not particular."

His unwonted wordiness inspirited me. I returned to the charge.

"Well, then, would you like to travel through the country collecting bills for the merchants? That would improve your health."

"No, I would prefer to be doing something else."

"How, then, would going as a companion to Europe, to entertain some young gentleman with your conversation—how would that suit you?"

"Not at all. It does not strike me that there is anything definite about that. I like to be stationary. But I am not particular."

"Stationary you shall be, then," I cried, now losing all patience, and, for the first time in all my exasperating connection with him, fairly flying into a passion. "If you do not go away from these premises before night, I shall feel bound—indeed I *am* bound—to—to quit the premises myself!" I rather absurdly concluded, knowing not with what possible threat to try to frighten his immobility into compliance. Despairing of all further efforts, I was precipitately leaving him, when a final thought occurred to me—one which had not been wholly unindulged before.

"Bartleby," said I, in the kindest tone I could assume under such exciting circumstances, "will you go home with me now—not to my office, but my dwelling—and remain there till we can conclude upon some convenient arrangement for you at our leisure? Come, let us start now, right away."

"No: at present I would prefer not to make any change at all."

215   I answered nothing; but, effectually dodging every one by the suddenness and rapidity of my flight, rushed from the building, ran up Wall Street towards Broadway, and, jumping into the first omnibus, was soon removed from pursuit. As soon as tranquillity returned, I distinctly perceived that I had now done all that I possibly could, both in respect to the demands of the landlord and his tenants, and with regard to my own desire and sense of duty, to benefit Bartleby, and shield him from rude persecution. I now strove to be entirely care-free and quiescent; and my conscience justified me in the attempt; though, indeed, it was not so successful as I could have wished. So fearful was I of being again hunted out by the incensed landlord and his exasperated tenants, that, surrendering my business to Nippers, for a few days, I drove about the upper part of the town and through the suburbs, in my rockaway; crossed over to Jersey City and Hoboken, and paid fugitive visits to Manhattanville and Astoria. In fact, I almost lived in my rockaway for the time.

When again I entered my office, lo, a note from the landlord lay upon the desk. I opened it with trembling hands. It informed me that the writer had sent to the police, and had Bartleby removed to the Tombs as a vagrant. Moreover, since I knew more about him than any one else, he wished me to appear at that place, and make a suitable statement of the facts. These tidings had a conflicting effect upon me. At first I was indignant; but, at last, almost approved. The landlord's energetic, summary disposition, had led him to adopt a procedure which I do not think I would have decided upon myself; and yet, as a last resort, under such peculiar circumstances, it seemed the only plan.

As I afterwards learned, the poor scrivener, when told that he must be conducted to the Tombs, offered not the slightest obstacle, but, in his pale, unmoving way, silently acquiesced.

Some of the compassionate and curious by-standers joined the party; and headed by one of the constables arm-in-arm with Bartleby, the silent procession filed its way through all the noise, and heat, and joy of the roaring thoroughfares at noon.

The same day I received the note, I went to the Tombs, or, to speak more properly, the Halls of Justice. Seeking the right officer, I stated the purpose of my call, and was informed that the individual I described was, indeed, within. I then assured the functionary that Bartleby was a perfectly honest man, and greatly to be compassionated, however unaccountably eccentric. I narrated all I knew, and closed by suggesting the idea of letting him remain in as indulgent confinement as possible, till something less harsh might be done—though, indeed, I hardly knew what. At all events, if nothing else could be decided upon, the almshouse must receive him. I then begged to have an interview.

220   Being under no disgraceful charge, and quite serene and harmless in all his ways, they had permitted him freely to wander about the prison, and, especially, in the inclosed grass-platted yards thereof. And so I found him there, standing all alone in the quietest of the yards, his face towards a high wall, while all around, from the narrow slits of the jail windows, I thought I saw peering out upon him the eyes of murderers and thieves.

"Bartleby!"

"I know you," he said, without looking round—"and I want nothing to say to you."

"It was not I that brought you here, Bartleby," said I, keenly pained at his implied suspicion. "And to you, this should not be so vile a place. Nothing reproachful attaches to you by being here. And see, it is not so sad a place as one might think. Look, there is the sky, and here is the grass."

"I know where I am," he replied, but would say nothing more, and so I left him.

225   As I entered the corridor again, a broad meat-like man, in an apron, accosted me, and jerking his thumb over his shoulder, said—"Is that your friend?"

"Yes."

"Does he want to starve? If he does, let him live on the prison fare, that's all."

"Who are you?" asked I, not knowing what to make of such an unofficially speaking person in such a place.

"I am the grub-man. Such gentlemen as have friends here, hire me to provide them with something good to eat."

230   "Is this so?" said I, turning to the turnkey.

He said it was.

"Well, then," said I, slipping some silver into the grub-man's hands (for so they called him), "I want you to give particular attention to my friend there; let him have the best dinner you can get. And you must be as polite to him as possible."

"Introduce me, will you?" said the grub-man, looking at me with an expression which seemed to say he was all impatience for an opportunity to give a specimen of his breeding.

Thinking it would prove of benefit to the scrivener, I acquiesced; and, asking the grub-man his name, went up with him to Bartleby.

"Bartleby, this is a friend; you will find him very useful to you."

"Your sarvant, sir, your sarvant," said the grub-man, making a low salutation behind his apron. "Hope you find it pleasant here, sir; nice grounds—cool apartments—hope you'll stay with us some time—try to make it agreeable. What will you have for dinner to-day?"

"I prefer not to dine to-day," said Bartleby, turning away. "It would disagree with me; I am unused to dinners." So saying, he slowly moved to the other side of the inclosure, and took up a position fronting the deadwall.

"How's this?" said the grub-man, addressing me with a stare of astonishment. "He's odd, aint he?"

"I think he is a little deranged," said I, sadly.

"Deranged? deranged is it? Well, now, upon my word, I thought that friend of yourn was a gentleman forger; they are always pale and genteel-like, them forgers. I can't help pity 'em—can't help it, sir. Did you know Monroe Edwards?" he added, touchingly, and paused. Then, laying his hand piteously on my shoulder, sighed, "He died of consumption at Sing-Sing. So you weren't acquainted with Monroe?"

"No, I was never socially acquainted with any forgers. But I cannot stop longer. Look to my friend yonder. You will not lose by it. I will see you again."

Some few days after this, I again obtained admission to the Tombs, and went through the corridors in quest of Bartleby; but without finding him.

"I saw him coming from his cell not long ago," said a turnkey, "may be he's gone to loiter in the yards."

So I went in that direction.

"Are you looking for the silent man?" said another turnkey, passing me. "Yonder he lies—sleeping in the yard there. 'Tis not twenty minutes since I saw him lie down."

The yard was entirely quiet. It was not accessible to the common prisoners. The surrounding walls, of amazing thickness, kept off all sounds behind them. The Egyptian character of the masonry weighed upon me with its gloom. But a soft imprisoned turf grew under foot. The heart of the eternal pyramids, it seemed, wherein, by some strange magic, through the clefts, grass-seed, dropped by birds, had sprung.

Strangely huddled at the base of the wall, his knees drawn up, and lying on his side, his head touching the cold stones, I saw the wasted Bartleby. But nothing stirred. I paused; then went close up to him; stooped over, and saw that his dim eyes were open; otherwise he seemed profoundly sleeping. Something prompted me to touch him. I felt his hand, when a tingling shiver ran up my arm and down my spine to my feet.

The round face of the grub-man peered upon me now. "His dinner is ready. Won't he dine to-day, either? Or does he live without dining?"

"Lives without dining," said I, and closed the eyes.

"Eh!—He's asleep, aint he?"

"With kings and counselors," murmured I.

There would seem little need for proceeding further in this history. Imagination will readily supply the meagre recital of poor Bartleby's interment. But, ere parting with the reader, let me say, that if this little narrative has sufficiently interested him, to awaken curiosity as to who Bartleby was, and what manner of life he led prior to the present narrator's making his acquaintance, I can only reply, that in such curiosity I fully share, but am wholly unable to gratify it. Yet here I hardly know whether I should divulge one little item of rumor, which came to my ear a few months after the scrivener's decease. Upon what basis it rested, I could never ascertain; and hence, how true it is I cannot now tell. But, inasmuch as this vague report has not been without a certain suggestive interest to me, however sad, it may prove the same with some others; and so I will briefly mention it. The report was this: that Bartleby had been a subordinate clerk in the Dead Letter Office at Washington, from which he had been suddenly removed by a change in the administration. When I think over this rumor, hardly can I express the emotions which seize me. Dead letters! does it not sound like dead men? Conceive a man by nature and misfortune prone to a pallid hopelessness, can any business seem more fitted to heighten it than that of continually handling these dead letters, and assorting them for the flames? For by the cart-load they are annually burned. Sometimes from out the folded paper the pale clerk takes a ring—the finger it was meant for, perhaps, moulders in the grave; a bank-note sent in swiftest charity—he whom it would relieve, nor eats nor hungers any more; pardon for those who died despairing; hope for those who died unhoping; good tidings for those who died stifled by unrelieved calamities. On errands of life, these letters speed to death.

Ah, Bartleby! Ah, humanity!

Bartleby's gradual descent into gloom—and ultimately death—because of his occupation is characterized by the same Gothic theme of entrapment in Edgar Allan Poe's "Fall of the House of Usher" (chapter 6). There's a similarity, too, between Bartleby's hopelessness and Gregor Samsa's transformation into an insect in Franz Kafka's *The Metamorphosis* (chapter 10).

GOING FURTHER   The themes of failed intentions and mortality explored by Melville in "Bartleby, the Scrivener" can also be found in the fiction of a number of modern American writers, such as the novels *The Moviegoer* (1961) and *Lancelot* (1977) by Walker Percy.

Ana Menendez (b. 1970)

ANA MENENDEZ WAS born in Los Angeles, the daughter of Cuban exiles. She is the author of two books of fiction: *In Cuba I Was a German Shepherd,* which was a 2001 *New York Times* Notable Book of the Year and whose title story won a Pushcart Prize, and the novel *Loving Che.* Her second novel, *The Last War,* was published in 2009 by HarperCollins. Since 1991, Menendez has worked as a journalist in the United States and abroad, including three years as a prize-winning columnist for *The Miami Herald.* She has a B.A. in English from Florida International University and an M.F.A from New York University. She was a 2008–2009 Fulbright Scholar in Cairo.

Traveling Madness (2009)

1   All the men on my father's side of the family have been mad in one way or another.

There was my great-uncle Panchito, who joined the communist party in 1934 when it was a nothing party of dreamers only to quit in 1965 when the party officially denied him permission to fly to the moon. He could have turned all those years of underground meetings and patriotic songs into something, he could have cashed in and finally helped his family. Instead, he spent the last years of his life writing angry letters to the Ministry for Travel and Culture, arguing that if the Russians could send a flea-bitten dog into space, certainly the Cubans ought to be able to fly a loyal party monkey to the moon. His latter letters were scrupulously ignored. And he ended up dying in a rented room in his niece's apartment, fighting her until the last for the right to his homemade rum. In the end, the party would not even allow him to be buried in the Patriot's cemetery.

There was a cousin named Severino who hanged himself from a banyan one spring morning after a passing traveler told him there was buried treasure on the other side of the mountain. Severino, who had never even traveled beyond the swamp. As a boy he had been happy to sit out by a stream for hours and launch paper boats, waiting until one disappeared downstream before sending out the next one. The passing traveler was never seen or spoken of again until many years later when miners discovered a silver vein hard against the mountain. The townspeople, in an act of remembering common to those times, named the mine after Severino.

And, most recently, there was my grandfather Solomon, who, as an exile in Miami, one cool winter morning began digging a tunnel beneath the azaleas with the intention of surfacing some day in Havana.

The first two stories have been passed down through the family and I can't vouch for the truth in them. The last one I saw with my own eyes and can tell you that nothing can match the image of a shirtless old man with a dream. He had it all planned out, my grandfather did, for he was a man who took great pride in logic and the scientific method. Before he even began to dig, he filled a great many notebooks with figures that explained precisely how many shovels of dirt it would take, how wide the hole should be, and how many years would have to pass before he finally broke through the sand on the other side. I was only eight years old then, but sometimes after school I helped him dig. My grandfather had barely made it under the property line when his project ended abruptly. It seems the neighbors had called the police to say the old man next door was digging what appeared to be a mass grave. It took some days to sort out the complications that followed. But my grandfather never recovered from his disappointment. He sank into a deep sadness that didn't lift even after my father, also prone to making mathematical calculations, pointed out a mistake in his figures and said that it actually would have taken 16,742 years to dig to Havana.

But perhaps the most tragically brilliant of this mad lineage was Matias Padron, a third great-cousin of my father's though marriage by way of his mother. The family connection is tenuous, I know. But I feel a certain pride in claiming Matias, for his story has passed into the island lore of Cuba; his story is all our story.

Matias, so it is told, was not a very big man. This is also true of most of the men on my father's side of the family. But unlike most of the men, who tend to make up in width for what they lack in height, Matias was slightly built all around. He was, it is well known, even smaller and thinner than his wife, who scandalously abused her advantage to keep Matias timid and soft-spoken at home. Matias didn't seem to mind this and often played along good naturedly, now and then repeating a favorite phrase he had heard about the greatness of a man being measured not from the ground to his head, but from the distance of his head to God. The literal-minded took this to be an even greater disadvantage. But Matias knew what he was talking about.

Since he had turned 18, Matias had been running the post office in Santiago de Cuba. By the time he was 40 years old, he had browsed 22 Christmas catalogs from El Encanto, leafed through dozens of Bohemias, and read several hundred letters of love, the great majority of which were not between husbands and wives. But the task that took up most of his time and the one, that by all accounts, he adored above all the others, was predicting the weather. In those years, the postmaster also ran the local telegraph service. This meant that the postmaster, in addition to being the telegrapher, was also a sort of informal meteorologist as the telegraph, for the first time in the Caribbean, was being used to give advanced warnings of storms developing off shore. It was a duty that all the previous postmasters had taken very seriously. But none had thrown themselves into it with anything approaching the passion that Matias brought.

Matias and his wife lived above the post office in a house that, according to tradition, was paid and kept up by the municipality for the use of the postmaster and his family. It was a large house, two stories, with a wide balcony that wrapped around all four sides. But as Matias and his wife had never had children, vast areas of the house remained dark and unused. It was in one such sealed room that Matias established a small office. When he wasn't below in the post office reading other people's mail or receiving telegraphs about the latest events around the world, Matias was in his little office trying to predict the weather. He had all matter of instruments, barometers, thermometers. Probably, it wasn't too different from the type of things amateurs keep the world over. But Matias's secrecy about his room, even from his wife, soon led to talk in the town that Matias was an alchemist dealing in nefarious activities. It was the first chatter about Matias's supposed eccentricity. And just because it prefigured the extraordinary act he was about to embark on, it doesn't mean that it was necessarily a fair assessment. At that moment, I believe that Matias had truly developed a scientific interest in the weather. After all, not too many years had passed since a hurricane had devastated Varadero, cutting the narrow peninsula in half until both oceans met over the sand. Matias, I think, was trying to save Santiago from the next cataclysm.

10   He ordered all manner of new equipment from New York and tore at the packages when they arrived weeks later. Soon he built an observation deck on the roof and in clear weather began sending up weather balloons. At first, the balloons didn't carry anything—Matias merely used them to calculate wind speeds and air pressure. But as technology improved and radio transmitters began to gain wider currency, Matias arranged for bigger and bigger balloons that could carry more and more equipment. Soon he was launching balloons as big as oil drums carrying thermometers, barometers, humidity detectors all wired to a radio that could send the information back to Matias in his little room.

Every Friday, he posted the results on the front door of the post office as well as a small assessment of what the coming week's weather was likely to be. He was right more often than he was wrong and except for a few lapses when, for example, he announced that yesterday "rain had been very heavy" (something the townspeople could know well enough without consulting any instruments other than their memories) the people grew to respect his forecasts.

Cuba had prospered in those years and along with it, Santiago, and along with Santiago, Matias. The memory of hunger was fading. Children grew healthy. And Matias entered middle age in the prime of health. Even the hurricanes that had assaulted Cuba the previous decade seemed to ease and everyone everywhere seemed relaxed and content as if the more malevolent workings of the world had finally passed them by.

Matias continued to go into his office every afternoon and every Friday he emerged with the forecast for the following week. And of course he also continued to send up his balloons, each more elaborate than the last. The weather was not always perfect, but it was predictable. Soon everyone knew the rains would come in August and the heaviest thunder would be reserved for the late afternoon, when the sun began to dip low in the sky. By October, the skies would clear and the blue days return. Winters, whether Matias said so or not, were generally dry and pleasant.

Some nights, couples out for a walk noticed a dark figure above the post office—Matias with his hands on the railing looking up into the sky. But otherwise, few people paid much attention to Matias or his forecasts, anymore. They met him once a week, sometimes touched their fingers lightly to his when he handed them their mail and that was that. It seemed there was nothing left to fear.

15   There are eddies that develop in time, places where histories converge, and individuals caught inside the current find themselves suddenly unable to act for themselves. Perhaps this is what happened to Matias. Maybe everything that followed was as inevitable as history. I have to say things like this because there is really no other explanation for what came to pass. Outside of a family connection, there was nothing in Matias's character to suggest madness. The reports that came out later pointed out that there was no history of despondency. And nothing in the days preceding the event gave anyone any reason to believe that Matias had suffered a sudden depression. The weather, moreover, had been pleasantly uneventful, with, as Matias himself had noted, an abundance of bright days somewhat unusual for springtime.

And yet, the truth is this: One morning Matias was handing a stack of letters to Consuelo Perez and the next he was floating high above Santiago, his office chair dangling beneath four giant weather balloons with him in it.

Santiago had been the first city in Cuba to be linked by telegraph to the rest of the Caribbean. Santiago had been the first city to pioneer the use of observation balloons during war time. The telegraph had connected Cuba to the world, but in the end, the country learned it could not stand alone. Its prosperity and health were forever tethered to history and geography. Did Matias sense this? In those last years he had developed a habit of linking ideas one to the next until he'd convinced himself that there was an inherent logic running through the universe, governing even the impossible. When his own mind finally became untethered, where did it fly to?

His wife was the first to notice Matias had gone. She ran up to the observation deck and when she saw him just clearing the tops of the palms she began to shout at him, You insolent madman, you flying fool! Her shouting brought out a handful of people whose shouting brought out still more people. And soon the whole town was pointing at the sky where Matias floated, sometimes rising suddenly and sometimes hanging in the air, swaying from side to side just over the tree line, every second becoming a little bit smaller in the distance. A few of the men started off after him and when they were directly under his path began shouting instructions at him, in the venerable Cuban tradition: Cut one of the balloons! Jump now, the fronds will break your fall! When you make it over the swamp let the helium out very slowly! They continued to run and shout even after it became clear that Matias was not coming back. One of the men said that just when he was becoming so small that one could hardly make out his person, Matias glanced down at the others and there was a wide, white smile on his face. He was like a saint or a martyr, the man said. And for days, the man could talk of nothing else but Matias's calm happy gaze as he floated away from Santiago forever.

Matias seemed to know right where he was going. All those years of tracing wind patterns had given him a pilot's confidence. It was April, when the winds blow east to west. Before an hour was out he was a tiny speck out over the sea and then he was impossible to make out in the haze. After a while most of the people stopped searching the sky for Matias and began walking back to their homes. A few gathered in silence outside the post office. Matilde locked herself in the house and didn't emerge until the governor arrived two weeks later to take a report. Some days later, the police came for his papers. They carted off hundreds and hundreds of notebooks filled with strange drawings and algebraic calculations. But among the more curious of his possessions was a stuffed owl and a rare Cuban tern preserved in a bottle of formaldehyde.

Today, people in Cuba still say of an elusive fellow, He vanished like Matias Padron.

I think of Matias now and then. I am also a traveler. And nowadays after I have taken off my shoes and put them back on, after I have retrieved my naked laptop from the conveyor and had my purse rifled through, after I have emerged safely on the other side of the security cabal, I like to take a seat up close to the windows and watch the planes come and go. How generous of airport architects to design such large windows. And how good of the staff to keep them so clean and shiny. Coming upon these portals is like stumbling onto a new and intricate explanation of the possible.

I sit in one of the soft functional chairs and watch the planes land and I watch them lift off from the earth. And each time it seems like a miracle. There are so many planes flying in so many different directions that it is difficult to follow a single one. Too often, the flight path takes them beyond my line of vision. But now and then a plane will take off just so and fly straight out in view of all the airport, fly off to that point that everyone calls infinity but is really just the limits of our perception.

I'll follow the plane until it is nothing and know that soon I will be on one just like it. And I wonder, do we still know what it's like to dream about the other side of the mountain? At what point does one cross the crest of forgetting? And this is when I think of Matias, who breached the space of the known for nothing more than a glimpse of the white-blind city on the other side.

If you like this story, you may like the fiction from Latin America by Borges and García Márquez (both in this section), along with the work of Kafka ("The Metamorphosis," chapter 10). You may also like other writers who take up the subject matter of first-generation Americans, such as Chinese-American writer Gish Jen ("Who's Irish?" chapter 5) and Sylvia Watanabe ("Talking to the Dead," chapter 12). You can read Junot Diaz's story "How to Date a Browngirl, Blackgirl, Whitegirl, or Halfie" (chapter 8) in a similar light.

GOING FURTHER   You may want to read Menendez in the company of her fellow Cuban-American writer Cristina Garcia (*Dreaming in Cuban*) or Haitian-American Edwidge Danticat, who, like Menendez, lives in Miami.

R. K. Narayan (1906–2001)

R. K. NARAYAN, born in Madras (the southern Indian city now known as Chennai) and educated in English-language schools, was one of the most prolific novelists and story writers of his generation. For a number of decades his work stood as the main source from which many thousands of readers in the West learned about life in India from a native perspective—as opposed, say, to that of a fascinated visitor such as E. M. Forster, in his *Passage to India*. Narayan's close attention to the lives of ordinary people, with all of their foibles and failings, lends his tales about India a universal appeal—and in some ways he is the first of a series of authors to make the subcontinent's culture vividly available in prose.

His creation of a town called "Malgudi" as the setting for a number of his works of fiction shows his affinity with the work of William Faulkner, whose imaginary southern U.S. Yoknapatawpha County served the same purpose of establishing a fictional location that had the air of real geography about it.

An Astrologer's Day (1947)

1   Punctually at midday he opened his bag and spread out his professional equipment, which consisted of a dozen cowrie shells, a square piece of cloth with obscure mystic charts on it, a notebook and a bundle of palmyra writing. His forehead was resplendent with sacred ash and vermilion, and his eyes sparkled with a sharp abnormal gleam which was really an outcome of a continual searching look for customers, but which his simple clients took to be a prophetic light and felt comforted. The power of his eyes was considerably enhanced by their position—placed as they were between the painted forehead and the dark whiskers which streamed down his cheeks: even a half-wit's eyes would sparkle in such a setting. To crown the effect he wound a saffron-coloured turban around his head. This colour scheme never failed. People were attracted to him as bees are attracted to cosmos or dahlia stalks. He sat under the boughs of a spreading tamarind tree which flanked a path running through the Town Hall Park. It was a remarkable place in many ways: a surging crowd was always moving up and down this narrow road morning till night. A variety of trades and occupations was represented all along its way: medicine-sellers,

sellers of stolen hardware and junk, magicians and, above all, an auctioneer of cheap cloth, who created enough din all day to attract the whole town. Next to him in vociferousness came a vendor of fried groundnuts, who gave his ware a fancy name each day, calling it Bombay Ice-Cream one day, and on the next Delhi Almond, and on the third Raja's Delicacy, and so on and so forth, and people flocked to him. A considerable portion of this crowd dallied before the astrologer too. The astrologer transacted his business by the light of a flare which crackled and smoked up above the groundnut heap nearby. Half the enchantment of the place was due to the fact that it did not have the benefit of municipal lighting. The place was lit up by shop lights. One or two had hissing gaslights, some had naked flares stuck on poles, some were lit up by old cycle lamps and one or two, like the astrologer's, managed without lights of their own. It was a bewildering crisscross of light rays and moving shadows. This suited the astrologer very well, for the simple reason that he had not in the least intended to be an astrologer when he began life; and he knew no more of what was going to happen to others than he knew what was going to happen to himself next minute. He was as much a stranger to the stars as were his innocent customers. Yet he said things which pleased and astonished everyone: that was more a matter of study, practice and shrewd guesswork. All the same, it was as much an honest man's labour as any other, and he deserved the wages he carried home at the end of a day.

He had left his village without any previous thought or plan. If he had continued there he would have carried on the work of his forefathers—namely, tilling the land, living, marrying and ripening in his cornfield and ancestral home. But that was not to be. He had to leave home without telling anyone, and he could not rest till he left it behind a couple of hundred miles. To a villager it is a great deal, as if an ocean flowed between.

He had a working analysis of mankind's troubles: marriage, money and the tangles of human ties. Long practice had sharpened his perception. Within five minutes he understood what was wrong. He charged three pies per question and never opened his mouth till the other had spoken for at least ten minutes, which provided him enough stuff for a dozen answers and advices. When he told the person before him, gazing at his palm, "In many ways you are not getting the fullest results for your efforts," nine out of ten were disposed to agree with him. Or he questioned: "Is there any woman in your family, maybe even a distant relative, who is not well disposed towards you?" Or he gave an analysis of character: "Most of your troubles are due to your nature. How can you be otherwise with Saturn where he is? You have an impetuous nature and a rough exterior." This endeared him to their hearts immediately, for even the mildest of us loves to think that he has a forbidding exterior.

The nuts-vendor blew out his flare and rose to go home. This was a signal for the astrologer to bundle up too, since it left him in darkness except for a little shaft of green light which strayed in from somewhere and touched the ground before him. He picked up his cowrie shells and paraphernalia and was putting them back into his bag when the green shaft of light was blotted out; he looked up and saw a man standing before him. He sensed a possible client and said: "You look so careworn. It will do you good to sit down for a while and chat with me." The other grumbled some vague reply. The astrologer pressed his invitation; whereupon the other thrust his palm under his nose, saying: "You call yourself an astrologer?" The astrologer felt challenged and said, tilting the other's palm towards the green shaft of light: "Yours is a nature . . ." "Oh, stop that," the other said. "Tell me something worthwhile . . ."

Our friend felt piqued. "I charge only three pies per question, and what you get ought to be good enough for your money . . ." At this the other withdrew his arm, took out an anna and flung it out to him, saying, "I have some questions to ask. If I prove you are bluffing, you must return that anna to me with interest."

"If you find my answers satisfactory, will you give me five rupees?"

"No."

"Or will you give me eight annas?"

"All right, provided you give me twice as much if you are wrong," said the stranger. This pact was accepted after a little further argument. The astrologer sent up a prayer to heaven as the other lit a cheroot. The astrologer caught a glimpse of his face by the match-light. There was a pause as cars hooted on the road, *jutka*-drivers swore at their horses and the babble of the crowd agitated the semi-darkness of the park. The other sat down, sucking his cheroot, puffing out, sat there ruthlessly. The astrologer felt very uncomfortable. "Here, take your anna back. I am not used to such challenges. It is late for me today . . ." He made preparations to bundle up. The other held his wrist and said, "You can't get out of it now. You dragged me in while I was passing." The astrologer shivered in his grip; and his voice shook and became faint. "Leave me today. I will speak to you tomorrow." The other thrust his palm in his face and said, "Challenge is challenge. Go on." The astrologer proceeded with his throat drying up. "There is a woman . . ."

10   "Stop," said the other. "I don't want all that. Shall I succeed in my present search or not? Answer this and go. Otherwise I will not let you go till you disgorge all your coins." The astrologer muttered a few incantations and replied, "All right. I will speak. But will you give me a rupee if what I say is convincing? Otherwise I will not open my mouth, and you may do what you like." After a good deal of haggling the other agreed. The astrologer said, "You were left for dead. Am I right?"

"Ah, tell me more."

"A knife has passed through you once?" said the astrologer.

"Good fellow!" He bared his chest to show the scar. "What else?"

"And then you were pushed into a well nearby in the field. You were left for dead."

15   "I should have been dead if some passer-by had not chanced to peep into the well," exclaimed the other, overwhelmed by enthusiasm. "When shall I get at him?" he asked, clenching his fist.

"In the next world," answered the astrologer. "He died four months ago in a far-off town. You will never see any more of him." The other groaned on hearing it. The astrologer proceeded.

"Guru Nayak—"

"You know my name!" the other said, taken aback.

"As I know all other things. Guru Nayak, listen carefully to what I have to say. Your village is two days' journey due north of this town. Take the next train and be gone. I see once again great danger to your life if you go from home." He took out a pinch of sacred ash and held it out to him. "Rub it on your forehead and go home. Never travel southward again, and you will live to be a hundred."

20   "Why should I leave home again?" the other said reflectively. "I was only going away now and then to look for him and to choke out his life if I met him." He shook his head regretfully. "He has escaped my hands. I hope at least he died as he deserved." "Yes," said the astrologer. "He was crushed under a lorry." The other looked gratified to hear it.

The place was deserted by the time the astrologer picked up his articles and put them into his bag. The green shaft was also gone, leaving the place in darkness and silence. The stranger had gone off into the night, after giving the astrologer a handful of coins.

It was nearly midnight when the astrologer reached home. His wife was waiting for him at the door and demanded an explanation. He flung the coins at her and said, "Count them. One man gave all that."

"Twelve and a half annas," she said, counting. She was overjoyed. "I can buy some *jaggery* and coconut tomorrow. The child has been asking for sweets for so many days now. I will prepare some nice stuff for her."

"The swine has cheated me! He promised me a rupee," said the astrologer. She looked up at him. "You look worried. What is wrong?"

25   "Nothing."

After dinner, sitting on the *pyol,* he told her, "Do you know a great load is gone from me today? I thought I had the blood of a man on my hands all these years. That was the reason why I ran away from home, settled here and married you. He is alive."

She gasped. "You tried to kill!"

"Yes, in our village, when I was a silly youngster. We drank, gambled and quarrelled badly one day—why think of it now? Time to sleep," he said, yawning, and stretched himself on the *pyol.*

If you like "An Astrologer's Day," you may also like "Interpreter of Maladies" by Jhumpa Lahiri (chapter 9).
GOING FURTHER Stories and novels by South Asian writers are plentiful these days, and such writers as Salman Rushdie and Amitav Ghosh sometimes reach the bestseller lists. Chitra Banerjee Divakaruni's *The Mistress of Spices* was, like Lahiri's *The Namesake,* made into a film.

Leo Tolstoy (1828–1910)

ONE OF RUSSIA'S most famous authors—both today and in his lifetime—Leo Tolstoy began life in the upper-class gentry and ended in self-elected poverty. As a young man he joined the army and fought in the Crimean War. During this period, he published his first works, which were largely about growing up or army life. Always introspective, Tolstoy grew frustrated with his youthful propensities for gambling and women; his struggle against these temptations led him to proclaim a fervent faith in God. The next period of his life was the happiest, the time in which he married, began a family of nine children, and wrote his two major masterpieces, *War and Peace* (1869) and *Anna Karenina* (1877).

While finishing *Anna Karenina,* however, Tolstoy became depressed to the point that he considered suicide, viewing his career and literary accomplishments as vanities. He renounced ostentation, simplified his life by dividing his property among his children, and became a vegetarian who wore peasant clothing. Although these actions estranged him from his family, many people, including Mohandas Gandhi, were inspired by "Tolstoyism"—Tolstoy's belief that goodness is achieved through passive resistance to evil, a dogma based on Christian teachings. His fiction is noted for its psychological realism in exploring both male and female characters in the face of great historical moments, moral crises, and death.

The Death of Ivan Ilych (1886)

I

1   During an interval in the Melvinski trial in the large building of the Law Courts, the members and public prosecutor met in Ivan Egorovich Shebek's private room, where the conversation turned on the celebrated Krasovski case. Fëdor Vasilievich warmly maintained that it was not subject to their jurisdiction, Ivan Egorovich maintained the contrary, while Peter Ivanovich, not having entered into the discussion at the start, took no part in it but looked through the *Gazette* which had just been handed in.

"Gentlemen," he said, "Ivan Ilych has died!"

"You don't say so!"

"Here, read it yourself," replied Peter Ivanovich, handing Fëdor Vasilievich the paper still damp from the press. Surrounded by a black border were the words: "Praskovya Fëdorovna Goloviná, with profound sorrow, informs relatives and friends of the demise of her beloved husband Ivan Ilych Golovin, Member of the Court of Justice, which occurred on February the 4th of this year 1882. The funeral will take place on Friday at one o'clock in the afternoon."

5   Ivan Ilych had been a colleague of the gentlemen present and was liked by them all. He had been ill for some weeks with an illness said to be incurable. His post had been kept open for him, but there had been conjectures that in case of his death Alexeev might receive his appointment, and that either Vinnikov or Shtabel would succeed Alexeev. So on receiving the news of Ivan Ilych's death the first thought of each of the gentlemen in that private room was of the changes and promotions it might occasion among themselves or their acquaintances.

"I shall be sure to get Shtabel's place or Vinnikov's," thought Fĕdor Vasilievich. "I was promised that long ago, and the promotion means an extra eight hundred rubles a year for me besides the allowance."

"Now I must apply for my brother-in-law's transfer from Kaluga," thought Peter Ivanovich. "My wife will be very glad, and then she won't be able to say that I never do anything for her relations."

"I thought he would never leave his bed again," said Peter Ivanovich aloud. "It's very sad."

"But what really was the matter with him?"

10   "The doctors couldn't say—at least they could, but each of them said something different. When last I saw him I thought he was getting better."

"And I haven't been to see him since the holidays. I always meant to go."

"Had he any property?"

"I think his wife had a little—but something quite trifling."

"We shall have to go to see her, but they live so terribly far away."

15   "Far away from you, you mean. Everything's far away from your place."

"You see, he never can forgive my living on the other side of the river," said Peter Ivanovich, smiling at Shebek. Then, still talking of the distances between different parts of the city, they returned to the Court.

Besides considerations as to the possible transfers and promotions likely to result from Ivan Ilych's death, the mere fact of the death of a near acquaintance aroused, as usual, in all who heard of it the complacent feeling that, "it is he who is dead and not I."

Each one thought or felt, "Well, he's dead but I'm alive!" But the more intimate of Ivan Ilych's acquaintances, his so-called friends, could not help thinking also that they would now have to fulfill the very tiresome demands of propriety by attending the funeral service and paying a visit of condolence to the widow.

Fĕdor Vasilievich and Peter Ivanovich had been his nearest acquaintances. Peter Ivanovich had studied law with Ivan Ilych and had considered himself to be under obligations to him.

20   Having told his wife at dinner-time of Ivan Ilych's death and of his conjecture that it might be possible to get her brother transferred to their circuit, Peter Ivanovich sacrificed his usual nap, put on his evening clothes, and drove to Ivan Ilych's house.

At the entrance stood a carriage and two cabs. Leaning against the wall in the hall downstairs near the cloak-stand was a coffin-lid covered with cloth of gold, ornamented with gold cord and tassels, that had been polished up with metal powder. Two ladies in black were taking off their fur cloaks. Peter Ivanovich recognized one of them as Ivan Ilych's sister, but the other was a stranger to him. His colleague Schwartz was just coming downstairs, but on seeing Peter Ivanovich enter he stopped and winked at him, as if to say: "Ivan Ilych has made a mess of things—not like you and me."

Schwartz's face with his Piccadilly whiskers and his slim figure in evening dress had as usual an air of elegant solemnity which contrasted with the playfulness of his character and had a special piquancy here, or so it seemed to Peter Ivanovich.

Peter Ivanovich allowed the ladies to precede him and slowly followed them upstairs. Schwartz did not come down but remained where he was, and Peter Ivanovich understood that he wanted to arrange where they should play bridge that evening. The ladies went upstairs to the widow's room, and Schwartz with seriously compressed lips but a playful look in his eyes, indicated by a twist of his eyebrows the room to the right where the body lay.

Peter Ivanovich, like everyone else on such occasions, entered feeling uncertain what he would have to do. All he knew was that at such times it is always safe to cross oneself. But he was not quite sure whether one should make obeisances while doing so. He therefore adopted a middle course. On entering the room he began crossing himself and made a slight movement resembling a bow. At the same time, as far as the motion of his head and arm allowed, he surveyed the room. Two young men—apparently nephews, one of whom was a high-school pupil—were leaving the room, crossing themselves as they did so. An old woman was standing motionless, and a lady with strangely arched eyebrows was saying something to her in a whisper. A vigorous, resolute Church Reader, in a frock-coat, was reading something in a loud voice with an expression that precluded any contradiction. The butler's assistant, Gerasim, stepping lightly in front of Peter Ivanovich, was strewing something on the floor. Noticing this, Peter Ivanovich was immediately aware of a faint odor of a decomposing body.

The last time he had called on Ivan Ilych, Peter Ivanovich had seen Gerasim in the study. Ivan Ilych had been particularly fond of him and he was performing the duty of a sick nurse.

Peter Ivanovich continued to make the sign of the cross, slightly inclining his head in an intermediate direction between the coffin, the Reader, and the icons on the table in a corner of the room. Afterwards, when it seemed to him that this movement of his arm in crossing himself had gone on too long, he stopped and began to look at the corpse.

The dead man lay, as dead men always lie, in a specially heavy way, his rigid limbs sunk in the soft cushions of the coffin, with the head forever bowed on the pillow. His yellow waxen brow with bald patches over his sunken temples was thrust up in the way peculiar to the dead, the protruding nose seeming to press on the upper lip. He was much changed and had grown even thinner since Peter Ivanovich had last seen him, but, as is always the case with the dead, his face was handsomer and above all more dignified than when he was alive. The expression on the face said that what was necessary had been accomplished, and accomplished rightly. Besides this there was in that expression a reproach and a warning to the living. This warning seemed to Peter Ivanovich out of place, or at least not applicable to him. He felt a certain discomfort and so he hurriedly crossed himself once more and turned and went out the door—too hurriedly and too regardless of propriety, as he himself was aware.

Schwartz was waiting for him in the adjoining room with legs spread wide apart and both hands toying with his top-hat behind his back. The mere sight of that playful, well-groomed, and elegant figure refreshed Peter Ivanovich. He felt that Schwartz was above all these happenings and would not surrender to any depressing influences. His very look said that this incident of a church service for Ivan Ilych could not be a sufficient reason for infringing the order of the session—in other words, that it would certainly not prevent his unwrapping a new pack of cards and shuffling them that evening while a footman placed four fresh candles on the table: in fact, that there was no reason for supposing that this incident would hinder their spending the evening agreeably. Indeed he said this in a whisper as Peter Ivanovich passed him, proposing that they should meet for a game at Fëdor Vasilievich's. But apparently Peter Ivanovich was not destined to play bridge that evening. Praskovya Fëdorovna (a short, fat woman who despite all efforts to the contrary had continued to broaden steadily from her shoulders downwards and who had the same extraordinarily arched eyebrows as the lady who had been standing by the coffin), dressed all in black, her head covered with lace, came out of her own room with some other ladies, conducted them to the room where the dead body lay, and said: "The service will begin immediately. Please go in."

Schwartz, making an indefinite bow, stood still, evidently neither accepting nor declining this invitation. Praskovya Fëdorovna recognizing Peter Ivanovich, sighed, went close up to him, took his hand, and said: "I know you were a true friend to Ivan Ilych . . ." and looked at him awaiting some suitable response. And Peter Ivanovich knew that, just as it had been the right thing to cross himself in that room, so what he had to do here was to press her hand, sigh, and say, "Believe me. . . ." So he did all this and as he did it felt that the desired result had been achieved: that both he and she were touched.

"Come with me. I want to speak to you before it begins," said the widow. "Give me your arm."

Peter Ivanovich gave her his arm and they went to the inner rooms, passing Schwartz, who winked at Peter Ivanovich compassionately.

"That does for our bridge! Don't object if we find another player. Perhaps you can cut in when you do escape," said his playful look.

Peter Ivanovich sighed still more deeply and despondently, and Praskovya Fёdorovna pressed his arm gratefully. When they reached the drawing-room, upholstered in pink cretonne and lighted by a dim lamp, they sat down at the table—she on a sofa and Peter Ivanovich on a low pouffe, the springs of which yielded spasmodically under his weight. Praskovya Fёdorovna had been on the point of warning him to take another seat, but felt that such a warning was out of keeping with her present condition and so changed her mind. As he sat down on the pouffe Peter Ivanovich recalled how Ivan Ilych had arranged this room and had consulted him regarding this pink cretonne with green leaves. The whole room was full of furniture and knick-knacks, and on her way to the sofa the lace of the widow's black shawl caught on the carved edge of the table. Peter Ivanovich rose to detach it, and the springs of the pouffe, relieved of his weight, rose also and gave him a push. The widow began detaching her shawl herself, and Peter Ivanovich again sat down, suppressing the rebellious springs of the pouffe under him. But the widow had not quite freed herself and Peter Ivanovich got up again, and again the pouffe rebelled and even creaked. When this was all over she took out a clean cambric handkerchief and began to weep. The episode with the shawl and the struggle with the pouffe had cooled Peter Ivanovich's emotions and he sat there with a sullen look on his face. This awkward situation was interrupted by Sokolov, Ivan Ilych's butler, who came to report that the plot in the cemetery that Praskovya Fёdorovna had chosen would cost two hundred rubles. She stopped weeping and, looking at Peter Ivanovich with the air of a victim, remarked in French that it was very hard for her. Peter Ivanovich made a silent gesture signifying his full conviction that it must indeed be so.

"Please smoke," she said in a magnanimous yet crushed voice, and turned to discuss with Sokolov the price of the plot for the grave.

35   Peter Ivanovich while lighting his cigarette heard her inquiring very circumstantially into the prices of different plots in the cemetery and finally decide which she would take. When that was done she gave instructions about engaging the choir. Sokolov then left the room.

"I look after everything myself," she told Peter Ivanovich, shifting the albums that lay on the table; and noticing that the table was endangered by his cigarette-ash, she immediately passed him an ashtray, saying as she did so: "I consider it an affectation to say that my grief prevents my attending to practical affairs. On the contrary, if anything can—I won't say console me, but— distract me, it is seeing to everything concerning him." She again took out her handkerchief as if preparing to cry, but suddenly, as if mastering her feeling, she shook herself and began to speak calmly. "But there is something I want to talk to you about."

Peter Ivanovich bowed, keeping control of the springs of the pouffe, which immediately began quivering under him.

"He suffered terribly the last few days."

"Did he?" said Peter Ivanovich.

40   "Oh, terribly! He screamed unceasingly, not for minutes but for hours. For the last three days he screamed incessantly. It was unendurable. I cannot understand how I bore it; you could hear him three rooms off. Oh, what I have suffered!"

"Is it possible that he was conscious all that time?" asked Peter Ivanovich.

"Yes," she whispered. "To the last moment. He took leave of us a quarter of an hour before he died, and asked us to take Vasya away."

The thought of the sufferings of this man he had known so intimately, first as a merry little boy, then as a school-mate, and later as a grown-up colleague, suddenly struck Peter Ivanovich with horror, despite an unpleasant consciousness of his own and this woman's dissimulation. He again saw that brow, and that nose pressing down on the lip, and felt afraid for himself.

"Three days of frightful suffering and then death! Why, that might suddenly, at any time, happen to me," he thought, and for a moment felt terrified. But—he did not himself know how— the customary reflection at once occurred to him that this had happened to Ivan Ilych and not to him, and that it should not and could not happen to him, and that to think that it could would be yielding to depression which he ought not to do, as Schwartz's expression plainly showed. After which reflection Peter Ivanovich felt reassured, and began to ask with interest about the details of Ivan Ilych's death, as though death was an accident natural to Ivan Ilych but certainly not to himself.

After many details of the really dreadful physical sufferings Ivan Ilych had endured (which details he learnt only from the effect those sufferings had produced on Praskovya Fĕdorovna's nerves) the widow apparently found it necessary to get to business.

"Oh, Peter Ivanovich, how hard it is! How terribly, terribly hard!" and she again began to weep.

Peter Ivanovich sighed and waited for her to finish blowing her nose. When she had done so he said, "Believe me . . ." and she again began talking and brought out what was evidently her chief concern with him—namely, to question him as to how she could obtain a grant of money from the government on the occasion of her husband's death. She made it appear that she was asking Peter Ivanovich's advice about her pension, but he soon saw that she already knew about that to the minutest detail, more even than he did himself. She knew how much could be got out of the government in consequence of her husband's death, but wanted to find out whether she could not possibly extract something more. Peter Ivanovich tried to think of some means of doing so, but after reflecting for a while and, out of propriety, condemning the government for its niggardliness, he said he thought that nothing more could be got. Then she sighed and evidently began to devise means of getting rid of her visitor. Noticing this, he put out his cigarette, rose, pressed her hand, and went out into the anteroom.

In the dining-room where the clock stood that Ivan Ilych had liked so much and had bought at an antique shop, Peter Ivanovich met a priest and a few acquaintances who had come to attend the service, and he recognized Ivan Ilych's daughter, a handsome young woman. She was in black and her slim figure appeared slimmer than ever. She had a gloomy, determined, almost angry expression, and bowed to Peter Ivanovich as though he were in some way to blame. Behind her, with the same offended look, stood a wealthy young man, an examining magistrate, whom Peter Ivanovich also knew and who was her fiancé, as he had heard. He bowed mournfully to them and was about to pass into the death-chamber, when from under the stairs appeared the figure of Ivan Ilych's schoolboy son, who was extremely like his father. He seemed a little Ivan Ilych, such as Peter Ivanovich remembered when they studied law together. His tear-stained eyes had in them the look that is seen in the eyes of boys of thirteen or fourteen who are not pureminded. When he saw Peter Ivanovich he scowled morosely and shamefacedly. Peter Ivanovich nodded to him and entered the death-chamber. The service began: candles, groans, incense, tears, and sobs. Peter Ivanovich stood looking gloomily down at his feet. He did not look once at the dead man, did not yield to any depressing influence, and was one of the first to leave the room. There was no one in the anteroom, but Gerasim darted out of the dead man's room, rummaged with his strong hands among the fur coats to find Peter Ivanovich's and helped him on with it.

"Well, friend Gerasim," said Peter Ivanovich, so as to say something. "It's a sad affair, isn't it?"

"It's God will. We shall all come to it some day," said Gerasim, displaying his teeth—the even white teeth of a healthy peasant—and, like a man in the thick of urgent work, he briskly opened the front door, called the coachman, helped Peter Ivanovich into the sledge, and sprang back to the porch as if in readiness for what he had to do next.

Peter Ivanovich found the fresh air particularly pleasant after the smell of incense, the dead body, and carbolic acid.

"Where to sir?" asked the coachman.

"It's not too late even now . . . I'll call round on Fĕdor Vasilievich."

He accordingly drove there and found them just finishing the first rubber, so that it was quite convenient for him to cut in.

II

Ivan Ilych's life had been most simple and most ordinary and therefore most terrible.

He had been a member of the Court of Justice, and died at the age of forty-five. His father had been an official who after serving in various ministries and departments in Petersburg had made the sort of career which brings men to positions from which by reason of their long service they cannot be dismissed, though they are obviously unfit to hold any responsible position, and for whom therefore posts are specially created, which though fictitious carry salaries of from six to ten thousand rubles that are not fictitious, and in receipt of which they live on to a great age.

Such was the Privy Councillor and superfluous member of various superfluous institutions, Ilya Epimovich Golovin.

He had three sons, of whom Ivan Ilych was the second. The eldest son was following in his father's footsteps only in another department, and was already approaching that stage in the service at which a similar sinecure would be reached. The third son was a failure. He had ruined his prospects in a number of positions and was now serving in the railway department. His father and brothers, and still more their wives, not merely disliked meeting him, but avoided remembering his existence unless compelled to do so. His sister had married Baron Greff, a Petersburg official of her father's type. Ivan Ilych was *le phénix de la famille*[1] as people said. He was neither as cold and formal as his elder brother nor as wild as the younger, but was a happy mean between them—an intelligent, polished, lively, and agreeable man. He had studied with his younger brother at the School of Law, but the latter had failed to complete the course and was expelled when he was in the fifth class. Ivan Ilych finished the course well. Even when he was at the School of Law he was just what he remained for the rest of his life: a capable, cheerful, good-natured, and sociable man, though strict in the fulfillment of what he considered to be his duty: and he considered his duty to be what was so considered by those in authority. Neither as a boy nor as a man was he a toady, but from early youth was by nature attracted to people of high station as a fly is drawn to the light, assimilating their ways and views of life and establishing friendly relations with them. All the enthusiasms of childhood and youth passed without leaving much trace on him; he succumbed to sensuality, to vanity, and latterly among the highest classes to liberalism, but always within limits which his instinct unfailingly indicated to him as correct.

At school he had done things which had formerly seemed to him very horrid and made him feel disgusted with himself when he did them; but when later on he saw that such actions were done by people of good position and that they did not regard them as wrong, he was able not exactly to regard them as right, but to forget about them entirely or not be at all troubled at remembering them.

60   Having graduated from the School of Law and qualified for the tenth rank of the civil service, and having received money from his father for his equipment, Ivan Ilych ordered himself clothes at Scharmer's, the fashionable tailor, hung a medallion inscribed *respice finem*[2] on his watch-chain, took leave of his professor and the prince who was patron of the school, had a farewell dinner with his comrades at Donon's first-class restaurant, and with his new and fashionable portmanteau, linen, clothes, shaving and other toilet appliances, and a traveling rug all purchased at the best shops, he set off for one of the provinces where through his father's influence, he had been attached to the Governor as an official for special service.

In the province Ivan Ilych soon arranged as easy and agreeable a position for himself as he had had at the School of Law. He performed his official tasks, made his career, and at the same time amused himself pleasantly and decorously. Occasionally he paid official visits to country districts, where he behaved with dignity both to his superiors and inferiors, and performed the duties entrusted to him, which related chiefly to the sectarians, with an exactness and incorruptible honesty of which he could not but feel proud.

In official matters, despite his youth and taste for frivolous gaiety, he was exceedingly reserved, punctilious, and even severe; but in society he was often amusing and witty, and always good-natured, correct in his manner, and *bon enfant*,[3] as the Governor and his wife—with whom he was like one of the family—used to say of him.

In the province he had an affair with a lady who made advances to the elegant young lawyer, and there was also a milliner; and there were carousals with aides-de-camp who visited the district, and after-supper visits to a certain outlying street of doubtful reputation; and there was too some obsequiousness to his chief and even to his chief's wife, but all this was done with such a tone of good breeding that no hard names could be applied to it. It all came under the heading

---

[1]French: "Paragon of the family"—the child most likely to succeed.
[2]Latin phrase meaning "Consider the end" (of one's life).
[3]French: "Good Child"—a phrase used to describe an amiable disposition.

of the French saying: "*Il faut que jeunesse se passe.*"[4] It was all done with clean hands, in clean linen, with French phrases, and above all among people of the best society and consequently with the approval of people of rank.

So Ivan Ilych served for five years and then came a change in his official life. The new and reformed judicial institutions were introduced, and new men were needed. Ivan Ilych became such a new man. He was offered the post of examining magistrate, and he accepted it though the post was in another province and obliged him to give up the connections he had formed and to make new ones. His friends met to give him a send-off; they had a group photograph taken and presented him with a silver cigarette-case, and he set off to his new post.

As examining magistrate Ivan Ilych was just as *comme il faut*[5] and decorous a man, inspiring general respect and capable of separating his official duties from his private life, as he had been when acting as an official on special service. His duties now as examining magistrate were far more interesting and attractive than before. In his former position it had been pleasant to wear an undress uniform made by Scharmer, and to pass through the crowd of petitioners and officials who were timorously awaiting an audience with the Governor, and who envied him as with free and easy gait he went straight into his chief's private room to have a cup of tea and a cigarette with him. But not many people had then been directly dependent on him—only police officials and the sectarians when he went on special missions—and he liked to treat them politely, almost as comrades, as if he were letting them feel that he who had the power to crush them was treating them in this simple, friendly way. There were then but few such people. But now, as an examining magistrate, Ivan Ilych felt that everyone without exception, even the most important and self-satisfied, was in his power, and that he need only write a few words on a sheet of paper with a certain heading, and this or that important, self-satisfied person would be brought before him in the role of an accused person or a witness, and if he did not choose to allow him to sit down, would have to stand before him and answer his questions. Ivan Ilych never abused his power; he tried on the contrary to soften its expression, but the consciousness of it and of the possibility of softening its effect, supplied the chief interest and attraction of his office. In his work itself, especially in his examinations, he very soon acquired a method of eliminating all considerations irrelevant to the legal aspect of the case, and reducing even the most complicated case to a form in which it would be presented on paper only in its externals, completely excluding his personal opinion of the matter, while above all observing every prescribed formality. The work was new and Ivan Ilych was one of the first men to apply the new Code of 1864.

On taking up the post of examining magistrate in a new town, he made new acquaintances and connections, placed himself on a new footing and assumed a somewhat different tone. He took up an attitude of rather dignified aloofness towards the provincial authorities, but picked out the best circle of legal gentlemen and wealthy gentry living in the town and assumed a tone of slight dissatisfaction with the government, of moderate liberalism, and of enlightened citizenship. At the same time, without at all altering the elegance of his toilet, he ceased shaving his chin and allowed his beard to grow as it pleased.

Ivan Ilych settled down very pleasantly in this new town. The society there, which inclined towards opposition to the Governor, was friendly, his salary was larger, and he began to play *vint,* which he found added not a little to the pleasure of life, for he had a capacity for cards, played good-humoredly, and calculated rapidly and astutely, so that he usually won.

After living there for two years he met his future wife, Praskovya Fëdorovna Mikhel, who was the most attractive, clever, and brilliant girl of the set in which he moved, and among other amusements and relaxations from his labors as examining magistrate, Ivan Ilych established light and playful relations with her.

While he had been an official on special service he had been accustomed to dance, but now as an examining magistrate it was exceptional for him to do so. If he danced now, he did it as if to show that though he served under the reformed order of things, and had reached the fifth official rank,

---

[4]French: "Youth must pass"—a phrase similar to "boys will be boys."
[5]French: "As it should be."

yet when it came to dancing he could do it better than most people. So at the end of an evening he sometimes danced with Praskovya Fĕdorovna, and it was chiefly during these dances that he captivated her. She fell in love with him. Ivan Ilych had at first no definite intention of marrying, but when the girl fell in love with him he said to himself: "Really, why shouldn't I marry?"

70 Praskovya Fĕdorovna came of a good family, was not bad-looking, and had some little property. Ivan Ilych might have aspired to a more brilliant match, but even this was good. He had his salary, and she, he hoped, would have an equal income. She was well connected, and was a sweet, pretty, and thoroughly correct young woman. To say that Ivan Ilych married because he fell in love with Praskovya Fĕdorovna and found that she sympathized with his views of life would be as incorrect as to say that he married because his social circle approved of the match. He was swayed by both these considerations: the marriage gave him personal satisfaction, and at the same time it was considered the right thing by the most highly placed of his associates.

So Ivan Ilych got married.

The preparations for marriage and the beginning of married life, with its conjugal caresses, the new furniture, new crockery, and new linen, were very pleasant until his wife became pregnant—so that Ivan Ilych had begun to think that marriage would not impair the easy, agreeable, gay, and always decorous character of his life, approved of by society and regarded by himself as natural, but would even improve it. But from the first months of his wife's pregnancy, something new, unpleasant, depressing, and unseemly, and from which there was no way of escape, unexpectedly showed itself.

His wife, without any reason—*de gaieté de coeur*[6] as Ivan Ilych expressed it to himself—began to disturb the pleasure and propriety of their life. She began to be jealous without any cause, expected him to devote his whole attention to her, found fault with everything, and made coarse and ill-mannered scenes.

At first Ivan Ilych hoped to escape from the unpleasantness of this state of affairs by the same easy and decorous relation to life that had served him heretofore: he tried to ignore his wife's disagreeable moods, continued to live in his usual easy and pleasant way, invited friends to his house for a game of cards, and also tried going out to his club or spending his evenings with friends. But one day his wife began upbraiding him so vigorously, using such coarse words, and continued to abuse him every time he did not fulfill her demands, so resolutely and with such evident determination not to give way till he submitted—that is, till he stayed at home and was bored just as she was—that he became alarmed. He now realized that matrimony—at any rate with Praskovya Fĕdorovna—was not always conducive to the pleasures and amenities of life, but on the contrary often infringed both comfort and propriety, and that he must therefore entrench himself against such infringement. And Ivan Ilych began to seek for means of doing so. His official duties were the one thing that imposed upon Praskovya Fĕdorovna, and by means of his official work and the duties attached to it he began struggling with his wife to secure his own independence.

75 With the birth of their child, the attempts to feed it and the various failures in doing so, and with the real and imaginary illnesses of mother and child, in which Ivan Ilych's sympathy was demanded but about which he understood nothing, the need of securing for himself an existence outside his family life became still more imperative.

As his wife grew more irritable and exacting and Ivan Ilych transferred the center of gravity of his life more and more to his official work, so did he grow to like his work better and became more ambitious than before.

Very soon, within a year of his wedding, Ivan Ilych had realized that marriage, though it may add some comforts to life, is in fact a very intricate and difficult affair towards which in order to perform one's duty, that is, to lead a decorous life approved of by society, one must adopt a definite attitude just as towards one's official duties.

And Ivan Ilych evolved such an attitude towards married life. He only required of it those conveniences—dinner at home, housewife, and bed—which it could give him, and above all that propriety of external forms required by public opinion. For the rest he looked for light-

---

[6]French: "To the heart's delight."

hearted pleasure and propriety, and was very thankful when he found them, but if he met with antagonism and querulousness he at once retired into his separate fenced-off world of official duties, where he found satisfaction.

Ivan Ilych was esteemed a good official, and after three years was made Assistant Public Prosecutor. His new duties, their importance, the possibility of indicting and imprisoning anyone he chose, the publicity his speeches received, and the success he had in all these things, made his work still more attractive.

More children came. His wife became more and more querulous and ill-tempered, but the attitude Ivan Ilych had adopted towards his home life rendered him almost impervious to her grumbling.

After seven years' service in that town he was transferred to another province as Public Prosecutor. They moved, but were short of money and his wife did not like the place they moved to. Though the salary was higher the cost of living was greater, besides which two of their children died and family life became still more unpleasant for him.

Praskovya Fĕdorovna blamed her husband for every inconvenience they encountered in their new home. Most of the conversations between husband and wife, especially as to the children's education, led to topics which recalled former disputes, and these disputes were apt to flare up again at any moment. There remained only those rare periods of amorousness which still came to them at times but did not last long. These were islets at which they anchored for a while and then again set out upon that ocean of veiled hostility which showed itself in their aloofness from one another. This aloofness might have grieved Ivan Ilych had he considered that it ought not to exist, but he now regarded the position as normal, and even made it the goal at which he aimed in family life. His aim was to free himself more and more from those unpleasantnesses and to give them a semblance of harmlessness and propriety. He attained this by spending less and less time with his family, and when obliged to be at home he tried to safeguard his position by the presence of outsiders. The chief thing, however, was that he had his official duties. The whole interest of his life now centered in the official world and that interest absorbed him. The consciousness of his power, being able to ruin anybody he wished to ruin, the importance, even the external dignity of his entry into court, or meetings with his subordinates, his success with superiors and inferiors, and above all his masterly handling of cases, of which he was conscious—all this gave him pleasure and filled his life, together with chats with his colleagues, dinners, and bridge. So that on the whole Ivan Ilych's life continued to flow as he considered it should do—pleasantly and properly.

So things continued for another seven years. His eldest daughter was already sixteen, another child had died, and only one son was left, a schoolboy and a subject of dissension. Ivan Ilych wanted to put him in the School of Law, but to spite him Praskovya Fĕdorovna entered him at the High School. The daughter had been educated at home and had turned out well: the boy did not learn badly either.

III

So Ivan Ilych lived for seventeen years after his marriage. He was already a Public Prosecutor of long standing, and had declined several proposed transfers while awaiting a more desirable post, when an unanticipated and unpleasant occurrence quite upset the peaceful course of his life. He was expecting to be offered the post of presiding judge in a University town, but Happe somehow came to the front and obtained the appointment instead. Ivan Ilych became irritable, reproached Happe, and quarreled both with him and with his immediate superiors—who became colder to him and again passed him over when other appointments were made.

This was in 1880, the hardest year of Ivan Ilych's life. It was then that it became evident on the one hand that his salary was insufficient for them to live on, and on the other that he had been forgotten, and not only this, but that what was for him the greatest and most cruel injustice appeared to others a quite ordinary occurrence. Even his father did not consider it his duty to help him. Ivan Ilych felt himself abandoned by everyone, and that they regarded his position with a salary of 3,500 rubles as quite normal and even fortunate. He alone knew that with the consciousness of the injustices done him, with his wife's incessant nagging, and with the debts he had contracted by living beyond his means, his position was far from normal.

In order to save money that summer he obtained a leave of absence and went with his wife to live in the country at her brother's place.

In the country, without his work, he experienced *ennui* for the first time in his life, and not only *ennui* but intolerable depression, and he decided that it was impossible to go on living like that, and that it was necessary to take energetic measures.

Having passed a sleepless night pacing up and down the veranda, he decided to go to Petersburg and bestir himself, in order to punish those who had failed to appreciate him and to get transferred to another ministry.

Next day, despite many protests from his wife and her brother, he started for Petersburg with the sole object of obtaining a post with a salary of five thousand rubles a year. He was no longer bent on any particular department, or tendency, or kind of activity. All he now wanted was an appointment to another post with a salary of five thousand rubles, either in the administration, in the banks, with the railways, in one of the Empress Marya's Institutions, or even in the customs—but it had to carry with it a salary of five thousand rubles and be in a ministry other than that in which they had failed to appreciate him.

90   And this quest of Ivan Ilych's was crowned with remarkable and unexpected success. At Kursk an acquaintance of his, F. I. Ilyin, got into the first-class carriage, sat down beside Ivan Ilych, and told him of a telegram just received by the Governor of Kursk announcing that a change was about to take place in the ministry: Peter Ivanovich was to be superseded by Ivan Semënovich.

The proposed change, apart from its significance for Russia, had a special significance for Ivan Ilych, because by bringing forward a new man, Peter Petrovich, and consequently his friend Zachar Ivanovich, it was highly favorable for Ivan Ilych, since Zachar Ivanovich was a friend and colleague of his.

In Moscow this news was confirmed, and on reaching Petersburg Ivan Ilych found Zachar Ivanovich and received a definite promise of an appointment in his former department of Justice.

A week later he telegraphed to his wife: "Zachar in Miller's place. I shall receive appointment on presentation of report."

Thanks to this change of personnel, Ivan Ilych had unexpectedly obtained an appointment in his former ministry which placed him two stages above his former colleagues besides giving him five thousand rubles salary and three thousand five hundred rubles for expenses connected with his removal. All his ill humor towards his former enemies and the whole department vanished, and Ivan Ilych was completely happy.

95   He returned to the country more cheerful and contented than he had been for a long time. Praskovya Fëdorovna also cheered up and a truce was arranged between them. Ivan Ilych told of how he had been fêted by everybody in Petersburg, how all those who had been his enemies were put to shame and now fawned on him, how envious they were of his appointment, and how much everybody in Petersburg had liked him.

Praskovya Fëdorovna listened to all this and appeared to believe it. She did not contradict anything, but only made plans for their life in the town to which they were going. Ivan Ilych saw with delight that these plans were his plans, that he and his wife agreed, and that, after a stumble, his life was regaining its due and natural character of pleasant lightheartedness and decorum.

Ivan Ilych had come back for a short time only, for he had to take up his new duties on the 10th of September. Moreover, he needed time to settle into the new place, to move all his belongings from the province, and to buy and order many additional things: in a word, to make such arrangements as he had resolved on, which were almost exactly what Praskovya Fëdorovna too had decided on.

Now that everything had happened so fortunately, and that he and his wife were at one in their aims and moreover saw so little of one another, they got on together better than they had done since the first years of marriage. Ivan Ilych had thought of taking his family away with him at once, but the insistence of his wife's brother and her sister-in-law, who had suddenly become particularly amiable and friendly to him and his family, induced him to depart alone.

So he departed, and the cheerful state of mind induced by his success and by the harmony between his wife and himself, the one intensifying the other, did not leave him. He found a delightful house, just the thing both he and his wife had dreamt of. Spacious, lofty reception rooms in the old style, a convenient and dignified study, rooms for his wife and daughter, a study for his son—it might have been specially built for them. Ivan Ilych himself superintended the arrangements, chose the wallpapers, supplemented the furniture (preferably with antiques which he considered particularly *comme il faut*), and supervised the upholstering. Everything progressed and progressed and approached the ideal he had set himself: even when things were only half completed they exceeded his expectations. He saw what a refined and elegant character, free from vulgarity, it would all have when it was ready. On falling asleep he pictured to himself how the reception-room would look. Looking at the yet unfinished drawing-room he could see the fireplace, the screen, the what-not, the little chairs dotted here and there, the dishes and plates on the walls, and the bronzes, as they would be when everything was in place. He was pleased by the thought of how his wife and daughter, who shared his taste in this matter, would be impressed by it. They were certainly not expecting as much. He had been particularly successful in finding, and buying cheaply, antiques which gave a particularly aristocratic character to the whole place. But in his letters he intentionally understated everything in order to be able to surprise them. All this so absorbed him that his new duties—though he liked his official work—interested him less than he had expected. Sometimes he even had moments of absentmindedness during the Court Sessions, and would consider whether he should have straight or curved cornices for his curtains. He was so interested in it all that he often did things himself, rearranging the furniture, or rehanging the curtains. Once when mounting a stepladder to show the upholsterer, who did not understand, how he wanted the hangings draped, he made a false step and slipped, but being a strong and agile man he clung on and only knocked his side against the knob of the window frame. The bruised place was painful but the pain soon passed, and he felt particularly bright and well just then. He wrote: "I feel fifteen years younger." He thought he would have everything ready by September, but it dragged on till mid-October. But the result was charming not only in his eyes but to everyone who saw it.

In reality it was just what is usually seen in the houses of people of moderate means who want to appear rich, and therefore succeed only in resembling others like themselves: there were damasks, dark wood, plants, rugs, and dull and polished bronzes—all the things people of a certain class have in order to resemble other people of that class. His house was so like the others that it would never have been noticed, but to him it all seemed to be quite exceptional. He was very happy when he met his family at the station and brought them to the newly furnished house all lit up, where a footman in a white tie opened the door into the hall decorated with plants, and when they went on into the drawing-room and the study uttering exclamations of delight. He conducted them everywhere, drank in their praises eagerly, and beamed with pleasure. At tea that evening, when Praskovya Fëdorovna among other things asked him about his fall, he laughed and showed them how he had gone flying and had frightened the upholsterer.

"It's a good thing I'm a bit of an athlete. Another man might have been killed, but I merely knocked myself, just there; it hurts when it's touched, but it's passing off already—it's only a bruise."

So they began living in their new home—in which, as always happens, when they got thoroughly settled in they found they were just one room short—and with the increased income, which as always was just a little (some five hundred rubles) too little, but it was all very nice.

Things went particularly well at first, before everything was finally arranged and while something had still to be done: this thing bought, that thing ordered, another thing moved, and something else adjusted. Though there were some disputes between husband and wife, they were both so well satisfied and had so much to do that it all passed off without any serious quarrels. When nothing was left to arrange it became rather dull and something seemed to be lacking, but they were then making acquaintances, forming habits, and life was growing fuller.

Ivan Ilych spent his mornings at the law courts and came home to dinner, and at first he was generally in a good humor, though he occasionally became irritable just on account of his house. (Every spot on the tablecloth or the upholstery, and every broken window-blind string, irritated him. He had devoted so much trouble to arranging it all that every disturbance of it distressed him.) But on the whole his life ran its course as he believed life should do: easily, pleasantly, and decorously.

He got up at nine, drank his coffee, read the paper, and then put on his undress uniform and went to the law courts. There the harness in which he worked had already been stretched to fit him and he donned it without a hitch: petitioners, inquiries at the chancery, the chancery itself, and the sittings public and administrative. In all this the thing was to exclude everything fresh and vital, which always disturbs the regular course of official business, and to admit only official relations with people, and then only on official grounds. A man would come, for instance, wanting some information. Ivan Ilych, as one in whose sphere the matter did not lie, would have nothing to do with him: but if the man had some business with him in his official capacity, something that could be expressed on officially stamped paper, he would do everything, positively everything he could within the limits of such relations, and in doing so would maintain the semblance of friendly human relations, that is, would observe the courtesies of life. As soon as the official relations ended, so did everything else. Ivan Ilych possessed this capacity to separate his real life from the official side of affairs and not mix the two, in the highest degree, and by long practice and natural aptitude had brought it to such a pitch that sometimes, in the manner of a virtuoso, he would even allow himself to let the human and official relations mingle. He let himself do this just because he felt that he could at any time he chose resume the strictly official attitude again and drop the human relation. And he did it all easily, pleasantly, correctly, and even artistically. In the intervals between the sessions he smoked, drank tea, chatted a little about politics, a little about general topics, a little about cards, but most of all about official appointments. Tired, but with the feelings of a virtuoso—one of the first violins who has played his part in an orchestra with precision—he would return home to find that his wife and daughter had been out paying calls, or had a visitor, and that his son had been to school, had done his homework with his tutor, and was duly learning what is taught at High Schools. Everything was as it should be. After dinner, if they had no visitors, Ivan Ilych sometimes read a book that was being much discussed at the time, and in the evening settled down to work, that is, read official papers, compared the depositions of witnesses, and noted paragraphs of the Code applying to them. This was neither dull nor amusing. It was dull when he might have been playing bridge, but if no bridge was available it was at any rate better than doing nothing or sitting with his wife. Ivan Ilych's chief pleasure was giving little dinners to which he invited men and women of good social position, and just as his drawing-room resembled all other drawing-rooms so did his enjoyable little parties resemble all other such parties.

Once they even gave a dance. Ivan Ilych enjoyed it and everything went off well, except that it led to a violent quarrel with his wife about the cakes and sweets. Praskovya Fĕdorovna had made her own plans, but Ivan Ilych insisted on getting everything from an expensive confectioner and ordered too many cakes, and the quarrel occurred because some of those cakes were left over and the confectioner's bill came to forty-five rubles. It was a great and disagreeable quarrel. Praskovya Fĕdorovna called him "a fool and an imbecile," and he clutched at his head and made angry allusions to divorce.

But the dance itself had been enjoyable. The best people were there, and Ivan Ilych had danced with Princess Trufonova, a sister of the distinguished founder of the Society "Bear My Burden."

The pleasures connected with his work were pleasures of ambition; his social pleasures were those of vanity; but Ivan Ilych's greatest pleasure was playing bridge. He acknowledged that whatever disagreeable incident happened in his life, the pleasure that beamed like a ray of light above everything else was to sit down to bridge with good players, not noisy partners, and of course to four-handed bridge (with five players it was annoying to have to stand out, though one pretended not to mind), to play a clever and serious game (when the cards allowed it), and then to have supper and drink a glass of wine. After a game of bridge, especially if he had won a little (to win a large sum was unpleasant), Ivan Ilych went to bed in a specially good humor.

So they lived. They formed a circle of acquaintances among the best people and were visited by people of importance and by young folk. In their views as to their acquaintances, husband, wife, and daughter were entirely agreed, and tacitly and unanimously kept at arm's length and shook off the various shabby friends and relations who, with much show of affection, gushed into the drawing-room with its Japanese plates on the walls. Soon these shabby friends ceased to obtrude themselves and only the best people remained in the Golovins' set.

110   Young men made up to Lisa, and Petrishchev, an examining magistrate and Dmitri Ivanovich Petrishchev's son and sole heir, began to be so attentive to her that Ivan Ilych had already spoken

to Praskovya Fĕdorovna about it, and considered whether they should not arrange a party for them, or get up some private theatricals.

So they lived, and all went well, without change, and life flowed pleasantly.

IV

They were all in good health. It could not be called ill health if Ivan Ilych sometimes said that he had a queer taste in his mouth and felt some discomfort in his left side.

But this discomfort increased and, though not exactly painful, grew into a sense of pressure in his side accompanied by ill humor. And his irritability became worse and worse and began to mar the agreeable, easy, and correct life that had established itself in the Golovin family. Quarrels between husband and wife became more and more frequent, and soon the ease and amenity disappeared and even the decorum was barely maintained. Scenes again became frequent, and very few of those islets remained on which husband and wife could meet without an explosion. Praskovya Fĕdorovna now had good reason to say that her husband's temper was trying. With characteristic exaggeration she said he had always had a dreadful temper, and that it had needed all her good nature to put up with it for twenty years. It was true that now the quarrels were started by him. His bursts of temper always came just before dinner, often just as he began to eat his soup. Sometimes he noticed that a plate or dish was chipped, or the food was not right, or his son put his elbow on the table, or his daughter's hair was not done as he liked it, and for all this he blamed Praskovya Fĕdorovna. At first she retorted and said disagreeable things to him, but once or twice he fell into such a rage at the beginning of dinner that she realized it was due to some physical derangement brought on by taking food, and so she restrained herself and did not answer, but only hurried to get the dinner over. She regarded this self-restraint as highly praiseworthy. Having come to the conclusion that her husband had a dreadful temper and made her life miserable, she began to feel sorry for herself, and the more she pitied herself the more she hated her husband. She began to wish he would die; yet she did not want him to die because then his salary would cease. And this irritated her against him still more. She considered herself dreadfully unhappy just because not even his death could save her, and though she concealed her exasperation, that hidden exasperation of hers increased his irritation also.

After one scene in which Ivan Ilych had been particularly unfair and after which he had said in explanation that he certainly was irritable but that it was due to his not being well, she said that if he was ill it should be attended to, and insisted on his going to see a celebrated doctor.

He went. Everything took place as he had expected and as it always does. There was the usual waiting and the important air assumed by the doctor, with which he was so familiar (resembling that which he himself assumed in court), and the sounding and listening, and the questions which called for answers that were foregone conclusions and were evidently unnecessary, and the look of importance which implied that "if only you put yourself in our hands we will arrange everything—we know indubitably how it has to be done, always in the same way for everybody alike." It was all just as it was in the law courts. The doctor put on just the same air towards him as he himself put on towards an accused person.

The doctor said that so-and-so indicated that there was so-and-so inside the patient, but if the investigation of so-and-so did not confirm this, then he must assume that and that. If he assumed that and that, then . . . and so on. To Ivan Ilych only one question was important: was his case serious or not? But the doctor ignored that inappropriate question. From his point of view it was not the one under consideration, the real question was to decide between a floating kidney, chronic catarrh, or appendicitis. It was not a question of Ivan Ilych's life or death, but one between a floating kidney and appendicitis. And that question the doctor solved brilliantly, as it seemed to Ivan Ilych, in favor of the appendix, with the reservation that should an examination of the urine give fresh indications the matter would be reconsidered. All this was just what Ivan Ilych had himself brilliantly accomplished a thousand times in dealing with men on trial. The doctor summed up just as brilliantly, looking over his spectacles triumphantly and even gaily at the accused. From the doctor's summing up Ivan Ilych concluded that things were bad, but that for the doctor, and perhaps for everybody else, it was a matter of indifference, though for him it was bad. And this conclusion struck him painfully, arousing in him a great feeling of pity for himself and of bitterness towards the doctor's indifference to a matter of such importance.

He said nothing of this, but rose, placed the doctor's fee on the table, and remarked with a sigh: "We sick people probably often put inappropriate questions. But tell me, in general, is this complaint dangerous, or not? . . ."

The doctor looked at him sternly over his spectacles with one eye, as if to say: "Prisoner, if you will not keep to the questions put to you, I shall be obliged to have you removed from the court."

"I have already told you what I consider necessary and proper. The analysis may show something more." And the doctor bowed.

120   Ivan Ilych went out slowly, seated himself disconsolately in his sledge, and drove home. All the way home he was going over what the doctor had said, trying to translate those complicated, obscure, scientific phrases into plain language and find in them an answer to the question: "Is my condition bad? Is it very bad? Or is there as yet nothing much wrong?" And it seemed to him that the meaning of what the doctor had said was that it was very bad. Everything in the streets seemed depressing. The cabmen, the houses, the passers-by, and the shops, were dismal. His ache, this dull gnawing ache that never ceased for a moment, seemed to have acquired a new and more serious significance from the doctor's dubious remarks. Ivan Ilych now watched it with a new and oppressive feeling.

He reached home and began to tell his wife about it. She listened, but in the middle of his account his daughter came in with her hat on, ready to go out with her mother. She sat down reluctantly to listen to this tedious story, but could not stand it long, and her mother too did not hear him to the end.

"Well, I am very glad," she said. "Mind now to take your medicine regularly. Give me the prescription and I'll send Gerasim to the chemist's." And she went to get ready to go out.

While she was in the room Ivan Ilych had hardly taken time to breathe, but he sighed deeply when she left it.

"Well," he thought, "perhaps it isn't so bad after all."

125   He began taking his medicine and following the doctor's directions, which had been altered after the examination of the urine. But then it happened that there was a contradiction between the indications drawn from the examination of the urine and the symptoms that showed themselves. It turned out that what was happening differed from what the doctor had told him, and that he had either forgotten, or blundered, or hidden something from him. He could not, however, be blamed for that, and Ivan Ilych still obeyed his orders implicitly and at first derived some comfort from doing so.

From the time of his visit to the doctor, Ivan Ilych's chief occupation was the exact fulfillment of the doctor's instructions regarding hygiene and the taking of medicine, and the observation of his pain and his excretions. His chief interests came to be people's ailments and people's health. When sickness, deaths, or recoveries were mentioned in his presence, especially when the illness resembled his own, he listened with agitation which he tried to hide, asked questions, and applied what he heard to his own case.

The pain did not grow less, but Ivan Ilych made efforts to force himself to think that he was better. And he could do this so long as nothing agitated him. But as soon as he had any unpleasantness with his wife, any lack of success in his official work, or held bad cards at bridge, he was at once acutely sensible of his disease. He had formerly borne such mischances, hoping soon to adjust what was wrong, to master it and attain success, or make a grand slam. But now every mischance upset him and plunged him into despair. He would say to himself: "There now, just as I was beginning to get better and the medicine had begun to take effect, comes this accursed misfortune, or unpleasantness. . . ." And he was furious with the mishap, or with the people who were causing the unpleasantness and killing him, for he felt that this fury was killing him but could not restrain it. One would have thought that it should have been clear to him that this exasperation with circumstances and people aggravated his illness, and that he ought therefore to ignore unpleasant occurrences. But he drew the very opposite conclusion: he said that he needed peace, and he watched for everything that might disturb it and became irritable at the slightest infringement of it. His condition was rendered worse by the fact that he read medical books and consulted doctors. The progress of his disease was so gradual that he could deceive himself when comparing one day with another—the difference was so slight. But when he consulted the doctors it seemed to him that he was getting worse, and even very rapidly. Yet despite this he was continually consulting them.

That month he went to see another celebrity, who told him almost the same as the first had done but put his questions rather differently, and the interview with this celebrity only increased Ivan Ilych's doubts and fears. A friend of a friend of his, a very good doctor, diagnosed his illness again quite differently from the others, and though he predicted recovery, his questions and suppositions bewildered Ivan Ilych still more and increased his doubts. A homeopathist diagnosed the disease in yet another way, and prescribed medicine which Ivan Ilych took secretly for a week. But after a week, not feeling any improvement and having lost confidence both in the former doctor's treatment and in this one's, he became still more despondent. One day a lady acquaintance mentioned a cure effected by a wonder-working icon. Ivan Ilych caught himself listening attentively and beginning to believe that it had occurred. This incident alarmed him. "Has my mind really weakened to such an extent?" he asked himself. "Nonsense! It's all rubbish. I mustn't give way to nervous fears but having chosen a doctor must keep strictly to his treatment. That is what I will do. Now it's all settled. I won't think about it, but will follow the treatment seriously till summer, and then we shall see. From now there must be no more of this wavering!" This was easy to say but impossible to carry out. The pain in his side oppressed him and seemed to grow worse and more incessant, while the taste in his mouth grew stranger and stranger. It seemed to him that his breath had a disgusting smell, and he was conscious of a loss of appetite and strength. There was no deceiving himself: something terrible, new, and more important than anything before in his life, was taking place within him of which he alone was aware. Those about him did not understand or would not understand it, but thought everything in the world was going on as usual. That tormented Ivan Ilych more than anything. He saw that his household, especially his wife and daughter who were in a perfect whirl of visiting, did not understand anything of it and were annoyed that he was so depressed and so exacting, as if he were to blame for it. Though they tried to disguise it he saw that he was an obstacle in their path, and that his wife had adopted a definite line in regard to his illness and kept to it regardless of anything he said or did. Her attitude was this: "You know," she would say to her friends, "Ivan Ilych can't do as other people do, and keep to the treatment prescribed for him. One day he'll take his drops and keep strictly to his diet and go to bed in good time, but the next day unless I watch him he'll suddenly forget his medicine, eat sturgeon—which is forbidden—and sit up playing cards till one o'clock in the morning."

"Oh, come, when was that?" Ivan Ilych would ask in vexation. "Only once at Peter Ivanovich's."

"And yesterday with Shebek."

"Well, even if I hadn't stayed up, this pain would have kept me awake."

"Be that as it may you'll never get well like that, but will always make us wretched."

Praskovya Fëdorovna's attitude to Ivan Ilych's illness, as she expressed it both to others and to him, was that it was his own fault and was another of the annoyances he caused her. Ivan Ilych felt that this opinion escaped her involuntarily—but that did not make it easier for him.

At the law courts too, Ivan Ilych noticed, or thought he noticed, a strange attitude towards himself. It sometimes seemed to him that people were watching him inquisitively as a man whose place might soon be vacant. Then again, his friends would suddenly begin to chaff him in a friendly way about his low spirits, as if the awful, horrible, and unheard-of thing that was going on within him, incessantly gnawing at him and irresistibly drawing him away, was a very agreeable subject for jests. Schwartz in particular irritated him by his jocularity, vivacity, and *savoir-faire*, which reminded him of what he himself had been ten years ago.

Friends came to make up a set and they sat down to cards. They dealt, bending the new cards to soften them, and he sorted the diamonds in his hand and found he had seven. His partner said "No trumps" and supported him with two diamonds. What more could be wished for? It ought to be jolly and lively. They would make a grand slam. But suddenly Ivan Ilych was conscious of that gnawing pain, that taste in his mouth, and it seemed ridiculous that in such circumstances he should be pleased to make a grand slam.

He looked at his partner Mikhail Mikhaylovich, who rapped the table with his strong hand and instead of snatching up the tricks pushed the cards courteously and indulgently towards Ivan Ilych that he might have the pleasure of gathering them up without the trouble of stretching out his hand for them. "Does he think I am too weak to stretch out my arm?" thought Ivan Ilych, and forgetting what he was doing he over-trumped his partner, missing the grand slam by three tricks. And what was most awful of all was that he saw how upset Mikhail Mikhaylovich was about it but did not himself care. And it was dreadful to realize why he did not care.

They all saw that he was suffering, and said: "We can stop if you are tired. Take a rest." Lie down? No, he was not at all tired, and he finished the rubber. All were gloomy and silent. Ivan Ilych felt that he had diffused this gloom over them and could not dispel it. They had supper and went away, and Ivan Ilych was left alone with the consciousness that his life was poisoned and was poisoning the lives of others, and that this poison did not weaken but penetrated more and more deeply into his whole being.

With this consciousness, and with physical pain besides the terror, he must go to bed, often to lie awake the greater part of the night. Next morning he had to get up again, dress, go to the law courts, speak, and write; or if he did not go out, spend at home those twenty-four hours a day each of which was a torture. And he had to live thus all alone on the brink of an abyss, with no one who understood or pitied him.

V

So one month passed and then another. Just before the New Year his brother-in-law came to town and stayed at their house. Ivan Ilych was at the law courts and Praskovya Fĕdorovna had gone shopping. When Ivan Ilych came home and entered his study he found his brother-in-law there—a healthy, florid man—unpacking his portmanteau himself. He raised his head on hearing Ivan Ilych's footsteps and looked up at him for a moment without a word. That stare told Ivan Ilych everything. His brother-in-law opened his mouth to utter an exclamation of surprise but checked himself, and that action confirmed it all.

140 "I have changed, eh?"

"Yes, there is a change."

And after that, try as he would to get his brother-in-law to return to the subject of his looks, the latter would say nothing about it. Praskovya Fĕdorovna came home and her brother went out to her. Ivan Ilych locked the door and began to examine himself in the glass, first full face, then in profile. He took up a portrait of himself taken with his wife, and compared it with what he saw in the glass. The change in him was immense. Then he bared his arms to the elbow, looked at them, drew the sleeves down again, sat down on an ottoman, and grew blacker than night.

"No, no, this won't do!" he said to himself, and jumped up, went to the table, took up some law papers, and began to read them, but could not continue. He unlocked the door and went into the reception-room. The door leading to the drawing-room was shut. He approached it on tiptoe and listened.

"No, you are exaggerating!" Praskovya Fĕdorovna was saying.

145 "Exaggerating! Don't you see it? Why, he's a dead man! Look at his eyes—there's no light in them. But what is it that is wrong with him?"

"No one knows. Nikolaevich said something, but I don't know what. And Leshchetitsky said quite the contrary . . ."

Ivan Ilych walked away, went to his own room, lay down, and began musing; "The kidney, a floating kidney." He recalled all the doctors had told him of how it detached itself and swayed about. And by an effort of imagination he tried to catch that kidney and arrest it and support it. So little was needed for this, it seemed to him. "No, I'll go to see Peter Ivanovich again." He rang, ordered the carriage, and got ready to go.

"Where are you going, Jean?" asked his wife, with a specially sad and exceptionally kind look.

This exceptionally kind look irritated him. He looked morosely at her.

150 "I must go to see Peter Ivanovich."

He went to see Peter Ivanovich, and together they went to see his friend, the doctor. He was in, and Ivan Ilych had a long talk with him.

Reviewing the anatomical and physiological details of what in the doctor's opinion was going on inside him, he understood it all.

There was something, a small thing, in the vermiform appendix. It might all come right. Only stimulate the energy of one organ and check the activity of another, then absorption would take place and everything would come right. He got home rather late for dinner, ate his dinner, and conversed cheerfully, but could not for a long time bring himself to go back to work in his room. At last, however, he went to his study and did what was necessary, but the consciousness that he had put something aside—an important, intimate matter which he would revert to when his work was done—never left him. When he had finished his work he remembered that this intimate matter was the thought of his vermiform appendix. But he did not give himself up to it, and went to the drawing-room for tea. There were callers there, including the examining magistrate who was a desirable match for his daughter, and they were conversing, playing the piano, and singing. Ivan Ilych, as Praskovya Fëdorovna remarked, spent that evening more cheerfully than usual, but he never for a moment forgot that he had postponed the important matter of the appendix. At eleven o'clock he said good-night and went to his bedroom. Since his illness he had slept alone in a small room next to his study. He undressed and took up a novel by Zola, but instead of reading it he fell into thought, and in his imagination that desired improvement in the vermiform appendix occurred. There was the absorption and evacuation and the re-establishment of normal activity. "Yes, that's it!" he said to himself. "One need only assist nature, that's all." He remembered his medicine, rose, took it, and lay down on his back watching for the beneficent action of the medicine and for it to lessen the pain. "I need only take it regularly and avoid all injurious influences. I am already feeling better, much better." He began touching his side: it was not painful to the touch. "There, I really don't feel it. It's much better already." He put out the light and turned on his side . . . "The appendix is getting better, absorption is occurring." Suddenly he felt the old, familiar, dull, gnawing pain, stubborn and serious. There was the same familiar loathsome taste in his mouth. His heart sank and he felt dazed. "My God! My God!" he muttered. "Again, again! And it will never cease." And suddenly the matter presented itself in a quite different aspect. "Vermiform appendix! Kidney!" he said to himself. "It's not a question of appendix or kidney, but of life and . . . death. Yes, life was there and now it is going, going and I cannot stop it. Yes. Why deceive myself? Isn't it obvious to everyone but me that I'm dying, and that it's only a question of weeks, days . . . it may happen this moment. There was light and now there is darkness. I was here and now I'm going there! Where?" A chill came over him, his breathing ceased, and he felt only the throbbing of his heart.

"When I am not, what will there be? There will be nothing. Then where shall I be when I am no more? Can this be dying? No, I don't want to!" He jumped up and tried to light the candle, felt for it with trembling hands, dropped candle and candlestick on the floor, and fell back on his pillow.

"What's the use? It makes no difference," he said to himself, staring with wide-open eyes into the darkness. "Death. Yes, death. And none of them know or wish to know it, and they have no pity for me. Now they are playing." (He heard through the door the distant sound of a song and its accompaniment.) "It's all the same to them, but they will die too! Fools! I first, and they later, but it will be the same for them. And now they are merry . . . the beasts!"

Anger choked him and he was agonizingly, unbearably miserable. "It is impossible that all men have been doomed to suffer this awful horror!" He raised himself.

"Something must be wrong. I must calm myself—must think it all over from the beginning." And he again began thinking. "Yes, the beginning of my illness: I knocked my side, but I was still quite well that day and the next. It hurt a little, then rather more. I saw the doctors, then followed despondency and anguish, more doctors, and I drew nearer to the abyss. My strength grew less and I kept coming nearer and nearer, and now I have wasted away and there is no light in my eyes. I think of the appendix—but this is death! I think of mending the appendix, and all the while here is death! Can it really be death?" Again terror seized him and he gasped for breath. He leant down and began feeling for the matches, pressing with his elbow on the stand beside the bed. It was in his way and hurt him, he grew furious with it, pressed on it still harder, and upset it. Breathless and in despair he fell on his back, expecting death to come immediately.

Meanwhile the visitors were leaving. Praskovya Fēdorovna was seeing them off. She heard something fall and came in.

"What has happened?"

160 "Nothing. I knocked it over accidentally."

She went out and returned with a candle. He lay there panting heavily, like a man who has run a thousand yards, and stared upwards at her with a fixed look.

"What is it, Jean?"

"No . . . o . . . thing. I upset it." ("Why speak of it? She won't understand," he thought.)

And in truth she did not understand. She picked up the stand, lit his candle, and hurried away to see another visitor off. When she came back he still lay on his back, looking upwards.

165 "What is it? Do you feel worse?"

"Yes."

She shook her head and sat down.

"Do you know, Jean, I think we must ask Leshchetitsky to come and see you here."

This meant calling in the famous specialist, regardless of expense. He smiled malignantly and said "No." She remained a little longer and then went up to him and kissed his forehead.

170 While she was kissing him he hated her from the bottom of his soul and with difficulty refrained from pushing her away.

"Good-night. Please God you'll sleep."

"Yes."

VI

Ivan Ilych saw that he was dying, and he was in continual despair.

In the depth of his heart he knew he was dying, but not only was he not accustomed to the thought, he simply did not and could not grasp it.

175 The syllogism he had learnt from Kiesewetter's Logic: "Caius is a man, men are mortal, therefore Caius is mortal," had always seemed to him correct as applied to Caius, but certainly not as applied to himself. That Caius—man in the abstract—was mortal, was perfectly correct, but he was not Caius, not an abstract man, but a creature quite, quite separate from all others. He had been little Vanya, with a mamma and a papa, with Mitya and Volodya, with the toys, a coachman and a nurse, afterwards with Katenka and with all the joys, griefs, and delights of childhood, boyhood, and youth. What did Caius know of the smell of that striped leather ball Vanya had been so fond of? Had Caius kissed his mother's hand like that, and did the silk of her dress rustle so for Caius? Had he rioted like that at school when the pastry was bad? Had Caius been in love like that? Could Caius preside at a session as he did? "Caius really was mortal, and it was right for him to die; but for me, little Vanya, Ivan Ilych, with all my thoughts and emotions, it's altogether a different matter. It cannot be that I ought to die. That would be too terrible."

Such was his feeling.

"If I had to die like Caius I would have known it was so. An inner voice would have told me so, but there was nothing of the sort in me and I and all my friends felt that our case was quite different from that of Caius. And now here it is!" he said to himself. "It can't be. It's impossible! But here it is. How is this? How is one to understand it?"

He could not understand it, and tried to drive this false, incorrect, morbid thought away and to replace it by other proper and healthy thoughts. But that thought, and not the thought only but the reality itself, seemed to come and confront him.

And to replace that thought he called up a succession of others, hoping to find in them some support. He tried to get back into the former current of thoughts that had once screened the thought of death from him. But strange to say, all that had formerly shut off, hidden, and destroyed his consciousness of death, no longer had that effect. Ivan Ilych now spent most of his time in attempting to re-establish that old current. He would say to himself: "I will take up my duties again—after all I used to live by them." And banishing all doubts he would go to the law courts, enter into conversation with his colleagues, and sit carelessly as was his wont, scanning the crowd with a thoughtful look and leaning both his emaciated arms on the arms of his oak chair; bending over as usual to a colleague and drawing his papers nearer he would interchange whispers with him, and then suddenly raising his eyes and sitting erect would pronounce certain words and open the proceedings. But suddenly in the midst of those proceedings the pain in his side, regardless of the stage the proceedings had reached, would begin its own gnawing work. Ivan Ilych would turn his attention to it and try to drive the thought of it away, but without success. *It* would come and stand before him and look at him, and he would be petrified and the light would die out of his eyes, and he would again begin asking himself whether *It* alone was true. And his colleagues and subordinates would see with surprise and distress that he, the brilliant and subtle judge, was becoming confused and making mistakes. He would shake himself, try to pull himself together, manage somehow to bring the sitting to a close, and return home with the sorrowful consciousness that his judicial labors could not as formerly hide from him what he wanted them to hide, and could not deliver him from *It*. And what was worst of all was that *It* drew his attention to itself not in order to make him take some action but only that he should look at *It*, look it straight in the face: look at it and, without doing anything, suffer inexpressibly.

And to save himself from this condition Ivan Ilych looked for consolation—new screens—and new screens were found and for a while seemed to save him, but then they immediately fell to pieces or rather became transparent, as if *It* penetrated them and nothing could veil *It*.

In these latter days he would go into the drawing-room he had arranged—that drawing-room where he had fallen and for the sake of which (how bitterly ridiculous it seemed) he had sacrificed his life—for he knew that his illness originated with that knock. He would enter and see that something had scratched the polished table. He would look for the cause of this and find that it was the bronze ornamentation of an album, that had got bent. He would take up the expensive album which he had lovingly arranged, and feel vexed with his daughter and her friends for their untidiness—for the album was torn here and there and some of the photographs turned upside down. He would put it carefully in order and bend the ornamentation back into position. Then it would occur to him to place all those things in another corner of the room, near the plants. He could call the footman, but his daughter or wife would come to help him. They would not agree, and his wife would contradict him, and he would dispute and grow angry. But that was all right, for then he did not think about *It*. *It* was invisible.

But then, when he was moving something himself, his wife would say: "Let the servants do it. You will hurt yourself again." And suddenly *It* would flash through the screen and he would see it. It was just a flash, and he hoped it would disappear, but he would involuntarily pay attention to his side. "It sits there as before, gnawing just the same!" And he could no longer forget *It*, but could distinctly see it looking at him from behind the flowers. "What is it all for?"

"It really is so! I lost my life over that curtain as I might have done when storming a fort. Is that possible? How terrible and how stupid. It can't be true! It can't, but it is."

He would go to his study, lie down, and again be alone with *It:* face to face with *It*. And nothing could be done with *It* except to look at it and shudder.

VII

How it happened it is impossible to say because it came about step by step, unnoticed, but in the third month of Ivan Ilych's illness, his wife, his daughter, his son, his acquaintances, the doctors, the servants, and above all he himself, were aware that the whole interest he had for other people was whether he would soon vacate his place, and at last release the living from the discomfort caused by his presence and be himself released from his sufferings.

He slept less and less. He was given opium and hypodermic injections of morphine, but this did not relieve him. The dull depression he experienced in a somnolent condition at first gave him a little relief, but only as something new, afterwards it became as distressing as the pain itself or even more so.

Special foods were prepared for him by the doctors' orders, but all those foods became increasingly distasteful and disgusting to him.

For his excretions also special arrangements had to be made, and this was a torment to him every time—a torment from the uncleanliness, the unseemliness, and the smell, and from knowing that another person had to take part in it.

But just through his most unpleasant matter, Ivan Ilych obtained comfort. Gerasim, the butler's young assistant, always came in to carry the things out. Gerasim was a clean, fresh peasant lad, grown stout on town food and always cheerful and bright. At first the sight of him, in his clean Russian peasant costume, engaged on that disgusting task embarrassed Ivan Ilych.

190   Once when he got up from the commode too weak to draw up his trousers, he dropped into a soft armchair and looked with horror at his bare, enfeebled thighs with the muscles so sharply marked on them.

Gerasim with a firm light tread, his heavy boots emitting a pleasant smell of tar and fresh winter air, came in wearing a clean Hessian apron, the sleeves of his print shirt tucked up over his strong, bare young arms; and refraining from looking at his sick master out of consideration for his feelings, and restraining the joy of life that beamed from his face, he went up to the commode.

"Gerasim!" said Ivan Ilych in a weak voice.

Gerasim started, evidently afraid he might have committed some blunder, and with a rapid movement turned his fresh, kind, simple young face which just showed the first downy signs of a beard.

"Yes, sir?"

195   "That must be very unpleasant for you. You must forgive me. I am helpless."

"Oh, why, sir," and Gerasim's eyes beamed and he showed his glistening white teeth, "what's a little trouble? It's a case of illness with you, sir."

And his deft strong hands did their accustomed task, and he went out of the room stepping lightly. Five minutes later he as lightly returned.

Ivan Ilych was still sitting in the same position in the armchair.

"Gerasim," he said when the latter had replaced the freshly washed utensil. "Please come here and help me." Gerasim went up to him. "Lift me up. It is hard for me to get up, and I have sent Dmitri away."

200   Gerasim went up to him, grasped his master with his strong arms deftly but gently, in the same way that he stepped—lifted him, supported him with one hand, and with the other drew up his trousers and would have set him down again, but Ivan Ilych asked to be led to the sofa. Gerasim, without an effort and without apparent pressure, led him, almost lifting him, to the sofa, and placed him on it.

"Thank you. How easily and well you do it all!"

Gerasim smiled again and turned to leave the room. But Ivan Ilych felt his presence such a comfort that he did not want to let him go.

"One thing more, please move up that chair. No, the other one—under my feet. It is easier for me when my feet are raised."

Gerasim brought the chair, set it down gently in place, and raised Ivan Ilych's legs on to it. It seemed to Ivan Ilych that he felt better while Gerasim was holding up his legs.

205   "It's better when my legs are higher," he said. "Place that cushion under them."

Gerasim did so. He again lifted the legs and placed them, and again Ivan Ilych felt better while Gerasim held his legs. When he set them down Ivan Ilych fancied he felt worse.

"Gerasim," he said. "Are you busy now?"

"Not at all, sir," said Gerasim, who had learnt from the townsfolk how to speak to gentlefolk.

"What have you still to do?"

210   "What have I to do? I've done everything except chopping the logs for tomorrow."

"Then hold my legs up a bit higher, can you?"

"Of course I can. Why not?" and Gerasim raised his master's legs higher and Ivan Ilych thought that in that position he did not feel any pain at all.

"And how about the logs?"

"Don't trouble about that, sir. There's plenty of time."

Ivan Ilych told Gerasim to sit down and hold his legs, and began to talk to him. And strange to say it seemed to him that he felt better while Gerasim held his legs up.

After that Ivan Ilych would sometimes call Gerasim and get him to hold his legs on his shoulders, and he liked talking to him. Gerasim did it all easily, willingly, simply, and with a good nature that touched Ivan Ilych. Health, strength, and vitality in other people were offensive to him, but Gerasim's strength and vitality did not mortify but soothed him.

What tormented Ivan Ilych most was the deception, the lie, which for some reason they all accepted, that he was not dying but was simply ill, and that he only need keep quiet and undergo a treatment and then something very good would result. He, however, knew that do what they would nothing would come of it, only still more agonizing suffering and death. This deception tortured him—their not wishing to admit what they all knew and what he knew, but wanting to lie to him concerning his terrible condition, and wishing and forcing him to participate in that lie. Those lies—lies enacted over him on the eve of his death and destined to degrade this awful, solemn act to the level of their visitings, their curtains, their sturgeon for dinner—were a terrible agony for Ivan Ilych. And strangely enough, many times when they were going through their antics over him he had been within a hairbreadth of calling out to them: "Stop lying! You know and I know that I am dying. Then at least stop lying about it!" But he had never had the spirit to do it. The awful, terrible act of his dying was, he could see, reduced by those about him to the level of a casual, unpleasant, and almost indecorous incident (as if someone entered a drawing-room diffusing an unpleasant odor) and this was done by that very decorum which he had served all his life long. He saw that no one felt for him, because no one even wished to grasp his position. Only Gerasim recognized it and pitied him. And so Ivan Ilych felt at ease only with him. He felt comforted when Gerasim supported his legs (sometimes all night long) and refused to go to bed, saying: "Don't you worry, Ivan Ilych. I'll get sleep enough later on," or when he suddenly became familiar and exclaimed: "If you weren't sick it would be another matter, but as it is, why should I grudge a little trouble?" Gerasim alone did not lie; everything showed that he alone understood the facts of the case and did not consider it necessary to disguise them, but simply felt sorry for his emaciated and enfeebled master. Once when Ivan Ilych was sending him away he even said straight out: "We shall all of us die, so why should I grudge a little trouble?"—expressing the fact that he did not think his work burdensome, because he was doing it for a dying man and hoped someone would do the same for him when his time came.

Apart from this lying, or because of it, what most tormented Ivan Ilych was that no one pitied him as he wished to be pitied. At certain moments after prolonged suffering he wished most of all (though he would have been ashamed to confess it) for someone to pity him as a sick child is pitied. He longed to be petted and comforted. He knew he was an important functionary, that he had a beard turning grey, and that therefore what he longed for was impossible, but still he longed for it. And in Gerasim's attitude towards him there was something akin to what he wished for, and so that attitude comforted him. Ivan Ilych wanted to weep, wanted to be petted and cried over, and then his colleague Shebek would come, and instead of weeping and being petted, Ivan Ilych would assume a serious, severe, and profound air, and by force of habit would express his opinion on a decision of the Court of Cassation and would stubbornly insist on that view. This falsity around him and within him did more than anything else to poison his last days.

VIII

It was morning. He knew it was morning because Gerasim had gone, and Peter the footman had come and put out the candles, drawn back one of the curtains, and begun quietly to tidy up. Whether it was morning or evening, Friday or Sunday, made no difference, it was all just the same: the gnawing, unmitigated, agonizing pain, never ceasing for an instant, the consciousness of life inexorably waning but not yet extinguished, the approach of that ever dreaded and hateful Death which was the only reality, and always the same falsity. What were days, weeks, hours, in such a case?

"Will you have some tea, sir?"

"He wants things to be regular, and wishes the gentlefolk to drink tea in the morning," thought Ivan Ilych, and only said "No."

"Wouldn't you like to move onto the sofa, sir?"

"He wants to tidy up the room, and I'm in the way. I am uncleanliness and disorder," he thought, and said only:

"No, leave me alone."

225   The man went on bustling about. Ivan Ilych stretched out his hand. Peter came up, ready to help.

"What is it, sir?"

"My watch."

Peter took the watch which was close at hand and gave it to his master.

"Half-past eight. Are they up?"

230   "No, sir, except Vasily Ivanovich" (the son) "who has gone to school. Praskovya Fёdorovna ordered me to wake her if you asked for her. Shall I do so?"

"No, there's no need to." "Perhaps I'd better have some tea," he thought, and added aloud: "Yes, bring me some tea."

Peter went to the door, but Ivan Ilych dreaded being left alone. "How can I keep him here? Oh yes, my medicine." "Peter, give me my medicine." "Why not? Perhaps it may still do some good." He took a spoonful and swallowed it. "No, it won't help. It's all tomfoolery, all deception," he decided as soon as he became aware of the familiar, sickly, hopeless taste. "No, I can't believe in it any longer. But the pain, why this pain? If it would only cease just for a moment!" And he moaned. Peter turned towards him. "It's all right. Go and fetch me some tea."

Peter went out. Left alone Ivan Ilych groaned not so much with pain, terrible though that was, as from mental anguish. Always and forever the same, always these endless days and nights. If only it would come quicker! If only *what* would come quicker? Death, darkness?. . . No, no! anything rather than death!

When Peter returned with the tea on a tray, Ivan Ilych stared at him for a time in perplexity, not realizing who and what he was. Peter was disconcerted by that look and his embarrassment brought Ivan Ilych to himself.

235   "Oh, tea! All right, put it down. Only help me to wash and put on a clean shirt."

And Ivan Ilych began to wash. With pauses for rest, he washed his hands and then his face, cleaned his teeth, brushed his hair, and looked in the glass. He was terrified by what he saw, especially by the limp way in which his hair clung to his pallid forehead.

While his shirt was being changed he knew that he would be still more frightened at the sight of his body, so he avoided looking at it. Finally he was ready. He drew on a dressing-gown, wrapped himself in a plaid, and sat down in the armchair to take his tea. For a moment he felt refreshed, but as soon as he began to drink the tea he was again aware of the same taste, and the pain also returned. He finished it with an effort, and then lay down stretching out his legs, and dismissed Peter.

Always the same. Now a spark of hope flashes up, then a sea of despair rages, and always pain; always pain, always despair, and always the same. When alone he had a dreadful and distressing desire to call someone, but he knew beforehand that with others present it would be still worse. "Another dose of morphine—to lose consciousness. I will tell him, the doctor, that he must think of something else. It's impossible, impossible, to go on like this."

An hour and another pass like that. But now there is a ring at the door bell. Perhaps it's the doctor? It is. He comes in fresh, hearty, plump, and cheerful, with that look on his face that seems to say: "There now, you're in a panic about something, but we'll arrange it all for you directly!" The doctor knows this expression is out of place here, but he has put it on once for all and can't take it off—like a man who has put on a frock-coat in the morning to pay a round of calls.

240   The doctor rubs his hands vigorously and reassuringly.

"Brr! How cold it is! There's such a sharp frost; just let me warm myself!" he says, as if it were only a matter of waiting till he was warm, and then he would put everything right.

"Well now, how are you?"

Ivan Ilych feels that the doctor would like to say: "Well, how are our affairs?" but that even he feels that this would not do, and says instead: "What sort of a night have you had?"

Ivan Ilych looks at him as much as to say: "Are you really never ashamed of lying?" But the doctor does not wish to understand this question, and Ivan Ilych says: "Just as terrible as ever. The pain never leaves me and never subsides. If only something . . ."

"Yes, you sick people are always like that. . . . There, now I think I am warm enough. Even Praskovya Fёdorovna, who is so particular, could find no fault with my temperature. Well, now I can say good-morning," and the doctor presses his patient's hand.

Then, dropping his former playfulness, he begins with a most serious face to examine the patient, feeling his pulse and taking his temperature, and then begins the sounding and auscultation.

Ivan Ilych knows quite well and definitely that all this is nonsense and pure deception, but when the doctor, getting down on his knee, leans over him, putting his ear first higher then lower, and performs various gymnastic movements over him with a significant expression on his face, Ivan Ilych submits to it all as he used to submit to the speeches of the lawyers, though he knew very well that they were all lying and why they were lying.

The doctor, kneeling on the sofa, is still sounding him when Praskovya Fёdorovna's silk dress rustles at the door and she is heard scolding Peter for not having let her know of the doctor's arrival.

She comes in, kisses her husband, and at once proceeds to prove that she has been up a long time already, and only owing to a misunderstanding failed to be there when the doctor arrived.

Ivan Ilych looks at her, scans her all over, sets against her the whiteness and plumpness and cleanness of her hands and neck, the gloss of her hair, and the sparkle of her vivacious eyes. He hates her with his whole soul. And the thrill of hatred he feels for her makes him suffer from her touch.

Her attitude towards him and his disease is still the same. Just as the doctor had adopted a certain relation to his patient which he could not abandon, so had she formed one towards him—that he was not doing something he ought to do and was himself to blame, and that she reproached him lovingly for this—and she could not now change that attitude.

"You see he doesn't listen to me and doesn't take his medicine at the proper time. And above all he lies in a position that is no doubt bad for him—with his legs up."

She described how he made Gerasim hold his legs up.

The doctor smiled with a contemptuous affability that said: "What's to be done? These sick people do have foolish fancies of that kind, but we must forgive them."

When the examination was over the doctor looked at his watch, and then Praskovya Fёdorovna announced to Ivan Ilych that it was of course as he pleased, but she had sent today for a celebrated specialist who would examine him and have a consultation with Michael Danilovich (their regular doctor).

"Please don't raise any objections. I am doing this for my own sake," she said ironically, letting it be felt that she was doing it all for his sake and only said this to leave him no right to refuse. He remained silent, knitting his brows. He felt that he was so surrounded and involved in a mesh of falsity that it was hard to unravel anything.

Everything she did for him was entirely for her own sake, and she told him she was doing for herself what she actually was doing for herself, as if that was so incredible that he must understand the opposite.

At half-past eleven the celebrated specialist arrived. Again the sounding began and the significant conversations in his presence and in another room, about the kidneys and the appendix, and the questions and answers, with such an air of importance that again, instead of the real question of life and death which now alone confronted him, the question arose of the kidney and appendix which were not behaving as they ought to and would now be attacked by Michael Danilovich and the specialist and forced to amend their ways.

The celebrated specialist took leave of him with a serious though not hopeless look, and in reply to the timid question Ivan Ilych, with eyes glistening with fear and hope, put to him as to whether there was a chance of recovery, said that he could not vouch for it but there was a possibility. The look of hope with which Ivan Ilych watched the doctor out was so pathetic that Praskovya Fёdorovna, seeing it, even wept as she left the room to hand the doctor his fee.

The gleam of hope kindled by the doctor's encouragement did not last long. The same room, the same pictures, curtains, wallpaper, medicine bottles, were all there, and the same aching suffering body, and Ivan Ilych began to moan. They gave him a subcutaneous injection and he sank into oblivion.

It was twilight when he came to. They brought him his dinner and he swallowed some beef tea with difficulty, and then everything was the same again and night was coming on.

After dinner, at seven o'clock, Praskovya Fëdorovna came into the room in evening dress, her full bosom pushed up by her corset, and with traces of powder on her face. She had reminded him in the morning that they were going to the theater. Sarah Bernhardt was visiting the town and they had a box, which he had insisted on their taking. Now he had forgotten about it and her toilet offended him, but he concealed his vexation when he remembered that he had himself insisted on their securing a box and going because it would be an instructive and aesthetic pleasure for the children.

Praskovya Fëdorovna came in, self-satisfied but yet with a rather guilty air. She sat down and asked how he was, but, as he saw, only for the sake of asking and not in order to learn about it, knowing that there was nothing to learn—and then went on to what she really wanted to say: that she would not on any account have gone but that the box had been taken and Helen and their daughter were going, as well as Petrishchev (the examining magistrate, their daughter's fiancé) and that it was out of the question to let them go alone; but that she would have much preferred to sit with him for a while; and he must be sure to follow the doctor's orders while she was away.

"Oh, and Fëdor Petrovich" (the fiancé) "would like to come in. May he? And Lisa?"

265   "All right."

Their daughter came in in full evening dress, her fresh young flesh exposed (making a show of that very flesh which in his own case caused so much suffering), strong, healthy, evidently in love, and impatient with illness, suffering, and death, because they interfered with her happiness.

Fëdor Petrovich came in too, in evening dress, his hair curled *à la Capoul*, a tight stiff collar round his long sinewy neck, an enormous white shirtfront, and narrow black trousers tightly stretched over his strong thighs. He had one white glove tightly drawn on, and was holding his opera hat in his hand.

Following him the schoolboy crept in unnoticed, in a new uniform, poor little fellow, and wearing gloves. Terribly dark shadows showed under his eyes, the meaning of which Ivan Ilych knew well.

His son had always seemed pathetic to him, and now it was dreadful to see the boy's frightened look of pity. It seemed to Ivan Ilych that Vasya was the only one besides Gerasim who understood and pitied him.

270   They all sat down and again asked how he was. A silence followed. Lisa asked her mother about the opera-glasses, and there was an altercation between mother and daughter as to who had taken them and where they had been put. This occasioned some unpleasantness.

Fëdor Petrovich inquired of Ivan Ilych whether he had ever seen Sarah Bernhardt. Ivan Ilych did not at first catch the question, but then replied: "No, have you seen her before?"

"Yes, in *Adrienne Lecouvreur*."

Praskovya Fëdorovna mentioned some rôles in which Sarah Bernhardt was particularly good. Her daughter disagreed. Conversation sprang up as to the elegance and realism of her acting—the sort of conversation that is always repeated and is always the same.

In the midst of the conversation Fëdor Petrovich glanced at Ivan Ilych and became silent. The others also looked at him and grew silent. Ivan Ilych was staring with glittering eyes straight before him, evidently indignant with them. This had to be rectified, but it was impossible to do so. The silence had to be broken, but for a time no one dared to break it and they all became afraid that the conventional deception would suddenly become obvious and the truth become plain to all. Lisa was the first to pluck up courage and break that silence, but by trying to hide what everybody was feeling, she betrayed it.

275   "Well, if we are going it's time to start," she said, looking at her watch, a present from her father, and with a faint and significant smile at Fëdor Petrovich relating to something known only to them. She got up with a rustle of her dress.

They all rose, said good-night, and went away.

When they had gone it seemed to Ivan Ilych that he felt better; the falsity had gone with them. But the pain remained—that same pain and that same fear that made everything monotonously alike, nothing harder and nothing easier. Everything was worse.

Again minute followed minute and hour followed hour. Everything remained the same and there was no cessation. And the inevitable end of it all became more and more terrible.

"Yes, send Gerasim here," he replied to a question Peter asked.

IX

His wife returned late at night. She came in on tiptoe, but he heard her, opened his eyes, and made haste to close them again. She wished to send Gerasim away and to sit with him herself, but he opened his eyes and said: "No, go away."

"Are you in great pain?"

"Always the same."

"Take some opium."

He agreed and took some. She went away.

Till about three in the morning he was in a state of stupefied misery. It seemed to him that he and his pain were being thrust into a narrow, deep black sack, but though they were pushed further and further in they could not be pushed to the bottom. And this, terrible enough in itself, was accompanied by suffering. He was frightened yet wanted to fall through the sack, he struggled but yet cooperated. And suddenly he broke through, fell, and regained consciousness. Gerasim was sitting at the foot of the bed dozing quietly and patiently, while he himself lay with his emaciated stockinged legs resting on Gerasim's shoulders; the same shaded candle was there and the same unceasing pain.

"Go away, Gerasim," he whispered.

"It's all right, sir. I'll stay a while."

"No. Go away."

He removed his legs from Gerasim's shoulders, turned sideways onto his arm, and felt sorry for himself. He only waited till Gerasim had gone into the next room and then restrained himself no longer but wept like a child. He wept on account of his helplessness, his terrible loneliness, the cruelty of man, the cruelty of God, and the absence of God.

"Why hast Thou done all this? Why hast Thou brought me here? Why, why dost Thou torment me so terribly?"

He did not expect an answer and yet wept because there was no answer and could be none. The pain grew more acute, but he did not stir and did not call. He said to himself: "Go on! Strike me! But what is it for? What have I done to Thee? What is it for?"

Then he grew quiet and not only ceased weeping but even held his breath and became all attention. It was as though he was listening not to an audible voice but to the voice of his soul, to the current of thoughts arising within him.

"What is it you want?" was the first clear conception capable of expression in words, that he heard.

"What do you want? What do you want?" he repeated to himself.

"What do I want? To live and not to suffer," he answered.

And again he listened with such concentrated attention that even his pain did not distract him.

"To live? How?" asked his inner voice.

"Why, to live as I used to—well and pleasantly."

"As you lived before, well and pleasantly?" the voice repeated.

And in imagination he began to recall the best moments of his pleasant life. But strange to say none of those best moments of his pleasant life now seemed at all what they had then seemed—none of them except the first recollections of childhood. There, in childhood, there had been something really pleasant with which it would be possible to live if it could return. But the child who had experienced that happiness existed no longer, it was like a reminiscence of somebody else.

As soon as the period began which had produced the present Ivan Ilych, all that had then seemed joys now melted before his sight and turned into something trivial and often nasty.

And the further he departed from childhood and the nearer he came to the present the more worthless and doubtful were the joys. This began with the School of Law. A little that was really good was still found there—there was lightheartedness, friendship, and hope. But in the upper classes there had already been fewer of such good moments. Then during the first years of his official career, when he was in the service of the Governor, some pleasant moments again occurred: they were the memories of love for a woman. Then all became confused and there was still less of what was good; later on again there was still less that was good, and the further he went the less there was. His marriage, a mere accident, then the disenchantment that followed it, his wife's bad breath and the sensuality and hypocrisy; then that deadly official life and those preoccupations about money, a year of it, and two, and ten, and twenty, and always the same thing. And the longer it lasted the more deadly it became. "It is as if I had been going downhill while I imagined I was going up. And that is really what it was. I was going up in public opinion, but to the same extent life was ebbing away from me. And now it is all done and there is only death."

"Then what does it mean? Why? It can't be that life is so senseless and horrible. But if it really has been so horrible and senseless, why must I die and die in agony? There is something wrong!"

"Maybe I did not live as I ought to have done," it suddenly occurred to him. "But how could that be, when I did everything properly?" he replied, and immediately dismissed from his mind this, the sole solution of all the riddles of life and death, as something quite impossible.

305   "Then what do you want now? To live? Live how? Live as you lived in the law courts when the usher proclaimed 'The judge is coming!' The judge is coming, the judge!" he repeated to himself. "Here he is, the judge. But I am not guilty!" he exclaimed angrily. "What is it for?" And he ceased crying, but turning his face to the wall continued to ponder on the same question: Why, and for what purpose, is there all this horror? But however much he pondered he found no answer. And whenever the thought occurred to him, as it often did, that it all resulted from his not having lived as he ought to have done, he at once recalled the correctness of his whole life and dismissed so strange an idea.

X

Another fortnight passed. Ivan Ilych now no longer left his sofa. He would not lie in bed but lay on the sofa, facing the wall nearly all the time. He suffered ever the same unceasing agonies and in his loneliness pondered always on the same insoluble question: "What is this? Can it be that it is Death?" And the inner voice answered: "Yes, it is Death."

"Why these sufferings?" And the voice answered, "For no reason—they just are so." Beyond and besides this there was nothing.

From the very beginning of his illness, ever since he had first been to see the doctor, Ivan Ilych's life had been divided between two contrary and alternating moods: now it was despair and the expectation of this uncomprehended and terrible death, and now hope and an intently interested observation of the functioning of his organs. Now before his eyes there was only a kidney or an intestine that temporarily evaded its duty, and now only that incomprehensible and dreadful death from which it was impossible to escape.

These two states of mind had alternated from the very beginning of his illness, but the further it progressed the more doubtful and fantastic became the conception of the kidney, and the more real the sense of impending death.

310   He had but to call to mind what he had been three months before and what he was now, to call to mind with what regularity he had been going downhill, for every possibility of hope to be shattered.

Latterly during that loneliness in which he found himself as he lay facing the back of the sofa, a loneliness in the midst of a populous town and surrounded by numerous acquaintances and relations but that yet could not have been more complete anywhere—either at the bottom of the sea or under the earth—during that terrible loneliness Ivan Ilych had lived only in memories of the past. Pictures of his past rose before him one after another. They always began with what was nearest in time and then went back to what was most remote—to his childhood—and rested there. If he thought of the stewed prunes that had been offered him that day, his mind went back to the raw shrivelled French plums of his childhood, their peculiar flavor and the flow of saliva when he sucked their stones, and along with the memory of that taste came a whole series of memories of those days: his nurse, his brother, and their toys. "No, I mustn't think of that. . . . It is too painful," Ivan Ilych said to himself, and brought himself back to the present—to the button on the back of the sofa and the creases in its morocco. "Morocco is expensive, but it does not wear well: there had been a quarrel about it. It was a different kind of quarrel and a different kind of morocco that time when we tore father's portfolio and were punished, and mamma brought us some tarts. . . ." And again his thoughts dwelt on his childhood, and again it was painful and he tried to banish them and fix his mind on something else.

Then again together with that chain of memories another series passed through his mind—of how his illness had progressed and grown worse. There also the further back he looked the more life there had been. There had been more of what was good in life and more of life itself. The two merged together. "Just as the pain went on getting worse and worse, so my life grew worse and worse," he thought. "There is one bright spot there at the back, at the beginning of life, and afterwards all becomes blacker and blacker and proceeds more and more rapidly—in inverse ratio to the square of the distance from death," thought Ivan Ilych. And the example of a stone falling downwards with increasing velocity entered his mind. Life, a series of increasing sufferings, flies further and further towards its end—the most terrible suffering. "I am flying. . . ." He shuddered, shifted himself, and tried to resist, but was already aware that resistance was impossible, and again, with eyes weary of gazing but unable to cease seeing what was before them, he stared at the back of the sofa and waited—awaiting that dreadful fall and shock and destruction.

"Resistance is impossible!" he said to himself. "If I could only understand what it is all for! But that too is impossible. An explanation would be possible if it could be said that I have not lived as I ought to. But it is impossible to say that," and he remembered all the legality, correctitude, and propriety of his life. "That at any rate can certainly not be admitted," he thought, and his lips smiled ironically as if someone could see that smile and be taken in by it. "There is no explanation! Agony, death. . . . What for?"

XI

Another two weeks went by in this way and during that fortnight an event occurred that Ivan Ilych and his wife had desired. Petrishchev formally proposed. It happened in the evening. The next day Praskovya Fëdorovna came into her husband's room considering how best to inform him of it, but that very night there had been a fresh change for the worse in his condition. She found him still lying on the sofa but in a different position. He lay on his back, groaning and staring fixedly straight in front of him.

She began to remind him of his medicines, but he turned his eyes towards her with such a look that she did not finish what she was saying; so great an animosity, to her in particular, did that look express.

"For Christ's sake let me die in peace!" he said.

She would have gone away, but just then their daughter came in and went up to say good morning. He looked at her as he had done at his wife, and in reply to her inquiry about his health said dryly that he would soon free them all of himself. They were both silent and after sitting with him for a while went away.

"Is it our fault?" Lisa said to her mother. "It's as if we were to blame! I am sorry for papa, but why should we be tortured?"

The doctor came at his usual time. Ivan Ilych answered "Yes" and "No," never taking his angry eyes from him, and at last said: "You know you can do nothing for me, so leave me alone."

"We can ease your sufferings."

"You can't even do that. Let me be."

The doctor went into the drawing-room and told Praskovya Fëdorovna that the case was very serious and that the only resource left was opium to allay her husband's sufferings, which must be terrible.

It was true, as the doctor said, that Ivan Ilych's physical sufferings were terrible, but worse than the physical sufferings were his mental sufferings, which were his chief torture.

His mental sufferings were due to the fact that one night, as he looked at Gerasim's sleepy, good-natured face with its prominent cheekbones, the question suddenly occurred to him: "What if my whole life has really been wrong?"

325   It occurred to him that what had appeared perfectly impossible before, namely that he had not spent his life as he should have done, might after all be true. It occurred to him that his scarcely perceptible attempts to struggle against what was considered good by the most highly placed people, those scarcely noticeable impulses which he had immediately suppressed, might have been the real thing, and all the rest false. And his professional duties and the whole arrangement of his life and of his family, and all his social and official interests, might all have been false. He tried to defend all those things to himself and suddenly felt the weakness of what he was defending. There was nothing to defend.

"But if that is so," he said to himself, "and I am leaving this life with the consciousness that I have lost all that was given me and it is impossible to rectify it—what then?"

He lay on his back and began to pass his life in review in quite a new way. In the morning when he saw first his footman, then his wife, then his daughter, and then the doctor, their every word and movement confirmed to him the awful truth that had been revealed to him during the night. In them he saw himself—all that for which he had lived—and saw clearly that it was not real at all, but a terrible and huge deception which had hidden both life and death. This consciousness intensified his physical suffering tenfold. He groaned and tossed about, and pulled at his clothing which choked and stifled him. And he hated them on that account.

He was given a large dose of opium and became unconscious, but at noon his sufferings began again. He drove everybody away and tossed from side to side.

His wife came to him and said:

330   "Jean, my dear, do this for me. It can't do any harm and often helps. Healthy people often do it."

He opened his eyes wide.

"What? Take communion? Why? It's unnecessary! However . . ."

She began to cry.

"Yes, do, my dear. I'll send for our priest. He is such a nice man."

335   "All right. Very well," he muttered.

When the priest came and heard his confession, Ivan Ilych was softened and seemed to feel a relief from his doubts and consequently from his sufferings, and for a moment there came a ray of hope. He again began to think of the vermiform appendix and the possibility of correcting it. He received the sacrament with tears in his eyes.

When they laid him down again afterwards he felt a moment's ease, and the hope that he might live awoke in him again. He began to think of the operation that had been suggested to him. "To live! I want to live!" he said to himself.

His wife came in to congratulate him after his communion, and when uttering the usual conventional words she added:

"You feel better, don't you?"

340   Without looking at her he said "Yes."

Her dress, her figure, the expression of her face, the tone of her voice, all revealed the same thing. "This is wrong, it is not as it should be. All you have lived for and still live for is falsehood and deception, hiding life and death from you." And as soon as he admitted that thought, his hatred and his agonizing physical suffering again sprang up, and with that suffering a consciousness of the unavoidable, approaching end. And to this was added a new sensation of grinding shooting pain and a feeling of suffocation.

The expression of his face when he uttered that "yes" was dreadful. Having uttered it, he looked her straight in the eyes, turned on his face with a rapidity extraordinary in his weak state and shouted:

"Go away! Go away and leave me alone!"

XII

From that moment the screaming began that continued for three days, and was so terrible that one could not hear it through two closed doors without horror. At the moment he answered his wife he realized that he was lost, that there was no return, that the end had come, the very end, and his doubts were still unsolved and remained doubts.

"Oh! Oh! Oh!" he cried in various intonations. He had begun by screaming "I won't!" and continued screaming on the letter *O*.

For three whole days, during which time did not exist for him, he struggled in that black sack into which he was being thrust by an invisible, resistless force. He struggled as a man condemned to death struggles in the hands of the executioner, knowing that he cannot save himself. And every moment he felt that despite all his efforts he was drawing nearer and nearer to what terrified him. He felt that his agony was due to his being thrust into that black hole and still more to his not being able to get right into it. He was hindered from getting into it by his conviction that his life had been a good one. That very justification of his life held him fast and prevented his moving forward, and it caused him most torment of all.

Suddenly some force struck him in the chest and side, making it still harder to breathe, and he fell through the hole and there at the bottom was a light. What had happened to him was like the sensation one sometimes experiences in a railway carriage when one thinks one is going backwards while one is really going forwards and suddenly becomes aware of the real direction.

"Yes, it was all not the right thing," he said to himself, "but that's no matter. It can be done. But what *is* the right thing? he asked himself, and suddenly grew quiet.

This occurred at the end of the third day, two hours before his death. Just then his schoolboy son had crept softly in and gone up to the bedside. The dying man was still screaming desperately and waving his arms. His hand fell on the boy's head, and the boy caught it, pressed it to his lips, and began to cry.

At that very moment Ivan Ilych fell through and caught sight of the light, and it was revealed to him that though his life had not been what it should have been, this could still be rectified. He asked himself, "What *is* the right thing?" and grew still, listening. Then he felt that someone was kissing his hand. He opened his eyes, looked at his son, and felt sorry for him. His wife came up to him and he glanced at her. She was gazing at him open-mouthed, with undried tears on her nose and cheek and a despairing look on her face. He felt sorry for her too.

"Yes, I am making them wretched," he thought. "They are sorry, but it will be better for them when I die." He wished to say this but had not the strength to utter it. "Besides, why speak? I must act," he thought. With a look at his wife he indicated his son and said: "Take him away . . . sorry for him . . . sorry for you too. . . ." He tried to add, "Forgive me," but said "forgo" and waved his hand, knowing that He whose understanding mattered would understand.

And suddenly it grew clear to him that what had been oppressing him and would not leave him was all dropping away at once from two sides, from ten sides, and from all sides. He was sorry for them, he must act so as not to hurt them: release them and free himself from these sufferings. "How good and how simple!" he thought. "And the pain?" he asked himself. "What has become of it? Where are you, pain?"

He turned his attention to it.

"Yes, here it is. Well, what of it? Let the pain be."

"And death . . . where is it?"

He sought his former accustomed fear of death and did not find it. "Where is it? What death?" There was no fear because there was no death.

In place of death there was light.

"So that's what it is!" he suddenly exclaimed aloud. "What joy!"

To him all this happened in a single instant, and the meaning of that instant did not change. For those present his agony continued for another two hours. Something rattled in his throat, his emaciated body twitched, then the gasping and rattle became less and less frequent.

"It is finished!" said someone near him.

He heard these words and repeated them in his soul.
"Death is finished," he said to himself. "It is no more!"
He drew in a breath, stopped in the midst of a sigh, stretched out, and died.

If you like this story, you may be interested in reading short fiction by other major foreign writers, such as Egyptian writer Naguib Mahfouz's "The Conjurer Made Off with the Dish" and the Indonesian writer Pramoedya Ananta Toer's "Circumcision" (both in chapter 4).

GOING FURTHER   Tolstoy's novels *War and Peace* and *Anna Karenina* stand at the summit of the greatest fiction in the Western world. The great tradition in Russia has been carried on by writers such as Aleksandr Solzhenitsyn (*Cancer Ward*), Vasily Aksyonov (*Generations of Winter*) and Victor Pelevin (*The Werewolf Problem in Central Russia*).

Alice Walker (b. 1944)

ALICE WALKER WAS born in rural Georgia, attended Spelman College in Atlanta and Sarah Lawrence College in New York, and worked in New York City as a welfare worker before returning to the South in the midst of the turmoil of the Civil Rights movement. In the late 1960s and early '70s she began to publish fiction and poetry. In 1982 her novel *The Color Purple,* became a great critical as well as commercial suc-

cess. Not only was it awarded the Pulitzer Prize for fiction, but it also became a movie directed by Stephen Spielberg. *The Color Purple* has become a central document in the literature of diversity—a book that celebrates black women in particular and the human spirit in general.

Alice Walker has lived for the past several decades in northern California.

Everyday Use

FOR YOUR GRANDMAMA

1   I will wait for her in the yard that Maggie and I made so clean and wavy yesterday afternoon. A yard like this is more comfortable than most people know. It is not just a yard. It is like an extended living room. When the hard clay is swept clean as a floor and the fine sand around the edges lined with tiny, irregular grooves anyone can come and sit and look up into the elm tree and wait for the breezes that never come inside the house.

Maggie will be nervous until after her sister goes: she will stand hopelessly in corners, homely and ashamed of the burn scars down her arms and legs, eyeing her sister with a mixture of envy and awe. She thinks her sister has held life always in the palm of one hand, that "no" is a word the world never learned to say to her.

You've no doubt seen those TV shows where the child who has "made it" is confronted, as a surprise, by her own mother and father, tottering in weakly from backstage. (A pleasant surprise, of course: What would they do if parent and child came on the show only to curse out and insult each other?) On TV mother and child embrace and smile into each other's faces. Sometimes the mother and father weep, the child wraps them in her arms and leans across the table to tell how she would not have made it without their help. I have seen these programs.

Sometimes I dream a dream in which Dee and I are suddenly brought together on a TV program of this sort. Out of a dark and soft-seated limousine I am ushered into a bright room filled with many people. There I meet a smiling, gray, sporty man like Johnny Carson who shakes my hand and tells me what a fine girl I have. Then we are on the stage and Dee is embracing me with tears in her eyes. She pins on my dress a large orchid, even though she has told me once that she thinks orchids are tacky flowers.

In real life I am a large, big-boned woman with rough, man-working hands. In the winter I wear flannel nightgowns to bed and overalls during the day. I can kill and clean a hog as mercilessly as a man. My fat keeps me hot in zero weather. I can work outside all day, breaking ice to get water for washing; I can eat pork liver cooked over the open fire minutes after it comes steaming from the hog. One winter I knocked a bull calf straight in the brain between the eyes with a sledge hammer and had the meat hung up to chill before nightfall. But of course all this does not show on television. I am the way my daughter would want me to be: a hundred pounds lighter, my skin like an uncooked barley pancake. My hair glistens in the hot bright lights. Johnny Carson has much to do to keep up with my quick and witty tongue.

But that is a mistake. I know even before I wake up. Who ever knew a Johnson with a quick tongue? Who can even imagine me looking a strange white man in the eye? It seems to me I have talked to them always with one foot raised in flight, with my head turned in whichever way is farthest from them. Dee, though. She would always look anyone in the eye. Hesitation was no part of her nature.

"How do I look, Mama?" Maggie says, showing just enough of her thin body enveloped in pink skirt and red blouse for me to know she's there, almost hidden by the door.

"Come out into the yard," I say.

Have you ever seen a lame animal, perhaps a dog run over by some careless person rich enough to own a car, sidle up to someone who is ignorant enough to be kind to him? That is the way my Maggie walks. She has been like this, chin on chest, eyes on ground, feet in shuffle, ever since the fire that burned the other house to the ground.

Dee is lighter than Maggie, with nicer hair and a fuller figure. She's a woman now, though sometimes I forget. How long ago was it that the other house burned? Ten, twelve years? Sometimes I can still hear the flames and feel Maggie's arms sticking to me, her hair smoking and her dress falling off her in little black papery flakes. Her eyes seemed stretched open, blazed open by the flames reflected in them. And Dee. I see her standing off under the sweet gum tree she used to dig gum out of; a look of concentration on her face as she watched the last dingy gray board of the house fall in toward the red-hot brick chimney. Why don't you do a dance around the ashes? I'd wanted to ask her. She had hated the house that much.

I used to think she hated Maggie, too. But that was before we raised the money, the church and me, to send her to Augusta to school. She used to read to us without pity; forcing words, lies, other folks' habits, whole lives upon us two, sitting trapped and ignorant underneath her voice. She washed us in a river of make-believe, burned us with a lot of knowledge we didn't necessarily need to know. Pressed us to her with the serious way she read, to shove us away at just the moment, like dimwits, we seemed about to understand.

Dee wanted nice things. A yellow organdy dress to wear to her graduation from high school; black pumps to match a green suit she'd made from an old suit somebody gave me. She was determined to stare down any disaster in her efforts. Her eyelids would not flicker for minutes at a time. Often I fought off the temptation to shake her. At sixteen she had a style of her own: and knew what style was.

I never had an education myself. After second grade the school was closed down. Don't ask me why: in 1927 colored asked fewer questions than they do now. Sometimes Maggie reads to me. She stumbles along good-naturedly but can't see well. She knows she is not bright. Like good looks and money, quickness passes her by. She will marry John Thomas (who has mossy teeth in an earnest face) and then I'll be free to sit here and I guess just sing church songs to myself. Although I never was a good singer. Never could carry a tune. I was always better at a man's job. I used to love to milk till I was hoofed in the side in '49. Cows are soothing and slow and don't bother you, unless you try to milk them the wrong way.

I have deliberately turned my back on the house. It is three rooms, just like the one that burned, except the roof is tin; they don't make shingle roofs any more. There are no real windows, just some holes cut in the sides, like the portholes in a ship, but not round and not square, with rawhide holding the shutters up on the outside. This house is in a pasture, too, like the other one. No doubt when Dee sees it she will want to tear it down. She wrote me once that no matter where we "choose" to live, she will manage to come see us. But she will never bring her friends. Maggie and I thought about this and Maggie asked me, "Mama, when did Dee ever *have* any friends?"

15   She had a few. Furtive boys in pink shirts hanging about on washday after school. Nervous girls who never laughed. Impressed with her they worshiped the well-turned phrase, the cute shape, the scalding humor that erupted like bubbles in lye. She read to them.

When she was courting Jimmy T she didn't have much time to pay to us, but turned all her faultfinding power on him. He *flew* to marry a cheap city girl from a family of ignorant flashy people. She hardly had time to recompose herself.

When she comes I will meet—but there they are!

Maggie attempts to make a dash for the house, in her shuffling way, but I stay her with my hand. "Come back here," I say. And she stops and tries to dig a well in the sand with her toe.

It is hard to see them clearly through the strong sun. But even the first glimpse of leg out of the car tells me it is Dee. Her feet were always neat-looking, as if God himself had shaped them with a certain style. From the other side of the car comes a short, stocky man. Hair is all over his head a foot long and hanging from his chin like a kinky mule tail. I hear Maggie suck in her breath. "Uhnnnh," is what it sounds like. Like when you see the wriggling end of a snake just in front of your foot on the road. "Uhnnnh."

20   Dee next. A dress down to the ground, in this hot weather. A dress so loud it hurts my eyes. There are yellows and oranges enough to throw back the light of the sun. I feel my whole face warming from the heat waves it throws out. Earrings, too, gold and hanging down to her shoulders. Bracelets dangling and making noises when she moves her arm up to shake the folds of the dress out of her armpits. The dress is loose and flows, and as she walks closer, I like it. I hear Maggie go "Uhnnnh" again. It is her sister's hair. It stands straight up like the wool on a sheep. It is black as night and around the edges are two long pigtails that rope about like small lizards disappearing behind her ears.

"Wa-su-zo-Tean-o!" she says, coming on in that gliding way the dress makes her move. The short stocky fellow with the hair to his navel is all grinning and he follows up with "Asalamalakim, my mother and sister!" He moves to hug Maggie but she falls back, right up against the back of my chair. I feel her trembling there and when I look up I see the perspiration falling off her chin.

"Don't get up," says Dee. Since I am stout it takes something of a push. You can see me trying to move a second or two before I make it. She turns, showing white heels through her sandals, and goes back to the car. Out she peeks next with a Polaroid. She stoops down quickly and lines up picture after picture of me sitting there in front of the house with Maggie cowering behind me. She never takes a shot without making sure the house is included. When a cow comes nibbling around the edge of the yard she snaps it and me and Maggie *and* the house. Then she puts the Polaroid in the back seat of the car, and comes up and kisses me on the forehead.

Meanwhile Asalamalakim is going through the motions with Maggie's hand. Maggie's hand is as limp as a fish, and probably as cold, despite the sweat, and she keeps trying to pull it back. It looks like Asalamalakim wants to shake hands but wants to do it fancy. Or maybe he don't know how people shake hands. Anyhow, he soon gives up on Maggie.

"Well," I say. "Dee."

"No, Mama," she says. "Not 'Dee,' Wangero Leewanika Kemanjo!"

"What happened to 'Dee'?" I wanted to know.

"She's dead," Wangero said. "I couldn't bear it any longer, being named after the people who oppress me."

"You know as well as me you was named after your aunt Dicie," I said. Dicie is my sister. She named Dee. We called her "Big Dee" after Dee was born.

"But who was *she* named after?" asked Wangero.

"I guess after Grandma Dee," I said.

"And who was she named after?" asked Wangero.

"Her mother," I said, and saw Wangero was getting tired. "That's about as far back as I can trace it," I said. Though, in fact, I probably could have carried it back beyond the Civil War through the branches.

"Well," said Asalamalakim, "there you are."

"Uhnnnh," I heard Maggie say.

"There I was not," I said, "before 'Dicie' cropped up in our family, so why should I try to trace it that far back?"

He just stood there grinning, looking down on me like somebody inspecting a Model A car. Every once in a while he and Wangero sent eye signals over my head.

"How do you pronounce this name?" I asked.

"You don't have to call me by it if you don't want to," said Wangero.

"Why shouldn't I?" I asked. "If that's what you want us to call you, we'll call you."

"I know it might sound awkward at first," said Wangero.

"I'll get used to it," I said. "Ream it out again."

Well, soon we got the name out of the way. Asalamalakim had a name twice as long and three times as hard. After I tripped over it two or three times he told me to just call him Hakim-a-barber. I wanted to ask him was he a barber, but I didn't really think he was, so I didn't ask.

"You must belong to those beef-cattle peoples down the road," I said. They said "Asalamalakim" when they met you, too, but they didn't shake hands. Always too busy: feeding the cattle, fixing the fences, putting up salt-lick shelters, throwing down hay. When the white folks poisoned some of the herd the men stayed up all night with rifles in their hands. I walked a mile and a half just to see the sight.

Hakim-a-barber said, "I accept some of their doctrines, but farming and raising cattle is not my style." (They didn't tell me, and I didn't ask, whether Wangero (Dee) had really gone and married him.)

We sat down to eat and right away he said he didn't eat collards and pork was unclean. Wangero, though, went on through the chitlins and corn bread, the greens and everything else. She talked a blue streak over the sweet potatoes. Everything delighted her. Even the fact that we still used the benches her daddy made for the table when we couldn't effort to buy chairs.

"Oh, Mama!" she cried. Then turned to Hakim-a-barber. "I never knew how lovely these benches are. You can feel the rump prints," she said, running her hands underneath her and along the bench. Then she gave a sigh and her hand closed over Grandma Dee's butter dish. "That's it!" she said. "I knew there was something I wanted to ask you if I could have." She jumped up from the table and went over in the corner where the churn stood, the milk in it clabber by now. She looked at the churn and looked at it.

"This churn top is what I need," she said. "Didn't Uncle Buddy whittle it out of a tree you all used to have?"

"Yes," I said.

"Uh huh," she said happily. "And I want the dasher, too."

"Uncle Buddy whittle that, too?" asked the barber.

Dee (Wangero) looked up at me.

"Aunt Dee's first husband whittled the dash," said Maggie so low you almost couldn't hear her. "His name was Henry, but they called him Stash."

"Maggie's brain is like an elephant's," Wangero said, laughing. "I can use the churn top as a centerpiece for the alcove table," she said, sliding a plate over the churn, "and I'll think of something artistic to do with the dasher."

When she finished wrapping the dasher the handle stuck out. I took it for a moment in my hands. You didn't even have to look close to see where hands pushing the dasher up and down to make butter had left a kind of sink in the wood. In fact, there were a lot of small sinks; you could see where thumbs and fingers had sunk into the wood. It was beautiful light yellow wood, from a tree that grew in the yard where Big Dee and Stash had lived.

55   After dinner Dee (Wangero) went to the trunk at the foot of my bed and started rifling through it. Maggie hung back in the kitchen over the dishpan. Out came Wangero with two quilts. They had been pieced by Grandma Dee and then Big Dee and me had hung them on the quilt frames on the front porch and quilted them. One was in the Lone Star pattern. The other was Walk Around the Mountain. In both of them were scraps of dresses Grandma Dee had won fifty and more years ago. Bits and pieces of Grandpa Jarrell's paisley shirts. And one teeny faded blue piece, about the piece of a penny matchbox, that was from Great Grandpa Ezra's uniform that he wore in the Civil War.

"Mama," Wangero said sweet as a bird. "Can I have these old quilts?"

I heard something fall in the kitchen, and a minute later the kitchen door slammed.

"Why don't you take one or two of the others?" I asked. "These old things was just done by me and Big Dee from some tops your grandma pieced before she died."

"No," said Wangero. "I don't want those. They are stitched around the borders by machine."

60   "That'll make them last better," I said.

"That's not the point," said Wangero. "These are all pieces of dresses Grandma used to wear. She did all this stitching by hand. Imagine!" She held the quilts securely in her arms, stroking them.

"Some of the pieces, like those lavender ones, come from old clothes her mother handed down to her," I said, moving up to touch the quilts. Dee (Wangero) moved back just enough so that I couldn't reach the quilts. They already belonged to her.

"Imagine!" she breathed again, clutching them closely to her bosom.

"The truth is," I said, "I promised to give them quilts to Maggie, for when she marries John Thomas."

65   She gasped like a bee had stung her.

"Maggie can't appreciate these quilts!" she said. "She'd probably be backward enough to put them to everyday use."

"I reckon she would," I said. "God knows I been saving 'em for long enough with nobody using 'em. I hope she will!" I didn't want to bring up how I had offered Dee (Wangero) a quilt when she went away to college. Then she had told me they were old-fashioned, out of style.

"But they're *priceless!*" she was saying now, furiously; for she has a temper. "Maggie would put them on the bed and in five years they'd be in rags. Less than that!"

"She can always make some more," I said. "Maggie knows how to quilt."

70   Dee (Wangero) looked at me with hatred. "You just will not understand. The point is these quilts, *these* quilts!"

"Well," I said, stumped. "What would *you* do with them?"

"Hang them," she said. As if that was the only thing you *could* do with quilts.

Maggie by now was standing in the door. I could almost hear the sound her feet made as they scraped over each other.

"She can have them, Mama," she said, like somebody used to never winning anything, or having anything reserved for her. "I can 'member Grandma Dee without the quilts."

75   I looked at her hard. She had filled her bottom lip with checkerberry snuff and it gave her face a kind of dopey, hangdog look. It was Grandma Dee and Big Dee who taught her how to quilt herself. She stood there with her scarred hands hidden in the folds of her skirt. She looked at her sister with something like fear but she wasn't mad at her. This was Maggie's portion. This was the way she knew God to work.

When I looked at her like that something hit me in the top of my head and ran down to the soles of my feet. Just like when I'm in church and the spirit of God touches me and I get happy and shout. I did something I never had done before: hugged Maggie to me, then dragged her on into the room, snatched the quilts out of Miss Wangero's hands and dumped them into Maggie's lap. Maggie just sat there on my bed with her mouth open.

"Take one or two of the others," I said to Dee.

But she turned without a word and went out to Hakim-a-barber.

"You just don't understand," she said, as Maggie and I came out to the car.

"What don't I understand?" I wanted to know.

"Your heritage," she said. And then she turned to Maggie, kissed her, and said, "You ought to try to make something of yourself, too, Maggie. It's really a new day for us. But from the way you and Mama still live you'd never know it."

She put on some sunglasses that hid everything above the tip of her nose and chin.

Maggie smiled; maybe at the sunglasses. But a real smile, not scared. After we watched the car dust settle I asked Maggie to bring me a dip of snuff. And then the two of us sat there just enjoying, until it was time to go in the house and go to bed.

If you like this story, you may be interested in reading Georgia-born Alice Walker in the context of the case study on the American South in chapter 12, with works by Flannery O'Connor, William Faulkner, and Ralph Ellison.

GOING FURTHER   Succeeding generations of young, black short-story writers have made their mark on American literature, many of them looking to Walker as their mentor. One of the foremost of these is the Pulitzer–Prize winner Edward P. Jones, author of *Lost in the City* (1992) and *All Aunt Hagar's Children* (2006).

A Handbook
for Writing
from Reading

Handbook Contents

1 Critical Approaches to Literature

1a APPROACH CRITICISM AS AN ONGOING CONVERSATION

Literary theorist Kenneth Burke famously described literary criticism as an ongoing conversation, one that began before we arrived and will continue after we leave. If the thought of engaging in literary criticism intimidates you, think of it instead as adding your voice to those of others who have read the same work of literature and want to talk about it. You need not interpret the work as if you've been the first to read it, and you certainly don't have to feel as though you must deliver the final response. You need only contribute to the conversation.

Whenever we discuss literature, whether we acknowledge our appreciation or disdain for a text, interpret its meanings and mysteries, or cite it as an example of a larger trend in culture, we engage in an act of **literary criticism.** Such responsiveness is all around us and probably has its origins in the genesis of literature itself. The classical philosophers Plato and Aristotle laid the foundations for studying the creation, interpretation, and impact of the written and spoken word—in a sense, they began the conversation we now join.

1b USE A CRITICAL APPROACH AS A LENS FOR EXAMINATION

While these classical theories are still relevant, approaches to literature have changed with new developments in human thought. Literary critics and theorists are almost inevitably influenced by major shifts in philosophy, politics, history, science, technology, and economics. For example, the advent of Freud's theories of psychology opened up a way of examining literature by applying psychoanalytic concepts to characters and authors. Later in the century, the feminist movement led critics to apply ideas about gender roles to literary criticism. These borrowings from other fields are particularly influential for twentieth-century theory and criticism, as our discussion of the major approaches to criticism will show.

It may be helpful to think of each of the critical approaches described here as a *lens* through which a piece of literature can be examined. Any work can be looked at from several different points of view, but the lens itself cannot do the interpreting—a reader must do that. Still, the lens provides the reader with a set of guiding principles with which to limit all of the possible questions the reader might ask. For students engaging in literary criticism for the first time, these lenses can be enormously helpful because they narrow down the overwhelming array of possibilities, providing specific approaches to take and questions to ask. Studying and understanding the work of readers who have come before us can make the task of coming up with our own ideas less daunting.

1c   CONSIDER MULTIPLE APPROACHES

Many of the critical schools described here initially defined themselves in opposition to the dominant theories of their times. It is important to keep in mind, though, that in current practice many critics are comfortable adopting methods from several critical approaches. For example, a reader who considers herself a Marxist critic may draw on historical and deconstructionist theories to help her analyze a work. Each approach described here has its own merits and shortcomings, proponents, and skeptics. These approaches are not necessarily mutually exclusive, and it is possible for critics to choose the most useful strategies from several approaches in their own writing. Though we will refer to "feminist critics" and "formalist critics" in the descriptions below, there are very few scholars who confine themselves solely to one theory without sometimes turning to other approaches.

What follows is an overview of different major critical methods.

Formalist Criticism

Formalist criticism emerged in Russia in the early twentieth century in the work of critics like Boris Eikhenbaum, Viktor Shklovsky, and Mikhail Bakhtin. Their ideas were adopted and further developed in the United States and Great Britain under the heading of **new criticism** by critics such as John Crowe Ransom, Allen Tate, Robert Penn Warren, I. A. Richards, William Wimsatt, T. S. Eliot, and Cleanth Brooks.

Formalists/new critics consider a successful text to be a complete, independent, unified artifact whose meaning and value can be understood purely by analyzing the interaction of its formal and technical components, such as plot, imagery, structure, style, symbol, and tone. Rather than drawing their textual interpretations from *extrinsic* factors such as the historical, political, or biographical context of the work, formalist critics focus on the text's *intrinsic* formal elements. As Cleanth Brooks explains in his article, "The Formalist Critic," published in 1951 in the *Kenyon Review*,

> . . . the formalist critic is concerned primarily with the work itself. Speculation on the mental processes of the author takes the critic away from the work into biography and psychology. There is no reason, of course, why he should not turn away into biography and psychology. Such explorations are very much worth making. But they should not be confused with an account of the work.

Formalist criticism relies heavily on **close reading** or explication of the text in order to analyze the ways in which distinct formal elements combine to create a unified artistic experience for the reader. A major tenet of formalism is the notion that form and content are so intertwined that in a successful work of art they cannot be dissevered or separated out.

For formalist or new critics the study and interpretation of literature is an intrinsically valuable intellectual activity rather than a means to advance moral, religious, or political ideologies. There are those who consider this approach to be a limited one—they have argued that formalism can be elitist, willfully dismissive of historical and biographical factors in the work. *All* study of literature has to include at least a component of close reading; the question other critics raise is whether it suffices as a way to approach a text.

Boris Eikhenbaum (1886–1959)
The Theory of the Formal Method (1926)

The organization of the Formal method was governed by the principle that the study of literature should be made specific and concrete. All efforts were directed toward terminating the earlier state of affairs, in which literature, as A. Veselovskij observed, was *res nullius*.[1] That was what made the Formalists so intolerant of other "methods" and of eclectics. In rejecting these "other" methods, the Formalists actually were rejecting (and still reject) not methods but the gratuitous mixing of different scientific disciplines and different scientific problems. Their basic point was, and still is, that the object of literary science, as literary science, ought to be the investigation of the specific properties of literary material, of the properties that distinguish such material from material of any other kind, notwithstanding the fact that its secondary and oblique features make that material properly and legitimately exploitable, as auxiliary material, by other disciplines. The point was consummately formulated by Roman Jakobson:

> The object of study in literary science is not literature but "literariness," that is, what makes a given work a *literary* work. Meanwhile, the situation has been that historians of literature act like nothing so much as policemen, who, out to arrest a certain culprit, take into custody (just in case) everything and everyone they find at the scene as well as any passers-by for good measure. The historians of literature have helped themselves to everything—environment, psychology, politics, philosophy. Instead of a science of literature, they have worked up a concoction of home-made disciplines. They seem to have forgotten that those subjects pertain to their own fields of study—to the history of philosophy, the history of culture, psychology, and so on, and that those fields of study certainly may utilize literary monuments as documents of a defective and second-class variety among other materials.

To establish this principle of specificity without resorting to speculative aesthetics required the juxtaposing of the literary order of facts with another such order. For this purpose one order had to be selected from among existent orders, which, while contiguous with the literary order, would contrast with it in terms of functions. It was just such a methodological procedure that produced the opposition between "poetic" language and "practical" language. This opposition [. . .] served as the activating principle for the Formalists' treatment of the fundamental problems of poetics. Thus, instead of an orientation toward a

---

[1]A legal term describing something that has no ownership.

> history of culture or of social life, towards psychology, or aesthetics, and so on, as had been customary for literary scholars, the Formalists came up with their own characteristic orientation toward linguistics, a discipline contiguous with poetics in regard to the material under investigation, but one approaching that material from a different angle and with different kinds of problems to solve.
>
> from *The Theory of the Formal Method*

Biographical Criticism

Biographical criticism emphasizes the belief that literature is created by authors whose unique experiences shape their writing and therefore can inform our reading of their work. Biographical critics research and use an author's biography to interpret the text as well as the author's stated *intentions* or comments on the process of composition itself. These critics often consult the author's memoirs to uncover connections between the author's life and the author's work. They may also study the author's rough drafts to trace the evolution of a given text or examine the author's library to discern potential influences on the author's work.

Knowledge of an author's biography can surely help readers interpret or understand a text. For example, awareness of Flannery O'Connor's devout Catholicism will make the religious elements of her stories and novels more meaningful to readers. However, as we have just seen, formalist critics reject biographical criticism, arguing that any essential meaning in a text should be discernable to readers purely through close reading. They reject the notion that an author's thought processes and stated *intentions* for a text necessarily define the work's meaning. They call this emphasis on discerning or trusting an author's own stated purpose the **intentional fallacy** and believe a text's meaning must be contained in and communicated only by the text as such.

While biographical criticism was once quite common, in recent decades it is more often used as *part* of a larger critical approach than as the primary critical strategy.

Gary Lee Stonum (b. 1947)
Dickinson's Literary Background (1998)

> Books and reading were [Emily] Dickinson's primary access to a world beyond Amherst. We can thus at least be reasonably confident that the cultural contexts of Dickinson's writing are primarily literary, particularly if that term is defined inclusively. Her surviving letters are filled with references to favorite authors, and some of the poems allude in one way or another to recognizable elements of her reading (Pollak, "Allusions"). To be sure, she is by no means a learned poet in the vein of Milton or Pope, writers who can hardly be appreciated without understanding their allusions and allegiances. Yet she is also surely not the unlettered author Richard Chase once unguardedly deemed her, uninfluenced by literary sources in either style or thought.
>
> A few cautions need to be kept in mind as we examine various claims about Dickinson's literary milieu. First, we know very little about how or even whether Dickinson imagined her work as participating in any public enterprise. By con-

trast to Keats, who dreamed of being among the English poets after his death, or a James Joyce, who schemed tirelessly to shape his own reputation, Dickinson hardly trafficked in any cultural arena. We do possess information about the books she read or admired, and we know from the persistent testimony of her letters and poems that she regarded poetry as an exalted calling. Yet, although we can reasonably infer from this a certain broad ambition, we simply do not know if Dickinson regarded her vocation as entailing some sense of a role in literary history or as obliging her to bargain in the cultural marketplace. We do not, for example, know whether or in what respect she regarded herself as a woman poet, in spite of a number of lively arguments supposing that she did.

[. . .] At the writerly end of the spectrum lie the sources Dickinson drew upon or referred to as she wrote, which are of varying importance. Dickinson's regard for Elizabeth Barrett Browning makes it likely that her "Vision of Poets" is a source of "I died for Beauty," as well as or even rather than Keats's now more famous "Ode on a Grecian Urn." On the other hand, the identification is by no means crucial to an understanding of the poem.

The more interesting cases are those in which the source is disputed and identification would make some difference to our reading. Dickinson was notably fond of exotic place-names, most of which she must have come upon in her reading and some of which may carry thematic associations. The reference to "Chimborazo" in "Love—thou are high" may well derive incidentally from Edward Hitchcock's *Elementary Geology,* where it stands among a list of the world's tallest mountains, or it may originate from similarly casual uses in Barrett Browning and Emerson. On the other hand, if we heed Judith Farr's investigations into the influence of contemporary painting, then we might recall that Frederic Church's mammoth painting of Chimborazo was one of the most celebrated luminist canvases of the day. If the poem is read in the latter context, then the "Love" addressed by the poem as like the mountain would function more insistently as a figure of sublime theophany. (The poem also clearly alludes to Exodus 33, the chief biblical commonplace for such an event.)

[. . .] Many of the references in Dickinson's writings are discussed in Jack Capps's indispensable *Emily Dickinson's Reading,* which includes a detailed index of the books and authors she mentions in poems or letters. Capps also surveys the contents of the family library, much of which is now at Harvard. Unfortunately, the usefulness of the library "is limited by the fact that books from the Austin Dickinson and Edward Dickinson household have been mixed and, in most cases, dates of acquisition and individual ownership are uncertain." Likewise, although these volumes include inscriptions, marginalia, and other evidence of use, few of the markings can be confidently traced to the poet herself.

from *Dickinson's Literary Background*

Historical Criticism

Historical criticism emphasizes the relationship between a text and its historical context. When interpreting a text, historical critics highlight the cultural, philosophical, and political movements and ideologies prevalent during the text's creation and reception. Such critics may also use literary texts as a means of studying or promoting a particular movement in history—cultural , political, or otherwise.

Historical critics do extensive research to uncover the social and intellectual trends that influenced the life and work of the author and his or her original audience. This research brings to light allusions, concepts, and vocabulary or word usage that would have been easily understood by the author or the original audience but may elude contemporary readers. Historical critics also study the ways in which the meanings of a given text change over time, looking, for example, at the ways in which Victorians staged or responded to Shakespeare's *A Midsummer Night's Dream*.

One frequent objection to historical criticism is that these methods can reveal more about the context surrounding a text than about the meaning or value of the text itself. Another objection is that historical criticism sometimes views literature simply as an expression of the historical trends of a given era, rather than viewing texts as autonomous, idiosyncratic expressions of a particular author's views. Historical criticism, some argue, oversimplifies the relationship between a text and the prevailing or dominant cultural context, overlooking the possibility that the text may have a subversive, distorted, distanced, or anachronistic relationship to the dominant culture of the author's time.

Carl Van Doren (1885–1950)
Mark Twain (1921)

Of the major American novelists Mark Twain derived least from any literary, or at any rate from any bookish, tradition. Hawthorne had the example of Irving, and Cooper had that of Scott, when they began to write; Howells and Henry James instinctively fell into step with the classics. Mark Twain came up into literature from the popular ranks, trained in the school of newspaper fun-making and humorous lecturing, only gradually instructed in the more orthodox arts of the literary profession. He seems to most eyes, however, less indebted to predecessors than he actually was, for the reason that his provenance has faded out with the passage of time and the increase of his particular fame. Yet he had predecessors and a provenance. As a printer he learned the mechanical technique of his trade of letters; as a jocose writer for the newspapers of the Middle West and the Far West at a period when a well established mode of burlesque and caricature and dialect prevailed there, he adapted himself to a definite convention; as a raconteur he not only tried his methods on the most diverse auditors but consciously studied those of Artemus Ward, then the American master of the craft; Bret Harte, according to Mark Twain, "trimmed and trained and schooled me"; and thereafter, when the "Wild Humorist of the Pacific Slope," as it did not at first seem violent to call him, came into contact with professed men of letters, especially Howells, he had already a mastership of his own, though in a second rank.

To be a "humorist" in the United States of the sixties and seventies was to belong to an understood and accepted class. It meant, as Orpheus C. Kerr and John Phœnix and Josh Billings and Petroleum V. Nasby and Artemus Ward had recently and typically been showing, to make fun as fantastically as one liked but never to rise to beauty; to be intensely shrewd but never profound; to touch pathos at intervals but never tragedy. The humorist assumed a name not his own, as Mark Twain did, and also generally a character—that of some rustic sage or adventurous eccentric who discussed the topics of the moment keenly and drolly. Under his assumed character, of which he ordinarily made fun, he claimed a wide license of speech, which did not, however, extend to indecency or to any very serious satire. His fun was the ebullience of a strenuous society, the laughter of escape from difficult conditions. It was rooted fast in that optimism which Americans have had the habit of considering a moral obligation. It loved to ridicule those things which to the general public seemed obstacles to the victorious progress of an average democracy; it laughed about equally at idlers and idealists, at fools and poets, at unsuccessful sinners and unsuccessful saints. It could take this attitude toward minorities because it was so confident of having the great American majority at its back, hearty, kindly, fair-intentioned, but self-satisfied and unspeculative. In time Mark Twain partly outgrew this type of fun—or rather, had frequent intervals of a different type and also of a fierce seriousness—but the origins of his art lie there. So do the origins of his ideas lie among the populace, much as he eventually outgrew the evangelical orthodoxy and national complacency and personal hopefulness with which he had first been burdened.

from The American Novel

Psychological or Psychoanalytic Criticism

Psychoanalytic criticism originally stemmed, like psychoanalysis itself, from the work of Sigmund Freud. That revolutionary thinker sought to analyze the conscious and subconscious mental workings of his patients by listening to them discuss their dreams, their erotic urges, and their childhoods. Psychoanalytical critics in a sense study characters and authors as they would patients, looking in the text for evidence of childhood trauma, repressed sexual impulses, preoccupation with death, and so on. Through the lens of psychology they attempt to explain the motivations and meanings behind characters' actions. Such critics have, for example, noted Hamlet's Oedipus complex, his desire to kill his (step)father and possess his mother.

At the same time, psychological critics use textual and biographical evidence as a means to better understand the *author's* psychology. They may attribute the somber tone of a group of poems to the poet's contemporaneous loss of a spouse, or may look for patterns in several texts to identify an author's subconscious preoccupations, fears, or motivations. Psychological critics have, for example, attributed sexist tendencies to Hemingway by arguing that women rarely play major roles in his fiction and are often manipulative or emasculating when they do. Others disagree, noting that Hemingway's female characters, while not dominant, frequently offer the story's wisest, most lucid perspectives through what are often the story's most memorable lines of dialogue. To relate these issues to Hemingway's conflicted love for his mother is to consider the work in psychological as well as biographical terms.

Finally, psychoanalytical critics also examine the process and nature of literary creation, studying the ways in which texts create an emotional and intellectual effect for readers and authors. Here too the strategy is most effective when inclusive as opposed to exclusive; this is a useful tool for reading when it's not the *only* approach to a text.

Kenneth Burke (1897–1993)
The Poetic Process (1925)

If we wish to indicate a gradual rise to a crisis, and speak of this as a climax, or a crescendo, we are talking in intellectualistic terms of a mechanism which can often be highly emotive. There is in reality no such general thing as a crescendo. What does exist is a multiplicity of individual artworks each of which may be arranged as a whole, or in some parts, in a manner which we distinguish as climactic. And there is also in the human brain the potentiality for reacting favorably to such a climactic arrangement. Over and over again in the history of art, different material has been arranged to embody the principle of the crescendo; and this must be so because we "think" in a crescendo, because it parallels certain psychic and physical processes which are at the roots of our experience. The accelerated motion of a falling body, the cycle of a storm, the procedure of the sexual act, the ripening of crops—growth here is not merely a linear progression, but a fruition. Indeed, natural processes are, inevitably, "formally" correct, and by merely recording the symptoms of some physical development we can obtain an artistic development. Thomas Mann's work has many such natural forms converted into art forms, as, in *Death in Venice*, his charting of a sunrise and of the progressive stages in a cholera epidemic. And surely, we may say without much fear of startling anyone, that the work of art utilizes climactic arrangement because the human brain has a pronounced potentiality for being arrested, or entertained, by such an arrangement.

[. . .] Whereupon, returning to the Poetic Process, let us suppose that while a person is sleeping some disorder of the digestion takes place, and he is physically depressed. Such depression in the sleeper immediately calls forth a corresponding psychic depression, while this psychic depression in turn translates itself into the invention of details which will more or less adequately symbolize this depression. If the sleeper has had some set of experiences strongly marked by the feeling of depression, his mind may summon details from this experience to symbolize his depression. If he fears financial ruin, his depression may very reasonably seize upon the cluster of facts associated with this fear in which to individuate itself. On the other hand, if there is no strong set of associations in his mind clustered about the mood of depression, he may invent details which, on waking, seem inadequate to the mood. This fact accounts for the incommunicable wonder of a dream, as when at times we look back on the dream and are mystified at the seemingly unwarranted emotional responses which the details "aroused" in us. Trying to convey to others the emotional overtones of this dream, we laboriously recite the details, and are compelled at every turn to put in such confessions of defeat as "There was something strange about the room," or "For some reason or other I was afraid of this boat, although there doesn't seem to be any good reason now." But the details were not the cause of the emotion; the emotion, rather, dictated the selection of the details. Especially when the emotion was one of marvel or mystery, the invented details seem inadequate—the dream becoming, from the standpoint of communication, a flat failure, since the emotion failed to individuate itself into adequate symbols. And the sleeper himself, approaching his dream from the side of consciousness after the mood is gone, feels how inadequate are the details for conveying the emotion that caused them, and is aware that even for him the wonder of the dream exists only in so far as he still remembers the quality pervading it. Similarly, a dreamer may awaken himself with his own hilarious laughter, and be forthwith humbled as he recalls the witty saying of his dream. For the delight in the witty saying came first (was causally prior) and the witty saying itself was merely the externalization, or individuation, of this delight. Of a similar nature are the reminiscences of old men, who recite the facts of their childhood, not to force upon us the trivialities and minutiae of these experiences, but in the forlorn hope of conveying to us the "overtones" of their childhood, overtones which, unfortunately, are beyond reach of the details which they see in such an incommunicable light, looking back as they do upon a past which is at once themselves and another.

The analogy between these instances and the procedure of the poet is apparent. In this way the poet's moods dictate the selection of details and thus individuate themselves into one specific work of art.

from *The Poetic Process*

Archetypal, Mythic, or Mythological Criticism

Archetypal or **mythological criticism** focuses on the patterns or features that recur through much of literature, regardless of its time period or cultural origins. The archetypal approach to criticism stems from the work of Carl Jung, a Swiss psychoanalyst (and contemporary of Freud) who argued that humans share in a **collective unconscious,** or a set of characters, plots, symbols, and images that each evoke a universal response. Jung calls these recurring elements **archetypes** and likens them to *instincts*—knowledge or associations with which humans are born. Some examples of archetypes are the quest story, the story of rebirth, or the initiation story; others are the good mother, the evil stepmother, the wise old man, the notion that a desert symbolizes emptiness or hopelessness, or that a garden symbolizes fertility or paradise.

Archetypal or mythological critics analyze the ways in which such archetypes function in literature and attempt to explain the power that literature has over us or the reasons why certain texts continue to hold power over audiences many centuries after their creation.

Northrop Frye (1912–1991)
The Archetypes of Literature (1951)

We say that every poet has his own peculiar formation of images. But when so many poets use so many of the same images, surely there are much bigger critical problems involved than biographical ones. As Mr. Auden's brilliant essay *The Enchafèd Flood* shows, an important symbol like the sea cannot remain within the poetry of Shelley or Keats or Coleridge: it is bound to expand over many poets into an archetypal symbol of literature. And if the genre has a historical origin, why does the genre of drama emerge from medieval religion in a way so strikingly similar to the way it emerged from Greek religion centuries before? This is a problem of structure rather than origin, and suggests that there may be archetypes of genres as well as of images.

It is clear that criticism cannot be systematic unless there is a quality in literature which enables it to be so, an order of words corresponding to the order of nature in the natural sciences. An archetype should be not only a unifying category of criticism, but itself a part of a total form, and it leads us at once to the question of what sort of total form criticism can see in literature. [. . .] the search for archetypes is a kind of literary anthropology, concerned with the way that literature is informed by pre-literary categories such as ritual, myth and folk tale. We next realize that the relation between these categories and literature is by no means purely one of descent, as we find them reappearing in the greatest classics—in fact there seems to be a general tendency on the part of great classics to revert to them.

[. . .] In the solar cycle of the day, the seasonal cycle of the year, and the organic cycle of human life, there is a single pattern of significance, out of which myth constructs a central narrative around a figure who is partly the sun, partly vegetative fertility and partly a god or archetypal human being. [. . .] I supply the following table of its phases:

1. The dawn, spring and birth phase. Myths of the birth of the hero, of revival and resurrection, of creation and (because the four phases are a cycle) of the defeat of the powers of darkness, winter and death. Subordinate characters: the father and the mother. The archetype of romance and of most dithyrambic and rhapsodic poetry.

2. The zenith, summer, and marriage or triumph phase. Myths of apotheosis, of the sacred marriage, and of entering into Paradise. Subordinate characters: the companion and the bride. The archetype of comedy, pastoral and idyll.

3. The sunset, autumn and death phase. Myths of fall, of the dying god, of violent death and sacrifice and of the isolation of the hero. Subordinate characters: the traitor and that siren. The archetype of tragedy and elegy.

4. The darkness, winter and dissolution phase. Myths of the triumph of these powers; myths of floods and the return of chaos, of the defeat of the hero[. . .] Subordinate characters: the ogre and the witch. The archetype of satire (see, for instance, the conclusion of *The Dunciad*).

from *The Archetypes of Literature*

Marxist Criticism

Marxist criticism is one of the most significant types of **sociological criticism.** Sociological criticism is the study of literary texts as products of the cultural, political, and economic context of the author's time and place. Critics using this approach examine practical factors such as the ways in which economics and politics influence the publishing and distribution of texts, shaping the audience's reception of a text and therefore its potential to influence society. Such factors, of course, may also affect the author's motives or options while writing the text. Sociological critics also identify and analyze the sociological content of literature, or the ways in which authors or audiences may use texts directly or indirectly to promote or critique certain sociological views or values.

Marxist or **economic determinist criticism** is based on the writings of Karl Marx, who argued that economic concerns shape lives more than anything else, and that society is essentially a struggle between the working classes and the dominant capitalist classes. Rather than assuming that culture evolves naturally or autonomously out of individual human experience, Marxist critics maintain that culture—including literature—is shaped by the interests of the dominant or most powerful social class.

Although Marxist critics do not ignore the artistic construction of a literary text, they tend to focus more on the ideological and sociological content of literary texts—such as the ways in which a character's poverty or powerlessness limits his or her choice of actions in a story, making his or her efforts futile or doomed to failure. These critics use literary analysis to raise awareness about the complex and powerful relationship between class and culture. At the same time, some Marxist critics also promote literature or interpretations of literature that can *change* the balance of power between social classes, often by subverting the values of the dominant class, or by inspiring the working classes to heroic or communal rebellion. As Marx wrote, "The philosophers have only *interpreted* the world in various ways; the point is to *change* it."

Leon Trotsky (1879–1940)
Literature and Revolution (1924)

The form of art is, to a certain and very large degree, independent, but the artist who creates this form, and the spectator who is enjoying it are not empty machines, one for creating form and the other for appreciating it. They are living people, with a crystallized psychology representing a certain unity, even if not entirely harmonious. This psychology is the result of social conditions. The creation and perception of art forms is one of the functions of this psychology. And no matter how wise the Formalists try to be, their whole conception is simply based upon the fact that they ignore the psychological unity of the social man, who creates and who consumes what has been created.

The proletariat has to have in art the expression of the new spiritual point of view which is just beginning to be formulated within him, and to which art must help him give form. This is not a state order, but an historic demand. Its strength lies in the objectivity of historic necessity. You cannot pass this by, nor escape its force. [. . .] It is unquestionably true that the need for art is not created by economic conditions. But neither is the need for food created by economics. On the contrary, the need for food and warmth creates economics. It is very true that one cannot always go by the principles of Marxism in deciding whether to reject or to accept a work of art. A work of art should, in the first place, be judged by its own law, that is, by the law of art. But Marxism alone can explain why and how a given tendency in art has originated in a given period of history; in other words, who it was who made a demand for such an artistic form and not for another, and why.

It would be childish to think that every class can entirely and fully create its own art from within itself, and, particularly, that the proletariat is capable of creating a new art by means of closed art guilds or circles, or by the Organization for Proletarian Culture, etc. Generally speaking, the artistic work of man is continuous. Each new rising class places itself on the shoulders of its preceding one. But this continuity is dialectic, that is, it finds itself by means of internal repulsions and breaks. New artistic needs or demands for new literary and artistic points of view are stimulated by economics, through the development of a new class, and minor stimuli are supplied by changes in the position of the class, under the influence of the growth of its wealth and cultural power. Artistic creation is always a complicated turning inside out of old forms, under the influence of new stimuli which originate outside of art. In this sense of the word, art is a handmaiden. It is not a disembodied element feeding on itself, but a function of social man indissolubly tied to his life and environment.

from *Literature and Revolution*

Structuralist Criticism

Structuralism emerged in France in the 1950s, largely in the work of scholars like Claude Levi-Strauss and Roland Barthes. They were indebted in part to the earlier work of the Swiss linguist Ferdinand de Saussure, who emphasized that the meanings of words or signs are shaped by the overarching structure of the language or system to which they belong. Similarly, structuralist literary critics work from the belief that a given work of literature can be fully understood only when a reader considers the system of conventions, or the *genre* to which it belongs or responds.

Structuralist critics therefore define and study systematic patterns or structures exhibited by many texts in a given genre. A classic example of this type of study is Vladimir Propp's *Morphology of the Folktale*, in which the critic identifies several key patterns in the plots of folk tales (the hero leaves home, the hero is tested, the hero gains use of a magic agent, etc.). Structuralists thus study the relationship between a given literary text and the larger system of meanings and expectations in the genre or culture from which that text emerges. They also look to literature to study the ways in which meaning is created across culture by means of a system of signs—for example, the pattern of associations that has developed around the images of light (purity, good) and darkness (evil, somber). Here the study of **semiotics** is germane; the way a thing looks to the individual reader or how and what a word *signifies* can change our understanding of a text.

The structuralist approach has been used more frequently and successfully in the study of fiction than poetry. Because of its emphasis on the commonalities within a genre, the structuralist approach has also been helpful to critics attempting to compare works from different time periods or cultures.

Vladimir Propp (1895–1970)
Fairy Tale Transformations (1928)

The study of the fairy tale may be compared in many respects to that of organic formation in nature. Both the naturalist and the folklorist deal with species and varieties which are essentially the same. The Darwinian problem of the origin of species arises in folklore as well. The similarity of phenomena both in nature and in our field resists any direct explanation which would be both objective and convincing. It is a problem in its own right. Both fields allow two possible points of view: either the internal similarity of two externally dissimilar phenomena does not derive from a common genetic root—the theory of spontaneous generation—or else this morphological similarity does indeed result from a known genetic tie—the theory of differentiation owing to subsequent metamorphoses or transformations of varying cause and occurrence.

In order to resolve this problem, we need a clear understanding of what is meant by similarity in fairy tales. Similarity has so far been invariably defined in terms of a plot and its variants. We find such an approach acceptable only if based upon the idea of the spontaneous generation of species. Adherents to this method do not compare plots; they feel such comparison to be impossible or, at the very least, erroneous. Without our denying the value of studying individual plots and comparing them solely from the standpoint of their similarity, another method, another basis for comparison may be proposed. Fairy tales can be compared from the standpoint of their composition or structure; their similarity then appears in a new light.

We observe that the actors in the fairy tale perform essentially the same actions as the tale progresses, no matter how different from one another in shape, size, sex, and occupation, in nomenclature and other static attributes.

This determines the relationship of the constant factors to the variables. The functions of the actors are constant; everything else is a variable. For example:

1. The king sends Ivan after the princess; Ivan departs.
2. The king sends Ivan after some marvel; Ivan departs.
3. The sister sends her brother for medicine; he departs.
4. The stepmother sends her stepdaughter for fire; she departs.
5. The smith sends his apprentice for a cow; he departs.

The dispatch and departure on a quest are constants. The dispatching and departing actors, the motivations behind the dispatch, and so forth, are variables. In later stages of the quest, obstacles impede the hero's progress; they, too, are essentially the same, but differ in the form of imagery.

The functions of the actors may be singled out. Fairy tales exhibit thirty-one functions, not all of which may be found in any one fairy tale; however, the absence of certain functions does not interfere with the order of appearance of the others. Their aggregate constitutes one system, one composition. This system has proved to be extremely stable and widespread. The investigator, for example, can determine very accurately that both the ancient Egyptian fairy tale of the two brothers and the tale of the firebird, the tale of *Morozka,* the tale of the fisherman and the fish, as well as a number of myths follow the same general pattern. An analysis of the details bears this out.

from *Fairy Tale Transformations*

New Historicism

Both **new historicism** and structuralism owe a debt to the work of the influential French philosopher Michel Foucault. Among other things, Foucault studied the ways in which power dynamics affect human society and, more important, the acquisition and spread of knowledge. Individuals and institutions in positions of power have greater potential to shape the discourse in their field and thus to influence human knowledge and shape the "truth." New historicists look in literary history for "sites of struggle"—developments or texts that illustrate or seek to shift the balance of power.

New historicism emerged as a reaction to new criticism's disregard of historical context, but also in response to the perceived shortcomings of older methods of historical criticism. Rather than focusing on canonical texts as representations of the most powerful or dominant historical movements, new historicists give equal or more attention to marginal texts and non-literary texts (newspapers, pamphlets, legal documents, medical documents, etc.). New historicists attempt to highlight overlooked or suppressed texts, particularly those that express deviation from the dominant culture of the time. In this way, new historicists study not just the historical context of a major literary text, but the complex relationship between texts and culture, or the ways in which literature can challenge as well as support a given culture.

A weakness of this method is implicit in its strength. Those who disagree with Foucault and his followers would stress that the plays of William Shakespeare are more important documents than laundry lists or tax rolls from Elizabethan and Jacobean England—that a work of individual excellence can tell us more about a period than does its census or burial records. Again, it's useful here to remember that critical approaches need not be exclusive, and a sophisticated critic will likely use more than a single strategy when dealing with a text.

Stephen Greenblatt (b. 1943)
The Power of Forms in the English Renaissance (1982)

The earlier historicism tends to be monological; that is, it is concerned with discovering a single political vision, usually identical to that said to be held by the entire literate class or indeed the entire population ("In the eyes of the later middle ages," writes Dover Wilson, Richard II "represented the type and exemplar of royal martyrdom" [p. 50]). This vision, most often presumed to be internally coherent and consistent, though occasionally analyzed as the function of two or more elements, has the status of an historical fact. It is not thought to be the product of the historian's interpretation, nor even of the particular interests of a given social group in conflict with other groups. Protected then from interpretation and conflict, this vision can serve as a stable point of reference, beyond contingency, to which literary interpretation can securely refer. Literature is conceived to mirror the period's beliefs, but to mirror them, as it were, from a safe distance.

The new historicism erodes the firm ground of both criticism and literature. It tends to ask questions about its own methodological assumptions and those of others [. . .].

Moreover, recent criticism has been less concerned to establish the organic unity of literary works and more open to such works as fields of force, places of dissension and shifting interests, occasions for the jostling of orthodox and subversive impulses. [. . .] The critical practice represented in this volume challenges the assumptions that guarantee a secure distinction between "literary foreground" and "political background" or, more generally, between artistic production and other kinds of social production. Such distinctions do in fact exist, but they are not intrinsic to the texts; rather they are made up and constantly redrawn by artists, audiences, and readers. These collective social constructions on the one hand define the range of aesthetic possibilities within a given representational mode and, on the other, link that mode to the complex network of institutions, practices, and beliefs that constitute the culture as a whole. In this light, the study of genre is an exploration of the poetics of culture.

from *The Power of Forms in the English Renaissance*

Gender Criticism

Feminist criticism also focuses on sociological determinants in literature, particularly the ways in which much of the world's canonical literature presents a patriarchal or male-dominated perspective. Feminist critics highlight the ways in which female characters are viewed with prejudice, are subjugated to male interests, or are simply overlooked in literature. They highlight these injustices to women and seek to reinterpret texts with special attention to the presentation of women. Feminist critics also study the ways in which women *authors* have been subjected to prejudice, disregard, or unfair interpretation. They attempt to recover and champion little-known or little-valued texts by women authors—who have been marginalized by the male establishment since the formal study of literature began.

Gay and lesbian studies are, if not directly related to feminist criticism, similar in operational strategy. Interpretation of recognized classics may bring a new vantage to bear and cast a new light on old writings; a discussion of "cross-dressing in Shakespeare" or "male bonding in Melville" would belong to this mode of analysis. Here the critic focuses on submerged or hidden aspects of a text, as well as more overt referents; here too a part of the project is to recover lost or little known works of art from earlier generations.

While the focus on overt prejudice is the easiest feature of feminist criticism to recognize, the approach as a whole actually involves much more subtle and nuanced interpretations of texts. As the passage below from Judith Fetterley indicates, feminist critics in some cases find the more subtle traces of male dominance in literature to be the most insidious, because they so easily can go overlooked and pass for the universal or true experience. This puts female readers in the awkward position of doubting the very validity of a female perspective.

Queer theory emerged from **gay and lesbian criticism** partly in response to the AIDS epidemic and owes much to Michel Foucault's work on power and discourse and how language itself shapes our sense of who we are. He argues that the idea of being a "homosexual" would have been impossible without psychoanalytic institutions and discourse that created the category of homosexuality. Sexuality is looked upon as straight (or *normative*) or queer (or *non-normative*) and as a social construction rather than an essential component of one's identity. Some believe this undermines a critique of oppression and prejudice toward gays and lesbians.

Judith Fetterley (b. 1938)
On the Politics of Literature (1978)

Literature is political. It is painful to have to insist on this fact, but the necessity of such insistence indicates the dimensions of the problem. John Keats once objected to poetry "that has a palpable design upon us." The major works of American fiction constitute a series of designs on the female reader, all the more potent in their effect because they are "impalpable." One of the main things that keep the design of our literature unavailable to the consciousness of the woman reader, and hence impalpable, is the very posture of the apolitical, the pretense that literature speaks universal truths through forms from which all the merely personal, the purely subjective, has been burned away or at least transformed through the medium of art into the representative. When only one reality is encouraged, legitimized, and transmitted and when that limited vision endlessly insists on its comprehensiveness, then we have the conditions necessary for that confusion of consciousness in which impalpability flourishes. It is the purpose of this book to give voice to a different reality and different vision, to bring a different subjectivity to bear on the old "universality." To examine American fictions in light of how attitudes toward women shape their form and content is to make available to consciousness that which has been largely left unconscious and thus to change our understanding of these fictions, our relation to them, and their effect on us. It is to make palpable their designs.

American literature is male. To read the canon of what is currently considered classic American literature is perforce to identify as male. Though exceptions to this generalization can be found here and there—a Dickinson poem, a Wharton novel—these exceptions usually function to obscure the argument and confuse the issue: American literature is male. Our literature neither leaves women alone nor allows them to participate. It insists on its universality at the same time that it defines that universality in specifically male terms. "Rip Van Winkle" is paradigmatic of this phenomenon. While the desire to avoid work, escape authority, and sleep through the major decisions of one's life is obviously applicable to both men and women, in Irving's story this "universal" desire is made specifically male. Work, authority, and decision making are symbolized by Dame Van Winkle, and the longing for flight is defined against her. She is what one must escape from, and the "one" is necessarily male. In Mailer's *An American Dream*, the fantasy of eliminating all one's ills through the ritual of scapegoating is equally male: the sacrificial scapegoat is the woman/wife and the cleansed survivor is the husband/male. In such fictions the female reader is co-opted into participation in an experience from which she is explicitly excluded; she is asked to identify with a selfhood that defines itself in opposition to her; she is required to identify against herself.

from *On the Politics of Literature*

Ethnic Studies and Postcolonialism

Ethnic studies emerged after the Civil Rights movement in the United States, but you can find its roots in the pioneering work of W.E.B. DuBois and others of the black arts movement and the Harlem Renaissance. Ethnic studies employs a cross-curricular analysis that is concerned with the social, economic, and cultural aspects of ethnic groups and an approach to literature that includes artistic and cultural traditions that are often pushed to the margins or considered only in relation to a dominant culture. Asian American, Native American, Afro-Caribbean, Italian American, and Latinos are a few of many examples of groups that ethnic studies might explore. Ethnic studies seeks to give voice to literature that has previously been overlooked in the traditionally Eurocentric worldview by reclaiming literary traditions and taking on subjects that explore identity outside the Eurocentric mainstream. But even works that are not written by ethnic writers lend themselves to ethnic studies. For example, a critic wishing to analyze William Faulkner's work from an ethnic studies perspective might focus on his portrayal of African Americans.

Ethnic studies has helped open the American literary **canon**—works deemed essential milestones in a literary tradition—to works by authors outside the white majority. Another far-reaching effect of ethnic studies is that it questions applying traditional modes of literary inquiry (such as feminist and Marxist approaches) to all literature. It suggests that we might be able to learn something more if we approach a text by examining the cultural and social conventions and realities out of which it was created. With the publication in the 1950s of work by Caribbean poet and legislator Aimée Césaire and North African writer Frantz Fanon, the discipline of **postcolonialism** found its beginnings, offering views of relations between the colonizing West and colonized nations and regions that differed sharply from the conventional Western perspectives. The field's modern American academic roots go back to the 1978 publication of *Orientalism* by the late Columbia University scholar Edward Said, a Palestinian by birth, who posits that the concept of the Orient was a projection of the West's ideas of the "other." Many of today's major writers have come out of the old British colonies, from Chinua Achebe to V.S. Naipal to Salman Rushdie, to name a few.

One of the major practitioners of this mode of criticism, Harvard scholar Henry Louis Gates, places such variety of study in a cultural context in which the urgency of the matter becomes plain to hear.

Henry Louis Gates (b. 1950)
Loose Canons: Notes on the Culture Wars (1992)

There's no denying that the multicultural initiative arose, in part, because of the fragmentation of American society by ethnicity, class, and gender. To make it the culprit for this fragmentation is to mistake effect for cause. [. . .] Perhaps we should try to think of American culture as a conversation among different voices—even if it's a conversation that some of us weren't able to join until recently. Perhaps we should think about education, as the conservative philosopher Michael Oakeshott proposed, as "an invitation into the art of this conversation in which we learn to recognize the voices," each conditioned, as he says, by a different perception of the world. Common sense says that you don't bracket 90 percent of the world's cultural heritage if you really want to learn about the world.

To insist that we "master our own culture" before learning others only defers the vexed question: What gets to count as "our" culture? What makes knowledge worth knowing? Unfortunately, as history has taught us, an Anglo-American regional culture has too often masked itself as universal, passing itself off as our "common culture," and depicting different cultural traditions as "tribal" or "parochial." So it's only when we're free to explore the complexities of our hyphenated American culture that we can discover what a genuinely common American culture might actually look like. Common sense . . . reminds us that we're all ethnics, and the challenge of transcending ethnic chauvinism is one we all face.

Granted, multiculturalism is no magic panacea for our social ills. We're worried when Johnny can't read. We're worried when Johnny can't add. But shouldn't we be worried, too, when Johnny tramples gravestones in a Jewish cemetery or scrawls racial epithets on a dormitory wall? It's a fact about this country that we've entrusted our schools with the fashioning and refashioning of a democratic policy; that's why the schooling of America has always been a matter of political judgment. But in America, a nation that has theorized itself as plural from its inception, our schools have a very special task.

The society we have made simply won't survive without the values of tolerance. And cultural tolerance comes to nothing without cultural understanding. In short, the challenge facing Americans in the next century will be the shaping, at long last, of a truly common public culture, one responsive to the long-silenced cultures of color. If we relinquish the ideal of America as a plural nation, we've abandoned the very experiment that America represents.

From *Loose Canons: Notes on the Cultural Wars*

Reader-Response Criticism

The **reader-response** approach emphasizes the role of the reader in the writer-text-reader transaction. Reader-response critics believe a literary work is not complete until someone reads and interprets it. Such critics acknowledge that each reader has a different set of experiences and views; therefore, each reader's response to a text may be different. (Moreover, a single reader may have several and contradictory responses to a work of art depending on the reading-context: a good dinner, a bad breakfast, a single flickering fluorescent bulb—all these affect the way we look at and absorb a page.) This plurality of interpretations is acceptable, even inevitable, since readers are not interpreting a fixed, completed text, but rather *creating* the text as they read it. Reader-response critics do stress that texts limit the possibilities of interpretation; it is not correct for readers to derive an interpretation that textual evidence does not support. So, for instance, it's inappropriate to claim that the character in a story is a vampire because she only ever appears during nighttime scenes in the story—but it's appropriate to compare the housewife in Susan Glaspell's play *Trifles* (chapter 30), to a "caged" bird once we understand the nature of her plight.

Reader-response criticism, moreover, acknowledges the subjectivity of interpretation and aims to discover the ways in which cultural values affect readers' interpretations. Rather than only emphasizing values embodied in an author or literary work, this approach examines the values embodied in the *reader*.

Wolfgang Iser (1926–2007)
Interplay between Text and Reader (1978)

Textual models designate only one aspect of the communicatory process. Hence textual repertoires and strategies simply offer a frame within which the reader must construct for himself the aesthetic object. Textual structures and structured acts of comprehension are therefore the two poles in the act of communication, whose success will depend on the degree in which the text establishes itself as a correlative in the reader's consciousness. This "transfer" of text to reader is often regarded as being brought about solely by the text. Any successful transfer however—though initiated by the text—depends on the extent to which this text can activate the individual reader's faculties of perceiving and processing. Although the text may well incorporate the social norms and values of its possible readers, its function is not merely to *present* such data, but, in fact, to use them in order to secure its uptake. In other words, it offers guidance as to what is to be produced, and therefore cannot itself be the product. This fact is worth emphasizing, because there are many current theories which give the impression that texts automatically imprint themselves on the reader's mind of their own accord. This applies not only to linguistic theories but also to Marxist theories, as evinced by the term "Rezeptionsvorgabe"[1] (structured

---

[1]See Manfred Naumann et al., *Gesellschaft—Literatur—Lesen. Literaturrezeption in theoretischer Sicht* (Aufbau-Verlag, Berlin and Weimar, 1973), p. 35.

prefigurement) recently coined by East German critics. Of course, the text is a "structured prefigurement," but that which is given has to be received, and the *way* in which it is received depends as much on the reader as on the text. Reading is not a direct "internalization," because it is not a one-way process, and our concern will be to find means of describing the reading process as a dynamic *interaction* between text and reader. We may take as a starting-point the fact that the linguistic signs and structures of the text exhaust their function in triggering developing acts of comprehension. This is tantamount to saying that these acts, though set in motion by the text, defy total control by the text itself, and, indeed, it is the very lack of control that forms the basis of the creative side of reading.

This concept of reading is by no means new. In the eighteenth century, Laurence Sterne was already writing in *Tristram Shandy:* ". . . no author, who understands the just boundaries of decorum and good-breeding, would presume to think all: The truest respect which you can pay to the reader's understanding, is to halve this matter amicably, and leave him something to imagine, in his turn, as well as yourself. For my own part, I am eternally paying him compliments of this kind, and do all that lies in my power to keep his imagination as busy as my own."[2] Thus author and reader are to share the game of the imagination, and, indeed, the game will not work if the text sets out to be anything more than a set of governing rules. The reader's enjoyment begins when he himself becomes productive, i.e., when the text allows him to bring his own faculties into play. There are, of course, limits to the reader's willingness to participate, and these will be exceeded if the text makes things too clear or, on the other hand, too obscure: boredom and overstrain represent the two poles of tolerance, and in either case the reader is likely to opt out of the game.

from *Interplay Between Text and Reader (1978)*

Poststructuralism and Deconstruction

The poststructuralist approach (**poststructuralism**) was primarily developed in France in the late 1960s by Roland Barthes and Jacques Derrida. Poststructuralists believe that texts do not have a single, stable meaning or interpretation, in part because language itself is filled with ambiguity, multiple meanings, and meanings that can change with time or context. Even a simple dictionary definition reveals several multiple uses for each word, and we know that context and tone can expand the number of possible meanings. Moreover, within any work of literature, authors intentionally and unintentionally create even more multiple meanings through sound sense, connotation, or patterns of usage. Poststructuralists revel in the possibility of so many interpretations not just for words but for every element of a text's construction.

Like formalists, poststructuralists use the technique of close reading to focus very precisely on the language and construction of a text. Yet whereas formalists do this in order to develop a sense of the text as a unified artistic whole, poststructuralists "deconstruct" the text, deliberately seeking to reveal the inevitable *inconsistency* or *lack of unity* in even the most successful and revered texts (**deconstruction**). Poststructuralists do not believe that interpretation can reconstruct an author's intentions; they do not even privilege an author's intentions, believing that the text stands apart from the author and may well contain meanings unintended by its maker. These meanings are, in the eyes of poststructuralists, as valid as any other, if textual evidence supports them.

---

[2]Laurence Sterne, *Tristram Shandy II*, 11 (Everyman's Library; London, 1956), p. 79.

Poststructuralists thus reject the notion of "privileged" or standard interpretations and embrace what might sometimes seem like a chaotic approach to literary interpretation. In his book *The Pleasure of the Text*, for example, Roland Barthes presents his random observations on narrative *in alphabetical order*, rather than in the form of a methodically unified argument, since the notion of textual unity is, in his eyes, an illusion.

Roland Barthes (1915–1980)
The Death of the Author (1967)

In his story *Sarrasine*, Balzac, describing a castrato disguised as a woman, writes the following sentence: "This was woman herself, with her sudden fears, her irrational whims, her instinctive worries, her impetuous boldness, her fussings, and her delicious sensibility." Who is speaking thus? Is it the hero of the story bent on remaining ignorant of the castrato hidden beneath the woman? Is it Balzac the individual, furnished by his personal experience with a philosophy of Woman? Is it Balzac the author professing "literary" ideas on femininity? Is it universal wisdom? Romantic psychology? We shall never know, for the good reason that writing is the destruction of every voice, of every point of origin. Writing is that neutral, composite, oblique space where our subject slips away, the negative where all identity is lost, starting with the very identity of the body of writing.

No doubt it has always been that way. As soon as a fact is *narrated* no longer with a view to acting directly on reality but intransitively, that is to say, finally outside of any function other than that of the very practice of the symbol itself, this disconnection occurs, the voice loses its origin, the author enters into his own death, writing begins. [. . .] The *author* still reigns in histories of literature, biographies of writers, interviews, magazines, as in the very consciousness of men of letters anxious to unite their person and their work through diaries and memoirs. The image of literature to be found in ordinary culture is tyrannically centered on the author, his person, his life, his tastes, his passions [. . .] The *explanation* of a work is always sought in the man or woman who produced it, as if it were always in the end, through the more or less transparent allegory of the fiction, the voice of a single person, the *author* "confiding" in us.

[. . .] We know now that a text is not a line of words releasing a single "theological" meaning (the "message" of the Author-God) but a multi-dimensional space in which a variety of writings, none of them original, blend and clash. The text is a tissue of quotations drawn from the innumerable centres of culture. [. . .] the writer can only imitate a gesture that is always anterior, never original. His only power is to mix writings, to counter the ones with the others, in such a way as never to rest on any one of them. Did he wish to *express himself*, he ought at least to know that the inner "thing" he thinks to "translate" is itself only a ready-formed dictionary, its words only explainable through other words, and so on indefinitely [. . .]. Succeeding the Author, the scriptor no longer bears within him passions, humours, feelings, impressions, but rather this immense dictionary from which he draws a writing that can know no halt: life never does more than imitate the book, and the book itself is only a tissue of signs, an imitation that is lost, infinitely deferred.

Once the Author is removed, the claim to decipher a text becomes quite futile. To give a text an Author is to impose a limit on the text, to furnish it with a final signified, to close the writing. Such a conception suits criticism very well, the latter then allotting itself the important task of discovering the Author (or its hypostases: society, history, psyche, liberty) beneath the work: when the Author has been found, the text is "explained"—victory to the critic. Hence there is no surprise in the fact that, historically, the reign of the Author has also been that of the Critic, nor again in the fact that criticism (be it new) is today undermined along with the author. In the multiplicity of writing, everything is to be *disentangled*, nothing *deciphered*; the structure can be followed, "run" (like the thread of a stocking) at every point and at every level, but there is nothing beneath: the space of writing is to be ranged over, not pierced; writing ceaselessly posits meaning ceaselessly to evaporate it, carrying out a systematic exemption of meaning. In precisely this way literature (it would be better from now on to say *writing*), by refusing to assign a "secret," an ultimate meaning, to the text (and to the world as texts), liberates what may be called an anti-theological activity, an activity that is truly revolutionary since to refuse to fix meaning is, in the end, to refuse God and his hypostases—reason, science, law.

from The Death of the Author

Cultural Studies

The critical perspective usually referred to as **cultural studies** developed mainly in England in the sixties by such New Left writers and sociologists as Raymond Williams, Richard Hoggart, and Stuart Hall. These critics took a sociological approach to literature and their views were colored by the philosophical leftism of such social philosophers as the Italian Antonio Gramsci. The movement grew mainly out of the desire to view social life and social movements from an analytical perspective somewhat akin to the analysis of film and literature.

The American academic branch of this form of criticism also incorporated (mainly in translation) the formal philosophical and critical approaches of a number of French academics including Foucault and other so-called deconstructionists. (Novelist Saul Bellow, affronted by this method, called these writings "Stale chocolates, imported from France. . . ."). Whatever good the English approach might have produced was muted, if not negated, by the French influence, which emphasized viewing society as comprised of various "texts" and imbuing everything from literature to the placement of traffic lights with equal value.

Twentieth-century sociological criticism has been a productive and interesting variety of criticism, as in, for example, studies of the relation of the literacy rate and the rise of the English novel or the effects of the rise of the dime novel in nineteenth-century America or the elevation of film studies to a high place within the university curriculum. Cultural criticism cheerfully blurs the boundaries among the disciplines and acts with a vengeance to blur the lines between high art and popular culture.

Vincent B. Leitch (b. 1944)
Poststructuralist Cultural Critique (1992)

Whereas a major goal of New Criticism and much other modern formalistic criticism is aesthetic evaluation of freestanding texts, a primary objective of cultural criticism is cultural critique, which entails investigation and assessment of ruling and oppositional beliefs, categories, practices, and representations, inquiring into the causes, constitutions, and consequences as well as the modes of circulation and consumption of linguistic, social, economic, political, historical, ethical, religious, legal, scientific, philosophical, educational, familial, and aesthetic discourses and institutions. In rendering a judgment on an aesthetic artifact, a New Critic privileges such key things as textual coherence and unity, intricacy and complexity, ambiguity and irony, tension and balance, economy and autonomy, literariness and spatial form. In mounting a critique of a cultural "text," an advocate of poststructuralist cultural criticism evaluates such things as degrees of exclusion and inclusion, of complicity and resistance, of domination and letting-be, of abstraction and situatedness, of violence and tolerance, or monologue and polylogue, of quietism and activism, of sameness and otherness, of oppression and emancipation, or centralization and decentralization. Just as the aforementioned system of evaluative criteria underlies the exegetical and judgmental labor of New Criticism, so too does the above named set of commitments undergird the work of poststructuralist cultural critique.

Given its commitments, poststructuralist cultural criticism is, as I have suggested, suspicious of literary formalism. Specifically, the trouble with New Criticism is its inclination to advocate a combination of quietism and asceticism, connoisseurship and exclusiveness, aestheticism and apoliticism. [. . .] The monotonous practical effect of New Critical reading is to illustrate the subservience of each textual element to a higher, overarching, economical poetic structure without remainders. What should be evident here is that the project of poststructuralist cultural criticism possesses a set of commitments and criteria that enable it to engage in the enterprise of cultural critique. It should also be evident that the cultural ethicopolitics of this politics is best characterized, using current terminology, as "liberal" or "leftist," meaning congruent with certain socialist, anarchist, and libertarian ideals, none of which, incidentally, are necessarily Marxian. Such congruence, derived from extrapolating a generalized stance for poststructuralism, constitutes neither a party platform nor an observable course of practical action; avowed tendencies often account for little in the unfolding of practical engagements.

from *Cultural Criticism, Literary Theory, Poststructuralism*

2 Writing from Reading

2a CONSIDER THE VALUE OF READING IN A DIGITAL AGE

If you want to savor a cup of coffee or a good meal, you will have to linger over it; you can't just gulp it down. In this supercharged world of instant access and the Internet, reading literature helps you slow down long enough to feel, almost firsthand, the experience of characters from nations, cultures, religions, genders, social classes, and temperaments different from your own. Complexity involves consciously sensing multiple aspects of an experience at one time, and reading literature is a training ground for understanding complex situations. In an era when the global economy makes the world smaller every day, this experience can enhance your ability to work with diverse groups of people—both in college and in your career—by helping you see others' points of view clearly. It will also help prepare you for most of the writing you will do in college, where understanding a variety of viewpoints is fundamental to academic thinking.

2b MASTER WRITING FROM READING FOR COLLEGE SUCCESS

Not only will you have required reading for almost all courses in college, you will likely be required to write about what you read. Your success will depend on how well you can turn your reading into writing. College writing assignments have a variety of specific purposes, but one of their main benefits is that when you write about what you read you become a better reader as well as a better writer. Your personal reaction causes you to be more attentive to the text, and this focused response contributes to your ability to remember what you've read, clarify your observations, and explore complex relationships. In this chapter you will find a step-by-step approach to any text-based writing assignment, from a short response to a research paper. In the handbook chapter 4, you will find several sample papers for a variety of common writing assignments.

2c USE READING STRATEGIES THAT SUPPORT WRITING

Critical reading is a process of digesting and understanding a text so you can appreciate not just the ideas it presents or the story it tells but how it presents those ideas, why it presents them, and the way those ideas exist in a certain context. Below are the three steps for successful critical reading.

1. Preview the text.   The process of gathering information about a piece of literature before you read it is called *previewing*. When you **preview,** look for information that will help you know how to approach the text. This information can be found in or on the book itself and includes:

- *Date of publication.* Check the copyright page—or, for older classics, you may need to consult the book's introduction or the author's biographical note—to find out when the book or story was published. This will help you determine whether the author was writing about his or her own time, or about a historical period. It might surprise you, for example, to find that Tolstoy wrote *War and Peace* more than fifty years after the time in which the story takes place.

- *Genre.* Sometimes you can tell genre simply from the cover. If it shows a shirtless man gazing at the attractive woman he holds in his arms, you can bet you're in for a romance novel. Knowing whether what you are about to read is fiction or nonfiction, and if it is science fiction, crime, literary, or another form of fiction will help you focus your expectations of your reading experience.

- *The foreword, preface, or other introductory material.* Read the introductory notices to help prepare for your reading. If the selection is part of an anthology or textbook, the surrounding text and questions will be especially helpful in giving your reading direction.

- *The epigraph,* if there is one. An epigraph is a quotation that the author selects and places at the beginning of a work, and it usually alerts you to an important theme.

TIP Previewing Non-Literary Works

If you are reading something that is not a piece of literature, say for another of your college courses or for research on a piece of literature, previewing is still an important step. For non-literary works,

- Try to identify the purpose of a work and the audience for which it was intended. This information can be found, often in great detail, in the foreword or introduction.

- Also, read the author's biographical note to see if you can identify a bias or school of thought, if the author has one.

- Finally, take note of the context of the work. Scan the copyright page to see where a work was published and by whom. Note how many editions the text has had and if the one you have is current.

2. Interact with the text: Annotate, keep a journal, take notes.   Reading closely is the first step to writing about literature. A careful reading and simple markup leads to observations that can form the basis of a written response. Annotating a text is a very basic process of noting impressions as they occur throughout a reading. Annotation should be as simple as circling repeated words, underlining interesting phrases, and jotting down brief sets of words. Remember that annotation is a process of *observation;* deeper analysis and interpretation will come later.

Look back at the student's annotation of Jamaica Kincaid's story "Girl" in chapter 3, and notice that this student does not come up with any actual *ideas* in his annotation. Instead, he makes *observations* about what he noticed as he read the story. This is an important distinction. For example, our student, Andrew, noticed that the narrator repeats certain phrases in the story, but he doesn't yet ask why. In fact, by comparing Andrew's original annotation to his final draft, you can see that most of his observations did not make their way into the final paper. He first had to notice many details about the story's tone, patterns, words, and his own reactions before he could start narrowing down the details that would be helpful in firming up his interpretation.

Annotation is a skill that improves with practice like any other. The skill of annotating is best described as learning to *notice what you notice.* Everyone has had the experience of reading a story, poem, or play for the first time and coming across something odd or jarring. Maybe while reading John Updike's "A&P" (chapter 1) you were surprised or even offended by the narrator's comparison of the female mind to a "little buzz like a bee in a glass jar." Students new to reading literature are often tempted to ignore that feeling of surprise, blaming themselves for the disruption. "I must not get what the author is trying to do," they tell themselves, or, "I just don't understand literature." In fact, those feelings are useful, the beginnings of your ideas. Don't ignore them. Even feeling bored by what you read is worth noticing.

Interactive Readings

Annotated selections can be found in the following chapters:

- Anton Chekhov's story "Rapture" (chapter 2)
- Jamaica Kincaid's story "Girl" (chapter 3)
- Carolyn Forché's poem "The Museum of Stones" (chapter 15)
- William Shakespeare's poem "My mistress' eyes are nothing like the sun" (chapter 16)
- Li-Young Lee's poem "Eating Alone" (chapter 17)
- Susan Glaspell's play *Trifles* (chapter 30)
- Edward Albee's play *Zoo Story* (chapter 31)

Keeping a reading journal is a great way to develop all kinds of skills—your observational skills, your writing skills, and even your skill for appreciating literature. Often, instructors will ask you to keep a journal and give you prompts to which you will respond. But whether or not you have that kind of guidance, you can keep your own journal in which you record what you have read, what you thought about it, and what you felt about it. There is no one right way to keep a journal; you may choose to fill it with personal reactions to literature, with ideas for paper topics, or with quotes that you liked and a description of what that quote means to you.

For samples of journal entries as part of the entire writing process, see chapter 3 (Writing about Fiction), chapter 17 (Writing about Poetry), and chapter 32 (Writing about Drama). Our student models from chapters 3 and 17 used their journals as a place to write a slightly more formal and focused response. Their strategy is worth emulating: By focusing their ideas in their journals, each student will be able to look back later in the semester if he or she has an exam—or later in their college career when they want to revisit literature that they enjoyed—and will immediately have a springboard into remembering the Jamaica Kincaid story or the Li-Young Lee poem and what makes it effective.

3. Read the text again for craft and context. Reading a good piece of literature is like getting to know somebody new: Your first impression is meaningful, but your second and third impressions can reveal to you entirely different aspects of the work. For a second reading, take into account how the elements of craft work together to create the selection you are reading, and for a third reading, put the selection into context. When was it written? What does its theme say about the perspective of the author on issues or circumstances of the day? It is important to make note of these impressions as well, because they will become the body of information you draw from when you write your responses. The practice of annotation and note taking will not only produce a fuller, more informed response, but will also save you time later.

2d MOVE FROM SUMMARY TO INTERPRETATION

When you start to write down your thoughts about a piece of literature, first make sure you understand the basics: What has happened in the selection, who is the main character or speaker, and whose point of view is at stake? This is a summary. Building on summary, you will want to think about the tone and style of the work, to analyze how the story, poem, or play is told. As you analyze, look for the role of the setting (particularly if you're reading a story), or important symbols, repeated words or sounds (which is critical when reading a poem), and the way dialogue pushes the plot forward (a central element in analyzing a play). Your analysis should take special note of who is telling the story; in a poem, identifying the speaker allows you to get underneath the hood of the "machine of words."

When you look at what was said (summary) and how it was said (analysis), you can put these together, bring in the context in which a work was written, and synthesize the work of literature to find themes and subthemes that the substance and style mutually support. You are now prepared to interpret the selection and support your interpretation with points taken from the selection itself. You may take a particular approach (see the preceding chapter on Critical Approaches to Literature) or point of view, and this framework can be useful as you interpret anything you read, whether it is literature or basic prose. Whether or not you take a particular point of view, this approach to reading will set you up to express your thoughts on what is important and meaningful to you in a literary work.

1. Summarize. After a first reading, solidify your understanding of the text by *summarizing* what you have read. **Summary** involves condensing a story, poem, or play into your own words, making sure to capture the text's main points. In the case of prose, a summary is much shorter than the original source and is often no more than a paragraph or two in length. For poetry, it may take a line-by-line paraphrase to result in the information you need to condense into the summary of a poem. Before summarizing, you might reread your annotations and notes with an eye toward picking out important points to include.

Remember that summary should be *objective*—focused more on what you saw happen in the work than on how you reacted to it. It should also not get bogged down with details and examples, but should focus on capturing the main events of the story or the main idea if it is a poem or an article.

One easy approach to summarizing is outlined below:

- *Pinpoint the main idea and write it in a sentence.* For a scholarly article, a main idea usually emerges in the thesis or is stated concisely in the conclusion. When you are summarizing a story, the main idea is often contained in the broad trajectory of the main character. For example: "In Alice Munro's *An Ounce of Cure*, the main character embarrasses herself while babysitting by getting drunk to ease her heartache."

- *Break the text into its sections.* Some scholarly sources might already have headings that divide the text for you. In a story or poem, identify the places where shifts occur—scene changes, a change in tone, or other points where the work takes a new direction.

- *Summarize each section's main idea.* As you did in the first step, write a sentence describing the key point the author makes in each section—or for a piece of literature, the key action or idea of the section. Think of this step as writing a topic sentence for each section. For example, the student who wrote the paper on Albee's *Zoo Story*, which appears in chapter 32, summarizes the beginning of Peter and Jerry's conversation and makes a point about the significance of animals in the play. In her discussion, she includes the following summary to support her point that Peter is associated with domesticated animals:

  > *After learning that Peter has a wife and two daughters, Jerry is eager to know what type of pets Peter owns. The animals he guesses are typical house pets: dogs and cats.*

Summaries are sometimes their own goal. See the chapter on Common Writing Assignments for help if your assignment is to write a **summary paper** or a **précis.** For that assignment, your professor is looking for a short paper that represents the main ideas of the text as the writer has presented it—*not* your own ideas or interpretation.

2. Analyze craft and voice.   Summary helps you understand *what* happened in the text, and you will likely use your summary to support a point. The next step is to **analyze** the text by determining *how* the author created the work. When you analyze, you take the text apart and examine its elements: the different writing devices the author uses (such as point of view, plot, and imagery) and the voice the author brings to the piece (tone, word choice).

3. Synthesize summary and analysis.   The goal of **synthesis** is to bring together the ideas and observations you've generated in your reading and analysis in order to make a concrete statement about the work you've read. The secret ingredients to synthesis are your own personal opinions and perspectives. (In a research paper, you will want to include the opinions and perspectives from academic sources as well.) Thus, synthesis takes the *what* happened from summary and the *how* it was accomplished from analysis and shapes them into an argument or statement.

4. Interpret the text.   By *analyzing* a text and *synthesizing* your thoughts into a statement on the text, you will set yourself up to **interpret** a particular element of a work by suggesting what that element means. **Interpretation** means striving to increase understanding of some aspect of a work to illuminate its meaning. Interpretation does not mean identifying one correct answer, one key to unlock a text. Rather, it means taking an argument or statement you've generated through synthesis and using it as an angle from which to enter a work and explore some new, insightful aspect. It is important to remember that an interpretation must have a strong foundation of evidence from the text itself.

Other Strategies for Exploring Ideas

A walkthrough of the entire writing process from exploring ideas to writing the final draft can be found in chapter 3 (Writing about Fiction), chapter 17 (Writing about Poetry), and chapter 32 (Writing about Drama). When you're stuck, here are some additional strategies that might get you going again.

Freewriting

1 It is all right to start with obvious impressions. Try to answer some of the questions that you asked yourself while annotating the text. Don't worry about finding the "right" answer, and don't limit yourself to just one—there are probably many possible interpretations. *Freewriting* is private writing, just for you. You need not worry about proper spelling or grammar, or even proper sentences and paragraphs.

Talking

2 Try explaining a story, poem, or play to someone who has never read it before, and encourage that person to ask you questions. If this sounds odd to you, consider what you do after seeing a new movie you had looked forward to seeing.

Brainstorming

3 If you find it simpler to think in diagrams, your freewrite might take the shape of a web or cluster of related or unrelated impressions. Start with a central idea, literary device, or character that you wish to explore and place that in the center. Then, draw lines to the elements or characteristics associated with your central term.

Charting

4 Another way to draw connections between your observations is by charting them. This is an especially helpful method if you have identified opposites of some sort in the text, whether it be a hero and a villain, rainy weather and fair weather, or light images and dark images.

2e   DEVELOP AN ARGUMENT

A literary analysis builds a complex argument around a particular aspect of a work of literature. Summarizing, analyzing, and synthesizing might help you come up with an interpretation that could be your paper's topic, but when you're looking for a topic for a paper, you probably wonder: Where do ideas come from? For all of us, coming up with ideas—and developing those ideas into claims worth writing about—is a challenge.

Claim: An argument is based on a claim that requires a defense. It isn't an opinion ("I liked the characters in this story"), and it isn't a fact or a generally recognized truth ("Langston Hughes is one of the most important American poets"). Your essay's claim will be reflected in your thesis (see the following section for guidance on creating a defendable thesis).

Persuasion: Aristotle, the same great philosopher who defined tragedy in ancient Greek theater (chapter 33) also defined logic and the art of persuasion. What we call *logic* today Aristotle would have called *analytics*, as in *to analyze*. When we refer to an academic argument, therefore, we are not referring to a fight but rather to a well-reasoned, logical analysis that is based on evidence.

Evidence: For literature, the text itself is your most convincing evidence; other kinds of evidence might be statistics, expert opinions, and anecdotes.

Different Kinds of Source-Based Evidence
Summary vs. Paraphrase vs. Quotation

Reference to a source is a form of evidence, and it can take many forms.

Summary: A boiled down analysis of the line of action or thought in a passage or full text, a summary is used not only to represent your understanding of a text but also as a point of reference that provides context for your argument. See the summary paper in the next chapter on Common Writing Assignments.

Paraphrase: Using your own words, a paraphrase is a restatement ("in other words") of someone else's language that makes a point more clearly than could be made by using the quotation itself. A paraphrase, therefore, may blend your own view with the words of the source. A paraphrase can help you understand a passage, particularly in poetry. Make sure you mention the source when you paraphrase. Use phrases like "According to," "As said in," "We know from."

Quotation: When the meaning of what was said would be distorted or changed in any other words, a quotation needs to be used to make your point. Do not avoid making a point by overusing quotations. A quotation is your evidence out of which you should build a point, using the quotation as a springboard for your own ideas.

You will need to show details, patterns, and ideas from the text when you present your evidence. The tips that follow are possible ways of developing or refining your ideas and then finding the evidence to support them. Together with the critical approaches outlined in the preceding chapter, they offer ways to generate new possibilities to develop an effective argument.

1. Follow your interests and expertise whenever possible.   If you are a psychology major and the family's interactions in *Death of a Salesman* (chapter 35) remind you of a theory you have just studied in a psychology seminar, don't be afraid to use that knowledge to aid in your interpretation. If you are an avid sailor and that makes you especially interested in analyzing the "open boat" scenes in Stephen Crane's short story (chapter 9), take advantage of your knowledge in creating your argument.

2. Acknowledge your gut reactions, but then analyze them.   If you found a given text or page extremely frustrating to read, it is absolutely legitimate to admit this to yourself and others. But don't stop there. Ask yourself,

- *What was it that frustrated me so much about this passage?*
- *Was it the slow pace of the action?*
- *Was it my own lack of familiarity with the language used at the time the piece was written?*
- *Was it the fact that the character I most identified with died in the previous scene?*
- *Was it the wordy prose style?*
- *What might have motivated the author to use such convoluted language?*
- *Are there any benefits to it?*

Certainly some works of art will appeal to you more than others; elements of taste and personal preference affect every reading. It is legitimate to say, "I hated that story," and intelligent analysis can come from that reaction if you analyze the ways in which the text creates specific impressions on readers.

Similarly, if you enjoy a text and feel a deep personal connection with it, keep in mind that you will have to ask yourself questions similar to those above to make sure you are being specific in examining the attributes you admire. You need not try to develop negative observations, but make sure that your affection isn't clouding your ability to see all aspects of the work clearly.

3. Choose a single aspect of the genre to examine.   For instance, look at meter in poetry, voice in fiction, or stage directions in drama. Reread the text closely, looking only at that one aspect. It may be counterintuitive, but it can be especially useful to choose an aspect of the genre that is *not* the most noticeable in the particular text. For instance, most readers notice right away that Elizabeth Bishop's poem "One Art" (chapter 23) is a villanelle, a tricky form that requires a complex rhyme scheme and repetition. It would be easy to comment on her use of the form, but it might be more fruitful, and certainly more original, to think about something less obvious, like the poem's use of images or its rhythm.

4. Pay attention to detail.   It is a convention of literary criticism to assume that *every* element of a text is potentially significant, no matter how small it seems. Whether or not the author specifically intended everything we notice, once it is written down, everything is fair game for interpretation. When a literary argument does go too far, it is generally *not* because the argument depended on minor details for its support but because it failed to present sufficient evidence or to form a coherent, logical argument. Some of the most insightful interpretations sound as though they are "reading too deeply" into the text until we hear all the supporting evidence and analysis.

Of course, this does not mean that we can arbitrarily assign meaning to any single detail in a text. It is not convincing, for instance, to argue that "Bartleby" (chapter 14) is Melville's rallying cry for Marxism, since there is little evidence for that interpretation in Melville's biography or his other works. The details, however, that might lead to this conclusion—Bartleby's escalating refusal to make copies, his boss's obliviousness to his condition, and the depressing metaphor of Bartleby staring at the brick wall—*could* work together to support a more subtle, complex claim about work and social class in the story. Each of these details on its own does not necessarily carry meaning, but a good paper will *note* them *and put them together* to form a meaningful interpretation.

So, do not be nervous about "reading too deeply" into a text. No claim is too outlandish, no detail too random or seemingly insignificant, no conclusion too farfetched or implausibly small if your literary argument provides sufficient evidence. "Did Herman Melville *really* mean to use the brick wall as a symbol of class struggle?" you might ask. "Is every tiny detail really so important?" Keep in mind that some interpretations that seemed to be reading too much into the text when they first appeared later became widely accepted. Today's audacious argument might be tomorrow's commonplace one, so don't be afraid to add to the conversation.

5. Compare the text with other things you have read.   Even if your assignment does not require or allow you to discuss more than one work of art, you may still find it helpful to compare your text to others while in the process of developing your topic. Comparing the spare, straightforward prose of Ernest Hemingway (chapter 7) with the more elaborate prose style of James Joyce (chapter 4), for example, may lead you to useful conclusions about the ways each of these authors uses language. It often helps to look at texts in juxtaposition or opposition; the differences are as important as the similarities.

6. Pay attention to the things a text does *not* contain.   Thinking about what an author decides to leave out of a text is as revealing as considering what he or she includes. Painters talk about the blank space surrounding an object in a composition, and literary critics often do the same. Looking at the blank space, or what *isn't there,* will cast our subject in relief, enabling us to see it more clearly. Consider which events a play summarizes through dialogue rather than staging; consider whose points of view are left out of a short story; consider why a poet writes without using rhyme. What are the possible motivations for and consequences of those decisions?

7. Try lumping ideas together.   Sometimes two (or more) minor ideas can combine into one strong one. Let's say your freewrite about Thomas Lynch's poem "Liberty" (chapter 29) turns up an interesting observation: the appearance of the "ex-wife" in line ten tells us that she and the speaker are divorced, which makes the light argument between them suddenly seem more serious. Much later in your freewrite, you notice that it was the great-great-grandfather who bought the plant, but it was "the missus" who planted it.

Neither of these ideas on its own is enough to generate much more, but what if you try putting them together? The ex-wife and the great-great-grandmother are the only two women in a poem about men taking the "liberty" of urinating outside. You find it interesting that the two women seem so different, and they might represent two different responses to male "nature," one American and one Irish. By *lumping* your two separate observations together, you stumble upon a complex and specific idea for an essay.

8. Or try splitting ideas apart.   You might *split* an unwieldy idea into two or more by narrowing or qualifying it. Narrow a broad observation to just one character, scene, or metaphor. For example, in Flannery O'Connor's "A Good Man Is Hard to Find" (chapter 12) you might notice that every scene in the story contains a moment of foreshadowing that the family will encounter the Misfit. This is a useful observation, but too broad for a short essay. If you instead concentrate on how descriptions of objects foreshadow the end (the car that looks like a hearse, for example), you will find it more manageable to gather evidence and make a clear argument.

9. Look for patterns.   If an author repeats an image, word, metaphor, gesture, or setting, make note of it. A poem might use words with "sh" sounds in many lines, a story might include images of animals repeatedly, or a play might have two important scenes set in kitchens. Notice these patterns and ask yourself how they are working—is the pattern emphasizing something, providing a sense of comfort, showing the ineffectuality of characters' attempts to change things? Repetition often works together with other aspects of the work and can serve as evidence that the author wanted to emphasize a point.

10. Look for breaks in the pattern.   Once an author establishes a given pattern, he or she may also disrupt that pattern in a way that compels a reader's attention. If there is a part that seems quite different from the rest of the text, don't ignore it! You can safely assume that such a passage merits special consideration. If a poem is in perfect sonnet form, conforming exactly to the traditional meter and rhyme scheme *except for one line,* it is likely the author wanted this line to disrupt the pattern and create a sense of surprise. If two characters seem alike in almost every regard, look more closely to discover what *distinguishes* them. If a play contains two scenes in the same setting, with nearly the same action, pay attention to the *differences* in these scenes.

Developing an Argument for Robert Pinsky's "Shirt" (chapter 23)

Follow your interests and expertise whenever possible.	Maybe your Gender Studies course has been discussing the treatment of women who work in sweatshops; a research paper could combine information about how clothes are made now with Pinsky's description of garment workers in the twentieth century. Or: Let's say your Journalism course has been studying newspaper stories from the turn of the twentieth century. You could use your new knowledge about how stories were written to compare and contrast the *New York Times* coverage of the Triangle Factory fire with the description of the fire in Pinsky's poem.
Acknowledge your gut reactions, but then analyze them.	This poem at first seems like a mishmash of depressing situations: the sweatshop workers, the girls jumping to their deaths in the Triangle fire, Scottish workers tricked into believing in a fake heritage, slaves growing cotton. All of this is disturbing when combined with the speaker's satisfaction with his new shirt—in the face of the workers' suffering, that satisfaction seems shallow. But these histories are not just tragic, because many of the people in the stories are behaving nobly (like the man who helped girls jump out of the burning building). Maybe Pinsky is saying that every object we own has this kind of tragic history or that our belongings' histories are also positive, because people like Irma are proud of doing good work even if they are exploited.
Choose a single aspect of the genre to examine.	Some of the more obvious aspects of this poem to write about are Pinsky's use of lists and his inclusion of stories and images from history. Those might lead to good essay topics, but it might be more interesting to look at a less obvious aspect of the poem, such as Pinsky's use of sound. For example, compare the hard, iambic words in the lists of objects with the longer, softer sounds of words in the stories.
Pay attention to detail.	The speaker's comparison of the matching pattern to "a strict rhyme" makes it seem as though he finds rhyme pleasing—but this poem does not rhyme, which would seem to suggest that its own speaker wouldn't like it. It would be going too far to argue that the speaker of "Shirt" dislikes the poem and is presenting it ironically, based on this one word. However, the observation of the word *rhyme* in an unrhymed poem is intriguing—maybe it could lead to looking for other kinds of rhyme, for instance combinations such as "the back, the yoke" and "sizing and facing."
Compare the text with other things you have read.	It might be useful to compare this poem to other poems by Robert Pinsky ("To Television," chapter 21) other poems about work ("The Fisherman," chapter 21), or to other poems that closely examine a single object ("The Red Wheelbarrow," chapter 20 and "Anecdote of the Jar," chapter 20).
Pay attention to the things a text does *not* contain.	You might notice that the poem doesn't contain any information about the speaker except that he has a new shirt. The poem offers no name, no history of the speaker, and no other people in the poem except those he imagines sewing shirts. You might come up with some ideas about what effect this anonymity has on the poem—how would it be different if we knew the speaker's name, his occupation, his tastes and preferences, etc.?
Try lumping and splitting your ideas.	Let's say you noticed the repeated use of jargon (vocabulary specialized to a specific profession)—terms like *yoke* and *navvy* that most readers will not be familiar with. You are also struck by the detail about Scottish workers being tricked into believing a false story about their heritage. Neither of these observations on its own is very useful, so you try *lumping* them: both the jargon and the lies about heritage are instances of people being left out of some important knowledge because of language.

continued

	Or you noticed that all the workers in the poem seem to be somehow exploited. Your first idea is to write a research paper exploring the situations of garment workers Pinsky mentions—Koreans and Malaysians, labor unions, the Triangle Factory, Scottish workers, and slaves in the American South. Then you realize this is too much even for a long essay and decide to *split* these possibilities and focus on only one, the Triangle Factory workers' union.
Look for patterns.	You might notice that most of the poem is made up of sentences that are not grammatically complete but just noun phrases—even some long sentences, like the second one (48 words) are just noun phrases, even though they span multiple stanzas.
Look for breaks in the pattern.	The pattern breaks in the fourth stanza with "One hundred and forty-six died in the flames . . ." The verb "died" jumps out and seems even more disturbing because it's the first verb in the poem.

2f FORM A DEFENDABLE THESIS

A thesis is not the topic of the paper or the topic sentence to the entire paper. Unlike a topic sentence, a thesis must be more than just a statement of fact. A **thesis** is the writer's argument about the topic of the paper, the controlling idea that he or she will show and develop in the body of the essay. Your interpretation will need to be set forth in a strong arguable thesis. Two strategies may be useful in developing your thesis:

- **Do a focused freewrite.** For example, if you are interested in how Shakespeare uses the seasons symbolically, you might want to highlight all the lines in the sonnets you are addressing that have to do with spring, summer, fall, or winter. It would also be a good idea to write a few sentences about your initial impressions of his handling of the seasons: Does he mention more than one season in a given poem, or does he limit it to one? What details of the season does he incorporate? Is the season mentioned a principal subject of the poem or a subpoint?

- **Write an observation as a sentence.** Then ask yourself which part of the observation you made is arguable. Try to imagine the opposite of your statement. If there is an opposite, you are well on your way to having a thesis. If not, you might try writing another of your observations as a statement, and then see if there is an opposite or argument in your new sentence.

Often, you may find it difficult to know exactly what your argument is until you have made it in the course of writing the paper. That's perfectly fine. Although you want to give yourself the best start possible with a well-planned thesis, don't worry too much about getting your thesis right the first time. Instead, look at the thesis in your first draft as a *working thesis*, one that serves as a diving board to launch you into a draft of your paper. At the end of the paper, chances are you'll have come to a more nuanced understanding of your topic. At that point, you'll want to revise your thesis so that it accurately reflects what you ended up saying in the paper itself. The defendable thesis that follows is arguable, supportable, complex, and purpose-driven.

1. A thesis must be arguable. A thesis is not just a statement of fact. Rather, a thesis is your argument, or to put it another way, a meaning you see in the story that not every other reader will necessarily see. Since your idea is not readily apparent to every reader, it is your job over the course of the paper to show why and how you have formed your interpretation. A good way to test whether you have a thesis statement or simply a statement of fact is to ask, "What is the opposite side of this statement? Is that opposite equally arguable?" If it is, you have a good thesis. If not, you either have a statement of fact or a weak argument, one that is widely accepted as true without needing to be explored in a paper.

INEFFECTIVE THESIS:

> Some of Langston Hughes's poetry was inspired by jazz.

➡ *The statement is a widely accepted fact. Although this particular sentence may function as a good topic sentence or a sentence in the introduction to the paper, it is not an effective thesis statement because there is nothing about it that the writer has to defend.*

ARGUABLE THESIS:

> Beyond being a jazz poet, Hughes understood the significance of jazz—even
>
> as it was being created—and used only those aspects of jazz that express the
>
> African-American experience.

➡ *As you will see this arguable thesis is also supportable, complex, and purpose driven. This statement takes a widely accepted fact—that Hughes is a jazz poet—and offers a particular and original interpretation of the significance of jazz in Hughes's poetry. Notice that the sentence is arguable: one could say that Hughes's interest in jazz was for another reason altogether—perhaps that it served the type of free verse he wanted to write or that it gave a popular appeal to his poetry. This thesis promises to show how race is the prominent factor in determining Hughes's use of jazz, and in so doing, it also promises a nuanced discussion of the elements of jazz present in Hughes's poetry.*

2. A thesis must be supported by the text.   In a good thesis, the writer puts forth a statement that is arguable, or, in other words, a statement of the writer's opinion. It may seem, then, that the writer can say whatever he or she wants in a thesis, but on the contrary, a thesis must be supportable. This support will come primarily from the text itself. You don't want to take your idea and quote the text in a way that misrepresents it, simply to make your idea work. Instead, your thesis should be a reflection of your broad and open reading of the text in question. Although you must ultimately settle on an opinion in your thesis, you must reach that opinion through observation, not through fabrication.

INEFFECTIVE THESIS:

> Beyond being a jazz poet, Hughes understood the significance of jazz—even
>
> as it was being created—and deliberately used very specific elements of jazz to
>
> exclude non-musical audiences.

SUPPORTABLE THESIS:

> Beyond being a jazz poet, Hughes understood the significance of jazz—even
> as it was being created—and used only those aspects of jazz that express the
> African-American experience.

➡ *You may choose to support this with poems that come from Hughes's* Montage of a
Dream Deferred *collection, which Hughes identified as being "like be-bop." Also, since
the thesis has to do with all of Hughes's jazz poetry, you would want to choose support from poems written at different times in Hughes's career. Whichever poems you
choose, you will need to explicate sections of those poems to show how their elements
are primarily influenced by race.*

3. A thesis must be complex, yet focused.   You may not perfect this aspect of your
thesis until a later draft, but your goal is to write a thesis that points you toward a
topic with enough material to fill a paper. However, it should also be refined enough
that the scope of your topic is manageable—that is, in a paper about Shakespeare's
sonnets, you need not address the entire evolution of the sonnet form, just one aspect
that interests you, such as Shakespeare's symbolic use of the seasons.

INEFFECTIVE THESIS:

> Beyond being a jazz poet, Hughes understood the significance of jazz—even as
> it was being created—and aspects of the jazz form can be found in every one of
> his poems.

COMPLEX, YET FOCUSED THESIS:

> Beyond being a jazz poet, Hughes understood the significance of jazz—even
> as it was being created—and used only those aspects of jazz that express the
> African-American experience.

➡ *This thesis has plenty of potential for a long paper. The author can easily limit the
scope, however, by choosing a few key poems to use in his or her discussion.*

4. A thesis must be purpose-driven and significant.   If your thesis is doing its job
well, it should lead the reader to answer the question "So what?" As the writer of the
paper, you'll want to answer this question yourself over the course of the paper and
perhaps more explicitly in your conclusion. But the seed of the answer to "So what?"
or "Why is this significant?" lies in the thesis. A good thesis leads the writer (and the
reader) to a particular perspective of an aspect of the text, or the writers' oeuvre, or
literature in general.

INEFFECTIVE THESIS:

> Beyond being a jazz poet, Langston Huges was also a big fan of listening to jazz music.

PURPOSE-DRIVEN THESIS:

> Beyond being a jazz poet, Hughes understood the significance of jazz—even as it was being created—and used only those aspects of jazz that express the African-American experience.

➡ *The purpose of this thesis is to better understand the role of race and jazz in Hughes's poems—an endeavor that may lead to a greater appreciation of Hughes's achievement and a deeper understanding of how to read his poems.*

2g CREATE A PLAN

If you have ever printed road directions from websites like MapQuest or Google Maps, you know that they provide step-by-step instructions for how to get from point A to point B. Some students may have such a finely tuned sense of direction that they are able to dive directly into writing a first draft. Or maybe a lucky few simply prefer to see where their writing takes them. Most, however, need some kind of a road map for their paper. An outline provides you with step-by-step instructions on how to get from your introduction (Point A) to your conclusion (Point B). It might help to sketch out an informal plan.

- introduction (includes your thesis and why the thesis is important to you and why you want to explore it in your paper)
- body (indicates the points you will use to support your thesis in a series of paragraphs)
- conclusion (adds a final comment that connects your thesis to a larger issue or places your thesis in a larger context that will make it more meaningful to the person who reads your paper)

Outlines can be very brief and simple or longer and in-depth. You might just write a **scratch outline,** or a list of topics you want to cover. If you're writing a shorter paper that analyzes one work, a **topic outline** might be enough. Topic outlines simply provide the order in which you plan to talk about your broad topics. Look at the student outline in chapter 17, Emma Baldwin's paper on Li-Young Lee's "Eating Alone."

    I.   Introduction
        A. confusing because last lines contradict
        B. thesis: A close reading shows the entire poem is created out of contradictory elements. Through contrasts of imagery, tone, and the literal events of the poem, Lee uses paradox to give full expression to the grief his speaker feels about his father's death.

   II. Imagery
       A. imagery that suggests life
       B. imagery that suggests death
  III. Tone
       A. plain language
       B. syntax is not complicated . . .
       C. . . . but subject matter is. This = understatement
  IV. Time/Literal Events
       A. present, past "years back," past "this morning"
       B. talk about contrast in time
   V. Conclusion
       A. address contrast in last lines
       B. we can understand them in context of poem

Notice how the major headers following the Roman numerals are the topics Emma plans to address: imagery, tone, and events. Supporting ideas can be listed with the alphabet (*A, B, C*). Evidence (quotations, for example) could be numbered in a third level as *1., 2., 3.*

    I. Topic
       A. Supporting Idea
          1. Evidence
          2. More Evidence
       B. Second Supporting Idea

Instead of single words or phrases, you might find it more helpful to state every idea in a complete sentence, giving you a **sentence outline** to work from.

Until you have written many papers and learned more about the way your own writing process works best for you, an outline can help you to organize your thoughts and to understand where your paper is headed. Generally, the longer or more complex your paper, the more useful a detailed outline will be. For example, before writing a research paper, you may want to make an outline so detailed that it includes the quotes you plan to integrate. In fact, you may find a full formal outline absolutely necessary.

A more detailed outline example follows for a research paper on Langston Hughes and jazz. The final draft is found in the chapter on Writing the Research Paper. Compare this slice of outline with the third and fourth paragraphs of that paper. Notice how the outline is so detailed that the author had only to flesh out the outline points into complete sentences when writing the actual paper.

   II. Blues in the Jazz Age
       A. "The Dream Keeper" and the Jazz Age
          1. Hughes's *The Weary Blues* published in 1925
             a. 1925 was middle of Jazz Age
                1. Marked by energy and optimism
                2. Jazz connoted rebellion
          2. "The Dream Keeper" influenced by blues, not jazz
             b. Part of *The Weary Blues* collection
                1. "The Dream Keeper" reads like abbreviated blues lyrics
                2. Compound words "cloud-cloth" and "too-rough" slow pacing to slow blues pace
       B. The Jazz Age and African-American experience
          1. Jazz Age and the blues have contrasting relationship
             a. Blues related to jazz; jazz grew out of blues roots
             b. Jazz exuberant, blues melancholy

2. Historical context is key
    a. Jazz Age "unprecedented prosperity" ("Roaring Twenties" article) for whites
    b. Great Migration—10% of blacks moved from South to North
       (1) low wages, poor housing conditions
       (2) disease

2h DRAFT YOUR PAPER

The word *draft* is used here to help keep the pressure down. Don't worry about spelling and grammar at this stage. Get your thoughts out on paper. *Draft* connotes that what you are writing is not final, that it is a work-in-progress. You will likely revise your first draft, so you will want to save your drafts early and often. Label your drafts so that you can retrace your steps (*draft l, draft 2* . . . or use specific dates to show what the most current draft is). Print the original. Having a hard copy may free you up to tinker and explore.

Introductions, Conclusions, and Body Paragraphs.   You may find you want to write your introduction last or right before your conclusion but after you've developed the supporting points of the paper. If you do, these two framing paragraphs can speak to each other more obviously, with the introduction stating your thesis and why it matters to you and the conclusion bringing in your thesis and why it might matter to your reader.

Drafting Body Paragraphs

- Focus each paragraph on one idea.
- State the main idea of each paragraph in a topic sentence.
- Connect the information clearly in each paragraph to support the topic.
- Make sure the paragraph clearly supports your thesis.

2i REVISE YOUR DRAFT

Once you've finished a draft you feel is complete, take a break from your paper—distance can sometimes help you see if your ideas flow as naturally as you thought when you first wrote them. Distance can also help you catch editing mistakes you miss in the heat of developing your ideas. It is also good to get some feedback from a fellow student in your class or a friend. When you come back to your paper, annotate the issues you find. (It is great if you can get your peer to annotate your paper as well.) As you write and revise your paper you have a chance to re-envision how to make your argument clearer and to support it more effectively. In the chapter on Writing the Research Paper you will find the entire final paper for the paragraphs that follow.

Draft Introductory Paragraph

Jazz poetry, according to the American Academy of Poets website, is "a literary genre defined as poetry necessarily informed by jazz music—that is, poetry in which the poet responds to and writes about jazz." By this definition, Langston Hughes was a jazz poet. Many critics point to specific techniques that Hughes employs to create the effect of jazz. Although the observations are true, such technical readings fail to show the full extent of Hughes's achievement in jazz poetry. More than just a jazz poet, Hughes understood the significance of jazz as it was being created, and he used only the aspects of jazz that expressed the African-American experience.

Which critics? What techniques? May be a good place for an outside source.

In what way? Back up this assertion.

Used how? Maybe back this up. Is there an existing critical argument my claim could respond to in order to create a stronger thesis?

Revised Introductory Paragraph

Jazz poetry, according to the American Academy of Poets website, is "a literary genre defined as poetry necessarily informed by jazz music—that is, poetry in which the poet responds to and writes about jazz." Langston Hughes was a jazz poet in that his poetry often captured jazz in a literary form. Many critics point to specific techniques that Hughes employs to create the effect of jazz. One such critic is Lionel Davidas, who writes:

> Langston Hughes, in his collection of poems, lavishly uses such characteristics of jazz as repetitions, choruses, riffs, scats, and nonsensical onomatopoeia to achieve musical success as well as audience participation. It is also significant to note that Hughes's poems are often marked by dissonance, discordance, and line irregularity, which all contribute to the representation of the jazz spirit in verse forms. (268)

Although these observations are true, readings like Davidas's fail to show the full extent of Hughes's achievement in jazz poetry. Beyond being a jazz poet, Hughes understood the significance of jazz—even as it was being created—and used only those aspects of jazz that express the African-American experience.

Draft Supporting Paragraph (Body)

Maybe need some more here—how did jazz, just a music form, connote rebellion?

The discussion here is a little unfounded . . . maybe I need a researched source.

This is too informal! Need to keep an eye out for these.

"The Dream Keeper" was published in 1925. At that time, America was in the midst of the "Jazz Age," the period from 1920-1930 marked by energy and optimism. Jazz itself was popular and connoted rebellion. However, Hughes's collection *The Weary Blues* was influenced more by (obviously) the blues than by this new form of jazz. While "The Dream Keeper" doesn't have as obvious a connection to the blues as Hughes's poems that copy blues lyrics directly—such as "Po' Boy Blues"—the repetition early in the poem bears echoes of the repetition characteristic of the blues. Consider the repetition of "Bring me all of your" in the first three lines; typical blues lyrics follow a pattern where the first couplet repeats before a third couplet resolves it, and here half the couplet is repeated and half resolved in both instances. Since Hughes was writing in the "Jazz Age," it may seem surprising that so many of his poems in *The Weary Blues* reflect the blues (lines 1, 3). His decision may in part have been informed by the fact that jazz grew out of the blues, and they were closely related enough that Hughes could use blues and be safe in the jazz realm. But whereas blues are "blue" and melancholy, jazz is "jazzy." The solution to this puzzle is in the historical context. The Roaring Twenties brought "unprecedented prosperity" to the United States ("Roaring Twenties") but it was also the era of the Great Migration, when many African Americans left the south and moved north. Times were difficult for blacks, who faced low wages and poor housing conditions (Marks). So, at the time that Hughes was writing these poems, jazz had two forms: the exuberant, new jazz, and the blues roots it came from. Hughes chose the form—the blues—that best reflected the state of the common black man at the time.

This explanation is cluttered and a bit confusing; illustrate or clarify.

Reads like a topic sentence. Break the paragraph here?

Cute, but is it meaningful?

Are these common knowledge? Maybe include a brief description.

Didn't I see a good image for this when I was researching online? That might help engage the reader here and enrich the discussion of historical context.

Maybe I need more research here, since understanding historical context is so important to my argument.

Could this point have its own paragraph?

Revised Supporting Paragraphs (Body)

Hughes first published "The Dream Keeper" in 1925 and included it in his collection *The Weary Blues* the following year (Rampersad 617). At that time, America was in the midst of the "Jazz Age," the period from 1920–1930 marked by energy and optimism. Jazz itself was popular and connoted rebellion as it was associated with nightclubs, sex, and drinking (Tucker, screen 4). But Hughes's collection was clearly influenced more by the blues than by this new form of jazz. The title of the collection suggests the blues takes center stage in these poems, and indeed, "The Dream Keeper" is no exception. While it does not have as overt a connection to the blues as Hughes's poems that replicate blues lyrics directly—such as "Po Boy Blues"—the repetition early in the poem bears echoes of the repetition characteristic of the blues. "Bring me all of your" is repeated twice within the first three lines; the object the addressee is told to bring, however, varies (lines 1, 3). In a way, lines one through three are a compounded version of blues lyrics. Typical blues lyrics follow a pattern where the first couplet repeats before a third couplet resolves it. Here, half the couplet is repeated and half resolved in both instances. Blues also has a hand in the pace of the poem. Compound phrases like "cloud-cloth" and "too-rough" slow the pace of reading, as does the high number of line breaks compared to the small number of words (6, 7).

Draft Concluding Paragraph

Too familiar, not the right tone for a research paper.

As you can see, "The Dream Keeper" and "Harlem [2]" demonstrate how Hughes effectively incorporated new forms of jazz as they arose. While he does successfully use technical elements of jazz music, to end a reading there would be to miss Hughes's larger achievement. He did not simply adopt jazz technique; he selected only

Embellish conclusion to include new arguments based on content. Remember to restate the argument.

the trends that reflected the African-American experience. He leaves out the "white" sounds of swing and opts instead for the forms of blues and bebop. In so doing, Hughes's poetry captures both the music, as it evolved from blues to bebop, and the African-American experience.

Elaborate or change wording; doesn't sound right.

Tie in history and time period with this, since it's the basis for the argument.

Revised Concluding Paragraph

As "The Dream Keeper" and "Harlem [2]" demonstrate, Hughes effectively incorporated new forms of jazz as they arose. While he does successfully use formal elements of jazz music, to end a reading there would be to miss Hughes's larger achievement. Hughes did not simply adopt jazz technique; he selected only those trends in jazz that reflected the African-American experience of the time in which he wrote. There is no room in his poetry for the smooth sounds of swing at the hands of whites; instead, he used the true African-American forms of blues and bebop. In so doing, Hughes's poetry captures both the music, as it evolved from blues to bebop, and the African-American experience, as it moved from the blues of the Great Migration to the bitter conflict of continued discrimination.

 TIP

Revising

- *Rethink your introduction:* Have you drawn your readers in by explaining how the topic of your paper is meaningful to you?
- *Rethink your thesis:* Have you changed your mind? Can you make your thesis clearer?
- *Rethink your structure:* Do you have a beginning, a middle, and an end? Do they flow naturally and logically into each other, with each paragraph focusing on an idea that supports your thesis? Are your transitions between ideas and paragraphs effective?
- *Rethink your argument:* Do you have sufficient and convincing evidence to prove your thesis? Does the evidence build logically to your conclusion?
- *Rethink your conclusion:* Have you made your case? Have you connected your thesis to a larger issue that gives it more meaning for your reader?

2i   EDIT AND FORMAT YOUR PAPER

After you have looked at your paper as a whole, take one more look at its sentence structure, spelling, and formatting. These simple matters, if not done correctly, can interfere with your instructor's good opinion of a well thought-out paper. You may have been making small corrections all along, but consider this last edit your dress rehearsal for making your paper public.

Questions to Guide Editing

1. Are my sentences wordy?
2. Have I dropped a word out of a sentence?
3. Is my point of view consistent?
4. Does each sentence make sense?
5. Do I have any sentence fragments?
6. Are my commas in the right places?
7. Do my subjects and verbs agree—*single to single/plural to plural?*
8. Are my apostrophe's used correctly—**'s** for singular possession (this *critic's* opinion; Hughes's work); **s'** for plural possession when the word ends in **s** (the *singers'* music)?
9. Do my quotation marks represent the exact words of the writer?
10. Have I paraphrased without giving credit to the source?

In addition to formatting your paper with a heading and a title, you will need to follow the formatting guidelines your professor prefers, particularly as you cite sources in your papers:

- *The Modern Language Association* (MLA) provides guidelines for formatting papers and citing sources for courses in the humanities (see handbook chapter 6, MLA Documentation Style Guide).

- *The Chicago Manual of Style* (Chicago or Turabian) is sometimes required for humanities courses where an instructor requires that footnotes be used.

- *The American Psychological Association* (APA) has a different set of formatting guidelines for citing sources in the social sciences.

- *The Council of Science Editors* (CSE) have put together guidelines for papers in mathematics, engineering, computer sciences, and the natural sciences.

Whatever form your instructor wishes you to follow, pay close attention to the conventions for quoting and citing sources that are provided. Mistakes can be misconstrued as plagiarism, and following the correct form will have the added benefit of making your paper consistent and clear. This is the effect you want your paper's design to convey. Variety is the spice of life but not the spice you need for your paper. Be consistent with the features of your design, and make your paper look clean, clear, and serious.

TIP

Formatting

1. Include a heading on the left with your name, the professor's name, your class, and the date.

2. Center your title (it can be larger than the rest of the type in your paper).

3. Headings within the paper should be the same style and typeface each time.

4. Make your margins wide enough to make the paper easy to read and not so wide as to make your professor suspect you are stretching out thin content.

5. Make your type big enough to be read easily (12-point type is fairly standard) and not so big your professor suspects you are stretching out thin content.

6. Select a common typeface that is easy to read (Times New Roman, for example).

7. Include a caption with any visual in the paper.

8. Double-space your paper.

9. Number the pages.

10. Print on standard 8½ by 11 paper with an ink-jet or laser printer.

3 Common Writing Assignments across the Curriculum

3a CONNECT WRITING IN COLLEGE TO WRITING BEYOND COLLEGE

In our digital age, we actually write more than ever, and our writing is quite public—on Facebook pages, blogs, or email. Writing after college becomes even more public. Writing for success—especially in the business world—must be succinct, logical, and persuasive. Most professions demand excellent writing skills, even if the job does not seem to depend on writing. According to a recent survey, more than half of major corporations say they take writing skills into consideration when hiring salaried employees—and exceptional writing skills are required for advancement. While it is unlikely you will be asked to write an essay on Coleridge's "Kubla Khan" or Shakespeare's *Hamlet* after graduation, you will very likely be asked to articulate an argument that reveals a better understanding of a complex situation and a complex text or set of texts. Writing about literature is a training ground in dealing with complexity and expressing yourself with clarity

3b WRITE TO LEARN ACROSS THE CURRICULUM

The ability to summarize, analyze, synthesize, and critique information is also essential for college writing. In almost all your college courses, you will be asked to respond to something you have read, whether it be a piece of literature, a textbook, a critical article or book, a primary source, a blog, or a website. You may find these sources in a library, in your bookstore, or on the Internet, but whatever the particular assignment, you will have to *show that you understand* the text and *explain* it clearly, and you will have to *develop your own ideas* about how it works and *persuade* your reader that your interpretation is correct.

As you interpret a work of literature, you will use critical thinking skills—from summary to analysis, synthesis, and critique—that require you to look more carefully at how the text has been put together and whether the text effectively accomplishes its purpose. You will use your critical thinking skills in a summary to determine what details to leave out and which ones to keep or in a research paper when you synthesize your research into your presentation. The interpretations that you create in writing about literature employ a number of strategic skills that will prepare you to write throughout your college career:

- Summary
- Analysis
- Synthesis
- Critique

3c   USE SUMMARY TO DISTILL A TEXT

Summary is used across the curriculum. It is used to condense a whole passage or text and may be a specific part of another paper (where a summary is a necessary reference point for your readers to understand your analysis) or the purpose of your paper as a whole. A summary is useful whenever you need to communicate the content of a text and represent the ideas behind any article or complex essay accurately. Summary is a mainstay of academic writing and is used in a variety of ways in all your courses, including some of the following:

- To summarize a source in order to critique it (as you would in a book review)
- To summarize several sources to reveal the body of knowledge on a particular topic (as in a report)
- To summarize the evidence you have compiled in an argument
- To summarize a critical perspective you are using to analyze a work

The goal of a summary paper (or précis or abstract) is to boil down into a few of your own words a whole text, without using your opinion or commentary. While you do have to decide what to include and what to leave out, your presentation should strive to be fair-minded and neutral. The summary paper is a way for you and your instructor to make sure you understand the main trajectory of action or thought in a reading.

Throughout this text, summary has been invoked to enhance learning, to help you make sure you have understood what has happened in a reading. The summary, therefore, needs to show that you have understood the overarching idea of what you've read. Begin by distilling the text to its single most compelling issue. Unlike a paraphrase, which is something said in another way (see the box on Summary vs. Paraphrase vs. Quotation in the handbook chapter 2 on Writing from Reading), a summary begins with a sentence that is a general condensation of all the *somethings* that were said and done in a text.

Your *interaction* with the text—the notes and annotations you have made while reading—will guide you as you identify how the story, play, or poem unfolds. You may find it useful to break the text into parts and write down each part's main idea. Use your notes or annotations to help you understand the text's twists and turns, its patterns and its allusions, and to explain comprehensively, concisely, and coherently how the main idea is supported by the entire reading.

Writing a Summary: Just the Facts

- Be neutral; don't include your opinion.
- Begin with a summary sentence of the whole text.
- Be concise; do not paraphrase the whole text.
- Explain how the elements in the reading work with the main idea.
- Look for repetitions and variations that provide insight into the main idea of the text.
- Check the text's context: When was it written? What form does it use?

Sample Student Summary

Solis 1

Lily Solis

Professor Bennett

Composition 102

30 September 2009

Précis of "Bartleby, the Scrivener"

Herman Melville's short story "Bartleby, the Scrivener" presents a businessman narrator who hires an unusual employee named Bartleby, and who consequently struggles with what to do about Bartleby's behavior. The first-person narrator introduces himself as an elderly gentleman who owns a law office. His three employees, Turkey, Nippers, and Ginger Nut, are so temperamental that the narrator is forced to hire a fourth man to fill in the gaps of their work. He hires Bartleby, who at first works industriously. However, when the narrator asks him to fulfill tasks beyond copying, Bartleby consistently replies "I would prefer not to." This pattern continues, with the narrator becoming more annoyed at Bartleby's refusals and yet feeling unwilling to turn him out. When the narrator discovers that Bartleby is living at the office, he makes an attempt at befriending Bartleby, which Bartleby evades with his usual "prefer not to" responses. Soon, Bartleby stops working entirely, due to damaged eyesight, but even when his eyes improve, Bartleby does nothing but stand all day in the office. The narrator gives Bartleby a friendly ultimatum that he must leave in six days. However, at the end of six days, Bartleby is still there, and the narrator—out of Christian charity—decides to let him remain. Still, Bartleby's presence is a nuisance, and the narrator at last decides to move his offices to another building. He receives complaints from the new tenants, asking him to remove the man he left behind. The narrator

[Margin annotations:]

Begins with a neutral statement that presents the basis for all plot elements in the story.

Important element identified specifically.

Concise statements introduce major characters and define their roles in the story.

Concise, neutral statements explain the sequence of action

Solis 2

returns to the old building and offers to Bartleby that he come to the narrator's private

home and live there, but Bartleby refuses. A short time later, the narrator learns that

Bartleby has been taken to prison as a vagrant. Although the narrator makes provisions

for Bartleby to be well-fed in prison, Bartleby refuses to eat, and the narrator visits

one day to find him dead. The narrator concludes the story by offering a rumor that

Bartleby previously worked in a Dead Letter Office.

Gives story's resolution without offering reader's interpretation.

Work Cited

Melville, Herman. "Bartleby, the Scrivener." *Literature: Craft & Voice*. Eds. Nicholas

Delbanco and Alan Cheuse. Vol. 1. New York: McGraw-Hill, 2009. 553–572. Print.

3d USE ANALYSIS TO EXAMINE HOW THE PARTS CONTRIBUTE TO THE WHOLE

Like summary, analysis is critical to college writing. In an analysis, you break the selection down into its parts and examine how the parts of a work contribute to the whole. Whether you are writing about irony in Flannery O'Connor or the impact of gunpowder on warfare, your analysis will look at how your source has put together its case, and you will use the source itself as evidence for your analysis. Your thesis will point specifically to the scope of your analysis. Possible analyses include:

- An explication of several aspects of how language is used—most often line by line—to point out the connotations and denotations of words as well as the reinforcing images that are used (see the following paper on William Blake's "The Garden of Love").

- An analysis of one aspect of a specific text, like dialect in Gish Jen's "Who's Irish?" or parallelism in The Museum of Stones by Carolyn Forché (see the Interactive Reading in chapter 15).

- A card report on the various elements of a story, generally only what you can fit on a 5" x 8" index card (see the sample card report at the end of this section).

1. Explication. An explication is a kind of analysis that shows how words, images, or other textual elements relate to each other and how these relationships make the meaning of the text clearer. Outside literature, an explication is a close reading of any text where the goal is to logically analyze details within the text itself to uncover deeper meanings or contradictions. According to *Merriam-Webster*, the definition of explicate is "to give a detailed explanation of" or "to develop the implications of; analyze logically." An explication paper does both of these things, as it *gives a detailed* *explanation of* the devices present in order to *analyze logically* the work in question. In other words, the goal of an explication is to unpack the elements of a poem, short passage of fiction or drama, or other text. The thesis statement in an explication is usually a summary of the central idea that all the devices combine to create.

Many explications take a line-by-line or sentence-by-sentence approach. Others organize the paper according to a few elements of craft that seem most meaningful to the work. However you decide to tailor your paper, remember that an explication should touch on more than one element. When explicating fiction or drama, pay attention to character, diction, and tone, and how those connect with larger thematic concerns. In the following paper on a poem, you will see an explanation of the significance of elements like rhyme, meter, diction, simile, metaphor, symbol, imagery, tone, and allusion. Although the author doesn't exactly move line by line through the poem, she does start where the poem starts and walks through it to the end. She organizes her paper in light of the shift she identifies in the poem, which she addresses in the introduction. Notice, too, that her thesis states the sum total of the devices explicated: an overall shift from an innocent state to a repressed state.

Sample Student Explication

Brown 1

Deborah Brown

Dr. Cranford

English 200

16 September 2007

Title introduces the poem and poet.

Repression and the Church: Understanding Blake's "The Garden of Love"

William Blake's "The Garden of Love" is seemingly appropriate for either *Songs of Innocence* or *Songs of Experience,* for it contains elements of both states. In publishing the poem under the latter, however, Blake suggests that beneath the singsong, child-like quality is a serious message. While the poem begins with colorful imagery and nursery-rhyme rhythm, there is a marked shift as it progresses with an increasingly dark setting and disrupted meter. This shift is triggered by the appearance of a chapel. It is only when considering how this shift occurs that we can fully appreciate how "The Garden of Love" inverts the idea of the church as good, aligning it instead with oppression.

Thesis statement that gives the central idea conveyed by the elements to be explicated.

At the beginning of the poem, several poetic factors work together to create the impression of youthfulness, and therefore a sense of innocence. The meter consists of an iamb followed by two anapestic feet, which makes a beat reminiscent of a nursery rhyme recitation. This nursery rhyme quality is supported by the rhyme scheme which, until the last stanza, follows a regular pattern of abcb. In addition to the structure of the poem, Blake's diction contributes to the child-like voice of the speaker, for he selects

Brown 2

simple words that are, for the most part, monosyllabic. At the most, the words contain two syllables, the longest being "garden" (lines 1, 7), "chapel" (3, 5), and "tombstones" (10). Furthermore, the syntax follows in accord with the simplicity of the diction, as the words are organized in a straightforward, sentence-like manner. The tone comes across as particularly child-like when we consider that seven of the twelve lines in this poem begin with "And," creating the effect of a child who is incapable of forming complex sentences and so advances his story by adding onto the same sentence time and again. The absence of simile and metaphor also lends a lack of complexity to the speaker (although this is certainly not to say that there is a lack of complexity in the poem). In fact, the seeming simplicity of the poem is furthered by the way in which the speaker offers observations rather than reflections. This is set up in the second line when the speaker says, "And saw what I never had seen." The rest of the poem, then, is merely a description of the scene without offering any interpretation. The innocence of the speaker is also established through the imagery at the beginning of the poem. Blake describes the Garden of Love as full of "so many sweet flowers" (8), and he also mentions "the green" (4). These images suggest growth and spring, both of which connote youth. Green especially holds connotations with innocence or a lack of maturity, since both wood that is not yet mature and un-ripened fruit are green.

All of these elements that are associated with childhood and innocence are found at the beginning of the poem. In the second stanza, there is a change in meter with the line, "And the gates of the Chapel were shut" (5). Here, just before the first hint of repression found in the word "shut," Blake has omitted the iamb and included three anapests instead of two. Although still predominantly anapestic, Blake continues to vary the meter, such as in lines 11 and 12 in which he alternates an iamb with an anapest and further deviates from his original form by changing from the abcb end rhyme scheme to internal rhyme—"And binding with *briars* my joys & *desires*" (emphasis added, 12). This altered structure is significant because it indicates that something has changed from the beginning of the poem. To understand this shift, we must first note where the disruptions occur.

The first major disruption of meter comes when Blake writes, "And 'Thou shalt not' writ over the door" (6). Because there are so many monosyllabic words, it is ambiguous where the stresses should lie, yet it is clearly impossible to read this as strictly anapestic. The result is that "thou shalt not" is emphasized, a message that contrasts the carefree state of "play" (4) in the first stanza. Blake again disrupts the meter when he writes, "And I saw it was filled with graves" (9), which draws attention to the word "graves." Here, too, Blake creates a stark contrast between the image of a garden full of life and the image of a garden filled with graves. Furthermore, the change in the color of Blake's imagery from the first stanza to the last represents a loss of the vibrant nature of youth. What began as a green is now filled with the bleak, monochromatic image of "tombstones where flowers should be" (10) while the priests add to the gloom of the scene by wearing "black gowns" (11). While all these changes are important to note, the key to understanding this poem can be found in the source that sparked this change of setting: a Chapel.

Discusses symbol.

The Chapel in the poem acts as a symbol, a metonymical device that can be taken as a representative of the church as an institution. The shut doors and the phrase "thou shalt not" written over them suggest that the Chapel represents repression. Blake writes that, "A Chapel was built [in the garden's] midst, / Where I used to play on the green" (3, 4), furthering the Chapel—a symbol of religion—as a repressive force by implying that it impedes playing and all the carefree ways that accompany playing. The Priests, who enter the scene with the Chapel, enforce the repression dictated by the church, for they are the ones who end up "binding with briars [the speaker's] joys & desires" (12). Blake's choice of the word "binding" is significant because it implies passivity and restraint; the same qualities are evoked in the idea of routine found in the image of the priests "walking their rounds" (11).

Topic sentence moves discussion towards the thesis.

In addition to the Chapel and the Priests, there are several religious elements that suggest that this poem is making a statement about the church. To begin with, the Garden of Love is in many ways reminiscent of the Garden of Eden. Both house abundant growth and are originally places of innocence. However, they each contain something forbidden which brings a loss of innocence and death. In Eden, it was the forbidden fruit from the Tree of Knowledge that led to sin and ultimately death. The forbidden part in the Garden of Love is the implication of "thou shalt not." The appearance of this forbidding message—a statement of repression—is accompanied by an appearance of graves (representative of death) instead of flowers (representative of growth/life). A second religious element in the poem is the phrase "thou shalt not"

Further explication of symbol.

Identifies allusion.

Brown 4

itself, which alludes to the Bible, and more specifically, the Ten Commandments. These commandments are statements of what man should not do; thus the phrase automatically echoes with connotations of restraint and repression. Another element reminiscent of religion is Blake's use of capitalization. Just as "He" is capitalized as a sign of respect when used in reference to God, so too does Blake capitalize only those words which are related to religion: Garden of Love, Chapel, and Priests. The poem becomes ironic when one considers that it is the Chapel and the Priests, the very objects that the capitalization suggests we should revere, that bring about the change from a place of life and play to a place of restraint and death. It is through these religious allusions that Blake allows the reader to connect the repressive, restrictive setting wrought by the appearance of a Chapel to the church at large as an institution.

> *Explains significance of Biblical allusions; ties elements previously discussed to thesis.*

The diction, imagery, symbols, and allusions used in "The Garden of Love" work together to create a contrast between the energy and youthfulness of innocence found in the first stanza and the repression and death that is increasingly present after the chapel's appearance. In this way, Blake shows that the church turns happy innocence into dark forbidding, creating in a mere twelve lines of poetry a statement against the repressive nature of the church in his time.

> *Reviews key points of the discussion; re-statement and refinement of thesis.*

Work Cited

Blake, William. "The Garden of Love." *Literature: Craft & Voice.* Eds. Nicholas Delbanco and Alan Cheuse. Vol. 2. New York: McGraw-Hill, 2009. 396. Print.

2. Card report.   A card report asks you to represent in a condensed space the various elements of a story. Most instructors require that your report not exceed the amount of information you can fit on a 5" x 8" inch note card, and therefore you must make every word count. As you take apart the pieces of the story, you will naturally forge a deeper understanding of it, and likely a new opinion of the work as a whole. Card reports are a great way to keep track of what you have read and can be an invaluable tool in preparing for exams.

In the following card report, our student, Tessa Harville, was instructed to include the list of information that appears below:

1.   Title of the story and date of publication

2. Author's name, dates of birth and death, and the nationality or region (if applicable) with which he/she is associated

3. The name and a brief description of the main character, especially important personality traits

4. Additional characters who play important roles and their major traits

5. The setting, including time and place

6. The type of narration or point of view

7. A summary of the story's major events in the order in which they occur

8. The tone or voice in which the author relates the story

9. The overall style of the work, including (if space allows) short quotes that exemplify the style

10. A brief analysis of irony in the story

11. The theme of the story

12. The major symbols in the story and a brief explanation of what you think each means

13. A critique of the story in which you give your evaluation or opinion of the story in question

As you look at the following model, note the amount of thought and effort to refine language that the student put into the "Critique" portion. Although it is brief, your critique should reflect the amount of thought you might put into a three-page paper.

Sample Student Card Report

Front of Card

Tessa Harville

English 101, Section 2

Title: "A Good Man Is Hard to Find" (1955)

Author: Flannery O'Connor, 1925-1964, American, Southern writer

Main Character: The grandmother, who lives with her son's family and refuses to be ignored. She considers herself a lady, but is stubborn, talkative, and insists on her own way.

Other Characters: Bailey, the father of the family, who is grumpy and sullen; Bailey's unnamed wife, who quietly tends the children and is ineffectual; John Wesley and June Star, Bailey's son and daughter who are typical children that bluntly speak their minds and are excited by adventure; and The Misfit, an escaped murderer who philosophizes with the grandmother.

Setting: Georgia, presumably around the 1950s, when the story was written. Much of the story recounts a car trip so the scenery changes.

Narration: Third-person omniscient; primarily follows grandmother.

Summary: 1. The grandmother tries to convince Bailey to take the family to Tennessee for vacation, rather than Florida, and uses the newspaper article she reads about The Misfit as a reason not to travel toward Florida. 2. The family leaves for Florida. The car trip is full of bickering and a restaurant stop where the grandmother talks with the owners about how bad people have become. 3. Back on the road, the grandmother convinces Bailey to take a detour so she can see a plantation she visited years ago. 4. The grandmother's cat, which she snuck into the car, causes an accident while they are on a deserted road looking for the plantation. 5. Three men arrive to help the family. The grandmother recognizes one as The Misfit, and as a result, he has his men shoot the family, one by one. The grandmother is shot last, after a moment of connection with The Misfit in which she sees him as "one of [her] own children" (437).

Tone/Voice: The tone is deadpan, with no comments from the narrator. This makes for a reportorial voice with the precision of an acute observer.

Back of Card

Style: The sentences are straightforward and often declarative: "The grandmother didn't want to go to Florida" (429). The description is vivid but concise: "The car raced roughly along in a swirl of pink dust" (433).

Irony: Becomes most apparent after reading the story and looking back, making it dramatic irony. The family does not know to heed the grandmother's preposterous warning about The Misfit before taking the vacation, but the reader knows she is right. The dramatic irony is aided by the large amount of foreshadowing, such as the grandma's remembering the plantation outside of "Toombsboro" (432). The grandmother's behavior is at times ironic—she is concerned with being a lady, but talks too much; she says people should be more respectful, but then uses biased language as she ogles a "pickaninny" (430). The way she causes her own trouble is ironic.

Theme: A feeling of connection can transcend the shocking reality of life's brutality.

Symbols: The grandmother could symbolize the South: her vanity and pretense to being a lady cause a violent downfall. The family burial ground with "five or six graves" seen from the car is both a foreshadowing tool and symbolic of the family's impending death (431).

Critique: Although the story relies on wild coincidence, elements including highly believable characters, perfectly placed description, and economic movement of the plot make this story gripping and a representation of life with all its vanity, surprises, and connections.

3e USE A SYNTHESIS TO SHOW RELATIONSHIPS

Synthesis requires two or more sources and shows significant relationships among those sources. The classic synthesis in college writing is the research project, which asks you to look at a topic in depth and from multiple perspectives. The next chapter will follow closely a research paper on the poetry of Langston Hughes, from finding a topic to selecting sources. Here we will look at how that research project is an argument. Another synthesis across the curriculum could be a report on a body of information (on, for example, the effect of AIDS on Africa). The comparison-contrast paper, like the research project, is found in almost every area of college study.

1. Argument.   The primary goal of an argument paper is to take a position on an issue or form an opinion about a piece of literature and defend that position/opinion using evidence. In a single-source paper (such as the critique of Chekhov's "Rapture" discussed under critique in this chapter), your evidence will be examples and quotations from the text itself. Most of the time, however, an argument paper will be an assignment that involves outside or secondary sources. Secondary sources, such as literary criticism, report, describe, comment on, or analyze a written work other than itself. You can use secondary sources to see what people have learned and written about a topic or an existing work of literature.

Nearly every sample paper cited in this chapter is an argument paper in some sense—a thesis statement in most papers is a type of argument because it posits an opinion that the writer must then support. The best examples of argument papers are the Chekhov student paper, which appears in chapter 2, and the model research project, which appears in the next chapter. In the Chekhov paper, the student argues that the story is incomplete and unsatisfying. Because the student responds to a single source, he supports his argument by citing Chekhov's text directly.

In the research paper on Langston Hughes in the next chapter, the student argues that Langston Hughes uses only those aspects of jazz that reflect the African-American experience. In that paper, the student uses multiple sources to make her argument. To support her points about jazz, she uses secondary sources that provide historical context. To support her reading of jazz devices in Hughes's poems, she relies on quotes taken directly from two of Hughes's poems.

2. Comparison and contrast. A compare/contrast paper asks you to consider two works side-by-side and highlight the similarities and differences between them in order to make a point about one or both texts. When you are selecting texts to compare, you must make sure that there is some basis for the comparison—perhaps the works share a common theme; or, they may be vastly different but both products of the same region.

Let's break that definition down a little bit, using the example of comparing *Beowulf* the epic poem with *Beowulf* the 2007 movie version (see chapter 13, Fiction and the Visual Arts, for these two works). The basis for comparison of these sources is self-evident: they are two versions of the same story. After reading the epic and watching the movie, you would ask yourself what the major similarities are and list them. In this case, you might make a list of the characters that the two have in common or the scenes that are common to both text and movie. Then, you should do the same for differences. In the *Beowulf* example, you might note the major plot change that Grendel's mother seduces King Hrothgar and Beowulf, so that they are the fathers of monsters.

As you make your lists, you might further think if some of the items you listed under similarities might in fact hold small differences when examined closely. Continuing with the *Beowulf* example, you might first have noted that Grendel appears in both versions and is a monster in both versions. But as you think about the movie, you might see that, in fact, he seems more distressed than evil.

The following student paper grew out of just such a comparison. Our author, Anthony Melmott, used the similarities and particularly the differences he saw in the two versions of Grendel to make a point about the role of the villain in today's world. Notice how he moves through the paper: after an introduction and an overview of the characters' similarities, Anthony delves into a detailed analysis of how the two differ. He then ties his entire discussion together in the concluding paragraph, and impressively broadens it to make a statement about contemporary society.

Sample Student Comparison/Contrast Paper

Melmott 1

Anthony Melmott

Professor Wallace

English 150

30 November 2008

Visions of the Villain:

The Role of Grendel in *Beowulf* the Epic and the Movie

In the movie version of *Beowulf,* directed by Robert Zemeckis and released in 2007, there are obvious deviations from the plot of the original epic. Most viewers who are familiar with the epic will readily recognize a major change: Beowulf does not kill Grendel's mother but is instead seduced by her. Clearly, Beowulf in the movie

Opening sentence establishes the works that will be compared.

Melmott 2

version is no longer the hero that he was in the original epic. But what many viewers might miss is that the movie changes more than the hero. Grendel, too, is no longer the evil villain he was in the original epic. Whereas the poem leaves no question that Grendel is a demon with evil intent, the movie portrays him as a tortured, childish soul through differences in his motivation, his power status, and his lineage.

Thesis statement. Also, the mention of three points sets up the organization of the paper.

Discussion of similarities.

The reason that many *Beowulf* movie viewers might miss the change to Grendel's character is that in many respects, he is similar to the original Grendel. In both versions, Grendel is a monster who eats and kills men. His overall trajectory does not change from the epic to the movie: in each, he attacks Hereot's hall and gets away with it until Beowulf comes and tears off his arm, thereby killing him. Even certain details of Grendel's portrayal in the movie echo the original epic. For example, the epic introduces Grendel by calling him an inhabitant of "the abode of monster kind" (14). The movie visually represents him as a monster by making him tall and hideous: his body—which drips with slime—looks as if it is turned inside out. As in the original epic, Grendel appears at night, thus aligning him with darkness in both versions. In these ways, he is meant to be seen as a terrible being in each.

Transition into discussion of differences.

But a little digging suggests otherwise. A major difference between the epic and the movie is that Grendel does not speak in the epic but does speak in the movie. Since Grendel does not speak, and since he is portrayed through narrative rather than visual effect, the epic uses a variety of language to describe Grendel. He is called a "fiend of hell"; "wrathful spirit"; "mighty stalker of the marches" (14); "creature of destruction, fierce and greedy, wild and furious" (15); and a "terrible monster, like a dark shadow of death" (17). All of this language reinforces Grendel's evilness and angry mode of existence. Grendel's fearsome appearance in the movie might lead a viewer to imagine him as the above list describes. However, the movie version allows Grendel to speak, and when he does, we hear a different story. Grendel speaks in Old English, even though the other characters speak in contemporary English, so his lines are difficult to understand. But listening closely reveals that when Beowulf says to Grendel, whose arm is caught in the door, "Your bloodletting days are finished, demon," Grendel replies, "I am not a demon."

Textual support.

Support from the movie.

Melmott 3

On its own, this example could be explained as Grendel lacking the self-awareness that he is a demon. But other details corroborate Grendel's statement. Both of Grendel's attacks are triggered by the loud rollicking of the men in Hereot. As the scene pans from the meadhall to Grendel's underground lair, the noise of the chanting sounds as if it has been submerged. The effect is that we are hearing the men as Grendel hears them—a constant, throbbing, bass line that makes Grendel's membranous ears quiver. When Grendel bursts into full view, his screams are more like cries of anguish than roars meant to frighten. The attention given to Grendel's sensitive ears, his clutching at his head as he screams, and his posture all suggest that he is in physical agony from the parties at Heorot, and thus bursts in to put a stop to it. This is a far less demoniac motivation than that cited in the epic.

In the original, Grendel's first attack reads, "The creature of destruction, fierce and greedy, wild and furious, was ready straight. He seized thirty thanes upon their bed" (15). Nothing in this suggests any sort of pain or anguish that Grendel experiences, as he appears to in the movie. Further, while the movie shows him as provoked, the epic clearly states after that first attack, "It was no longer than a single night ere he wrought more deeds of murder; he recked not of the feud and the crime—he was too fixed in them!" (16). According to the *Oxford English Dictionary*, "reck" means "To take heed or have a care of some thing (or person), so as to be alarmed or troubled thereby, or to modify one's conduct or purpose on that account." In other words, this quote shows that Grendel's killings do not bother him or give him pause because he is so set in his evil ways. Hence, even if Grendel could speak in the original epic, he certainly wouldn't say "I am no demon" and even if he did, we would know by his actions that this was not true. On the contrary, when Grendel utters that line in the movie, we have seen that, indeed, his motivation is not naturally demonic but provocation.

Consistent with the change in motivation is the change in Grendel's power status from the epic to the movie. In the epic, Grendel holds a reign of terror. Although it is difficult to analyze language in a translation, it is safe to say that the text refers to Grendel in several places as a ruling authority of sorts. One example follows Grendel's

Defines unknown word to add textual support.

Transition sentence that leads into the second point of the thesis.

Textual support.

first series of attacks in which the poem reads, "Thus he tyrannized over them" (16). In another translation, that of Seamus Heaney, the same line reads "So Grendel ruled" (35). Both "rule" and "tyranny" are ways of describing an all-powerful governing body. Later, when he fights Beowulf, Grendel is described as the "master of evils" (43), and in the Heaney translation as "the captain of evil" (47). "Master" and "captain" both refer to someone in charge, someone with power, and both are applied to Grendel in the original epic.

Yet for all the power the epic accords to Grendel, the movie portrays Grendel as child-like. While Grendel has a mother in both versions, only the movie shows Grendel interact with her like a child. After his first attack in the movie, he returns to his lair and speaks with his mother. Throughout their dialogue, he lays on the floor of the cave in a position reminiscent of a fetus. The words he speaks are likewise childish; at one point, he cries out, "The men screamed! The men bellowed and screamed! The men hurt me, hurt my ear." Not only do his simple, repetitive sentences suggest a child's voice, but his fear of and dismay at the men show him to be the opposite of their tyrant, ruler, master, or captain.

Support from the movie.

The reduction of Grendel's evilness and power can perhaps be traced to the biggest difference between the epic and the movie's Grendel: that of Grendel's lineage. As mentioned in the introduction, the movie portrays Grendel's mother as a seductress, with the premise that she once seduced King Hrothgar, making Grendel the offspring of Hrothgar and the mother. On the other hand, the original epic is very clear—and frequently emphasizes—that Grendel is a descendent of Cain, who committed the first murder. Referring to Cain, the epic reads, "From him there woke to life all the evil broods, monsters and elves and sea-beasts, and giants too, who long time strove with God" (14–15). There is no room for a human in this description, and certainly not Hrothgar, whom the epic praises as being a "good king." By changing Grendel's parentage, the movie shifts the root of evil from Grendel to Hrothgar. It is because of Hrothgar's past weakness that his kingdom is plagued by the fruit of that very weakness. Grendel, then, is a by-product, a mere pawn in the struggle between Hrothgar's kingdom and the mother's corrupting ways. The mother uses Grendel's

Transition sentence that leads into the third point of the thesis.

Melmott 5

death as a way to further corrupt the kingdom through her seduction of Beowulf—and Beowulf succumbs.

In the retelling of an existing story—whether that retelling be in the form of a story, a poem, or a movie—there will always be similarities and differences. But the difference in the role of the villain between an epic written in 1000 and a movie filmed in 2007 tells us something about our contemporary society. As we noted briefly in the introduction, Beowulf's seduction makes him less heroic; likewise, we have seen that the movie makes Grendel less villainous in motivation, in power, and in lineage. We might ask ourselves: What does it mean to live in an age where we see heroes as fallible and villains as innocent? The difference between the epic Grendel and the movie Grendel offers an answer: the original villain has been turned into a product of human vice, suggesting that true villainy lies in human behavior. Or, to put it another way, in a world where human deeds are monstrous, there isn't much room for a monster.

Brief reiteration of the three points made in the paper.

Conclusion broadens significance to our own society.

Conclusion explains the implication of the thesis; answers the "so what?" question.

Works Cited

Beowulf. Dir. Robert Zemeckis. Perf. Crispin Glover, Anthony Hopkins, Angelina Jolie, and Ray Winstone. Paramount Pictures, 2007. Film.

Beowulf. Trans. Seamus Heaney. *The Norton Anthology of English Literature.* 7th ed. Ed. M.H. Abrams and Stephen Greenblatt. New York: W.W. Norton, 2000. 32–99. Print.

Beowulf. Trans. Chauncey Brewster Tinker. New York: Newson & Co., 1902. Print.

"Reck." Def. 1b. *The Oxford English Dictionary.* 2nd ed. 1989. Print.

3f USE CRITIQUE TO BRING IN YOUR OWN EVALUATION

We define a critique as a summary with your own reasonable opinion. Whether you are asked to critique a reading for an essay exam, the accuracy of a website as a source, or respond to an argument, in most of your courses, you will be required to evaluate the presentation of information.

- What is the work (or performance) trying to accomplish?
- Does it achieve its purpose?
- Do you agree or disagree with the piece, like or dislike it?
- How has the piece created this reaction in you?

Review.   A critique is a formal evaluation of a text, and one of the most common forms of critique in literature is the review. In a review, you—as the reviewer—get to evaluate the text or, in the case of live theatre, a performance. For an example of a review, see the response to Anton Chekhov's early story "Rapture" in chapter 2. After a few general, opening sentences, the discussion becomes more specific as the student asserts that the main character's lack of change makes the story unsatisfying. The student continues by analyzing the various parts of the story. As your review progresses and you begin to make evaluative statements—such as *The story begins on a strong note but deteriorates; The casting was so well-done that it carries the play from start to finish; The poem's sonnet form is perfect for its content*—you will also need to analyze why you are reacting to the text in that particular way. Particularly strong is his division of the story into three parts:

> *Part one: the clerk runs in, announcing himself, disrupting the household, waking his brothers. Part two: Mitya takes out the newspaper and urges his father to read it aloud. In the closing sequence, a reader may expect something to happen as a result of Mitya's "rapture" that he has become famous because his name is in the paper and on the police record. However, as the ancient philosopher and critic Aristotle might put it, what is the dramatic purpose here? . . . His parents and his siblings humor him instead of contradicting or berating him; thus making change less likely for Mitya. The reader is left to wonder what the point is, and without that concluding action, the dramatic purpose is unclear, and the story is incomplete and ultimately unsatisfying.*

Notice here that the author is not afraid to make bold claims: that the story is incomplete and unsatisfying. You may feel a little intimidated the first time you write a review, especially if the author is well known. Take the Chekhov paper to heart; the validity of an evaluation rests not on how highly you are ranking a noted author but on how your analysis of the story supports your evaluation. In this case, the student has analyzed the structure of the story, and found that in a story set up for a three-part movement, the third part is missing. Therefore, when he claims that the story is incomplete and unsatisfying, we see the author's point.

Guidelines for Writing Reviews

Introduce What You Are Evaluating

- Include the title and author.

- For a live performance, include who performed, when, and under what circumstances (a full house? an outdoor amphitheater?).

- Be clear about what you are evaluating.

Set Up Your Review with a Summary

- Your summary is to be used as a reference point for your discussion; you may not want to give the ending away, however.

Put the Piece into Context

- What type of work is it? A comedy? A tragedy?

- When was it written?

- If it is a well-known play such as Shakespeare, include any unusual information on the "take" of the director (what's the director's purpose in staging Shakespeare's "Hamlet" in Pakistan, for example).

Analyze the Text

- For a play, note the staging, lighting, and costuming as well as the acting.

- Note how the work is structured.

- Look at the individual elements: plot, character, dialogue.

- Determine the purpose of the work.

Include Your Reasoned Opinion: This Is Your Evaluation

- Did the work achieve its purpose?

- What is your response to the selection and why?

- Agree or disagree with the presentation of information (whether or not it achieved its purpose).

- Base your agreement or disagreement on evidence.

End with a Balanced Conclusion

- Recap the pros and cons of the piece.

- Give your overall reaction.

3g FIND AN EFFECTIVE APPROACH TO THE ESSAY EXAM

Timed writing on an exam may seem like an intimidating prospect. Reviewing the tips below will help you learn an effective approach to essay exams, whether you are taking one for a class in English, political science, or psychology.

1. Prepare.   If you have been diligent in annotating the texts you read and keeping a journal or freewriting exercises, be sure to review these materials before the day of your exam. Jog your memory about each story, poem, novel, or play you have read for the class by reviewing major characters and events of the work, as well as any important information about the authors.

2. Pace yourself.   When you receive the exam, glance through it to see approximately how much time you should spend on each section. Remember that if an essay is worth, say, 70 percent of the grade, you want to make it a priority to spend sufficient time on it.

3. Read the assignment carefully.   When you arrive at the essay question, circle key words as you read the assignment. Pay particular attention to the verbs your instructor uses: common choices are *explain, discuss, analyze, compare, contrast, interpret,* and *argue.* Your understanding of the different types of assignments addressed in this chapter can help you here.

Understanding Essay Exam Assignments

The words explain *or* discuss *ask you to engage in a detailed way, much like an explication or a close reading.*

Analyze *should remind you of what you know about an analysis paper—that your job is to explore one element of the text and show how it contributes to the overall work.*

Compare *and* contrast *asks you to find similarities and differences between two items and to suggest what those similarities or differences emphasize or illuminate.*

Argue *is a way of asking you to take a position about an issue, or in the case of a literary text, to defend what you see in the work that may not be readily apparent to others.*

4. Form a thesis.   In an essay exam, your thesis will likely be a simpler statement than the type of complex argument you would form in a longer research paper or analysis. Look at the phrasing of the question itself to help you shape your thesis.

EXAMPLE OF AN ESSAY EXAM ASSIGNMENT

➡ *Analyze Frost's use of imagery in "Stopping By Woods on a Snowy Evening."*

EXAMPLE OF A THESIS THAT RESPONDS TO THE ASSIGNMENT

Frost uses idyllic, New England imagery to disguise a more serious statement about death.

5. Outline briefly.   Even if you don't typically work from an outline when writing a paper, take a few moments to jot down a brief outline. In an essay exam, even a brief outline will keep you from freezing up entirely. And, if you find you are spending too much time on the first paragraph, you can quickly wrap it up to move on to the next point in your outline. In short, an outline can help you budget time and space in your essay while eliminating the stressful feeling of not knowing where to go next.

6. Check your work.   Try your best to allow a little extra time in which to read over what you have written. Time constraints often make even the best students leave out words or write sentences that make no sense. Rereading your work will allow you to fix these problems.

Follow our model student, Renee Knox, as she completes the following essay assignment on a timed exam.

Notes for a Sample Student Essay Exam

Renee identifies key words in the prompt. Already, she knows her paper must focus on the significance of the imagery.

Renee underlines the imagery in the poem and highlights phrases she finds significant.

Assignment: Analyze Frost's use of imagery in "Stopping By Woods on a Snowy Evening," reproduced below.

Stopping By <u>Woods</u> On A <u>Snowy</u> Evening

Whose <u>woods</u> these are I think I know.	1
His <u>house</u> is in the <u>village</u> though;	2
He will not see me stopping here	3
To watch his <u>woods fill up with snow.</u>	4
My <u>little horse</u> must think it queer	5
To stop <u>without a farmhouse near</u>	6
<u>Between the woods and frozen lake</u>	7
<u>The darkest evening of the year.</u>	8
He gives his harness bells a shake	9
To ask if there is some mistake.	10
The only other <u>sound's the sweep</u>	11
<u>Of easy wind and downy flake.</u>	12
<u>The woods</u> are <u>lovely, dark and deep.</u>	13
But I have promises to keep,	14
And miles to go before I sleep,	15
And miles to go before I sleep.	16

Renee numbers the lines for easy reference when she quotes in the essay.

Important images: woods, snow, horse, house, village, dark, wind, snowflakes, dark

> woods, snow, horse, farmhouse, village=New England; ideal Christmas scene
>
> no farmhouse near, dark, deep, winter=cold, alone, death??
> sleep=death?

Renee notes that many of her underlined phrases bring to mind a farm-like, New England setting. Then she separates out the other images and names their connotations.

Thesis: Frost uses pretty New England imagery to disguise a more serious statement about death.

Renee formulates a thesis based on her observations.

Renee generates a brief outline to follow. In constructing her essay, she will use a 5 paragraph structure.

I.   Introduction and thesis
II.   Set up "pretty" imagery
    A. Mention horse
    B. Mention farmhouse
    C. Mention woods
    D. Mention snow
    E. Adds up to ideal Christmas village scene
III. Set up dark imagery and cold effect
    A. Snow
    B. Woods
    C. Wind
    D. Solitary
IV.   Discuss symbolic significance of images
    A. Snow=winter=death
    B. Woods=wild, easily lose your way
    C. Sleep=form of death
V.   Conclusion—why would Frost do this?

Sample Student Essay Exam

Knox 1

Renee Knox

Professor Giordano

ENGL 1203

5 November 2008

Imagery in Frost's "Stopping By Woods on a Snowy Evening"

Many times in literature, as in life, something appears to be one thing but is actually another. One need only think of tales like "Little Red Riding Hood" in which the woman who appears to be her grandmother turns out to be a wolf. In a similar way, Robert Frost's "Stopping By Woods on a Snowy Evening" appears to be a simple and charming experience. Instead, Frost uses idyllic New England imagery to disguise a more serious statement about death.

Even in the poem's title, Frost is already using imagery, for the title presents woods, snow, and evening. We can picture an evening scene in which snow is softly falling on woods. And indeed, the speaker is there with his "little horse" (line 5) that wears "harness bells" (9). The mention of a village (2) and a farmhouse (6), even though the speaker is not near them, suggests that villages and farmhouses dot the landscape in which the speaker moves. Put all together—snow, a horse with harness bells, a village, and a farmhouse—Frost's imagery conjures a New England scene that is so quaint, it is exactly the type of scene many people replicate with porcelain villages at Christmas time—it is that perfect.

However, if we look at the nature imagery, we get a much darker picture. While evening might connote a soothing time of leisure after the day's work is done, it is also the time of oncoming dark, as Frost's imagery indicates when he describes it as "the darkest evening of the year" (8). In fact, Frost calls attention to the fact that it is the darkest evening by placing that description in line 8, the exact center of the 16-line poem. Furthermore, he repeats "dark" again when he describes the woods as "dark and deep" (13), adding emphasis to the imagery of dark through repetition. We also know that the evening is cold, and although snow is a part of an idyllic New England Christmas scene, it is equally an unpleasant feeling with bleak connotations. If the world is cold, it means that it is not treating you well. Beyond this kind of cold, there

Renee uses a simple but complete title, in order not to spend too much time on it.

Thesis statement. When Renee reread her essay, she changed "pretty" to "idyllic" for more sophisticated diction.

Renee stays on topic by following her outline.

Renee helps her paper flow by using "however" to signal her transition to her next point.

Knox 2

Renee further analyzes the imagery she set up in the previous paragraph to ensure she sufficiently answers the prompt.

is the sensory imagery of the only sound being "the sweep / of easy wind and downy flake" (11-12). In other words, the narrator is not only out in the cold, but he is so alone that he actually hears the snowflakes falling in the wind. When put together with the dark, this is a bleak and lonely scene.

Renee supports her point with specific examples from the text.

Beyond the sensory unpleasantness of dark and cold, these images have symbolic meaning when placed in the context of other literature. Frost's imagery clearly places this moment in winter, which traditionally symbolizes death, much as spring symbolizes rebirth. Moreover, even though the woods are "lovely," they are also "dark and deep," a place where in much of literature, like Shakespeare's "A Midsummer Night's Dream," characters easily lose themselves or succumb to supernatural forces. Perhaps the woods are "lovely" because their darkness tantalizes the narrator to lose himself, but if you followed such an idea through, the speaker would end up lost and frozen in the dark woods. The last lines reinforce the idea that he is being tempted by death. When recalling himself from gazing into the cold, dark woods, the speaker gives his reason as having "miles to go before I sleep" (15). Sleep, like winter, is another way of suggesting death, for much of literature speaks of death as a type of eternal sleep.

Renee transitions to a brief but insightful conclusion.

Thus, while the scene's first impression is one of a quaint New England night— an impression built through imagery of horse, village, farmhouse, and snow—the cold and dark nature imagery tells another story of death and the temptation to remain in the presence of death. By bringing these two types of imagery together in one poem, Frost perhaps suggests that death is always near, even when we think we are looking at a vivid scene of comfort. Or, to put a more optimistic spin on things, since some of the images overlap (snowy woods are both beautiful and dangerous), Frost might be trying to tell us that death is nothing to fear, that even on the darkest evening, there is still loveliness in the dark of the woods and the sweep of the flake.

In reading Renee's essay, you may have noticed that there were places that sounded a little rough or colloquial and other spots that weren't perfectly explained, such as the end of the fourth paragraph. However, her main ideas are clear and her conclusion compelling. She also used specific support and stayed exactly on topic with what the assignment asked her to do. For these reasons, Renee's essay is well done because the constraints of a timed setting often force the writer to leave a few rough spots. If you have time, do your best to revise, but remember that a timed essay will almost never have the same polished quality as a paper you have had time to think about, draft, and revise.

4 Quoting, Paraphrasing, Summarizing, and Avoiding Plagiarism

4a KNOW WHAT INFORMATION REQUIRES DOCUMENTATION

When writing from sources—whether a single source, as when you respond to a story, poem, or play you have just read, or multiple sources, as when you include research—you will need to effectively use quotation, paraphrase, and summary in your paper. Quotation, paraphrase, and summary are the evidence you use for your interpretation of a work, and it is common for all three to be employed in the same paper. **Plagiarism** occurs when this material isn't presented accurately. In this chapter, you will find information on how to keep track of the author, title, or URL for any source you have consulted (see also Writing the Research Paper, Avoiding Plagiarism, and Documenting Sources). Keeping track of sources is critical, because how you present your evidence determines more than just how convincing your paper is; it keeps your paper honest by giving your readers

- A framework (who, what, when, where, and how) for your response.
- The specifics in the source that led you to your observations, thoughts, and connections.

Marginal annotations, underlined and highlighted passages, or notes in a reading journal help you trace your response back to specific source material. Your interaction with one text or many provides the basis of your interpretation and the thesis of your paper. Whether you base your paper on a single source or you work with multiple sources, you will likely need to summarize a work to provide your reader with a framework for your analysis. When working with multiple sources, you may also need to summarize a number of critical opinions. It is likely you will paraphrase a short passage to give your reader context for your assessment or the point of view of a scholarly work. Should you be writing about drama, you'll likely quote from the play; should you be discussing a poem, it's almost inevitable that several lines of poetry will be included in your discussion. The guidelines provided here will keep you from plagiarizing when you have summarized, paraphrased, or quoted sources. You will always want to document in your paper where you found the kinds of information listed in the following box.

Information Requiring Documentation

- Lines from a story, poem, or play
- Opinions, observations, interpretations by writers, critics, and scholars
- Information from expert and/or sponsored sites
- Visual materials, including tables, charts, or graphs
- Footnotes from printed sources
- Statements that are open to debate
- Historical information that is not commonly known
- Statistics, or surveys, census or poll results if you use them

SAMPLES OF TYPES OF INFORMATION REQUIRING DOCUMENTATION

The whaling industry in nineteenth-century America collapsed when flexible steel hoops replaced whalebone in women's corsets.

A twenty-year Swiss study of organic farming found that organic farms yielded more produce per unit of energy consumed than farms that did not use organic farming methods.

Smoking kills over 418,000 people every year in the United States.

The easiest way to avoid plagiarism is to remember that you must tell your reader the sources of all facts, ideas, and opinions that are taken from others that are not considered common knowledge. If a number of sources contain the same information and that information is widely considered to be true, it is considered common knowledge. For example, in biology, the structure of DNA and the process of cell division or photosynthesis are considered common knowledge. A recent scientific discovery about genetics, however, would not be common knowledge, so you would need to cite the source of this information. When in doubt cite your source; citing is never incorrect.

COMMON KNOWLEDGE (DOCUMENTATION NOT REQUIRED)

Millions of soldiers died in the trenches of the Western front in World War I.

Mohandas K. Gandhi was assassinated in 1948.

The cheetah is the fastest-moving land animal.

Tip for Avoiding Plagiarism and the Web.   What you find on the Web requires extra precaution to make sure you document correctly where you got your information. Do not assume that what you find on the Web is common knowledge. Write in your notes the URL as well as *the date* that you accessed the site. Websites are notoriously prone to change, so this helps you keep your source clear. In your notes, put quotation marks around anything that is a direct quotation (wherever you found the information, print or online) so that you can easily see when you are using another's words. It is easy to cut whole passages from the Internet and paste them into your paper, or to think you have paraphrased when you have quoted if your notes aren't effective. This is plagiarism. Diligence is needed to avoid cobbling together a patchwork of sources without complete and accurate source information.

4b USE SOURCES TO SUPPORT YOUR COMMENTARY

Your paper is your own independent thought. A quotation, paraphrase, or summary should be used only if you are going to comment on it in your paper. You can expand upon a quotation, paraphrase, or summary. You can interpret it. You can indicate what you believe the work implies. You can refer to a quotation, paraphrase, or a summary. You can even disagree. Your instructor is looking at your work to make sure you have understood a selection and to see what you have discovered for yourself. So, do not worry that you don't have anything original to say. Few do, even among professionals. *How* you say what you have to say is original to you. Don't apologize by suggesting this is only your opinion ("it seems to me" or "in my opinion"). Make your case. Be confident that, if you have discovered something that is interesting to you, it will also be interesting to your reader.

- A paper with too few references to sources does not provide the evidence you need to support your case.
- A paper with too many references to sources prevents you from making your case because it is overshadowed by the ideas of others.

Use Quotation, Summary, Paraphrase

- To support a point
- To present your source's point of view
- To disagree with your source
- To generalize from examples
- To reason through examples
- To make comparisons
- To distinguish fact from opinion
- To provide context

1. Quotation: *A word-for-word copy from an original source.* Direct quotation is especially useful when you are writing about literature because the way a writer uses words is central to an understanding of the text You will use quotations as examples of the way a writer uses language. However, you can also use a quotation from another source if a technical term is used that is not easily rephrased or if rephrasing it would change its meaning. You may want to use a quotation when the ideas are so vividly and beautifully expressed that you prefer to avoid paraphrase. Even if you do, a direct quotation is not to be used as a conclusion or summation of your main point in your work. It doesn't stand on its own. You must expand upon any quotation—or paraphrase or summary—that you include in your paper.

Tip on Avoiding Plagiarism in a Quotation: Using quotation marks around information from a source while changing or omitting information from that source is a serious error. Use *brackets* [ ] around a word or words you insert in a quotation. Use three periods in succession (**ellipses**) . . . to show that you have omitted something that was in the original quotation: "He turned green . . . but he went on [to steer the ship]."

ORIGINAL SOURCE (from page 7 of *The Metaphysical Club* by Louis Menand).

> We think of the Civil War as a war to save the union and to abolish slavery, but before the fighting began most people regarded these as incompatible ideals. Northerners who wanted to preserve the union did not wish to see slavery extended into the territories; some of them hoped it would wither away in the states where it persisted. But many Northern businessmen believed that losing the South would mean economic catastrophe, and many of their employees believed that freeing the slaves would mean lower wages. They feared secession far more than they disliked slavery, and they were unwilling to risk the former by trying to pressure the South into giving up the latter.

➡ *For more practice with quotation, paraphrase, and summary using this example and many others, visit www.mhhe.com/delbancole.*

SERIOUS ERROR

Menand notes that "many Northern businessmen and many of their employees feared secession far more than they disliked slavery, and they were unwilling to risk the former by trying to pressure the South into giving up the latter" (7).

➡ *This sentence is unacceptable because the writer has not used ellipses to indicate where words have been omitted from the quotation.*

CORRECT QUOTATION

Menand notes that "many Northern businessmen . . . and many of their employees . . . feared secession far more than they disliked slavery, and they were unwilling to risk the former by trying to pressure the South into giving up the latter" (7).

2. Paraphrase: *Someone else's ideas in your own words.* When writing about literature, you may paraphrase some of the story line in order to get to the point you want to make. In research, paraphrase is most often used when you are referring to the work of critics and scholars. If you find that the language you are trying to put into your words is already broken down to its most simple form, or that the language is too perfectly worded to change, you may want to use a quotation instead of a paraphrase. Don't paraphrase if you are not entirely sure you understand the original or you risk misrepresenting its original meaning. One test of a good paraphrase is if you can restate what you are trying to paraphrase without looking at the source.

Tip on Avoiding Plagiarism in a Paraphrase: A true paraphrase is not just a few different words, even if you feel the scholar has said something better than you could have said it yourself. *Your words* are the words that matter to your instructor. Just changing a few words—*even when you indicate the source of the paraphrase*—is still plagiarism. In a true paraphrase, the sentence structure is your own. It doesn't sound like the original; it sounds like you.

PLAGIARISM

Menand observes that before the Civil War, many Northerners feared secession far more than they disliked slavery, and they were unwilling to risk the former by trying to pressure the South into giving up the latter (7).

➡ *This quotation is plagiarized because it uses the exact words of the source—most of a sentence—without quotation marks.*

CORRECT PARAPHRASE

> Menand observes that before the Civil War, many Northerners were afraid that secession would be worse for the country than slavery, and they were not willing to try and force the South to give up slavery for fear that a disastrous Southern secession would follow (7).

3. Summary: *A condensation of the main idea or action that includes only the supporting details related directly to that main idea.* Unlike a paraphrase, where a concept or action from a brief passage is explained in your own words, a summary lays out a long passage (such as an act in a play or a whole poem, story, play, or other work). When writing about literature, a plot summary is not enough. A summary sets the stage for an analysis, providing your readers with enough information for them to understand your commentary. In a research paper, summary can also be used to provide examples of a variety of points of view on your topic. Make comparisons between two points of view, then summarize several sources to build upon for your conclusion. (See the chapter on Common Writing Assignments for a discussion of the summary paper.)

Tip on Avoiding Plagiarism in a Summary: When you summarize information, you must include information on the source or it will appear as if you are using someone else's ideas as your own. Omitting information in a summary that alters the source's meaning is also unacceptable. Offering an inaccurate interpretation of your source in a summary is not satisfactory either. If the source's words or meaning do not support your argument as fully as you might like, find another source that does.

PLAGIARISM

> People believed that the Civil War was a war to save the union and to abolish slavery, but before the fighting began most people regarded these as incompatible ideals.

➡ *The sentence does not acknowledge that the idea comes from a source and is, therefore, an example of plagiarism. Ideas and words from a source cannot be included as if they are your own. You must give credit to the original writer.*

CORRECT SUMMARY

> According to Menand, during the Civil War people did not believe both that slavery could be abolished and the union could be saved (7).

4c ACKNOWLEDGE YOUR SOURCES

In the case of paraphrases, summaries, and direct quotations, your paper itself must include information about your source (an in-text citation), including an introductory phrase with the author and title, and the page number(s), URL, or line numbers (for a poem or play) placed immediately following the cited material and usually preceding any punctuation marks that divide or end the sentence. (See block quotation later in the next section, p. H-79.)

IN-TEXT CITATION

According to Louis Menand in his book on the Civil War, *The Metaphysical Club*, people believed that "the Civil War was a war to save the union and to abolish slavery, but before the fighting began most people regarded these as incompatible ideals" (7).

Professional organizations (such as the Modern Language Association or the American Psychological Association) provide guidelines for how sources should be acknowledged in a paper. MLA guidelines are commonly used in writing for the humanities, and those guidelines are followed here. For more information on how to properly cite electronic and print sources using the MLA documentation styles, see the chapters on Writing the Research Paper and MLA Documentation.

Keep a running list of your sources. The more accurate and complete the information on your sources, the easier it will be to present that source accurately and completely in your paper. In addition to in-text citation, you must also provide a complete and accurate list of all the texts you have consulted in a list at the end of your paper called a **bibliography.** Anything you have cited in your paper must be included in the final bibliography for that paper. Other works, not referenced in your paper, can be included as well. The best way to prevent plagiarism is to make sure you keep precise records of the sources you consult while preparing your paper in a **working bibliography**—a list of all the sources you've used, as well as all the information you'll use to cite them later. For your working bibliography, make sure to include this information:

- The names of all the authors, editors, and/or translators of the piece
- The complete title of the work and relevant chapter title or heading; for Web pages, the name of the site and the page on which the information appears
- The publisher, copyright date, edition, and place of publication should be recorded for sources from books.
- The date, volume, issue, and page number should be included for all sources from periodicals or journals (including those you have pulled up from an online database).
- The URL (complete web address), the date the page was updated, and the date you viewed the page should be recorded for all sources from the Internet.

Plagiarism can be intentional or unintentional. Professors are adept at recognizing papers obtained via the Web—they've likely seen them before! However, unintentional plagiarism carries the same penalties. This chapter should help you avoid plagiarizing unintentionally, and you will soon be found out if your plagiarism is of the other kind.

Two Kinds of Plagiarism

Intentional plagiarism	Intentional plagiarism occurs when you buy someone else's work or copy something from a source, usually word for word, and use it without quotation marks or acknowledgment of the source, as if it were your own words.
Unintentional plagiarism	Unintentional plagiarism can result from careless note taking, such as forgetting to put quotation marks around material you copy, cutting and pasting from the web, and using material you have summarized or paraphrased and forgetting to tell readers the source of that material.

4d FORMAT QUOTATIONS TO AVOID PLAGIARISM

When you integrate your ideas with those of your sources, you will want to format your quotations so that they flow naturally into your sentences and build toward your conclusion. Where possible, keep your quotation brief, four or fewer lines for prose and no more than three for poetry or drama, since you will comment on the entire quotation in your paper. If you include a long quotation (five lines or more for prose or four or more for poetry or drama) make sure you include the entire quotation for your interpretation or analysis. Otherwise, the quotation overshadows your argument instead of supporting it. Introducing a direct quotation into a text can happen in two ways depending on whether it is short or long; each is formatted differently.

- A short quotation within a sentence is identified by quotation marks.
- A long quotation formatted in an indented block of text separated out from a sentence does not use quotation marks.

1. Refer to your source in an introductory phrase.   Whether your quotation is short or long, however, you will need to introduce it with an introductory (*signal*) phrase. You need to identify the source and the author *before* the quotation. An in-text citation requires that you include the author's full name (without Mr., Miss, Mrs., or Ms.) the first time you quote from the source. Unless there is a long lapse between references to the source, the second time you quote from the same source you should use only the author's last name. Treat women and men equally when you cite them as authors, using the last name only for the second citation and no *Miss, Mrs.*, or *Ms.* Avoid the repetition of *the author says.*

Verbs to Use in an Introductory Phrase

according to	considers	notes
adds		
admits	declares	observes
aknowledges	denies	
agrees	describes	points out
asks	disagrees	proposes
asserts		proves
argues	emphasizes	
	establishes	refutes
believes	explains	rejects
	expresses	remarks
charges		reports
claims	finds	responds
comments		
compares	holds	shows
complains		states
concedes	implies	speculates
concludes	insists	suggests
contends	interprets	
continues		warns
	maintains	

2. Integrate a short quotation in a sentence and always use quotation marks. Always put a short quotation into quotation marks. Not to do so constitutes plagiarism. Keep your quotations to the point. The source material you quote as a reference should provide backup for the argument you have made. Avoid the temptation to use sources to make your arguments for you, however well the source is worded. References from outside sources, whether they are paraphrased or quoted, are *evidence* or *support* for your own arguments.

You should not use outside sources to make arguments for you.

- Use an introductory phrase to identify the source.
- If the quotation flows into the natural wording of the sentence, begin the quotation with a lowercase letter whether or not the original is capitalized.
- If your introductory phrase ends with a comma, use a capital letter.
- Use quotation marks.
- When quoting poetry in a sentence, use the format of the lines in the poem and break the lines exactly as they appear in the poem with a slash / mark.
- Place periods and commas inside the quotation marks.
- Semicolons, colons, and dashes are placed outside the quotation marks.
- Question marks and exclamation points are sometimes placed inside the quotation marks and sometimes placed outside. If the quotation is itself a question or exclamation, the question mark/exclamation point goes inside the quotation marks.
- Include page numbers for prose, line numbers for poems, act, scene, and line numbers for plays written in verse and page numbers for plays written in prose.

A SHORT QUOTATION FROM A POEM

In Robert Frost's "Stopping by Woods on a Snowy Evening," the hypnotic rhythm of the poem is reinforced through the repetition of the speaker's last lines, "And I have miles to go before I sleep / And I have miles to go before I sleep" (lines 15-16).

INTEGRATING A QUOTATION WITH A LOWERCASE LETTER

Even certain details of Grendel's portrayal in the movie echo the original epic. For example, the epic introduces him by calling him an inhabitant of "the abode of monster kind" (line 14).

PERIOD INSIDE QUOTATION MARK

Blake again disrupts the meter when he writes, "And I saw it was filled with graves" (line 9), which draws attention to the word "graves."

—from the student paper on William Blake's "The Garden of Love" in Common Assignments across the Curriculum.

SEMICOLON OUTSIDE QUOTATION MARKS

> He is called a "fiend of hell"; "wrathful spirit"; "mighty stalker of the marches"
> (line 14); "creature of destruction, fierce and greedy, wild and furious" (15); and
> a "terrible monster, like a dark shadow of death" (17).
>
> > —from the student paper on the role of Grendel in *Beowulf*, the epic and
> > the movie, in Common Assignments across the Curriculum.

3. Set off a long quotation in a block, and don't use quotation marks. Quotations in block format should be used sparingly because they break up your discussion and can be distracting. If you find that you do not need to refer back to a long quote in several instances, consider using a paraphrase or more precise direct quotation to present the information. If you use a long quotation to support your point, you must set the quote apart:

- Use an introductory phrase to identify the source.
- Punctuate the end of an introductory phrase with a comma or a colon.
- Leave a line of space before and after the long quotation.
- Do not use quotation marks.
- Indent each line of the quotation by ten spaces from the left margin (right margin is not indented).
- Capitalize the first word whether or not it is capitalized in the original unless quoting poetry.
- When quoting poetry, follow the line format exactly as it appears in the poem.
- Double-space.
- Include a page number (or line numbers for a poem) in parentheses after the final punctuation in the quotation.

BLOCK QUOTATION

> As her spirit wanes, our heroine in Charlotte Perkins Gilman's "Yellow
> Wallpaper" gives her soliloquy:
>
> > I lie down ever so much now. John says it is good for me, and to sleep
> > all I can. Indeed he started the habit by making me lie down for an hour
> > after each meal. It is a very bad habit, I am convinced, for you see, I don't
> > sleep. And that cultivates deceit, for I don't tell them I'm awake—oh, no!
> > The fact is I'm getting a little afraid of John. (226)

4e FORMAT A PARAPHRASE TO AVOID PLAGIARISM

Using paraphrase in your paper is similar to using quotation, but there are some areas that require extra care. Make sure you have understood the text you are paraphrasing; your paraphrase must be true to the original meaning of the text. Don't guess at the meaning of a text by changing a few words and letting it stand for your own idea. This is plagiarism. Even if one part of the text can be construed to support your argument, don't use it if that part doesn't represent the whole source accurately. Make it clear where your ideas end and the ideas of others begin. In addition to giving credit to others for their ideas, a clear transition from your own work to your source materials gives your writing credibility.

- Keep your paraphrase brief.
- Refer to the source in an introductory phrase.
- Include the page number in parentheses after the paraphrase.
- A period, question mark, or exclamation point goes after the page number when the page number is at the end of a sentence.

ORIGINAL SOURCE MATERIAL

Although Emily Dickinson was a noted wit in her circle of friends and family, and although her poetry is surely clever, frequently downright funny, and as we shall argue, throughout possessed of a significant comic vision, criticism has paid little attention to her humor. Dickinson's profound scrutiny of life-and-death matters has usually taken precedence in the analysis and evaluation of her work. Yet comedy is a part of that profundity.

—from "Comedy and Audience in Emily Dickinson's Poetry" by Suzanne Juhasz, Cristanne Miller, and Martha Nell Smith (See the McGraw-Hill website for the full text of this article that accompanies the Frost/Dickinson case studies.)

PARAPHRASE

Because Emily Dickinson's poetry concerns itself with serious issues like mortality, critics have long overlooked the comedy that aids her poems' success. Those who knew Dickinson personally recognized her smart humor, which shines through her poems but has since gone unnoticed. The authors of the article wish to reverse this trend of neglect, as Dickinson's witty touches are important to understanding her oeuvre.

4f FORMAT SUMMARY TO AVOID PLAGIARISM

Summary and paraphrase are certainly related, but they are not the same thing. In general, paraphrase is used for a smaller portion of the original source, and your goal is to capture the spirit of the passage you are paraphrasing, without exactly copying the sentence structure or word choice. Summary is useful for relating a larger idea that you gained from a longer passage of text, as the above example shows.

Paraphrase	Summary
• a relatively short passage	• a passage of any length
• covers every point in the passage	• condenses main idea and support
• takes up points consecutively	• changes order when necessary
• includes no interpretation	• explains point of passage

When you write a summary, introduce your source and identify the main ideas of the text. Break the discussion of those ideas into sections, and then write a sentence or two in your own words that captures each section.

ORIGINAL SOURCE

A figure who played a major role in popularizing swing in the mid-1930s was Benny Goodman. Like Whiteman earlier and Elvis Presley a few decades later, Goodman was a white musician who could successfully mediate between a black American musical tradition and the large base of white listeners making up the majority population in the USA. Wearing glasses and conservative suits—"looking like a high school science teacher," according to one observer (Stowe 45)—Goodman appeared to be an ordinary, respectable white American. Musically he was anything but ordinary: a virtuoso clarinetist, a skilled improviser who could solo "hot" on up tempo numbers and "sweet" on ballads, and a disciplined bandleader who demanded excellence from his players. [. . .]

In the guise of swing, jazz became domesticated in the 1930s. Earlier, jazz had been associated with gin mills and smoky cabarets, illegal substances (alcohol and drugs) and illicit sex. Swing generally enjoyed a more wholesome reputation, although some preached of the dangers it posed to the morals of young people. This exuberant, extroverted music performed by well-dressed ensembles and their clean-cut leaders entered middle-class households through everyday appliances like the living-room Victrola and the kitchen radio. It reached a wider populace as musicians transported it from large urban centers into small towns and rural areas. Criss-crossing North America by bus, car, and train, big bands played single night engagements in dance halls, ballrooms, theatres, hotels, night clubs, country clubs, military bases, and outdoor pavilions. They attracted hordes of teenagers who came to hear the popular songs of the day and dance the jitterbug, lindy hop and Susie Q. The strenuous touring schedule of big bands was far from glamorous. Nevertheless, musicians who played in these ensembles could symbolize achievement and prove inspirational, as the writer Ralph Ellison recalled from his early years growing up in Oklahoma City. . . .

Mark Tucker and Travis A. Jackson. "Jazz." *Grove Music Online.* Oxford UP. Web. 11 May 2008.

EXAMPLE OF SUMMARY

Swing, which became the popular dance music in more reputable venues than just bars and clubs, was usually performed by big bands under the direction of white leaders like Benny Goodman and Glenn Miller. Thus, jazz became mainstream and middle class, unlike the "hot jazz" of the twenties.

5 Writing the Research Paper, Avoiding Plagiarism, and Documenting Sources

5a UNDERSTAND RESEARCH TODAY

Research today often makes its first stop at the World Wide Web. You might even access the library through your computer. Navigating the research process, therefore, requires critical skills not asked of your predecessors for one of the most common assignments across the curriculum. While the Web makes it more convenient to do your research at three o'clock in the morning if you like, it also brings with it a new set of challenges. Today you don't just find sources, you have to manage the thousands of hits you might get when you google a topic. The Web also makes it more difficult to see what is credible and valid when every site looks largely the same on the computer screen. Plus, the Web makes it easy to create a patchwork cut-and-paste of sources that can lead to unintentional plagiarism. Plagiarism occurs when a source is not properly acknowledged, and whenever you conduct research from outside sources, you run the risk of taking credit for another person's ideas. For more information on acknowledging sources, see our chapter on Quoting, Paraphrasing, Summarizing, and Avoiding Plagiarism.

This chapter will get you started on your research project and also provide guidelines for documentation that keep you from unintentionally plagiarizing someone else's work. How you take notes is more important than ever if you are to distinguish your own work from the work you have found online (or in print). In literature, your instructor is likely to want a variety of sources, not just online references. There are three basic kinds of sources with which you will be working:

- Books
- Print magazines, newspapers, or scholarly journals
- Non-print online sources

The type of source you want to use depends on the type of project you are working on. If you are approaching a piece of literature from a particular critical perspective—like the feminist, Marxist, or psychoanalytical schools of thought discussed in our chapter on Critical Approaches to Literature—your research will likely involve reading literary criticism. If you are embarking on historical criticism or biographical criticism, you will need to gear your research to sources that inform you about a time period or your author's life. This chapter provides a step-by-step walkthrough of the research process. Read the student research paper on Langston Hughes at the end of this chapter to see how these steps look in action.

5b CHOOSE A TOPIC

Often, your instructor will assign a topic or provide some guidance. Or, you can find several research topics in this textbook, especially at the end of each case study. We have provided not only the topics, but also a list of good sources to get you started. In addition, there are many relevant secondary sources that you can find for each case study on our website at www.mhhe.com/delbanco1e. Research projects require a considerable amount of reading and a good deal of thinking. Your job is to make your process and the research project fun. Explore a topic that interests you, and discover new ideas that will help inform your own idea. Break the topic down so that you can manage your research and create a project that teaches you about a subject you enjoy.

1. Identify what interests you.   Choose your topic, or choose how you want to address your assigned topic, by considering what strikes you as important or interesting in the work of literature you are researching.

> **Example:** Our student author, Christine Keenan, was assigned to write a research paper on Langston Hughes. To find a topic, she thought of what she knew about Hughes that interested her. Since Christine loves music, she decided she would like to know more about how jazz influenced Langston Hughes.

2. Form a question.   Once you have a topic in mind, explore how that aspect of the work is meaningful to you. Do some of the brainstorming exercises that students used to get started in chapter 3, Writing about Fiction, chapter 17, Writing about Poetry, and chapter 32, Writing about Drama. Turn this aspect into a question. Christine made a list of words that she associated with jazz.

> *improvisation, be-bop, Duke Ellington, and nightclubs*

She also considered that jazz has several forms including blues, swing, be-bop, and cool jazz. Based on this, she formed the question.

> **Example:** "What elements of jazz influenced Langston Hughes when he wrote his poems?"

3. Narrow your topic.   She then decided to narrow her question further by picking two poems influenced by jazz, an early poem, "The Dream Keeper," and a later poem, "Harlem [2]."

5c   FIND AND MANAGE PRINT AND ONLINE SOURCES

The sources you cite in your research should be *reliable* and *relevant*—significant in the context of your current discussion. Refining your keyword search can help prevent information overload and find sources that are pertinent to your topic. Your instructor may have some recommendations for good sources on a topic, and there are also sources listed in this textbook as good starting places. The Web does not offer any guarantees about the accuracy of its content. However, some websites and search engines are better than others for trustworthiness. If your website ends in *.org, .edu,* or *.gov,* it's like having a good character reference for the content on the site. If your search engine has preselected source material (such as GoogleScholar) or if you have accessed a library database, you will have saved yourself the painful weeding through of hits that cannot help you. Some tips for finding reliable and relevant sources include:

- *Title.* In a scholarly article or book, the title and subtitle will usually be designed to convey the topic of the piece as specifically as possible. If the title doesn't seem relevant to your topic, that author or piece of work might not be the best source for your discussion.
- *Date of publication.* For print sources, this will often be found on the copyright page of the book. Note not just the copyright of the current edition, but the original copyright. Journals will have dates printed with their issue numbers and often on individual articles themselves to inform the reader when the article's research was originally conducted. A reliable web page will usually print the date last modified at the bottom of the page. Bear in mind that "relevant" doesn't always mean "current." A classic source is one that is a hallmark in the field. If you see a source cited when you're reading sources elsewhere, you've likely come upon a classic work. A current source is just what the word suggests, something written about a topic within the past five years.
- *Abstract.* Most research papers in journals will have **abstracts,** or summaries, that explain the research done, briefly detail the findings, and state the conclusion of the research.
- *Chapter titles or headings.* A perusal of a print source's detailed table of contents can help you determine if the source will contain information useful and relevant to your research. If you are searching for an interpretation of Shakespeare's *Romeo & Juliet* and the index of the book indicates that all mentions of that play occur in a chapter called "Shakespeare: The Fraud," that text might be biased toward a perspective beyond the scope of your paper.

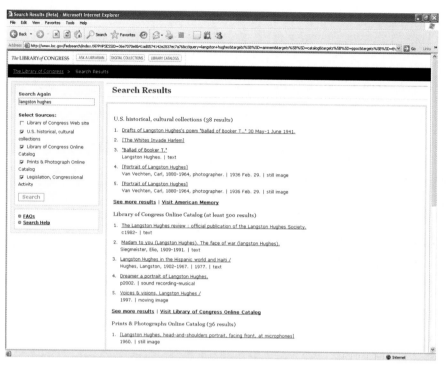

(Library of Congress search for "Langston Hughes")

1. Refine your keyword search. Whether you are searching one of your library's databases or the Web, refine your key words by grouping words together, e.g. "Harlem Renaissance." Use *and* or + to bring up sites that have both topics together. Use *or* when you list sites that are for either topic. Two words are better than one to help you narrow the number of sites that come up; use quotation marks around titles or parentheses around key phrases to manage the number of hits as well. To find information on Web pages and avoid the information flood, a good key word search is essential. Experiment with the phrasing of your keyword.

2. Use more than one search engine. The Internet brings the world to your door, but don't just google. Use at least three general search engines to locate the sources you need. In addition to Google, you may want to try Yahoo! (http://www.yahoo.com) or WebCrawler (http://www.webcrawler.com). Some sites search several different search engines at once: Library of Congress (http://www.loc.gov) or the Librarian's Index to the Internet (http://www.lii.org). You even have search sites that have already been vetted by experts, such as GoogleScholar (http://scholar.google.com), About.com (http://www.about.com), and Looksmart (http://www.looksmart.com).

3. Use the library, on campus and online. Check out your library's website. Talk to your librarian. The library is not just a collection of printed texts anymore. Your librarian can help you find the library's computerized catalog of books and discipline-specific encyclopedias, bibliographies, and almanacs, such as the *MLA International Bibliography of Books and Articles on Modern Language and Literature* (also available online) or the *Oxford History of English Literature*. In addition, the librarian can help you locate the library's database of scholarly journals and other electronic resources.

(Google Scholar Advanced Search Page)

Databases, Online Periodicals

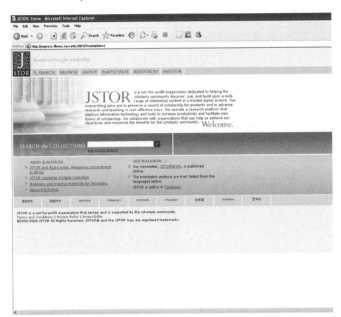

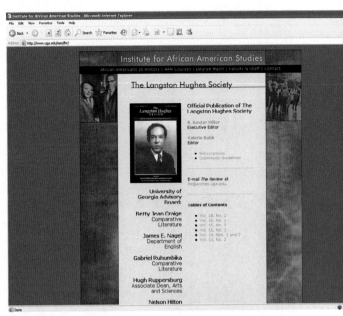

(JSTOR Online Database) *(Langston Hughes Society online Periodical)*

Library searches can help you find the kinds of sources your professor wants to see on your topic.

Example: Christine used a database through her university's library to do keyword searches using the words "Langston Hughes" and "jazz." She skimmed the results and picked a few that seemed most related to her topic.

Searching the Internet

When you go online for help, you may feel all the information is the same. It only looks that way. The Internet serves up information in a couple of ways that it is important for you to differentiate.

- A *general search* from the entire World Wide Web includes everything that anyone has posted on your topic, from very personal blogs to news groups. You will need to carefully evaluate anything you find in a general search to determine if it is providing information that is reliable.

- An *online database* from your library searches through a collection of reliable published articles and electronic journals. The results of a database search will include only publications and will connect you to abstracts, summaries, or full text (that is, the entire article).

These film shots illustrate portrayals of the Grendel monster and the Beowulf hero in the movie Beowulf *(top) and the movie* The 13th Warrior *(bottom).*

5d EVALUATE VISUAL SOURCES

A picture is worth a thousand words, or so the old proverb goes. We live in a visual world and visual data is now as easy as a cut-and-paste job off GoogleImage. Like all source information, however, it must be relevant and reliable. Visuals must serve a specific purpose in your paper. A graph or chart can be a useful snapshot of quantitative data. A diagram is a useful flowchart to explain a process. A picture is qualitative evidence that is used to strengthen or amplify your point. If you have taken your visual from the Web or another source, it must be documented in your bibliography and identified in your paper with a caption. The example here is evidence for a paper on adapting the *Beowulf* epic.

5e EVALUATE TEXT SOURCES

Sources can be popular or scholarly. A popular source is something you could buy easily at a store, such as *Time* magazine. It will likely have advertisements in it or be advertised to the general public (such as a self-help book like *Rich Dad, Poor Dad*). A scholarly source is generally found through a library rather than a store. The writers focus on discipline-specific rather than broad, general topics and are usually affiliated with a university. These books are likely to have footnotes or include citations to sources and bibliographies. When considering whether a print publication is popular or scholarly, follow these guidelines:

- *Note the publisher of the book, magazine, or journal.* A commercial publisher will probably suggest a popular aim, whereas an academic publisher such as a university press will suggest a scholarly aim.

- *Consider the authors of the articles.* Take note of both the authors' names and their affiliations (generally universities for scholarly articles), and consider how their titles match up with the topic of their article. For instance, Alton Brown might be a name you recognize as an authority from The Food Network, but he would not be a trustworthy expert to cite in a paper on comparative politics.

- *Notice the range of topics in the publication.* A popular publication will usually cover a range of topics to appeal to a wide readership, whereas a scholarly publication will focus on various aspects of one topic.

- *Observe the visual presentation of the publication.* Is it flashy and full of ads and cartoons? Or is it mostly text-based, with fewer but higher quality captioned images?

- *Evaluate the articles themselves.* Academic articles will often be preceded by abstracts that summarize their findings and followed by bibliographies or listings of works cited. Popular articles, on the other hand, may lead in with a catchy line that leaves an unanswered question and will seldom list references.

- *Ask whether the source is refereed or peer reviewed.* A publication may or may not specify this, but most trustworthy scholarly publications accept articles only after they have been reviewed, debated, and accepted by a body of experts in the field. Some research databases will allow you to filter for peer-reviewed publications; or, when in doubt, you can ask your librarian whether a publication has been refereed.

You may find it difficult when using the Web to tell the difference not only between a popular and a scholarly site, but also between a reliable site and one that is biased. The Library of Congress website can be counted on, as can its search engine, so don't just google. Find search engines that will save you the time by leading you to reliable sites. Many of the same guidelines you use for evaluating print sources can apply to evaluating an online publication as well. Some other things you can pay attention to when considering whether an electronic source like a website is reliable include

- *The Web address.* As mentioned earlier, often reliable content will be found on websites with the domains *.org* (non-profit organization), *.edu* (educational institution), *.mil* (military), or *.gov* (United States government). Keep in mind that not all information on a *.org* or *.edu* (or sometimes *.gov* or *.mil*) is reliable. Information on these pages may be biased; or, sometimes, the information might be from a personal page hosted by that specific domain. In this case, you will often notice a tilde (~) followed by a name or personalized "handle" (such as your school ID or AIM screen name) in the Web address.

- *The host of the page.* Is the Web page hosted by a university or academic association? Is it an article of an online encyclopedia? Be careful of sites like Wikipedia, which can claim to be "encyclopedias" or "dictionaries" but may not be accurate. Do not use Wikipedia as a citation in a college paper. You will need to verify the content you find on Wikipedia through another source, and if it is common knowledge (a birth date, for example), it won't need a citation.

- *The visual presentation.* As with print sources, you can tell a lot about a Web page's content and intended audience just by looking at how it is presented. Flashy ads, pop-up windows, intricate backgrounds, complex layouts, and funky colors are all indications that a website might not contain reliable content. A reliable Web page, created by an academic for academic use, will be laid out functionally, without intricate designs or distracting colors.

- *The tone of the information.* Tone is a major indicator of scholarliness and bias. Avoid Web pages that use poor grammar or punctuation or employ colloquial Internet shorthand. Scholarly information will seldom be presented so informally. Also take note of aggravated tone of voice, or hyperbolic claims, or a failure to consider more than one point of view. These are indicators of bias—which might support your point of view, but will detract from the legitimacy of the source as support.

Whenever you are conducting research, if an opinion or piece of information seems fishy or flimsy, you should double-check. If you find that information or point of view in only one place, there's a good chance it is unsupported or not widely agreed upon by the academic community. Many databases now provide information on where an article or book has been cited by other academics in their research; this can be a valuable resource in confirming the reliability of a research source.

5f RECOGNIZE UNRELIABLE WEBSITE WARNING SIGNS

The following example shows two websites containing the text of Langston Hughes's poem "Harlem," one unreliable and one reliable. Note the striking differences between the two. Likely your eye will go first to the unreliable site; whereas the reliable site by the Poetry Foundation is designed as a resource, the unreliable site hosted by PoemHunter. com is designed to attract attention and amass visits to the page.

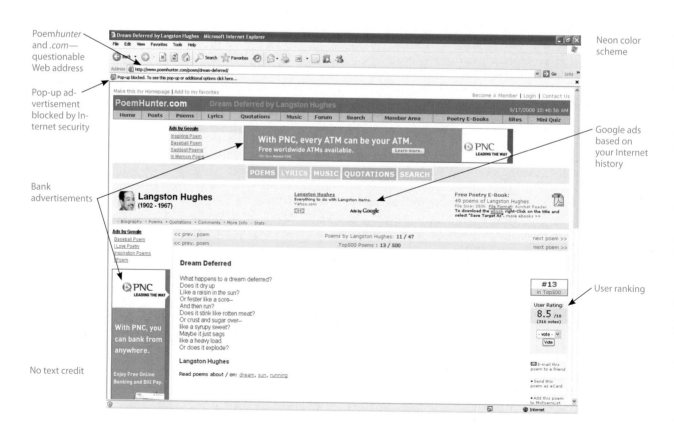

Poem*hunter* and *.com*—questionable Web address

Pop-up advertisement blocked by Internet security

Bank advertisements

No text credit

Neon color scheme

Google ads based on your Internet history

User ranking

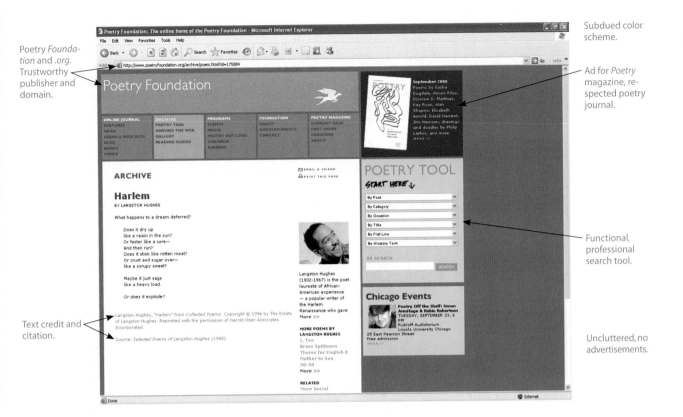

Poetry *Foundation* and *.org*. Trustworthy publisher and domain.

Subdued color scheme.

Ad for *Poetry* magazine, respected poetry journal.

Functional, professional search tool.

Text credit and citation.

Uncluttered, no advertisements.

Besides flashy colors and design, there are other major differences between the two. Whereas PoemHunter.com has bank ads (don't ignore that blocked pop-up ad, it's a major clue to unreliability), the Poetry Foundation website advertises only its own publication, *Poetry* magazine, a well-known and respected journal of poetry. Notice also the references that follow the poem text: PoemHunter.com does attribute the author of the poem but does not cite any permission or original publication information.

It will save you time if you can quickly recognize the difference between reliable and unreliable sites. A google search for Langston Hughes's "Harlem" will list PoemHunter.com before the Poetry Foundation, so strong searching skills and judgment are your keys to efficient, effective Web research.

5g WORK WITH SOURCES TO AVOID PLAGIARISM

As you collect your sources for your papers, your source notes will protect you from plagiarism. Take careful notes as you read your sources. You may want to use sticky notes to flag specific quotes or passages that you find interesting or of particular relevance to your topic. A necessary part of writing a research paper is the inclusion and citation of outside sources, usually scholarly works from books, journals, and trustworthy Web pages. Because of the risk of plagiarism (taking credit for another's words or ideas), it is important to know the several appropriate ways to include outside information.

There are two different approaches to including outside information into your own research paper, and both require **in-text parenthetical citation** and documentation in the **Works Cited** (or **Bibliography,** depending on the documentation style you are working within) at the end of your paper. Always be sure to copy the bibliographical information of the source so you can easily return to it when writing your paper and properly cite it (for more on this, see the MLA Documentation Style Guide that follows this chapter). All works that have been included in your paper with in-text parenthetical citations must be included in your Works Cited page. Some general tips to avoid plagiarism during research are:

- **Take notes on your sources.** First, when taking notes, make sure to underline or put into quotation marks all direct quotations you copy from books or journals. Record the page numbers and other source information that you'll need for your in-text parenthetical citation. This will help you distinguish your own impressions and conclusions from those that you copied directly and to avoid plagiarism by correctly citing your sources.

- **Do not copy and paste directly into your paper.** Next, when working with Web sources, try not to copy and paste directly into the body of your work; consider instead pasting into a separate document and printing it out to consult alongside your other notes. It's much easier to catch yourself retyping whole passages from another source.

- **Keep bibliographical information.** Finally, choose a documentation style (MLA, APA) early and stick to it as you create the body of your work. Usually your instructor will have assigned you a style for the assignment. If you cannot cite as you write, make sure to note "citation needed" in appropriate places, such as after paraphrases, figures, or direct quotations.

5h REFERENCE CITATIONS WITHIN THE PAPER IN THE END-OF-PAPER WORKS CITED PAGE

When you use sources in an MLA -style paper, you must include a parenthetical reference in the body of your paper (for more information, see our chapter on Quoting, Paraphrasing, Summarizing, and Avoiding Plagiarism) and a corresponding entry in a Works Cited page at the end of your paper. The idea is simple: full information about the books, journals, or websites you used in writing your paper appears in a list (the Works Cited page) at the end of your paper. Including all that information in the body of your paper would bog down both you and your reader. Instead, insert a brief reference in parentheses after the word or idea you have borrowed from an outside source. This parenthetical citation does two jobs: (1) It shows your reader exactly which sentences of your paper include ideas that are not your own, and (2) It points the reader to the original source by corresponding with the full citation that occurs in the Works Cited page.

1. In-text parenthetical reference. Here, the parenthetical citation tells the reader that the student author has summarized or paraphrased an idea that she found on pages 61 and 62 of a source with an author whose last name is Borshuk.

SENTENCE FROM STUDENT PAPER:

Also, the traditionally African-American art form had now been taken over and turned into a commercial success largely by whites, with a few exceptions like Duke Ellington and Count Basie (Borshuk 61-62).

2. Corresponding entry from works cited page.   Turning to the Works Cited page at the end of the paper, the reader can find the entry beginning with "Borshuk" and know that the information following it is the source from which it came. In this case, the source is a book called *Swinging the Vernacular* by Michael Borshuk. The parenthetical citation and the works cited entry have worked together to inform the reader of the original source of the idea.

Borshuk, Michael. <u>Swinging the Vernacular.</u> New York: Routledge, 2006.

5i ORGANIZE YOUR RESEARCH AND DEVELOP A THESIS

1. Connect your interpretation of a text to various sources.   Consider what each source tells you about your topic. Particularly if you are reading literary criticism, decide whether or not you agree with the critic. If you agree, you may want to use what that critic says to corroborate your reading. If you disagree, use that critic's perspective as a springboard into talking about your own perspective.

Example: Christine read the following quote in one of her sources:

Langston Hughes, in his collection of poems, lavishly uses such characteristics of jazz as repetitions, choruses, riffs, scats, and nonsensical onomatopoeia, to achieve musical success as well as audience participation. It is also significant to note that Hughes's poems are often marked by dissonance, discordance, and line irregularity, which all contribute to the representation of the jazz spirit in verse forms.

Although this quote directly related to her topic, Christine found that she was dissatisfied with the vague way in which most sources—like this one—talked about the jazz elements in Hughes's poems. She began to consider the historical reasons why Hughes might have chosen these specific elements.

2. Form a working thesis.   Once you have gathered your own ideas and taken notes on your sources, try to state your overall idea in a sentence or two. Most likely, your thesis will have the kernel of the idea that you started with, but it will have become more nuanced by your research. (See more on thesis in our chapter on Writing from Reading.)

> **Example:** Christine's original idea was to talk about jazz elements in Hughes's poems. Her research showed her that most critics approach his jazz poetry from a general angle. As a result, she formed the following thesis, which shows a very specific interpretation of why Hughes chose certain jazz elements.
>
> **Working thesis:** Hughes used jazz in a significant way. More than simply feeling jazz's influence generally, Hughes felt the influence of African-American jazz specifically.

3. Choose your best support.   Review the notes you took on your sources and on the primary text. Select a few quotes that best illustrate a point you want to make. Note ideas that you will want to paraphrase or summarize in your paper, and remember that these are important forms of support as well. For examples of successful summary, paraphrase, and direct quotation refer to our chapter on Quoting, Paraphrasing, Summarizing, and Avoiding Plagiarism and the sample research paper in this chapter.

5j   DRAFT AND REVISE YOUR DRAFT

Now that you have conducted your research and developed a thesis, you are ready to draft your paper. This is just a first draft, so leave yourself time to revise.

- **Introduction.** Your introduction sets up the rest of your paper.
- **Body.** The body of your paper presents your supporting evidence.
- **Conclusion.** Your conclusion relates your paper to a larger issue.

You may want to share your first draft with a friend or classmate. Then put your draft away and return to it fresh. You may see things you hadn't seen before. When you think through your thesis and look at the supporting evidence for your thesis, you may even find that you've changed your mind. Your thesis can be refined in response to your writing. To see revisions of the introduction, body, and conclusion in the paper on Langston Hughes, go to our Chapter on Writing from Reading. There you will find more on the drafting and revising process.

You can see in-text references and a properly formatted Works Cited page by looking at the student research paper that follows. Other student papers, like the explication of William Blake's "The Garden of Love," which appear in Common Writing Assignments, can also serve as models for in-text references. In that particular paper, note the proper parenthetical citation of lines of poetry rather than page numbers.

Remember, too, that even if you respond to a single source, you should still cite that work. This is especially important when many versions of the same text exist—for example, if you are reading Charlotte Bronte's classic *Jane Eyre* from a Penguin Classics edition, the pagination will be different from the *Jane Eyre* edition published by Oxford World's Classics. Only a full citation in a Works Cited page will tell your reader from which version you are reading. For an example of a single source, see the final draft of the student paper in chapter 3 on Jamaica Kincaid's "Girl."

Sample Student Research Paper

Christine Keenan

Professor Jackson

English 200

15 May 2008

From Dream Keeper to Dream Deferred:

Langston Hughes and Jazz Poetry

Jazz poetry, according to the American Academy of Poets website, is "a literary genre defined as poetry necessarily informed by jazz music—that is, poetry in which the poet responds to and writes about jazz" ("A Brief Guide to Jazz Poetry"). Langston Hughes was a jazz poet in that his poetry often captured jazz in a literary form. Many critics point to specific techniques that Hughes employs to create the effect of jazz. One such critic is Lionel Davidas, who writes:

> Langston Hughes, in his collection of poems, lavishly uses such characteristics of jazz as repetitions, choruses, riffs, scats, and nonsensical onomatopoeia, to achieve musical success as well as audience participation. It is also significant to note that Hughes's poems are often marked by dissonance, discordance, and line irregularity, which all contribute to the representation of the jazz spirit in verse forms. (268)

Although these observations are true, readings like Davidas's fail to show the full extent of Hughes's achievement in jazz poetry. Beyond being a jazz poet, Hughes understood the significance of jazz—even as it was being created—and used only those aspects of jazz that express the African-American experience.

Two of Hughes's collections that have an overt connection to music are *The Weary Blues*, published in 1926, and *Montage of a Dream Deferred*, published in 1951. In the twenty-five years between their publications, jazz music changed dramatically. Two poems, "The Dream Keeper" from *The Weary Blues* and "Harlem [2]" from *Montage of a Dream Deferred*, show how Hughes effectively responded to the current trends in jazz from an African-American perspective.

Margin annotations:

Title centered; no underline.

Quote from website source.

Block quote (more than four lines long) from a periodical source.

Establishes a critical reading to which the student responds.

Thesis statement

Author maps out how she will support her thesis.

Topic sentence
introduces first
poem to be
analyzed.

Hughes first published "The Dream Keeper" in 1925 and included it in his collection *The Weary Blues* the following year (Rampersad 617). At that time, America was in the midst of the "Jazz Age," the period from 1920-1930 marked by energy and optimism. Jazz itself was popular and connoted rebellion as it was associated with nightclubs, sex, and drinking (Tucker, screen 4). But Hughes's collection was clearly influenced more by the blues than by this new form of jazz. The title of the collection suggests the blues takes center stage in these poems, and indeed, "The Dream Keeper" is no exception. While it does not have as overt a connection to the blues as Hughes's poems that replicate blues lyrics directly—such as "Po Boy Blues"—the repetition early in the poem bears echoes of the repetition characteristic of the blues. "Bring me all of your" is repeated twice within the first three lines; the object the addressee is told to bring, however, varies (lines 1, 3). In a way, lines one through three are a compounded version of blues lyrics. Typical blues lyrics follow a pattern where the first couplet repeats before a third couplet resolves it. Here, half the couplet is repeated and half resolved in both instances. Blues also has a hand in the pace of the poem. Compound phrases like "cloud-cloth" and "too-rough" slow the pace of reading, as does the high number of line breaks compared to the small number of words (6, 7).

Example of
paraphrase.

Student's own
analysis.

Since Hughes was writing in the Jazz Age, it may seem surprising that so many of his poems in *The Weary Blues* reflect the blues. In part, his decision may have been informed by the fact that jazz grew out of the blues, and the close relationship of the two forms of music allowed Hughes to use blues and still be in the realm of jazz. But blues is marked by a "blue" or melancholy frame of mind (Oliver, screen 1), not the exuberance of the Jazz Age. Examining the historical context offers an answer for why Hughes chose blues over jazz. While the Roaring Twenties brought "unprecedented prosperity" to the United States ("Roaring Twenties"), it was also the era of the Great Migration, the movement in which ten percent of African Americans left the South and moved North. These were difficult times for blacks, as they faced low wages, poor housing conditions, and disease in the northern cities to which they relocated (Marks). Also, while positive advances did occur in the African-American community, such as the Harlem Renaissance, Emily Bernard has noted that most blacks were not affected

Example of
summary.

by the Renaissance—only a so-called talented tenth participated, leaving most blacks to face everyday problems (Bernard xvi-xvii).

To put it simply, jazz at the time that Hughes was writing poems for *The Weary Blues* had two forms: the exuberant new jazz and the blues roots from which it came. Hughes chose the form of music—the blues—that best reflected the state of the common black man. By the time Hughes was writing the poems for *Montage of a Dream Deferred,* however, jazz had changed and once again offered two new forms.

The 1930s and 40s brought a change to jazz: ensembles of about twelve players began to change the rhythms of jazz into swing. Swing, which became the popular dance music in more reputable venues than just bars and clubs, was usually performed by big bands under the direction of white leaders like Benny Goodman and Glenn Miller.[1] Thus, jazz became mainstream and middle class, unlike the "hot jazz" of the 20s (Tucker, screen 5). Also, the traditionally African-American art form had now been taken over and turned into a commercial success largely by whites, with a few exceptions like Duke Ellington and Count Basie (Borshuk 61-62).

Transition paragraph. The first two sentences conclude the blues discussion. The last sentence segues into discussion of the second poem.

Example of summary.

Example of paraphrase.

Fig. 1 The Glenn Miller Orchestra Source: Photo Gallery. Glenn Miller Orchestra Online. Glenn Miller Productions, Inc. Web. 12 May 2008.

Jazz underwent another major change in the 1940s. Young African-American musicians in Harlem met in informal jam sessions where they began to experiment with nearly every aspect of the music—melody, harmony, and rhythm.[2] Musicians such as Dizzy Gillespie, Thelonious Monk, and Charlie Parker increasingly championed improvisation and creativity over the organized big band aesthetic. Their innovations included "rapid tempo, irregular phrase groups . . . sudden, sharp drum accents, [and] chromatically altered notes" (Tucker, screen 7). This new form of jazz became known as bebop, a form of music that many critics see as "the revolt of young black musicians of the ghetto against the commercialization of 'swing music' of the time" (Lenz 274). In other words, bebop made jazz into a predominantly African-American art once more.

Citation of both para-phrase and direct quote.

Fig. 2 Tommy Potter, Charlie Parker, Dizzy Gillespie, and John Coltrane—leaders of the bebop movement—pictured at the famous jazz club Birdland, c. 1951. Source: "Charlie Parker, Uptown and Down." *New York Times on the Web. The New York Times.* Web. 12 May 2008.

Topic sentence introduces the second poem to be analyzed.

When Langston Hughes penned "Harlem [2]," two types of jazz existed: the mellow, organized sound of swing and the creative, frantic sound of bebop. For *Montage of a Dream Deferred,* Hughes chose to use the latter jazz form, as his preface to the collection suggests:

> In terms of current Afro-American popular music and the sources from which it has progressed—jazz, ragtime, swing, blues, boogie-woogie, and be-bop—this poem on contemporary Harlem, like be-bop, is marked by conflicting changes, sudden nuances, sharp and impudent interjections, broken rhythms, and passages sometimes in the manner of the jam session, sometimes the popular song, punctuated by the riffs, runs, breaks, and disc-tortions [sic] of the music of a community in transition.
> (Rampersad 387)

Example of paraphrase.

Indeed, these bebop-like traits are present in "Harlem [2]": "conflicting changes" and "sudden nuance" can be seen in the series of images Hughes selects; "sharp and impudent interjections" occur in the form of the last line, *"Or does it explode?"* (line 11); and "broken rhythms" are created by the space after the first line and the space before the last line. Hughes, then, successfully reflects bebop technique in his poetry, and in so doing, uses the form of jazz aligned with African Americans, rather than the form of mainstream, middle-class whites.

Citation of line in poem.

Conclusion that shows significance of student's preceding analysis.

More significant than the blues and bebop form, however, is Hughes's use of blues and bebop content. "The Dream Keeper" and "Harlem [2]" share the theme of dreams, yet each reflects the mindset of the music that influenced it—music that in turn was influenced by the historical events of its day. "The Dream Keeper" is itself dreamy in its imagery of "blue cloud-cloth" and the diction of phrases like "heart melodies" (6, 7). Despite these whimsical elements, the act of tucking away one's dreams so the world will not harm them is a sad one. In fact, the tone of the poem is melancholy, or "blue." Even the one color mentioned in the poem is "blue," which

Topic sentence that introduces a new thread of discussion and analysis.

Reiteration that citation is to poetic line. Avoids confusion with source page numbers found in other citations.

Student's analysis.

Example of summary.

guides the reader toward blue (i.e., sad) feelings (6). This laying aside of dreams is more than the material of blues music; it was also, for many blacks, the reality of the Great Migration. Reading "The Dream Keeper" with the Great Migration in mind makes the poem seem as if it is directly about the blues created by the migration. Blacks were motivated to migrate by the promise of opportunity and freedom from the South's discrimination; once in the North, however, blacks often found limited advancement possibilities in their jobs and continued to suffer from segregation (Marks). In a sense, then, African Americans of the Great Migration often had to lay aside their dreams from the "too-rough fingers" of reality (7).

Student's synthesis of poem and historical context.

Similarly, "Harlem [2]" captures the mindset and historical context that gave rise to bebop. Although the dream theme is the same as in "The Dream Keeper," its imagery of "fester[ing] like a sore" and "stink[ing] like rotten meat" suggests an uglier, bitterer side of dreams than anything that appears in "The Dream Keeper" (4, 6). John Lowney's characterization of Harlem is helpful in understanding this shift; he writes, "By the 1940s, Harlem was of course no longer the center of refuge and hope associated with the New Negro Renaissance. Although still a major destination for poor migrant blacks during the Great Depression, Harlem had become better known nationally as an explosive site of urban racial conflict, first in 1935 and then in 1943" (362). Those years saw race riots in Harlem, and racial tension continued to grow as blacks faced discrimination even in the World War II era (362). Lowney notes that "the agitated sound of *Montage* struck many of [Hughes's] contemporaries as a radical departure from the more straightforward 'populist' rhetoric of his best-known work" (369). Indeed, in reflecting bebop's dramatic change from swing, Hughes's poetry also takes a dramatic shift from earlier modes. This shift shows the rising frustration of

Student's analysis.

Example of direct quotation.

Student's synthesis of poem and historical context.

African Americans whose dreams were no longer the root of melancholy from being tucked away, but were now the product of dreams that continued to be deferred, nearly halfway into the twentieth century.

As "The Dream Keeper" and "Harlem [2]" demonstrate, Hughes effectively incorporated new forms of jazz as they arose. While he does successfully use formal elements of jazz music, to end a reading there would be to miss Hughes's larger achievement. Hughes did not simply adopt jazz technique; he selected only those trends in jazz that reflected the African-American experience of the time in which he wrote. There is no room in his poetry for the smooth sounds of swing at the hands of whites; instead, he used the true African-American forms of blues and bebop. In so doing, Hughes's poetry captures both the music, as it evolved from blues to bebop, and the African-American experience, as it moved from the blues of the Great Migration to the bitter conflict of continued discrimination.

Reiteration of thesis and broadening to encompass Hughes's overall achievement.

Topic sentence that signals conclusion.

Broadens thesis to include histori-cal discussion presented in the body of the paper

Notes

Properly formatted "Notes" section for additional information.

[1]Fig. 1 shows Glenn Miller's orchestra, which exemplifies the white, mainstream big band associated with swing of the 1930s and 1940s.

[2] Fig. 2 represents the smaller, black ensembles associated with bebop in the early 1940s. Comparing the two figures gives a visual representation of the stark difference between the two forms of jazz.

Works Cited

Introduction to a book. — Bernard, Emily. Introduction. *Remember Me to Harlem: The Letters of Langston Hughes and Carl Van Vechten, 1925-1964.* Ed. Bernard. New York: Knopf, 2001. Print.

Book. — Borshuk, Michael. *Swinging the Vernacular.* New York: Routledge, 2006. Print.

"A Brief Guide to Jazz Poetry." *Poets.org.* The American Academy of Poets. Web. — Article on a website. 8 May 2008.

Visual from Web. — "Charlie Parker, Uptown and Down." *New York Times on the Web. The New York Times.* Web. 12 May 2008.

Davidas, Lionel. " 'I, Too, Sing America': Jazz and Blues Techniques and Effects in — Print periodical. Some of Langston Hughes's Selected Poems." *Dialectical Anthropology* 26 (2001): 267-272. Print.

Book. — Hughes, Langston. *Montage of a Dream Deferred.* New York: Henry Holt, 1951. Print.

Hughes, Langston. *The Weary Blues.* New York: Knopf, 1926. Print. — Book.

Article from a database. — Lenz, Gunter. "The Riffs, Runs, Breaks, and Distortions of the Music of a Community in Transition." *The Massachusetts Review* 44.1-2 (Spring 2003): 269-282. *ProQuest.* Web. 11 May 2008.

Lowney, John. "Langston Hughes and the 'Nonsense' of Bebop." *American Literature* — Online periodical. *Online.* Duke University. Web. 11 May 2008.

Article on a scholarly website. — Marks, Carole. "The Great Migration: African Americans Searching for the Promised Land, 1916-1930." *In Motion: The African-American Migration Experience.* Ed. Howard Dodson and Sylviane A. Diouf. Schomburg Center for Research in Black Culture. Web. 11 May 2008.

Oliver, Paul. "Blues." *Grove Music Online.* Oxford UP. Web. 11 May 2008. — Online music dictionary.

Visual from web. — Photo Gallery. *Glenn Miller Orchestra Online.* Glenn Miller Productions, Inc. Web. 12 May 2008.

Rampersad, Arnold, ed. *The Collected Poems of Langston Hughes.* New York: Knopf, — Book, emphasis on editor. 1995. Print.

Article on a website. — "Roaring Twenties." *JAZZ: A Film by Ken Burns.* PBS. Web. 11 May 2008.

Tucker, Mark and Travis A. Jackson. "Jazz." *Grove Music Online.* Oxford UP. Web. 11 — Online music dictionary. May 2008.

6 MLA Documentation Style Guide

6a DOCUMENT SOURCES CONSISTENTLY IN APPROPRIATE STYLE

Anytime you use a direct quotation, paraphrase, or summary from a source—in other words, any text or idea that is not your own—you must indicate the author and work from which it came. This is called citing your sources. Different fields of study follow different guidelines for how to format citation. Psychology, for example, requires APA style, while anthropology typically uses the *Chicago Manual of Style*. English and most humanities, however, use MLA style, a format developed and maintained by the Modern Language Association. (For more on documentation styles, see p. H-108.)

This chapter will provide a quick overview and an abbreviated guide to MLA style. For a full description of how to properly cite works, you will want to consult the *MLA Handbook for Writers of Research Papers* (often referred to as simply the *MLA Handbook*), which is the authoritative guide to MLA style. Be sure to consult the 6th edition, which is the most current, as the rules vary slightly from edition to edition.

6b DOCUMENT IN-TEXT CITATIONS, MLA STYLE

1. Author Named in Parenthesis

A parenthetical reference in MLA consists of the author's last name and the page number from which you are quoting, summarizing, or paraphrasing. The reference comes at the end of the sentence *before* the period. Do *not* insert a comma, hyphen, or other punctuation between the last name and the page number.

> **Example:** While documenting sources may take extra time, it is worth it because "your reader might want to see the source for his or her own research" (Smith 42-43).

When you need to cite a page range, simply put a hyphen between the start and end pages, as in the example above. When citing two different pages, separate them with a comma.

> **Example:** (Smith 42, 51)

2. Author Named in Sentence

If you mention the author's name in the text surrounding the sentence, you need insert only the page number in parentheses.

> **Example:** As John Smith points out, "Your reader might want to see the source for his or her own research" (42).

3. Two or More Works by the Same Author

If you use two books or articles by John Smith in your paper, you must let your reader know which source you are using by inserting the title of the work into your sentence *or* by abbreviating the title and inserting it in the parenthetical reference as shown below.

> **Example:** As John Smith points out in his article "Using Sources," "Your reader might want to see the source for his or her own research" (42).

> **Example:** While documenting sources may take extra time, it is worth it because "your reader might want to see the source for his or her own research" (Smith, "Sources" 42).

*For parenthetical references for works with two, three, or more authors, see p. H-108.

4. Source of a Long Quotation

When citing a block quotation—one that is four lines or longer in poetry or five lines or longer in prose—indent by one inch and do not include quotation marks. The citation comes *after* the period.

> **Example:** Many critics point to specific techniques that Hughes employs to create the effect of jazz. One such critic is Lionel Davidas, who writes:
>
> > Langston Hughes, in his collection of poems, lavishly uses such characteristics of jazz as repetitions, choruses, riffs, scats, and nonsensical onomatopoeia to achieve musical success as well as audience participation. It is also significant to note that Hughes's poems are often marked by dissonance, discordance, and line irregularity, which all contribute to the representation of the jazz spirit in verse forms. (268)

6c DOCUMENT LIST OF WORKS CITED, MLA STYLE

To properly format a Works Cited page:

- Begin on a new page, following the end of your paper. If your paper ends on page 5, your Works Cited page will begin on page 6.
- Just like your paper itself, a Works Cited page should be double spaced with one-inch margins.

- At the top of the page, type "Works Cited" and center it. Do not include quotation marks around the words "Works Cited."
- Do not skip spaces. Drop down one double-spaced line, and align your entry to the left.
- If an entry runs longer than one line, indent every line one-half inch (or five spaces) after the first line.
- Put a period at the end of each entry.
- Alphabetize your Works Cited list by the first word of the entry. In most cases, this will be the author's last name.

For an example of a Works Cited page, see the model research paper in the previous chapter on Writing the Research Paper.

Common Formatting Errors

- Single spacing a Works Cited page
- Adding extra spaces between entries
- Numbering entries

What goes in an entry on a Works Cited page? First determine what type of source it is—a book, a periodical, an online resource. Then follow the instructions in the appropriate section, as follows:

Citing Book Sources

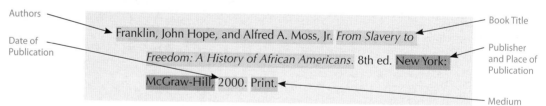

Authors → Franklin, John Hope, and Alfred A. Moss, Jr. *From Slavery to Freedom: A History of African Americans.* 8th ed. New York: McGraw-Hill, 2000. Print. ← Book Title / Publisher and Place of Publication / Date of Publication / Medium

1. Book with One Author.   Reverse the author's name for alphabetizing, adding a comma after the last name and a period after the first name. The book title follows in italics, followed by a period. Then list the city of publication, followed by a colon. Then the publisher, followed by a comma, then the year, followed by a period. Then list the medium. For how to abbreviate the publisher's name, see Additional Tips, p. H-111.

Borshuk, Michael. *Swinging the Vernacular.* New York: Routledge, 2006. Print.

Elements in Works Cited Entry: Books

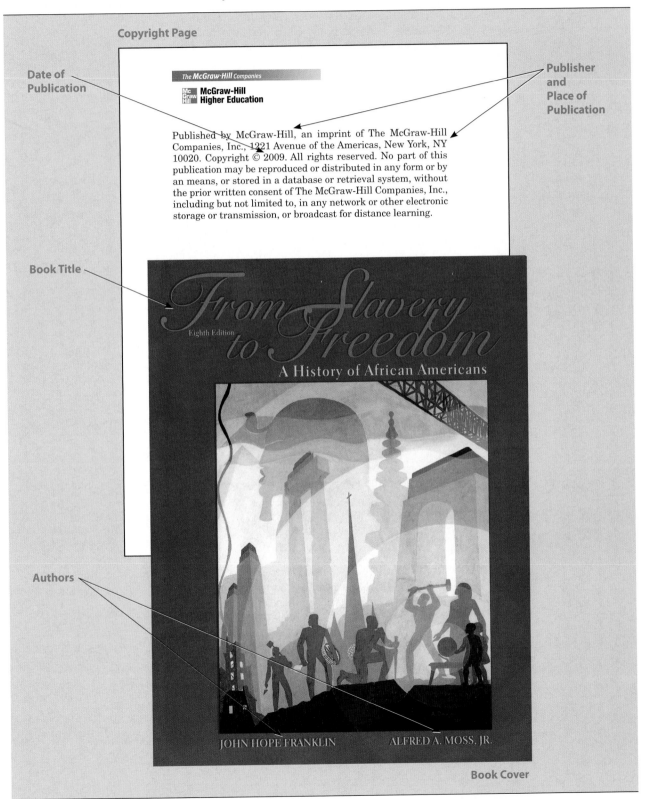

Copyright Page

Date of Publication

Publisher and Place of Publication

The McGraw-Hill Companies

McGraw-Hill
Higher Education

Published by McGraw-Hill, an imprint of The McGraw-Hill Companies, Inc., 1221 Avenue of the Americas, New York, NY 10020. Copyright © 2009. All rights reserved. No part of this publication may be reproduced or distributed in any form or by an means, or stored in a database or retrieval system, without the prior written consent of The McGraw-Hill Companies, Inc., including but not limited to, in any network or other electronic storage or transmission, or broadcast for distance learning.

Book Title

From Slavery to Freedom
Eighth Edition
A History of African Americans

Authors

JOHN HOPE FRANKLIN   ALFRED A. MOSS, JR.

Book Cover

2. Book with Two or Three Authors.   This entry follows the same formula as a book with a single author *except* that you will name the authors in the order listed on the title page. Reverse only the name of the first author. Then add a comma and list additional authors by first name followed by last name. Separate each author's complete name from the next author by a comma.

> Gilbert, Sandra M., and Susan Gubar. *The Madwoman in the Attic: The Woman Writer and the Nineteenth-Century Literary Imagination.* New Haven: Yale UP, 2000. Print.

*A parenthetical reference for **two** authors should look like this:

> (Gilbert and Gubar 34)

*A parenthetical reference for **three** authors should look like this:

> (Gilbert, Gilbert, and Gubar 34)

3. Book with Four or More Authors.   Indicate the name of the first author appearing on the title page, followed by "et al." (the Latin abbreviation for "and others"). As an alternative, however, you may list the names of all the authors *if convenient.*

> Jordan, Frank, et al. *The English Romantic Poets: A Review of Research and Criticism.* New York: MLA, 1985. Print.

*A parenthetical reference for **four or more** authors would look like this:

> (Gilbert et al. 34)

4. Two or More Books by the Same Author.   Follow the same formula as the single book entry, but in this case, you need not repeat the author's name. Instead, indicate the same author with three hyphens and a period.

> Bloom, Harold. *The Art of Reading Poetry.* New York: Perennial, 2005. Print.
>
> ——. *How to Read and Why.* New York: Scribner, 2000. Print.

5. Book with an Editor.   In place of an author's name, put the editor's name, followed by a comma and the abbreviation "ed." If there is more than one editor, follow the format for "Book with more than one author" but place a comma and the abbreviation "eds." after the final editor's name listed.

> Rampersad, Arnold, ed. *The Collected Poems of Langston Hughes*. New York:
>
> Knopf, 1995. Print.

6. Book with Two Editors.   Use the abbreviation "eds." after the names of the editors.

> Opie, Iona, and Peter Opie, eds. *The Oxford Book of Children's Verse*. New
>
> York: Oxford, 1973. Print.

7. Book with an Author and an Editor.   Start with the name of the author, followed by the book title and a period. Then write "Ed." followed by the editor's name in normal order.

> Twain, Mark. *Adventures of Huckleberry Finn*. Ed. Henry Nash Smith. Boston:
>
> Houghton, 1958. Print.

8. Book by an Unknown Author.   Begin with the title of the book, followed by the translator or editor (if appropriate). Follow with the publication information. Remember to alphabetize such a book in your Works Cited list by the first major word in the title, *not* by an article (*a, an,* or *the*).

> *The Bhagavad Gita*. Trans. Eknath Easwaran. Berkeley: Blue Mountain Center for
>
> Meditation, 2007. Print.

9. Work in an Anthology or Chapter in an Edited Book.   Selection author's last name, first name. "Selection or Chapter Title." *Book Title*. Editor's name. City: Publisher, Year. Page numbers of selection. Medium.

> Fox, Paula. "The Broad Estates of Death." *The O. Henry Prize Stories*. Ed. Laura
>
> Furman. New York: Anchor, 2006. 46-58. Print.

10. Translation of a Text.   Author's last name, first name. *Title of Book*. Abbreviation "Trans." for "translator." City of publication; publisher, year. Medium.

> Alighieri, Dante. *The Divine Comedy*. Trans. John Ciardi. New York: Norton,
>
> 1970. Print.

11. Introduction/Preface/Foreword/Afterword to a Text   If the introduction, preface, foreword, or afterword was written by *someone other than the book's author,* start with the writer and the title of *this* part. Then, indicate the book's title, followed by the word "By" and the name of the book's author in normal order. In the following example, Anita Brookner wrote the introduction to Edith Wharton's novel *The House of Mirth.*

> Brookner, Anita. Introduction. *The House of Mirth.* By Edith Wharton. New York:
>
> Scribner, 1977. ii- ix. Print.

If the introduction, preface, foreword, or afterword *was written by the author,* use **only** his or her last name preceded by the word "By." In the following example, Thomas Hardy wrote both the book itself and the introduction.

> Hardy, Thomas. Introduction. *Tess of the D'Urbervilles.* By Hardy. New York:
>
> Barnes and Noble, 1993. Print.

12. Multivolume Work   If you have taken information from only one of the work's volumes, indicate the number of that volume and abbreviate to "Vol" (no period after "Vol").

> Poe, Edgar Allan. *The Collected Works of Edgar Allan Poe.* Ed. Thomas Ollive
>
> Mabboth. Vol 2. Cambridge: Harvard UP, 1969. Print.

If you have taken information from more than one volume, indicate the total number of volumes used, abbreviate to "vols" and follow with a period.

> Poe, Edgar Allan. *The Collected Works of Edgar Allan Poe.* Ed. Thomas Ollive
>
> Mabboth. 2 vols. Cambridge: Harvard UP, 1969. Print.

13. Book in a Series   Place the name of the series after the medium. Indicate the book's number in the series if available.

> Franchere, Hoyt C., ed. *Edwin Arlington Robinson.* New York: Twayne, 1968.
>
> Print. Twaynes's United States Authors Series 137.

14. Encyclopedia Article

Signed A signed article is one that is attributed to an author.

Invert author's name. "Title of the Article." *Title of the Encyclopedia.* Editor(s). Volume number (if appropriate). City of publication; publisher, year. Page number(s). Medium.

> Merlan, Philip. "Athenian School." *The Encyclopedia of Philosophy.* Ed. Paul
>
> Edwards. Vol. 1. New York: Macmillan, 1967. 192-93. Print.

Unsigned An unsigned article is not attributed to an author. Start with the title of the article. Then proceed as above.

> "Pericles." *The Columbia Concise Encyclopedia.* Eds. Judith S. Levey and Agnes
>
> Greenhall. New York: Columbia UP, 1983. 655. Print.

15. Dictionary Definition   "Title of Entry." *Title of Dictionary.* Edition. Year of publication. Medium.

> "Fresco." *Merriam-Webster's Collegiate Dictionary.* 11th ed. 2003. Print.

Additional Tips

When a book lists multiple cities in which the publisher exists, choose the closest one geographically to put in your citation. For W. W. Norton & Company, which lists New York and London, you would use New York as the city for publication. Also, if the city is relatively unknown, or if there is more than one U.S. city with the same name, indicate the state in addition to the city, as in the following examples:

> Durham, NC: Duke UP
>
> Springfield, IL: Charles C Thomas

You will want to abbreviate or condense the publisher's name. Anytime you see "University Press," you can abbreviate it as "UP." For Southern Methodist University Press, write Southern Methodist UP. Alfred A. Knopf can be condensed to simply "Knopf."

If a book has multiple years on the copyright page, put only the most recent year in your Works Cited entry.

Citing Periodical Sources

Author → Davidas, Lionel. "'I, Too, Sing America': Jazz and Blues Techniques ← Article Title

and Effects in Some of Langston Hughes's Selected Poems." ← Date / Pages

Journal Title → *Dialectical Anthropology* 26 (2001): 267-272. Web. ← Medium

Volume number

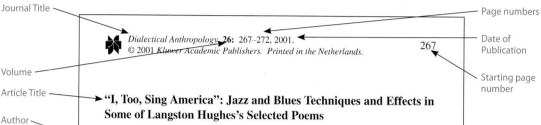

Journal Title → *Dialectical Anthropology* **26:** 267–272, 2001. ← Page numbers / Date of Publication

© 2001 *Kluwer Academic Publishers.* Printed in the Netherlands.

267 ← Starting page number

Volume

Article Title → **"I, Too, Sing America": Jazz and Blues Techniques and Effects in Some of Langston Hughes's Selected Poems**

Author →

Author Affiliation → LIONEL DAVIDAS
Université des Antilles et de la Guyane, Martinique, West Indies

It is commonly accepted that oral poetry has been greatly influenced by jazz and blues, a phenomenon that developed mainly in the USA. In light of this, we may infer that such poems should logically be considered as mere scores to be deciphered and performed, or records that should be heard rather than read, and that have many of the dynamics of "the music" about them.[1] In point of fact, a significant number of jazz techniques are to be found within the framework of poetry and combine with it to produce a highly personalized mode of free expression, which is the essence and spirit of of jazz creation. As it appears, Langston Hughes's outstanding collection of poems exemplifies the greatest of those qualities of jazz and blues, and his talent truly makes these poems come alive in the same way that jazz and blues music comes alive for the audience as well as for the musicians.

To those who are familiar with such music, it is quite clear that *Selected Poems of Langston Hughes*, a book which reveals the author's personal choice, unquestionably includes blues poetry, as evidenced by the many characteristics of blues music that pervade most of the selected pieces. To start with, it is significant to note that Hughes's poems are not at all static. They are pervaded with lively and active repetitions, and we notice a series of variations within each poem which closely resemble the variations present in a blues song. Many of Hughes's poems exhibit a slow tempo and rhythm which is a common trait to most styles of blues. What is more, there exists some degree of internal variation in breath rhythm that contributes to the blues effect. In addition, those poems definitely seek the interaction of call-and-response, making the reader feel an active participant in the "concert" provided by the poet as musician, as performer.

Periodicals include scholarly journals, magazines, and newspapers. For print periodicals (as opposed to online periodicals), use the following citation formulas.

1. Article in a Scholarly Journal   Author's last name, first name. "Article Title." *Journal Title* Volume. Issue (Year): Page numbers of article. Medium.

> Davidas, Lionel. "'I, Too, Sing America': Jazz and Blues Techniques and Effects
>
>   in Some of Langston Hughes's Selected Poems." *Dialectical Anthropology*
>
>   26 (2001): 267-272. Print.

Note that not all journals have an issue number, as in the example above. If that is the case, simply include the volume and the year.

2. Article in a Magazine   Author's last name, first name. "Article Title." *Magazine Title* Day Month Year: Page numbers of article. Medium.

> Lehrer, Jonah. "The Eureka Hunt." *The New Yorker* 28 July 2008: 40-45. Print.

Note that monthly magazines will not have a day with the month; in that case, simply list the month. Also, abbreviate months except for May, June, and July.

3. Article in a Newspaper   Author's last name, first name. "Article Headline." *Newspaper's Name* Day Month Year: Section letter Page number +. Medium.

> Svrluga, Barry. "Phelps Earns Eighth Gold." *The Washington Post* 17 Aug. 2008:
>
>   A1+. Print.

Use the plus sign after the page number only if the article is continued on nonconsecutive pages.

4. Book Review   Start with the reviewer's name, followed by the title of the review (if it has one) in quotation marks. Follow with "Rev. of" (the abbreviation for "review of"), the title of the book, and the name of the book's author preceded by the word "by." The author's name should be in normal order.

In the following example, the reviewer is Robert Kelly; the author of the book is Umberto Eco.

> Kelly, Robert. "Castaway." Rev. of *The Island of the Day Before,* by Umberto Eco.
>
>   *New York Times* 22 Oct. 1995: BR7. Print.

Citing Online Resources

Author —
Article Title —
Journal Title —
Name of Database —
Volume number —

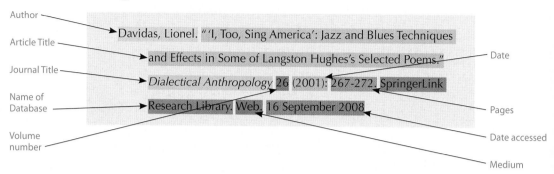

Davidas, Lionel. "'I, Too, Sing America': Jazz and Blues Techniques and Effects in Some of Langston Hughes's Selected Poems." *Dialectical Anthropology* 26 (2001): 267-272. SpringerLink Research Library. Web. 16 September 2008

— Date
— Pages
— Date accessed
— Medium

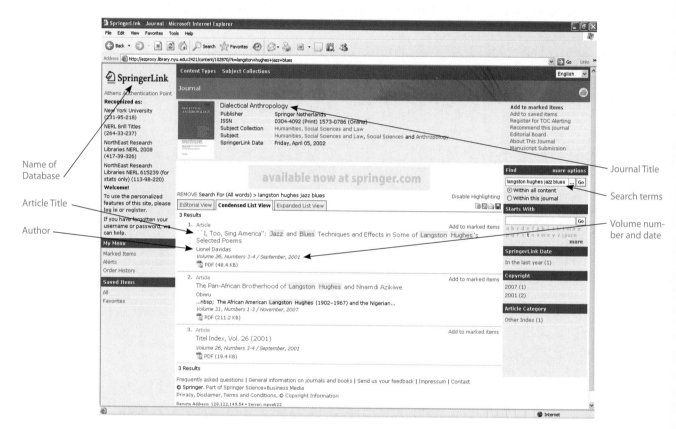

1. Web Site. The amount of source information provided varies from Web site to Web site. Include as much of the information below as you can. Remember, too, to choose your online resources wisely. If there is little or no information on the person or institution that created it, you may want to reconsider using it in your paper.

Last name of person responsible for site, first name. *Name of Web site*. Name of publisher, date of publication or last update. Medium. Day you accessed site—Month Year. Note: If no publisher is listed, use the abbreviation "n.p."

> Souther, Randy. *Celestial Timepiece: A Joyce Carol Oates Homepage.* N.p., Web.
>
> 8 Oct. 2007.

2. Article on a Web Site/Part of an Online Scholarly Project. Segment author's last name, first name. "Title of the Part of the Project." Ed. Name of person responsible for project. Date of publication or update. Name of sponsoring institution. Medium. Date you accessed site.

> "Roaring Twenties." *JAZZ: A Film by Ken Burns.* PBS. Web. 11 May 2008.

*Note that in the above example, the date of the Web site's publication was not available, so the student simply put the date she accessed the site.

3. Article in an Online Periodical. Article author's last name, first name. "Article Title." *Periodical's Web site*. Web site sponsor (if available). Day Month Year of publication. Medium. Date you accessed site.

> Lowney, John. "Langston Hughes and the 'Nonsense' of Bebop." *American*
>
> *Literature Online.* June 2000. Web. 11 May 2008.

4. Article from a Database. Cite the article as you normally would for a print article, but at the end of your entry add the following information:

Database Name. Medium. Date of access.

> Lenz, Gunter. "The Riffs, Runs, Breaks, and Distortions of the Music of a
>
> Community in Transition." *The Massachusetts Review* 44.1-2 (Spring
>
> 2003): 269-282. *ProQuest.* Web. 11 May 2008.

5. Online Book.

The entire online book. Start with the information you would include for any printed book. Follow with the name of the database, project, or other entity in which you found the book. Then, indicate the medium and the date you accessed the book.

> Hardy, Thomas. *Wessex Poems and Other Verses.* New York: Harper, 1898.
>
> *Bartleby.com.* Web. 30 Sept. 2008.

Part of an online book. Start with the name of the author, followed by the title of the part of the book you have cited. Then, proceed as above. The following example is an entry for Thomas Hardy's poem "Neutral Tones," which appears in an online book entitled *Wessex Poems and Other Verses*.

> Hardy, Thomas. "Neutral Tones." *Wessex Poems and Other Verses*. New York:
>
> Harper, 1898. *Bartleby.com*. Web. 30 Sept. 2008.

6. Online Posting.   Treat an online posting as you would a Web site.

> Brantley, Ben. "London Theater Journal: Hitting Bottom." *Artsbeat. New York*
>
> *Times*. 17 July 2008. Web. 29 Sept. 2008.

Citing Other Media

1. Audio Recording.   Start with the name of the composer, performer, or conductor—depending on whom you have discussed in your paper. Then, indicate the title of the recording, followed by the name(s) of the composer (s), performer(s), and/or conductor (if they were not mentioned earlier). Follow this with the distributor, the date, and the medium.

> Chopin. Frederic. *Chopin: Etudes*. Maurizio Pollini. Deutsche Grammaphon,
>
> 1972. CD.

2. Film.   Begin with the title of the film. Then, write the name of the director preceded by "Dir." (the abbreviation for "director"). Next indicate the name(s) of the principal performer(s) preceded by "Perf." (the abbreviation for "performers"). Follow this with the distributor, the date, and the medium.

> *Cinema Paradiso*. Dir. Giuseppe Tornatore. Perf. Phillipe Noiret, Jacques Perrin,
>
> Antonella Attilli, Pupella Maggio, and Salvatore Cascio. Miramar, 1988.
>
> Film.

3. Television Program.   Start with the title of the episode in quotation marks. Then, list the title of the program. Follow with the name of the network or channel, the city, the date you viewed the program, and the medium.

> "Noah: Myth or Fact." *Into the Unknown with Josh Bernstein*. Discovery
>
> Channel, Silver Springs, MD. 15 Aug. 2008. Television.

Glossary of Literary Terms

Abstract   A short **summary** at the beginning of a scholarly article that states the **thesis,** the major points of **evidence,** and the **conclusion** of the article.

Abstract Diction   Language referring to a general or conceptual thing or quality, such as *progress,* or *justice.*

Accent   The vocal emphasis on a syllable in a word. Often used interchangeably with **stress,** which sometimes refers to emphasis within a line of poetry, rather than a single word.

Accentual Meter   A kind of **meter** or verse measure that uses a fixed number of stressed syllables in each line, although based on a number of unstressed syllables may vary. Accentual meters often can be heard in rap music and children's rhymes.

Accentual-Syllabic Verse   A verse form that uses a fixed number of **stresses** and syllables per line. This is the most common verse form in English poetry, and includes, for example, **iambic pentameter,** where each line has five **stressed** syllables and five unstressed syllables.

Act   A subdivision of the action of a play, similar to a chapter in a book. Acts generally occur during a change in **scenery,** cast of **characters,** or mood, and the end of an act usually suggests the advancement of time in the play. Acts are often divided into subunits called **scenes.**

Allegory   A story in which major elements such as **character**s and settings represent universal truths or moral lessons in a one-to-one correspondence.

Alliteration   The repetition of the initial consonant sounds of a sequence of words.

Allusion   A reference to another work of art or literature, or to a person, place, or event outside the text.

Amphibrach   A syllable pattern characterized by three syllables in the order *unstressed, stressed, unstressed.*

Amphitheater   A stage surrounded on all sides by the audience, who watch the action from above.

Anagnorisis   In **tragedy,** a change from ignorance to knowledge, producing love or hate between the persons destined by the poet for good or bad fortune.

Anagram   A word or phrase created using the letters that spell a different word or phrase. For example, *dirty room* is an anagram for *dormitory.*

Analyze   To take a text apart and examine its elements: the different written devices the author uses (such as **point of view, plot,** and imagery) and the **voice** the author brings to the piece (**tone,** word choice).

Anapestic Meter   A **meter** using feet with two unstressed syllables followed by a **stressed** syllable.

Anecdote   A personal remembrance or brief story.

Antagonist   A **character** in **conflict** with the **protagonist.** A story's **plot** often hinges on a protagonist's conflict with an antagonist.

Anticlimax   The opposite of a **climax;** a point in a narrative that is striking for its *lack* of excitement, intensity, or emphasis. An anticlimax generally occurs at a point of high action where a true climax is expected to occur.

Antihero   A main **character** who acts outside the usual lines of heroic behavior (brave, honest, true).

Apostrophe   A **figure of speech** in which a writer directly addresses an unseen person, force, or personified idea. The term *apostrophe* derives from the Greek term meaning *turning away* and often marks a digression.

Approximate Rhyme   *See* **Slant Rhyme.**

Archetypal Criticism   *See* **Mythological Criticism.**

Archetype   An **image** or **symbol** with a universal meaning that evokes a common emotional reaction in readers.

Arena Theater   Also called *Theater in the Round,* an arena stage is surrounded on all sides by the audience, with all the action taking place on a stage in the center.

Argument   A position or perspective based on a **claim** that can be supported with **evidence.**

Aside   In drama, a remark made by an actor to the audience, which the other **characters** do not hear. This convention is sometimes discernable in fiction writing, when a self-conscious **narrator** breaks the flow of the narrative to make a remark directly to the reader.

Assonance   A repetition of vowel sounds or patterns in neighboring words.

Auditory Imagery **Images** that appeal to a reader's sense of hearing.

Augustan Age A distinct period in early-eighteenth-century neo-classical English literature characterized by formal structure and diction. This Augustan Age is named after the great period of Roman literature during Emperor Augustus's reign, when Ovid, Horace, and Virgil were writing. Famous writers of the English Augustan Age were Alexander Pope, Thomas Gray, and Jonathan Swift.

Authorial Intrusion *See* **Editorial Omniscience.**

Ballad Stanza A **quatrain** in which the first and third lines possess four stresses, while the second and fourth have three stresses. The **rhyme scheme** is often *abcb.*

Ballad A song or poem that tells a lively or tragic story in simple language using rhyming four-line **stanzas** and a set **meter.**

Bathos An error that occurs when a writer attempts elevated language but is accidentally trite or ridiculous; a sort of **anticlimax.**

Beat Generation A group of writers in the 1950s and '60s who represented the counterculture to 1950s American prosperity. The word "beat" comes from the slang for being down and worn out, suggesting their weariness with mainstream culture and their adoption of a freespirited attitude. Jack Kerouac's *On the Road* and Allen Ginsberg's poem "Howl" are major works of the Beat Generation.

Bibliography A list of the works consulted in the preparation of a paper, containing adequate information for readers to locate the source materials themselves.

Bildungsroman A **coming of age story** that details the growth or maturity of a youth, usually an adolescent. The term is German, meaning "**novel** of formation."

Biographical Criticism **Literary criticism** that emphasizes the belief that literature is created by authors whose unique experiences shape their writing and therefore can inform our reading of their work. Biographical critics research and use an author's biography to interpret the text as well as the author's stated intentions or comments on the process of composition itself. These critics often consult the author's memoirs to uncover connections between the author's life and the author's work. They may also study the author's rough drafts to trace the evolution of a given text or examine the author's library to discern potential influences on the author's work.

Biography The factual account of a person's life.

Blank Verse Unrhymed **iambic pentameter,** often used in Shakespeare's plays or for epic subject matter, as in Milton's *Paradise Lost.*

Blues A form of music that originated in the Deep South. Descended from African-American spirituals and work songs, the blues reflects the hardships of life and love in its lyrics. Most blues songs follow a form made of three phrases equal in length: a first phrase, a second that repeats the first phrase, and a third phrase different from the first two that concludes the verse.

Box Set *See* **Proscenium Stage.**

Brainstorming A process of generating and collecting ideas on a topic.

Burlesque A work of drama or literature that ridicules its subject matter through exaggerated mockery and broad **comedy.**

Cacophony Harsh-sounding, grating, or even hard-to-pronounce language.

Caesura A pause, usually in the middle of a line, that marks a kind of rhythmic division.

Canon In a literary context, the group of works considered by academics and scholars to be essential to and representative of the body of respected literature.

Carpe diem Latin for *seize the day.* A phrase used commonly in poetry that emphasizes the brevity of life and the importance of living in the moment.

Catharsis The purging of emotions which the audience experiences as a result of the powerful **climax** of a classical **tragedy;** the sense of relief and renewal experienced through art.

Central Intelligence Henry James's term for the **narrator** of a story—distinct from the author—whose impressions and ideas shape the telling of the story and determine the details revealed.

Character The depiction of human beings (and nonhumans) within a story.

Characters The actors (human and nonhuman) in a story.

Characteristics The physical and mental attributes of a **character,** established through **characterization.**

Characterization The way a writer crafts and defines a **character's** personality to give an insight into that character's thoughts and actions.

Charting A technique for generating ideas that involves placing related concepts and themes in a chart to view their relationships.

Chorus A group of amateurs and trained actors who participated in traditional Greek plays. The chorus represents a group of citizens with worries and questions, expressed in poetry and music and dance movement.

Claim An idea or stance on a particular subject; a defendable claim is necessary for a strong **thesis.**

Classifications of Drama These four categories are generally assigned to Shakespeare's theater, but are commonly used in reference to the works of other **playwrights. Histories** focus on the reign of kings from the past, from Julius

Caesar to Henry V. Because histories naturally contain very astute and sometimes troubling political commentaries, playwrights had to limit their subjects to rulers of the distant past. **Comedies** are plays for entertainment, and as a convention end in the marriage of two main **characters.** A comedic **plot** generally begins with a complication or misunderstanding between two lovers, which is complicated by further scheming and misunderstandings until finally a **resolution** is attained and the two are wed. **Tragedies** are darker plays, with more complex **characters** and more dire consequences, usually dramatizing the fall from a high state of life of a royal or special **character. Romances** (from the French *roman*, which means an "extended narrative") involve lovers whose potential happiness is complicated by misunderstandings, mistaken identities, and any number of other difficulties. Although similar in plot to a **comedy,** a romance play does not guarantee a happy ending.

Cliché   A **figure of speech** that has been used so commonly that it has become trite. The use of cliché may suggest an ironic tone.

Climax   The narrative's turning point in a struggle between opposing forces. The point of highest **conflict** in a story.

Close Reading   The **explication** of a text in order to **analyze** the ways in which distinct formal elements interact to create a unified artistic experience for the reader.

Closed Couplet   A pair of rhymed lines that capture one complete idea. If the couplet is **end-stopped** and in **iambic pentameter,** it is called a **heroic couplet.**

Closed Denouement   A **resolution** to a story that leaves no loose ends.

Closed Form   *See* **Fixed Form.**

Closet Drama   A piece of literature written as though for the stage, but intended only to be read.

Collective Unconscious   A set of **characters, plots, symbols,** and **images** that each evoke a universal response.

Colloquial Speech   Familiar and conversational speech.

Comedy   A type of drama that deals with light or humorous subject matter and usually includes a happy ending. The opposite of **tragedy.** *See* **Classifications of Drama.**

Comedy of Manners   A work of **satire** that pokes fun at human behavior in particular social circles. Since a comedy of manners concerns itself with social interactions, it tends to reveal the **characters'** foibles or follies as they try to appear or act in a certain way.

Comic Relief   A **character** or situation that provides humor in the midst of a work that is predominantly serious. A classic example is the bumbling Falstaff, a character in Shakesepeare's *Henry IV* who makes the audience laugh, even as England's fate hangs in the balance.

Coming of Age Story   A story that follows a **character's** physical, emotional, or spiritual maturation, often from youth into adulthood. *See* ***Bildungsroman.***

Common Measure   A variation on **ballad** meter that uses **iambic quatrains** with the first and third lines containing four feet (**tetrameter**) and the second and fourth containing three feet (**trimeter**). The rhyme scheme is often *abab* rhyme. Common measure, also called *common meter,* is the **meter** most associated with hymns.

Comparison   Looking at two or more texts, **characters,** authors, or other items side by side to draw similarities between them.

Conceit   A complex comparison or **metaphor** that extends throughout a poem

Conclusion   The final idea and **resolution** of a text. In a good essay, the conclusion not only reiterates the **thesis** but offers a reason for its significance or a reflection that pushes it toward a broader meaning beyond the essay itself. In a story or play, the conclusion refers to the resolution or **dénouement.**

Concrete Diction   Language referring to a specific, definite thing or quality, such as *lawn mower* or *street light.*

Concrete Poetry   Also called *visual poetry.* Poetry written in the shape of something it describes.

Confessional Poetry   Poetry that includes pieces of a poet's autobiography or personal experience. This mode of poetry was prevalent in the mid-twentieth century with poets like Sylvia Plath, Anne Sexton, and Robert Lowell.

Conflict   The central problem in a story. The source of tension between the **protagonist** and **antagonist.**

Connotation   The associations a word carries beyond its literal meaning. Connotations are formed by the context of the word's popular usage; for example, *green,* aside from being a color, connotes money. The opposite of **denotation.**

Consonance   A repetition of consonant sounds or similar patterns in neighboring words.

Context   The literary, historical, biographical, or poetical situation that influences the writing of a work of literature.

Contextual Reading   Reading and interpreting a story while mindful of its author, the time and place it was written, the traditions of its form, and the criticism it explicitly or implicitly responds to.

Contrast   Looking at two or more texts, **characters,** authors, or other items side by side to highlight the differences between them.

Convention   In literature, a feature or element of a **genre** that is commonly used and therefore widely accepted—and expected—

by readers and writers alike. For example, it is a convention of Shakespearean **comedy** to end with a marriage.

Conventional Symbols **Symbols** that have accrued a widely accepted **interpretation** through their repeated use in literature and the broader culture. For example, spring and winter are conventional symbols of birth and death, as they appear with that meaning in Shakespeare's works through Frost's poetry. Colors, too, can be used as conventional symbols; in contemporary society, a pink ribbon is a conventional symbol of breast cancer awareness.

Cosmic Irony A literary convention where forces beyond the control of **characters**—such as God or fate or the supernatural—foil plans or expectations.

Couplet Two lines of poetry forming one unit of meaning. Couplets are often **rhymed,** strung together without a break, and share the same **meter.**

Cothurni Tall boots, worn by actors in the Ancient Greek theater, which served both to elevate an actor and make him more visible to the massive crowds, and also to make the **character**s seem larger than life.

Craft As a noun, craft refers to the elements that comprise a story; as a verb, craft refers to the process of making or fashioning a story out of those elements.

Cretic Also called *Amphimacer.* A syllable pattern characterized by three syllables in the order *stressed, unstressed, stressed.*

Crisis See **Climax.**

Critical Reading A process of digesting and understanding a text so you can appreciate not just the ideas it presents or the story it tells, but how it presents those ideas, why it presents them, and how those ideas exist in a certain context. Critical reading involves **summary, analysis, synthesis,** and **interpretation.**

Critique A **summary** accompanied by one's own personal opinion and perspectives.

Cultural Studies This critical perspective was developed mainly in England in the sixties by New Left writers, social philosophers, and sociologists. Cultural studies incorporates the techniques of literary analysis to **analyze** social life and social movements as though they were written texts.

Dactylic Meter A **meter** in which the foot contains a stressed syllable followed by two unstressed syllables.

Deconstruction A critical approach to analyzing literature based on the idea that texts do not have a single, stable meaning or **interpretation.** Deconstructionists seek to break down literature to reveal the inevitable inconsistency or lack of unity in even the most successful and revered texts, believing that the author's intentions have no bearing on the meaning of the text to the reader.

Decorum A certain level of propriety appropriate to a given text. As well as demanding a certain level of **diction,** decorum can also have bearing on the **characters, setting,** and **plot** events of a piece of literature.

Denotation The literal meaning of a word. The opposite of **connotation.**

Denouement The period after the story's **climax** when **conflicts** are addressed and/or resolved. Includes the **falling action** and **resolution** of a story.

Deus ex machina Latin for *God from the machine;* a literary device, often seen in drama, where a **conflict** is resolved by unforeseen and often far-fetched means.

Dialect **Dialogue** written to phonetically or grammatically replicate a particular **sound,** cadence, **rhythm,** or emphasis in a **character's** speech.

Dialogue Spoken interaction between two or more **characters.** A **characterization** technique that can signal class, education, intelligence, ethnicity, and attitude in the characters involved.

Diction An author's or **character's** distinctive choice of words and style of expression.

Didactic Literature Literature, such as a fable or **allegory,** written to instruct or teach a moral.

Dimeter A poetic **meter** comprised of two poetic feet.

Dirge A funeral song.

Doggerel An obviously patterned piece of **rhyme,** often lunging or twisting word order in order to get a rhyme. Doggerel can sometimes seem almost childish and, when extensive, boring.

Drama A term that comes from the Greek word for doing or acting and refers to a literary work that is represented through performance.

Dramatic Irony A situation in which an author or **narrator** lets the reader know more about a situation than a **character** does.

Dramatic Monologue A poem in which a **character** addresses another character or the reader. Dramatic monologues are offshoots of the epic form.

Dramatic Poetry Poetry in which the speaker of the poem is not the poet. Dramatic poetry often tells a story.

Dramatic Point of View A **third-person point of view** in which the **narrator** presents only bare details and the **dialogue** of other **characters.**

Dramatic Question The overarching challenge or issue in a piece of drama—the complication which the events of a play work to resolve.

Dynamic Character A **character** whose personality and behavior alter over the course of the action in response to challenges and changing circumstances.

Dramatis Personae "People of the play"; a list of the **characters** in a play, usually one of the first elements of a script.

Echo Verse Poetry in which words at the ends of lines or **stanzas** are repeated, mimicking an echo.

Economic Determinist Criticism *See* **Marxist Criticism.**

Editorial Omniscience A **narrator** inserts his or her own commentary about **characters** or events into the narrative.

Electra Complex The female version of the **Oedipus Complex,** the Electra Complex suggests that female children are hostile toward their mothers because of subconscious sexual attraction to their fathers.

Elegy A poem of lamentation memorializing the dead or contemplating some nuance of life's melancholy. Early Greek elegies employed a fixed form of **dactylic hexameter** and **iambic pentameter couplets.**

Elision The omission of a vowel or consonant sound within or between words, such as "ne'er" for "never" and "o'er" for "over." Elision dramatizes language and allows for flexibility within a poem's **meter.**

Ellipses Three periods placed in succession (. . .) to illustrate that something has been omitted.

End Rhyme **Rhyme** that occurs at the end of two or more lines of poetry. An example of end rhyme can be found in "The Love Song of J. Alfred Prufrock": "Let us go through certain half-deserted streets, / The muttering retreats."

End-stopped Line A line that ends with a full stop or period.

Endnote Information placed at the end of a text in an explanatory note. In a research paper, endnotes are used to comment on sources or provide additional analysis that is slightly tangential to the focus of your paper. An endnote is indicated by a superscript number ([1]) in the text itself, which corresponds to a numbered explanatory note at the end.

English Sonnet *See* **Shakespearean Sonnet.**

Enjambment The running over of a phrase from one line into another so that closely related words belong to different lines.

Envoi The final **stanza** of a **sestina,** which summarizes the entire poem. Envoi is French for *farewell.*

Epic A long **narrative poem,** traditionally recited publicly, whose subject matter reflects the values of the culture from which it came by portraying important legends or heroes. Classical epics include the *Odyssey* and the *Aeneid,* while English epics include *Beowulf* and *Paradise Lost.*

Epigram A short, often satirical observation on a single subject.

Epigraph A quotation or brief passage from another source, included at the beginning of a piece of literature. Writers use epigraphs to suggest a major theme or idea in their work.

Epiphany A sudden realization or new understanding achieved by a **character** or speaker. In many short stories, the character's epiphany is the **climax** of the story.

Episode A unified event or incident within a longer narrative.

Episodia The scenes of a Greek tragedy, divided by **stasimon** from the **Chorus.**

Epistolary Novel A novel written in the form of letters between two or more **characters,** or in the form of diary entries. Epistolary novels were particularly popular in the eighteenth century.

Ethnic Studies A critical approach to literature that seeks to give voice to literature that has previously been overlooked in the traditionally Euro-centric worldview—not simply by including ethnically diverse literature in the **canon,** but by attention to historically underrepresented groups, like African Americans and Native Americans.

Euphony Musically pleasing poetic language.

Evidence Reliable information, such as statistics, expert opinions, and anecdotes, used to support a **claim** in an **argument.**

Exact Rhyme A rhyme in which the final vowel and consonant sounds are identical, regardless of spelling. Also called *pure rhyme, perfect rhyme,* and *true rhyme.*

Exodos The concluding scene of a Greek **tragedy.**

Explication a **close reading** of any text where the goal is to logically **analyze** details within the text itself to uncover deeper meanings or contradictions.

Exposition: The narrative presentation of necessary information about the **character, setting,** or character's history provided to make the reader care what happens to the characters in the story.

Expressionism A mode of theater in which the playwright attempts to portray his or her subjective emotions in a symbolic way on stage.

Extended Metaphor A figurative analogy that is woven through a poem.

Eye Rhyme Words that share similar spellings but—when spoken—have different sounds. For example, *lint* and *pint.* Also called *Sight Rhyme.*

Fables A short narrative in which the **characters** (often animals or inanimate things) illustrate a lesson. The characters in fables are *actors* rather than **symbols.**

Fairy Tale A story, usually for children, that involves magical creatures or circumstances and usually has a happy ending.

Falling Action The events following the **climax** and leading up to the **resolution.** These events reveal how the **protagonist** has been impacted by and dealt with the preceding **conflicts** of the story.

Falling Meter A **meter** comprised of feet that begin with a stressed syllable, followed by an unstressed syllable or syllables. **Trochaic** and **dactylic** feet both create falling meter, which is named for the effect of *falling* from the initial stressed syllable to the unstressed.

Fantasy A literary **genre** that uses magical **characters** or circumstances.

Farce A work of drama or literature that uses broad, often physical **comedy,** exaggerated **characters,** absurd situations, and improbable **plot** twists to evoke laughter without intending social criticism.

Feminine Rhyme Rhymes between multisyllable words in which the final syllable is unstressed, such as *bother* and *father.* Also called *falling rhyme.*

Feminist Criticism An approach to literary criticism that highlights literature written by women and the exploration of the experience of female **characters**; also a critical examination of the ways in which female characters are viewed with prejudice, are subjugated to male interests, or are simply overlooked in literature.

Fiction A genre of literature that describes events and **characters** invented by the author.

Figurative Language Language that describes one thing by relating it to something else.

Figure of Speech A technique of using language to describe one thing in terms of another, often comparing two unlike objects, such as *the sun* and *the face of the beloved,* to condense and heighten the effect of language, particularly the effect of **imagery** or **symbolism** in a poem.

First-Person Narrator The story is narrated by a **character** in the story, identified by use of the pronoun *I* or the plural first-person, *we.*

Fixed Form An arrangement of text that requires a poet to obey set written combinations, including line length, **meter, stanza** structure, and **rhyme scheme.** Also called *closed form.*

Flashback The device of moving back in time to a point before the primary action of the story.

Flat Character A **character** with a narrow range of speech or action. Flat characters are predictable and do not develop over the course of the **plot.**

Foil A **character** who contrasts with the central character, often with the purpose of emphasizing some trait in the central character. For example, a cruel sister emphasizes the other sister's kindness.

Folklore A traditional **canon** of stories, sayings, and **characters.**

Folktale A short, often fantastic tale passed down over time.

Foot The smallest unit of measure in poetic **meter.** A foot usually contains a stressed syllable and one or two unstressed syllables. **Meter** is formed when the same foot repeats more than once. For example, in **iambic pentameter,** *iambic* refers to the type of foot (an unstressed syllable followed by a stressed syllable), while *pentameter* tells us that there are five (pent) iambic feet in each line.

Footnote Like an **endnote,** a way to include commentary on sources or other information tangential to the focus of a text. A footnote occurs at the bottom of the page on which the subject is most closely addressed. To create a footnote, a superscript number ([1]) is placed in the text itself and corresponds to the number of the explanatory note at the bottom of the page.

Foreshadowing A hint about **plot** elements to come, both to advance the plot and build **suspense.**

Form The shape, structure, and style of a poem, as distinguishable from, but integral to, the content or substance of the poem.

Formal Diction Complex, grammatically proper, and often polysyllabic language in writing. It sounds grandiloquent—a *formal* word—and tends not to resemble the sort of talk heard in daily life.

Formalist Criticism An approach to literary criticism that considers a successful text to be a complete, independent, unified artifact whose meaning and value can be understood purely by analyzing the interaction of its formal and technical components, such as **plot, imagery,** structure, style, **symbol,** and **tone.** Rather than drawing their textual interpretations from *extrinsic* factors such as the historical, political, or biographical context of the work, formalist critics focus on the text's *intrinsic* formal elements.

Found Poem A poem created from already existing text that the poet reshapes and presents in poetic form. Text may come from advertisements, labels on household items, newspapers, magazines, or any other printed source not intended originally as poetry. A poet may piece together several sources like a collage, or he/she might take a short text exactly as it is and insert line breaks.

Fourth Wall The *invisible wall* of the stage, through which the audience views the action.

Free Verse Poetry in which the poet does not adhere to a preset metrical or **rhyme scheme.** Free verse has become increasingly prevalent since the nineteenth century, when it was first used. *See* **Open Form.**

Freewrite Writing continuously to generate ideas, without worrying about mistakes.

Gay and Lesbian Criticism A critical approach that is similar to **feminist criticism** in its quest to uncover previously overlooked undertones and themes in literature. Gay and lesbian criticism seeks to identify underlying homosexual themes in literature.

Gender Criticism A critical approach to literature that seeks to understand how gender and sexual identity reflect upon the interpretation of literary works. Feminist criticism and gay and lesbian criticism are derivatives of gender criticism.

Genre A literary category or form, such as the short story or novel, or a specific type of fiction, such as science fiction or mystery.

Groundlings "Standing room only" spectators in the Elizabethan theater who paid a penny to stand on the ground surrounding the stage.

Haiku A poetic form containing seventeen syllables in three lines of five, seven, and five syllables each. Haiku traditionally contain a natural-world reference or central **image.**

Hamartia A tragic flaw or weakness in a tragic **character** that leads to his or her downfall. **Hubris** is a type of *hamartia.*

Heptameter A poetic **meter** that consists of seven feet in each line.

Hero/Heroine The **protagonist** of a story, often possessing positive traits such as courage or honesty.

Heroic Couplet Two successive rhyming lines in **iambic pentameter.**

Hexameter A poetic **meter** that consists of six feet in each line. If the six feet are **iambic,** the line is known as an alexandrine, which was the preferred line of French epic poetry.

High Comedy **Comedy,** often a satire of upper-class society, that relies on sophisticated wit and **irony.**

Hip Hop An intensely rhythmical form of popular music developed by African-Americans and Latinos in the 1970s in which vocalists deploy rhyme—known as rap—over the rhythm.

Historical Criticism An approach to **literary criticism** that em-

phasizes the relationship between a text and its historical context. When interpreting a text, historical critics highlight the cultural, philosophical, and political movements and ideologies prevalent during the text's creation and reception.

Historical Fiction A type of fiction writing wherein the author bases his or her **characters, plot,** or **setting** on actual people, events, or places.

Histories *See* **Classifications of Drama.**

Hubris Excessive arrogance or pride. In classical literature, the hero's tragic flaw was often hubris, which caused his downfall in the tragedy.

Hyperbole A type of figurative speech that uses verbal exaggeration to make a point. Hyperbole is sometimes called *overstatement.*

Iamb A poetic **foot** consisting of an unstressed syllable followed by a stressed syllable.

Iambic Meter A poetic **meter** created when each line contains more than one **iamb** (a unit with an unstressed syllable followed by a stressed syllable).

Iambic Pentameter A poetic **meter** in which each line contains five feet, predominantly iambs. Iambic pentameter is the most commonly used meter in English poetry, comprising **sonnets,** much of Shakespeare's plays, Milton's *Paradise Lost,* Wordsworth's *The Prelude* and Wallace Stevens' "Sunday Morning."

Iconography **Symbols** that commonly engender a certain meaning. For example, a skull equals *death,* and a dove equals *peace.*

Image A sensory impression created by language. Not all images are visual pictures; an image can appeal to any of the five senses, emotions, or the intellect.

Imagism A poetic practice wherein the *thing itself*—the object seen and not discussed or **analyzed**—

becomes the poet's focus and the poem's primary concern. Imagism is associated with poets like Ezra Pound and William Carlos Williams.

Impartial Omniscience A **narrator** who remains neutral, relating events and **characters'** thoughts without passing judgment or offering an opinion.

Implied Metaphor A suggested comparison that is never stated plainly.

Impressionism In literature, a style of writing that focuses on a **protagonist**'s reactions to external events rather than the events themselves.

Indirect Discourse A **narrator**'s description of an action or event as experienced by a **character** in the story.

Informal Diction An author's use of words that are conversational or easily understood, as opposed to elevated or formal language. For example, using *you* instead of *thou.*

Initial Alliteration The repetition of consonant or vowel sounds in the middle of a line of poetry.

Initiation Story *See* **Coming of Age Story** and *Bildungsroman.*

In medias res Latin for *in the middle of things.* A term applied when a story begins with relevant story events already having occurred.

Innocent Narrator *See* **Naïve Narrator.**

Intentional Fallacy The practice by **formalist** critics of discerning or trusting an author's own stated purpose for the meaning of a text.

Interior Monologue A **character**'s conscious or unconscious thought processes, narrated as they occur, with only minimal-seeming guidance from the **narrator.**

Internal Alliteration The repetition of consonant or vowel sounds in the middle of a line of poetry.

Internal Refrain The repetition of words or phrases within the lines of a poem.

Internal Rhyme **Rhyme** that occurs within a line. The placement of internal rhyme can vary; for example, a word in the middle of the line might rhyme with the word at the end of that same line, or both rhyming words might occur in the middle of two consecutive lines.

Interpret The act of **interpretation.**

Interpretation The process of contributing to the overall understanding of some aspect of a work in order to illuminate its meaning.

In-Text Parenthetical Citation A reference within the body of a paper that links a **quotation, paraphrase,** or **summary** from another source to its full citation in the list of **works cited.**

In the Round *See* **Arena Theater.**

Inverted Syntax A reversal of expected or traditional word order, often used to aid a poem's sounds, **rhyme,** and/or **meter.**

Ironic Point of View Describes a **narrator** who does not understand the significance of the events of a story.

Irony A **tone** characterized by a distance between what occurs and what is expected to occur, or between what is said and what is meant.

Italian Sonnet *See* **Petrarchan Sonnet.**

Jargon Words used with specific meaning for a particular group of people. For example, *starboard* in nautical jargon refers to the right side of a ship.

Journal Entry A writing exercise that expands **freewriting** into a more focused discussion that reflects a growing understanding of a topic.

Language, Tone, and Style The elements that conjure a story's particular flavor and **voice,** as achieved by means of the words the author chooses and the **rhythm** with which he or she puts the words together

Language The words of a story, including **syntax** (how words or other elements of the sentence are arranged) and **diction** (what words the author chooses).

Levels of Diction Refers to the three major categories of diction: high, middle, and low diction. The level of diction a writer uses determines whether the words in the work will be formal or informal, poetic or conversational, etc.

Limerick A light, often humorous verse form consisting of five **anapestic** (two short syllables followed by one long one) lines, with a rhyme scheme of *aabba*. The first, second, and fifth lines consist of three feet, while lines three and four consist of two feet.

Limited Omniscient Narrator A **third-person narrator** who enters into the mind of only one **character** at a time. This narrator serves more as an interpreter than a source of the main **character's** thoughts.

Line A row of words containing phrases and/or sentences. The line is a defining feature of poetry, in which there are often set amounts of syllables or poetic feet in each line.

Literary Ballad A story told in **ballad** form.

Literary Criticism The acts of analyzing, interpreting, and commenting on literature.

Literary Epic *See* **Epic.**

Literary Theory The body of criticism and schools of thought (such as **Feminist, Deconstructionist,** or **Biographical** Criticism) that govern how we study literature.

Low Comedy An informal brand of **comedy** that uses crude humor and **slapstick.**

Lyric A short poem with a central pictorial **image** written in an uninflected (direct and personal) **voice.**

Madrigal A variety of contrapuntal song that originated in 16th-century Italy. Madrigal features

secular verse sung by two or more voices without instrumental accompaniment.

Magic Realism A type of fiction in which something "magical" happens in an otherwise realistic world. The form is particularly associated with Latin American writers like Gabriel García Márquez. Unlike **fantasy** or science fiction, magic realism generally has only one fantastical element and the rest relies on realistic **characters** and settings. Notable examples in this book are Franz Kafka's *The Metamorphosis* and Aimee Bender's "The Rememberer."

Marxist Criticism Marxist or Economic Determinist Criticism is based on the writings of Karl Marx, who argued that economic concerns shape lives more than anything else, and that society is essentially a struggle between the working classes and the dominant capitalist classes. Rather than assuming that culture evolves naturally or autonomously out of individual human experience, Marxist critics maintain that culture—including literature—is shaped by the interests of the dominant or most powerful social class.

Masculine Rhyme The **end rhymes** of multisyllable words with a stressed final syllable, such as *remove* and *approve*. Also called rising rhyme.

Melodrama A literary work, mainly a stage play, movie, or television play or show in which **characters** display exaggerated emotions and the **plot** takes sensational turns, sometimes accompanied by music intended to lead the audience's feelings.

Melody The linear succession of various musical pitches recognized as a unit.

Metafiction A work of fiction that self-consciously draws attention to itself as a work of fiction. Rather than upholding the standard pretense, prevalent in realist fiction, that a story creates or refers to a "real world" beyond the text, metafiction self-consciously reveals the fact and sometimes the manner of its own construction. Metafiction is often associated with **postmodernism,** but examples of metafiction also occur in many other literary movements.

Metaphor A close comparison of two dissimilar things that creates a fusion of identity between the things that are compared. A metaphor joins two dissimilar things *without* using words such as *like* or *as*. While a **simile** suggests that X is *like* Y a metaphor states that X *is* Y.

Meter A measure of verse, based on regular patterns of sound.

Metonymy A **figure of speech** that uses an identifying emblem or closely associated object to represent another object. For example, the phrase *the power of the purse* makes little sense literally (there is no purse that has power), but in the metonymical sense, *purse* stands for money.

Middle Diction Poetic language characterized by sophisticated word usage and grammatical accuracy. Middle diction reads as educated, cultured language but is not extravagant like **poetic diction.**

Mime The act of performing a play without words.

Miracle Plays During the tenth century, when drama was suppressed by the church, these anonymous plays were acted out as religious instruction for the benefit of spectators who could not read the Bible.

Mixed Metaphor A failed comparison that results when a writer uses at least two separate, mismatched comparisons in one statement—to confusing, and sometimes comical effect. For example, *The early bird strikes when the iron's hot!*

Monologue A single **character's** discourse, without interaction or interruption by other **characters.**

Monometer A poetic **meter** comprised of one poetic foot.

Monosyllabic A word with one syllable.

Moral The lesson taught by a piece of **didactic literature** such as a fable. A moral is often phrased simply and memorably.

Morality Play A form of drama in which the figures on stage taught right and proper behavior—morality—to those who watched.

Motif A pattern of **imagery** or a concept that recurs throughout a work of literature.

Motivation A **character's** reason for doing something.

Mystery Play A play that enacted stories of the Bible, such as the Creation or the Crucifixion. These plays appeared during the tenth century, when drama was suppressed in England.

Myth The pre-Classical Greek word for sacred story or religious narrative, which by the Classical period had come to mean **plot,** as used in Aristotle's *Poetics*.

Mythological Criticism Also called the *archetypal approach*, mythological criticism stems from the work of Carl Jung, a Swiss psychoanalyst (and contemporary of Freud) who argued that humans share in a **collective unconscious,** or a set of **characters,** plots, symbols, and **images** that each evoke a universal response. Jung calls these recurring elements **archetypes,** and likens them to *instincts*—knowledge or associations with which humans are born. Mythological critics **analyze** the ways in which such archetypes function in literature and attempt to explain the power that literature has over us or the reasons why certain texts continue to hold power over audiences many centuries after their creation.

Naïve Narrator An unreliable **narrator** who remains unaware of the full complexity of events in the story being told, often due to youth, innocence, or lack of cultural awareness.

Narrative Poem A poem that tells a story. Examples include Tennyson's "The Charge of the Light Brigade," Longfellow's "The Midnight Ride of Paul Revere," and most ballads.

Narrator The **character** or consciousness that tells a story. For specific types of narrators, see **First-Person Narrator, Second-Person Narrator, Third-Person narrator, Omniscient Narrator, Limited Omniscient Narrator, Impartial Omniscience, Editorial Omniscience, Naïve Narrator,** and **Unreliable Narrator.**

Naturalistic Theater Drama that shines a light on the painful realities and problems of everyday life.

Near Rhyme *See* **Slant Rhyme.**

New Criticism *See* **Formalist Criticism.**

New Historicism A critical approach that emerged as a reaction to **new criticism's** disregard of historical context, but also in response to the perceived shortcomings of older methods of **historical criticism.** Rather than focusing on texts in the **canon** as representations of the most powerful or dominant historical movements, new historicists give equal or greater attention to less dominant texts and non-literary texts (newspapers, pamphlets, legal documents, medical documents, etc.). New historicists attempt to highlight overlooked or suppressed texts, particularly those that express deviation from the dominant culture of the time. In this way, new historicists study not just the historical context of a major literary text, but the complex relationship between texts and culture, or the ways in which literature can challenge as well as support a given culture.

Nonfiction Novel   A presentation of real events using the craft and technique of a fiction novel.

Novel   A long fictional work. Because of their greater length, novels are typically complex and may follow more than one **character** or **plot**.

Novella   A short novel, which generally means it has more complexity than a short story but without the usual length of a novel.

Objective Point of View   The story is told by an observer who relates only facts, providing neither commentary nor insight into the **character's** thoughts or actions.

Observer   A **first-person narrator** who does not participate in the action of the story.

Octameter   A poetic **meter** that consists of eight feet in each line.

Octave   Eight lines of poetry grouped together in a **stanza** or a unit of thought, as in the **Petrarchan sonnet** where the octave sets up a thought or feeling that the following **sestet** resolves.

Ode   An elevated, formal **lyric** poem often written in ceremony to someone or to an abstract subject. In Greek **tragedy**, a song and dance performed by the **Chorus** between *episodia*.

Oedipus Complex: Sigmund Freud's theory of behavior (derived from the **plot** of Sophocles's *Oedipus the King*) which holds that male children are jealous of the father because of their sexual attraction to the mother. In *Oedipus the King*, Oedipus kills his father and sleeps with his mother.

Off Rhyme   *See* **Slant Rhyme.**

O. Henry Ending   A short story ending that consists of a sudden surprise, often ironic or coincidental in nature, named for the short story writer O. Henry, who frequently ended his stories in this way. A classic example is O. Henry's "The Gift of the Magi" in which a husband and wife each give something precious of theirs to purchase a gift for the other; the ending reveals that each has sacrificed the very thing that would have allowed him or her to enjoy the gift received from their spouse.

Omniscient Narrator   A **third-person narrator** who observes the thoughts and describes the actions of multiple **characters** in the story. The omniscient narrator can see beyond the physical actions and **dialogue** of **characters** and is able to reveal the inner thoughts and emotions of anyone in the story.

One-Act Play   A play that consists of a single act that contains the entire action of the play. One-act plays usually portray a single **scene** with an exchange among a smaller number of **characters**; for example, Edward Albee's *The Zoo Story*.

Onomatopoeia   The use of words that imitate the sounds they refer to, such as *buzz* or *pop*.

Open Denoument   A **resolution** to a story that leaves loose ends and does not completely resolve the overarching **conflict.**

Open Form   Poetry ungoverned by metrical or rhyme schemes. Also called free verse.

Orchestra   The open area in front of the stage (or *skene*) in the Greek **amphitheater.**

Overstatement   *See* **Hyperbole.**

Oxymoron   A version of **paradox** that combines contradictory words into a compact, often two-word term, such as *jumbo shrimp* or *definitely maybe.*

Paean   The final choral **ode** of a Greek **tragedy.**

Pantoum   A variation on the **villanelle,** consisting of an unspecified number of **quatrains** with the rhyme scheme *abab*. The first line of each quatrain repeats the second line of the preceding quatrain, and the third line repeats the final line of the preceding quatrain. In the final quatrain, the second line repeats the third line of the first quatrain, and the last line of the poem repeats the first line of the poem.

Parable   A short narrative that illustrates a lesson using comparison to familiar **characters** and events. The characters and events in parables often have obvious significance as **symbols** and **allegories.**

Parados   The **Chorus'** first **ode** in a Greek **tragedy.**

Paradox   Seemingly contradictory statements that, when closely examined, have a deeper, sometimes complicated, meaning.

Parallelism   The arrangement of words or phrases in a grammatically similar way.

Paraphrase   Condensing a passage or idea from an existing text into your own words. Paraphrase does not mean simply changing the words from the original; rather, it should re-present the original in a way that demonstrates your understanding of it.

Parody   Mimicking another author or work of literature in such a way as to make fun of the original, often by exaggerating its characteristic aspects.

Participant narrator   A **first-person narrator** who takes part in the action of the story.

Pastoral Poetry   A variety of poem in which life in the countryside, mainly among shepherds, is glorified and idealized.

Pentameter   A poetic **meter** that consists of five feet in each line.

Peripeteia   An element of Greek **tragedy,** *peripeteia* occurs when an action has the opposite result of what was intended. In a **tragedy,** this generally occurs at a turning point for the **hero** and signals his downfall.

Persona   A poem's speaker, which may or may not use the **voice** of the poet.

Personae Masks, often representative of certain **iconography** and familiar **characters,** worn by actors in the Ancient Greek theater to enable one actor to perform as many **characters.** *Personae* often were designed to project an actor's voice to the far rows of the **amphitheater.**

Personification A **figure of speech** in which a writer ascribes human traits or behavior to something inhuman.

Persuasion The process of using **analysis** and logical **argument** to prove the validity of a certain **interpretation** or **point of view.**

Petrarchan (Italian) Sonnet A sonnet consisting of an **octave** and a **sestet,** all in **iambic pentameter,** with the rhyme scheme *abbaabba cdecde* or *abbaabba cdcdcd.* The **volta,** or turn, typically occurs between the octave and sestet, around line nine of the poem.

Plagiarism The act of taking credit for another's work or ideas.

Play A work of drama, usually performed before an audience.

Players Traveling actors, men and boys, who spoke their lines for pay.

Play Review The critique of a play.

Playwright The author of a dramatic work.

Plot The artful arrangement of incidents in a story, with each incident building on the next in a series of causes and effects.

Poetic Diction Lofty and elevated language, used traditionally in poetry written before the nineteenth century to separate poetic speech from common speech.

Point of View The perspective from which the story is told to the reader.

Polysyllabic A word that has many syllables.

Portmanteau Word A word invented by combining two other words to achieve the effect of both. Lewis Carroll's poem "Jabberwocky" is comprised largely of portmanteau words such as *slithy,* which means *slimy* and *lithe.*

Postcolonialism A critical approach to **literary criticism** that seeks to offer views of relations between the colonizing West and colonized nations and regions that differed sharply from the conventional Western perspectives.

Poststructuralist Criticism Criticism based on the belief that texts do not have a single, stable meaning or **interpretation,** in part because language itself is filled with ambiguity, multiple meanings, and meanings that can change with time or context.

Precís *See* **Summary Paper.**

Preview The process of gathering information about a piece of literature before you read it.

Problem Play A play about a social problem, written with an aim to create awareness of the problem.

Prologue The introduction to a literary work.

Proscenium Stage A realistic **setting** with three flat walls (two flat sides, and a ceiling) that simulates a room; the audience views the action through the missing **fourth wall.**

Prose Poem A poem that uses the devices and **imagery** characteristic of traditionally lined poetry, but in compact units without clearly defined line breaks.

Prosody The analysis of a poem's rhythm and metrical structures.

Protagonist The main figure (or principal actor) in a work of literature. A story's **plot** hinges equally on the protagonist's efforts to realize his or her desires and to cope with failure if and when plans are thwarted and desires left unfulfilled.

Psalm A sacred song, usually written to or in honor of a deity.

Psychoanalytic Criticism Also called *psychological criticism,* this approach in a sense studies **characters** and authors as one would patients, looking in the text for evidence of childhood trauma, repressed sexual impulses, preoccupation with death, and so on. Through the lens of psychology critics attempt to explain the motivations and meanings behind characters' actions. Psychological critics also use textual and biographical evidence as a means to better understand the author's psychology, as well as examine the process and nature of literary creation, studying the ways in which texts create an emotional and intellectual effect for their readers and authors.

Pun A play on words that reveals different meanings in words that are similar or even identical.

Pyrrhic A poetic foot characterized by two unstressed syllables.

Quantitative Meter A type of poetry that counts the length of syllables, rather than the emphasis they receive (as in **accentual meter** and syllabic verse). Quantitative meter primarily appears in Greek and Latin poetry and is rarely used in English since English vowel lengths are not clearly quantified.

Quatrain A four-line **stanza.** Quatrains are the most popular stanzaic form in English poetry because they are easily varied in **meter,** line length, and **rhyme scheme.**

Queer Theory The idea that power is reflected in language and that discourse itself shapes our sense of who we are and how we define ourselves sexually.

Rap An oral form of poetry that is akin to spoken word, but distinguished by musical qualities and choral repetitions. *See* **Hip Hop.**

Reader-Response Criticism The reader-response approach emphasizes that the reader is central to the writer-text-reader interaction. Reader-response critics believe a literary work is not complete until someone reads and **interprets** it.

Such critics acknowledge that because each reader has a different set of experiences and views, each reader's response to a text may be different.

Realism A mode of literature in which the author depicts **characters** and scenarios that could occur in real life. Unlike **fantasy** or **surrealism**, realism seeks to represent the world as it is.

Recognition The moment in a **tragedy** when the **hero** comes to recognize the actuality of events and is no longer under illusion.

Refrain A line or **stanza** that is repeated at regular intervals in a poem or song.

Resolution The end of the story, where the **conflict** is ultimately resolved and the effects of the story's events on the **protagonist** become evident.

Restoration Comedy A bawdy play about fallen virtue and infidelity that became popular after the Puritans were displaced in England in the mid-seventeenth century.

Retrospect *See* **Flashback.**

Reversal *See* *Peripeteia.*

Rhyme The echoing repetition of sounds in the end syllables of words, often (though not always) at the end of a line of poetry.

Rhyme Scheme The pattern of **rhyme** throughout a particular poem.

Rhythm The sequence of stressed and unstressed sounds in a poem.

Rising Action Story events that increase tension and move the plot toward the climax.

Rising Meter A **meter** comprised of feet that begin with an unstressed syllable, followed by a stressed syllable or syllables. **Iambic** and **anapestic** feet both create rising meter, which is named for the effect of *rising* from the initial unstressed syllable to the stressed.

Romance *See* **Classifications of Drama.**

Romantic Comedy A type of **comedy** in which two would-be/should-be lovers find each other after a series of misunderstandings and false starts.

Round Character A **character** with complex, multifaceted characteristics. Round characters behave as real people. For example, a round **hero** may suffer temptation, and a round **villain** may show compassion.

Run-On Line A line of poetry that, when read, does not come to a natural conclusion where the line breaks. *See* **Enjambment.**

Sarcasm Verbal irony that is intended in a mean-spirited, malicious, or critical way.

Satire An artistic critique, sometimes heated, on some aspect of human immorality or absurdity.

Satiric Comedy A derisive and dark **comedy** in which there is no promise that good will prevail.

Satyr Play An often obscene satirical fourth play, provided after a trilogy of tragedies, meant to provide **comic relief.**

Scansion The process of determining the metrical pattern of a line of poetry by marking its stresses and feet.

Scene A defined moment of action or interaction in a story usually confined to a single **setting.** Scenes are the building blocks of a story's **plot.**

Scenery The set pieces and stage decorations onstage during the performance of a play.

Scratch Outline A multi-tiered, ordered list of topics that should be covered in a paper. A scratch outline goes into deeper detail than a topic outline.

Screenplay A script that is specifically tailored and structured for television or film rather than the stage.

Script The written text of a play, which may include set descriptions and actor cues.

Second-Person Narrator A **narrator** who addresses the character as *you*, often involving the reader by association.

Semiotics The study of how meaning is attached to and communicated by symbols.

Sentence Outline An outline that uses complete sentences instead of brief words or phrases.

Sestet Six lines of poetry grouped together in a stanza or a unit of thought, as in the **Petrarchan sonnet** where the last six lines of the poem resolve the idea or question set up by the initial **octave.**

Sestina A poem of six six-line **stanzas** and a three-line **envoi,** usually unrhymed, in which each stanza repeats the end words of the lines of the first stanza, but in different order, the envoi using the six words again, three in the middle of the lines and three at the end.

Setting The time and place where the story occurs. Setting creates expectations for the types of **characters** and situations encountered in the story.

Shakespearean (English) Sonnet A **sonnet** form composed of three quatrains and a final couplet, all in **iambic pentameter** and rhymed *abab cdcd efef gg.* The **volta,** or turn, occurs in the final **couplet** of the poem.

Short Story A brief fictional narrative that attempts to dramatize or illustrate the effect or meaning of a single incident or small group of incidents in the life of a single **character** or small group of characters.

Simile A direct comparison of two dissimilar things using the words *like* or *as.*

Situational Irony A situation portrayed in a poem when what occurs is the opposite or very different from what's expected to occur.

Skene The stage in the Greek **amphitheater.**

Slam Poetry in a variety of styles, performed competitively in clubs and halls.

Slant Rhyme   A case in which vowel or consonant sounds are similar but not exactly the same, such as *heap* and *rap* and *tape*. Also called *near rhyme, imperfect rhyme* and *off rhyme*.

Slapstick   A type of low **comedy** characterized by unexpected, often physical humor. A classic example of slapstick is the man walking along who accidentally slips on a banana peel.

Social Environment   A study of **setting** that considers era and location as well as a **character's** living and working conditions.

Sociological Criticism   The study of literary texts as products of the cultural, political, and economic context of the author's time and place.

Soliloquy   A **monologue** delivered by a **character** in a play who is alone onstage. Soliloquies generally have a **character** revealing his or her thoughts to the audience.

Sonnet   A poem of fourteen lines of **iambic pentameter** in a recognizable pattern of **rhyme.** Sonnets contain a **volta,** or turn, in which the last lines resolve or change direction from the controlling idea of the preceding lines.

Sound   The rhythmic structure of the lines of a poem, which draws the reader in, often utilizing **rhyme** and created through word choice and word order.

Spoken Word Poetry   Poetry that derives from the **Beat** poets, characterized by emphasis of the *performance* of a poem over the written form. Spoken word often employs improvisation.

Spondee   A poetic foot characterized by two stressed syllables.

Stage Directions   Cues, included by the playwright in the script of a play, which inform the actions of the actors during the play.

Stanza   A unit of two or more lines, set off by a space, often sharing the same **rhythm** and **meter.**

Stasimon   In Greek **tragedy,** an ode performed by the **Chorus** which interprets and responds to the preceding scene.

Static Character   A **character,** often flat, who does not change over the course of the story.

Stock Character   A **character** who represents a concept or type of behavior, such as a "mean teacher" or "mischievous student," and offers readers the comfort of repetition and reliability.

Stream of Consciousness: A **character's** thoughts are presented flowing by in free association, and the literary convention that rules is that there is no writer mediating the consciousness of the subject.

Stress   The vocal emphasis on a syllable in a line of verse, largely a matter of pitch.

Structuralism   Structuralist literary critics work from the belief that a given work of literature can be fully understood only when a reader considers the system of conventions, or the *genre* to which it belongs or responds.

Style   The characteristic way in which any writer uses language.

Subplot   A **plot** that is not the central plot of the work, but nonetheless appears in the same work. Longer works, like **novels** and plays, tend to have subplots that might follow side **characters** or somehow affect the action of the main plot.

Summary   Restating concisely the main ideas of a text without adding opinion or commentary. The best approach to summary is to divide the text into its major sections and then write a sentence for each section stating its main idea.

Summary Paper   A short paper that represents the main ideas of the text as the author has presented them, excluding any subjective ideas or interpretations.

Surrealism   A technique of the modern theater in which the realms of conscious and unconscious experience are fused together to create a total reality. In this way the fiction writer, poet, and **playwright,** tap into the resources of the unconscious mind and the imagination and portray in story on the page or on the modern stage the stuff of human desire, hope, and dreams.

Suspense   A sense of anticipation or excitement about what will happen and how the **characters** will deal with their newfound predicament.

Syllabic verse   A verse form that uses a fixed number of syllables per line or stanza, regardless of the number of stressed or unstressed syllables.

Symbol   Any object, **image, character,** or action that suggests meaning beyond the everyday literal level.

Symbolic Act   A gesture or action beyond the everyday practical definition.

Synecdoche   A **figure of speech** that uses a piece or part of a thing to represent the thing in its entirety. For example, in the Biblical saying that man does not live by bread alone, *bread* stands for the larger concept of food or physical sustenance.

Synopsis   A **summary** or **précis** of a work.

Syntax   The meaningful arrangement of words and phrases. Syntax can refer to word placement and order, as well as the overall length and shape of a sentence.

Synthesis   The act of bringing together the ideas and observations generated by reading and analysis in order to make a concrete statement about a work.

Tactile Imagery   Imagery that appeals to a reader's sense of touch.

Tercet   A group of three lines of poetry, sometimes called a **triplet** when all three lines rhyme.

Terminal Refrain Repeated lines which appear at the end of each **stanza** in a poem.

Terza Rima A **tercet** fixed form featuring the interlocking rhyme scheme *aba, bcb, cdc, ded,* etc.

Tetrameter A poetic **meter** that contains four feet in each line.

Theme The central or underlying meanings of a literary work.

Thesis Statement A sentence, usually but not always included in a paper's introductory paragraph, that defines a paper's purpose and argument.

Thesis A paper's purpose and **argument,** defined by the **thesis statement** and proved by the paper's **conclusion.**

Third-Person Narrator A **narrator** who is outside the story. The narrator refers to all the **characters** in the story with the pronouns *he, she,* or *they.*

Tiring House In the Elizabethan theater, a room, adjoined to the stage, in which actors changed their costumes.

Tone The author's attitude toward his or her **characters** or subject matter.

Topic Outline A multi-tiered organization of a paper's topics and **arguments,** used to structure a paper.

Tragedy A dramatic form in which **characters** face serious and important challenges that end in disastrous failure or defeat for the **protagonist.** *See* **Classifications of Drama.**

Tragic Flaw In classical literature, the hero's weakness that causes his downfall.

Tragic Hero A heroic **protagonist** who from the beginning, due to some innate flaw in his **character** or some unforeseeable mistake (*see* **Tragic Flaw**), is doomed. The inevitability of a tragic hero's demise inspires sympathy in the audience.

Tragic Irony The situation in a **tragedy** where the audience is aware of the **tragic hero's** fate although the **character** has not yet become aware.

Tragicomedy A play with the elements of **tragedy** that ends happily.

Transferred Epithet A description that pairs an adjective with a noun that does not logically follow, such as *silver sounds.*

Trimeter A poetic **meter** that contains three feet in each line.

Triplet A **tercet** of three rhymed lines.

Trochaic Meter: A poetic **meter** created when each line contains more than one **trochee** (a unit with a stressed syllable followed by an unstressed syllable). Trochaic meter is a type of **falling meter.**

Trochee A poetic **foot** consisting of a stressed syllable followed by an unstressed syllable. The opposite of an **iamb,** and so sometimes called an "inverted foot," often beginning a line of **iambic pentameter.**

Understatement A purposeful underestimation of something, used to emphasize its actual magnitude.

Unreliable Narrator A **narrator** who cannot be trusted to present an undistorted account of the action because of inexperience, ignorance, personal bias, intentional deceptiveness, or even insanity.

Verbal Irony A statement in which the stated meaning is very different (sometimes opposite) from the implied meaning.

Verisimilitude How alike an imitation is to its original. The goal of literature, especially when written in the mode of realism, is to provide a likeness, or a verisimilitude, of real life.

Verse A broad term to describe poetic lines.

Vers libre See **Free Verse.**

Villanelle A poem consisting of five **tercets** and a concluding **quatrain.** Each tercet rhymes *aba* and the final quatrain rhymes *abaa.* The poem's opening line repeats as the final line of the second and fourth stanzas, and in the second-to-last line of the poem. The last line of the first **stanza** repeats as the final line of the third and fifth stanzas and is also the final line of the poem overall.

Visual imagery **Imagery** and descriptions that appeal to a reader's sense of sight.

Voice The unique sound of an author's writing, created by elements such as **diction, tone,** and sentence construction.

Volta In a sonnet, the turn where a shift in thought or emotion occurs. In the **Petrarchan sonnet,** the **volta** occurs between the **octave** and the **sestet;** in the **Shakespearean sonnet,** the ending couplet provides the volta.

Vulgate A term to describe the common people, often used in reference to a level of speech or **diction.**

Well-made Play A type of theater popularized in France. Well-made plays feature a three-act sequence that *poses* a problem, *complicates* and then *resolves* it; usually that **resolution** comes when a **character's** past is revealed. The first act offers *exposition,* the second a *situation,* the third an unraveling or *completion.* Meticulous plotting and **suspense** are components of this mode of theater.

Working Bibliography A list of all the sources consulted in preparing a paper, as well as all the information necessary to cite them in the final list of works cited.

Works Cited A list of all the primary and secondary sources consulted in the creation of a paper.

Credits

Adichi, Chimamanda Ngozi. "Cell One" first published in *The New Yorker*, January 29, 2007. Copyright © 2007 by Chimamanda Ngozi Adichie, reprinted with permission of The Wylie Agency, Inc.

Alexie, Sherman. "What You Pawn I Will Redeem" from *Ten Little Indians* by Sherman Alexie. Copyright © 2003 by Sherman Alexie. Used by permission of Grove/Atlantic.

Atwood, Margaret. "Happy Endings" from *Good Bones and Simple Murders* by Margaret Atwood, copyright © 1983, 1992, 1994, by O.W. Toad Ltd. A Nan A. Talese Book. Used by permission of Doubleday, a division of Random House, Inc. and McClelland & Stewart.

Baldwin, James. "Sonny's Blues" © 1957 by James Baldwin was originally published in *Partisan Review*. Copyright renewed. Collected in *Going to Meet the Man*, published by Vintage Books. Used by arrangement with the James Baldwin Estate.

Barthes, Roland. Excerpt from "The Death of the Author" from *Image/Music/Text* by Roland Barthes, translated by Stephen Heath. English translation copyright © 1977 by Stephen Heath. Reprinted by permission of Hill and Wang, a division of Farrar, Straus & Giroux, LLC.

Bender, Aimee. "The Rememberer" from *The Girl in the Flammable Skirt* by Aimee Bender, copyright © 1998 by Aimee Bender. Used by permission of Doubleday, a division of Random House, Inc.

Borges, Jorge Luis. "The Circular Ruins" from *Collected Fictions by Jorge Luis Borges*, translated by Andrew Hurley, copyright © 1998 by Maria Kodama; translation copyright © 1998 by Penguin Putnam Inc. Used by permission of Viking Penguin, a division of Penguin Group (USA) Inc.

Boyle, T. Coraghessan. "Greasy Lake" from *Greasy Lake and Other Stories* by T. Coraghessan Boyle, copyright © 1979, 1981, 1982, 1983, 1984, 1985 by T. Coraghessan Boyle. Used by permission of Viking Penguin, a division of Penguin Group (USA) Inc.

Burke, Kenneth. Excerpt from "The Poetic Process" from *Counter-Statement* by Kenneth Burke, second edition, University of California Press. Reprinted by permission of the Kenneth Burke Literary Trust.

Carver, Raymond. "Cathedral" from *Cathedral* by Raymond Carver. Copyright © 1981, 1982, 1983 by Raymond Carver. Used by permission of Alfred A. Knopf, a division of Random House, Inc.

Chekhov, Anton. "The Lady with the Pet Dog" translated by Avrahm Yarmolinsky, from *The Portable Chekhov by Anton Chekhov*, edited by Avrahm Yarmolinsky, copyright 1947, © 1968 by Viking Penguin, Inc., renewed © 1975 by Avrahm Yarmolinsky. Used by permission of Viking Penguin, a division of Penguin Group (USA) Inc.

Chekhov, Anton. "Rapture" translated by Patrick Miles and Harvey Pitcher. Reprinted from *Chekhov: The Comic Stories*, published by Andre Deutsch by permission of Carlton Publishing Group.

Crichton, Michael. Excerpt from *Eaters of the Dead* by Michael Crichton, copyright © 1976 and renewed 2004 by Michael Crichton. Used by permission of Alfred A. Knopf, a division of Random House, Inc.

Diaz, Junot. "How to Date a Browngirl, Blackgirl, Whitegirl, or Halfie" from *Drown* by Junot Diaz. Copyright © 1996 by Junot Diaz. Used by permission of Riverhead Books, an imprint of Penguin Group (USA) Inc.

Eikhenbaum, Boris. Excerpt from "The Theory of the Formal Method" by Boris Eikhenbaum collected in *Readings in Russian Poetics: Formalist and Structuralist Views*, edited by Ladislav Matejka and Krystyna Pomorska (Michigan Slavic Publications, 1998). Reprinted by permission.

Ellison, Ralph. "Battle Royal" copyright 1948 by Ralph Ellison, from *Invisible Man* by Ralph Ellison. Used by permission of Random House, Inc.

Ellison, Ralph. "A Party Down at the Square" copyright © 1996 by Fanny Ellison, from *Flying Home and Other Stories* by Ralph Ellison. Used by permission of Random House, Inc.

Faulkner, William. "Barn Burning" copyright 1950 by Random House, Inc. Copyright renewed 1977 by Jill Faulkner Summers. "A Rose for Emily" copyright 1930 and renewed 1958 by William Faulkner, from *Collected Stories of William Faulkner* by William Faulkner. Used by permission of Random House, Inc.

Fetterley, Judith: Excerpt from the Introduction to *The Resisting Reader: A Feminist Approach to American Fiction* by Judith Fetterley. Indiana University Press.

Ford, Richard. "Optimists" from *Rock Springs* by Richard Ford. Copyright © 1987 by Richard Ford. Used by permission of Grove/Atlantic, Inc.

Frye, Northrup. Excerpt from *Anatomy of Criticism* by Northrup Frye. Copyright © 1957 Princeton University Press, 1985 renewed Princeton University Press, 2000 paperback edition. Reprinted by permission of Princeton University Press.

García Márquez, Gabriel. "The Handsomest Drowned Man in the World" from *Leaf Storm and Other Stories* by Gabriel García Márquez. Copyright © 1971 by Gabriel García Márquez. Reprinted by permission of HarperCollins Publishers.

Gardner, John. Excerpt from *Grendel* by John Gardner, copyright © 1971 by John Gardner. Used by permission of Alfred A. Knopf, a division of Random House, Inc.

Photo Credits

Index

List of Authors and Selections for Fiction, Poetry, Drama, and Critical Approaches

FICTION

CHIMAMANDA NGOZI ADICHIE, *Cell One*
SHERMAN ALEXIE, *What You Pawn I Will Redeem*
MARGARET ATWOOD, *Happy Endings*
ROGER AVERY AND NEIL GAIMON, *Interview on Adapting the Beowulf Story for Film*
JAMES BALDWIN, *Sonny's Blues*
AIMEE BENDER, *The Rememberer*
BEOWULF [GRENDEL'S ATTACK AND THE FIGHT WITH BEOWULF], *translated by CB Tinker*
BEOWULF: THE MOVIE (FILM STILLS OF BEOWULF AND GRENDEL)
J.L. BORGES, *The Circular Ruins, translated by Anthony Bonner*
T. CORAGHESSAN BOYLE, *Greasy Lake*
RAYMOND CARVER, *Cathedral*
WILLA CATHER, *Paul's Case*
ANTON CHEKHOV, *The Lady with the Pet Dog, translated by Avrahm Yarmolinsky*
——, *Rapture, translated by Patrick Miles and Harvey Pitcher*
KATE CHOPIN, *The Story of an Hour*
STEPHEN CRANE, *The Open Boat*
MICHAEL CRICHTON, *Eaters of the Dead [First Glimpse of Buliwyf; Battle with the Wendol]*
——, *A Factual Note on Adapting Beowulf for Eaters of the Dead*
JUNOT DIAZ, *How to Date a Browngirl, Blackgirl, Whitegirl, or Halfie*
RALPH ELLISON, *Battle Royal*
——, *A Party Down at the Square*
WILLIAM FAULKNER, *A Rose for Emily*
——, *Barn Burning*
RICHARD FORD, *Optimists*

JOHN GARDNER, *Grendel [Grendel's Isolation; Beowulf's Arrival; Fight with Beowulf]*
DAGOBERTO GILB, *Romero's Shirt*
CHARLOTTE PERKINS GILMAN, *The Yellow Wallpaper*
NATHANIEL HAWTHORNE, *Young Goodman Brown*
ERNEST HEMINGWAY, *The Short Happy Life of Francis Macomber*
AMY HEMPEL, *San Francisco*
GARETH HINDS, *Beowulf: The Graphic Novel [Grendel's Attack]*
ZORA NEALE HURSTON, *The Gilded Six-Bits*
GISH JEN, *Who's Irish?*
HA JIN, *Saboteur*
JAMES JOYCE, *Araby*
FRANZ KAFKA, *The Metamorphosis*
JAMAICA KINCAID, *Girl*
WILLIAM KITTREDGE, *Thirty-Four Seasons of Winter*
JHUMPA LAHIRI, *The Interpreter of Maladies*
D. H. LAWRENCE, *The Odour of Chrysanthemums*
URSULA K. LE GUIN, *The Kerastion*
JACK LONDON, *A Wicked Woman*
BARRY LOPEZ, *The Location of the River*
NAGUIB MAHFOUZ, *The Conjurer Made Off with the Dish, translated by Denys Johnson-Davies*
BERNARD MALAMUD, *The Magic Barrel*
KATHERINE MANSFIELD, *Miss Brill*
GABRIEL GARCÍA MÁRQUEZ, *The Handsomest Drowned Man in the World, translated by Gregory Rabassa*
HERMAN MELVILLE, *Bartleby, the Scrivener: A Story of Wall Street*
ANA MENENDEZ, *Traveling Madness*
LORRIE MOORE, *How to Become a Writer or, Have You Earned This Cliché?*

POETRY

——, *Saturday at the Canal*
WILLIAM STAFFORD, *Traveling Through the Dark*
WALLACE STEVENS, *Anecdote of the Jar*
——, *Disillusionment of Ten O'Clock*
——, *The Emperor of Ice-Cream*
——, *Sunday Morning*
——, *Thirteen Ways of Looking at a Blackbird*
ROBERT SWARD, *God Is in the Cracks*
SARAH TEASDALE, *I Am Not Yours*
ALFRED, Lord TENNYSON, *Ulysses*
DYLAN THOMAS, *Do not go gentle into that good night*
——, *Vision and Prayer (I)*
JEAN TOOMER, *Reapers*
NATASHA TRETHEWEY, *Letter Home—New Orleans, November 1910*
QUINCY TROUPE, *Poem Reaching towards Something*
DIANE WAKOSKI, *Inside Out*
ANNE WALDMAN, *Bluehawk*
PHYLLIS WHEATLEY, *On Being Brought from Africa to America*
WALT WHITMAN, *A Noiseless Patient Spider*
——, *Crossing Brooklyn Ferry*
——, *Song of Myself [I Celebrate myself, and sing myself]*
RICHARD WILBUR, *The Writer*
NANCY WILLARD, *Saint Pumpkin*
C. K. WILLIAMS, *Tar*
WILLIAM CARLOS WILLIAMS, *The Red Wheelbarrow*
——, *Spring and All*
——, *This Is Just To Say*
DAVID WOJAHN, *The Assassination of John Lennon as Depicted by the Madame Tussaud Wax Museum, Niagara Falls, Ontario, 1987*
WILLIAM WORDSWORTH, *Composed Upon Westminster Bridge, September 3, 1802*
——, *I Wandered Lonely as a Cloud*
——, *London, 1802*
——, *The World Is Too Much with Us*
——, *The Solitary Reaper*
JAMES WRIGHT, *A Blessing*
——, *Autumn Begins in Martins Ferry, Ohio*
——, *Lying in a Hammock at William Duffy's Farm in Pine Island, Minnesota*
EMILY XYZ, *Ship of State of Fools*
WILLIAM BUTLER YEATS, *Crazy Jane Talks with the Bishop*
——, *Leda and the Swan*
——, *Sailing to Byzantium*
——, *The Fisherman*
——, *The Second Coming*
——, *When You Are Old*
AL YOUNG, *Doo-Wop: The Moves*
KEVIN YOUNG, *Jook*

DRAMA

JOAN ACKERMANN, *The Second Beam*
EDWARD ALBEE, *Zoo Story*
DENISE CHAVEZ, *Guadalupe X3*
SUSAN GLASPELL, *Trifles*
JULIANNE HOMOKAY, *The Wedding*
DAVID HENRY HWANG, *Dance and the Railroad*
HENRIK IBSEN, *A Doll House, translated by R. Farquharson Sharp*
DAVID IVES, *Moby Dude, OR: The Three-Minute Whale*
ARTHUR KOPIT, *Wings*
ARTHUR MILLER, *Death of a Salesman*
RUBEN SANTIAGO-HUDSON, *Lackawanna Blues [Film stills and discussion]*
WILLIAM SHAKESPEARE, *Hamlet*
——, *Othello*
——, *A Midsummer Night's Dream*
SOPHOCLES, *Oedipus the King, translated by Robert Fitzgerald*
TENNESSEE WILLIAMS, *The Glass Menagerie*
AUGUST WILSON, *Fences*

CRITICAL APPROACHES TO LITERATURE

ROLAND BARTHES, *Death of the Author*
KENNETH BURKE, *The Poetic Process*
BORIS EIKHENBAUM, *The Theory of the Formal Method*
JUDITH FETTERLEY, *Introduction to On the Politics of Literature*
NORTHROP FRYE, *The Archetypes of Literature*
HENRY LOUIS GATES, *Loose Canons: Notes on the Culture Wars*
STEPHEN GREENBLATT, *The Introduction to the Power of Forms in the English Renaissance*
WOLFGANG ISER, *Interplay between Text and Reader*
VINCENT B. LEITCH, *Cultural Criticism, Literary Theory, Postculturalism*
VLADIMIR PROPP, *Fairy Tale Transformations*
GARY LEE STONUM, *Dickinson's Literary Background*
LEON TROTSKY, *Literature and Revolution*
CARL VAN DOREN, *Mark Twain*

Bringing Writers to Students, Bringing Students to Writing

Conversations on Writing

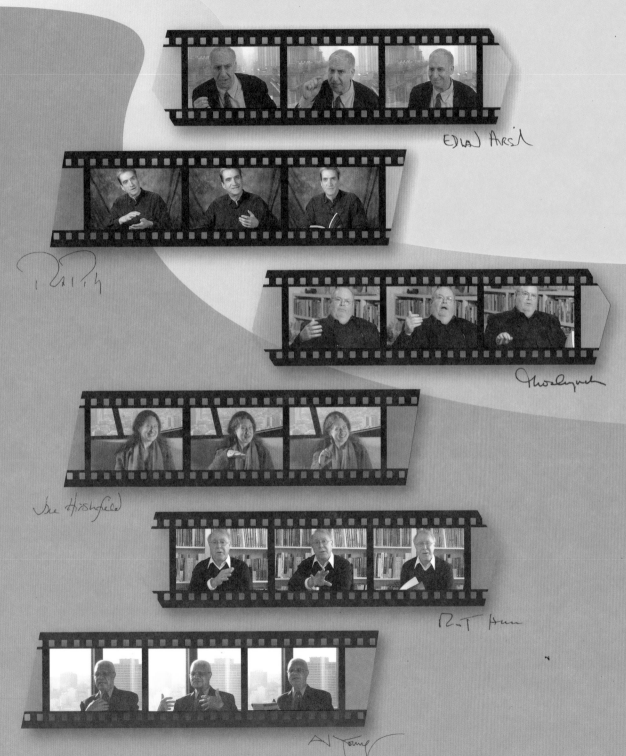

It looks like a great story is about to take place.

Like the cover of this book, every chapter opens your imagination, your curiosity, your interest—visually. And *Literature: Craft and Voice* will go wherever students go in a portable three-volume set of fiction, poetry, and drama. The format and design of *Literature: Craft and Voice* invites students to read, inspires independent critical analysis, and engages them in writing for college success.

visually rich

easy to carry

designed for reading

ISBN for three volume set:
0-07-732633-4

The McGraw·Hill Companies

McGraw Hill **Higher Education**

ISBN 978-0-07-310444-7
MHID 0-07-310444-2

EAN

90000

9 780073 104447

www.mhhe.com